GENDER IN CANADA

E. D. Nelson
University of Waterloo

Barrie W. Robinson

Prentice Hall Allyn and Bacon Canada
Scarborough, Ontario

Canadian Cataloguing in Publication Data

Nelson, Adie, 1958–
    Gender in Canada

Includes bibiographical references and index.
ISBN 0-13-375767-6

1. Sex role – Canada. 2. Sexism – Canada. I. Robinson, Barrie W.,
1944–   . II. Title.

HQ1075.5.C3N44 1998   305.3/0971   C98-931010-8

Allyn and Bacon, Inc., Needham Heights, MA
Prentice-Hall, Inc., Upper Saddle River, New Jersey
Prentice-Hall International (UK) Limited, London
Prentice-Hall of Australia, Pty. Limited, Sydney
Prentice-Hall Hispanoamericana, S.A., Mexico City
Prentice-Hall of India Private Limited, New Delhi
Prentice-Hall of Japan, Inc., Tokyo
Simon & Schuster Southeast Asia Private Limited, Singapore
Editora Prentice-Hall do Brasil, Ltda., Rio de Janeiro

ISBN 0-13-375767-6

Vice President, Editorial Director: Laura Pearson
Acquisitions Editor: Nicole Lukach
Marketing Manager: Kathleen McGill
Developmental Editor: Jean Ferrier
Production Editor: Kelly Dickson
Copy Editor: Dawn Hunter
Production Coordinator: Peggy Kakaflikas
Marketing Coordinator: Dayna Vogel
Marketing Assistant: Kathie Kirchsteiger
Cover Design: Dave McKay
Cover Image: Photodisc
Page Layout: Dave McKay

1 2 3 4 5   03 02 01 00 99

Printed and bound in Canada

Visit the Prentice Hall Canada web site! Send us your comments, browse our catalogues, and more at
www.phcanada.com. Or reach us through e-mail at **phabinfo_pubcanada@prenhall.com**.

Every reasonable effort has been made to obtain permissions for all articles and data used in this edition. If errors or omissions have occurred, they will be corrected in future editions provided written notification has been received by the publisher.

Statistics Canada information is used with the permission of the Minister of Industry, as Minister responsible for Statistics Canada. Information on the availability of the wide range of data from Statistics Canada can be obtained from Statistics Canada's Regional Offices, its World Wide Web site at **http://www.statcan.ca**, and its toll-free access number 1-800-263-1136.

To my sister, Reena Kreindler, for being totally kind.

A.N.

To Darcie and Tracie. It's in your hands now.

B. W. R.

Contents

Chapter 3: Historical And Structural Perspectives

Chapter 4: Development and Socialization in Childhood and Adolescence

Chapter 5: Symbolic Representations of Gender

Chapter 6: Work

Chapter 8: Marriage and Parenting

Chapter 9: Gender and Aging

Chapter 10: Equality and Social Gender Movements

Preface

This book has been fertilized by a combined quarter of a century spent teaching courses on the sociology of gender at the Universities of Alberta, British Columbia, and Waterloo. Although we had previously published two edited collections of readings on gender (Salamon and Robinson, 1987; Nelson and Robinson, 1995), we felt there still existed a need for a text that was comprehensive in scope, inclusive in treatment, and coherent and accessible in writing style. Too often, we have found, instructors teaching courses in the area of gender are confronted with materials prepared for an American audience, or that offer an analysis that focuses exclusively on either girls or women, or boys or men, or that mute discussion of how gender as a status variable intersects with other variables such as "race," ethnicity, social class, sexual orientation, and ableness. In preparing this book, we have attempted to provide students with a treatment that is as inclusive as the available literature allows. We present up-to-date materials drawn from interdisciplinary sources and the most recent Canadian census and General Social Survey findings. We introduce students to the rich body of research, both qualitative and quantitative, and empirical and theoretical, that has been undertaken in this area. We take special care to ensure that both theory and data are presented in ways that engage, rather than bemuse, our readers. Our coverage of topics is purposefully broad and we focus on how the social construction of gender affects the behaviour, beliefs, attitudes, and interpersonal relationships of women and men throughout their lives.

Like all expectant parents, we have planned for and pondered over our creation and considered whether we could do well by it, consulted the writings of various experts to guide us along the way, bandied about names for its title and chapter headings, and grumbled, to all who would listen, that the other parent had been assigned the easier tasks involved in the labour of its birth. We also wish to remind our readers that any flaws in our creation are, of course, due solely to the inferior genes of the other author.

We have organized our text into 10 chapters, each designed to introduce the reader to the core concepts, theorists, theories, and controversies that surround the topic under discussion. In Chapter 1, we direct attention to the three concepts, sex, gender, and sexuality, that form the foundation for this text, and to the complexities involved in their definition. We introduce the concept of gender stereotypes, review the major methods used to ascertain the content of these stereotypes, and explore the double or multiple jeopardies that occur when stereotypes about men and women are enmeshed with stereotypes of "race," social class, disability, sexual orientation, age, and attractiveness. The power of gender stereotypes is forcefully illustrated with a discussion of sex (re)assignment and transsexualism. We additionally discuss the ways in which gender has influenced the development of research and theory, and the conclusions reached.

In Chapter 2, we consider each of the basic variables of sex (chromosomal, gonadal, hormonal, reproductive, genital, brain, and assigned) and gender (identity and social behaviour) independently and then in relation to one another. Within this chapter, we explore a number of theories and theoretical perspectives whose explanations are anchored within the biological basis of human existence, and argue, directly or indirectly, that gender behaviour is ultimately a product of human biological nature. We then turn our attention to several theories within psychology that consider the processes by which sex typing occurs and examine a social psychological theory, symbolic interactionism. We conclude this chapter with a discussion of the gender perspective that attempts to combine elements from several social psychological and structural feminist theories.

In Chapter 3, we explore how the structure of a society exerts influence upon the ways in which gender is experienced and expressed. We provide a brief overview of the historical development of Canada, from preindustrial times through to the mid 1960s, to illustrate how conceptions and guidelines for masculinity and femininity in our society are constructed relative to time and place. We review the central tenets of both functionalism and conflict theory, and provide a comprehensive review of feminist theories and perspectives on men and masculinity.

Development and socialization in childhood and adolescence are the foci of Chapter 4. Within this chapter, we examine various ways in which messages about gender are transmitted and reinforced within the family, the peer group, and the school. We explore the dominant themes of gender socialization during childhood and adolescence that prevail in Canada, discuss a variety of mechanisms that contribute to a child becoming gendered, and suggest how gender ideologies and gender strategies may have an impact upon the future aspirations of young men and women.

In Chapter 5, we extend our discussion of socialization influences to consider symbolic representations of gender that are found within language and speech patterns, nonverbal communication, and the media. We examine the socialization messages conveyed through such mediums as children's books, comics, television, advertising and commercials, teen magazines, popular music, computers, and the Internet. Although our list of socialization influences does not presume to be exhaustive, we believe that it will provoke and stimulate thought and discussion on the myriad of subtle ways through which the "reality" of gender is created and sustained.

Gender in our society is inextricably intertwined with work and the family or intimate relations. These social institutions create and sustain gender as much as they are created and sustained by gender. In Chapter 6, we focus upon both paid and unpaid work. Some of the topics discussed within this chapter include age and sex differentials in labour-force participation rates; the impact of marital status and parenting upon paid work; occupational distributions and segregations; the impact of "family-friendly" benefits; multiple jeopardies, unemployment, and underemployment; earning differentials; self-employment and home-based employment; part-time work; and the problems of sexual harassment and the chilly climate. We pay particular attention to the gendered nature of housework, and examine various explanations for the unequal distribution of housework responsibilities and labour expenditures. The notion of female responsibility for housework has been captured in a popular slogan: "It starts when you sink into his arms and ends with your arms in his sink" (Jackson and Scott, 1996:13). This slogan summarizes and satirizes the course of idealistic romantic love relationships within our society, as they confront the everyday reality of a woman's household life.

In Chapter 7, we discuss intimate relations. We begin our exploration by reviewing findings on gender differences in friendship, courtship, and mate-selection practices. Although we might prefer to think of our quest for an intimate partner as an intensely "unique" odyssey, sex ratios, mating gradients, and changing gender expectations and behaviours all place different, yet interrelated, constraints on the options we confront. Similarly, although relationships vary in terms of how explicitly or obviously power is expressed, a power dimension is always present. Within this chapter, we also discuss experienced sexuality and sexual scripts and suggest that, rather than being driven by human biology, observable differences in human sexuality are socially constructed through active and passive participation in lifelong differential socialization processes within variable sociocultural contexts. Part of this socialization, we emphasize, involves being exposed to social definitions, which privilege some forms of sexuality as acceptable and others as disreputable, and constructs sexuality scripts for men and women. We conclude this chapter with an examination of violence in intimate relationships.

Although it has long been a central tenet of family sociologists that one of the major functions of the family is to provide protection for family members from bodily harm by outsiders, the dangers posed by family members to each other have, until relatively recently, escaped scrutiny. We provide a brief historical review of the laws and informal social norms that, in the past, promoted the illusion of tranquillity within intimate relationships. We also note the controversies that currently surround attempts to name and frame the problem of intimate violence, to define its parameters, and to measure its incidence.

In Chapter 8, our topic is marriage and parenting. Unlike many other types of intimate relations in our society, husband-wife and parent-child relationships are governed by laws in addition to other unique informal expectations and conventions. We suggest how marriage and gender create and recreate one another in a continually interacting fashion and how gender and gender inequalities become organizing principles in heterosexual marriages. We challenge our readers to consider the far-reaching significance of our social constructions of motherhood and fatherhood and invite them to contemplate what the new assisted reproductive technologies can or will mean for families, parenting, and some of our most basic understandings and expectations of gender.

Our attention in Chapter 9 is devoted to selected events associated with aging and, more important, upon the social meanings of aging for each gender. Among the topics discussed in this chapter are sex ratio and life expectancy differentials; gender differences in mortality and morbidity; adult development during adulthood and old age; menopause, men's pause, and sociophysical aging; gender depolarization; retirement; the experience of displaced homemakers and displaced providers; adult-elder caregiving; and the double standard of aging.

Our final chapter, Chapter 10, focuses upon social movements and gender. We chronicle the struggles and accomplishments of the first and second waves of the women's movement in Canada, examine the resistance to feminism and antifeminist movements, and note some of the challenges confronting feminists organizing for change in Canada in the 1990s.

A.N. would like to thank Ronald and Marilyn Lambert, Robert Hiscott, Robert Prus, and Jim and Penny Curtis, for their help in various ways. She would also like to thank her son, Joshua Paul ("Josh") who, over the course of preparing this book, graduated from dinosaurs to Godzilla (and his family), and her daughter, Veronica Brittany ("Ronnie"), who transferred her affections for Mickey Mouse to the Spice Girls.

B.W.R. wishes to thank his mother, Peggy Robinson, his colleague and close friend Wayne McVey Jr., and his close friend, Barbara Smith, for their financial, technical, and moral support over the long course of the writing of this text.

We both wish to thank the capable staff at Prentice Hall Canada for their incredible helpfulness and infinite patience, especially Lisa Berland, Rebecca Bersagel, Kelly Dickson, Jean Ferrier, Shoshanna Goldberg, Dawn Hunter, Nicole Lukach, Marjorie Munroe, Laura Forbes Patterson, Laura Pearson, and David Stover.

Acknowledgments

The authors and the publisher have made every attempt to trace ownership of all copyrighted material reprinted herein. While expressing regret for any error unintentionally made, the publisher will be pleased to make necessary corrections in future editions of this book.

For permission to reprint copyrighted material, the following acknowledgments are gratefully made:

FARCUS © is reprinted with permission from LaughingStock Licensing Inc. Ottawa, Canada. All rights reserved.

The excerpt from Sherene Razack's "Exploring the Omissions and Silence in law Around Race" reprinted by permission of Thompson Educational Publishing.

The excerpt from Mark Snyder's "Self-fulfilling Stereotypes" is reprinted with permission from *Psychology Today* magazine, copyright © 1982.

The excerpt from Suzanne Kessler's "The Medical Construction of Gender: Case Management of Intersexed Infants" reprinted by permission of University of Chicago Press.

The excerpt from Jean Lipman-Blumen's *Gender Roles and Power* reprinted by permission of Prentice-Hall.

The excerpt from John Crewdson's "Second thoughts on 'gay genes.'" reprinted by permission of the Chicago Tribune.

The excerpt from Carol Tavris' *The Mismeasurement of Women* is reprinted by permission of Simon & Schuster © 1992 by Carol Tavris.

The excerpts from William Masters and Virginia Johnson's *Masters and Johnson on Sex and Human Loving* reprinted by permission of Little Brown.

The excerpt from Hilary Lips' *Sex & Gender: An Introduction,* 2nd ed., reprinted by permission of Mayfield Publishing Company.

The excerpts from Gloria Steinem's *Moving Beyond Words* are reprinted by permission of Simon & Schuster © 1994 by Gloria Steinem.

The excerpt from Steve Pagani's "Virgins' take men's place in vendetta-torn Albania" reprinted by permission of Reuters.

The excerpt from Salome Lucas et al.'s "Changing the Politics of the Women's Movement" is reprinted by permission of Resources for Feminist Research.

The excerpt from William Gairdner's *The War Against the Family: A Parent Speaks Out* reprinted by permission of Stoddart.

The excerpt from Robert Bly's *Iron John: A Book About Men* reprinted by permission of AddisonWesley.

THE SOCIAL CONSTRUCTION OF SEX, GENDER, AND SEXUALITY

BASIC CONCEPTS: SEX, GENDER, AND SEXUALITY

Three concepts, each part of our everyday language, form the foundation for this text. Unfortunately, these basic terms are often used in imprecise and, subsequently, confusing ways. "[Much] like Humpty Dumpty's words ('When I use a word,' Humpty Dumpty said, 'it means what I choose it to mean—neither more nor less.' [Carol, *Alice Through the Looking Glass*]), they mean whatever one chooses them to mean" (Lipman-Blumen, 1984: 1). Because meaningful communication requires that participants achieve a basic level of agreement about the scope and content of the key terms they will be exchanging, we must first devote ourselves to some definitional issues.

Sex

Sex refers to the designation of being *male* or *female* as identified from a biological stand-point. At first glance, it would appear that this is an obvious determination and a simple distinction. However, as we shall explore in more detail later, the designation of a person as either female or male is neither simple nor obvious; it requires making determinations on a number of variable dimensions. We shall begin with a simplistic distinction. The division of the human population into either female or male, sometimes referred to as **sex dimorphism**, rests upon the notion of a *dichotomy*, that is, the assumption that a given phenomenon can be categorized as located within either one or the other of two mutually exclusive categories. This assumption provides the basis for a commonly held belief that only two categories exist—male or female—and, furthermore, that all persons must be, and can be, categorized as belonging to one or the other.

The notion of dichotomies is an integral part of the philosophical thought patterns predominant in Canada and other Western societies. Dichotomies are applied as both descriptions and evaluations. Thus, phenomena are classified in "either/or" terms such as either male or female, good or bad, right or wrong, black or white, yes or no, and so on. Such reductions of complexity into seeming simplicity are designed to allow us to navigate quickly through social life, without having to take into consideration all facets and shadings of every aspect of life, a situation which could ultimately render us immobile. However, engaging in dichotomous thinking sets the stage for a series of consequences.

If a phenomenon can, and should be, categorized as belonging in only one of two categories, it follows that no middle ground of ambiguity will be tolerated. The category contents must be, or must be made to be, substantially different from one another. In fact, dichotomous thinking encourages us to believe that the contents of each category are different to the point of being complete opposites. For example, this notion of dichotomies representing *diametrical opposites* is captured in the everyday use of the term "opposite sex." A legitimate question to ask immediately is "who is the opposite sex?" At first glance, this question might seem downright silly, but it is a meaningful question whose answer is full of implications for the lives of women and men. Males, traditionally, within our own and many other cultures, have been, and to a very large extent still are, considered to be the central or standard sex. Females have been, and still are, defined, analyzed, and seemingly understood with reference to males—and not the other way around. Consequently, it is females who have been considered as the opposite, the different, the deviant, or the "Other" (de Beauvoir, 1961: xvi).

In those two simple words, "opposite sexes," are contained beliefs and expectations that whatever females are, males are not, and whatever males are, females are not. While such simplicity is not the case, the existence of dichotomies and dichotomous thinking leads us to search for, and focus upon, differences rather than similarities between the sexes. To return to our original point, we shall use the concept of "sex" to refer to being biologically male or female.

Gender

Gender refers to the designation of *feminine* and *masculine,* as identified from a sociocultural standpoint. The term "gender" is of relatively recent origin, having been introduced into our vocabulary by psychoneuroendrocrinologist John Money in 1955. (One wonders how he responds to questions on various forms asking for his occupation.) While "there is no linguistic magic that can isolate the strictly social and cultural components of femininity and masculinity in a single operative term" (Komarovsky, 1988: 586), "gender" is the best available term that focuses our attention upon the vital contribution of those components. Throughout its relatively brief history, the term "gender" has been used, generally, as we indicated above, although a tendency is developing to use the term in a more inclusive, and possibly misleading, way. For example, Hyde (1995), in her textbook on human sexuality, uses "gender" to include both sex and gender as we have used the terms here. Udry (1994: 561) comments that editors of scientific journals regularly strike out his use of the term "sex" and insert the term "gender," even in those places where he is specifically referring to the biological designation. This unfortunate lack of precision in the use of our basic concepts is confusing to researchers, theorists, textbook authors, and students alike.

A major part of this confusion stems from uncertainty as to precisely what it is that we are focusing upon in a specific instance. It is not always clear whether social scientists are examining a biological or a cultural phenomenon when conducting empirical studies and generalizing either their own findings, or those of other researchers. When we simply note that some respondents or participants in a study are "female" while others are "male," and then compare their average differences or similarities on some task or issue, the question still remains as to whether we are noting and measuring something that is the product of experiences and behaviours associated with being feminine or masculine (and, therefore, best captured by the term "gender") or something that is directly associated with, and derived from, being biologically male or female (and, therefore, best captured by the term "sex"). Since biology and culture do overlap and interact and are not separate and distinct from one another, the decision whether to use the term "sex" or "gender" is not an immediately obvious one.

In keeping with the conventional usage of the term, "gender" will be used throughout these pages to refer to *all expected and actual thoughts, feelings, and behaviours associated with masculinity and femininity*. Achieving consensus upon the meaning of gender is relatively less arduous than the larger questions that can be raised regarding this basic concept. For example, some of the fundamental questions before us have been identified as follows:

> What is gender? How is it related to anatomical sexual differences? How are gender relations constituted and sustained (in one person's lifetime and, more generally, as a social experience over time)?...What causes gender relations to change over time? What are the relationships between gender relations, sexuality, and a sense of individual identity? What are the relationships between heterosexuality, homosexuality, and gender relations? Are there only two genders?...Are gendered distinctions socially useful or necessary? (Flax, 1990: 43)

We shall consider all of these questions throughout this text.

How Many Genders?

In addition to inconsistencies in the use of the term "gender," further disagreement exists regarding how many genders actually exist. Our reference to gender as denoting masculinity and femininity suggests the existence of only two separate discrete gender categories. Many standard psychological tests, such as the commonly used *Minnesota Multiphasic Personality Inventory* or MMPI (Hathaway and McKinley, 1943), are based upon an assumption of dichotomous genders. However, Bem (1974), when introducing the concept of "androgyny," suggests that masculinity and femininity represent two continua. She further suggests that individuals can be located along each continuum and that these positions provide an indication of their personal combination of masculinity and femininity. Bem developed a methodological test (the Bem Sex Role Inventory) whose results yielded a fourfold classification system: (1) **androgynous** individuals rank high on both femininity and masculinity, (2) **feminine** individuals rank high on femininity and low on masculinity, (3) **masculine** individuals rank high on masculinity and low on femininity, and (4) **undifferentiated** individuals rank low on femininity and masculinity. Bem's research provided empirical support for the possible existence of four genders. However, partly due to limitations of the English language and partly due to the necessity of linking this research with a larger research tradition, Bem's classification types are discussed using only the terms of masculinity and femininity, thereby reinforcing the notion that only two basic genders really exist.

As Heilbrun (1973: xv) acknowledges, "so wedded are we to the conventional definition of 'masculine' and 'feminine' that it is impossible to write about androgyny without using these terms in their accepted, received sense." The Sapir-Whorf hypothesis (to be presented more fully in a later chapter) proposes that, until a term is constructed for something, it is impossible to think about, communicate about, and fully understand. Without the luxury, or necessity, of an available, truly neutral nongendered language, it is difficult to describe actions, thoughts, and feelings in other than stereotypical terms. We live within a linguistic reality whereby most, if not virtually all, behaviour is identified by dichotomous gender labels.

The concept of androgyny, a term stemming from the Greek words *andros* (man) and *gune* (woman), suggests the possible attainment of an additional gender (actually a "nongender"), a human hybrid that, except for a few reproductively related differences, encourages and allows persons of both sexes to integrate and acknowledge "the realization of man in woman and woman in man" (see Bem, 1975, 1978; Bem et al., 1976; Bem and Lenney, 1976; Castro, 1990: 163; hooks, 1992). The difficulty of translating this ideal into reality lies in the fact that "masculinity" and "femininity" are situated within the context of male power and female subordination. Within this context of structured inequities, our stereotypes of gender define certain styles (typically associated with masculinity) as "normal" and admirable, while dismissing others (typically associated with femininity) as deviant, irrational, and inferior (see also Archer, 1989; Binion, 1990; Daly, 1990). While in Western society a woman may receive rewards for displaying such supposedly masculine characteristics as being assertive (versus timid), logical and rational (versus emotional or irrational), or active (versus passive), a male demonstrating feminine qualities may be only psychologically benefited and not socially rewarded. Indeed, reactions from outsiders may be equivocal at best, and typically range from bemusement to ridicule and antipathy.

However, the problems we experience in our Western society are not universally shared. The anthropological record provides evidence of the existence, within a variety of cultural contexts, of distinctive gender types, in addition to our own limited everyday understanding of masculine and feminine. The North American First Nations *berdache* ("ber-dash") (Callender and Kochems, 1983) is a person, usually a biological male, who effects a change in his or her gender status by adopting the clothing styles, occupations, and behaviours of the other sex. This is not simply a case of transvestitism, which occurs when a person's outward appearance and mannerisms shift from one apparent gender to another. By acknowledgment from all those in the social environment, this person now occupies an intermediate gender status. *Berdaches* or "two-spirits," are designated within specific First Nations-language groups by a term that has been translated into English as a "halfwoman-halfman" or "man-woman." Since no change of biological state is involved, and in keeping with our usage of terms here, this intermediate status would more accurately be stated as "halffeminine-halfmasculine" or "masculine-feminine." You can see how our language customs constrain our ability to designate this intermediate status in any words other than feminine and masculine. *Berdaches* occupy a separate status and a standing within a First Nations community equivalent to those people of masculine and feminine genders. No sense of deviance or disrepute is associated with this intermediate, or other, gender state. Rather, the person is treated as simply belonging to another acceptable category (Williams, 1996: 73).

Jacobs (1983), recounting her experiences among the Tewa of New Mexico, and the role of what was referred to in their language as the *quetho*, illustrates how our language constrains us from conceptualizing the role of *berdache*s and their significance among the more than 113 First Nations cultures which recognize their status.

> Among the Tewa elders with whom I have spoken who would not assign a male or female sex to *quetho*, I pushed the point further on a number of occasions, asking if women were ever *quetho*s. The answer was no. Then I asked if men were the only ones who were *quetho*s. Again, the answer was no. In trying to force a categorization of *quetho*s as women or men (or female or male), I only exasperated my Tewa friends, who do make a clear distinction between *quetho*s, homosexuals (gay men and women), women, men, and those who on ceremonial occasion dress in the attire of their opposite sex. If the Tewa do this, is it not possible that we are still asking the wrong questions because in Euro-American culture we have a difficult time accepting that there can be a genuinely conceptualized third gender that has nothing to do with transvestism or homosexuality? (1983: 460)

As Jacobs' comments suggest, not only do *berdache*s transcend our ideas about gender, they also challenge many of our notions about sexuality as well.

Despite the absence of any solid evidence in either direction, a significant debate has ensued about whether or not *berdache*s engage in homosexual acts. The debate appears to suggest more about the preoccupation of the writers than about *berdache*s themselves. For nineteenth-century missionaries, the "evidence" was quite clear. "Of course" *berdache*s engaged in homosexual acts; missionaries described *berdache*s as "disgusting sodomites" and "savages." As Callender and Kochems (1983: 443) observe, these early descriptions of *berdache*s "sometimes contained much more denunciation than data." Anthropologists who followed the missionaries tended to be more liberal on value judgments about "race," but not so on matters of sexuality. They preferred, by and large, to delicately and selectively ignore the possibility of homosexuality altogether and reported that *berdache*s were ceremonial cross-dressers who *never* performed homosexual acts. In contrast, writers active in the modern gay movement, have depicted *berdache*s as spiritually and communally powerful homosexuals, whose existence suggests that First Nations cultures were, and are, more liberal about homosexuality than is our own (Roscoe, 1988). Indeed, the *berdache* has been revived by some contemporary gay American First Nations people who have also, in a sense, possibly "reinvented" them to contain an explicitly acknowledged homosexual component.

Whitehead (1981) argues that the reason why there is very little evidence on whether or not *berdache*s engaged in homosexual acts stems from the fact that sexuality was not all that important as a defining feature in First Nations culture. She suggests that *berdache*s were defined in terms of their occupational and kinship status. It was these two statuses, she maintains, that were important—not whether or not they engaged in genital homosexuality. She argues that it is only in the West, and reflective of a Western cultural obsession, that we find a preoccupation with sexuality, or more specifically with genital sexuality, to define a person's **master status**, the status by which a person is chiefly identified. Whitehead's views came out at approximately the same time as Rich's (1980/1984: 227) concept of the "lesbian continuum"—that is, the idea of lesbians as "women-defined women," rather than simply as women who engage in specific types of genital sexuality. According to Rich, "lesbian" should not be thought of as simply the experience of or desire for a specific type of genital sexual experience; rather "lesbianism" is thought to encompass a "range of 'woman-identified' experience, including the sharing of a rich inner life, bonding against male tyranny, and practical support" (Frith, 1993: 157).

What, if anything, *berdaches* actually did, and do, in terms of genital homosexuality is up for question. What is not debatable is the fact that *berdache*s, a third gender, were, and are, very much respected and in possession of a great deal of ceremonial and spiritual power. While a *berdache* is unambiguously biologically either a male or a female, *nadle* (nad-leh) in First Nations communities is a gender status assigned to a person born with an ambiguous genital configuration. According to Olien (1978), the *nadle* adopts the clothing styles deemed consistent with performing sex-linked work in the community, donning women's clothing to perform what is considered to be "women's work" and then donning men's clothing to perform what is designated as "men's work." A *nadle* is free to switch back and forth between different work and clothing styles at will. Although prevented from engaging in hunting and warfare, *nadles* are treated by their communities with deference, not disdain, and are considered to be valuable, even gifted, members of their social groups.

The *hijras* (HIJ-ras) of India are a religious community of men whose culture focuses on the worship of *Bahuchara Mata*, one of the many Mother Goddesses. Both Indian mythology and culture have long recognized gender transformations and a third gender. According to Nanda (1990: xi), the special status of *hijras* within Indian society is based on their identification with the Mother Goddess, who is seen as the embodiment of female creative power. *Hijras* are biological men who wear female apparel and behave like women. Undergoing surgical emasculation to remove their penis and testicles defines them as *hijras*— "neither men nor women" (Nanda, 1990: xv). Hijras occupy a recognized place within Indian society as an "institutionalized third gender," performing songs and dances at festivals, after the birth of a child, and at weddings.

The *xanith* (han-eeth) in Islamic Oman provide further evidence of yet another "intermediate gender" (Wikan, 1977). Regarded as neither men nor women, *xanith* are males who enjoy all the rights of a man under law, worship in mosques with other men, have male names, and are referred to with the use of masculine grammatical form. However, *xanith* perform the role of women within their households and their attractiveness is judged by standards of female beauty. In this Saudi Arabian setting where the practice of *purdah,* or seclusion, ensures the segregation of women and men, *xanith* are classed with women for most festive occasions and social activities (e.g., eating with women, visiting with women and so on). Although prohibited by law from dressing in women's clothing or adopting the mask and veil that adult women in Oman must wear, the clothing of *xaniths* is an admixture of male and female styles. Although both men and women in Oman generally cover their heads, the *xanith*, in contrast, goes bareheaded. And while both men and women scent themselves with perfume, the *xanith* applies perfume more heavily than is typical for either (Nanda, 1990: 131).

Xaniths serve as homosexual male partners, taking the passive role. In Oman, "being a man," or masculinity, is defined by sexual potency in marriage and a bloodied handkerchief is publicly displayed after one's wedding night, to prove, simultaneously, the wife's virginity upon marriage and the husband's ability to consummate the union. However, inasmuch as being a man is linked to the aggressor role within sexual intercourse, a *xanith* may become a man, despite his former status, should he marry and demonstrate his potency in the male sexual role. Upon this demonstration of masculinity, a former *xanith* will become subject to the constraints operating on other men, which will generally bar him from interacting with women festively and socially.

Although the term *mahu* (ma-hoo) is used in modern-day Hawaii as one designation for homosexuals, the *mahu* of traditional Tahiti were, and are, a third gender. *Mahu* is a culturally available role within traditional Tahitian villages comparable to a cross between a *berdache* and a *nadle*. Unambiguously biologically male, there is always one *mahu*— never more nor less—who adopts this role voluntarily and publicly takes on both the work and dress of a woman. As in the case of *xaniths*, *hijras*, and *berdache*s, the sexual partners of a *mahu* are not viewed as homosexual, nor is this thought to be the primary determining characteristic of a *mahu*. Tahitians distinguish between homosexuality (termed *raerae*) and the sexual activity engaged in by *mahu*s and their partners. If, at any time, a *mahu* feels that he no longer has the calling to be a *mahu*, he can simply stop, cast off the role, and resume everyday life as a heterosexual man performing what are viewed in the village as masculine duties (Nanda, 1990: 134–136).

The existence of these other genders illustrates the likelihood that our understanding in Western society of the nature and number of genders is limited and constrained by social convention, and by the English language, to thinking in terms of only two genders: feminine and masculine. For the moment, and for the sake of simplicity, we shall think of gender as existing along two continua—one of masculinity and the other of femininity. Individuals can, and do, array themselves along each continuum in terms of their high-to-low conformity to a set of standards for ideal behaviour found within a given society, possessing a given culture and subcultures, at a particular point in historical time.

Sex and Gender

A fundamental issue confronting a sociology of gender lies in identifying the nature of the connection between sex and gender. Logically, three types of relationships are possible. In no particular order of importance, they are:

1. sex *determines* gender

2. sex is *arbitrarily* related to gender

3. sex *influences* gender

(A fourth possibility, namely, that gender determines or influences sex, is applicable only in exceptional cases, as we shall see in a later section of this chapter, and will not be considered further here.)

The first relationship attributes a causal role to sex and assumes that one's biological state dictates one's thoughts, feelings,

Farcus

by David Waisglass
Gordon Coulthart

6-1
© 1995 Farcus Cartoons/dist. by LaughingStock Licensing Inc.   WAISGLASS/COULTHART

"I had five ... one of each."

and behaviours on the gender continua. In other words, sex is assumed to be both a necessary and a sufficient cause of gender. The second relationship suggests that any apparent connection existing between sex and gender is random, accidental, or arbitrary. Some correlation may be found between, for example, being female and being feminine but, as we know, correlation is not the same as causation. A correlation may be a statistical artifact and thus an inaccurate reflection of "reality." In this case, sex is deemed to be neither a necessary nor a sufficient cause of gender. Other factors, such as certain features of the social environment for example, must be identified and analyzed as the actual cause(s) of gender. The third relationship suggests that sex and gender are related to each other in some necessary fashion, but that gender cannot fully nor sufficiently be explained, or caused, by sex. Additional factors must, therefore, be taken into account if our goal is to achieve as complete an understanding of the nature of gender as possible.

It is difficult to state with any absolute confidence which of the three positions is held by what proportion of the general Canadian population. However, impressionistic evidence suggests that the first, determinist, position is the most common. Fueled by information obtained from a variety of sources including folk wisdom, superstition, common sense, philosophy, religious beliefs, and persuasions of varying origins from persons significant to our lives (collectively referred to as *received wisdom*), most Canadians appear to believe that being born male or female determines whether one will be masculine or feminine. We live within a society that proceeds on the presumption that sex determines gender and that the two terms are interchangeable (that is, either term can be used in place of the other). This deterministic linkage of sex and gender in itself perpetuates a belief in the dichotomization of gender. According to this line of thought, if there are only two sexes, then there must be only two genders. Masculinity and femininity are thus cast into opposite categories that are anchored in biology and explained in the rhetoric of "doing what comes naturally." Once again, complexity is reduced to apparent simplicity.

Canadians typically use the simple one-word designations of either "masculine" or "feminine" to describe themselves or other people (e.g., "He's very masculine. A regular 100 percent Canadian stud-muffin."). We rarely hear people use qualifying adjectives indicating degrees of masculinity or femininity or both to describe themselves or others (e.g., "He's about 75 percent masculine, charmingly blended with about 25 percent feminine."). This greater degree of precision would probably make most Canadians uncomfortable as it threatens our conventional received wisdom and would require providing a recipe list of the distribution of masculine and feminine ingredients. Many, and perhaps most, people would like to continue thinking that sexes and genders come "two by two." Throughout this text, we will be challenging you to avoid such simplistic thinking and to acknowledge greater complexity in both sex and gender.

Reduced to their essential elements, the first and second positions reflect the long-standing "either/or" controversy of "nature" versus "nurture" (yet another dichotomy). The first position is generally referred to within the social sciences as a **biological determinist** position, while the second is generally referred to as the **social constructionist** position. The third position rejects the "either/or" reductionist thinking of the first two in favour of more complex and ambitious thinking that stresses both: biology and the social environment combine to produce gender. This third position is often referred to as the **interactionist** position. Money's comments are relevant here when he notes:

> Reductionist theory is popular on both sides of the false fence that erroneously claims to separate biology from social learning. It allows its proponents on either side to earn a living by ignoring each other's specialty knowledge, training, and certification. The bureaucracy of scholars is not well suited to inter-disciplinary knowledge, nor to the concept of multivariate,

sequential determinants that cross the boundaries of scientific specialities. (Money, 1988: 54)

In other words, an important factor contributing to the endorsement of the first and second positions, and working against full acceptance and implementation of the third position, lies in the very nature of academic specialization and the bureaucratic structure of the academy itself. Undergraduate, graduate, and professional training, with increasing specialization at each level, are all structured within disciplinary lines, which do not promote the full development of multidisciplinary knowledge.

Udry speculates about the reasons why social scientists do not take biological theory into consideration in their search for a full understanding of the nature of gender and suggests that "[f]irst, most do not know about it" (Udry, 1994: 563). This is not intended as an indictment of individual theorists, but rather as further indication of the difficulties of being conversant with developments in disciplinary areas outside of one's own area of specialization. Adoption of one of the "either/or" biological determinist or social constructionist positions is thus largely a consequence of academic specialization. Even when a researcher, theorist, or author states a preference for an interdisciplinary interactionist position, the resultant product typically places a greater emphasis upon either biological or social factors, reflective of the person's academic roots.

To the best of our awareness and ability we will present theories and research from as many perspectives as possible within the confinements of a book-length text. However, since we are both sociologists by avocation and training, and since this text is intended primarily for a student audience in sociology or related courses, we feel that it is necessary and desirable to introduce you to, and emphasize, the social construction perspective throughout these pages.

Sexuality

To our list of basic concepts, we now add **sexuality** and the shorter term of **sexual**. In everyday spoken and written communication, these two terms are very frequently subsumed under the even shorter term of *sex*. Unfortunately, the ways we use the term "sex" in our everyday attempts to communicate creates three confusingly different meanings. Reiss provides the following illustrations:

1. Her sex is female

2. Her sex role is that of a woman

3. She had sex with her partner (Reiss, 1986: 18)

The first sentence uses sex in the manner we used earlier, and will continue to use, to refer only to a biological designation. The second sentence uses sex in a way we would prefer to designate as gender. (We will introduce the concept of *role* in relation to sex and gender in a later section, and explain why the preferred concept is that of gender role.) The third sentence refers to something that is part of the constellation of feelings, thoughts, and behaviours comprising human sexuality.

Following Reiss, we will use the words "sexuality" and "sexual" to refer to a limited human activity or set of activities likely, but not guaranteed, to produce physical pleasure and self-disclosure (Reiss, 1986: 31). Reiss defines the universal, shared, meaning of human sexuality as "*those scripts shared by a group that are supposed to lead to erotic arousal and in turn to produce genital response*" (Reiss, 1986: 20; emphasis in original). The *scripts* being referred to are culturally created guidelines that represent a society's or group's shared definitions of the types of situations, people, and behaviours considered to be appropriate in any social situation. More specifically, sexuality scripts provide definitional guidelines as to where, with whom, in response to which conditions, and how (emotionally, cognitively, and physically), to be or behave as a sexual being.

As has been the case with the other basic concepts, "sex" and "sexual" have unfortunately been used imprecisely and often interchangeably with biological sex and social gender to produce confusing outcomes regarding the meaning of phrases. For example, a commonly used phrase within the gender literature is that of the "sexual division of labour" (e.g., Steuter, 1992: 292; Wilson, 1991: 5). Although not intended, the phrase would most accurately refer to task specialization in the (presumably) unpaid work performed by partners in a sexuality scenario of some kind. In this instance, greater precision in the original phrase can be gained by changing it to the "*sex-linked* division of labour," that is, task-specialization assignments attached either meaningfully or arbitrarily to one's biological sex. When "sexual" and "sex" are used interchangeably, or are implied to be interchangeable terms, the impression is casually fostered that sexuality is biologically determined. Whether sexuality is biologically determined or social constructed is an issue we shall examine momentarily.

How Many Sexualities?

First, we must confront the question of how many sexualities exist. Fortunately, we do have agreement about the existence of **homosexuality** (following a sexuality script oriented towards a member of the same sex), **heterosexuality** (following a script oriented towards a member of the other sex), and **bisexuality** (following a script towards members of both sexes), although the precise terms used to designate these three forms vary from one author to another, such as the more colloquial "gay," "straight," and "in-between" (Money, 1988). Lips (1993: 202) notes that heterosexuality, bisexuality, and homosexuality "seem to be points on a continuum rather than completely discrete categories."

The research of Kinsey et al. (1948; 1953), and others to follow, demonstrates the futility of attempts to divide human beings into only two dichotomous, polar-opposite, categories: "heterosexual" and "homosexual." Rather, as Figure 1.1 illustrates, the Kinsey findings and subsequent development of a seven-point scale of sexual behaviour emphasize the fluidity of human sexual experience. While 60 percent of their nonrandom sample of white males had had some form of same-sex experience prior to adulthood, and approximately 37 percent had had at least one same-sex experience leading to orgasm (including those in adolescence), only 4 percent continued into an exclusively homosexual pattern of sexuality. Kinsey et al. (1953) estimate that approximately 13 percent of women had experienced at least one same-sex experience leading to orgasm. The researchers report that only 2 to 3 percent of women were mostly or exclusively same-sex in their sexuality on a lifelong basis. Bisexuality (having sexual relations with both males and females—positions one through five on the continuum) was much more common than exclusive homosexuality (position six). Six to 14 percent of unmarried women, 2 to 3 percent of married women, and 8 to 10 percent of previously married women were found to have had more than incidental same-sex along with predominantly other-sex sexuality experiences. The comparable statistics for men given by Kinsey et al. were 2 to 6 percent, 1 percent, and 1 to 6 percent, respectively. All of these statistics refer to sexual behaviour only and do not include unacted-upon sexual feelings nor sexuality identity.

The provision of statistics on the incidence of the varied forms of sexual behaviour was only half the message Kinsey et al. sought to convey. In their words:

> The world is not divided into sheep and goats....Only the human mind invents categories and tries to force fit individuals into separated pigeon holes. The living world is a continuum in each and every one of its aspects. The sooner we learn this concerning human sexual behaviour the sooner we will reach a sound understanding of the realities of sex. (Kinsey et al., 1948: 639)

FIGURE 1.1 The Kinsey Continuum of Heterosexuality-Homosexuality

Exclusively heterosexual			Bisexual			Exclusively homosexual
0	1	2	3	4	5	6

0   Exclusively heterosexual

1   Predominantly heterosexual, only incidentally homosexual

2   More heterosexual than homosexual

3   Equally heterosexual and homosexual

4   More homosexual than heterosexual

5   Predominantly homosexual, only incidentally heterosexual

6   Exclusively homosexual

Ellis et al. (1987) investigated sexual orientation by focusing on both sexual fantasies and sexual experiences within a sample of adults. They find that one-third of men and women report that they have fantasized about same-sex sexual encounters on occasion; a further one-third of the men in the sample reported that they have had at least one sexual experience with a same-sex partner (versus one-tenth of the females within this study). This study is useful in that it acknowledges that homosexuality may remain in the realm of fantasy. Fantasies, of course, may or may not be translated into actual sexual behaviour. The nationwide research of Michael et al. (1994: 174–177) on 3432 American adults aged 18 to 59 focuses attention, in part, on three different aspects of homosexuality: sexual attraction to others of the same sex (a desire measure); engaging in same-sex sexual acts (a behavioural measure); and self-identification as being homosexual. "The three categories are distinct...and produce three different estimates of homosexuality....[E]stimates of the prevalence of homosexuality depend very much on what question you ask and what you think it means to be a homosexual" (Michael et al., 1994: 174).

Their research, not unexpectedly, notes that there are more people who find others of the same sex sexually attractive than there are people who actually engage in homosexual acts. Thus, while 5.5 percent of women report that they find the *thought* of a lesbian sexual experience very appealing or appealing, only 4 percent report themselves to be attracted sexually to other women, and less than 2 percent report having had a sexual encounter with another woman in the preceding year (Michael et al., 1994: 174–175). Of their sample, slightly more than 4 percent of their respondents report having had a sexuality experience with another woman at some point in their lives. Such experiences rarely occurred prior to age 18 (Michael et al., 1994: 175,176). Only 1.4 percent of the women in their sample, however, identify themselves as homosexual or bisexual. Among the men, approximately 6 percent indicate being attracted to other men although only 2 percent report having had a sexual experience with another man in the past year. Nine percent of the men had a homosexual encounter at some point in their lives since puberty. Sixty percent of the men who report having had a sexual experience with another man prior to the age of 18, continued to engage in homosexuality during their adult years. Only 2.8 percent of the male sample identify themselves as either homosexual or bisexual (Michael et al., 1994: 176). Generally, men who find same-sex others sexually attractive are more likely than women to act upon their desire and to identify themselves as homosexual.

As we have just seen, heterosexuality, bisexuality, and homosexuality differ from one another in what has been termed as their **sexual orientation**, which can be defined as "the manner in which people experience sexual pleasure or achieve sexual arousal" (Lindsey, 1994: 3). This definition suggests that each sexual orientation reflects a different sexuality script for erotic arousal and genital response with another partner that is likely to produce pleasure and/or self-disclosure. The term **sexual preference** has sometimes been used interchangeably with sexual orientation, but the former is a highly contentious and politically disfavoured term at present, as it implies the existence of choice or voluntary selection. Since the early 1970s, gay and lesbian communities have discerned that the element of choice is an additional liability to themselves within our generally homophobic society.

Canada is not guided by any concept of "different, but equal" when it comes to sexual orientation. Rather, the opposite would seem to pertain. For example, a recent Gallup Poll reports that less than half (49 percent) of Canadians believed that homosexual couples should be entitled to the same benefits (e.g., dental, health, survivor) as heterosexual couples; less than one-third (31 percent) of Canadians feel that gay or lesbian couples should be permitted to adopt children (Schaefer et al., 1996: 254). Heterosexuality is considered to be prescriptively normative and any and all divergence from the heterosexual norm is classified as deviant at best, and threatening to our entire cultural way of life at worst. The widespread existence of **homophobia** (an irrational fear and consequent hatred of homosexuals and homosexuality), surely makes the term "gay" an ironic misnomer in contemporary Canadian society.

Human rights, sometimes referred to as civil rights, are extended essentially in both Canada and the United States as guarantees of equal-rights protection to individuals who could be singled out for prejudicial and discriminatory treatment based solely upon their possession of a quality over which they have no control. Prior to 1986, the Quebec *Charter of Human Rights and Freedoms* established Quebec as the only jurisdiction in Canada to include "sexual orientation" as a prohibited ground of discrimination under statute law (Yogis et al., 1996: 1). Since that time, seven other provinces have enacted comparable legislation. Alberta was forced by the Supreme Court of Canada to include sexual orientation in existing human rights legislation and, at the time of printing, Prince Edward Island was about to revise its legislation.

Although on May 9, 1996, the passage of Bill C-33 by a 153 to 76 free vote in the House of Commons paved the way for the Canadian *Human Rights Act* to include "sexual orientation" as a prohibited ground of discrimination (pending the Bill's approval in the Senate), an amendment to the federal human-rights legislation cannot eradicate stereotypes or militate an end to prejudice. Prior to, and following, the debate in the Canadian House of Commons, various Canadian MPs voiced comments that evidenced misinformation and intolerance towards homosexuals. Reform MP Bob Ringma argued that it was acceptable for businesses to fire gay or black employees or relegate them "to the back of the shop" to placate bigoted customers—a position similarly endorsed by Reform MPs Myron Thompson and Leon Benoit. Reform MP Dave Chatters argued that "it's in the interest of society to have the right to discriminate against" gays and lesbians. Reform MPs maintained that extending rights to gays and lesbians under the *Canadian Charter of Rights and Freedoms* "would encourage a lifestyle that spreads disease." Similarly, 28 Liberals voted against their own party's policy, with Liberal Roseanne Skoke commenting to the press that "[w]e're asking Canadians to condone and accept homosexuality as natural and moral. It's my position that it is unnatural and it is immoral," while Liberal MP Dan McTeague suggested that "Canadians and families in general ought to be very concerned" over the passage of Bill C-33 (*Toronto Star*, 10 May 1996: A1, A14, A26). Bill C-33, the Canadian *Human Rights Act*, received royal assent on 20 June 1996.

Equal rights, in theory and in practice, have been difficult, if not impossible, to attain for homosexuals and bisexuals, when opponents claim that these sexual preferences are simply unacceptable "lifestyle choices" (Davis, 1993; Yogis et al., 1996). Demanding equal rights protection for an orientation over which they claim to have no control (comparable to, for example, age, sex, race, ethnicity, and disability) is believed by members of lesbian and gay communities to stand a better political chance of acceptance (*Newsweek*, 1993).

Heterosexuality, homosexuality, and possibly even bisexuality, are concepts that could be generalized to involve more than just sexual orientations and to include entire subcultural ways of life. Once again, we run into an issue of language where we must also confront the two most-often-used terms of **gay** and **lesbian**, terms which go beyond the sexual. As Thompson notes, "gay implies a social identity and consciousness actively chosen, while homosexual refers to a specific form of sexuality. A person may be homosexual but that does not necessarily imply that he or she would be gay" (Thompson, 1987: xi). You can see that Thompson includes both men and women under his use of the term "gay." Rather than follow Thompson's generic use of the term, we prefer to use both gay and lesbian when focusing beyond the explicitly sexual, and homosexuality, heterosexuality, and bisexuality when limiting ourselves to just the sexual.

The French theoretician Wittig (1992) has claimed that lesbians are not women and, on at least one public occasion, maintained that she did not have a vagina. In doing so, she sought to draw attention to the construction of the category "women" as subordinate to men within our society. Accordingly, her claim that lesbians are not women is intended to indicate the noncompliance of lesbians to norms dictating that "being a woman" entails remaining socially, sexually, economically, and legally subordinate to men. In like fashion, Wittig's assertion that she does not have a vagina is meant to convey her refusal to participate in the dissection of women into body "parts" and, "a refusal to participate in the naming which situate[s] the female body into heterosexuality: vagina, from Latin, means sheath (for the penis)" (Cottingham, 1996: 13).

The Etiology of Sexuality

The social sciences have developed a lengthy (too lengthy to consider here) theoretical and empirical record attempting to discern the nature of the connections between biology, culture and the social environment, and sexuality. In terms of the language we introduced earlier, the basic questions once again seem to be whether sexuality is determined by, arbitrarily related to, or is only influenced by one's biological makeup. Proponents and opponents line themselves up principally along either side of the biology versus social construction fence. Our everyday use of language clearly demonstrates a prevalent belief in a biological cause for human sexual behaviour. For example, in print and in conversations, we see and hear reference to our "sex hormones," our "sex instinct," or our "sex drive." Each phrase contains a double meaning. First, we have the suggestion that sexuality is caused by something originating from within and, therefore, ultimately determined by our bodies. Second, through use of the word "sex" comes a suggestion that the sexuality of women and men is different.

The actual empirical research attempting to isolate a biological-cause basis for sexuality is less than convincing in its findings. For example, science has yet to identify a "homosexuality" gene despite the assertions of some researchers, such as Hamer et al. (1993), who claim to have discovered *statistical* evidence for its existence. In their examination of 40 pairs of gay brothers, Hamer et al. note a significantly higher number (33 out of 40) than expected (20 out of 40) of the pairs shared matching DNA in a region called **Xq28** at the tip of the X chromosome, a chromosome males genetically inherit from their biological mothers. The researchers focused upon this chromosome after noting in previous research that more gay male relatives appear to be found on the mother's side of the family. Hamer and his research team have not actually isolated a specific gene, or even a specific set of genes, that exist within that chromosomal region: they only provided the statistics-based suggestion that such genes must be there. Nor do they specifically account for the homosexuality of those brothers who do not possess the matching DNA. Nor has Hamer et al. examined heterosexual brothers for the existence or nonexistence of matching DNA in the Xq28 region to determine if heterosexual brothers are similar to or different from homosexual brothers (Peele and DeGrandpre, 1995: 64).

Hamer et al.'s findings have come under serious scrutiny in the scientific community and by a government regulatory agency (see Box 1.1). The lack of independent replication of Hamer et al.'s findings and the possibility that the presented data may have been selectively created have raised serious questions about this study's claims of a genetic basis for homosexuality. At the time of printing, no judgments have been made by the Office of Research Integrity as to the validity of Hamer et al.'s research findings. Should any be forthcoming, it is unlikely that the investigators' conclusions will receive the headlines or T-shirts that greeted the original claim. Our culture's apparent hunger for simple genetic solutions for complex issues (surrounding, for example, homosexuality, obesity, eating disorders, alcoholism, or violence) often outweighs our willingness to consider more complex causes (Henry, 1993; Peele and DeGrandpre, 1995). As Minas (1993: 306) has observed, "we only question what we consider deviant."

Just as with homosexuality, researchers have yet to discover, and in the opinion of many are unlikely to ever find, the existence of a heterosexuality, or a bisexuality gene or genes. As Peele and DeGrandpre (1995: 51) note, "the search for single genes for complex human traits, like sexual orientation…is seriously misguided." Furthermore, the evidence regarding any linkage (and the direction of any connection; see Saxton, 1990: 94) among humans

Box 1.1	Second thoughts about "gay genes."

In the summer of 1993, an obscure National Cancer Institute researcher named Dean Hamer reported what he describes as "the first concrete evidence that gay genes really do exist." Overnight, the 45-year-old Harvard PhD was transformed from an expert on the genetics of yeast into a featured guest on *Nightline* and *The MacNeil/Lehrer News Hour*. Within days of Hamer's announcement, T-shirts reading "Thanks for the genes, Mom!" began appearing in gay and lesbian book stores....Nearly two years later, no other laboratory has confirmed Hamer's findings. Now, Hamer and his lawyers are defending his study before the Office of Research Integrity, which is investigating allegations by one of Hamer's collaborators that he selectively reported his data in ways that enhanced the study's conclusions. Hamer did not respond to requests for comment. His accuser, a junior researcher who performed the computerized genetic mapping that is at the heart of Hamer's claimed discovery, also refused to speak about the investigation.

Questions about Hamer's choice of data were first raised in March of last year by the researcher, a 38-year-old post-doctoral fellow in the NCI's Laboratory of Biochemistry, where Hamer is chief of the section on gene structure and regulation. Shortly after voicing her questions, the woman was abruptly ordered to leave the laboratory without even removing her personal effects. It could not be learned who ordered her to leave the lab or the reason for the action.

The woman then took her concerns to higher-ups at the National Institutes of Health, the federal biomedical research complex of which the NCI is a part. NIH officials referred the matter to the Office of Research Integrity, the federal agency charged with investigating possible scientific misconduct. A formal ORI investigation was begun in January after a preliminary inquiry found that the researcher's allegations had sufficient substance to merit a full-scale examination that could include scrutiny by a panel of experts in Hamer's field . ....

It could not be learned exactly what data are alleged to have been omitted from Hamer's article, or how the inclusion of that data might have affected his results. But J. Michael Bailey, a Northwestern University psychologist who has collaborated with Hamer on some aspects of his research, said that, in general, "selective reporting of data is a big problem, if it's selective in order to find the effect."...

Bailey said his skepticism over Hamer's initial findings had lessened following Hamer's announcement, at a scientific meeting in North Dakota in May, that he had reproduced the data in the *Science* article on a different group of gay brothers but with a lower level of statistical significance. "Given Hamer's replication, I'd say his finding is in fairly good shape," Bailey said. But Hamer's new data have not yet been published, and Bailey concedes that "I wish another lab had replicated" the finding.

Only one independent laboratory has reported attempting such a replication and it has found no evidence to support Hamer. "We can't reproduce Hamer's data," said Dr. George Ebers, a neurogeneticist from the University of Western Ontario, who has searched unsuccessfully for a Hamer-style genetic link to homosexuality in more than 50 pairs of gay Canadian brothers.

Hamer had reported in *Science* that the 76 gay men he studied for patterns of inherited homosexuality had significantly more gay cousins and uncles on the mother's side of their families than on the father's side. "He went from this finding that there was a difference on the maternal side," Ebers said, "to the sort of Eureka-like conclusion that this must mean it's on the X chromosome, and set about to prove it and, to his own satisfaction, did."

Ebers said his group found no such disparities in the families of gay Canadian brothers. He suggested that the apparent difference seen by Hamer was attributable to the fact that women know more about their relatives than men do....."Most males are poorer at reporting information about the medical histories of their families. There's a ton of literature on this. If you want to find information about a male's medical history, you're much better off talking to his wife."

Despite fears that Hamer's discovery might lead to genetic screening for homosexuality by employers and to prenatal testing for pregnant women who did not want to bear homosexual children, the notion that there is a genetic component to homosexuality was enthusiastically received by most homosexual organizations.

NIH Director Harold Varmus [noted] that the object of Hamer's research had been the study of whether homosexuals had a genetic susceptibility to Kaposi's sarcoma, a rare form of cancer that afflicts some gay men with AIDS. Only a few of the gay brother pairs studied by Hamer were infected with the AIDS virus however, and Hamer's *Science* article contains no mention of Kaposi's sarcoma, describing the goal of Hamer's research as "to determine whether or not male sexual orientation is genetically influenced."

Richard Lewontin, a professor of zoology and biology at Harvard University, is one of a number of well-known geneticists who predict Hamer's findings on genes and homosexuality will remain unconfirmed. He recalled that the way Hamer presented his research to a Harvard audience suggested to him that Hamer's science was also political: "What he says is, 'I am gay'—he makes no secret about that—'and I believe that it's important to do this research because I want to show that homosexuality is just one of the natural genetic variations, just like blue eyes or hair color.' That was his argument. He had a very explicit social-political agenda, and he didn't make any bones about it."

Source: John Crewdson, "Second thoughts about 'gay genes,'" *Chicago Tribune*. Reprinted in *Edmonton Journal*, 2 July 1995: E7.

between hormones, such as testosterone, and sexuality behaviour is very unclear. Also, even if analogous to hunger or thirst, what actually "drives" the sexual drive has yet to be identified. Most important, any attempts to isolate a biological basis for human sexuality cannot account for the tremendous variations in actual, and in acceptable and unacceptable, sexual behaviour across the cultures of the world, both currently and historically, nor even changes in sexuality behaviour within the same individual over her or his lifetime. It appears that "sexual behaviour is shaped by our social surroundings. We behave the way we do, we even desire what we do, under the strong influence of the particular social groups we belong to" (Michael et al, 1994: 16). Moreover, as Cottingham (1996: 15) has remarked, "the pervasiveness of legal and social customs that are maintained to orchestrate and proliferate cross-gender relationships while prohibiting, punishing and otherwise penalizing" same-sex relationships must be considered significant. She rhetorically asks, "If the heterosexual process is so natural, why is it so coercive?" (1996: 15).

Regardless of the state of empirical research on the etiology of sexuality, there is clear consensus about the existence of our culture's differential valuation of heterosexuality, homosexuality, and bisexuality. Wittig (1992) observes that even when lesbianism and homosexuality may be considered "sexual preferences"—a supposedly "neutral designation"—heterosexuality is regarded as both "natural" and "normal." We must constantly bear this cultural climate in mind as we consider sexual orientation throughout the text. For the moment, our focus here has simply been on clarifying our meaning when we use the terms "sexuality" and "sexual."

In summary, you should now have a basic grasp of our central terms: sex (biologically male or female), gender (culturally feminine or masculine), and sexuality (scripted behaviour designed to produce erotic response, pleasure, and self-disclosure). Of the three, gender will be at the centre of our focus throughout the remainder of this text.

THE POWER OF GENDER

Widely held beliefs about the defining characteristics of masculinity and femininity, known as **gender stereotypes**, exert a very powerful influence within a society such as ours. When translated into expectations for gender-appropriate behaviour, constraints and limitations are placed not only upon the actions of women and men from birth onwards, but also upon our ability to conceive of alternatives to our present-day understandings of both sex and gender. Gender ultimately becomes self-perpetuating in a number of ways that we shall briefly explore.

Gender Stereotypes

Based upon their review of the literature on both gender and ethnicity, Ashmore and Del Boca propose the following simple definition of gender stereotypes: "the structured set of beliefs about the personal attributes of women and men" (1979: 222). In other words, stereotypes contain notions about the qualities possessed by individuals who belong to a specified social category, in this case the gender categories of women and men. Empirical research on what is varyingly referred to as "gender stereotypes," "sex stereotypes," or "sex-role stereotypes" has developed rapidly since the early 1960s. While the methodologies used for gaining access to stereotypes vary somewhat, the sampling techniques used demonstrate a high level of consistency. The vast majority of studies utilize *convenience* samples, that is, groups of potential respondents to whom a researcher has easy and available access. These samples overwhelmingly comprise what researchers ostensibly regard as the human equivalents of laboratory white rats, namely, university and college students. While such samples permit comparability of research findings across studies, their consistent use does raise questions regarding the pervasiveness of the identified stereotypes throughout our culture (Ashmore et al., 1986: 84).

The three major methodologies used to learn respondents' stereotypes involve open-ended questions, rating scales, and adjective checklists. *Open-ended questions* ask subjects to describe, in their own words, the qualities they believe characterize women and men in general. *Rating scales* typically present a list of personality attributes and respondents are asked to indicate, using a five- or seven-point scale ranging from "very much" to "very little," the extent to which they believe this quality is characteristic of men and women. Both of these methods are often used as a preliminary step towards the creation of a more structured adjective list.

As the name implies, the *adjective checklist* presents a preselected list to subjects who are asked to simply indicate if each adjective is more frequently associated with women, or with men, or is neutral and not associated with either gender. Several such checklists are available to researchers and all have the same benefits and drawbacks associated with their use. The greatest benefit is that research findings can be compared across different studies when the same checklist is used. The greatest drawback is that such lists limit the respondents' focus to only certain specified qualities. A checklist will contain words that might not readily come to mind when a respondent is thinking about characteristic gender qualities. While a respondent could always indicate "don't know," the possibility exists that the checklist will promote the creation of a more elaborate stereotype within the mind of a respondent. At the same time, checklists might not contain descriptive characteristics that do come readily to a respondent's mind. In this case, the researcher is denied access to the full content of the respondent's stereotyped picture of one gender or the other. Despite these drawbacks, checklists continue to be the most commonly used method in research to date (Ashmore et al., 1986: 72; Six and Eckes, 1991: 59).

Table 1.1 presents an abbreviated list of characteristics identified by respondents in two of the most well known series of gender stereotype studies. Rosenkrantz and his colleagues (Rosenkrantz et al., 1968; Broverman et al., 1972) developed a pool of stereotype items from an initial open-ended request of subjects to "list behavior, attitudes, and personality characteristics which they considered to differentiate men and women" (Rosenkrantz et al., 1968: 287). From this pool, the researchers eventually created the Sex-Role Stereotype Questionnaire (SRSQ) and were able to identify 41 items on which 75 percent of respondents agreed that the items characterized one gender more than the other. Many of these items are found in Table 1.1.

Williams and Bennett (1975) administered the Gough and Heilbrun Adjective Check List (ACL), containing 300 items, to 100 psychology students (50 men and 50 women) attending a private American university. Adjectives that 75 percent of each set of subjects agreed characteristic of men or of women comprised part of what the authors termed as "focused sex stereotypes," many of which are also contained in Table 1.1. These results were found to be highly consistent with the findings from other studies conducted in the United States during the 1970s. Williams and Best (1982) administered the same checklist between 1975 and 1980 to equal numbers of male and female students in 30 countries, including Canada (at the University of Lethbridge in Alberta and St. Francis Xavier University in Nova Scotia). Their results indicate a high level of similarity among the stereotypes attributed to women and men in most of the countries, with the Canadian results strongly paralleling those obtained for the United States.

More recently, Bergen and Williams (1991) replicated the original study (Williams and Bennett, 1975) by administering the same checklist to a matched sample of students at the same American university. The results obtained are essentially the same, despite the significant changes in women's lives in particular over the intervening years, indicating a high level of persistence of the stereotypical qualities attributed to women and men over the 1970s and the 1980s.

TABLE 1.1	Gender Stereotypes

Men	Women
Active	Affectionate
Adventurous	Appreciates art and literature
Aggressive	Appreciative
Ambitious	Attractive
Boastful	Aware of the feelings of others
Coarse	Charming
Competitive	Complaining
Confident	Dependent
Courageous	Does not use harsh language
Cruel	Dreamy
Daring	Emotional
Disorderly	Excitable
Dominant	Expresses tender feelings easily
Enterprising	Fickle
Feelings not hurt easily	Flirtatious
Forceful	Fussy
Hides Emotions	Gentle
Independent	High-strung
Knows the ways of the world	Interested in own appearance
Likes math and science	Meek
Logical	Mild
Loud	Nagging
Not concerned about appearance	Neat in habits
Not uncomfortable about being aggressive	Prudish
Objective	Quiet
Rational	Religious
Realistic	Sensitive
Self-confident	Sentimental
Stable	Soft-hearted
Steady	Sophisticated
Strong	Strong need for security
Talks freely about sex with men	Submissive
Thinks men are superior to women	Tactful
Tough	Talkative
Unemotional	Weak
Worldly	Whiny

Source: Adapted from Ashmore et al., 1986: 70–71.

DeLisi and Soundranayagam (1990) adopt a method that allows their respondents to indicate the degree to which various traits represent "typical" men and women. While considerable overlap is found, findings suggest that the "core" traits for women reside on a niceness/nurturance dimension. For men, the "core" traits belong to a potency/power dimension. Suggesting an overlapping of traits between men and women, those adjectives that are thought to form the core traits for one gender, are found in the periphery of the other. However, while female respondents augment the female "core" of niceness/nurturance with a second group of adjectives (competent, dependable, intelligent, responsible, capable), male respondents do not. Rather, male respondents select as additional identifiers of the female "core" such adjectives as attractive, good-looking, sexy, and soft (in Lips, 1993: 7). This study not only reminds us that some stereotyped qualities attributed to each gender are considered to be more important than others, but also demonstrates that the meanings of attributed qualities are to be found within larger and different clusters of descriptive terms. For example, the niceness and nurturance qualities of women obviously have different meanings for women than for men.

Ruble (1983), administering a different adjective checklist to a sample of American college students, finds that while the qualities attributed to women and men remain remarkably stable, the *desirability* of those qualities has undergone change. Students still believe that "typical" women and men differ from one another in terms of their identifying qualities, although they do not believe that these qualities are necessarily good or beneficial for either sex. Bear in mind that such studies typically focus upon respondents' perceptions of general beliefs held within their culture about men and women, using instructions such as:

> In participating in this study, you are being asked to serve as an observer and reporter of the characteristics generally said to be associated with men and women in our culture. You are *not* being asked whether you believe that it is true that men and women differ in these ways...(Bergen and Williams, 1991: 417, emphasis in original)

In other words, each respondent reports on the beliefs he or she thinks others hold and not necessarily on his or her own personal beliefs. Similarly, respondents are not asked whether the qualities presented in the checklists are descriptive of themselves. In fact, we know very little about the extent to which respondents' self-concepts reflect the stereotypical qualities they attribute to the perceptions of others.

Such research would be invaluable, since it is assumed that not only are stereotypes **descriptive** of women and men (what they *are*), but they are also **prescriptive** (what they *should be*). Stereotypes provide us with a set of predictive guidelines for what we can and generally should expect from a person who belongs to a given social category. These expectations are necessary, and perhaps even desirable, as aids to enable us to navigate within our social world where it is impossible to take the time required to fully get to know each person we encounter. At the same time, however, such expectations can limit and constrain the behaviour of the other person to conform to our expectations. By setting in motion a **self-fulfilling prophecy** (Merton, 1968: 475–480), stereotypes ultimately deny individuality.

To understand the self-fulfilling prophecy, we begin with the famous theorem created by one of the founders of what came to be known as symbolic interactionism theory, W. I. Thomas: "[i]f men define situations as real, they are real in their consequences" (1928). Thomas, a product of his historical time, uncritically uses the term "men" in the supposedly generic sense of the term. His argument is relatively simple: if people believe something is real and true, regardless of whether this is objectively the case, they will act upon their belief (or definition of the situation) in such a way as to produce real consequences. More specific to our focus here, if people *believe* that men and women possess different qualities, these people will consequently *expect* and even *pressure* men and women to demonstrate those properties. To the extent that men and women conform to these gender expectations, their *behaviour* will then be used as evidence to reinforce and justify the existence of the beliefs in the first place. Thus the prophecy (the belief that genders are different) creates and supports the existence of differences that are emphasized and then used to fulfill and maintain the original prophecy.

Stereotypes, therefore, powerfully constrain gender behaviour by prescriptively limiting how women and men will receive approval for acting in gender-appropriate ways. Departures from stereotyped expectations are judged deviant and labeled as either unmasculine (or effeminate) or unfeminine (or masculine). Notice how our language still preserves the power of the word "masculine" as a standard of judgment and modifies only the word "feminine." We have no word such as "emasculinate," while the word "emasculate" has an entirely different meaning. These negative judgments are intended to both force a modification of the deviant behaviour and to reinforce the stereotyped standards themselves.

Variations in Gender Stereotypes

Adrienne Shadd, a fifth-generation black woman who grew up in Buxton, Ontario, has reflected upon the stereotypical and derogatory images she was exposed to during her childhood. She comments that, in the media, "Africans were portrayed as backward heathens in the Tarzan movies....[and] depicted through the characters of Step 'n Fetchit, Amos 'n Andy, Buckwheat of 'Our Gang' fame, or the many maids who graced the television and movie screens in small bit parts." She remarks, "I used to wonder if it could really be true that black people the world over were so poor, downtrodden, inarticulate, and intellectually inferior, as the depictions seemed to suggest" (in Schaefer et al., 1996: 196). As Higginbotham (1992) remarks about women of colour, "we were never on a pedestal." For Yee (1993: 15), who immigrated to Toronto from Hong Kong at age two, the Western stereotype of Asian women as "both passive/submissive 'china dolls' and 'dragon ladies' who use their 'exotic' sexuality to manipulate" did not even hint at the strength of Asian women, "the carriers of incredible burdens of family and work, and age-old traditions."

As we have seen, the commonly used method for conducting research on gender stereotypes asks respondents to mentally construct a "typical" man or woman and identify the traits that are thought to characterize them. This universal man or woman is, according to Lips (1993: 14) "someone who is relatively young, white, able-bodied, neither too fat nor too thin, neither too short nor too tall, and of average physical attractiveness." However, as Razack (1993: 39–40) argues,

> if you isolate gender from race and class (among other things)...you will miss some very important insights into how gender is constructed in specific context....[O]ne can afford to have no clear sense of one's racial or class identity only when those identities never pose a problem, that is to say when one lives close to centre. White, middle-class, heterosexual, non-disabled women can be "simply women," in the same way that white, middle-class, heterosexual, non-disabled men can be simply "human beings."

Inasmuch as "gender is clearly not one identity but a set of relations" (Razack, 1993: 47), it becomes essential to explore the "double" or "multiple jeopardies" created when stereotypes about men and women are enmeshed with stereotypes of race, social class, disability, sexual orientation, age, and attractiveness. Unfortunately, research on multifaceted stereotypes is virtually nonexistent.

Stereotypes must be recognized as consequential, especially for those who must confront their subordinate status twice or more defined. For example, an extreme, but telling, illustration of the "double jeopardy" faced by First Nations women in Canada was provided with the 1971 murder of a 19-year-old Cree high-school student, Helen Betty Osborne (Priest, 1990). Osborne was abducted by four young white men, from the main street of The Pas, Manitoba, in a practice known as "squaw-hopping," driven to a remote area, stabbed more than 50 times with a screwdriver when she resisted being raped, and left to bleed to death. For more than 16 years, no charges were laid, although "it was felt that perhaps the majority of people in the town knew about the youths' involvement in the murder" (Griffiths and Yerbury, 1995: 394). Elliott and Fleras (1992: 117) observe that "[i]n the community at the time of the crime, it was an acknowledged practice for white men to harass and sexually assault native women. By applying this derogatory label [squaw-hopping] to the behaviour, the men distanced themselves from its immoral and criminal nature. In effect, they were not with women but with 'squaws.'"

It has been argued that the stereotypes constructed by respondents utilizing adjective checklists may be implicitly racist and based upon the construct of a ideal-typical white, middle-class woman. To test this suggestion, Landrine (1985) asked her sample of undergraduate students to describe four "types" of women—a black middle-class woman, a white middle-class woman, a black lower-class woman, and a white lower-class woman—drawing upon a list of 23 adjectives. She reports that while all four subtypes were described in ways consistent with the stereotype of "femininity," white women and middle-class women were most likely to be defined in stereotypical "feminine" ways. For example, white women are more likely than black women to be described as dependent, emotional, status conscious, passive, and concerned about their appearance. Since the cues provided by physical appearance have an impact upon our evaluations of a person's likely traits, occupation, or role behaviours (Deaux and Lewis, 1983), we might expect stereotypes of race to modify stereotypes of gender. You might wish to return to Table 1.1 and reflect upon the extent to which the stereotyped attributes reported by respondents may be "racially" or ethnically biased.

It may or may not be true that "blondes have more fun"; however, physical appearance is undoubtedly not only a critical aspect of stereotyping, particularly for and about women (Rodin et al., 1985), but also the basis for a self-fulfilling prophecy. If our referent for "femininity" is based on the prototype white middle-class woman, it is evident that women of colour, women with disabilities, or women who occupy an other-than-middle-class socioeconomic status, will be seen as flawed, inadequate, or less than truly "feminine." As Wolf (1991:264) observes, in our society, nonwhite "racial" features have been portrayed as "deformities" to be cosmetically altered in the quest for prototypical feminine beauty.

Research has noted that the stereotypes held of black American females and males in relation to expressiveness and competence are more similar to each other than are the stereotypes of white American males and females (Smith and Midlarsky, 1985). In comparison with white men, black men are more likely to be described as emotionally expressive and less likely to be viewed as competitive, independent, or status conscious (Basow, 1992: 4). While less research has been conducted on the gender stereotypes of other racial or ethnic groups, the stereotypes of the "JAP" or "Jewish American Princess" (Beck, 1992; Schneider, 1986), the "ultrafeminine" Hispanic or South Asian woman (Vazquez-Nuttall, Romero-Garcia and DeLeon, 1987), and the "macho" Hispanic man (Garcia, 1991) are all, unfortunately, too well known.

Gender stereotypes may, of course, also be influenced by variables other than that of race. Baldus and Tribe (1995) observe that by the time Canadian school children reach grade six, the majority have "learned to recognize and classify people and their environment in a context of social inequality." The content of this learning, they suggest, entails cognitive and affective predispositions that lead them to anticipate that lower-class individuals are more likely to possess unlovely and unloveable qualities than those persons of a higher social status. Landrine (1985) notes that among her sample of middle-class university students, lower-class women were more likely than middle-class women to be seen as "confused, dirty, hostile, illogical, impulsive, incoherent, inconsiderate, irresponsible, and superstitious" (in Lips, 1993: 18). Similarly, working-class males have been stereotyped as chauvinistic, inarticulate, aggressive, and defiant (see Basow, 1992).

Snyder and Uranowitz (1992) examine the impact of sexual orientation upon students' evaluations of a hypothetical female. In their study, student respondents were asked to read a biography of a fictitious woman named "Betty K." The researchers were careful to construct the story of her life so that it could accommodate the stereotyped images of both heterosexual and lesbian women. Thus, Betty had never had a steady boyfriend in high school, but did date, and while she acquired a steady boyfriend in college, it was emphasized that he was more a "close friend" than anything else. A week after distributing this biography to their student participants, Snyder and Uranowitz added an additional detail; some students were informed that Betty was involved in a lesbian relationship, while others were informed that Betty was living with her husband. They then asked students a series of questions about Betty's life.

Students' responses revealed that they had retrospectively appropriated the "facts" of Betty's life to "fit" with her identification as, variously, lesbian or heterosexual.

> Those who believed that Betty was a lesbian remembered that Betty had never had a steady boyfriend in high school, but tended to neglect the fact that she had gone out on many dates in college....The students showed not only selective memories but also a striking facility for interpreting what they remembered in ways that added fresh support for their stereotypes. One student who accurately remembered that a supposedly lesbian Betty never had a steady boyfriend in high school confidently pointed to the fact as an early lack of romantic or sexual interest in men....Clearly, the students had allowed their perceptions about lesbians and heterosexuals to dictate the way in which they interpreted and reinterpreted the facts of Betty's life. (in Snyder, 1982/1992: 328–329)

Storms et al. (1981) suggest the subtle ways in which stereotypes may operate. In their study, subjects were given written and tape-recorded descriptions of the following "types" of women: a "feminine" woman (described as emotional, warm towards others, kind, and feminine) or a "masculine" woman (described as someone who felt superior, and who was active, competent, and masculine). The descriptions of both types of woman varied whether her sexual orientation was lesbian or heterosexual. Subsequently, respondents rated their perceptions of the woman so described. The woman who was described as being lesbian was rated as more "masculine" than the heterosexual woman, even though the rest of the descriptions of the two "types" of women were identical. Moreover, the woman who was described as feminine and homosexual was perceived as having a confused, unstable sexual identity. Even when lesbians do not possess these stereotypical characteristics, Storms et al.'s study would suggest that, nevertheless, deviance is imputed to their behaviour and personality characteristics. The study also suggests that sexual orientation overrides gender in the construction of stereotypes. As we shall see later, an important issue yet to be resolved is whether gender is always, most times, or only some times the most important attribute a person possesses in our society. Expanding our research to examine the intersection of multiple stereotypes will help us to clarify this issue.

CONSTRAINTS AND LIMITATIONS OF GENDER UPON SEX

The power of gender stereotypes is illustrated even more forcefully regarding the phenomenon of sex (re)assignment and transsexualism, where gender expectations and beliefs ultimately shape biological sex. For reasons to be identified in a moment, a number of infants and children involuntarily undergo some changes in their biological sex. Other persons, usually adults, voluntary choose to alter various aspects of their biological sex. All such transformations of biological sex are generically referred to as **sex (re)assignment**. However, in the case of those voluntarily seeking medical intervention, the tendency within the literature is to treat this as a separate case and to use the term **transsexualism**. Regardless of the degree of voluntary or involuntary choice involved, we have the opportunity in both situations to observe the power of gender beliefs in constraining and limiting the available options.

Sex (Re)assignment

Two different conditions occasion sex (re)assignment. In the first instance, infants born with ambiguous (or not clearly male nor female) genital configurations (estimated to be 2 to 3 percent of all infants; Abu-Laban et al., 1994: 231) are assigned to one sex or the other, based upon the decisions of an attending medical team. These decisions usually result in surgical alteration of the child's genitals. In the very rare second instance, infants or children initially assigned to one sex must, due to accidents or other events surrounding the conditions of their birth, be (re)assigned to the other sex. Once again, further alterations to their biological sex are required.

The biological condition of children born with ambiguous genitalia has been referred to traditionally as **hermaphroditism** or, more recently, **intersex** (Kessler, 1990/1995; Money, 1988: 28). True hermaphroditism, or a true intersexed condition, is statistically very rare and occurs when an infant is born with both ovarian and testicular tissues and a genital structure that is unclear upon simple observation by the attending medical team. What is observable looks like either a diminutive penis (sometimes referred to as a micropenis) or an enlarged clitoris. The urethral opening is often found somewhere along the shaft of the penis/clitoris. In addition, either the scrotum has not fully closed or the vagina has not fully opened. The more frequently occurring cases, involving ambiguous genitalia along with the presence of either two ovaries or two testes, are referred to, respectively, as female **pseudohermaphroditism** and **male pseudohermaphroditism**. Regardless of the preferred terminology, and regardless of the causes, being born with ambiguous genitalia is rarely, in itself, harmful to a person's physical health. As we saw earlier with regard to *nadles*, some societies have accepted persons with ambiguous genitalia as integral members of their communities.

Within our own society, persons now born with ambiguous genitalia are considered to possess a problematic condition which can, and should, be "remedied" medically. The available evidence (e.g., Kessler, 1990/1995) indicates that several factors beside biological ones assist physicians in determining, assigning, and announcing the sex of an infant including "ultimately...cultural understandings of gender" (Kessler, 1990/1995: 8). The most important of these understandings is the belief that only two genders and two biological sexes exist and should be allowed to exist; "physicians hold an incorrigible belief in and insistence upon female and male as the only 'natural' options" (Kessler, 1990/1995: 8).

Attitudes towards the intersexed condition have been shaped by three developments (Kessler, 1990/1995: 9). First, we now possess, and continue to rapidly develop, medical technologies that can alter genital anatomy and reproductive systems, along with hormonal balances and their influences upon body tissues. Female genitalia (labia and vaginal opening) and male genitalia (penis, scrotum, and testes) can now be constructed that are both functional, to varying degrees, and authentic in appearance.

Second, the feminist movement has been instrumental in challenging traditional gender beliefs that defined women solely in terms of their reproductive ability and their possession of an apparently functional pair of ovaries. Based upon those beliefs, newborns with ambiguous genitalia and a pair of ovaries were automatically assigned female status, with attempts made to reconstruct "her" genitals into the appropriate form. The current basis for gender (re)assignment has been expanded and other criteria have come into existence, as we shall soon see.

Third, a number of social-psychological theories stress the important role of a child's gender identity for subsequent gender behaviour. These theories, based upon examination of children who presumably did not possess ambiguous genitalia, claim that gender identity develops in some form by approximately 18 months of age. Since gender identity is assumed to be based partly upon one's genital configuration, the existence of these theories increases pressure upon attending physicians to establish unambiguous genitalia, contributing to "healthy" gender identities, as soon as possible after birth.

Medical decisions regarding the management of intersexed conditions appear to be based overwhelmingly upon the model created by Money and Ehrhardt (1972), who propose that gender identity is changeable until approximately 18 months of age (Kessler, 1990/1995: 9–10). This proposal contributes to the urgency to "resolve" the intersex "problem." It is also believed that parents need and want a child with an obvious genital configuration. A lack of ambiguity will help parents begin appropriate gender socialization and will influence interactions of all kinds between parents and the child. Parents' assumed gender beliefs, therefore, indirectly become an important part of the physician's decision-making processes.

These decisions are made as quickly as possible after an infant's birth. If the decision is made to assign an infant to the male sex, penis repair is undertaken within the first year. In the case of a female-sex decision, vulva repair, including surgical reduction of the clitoris, is begun within three months after birth. Further surgery, if necessary, is performed during early childhood, followed by hormone therapy, particularly around puberty (and for life in some cases). Parents are counseled on what has happened and will happen. Eventually, the children or adolescents themselves are counseled with either full or partial explanations for what has already occurred and what will eventually occur (Kessler, 1990/1995: 10–11, 15–17).

What are the medical decisions based upon? While tests are frequently conducted to determine the infant's chromosomal sex, the results do not appear to play a decisive role in the ultimate genital sex assignment. Rather, the size and functionality of the real or potential penis appears to be the deciding factor now.

> Money's case management philosophy assumes that while it may be difficult for an adult male to have a much smaller than average penis, it is very detrimental to the morale of the young boy to have a micropenis. In the former case the male's manliness might be at stake, but in the latter case his essential maleness might be. Although the psychological consequences of these experiences have not been empirically documented, Money and his colleagues suggest that it is wise to avoid the problems of both the micropenis in childhood and the still undersized penis postpuberty by reassigning many of these infants to the female gender....This approach suggests that for Money and his colleagues, chromosomes are less relevant in determining gender than...the aesthetic of having an appropriately sized penis. (Kessler, 1990/1995: 13)

Existing gender stereotypes about the importance of penis size for masculine identity and behaviour clearly form an important part of the medical decision-making process.

The criterion for sex assignment has shifted from one where ovaries equals female to one where penis equals male. Should the ambiguous genitalia not seem to have the potential to allow for creation of a sufficiently large penis, the infant will be surgically transformed into a genital female. As Money (1988: 41) notes, "[s]urgically it is technically more feasible to demasculinize and feminize the external genitalia than it is to defeminize and masculinize them." Kessler (1990/1995: 16) notes that doctors claim to "reconstruct," not construct, the genitals of intersexed infants. They perceive their actions as being objective and involving only the surgical alteration of genitals to conform more accurately to what was already there. In this way, they maintain their illusion that subjective beliefs surrounding gender do not play a role in the decision-making process.

The assumption that surgical intervention is necessary reflects cultural beliefs about the dichotomous nature of sex. Ambiguous genitals are perceived to be unnatural, and surgical alteration is believed necessary to create genitals that conform to either a male or female state. Despite doctor's denials, the direction of their alterations reflect cultural beliefs about gender. In addition,

> an emphasis on the good phallus above all else could only have emerged in a culture that has rigid aesthetic and performance criteria for what constitutes maleness. The formulation [is] "good penis equals male; absence of good penis equals female."...There is a striking lack of attention to the size and shape requirements of the female genitals, other than that the vagina be able to receive a penis. (Kessler, 1990/1995: 19)

These cultural beliefs inform decisions regarding biological sex (re)assignment and ultimately reinforce the power of our beliefs about gender by removing ambiguities that could complicate the belief system.

Mackie (1987: 22–23) notes the importance of gender beliefs in the 1984 case of doctors at a Toronto hospital who had to decide the consequences of surgically separating genetically male conjoined twins, who shared a common penis. In this case, the more aggressive and physically active twin was "awarded" the penis, while the other twin, who now did not possess a penis, was surgically fitted with an artificial vagina and raised as a female. Both decisions reflect dominant beliefs about gender. Masculinity is associated with activity, aggression, and possession of a penis. Femininity, at its base, is associated with the lack of a penis.

A somewhat similar case is reported by Money and his associates (Money and Tucker, 1975: 91–92; Money and Ehrhardt, 1972). During the routine circumcision of seven-month-old identical genetically male twins, an accident with the electric cauterizing machine almost completely burned off the penis of one of the boys. The damage was so severe that no attempt could be made to construct a penis from the remaining tissue. However, an artificial vagina could be created and inserted in place of a penis. After consultation with physicians, the parents agreed to have this boy's sex reassigned. Female external genitals were surgically constructed when the "girl" was 17 months of age. The child's hairstyle, clothing styles, and name were all feminized and a lifelong regimen of hormone therapy was planned. The parents were then coached on how to raise their twins, one as a boy and the other as a girl. The preliminary follow-up report compiled by Money and Ehrhardt (1972: 119) from self-reports provided by the mother when the children were approximately six years old, indicates that her "daughter" preferred and took pride in her feminine clothing, played a small part in housekeeping chores (while her son did not), was neat and tidy (in contrast to her brother), and preferred feminine toys and play activities. These preferences and activities were all taken as indicators of successful conformity to a feminine gender and of the power of gender to override biological sex.

A later study by a psychiatrist of the reassigned twin at age 13 (Diamond, 1982), cast some doubt on the success of the transformation. Diamond suggests that the twin, who had not yet been informed about her circumcision accident, was experiencing emotional problems associated with teasing from her peers over her somewhat "masculine" appearance. More recently, Unger and Crawford (1992) report that the reassigned twin has chosen to be re-reassigned, to have an artificial penis constructed, and to live as a man rather than as a woman. Questions about optimal conditions in the social environment required for successful (re)assignment obviously still need to be raised and answered.

Transsexualism

The most recent change requested by the reassigned twin reported above is similar to that made by the majority of individuals who chose to undergo a transsexual (literally meaning to cross over from one sex to another—although, technically, the proper term should be "transsex") transformation, or what is more commonly referred to as a "sex change." Transsexuals are individuals who initially have been assigned to one biological-sex status, possess unambiguous genitalia, and have received a socialization experience consistent with their sex assignment. At some point in their adult lifetime, they choose to be surgically transformed to become as much a member of the other biological sex as possible. Both prior to and accompanying the various required medical procedures, transsexuals also engage in a self-socialization process consistent with their new sex status.

Transsexuals claim that they have always felt strongly that their gender identity was at odds with their sex assignment and subsequent socialization (a condition referred to in the clinical literature as **gender dysphoria**). In other words, they believe they are either a woman trapped in a man's body, or a man trapped in a woman's body. If individuals may have felt themselves to be "trapped in the wrong body" historically, it is only within the last 50 years that medical technology has provided individuals with a medical "solution" to such feelings of discomfort and unease (Benjamin, 1966; Green, 1969). The solution the medical establishment has provided for this conundrum (the title of the autobiography by trans-sexual, Jan Morris, 1974) is to surgically adjust their bodies to fit their identities. In our gender-dichotomous society, it seems to make perfect sense that if one cannot change one's mind to fit one's body, one changes one's body to fit one's mind (Raymond, 1982). The surgery, along with attendant hormonal treatments, will, at least in theory, release the previously hidden inner "person," and allow him or her to present themselves to others in a consistent and integrated manner.

> The transexual [*sic*] applicant has two dogmatic fixations. One is to forfeit those parts and functions of the body that are the somatic insignia of the sex of birth. The other is to simulate the other sex and to pass as a member of that sex, naked and clothed. (Money, 1988: 88)

Individuals who contact the Clarke Institute of Psychiatry in Toronto, or equivalent facilities elsewhere, and apply for a sex change operation must, usually, first undertake a real-life test period of approximately two years (the length varies somewhat from clinic to clinic) before a decision is made about whether they will be permitted to undergo surgery. Transsexual surgery is not "elective surgery" per se. Unlike those who would decide to undergo rhinoplasty (to surgically alter the shape or contours of one's nose), or breast augmentation, the would-be transsexual cannot be assured that their possession of sufficient money or medical coverage will entitle them to the procedure. Rather, the person must demonstrate to the satisfaction of the medical community that he or she is, indeed, someone who suffers from, or is afflicted with, the preoperative condition of gender dysphoria. Through the administration of psychological tests, it is assumed by medical experts that they will be able to distinguish true gender dysphorics from false claimants, such as masochists (who desire the pain incurred by major surgery), or others who might suffer delusions about changing sex as a byproduct as being in a psychotic state such as schizophrenia. However, the tests themselves may simply measure a would-be transsexual's willingness to abide by gender-role stereotypes.

The California Sex Role Inventory is one of many psychological tests that purport to measure masculinity and femininity. Within this test, a series of statements are given, to which the respondent is to answer "true" or "false" in relation to their own beliefs. Statements such as: "I am somewhat afraid of the dark," "I would find the work of a librarian enjoyable," "I am afraid of snakes" are believed to indicate femininity. Questions such as "I could do a better job than most of the politicians in office today," or "I want to be an important person in the community," supposedly indicate masculinity. Should the male-to-constructed-female applicant answer "true" to the questions which purportedly measure "femininity" and "false" to questions which supposedly measure "masculinity," their chances of qualifying as a gender dysphoric are heightened. Ironically, applicants whose answers demonstrate gender rigidity and a reluctance to trespass on conventional boundaries of masculinity and femininity fare better on such tests than those whose answers indicate an acceptance of androgynous or undifferentiated gender. Indeed, Kando's research on male-to-constructed-female transsexuals finds that, in many ways, those selected for transsexual surgery are more stereotypically "feminine" than most females.

> Elizabeth: "I feel that everything should be distinctly masculine or feminine. My boyfriend has to look like a real man."

Elinor: "The ultimate criterion of being a woman is being a good wife, being able to make a
man happy."

Maryjo: "I feel that a man should make more than a woman." (in Raymond, 1982: 24–26)

Research suggests that transsexuals are reactionary individuals, despite their seeming non-
conformity. As a group, they maintain highly conventional notions as to gender-appropriate
and inappropriate behaviour, and define their being "trapped in the wrong body" in ways that
reiterate stereotypic notions of males and females. The following comments of a male-to-constructed-female transsexual (M-F TS) and a female-to-constructed-male (F-M TS) are illustrative:

M-F TS: I used to like to play with girls. I never did like to play with boys. I wanted to play
jacks. I wanted to jump rope and all those things. The lady in the schoolyard used to always
tell me to go play with the boys. I found it distasteful. I wanted to play with the girls. I wanted
to play the girl games....

F-M TS: I have wanted to be a boy ever since I can remember, but there are no logical reasons
for what I feel inside....Part of the time it used to be if you were a boy you could do more
things. It was just sort of the way I felt. I used to like playing football. I didn't like being a girl
and doing things girls do, and lately, it's gotten more so. I feel very awkward being dressed
up and going places as a girl....[My family] always considered me a tomboy. My mother
used to always try to get me to play with dolls and everything, and I wouldn't do it. I played
cowboys and Indians with the boys, climbed trees and rode horses, went hunting and fishing
with my brothers. I was always out wrestling with the boys. (Green, 1992: 100–102)

During the qualifying period, candidates for transsexual surgery are also required to hormonally and socially experience themselves as, and behave with comfort in ways deemed consistent with, their desired other gender. The "real-life test," as it is termed, is premised on the
understanding that the most reversible forms of changing one's gender should precede the
most irreversible (Green, 1992: 104). The mandates of the real-life test require that, for example, the would-be male-to-constructed-female transsexual demonstrate their facility and
ease in adopting "female-appropriate" patterns of dress (including the use of the "tuck," or
the folding of the penis back between one's legs and eliminating any tell-tale bulge by wearing tight undergarments), deportment, employment, and sexual role (including, the "passive" position within acts of sexual intercourse). Candidacy for surgery will be evaluated as
favourable or unfavourable depending upon their ability to negotiate their way over these gender hurdles.

The first medical intervention involves hormonal treatments which yield relatively consistent effects (Money, 1988: 57–58, 89–90). A female-to-male transsexual is treated with
testosterone, which promotes the growth of facial and body hair, enlargement of the Adam's
apple (with attendant lengthening of the vocal cords and subsequent deepening of the voice),
lessening of subcutaneous body fat (making the body appear more angular), increasing
muscle mass, some shrinkage of the breasts, eventual dormancy of the ovaries and cessation
of menstruation (so long as the dosage of testosterone is maintained, and unless a hysterectomy and ovariectomy are not performed later), and some enlargement of the clitoris.
If the hormonal treatments are begun following puberty, as is almost always the case, no alterations will occur to the person's bone structure.

Male-to-female transsexuals are treated with estrogen which has the eventual effect of promoting breast growth (within the limitations of available glandular tissue), decreasing muscle mass, increasing subcutaneous body fat (thus adding to a "softer" or more "rounded" appearance), retarding but not stopping the growth of body and facial hair (complete removal must be accomplished with electrolysis), as well as causing shrinkage and dormancy of the testicles, shrinkage of the penis with subsequent loss of erectile capacity, and shrinkage of the prostate and seminal vesicles (with subsequent loss of the ability to ejaculate). Once again, if the treatment occurs after puberty, bone structure will not change. In addition, voice register and tone will not be affected by hormonal treatments following puberty, thus accounting for the tendency of male-to-female transsexuals to retain a lower register voice. Any further modifications to one's voice must be accomplished through self-conscious and willful efforts.

While the transsexual applicant learns to live with the effects of the hormone treatments, deciding if these bodily changes are comfortable and consistent with expectations, behavioural changes must either begin or continue. In essence, each transsexual must learn how to conceal who they once were, biologically and via socialization, and how to reveal who they wish to be acknowledged as, by themselves and others. As we mentioned earlier, this necessitates learning how to present themselves in public as a person of the other gender. A number of authors (e.g., Garfinkel, 1967; Mackie, 1991: 14; Richardson, 1988: 14) note that transsexuals tend to "go overboard" in their portrayal of an other-gendered person, in such things as clothing, cosmetics, and body gestures. While exchanging one sex's body for another, they also exchange one gender's stereotypes for another. In many ways, they effect a caricature of the other gender's behaviour, while simultaneously reaffirming the validity of existing stereotypes (a subject to which we shall return shortly).

If, at the end of the waiting period, the applicant still wishes to continue and the medical team at the sex (re)assignment clinic agree, the final, and usually irrevocable, surgical step will be undertaken. Up to this point, the changes instigated by hormones can be reversed with the cessation of treatment, and the behavioural changes can be unlearned. The surgical changes usually cannot be reversed. Male-to-female transformation is a relatively quick one- or two-stage process, while female-to-male involves a lengthier multistage series of procedures (Money, 1988: 90–91).

To surgically construct a female, the spongy tissue within the penis is removed and the remaining skin of the empty penis is turned outside in, "like the inverted finger of a glove" (Money, 1988: 90), to provide the lining for the new vaginal cavity. If, in the opinion of the surgeons, insufficient skin exists to create a satisfactory vagina, a skin graft from the thigh will be used to lengthen the cavity. The testicles will be removed and skin from the scrotum will be used to fashion the appearance of labia majora, although labia minora will not be created. Due to the contraction of perineum muscles surrounding the newly formed vagina, a dilator or "spacer" will have to be used constantly should the transsexual wish to experience vaginal penetration during sexual relations. If desired, implants will be inserted to enlarge the breasts (no data have been provided to date regarding the number of male-to-female transsexuals who sought financial compensation in conjunction with the silicone-breast-implant legal actions of the mid-1990s).

For a female-to-male transformation, breast flattening is accomplished with mastectomies. Hysterectomy and ovariectomy accomplish a complete cessation of menstruation, or the person may wish to use hormone treatments continuously until menopause. The "inverted finger" of a vaginal glove cannot be turned inside out. Therefore, the vagina is removed and skin-grafting is used to fashion a penis that is usually "numb and without tactual, painful, or erotic sensory feeling" (Money, 1988: 91). The resultant penis is flabby and, without the insertion of a hydraulic device, is incapable of erection. It is not possible, at present, to transplant erectile spongy tissue from another penis into the constructed penis of a transsexual. The urethral canal is typically left intact with an opening at the base of the new penis— meaning that use of a urinal in the men's washroom is not among the newly available options. The intact clitoris is typically not removed and will also remain at the base of the penis, thus providing for the possibility of orgasm. The labia majora can be used to fashion a scrotum and simulated testes can be implanted within. Ejaculation will be impossible unless a hydraulic device, filled with replenishable fluid and complete with a push-button attached to either the groin or the scrotum, is also implanted in the penis.

As you have just seen, the surgical procedures required for transsexualism involve the mutilation, removal, and eventual destruction of healthy body tissues for social, psychological, and cosmetic reasons (Eichler, 1980/1995: 30; Richardson, 1988: 13). The surgery is "expensive, time-consuming, arduous, and *painful*" (Richardson, 1988: 12; emphasis in original). Undergoing a transsexual transformation requires a high level of commitment and very strong beliefs that no other alternative will resolve the personal conundrum of being trapped in the wrong-sexed body.

While researchers have sought explanations for this phenomenon in hormonal imbalances and dysfunctional parenting patterns, the most compelling explanation appears to lie within our culture's rigid system of dichotomous gender stereotypes. Transsexual applicants and the team of clinicians and physicians who approve the applications and perform the surgery all endorse a belief that the dichotomy must be upheld and ambiguity must not be tolerated. As Eichler notes,

> were the notions of masculinity and femininity less rigid, sex change operations should be unnecessary. Rather than identify somebody with a "gender identity problem" as sick, we could define a society which insists on raising boys and girls in a clearly differentiated manner as sick. What should be treated as a *social* pathology is treated as if it were normal and when it manifests its effect in individuals it is treated as an *individual* pathology, and is "corrected," rather than any attempts being made to combat the issue at its root: the oppressive (non-human) definition of sex roles, and the lack of recognition of intermediate sexes in Western society. (1980/1995: 31; emphasis in original)

The vast majority of transsexualism involves male-to-female, rather than female-to-male, transformations. In addition to noting some contributing factors, such as less financial cost and surgical complexity, as well as a lack of social-movement alternatives for men (i.e., a comparative lack of available men's groups to support a man seeking an expanded range of gender behaviour), Richardson suggests that the "greater sex role rigidity...expected of men in this society" accounts for the greater preponderance of male-to-female sex changes (1988: 14). If men cannot live up to the narrow range of gender stereotypes expected of them, a sense of failure becomes a major motivating factor in their search for alternatives. Within a dichotomous gender system, if one believes that one's behaviours and feelings "naturally belong" to the other gender, and that sex and gender must be consistent, the only perceived alternative is to change one's hormonal and genital sex, and adopt even more of the behaviours attributed to the other (now one's hoped-for) gender.

The participants involved in transsexual transformations clearly hold rigid and highly stereotypical views of gender-appropriate behaviour. (The same views have also been noted among transvestophiles who engage in cross-dressing [Money, 1988: 95], but apparently are not held by most contemporary butch/femme lesbians [Faderman, 1992/1995], nor gay males into "camp" [see Blachford, 1981/1995]). Rather than explore the possibilities of expanding social expectations for gender behaviour, transsexual applicants and their clinicians and surgeons all conclude that it is not only necessary, but also right and proper to change individual bodies rather than social beliefs. As we have already mentioned, they consequently endorse and reinforce those beliefs by treating transsexualism as a medical, rather than as a social, issue. As the general population becomes aware of the phenomenon of transsexualism (primarily, unfortunately, from television talk shows), even if it does not affect them directly, their beliefs in the link between sex and gender, and in narrow guidelines for gender-appropriate behaviour are also reinforced. While initially appearing to be highly deviant, transsexuals and their support team ultimately demonstrate themselves to be highly conformist. Once again, we witness the power of gender within our culture.

The construction of a condition referred to as **childhood transsexualism** also demonstrates the continuing tenacity of gender stereotypes in the 1990s. The most recent edition of the *Diagnostic and Statistical Manual* (DSM-IV), the penultimate source for all identifications and classifications of psychological disorders published by the American Psychiatric Association, includes childhood transsexualism, also termed the "sissy boy syndrome" (Green, 1987). The inclusion of this diagnostic category would seem to legitimate the anxiety of those parents who hold rigid expectations of how young boys should, or ought to, act. Although some parents may also be alarmed at young girls who evidence "tomboyism" and veer from the path of stereotypical feminine behaviour, an interesting thing happened in the construction of childhood transsexualism within the DSM-IV. Feminists were aghast at the possibility that young girls who evidenced nontraditional behaviour would be labeled as pathological for doing so. Their opposition proved effective and the American Psychiatric Association amended their original plan to include both tomboy and sissy behaviour as evidence of childhood gender dysphoria. Unfortunately, nobody seemed sufficiently concerned about medicalizing deviation from the "snakes and snails" stereotype of what little boys are made of to prevent "sissy" boys from being diagnosed as suffering from a mental disorder (see Caputi and MacKenzie, 1992: 77).

The Tyranny of Gender

Our focus in this section is primarily upon a variety of ways in which the gender of researchers and their subjects, and certain aspects of gender beliefs, contaminate the research process itself and the products of that research. As we shall soon see, the male-created and male-dominated social sciences tended, historically, to be unaware of the ways in which gender influenced both the development of research and theory and the conclusions reached and disseminated, particularly with regard to women. We shall also explore some related issues along the way.

Gender was, at first, seemingly invisible and its influence was largely ignored. However, as we become more aware of the impact of gender in areas previously thought to be untouched by its influence, we now must recognize a relatively new danger of attributing gender as a central causal factor in areas of social behaviour where it is only a minor factor. Whether invisible or all too visible, finding a balanced perspective continues to be a major challenge.

Sexism in Science

Sexism refers to singling out a person or group for either preferential or detrimental treatment, based solely upon their possession of a specific characteristic, in this case their biological sex. Although recognized earlier (Oakley, 1974: 1–29), Eichler (1984) was among the first sociologists in Canada to write specifically on a variety of ways in which sex, gender, and our beliefs about sex and gender produce a sexist outcome in the scientific enterprise. According to Eichler (1984: 20), sexism can influence the research process in any one of at least five ways through the use of (i) sexist language, (ii) sexist concepts, (iii) an androcentric perspective, (iv) sexist methodology, and (v) sexist interpretations of results produced by that methodology.

We have already seen some examples of how the English language constrains our imaginations when we attempt to conceptualize alternatives to our dual-sex, dual-gender system. Eichler claims that both English and French are "profoundly sexist languages" (Eichler, 1984: 21) and their uncritical use will continue to lead us into making, and accepting, sexist statements that are misleading. One long standing problem involves the use of male terms such as *man, he,* and *his* to supposedly and generically refer to humanity in general. Their use represents an archaic stylistic linguistic device, which is often contradictory and confusing. The reader is left to ponder whether the referent is indeed all of humanity or solely men, and whether the penned, or keyboarded, theory includes—or ignores—women.

Throughout this text, and particularly in Chapter 5, we will examine how our language directs our attention in some directions, while simultaneously making us blind to other possibilities. We will also keep drawing your attention to sexist, or possibly sexist, phrases within quotations used through the text. Sometimes we will focus explicitly upon the implications of a particular word or phrase, and other times we will simply use the designation [*sic*], which indicates that our reproduction of the phrase is accurate, but the meaning is debatable. You are then free to consider the possibilities in your own mind. We will also devote attention to the second of Eichler's noted sexisms in science, namely, concepts which have sexist connotations or denotations, such as "to impregnate" or "work."

A third way in which sexism enters the scientific process is via use of an **androcentric** perspective. in which males are assumed to be the centre of all aspects of social and scientific life. We have already noted how women have been assumed to be the "opposite" sex, a use of language that places men at the centre and women at the margins in some way. You will be reading about theories in the next chapter in which the experiences of men were assumed to be representative of both women and men (see Freud and also Kohlberg). Supposedly, if men are generic, then their lives are also assumed to be generic and, once understood, the lessons learned are generalized to all persons. Through the use of androcentric perspectives, gender appears to be rendered invisible. What is actually invisible and lacking is a self-conscious awareness on the part of many, or most, male researchers and theorists of how their own gender shapes their interpretations and understandings of the social world.

Androcentrism also operates in another, unanticipated, sexist fashion. When men are taken to be representative of humanity, many aspects of men's lives are ignored or distorted to fit the all-humanity mold. Consequently, our understanding of men, simply *as men*, is incomplete. Researchers have historically tended to focus upon the public worlds of men and the private worlds of women, without a coherent awareness of these gender biases, and without realizing how little we know, consequently, about the public and private lives of women (a gap in knowledge we are rapidly filling), and about the private worlds of men (a gap which still largely remains today).

A growing awareness of the androcentric bias in science has also heightened our awareness of many of the ways in which gender itself, and beliefs about gender, influence the methodology and actual conduct of research (Eichler's fourth point). Male-dominated science emphasizes the importance of **objectivity**, and devises methods that permit and promote emotional distance between researchers and subjects. Surveys and laboratory experiments have been developed to obtain data that can be *quantified*, or reduced to numbers and mathematical formulae, and impersonally manipulated through the use of computers and statistics. This traditional model of science can be seen "as establishing mastery over subjects, as demanding the absence of feeling, and as enforcing separateness of the knower from the known" (Hess and Ferree, 1987: 13).

Partly as a means of filling in the gaps in the scientific record by allowing previously ignored respondents to express the substance of their lives, feminists have tended to prefer methods designed to reduce the distance between researchers and subjects (Dilorio, 1989; Reinharz and Davidman, 1992). Case-study approaches (in which a small number of subjects are examined intensively over a wide variety of topics) and the use of nondirective, or open-ended, interview strategies are preferred as a means of permitting respondents to express themselves to researchers as fully as possible (Hess and Ferree, 1987). Obtained findings are then presented using the respondents' own words as much as possible, with a minimum of statistical manipulation or mathematical modeling. We will consider next how assumptions about the genders and gender itself can influence the interpretation of results (Eichler's fifth point).

Emphasis on Differences

Throughout the history of research on gender, the main focus has been upon identifying differences between men and women. This emphasis is partly due to the "politics of publication" and partly due to the nature of the scientific enterprise itself. The politics of publication refers to the editorial decision-making process. Decisions about which empirical or theoretical articles submitted to scholarly periodical journals will eventually be printed are made by the editors and a number of reviewers selected from scholars in the same field of specialization as the authors of the article. Reviewers make their decisions based upon whether accepted procedures have been used, whether the submitted product is coherently presented, and whether the article makes a scholarly contribution to knowledge. Until very recently, articles that featured sex and gender differences were significantly more likely to find their way into print than articles that stressed a lack of differences. Just as with newspapers, radio, and television news programs, something different is more newsworthy than nothing different. In the fashion of a self-fulfilling prophecy, beliefs in sex and gender differences led to the search for differences, and increased the likelihood that studies claiming to find differences would get into print, which in turn reinforced our belief in the existence of gender differences.

Focus on Group Averages

This leads us to briefly consider what kinds of differences are more likely to be brought to our attention. Within the realm of empirical research, the focus, both in the past and today, is on the existence of group-average differences. In other words, measurement scales are created to elicit responses along various dimensions of interest to research scientists. Results are gathered from selected samples and then tabulated, charted, and graphed where necessary or desirable, and submitted to various tests to determine if any revealed differences are statistically significant (i.e., beyond chance).

These tests are typically performed on the average scores obtained from the groups or social categories under study. If the tests come out positive, the existence of a group difference is proclaimed. Attention is less often focused upon the range of variation found within each group or category, or upon a comparison of these ranges between the groups, and the meanings of such variations for our understanding of the groups. To give a typical example, measurements can be taken of the heights of a random sample of adult males and a random sample of adult females. Most likely, the average height of the males will be found statistically to be significantly different from the average height of the females, with the males, on average, taller than the females by approximately four inches. At the same time, many females may be found in the sample to be taller than the average male, and many males may be found to be shorter than the average female. While the average differences are significant, considerable overlap exists in the heights of women and men. Most researchers and readers of the research will focus their attentions on the between-group average differences and pay less attention to the within-group variations and the between-group overlapping.

This issue of focus applies not only to physical characteristics, such as height, weight, musculature, endurance, susceptibility to disease and death, activity levels, and manual dexterity, but also to personal and social characteristics, such as verbal ability, mathematical ability, visual-spatial ability, empathy, emotionality, dependence, nurturance, and aggressiveness. Research on physical attributes consistently find that men are, on average, taller, heavier, and more muscular, while women are less susceptible to a variety of diseases and illnesses and tend to live longer. Surveys (such as Maccoby and Jacklin, 1974) of hundreds of published and unpublished studies focusing upon personal and social qualities find that, in the final analysis, women and men demonstrate very few consistent average differences. Maccoby and Jacklin conclude that females, from late childhood onwards, tend to excel on tests of *verbal ability,* and males, from late childhood onwards, tend to excel on tests of *mathematical* and of *visual-spatial ability*. Males are also found to be more *aggressive* from early childhood. (As we shall see shortly, however, most of these average differences have been found more recently to have either declined to the point of nonexistence, or to be attributable to something other than gender). In all cases, studies reporting difference findings also observe considerable overlap to exist between their female and male subjects. None of the differences are what could be termed *absolute* differences where, for example, all females score higher on some test than do all males. As a result, whenever we refer to sex differences in personal and social qualities, we are referring to *average* differences.

You can quickly see a connection between stereotypes and empirical research on gender differences. Both focus upon the average differences between men and women, while essentially ignoring considerable overlap between the sexes in terms of their various physical, personal, and social qualities. People who believe in a particular stereotype will, most frequently, when confronted with a person who does not conform to expectations, dismiss the potential challenge to the stereotype with a vague statement about the "exception proves the rule." A focus on gender differences leads to a tendency to ignore gender similarities or the existence of overlap in the possession of various qualities.

Sex Irreducible Differences

Money indicates that absolute, or what he prefers to term **sex-irreducible**, differences between the sexes are very few, and relate solely to biological reproduction. The term "irreducible" is borrowed from mathematics and refers to something that exists as a basic unit and cannot be broken down or reduced further.

> [M]en impregnate, and women menstruate, gestate, and lactate. Ovulation is omitted insofar as gestation does not take place without it. Lactation might be omitted insofar as modern nutritional technology has made it possible, though not desirable, for maternal neonatal breast-feeding to be replaced by a formula-milk substitute....Immutability of the procreative sex difference will undoubtedly remain as if absolute for most men and women forever. However, in the light of contemporary experimental obstetrics, being pregnant is no longer an absolutely immutable sex difference. (Money, 1988: 54)

We will demonstrate how the term "impregnate" is sexist, misleading, and, technically, somewhat inaccurate. However, for the moment, we shall continue to use this term as we summarize the existence of the most basic, fundamental, absolute, currently unchangeable (given present technologies) differences between men and women. Only men impregnate and only women menstruate, gestate, and lactate. No overlap between the sexes exists regarding these factors.

These abilities, for lack of a better term, are all fraught with social meanings and gender implications. What are the ramifications for masculinity for men who cannot "impregnate," and for femininity for women who cannot menstruate, gestate (carry a pregnancy to near full term), or lactate (produce sufficient breast milk to permit breast-feeding)? Historically and currently, two of the most powerful epithets we could hurl at a man or woman was to call them, respectively, either "impotent" or "barren." Our everyday use of "impotent" is most often inaccurate when the term is used to refer to a man who cannot impregnate a woman. The accurate technical term is "infertile." Impotency refers to an inability to attain and/or sustain a penile erection. A man can ejaculate sufficient sperm to contribute to conception without having an erection. Therefore, the term "impotent" is most often used in everyday language in an overgeneralized manner. We also tend to use the term beyond the scope of fertility and the sexual to include nonsexual situations where impotence is equated with a sense of powerlessness. It is not at all uncommon to hear a man claiming to have felt impotent, unable to do something or anything, in a situation having nothing to do with sexuality. Since our stereotypes attribute the qualities of "powerful" and "sexual potency" to masculinity, he who is not powerful, or potent, is not masculine.

In cultures dominated by the belief that pregnancy is determined solely by a female's capabilities, the term "barren" is used to refer to a woman who can either not get pregnant or not produce a live birth. The word "barren" conjures up images of an arid desert incapable of, or inhospitable to, sustaining life. Barrenness was sufficient grounds for termination of a marriage in early Judeo-Christian, and other, cultures. A barren woman was a woman who failed to live up to her feminine potential, particularly in a pronatalist culture dependent upon biological reproduction for family and social survival. Despite the greater element of reproductive choice available in our society today, a major distinction is still seen to exist between choosing not to reproduce versus being unable to reproduce, with the latter still containing implications of failure. Similar connotations surrounding lactation vary in severity, depending upon current fashions in the mother's-milk-versus-formula debates.

Unlike "impotent," we do not see use of the term "barren" generalized from reproductive to nonreproductive areas of women's social life. However, we often observe women being described in sexually implicit imagery regarding actions perceived by men to have potentially threatening implications for men's ability to assert power. The terms "emasculators," "castrators," and/or "ball-breakers," all suggest threats to men's "potency," regardless of whether or not the alleged actions of a women have anything to do with a specifically sexual situation. Once again, the use of sexual imagery in nonsexual situations is testimony to the important linkage of sexuality and power within our stereotypes of masculinity. In generalizing beyond the sex-irreducible differences, our cultural expectations produce tyrannical pressures upon Canadians to act in gender-appropriate ways.

Statuses and Multiple Occupancy

One of the most commonly used concepts in sociology is that of **status**, which refers to a position or location within a group or society. We can view a society or a group as composed partly of a system of interrelated statuses. Two characteristics of statuses are important for our purposes here. First, each status has a socially constructed meaning only in relation to one or a number of other statuses. No status exists in isolation from all others. To understand the meaning of one status, we have to examine it in the context of its relationship to other statuses. The meaning of the status of husband is unknown until we examine its relation to the status of wife. The same applies to student and instructor, child and parent, male and female. While it is theoretically possible to focus our attentions upon one status for analytical purposes only, it is impossible to meaningfully describe and discuss that status without any reference whatsoever to other related statuses. Males cannot be understood without reference to females and females cannot be understood without reference to males. As Flax (1990: 44) notes in relation to gender relations, "each part can have no meaning or existence without the others."

This brings us to the second characteristic of status: *simultaneous occupancy*. Each person in a society occupies a number of statuses at any one moment in their lives, and through their entire lifetime. At this point in your lifetime, you occupy at least a marital status (single, married, separated, divorced, widowed), a family status (husband, wife, son, daughter, brother, sister), a kinship status (aunt, uncle, nephew, niece, cousin), a religious status (which also includes atheist and agnostic), an ethnicity status (which also includes "racial" status), a citizenship status, a social-class status, an occupational status (which also includes student), an age status (measured by chronological age or, colloquially, by decade since birth, such as "forty-something"), a sex status, and many others too numerous to list here. If you were to make up a list of all of the people you know and relate to, regardless of how well you know them or how superficial or intimate your relationship is, you would be making up a list of all the statuses you occupy, however temporarily, at this point in your lifetime.

At any given moment, only some of those multiple statuses you occupy will be important or relevant. Linton distinguishes between *active* and *latent* statuses and notes that "the status in terms of which an individual is operating is his [*sic*] active status at that particular point in time. His [*sic*] other statuses are, for the time being, latent statuses" (Linton, 1945: 78). One intriguing question confronting us is whether sex is ever a latent, or irrelevant, status in any situation. Are there situations where the sex of any of the participants are ignored? Freud observes, "when you meet a human being, the first distinction you make is 'male' or 'female'" (1933/1964: 113). Presumably, once made, that distinction remains active for as long as you relate to that person. Sarbin and Allen (1968: 537) claim that sex, and age, are probably always active.

Being either female or male is an example of a master status, "one which will affect almost every aspect of our lives" (Lindsey, 1994: 2). However, it is unlikely that the sex (or age) of a person is the only active status in any situation. At least one, and most likely more, of the other simultaneously occupied statuses will be relevant and will exert some influence upon the perceptions and behaviours of all parties in a situation. Recall how the status of "lesbian" influenced people's perceptions of a hypothetical female. The next question confronting us is to determine the extent to which a person's sex exerts an influence upon their actions. Stated simplistically, how much of what we do is because of our sex, and how much is due to any or all of the other statuses we occupy simultaneously? What proportion of our behaviour is accounted for by our sex and what proportion of our behaviour is accounted for by our other statuses?

Researchers can approximate an answer to the last question using statistical techniques to account for the contribution of the sex of respondents to variations in the data obtained in a study. For example, Hyde (1981) reanalyzed the studies that led Maccoby and Jacklin (1974) to conclude that sex differences exist with regard to verbal, quantitative or mathematical, and visual-spatial ability. Hyde's (1981) analysis, formally known as a **meta-analysis**, found that respondents' sex accounted for approximately 1.0 percent of the variance in verbal ability, 1.0 percent of the variance in qualitative ability, and 4.5 percent of the variance in visual-spatial ability. At most, 5 percent of the variation in test scores related to these abilities is attributable to the sex of the tested subjects. Other factors, many, or most, of which are related to the other statuses the subjects occupied at the time account for the rest. We cannot reduce everything to being either female or male. We must remember that one is male or female *and* in possession of other statuses as well. Some portion of what we call masculine and feminine behaviour is actually the product of our enacting portions of the requirements associated with our other simultaneously occupied statuses.

Since the time of the Maccoby and Jacklin (1974) review, and Hyde's (1981) initial meta- analysis, subsequent studies have suggested that gender differences in verbal abilities have been dramatically declining to the point where there now appears to be no overall differences (Hyde and Lynn, 1988). Research on visual-spatial ability (Deaux and Kite, 1987) now finds gender differences to be relatively small. Equally important are the findings that neither women's supposed superiority in verbal ability (Harmatz and Novak, 1983; Safir, 1986) nor men's supposed superiority in visual-spatial ability (Harmatz and Novak, 1983) are supported in cross-cultural research. The latter findings point to the cultural context as an important contributing factor for any observed gender behaviour differences.

A statistical meta-analysis of 259 gender comparisons reported in the empirical literature (Hyde et al., 1991) concludes that boys no longer have an overall superiority in math skills. Earlier findings of gender differences are now believed to be mainly attributable to differences in family income, parental education, and students' occupational aspirations. In other words, the *social-class* status that male and female students occupy, and aspire to, has the most significant influence upon mathematical ability. Overall, the persistent tendency to focus on gender differences, rather than upon gender similarities, is attributable more to the power and tyranny of gender stereotypes than to the findings of available research.

New theories are being constructed in an attempt to understand how a person's gender interacts with, for example, his or her age, social class, race/ethnicity, sexual orientation, and able-bodiedness, to influence his or her experience of, and participation in, Canadian society. As these theories become more coherent and sophisticated, we will become less simplistic in our thinking about sex and gender. We should be in a more knowledgeable position to indicate when a behaviour or experience is attributable to a person's gender and when it is not.

Sex Roles and Gender Roles

It is time to be more specific with regard to what we have been referring to generally as "behaviour." Attached to each status is a dynamic element formally known as a **role**. Roles are comprised of duties and responsibilities as well as rights and privileges associated with the occupancy of a status. These duties, responsibilities, rights, and privileges are socially constructed in conjunction with the values and beliefs of a culture. Generally, the concept of "role" is used to refer to the *expectations* of what one is supposed to do, and modified concepts, such as "role performance," "role enactment" (Sarbin and Allen, 1968: 489), or "role behaviour" are used to refer to what one actually does.

Unfortunately, once again, some confusion and inconsistency surrounds attempts to apply the concept of roles to the study of sex and gender. Lipman-Blumen attempts to make the following distinction:

> We shall use the better-known term, sex *roles,* to refer specifically to behaviors determined by an individual's biological sex, such as menstruation, pregnancy, lactation, erection, orgasm, and seminal ejaculation. At the same time, we should not forget that even biologically determined phenomena do not escape the influence of cultural attitudes, norms, and values....Gender roles...are socially created expectations for masculine and feminine behavior. Exaggerating both real and imagined aspects of biological sex, each society sorts certain polarized behaviors and attitudes into two sets it then labels "male" and "female." Gender roles are social constructions; they contain self-concepts, psychological traits, as well as family, occupational, and political roles assigned to members of each sex....In all societies, gender roles and sex roles intertwine in a dynamic doublehelix that feminist theorists have labeled the sex-gender system. (Lipman-Blumen, 1984: 2–3; emphasis in original)

As you can see, trying to disentangle and keep sex and gender roles analytically separate is very difficult. Lipman-Blumen suggests that sex roles are biologically determined, but acknowledges the influence of culture upon biology. Gender roles are defined as social constructions of behaviours labeled "male" and "female," terms referring to biological sex. The conceptual difficulties found in the material just quoted are not limited only to Lipman-Blumen. For example, Lindsey defines gender roles as "those expected attitudes and behaviors which a society associates with each sex" (Lindsey, 1994: 4).

Efforts to keep sex and gender separate often rely upon a characteristic distinction associated with the concept of status. **Ascribed** statuses are those statuses over which an individual has no control (Linton, 1945). These statuses are assigned to individuals either immediately after birth or over the course of their lifetime. Ascribed statuses can include social class (where social mobility is not permitted), race and ethnic heritage, kinship, and age. **Achieved** statuses are those over which individuals have some degree of control and attain primarily by virtue of their own efforts (Linton, 1945). Achieved statuses can include occupation (in a society such as ours), adult social class location, and marital status.

Adopting this distinction leads to the suggestion that sex is ascribed and gender is achieved. However, ascribed and achieved statuses are not a dichotomous distinction. They are best thought of as existing along a continuum. Many of you probably thought of some exceptions or had some questions when you read the previous paragraph containing examples of ascribed and achieved statuses. Richardson suggests that we may be further ahead in our understanding if we consider that

> Gender behavior is both *prescribed* and *chosen*. On the one hand, appropriate behavior is socially shared and transmitted through the culture: People learn what is appropriate for their gender. But, on the other hand, they choose how to present themselves. Therefore, persons have the option to accept or reject cultural definitions of appropriate gender behavior and, consequently, the ability to change either themselves or the culture. (Richardson, 1988: 9; emphasis in original)

Therefore, gender has elements of both ascription and achievement—as does sex, demonstrated by transsexualism.

Given that gender is a social construction, and that sex (including for example, pregnancy and menstruation) is strongly influenced by sociocultural forces, the tendency within the literature is to use one general term, "gender roles," to refer to all expectations and behaviour associated with sex and gender. Unfortunately, the concept of "sex roles" is still in use; one of our major periodical journals is still named *Sex Roles*. Most courses taught in colleges and universities throughout Canada were first named, and many still remain named, the *Sociology of Sex Roles*. We prefer to use "gender roles" as our general concept and suggest that you mentally substitute "gender" for "sex" whenever you come across the term "sex roles" in other written materials.

Use of the concepts of roles and role behaviour could easily lead to the suggestion that everything is predetermined for gendered beings. When occupying the relevant statuses, we simply follow the expected guidelines to be rewarded for appropriate gender behaviour, and all, or almost all, people consequently behave in similar ways. Casual observation of women and men demonstrates that social life is not quite so simple. Role behaviour is partly dependent upon a status occupant's command of cognitive and motor skills (Sarbin and Allen, 1968). Each of us is capable of thinking about and accepting or rejecting the gender expectations of which we are aware. This is part of what Richardson (1988) means when she writes that gender is chosen. In addition, we have to perform our roles within the limitations of our verbal and movement skills, skills that are not equally and evenly distributed throughout the population.

Gender expectations also demonstrate variations across age groups, social classes, and race/ethnic groups, to name just a few of the major distinctions. Consequently, guidelines for gender behaviour are not uniform throughout an entire culture such as ours. As we noted earlier, each of us occupies a number of statuses and, therefore, perform any number of roles simultaneously. We are highly unlikely to ever find that only our gender status and role are active, that we must solely "be a man" or "act like a lady." Rather, our gender role is intertwined with other roles related to, for example, age, race/ethnicity, social class, and sexual orientation. Each of us creates his or her own personal style for gendered behaviour, combining the expectations of the social groups and status categories to which we belong, or aspire to, with our own role skill capabilities. The resulting gender behaviours are not totally diverse, but, overwhelmingly, represent variations upon certain themes. We will identify and explore these themes in subsequent chapters.

BIOLOGICAL, PSYCHOLOGICAL, AND SOCIAL PSYCHOLOGICAL PERSPECTIVES

SEX AND GENDER: BASIC VARIABLES

Women's track star Stella Watson won numerous medals in international competitions during the 1930s: five gold (including one for a record-breaking 100-metre dash in the 1932 Olympics), three silver, and one bronze. She was the United States women's pentathlon champion in 1954. Following her death at age 69 in 1980, the coroner's report revealed that some of her body cells contained an XY male-sex chromosome pattern and others an XX female-sex chromosome pattern. Her external (and nonfunctional) sex organs were male. Further investigation revealed that "Stella" was born in Poland as Stanislawa Walasiewicz. Her former, and dumbfounded, husband from a 1956 two-month-long marriage commented that their infrequent sex life had always occurred with the lights out. The International Olympic Committee has yet to resolve its dilemmas: Was Stella male or female? Should her medals be returned and her championships deleted from the official records (or at least modified with an asterisk)? Should the silver medalist, who came in second by mere centimetres, Hilda Strike of Montreal, be posthumously (she died in 1989) awarded a gold medal for *truly* being the world's fastest woman at the 1932 Olympics? Do not be concerned if you cannot make up your mind quickly. After all, it took until December of 1996 for France's Marielle Goitschel to receive her gold medal for winning the 1966 World Championship downhill-skiing race at Portillo, Chile. The medal was originally awarded to first-place finisher Erika Schinegger of Austria. Two years later, at the 1968 Winter Olympics in Grenoble, France, Schinegger was discovered to have "male" internal organs and a preponderance of "male" hormones. She later underwent a transsexual operation, married, and became a father. Erik Schinegger gave his gold medal to Goitschel in 1988, but the

International Ski Federation did not change its mind and make the official medal presentation until late-1996.

Dr. Richard Henry Raskind, an ophthalmologist and avid tennis player, was married and the father of a son. However, in his own mind, a central portion of his life was a lie. He successfully underwent a transsexual transformation to become Dr. Renée Richards. Dr. Richards continued with her interest in tennis, even coaching world champion Martina Navratilova, and competed in professional women's tennis tournaments until 1976 when a protest was lodged that she held an unfair competitive advantage. Organizers decided to use a buccal smear (in use since 1966 as a screening device for Olympic competition), to establish eligibility for participation in their tournament. The smear, a scraping of cells taken from the inside of the mouth, would be subjected to a chromosome test. Since transsexual transformation does not alter sex chromosomes, Richards could be prohibited from participation in women's play. Richards objected that this was an inappropriate test because, psychologically, she was female, in possession of (albeit reconstructed) female genitals, and capable of successfully functioning socially as a female. She argued that these were all more appropriate tests. However, since the transsexual transformation was undertaken after puberty, Renée Richards still possessed a male bone structure, which could affect her athletic performance. Which test would have been more appropriate to determine Renée Richard's sex and eligibility? (Incidentally, the buccal smear test was dropped prior to the 1996 summer Olympics.)

As we noted briefly in Chapter 1, biological sex is not a single variable divided into two simple all-encompassing dichotomous categories. The most accurate designation of "male" or "female" depends upon a person's location within at least six, perhaps seven, different variables considered together. Instances of inconsistent positioning across different variables raise serious social and scientific issues. We also have at least two variables (one of which can be subdivided into many dimensions) that are considered to comprise gender. Programs and courses of study, textbooks, reference books, periodical journal articles, conference presentations, and decades of empirical research have been devoted to considering each of these variables separately and the relationships among all of the variables of sex and gender. In the following sections, we will first consider each of the basic variables of sex (chromosomal, gonadal, hormonal, reproductive, genital, brain, and assigned) and gender (identity and social behaviour) independently, and then in relation to one other. We will consider gender initially, via consideration of various biological, psychological, and social psychological theoretical perspectives. Other approaches will be presented in subsequent chapters.

Biological Sex: Chromosomal and Hormonal Influences

The process of biological sex differentiation begins at the moment of conception, when a male sperm and a female egg (or ovum) unite to form a zygote. Traditional scientific depictions of this unification process typically utilize words that conform to existing gender stereotypes. In its simplest and least romanticized form, the union is captured with the statement "men impregnate women," words that imply an active male and a passive female unequally participating in conception. We immediately conjure up cartoon-like images of mighty male sperm vigorously swimming upstream, like spawning salmon, against monumental odds through the vagina, past the cervix, valiantly onwards through the uterus towards the

Fallopian tubes, to finally capture, penetrate, and fertilize a female egg. This egg, by contrast, is visualized as an entity that merely emerges from a ruptured ovarian follicle and then passively allows herself to be pushed by fimbria to a Fallopian tube where, all dressed up with nowhere to go, she lounges around, waiting to be conquered by a sperm suitor. In apparent support of this imagery, an advertisement for First Response™, a home pregnancy test, which appeared in the December 1995 issue of *Canadian Living*, featured a cartoon drawing in which dozens of baby-blue sperm were shown competing in a type of sperm Olympics, swimming purposefully upstream in a pink ocean, towards a yellow egg. The caption for the product read: "It's our job to tell you if any of them did theirs" (p. 57).

Martin (1987, 1994) challenges the imagery of sperm as "the nuclear war-head of paternal genes" by arguing that not only do sperm actually move quite slowly, with more side-to-side than straight-ahead motion, but also that both sperm and egg are best thought of as mutually interdependent agents. The egg's adhesive surface aids in the attachment of the sperm, whereupon the egg actively participates in incorporation of the sperm's genetic material. The commonly used active/passive imagery is but a figment of traditional gender-stereotypical imaginations. As Wajcman (1991: 67–68) observes, the cultural grammar and the dominant metaphors used within the language of the biomedical sciences today remains "suffused with implicit assumptions about and imagery of sexual [*sic*] difference."

Chromosomal Sex

Sperm carries among its genetic material either an X or a Y sex chromosome while each egg always carries an X sex chromosome, among its genetic package. The most frequently occurring newly formed zygote contains a total of 46 chromosomes: 23 obtained from the sperm and 23 from the egg. Forty-four of the chromosomes (known as autosomes) provide genetic instructional material for creation of various hereditary physical qualities such as height, eye colour, skin colour, internal organs, skeletal formations, and so on. The 46,XX chromosome pattern (meaning a total of 46 chromosomes, including an XX sex chromosome configuration) is the usual genetic code for a female; the 46,XY pattern is the genetic code for a male. Since the larger X chromosome carries more genetic material than does the Y chromosome, the XX pattern is believed to provide additional benefits to female immune systems, which has important ramifications for morbidity and mortality differentials between the sexes. In terms of fetal development, other than these differences in *chromosomal sex*, male and female embryos are anatomically identical in the initial weeks following conception.

Further sex differentiation appears to follow what has been characterized as the *Eve first, then Adam principle* (Money, 1988: 15). The term "appears to" is used here deliberately, because researchers have focused their attention overwhelming upon explaining male fetal development and have simply assumed that female development is nonproblematic, straight forward, and not in need of a separate explanation (Fausto-Sterling, 1985). This possible androcentric bias may need to be reviewed and scrutinized more closely in future years, as researchers focus specifically upon female fetal development itself. According to the principle of Eve first, then Adam, the "natural" tendency in fetal development is towards creation of a biological female. Consequently, to differentiate a fetus into a biological male, something must be added. In the absence of that something, a female fetus will be differentiated. The "something" varies depending upon the particular aspect of fetal development being considered.

Gonadal Sex

The **gonads** (often referred to in everyday language as the sex glands) begin to develop around the sixth to seventh week following conception. Male testes and female ovaries are homologous sex organs, meaning that they develop from the same embryonic tissue known as the **primordial**, or "indifferent," **gonad**. Scientists are continually searching for the "something" that triggers the differentiation of the primordial gonad into testes.

For a considerable period of time, a chemical protein substance controlled by the Y chromosome, known as H-Y antigen, was thought to be the key factor (Money, 1988; Watchel, 1979). After some laboratory animals were found to possess testes, but no H-Y antigen, attention shifted to a gene referred to as testis-determining factor (TDF). Unfortunately, to complicate matters scientifically, TDF has been found on both the X and the Y chromosomes, thus making the contribution of this gene unclear (Roberts, 1988). Research is also focusing upon the contribution of the molecule SRY produced by the Y chromosome (SRY means "sex-determining region of the Y") which is activated at 35 days following conception. SRY is now believed to set off a cascade of events leading to masculinization of various tissues, including transformation of the primordial gonad into testes (McLaren, 1990). Based upon current understandings, if SRY is not present, the primordial gonad will differentiate into ovaries at a later point in fetal development. The delay between formation of either testes or, eventually, ovaries, appears to provide for a late arrival of that necessary gonadal-differentiating something—akin to a waiting period in case the something gets held up in fetal development traffic.

Hormonal Sex

Subsequent sex differentiation is controlled largely by hormonal mechanisms (Money and Ehrhardt, 1972). **Androgens** are commonly referred to in our everyday vernacular as the "male sex hormones," while **estrogens** (including progesterone) are referred to as the "female sex hormones." Such language implies that only males produce androgens and only females produce estrogens. Testes and ovaries produce both estrogens and androgens. Individuals are arrayed along a hormonal-sex continuum depending upon their proportional balance of these produced hormones. Males generally produce proportionally and significantly more androgens to estrogens, while females generally produce proportionally and significantly more estrogens than androgens. During fetal development, the absolute amounts of androgens and estrogens produced by males and females are actually very small. Greater amounts are produced later in developmental life, around the time of puberty. However small the amounts of sex hormones created during fetal development, the proportional imbalance is either sufficiently or not sufficiently great enough to exert an influence in the appropriate time frame.

Internal Reproductive Sex

Meanwhile, other genes have already created two sets of duct systems, the Müllerian and the Wolffian, which have the potential to develop, or proliferate, into internal reproductive systems. By the eighth week following conception, testes begin to secrete two products. Müllerian inhibiting hormone (MIH) causes the Müllerian ducts to atrophy, or vestigiate, rather than form female internal organs. Androgens—particularly testosterone—stimulate the development of the Wolffian ducts into *male reproductive-sex* features such as the epididymis, vas deferens, seminal vesicles, and prostate gland.

If masculinization of the primordial gonad has not occurred around the seventh week, ovaries will typically develop at about the 12th week of pregnancy. Later, and in the absence of MIH and sufficiently large quantities of androgens, the Müllerian duct system differentiates into the *female reproductive-sex* features of the uterus, fallopian tubes, and inner third of the vagina. Unstimulated by sufficiently large amounts of testosterone, the Wolffian duct system in the female atrophies, or vestigiates, into minute fragments, and is absorbed into the bloodstream.

External Genital Sex

Little differentiation exists in the external genitals of a male and female fetus until after the seventh week of development. It would appear that androgens, and particularly testosterone, which is converted by some body tissues into dihydrotestosterone, are key determining factors in development of the *male genital-sex* features of the penis and scrotum (Imperato-McGinley and Peterson, 1976). The lack of sufficient androgens in the female embryo lead to the development of the *female genital-sex* features of the clitoris, inner and outer labia, and outer portion of the vagina.

Androgen stimulation in the male causes the folds, which would develop into the inner vaginal lips (or labia minora) of a female, to grow together and form the tubular urethra of the penis. The homologous *genital tubercle*, which in the female develops into the clitoris, becomes the glans of the penis in the male. Dependent upon the presence or absence of sufficient androgens, the labioscrotal swellings either differentiate into the scrotum in the male, or the outer vaginal lips (labia majora) in the female. The testes later descend into the scrotum of the male. As a consequence of these developments, visible genital differences between the male and female fetus are observable, suitable for an ultrasound snapshot for the family album, by the 14th week following conception.

Brain Sex

Considerable uncertainty surrounds a variety of issues on whether *brain sex* should be added to the list of biological sex variables. During the great brain controversy of the early 1900s, scientists, assuming that brain size and intelligence were positively correlated, debated the issue of which sex had the larger brain. Researchers initially concluded that males possessed greater intelligence due to their possession of larger brains. Once it was determined that global brain size was a function of height and weight, which are not sex irreducible, attention then shifted to the portions of the brain. As knowledge of these locations changed, so too did the supposed attributes of each sex. Mackie (1991: 32) notes:

> At first, the frontal lobes were viewed as the seat of the intellect. Not surprisingly, "research" showed that men had larger frontal lobes, relative to the parietal lobes, than did women. Later on, the parietal lobes came to be regarded as the source of higher intellectual functions. Scientific opinion reversed itself; studies began to report than men had relatively larger parietal lobes than women. Today scholars agree that neither overall brain size, nor proportions of brain parts, differ by sex.

Hypothalamic development

The least controversial issue currently focuses upon how the presence or absence of fetal androgens influences development of the number and location of certain types of nerve-cell connections (synapses) in the hypothalamus portion of the brain (Carter and Greenaugh, 1979; Goldman, 1978) and eventually effects its sensitivity to estrogen. The hypothalamus functions, in part, along with the pituitary gland and the gonads in a complex feedback loop that becomes operational during puberty. The presence of sufficient amounts of fetal androgens "masculinize" (the commonly used term; the nonexistent term "maleize" would be more appropriate) the hypothalamus to become essentially insensitive to estrogens, resulting in a relatively constant, or *acyclic*, level of sex hormone production in men after puberty. A lack of sufficient fetal androgens promotes hypothalamic estrogen sensitivity, which eventually contributes to the *cyclic* estrogen and progesterone sex-hormone production patterns that are responsible for creating menstrual cycles in women. Despite what you may have read in an abundance of ill-founded speculations in the popular press, due to the development of their hypothalamus and consequent acyclic hormone production, men do not have an analogous menstrual cycle, nor do they undergo a biologically based "male menopause" at midlife. We will return to this latter subject in Chapter 9.

Brain lateralization

The most controversial issue related to brain sex is related to the fact that the brain is composed of two hemispheres connected by a bundle of fibres known as the *corpus callosum*. Considerable research has focused upon whether each hemisphere is responsible for specific functions, and whether females and males have different dominant hemispheres. More specifically, the fundamental questions have been whether male brains are more *lateralized* (i.e., specialized), with the left hemisphere responsible for verbal ability and the right hemisphere for visual-spatial ability, and whether female brains are less lateralized and more *symmetrical*, meaning that each hemisphere contributes to these abilities.

Bleier (1984: 93) notes that existing research findings on brain lateralization are either inconsistent or inconclusive. Some of the most tantalizing supportive research comes from studies of brain-damaged individuals (Inglis and Lawson, 1981; McGlone and Kertesz, 1973; Witelson, 1989), wherein it has generally been found that women recover more quickly from strokes than do men, and appear to suffer less impairment to their verbal or visual-spatial abilities following localized damage to one side or the other of their brain. The possibly greater hemispheric symmetry among women may be due to their apparently larger corpus callosum (Allen and Gorski, 1992), which could permit greater synaptic communication between their brain hemispheres. A lesser number of connecting fibres may impede the ease with which one hemisphere learns to compensate for damage in the other hemisphere.

Despite these findings, and despite hypotheses from researchers such as Levy (1976) that higher levels of testosterone washing over the male fetus produces hemispheric specialization, leading to superiority in certain abilities, we must bear in mind the research findings indicating that sex differences in verbal, mathematical, and visual-spatial abilities have all been reduced substantially in recent years. These reductions suggest that brain lateralization, to the extent it does exist, is not the sole determining factor for certain abilities. As well, we cannot as yet assume that brain research and the presentation and interpretation of findings, is now unbiased and nonsexist. Tavris (1992: 48, emphasis in original) notes that

> just like the nineteenth-century researchers who kept changing their minds about which *lobe* of the brain accounted for male superiority, twentieth-century researchers keep changing their minds about which hemisphere of the brain accounts for male superiority. Originally, the left *hemisphere* was considered the repository of intellect and reason. The right hemisphere was the sick, bad, crazy side, the side of passion, instincts, criminality and irrationality. Guess which sex was thought to have left- brain intellectual superiority? (Answer: males.) In the 1960s and 1970s, however, the right brain was resuscitated and brought into the limelight. Scientists began to suspect that it was the source of genius and inspiration, creativity and imagination, mysticism and mathematical brilliance. Guess which sex was now thought to have right-brain specialization? (Answer: males.)

Kinsbourne, a leader in brain hemisphere research remarks that "[u]nder pressure from the gathering momentum of feminism, and perhaps in backlash to it, many investigators seem determined to discover that men and women 'really' are different. It seems that if sex differences (e.g., in lateralization) do not exist, then they have to be invented." (in Tavris, 1992: 53). *If* differences do exist in brain lateralization, the connections between these differences and subsequent behavioural abilities have yet to be clearly and consistently determined. In particular, the *direction* of influence between brain and behaviour is not all that clear. Walsh and Cepko (1992) suggest that genes may not determine brain cell functions, but rather that neurons in the brain may adjust and adapt to other inputs produced by changes occurring in other parts of the body—changes that can be caused by environmental factors. Learning may effect brain chemistry and functioning and, subsequently, any lateralization which may or may not exist.

Today, it appears that we can safely conclude that a sex difference does exist regarding the structure and functioning of the hypothalamus. Regarding the degree of brain hemispheric lateralization and the meaning of any lateralization that may exist, the only conclusion we can reach is that it is too early to conclude anything. More specific to the focus of this entire section, the nature and influence of genes and prenatal hormones on the brain remains unclear (Bleier, 1988; Hubbard, 1990; Lott, 1994:26–27; Rubin et al., 1981).

Thus far, we have seen that the hormonal balance during fetal development influences internal reproductive sex and genital sex. Hormone production remains basically unchanged during infancy and childhood. However, during the processes of puberty, the amount of sex hormones produced increases substantially and influences, among other things, the proportional hormonal balance (further increasing the range of the continuum along which individual males and females are arrayed), subsequent development of female and male secondary sex characteristics, and the onset of menses among females. Hormones are also involved in the processes of menopause, a topic to be considered in Chapter 9. Finally, we shall also investigate the possible relationship between hormones and various social attributes of males and females in some of the subsequent chapters. See Table 2.1 for a summary of the known differentiating variables of biological sex.

Assigned Sex

For the vast majority of Canadians, a visual inspection of the genitals, either immediately upon birth or earlier via ultrasound pictures, provides the basis for their *assigned sex*. In the absence of any noticeable problems, the apparent presence of a penis and scrotum is deemed sufficient to pronounce "it's a boy!" Similarly, the observable presence of labia and a vagina is considered sufficient evidence that "it's a girl!" Only in somewhat rare situations, as we saw in Chapter 1, are further investigations instigated to determine an individual's chromosomal, gonadal, hormonal, and internal reproductive sex. It is simply, and most often accurately, assumed that all the variables of an individual's biological sex are *concordant* (i.e., consistent). In other words, it is assumed that an infant possessing an apparent penis and scrotum also possesses a fully developed Wolffian system of a vas deferens, epididymis, seminal vesicles, prostate gland, a proportionally greater balance of androgens to estrogens, testes, and an XY sex-chromosome profile. Similarly, it is assumed that an infant possessing an apparent vaginal opening, labia, and a clitoris also possesses a fully developed Müllerian system with an inner third of a vagina, uterus and fallopian tubes, as well as ovaries and an XX sex-chromosome pattern. However, what if the assumption of concordance is incorrect and the individual is characterized instead by *discordance* between certain variables of biological sex?

TABLE 2.1	Summary of Biological Sex Dimorphism Variables During Typical Fetal Development	
Variable	**Female**	**Male**
Chromosomal	XX	XY
Gonadal	Ovaries	Testes
Hormonal	More estrogens than androgens	More androgens than estrogens + MIH
Internal Reproductive	Uterus, fallopian tubes, inner third of vagina	Epididymis, vas deferens, seminal vesicles, prostate
External Genital	Clitoris, labia, vagina	Penis, scrotum
Brain	Estrogen-sensitive hypothalamus	Estrogen-insensitive hypothalamus

Sex Discordance

In Chapter 1, we examined some examples of individuals born with ambiguous external genitalia. These hermaphrodites, or intersexed individuals, appear to defy easy designation as being either biologically male or female. We can now be more precise here in identifying some of the causes of these discordant conditions. In addition, a number of other instances of discordance, not characterized by ambiguous genitalia, have been identified in the clinical literature. We shall describe them only briefly.

In the case of **androgen-insensitivity syndrome** (AIS), either an enzyme necessary for the production of androgens is missing or, in the more frequently occurring situation, a substance toxic to androgens is present. Regardless of the etiology, the result is a genetic male (46,XY), with testes that produce MIH, but whose body fails to masculinize further. Consequently, neither the Müllerian nor the Wolffian systems proliferate. The person is born with ambiguous genitalia that frequently appear to be more female than male. He or she, depending upon how the infant is (re)assigned, typically develops female secondary sex characteristics during puberty, but does not possesses the ability to menstruate and is, of course, infertile.

A variation of AIS is known as **5-alpha-reductase deficiency.** In this instance, the enzyme (5-alpha-reductase) responsible for converting testosterone into dihydrotestosterone is missing. Consequently, 46,XY males are born with undescended testes and complete male reproductive organs, but the external genitalia are ambiguously formed with what initially appears to be an enlarged clitoris and either partially fused labia, forming an incomplete scrotum, or fully fused labia forming an empty scrotum. At birth, such individuals are typically assigned the female sex and are reared as females. At puberty, when the testes begin to secrete larger amounts of androgens, the "clitoris" enlarges further to more closely resemble an appropriately-sized penis.

Androgenital syndrome (AGS), also known as **congenital virilizing adrenal hyperplasia** (CVAH), occurs among both males and females, but its effects are most noticeable among genetic females (46,XX), when abnormal amounts of androgens are secreted by either the mother's or the fetus's adrenal glands. These androgens do not effect the internal reproductive organs, but do effect the external genitalia, most often producing ambiguous genitalia with an enlarged clitoris. Included in this instance of discordance are those females whose mothers were (erroneously, in hindsight) prescribed a synthetic hormone, diethylstilbestrol (DES), during the 1940s through to the early 1960s as a means of preventing miscarriages.

In all of the above instances, discordance occurs at other than the genetic or chromosomal level. There are, however, a number of categories of discordance that begin with the chromosomal level. As we noted at the beginning of this chapter, sperm typically carry either an X or a Y chromosome. As a consequence of the failure of sperm to divide properly, they may, depending upon the precise stage of the division process where the error occurs, carry an XX or an XY chromosomal combination or no sex chromosome at all. At the mystical moment of conception, when these sperm are united with an X-bearing egg, the resulting zygote could carry an XXX, XXY, or XO combination. About "1 in 400 children is born with SCA [sex chromosome abnormality], although most will never be diagnosed" (Berch and Bender, 1987: 54).

Turner's syndrome occurs when a genetic female (45,XO) does not develop gonadal tissues (ovaries) and, therefore, no sex hormones are produced. Due to the absence of androgens, the external genitalia appear as female and individuals experiencing this form of discordance are identified and raised as females. The discordance is most likely to be diagnosed when no onset of puberty occurs. **Klinefelter's syndrome** occurs among genetic males (47,XXY) who are born with underdeveloped testes, a scrotum, and a small penis. "At puberty, they grow taller than average, their hips tend to feminize, they may have some breast development, their testes do not enlarge, they do not produce sperm, their voices do not deepen, and they develop little or no pubic and facial hair" (Renzetti and Curran, 1995: 26). Women born with an extra sex chromosome (47,XXX) do not appear to display any other variations regarding their hormones, internal reproductive organs, or external genitalia either at birth or at puberty.

As each of these instances of sex discordance has been clinically isolated and identified, researchers have been interested in determining if any of the conditions can be linked to specific variations in social or psychological gender behaviour. Rather than bore, or possibly confuse, you with any listing of claims and counterclaims, including all of the specific methodological problems and issues raised by the research, we prefer to simply note that the results are inconclusive overall. The conclusions of one researcher that "the history of research on prenatal hormones and human behavior has been typified by reports of suggestive results, followed by realization of potential methodological problems" (Hines, 1982: 73), are still appropriate today and can be generalized to include chromosomal anomalies as well. In other words, initial studies frequently suggest possible behavioural outcomes of discordant hormonal or chromosomal conditions (and any related genital ambiguities), but when these studies are held up to scrutiny, the results have ultimately been deemed to be inconclusive at best. In the final analysis, the existence of discordance is important to us mainly for the analytic questions that can be raised regarding any erroneous assumptions individuals may hold that biological sex is always a simple concordant variable.

We stress once again that assigned (or labeled or named) sex, with all of its attendant deliberations about given names, the purchasing of cards, birth announcements, perhaps cigars, toys, clothing, room furnishings, government bonds and tuition endowment plans, and the development of hopes, dreams, and aspirations are all based upon a visually apprehended genital configuration. Genital sex dictates assigned sex and the resulting label remains unchanged for the lifetimes of almost all of the Canadian population.

Gender Identity

The important variable of **gender identity** is typically and generically defined as a sense of oneself as being either male or female. As the definition uses the terms "male" and "female," *sex identity* would appear to be a more logically consistent concept. However, since such logical usage has not been adopted to any significant extent throughout the gender-studies literature, we shall keep with tradition and use the phrase "gender identity" to refer to this variable. Regardless of which term is used, numerous researchers and theorists, such as Saxton (1990: 28–31) and Money (1988), and proponents of theories, such as the cognitive-developmental (e.g., Martin and Little, 1990; Kolhberg, 1966), all argue that gender identity is the key variable in the ultimate determination of subsequent gender behaviour, as we shall see later.

Gender Behaviour

This general, and somewhat vague, concept represents the last of our basic variables of sex and gender. It is obviously impossible to list all of the components that could be contained under the umbrella of gender behaviour. The bulk of this textbook is devoted to exploring various dimensions of many, but not all, of these components. For the moment, we shall just note that the fundamental issue for researchers and theorists of all persuasions lies in trying to determine the nature of the connections between the variables of biological sex, assigned sex, gender identity, and gender behaviour.

Before we shift our attention to considerations of various theoretical perspectives that attempt to shed analytic and descriptive light on the essential relationships, if any, between what we can loosely refer to as sex and gender, we ask you to briefly consider one issue you confront in everyday life. When you meet a stranger for the first time, upon what basis do you determine that person's sex? Unless you are meeting in a nudist camp or some other nudity-required situation, visual determination of genital sex is probably out of the immediate question. So what cues do you rely upon? In all probability you must rely upon apparent physical appearance and the apparent display of secondary sex characteristics.

We state "apparent," since we all know that cosmetics and clothing can be selectively applied and donned to conceal and reveal whatever we wish to visually communicate to others, as anyone who has ever observed a transvestite or hopeful transsexual can readily attest. Recall from Chapter 1 that an important part of the "real-life test" waiting period before transsexual surgery is approved is devoted to an applicant's attempts at deceiving observers about their current sex designation. What you see isn't necessarily what you get. The use of clothing and cosmetics can be considered under the heading of gender behaviour, as can be diet, elective surgery, exercise programs, the selective application of alcohol and other recreational drugs, and any other behaviours we engage in to influence our physical appearance and/or other people's perceptions of that appearance.

Depending on the situation, you may have the opportunity to study a person prior to actually interacting with them. In addition to their appearance, you may also focus your attention upon their general demeanor, the way they stand and physically carry themselves, and their kinesics, or body-part movements, such as their facial expressions, hand and arm movements, and leg positions and movements. These gender-behaviour attributes are learned and can be manipulated, with greater or lesser success, to reinforce impressions of gender and, ultimately, of one's sex. From the imagery created by gender-display behaviour, you infer the observed's gender identity, genital sex, internal reproductive sex, hormonal sex, and chromosomal sex. All of this is done in a cursory taken-for-granted manner, as if the issue is neither problematic nor in need of further investigation. Only if we somehow acquire contradictory information, will we be motivated to delve beyond our initial assumptions.

It is, therefore, interesting to the sociologist of everyday life that the vast majority of the Canadian population identify each other's apparent biological sex based upon observation of something which is highly variable and alterable. Indeed, "it is quite likely that appearance is a core aspect of gender stereotyping" (Lips, 1993: 8). The research of Deaux and Lewis (1984) finds that the cues provided by an individual's physical appearance (e.g., strong and sturdy versus dainty and graceful) invariably outweigh the label "male" or "female" when respondents are inferring what a hypothetical person would be like, what roles she or he would engage in, and what traits the person would possess. In like fashion, we may presume to judge the sexual orientation of another person based upon little more than their facial appearance. Thus, males with "feminine" faces and females with "masculine" faces are more likely than others to be judged as homosexual (Dunkle and Francis, 1990).

Of all the variables of sex and gender we have considered thus far, only chromosomal sex, once established at conception, is unalterable. We possess the ability today to alter a person's gonadal sex (primarily through removal and through implants of nonfunctioning replicas), hormonal sex, internal reproductive sex (principally through removal), genital sex, assigned sex, and gender behaviour. As we saw in Chapter 1, regarding transsexualism and sex (re)assignment, the issue of the immutability of gender identity is still somewhat controversial. With the increased use of various technologies, including our improved abilities to identify more instances of sex discordance, the variability of sex and gender will continue to increase. This increase poses further challenges to the explanatory power of each theoretical perspective as it attempts to become either a grand-scale theory offering an

Box 2.1   The Vowed Virgins Of Albania

[Author's note: please bear with the journalist's obvious difficulties in comprehending cultural differences. This "outsider" hasn't had the benefit of a social-science upbringing.]

Deep in the barren mountain region of northern Albania, a group of women cling to an ancient tradition as old as the blood feuds that have returned to haunt this tiny corner of the Balkans. Searing poverty, war and bloody vendettas wiping out the male line of a family in feud meant women—sometimes girls—took control of the household. It is a custom that many even in Albania believed had died out with the feudal system that Communist leaders tried to eradicate during 45 years in power. But the women live on. They are known as the "vowed virgins" of Albania.

When a girl adopts the mantle of "paterfamilias," she cuts her hair short, dresses as a boy and takes on a man's job, which can mean back-breaking work toiling in the fields. With a fervor similar to that of an order of Roman Catholic nuns, the "virgins" stick to the unwritten rule that requires them never to marry or have children. What surprises the outsider is that the men and village elders in this staunchly chauvinistic society accord the "virgins" all the rights and privileges of fellow males. No bar falls silent when one of the women walks in for a glass of throat-scorching raki (local brandy). They negotiate deals on behalf of the family and are consulted on village affairs.

Lula Ivanaj is one such woman. At age 15, her destiny was laid before her. She willingly accepted her widowed mother's plea to head the family of 10 daughters and one son. The boy was considered too weak to take on the job. "I am never regarded as a woman but as a man," said Lula, 41, sitting in the one-room home of her elder sister in the rural town of Bajza, 150 kilometres north of Tirana. "Usually if the men have been killed either through war or blood feud, then a woman has the power to take over the defence of the family," said the chain-smoking Lula, surrounded by family members assembled to mark a Roman Catholic feast day.

Family vendettas have made a comeback since the Communist dictatorship

---

all-encompassing explanation of the relationship between all aspects of sex and gender, or become a middle-range explanation for a selected set of relationships between limited sex and gender variables. We turn now to consideration of some of those perspectives.

BIOLOGICALLY GROUNDED THEORIES

A number of theories and theoretical perspectives anchor their explanations within the biological basis of human existence. Directly and indirectly, these theories argue that gender behaviour is ultimately a product of human biological nature (see Box 2.2). In simple words, sex determines gender. The three theories selected for consideration here vary in terms of the specific aspects of biology used as a cornerstone for explaining sex and gender differences.

collapsed in 1990, and the Bajza area is serious blood-feud country. Lula's sister, Marje, herself a mother of 11 children, and other female family members, wear long dark dresses, black scarves or white headwraps characteristic of the region. Lula wears a sweatshirt and trousers.

"I've never worn a dress or scarf. At weddings and on special occasions, I put on a suit, shirt and tie," Lula said with a loud laugh, shaking her crop of short, wavy hair. After years in male company, Lula sits and gesticulates as a man, while her sisters display rural hospitality, offering olives, mutton and bread. Outside, pigs and chickens scratch the earth around fig and plum trees. Does Lula talk to her sisters as a woman would? "No, I never discuss women's affairs. Nor do they expect me to," she answered. Marje shook her head in agreement—confusingly, Albanians nod their head for "No" and shake it for "Yes." "We don't talk about women's subjects. I regard Lula as my brother," said Marje, who had never seen her husband until her wedding day.

Although Lula knows how to cook and sew, she has spent most of her working life driving a tractor. She is now an experienced welder—a job unthinkable

for a "non-virgin" in the region—and hires out welding equipment to supplement a meagre income.

Residents of the region talk of a place called Kelmendi, a community accessible only by donkey or four-wheel drive vehicle, as the birthplace of the "warrior virgin" Nora—a legendary heroine who for a time fought back the Turks in the seventeenth century. Folklore has it that a conquering Ottoman pasha wanted Nora for his wife. Instead, she stabbed him to death, fled into the hills and led local resistance against the Turks. She was eventually caught, but the Turks, acknowledging her status, accorded her the "privilege" of being executed as a man. Lula recalls the story of Nora of Kelmendi and is proud her family came from the nearby village of Shkreli. The tradition at least will live on with her. "I started my career as a boy and my life will end as a man," she said.

Source: Steve Pagani, "Virgins' take men's place in vendetta-torn Albania," *Reuter.* Reprinted in *Edmonton Journal*, 13 May 1996: C7.

Sociobiology

First proposed by entomologist Edward O. Wilson in 1975 as a blend of genetics, animal studies, psychology, anthropology, and sociology, **sociobiology** is defined as "the systematic study of the biological basis of all forms of social behavior" (Wilson, 1978: 16). Sociobiologists attempt to link the long sweep of biological evolution to human cultural evolution by searching for the biological causes of existing culturally universal social behaviour in general, and gender behaviour in particular. Much of sociobiological theory was anticipated earlier by ethnologists, such as Morris (1969) and Tiger (1969) who attempted to link human behaviour to the behaviour of specific animal species. Sociobiologists extend this argument by claiming that, at some point in human evolutionary history, certain forms of behaviour (e.g., territoriality, aggressiveness, mate selection, male dominance) maximized the reproductive success of the organisms who exhibited them and subsequently

Box 2.2	Biology Versus Culture—Biology is the Answer

Steven Goldberg (1974, 1986, 1989) finds it astonishing that anyone should doubt "the presence of core-deep differences in males and females, differences of temperament and emotion we call masculinity and femininity." Goldberg's argument, that it is not environment but inborn differences that "give masculine and feminine direction to the emotions and behaviors of men and women," is summarized as follows.

1. The anthropological record shows that all societies for which evidence exists are (or were) **patriarchies** (societies in which men dominate women). Stories about past **matriarchies** (societies in which women dominate men) are myths.

2. In all societies, past and present, the highest statuses are associated with males. In every society, politics is ruled "by hierarchies overwhelmingly dominated by men."

3. The reason for this one-way dominance of societies is that males "have a lower threshold for the elicitation of dominance behavior…a great tendency to exhibit whatever behavior is necessary in any environment to attain dominance in hierarchies and male-female encounters and relationships." Males are more willing "to sacrifice the rewards of other motivations—the desire for affection, health, family life, safety, relaxation, vacation and the like—in order to attain dominance and status."

4. Just as a six-foot woman does not prove the social basis of height, so exceptional individuals, such as a highly achieving and dominant woman, do not refute "the physiological roots of behavior."

In short, only one interpretation of why every society from that of the Pygmy to that of the Swede associates dominance and attainment with males is valid. Male dominance of society is simply "an inevitable resolution of the psychophysiological reality." Socialization and social institutions merely *reflect*—and sometimes exaggerate—inborn tendencies. Any interpretation other than inborn differences is "wrongheaded, ignorant, tendentious, internally illogical, discordant with the evidence, and implausible in the extreme." The argument that males are more aggressive because they have been socialized that way is the equivalent of a claim that men can grow moustaches because boys have been socialized that way.

To acknowledge this reality is *not* to defend discrimination against women. Whether or not one approves of what societies have done with these basic biological differences is not the point. The point is that biology leads males and females to different behaviors and attitudes—regardless of how we feel about this or wish it were different.

Source: Henslin and Nelson, 1996: 285.

became genetically encoded within the species through the operation of Darwinian "survival-of-the-fittest" natural selection.

According to Darwin (1859), natural selection is based on four principles. First, reproduction occurs within a natural environment. Second, the genes of a species, the basic units of life that contain the individual's traits, are passed on to offspring. These genes have a degree of random variability; that is, characteristics are differentially distributed among the members of a species. Third, because the members of a species possess different characteristics, some members have a better chance of surviving in the natural environment than do others—and of passing their particular genetic traits on to the next generation. Fourth, over thousands of generations, those genetic traits that aid survival in the natural environment tend to become common in a species, while those that do not tend to disappear.

Natural selection is used to explain not only the physical characteristics of animals, including humans, but also behaviour, through the emergence of instincts over countless generations. Wilson (1975), an insect specialist, claims that human behaviour is no different from the behaviour of cats, dogs, rats, bees, or mosquitoes—it has been bred into *Homo sapiens* through evolutionary principles. According to Wilson, religion, competition and cooperation, slavery and genocide, war and peace, envy and altruism—can all be explained through sociobiology.

"The fundamental assertion of sociobiology is that we are structured by nature with a desire to ensure that our individual genes pass to future generations and that this is a motivating factor in almost all human behavior" (Lindsey, 1994: 41). Although our behaviour is thought to be limited by the physical capacity imposed by our genes (e.g., humans cannot soar in the skies like birds, nor dwell underwater without mechanical devices), sociobiology suggests that characteristics such as competitiveness, sexual selection, and so on, have become part of the human "biogram" or genetically encoded biological program. The basic message of sociobiology can be stated, using improper grammar, as "genetics is destiny."

Various human social behaviours have been examined by sociobiologists searching for an underlying genetic basis. For example, Wilson claims that the division of labour, wherein women look after the home and men assume responsibilities outside of the home, is genetically coded and, therefore, in future societies "even with identical education and equal access to all professions, men are likely to continue to play a disproportionate role in political life, business and science" (Wilson as quoted in Doyle and Paludi, 1995: 57). Other sociobiologists suggest that the concept of *parental investment* explains why women in all societies care for children. Parental investment refers to actions undertaken by the parent that increase a child's chances of survival.

According to this theory, a woman has the greater investment in the survival of a child because she contributes more than a man does from the moment of conception. Whereas sperm are "cheap" (each ejaculation typically contains between 200 and 500 million sperm, but may contain as many as a billion sperm cells [Saxton, 1990: 94–95]; this number can be replicated within 24 to 48 hours), eggs are "precious," not only because just one egg "ripens" per month, unless a woman takes a fertility drug, but also because each female possesses only a finite number of eggs and cannot manufacture new eggs during her lifetime.

Before a baby girl is born, development of future eggs begins in her just-forming ovaries. About halfway through her mother's pregnancy, the girl's ovaries contain 6 or 7 million future eggs, most of which degenerate before birth. About 400,000 immature eggs are present in the newborn girl, and no new eggs are formed after this time. During childhood, continued degeneration reduces the number of eggs still further....Fewer than 400 follicles [which rupture and release one egg each] are usually involved in ovulation during the female's reproductive years. (Masters et al., 1986: 38, 39)

In addition, eggs provide nourishment for the developing zygote while sperm do not. Eggs are, therefore, larger and more precious than sperm (Dawkins, 1976) and represent a greater genetic investment for the female than for the male biological parent. Add to this the fact that a woman invests nine months of her time (as opposed to only a few minutes of a man's time) as well as all of her bodily resources from conception through gestation of the fetus, and the conclusion is reached that it would be "evolutionary insanity" (Hyde, 1985: 68) for a woman to relinquish primary responsibility for her genetic child after birth. Hence, according to this theory, women necessarily assume primary responsibility for childrearing to protect their investments.

The combination of cheap sperm and the precious egg is also used to explain and legitimate the double standard of sexual behaviour and morality. According to sociobiology, it is evolutionarily adaptive for a man to attempt to impregnate as many women as possible to increase the likelihood that his genes will contribute to the next generation (Symons, 1979). However, a woman's sexual "promiscuity" (a vague and value-laden term) is not adaptive; she must be carefully selective regarding mating to find the one best partner with whom to intermix her precious genes. Sociobiologists also claim that the monogamous (one person at a time) mating system produces the greatest likelihood of infant survival. Given that a child is particularly helpless and dependent, the presence of two adults who are pledged to each other is considered genetically adaptive and desirable if the child is to survive. Sociobiologists also claim that female orgasm evolved to hold this dyad together, because it sustains the woman's interest in sexuality during non-ovulation times and solidifies the monogamous bond.

Numerous criticisms have been raised against sociobiology and the sociobiological argument. Essentially, it is considered to be simplistic, tautological (repetitive and circular in its logic), extremely reductionist, untestable and, therefore, unfalsifiable, and inherently conservative (Doyle and Paludi, 1995: 58–59; Lindsey, 1994: 42; Mackie, 1990: 59–61). Perhaps the most significant criticism is that sociobiologists have not been able to identify any of the specific genes that supposedly determine social behaviours such as nurturance, domestic labour, promiscuity, or monogamy. We are simply expected to assume, along with the sociobiologists, that such genes exist. Perhaps sociobiology will be vindicated when, or if, the Human Genome Project succeeds in locating and mapping the contributions of all human genes, but for now the basic tenets of the theory remain highly speculative.

Critics note that sociobiology fails to confront a fundamental problem in its attempts to link biological evolution to cultural evolution. The pace of change in the evolutionary histories of biological organisms and of cultures is by no means identical (Doyle and Paludi, 1995: 58). While cultures are capable of rapid social change, such is not the case for genetic change. Sociobiologists cannot easily incorporate genetic explanations for rapid sociocultural changes in infant-nurturing behaviour, marital behaviour patterns, labour-force participation rates, and so on. Even if behavioural change can be demonstrated to be adaptive, it cannot be assumed automatically that such change is genetically based (Mackie, 1991: 60). Sociobiology cannot easily account for cultural variations in behaviour patterns existing among contemporary and historical peoples, all of whom are members of the same human genetic species (Lindsey, 1994: 42). Furthermore, confirmation of this theory would require empirical evidence of human genes taken from our biological ancestors of long ago, something that is unattainable. Sociobiological theory is, therefore, scientifically unverifiable.

Critics have also observed that sociobiology is inherently conservative. The method of sociobiology involves focusing upon a currently existing behaviour pattern and then searching for an evolutionary biological reason to account for why things are now the only way they could possibly be. Present-day gender differences of whatever form are held to be immutable and unalterable in the absence of biological change. "By restating age-old claims that human nature is fixed and unchangeable, and that efforts to ameliorate social woes by changing the social environment are doomed to fail, sociobiology gives aid and comfort to supporters of the status quo" (Kamin, 1985: 78).

Sociobiology has also been criticized for being highly selective in the use of specific species selected to provide supposedly supportive evidence. Hyde (1985) notes that both the examples given and the theory itself are blatantly androcentric and sexist; examples that appear to support current social arrangements advantageous to males are stressed, while those that contradict it are ignored. For example, female chimpanzees are indiscriminately promiscuous when in estrous and mate with many males. This could be construed as a biologically determined behaviour pattern designed to maximize the female's chances of pregnancy and of ensuring that her genetic material is reproduced in future generations by taking advantage of all the cheap, but often ineffective (considering how few of the millions per ejaculate ever contribute to conception), male sperm available. However, since such behaviour would be supportive of female promiscuity and would challenge the double standard of morality advocating restricted female sexual behaviour, sociobiologists typically ignore female chimpanzee sexual behaviour (for further examples, see also Bleier, 1984; Fausto-Sterling, 1985; Hubbard, 1994; Udry, 1994).

This criticism of selective-species use has also been leveled against all animal studies research and theorizing, which claim to generalize from animal behaviour to explain human behaviour (Tavris and Wade, 1984: 133–135). Sociobiology has also been chided for its application of anthropomorphic language (i.e. language which refers to human characteristics or behaviour) to animals and even vegetation.

> A widely cited example of this practice is Barash's (1979) use of the term *rape* to describe what appears to be a male's forcing of sexual advances on an unwilling female among a variety of species, including mallard ducks and even plants! Although the use of the word *rape* in such contexts may have an attention-getting function for the scientist, it does little to clarify what is indeed going on. How, for instance, does the researcher establish that a female flower or a female duck is "unwilling"? (Lips, 1993: 91)

Even apparent universality of a behaviour need not imply that the behaviour is genetically encoded. Although birds raised in soundproof chambers will sing the songs unique to their species, a bullfinch raised with canaries will sing like a canary (Eibl-Eibesfeldt, 1970). Research conducted among primates suggests that their mating behaviour is learned. Gorillas, for example, are notorious for not mating in captivity and zookeepers have to replenish their supply of these animals from the wild. When there was a seemingly endless supply of wild animals, the apparent bashfulness of gorillas in zoos was but a minor nuisance. With growing international restrictions on capturing and importing animals, finding ways to sexually arouse captive gorillas and entice them into mating becomes a more serious issue. Zookeepers in Sacramento, California, noting their young gorillas seemed to want to mate,

Box 2.3 — Biology Versus Culture—Culture is the Answer

For sociologist Cynthia Fuchs Epstein (1986, 1988, 1989), differences between males' and females' behaviour are solely the result of social factors—specifically, socialization and social control. Her argument follows.

1. A re-examination of the anthropological record shows greater equality between the sexes in the past than we had thought. In earlier societies, women as well as men hunted small game, devised tools for hunting and gathering, and gathered food. Studies of today's hunting and gathering societies show that "both women's and men's roles have been broader and less rigid than those created by stereotypes. For example, the Agta and Mbuti are clearly egalitarian and thus prove that hunting and gathering societies exist in which women are not subordinate to men. Anthropologists who study them claim that there is a separate but equal status of women at this level of development."

2. The types of work that men and women perform in each society are determined not by biology but by rigidly enforced social arrangements. Few people, whether male or female, can escape these arrangements to perform work outside their allotted narrow range. This gender inequality of work, which serves the interests of males, is enforced by informal customs and formal systems of laws. Once these socially constructed barriers are removed, women can and do exhibit similar work habits as males.

3. The human behaviours that biology "causes" are limited to those involving reproduction or differences in body structure. These differences are relevant for only a few activities, such as playing basketball or "crawling through a small space."

4. Female crime rates, which are rising in many parts of the world, indicate that displays of aggressiveness, often considered a biologically dictated male behaviour, are related to social rather than biological factors. When social conditions permit, such as in the practice of female lawyers, females also exhibit "adversarial, assertive, and dominant behavior." Not incidentally, this "dominant behavior" also appears in scholarly female challenges to the biased views about human nature that have been proposed by male scholars.

   In short, rather than "women's incompetence or inability to read a legal brief, perform brain surgery, [or] predict a bull market," social factors - socialization, gender discrimination, and other forms of social control - are responsible for gender differences in behavior. Arguments that assign "an evolutionary and genetic basis" to explain gender differences in sex status are simplistic. They "rest on a dubious structure of inappropriate, highly selective, and poor data, oversimplification in logic and inappropriate inferences by use of analogy."

Source: Henslin and Nelson, 1996: 284.

but did not seem to know how, successfully solved the problem by showing their young charges a movie (gorillography?) of two adult gorillas mating (Stark, 1989).

Obviously, most sociologists find the sociobiological position unpalatable. Not only is it a direct attack on their discipline, but it also bypasses the essence of what sociologists focus on: humans designing their own cultures, their own unique ways of life (see Box 2.3). Sociologists do not deny that biology underlies human behaviour—at least not in the sense that it takes a highly developed brain to develop human culture, that there would be no speech if humans had no tongue or larynx, or that abstract thought could not exist if we did not have a highly developed cerebral cortex. But sociologists find the claim that human behaviour is due to genetic programing to be quite another matter (Howe et al., 1992). Humans, they argue, are not driven by instincts. Humans possess a sense of self and have abstract thought. They create and discuss principles that underlie what they do. They develop purposes and goals. They decide on courses of action that seem rational to them. They consider, reflect, and make choices. While their creative choices may appear to demonstrate universalities at the most general and superficial level, close examination reveals a wealth of differences in meaning and intent that defy reduction to a simple biological cause.

Evolutionary Psychology

Recently, a "new" blend of biology, anthropology, psychology, and psychiatry has developed under the heading of **evolutionary psychology**. The general theoretical and empirical approach being offered here is very similar to that of sociobiology, except that, for the moment, the focus of evolutionary psychology appears to be limited to identifying and explaining sexual strategies used by males and females in mating behaviour.

Based primarily upon the work of psychologist David Buss (1994), evolutionary psychology proposes that males and females are virtually identical in evolutionary terms except for the strategies they use to ensure survival of their sperm and eggs. The strategies identified are essentially the same we presented from sociobiologists, wherein males seek to spray their sperm as far and wide as they possibly can, in the hopes of contributing to conception and ensuring the survival of their genes. Females, in contrast, use a variety of techniques to reject inappropriate, and attract appropriate male, suitors who appear to provide the best genetic bet for her genes', her egg's, and her child's survival. Once again we have a theory that attempts to identify a genetic basis, based upon deliberately selected cross-cultural evidence and selected animal species, for male promiscuity, female monogamy, male infidelity (e.g., Fisher, 1992), and differential gender strategies utilized in the sexual seduction game (see also Givens, 1983).

Despite the obvious links to sociobiology, evolutionary psychology is so new that it is difficult to determine the ultimate scope of inquiry and shape of the theory being advanced. Whether it will remain a separate and distinct theory or become integrated into the sociobiological fold will be determined in the future. Today, the criticisms noted for sociobiology appear to be relevant for evolutionary psychology.

Psychoanalytic Theory

Psychoanalytic theory was initially and essentially formulated by Freud (1856–1939), who has been referred to as the "father of Western masculinist psychology" (Gerrard and Javed,

1995: 131). We locate the theory at this point in the text because Freud's formulations rely upon anatomical-sex differences to explain other differences between men and women. A basic message of psychoanalytic theory is, "anatomy is destiny." Before presenting Freud's theory, we draw your attention to the fact that his views on the origins of these subsequent gender differences, and on the nature of female personality in particular, were derived almost exclusively from his work with adult patients who sought relief from personal difficulties through his controversial newly developed "talking" therapy.

According to the basic tenets of psychoanalytic theory, human beings experience thoughts and feelings at both the conscious and unconscious levels of awareness. According to Freud, most of the thoughts and motivations of children, presented below, occur at the unconscious level. Freud further hypothesized the existence of three mental structures: the **id**, which represents biological influences or drives, governed by the "pleasure principle," the **ego**, which seeks to impose limits on the id; and the **superego**, which represents society's standards as incorporated into what may be termed as the individual's conscience. Although the id is present from birth, every individual must pass through five invariantly sequenced *developmental stages* (oral, anal, phallic, latency, and genital) to acquire an ego and a superego, and subsequently achieve a mature adult personality and behaviour patterns.

Freud believed that human beings are dominated by instincts, and that sexuality, fueled by **libido** (an instinctual craving for sensual pleasure), is one of the key forces motivating behaviour throughout childhood (a very radical notion at the time) and beyond. During each of the five developmental stages of childhood, libido is centred in a different *erogenous zone*, an area of the body sensitive to sensual stimulation. In the **oral** stage of the first 18 months of life, the infant's mouth acts as the major focus of sexual energy and gratification. In the **anal** stage, from eighteen months to three years, sensual pleasure is derived from the region of the anus. Allowing or restricting bowel movements gives the child physical and psychological pleasure, and provides the first opportunity for expressing freedom from the control of the mother, who is the child's primary love object during both of the first two stages. According to Freud, boys and girls pass through the oral and anal stages of psychosexual development in the same fashion. Their experiences are so similar that Freud androcentrically referred to both sexes as "little men" (Frieze et al., 1978: 30). However, during the **phallic** stage (ages three to five), when libido focuses on the genitals and masturbation is the source of sexual gratification, boys and girls diverge and follow separate developmental pathways.

The young boy becomes fascinated with his penis and develops an unconscious fantasy of possessing his mother sexually. This fantasy creates an **Oedipal complex**, which Freud named after the Greek myth of Oedipus, who unwittingly killed his father and married his mother. During the time of the Oedipal complex, the boy is intensely attached to his mother and resents the presence of his father, whom he unconsciously perceives to be a rival for his mother's sexual and nonsexual affections. The boy considers his father to be a formidable opponent. He becomes anxious that his father will retaliate by depriving him of his source of sexual pleasure by castrating him. The boy's anxiety over castration is further fueled partly by his startling observation that girls do not possess a penis, which the boy assumes is a superior sexual organ and, therefore, that girls and women are inferior, and partly by his belief that girls must have once possessed a penis and later been castrated. Since it happened to them, it could happen to him and no one is more likely to do this than his father, the rival.

Freud considered *castration anxiety* to be a powerful motivating force in male psycho-sexual development. The young boy, fearful of his father, represses his sexual desires for his mother and comes to identify with his father as a way of avoiding castration. In seeking to become as much like his father as possible, so that he too will some day be able to satisfy his own sexual cravings, the boy takes on the values, ideas, and gender identity of his father, which leads to his development of an ego, superego, and a masculine personality.

The counterpart, but more complex, female experience during the phallic stage is that of the **Electra complex**, named initially by Jung (Stockard and Johnson, 1980: 206) after the Greek legend of the princess who helped kill her mother. The first critical event for the young girl during the phallic stage is her realization, upon visual inspection of young boys, that she does not possess a penis. This awareness immediately creates unconscious feelings of inferiority about herself and envy of boys and men. *Penis envy,* coupled with the girl's belief that her mother must have mutilated the penis the girl once possessed, leads her to reject her mother and to unconsciously desire her father sexually and to desire to be impregnated by him.

Freud claimed that a girl can never fully resolve her Electra complex because she can never physically possess her own penis. Whereas the boy's powerful fear of castration is resolved by the critical process of identification with his father, the girl is motivated by envy, which is less powerful than fear. Eventually realizing that she can never actually possess her father sexually, the girl comes to identify with her mother as a way of vicariously acquiring her father's penis, a wish that is eventually transformed in the mature woman into a desire to bear children. Through this weaker identification she takes on her mother's values, ideas, and gender identity and acquires an ego, superego, and feminine personality. The girl's partial resolution of her Electra complex leaves her, according to Freud, with lifelong feelings of inferiority, psychological immaturity, a predisposition to jealousy, intense maternal desires with attendant masochism, a dependence upon men for values, and a less mature sense of conscience or morality (an "immature" superego). In other words, her anatomical inferiority leads to a moral-ethical inferiority (Mackie, 1991: 63).

According to Freud's theory, after passing through the phallic stage by age six, every child then enters the **latency** stage in which sexual impulses recede in importance and both boys and girls focus on nonsexual interests. In the **genital** stage, precipitated by instinctual forces at puberty, the adolescent directs his or her sexual interests towards heterosexuality, although Freud did believe that all persons were capable of heterosexuality, homosexuality or bisexuality (Lee and Hertzberg 1978: 29), and a mature genital sexuality expressed in different sex-linked forms, such as the shift of emphasis by women from their clitoris to their vagina as the mature source of sexual pleasure (Lee and Hertzberg, 1978: 31).

We should note that evaluations and criticisms are typically based upon a presumed understanding of what a theorist actually claims. In the case of Freud, a significant problem exists in determining what his theory states.

> The difficulty in finding the "real" Freud...is that we must get through a series of layers: what Freud himself said originally, what he said later, what his followers did with what he said, what his detractors thought he said, and what his defenders wish he had said. (Tavris and Wade, 1984: 176)

Despite these difficulties, a general consensus exists that Freudian theory is subject to a number of criticisms. Several authors have challenged the basis for certain of Freud's formulations. For example, Masson (1985) observes that Freud presented a paper in 1896, to the Society for Psychiatry and Neurology in Vienna on the alarming prevalence of childhood rape and incest and its pathogenic effects on adult women. Although his professional peers advised him never to publish this paper, Freud defied them and "The Aetiology of Hysteria" appeared that year. Masson concludes from his review of Freud's personal documents, including letters from his colleagues, that Freud experienced such severe professional ostracism following publication of the paper that he later retracted his views that actual childhood sexual traumas formed the basis of hysteria in women. Childhood sexual trauma was now reformulated into the supposedly unconscious workings of the Electra complex and allegations of childhood sexual abuse were now considered to be a consequence of repressed, unfulfilled, and unconscious childhood longings during the phallic stage of development. Masson asserts that this decision was simply the result of professional expedience and notes that, in a letter written to his friend and colleague Wilhelm Fleiss, Freud acknowledged that "[m]y own father was one of these perverts and is responsible for the hysteria of my brother…and those of several younger sisters."

While Masson attributes Freud's reformulation to a lack of moral courage in the face of professional censure, Miller (1990) suggests that Freud suppressed his theory out of a desire to protect himself and his friends from the pains of self-examination. She states that Fleiss's son, psychiatrist Robert Fleiss, discovered decades after the event that "at the age of two, he had been sexually abused by his father and that this incident coincided with Freud's renunciation of the truth" (Miller, 1990: 56). If Masson and Miller are correct, the portion of Freudian theory dealing with the phallic stage of psychosexual development in women requires careful re-examination.

Three other major criticisms have been leveled at Freudian theory. First, the theory is not just androcentric but, more specifically, **phallocentric**. Profound gender differences in personality and behaviour rest upon a cornerstone of anatomical-sex differences observed by three-year-old children, who immediately and uncritically recognize the superiority of the penis and of the person attached to it. Freud wrote that

> [girls] notice the penis of a brother or playmate, strikingly visible and of large proportions, at once recognize it as the superior counterpart of their own small and inconspicuous organ, and from that time forward fall a victim to envy for the penis.…She has seen it and knows that she is without it and wants to have it. (Freud, 1925, in Steinem, 1994: 50)

Bigger is apparently better in Freud's interpretation, even though he attributes this judgment to young children, and despite the fact that he studied troubled adults and few children. Anxiety over possibly losing a penis, or envious desire to obtain a penis, provide the important motivations to resolve developmental issues during the phallic stage. This supposedly human developmental stage is named after male, not female, anatomy, thus equating male with human, and female with something less, or other, than human. You are invited to speculate on the possible form of Freud's theory, and subsequent interpretations and criticisms, had he centred it upon the clitoris, that erogenous organ of the female body, whose sole function, unlike the phallus, is the provision of sensual pleasure. If your imagination is too weary, see Box 2.4 for a gynocentric revision of certain elements of Freud's theory.

Second, Freud has been criticized for making extremely biased over-generalizations. In proclaiming that biological differences ultimately determine human social and psychological behaviour ("anatomy is destiny"), Freud ignored sociocultural influences on both the development of gender differences and the creation of his own theory (Lee and Hertzberg, 1978: 34; Mackie, 1991: 63). Freud was seemingly oblivious to the fact that his patient

| Box 2.3 | **What if Freud were Phyllis?** |

The following presents a speculative fictional gynocentric rewrite of Freudian theory, placing women centre stage and men at the problematic margins of social and psychological life.

It's important to understand that when Phyllis was growing up in Vienna, women were considered superior because of their ability to give birth. From the family parlor to the great matriarchal institutions of politics and religion, this was a uniform belief....

Women's superior position in society was so easily mistaken for an immutable fact of life that males had developed exaggerated versions of such inevitable but now somewhat diminished conditions as *womb envy*. Indeed, these beliefs in women's natural right to dominate were the very pillars of Western matriarchal civilization....

In addition, men's lack of firsthand experience with birth and nonbirth—with choosing between existence and nonexistence, conception and contraception, as women must do so wisely for all their fertile years—severely inhibited their potential for developing a sense of justice and ethics. This tended to disqualify them as philosophers, whose purview was the "to be or not to be" issue, the deepest question of existence versus nonexistence, that dominates serious human discourse. Practically speaking, it also lessened men's ability to make life-and-death judgements, which explained their absence from decision-making positions in the judiciary, law enforcement, the military, and other such professions. True, one or two exceptional men might ascend to a position requiring high moral judgement, but they had been trained to "think like a woman" by rare contact with academia or because they had no sisters and their mothers were forced to burden their tender sons with matriarchal duties.

Finally, as Phyllis Freud's clinical findings showed, males were inclined toward meanness and backbiting, the inevitable result of having been cut off from the coveted sources of life and fulfillment to which their mates had such ready access within their bodies....

After life-giving wombs and sustenance-giving breasts, women's ability to menstruate was the most obvious proof of their superiority. Only women could bleed without injury or death; only they rose from the gore each month like a phoenix; only their bodies were in tune with the ululations of the universe and the timing of the tides. Without this innate lunar cycle, how could men have a sense of time, tides, space, seasons, movement of the universe, or the ability to measure anything at all? How could men mistress the skills of measurement necessary for mathematics, engineering, architecture, surveying—and so many other professions? In Christian churches, how could males, lacking monthly evidence of Her death and resurrection, serve the Daughter of the Goddess? In Judaism, how could they honor the Matriarch without the symbol of Her sacrifices recorded in the Old Ovariment? Thus insensible to the movements of the planets and the turning of the universe, how could men become astronomers, naturalists, scientists—or much of anything at all?...

As Phyllis observed...there was "yet another surprising effect of womb envy, or of the discovery of the inferiority of the penis to the clitoris, which is undoubtedly the most important of all…that masturbation…is a feminine activity and that the elimination of penile sensuality is a necessary pre-condition for the development of masculinity."

In this way, Phyllis Freud wisely screened all she heard from her testyrical patients through her understanding, still well accepted to this day, that men are sexually passive, just as they tend to be intellectually and ethically. After all, the libido is intrinsically feminine, or, as she put it with her genius for laywoman's terms, "man is possessed of a weaker sexual instinct."

This was also proved by man's mono-orgasmic nature. No serious authority disputed the fact that females, being multiorgasmic, were better adapted to pleasure and thus were the natural sexual aggressors. In fact, "envelopment," the legal term for intercourse, was an expression of this active/passive understanding. It was also acted out in microcosm in the act of conception itself. Consider these indisputable facts of life: The large ovum expends no energy, waits for the sperm to seek out its own destruction in typically masculine and masochistic fashion, and then simply envelops this infinitesimal organism. As the sperm disappears into the ovum, it is literally eaten alive—much like the male spider being eaten by his mate. Even the most quixotic male liberationist will have to agree that biology leaves no room for doubt about intrinsic female dominance.

What intrigued Freud was not these well-known biological facts, however, but their psychological significance: for instance, the ways in which males were rendered incurably narcissistic, anxious, and fragile by having their genitals so precariously perched and visibly exposed on the outside of their bodies. Though the great Greek philosopher Aristotelia had been cruel to say that men were simply mutilated women, men's womblessness and the loss of all but vestigial breasts and odd, useless nipples were the end of a long evolutionary journey toward the sole functions of sperm production, sperm carrying, and sperm delivery. Women did all the rest of reproduction. Thus, it was female behavior, health, and psychology that governed gestation and birth. Since time immemorial, this disproportionate reproductive influence had unbalanced the power of the sexes in favor of women.

Finally, there was the unavoidable physiological fact of the penis. Its very existence confirmed the initial bisexuality of all humans. All life begins as female, in the womb as elsewhere (the only explanation for men's residual nipples), and penile tissue had its origin in the same genital nub, and thus retained a comparable number of nerve endings as the clitoris. But somewhere along the evolutionary line, the penis had acquired a double function: excretion of urine and sperm delivery. Indeed, during the male's feminine, masturbatory, clitoral stage of development before young boys had seen female genitals and realized that their penises were endangered and grotesque compared to the compact, well-protected, aesthetically perfect clitoris—it had a third, albeit immature, function of masturbatory pleasure….

It was almost as if Father Nature himself had paid "less careful attention" to the male. His unique and most distinctive organ had become confused. Was the penis part of the reproductive system or the urinary tract? Was it intended for conception or excretion? How could males be trusted to understand the difference?…

Nonetheless, Freud continued to extend her "Anatomy is destiny" thesis beyond previous boundaries. With the force of logic in combination with clinical evidence of men's greater tolerance for physical as well as psychological pain, she demonstrated that the suicide run of tiny, weak male sperm toward big, strong female ova was the original paradigm of male masochism. There was also the chronic suffering caused by burning urine forced through the residual clitoral nerve endings within the penis. For the next century and perhaps the future of womankind, Freud had brilliantly proved why the pleasure/pain principle of masochism was a hallmark of masculinity. (Though, as she well knew, it also occurred in females who were put in a masculine position.)...

Male sexuality became mature only when pleasure was transferred from the penis—which was desensitized and rendered unpleasant by its dual function anyway—to the mature and appropriate areas: the fingers and the tongue. Immature *penile* orgasms had to be replaced by mature *lingual and digital* ones....

...after her mother's death, Phyllis Freud had realized that *all* children feel hostility toward their parents and want them to die....As she wrote, "in sons this death wish is directed against their father, and in daughters against their mother." It was not only a comforting confirmation of her own normalcy but the moment many Freudian scholars have pinpointed as the discovery of the Electra and the later-discovered less important Oedipus complex.

Source: Steinem, 1994: 32, 33, 35, 36, 48–50, 51, 52, 69.

sample, and he himself, lived in a particular historical time (late 1800s and early 1900s) and societal place (Victorian Austria, characterized by a patriarchal authority structure and a strict sex-linked division of labour). From this time and place, he generated a polarized depiction of women as "weak, inferior, passive, fragile, soft, vacillating, dependent, unreliable, intuitive rather than rational, castrated and handicapped" and men as "aggressive, controlling, strong, superior, proud, independent, venturesome, competitive, hard and athletic" (Miller, 1974: 367). Furthermore, such characteristics are depicted as being universal for all women and men in all cultures at all points in historical time. The findings of cultural anthropologists (e.g., Mead, 1935; 1949) and researchers from numerous other perspectives referred to throughout this text strongly dispute those characterizations.

Before leaving this point, we must point out that Freud's theory was not completely biologically determinist. Resolution of the Oedipus and Electra complexes was portrayed as ultimately resting on a child's identification with the same-sex parent. Such identification would incorporate environmental influences through imitative learning. Freud provided the basis for a later-developed branch of social learning theory known as identification theory (Tavris and Wade, 1984: 218). In addition, the "neo-Freudians," such as Erikson (1963) and Horney (1967), modified Freud's original theory to give more emphasis to the contributions of the sociocultural environment to child development and adult personality.

Third, from an empirical viewpoint, a major problem with psychoanalytic theory is that its concepts cannot easily be evaluated scientifically. The limited available research evidence has not been supportive. Greenglass (1982: 49–50) notes, "[e]mpirical work on many of Freud's assumptions about women has not given support to such ideas as penis envy and the Oedipus complex. For example, little evidence exists that girls and women envy male anatomy, while there is considerable evidence that women and girls envy the masculine role for its greater power and privilege—its greater sociocultural advantages." Lindsey (1994: 38) notes that "[a]lmost a century of empirical research on the foundations of Freud's work has produced more questions than answers and more inconsistencies than agreement." In summary, since Freud's major concepts do not lend themselves to testing, they must, like a secular religion, be accepted or rejected on the basis of faith or lack thereof.

Psychoanalytic Feminism

Feminists generally rejected Freudian theory in its entirety and devoted themselves to advancing critiques of the theory, its therapy (psychoanalysis), as well as its historical influence on various sectors of society (e.g., Clark and Lewis, 1977, on violence towards women; Edwards, 1981, on the law). However, by the late 1970s, some feminist theorists began to utilize portions of Freud's psychoanalytic theory in their own formulations. We will briefly focus here upon one strand of theorizing, **object relations theory**. For an overview of other strands, particularly those of the "French school," see Elliot and Mandell (1995: 20–23) and Code (1993: 44–47).

Psychoanalytic feminists, also referred to as *gynocentric theorists* (Stockard and Johnson, 1980: 214), of the object-relations school, trace their origins to the works of Klein (1957) and the more recent formulations by Dinnerstein (1976), Chodorow (1978), and Rubin (1983). The impetus for this psychoanalytic revival appears to be a growing awareness that, despite considerable ideological and structural changes in our society, significant gender divisions persist that have not been explained adequately by other theories (Elliot and Mandell, 1995: 13). Rubin notes that

> cultural ideals are powerful forces, shaping not only our ways of thinking and doing but our ways of being as well, giving form to both the conscious and unconscious content of our inner lives. Change, therefore, comes slowly, meeting enormous resistance both inside us and in the system of social institutions that supports our society's mandates about femininity and masculinity….[C]hange generally outruns consciousness, and, for most of us, change in consciousness lags well behind the changing social norms, sometimes even behind changing personal behaviors." (Rubin, 1983: 2–3)

These psychoanalytic feminists acknowledge that Freud's theory, his patients, and Freud himself were all the products of living within a patriarchal society at a specific point in time. Clearly, the social environment or context that structures the nature of family life plays an important role in determining the experiences of children living in a certain time and place. Chodorow (1978), Dinnerstein (1976), Klein (1957), and Rubin (1983) all argue that the key events of childhood that shape adult personality occur in the "pre-Oedipal" stage of developmental life. They assert that the central feature of this stage, both now and in the past, is that it is women who mother boys and girls. According to these theorists, childcare by mothers produces daughters who want to become mothers and sons who dominate and devalue women.

Chodorow (1978) argues that a girl's intense bond with her mother is never severed, with the consequence that girls and women unconsciously define themselves primarily in relational terms. To achieve masculinity, however, boys must sever their attachment to their mothers and develop a sense of separateness, which leads them to devalue women and makes later attachments with women difficult to achieve. Adult-women's relational needs are consequently not satisfied within relationships with men, leading to the intense desire to reproduce the more satisfying mothering experience. It is implicit within Chodorow's formulations that the strongest desire would be for a mothering relationship with a daughter, not a son.

Rubin argues that the lack of obvious differences between girls and women makes it easier for girls to establish their gender identity. One consequence of this developmental path is that women's sense of ego boundaries are more permeable, which largely accounts for women's greater empathetic abilities (Rubin, 1983: 58). The apparent differences between boys and their mothers makes the development of strong male-ego boundaries easier, but, since their closest previous attachment is with mothers, establishment of a gender identity is more difficult for boys (Rubin, 1983: 57). As a result of these different developmental experiences, women have difficulties in maintaining their ego boundaries within a relationship, while men have difficulties in breaching their own ego boundaries (Rubin, 1983: 92–96).

Full exploration of the consequences of gender development based upon the fact that it is women who mother is beyond our present scope. These psychoanalytic feminists propose, as a solution to gender developmental problems, a fundamental reorganization of parenting, where men become more involved in the nurturing process during the pre-Oedipal period. If the consequences of past and present childcare arrangements are as these feminists claim, how such a reorganization can occur in the context of a women-mothering society is unclear. In addition to this practical problem, psychoanalytic feminism also faces the same problems as Freud's work does; it is not verifiable empirically. Regardless of these problems, Freud's work has clearly been provocative to admirers and critics alike, hence his inclusion here as a pivotal theorist on the issues of the nature of sex and gender.

PSYCHOLOGICAL THEORIES

It is generally agreed that, at least by the age of four or five, girls and boys demonstrate a preference for being with their same-sex peers, and generally seem to prefer activities defined by their culture as being sex-appropriate. "The acquisition of sex-appropriate preferences, skills, personality attributes, behaviors, and self-concept is typically referred to within psychology as the process of 'sex typing' (Bem, 1983/1995: 83). Several theories within psychology consider the processes by which such sex typing occurs. We next briefly consider social learning theory, cognitive developmental theory, and gender lens/gender schema theory. Following them, we shall also explore a social psychological theory, symbolic interactionism, which possesses several insights relevant to our subject matter.

Social Learning Theory

Social learning theory (Bandura, 1986, 1977; Bandura and Walters, 1963; Mischel, 1966) focuses upon the impact of the social environment on human behaviour. The theory has been applied to the development of gender differences, based upon the assertion that learning gender follows the same principles as learning any other social behaviour. In explaining the acquisition of gender behaviour, social learning theory stresses the operation of two basic processes. One is the process of **direct reinforcement**, or the differential rewarding of gender-appropriate, and the punishing of gender-inappropriate, behaviour. According to social learning theory, behaviour is determined by its consequences. Individuals are likely to repeat behaviours that have been responded to in a positive manner (such as praise, smiles of approval, material gifts) and to cease engaging in behaviours that have been responded to in a negative manner (such as criticism, angry looks, removal of privileges, lack of attention). The second basic process is that of **modeling**, which can take either of two forms. *Direct imitation* involves immediately patterning one's behaviour upon what one sees others doing. *Observational learning* involves observing other people's behaviour, and the reactions to that behaviour, even though this information may not be acted upon until a much later time. Social learning theorists assume that "knowledge about gender roles either precedes or is acquired at the same time as gender identity" (Intons-Peterson, 1988: 40).

Specifically, with respect to gender learning, some social learning theorists (Levy, 1989: 12; Lynn, 1969, 1959) assert that the mother is the initial and central reinforcer of gender-appropriate behaviour. Consequently, a child learns early in life to exhibit those actions that will bring forth a mother's approval. The mother supposedly rewards feminine and punishes masculine behaviour in a girl, and rewards and punishes the opposite behaviours in a boy, thus differentially reinforcing gender-appropriate behaviour in her children. *Stimulus generalization* occurs later, when others (such as a father, other adults, or peers) reinforce gender-appropriate behaviour in a manner similar to the original stimulus, the mother. A child, therefore, learns that the reinforcements anticipated from one source can generally be expected to be forthcoming from others. Appropriate behaviour is consequently maintained.

In addition to the direct shaping of behaviour, according to this theory, children tend to imitate their same-sex parent and other same-sex adults. Imitation may explain the acquisition of certain, particularly subtle, aspects of gender behaviour that have not been the object of direct reinforcement from others. Finally, through observing people in the immediate environment or in the media, children incorporate into their behavioural repertoire gender behaviours that may be replicated during a later stage of life. For example, a young girl may observe her mother tending to the needs of a younger sibling and store this information for later use when she is a mother. At that point, she will probably announce to herself or her friends, and not always with pride, "Good grief, I've become just like my mother."

Although laboratory experiments support learning theory's suggestion that aggressive behaviour can be promoted or inhibited through selective application of rewards or punishments, Baldwin (1967) suggests that these results cannot be posited pre-emptorily as the mechanisms underlying the acquisition of gender differences. The reality of the process may be more complex in naturalistic, or nonlaboratory, settings. Evidence indicates that parents treat boys and girls differently and, in specific instances, differentially reinforce them for exhibiting the same behaviour (Block, 1978; Sherman, 1978). Parents, particularly fathers, engage in "roughhouse" activities with their sons, but treat their daughters as if they were more fragile (Maccoby and Jacklin, 1974). Block (1978) notes that parents emphasize different values for boys and girls, stressing the demonstration of achievement and assertion in boys and controlling these characteristics in girls, emphasizing instead a concern for relationships with other people. The direct use of rewards and punishments by parents appears to be most obvious in areas of their children's clothing and aggressive behaviour (Losh-Hesselbart, 1987: 545).

The available evidence suggests that, during childhood, parents monitor the behaviours of boys more closely than those of girls. Sons are found to be the recipients of both more rewards and more punishments than are daughters (Losh-Hesselbart, 1987: 545; Lynn, 1976).

Could being the centre of greater attention during childhood at least partly explain the tendency of men to consider themselves the centre of attention, the "star" (Hite, 1987: 79–83) in adult life?

Regardless of that speculation, it appears that parents are more concerned generally about ensuring the presence of masculine behaviour in boys than of ensuring feminine behaviour in girls during childhood (Losh-Hesselbart, 1987: 546). Cross-sexed "sissy" behaviour in boys is responded to more negatively than is cross-sexed "tomboy" behaviour in girls, although women are more accepting of cross-sexed behaviour in their children than are men (Fagot, 1985; Martin, 1990). Fathers, more so than mothers, attempt to inhibit gender-inappropriate behaviour in their children (Block, 1978; Lansky, 1967; Rekers and Varni, 1977). These findings suggest that mothers are more likely to focus upon behaviour that is gender appropriate, while fathers mainly focus upon behaviour that is gender inappropriate. Clearly, more research is needed to inquire into the dynamics of an apparent parental "division of labour" in childhood gender learning. Pressures for girls to act more feminine do not appear to intensify until around the time of puberty, in late childhood or early adolescence (Losh-Hesselbart, 1987: 546).

If, as asserted by social learning theory, fathers are not generally a meaningful part of a boy's life (Hartley, 1959; Levy, 1989; Lynn, 1969), yet imitation of a same-sex parent is important for learning appropriate masculine behaviour, boys' repertoire of gender-appropriate behaviour could consequently be incomplete. Despite her comparatively more accepting orientation, the reinforcements boys receive from mothers, as the primary caregivers, may still be of a more punishing than a rewarding nature. Being told that "boys don't cry" or "boys don't act like sissies" leaves unanswered the question of what it is that boys are supposed to do. In contrast, girls receive more rewarding reinforcements from a comparatively more available imitative role model. Lynn (1969) suggests that the absence of a male role model accounts for the tendency of boys to view masculinity in highly stereotypical terms, and the tendency for men to be more anxious and insecure than women about their gender identity and behaviour. These suggestions may account, in part, for the greater concern of fathers, when they are physically present, to observe and monitor whether their sons display gender-appropriate behaviour.

The social learning theory assertion that boys acquire masculinity through imitating their fathers and girls acquire femininity through imitating their mothers, appears to be too simplistic, even though it has obvious appeal for advocates of the dual-sex parental family, who argue that lone parent families, and gay or lesbian families, do irreparable harm to children by not providing appropriate sex- and gender-role models for children to imitate. Maccoby and Jacklin (1974) suggest that very young children *do not* imitate people of their own gender more than they imitate people of the other gender; their behaviour seems fairly random regarding the gender of the model. Social learning theory has been unable to untangle whether it is the qualities of nurturance or power in potential models, and under what conditions, that makes them more likely to be imitated. We must keep in mind that imitation refers essentially to mimicking behaviour. Observational learning, in contrast, need not translate into immediate behaviour patterns, as actual responses may be delayed indefinitely. Children could learn equally from models of both sexes, but selectively perform what they have learned, depending on their perceptions at a later time of how others' actions are rewarded or punished (Goldberg and Lewis, 1969; Hyde, 1985: 66; Rheingold and Cook, 1975).

It would appear that additional, more complex, processes may be involved in the acquisition of gender differences (Beal, 1994; Lott and Maluso, 1993). Perhaps the most persistent criticism of social learning theory is that it views humans in general, and children in particular, as passive vessels shaped simply by the application of rewards and punishments (Davidman, 1995; Lindsey, 1994: 53). The active participation of children in their own socialization is seemingly neglected. We should also note that social learning theory does not explicitly address the question of how children learn that they are female or male (Losh-Hesselbart, 1987: 549), nor how this knowledge relates to other lessons about gender appropriate, or inappropriate, behaviour. In addition, social learning theory does not address the question of why some behaviours are considered appropriate for one sex and not the other, nor why some behaviours are rewarded and others punished for each sex. In other words, social learning theory simply assumes the gendered context for learning exists, accepts it uncritically, and focuses only upon how learning takes place within that context.

Cognitive Development Theory

Cognitive development theory was formulated by Kolhberg (1966), based upon the theoretical framework created by Piaget (1968, 1954, 1950). Piaget concludes from his own empirical research that not only do children possess a cognitive organization that is different from adults, but also that children's cognitive organization changes systematically over time, in a developmental sequence. Unlike social learning theory, which suggests that people (children and adults) learn the same way, Piaget's theory suggests that learning will occur differently, dependent upon the type of thinking, or cognitive ability, the individual possesses at any particular point in time. Using Piaget's theory as a foundation, Kolhberg presents his own evidence to claim that children's understanding of gender and appropriate gender roles is based upon their developmentally changing cognitions of gender identity. As Kolhberg's sample comprised boys only, we shall accordingly provide only male examples in the first portion of our presentation and, in the process, demonstrate an all-too-common proclivity of traditional theorists to generalize male experiences to include all of humanity.

According to cognitive developmental theory, children acquire a rudimentary sense of gender identity, the sense that they are either male or female, and a sense of the gender identity of others sometime between eighteen months and three years of age, as part of their general attempt to understand the world around them. This initial gender identity is considered to be rudimentary, since, despite knowing what his current identity is, a young child is uncertain as to what his identity will be in the future and uncertain of the connections between current gender identity and future behavioural possibilities. Initial gender identity is based upon visible cues such as hair length and style and clothing styles. According to childhood "logic" at that stage of cognitive development, should those visible cues change, so too would gender itself. Put a dress on a boy and he becomes a girl, or cut a girl's long hair into a short style and she then becomes a boy. Until a child can understand the principle of conservation despite transformation (i.e., despite superficial changes, underlying features remain the same—such as the constancy of water volume despite changes in the shape of a container), a sense of unchangeable gender is not possible.

Kolhberg provides the following example of a child's incomplete conceptualization of gender:

Johnny: [age four and a half]: I'm going to be an airplane builder when I grow up.
Jimmy: [just turned four]: When I grow up I'll be a mommy.
Johnny: No, you can't be a mommy. You have to be a daddy.
Jimmy: No, I'm going to be a mommy.
Johnny: No, you're not a girl, you can't be a mommy.
Jimmy: Yes, I can. (1966: 95)

According to this example, Johnny demonstrates a sense of **gender constancy**: an awareness that one's gender identity is permanent or unchanging. In other words, gender constancy refers to a cognitive awareness that whatever one's gender identity is now is the same as one's gender identity will be in the future, regardless of whatever other superficial changes may occur. In contrast, Jimmy's sense of gender identity is still rudimentary and he demonstrates a belief that gender identity can change. Gender identity and gender constancy are inferred in this example from the children's statements about which parental status (mommy or daddy) they will occupy in the future.

Kolhberg claims that gender constancy is generally acquired around the ages of five or six (Marcus and Overton [1978] suggest ages five to seven), and is crucial as a motivating factor for the eventual acquisition and display of gendered behaviour. In other words, gender constancy is necessary to function in a consistently gender-appropriate way (Stockard and Johnson, 1980: 196). According to cognitive development theory, gender identity becomes a central part of a child's self-concept and is invested with a positive emotional attachment. Once gender constancy is attained, according to this theory, children then engage in what is essentially a **self-socialization** process. A child is self-motivated to seek out behaviour which is appropriate to, or consistent with, his or her understanding of gender. "I am a boy, therefore I want to do boy things" (Kolhberg, 1966: 89). Learning how to conduct oneself as a gendered being is, therefore, not something imposed on the child via reinforcement by external sources, such as parents, but rather is something actively sought by the child.

Once gender constancy has been acquired, children are then said by Kolhberg to accumulate gender stereotypes of supposedly appropriate behaviour for males and females and, furthermore, of societal evaluations of males and females. These stereotypes guide the self-socialization process and provide content for subsequent gender behaviour. The self-socialization process is supposedly easier for boys than for girls, because of the more positive evaluations of males in our society. "In the reality of the young child, 'male' is identified with 'big' and synonymous with 'more powerful'" (Kessler and McKenna, 1978: 97). During early childhood, both boys and girls identify to some extent with male role models in their environment. However, girls eventually come to see the female gender role as attractive, because of its "niceness" (Kolhberg, 1966: 121–122), and identify with their mothers as a readily available role model.

Although Kolhberg's theory is based upon examination of boys only, and then generalized as depicting the cognitive developmental process of girls, some evidence supports the existence of the same process occurring in girls (Coker, 1984). However, the precise sequencing of the developmental process has been questioned by research that claims that gender-typed interests (for example, in toys) appear in children when they are too young to have acquired gender constancy (O'Keefe and Hyde, 1983). While this finding appears to contradict Kolhberg's hypothesis that such interests should not appear until after gender constancy emerges, Martin and Little (1990) conclude that only a rudimentary knowledge of gender need exist before gender stereotypes and preferences are acquired. "Once children can accurately label the sexes, they begin to form gender stereotypes and their behavior is influenced by these gender-associated expectations" (Martin and Little, 1990: 1438). This finding suggests that Kolhberg's cognitive development model needs to be modified regarding the precise sequencing of initial gender identity, gender constancy, sex stereotypes, and sex-typed interests and preferences. Kolhberg's suggestion that children, particularly boys, value their own sex and prefer same-sex individuals for gender-based reasons has been substantiated by other researchers (Geller et al., 1979; Zuckerman and Sayre, 1982). However, the mechanisms responsible for this development in girls still remain somewhat speculative and problematic for this theoretical perspective. As with social learning theory, cognitive development theory does not address the issues of how and why stereotypes and differential standards of gender-appropriate toys, clothes, and behaviours exist. The sociocultural context of sex and gender is simply taken for granted.

Gender Lens/Gender Schema Theory

Bem (1974) was one of the modern-day pioneer researchers and theorists on the concept of psychological androgyny. She later (1983/1995) renounced her advocacy of androgyny and shifted her focus to the theoretical and practical implications of how we conceive of and perceive gender, with her development of **gender schema** theory. With her more recent **gender lens** theory, Bem (1993) elaborates upon earlier-developed themes, arguing that cultures are founded upon a limited number of assumptions (the "lenses") that shape perceptions of gender.

Three gender lenses found in all western societies are: polarization, androcentrism, and biological essentialism. *Polarization*, as Bem (1993) uses the concept, refers to what we have already termed as dichotomization of the sexes. Similar to what we presented in Chapter 1, *androcentrism* refers not only to a belief in male superiority, but also to the assumption that men's lives and ways of being are normative. *Essentialism* legitimates the first two lenses by suggesting that they are the inevitable by-products of inherent differences between the sexes. Since further elaboration of Bem's (1993) work would involve treating topics already covered in the previous chapter, we will focus here upon her more-limited theory of gender schema.

A **schema** is a cognitive information-processing system that guides and organizes, or structures, our perceptual processes, as well as our cognitive acquisition of knowledge about the world around us. Gender schema develop in people living in cultures that assert the primacy of the sex dichotomy and its elaboration into gender dichotomies. These cultures do not limit the application of gender labels or the attribution of gender-linked qualities only to humans. Even inanimate objects in a culture such as ours are invested with gender attributes, so that straight lines and sharp angles are considered to be masculine, while curves and circles are feminine. Nature and earth are anointed "Mother," while sky and impersonal time are called "Father." Ships are "shes" and flags are "hes" and very little in our culture is considered to be gender neutral or gender irrelevant.

Bem (1981, 1983/1995) blends elements from the cognitive development and social learning theories to create a theory about the processing, but not the content, of gender schema. According to Bem, a child's gender identity, once acquired within a gendered culture such as ours, forms the foundation for learning a gender schema. Martin and Halverson (1983) provide supportive evidence when they claim that one's own-sex gender schema develops first, followed by the development of an other-sex gender schema. Not surprisingly, the own-sex schema possesses more detail and complexity than the other-sex schema. Bem (1983/1995) suggests that a gender schema, once formed, creates a state of readiness within a child to organize and understand all subsequently received information about the social and physical world, in terms of its apparent male or female, masculine or feminine, properties. In other words, one learns to make sense of incoming information in schema-relevant terms.

Gender properties become more salient than any other properties the information may possess, so that, for example, the actions of a person will be attributed to their gender, regardless of whether gender was the sole, or even the major, motivating force behind them. For example, the way in which an automobile is being manoeuvred is much more likely to be attributed to the gender of the operator ("typical woman driver") than to any road conditions or vehicle-equipment problems that may be more relevant. Only by nesting those actions within the context of gender do the actions "make sense" to the perceiver. Possession of a gender schema also heightens one's sensitivity to existing gender stereotypes. Once integrated into a gender schema, these stereotypes gain a tenacious hold, because they support and maintain the schema itself. The larger gender-schematic culture reinforces individual beliefs, perceptions, and thought processes about gender, through the perpetuation of these stereotypes.

Bem (1983/1995) and others (Crane and Markus, 1982; Markus et al., 1982) suggest that gender schema are highly salient in "masculine" boys, "feminine" girls, and even androgynous individuals. Possibly only the "undifferentiated," as measured on the Bem Sex Role Inventory, who do not consider their personality qualities to be related to gender, are "aschematic," although Bem (1983/1995) claims that, since schema are learned, it is possible to raise aschematic children in a schematic world. Similar to Kolhberg, Bem suggests that children are internally motivated to conform to their gender-appropriate roles, since their gender schema become closely allied with both their gender identity and their self-concept. Matching one's behaviour to one's gender schema forms the basis for evaluating oneself as adequately masculine or feminine.

Some empirical evidence has been generated to support gender schema theory. Bem (1981) finds that gender-typed college students tend to cluster and recall words according to their perceived gender content, indicating that they use a gender schema to organize incoming information. Martin and Halverson (1983) find that children use their gender schema to filter out inconsistent information and selectively reorder their memories. Fagot and Leinbach (1989) demonstrate that parent's gender schemas influence how they relate to their children, which, in turn, influences the development of the children's gender schemas. The primary value of Bem's gender schema lies in its ability to integrate many of the concepts and principles of social learning and cognitive developmental theories, and to provide us with a better understanding of how gender-related information is cognitively processed. Bem's (1993) gender lens theory addresses limitations of other psychological theories by providing insight into the sociocultural conditions that promote development of certain gender schemas as opposed to others.

SOCIAL PSYCHOLOGICAL THEORY

The previous three theories have all been developed by psychologists. We now turn to a brief examination of the central tenets of a theory developed within sociology. Once again, the primary focus of this theory is on the process of becoming gendered, and not upon the actual content of gender.

Symbolic Interactionism

Symbolic interactionism is a social psychological theory, whose roots can be traced to sociologist/philosophers, such as Max Weber and George Herbert Mead, and early twentieth-century sociologists, such as Charles Horton Cooley and W. I. Thomas. Addressing the questions of the relationships between individuals and society, how society gets inside the individual, how individuals sustain or change society, and how individuals relate to one another, this theory focuses upon interpersonal interaction as a key explanatory variable and a basic unit of analysis.

Interactionists assert that human social behaviour is basically symbolic behaviour. A **symbol** is something which stands for, or represents, something else. Virtually anything and everything can be, and are, symbols, including written and spoken words, nonverbal gestures, and physical signs. Through agreement negotiated from interaction between humans over a period of time, symbols are assigned *meanings*, or shared definitions, and the symbols come to be responded to in terms of those, more or less agreed upon, meanings. In social interaction,

> human beings interpret or 'define' each other's actions instead of merely reacting to each other's actions. Their 'response' is not made directly to the actions of one another but instead is based on the meaning which they attach to such actions. Thus, human interaction is mediated by the use of symbols, by interpretation, or by ascertaining the meaning of one another's actions. (Blumer, 1969: 79)

Symbolic interactionists focus their analyses upon the symbols exchanged in interactions and the meanings these symbols have for the participants. These meanings may vary according to the particular cultural or subcultural (e.g., social class, race/ethnic) context within which they are embedded.

Human symbolic interaction occurs mainly through the mechanism of **role taking,** sometimes referred to as "taking the role of the other." In role taking, each person is "imaginatively assuming the position or point of view of another person" (Lindesmith and Strauss, 1968: 282). Through role taking, each person attempts to predict or anticipate the likely actions and reactions of other persons in an interaction situation. Furthermore, social interactionists argue that role taking is the principal means through which the socialization process occurs, and by which each individual develops a **self**.

The self and self-awareness emerge, or is presumed to emerge, by approximately two years of age (with a range of eighteen months to three years), as demonstrated by a child's accurate use of words such as "I," "me," and "mine." According to symbolic interactionists, self-development and language development evolve simultaneously (Mackie, 1991: 92). A central element of the self is a person's gender identity, the awareness that not only is one either male or female, but also that the labels "male" and "female" have certain meanings. So, in addition to recognizing that "I," the self, exists as a separate and distinct object, children also label that self as either male or female, boy or girl, and incorporate into their self-concept what it means to be a boy or a girl.

Initial acquisition of language in general, and sex/gender words in particular, as well as self-awareness in general, and gender identity in particular, occur during the early stages of socialization through role-taking interaction between a child and her or his *significant others* (Mead, 1934/1962). Significant others are those important individuals in the social environment with whom a child (and later an adolescent and adult) has an emotional bond, including one's parents, siblings, and kin, and eventually one's teachers, peers, friends, spouse(s), children, and coworkers. Parents, as significant others, help children to acquire language and to form connections between names (word labels) and things (including self) in their social and physical environment. As we have already noted, in acquiring names children also acquire knowledge about the meanings of those things being named. Learning the meaning of male and female, and the meaning of gender-appropriate behaviour, are important components of interactions with significant others.

Through role taking with these significant others, a child learns to see his or her self as these others see her or him. The perspective of these others becomes part of the perspective one takes towards one's self, including positive and/or negative feelings about oneself, a process captured in Cooley's (1902) concept of the *looking-glass self.* Consequently, if a person perceives that others consider him to be a worthwhile individual because he is a male and not a female, and because he does masculine and not feminine things, this person will develop positive feelings about his maleness and possible feelings of superiority to females and femininity. While initial role taking is limited to significant others, eventually, with exposure to an expanded world of the school system and to other less-personal relationships, individuals learn to take the role of the *generalized other* (Mead, 1934/1962). The generalized other is a more abstract and impersonal viewpoint, supposedly representative of the general society. "Instead of a child thinking, 'Dad says I mustn't cry when I don't get my own way,' the more mature youngster can now think, '*They* say boys mustn't cry'" (Mackie, 1991: 94 emphasis in original). Being able to generalize rules, understandings, and meanings beyond one's close circle of significant others is an important part of the socialization process by which an individual is able to adopt the perspective of the larger society and to monitor and control his or her behaviour in accordance with societal expectations and in anticipation of general societal reactions.

While symbolic interactionism initially appears to be a social determinist theory promoting a model of a passive individual shaped entirely by society (somewhat similar to the social learning theory model), such an interpretation is incorrect for three reasons. First, the self is not completely socially defined. Mead (1934/1962: 173–178) argues that the self is comprised of the "Me" (which represents the stable self, developed through interaction with others) and the "I" (which represents the spontaneous, autonomous, impulsive self). The commonly uttered phrase "I don't know why I did that. It's not at all like me," somewhat simplisticly illustrates that not all of our actions are predetermined by real or anticipated reactions of others. Even though we acquire the social meanings of male and female, masculinity and femininity, our behaviours are not necessarily dictated by those meanings. We are capable of independently creating our own thoughts, feelings, and actions.

Second, role taking, a central ingredient of human social interaction, is an active process, fraught with possibilities for understandings or misunderstandings. The more individuals find themselves in interactions with people from other social classes, ethnicities, sexual orientations, and abilities, the more likely they are to actively change their self-concepts, actions, feelings, and thoughts. As humans interact, they actively negotiate how they will conduct themselves in relation to one another, making their own interpersonal roles.

Finally, meanings that are socially constructed can be socially changed and reconstructed. Since meaning is not inherent in symbols, but is created out of interaction, meaning can be changed. The meanings (including evaluations) of male and female and of masculinity and femininity are not permanent and can be altered.

You can see that symbolic interactionist theory is compatible with the psychological theories already presented. To note just a few examples, the acquisition of meaning is clearly influenced by the system of rewards and punishments used by significant others in our environment. How we incorporate and organize those meanings will partly depend upon the schemas we acquire through interaction with others. Our concept of self will change with our stage of cognitive development. Finally, the "I" represents the active self, which can seek out traditional or new meanings of male and female and of masculine, feminine, or nongendered human behaviours. Each of these theories has a slightly different focus of questioning, and each produces slightly different answers to enhance our understanding of gender.

THE GENDER PERSPECTIVE

Our placement of the next perspective at this point in the text is somewhat arbitrary. Since it has been generated mainly by feminists, with many roots going back further than the recent wave of feminist theorizing, the perspective could be placed near the end of the next chapter, where we discuss feminist theories. However, since it is partly derived from a rejection of some, and an acceptance of other, ideas both implicitly and explicitly contained in several of the theories we have just examined, the present location appears to be best. We can review some elements presented in earlier theories and anticipate elements to be presented later. The new perspective rejects a central theme of all biologically based theories and an implicit theme flowing from aspects of social learning and symbolic interactionism theories in particular. At the same time, the perspective also attempts to combine elements from several social psychological and structural feminist theories.

Unlike many of the theories examined in this chapter, no single researcher or theorist can be named as synonymous with the gender perspective. In large part, this is because the perspective in still in its developmental infancy. We are dealing with a perspective that has yet to attain the status of theory, as some of its proponents readily acknowledge (e.g., Connell, 1985: 261; Thompson, 1993: 558, 567). The gender perspective has yet to attain a level of development wherein its constituent elements are logically organized and interrelated, forming a coherent whole. Consequently, our presentation will be as incomplete as is the perspective itself. The gender perspective may become the most comprehensive multilevel theory developed in gender studies thus far. However, since the road to scholarly hell is paved with the best of theoretical aspirations, success, or failure to live up to that promise, awaits future judgment. By the time we are finished, you should have some sense of the basic scope of the perspective, its major criticisms of existing theories, and some of its intended goals. Like ourselves, you should also have more questions about the gender perspective than answers.

The gender perspective arose partly in reaction to theories such as sociobiology and psychoanalytic theory that treat gender as an individual property rooted in biology (Thompson,

1993: 557; Zvonkovic et al., 1996: 91). These theories, both directly and indirectly, promote the notion that biologically based sex differences are responsible for creating stable properties of men and women that will manifest themselves in any and all institutions over the course of their lifetimes in Canadian society. As we noted in Chapter 1, these essentialist theories direct our attention towards emphasizing differences between men and women, while ignoring their similarities.

The gender perspective also arose in reaction to social psychological theories that stress the role of socialization as the ultimate mechanism by which gender is accomplished. Throughout the 1970s and 1980s, many feminist and nonfeminist sociologists and psychologists promoted a generic "sex-role" theoretical model to capture the social basis of gender. Sex roles, or its replacement term, gender roles, were "assumed to be dichotomous, complementary but unequal, relatively consistent internally, deeply internalized during the process of childhood socialization, and susceptible to only limited change in adulthood" (Potuchek, 1992: 548). Similar to the biologically based theories, socialization-based models anchored in social learning theory, and elements of symbolic interaction theory, also promoted a viewpoint that described gender as an individual property that, once attained through childhood socialization, retained an essential continuity throughout an individual's life. Attention was consequently focused upon identifying those properties of the socialization process and content that account for why women and men behave as they do within our society. Alternative behavioural patterns found in other subcultures, other cultures, or our own general culture at different points in historical time, were simply attributed to the existence of different role expectations into which individuals were socialized.

The sex-role socialization model began to receive critical appraisal (e.g., Breines, 1986; Lopata and Thorne, 1978; Stacey and Thorne, 1985; Vannoy-Hiller and Philliber, 1989) for its neglect of power and inequality, contradictions and inconsistencies in social expectations, and its inability to easily explain changes later in adults' lives. For example, predictions of female behaviour, based upon their childhood socialization, regarding paid employment and motherhood are not necessarily borne out in their adulthood (Gerson, 1986/1987). While participating in that critique (e.g., Ferree, 1990; Lero, 1996; Potuchek, 1992; Thompson, 1993), the gender perspective offers in place of the sex-role socialization model an alternative **social construction** approach (Osmond and Thorne, 1993; Thompson and Walker, 1995). The approach combines certain elements from a social role model (Thompson, 1993: 558) with elements of symbolic interactionism theory (Zvonkovic et al., 1996: 91), as well as conflict theory and ethnomethodology (Poutchek, 1992: 557; West and Zimmerman, 1987), and structural theories that we will explore in the next chapter.

We have already pointed out the presence of great similarities between the sexes and great variability within each sex. We have also noted that numerous possibilities exist for the social acceptance of more than two sexes and more than two genders. Despite these realities and possibilities, our society has chosen to construct and differentiate only two sexes and two genders. The gender perspective argues that apparent sex and gender differences are not the product of individual properties, but rather the product of ongoing multilevel social construction and reconstruction processes. Although the number of identified levels varies (Ferree, 1990; Thompson, 1993), four distinct-yet-related levels are becoming apparent: sociocultural, institutional, interactional, and individual. As each of these levels exhibits periods of stability and change, so too do the social construction processes and the contents of the constructions themselves.

The sociocultural level includes the symbolic conditions within which men and women live. Included here are the "systems of meaning" (Thompson, 1993: 559) incorporating values, specific beliefs, and ideologies that support social arrangements pertaining to gender (that only two genders exist and how they are to be experienced and demonstrated) and gender relations. Although not yet specifically included within the gender perspective, Bem's (1993) identified gender lenses of polarization, androcentrism, and biological essentialism are important components of our sociocultural context. In this mix we could also include the meaning system of patriarchalism, the cultural belief in the superiority of men over women. Belief systems change over time and we will examine, at the beginning of the next chapter, some specific changes in Canadian beliefs regarding the proper "spheres" for each gender, brought about by the transition of industrialization. We will also examine in later chapters how the "separate-spheres" belief systems have slowly been modified.

The institutional level focuses upon the fundamental structural basis of Canadian society. Institutions are informed by the sociocultural environment. According to the gender perspective, each institution within our society, such as the economy, the family, the polity, or religion is then structured to have different consequences for each gender. For example, with the industrialization of our society, the institution of the economy came to be defined as a masculine institution. Controlled and shaped by males, participation in the world of paid work also bestows key ingredients that help to construct and confirm masculinity. Increases in women's labour-force participation in Canada this century have been accompanied by concerns that such participation could "masculinize" females. In contrast, the institution of the family has been defined by our culture as a feminine institution, and concerns have been raised about the possibility that intensive participation within all facets of family life could "feminize" men. As we shall see in Chapter 3, a number of other feminist theories also point to the institution of the economy as a major structural feature limiting the possibilities for women within our society.

The interactional level focuses upon the impact of immediate situations of everyday interaction as they shape the gendered actions, thoughts, and feelings of men and women (Thompson, 1993: 562). Social expectations combine at the interactional level with practical situational demands and constraints to promote and restrict the presentation of a gendered self. Private intimate contexts call for different expressions of gender than do public impersonal contexts. New situations sometimes call for unanticipated changes. For example, an adult woman's combination of motherhood and paid work may be very different from what her early socialization had lead her to anticipate (Gerson, 1986/1987), or her orientation towards breadwinning may change dramatically from what she had once expected (Potuchek, 1992). These changes reflect the impact of the immediate situation overriding general social expectations.

In their everyday interactions, individuals negotiate boundaries between what is viewed as gender-appropriate and gender-inappropriate behaviour (Gerson and Peiss, 1985). They also give meaning to their own actions and the actions of others. Through their negotiated behaviour, interacting individuals either confirm or challenge each other's gender, and construct or reconstruct their gender on a daily basis (Zvonkovic et al., 1996). Many of the concepts of symbolic interactionism are particularly relevant for analyzing and understanding the interactional level.

The individual level primarily involves the form and shape of gender identity, gender consciousness, and gender behaviour (Thompson, 1993: 566). We noted in the last chapter that most research in search of differences simply notes the "sex" of study participants and subsequently implies that they have captured the essential biologically based properties of individuals that cause the certain social or psychological behaviours under examination. The gender perspective argues that what is being measured is a part of gender, and is contingent upon how a person defines him or herself and whether or not she or he believes that their gender is relevant to the performance of a certain task. How an individual constructs her or his sense of gender influences their behaviour and should influence how we analyze and interpret the results of our research.

As well, individual women and men vary in the extent to which they are aware or conscious of gender in our society (Gerson and Peiss, 1985). The higher the level of gender consciousness, the greater the likelihood that a person will try to deliberately shape her or his own gender behaviour and the gender behaviour of others. Low consciousness levels lead to taken-for-granted unquestioned gender behaviour. A constant theme running throughout this text is that the gender self-consciousness of women was raised higher and earlier in Canadian society than was the gender self-consciousness of men. We are now witnessing consciousness-raising efforts among men to reconstruct their own gender ideals, sense of identity, and behaviour, reminiscent of the efforts of Canadian women over the past 25 years.

The description of these different levels has necessarily been cursory at best. This is partly due to the fact that the gender perspective is still, as mentioned earlier, in its infancy. The major contribution of this perspective thus far has been to focus our attention upon the contributions of different levels to the social construction of gender. Not only will each level have to be examined in more detail, but a major challenge lies ahead in describing and analyzing connections between the different levels (Thompson, 1993: 567). The task is similar to what Reigel (1975) envisioned in his call for a dialectical theory to explicate the interconnected multilevel processes contributing to human aging and development, a task that has yet to be fully accomplished.

Individual men and women construct their gender through interacting with other gendered beings in the situational contexts of basic institutions within a particular society possessing a particular culture at a particular point in historical time. How institutions are shaped by sociocultural meanings of gender and how those institutions, in turn, shape gender interactions and relations is not yet clear. How individuals construct, confirm, and reconstruct gender in relation to each and all of these other levels is yet to be determined. Nonetheless, the gender perspective argues that individual gender behaviour is not a consequence of biology, nor simply conformity to role expectations learned during childhood socialization. According to one of its leading proponents (Thompson, 1993: 567), "[t]he perspective encourages researchers to ask new questions and discourages us from too-easy answers that blame [biology], society, women, or men for current gender arrangements."

3

HISTORICAL AND STRUCTURAL PERSPECTIVES

In this chapter, we shall explore how the structure of a society exerts major influences on the ways in which gender is experienced and expressed. We begin with a very brief overview of the historical development of Canada, from preindustrial times through to the mid-1960s, to illustrate how conceptions of, and guidelines for, masculinity and femininity in our society are constructed relative to time and place. Modern feminists theories, and the even more recently developed perspectives on masculinity, have all been generated against the backdrop of our history and take various elements of these social constructions into account, differing from one another primarily by what each identifies as the most important precipitants and consequences of those constructions.

A BRIEF HISTORY OF GENDER IN CANADA

Early First Nations Peoples

Before we examine historical developments in what is now known as Canada, we should first note that our focus will be primarily upon European settlers and their descendants. Unfortunately, our knowledge of their history, relative to gender, is significantly greater than our knowledge of First Nations cultures prior to the arrival of Europeans. By the time any systematic study of First Nations cultures had begun, these cultures had already been altered to varying degrees as a consequence of contact with European cultures, represented by explorers, fur traders (see Van Kirk [1986] for insights into the role of First Nations women in the fur trade), religious missionaries, and early settlers. Our knowledge is consequently contaminated by such contacts and also by the sometimes blatant, and sometimes subtle, biases of early European observers. In addition, First Nations peoples were considerably more diverse in their cultural heritages than were the first English and French colonizers, a diversity that restricts the number of generalizations we can make.

The majority of traditional First Nations cultures were centred upon fishing, hunting, and gathering activities. With the exception of the Inuit, a high percentage of the daily sustenance within these cultures was provided by women (Nett, 1993: 45), given the unpredictable, and often erratic, nature of hunting and fishing. In the eastern regions of Canada, many groups of First Nations peoples attained self-sufficiency through horticulture, or the domestication and cultivation of plants, supplemented by hunting and fishing where possible. Men cleared the land and were responsible for hunting and fishing, while women assumed primary responsibility for planting, tending, and harvesting the plant crops. The activities of both men and women were woven into an interdependent social fabric, ensuring tribal or group survival.

While some traditional First Nations cultures that depended upon hunting and fishing, such as the Inuit, were patriarchal (or arguably egalitarian) and patrilocal (wives moved in with their husbands [Peters, 1990: 175]), many of the eastern First Nations peoples, such as the Iroquois and Huron, existed within a social organization that was matrilocal (husbands moved in with their wives), matrilineal (descent was traced through the female line), and matrifocal (the central and strongest bonds within the community existed between mothers and their children) (Cassidy et al, 1995; Peters, 1990). Among the Iroquois, women owned the fields and the crop seeds. "[E]ven though Iroquois men gained and held power only with female approval, it was males who composed the council of chiefs that led the Iroquois League" (Nett, 1993: 46).

These traditional forms of social organization have undergone significant changes as a consequence of contact with European cultures (see Cassidy et al, 1995: 33–39; Peters, 1990: 175–182, for brief histories). For example, the introduction of European law, which supported patrilineality and, by implication, patrilocality, forcibly changed the descent rules and residence patterns among many First Nations cultures. This disruption of traditional customs has only been recently addressed by the government of Canada in the 1985 amendments to the Indian (a legal designation only) Act, regarding the statuses of First Nations women who married non-First Nations men and of the children they produced. This amendment remains a highly contentious issue among many First Nations groups across the country (Weaver, 1993). As the diversity of our traditional cultures makes further generalizations difficult and even tenuous, we shall turn our attentions to identifying patterns among the European settlers who eventually became the dominant ethnic groups in Canada.

The Preindustrial Period

Prior to the nineteenth century, Canada was essentially an agrarian society, whose economy was dependent upon, and equal to, the sum of the economies of its resident families (Gaffield, 1990: 23). The bulk of productive economic activities, for most European settlers, took place in, or on areas adjacent to, family households. The family home was, therefore, both a place of residence and a place of work (Bernard, 1981/1995; Gaffield, 1990: 26). Age, being generally commensurate with physical capabilities, was a more important determinant of an individual's work contribution than was gender. Family survival depended upon the interdependent and collective labours of all household members. Households of the time included servants, seasonal labourers, and boarders, in addition to family and kin-related members (Anderson, 1987: 28; Wilson, 1996: 8). Regardless of the combination of family and nonfamily household members, men, women, and children were all active producers, contributing to the family economy (Gaffield, 1990: 28; Wilson, 1996: 17). Despite the fact that everyone's labour was necessary for family survival, the family itself was not egalitarian, but was patriarchal in that power and authority were invested in the husband/father; wives were expected to be subordinate to their husbands, and children were expected to obey their parents.

Given that the survival of individuals in preindustrial Canada was dependent upon family survival, we find that the vast majority of people married (and remarried in the event of the death of a spouse), fertility was high (as was infant mortality) compared to today, and life expectancy was short (pioneers born in 1700 lived 30 to 35 years on average; Lavoie and Oderkirk, 1993: 3) with few women surviving to see all of their children grow to adulthood. The sex-linked division of labour within the family was such that mothers had sole responsibility for the physical care of infants. Fathers assumed responsibility for raising their sons after infancy by integrating them into farming activities, while mothers continued to raise their daughters and quickly integrated them into certain housekeeping management chores (such as cooking, clothes-making, and laundry), livestock maintenance, gardening, and caring for younger siblings (Wilson, 1996: 18).

Based upon his historical examination of middle-class males in the Northern United States, Rotundo claims that masculinity, during the preindustrial period prior to 1800, was guided by a model of *communal manhood,* in which a "man's identity was inseparable from the duties he owed to his community" (Rotundo, 1993: 2). Public usefulness was deemed to be more important than economic success. As status within an agrarian communal society was ascribed at birth based upon one's family standing, a man's achievements in economic matters were not as important as ensuring that his family did not disrupt, but rather contributed to, the functioning of his community. In contrast with womanhood, manhood was invested culturally with greater reason, lesser passion, and greater virtue (Rotundo, 1993: 3). These stereotypical attributions provided the foundation for the existence of the patriarchal society and family. Doyle (1989: 37), borrowing the historical classification scheme developed by Pleck and Pleck (1980), suggests that, prior to the early 1800s, landowners in the New World provided the ideal model for colonial men's masculinity. These "aristocrats" displayed and promoted the masculine ideals of "independence, self-confidence, intelligence, and a spirit of individualism" (Doyle, 1989: 37) expressed primarily in the context of the patriarchal agrarian family setting.

The Industrializing Period

The process of industrialization, which began in the early 1800s, and the accompanying urbanization eventually produced by the mechanization of farm labour, proceeded unevenly throughout Canada, varying across different regions of the country in terms of timing, but not in terms of its consequences. The manufactory stage initially brought various kinds of craftsmen and, eventually, all kinds of labourers to centralized work sites (Gaffield, 1990: 26–28). Economic production processes were slowly removed from the home and transferred to those sites where workers were paid a wage for their labours. The introduction of a wage economy lead to the word **work** being redefined to refer to the narrow area of paid labour only (Gaffield, 1990: 30). Consequently, unpaid labour conducted within the home was devalued as something less than "real" work. This marginal status was indicated by the addition of a modifying adjective to form "housework," a word introduced into the English vocabulary in the mid-1800s (Wilson, 1996: 64). As a result of these trends, paid occupations became idealized, while housework became trivialized (Zaretsky, 1976).

Industrialization thus brought about a physical separation of the public "work" place from the private home place, generally referred to now as the *separate spheres*, only in the sense of the new definition of work itself. The concept of "separate spheres" actually promotes a false notion of a dichotomy, as it implies the existence of two distinct and unconnected geographical locations. It is more accurate to think of the spheres as represented by two overlapping circles. Unpaid labour in the home provides crucial support for paid labourers in the workplace and "makes industrial society possible" (Nett, 1993: 51), while events in the workplace have significant impact upon the life of the homeplace. For the sake of simplicity, we shall treat the separate spheres in the following pages *as if* they were physically distinct and unrelated, and then revisit the connections between them in a more complete and complex form in later chapters.

Initially, since the wages paid to an individual worker were very low (Nett, 1993: 50), wage earners included whole families working either together or separately at different work sites. Fathers, mothers, and children entered the paid-labour force to generate sufficient income to support their family. Families now pooled wages, not productive labours, in this newly developed *family wage economy*. Wage pooling was not simply an expedient process necessitated by financial needs of the family as a whole. Under British law, which governed all of the colonies except New France (i.e., Lower Canada or, eventually, Quebec), when two people married, husband and wife became as one and that one was the husband. Wives did not exist as independent beings under the law. Consequently, Canadian wives, during the earliest stages of industrialization, had no option but to contribute their wages to the family financial pool. Not until the passage, in 1870, of the Married Women's Property Act in Britain were wives allowed to keep their own earnings and not required to turn them over to their husbands (Fowler, 1993: 40). Wives in Ontario received the right to own their earnings independent of their husband's control in 1872 (Whitla, 1995: 320). Wives in Quebec were not granted control over their own earnings until after the publication of the Dorion Report in 1929–30 (Krull, 1996: 378). However, Canadian women still could not own property independently.

In summary, during Canada's industrializing period, survival depended upon the new family wage economy where husbands, both in law and in custom, exercised sole control over disposal of all financial assets accruing to the family. As the production of goods, and eventually services, moved outside of the family household, those assets were used increasingly to purchase the necessities of family life. The family, consequently, became essentially a unit not of producers, but of consumers.

Rotundo suggests that, during the early stages of industrialization at the beginning of the nineteenth century, a new model of masculinity developed, namely that of *self-made manhood*, where "a man took his identity and his social status from his own achievements, not from the accident of his birth" (Rotundo, 1993: 3). Early industrialization ushered in an era in which a man's newly defined work role, not his family role, became central to his personal and social identity. This new emphasis upon individualism permitted men to give free rein to ambition and aggression, so long as they were used constructively within business and the professions. Doyle (1989: 38–39) claims that, with the development of the separate spheres and the growing presumption that men were best suited to the public sphere of work, the ideal of the landed aristocrat gave way to a new masculine ideal of the *common man,* which dominated between 1820 and 1860. This new masculinity was characterized by "common sense, success in business, personal ingenuity, [and] heightened sexual interests" (Doyle, 1989: 38). Men were expected to channel or sublimate their sexual interests and energies into their work, which was considered to be ideally more "worthwhile than mere sexual release" (Doyle, 1989: 39).

Hochschild (1990) argues that early industrial development probably altered the lives of men more than it did the lives of women. Women's lives were still centred on the familiar surroundings and tasks of the home, while men had to make the adjustment of physically and mentally moving themselves out of the home and into a centralized work place. In the early stages of industrialization, many men still owned land and experienced a double shift of working in some form of manufacturing during the day, and then returning home to continue working their land. It was men who initially had to shift the foundation for their self-concept from one based upon the possession of land, to one based upon the possession of money. In addition, as noted by Bly (1990) and Pittman (1993), when fathers began to leave the home to go to work, young sons lost a visible role model with whom to identify and relate during daily life.

With the advent of a new form of an ideal masculinity, based upon the pursuit of success in the paid-work sphere, and the societal changes accompanying continued urbanization and industrialization, concern among politicians and public leaders about family and societal stability lead to the promotion of a new ideal of femininity from the 1820s to the mid-1860s. Books, most written in Britain and reprinted in Canada and the United States (Fowler, 1993: xvi), and magazines began to extol the virtues of *true womanhood* (Gaffield, 1990: 37).

> True Women…were pious, their lives being one long act of devotion to God, husband, children, servants, the poor, humanity. Second, they were passive, without any desire to strive or achieve for themselves. Third, they were 'pure.' Marriage was their career—spinsters were pitied and regarded as failures—and virginity and total sexual ignorance were crucial…(Fowler, 1993: xvi)

The cult of true womanhood asserted a belief that women could best serve family and society by restricting themselves to the domestic sphere, and devoting their energies to caring for their husbands and children. Love and the satisfaction of interpersonal needs were now slowly becoming important institutionalized elements of the marital relationship (Anderson, 1987: 33–34). Canadian women in those times gave birth to an average of 6.6 children, beginning in their mid-twenties and continuing through to their early forties (Gee, 1986: 269, 273). Newly created beliefs regarding the special emotional needs of children claimed that full-time mothering was necessary for optimal child development. Mothers were expected to be the "custodians" (Anderson, 1987: 35) of their children's happiness and well being. The domestic sphere was now "venerated as a retreat, a place where individuals could truly express their innermost being" (Anderson, 1987: 36), and women were to follow their "natural" calling and assume primary responsibility for creating an environment conducive to optimal emotional expression. After all, the True Woman, the "angel of the hearth" (Hayford, 1987: 7), knew that "domesticity is her honor and glory" (Fowler, 1993: xvii).

The imagery of the true woman provided the basis for the stereotype of the "fragile" woman who was so pure and delicate that she must be placed upon a pedestal to be worshiped by men. Being fragile, she had to be kept in the home, literally placed under house arrest and protected first by her father and later by her husband. As we shall see shortly, since this ideal was more compatible with the economic circumstances of upper- and middle-class families, the true woman was most often a lady of significant financial refinement as well. Nevertheless, regardless of her social-class position, the true wife and mother was expected to be the glue that held her family together in the face of personal and social changes wrought by industrialization.

Beginning in the 1840s and 1850s, Canadians became increasingly more favourably inclined towards establishing compulsory formal education as a solution to the problems of youth made idle by continuing mechanization of the workplace (Gaffield, 1990: 34) and the steadily growing influx of migrants, including young children, from other cultures. Industrialization required a labour force skilled in literacy and numeracy, and schools were seen as the solution. Consequently, in addition to laws prohibiting child labour, school attendance laws were enacted slowly over the latter part of the nineteenth and the early part of the twentieth centuries. As well as providing physical care and emotional nurturance, mothers were also expected to provide support for their children when they returned each day from school (as in supervising their *home*work). The school curriculum eventually began to include domestic science courses to prepare girls for their future familial role (Gaffield, 1990: 37). The removal of children from the paid-labour force had an additional consequence of transforming children from economic assets into economic liabilities. Even as their emotional value was increasing, their economic value was decreasing. This latter change was a major contributor to further declines in the Canadian birth rate during the late 1800s.

As we have seen, with the development of the separate spheres, the sites of unpaid and paid labour became firmly gendered. A woman's place was in the home, married to it, as implied by the term "housewife," where she performed unpaid labour. A man's place was on the job where he performed paid labour. Work (depending upon whether it was paid or unpaid) defined gender and gender defined work. The creation of the separate spheres also lead to the establishment of the ideal "good provider" role for men (Bernard, 1981/1995). A good provider was a man who, by virtue of his economically productive labour, earned sufficient income to ensure his family had the basic necessities of life, at least. As such, he was also considered to be the "head" of the household, an entitlement that lasted until the late 1970s (Bernard, 1981/1995). However, only middle- and upper-class Canadian families could financially afford to have married women remain in the home. Despite demands, emanating initially from the trade union movement, for business and industry to provide men with a *family wage* (Wilson, 1996: 21), working-class men typically did not earn sufficient income to permit their wives to leave the paid-labour force. Working-class families remained dependent upon the wage earnings of wives and mothers.

The Industrial Period

Canada possessed an industrialized economy by the 1870s (Gaffield, 1990: 27) with the growth of large factories permitting fully mechanized and centralized economic production. A substantial proportion of the population was still involved in agricultural occupations, but more and more workers left farming and moved into sectors of the economy devoted to manufacturing goods and, increasingly, providing services to others. These trends would continue for the next hundred years. Opportunities for female paid-labour-force participation were limited essentially to occupations such as factory workers, domestics, secretaries, teachers, and nurses. With women's wages being comparatively less than men's (between one-half and two-thirds that of men since the seventeenth century [Phillips, 1991: 249]), women's chances for attaining financial independence were limited. Women workers were more likely to be single, as married women were excluded from most jobs and were often fired from their jobs when they married. More and more women became dependent upon the wages of men, with marriage seen as an attractive alternative compared to the bare subsistence of living alone, or to living permanently in one's parental home, or to becoming a long-term live-in domestic for another family. The ideal roles of the patriarchal family in industrial times, from the late 1800s to the 1960s, were now defined with men as providers, women as homemakers, and children as dependents.

"In the late eighteenth and early nineteenth centuries, women's lives were devoted to motherhood" (Lavoie and Oderkirk, 1993: 4). The average life expectancy for women born in 1861, compared with women born in 1831, rose to 45 years from 42 years while men's life expectancy of 43 had increased from 40 for those born in 1831 (Lavoie and Oderkirk, 1993: 5). As in earlier times, the adult lives of most women were devoted mainly to child-bearing and childrearing. The average man born in eighteenth-century Canada would work for 23 years before he died (Lavoie and Oderkirk, 1993: 4). The average Canadian family size in 1871 was 5.9 persons with the average of four of a woman's six or seven children surviving beyond infancy (Anderson, 1987: 28).

Until the late 1800s, married women could not control any property they might have possessed either as a consequence of inheritance from their fathers or their husbands, or by virtue of their own efforts. Twelve years after women were granted the right to control their own wage earnings, the Married Women's Property Act was passed in England in 1882, granting wives the right to independently acquire and own property (McKie et al., 1983: 188). The passage of this law was part of a trend permitting economic independence to women throughout Western societies, during the latter part of the nineteenth century (Phillips, 1991: 230). The majority of states in the United States passed married women's property legislation between the mid- to late 1800s (Fowler, 1993: 155; Phillips, 1991: 230). At the time of the Union of Canada (1840), wives could not give away or contract out their property, since it lawfully belonged to their husbands. During the last few years of the 1800s and the first two decades of the 1900s, provinces passed property legislation granting married women the right to own and dispose of their property without having to obtain their husband's consent (McKie et al., 1983: 33, 42–43).

These legislative acts, however, did not give married women entitlement to a share of any property acquired by the couple during their marriage (Nett, 1993: 124). The dominant expectation remained encoded in law that women, being legally incapable of caring for themselves, were to be cared for first by fathers, then by their husbands, and later by their sons. Further legislation, such as the 1911 dower legislation in Alberta permitting a wife to inherit one-third of her husband's estate (McKie et al., 1983: 43), was eventually passed in most provinces during the early decades of this century, providing women with some access to marital property. However, the Civil Code of Quebec created in 1866 included married women in the same category as "minors and the feeble minded" (McKie et al., 1983: 34). Married women were not allowed to own or dispose of property and "political participation and economic support were the responsibility of the husband" (McKie et al., 1983: 44). Rights over property were not granted to women in Quebec until much later.

During the late 1800s and early 1990s, a new model of masculinity developed: *passionate manhood* (Rotundo, 1993: 5). Competitiveness, aggression, and ambition all became ends in themselves and were no longer restricted to the economic sphere. Toughness, physical strength, athletic skill, and personal appearance rose to prominence as desired masculine qualities. Tenderness, self-restraint, and self-denial were no longer considered virtues. Play and leisure pursuits were elevated to acceptable areas for masculine self-fulfillment and self-expression, and men were no longer expected to limit themselves solely to the pursuit of economic success. Doyle describes the male ideal of this time period as *he-man* masculinity characterized by "strenuous activity, involvement in sports, [and] two-fisted preparedness" (Doyle, 1989: 38). A combination of the monotony of factory work, reduced opportunities for business success, and a need to find new ways to validate their masculinity lead men to "all-male activities in which they could play at being rough and tough" (Doyle, 1989: 40). Both Doyle and Rotundo note the significant increase during the late 1880s and early 1900s of organized spectator sports, and the proliferation of all-male fraternal organizations including the Boy Scouts, and men-only clubs and drinking establishments as gathering places for the expression of masculine solidarity (Doyle, 1989: 40–41; Rotundo, 1993: 222–246).

At the same time, middle-class female proponents of the virtues of true womanhood began to claim that these virtues need not be restricted solely to the domestic sphere but had applicability beyond the family (Gaffield, 1990:38). Later known as **maternal feminists**, these women felt "morally responsible to extend their mothering to society" (Wilson, 1996: 23). Initially forming groups to focus upon social issues of the day such as temperance (abstaining from alcohol consumption), equality (particularly antislavery), and poverty, they eventually turned their attentions to issues that affected themselves more directly as women, such as the need for greater child-welfare protections, and the right of women to vote (suffrage or enfranchisement). This latter issue was seen as particularly important, partly as a means to tame the aggressive tendencies of men, and partly as a means to exert more control over their own destinies. Most suffragettes still accepted the prevalent beliefs that posited the existence of essential differences between men and women and sought to assert feminine values into the public sphere.

Concurrently, a different model of femininity arose in the late 1800s, in response to writings such as John Stuart Mill's *On the Subjugation of Women* in 1869. The *New Woman* "demanded the right to have a proper career outside the home, to remain unwed from choice....to vote and smoke and ride a bicycle....The New Woman jettisoned piety, submissiveness and domesticity but hung on to her moral purity" (Fowler, 1993: xvii). Middle- and upper-class new women challenged existing beliefs regarding many of the supposed gender differences, and particularly campaigned against the restrictions they believed that ideologies such as true womanhood had created for women.

Both of these groups, each in their own way, contributed to the "first wave" of feminism that formed during the late 1800s and lasted into the early 1920s. Arguably the most prominent public achievements of this movement in Canada were the right to vote and the right (granted in 1929) to be considered *persons*, and not chattels, under Canadian law. Women over the age of 21 were granted the right to vote in provincial elections in 1916 in Alberta, Manitoba, and Saskatchewan; in 1917 in British Columbia and Ontario; in 1918 in all of Canada and in provincial elections in Nova Scotia; in 1919 in New Brunswick; in 1922 in Prince Edward Island; in 1925 in Newfoundland (initially only for women over the age of 25); and in 1940 in Quebec (Whitla, 1995: 320–332). These rights were first granted to white women; women from certain other ethnic groups did not receive the franchise until later years.

Single women continued to form a significant proportion of the paid-labour force in Canada during the early 1900s. With the increasing demand for clerical and sales workers, more married women entered, and stayed in, the labour force. Professional employment for women was limited primarily to teaching, social work, and nursing—all extensions of the socially defined motherhood role. World War I, the Great Depression, and World War II all generated social conditions conducive to increasing female labour-force participation. The primary condition during the wars was a shortage of male labourers as men were conscripted in the armed services. Despite the significant economic downturn of the Depression, and the still prevalent beliefs that motherhood and paid employment were incompatible and that every employed woman took a job away from a man, the lower wages paid by employers to women contributed to increasing proportions of married wives and mothers entering the labour force during the Depression years.

During the years spanning each of the World Wars, and declining during the Korean and later Vietnam wars, the vision of the *Warrior* was added, temporarily, to existing images of an ideal masculinity in Canada. Through either conscription (compulsory enrolment in the armed forces) or voluntary enlistment, substantial numbers of young men found themselves defenders of their country (albeit while fighting in foreign lands), homes, families, and way of life. Canadian men born since the mid-1930s have not personally faced conscription and, subsequently, have been most likely to confront warlike images of masculinity only in the form of exposure to television documentaries and, overwhelmingly American-made, motion pictures. The Warrior established only shallow roots in Canadian soil. Our experience stands in sharp contrast to that of all American men between the ages of 19 and 25 who were required, since early in this century until 1969, when the lottery draft system was introduced, to undergo two years of some form of compulsory military service. As in Canada during the World Wars, some American men could obtain deferments from the draft, although these tended to be granted primarily to men from the "influential, wealthy, and educated classes" (Jones, 1980: 108). The entire American system was changed to one comparable to that of Canada, namely a voluntary military system, only fairly recently. Still, the image of the Warrior as a central element of masculinity has long been, and still remains, entrenched in the United States.

Beliefs in the centrality of marriage and motherhood for femininity in Canada remained strong through the first half of the twentieth century, as the wars and the Depression were all considered to be exceptional times requiring exceptional alterations to social life. When conditions returned to "normal" after each war (there being no such return following the Depression as it ended with the beginning of World War II), women and men were expected to return to their "normal" spheres of home and work, respectively. Women working for the peacetime Canadian federal civil service in 1921 were obliged to resign when they married (Whitla, 1995: 329). Special services and legislation created to facilitate the entry of wives and mothers into the labour force during World War II were all disbanded and repealed following the war (McKie et al., 1983: 49). The Income Tax Act had been changed during World War II to allow husbands a full tax exemption for working wives, regardless of the amount of income their wives earned. After World War II, that exemption was rescinded and men were only allowed to claim as dependents wives who earned below a minimum income level. The structure of the income tax laws before and after the war reinforced the notion of husbands as providers and wives as financial dependents. The Nurseries Agreement passed during the World War II, which saw the federal and provincial governments split costs for nursery care, foster care, and day care for children from infancy to age 16, so that mothers could work full-time, was rescinded immediately after the war and existing nurseries and day-care centres created under these agreements were all disbanded. These examples all serve to illustrate how gender expectations, promoted as based upon the essential natures of women and men, could conveniently be suspended when pragmatic circumstances warranted, and then be reinstituted when those circumstances changed.

Mid-1940s to Late 1960s

Post-World-War-II Canadian society expected men and women to settle down into their separate, and supposedly natural, spheres, despite the fact that women in general, and middle-class women in particular, had expanded their participation beyond the domestic sphere for almost half of the first four decades of the twentieth century. Women, in changing and enlarging their behavioural repertoires, had demonstrated to themselves and to men that they were capable of holding down jobs while managing a home and family at the same time. They had experienced a greater sense of independence, which, despite its being called "exceptional," would remain locked in their memories. However, extraordinary social pressures were set in motion immediately following World War II to erase those memories in older women and to prevent any similar developments in women born after the war years.

The most significant demographic event occurring after the war and through the 1950s was the **baby boom**, an event that defied the long-term trend of declining fertility in Canada since at least the middle of the nineteenth century. Canada, the United States, Australia, and New Zealand were the only four Western countries to experience a significant and sustained upsurge in births, lasting far beyond the short-term increase commonly experienced in countries following periods of war. The baby boom in the United States lasted from 1946 to 1964 (Jones, 1980: 6) and is generally considered to have occurred in Canada from 1946 to 1959 (McVey and Kalbach, 1995: 271), with some dissenting writers claiming that the term "baby-boom generation" belongs either to those born between 1951 and 1966 (Kettle, 1980: 19) or those born between 1947 and 1966 (Foot, 1996). Unlike many European countries that had to devote their immediate postwar efforts to physically rebuilding cities and countrysides ravaged by invasion, Canada was able to forge ahead immediately with a peacetime economy buoyed by an optimism or "euphoria" (Kettle, 1980: 34) born of a sense of victory. Aided by the growing power of the mass media, including the new technology of television, government, manufacturers, and advertisers commenced disseminating a vision of the good life in our country, and particularly in the Canadian family.

A dominant part of this vision focused upon the desirability of expressing femininity through becoming a wife and mother. A major mass-circulation magazine of the time, *Look*, offered the following words of praise:

> The wondrous creature married younger than ever, bears more babies and looks and acts far more feminine than the "emancipated" girl of the twenties or thirties. If she makes an old-fashioned choice and lovingly tends a garden and a bumper crop of children, she rates louder Hosannas than ever before. (Quoted in Jones, 1980: 24)

Echoing the call of the previous century for true womanhood, femininity was to reside *solely* in becoming a wife and mother (Friedan, 1963: 11; Jones, 1980: 25).

The power of these messages cannot be underestimated. The generation who spawned the baby boom were born primarily during the Depression years of the 1930s, and grew up during the war years. They were imbued with a strong sense of duty to follow societal expectations and have been characterized as possessing "rather narrowly conformist values" (Kettle, 1980: 29). Self-fulfillment came not from an expression of individualism, as it did during the 1970s and later, but rather from a sense of conforming to what was expected. Consequently, they took to heart the messages inundating them from all directions including government rostrums, preacher's pulpits, school classrooms, television situation comedies, and the pages of mass circulation magazines and newspapers.

Bernard (1973: 244) notes that during the 1950s, "women had been convinced that not to get married was indeed a fate worse than death, for without marriage, one could not be completely fulfilled." Friedan claims that the number of women attending institutions of higher learning declined significantly during the 1950s. "A century earlier, women had fought for higher education; now girls went to college to get a husband. By the mid-fifties, 60 per cent dropped out of college to marry, or because they were afraid too much education would be a marriage bar" (Friedan, 1963: 12). During this time, a variety of factors lead to the development of the **Procreation Ethic**, a belief system that fostered a climate conducive to creating and prolonging the baby boom. According to the Procreation Ethic,

1. It was preferable to marry than not to marry. If a person chose to remain single, the onus was on him or her to explain why.

2. It was preferable to be a parent than a nonparent. A couple that did not have children would be considered unconventional and tacitly pressured to make an explanation. The only excuses accepted were medical or financial.

3. It was preferable not to have an "only" child, especially in the suburbs. (Jones, 1980: 31)

The demographic evidence indicates that Canadians complied with the expectations of the Procreation Ethic. The average age at first marriage in Canada dropped from 24.4 years for brides and 27.6 for bridegrooms in 1941, to 22.6 and 25.2 years, respectively, by 1966 (McVey and Kalbach, 1995: 225), and fell to approximately two years lower for men and women in the United States during that same period. Between 1941 and 1966, the proportion of the total Canadian population aged 15 and over who were single (never married) dropped from 36.5 percent to 28.0 percent, while the proportion married increased from 57.0 to 65.0 percent. More specifically, among Canadians aged 20 to 29, the proportion of singles decreased from 59.9 percent in 1941 to 40.5 percent in 1966, while the proportion married rose from 41.7 percent to 59.0 percent. Simply stated, more Canadians were marrying and were married at earlier ages.

These young marrieds, along with older married couples who had deferred childbearing during the war years, all contributed to the baby boom. Table 3.1 presents data for the number of live births and the crude birth rates in Canada spanning the period of 1941 to 1966. You can discern from the table that the number of live births continued to increase from 1941 to 1961 and then declined by 1966. The crude birth rate, expressed as the number of births per 1000 population, rose from 1941 to 1956 (actually peaking in 1954; McVey and Kalbach, 1995: 269) and then declined.

TABLE 3.1	Number of Live Births and Crude Birth Rates, Canada: 1941–1966*	
Year	**Number of Live Births**	**Crude Birth Rate**
1941	263 993	22.4
1946	343 504	27.2
1951	381 092	27.2
1956	450 739	28.0
1961	475 700	26.1
1966	387 710	19.4

* Data for Newfoundland not available. Yukon and Northwest Territories excluded prior to 1951.

Source: Statistics Canada (1976). Vital Statistics 1974. Vol. 1. Ottawa.

During this time, contraception was often ineffective and limited in availability. The Pill was not authorized for public use until 1960, was not in general use until around 1963, and doctors were not legally allowed to prescribe birth control pills in Canada until 1970. Most younger couples had, therefore, not yet learned about, or used, the methods that did exist (Kettle, 1980: 35; Jones, 1980: 33). Economic deterrents to fertility were also relatively weak in our financially booming economy. Consequently, in keeping with the third dictate of the Procreation Ethic, Canadian couples tended not to limit themselves to having only one child. From 1946 to 1961, the average Canadian woman had between 3.4 and 3.9 children during her lifetime (McVey and Kalbach, 1995: 270). The baby boom was, therefore, a boom in small, not large, families. (In contrast, the average Canadian women in the early 1990s is expected to have approximately 1.8 children during her lifetime, assuming current rates remain basically constant.) Regardless of the measurement being used, and in contrast to prior long-term historical trends, marrying and birthing and childrearing were all important elements of the social fabric of Canadian life during the late 1940s, the entire 1950s, and the early 1960s.

Not only were more Canadians marrying earlier and giving birth to more children, all under the umbrella of the Procreation Ethic, but Canadian women were also changing their paid-work patterns. Following a relatively brief departure from the work force after the World War II (Statistics Canada, 1983) and a return to the home, women's labour-force participation began to increase slowly during the 1950s and 1960s. As can be noted from Table 3.2, the greatest increases occurred among married women whose paid-labour-force participation rates increased from 11.2 percent in 1951 to 37 percent by 1971. The proportion of single women in the labour force remained essentially the same, with a slight drop over the 20-year period attributable to an increase in the proportion of younger women remaining within the educational system for longer periods of time. Men's overall labour-force participation rates generally declined, attributable to a combination of earlier retirement and a longer time spent in education.

Despite these changes within each sex, Table 3.2 documents significant differences between the sexes in their participation within the paid-labour force. Of particular note are the differences between the married groups. In keeping with the Procreation Ethic and the dominant cultural beliefs that a "(married) woman's place is in the home" and a "man's

TABLE 3.2	**Percentage of the Population, 15 Years of Age and Over, in the Labour Force, by Marital Status and Sex, Canada: 1951–1971**		
Sex and Marital Status	**1951**	**1961**	**1971**
Males:			
Single	76.6	63.5	63.5
Married	90.0	86.9	84.4
Widowed and Divorced	46.9	39.2	46.8
Total	84.0	78.1	76.4
Females:			
Single	58.4	54.9	53.5
Married	11.2	22.1	37.0
Widowed and Divorced	19.3	23.1	26.6
Total	24.1	29.7	39.9

Source: Statistics Canada (1974). *1971 Census of Canada.* Bulletin 3.1-2, Table 3. Ottawa: Information Canada.

place is at (paid) work," married men were significantly more likely than married women to be working for pay. This sex difference is clearly demonstrated in 1961 (not shown in the table), when 68.3 percent of all husband-and-wife families in Canada had only the husband in the labour force, 19.5 percent were dual-income families with both husband and wife in the labour force, 3.2 percent had only the wife in the labour force, most likely earning her "PHT" (Putting Husband Through his education), and 9.0 percent had neither the husband nor the wife being paid for work (McVey and Kalbach, 1995: 253). A single-income marriage and family unit was the statistical and social norm in Canada, and that income was overwhelmingly, but not exclusively, generated by men, in keeping with the powerful dictates of the good-provider role.

When women were in the paid-labour force, they tended to be concentrated within a restricted number of occupations. Between 1951 and 1971, approximately 60 percent were clustered in clerical, sales, and service occupations (Kalbach and McVey, 1979: 290). By 1971, women comprised more than 70 percent of all clerical workers in Canada and 60 percent of all service workers (Kalbach and McVey, 1979: 289). During that 20-year period, the proportion of women in professional and technical occupations increased from 10.2 to 17.5 percent, with the overwhelming majority of these women concentrated in the teaching and health (especially nursing) professions (Kalbach and McVey, 1979: 290, 294). All of these trends reiterate patterns found in the earlier part of this century.

The general life-course pattern of Canadian women during these times was fairly consistent. Upon completing their education, women who did not go immediately from graduation to wedding ceremonies entered the paid-labour force and remained there until their wedding or until they were prepared to start a family, usually less than two years later. With the impending or actual arrival of their first child, these women tended, in overwhelming numbers, to drop out of the labour force and concentrate their energies upon home management (a continuation of something they had already assumed upon marriage) and childrearing. Existing social beliefs stressed the crucial importance of mothers being physically present

TABLE 3.3	Female Labour-Force Participation Rates by Age, Canada: 1951 and 1961	
Age Group	**1951 (%)**	**1961 (%)**
15–19	37.8	34.2
20–24	46.9	49.5
25–34	24.2	29.6
35–44	21.8	31.1
45–54	20.4	33.4
55–64	14.5	24.4
65+	5.1	6.7
Total	24.1	29.7

Source: Adapted from McVey and Kalbach, 1995: 251. Based upon *1971 Census of Canada*, Vol. 3, Part 1, Economic Characteristics, Table 2.

for their children from the moment of birth until these children were ready to leave their parental home. Only severe financial hardship was considered sufficient grounds for a married woman with children present in the home to remain in or to re-enter the labour market. Following the real or imminent departure of their children, a small proportion of married women then re-entered the labour force.

Table 3.3 documents the changing labour-force participation rates for women by age in 1951 and 1961, and demonstrates the bimodal pattern evidenced during that period. Younger women (particularly those between the ages of 15 and 24) show the highest rates. Women in the typical childbearing and childrearing years, between 25 and 34, demonstrate a significant and noticeable decline in their labour-force participation. Close comparison of the rates between 1951 and 1961 reveals the increasing tendency of women, by 1961, to return to the labour force, especially between the ages of 35 and 54. These comparatively higher rates signal the beginning of changes, which accelerated throughout the 1970s, that saw women balancing the demands of childrearing with a combination of inflationary pressures and greater available social and economic opportunities. It is sufficient to note for now that less than one-third of all women were in the paid-labour force in 1951 and 1961.

Belief in the appropriateness of the separate spheres, although not referred to by that name at the time, reinforced the companion belief in separate gender destinies. As noted earlier, men were to demonstrate their masculinity in the public sphere through paid work and the good-provider role, and we have seen that the overwhelming majority of men were in the labour force. Bernard (1973: 76) notes an unspecified study from the 1960s of 600 suburban housewives wherein two-thirds of the women viewed men as "breadwinners first, as fathers second, and as husbands third." Success as a breadwinner, with all of the characteristics needed to ensure that success, such as competitiveness, confidence, ambition, and independence, were all dominant themes of masculinity in postwar Canadian society. Perhaps not too surprisingly, studies also indicated that men cited "economic responsibilities," along with "sexual restrictiveness," as their two greatest grievances about marriage as it was constructed at the time (Bernard, 1973: 24).

The gender destiny of women was to demonstrate their femininity in the private sphere through their wife and mother roles. The impact of marriage and family upon women's lives came under increasing scrutiny during the 1960s. Bernard (1973: 41) suggests that postwedding life held at least two "shocks" for women. First, many women discovered that their husbands were not as strong and confident as suggested by the popular stereotypes of masculinity, and that a considerable amount of a wife's energies had to be devoted to propping up her husband's self-concept. Second, many women had to adjust to an important shift from being the one catered to prior to marriage, to the one who did the catering forever after. The pedestal upon which they had been placed shrank very quickly after the wedding ceremony. This latter shift was part of a larger and longer lasting process of "dwindling" into a wife, whose sphere of life was limited to home, children, and husband.

The phenomenon of the "trapped housewife" became a popular topic of discussion in the mass media during the late 1950s and early 1960s. Columnists, marriage counselors, and psychotherapists all offered advice to women on how to adjust to the dictates of contemporary wife and mother roles. Implicit within this advice was the notion that the ideal roles were sacrosanct and not to be challenged. Any difficulties experienced by individual women was considered to be testimony to their own inadequacies or lack of femininity. However, author Betty Friedan amassed considerable interview data, and performed an intensive examination of existing media messages and social-science theories. She suggests that the "problem that has no name" resided not within women, but rather within the gender expectations themselves. "There was a strange discrepancy between the reality of our lives as women and the image to which we were trying to conform, the image that I came to call the feminine mystique" (Friedan, 1963: 7). She further asserted that it was no longer possible to ignore the increasing numbers of women who felt "I want something more than my husband and my children and my home" (Friedan, 1963: 27).

The publication of Friedan's work signaled the beginning of intense examination of the generating conditions for women's gender roles and expectations and, later, men's roles and expectations, all of which had been accepted uncritically for most of the postwar period. Contributing to this climate of questioning were an increasing quest for personal freedom, a concern about over-population and the contribution of the baby-boom phenomenon to the problem, and a general challenging of the structure of all major social institutions and the content of existing belief systems. Bernard summarizes the thinking of many social critics writing about women in the 1960s when she notes that,

> From the very earliest years, girls will have to learn that however large marriage may loom in their lives, it is not nirvana, that it does not mark the end of their growth, that motherhood is going to be a relatively transient phase of their lives, that they cannot indulge themselves by investing all their emotional and intellectual resources in their children, that they cannot count on being supported all their lives simply because they are wives. They will have to prepare for loving autonomy rather than symbiosis or parasitism in marriage. (Bernard, 1973: 321–322)

Further exploration of many of these issues were to become central components of the women's movement and various feminist theories that began to be articulated during the mid- to late 1960s.

It can be argued that the "second wave" of the feminist movement was formed largely in reaction to the events and social beliefs characteristic of Canada and the United States in the mid-1940s to mid-1960s. This period saw the culmination of a series of processes set in motion with the industrialization of our society, beginning in the early 1800s. No longer constrained by slowly and erratically developing industrial processes, World Wars, or a major economic depression, gendered separate spheres were experienced in almost a pure form. It is this time period that many speakers during the 1990s call a time of "traditional family values." Most of those who sound the clarion call today for traditional values were either parents, or children, who experienced the 1940s, 1950s, and 1960s in families with homemaker mothers and breadwinner fathers. In essence, they seek to recreate the families and society of either their early adulthood or their childhood, usually without an awareness of the social and economic climate that made those times possible, a climate that no longer exists as we approach the twenty-first century.

Whether a focal point for nostalgia, with all of its attendant simplifications, or for derision as the modern day epitome of gender restrictions, the period from the mid-1940s to the mid-1960s represents a relatively unique phase in Canadian history. It spawned the development of additional theories and perspectives that enrich our understanding of the social context of gender. Before we examine those feminist theories and masculinity perspectives, we must first review the central elements of mainstream sociological theory, which also provides an important point of departure for future theorizing.

MAINSTREAM SOCIOLOGICAL THEORIES

Mainstream theory in sociology is derived from what is referred to as the positivist model that originated within the natural sciences. According to mainstream sociology, the social scientist, like the natural scientist, is expected to take a value-neutral (unbiased) and objective (nonjudgmental) approach towards his or her subject matter. Theories may either be created from empirical observations (the *inductive method*), or derived from assumptions about the nature of humans and human societies (the *deductive method*) (Burr et al., 1979: 4). Regardless of the method used, the resulting theory is designed to provide an explanation (Lindsey, 1994: 4) or to increase human understanding (Burr, 1973: 3) about a specified social phenomenon. One major criticism leveled against traditional mainstream theories in the social sciences in general, and sociology in particular, (Eichler, 1984) is that they have focused primarily on subjects of interest to men and have consequently been described as "malestream" (O'Brien, 1981) theories.

More specific to the study of gender, "few men showed any interest in women's studies: they 'rarely attended gender sessions at professional meetings, showed little awareness of research on the topic…and rarely cited work about women' [Ward and Grant, 1985: 143]" (in Wilson 1996: 7). To the extent that theory informs research, which, in turn, reflects back on theory, feminist scholars claim that most sociological theorizing has treated women as if they are invisible, insofar as the topics studied focused overwhelmingly on the public sphere of social life. One mainstream theory, however, did extend its analysis to marriage, the family, and gender.

Functionalism

Known also as *structural-functionalism*, this theory argues that human societies are composed of a number of interrelated parts, each of which contributes in some way to the stable functioning of the whole. "Functionalists seek to identify the basic elements or parts of society, determine the functions these parts play, and then consider how the entire society operates or functions" (Lindsey, 1994: 4). The "parts" can comprise, for example, basic social institutions, social groups, statuses (positions within society), and roles (either ideal expectations or actual patterns of behaviour), all depending upon the breadth of a particular functionalist focus. Since functionalism assumes that societies naturally tend to achieve a state of homeostasis or equilibrium, explanations are offered for how the part under examination contributes to stable functioning of the societal whole.

Parsons and Bales (1955), building on an earlier work of Parsons (1942), present a functionalist analysis of the traditional two-parent nuclear family when they argue that having women and men perform separate specialized and complementary roles contributes to family cohesiveness and stability. The *instrumental* role specializes in providing food and shelter for the family, making "managerial" (Parsons and Bales, 1955: 317) decisions, and providing a link between the family and the larger society. The *expressive* role specializes in providing emotional support and nurturance to all family members, cementing relations between family members, and running the family household smoothly and efficiently (Parsons and Bales, 1955: 317–319). Parsons and Bales argue that such a "division" (a highly contested term in that it implies equality) of labour into these two basic roles is functional to both family and societal equilibrium for two reasons. First, specialization promotes the interdependence of women and men. Each contributes what the other lacks: domestic skills and emotional support in exchange for economic support and protection. Second, well defined and clearly distinct roles reduce confusion and conflict over marital and gender expectations.

Parsons and Bales (1955) present evidence drawn from anthropological research to demonstrate that males in preindustrial societies tended to assume the instrumental role, and females to assume the expressive role, as a consequence of biological-sex differences pertaining to childbearing and early childrearing. The lesser physical mobility associated with pregnancy and child nursing led to female roles being concentrated within or close to the home. The greater physical mobility of males led to a concentration of their roles outside of the home, such as hunting and protection of the home through warfare. Parsons and Bales argue that not only did such a division of labour became institutionalized (or customarily expected) in early societies, but also that the functionality of this sex-linked division of roles is equally applicable to modern-day family and society.

Men and women, performing their complementary roles, are considered by functionalists to be providing different, but equal, functions for family and society. Directly and indirectly, functionalists further suggest that large-scale departures from the sex-linking of these roles, such as blurring them by having men and women share both roles, are inefficient (or *dysfunctional*), since they place women and men in competition with one another, cause not only confusion, inefficiency, instability, and a lack of family cohesion, but also lead eventually to disequilibrium or destabilization of the society as a whole. Parsons argues that "it is scarcely conceivable that the main lines of the present situation could be altered without consequences fatal to the total of our unique society" (Parsons, 1949: 268).

As you can readily see, functionalist theory is inherently conservative. Indeed, Abramovitz (1988) has suggested that functionalism is supportive of and promotes a "traditional, white middle-class family ethic." Stability, defined as conformity to traditional roles, is presumed to be functional, while change, defined as departure from convention, is presumed to be dysfunctional. Conservative writers (e.g., Gilder, 1973; Meilaender, 1990; Schlafly, 1977), drawing upon religious beliefs and appeals to tradition, continue to argue than any departures from convention weaken the commitment of men and women to their historical roles, contribute to family instability, and place children at risk.

In claiming that instrumental and expressive roles make "different, but equal" contributions to the continued smooth operation of a modern family and society, functionalists suggest that each of these roles is socially rewarded to an equal degree and that no significant gender differences exist in prestige, material benefits, or power, or if any do exist (such as decision-making power within families), these differences are functionally necessary. Functionalists tend to ignore issues of power and consider conflict within families and societies to be only destabilizing and dysfunctional. Subsequently developed theories seriously challenge these assumptions and implications. It is important to bear in mind that this theory was largely developed in the context of the postwar late 1940s and 1950s, that period of time whose characteristic family structure and gender roles is now considered to be an historical aberration (Cherlin 1992; Oppenheimer 1994).

Conflict Theory

During the 1960s, another theory emerged within sociology to challenge the functionalist point of view. *Conflict theory* has its roots in the earlier writings of social philosophers Karl Marx (1848/1964; 1867–1894/1967) and Frederich Engels (1884/1902). In sharp contrast to the functionalist emphasis upon consensus and equilibrium, conflict theory assumes that human societies are characterized by struggles between social groups for scarce physical and social resources, including power, wealth, and prestige. These struggles provide the major source of inevitable social change. As used within the context of this theory, conflict does not necessarily refer to violence, but also includes competition, disagreements, and tensions over group goals and values.

Marx was concerned primarily with the conflicts between those social classes who own and control the means of economic production (e.g., factories, machinery, raw materials, and labour) and the distribution of scarce resources (e.g., natural resources, manufactured goods, and services), and those classes who do not. To him, economic control meant social control, since the economic system was the structural basis for all social life. Any apparent stability in the relations between social groups within a society is the product of one group's ability to exert their will over other group(s) through the use of legitimized authority, and the construction of belief systems (ideologies) that make such domination seem palatable. Underneath the surface of that stability, social forces in the form of conflicts among different groups with different goals are inevitably at work, either to reinforce or to change existing power differentials. The dominant group attempts to consolidate even greater power and control over the economic system, while the subordinate groups attempt to wrestle power away from their dominators and to empower themselves.

Smelser (1981: 14) identifies the central assumptions of modern conflict theory as follows:

1. the main features of society are change, conflict, and coercion;

2. social structure is based on the dominance of some groups by others;

3. each group in society has a set of common interests, whether its members are aware of it or not;

4. when people become aware of their common interests, they may become a social class;

5. the intensity of class conflict depends on the presence of certain political and social conditions (e.g., freedom to form coalitions), the distribution of authority and rewards, and on
the openness of the class system.

Modern theorists, such as Mills (1956; 1959), Dahrendorf (1959), and Collins (1975), have
broadened and refined conflict theory to reflect conditions existing within our contemporary
society. Instead of limiting their focus to relations between various social classes as a consequence of the relations between employers and employees to the means of production
and distribution of resources, many sociologists argue that the basic elements of conflict
theory are equally applicable to relations between, for example, the younger and the older
members of society, parents and children, the able-bodied and people with disabilities, different ethnic groups, and women and men.

Applying conflict theory to the study of gender, for many theorists, means redefining
"class," as used by Marx and Smelser above, to refer to groups identified principally by
sex and/or gender, and then examining their access to and control over scarce resources
such as political and economic power. Doing so has lead to the following explanation of
women's inequality in structural terms:

> A glance at the Canadian social structure indicates that it is men who own and control the
> essential resources....Ownership of the most important resource, the means of production,
> is mainly in the hands of a few men who have power over almost all women as well as other
> men....Men also have control of the next most important resources, access to the occupa-
> tional structure and control of policy making in the major areas of social life. (Connelly and
> Christiansen-Ruffman, 1977/1987: 283)

As can be seen in the above quotation, modern conflict theorists emphasize *power* and
have moved beyond the comparatively limited economic focus of Marx to include analysis
of other sources of power that affect the relative positions of women and men in Canadian
society. While women possess less economic and political power than do men, they are not
without access to those sources, nor are they lacking in other forms of social power, as we
shall see in Chapter 7.

Conflict theorists are lead to investigate existing social arrangements in an attempt to determine who benefits, who suffers, and by what mechanisms those outcomes are distributed. Applying this theory to an analysis of the structural positions and socially defined
roles of women and men offers very different interpretations from that promoted by functionalism. However, just as functionalism tends to overemphasize social cohesion and stability and essentially ignores conflict and social change, conflict theory tends to overemphasize
the latter and ignores the former. We turn now to an examination of a number of theories that
focus exclusively upon issues of gender.

FEMINIST THEORIES

As we noted in Chapter 1, feminists challenge the theorizing and research enterprises within
sociology by questioning whether the social sciences can ever be objective and value-neutral, and whether they should be kept separate and distinct from policy advocacy and application at either the individual or societal level (Eichler 1984). Claims of objectivity and
value-neutrality have generally been replaced in feminist theory with **value-specification**
(Lindsey 1994: 14), wherein the writer clearly states her or his values, thereby acknowledging possible, and probable, biases. For example, Bart begins her editorial article in a

mainstream academic journal with: "I should explain the reasons for the personal, informal and emotional quality of this editorial. In the women's movement we believe that the personal and the political cannot be separated" (Bart 1971: 734). Readers are then invited to assess a presentation in light of the author's acknowledged value premises. Of course, this approach assumes that writers can be, and are, aware of their values and possible biases.

The rejection of value-neutrality appears to pit feminist theories against mainstream "scientific" research and theory and to create competing claims for legitimacy. However, since mainstream theories throughout the social sciences (including sociology), supposedly founded upon a bedrock of objectivity, have been found to contain biases in varying degrees towards male values, self-images, and desires (Eichler, 1984; Mandell, 1995: x; Nicholson, 1990: 3), feminist theories obviously cannot be ignored or summarily dismissed because of possible value contamination. The challenge posed by our increasing awareness of the values underlying all theories will eventually lead us to a more comprehensive understanding of the nature of gender.

Before we present an overview of each perspective, bear in mind that the major perspectives (e.g., liberal, Marxist, radical, socialist) are not mutually exclusive. While each has a dominant focus, overlap of content themes, proposals, and contributing authors can be observed. You are not required to choose which theory is best in terms of comprehensive explanatory power and then consequently exclude or ignore the others. Even though adoption of a single all-explanatory theoretical framework can appeal to, and seemingly provide for, one's intellectual comfort, no one theory can be considered all-powerful.

> Recent criticisms of feminist theory have demonstrated conclusively, in our view, that universal generalizations about women are almost certain to be false; that different groups of women experience subordination in very different ways—and that some may not even be conscious of or concerned about subordination at all; that some women exercise power over others—as well as over some men....(Jaggar and Rothenberg, 1993: 113)

Consequently, each theory and all theorizing is best thought of as a work-in-progress.

While some theorists are committed to one perspective exclusively, most shift from one to another, depending upon the issue under examination, drawing from the insights provided by any source. Consequently, you will find some author's names appearing under the heading of more than one theory. In addition, feminists from all theoretical persuasions frequently work together on practical issues. This cooperation and flexibility stems from a realization that each perspective is perhaps best thought of as a "lens" (Jaggar and Rothenberg, 1993: xvi, borrowing a metaphor from Bem, 1993) through which one views a subject matter. Selecting a particular lens may sharpen one's insight in certain ways but, as Burke (1945) notes, "[a] way of seeing is a way of not seeing" (in Downes and Rock, 1982: 6). A lens can blinker as well as improve sight at the same time. Jaggar and Rothenberg observe that, "different theoretical approaches are likely to be useful in different circumstances and for different purposes....[F]eminist theories ultimately are tools designed for a practical purpose—the purpose of understanding women's subordination in order to end it" (1993: xvii).

A recent summary by two Canadian sociologists suggests that feminist theories are intended to "deconstruct errors and myths about women's abilities, add to knowledge about women's empirical realities...construct theory by and about women...[and] tend to be explicitly political in their advocacy of social change" (Elliot and Mandell, 1995: 4). While much of the quotation accords well with what we have stated earlier, we wish to draw attention to the phrase "construct theory *by* and *about* women" (emphasis ours) for two reasons. First, we have the claim that only theories created by women qualify as feminist. This statement implies that men need not apply for consideration as feminist theorists. Morra and Smith (1995) assert that most feminists agree. Even though it may be a bit early in your career as a student in formal studies of gender, do you agree with this exclusionary statement? Can men be feminist theorists, or feminists in general? Second, to suggest that feminist theories are only about women is misleading, particularly considering the relational nature of statuses that we referred to in Chapter 1. We agree that feminist theories explicitly focus upon women but, by implication at the very least and often by direct statement, they also offer claims about men as well.

Although feminist theories advance from the premises that men and women in all societies are not evaluated similarly, that women live under conditions of subordination and even oppression, and that these conditions are neither natural nor inevitable, each type of feminist theory begins with an identification and examination of what it considers to be the primary or root cause(s) of oppression and provides guidelines for eliminating inequality. Bear in mind that many of the insights presented here were once considered to be new and innovative, but are now accepted as part of feminist, and even our own society's, mainstream thought. We shall present, but not be limited to, the basic frameworks first identified and named by Jaggar and Rothenberg (1984). Throughout this text, and from other sources as well, you are likely to be confronted with many additional labels (e.g., materialist feminism) as writers and analysts attempt to name a specific theoretical or empirical focus. With your knowledge of some of the basic approaches, you should be able to discern their background assumptions and to make links between wider and narrower theoretical frameworks.

Liberal Feminism

This is the most moderate, as well as the "most mainstream and popular" (Elliot and Mandell, 1995: 8), of all the feminist theories. *Liberal feminism,* or *egalitarian feminism* as it is sometimes called, identifies its goal as the creation of "a just and compassionate society in which freedom flourishes" (Wendell in Tong, 1989: 13). Similar to other liberal discourses on equality, this theory is grounded on the assumption that a society based upon the principles of equality of opportunity and freedom will provide the most positive environment for all persons to achieve the best of their potential. Should these conditions not be present, education devoted to enhancing technical skills, knowledge, and the power of rational thought, will lead to the social changes necessary for creating a **meritocracy** society, where social rank is based on merit and in which inequality and hierarchy are both inevitable and acceptable, since not all individuals possess equal potential. Liberal feminism maintains that women have received a lesser share of social rewards because of their unequal participation in institutions outside the family domestic sphere—in particular, education and paid work. "Liberal feminists usually are…committed to major economic re-organization and considerable redistribution of wealth, since one of the modern political goals most closely associated with liberal feminism is equality of opportunity, which would undoubtedly require and lead to both" (Wendell in Tong, 1989: 12).

According to liberal feminists, who strongly believe that gender is not determined by sex, women are unequally distributed within the economic institution because of a combination of gender discrimination and a lack of equal-quality education. The reasonable or rational solution to women's subordination, first proposed by Mary Wollstonecraft in 1792 (Code, 1993: 26) and still endorsed today, requires that such obstacles be eliminated, and equality, defined as equality of opportunity, be assured for both women and men. Historically, liberal theorists emphasized the distinction between public and private spheres and the notion that, while the government should pass legislation promoting equality in the public sphere, it had no authority to interfere in the daily life of the private sphere. These latter sentiments were echoed during the 1960s, when then-Justice Minister Pierre Trudeau pronounced that the Canadian government has no place in the bedrooms of the nation. Liberal feminists today generally support these positions with the exception of asserting that limited government intervention is necessary to ensure financial and physical security and safety for women within the domestic realm (Jaggar and Rothenberg, 1993: 118).

Much of the practical agenda for liberal feminists in Canada was established by the 1970 Royal Commission on the Status of Women, whose recommendations were designed to "ensure for women equal opportunities with men in all aspects of Canadian society" (in Wilson, 1996: 10). The recommended programs of action, known by various names in different locales and jurisdictions, including affirmative action quotas in business and education, equal opportunity employment, employment equity, pay equity, parental leave, and subsidized day-care centres are all consistent with the liberal feminist orientation. Such programs are considered necessary to provide women with freedom from oppression and equality of opportunity to develop as human beings. These outcomes are argued to be, ultimately, in the best rational interests of both women and men. Men and women would, as a result of the implementation of these programs, rise or fall within the existing system of social stratification based solely on their talents (hence, society as a meritocracy). Liberal feminist theory is considered to be relatively moderate because, while it does advocate social changes, it does not propose to radically restructure the nature of basic institutions in Canadian society, but instead stresses the need to restructure the distribution of individuals within those slightly-modified institutions. You can see, however, that liberal feminists accept a reality in which inequalities of power, prestige, and material benefits are still found between individuals of both sexes.

While aimed at eliminating gender oppression, other forms of subordination, such as those stemming from class and "race"/ethnic distinctions, may still remain in effect. The perspective appeals primarily to white middle-class professional women who are considered to be the main beneficiaries of the suggested policy interventions (Elliot and Mandell, 1995: 9; Lindsey, 1994: 15). Liberal feminism has been derisively referred to as "assimilationism" (Williams, 1991: 95) for its moderate stance, for its focus on providing opportunities for women to gain equal access to areas that were traditionally reserved for men, and for its focus on "sameness." The theory asserts that women are essentially the same as men, with any observable gender differences being the product of social construction and not genetics, and are, therefore, capable of benefiting from needed programs of intervention. Furthermore, liberal feminism does appear to suggest that, with the aid of those programs, women ultimately should, and will, become more like men.

Marxist Feminism

In contrast to the liberal viewpoint, *Marxist feminism* insists that the entire structure of our society must be changed before true gender equality can be attained. The Marxist approach focuses on the public sphere of formal economic production processes and argues that the economic institution, as it is organized in a particular society, determines the nature of all other institutions. Furthermore, one's position within the economic institution determines one's relationship to all other aspects of social life. The capitalist economic system, organized as it is around the principles of private property and the pursuit of profit, ensures the existence of unequal distributions of material rewards and is viewed as the primary source of female oppression in Canada.

Engels (1884/1902), Marx's collaborator, argued that women's subordination was a consequence of the introduction of private property, which lead property-owning men to institute tight control over women in an attempt to ensure the paternity of potential heirs. Women thus became the property of men and the first oppressed class. Engels further believed that the solution to such oppression required women's equal participation in the economic production process with a resulting equal share of economic rewards. He also called for the creation of collective or communal systems for household labour and childrearing, to free more of women's energies for economic production. Unlike Marx, Engels recognized that significant reorganization of the private sphere was needed to achieve the restructuring of the public sphere necessary for gender equality. However, as the name implies, Marxist feminists have followed the teachings of Marx more closely than those of Engels.

Tong (1989: 51) observes that Marxist feminism has overwhelmingly focused its attention on women's work-related concerns, including "how the institution of the family is related to capitalism; how women's domestic work is trivialized as not real work; and, finally, how women are generally given the most boring and low-paying jobs." The family is related to capitalism in numerous ways, in that women's unpaid labour in the home physically, psychologically, and emotionally raises the next generation of workers and recreates the adult male worker at the end of each work day. While these activities support and maintain the capitalist system, they are detrimental to women, since unpaid labour is not considered to be "real work" and is not formally rewarded financially. Marxist feminists, therefore, advocate the necessity of developing a system for paying women directly for their household work.

Marxist feminists have also contributed to our understanding of the importance, for male capitalists and the capitalist system, of keeping women poorly paid so that they exist as an exploitable "reserve labour force" (Benston, 1969; Connelly, 1978; Lindsey, 1994: 15; Wilson, 1996: 118). This concept refers to a pool of women who can be pulled into and pushed out of the labour force when economic circumstances, such as wars and economic depressions, supposedly warrant it. The existence of a reserve pool of cheap labour operates to depress male workers' wages (under threat of being replaced by lesser-paid female workers) and to support the capitalist's, but not women's, pursuit of profit. These social arrangements further promote women's economic dependence on men and perpetuate female exploitation and subordination.

Accordingly, from the perspective of this theory, the only solution to eliminating women's oppression is to radically transform the economic institution from one based on capitalism, to one based on socialism and, eventually, communism. With the eventual abolition of private property, the economic production process would, thereafter, belong to society as a whole; every individual would have essentially the same relationship to the process, and would thus receive the same economic rewards. Once the fundamental economic oppression inherent in capitalism has been eliminated, the oppression of women would necessarily disappear. From the basic Marxist perspective, the unequal status of women is analogous to that of any other disadvantaged group in our country, such as First Nations people or the poor. Sex, ethnic, and class inequalities are all believed to be byproducts of the same underlying cause: the capitalist economic system. For most Marxists, the situation of women is not considered to be a special case requiring a separate explanation or solution, but rather is simply another example of how the capitalist economic system works.

Radical Feminism

Originating in the 1960s, primarily among women dissatisfied with their treatment in New Left socialist and civil rights groups, *radical feminism* came to be most strongly identified with the women's movement of the 1970s (Wilson, 1996: 13). Unlike Marxist feminists, radical feminists do not identify the capitalist economic system as the sole, or even primary, source of female subordination, but instead suggest that women live under conditions of inequality in most systems of economic production, whether they be capitalist, socialist, or communist. The most fundamental oppression, according to radical (meaning root) feminists, in terms of its temporal priority, near-universality across societies, pervasiveness throughout entire societies, and depth of inflicted suffering, is the subordination of women specifically by men.

This oppression is ultimately founded on a system of ideas referred to as *patriarchy* (sometimes as "patriarchalism" or "sexism"). Patriarchy promotes a belief in male superiority that supports and justifies the domination of women by men (see Caputi, 1989; Cottle et al., 1989; Roberts, 1990).

> Patriarchal societies are those in which men have more power than women and readier access than women to what is valued in the society or in any social sub-group. In consequence of this power and privilege, men in such societies or groups occupy positions that permit them to shape and control many, if not most, aspects of women's lives. (Code, 1993: 19–20)

According to radical feminists, patriarchy pervades not only the public world of formal economic production processes, but also, and more oppressively, the private worlds of the family, marriage, sexuality, and biological reproduction. Social change is, therefore, necessary in both the public and private domains. Patriarchal ideology, and all behaviour based upon this belief system, must be eliminated before any meaningful change in women's subordination can occur. Since radical feminists suggest that gender is the fundamental form of difference, their theory initially placed little emphasis on ethnicity and social-class differences.

Perhaps more than any other branch of feminist theory, early radical feminism was deeply influenced by insights derived from women's consciousness-raising (CR) groups formed during the middle to late 1960s and early 1970s. Eisenstein notes that "[a] first assumption of consciousness raising was that what women had to say about the details of their daily lives, about their personal experiences and histories, mattered, it had significance, and above all it had validity" (in Wilson, 1996: 8). These experiences and concerns came to be viewed as more than limited personal problems in need of private solutions. Since they were found to be common to so many other women, they were redefined as public issues with societal causes that could only be altered by collective-action movements through formal and informal political processes. The transformation of these experiences was captured in the phrase, "the personal is political," an insight that some suggest is the most significant contribution of radical feminism (Jaggar and Rothenberg, 1984: 219).

While the phrase "the personal is political" was initially descriptive in nature, it contained the possibility of becoming prescriptive. As the radical feminist movement began to grow in size and strength, segments of the movement began to emphasize the prescriptive, essentially reversing the phrase to become "the political is personal," and to exhort adherents of radical feminism to transform their private lives to reflect their politics. "Politically correct behavior...is that which adheres to a movement's morality and hastens its goals" (Dimen, 1984: 139). Ironically, the notion of politically correct behaviour created a fundamental tension within radical feminism (and other feminisms that adopted the slogan) between, on the one hand, the individualism of freedom of choice and the validity of personal experience and, on the other hand, the movement's emphasis on collectivism, personal sacrifice, and unity in pursuit of political goals.

Dimen (1984) suggests that the phrase "politically correct" originated within the general leftist political movement, while Echols (1984: 56) attributes its inception to lesbian separatists. Regardless of the initial source, the concept of *political correctness* has become part of our everyday language in Canada in the 1980s and 1990s. During the 1990s, the phrase has also become a favourite pejorative epithet used by conservatives (replacing "knee-jerk" and "bleeding-heart liberal") to oppose any social change they consider to be undesirable (Fekete, 1994; Richer and Weir, 1995; for examples of its use, see Fekete, 1994). Critics usually manage to condemn change-oriented practices and programs as indicative of the "evil" of feminist political correctness. Under the heading of *The Feminist Mistake*, a Canadian conservative writes: "In our present society...is the presence on every campus of thought-control police in the form of human rights tribunals, gender committees, and `political correctness' officers, whose work it is to control the acceptability of social expectations while creating new ones via educational courses" (Gairdner, 1992: 304–305). It is more than mildly interesting to observe that a widely used, male-created, comparable saying from the Vietnam-war era "if you're going to talk the talk, you have to walk the walk" has never been similarly disparaged. Is this due to "political correctness" being a shorter catchy easier-to-use phrase, or simply another example of a patriarchal double standard of evaluation that discriminates against anything associated with women? But, we digress....

While radical feminists generally agree upon the fundamental cause of female subordination—patriarchy—individual proponents of the perspective focus their attentions upon different aspects of patriarchy-at-work in need of social change. Some radical feminists claim that patriarchy justifies the differential valuation of men and women by promoting the belief that the sexes are inherently different. These feminists take the contrary position that most apparent differences between men and women are not innate and immutable, but rather are the product of a social construction process predicated on patriarchy itself. The elimination of patriarchy would lead to the eventual disappearance of these socially created gender differences. In essence, they seek to eradicate gender as a meaningful social category (Echols, 1983: 50) and to replace existing gender roles with androgyny (Decker, 1983: 331, 459). Any resulting differences between women and men would then be considered "human," and not gender, differences.

A more limited focus can be found in the writings of theorists, such as Rich (1980), that centre upon male physical, psychological, and social control of female sexuality as the basic cause of female subordination. In contrast to this focus upon sexuality, Firestone (1970) argues that women must be liberated from the "tyranny of their reproductive biology" that necessitates their dependence during pregnancy upon men, and, in her opinion, forms the foundation of patriarchy. As long as women's roles and rewards are tied to reproductive differences and the beliefs surrounding them, true gender equality cannot be realized. The goal of this radical feminist is to seek the elimination of biological sex as a basis for social differentiation. Firestone was optimistic that reliable birth-control measures, technological developments for extra-uterine gestation of a fetus, and the creation and widespread use of alternative forms of childcare (so that the childbearer need not be the childrearer), would eliminate women's dependence upon men and create conditions of gender equality. As you are probably aware, such optimistic faith in the positive power of technology has recently given way to significant concern over possible negative impacts of new, asexual or assisted, reproductive technologies upon women (Achilles, 1995; Grant, 1994; Hartouni, 1995; Mann, 1995; McDaniel, 1988a; Royal Commission on New Reproductive Technologies, 1993). Radical feminists were among the first (to be joined by liberal and socialist feminists) to define such issues as reproductive and contraceptive rights, abortion, reproductive technologies, sexuality expression and experience, and sexual and physical violence against women as being feminist issues.

By the early 1980s, another branch of radical feminism became discernible. It originated among feminists who grew increasingly pessimistic about the likely occurrence of the radical changes needed to eliminate patriarchy and who, furthermore, viewed the liberal feminist emphasis upon assimilation into patriarchal culture as unacceptable. Their proposed alternative was one of separation from the entire patriarchal system. Since the focus of this segment of feminism is sufficiently different, we believe it deserves consideration as a distinct category.

Cultural Feminism

While other names have been suggested, such as *integrative feminism* (Miles, 1985), *relational feminism* (after Gilligan, 1982), and *difference feminism* (an application which is problematic and subject to debate as to its referent), we have elected to use the label of *cultural feminism* for reasons to be noted later. Cultural feminists identify the suppression of distinctive or different female qualities, experiences, and values as the primary cause of women's subordination. Rather than direct immediate attention to the elimination of patriarchy, their proposed solution is the identification, rehabilitation, and nurturance of women's qualities, such that they will ultimately supersede the currently dominant patriarchal system. Indicative of this orientation, Mackie (1991: 34) notes a "perceptible shift in feminist thinking," away from an interest in disproving, and towards an interest in stressing, the existence of gender differences. "Alleged feminine distinctions are now being proclaimed with pride, rather than denied or minimized" (Mackie, 1991: 34). Some feminists (e.g., Daly, 1978) seek to build on women's shared or unique qualities and create an "alternative female consciousness" (Echols, 1984: 53). To that end, Belenky et al. (1986) devote an entire volume to description and celebration of "women's ways of knowing."

To create an alternative female consciousness, women-centred cultural or subcultural environments must be established to facilitate the promotion of women's accomplishments and sense of unity. A hallmark characteristic of these "women's cultures" (hence our preference for naming this theory), according to cultural feminists, would be an emphasis upon consensual nonhierarchical decision-making processes (Worell, 1996: 360). Gilligan (1982) claims that women speak "in a different voice" from men, and that a culture based on "womanly values" would stress responsibility, connection, community, negotiation, altruism, and nurturance, in contrast to a culture based on male values emphasizing separation, self-interest, combat, autonomy, and hierarchy.

The etiology of these posited gender differences does not appear to be a focal issue for the majority of cultural feminists, although they generally seem to favour a biological, or innate and immutable, basis, which puts them at odds with earlier radical feminists. For example, Echols (1984: 51) notes that *eco-feminists* (see Armstrong, 1993; Sturgeon, 1997) and *pacifist feminists* claim that women's "bond with the natural order" (Rich, 1976) makes them uniquely qualified to resolve threats of ecological disaster and nuclear holocaust. In this vein, Caldicott (1984: 294) argues that "[o]ne of the reasons women are so allied to the life processes is their hormonal constitution" and that males are "naturally" more fascinated by killing (1984: 296). Russell (1987: 15) claims that "the nuclear mentality and the masculine mentality are one and the same. To rid ourselves of one, we must rid ourselves of the other." However, Jane Flax (1990: 55), a proponent of postmodernist feminism (to be presented later), cautions against claims that assert the assumed "superiority of the opposite." She further notes that "perhaps women are not any less aggressive than men; we may just express our aggression in different, culturally sanctioned (and partially disguised or denied) ways" (Flax, 1990: 55).

The belief among cultural feminists that male sexuality is "selfish, violent, and woman-hating" (Echols, 1984: 60) leads to the premise that "pornography is the theory, rape is the practice" (Morgan in Echols, 1984: 58), thus linking male sexuality, violence towards women, and pornography. Rich (1980/1984) provides provocative insights into the patriarchal control of heterosexual relations and offers lesbianism (loosely defined) as the paradigm for female-controlled sexual (although she de-emphasizes genital sexuality) and social life. Lesbianism is described as a personal and political choice (not biologically determined) that expresses the ultimate rejection of patriarchy. According to Martindale's (1995: 75) summary of Rich's argument, "lesbian/feminism is industrial-strength feminism….If all women became lesbians, the patriarchy would crumble." Reminiscent of MacKinnon's (1982: 515) assertion that sexual relations are the quintessential site of female subordination ("sexuality is to feminism what work is to Marxism"), lesbian separatists advocate women's separation from men in every way. Nonlesbian cultural feminists, seeking to avoid estrangement of heterosexual feminists, prefer to advocate separation only from male values.

Echols (1984: 53) notes that "cultural feminists insist that feminism and the [political] left are intrinsically incompatible." Given that Marxist, radical, and socialist feminists all seek to eliminate gender differences, albeit each according to their own preferred solutions, the incompatibility of cultural feminism with the others is not in itself surprising. As a consequence of its orientation, cultural feminism is subject to the criticism of being *matriarchalist* and *essentialist*. Positing the existence of selected features, such as nurturance or relatedness, as part of the essential nature of all women supports basic stereotypes and the stereotyping process, which are seen by other feminists as forming part of the roots of female subordination. Essentialist and romanticized conceptions of women can pose analytical and political dangers to feminism that have yet to be fully explored (Tong, 1989). Whether cultural feminism will eventually be recognized as a separate and distinct feminist theory or will remain embedded within descriptive analyses of radical feminism (e.g., Elliot and Mandell, 1995; Jaggar and Rothenberg, 1993; Wilson, 1996) is still uncertain.

Socialist Feminism

Seeking to address the "gender-blindness of traditional Marxism and the class-blindness of early radical feminism" (Jaggar and Rothenberg, 1993: 122), *socialist feminism* attempts to extend and enrich Marxist analysis by incorporating radical feminist insights. Since socialist feminism evolved from two previously developed frameworks, it has attracted both Marxist feminists and radical feminists into its theoretical fold. As we have seen, Marxist feminism seeks to eliminate class oppression, while radical feminism seeks to eliminate gender oppression. These different solutions are predicated on identification of different root causes of female subordination. Socialist feminism argues than an historical combination of capitalist political economy with patriarchal ideology leads to the oppression of women both inside and outside the home. Gender equality, therefore, requires the elimination of both capitalism and patriarchy.

Mitchell (1973) was one of the first feminists to identify four major focal points for a socialist feminist analysis of the problems confronting women, and their solutions. From this perspective, not only must the socially organized system of (i) producing goods and services to meet human needs for food, shelter, clothing, and other material necessities be restructured, but so must the systems of (ii) sexuality, (iii) childbearing and ministering to the physical and emotional needs of children, husbands, aging parents, the sick, and the infirm, and (iv) childrearing in general and gender socialization in particular. Egalitarian solutions must also be examined in relation to one another, to ensure that one system's solutions do not become another system's problems.

Socialist feminists' attention has been directed to further exploration of the nature and importance of domestic labour (e.g., Luxton, 1980), the nature and location of women's paid-labour experiences (e.g., Armstrong and Armstrong, 1978; Duffy et al., 1989; Martin, 1995), and the interface between women's paid-labour and domestic-labour lives (Lynn and Todoroff, 1995). The traditional sexuality script, emphasizing aggressive male and passive female behaviour, has been examined as being emblematic of gender power relations. For example, McKinnon (1982: 531) suggests that "gender socialization is the process through which women come to identify themselves as sexual beings, as beings that exist for men." Not only do sexuality roles need to be restructured to promote gender equality, but also a new female-generated model of sexuality and socialization must be created.

Following Hartmann (1981) and others who view the nuclear family in North America as a central site of women's oppression, socialization within the family has also been examined to observe how girls and boys are prepared for differential participation in the domestic and paid-labour spheres. Despite the proliferation of work developed by socialist feminists that explicitly acknowledges subordination based upon both gender and social class, oppression based upon ethnicity, sexuality, able-bodiedness, and age have all tended to receive a lesser emphasis.

Inclusive Feminism

We have chosen to use the term *inclusive feminism* to refer to a newly evolved body of thought that addresses a claim now being made for all feminism: "Feminists challenge what they call traditional race-class-sexuality-power arrangements which favour men over women, whites over non-whites…able-bodiedness over non-able-bodiedness…and the employed over the non-employed" (Elliot and Mandell, 1995: 4–5). This depiction of feminism arose in response to criticisms voiced during the 1980s and 1990s that early feminist theory was derived from, and directed towards, a privileged white middle-class feminism that "denied, dismissed, and denigrated the experiences of differently raced, abled, and classed women" (Cassidy et al., 1995: 32). For example:

> To this day, white feminists cling to the false assumption that the women's movement is a homogeneous group experiencing the same forms and degree of oppression. With this assumption, white feminists have not only monopolized the movement with their interests and privileges, but have also carried their quality struggle, in the name of gender, at the expense of aboriginal, black women and women of colour. (Lucas et al., 1991/1995: 534)

In other words, in its search for the essential experience of generic "woman," not only did early feminists tend to treat all women as a singular entity, they also tended to presume that white middle-class heterosexual women were synonymous with, and representative of, that entity. Inclusive feminism, as it incorporates a multiplicity of experiences, is increasingly rendering the notion of a generic "woman" problematic (Code, 1993: 48; Elliot and Mandell, 1995: 26–27; Jaggar and Rothenberg, 1993: xiv). Arguments increasingly are being put forth that it may no longer be possible to create meaningful generalizations about the experiences of "woman," if indeed it ever was (see Box 3.1).

The scope of inclusive feminism is subject to variable interpretation. Jaggar and Rothenberg (1993: 123) use the term *multicultural feminism* to refer to a framework developed in the United States that explicitly focuses upon the interstices of "sex/gender, sexuality, class, and race." The counterpart framework developing within Canada appears to cast a wider and more inclusive net to envelop, in addition to the aforementioned, women with disabilities, elderly women, and women from minority ethnic groups who may not be visibly different from privileged women.

More is involved within this framework than simply adding to existing theory an understanding of the experiences of women from previously ignored (often referred to as "silenced") social categories and groups. Acknowledging these groups as "different" contains within itself the possibility for promoting what we shall refer to here as the doctrine of *different means deficient*. If white, middle-class, Anglo-Saxon, heterosexual women are still represented as having the standard women's experience, while women from other social categories are presented as possessing different experiences, these latter women are likely to be marginalized, just as all women are when men are assumed to be *the* standard and women are considered to be different and consequently deficient somehow.

Increasingly, representatives of, and advocates for, these identifiable groups are claiming a right to reshape feminist theory and feminism itself. The ultimate goal is to create a more inclusive feminism that renders comprehensible the interactive or multiplicative impacts of numerous "isms" such as, sexism, racism, ethnism, classism, heterosexualism, ableism, and ageism. The challenge is to develop an understanding of the commonality of women's subordination, without asserting that this subordination is necessarily more fundamental than other forms of subordination women confront due to their "race"/ethnicity, class, and so on. In some instances, issues of gender transcend issues of race, ethnicity, class, sexuality, or ability. In other instances, gender is a background issue. Gender status may be active or latent in comparison to other statuses. With further refined analysis and understanding, according to inclusive feminism, subordination of women as women will eventually be seen as more, or less, crucial in comparison to other forms of subordination occurring in certain times and places.

| Box 3.1 | **Ain't I A Woman?** |

Sojourner Truth (1797–1883), born into slavery, became well known as a preacher and as an antislavery lecturer after she gained her freedom in 1827. The speech that follows was given by Truth extemporaneously at a woman's right convention in Ohio in 1851, in response to audience jeers and arguments that all women, the universal woman, are by nature, delicate creatures who require protection—not the vote. Gage, a feminist activist, recorded Truth's powerful speech as she challenged this depiction of women. Truth's speech reminds us that cultural constructs of "woman" may only reflect certain segments of our society. We reproduce the speech as it is given in Stanton, Anthony, and Gage's (1889) edited work, *History of Woman Suffrage.* 2nd ed. Vol. 1. Rochester, New York: Charles Mann.

When, slowly from her seat in the corner rose Sojourner Truth, who, till now, had scarcely lifted her head. "Don't let her speak!" gasped half a dozen in my ear. She moved slowly and solemnly to the front, laid her old bonnet at her feet, and turned her great speaking eyes to me. There was a hissing sound of disapprobation above and below....

"Wall, chilern, whar dar is so much racket dar must be somethin' out o' kilter. I tink dat 'twixt de niggers of de Souf and de womin at de Norf, all talkin' 'bout rights, de white men will be in a fix pretty soon. But what's all dis here talkin' 'bout?

"Dat man ober dar say dat womin needs to be helped into carriages, and lifted ober ditches, and to hab de best place everywhar. Nobody eber helps me into carriages, or ober mud-puddles, or gibs me any best place!" And raising herself to her full height, and her voice in a pitch like rolling thunder, she asked. "And a'n't I am woman? Look at me! Look at my arm! (and she bared her right arm to the shoulder, showing her tremendous muscular power.) I have ploughed, and planted, and gathered into barns, and no man could head me! And a'n't I a woman? I could work as much and eat as much as a man—when I could get it—and bear de lash as well! And a'n't I am woman? I have born thirteen chilern. And a'n't I a woman? I have borne thirteen chilern, and seen 'em ms' all sold off to slavery, and when I cried out with my mother's grief, none but Jesus heard me! And a'n't I a woman?

"Den dey talks 'bout dis ting in de head; what dis dey call it?" ("Intellect," whispered some one near.) "Dat's it, honey. What's dat got to do wid womin's rights or nigger's rights? If my cup won't hold but a pint, and yourn holds a quart, wouldn't ye be mean not to let me have my little half-measure full?"

The quest for a more inclusive feminism in the 1990s has created somewhat of a paradox, wherein "feminism seems, still, to require the consciousness-raising that enables women to claim some measure of unity 'as women' even while they concentrate on understanding differences" (Code, 1993: 48). Not surprisingly, given the recency of an explicit emphasis on inclusiveness, reclaiming the voices of ignored and neglected groups is still in the early stages of development. Incorporating these voices into an integrated feminist theory that acknowledges both the difference (hence the use of "difference feminism") and the commonality of women's experiences and the relationships between the two, will continue for decades to come. Rather than inventory a list of supposedly representative experiences recently identified with various categories of women, we shall endeavour to integrate the research and the "voices" into various chapters through this text.

Postmodern Feminism

Recently derived in large part from architecture and philosophy, *postmodern feminism* exists both as a form of admonition to all statements of claim made by other branches of feminist thought, and as a perspective in its own right. In simple terms, postmodernists extend inclusive feminism even further. Elliot and Mandell (1995: 23) note that considerable debate exists as to exactly what "postmodern" means and to whether feminism should either incorporate or distance itself from postmodern theory and politics.

Postmodernists challenge still-prevalent modern beliefs, derived from the period of the Enlightenment, regarding the constituent nature, causes, and consequences of the emphasis placed upon knowledge, reason, and science (see Nicholson, 1990: 2–4). Modernist ideals and beliefs include:

> the idea that individuals comprise stable, coherent, and rational subjects; that reason, with its scientific laws, provides an objective, reliable, and universal basis for knowledge; that the rational use of knowledge is neutral and socially beneficial. (based on Flax, 1990, in Elliot and Mandell, 1995: 23–24)

Postmodernist criticism suggests that such ideals and beliefs are not now, nor have they ever been, obtainable. Furthermore, the argument is advanced that these beliefs are also oppressive, since they demand that other beliefs be deemed irrational and unscientific. "Knowledge" is subsequently limited to that which meets a narrow and highly debatable set of criteria. In contrast, postmodernists beliefs include:

> a conception of the individual as unstable, contradictory, and socially constructed; a conception of what forms of authority or knowledge are legitimate, namely multiple, anti-hierarchical, and participatory forms; a conception of history as non-linear, not necessarily progressive, and as always read through the limited perspective of the present, as well as through particular contexts; and a conception of community as an achievement based on valuing differences without opposition. (Elliot and Mandell, 1995: 24)

Postmodern feminism is not alone when it also claims that our ideals emphasizing rationality and scientific objectivity are congruent with socially constructed conceptions of masculinity (Nicholson, 1990: 5). These masculinist conceptions are rejected along with what they depict as the narrow, unself-conscious, white, middle-class feminisms that attempt to universalize experiences of one "privileged" group to all women. Postmodern feminists argue that the theoretical claims emanating from liberal, Marxist, radical, cultural, and socialist feminisms, which assert a single or even a limited plurality of causes for women's oppression, are flawed, inadequate, and typically based upon suppression of female experiences that are incompatible with each theory (Flax, 1990: 46–49). Any theory claiming to be fully explanatory is necessarily assuming a dominant and oppressive stance. Postmodernist feminists seek to acknowledge the perspectives and experiences of women from all classes, "races," ethnicities, differently-abled groups, sexualities, and ages, without generalizing to all women, nor representing any one or all of these groups as possessing "essential" components of women's lives. For postmodern feminists, *a* feminist theory is not possible.

Critics suggest that postmodernism would lead to an ultimate reduction of pure individualism. If every woman's experience is unique, as postmodernists claim, then generalizations and the theories that contain them are not possible. Existing feminist theories would all be invalid. Acceptance or rejection of any of these theories, including the postmodernist, would ultimately be based upon whichever feminist group(s) holds the most power. Furthermore, any feminist politics derived from feminist theory, any proposed plan of action and advocacy, on behalf of any group of women or women in general would be impossible, since it would be oppressive to some specific group of women (Di Stefano, 1990: 76).

We agree with postmodernists that many statements made by feminists during the 1970s and 1980s contained overgeneralizations based on privileged women and ignored or marginalized important claims from, and about, women living in other groups and social categories. We do not agree, however, that all generalizations are inappropriate and masculinist (an ultimate epithet within feminism). Postmodernism appears to suggest that gender textbooks should be limited to providing only specific, nongeneralized, descriptions of the lives of women and men belonging to, for example, different "races," ethnicities, or classes, both today and in the past (as currently understood). While such a limited set of descriptions might be inherently fascinating, they would be of value only at the present moment. We believe that a textbook should provide an understanding of gender that is portable beyond the here and now. As long as we recognize their limitations, carefully crafted generalizations provide the basis for such an understanding.

The "we" referred to in the last sentence includes authors, theorists, and researchers, as well as you, the reader. Generalizations are "statements that apply not just to a specific case but to *most* cases of the same type" (Robertson, 1987: 6, emphasis ours). They are not intended to be applied to everyone. If you cannot recognize yourself in certain statements made within these pages, this neither invalidates the generalizations nor your own personal experiences. The generalization is not necessarily wrong, nor are you necessarily weird, different, or special. Your experience may demonstrate the limitations of a generalization, which, we hope, will be addressed in time. Feminists have devoted themselves to the task of noting disparities between experience and theory (Code, 1993: 52), of naming and elaborating upon the nature and meaning of those experiences, and of modifying existing theories or creating new ones to develop a better fit between theoretical generalizations and lived experience.

PERSPECTIVES ON MEN AND MASCULINITY

In contrast to many feminist theories, theorizing on men *as* men, and on the nature of masculinity in our society, has yet to achieve systematic coherency. It could be argued that traditional theories, such as classical liberalism, while claiming (erroneously) to exemplify generic humanity with concepts such as "rational man," have already developed models of men. However, in lacking a self-conscious focus upon men per se, these theories would require considerable refinement before specific statements on men and masculinity could be produced. Present-day theorizing on men has largely evolved in response to feminist theories and to various social changes initiated by the women's movement. For the moment, what does exist should most accurately be considered as *perspectives* on men and masculinity. Following the classification scheme put forth by Clatterbaugh (1990), we will briefly survey six perspectives that vary in terms of their current level of theoretical sophistication.

The Conservative Perspective

Drawing inspiration from classical thought, the *conservative perspective* argues that the essential nature of men and masculinity is different from that of women and femininity. Two strands of thought exist within conservatism regarding the basis for essential masculinity. One locates the roots in biology, as outlined initially by Charles Darwin (1809–1882), while the other locates them in the moral order of civilization, as outlined by Edmund Burke (1729–1797). *Biological conservatives* of today primarily support and advocate the sociobiology argument put forth by Wilson (1978) that we have already presented in Chapter 2. Current *moral conservatives* such as Gilder (1973: 103–114) argue that masculinity is a manifestation of society's civilizing veneer, which harnesses men's nature to become providers and protectors of women and children. More specifically, Gilder suggests that men are by nature antisocial, as exemplified by the irresponsible actions of single men, in the forms of drunkenness, criminality, violence, and indebtedness (Gilder, 1973: 5, 30, 208). By exercising the powers of their sexuality, women tame and civilize men, bringing out their best and most noble qualities (Gilder, 1973: 38, 98).

Moral conservatives argue in favour of restoring the "traditional" male-dominated nuclear family to supremacy. Gilder targets the liberal feminist agenda (e.g., affirmative action, increased availability of contraception, abortion, and day-care facilities) as threatening men's ability to perform their traditional masculine role. In the face of such threats, men are likely to flee their responsibilities, abandon their families, and revert to their antisocial tendencies (Gilder, 1973: 265–267). In his defence of the "natural family," one of Canada's most prominent moral conservatives essentially parrots Gilder while mixing in a little sociobiology (Gairdner, 1992: 85–87), and then adds a highly selective interpretation of psychological and biological research findings (Gairdner, 1992: 313–317) to uphold the conservative interpretation of men and masculinity:

> Unless some social pressure is imposed to recruit men and their energies for a purpose higher than themselves and their appetites—in particular, if women are not present, or not willing, or lack confidence, or are afraid to tame errant male proclivities—then "over the whole range of human societies, men are over-whelmingly more prone to masturbation, homosexuality, voyeurism, gratuitous sexual aggression, and other shallow and indiscriminate erotic activity" [Gilder, 1986: 5]. They are also more prone to violent crime. (Gairdner, 1992: 85)

In other words, if masculinity, the family, and society itself are on the brink of moral decay, it is all women's, especially feminist women's, fault. When women discard the civilizing roles of their traditional femininity, men forgo the moral dimensions of traditional masculinity. However, feminist-initiated social reforms are doomed to failure, in the opinion of conservatives, either because of the "natural" biological basis for male and female behaviour, or because right-minded men recognize the importance of the moral order for the continued progress of civilization.

The Profeminist Perspective

Possibly the most popular of the six perspectives (Clatterbaugh, 1990: 40), *profeminists* argue that, since current masculinity is neither biologically nor morally inevitable, a new masculinity can be socially constructed. In contrast to the conservative perspective, profeminists claim that the traditional family is not a civilizing institution, but rather an institution "oppressive to women and destructive of men's ability to be caring, loving partners to women" (Clatterbaugh, 1990: 59). Two types of profeminism are discernible, each developing as a response to two major branches of early feminism.

Liberal profeminists tend to find symmetry in the situations of men and women, wherein both are equally, but differently, restricted by existing gender prescriptions (Clatterbaugh, 1990: 45). Arguing that the expectations for masculinity prevent men from attaining their full potential as human beings (Sawyer, 1974), liberal profeminists focus primarily upon the costs to men created by their traditionally limited gender role within our society. Farrell (1974: 30) lists the 10 commandments of masculinity that require men to be unemotional, invulnerable, unresponsive, controlling, condescending, egotistical, nonintrospective breadwinners who disdain housework. Other liberal profeminists focus upon describing the socialized constraints placed upon masculinity in, for example, athletics (Lester, 1976), the provider role (Gould, 1976), and parenting (Fasteau, 1975). While early liberal profeminists tended to depict a monolithic image of masculinity, more recently a plurality of "masculinities" (Brod, 1987a) have been acknowledged that vary by subculture (for example, ethnicity or social class) and historical time period (Dubbert, 1979; Rotundo, 1993). Liberal profeminists argue that removal of gender restrictions from men would be of benefit not only to men, but also to women.

Radical profeminists view contemporary masculinity as the byproduct of a patriarchal society based upon a system of power designed to benefit and privilege men (Kaufman, 1987b). According to this perspective, masculinity is characterized by *misogyny* (hatred of women) and violence towards women, other men, and even each man himself. These qualities are deemed to be neither natural nor essential, but are imposed on men by our patriarchal society. Whereas moral conservatives claim that women hold sexual power over men, radical profeminists argue that men use their greater power to sexually oppress women (Clatterbaugh, 1990: 42). To attain a new masculinity existing "beyond patriarchy" (Kaufman, 1987a; 1993), radical profeminists promote the deprograming of men to eradicate misogyny, male violence against women, the taken-for-granted assumption of male superiority, men's emotional isolation from one another, and male competitiveness. In their place, men should be socialized into the values of nonviolence, cooperation, and nurturance (Clatterbaugh, 1991: 10).

Both liberals and radicals advocate and utilize consciousness-raising group techniques as a means of sensitizing men to their own sexism, and providing emotional support for, and from, other men (Hornacek, 1977). Some profeminists promote the development of men's studies programs as a way of furthering analysis and understanding of masculinity and of combating sexism (Brod, 1987b). The tactic of combating sexism against men through political channels has largely been taken up by men's rights groups, as we shall see shortly. For alternatives to traditional and current masculinity, liberal profeminists view androgyny as the ideal solution (Fasteau 1975: 196), while radical profeminists are divided on this issue insofar as androgyny still incorporates elements of traditional masculinity. Most radicals would endorse an androgyny that transcends traditional masculinity.

The Men's Rights Perspective

Evolving from a liberal profeminist position, and incorporating a proliferating number of father's rights groups in the 1980s and 1990s, the *men's rights perspective* argues that the current gender system, rather than privileging men, is oppressive and devastating to them. "In short, masculinity is riddled with guilt, shaped by guilt, and maintained by guilt" (Clatterbaugh, 1990: 66). Expectations for masculinity create no-win situations for men that lead ultimately to lethal consequences in the form of disease, disability, and premature death (Farrell, 1993, 1986; Goldberg, 1976).

Men's rights advocates note contradictions incorporated within contemporary masculine roles:

> Men are told to be gentle, while gentle men are told they are wimps. Men are told to be vulnerable, but vulnerable [men] are told they are too needy. Men are told to be less performance oriented, but less successful men are rejected for lack of ambition. This list of contradictions is seemingly endless. (Hayward, 1987: 12)

Since there are no correct choices, failure is a foregone conclusion. When men fail, guilt turns to self-hate, which leads to emotional and physical self-neglect (Goldberg, 1976: 6, 181–182), culminating in higher suicide, alcoholism, disease, drug addiction, and crime (especially violent crime) rates (Farrell, 1993).

Similar to conservatives, men's rightists claim that men want to enter into an exchange of economic provision and protection for sexual favours because they are raised to be sexually and emotionally dependent upon women. But, unlike conservatives who praise women for their civilizing influence, men's rights advocates are not as charitable. They argue that the feminist movement has altered conditions such that the dynamics of men's lives have worsened, not improved. According to the men's rights perspective, feminism and "Feminazis" have intensified the contradictions in the masculine gender role by promoting a new sexism. "Sexism is discounting the female experience of powerlessness; the new sexism is discounting the male experience of powerlessness" (Farrell, 1986: 196).

"Whereas many in the profeminist movement consider the men's rights perspective to be anti-feminist, men's rights partisans claim to be the *true* antisexist movement" (Clatterbaugh, 1990: 63, emphasis in original). Proponents of the men's rights perspective argue that programs designed to promote women's equality, such as affirmative action, actually further disadvantage and victimize men. Not surprisingly, men's rightists are among the most vocal members of the "whitelash" phenomenon (activism on behalf of white, middle-class males said to be the casualties of affirmative action). They also draw attention to family issues, such as child custody decisions, they believe are based on sexism against men, and alternatively advocate the creation of joint-custody presumption laws. As part of itemizing the lethal hazards of being male in our society and the cheapness of men's lives (Farrell, 1993), the men's rights perspective focuses particularly upon domestic and societal violence against men. The goal here is to expose existing practices that are perceived as sexist and detrimental to men.

Men's rights attention is also directed towards exposing negative images of men ("male-bashing") they believe are promoted by feminists (Clatterbaugh, 1990: 71; Farrell, 1993, 1987). Every facet of economic, political, and sexual male privilege identified by feminists is transformed by men's rights analysis into examples of equal or greater oppression of men (e.g., burdens of the provider role that turn men into success objects, burdens of leadership, and burdens of sexual initiation and rejection; see Farrell, 1993, 1986). These analyses adopt a technique from feminism by attempting to create a sense of outrage and anger in men. Such feelings are then directed towards women and feminism as a means of escaping restrictive social roles and unwanted stereotyped images (Clatterbaugh, 1990: 70–71).

A major stumbling block confronting proponents of the men's rights perspective lies in attempting to generate understanding, sympathy, and political action for a social category (i.e., men) perceived to be generally privileged. It is much easier to produce sympathy for the underdog than it is for the top dog. As Richardson (1988: 247) notes, "[t]heir privileged position within the system does not give them the structural advantage of challenging their own treatment as unfair. Most of the goals…are not easily politicized." Aside from gaining an increasing number of followers, perhaps the most significant political achievements reached by men's rights advocates thus far have been highly contentious changes to child custody laws in Canada (see Drakich, 1998/1995).

The Spiritual Perspective

This nonscientific, and essentially nonpolitical, perspective maintains that masculinity arises out of psychospiritual patterns anchored in mystical origins best uncovered through examination of ancient myths and through immersion in the spiritual energies accessed through symbolic rituals. The perspective promotes an essentialist argument that the fundamental qualities of masculinity have remained unchanged for all time. Spiritualists owe an intellectual debt to Jung (1875–1961) who broke from Freud and developed his own theory of a genetically transmitted *collective unconscious*, a universally shared storehouse of human memories containing thoughts and feelings existing since ancient times. Jung also claimed that men are born whole, but sometime during childhood, they become fragmented and lose their psychospiritual sense of unity. This unity can only be restored through getting in touch with their *archetypes*. Archetypes are focal points for organizing the contents of the collective unconscious. The most important archetypes include primordial patterns of femininity (the *anima*), masculinity (the *animus*), and the darker instinctual side of the self, the *shadow* (Potkay and Allen, 1986: 85–86). A person gains access to these ancient archetypes through participation in rituals and exposure to myths and storytelling.

Although Jungian analysis has become increasingly popular as a potential source of insights into masculinity (e.g., Johnson, 1989; Moore and Gillette, 1990), we shall focus upon the approach that is most synonymous with the spiritual perspective. The principal architect of the *mythopoetic movement* is Bly (1990, 1988, 1987), whose interview in *New Age* magazine during the early 1980s appears to have provided the foundation for the contemporary movement (Clatterbaugh, 1990: 87), although Lindsey (1994: 23) attributes the birth of the movement to a 1990 television documentary on Bly. Bly examines ancient myths to discern the missing component of masculinity and claims that men in modern society have lost their roots because of the absence of symbolic rituals, conducted by male elders, initiating men into masculinity. The current mythopoetic movement is remarkably similar to an earlier movement in the 1890s searching for "primitive masculinity" (Rotundo, 1993: 227–232, 287) through examination of ancient tales for rituals to restore connections between men.

According to Bly, who is vague about any underlying biological or cultural causes, masculinity is the product of psychological scripts played out against the canvas of a society at any given historical moment. The man of the 1970s to the present, different from the 1950s and 1960s man, is the "soft," "feminized," male.

> They're lovely, valuable people—I like them—they're not interested in harming the earth or starting wars. There's a gentle attitude toward life in their whole being and style of living. But many of these men are not happy. You quickly notice a lack of energy in them. They are life-preserving but not exactly life-giving. Ironically, you often see these men with strong women who positively radiate energy. (Bly, 1990: 2–3)

To Bly's mind, these men have failed to connect with archetypal masculinity for a number of reasons. "The Industrial Revolution, in its need for office and factory workers, pulled fathers away from their sons and, moreover, placed the sons in compulsory schools where the teachers are mostly women" (Bly, 1990: 19). Women cannot properly initiate men into masculinity. "[O]nly men can initiate men, as only women can initiate women. Women can change the embryo to a boy, but only men can change the boy to a man....[B]oys need a second birth, this time a birth from men....One could say that the father now loses his son five minutes after birth" (Bly, 1990: 16, 21). In addition to this absence of fathers, the isolated nuclear family of today does not provide boys with access to elderly men, who could perform a connective initiation into masculinity. "The ancient societies believed that a boy becomes a man only through ritual and effort—only through the 'active intervention of the older men'" (Bly, 1990: 15).

Bly views feminism as a positive force for women, but only a mixed blessing for men, insofar as it permits men to get in touch with their feminine side (the anima), but prevents them from finding the deeply masculine within themselves (Bly, 1987: 2–3). Bly's solution is to help men explore the missing elements of their masculinity by drawing upon the symbolism found in the Grimm brothers' tale of *Iron Hans*, written in the early 1800s, which he renames *Iron John*. "The Iron John story retains memories of initiation ceremonies for men that go back ten or twenty thousand years in northern Europe. The Wild Man's job is to teach the young man how abundant, various, and many-sided his manhood is" (Bly, 1990: 55). The "Wild Man" is the symbolic embodiment of the archetypal shadow, the darker, primitive, but also creatively nourishing (Bly, 1990: 6) imagery that Bly considers necessary to balance the "softer" masculinity of today. "The aim is not to *be* the Wild Man, but to be *in touch with* the Wild Man" (Bly, 1990: 227, emphasis in original).

The agenda of the spiritual, especially mythopoetic, perspective is to provide men with all-male therapeutic settings, in workshops and weekend retreats, for learning ancient myths and stories, such as *Iron John* and the Wild Man, and gaining exposure to masculinity initiation rituals. These rituals, lead by older men, provide opportunities for younger men to resolve their separation issues with absent fathers and other men, get in touch with their darker, yet spontaneously playful self, and provide mentors with whom to identify. The result, they hope, will be stronger men-defined men, capable of acting with forceful resolve, as opposed to "softer" men who are women-defined.

The spiritual perspective does not advocate social change of a political nature, but instead focuses upon the necessity for self change. The suggestion that men are overwhelmed by feminism appeals to adherents of the men's rights perspective, while the suggestion that men can benefit from the creative energies of a men's movement, just as women have benefited from the women's movement, appeals to liberal profeminists (Clatterbaugh, 1990: 102). Being based largely upon spiritualism, this perspective cannot be evaluated according to any scientific criteria. Ironically, the appeal of this approach is intuitive and emotional—qualities not normatively associated with masculinity in our culture.

The Socialist Perspective

The *socialist perspective*, derived from classical Marxism, considers masculinity to be the product of the capitalist economic system. Under capitalism, a small proportion (exact figures vary with each analysis) of the male population own and control the means of production, while the vast majority of men do not. Furthermore, socialists argue, within each class, men control the labour of women (Clatterbaugh, 1990: 108). "[M]asculinity is…a product of the power relations that exist among men and between men and women in the relations of production" (Clatterbaugh, 1990: 124). A central characteristic of all men in capitalist societies, and, therefore, of masculinity, is *alienation,* or a lack of control and a sense of estrangement from their environment. However, the causes, experiences, and consequences of alienation differ for owners and workers.

The socialist perspective focuses primarily upon the life experiences of workers, but has directed some attention towards the general class of "owners," which includes not only actual owners, but also managers and professionals who represent them and their interests. While their work environments do not induce any fears concerning physical safety, the working life of owners is characterized by long hours, intense competition, career insecurity, and the pursuit of money and promotions (Clatterbaugh, 1990: 114). Even though owners control the lives of male and female workers, they cannot fully control the marketplace itself, nor fully control whether they will be able to maintain power. This lack of full control, as well as the use of power to reduce others to the equivalent of machines or property, is alienating (Clatterbaugh, 1990: 119).

As portrayed by the socialist perspective, the lives of workers stand in stark contrast to members of the owner class. Workers, by definition, cannot control their own labour. Their productivity and the outcome of that productivity are basically determined by those to whom they sell their labour. Working conditions, including physical hazards, length of working days and weeks, pay and benefits scales, employment security, are all beyond the control of workers, especially the approximately two-thirds who do not enjoy union protection in Canada (Statistics Canada, 1995: 35). Tolson (1977: 59, 63) and Gray (1987: 219) suggest that a shared sense of masculinity enables men to develop worker solidarity in an attempt to resist the power of owners over their lives. Gray (1987: 221–223) further suggests that working men's attempt to exclude women from the work force, or restrict women's participation to only selected work areas, is an exertion of masculine control. As well, male workers consider their homes to provide a respite from the alienation of work, because within the home they can exercise a degree of control and power over their wives and children (Clatterbaugh, 1990: 111; Tolson, 1977: 70–71). Working-class masculinity, therefore, reflects a combination of general powerlessness over self in the workplace, with some degree of power and privilege over women of the same class, both at work and, especially, at home (Clatterbaugh, 1990: 118).

Proponents of the socialist perspective argue that masculinity is class-specific. Furthermore, they claim that proponents of other perspectives tend to present a monolithic image of masculinity that is class biased.

Most of the literature on masculinity focuses on men who are owners, managers, and professionals. As the lives of these men are taken as representative, masculinity becomes identified with competitiveness, not solidarity; making ever more money, not getting-by; promotion, not fear of being laid off; learning to live in healthy ways, not being maimed at work; how to spend leisure time, not the exhaustion of compulsory overtime. (Clatterbaugh, 1990: 113)

The socialist perspective not only attempts to redress this class bias, but also adds a cautionary note regarding the success of any men's movement promoting social change, stressing that agendas to alleviate costs of masculinity, such as alienation, must vary by social class. Not surprisingly, the socialist approach is itself monolithic in focusing solely upon economic determinants of masculinity. According to this perspective, only a radical transformation of the economic system to eliminate the division of workers and owners will bring about equality between men, and between men and women, and an end to alienation.

The Group-Specific Perspective

With a focus similar to inclusive feminism, the *group-specific perspective* describes masculinity not as a singular whole, but rather as specific to men's various social locations. By focusing upon the "experiences and realities of men of different religions, races, sexual affections" (Clatterbaugh, 1990: 128), this perspective raises numerous challenges to images of masculinity depicted by other perspectives, and contributes to our understanding of various forces influencing masculinity.

Liberal profeminists unself-consciously proclaim a universality of the experiences of white, middle-class, presumably heterosexual men. In part, this is due to the fact that a majority of the proponents of this perspective are white, middle-class, heterosexual men. As we noted regarding inclusive feminism, whites within our society generally tend not to conceive of themselves as a unique social group and, therefore, assume that their own experiences are typical of everyone. Other perspectives offer alternative explanations of masculinity that, while seemingly trying to avoid overgeneralizations, are still open to various challenges.

The socialist perspective views masculinity as founded on the basis of economic power, yet working-class men clearly possess less economic power than owner-class men, while men of colour generally possess less economic power than do white men in our society. Does this make working- class men or men of colour less masculine by contrast? The spiritual mythopoetic perspective considers a lack of initiation rites as particularly problematic for masculinity today, yet men from certain religious groups, such as members of the Jewish faith, or from certain First Nations communities, will not recognize themselves within this perspective.

We noted earlier that radical profeminists contend masculinity exists primarily by virtue of the sexual oppression of, or violence committed against, women. This conception of masculinity is challenged by insights from a gay perspective. "[W]hile we share with straight men the economic benefits of being men…we do not participate as regularly in the everyday interpersonal subordination of women in the realms of sexuality and violence" (Kinsman, 1987: 104–105). In other words, the masculinity of gay men is forged without benefit of physical and sexual power over women. Either gay masculinity is (i) substantially different from that of heterosexual men, or (ii) gay masculinity is somehow based upon a latent sexual power of all men over women, regardless of whether that power is ever acted upon, or

(iii) explanations of heterosexual masculinity are incomplete in overemphasizing the role of sexual power. The issue of sexual power in relation to masculinity obviously needs to be examined further.

Another important insight from the gay perspective is that the "dominant form of masculinity is substantially shaped and maintained by homophobia, a generalized fear of homosexuality embedded in the masculine gender role, stereotype, and ideal" (Clatterbaugh, 1990: 131). In other words, heterosexual masculinity, considered by many within our society to be the only true masculinity, exists largely by virtue of a feared alternative. In his classic article on homophobia, Lehne (1976: 66, 78) argues that the taunt: "What are you, a fag?" is used to inhibit some, and encourage other, forms of behaviour among men, and, consequently, restricts masculinity to narrow "acceptable" limits. For "fag," we could also substitute "queer," "faggot," or "sissy" and then compare the implications of this phrase for masculinity with: "What are you, an athlete?" (Lehne, 1976: 66) or "What are you, a sociologist?" In equating certain behaviours with nonmasculinity, such as choice of certain occupations, or not evidencing sexual interest in women (Lehne, 1976), heterosexual masculinity is further promoted as a prescriptive norm. This singular ideal of masculinity is also reinforced by the existence of verbal and physical violence against actual or presumed homosexuals (Kinsman, 1987: 106).

Homophobia contributes to the costs of masculinity identified by the liberal profeminist and men's rights perspectives. A fear of being labeled as homosexual promotes hypermasculine behaviour and inhibits the development, and expression, of close bonds between men, as well as the general emotional inexpressivness of men with women (Lehne, 1976: 82). "Even the lack of affection between fathers and sons has been attributed to the phobic fear of being seen as homosexual males" (Clatterbaugh, 1990: 135). Neither the socialist nor the spiritual perspectives confront the issue of homophobia in their understandings of masculinity. The conservative viewpoint considers homophobia to be both justifiable and necessary in defence of natural masculinity and the natural family (Clatterbaugh, 1990: 137; Gairdner, 1992: 361–365). It is only from the group-specific perspective that we learn how homophobia is a major factor in the forging of heterosexual masculinity.

The masculinity experiences of men of African origins appears to be the most well developed perspective on men of colour in North America. To the extent that African males are an accurate paradigm for men of colour, in itself an issue that needs to be addressed in more detail, the group-specific perspective raises issues about racism and about poverty in shaping masculinity.

> The white patriarchal gender ideals that are held out to black men in a racist society create double binds: Black men are taught that men should be providers and should create their own opportunities, but poverty and racism block many black men from provider roles. The message to black men from patriarchy is to "be a man"; the message from capitalism is "no chance." (Clatterbaugh, 1990: 143)

The extent to which the above quote could be applied to First Nations men in Canada is unclear, but obvious parallels do exist. The impact of racism upon opportunity and ability to perform the provider role, upon the relationship between the provider role and masculinity, and upon the relationship between the provider role, masculinity, and other domains, such as family and intimate relations, are all brought into question by the experiences of men of colour. Nonetheless, racism is an important factor forging the masculinity of both white men and men of colour in our society.

The future contributions of the group-specific perspective should aid us in resolving some key questions. Are the effects of membership in different groups and location in different positions within the social structure additive or multiplicative for experienced masculinity? Does a standard masculinity exist that is experienced with only minor variations among men located throughout various social categories such as "race," ethnicity, social class, and sexual orientation? Does gender transcend those social categories? Or do we have a number of masculinities whose experiences cannot be generalized to each other and, therefore, must be described and analyzed separately? Do masculine genders uniquely reside within each of the other socially defined categories?

Since the experiences of previously marginalized men will, fortunately, continue to be even more thoroughly explored, we must end our presentation here with a cautionary note similar to the one issued regarding inclusive and postmodernism feminist theories. Once again, the danger lies in the possibility of assuming the existence of many specific "masculinities," each separate and distinct from the other. Just as other perspectives may err on the side of overgeneralizing a universal and essential masculinity, the group-specific perspective may err on the side of overparticularizing unexceptional masculinities. These issues of difference and similarity promise to become even more controversial as this perspective develops over time.

DEVELOPMENT AND SOCIALIZATION IN CHILDHOOD AND ADOLESCENCE

Human **development** has been defined simply as "any age-related change in body or behavior from conception to death" (Perlmutter and Hall, 1985: 11). All of the developmental changes occur in the context of three interacting dimensions: historical time, social time, and individual life time (Clausen, 1986: 2–3). The broadest dimension is **historical time** framed by cultural eras and interspersed with watershed events and processes. We have already examined in Chapter 3 some important changes in gender expectations and experiences associated with the processes of industrialization in Canada during the latter half of the nineteenth and the first half of the twentieth centuries. Our focus here will be upon Canada in the contemporary period, from the end of World War II to the beginning of the twenty-first century. Within this time context, sequences of events, such as the most recent women's movement, changes in the economy and the law, perhaps the invention and mass production of the computer, changes in family formation and dissolution, to name just a few, help frame the current historical context within which individual women and men live out their lives.

Social time refers to the socially constructed division of the human lifespan into meaningful age categories, such as childhood, adolescence, adulthood, and old age. Not only are the boundary lines between these categories socially constructed, but so are the meanings of each category, and the expectations associated with category membership. The number of categories and their boundary lines, meanings, and expectations can and do vary from one historical epoch to another, both within and across societies. For example, the meanings of children and childhood (Fasick, 1994; Howe and Bukowski, 1996: 175–183) and parenting (Ambert, 1994) have varied in significant ways over historical time. The same can be said for adolescence (Offer et al., 1988; Schlegel and Barry, 1991), adulthood (Bly, 1996; Fasick, 1979; Sheehy, 1995), and old age (Achenbaum, 1979; Butler, 1985; Cotton, 1979; Cowgill, 1974; Fisher, 1979; MacPherson, 1990; Palmore, 1985) during the present century. *Gender and age interact,* such that gender expectations and expressions vary as men and women move through the age categories of social time (Bell, 1989; Gee and Kimball, 1987).

Life time relates to the movement of individuals over the life course from conception to death. We have already examined the fetal development of sex in Chapter 2. Our focus now shifts from birth through old age. Lifetime development is obviously influenced by varying combinations of biological and sociocultural factors. Not surprisingly, we shall pay scant attention to the biological factors associated with early human maturation and later physical deterioration. Instead, we shall examine the influence of sociocultural factors.

Neugarten and Hall (1980) liken human lives over the life course to the spreading wings of a fan. Human development demonstrates remarkable similarities during the earliest years as it is strongly influenced by biological maturation. Although not stressed by these psychologists, great similarities also exist in social expectations for infants and toddlers. Despite these similarities, some differences in gender expectations and behaviour can still be observed. As humans age, the wings of the fan begin to spread with the increasing differential influence of sociocultural factors. One of the most important sociocultural factors influencing the social construction of gender is socialization.

SOCIALIZATION

Socialization can be defined as *"the process by which we learn the ways of a given society or social group so that we can function within it"* (Elkin and Handel, 1989: 2, emphasis in original). You can see that the emphasis in this definition is upon the *process* of learning and not upon the actual *content* of what is being learned. We have already presented various theories in Chapter 2 that focus primarily upon elucidating how the general processes of socialization accomplish their outcome. In the present chapter, we shall be more concerned with specific contexts and contents of socialization as revealed by existing empirical research.

Unlike many other species, humans today are not born with a genetically determined understanding of how to conduct themselves in social life. We must learn the appropriate rules and expectations of conduct. The definition already presented suggests that socialization is formed by a very practical purpose of preparing an individual to function appropriately within specific social groups and within society generally. The notion of what is "appropriate" and the success or failure of socialization is ultimately determined by whether an individual acts, thinks, and feels in ways deemed acceptable to some group's or individual's standards of judgment. Since societies, social groups, and individuals are rarely completely consistent or in agreement on their standards, the success of socialization efforts will always be subject to some debate.

More specifically, socialization attempts to prepare persons for the statuses they either now occupy or will occupy sometime in the future and for the roles attached to those statuses. This preparation does not begin randomly or haphazardly, but is based upon assumptions made about an individual's future given his or her circumstances at birth, within a specific society, possessing a certain culture, at a particular point in historical time. Those circumstances include a person's gender, ethnicity, social class, and degree of ableness. With increasing age, individuals become less passive recipients and begin to take a more active part in constructing their own socialization.

Socialization is not only direct and *intentional*, but also indirect and *accidental*. Socializers self-consciously and knowingly teach the recipient materials believed necessary for functioning in a society or social group. At the same time, however, socializers are also unaware of the socialization impact of many, if not most, of their own words or behaviours. Parents are often unaware of the extent to which they model behaviour that may be absorbed by a child and displayed at a later time. Anything and everything can be utilized as raw data by individuals acquiring information and guidelines on how to conduct themselves. Even though mommy is perfectly capable of driving the family minivan on her own, every time daddy comes along, he drives. The implicit message accompanying this continually played out scenario is that women are rendered incompetent in the presence of men. Since having these and other messages reflected back is sometimes embarrassing, socializing parents quickly learn to recite the mantra: "Do what I say, not what I do."

As well, socialization messages may be *blatant* or *subtle*. In the case of the former, a parent or teacher may explicitly state that a child should learn a specific lesson well as it will be important when she becomes an adult. In the case of the latter, exposing a young daughter to the bedtime story of *Sleeping Beauty* can subtly transmit a socialization message that women exist in a coma-like state until they are awakened by a man and, therefore, men are important for defining women's existence (Kolbenschlag, 1988). Given that most socialization is indirect and accidental, this means that it also occurs mainly on a subtle level. The subtle nature of socialization messages accounts for the fact that most of us cannot easily attribute a specific source for lessons we somehow learned somewhere during our lifetimes.

Socialization is also a *lifelong* process, beginning at the moment of birth and ending moments before death. The early socialization experiences of childhood and early adolescence are referred to as **primary** socialization (Elkin and Handel, 1989: 7). Subsequent socialization over the remainder of the life course has been referred to as **secondary** or, where appropriate, **adult** socialization (Elkin and Handel, 1989: 5). Our relatively greater emphasis in this text upon socialization during childhood and adolescence reflects the greater attention focused by sociologists and psychologists, operating out of a variety of theoretical and research perspectives, upon this portion of the life course.

Socialization is not the sole responsibility of one social group. Rather, a number of groups, or what we refer to as **agencies of socialization**, are involved in various aspects of the process. Four of the major agencies in our society are: the family, the school, the peer group, and the mass media. Although some variations exist between specific families, schools, peers, and media regarding the particular processes they use and the content of socialization they impart, sufficient similarities exist that enable us to make generalizations about the general characteristics of each agency.

The Family

The family is considered to be the primary agency of socialization for two reasons. One, the family is the typical example of a primary group, one characterized by highly personal, intimate, relationships. Two, it is the first agency a child comes into contact with and, therefore, it exerts a **primacy effect**: the family's world is the only world a child first knows. The family represents a society and culture for at least the first three years of life for a developing child, before other agencies begin to exert some influence. However, the family is not necessarily a direct, accurate, mirror representation of the outside world. The family acts more as a prism, bending and refracting outside influences to suit its own immediate purposes, goals, and desires (Elkin and Handel, 1989: 140).

The impact of the family can be profound. Most important for our purposes, it is within the context of our family that we develop our gender identity, our self-definition as male or female, and begin acquiring actions, thoughts, and feelings to demonstrate our masculinity and femininity. Our family also provides us with our earliest, often enduring, feelings about ourselves as smart or stupid, strong or fragile, attractive or ugly, worthy or unworthy—or somewhere in between. As well, many of our early family experiences shape our initial motivations, values and beliefs (Gecas, 1990).

The School

Before examining the formal educational system in Canada, we must note that considerable debate, but little consensus, surrounds the socialization impact of nursery schools, preschool-age day care, and after-school centres. The need for such childcare facilities is readily apparent. "In 1991, there were 2.2 million children twelve years of age and younger who required care for at least twenty hours each week while their parents worked or studied. Yet there were only 333,000 licensed spaces for children in Canada, which suggests that only 15 percent of these children could be served by licensed care arrangements" (Baker and Lero, 1996: 91). Existing centres are not simply warehouses intended solely for the provision of physical care. Holmes (1990) suggests that day-care centres act to supplement some of the functions traditionally associated with the family, including nurturance and socialization of the young. Due to variations in the size of such childcare institutions, ratios of adults to children, qualifications of attending personnel, and quality of the facilities, the short- and long-term socialization consequences of such care are unclear.

Our focus here lies primarily upon the public school system as opposed to private schools (based either upon religious values or academic teaching goals and methods) or what is often identified as "home schools." The organization of school systems lies within provincial jurisdiction in Canada, with some variation existing across provinces along a few dimensions. Over the late nineteenth and early twentieth centuries, school attendance eventually became compulsory for all Canadian children between the ages of six and sixteen. The rhythms of the school calendar year were based upon the demands of farming life and this calendaring of events is basically with us still, although year-round trimester schooling is slowly being introduced throughout this country.

Most students attend a publicly funded school system characterized by a standardized curriculum spanning a sequence of grades from kindergarten (optional in Alberta since 1994 and under threat of becoming so in other provinces with attempts to curb government spending) to grade 12 or 13 (the latter also under threat of being abolished as a cost-cutting measure). Many provinces divide academic life into three divisions: elementary (grades 1 through 6), junior high or middle school (grades 7 through 9), and high school (grades 10 through 12 or 13). Some provinces, such as British Columbia, have maintained only two divisions: elementary (grades 1 through 8) and high school (grades 9 through 12). Others, such as Ontario, employ cutoff points that define grades 6 through 8 as "senior public school" and grade 9 as the initial year of high school. Despite these divisional variations, and although the curriculum content for each grade may vary somewhat between provinces, curricula are fairly constant across all private- and public-school jurisdictions within each province and between provinces. Despite these potential variations, schools possess sufficient commonalities to permit a few opening generalizations.

In contrast to the family, the school is an *impersonal* agency of socialization characterized by secondary formal relationships. Within a school, each child learns that, in sharp contrast to the primary relationships of the family, she or he is but one person among many whose unique needs and interests may not be recognized or accepted. Ideally, he or she will be treated more or less equally along with all other students. Even though the public school system was created to represent and to mirror the larger society, considerable evidence has been accumulated over the years to indicate that schools typically reflect white middle-class Canadian society. Still, a school, among its many functions, is expected to expand the relatively limited horizons of a child created by his or her immediate family, to promote allegiances to the larger society, and, therefore, to integrate a child into a larger societal and cultural context (Elkin and Handel, 1989: 160).

While formally devoted to an official school curriculum of studies, schools also informally promote a number of hidden agendas that include learning respect for authority as represented by the teachers, how to get along with others, and how to accommodate one's own needs to the needs of others. Although gender socialization is typically not part of the formal curriculum, significant socialization messages are transmitted to female and male students as part of the hidden curriculum (Elkin and Handel, 1989: 168), mainly in subtle and unintentional ways.

The Peer Group

The peer group basically comprises one's age equals, or peers, usually drawn initially from the same or perhaps an adjacent grade at school. Consequently, the age range of variation is usually limited to less than four years (Santrock, 1981: 242). While preschool age children may play in groups, their play typically takes the form of parallel, highly egocentric, experiences requiring minimal coordination among the participants and minimal awareness of the needs of others. In light of the relatively small numbers of Canadian children who attend formal day care and nursery schools, the large majority of children first experience membership in a group of peers upon entry into the formal school system. Initially, these groups do not appear to exert an important influence on the life of a child outside of providing new playmates with new interests.

The influence of the peer group becomes noticeable by around ages seven to eight and reaches an apex of influence by ages fourteen to sixteen (Berndt, 1978 in Santrock, 1987; Rice, 1996; Thornburg, 1982: 124). Beyond these years, peer group influence varies with the length of schooling which is itself associated with social class. Elementary and secondary school-based peer groups tend to break up or disperse after high-school graduation, with new groups forming among those continuing to attend postsecondary educational institutions, among work mates, and sometimes around residential neighbourhoods. Our focus here will be upon the role of peer groups during their peak years of childhood and adolescent influence.

Peer groups, in contrast to the family and the school, provide a child with experience in **egalitarian** relationships (Elkin and Handel, 1989: 184), of an intimate nature, and, perhaps most importantly, of one's own choosing. Within a peer group, one is surrounded with people who are more or less equal (although power differentials do exist), who relate in a personal manner based upon personal qualities and characteristics, and who exist in a relationship that is largely voluntary in nature. Young children can frequently be observed exercising their new-found power of choice as they pronounce each other as a best friend one day and not a friend the next. The seemingly fragile nature of early childhood peer relationships is due primarily not to fickleness, but to learning how to exercise choice in developing, maintaining, and terminating friendships.

While both the family and the school are strongly future oriented in their socialization intentions, preparing children for their eventual participation as adults in the larger society (a process known as *anticipatory socialization*), the peer group is not self-consciously focused upon either socialization or the future. Most socialization experiences in the peer group are of the accidental or unintentional nature (Elkin and Handel, 1989: 178), yet while the focus appears to be upon the immediate moment, peer groups do exert important long-term influences upon their members.

The Mass Media

While the media educate, entertain, portray role models, and present guidelines for behaviour, debate continues over the socialization potential and actual influence of the media. In large part, the debate is a consequence of the fact that the media are very different from the other agencies of socialization along several important dimensions. The mass media are more *diverse* in nature, being composed of a number of different communication mediums, such as the print media of newspapers, magazines, and books, and the electronic media of movies, radio and, perhaps most important, television. Due to the diversity found within the media, our comments here will be brief.

The media, despite their advertising claims to being our best friends and companions, are an *impersonal* agency of socialization (Elkin and Handel, 1989: 188) in that messages are transmitted to as many consumers as possible. While various media may orient certain messages towards specific "demographics" to the exclusion of others, each medium still attempts to reach all members of a demographic category. Consequently, individual distinctions and other statuses an individual may simultaneously occupy are essentially ignored. The media, therefore, have the potential to be a great "leveler," ignoring social distinctions that differentiate individuals and groups from one another. The question remains as to where that level is drawn since the media often appear to be oriented to the "lowest" common denominator shared by audience members.

The impersonality of the mass media is very different from that of the school because mass media socialization is *unidirectional* (or one-way) and not interactional or interpersonal. The media transmit messages but do not receive direct and immediate feedback. While it could be argued that consumers do provide feedback in the form of sales purchases and viewer or listener ratings, such feedback is delayed for a relatively long period of time, and stands in stark contrast to the immediate interactional nature of relationships occurring within the family, school room, and peer-group setting. Neither the mass media, nor its audience, can immediately reward, punish, or observe and monitor the behaviour of those they seek to influence. Whether that influence is mainly deliberate and intentional or accidental and unintentional is subject to debate.

The Agencies in Relation to One Another

We have briefly considered the main characteristics of each of the basic agencies of socialization in isolation from one another. However, these agencies do not exert their own influence independent of one another. An important point to remember is that no one agency is designated by our society as the sole agency for gender socialization. Nor has the government of Canada created a Ministry of Gender to oversee and coordinate the efforts of gender socializers to ensure that every individual can function as a gendered person within our society and its constituent social groups. Consequently, the potential exists for various agency-transmitted gender socialization messages to be either mutually reinforcing or contradictory and conflicting.

As well, each agency provides socialization for a number of statuses and roles in addition to gender. No agency exists solely for the purpose of providing gender socialization. Thus, gender messages are transmitted along with any number of other messages directed at, for example, religion, social class, ethnicity, and, particularly, age. Contradictions between messages are entirely possible and socializers may be unaware of the extent to which they are inconsistent as they shift their focus between one status and another.

Due to the fact that Canada lacks a master plan for gender socialization, each individual family, school system, and media outlet must determine the desirable and/or acceptable general and specific expectations and skills they wish to promote and endorse. Ironically, the peer group appears to be the least self-conscious agency in arriving at decisions about what socialization messages will be transmitted. It would be inaccurate to conclude that families, schools, and the media rationally plan all of their socialization processes and contents. As we have suggested a number of times in this chapter, gender socialization, like other forms of socialization, is often accidental, unintentional, and inconsistent. This would appear to be the case particularly when a society, such as our own at the present moment, experiences a period of transition regarding ideal standards for masculinity and femininity.

Finally, we must also bear in mind that socialization agencies also exist for other reasons in addition to socialization; they "have a life of their own" (Elkin and Handel, 1989: 136). Families exist for companionship, protection against the social and physical environment, and satisfaction of other adult needs. Schools exist to keep teachers, administrators, and support staff in the labour force and children and adolescents out of the labour force, and also perform an important "baby" sitting function. The mass media exist first and foremost for the pursuit of profit and depend upon pleasing their advertisers to survive financially (Richardson, 1988: 69). Entertainment or educational materials are, therefore, designed to serve a profitable end. The peer group exists for fun and companionship away from the prying and judgmental eyes of adult society. All of these other purposes can reduce the effectiveness of an agency in accomplishing any one of them. While attempting to accomplish one purpose, an agency may accidentally transmit socialization messages associated with its other purposes. Some of the time agencies knowingly focus upon gender, and some of the time, while focusing upon other purposes, they accidentally influence the process or content of gender socialization.

Dominant Themes of Gender Socialization

Gender socialization can be defined as the process through which an individual acquires a gender identity, as well as gendered ways of acting, thinking, and feeling considered appropriate within the culture and subcultures of his or her society and relevant social groups. More than 25 years ago, Udry (1971) identified several basic themes of gender socialization during childhood and adolescence that are equally prevalent in Canada today. Although presented in the context of peer- group interaction by Udry, these themes are also emphasized in socialization experiences occurring within the family and within various hidden curricula that underlie the formal school experience, and also constitute important elements of messages transmitted by our mass media.

Udry (1971: 82) argues that the focal themes of female socialization centre upon "sociability, popularity, and attractiveness." Being sociable is often referred to today as possessing "people skills," such as being interested in relating to people, adept at verbal and nonverbal communication, comfortable at giving and receiving self-disclosures, and being sensitive to and appropriately empathetic with other people's thoughts and feelings. Popularity is one of the byproducts of being a successfully sociable person. To be popular also requires being aware of, and often possessing, the latest trends in things that matter to members of various groups. Perhaps the dominant theme of female gender socialization within our culture is the equation of femininity with physical attractiveness as measured by the dominant standards of the times. To this list we can add another theme increasingly emphasized as a girl moves through childhood into adolescence and adulthood: the equation of femininity with becoming a wife and mother.

Udry also argues (1971: 76) that male socialization in childhood and adolescence centres around "independence, emotional control, and conquest." Being independent means being autonomous, self-motivated, and in control of oneself and one's environment. These characteristics are admittedly difficult to acquire and demonstrate during developmental periods of childhood dependency within a family, power imbalances vis-à-vis school teachers, and almost slavish conformity to the demands of peers. Yet young males are expected to find ways to demonstrate their independence even within those limitations. Control over emotions for males is selective in that only demonstrations of emotions defined as "feminine" within our culture, such as tenderness, compassion, vulnerability, or crying, are supposed to be suppressed. Emotions such as pride or anger, and its behavioural counterpart, aggression, are considered to be consistent with and indicative of masculinity. Feelings of vulnerability and tenderness are supposed to be hidden or masked and then channeled into feelings of anger. Conquest is the desired successful outcome of being competitive at anything and everything. Whether it be competing against other males, females, or oneself (as in the search for a "personal best"), conquering all odds and winning are expected demonstrations of being a competent man. To these themes we can add another that becomes increasingly more important as a boy moves through childhood into adolescence and young adulthood: the equation of masculinity with becoming a paid worker and provider.

These themes and related equations all spring from our society's expectations for successful adult outcomes of early gender socialization. Believing that men and women must be prepared for different gender destinies (fashioned since the time of the Industrial Revolution), socializers attempt to provide developing individuals with the necessary actions, thoughts, and feelings deemed appropriate to function successfully as gendered beings within our society.

THE FAMILY

Family Structure

The family within which we are born, or adopted, are socialized, and develop from infancy through childhood and adolescence, and sometimes well into adulthood, is known as the **family of orientation**. For the vast majority of individuals in Canada, this family, comprising two generations, is also known as a **nuclear** family. Over the past 25 years, nuclear families in Canada have become increasingly diversified in form and content. For example, families may be headed by either two parents or a lone parent. According to the 1996 Census, 52 percent (a little over 3.9 million) of the 7.8 million families living in Canada in 1996 were composed of a cohabiting (or "common-law") or married couple with never-married sons and/or daughters currently living at home. The two parents may be a heterosexual, bisexual, gay, or lesbian couple. Although no official statistics are available for Canada, we estimate that a little more than 444 000 families in our country have gay or lesbian parents. According to the 1996 Census, 1 137 505 Canadian families are composed of a lone parent with never-married children still living at home; 83.1 percent are female-headed and 16.9 percent are male-headed families (Statistics Canada, 1997b: 1–4). The proportion of lone-parent families has increased since 1966, when 8 percent of all families were headed by a lone parent, but is approximately equal to the proportion in 1941 of 12 percent (Ram, 1990: 51).

Lone Parent Families

Elements of psychoanalytic and social learning theories (see Chapter 2) suggest that adequate gender development requires the presence of, and eventual identification with, a same-sexed parent. Custody battles following the dissolution of a marital or cohabiting relationship have often been fought on the basis of these theories, as have battles regarding the competence of gay or lesbian parents. Although they could not address the sexual orientation issue due to data limitations, Downey and Powell (1993) find no evidence regarding gender outcomes to support the same-sex deficit argument. In part, this lack of support is due to the fact that lone parents of either sex are highly unlikely to populate their children's environment only with people of the same sex as the parent. Close friends of varying degrees of intimacy, acquaintances, other extended family members, all of the other sex, interact frequently and often intensely with children in lone-parent family situations. As well, a lone parent can, and does, model and explicitly socialize, via both words and deeds, characteristics stereotypically associated with the other sex. Weisner et al. (1994) report that parents who reside in nontraditional households are less likely to gender stereotype their children than parents living in traditional families. Finally, as demonstrated throughout this entire chapter, the family is not the sole agency involved in gender socialization.

One aspect of lone-parent family life that may have an impact upon gender development and socialization relates to economic standard of living. Currently, the best single predictor of whether a family is poor is the sex of the family head. Most poor families in Canada now are headed by women (National Council of Welfare, 1992). Ninety percent of Canadian lone-parent families headed by women under the age of 25, and 58 percent of those families headed by women aged 25 to 33, exist below the "poverty line." More than a third of these families live far below that line (Oderkirk and Lochhead, 1992: 19). Among the main causes of what is often called the **feminization of poverty** are divorce (and the consequent low compliance of noncustodial parents with child- maintenance awards), births to unwed mothers of limited financial means, and the lower wages paid to women in the labour force, particularly women with lower levels of education. Another major cause, the increasingly large numbers of elderly widows living on low incomes, will be discussed separately in Chapter 9.

In passing, we must note that the "feminization" of poverty is not in itself a new phenomenon, nor is it a new social issue (Eitzen and Baca Zinn, 1994: 163). Women in certain social categories, such as older women and women of colour, have always been at risk to experience conditions of poverty. For the most part, their lives tended to be invisible to mainstream Canadian society. What is relatively new are the increasing numbers of white women, and women formerly living in comparative middle-class "luxury," who are now living in poverty. Their conditions and experiences have made the entire problem more visible to politicians, members of the general public, and even academic researchers and theorists who created the feminization label as if women in poverty was an entirely new occurrence.

Living in conditions of poverty or near-poverty significantly affects the life opportunities and even the motivation to utilize the fewer opportunities parents can provide for their children. Ambert (1990: 204) suggests that many of the negative consequences for children previously attributed to divorce may actually be consequences of trying to live with the reduced, often impoverished, standard of living more likely experienced by female, as opposed to male, lone parents. A lower social-class standing is associated with more traditional orientations towards gender roles and the practice of socialization techniques directed towards more traditional gender outcomes.

Social-Class Location

Among the ascribed statuses we inherit from our socializing parent(s) is their social class. Social class has a profound impact upon our mental and physical health and our chances of living and dying (Freedman, 1990; Lundberg, 1991), our likelihood of becoming politically active (Gilbert and Kahl, 1993; Grabb and Curtis, 1992); or being arrested (Hurst, 1992), our prospects for social mobility (Creese et al., 1991), and the kind and content of socialization we receive (Kohn, 1977).

Socialization practices vary by a family's social-class position. Kohn (1959, 1963, 1976; Kohn and Schooler, 1983; Kohn et al., 1986) reports that working-class parents are mainly concerned with the external qualities of their children as expressed in outward conformity. These parents want children who appear neat and clean, obey rules, and stay out of trouble. Working-class parents are most likely to use "power-assertive" techniques (Langman, 1987: 239) such as physical punishment to achieve these ends. In contrast, middle-class parents are more concerned with their children's motivations for behaviour and focus upon developing their children's inner qualities of curiosity, self-expression, and self control. These parents are less likely to use physical punishment, preferring instead to use "psychological" techniques (Langman, 1987: 239) such as reasoning with their children and either providing or withdrawing privileges, love, and affection.

Kohn (see also Kohn and Schooler, 1969; Pearlin and Kohn, 1966) attributes these differences in childrearing practices to differences in the work environments experienced by parents. Working-class parents are often closely supervised in a controlled work environment that rewards conformity to strict rules, while middle-class parents enjoy greater independence and are rewarded for being imaginative and taking initiative. Expecting their children's lives to be similar to their own, parents of each class attempt to prepare their children accordingly.

Upper-middle-class families are the most likely to endorse and express relatively egalitarian gender relations and opportunities (Lackey, 1989; Langman, 1987: 224–229; Lips, 1993). In contrast, upper-class, lower-middle-class, working-class, and poor families are all more likely to endorse and express more traditional, less egalitarian, gender roles. Ironically, families at the highest and lowest strata levels can be observed to contain contradictions between their ideals and actual behaviours. Upper-class families place great emphasis upon extended family linkages (Baca Zinn, 1993: 107; Langman, 1987: 223–224), espouse a traditional sex-segregated division of labour, and a male-dominated family life, yet these families are often headed by a powerful matriarch who is the final authority on the educations, occupations, and marriages of sons, grandsons, daughters, and granddaughters (Cavan, 1969: 88). Lower-middle- and working-class families also verbally endorse a traditional sex-linked division of paid work and family-work labour, yet these families are increasingly dependent upon the wages earned by both parents simply to maintain their standard of living (Glossop, 1994: 7). In other words, important gender boundaries are crossed despite attempts by parents to verbally uphold the validity of gender distinctions.

Even though families in all social classes engage in differential gender socialization, the *degree* to which gender differences are emphasized increases towards the lower levels of the social- class hierarchy (Brooks-Gunn, 1986; Canter and Ageton, 1984; Langman, 1987: 243). Consistent with Kohn's findings on social class and socialization goals and practices, it appears that children raised in working-class homes are more likely to conform to traditional conceptions of masculinity and femininity while middle-class (particularly upper-middle class) children are likely to conform less to tradition and more likely to embrace newer, more egalitarian, models of gender. Tuck et al. (1994) report that children raised in homes with career-oriented middle-class mothers are provided with gender role choices that are less stereotypical in terms of behavioural expectations, career choices and, in consequence, display more egalitarian attitudes (see also Betz, 1993).

Confirming findings from the United States (e.g., Blau and Duncan, 1967), Creese et al. (1991) find that Canadians are more likely to move up the social-class ladder if they come from families in which fathers have been well educated and employed in high-status occupations. Comparing the present generation with the parental generation, these researchers find that 39 percent of younger men moved up the social-class ladder and 36 percent moved down. Among women, 48 percent moved up, while 40 percent moved down. The remaining percentages remained at the same social-class position as their parents. The higher percentages of mobility for women than men reflect the greater consequences of marriage upon social mobility for women. Until recently, women had little opportunity to climb the social class ladder except through marriage.

Social class of origin has a significant impact upon educational opportunities and attainment, which, in turn, significantly affects occupational opportunities and attainments. More well-to-do families are likely to create opportunities for their children, regardless of their abilities, to be placed on university-bound tracks, while children from working-class and poor families are more likely to be streamed towards vocational tracts, each inheriting life opportunities established by their elders (Bowles, 1977; Guppy and Arai, 1993; Manski, 1992,

1993; Porter et al., 1982). However, within these general social-class differences, parents have also traditionally varied in the extent to which they differentially encourage or discourage their sons or daughters to make use of available educational opportunities.

Epstein and Coser (1981) note that parents have been more willing to underwrite the educational costs of their sons (even academically undistinguished sons) than those of their academically gifted daughters. They also suggest that parents tend to encourage their daughters to set their sights on career aspirations that are considered to be gender appropriate and of a lower occupational status (e.g., nurse rather than doctor, elementary school teacher rather than professor). Since their daughters were expected to climb the social ladder through marriage, too much education was considered threatening to a daughter's marital prospects. A postsecondary degree in the arts and humanities might be useful only for enhancing communication with a well-educated husband.

These orientations maintain the traditional notion of gendered social spheres. If women are to remain restricted basically in the domestic sphere, only men will be encouraged by parents to pursue educational opportunities leading to more prestigious occupations and subsequent social mobility that enhances an entire family's social standing in the community. However, as the gender boundaries of the separate spheres become more permeable, some signs of change in parental orientations to their daughter's education are becoming evident. Higginbotham and Weber's (1992) research on 200 women professionals, managers, and administrators from working-class backgrounds find that the parents of these women played a significant role in encouraging them to take advantage of their opportunities. Almost uniformly, these parents urged their daughters at an early age to strive towards a better life, stressing that the way to succeed was not only through education but also through postponing marriage.

Ethnicity

In addition to social-class location, being born into a particular family also means being ascribed the ethnicity of one's parents. At some later point in adolescence or adulthood, a person can actively choose to retain and identify with or to ignore and even conceal selected aspects of her or his ethnic origins. For example, distinctive accents or birth names that may be suggestive of an ancestor's country of origin can be altered. As well, religious membership can be changed or simply be allowed to lapse. The most enduring of the three basic components ("race," religion, and national origin, according to Gordon, 1964) of one's ethnic origins is the colour of one's skin and other features of physical appearance.

Although the issue remains highly contested, several researchers (see Langman, 1987: 232) argue that social-class status and related available resources exert a greater influence over socialization patterns than do "race" or ethnicity. In other words, within each ethnic category, variations in socialization patterns seem to accord with the social-class position of each ethnic family. However, Hale-Benson (1987) takes the contrary position that "race" overrides social class and, therefore, "racial" (especially black-white) differences will be found, regardless of social-class location. Resolving these divergent positions will have important implications for addressing key questions raised by inclusive feminism, as noted briefly in the previous chapter.

Basic issues and theoretical frameworks regarding ethnicity and gender were first generated by American feminists anchored in the American experience (e.g., see Jaggar and

Rothenberg, 1984). While Canada shares many of the same tenets of racism as the United States, our own social history and demography raises questions regarding the extent to which American experiences and concepts can be generalized to the Canadian scene. For example, the impact of geographical region upon social class, ethnicity, and gender in Canada is unclear. Since members of visible minority groups are unevenly distributed across our country, issues of practical concern and even researcher interests vary widely by region. Concerns regarding the interstices of gender and ethnicity for African or Caribbean blacks and southeast or east Asians, frequently using the generic language of "people of colour," are most likely to be raised in southern Ontario, parts of southern Quebec and Nova Scotia, and the lower mainland of British Columbia, reflecting the more complex "racial" palette of those regions. This language is less likely to be voiced with reference to northern and interior British Columbia, the prairies, Territories, northern Ontario, northern Quebec, or the Atlantic regions, where interest focuses more specifically on the implications of being a man or woman of First Nations, or Aboriginal, or Métis origins. Generalizing within ethnic groups in problematic: generalizing across ethnic boundaries is fraught with even greater difficulties at this point in our research history. For the moment, attention tends to focus either upon describing gender experiences within various ethnic contexts, or upon comparing white Canadians with specific other ethnic groups along various dimensions.

For example, growing up as a Chinese woman in Toronto, Yee (1993) writes that she experienced "living in two worlds" (p. 10), being "homesick for the home I never had, home I never knew" (pp. 20–21), yet feigning an inability to speak Chinese. She describes going "through painful contortions to try to act `white'" (p. 25), distancing herself from family members and peers who were visibly "different," and finding the term "visible minority" ironic when she craved the invisibility that "whiteness" seemingly afforded. She further observes that, despite Canada's status as a "multicultural society," visible-minority children may face special difficulties because of contradictory socialization messages stemming from within their family of origin and from their broader social environment.

Maracle (1996: ix), a member of the Sto:lo nation, argues that to understand the childhood and adult experiences of women within both contemporary First Nations society and the broader society, it is necessary to focus the discussion on the impacts of colonialism. She writes that as a child, visiting among the elders, she observed "a quiet and deep respect for thinking which extended to men, women and children" and "was shocked as a twenty-year-old by concepts of sexism coming from the mouths of young Native men; no one would have dared doubt the intelligence of women ten years earlier." However, she remarks, "Sexism, racism and the total dismissal of Native women's experience has little to do with who does dishes and who minds babies. These oppressions result from the accumulation of hurt sustained by our people over a long period of time."

Until relatively recently, a number of studies supported the suggestion that francophones were likely to hold traditional attitudes towards gender, particularly in relation to the role of women as wives and mothers (Boyd, 1975). Lambert (1971) reports that although French-Canadian parents are more traditional than their English-Canadian counterparts, French-Canadian children hold less differentiated views of appropriate gender behaviour than do English-Canadian children. More recently, findings from the national study conducted by Ponting (1986) indicate that francophones' gender attitudes are more egalitarian than those expressed by anglophones. Eighty percent of francophones (versus 72 percent of anglophones) agreed with the statement "There should be more laws to get rid of differences in the way women are treated, compared to men," and 87 percent of francophones (versus 73 percent of anglophones) agreed that "In the business world more women should be promoted into senior management positions." However, Ponting also reports that 62 percent of francophones (versus 63 percent of anglophones still agree that "When children are young, a mother's place is in the home" (as cited by Mackie, 1991: 30). Presumably women are to be granted these legal protections, and employment opportunities, only when their children are older.

Socialization in the Family: A Developmental Perspective

Our presentation in the following pages reflects the fact that the vast majority of empirical studies to date have been conducted with white, heterosexual, middle-class, two-parent families. Clearly, generalizing from these studies to families located in other ethnic groups and social classes, or comprising parents of other sexual orientations, or composed of a lone parent, is risky. Despite these limitations, the available findings provide a starting point in our quest for understanding important elements of the social construction of gender within our society.

Research indicates that in North America, as in most other societies (Carmody, 1989; Miller, 1993; Moen, 1991; Watson, 1993), the majority of couples express a preference for sons as either their only-born or their first-born, and a preference for more sons than daughters overall (Lindsey, 1996: 64; Richardson, 1988: 36). While it is currently fashionable to claim, during pregnancy, that the only preference is for a healthy child regardless of its sex, couples still demonstrate a greater likelihood of trying to have another child if only daughters have been born into the family. Among American women stating a desire to have daughters, the most commonly offered reason was that a daughter would not only be a good companion but she would also be fun to dress (Hoffman, 1977). Based on survey research conducted on American college students in 1985 and 1988, which posed the question "If you could have only one child, which one would you prefer?" Pooler (1991) reports that 80 percent of male students in both years expressed a desire for a son while female students reported a slight preference for a daughter (54 percent in 1985 and 58 percent in 1988). Pooler suggests that the preference for daughters indicated by female students reflects their awareness of the potential difficulties the mothering role poses for the retention of an independent sense of self and, as well, their stereotyped assumptions that daughters will be easier to raise than sons, will develop close, affectionate ties with their mothers, and will act in a nurturant manner towards them.

Parents undergo a form of anticipatory socialization before their child is born when they and other interested parties speculate on its sex. Our folk wisdom, often wrongly referred to as "common sense," (wrong since it is rarely that common, most often does not make sense when subjected to empirical verification, and typically is used as a euphemism to mask a speaker's own personal beliefs) attempts to provide guidelines for parents on how to anticipate the birth of a baby of a particular sex. For example, in conformity to our stereotypes regarding physically more active males, the amount of activity a fetus engages in is supposed to be one prime indicator (Lewis, 1972). The greater the activity, such as kicking, the greater the supposed likelihood that the fetus is male.

The prenatal position of the fetus is another indicator stressed by our folk wisdom. Boys are supposedly carried "high" in the expectant mother's abdomen, while girls are carried "low." Girls are also supposedly carried "neatly" in front—conveying the image of a basketball tucked compactly under a woman's blouse—while boys are supposedly carried in a "messy," more "obvious" fashion—conveying the image of a sprawling (male) innertube wrapped around a woman's torso. Unfortunately, we do not possess any data regarding the reactions of parents, nor the gender socialization consequences if any, among those who discover that relying upon folk wisdom is not always that wise. Presumably, a number of baby's rooms throughout our country have been hastily redecorated immediately following a child's birth.

Medical technology, where accessible, can aid parents more precisely in knowing the sex of a fetus. Ultrasound is now in common use throughout Canada. This technique provides a picture-like image (copies of which often find their way into wallets or baby books) of a fetus that can be interpreted with a high, but not perfect, degree of accuracy regarding the fetus' genital sex. Amniocentesis and chorionic villus sampling (CVS), less commonly used methods designed for identifying possible genetic problems in a fetus during early pregnancy, can also reveal the fetus' chromosomal sex. No statistics have been published regarding how many parents avail themselves of the knowledge of a fetus' sex, nor how many use that knowledge to prepare for socializing their known-sex child.

Infancy

Gender socialization begins at birth upon the pronouncement by the attending medical team of a baby's genital sex. This announcement is almost immediately followed by the first official and deliberate postpartum act of parents fraught with gender implications in our society — naming an infant. While most Canadians observe their pets for a short period of time until some physical or behavioural characteristic suggests an appropriate name, few parents feel they can wait to apply the same principle to naming their child. Consulting books of baby names (which helpfully divide their selection into separate lists for boys and girls) or developing their own lists is a common pastime among expectant parents. Lists are sometimes generated out of an idiosyncratic desire to begin each child's name with the same first letter, or the same name (as in the case of heavyweight boxing champion George Foreman who named all five of his sons "George"), or dictated by ethnic and/or family customs wherein one or more of the newborn's names must follow certain traditions, such as incorporating parental or grandparental names. (We'll ignore the predilections of parents in the 1970s to create unique names such as "Moon Unit," "River," "Rain," "Storm," "Blue Sky," or "Pickle.")

Similar to the principles applied to personalizing license plates, limitations are placed on the naming process by provincial-registry-system lists of forbidden names that cannot be applied, typically names of a religious deity (we have never met a student named "God," "Allah," or "Buddha," for example, although we have met one named "Christ"), or names of a scatological or obscene nature (we have never met a student with a formal name contained within what *Time* magazine once referred to as the "famous-but-forbidden-four-letter" vocabulary). Within these ethnic, familial, and legal limitations, parents in Canada are free to select the name, and its spelling, of their own choosing.

First, or given, names are typically sex-linked and serve as sex identifiers in the absence of any other information about a person. Male names in Anglo-Saxon Canada usually have harsher cutting-edge sounds (e.g., Jack, Jordan, Michael, Matt, Ridge, Spike, Stone) or

Box 4.1 Naming Babies

University of Waterloo professors Naomi Nishimura and Prabhakar Ragde, both of the Department of Computer Science, intentionally gave their babies first names devoid of gender implications and "family" names in alternating order. With the permission of the parent-authors, we reproduce their birth announcements, complete with an accompanying bibliography, as they appeared on the World Wide Web. We also reproduce, again with permission, comments from Professor Ragde on the reactions the proud parents have received to the announcements.

Naomi Nishimura and Prabhakar Ragde would like to announce the birth of Arju Ragde Nishimura, who arrived at 14:37 EDT on 17 September 1992, at Kitchener-Waterloo Hospital, weighing 3080 grams and measuring 51 cm from head to toe. Naomi went through twenty-six hours of pre-labour and seven hours of active labour at home before going to the hospital; after another nine hours of labour there, our natural childbirth was facilitated by the team of Robert Annis (our family doctor), Evelyn Cressman (our midwife), and Set Len Yau (the duty nurse). We left the hospital six hours after the delivery, and we are all resting at home, with all the phones unplugged.

Some answers to questions you may have: Arju (pronounced Are—jew, factually if not grammatically correct, accent on the first syllable) doesn't mean anything. It's a nice sounding pair of syllables, nothing more, and we made it up more than a year ago, after trying lots of different combinations. We wanted a name that was short, sounded good with Nishimura, and didn't lead to any obvi-

ous derogatory nicknames. (If you can think of one...well, it's too late.)

Please don't rush out and buy a gift. We stocked up on the basics before the birth, and it will take us a while to figure out what else we need, or what might prove useful or entertaining. If you still have the gift-giving urge a few weeks from now, we may be able to suggest some possibilities to you. But really, don't feel obligated to do anything more than smile and coo when you first meet Arju (and you don't even have to do that, if you're really in a bad mood).

No, we didn't forget to mention whether Arju was a boy or a girl. We deliberately left it out — another decision made many months ago. We are concerned about early gender stereotyping. Studies have shown (see the bibliography at the end of this announcement) that adult perception of infant behaviour is affected more by the perceived sex of the child than the actual behaviour of the child. There is a difference in the way adults talk to girl babies and boy babies; there is a difference in the way adults hold and play with girl babies and boy babies. We think that the sex of a newborn child who will still be sorting out its senses and perceptions for weeks if not months after birth is the least interesting bit of information about that child. We hope you'll help us in our task of raising our child properly by focusing on Arju as a developing human being, with all the wonder that entails.

No, we don't know when we're going to have a second child. Shame on you for even thinking of asking!

Bibliography:
Pomerleau, Bolduc, Malcuit, and Cossetta."Pink or Blue: Environmental Gender Stereotypes in the First Two Years of Life." *Sex Roles*, v.22 (1990), nos.5–6, pp.359–367.

Stern and Karraker. "Sex Stereotyping of Infants: A Review of Gender Labeling Studies." *Sex Roles*. v.20 (1989), nos.9–10, pp.501–522.

Sidorowicz and Lunney. Baby X Revisited. *Sex Roles*, v.6 (1980), no.1, pp.67-73.

[Approximately three years later, a second birth announcement appeared as follows.]

We would like to announce the birth of Zazuki Nishimura Ragde, who arrived at 08:06 EST on 24 March 1995, at Kitchener-Waterloo Hospital, weighing 4160 grams and measuring 52 cm from head to toe. The birth was assisted by our midwife, Elsie Cressman, and duty nurse Joan Becker. Labour started at 02:00, Elsie arrived at 06:00, we left for the hospital at 07:00. We've been home since 11:00 and are resting comfortably with the phones unplugged, happy and healthy.

Some answers to questions you may have: Zazuki is pronounced "Zah-ZOO-key". Like "Arju", it doesn't mean anything in any language we know or have checked. We tried a lot of combinations of syllables until we found one that sounded nice to us.

Please don't rush out and buy a gift. We have everything we need and plenty that is sheer luxury, and there are Arju's feelings to consider. If you feel the urge to mark the occasion, please consider a donation to Planned Parenthood. Local councillors blocked a provincial grant to our local branch and they could use the money, but wherever you are located,

there's likely to be a branch near you. You get a nice tax deduction and you can feel good about helping others. (Yes, Zazuki was planned, and we don't plan to have any more.)

As we did with Arju, we are not announcing Zazuki's sex. We think it worked out just fine in Arju's case, and we're used to dropping sex-specific pronouns out of our speech now. If you can't understand why we're doing this, we'll be happy to pass on a copy of Arju's birth announcement, which includes a bibliography containing the articles which inspired us.

Naomi Nishimura
Prabhakar Ragde
Arju Ragde Nishimura

Not everyone viewed these birth announcement in a positive light. As the children's' father commented in a letter to one of the authors about the announcements: "The first one of course caused quite a stir. We got almost no gifts (except from people who could handle the situation) because people couldn't think of what to buy without knowing Arju's sex! Others worried about the effect on Arju of being handled by people ignorant of this crucial fact — even on Arju's sexual orientation....For months afterwards people would ask us if we'd 'announced it yet.' Strangers would quiz us carefully, hoping to catch a slip. (I slipped four times that I remember — twice for each pronoun 'he' and 'she'!)." Regarding the second child, Ragde observed "there was much less fuss; everyone was resigned to our eccentricities by then, and Arju would tell anyone who was really curious."

are associated with Biblical references or authorative names drawn from the Royal Family (John, Luke, Andrew, Charles). In contrast, female names tend to reflect stereotypical qualities of softness and gentleness in their sound and often incorporate male names enhanced with diminutive endings (e.g., Ashley, Brittany, Tracie, Danielle, Ericka, Jackie, Jessie, Michelle) or are also associated with Royalty or Biblical references (e.g., Angela, Diana, Elizabeth, Faith, Hope, Charity – Chastity does not appear to be very popular at this point in our history). In contrast to male names, female names contain more sounds and syllables, are more likely to end in either a vowel or resonant sound, and to involve a variation of the syllable commonly emphasized such as, for example, "Aye-li-son" versus "Alison" (Slater and Feinman, 1985).

Nicknames, where given, are also linked to gender-related stereotypes; "male nicknames related typically to connotations of strength, hardness, and maturity [e.g., Grenade, T-Rex, Dude], while female nicknames related more to beauty, pleasantness, kindness and goodness" [e.g., Bunnikins, Baby] (de Klerk and Bosch, 1996: 526). Although males, generally, are more likely to have nicknames than females, male nicknames are more likely to be coined at later ages and by male peers, especially in sports, than are female nicknames. Female nicknames are more likely to be given by family members as a term of endearment, to spread to wider circles of usage than male nicknames, and to be "gentler, more childish and more affectionate than male nicknames" (de Klerk and Bosch, 1996: 540; see also Phillips, 1990).

Once names have been decided upon, the next significant gender event is the birth announcement made via newspapers, greeting cards, and personal communications of various kinds. Overwhelmingly, such announcements contain information such as date and time of birth, height, weight, perhaps Apgar rating (based upon muscle tone, respiratory function, reflexes, heart rate), the names of the parent(s), names of any siblings, and the names of the newborn. Prominently displayed near the beginning of the announcement will be the seemingly most important piece of information: the sex of the new arrival. When was the last time you saw a card or birth notice that simply stated: "It's Alive," or "It's Healthy," and made absolutely no mention of the infant's sex nor provided a name clue that could aid in the sex-identifying process?

Gould (1980/1995) wrote a story about "X," a "fabulous child," whose sex was purposefully concealed from others. This fictional account was designed to draw our attention to the importance of names as well as subsequent related elements of gender socialization. Few parents in our society appear to be willing to risk surrounding their children with potential confusion stemming from use of gender neutral names (e.g., Pat or MacKenzie) and, even then, are more likely to give such names to their daughters than to their sons, as is often indicated by the preferred spellings (e.g., Kerri, Lori, Robyn). Even fewer parents deliberately select names devoid of any gender implications (but see Box 4.1).

In their classic review of empirical research, Maccoby and Jacklin (1974: 338–339) find "surprisingly little differentiation in parent behavior according to the sex of the child" during infancy and early childhood. While Greenglass (1982: 39) suggests that physical and intellectual limitations of infants curtail the differential socialization parents can provide, Block (1978) suggests that researchers' measuring devices are insensitive to the often subtle and pervasive methods that parents do use (Stenberg and Campos, 1990). When asked if they socialize infant sons differently than daughters, the majority of parents will respond in the negative, believing they are essentially gender neutral in their interactions with their children.

Yet parents do model different behaviours that may leave an impression upon even the youngest children. For example, research on the "stroller effect" (Mitchell et al., 1992) finds that, when both parents are present, fathers are more likely to push a stroller when the child is in it, while the mother pushes when the stroller is empty. In addition, when both parents are present, the father is more likely to carry a child than is the mother. Such behaviours convey subtle messages about expected differences between men and women when they are in each other's company as well as about their respective dominance, strength, and power within families and the broader society. As well, Lewis (1972) finds that boys receive more physical contact and less nonphysical contact (such as being looked at or being talked to) than do girls during the first six months of life. Greenglass (1982: 38) suggests that this greater physical contact accounts in part for the greater gross motor development found in boys.

During the first year or two following birth, meaningful interaction between parent and infant occurs primarily on the nonverbal level, with the parent most often reacting to the actions of the newborn. Research indicates that parents (among others) differentially interpret an infant's actions depending upon their perception of the sex of the infant. Rubin et al. (1974) report findings from interviewing parents within 24 hours of their infant's birth. Even though the infants did not differ in average length, weight, or Apgar scores, depictions provided by both parents in general, and fathers in particular, were highly stereotypical. Daughters are described as delicate, weak, beautiful, and cute, while sons are identified as strong, alert, and well coordinated. In a novel offshoot of this classic study, Stern and Karraker (1989) observed that young children were even more likely than adults to describe infants in gender-stereotyped ways with boy babies described as "tough" and "big" and girl babies described as "gentle" and "cheerful."

Condry and Condry (1976), whose respondents observed a videotape of a nine-month-old infant reacting to different stimuli, report that an infant's reactions are differently interpreted depending upon the identified sex of the infant. The same action was described as, for example, either anger in boys or fear in girls. This differential attribution of emotion would appear to begin early in life; Leinbach and Hort (1995) report that when three-year-old children were asked to assign gender to pictures of animal faces, they were more likely to label a happy animal face "female" and an angry animal face "male." Complimenting this, Birnbaum and Croll (1984) observe that their sample of preschool-aged children held the beliefs that while males were prone to feelings of anger, such emotions as happiness, sadness, and fear were more characteristic of females.

Sidorowicz and Lunney (1980) find that university students differentially react to young children depending upon what sex they perceive a child to be (in this case, the same child was used with different subjects being informed the child was either male or female). Thus, the known sex of infants appears to influence gender filters of parents and others so that identical appearances and actions are selectively and unknowingly perceived to conform to prevailing stereotypes (Stern and Karraker, 1989). Zahn-Waxler et al. (1991) report that even when their children are very young, parents appear to have a greater tolerance for their son's displays of anger than for similar behaviour in their daughter. Malatesta and Haviland (1982) observe that anger expressions in female infants are more likely to be met with negative maternal responses (e.g., frowning and anger) and less empathetic responses than those made in response to male infants.

Childhood

Despite parental claims of being gender neutral, researchers find that fathers and mothers become increasingly more gender differentiating as their sons and daughters develop through infancy, toddlerhood, and young childhood. Ironically, sons are granted more freedoms and yet at the same time are more closely monitored than are daughters. Lytton and Ronney (1991) note that sons are allowed more independence and physical freedom to explore their environment. Sidorowicz and Lunney (1980) find that parents treat daughters as being more physically fragile and more in need of protection than sons and consequently restrict their daughters' physical movements more (see also Bronstein, 1988 and Snow et al., 1983). Mitchell et al. (1992) observe that the parents of male toddlers are more likely to allow their child to walk on their own through public places than are the parents of female toddlers. Echoing Block's (1984) contention that boys develop "wings" that allow them to explore vistas beyond the home, while girls develop "roots" that anchor them to the home, Lindsey (1997: 64) comments that "[w]hile Dick is allowed to cross the street, use scissors, or go to a friend's house by himself, Jane must wait until she is older."

Whereas parents, particularly fathers, are more likely to engage their sons in rough-housing active play (MacDonald and Parke, 1986; Ross and Taylor, 1989; Tauber, 1979) and to discourage their daughters from engaging in boisterous and rowdy play (MacDonald and Parke, 1986; Power and Parke, 1986), these parents, particularly mothers, are more likely to talk with their daughters (Tauber, 1979). In an examination of conversations about past events between mothers and their two- to three-year-old children, Fivush (1991) reports that mothers only accepted anger and retaliation as appropriate responses from their sons and spent more time talking about sadness with their daughters. Fivush suggests that the lesson conveyed to girls may be that anger is not an acceptable emotional response.

Hay et al. (1992) report that in their research on peer conflict, which was based on a simulated dispute between puppets, five-year-old girls were more likely to advance such socialized tactics as "asking nicely" than were same-aged boys. In a study of how children between three-and-a-half and five-and-a-half years of age attempted to influence their play partners' behaviour, Serbin et al. (1984) found that while girls attempted to use polite suggestion, boys more often used direct demands. Among children aged nine to eleven, boys were more likely than same-aged girls to report that they would use confrontational behaviour such as hitting or yelling as a preferred strategy when angry with a same-sex peer.

When engaging in physically active play, parents implicitly encourage boys to be tough, to fight back and win, and, in the event of losing, not to whine or "act like a baby." In contrast, because conversation requires aligning one person's conduct with that of others (i.e., taking turns speaking, allowing the speaker to complete his or her message before proceeding, then responding to the message), parents encourage cooperative skills when emphasizing talking with their daughters. The emphasis placed on females demonstrating cooperative play may explain why observational studies have noted that girls are more likely than boys to refrain from the use of physical aggression when adults are watching (Loeber and Hay, 1997) and to mask their anger, particularly when in the presence of adults (Underwood et al., 1992). Among children as young as two years of age, girls appear to be more uncomfortable than boys when in an angry environment, show more overt distress when witnessing interadult anger, and are more likely to express a desire to stop such arguments, whereas boys are more likely to respond with aggression (El-Sheikh and Reiter, 1995).

Fagot et al. (1986) report that young male and female children are differentially reinforced for their attention-seeking behaviour. Parents pay greater attention to boys whose conduct is assertive and aggressive, while they are more apt to respond only to daughters who request help in a soft-spoken or gentle tone. Observing these same children nearly a year later, the researchers found that the girls were more talkative than the boys and the boys were more aggressive than the girls. Kerig et al. (1993) observes that boys are more likely than girls to be praised for assertiveness and that fathers, in particular, were more likely to reward their daughters for compliant behaviour while rewarding their sons for assertiveness. Similarly, Kerig et al. (1993) found that both mothers and fathers of three-and-a-half-year-old children were more likely to override and negate daughters more than their sons, especially when daughters attempted to assert themselves. While parents respond to shyness in daughters with warmth and affection, this behaviour in boys is responded to with disapproval (Hinde and Stevenson-Hinde, 1987; Radke-Yarrow et al., 1988).

Although not all research finds strong differences in the way parents treat their sons and daughters on such dimensions as discipline, warmth, or amount of interaction (Bee et al., 1982; Jacklin, 1985), many studies do. For example, Ross and Taylor (1989) find that both mothers and fathers in their research are more likely to encourage independent achievement and to discourage demonstrations of emotions from their sons. Perhaps in consequence, these parents are more likely to identify relationships with their daughters as having greater warmth and physical closeness, more likely to perceive their daughters as being more truthful, and are more reluctant to discipline their daughters. Finally, mothers take a more positive-reinforcing approach of posing questions to, and explicitly teaching, their sons, while modeling appropriate behaviour for their daughters (Weitzman et al., 1985). In contrast, fathers take a more negative reinforcing approach aimed at punishing or inhibiting gender inappropriate behaviour from their children, particularly their sons (Block, 1978; Fagot and Leinbach, 1995; Hardesty et al., 1995; Huston, 1983: 430; Roopnartine, 1986).

Especially during childhood, parents exert a significant influence over the kinds and contents of mass media entering the family home, a subject we shall explore in the next chapter. Parents also structure their child's environment through the creation and decoration of rooms to play in, the provision of toys to play with, and the selection of clothes to wear. Room decorations in themselves do not determine the gendered direction of a life course, but they do provide constant, yet subtle, visual messages beginning with the gendered style and colours of mobiles suspended over a baby's crib or bassinette. Studies of middle-class children's bedrooms in Canada and the United States find that the decor of girls' rooms is apt to be pink and to feature floral designs, the extensive use of ruffles and lace in bedding and curtains, miniature furniture, and an abundance of dolls. Boys' rooms, in contrast, are more likely to be brightly painted in red, blue, or white, and to decorated with a more spartan decor dominated with animal or sports motifs (Pomerleau et al., 1990; Rheingold and Cook, 1975; Stoneman et al., 1986). Within those rooms, these studies also find that boys not only have more toys, but also more categories of toys, than do girls. It is not, perhaps, surprising, that children develop preferences for gender-typical toys, even thought this preference in girls decreases with age (Etaugh and Liss, 1992).

Toys

Toys entertain, amuse, develop skills, and encourage play-acting of roles that might be adopted some day in the future. While boys' toys emphasize aggressive competition, visual and spatial manipulation, and activities oriented towards the world outside of the home, toys for girls are typically more passive, emphasize nurturance and physical attractiveness, and are significantly more oriented towards the world inside the home (Hughes, 1994; Leaper, 1994). Within our culture, boys who prefer to play indoors and girls who prefer to play outdoors are highly likely to be respectively labeled as sissies or tomboys. Not only are the toys oriented differently, but they also lend themselves to being played with in different locations. Boys' toys are more portable and conducive to being carried to outdoor settings. Girls' toys are more firmly anchored, by structure, fragility of design, or by cost, to the household, particularly a bedroom setting. In a study of parents interacting with children playing with masculine-typed, feminine-typed, and neutral toys, Idle et al. (1993) report that parents spend the least amount of time interacting with children with feminine-typed toys.

If toys are the building blocks of the future, the blueprint for women is consistent with older, traditional messages (Etaugh and Liss, 1992; Caldera et al., 1989; McAninch et al., 1996). A dollhouse may be of the "starter home" variety, with the basic amenities of chairs and dish sets, but the possibility exists to furnish it with an increasingly elaborate array of miniature gadgets essential to the comfort of the well-heeled doll, such as microwaves, blenders, Jacuzzi™, vanity tables, and candelabras. A young girl can acquire her own miniature domestic world of larger toys, such as single or tandem strollers, stoves, fridges, and Easy-Bake Ovens™. There being no such thing as an age too young to form name-brand loyalties, her parent(s) can buy her a shopping cart and a seemingly infinite selection of empty boxes and cans boasting brand name foods. She can grocery shop and cook for a variety of her own toy families including Little Ponies™, Kissing Cubs™, Bunny Bunny Bunnies™, Kitty Kitty Kittens™, Playtime Newborns™ (a collection of cats and dogs that can be pandered to with the additional purchase of a Bow Wow Boutique™ of their very own), Baby Baby Farm Animals™ and Polly Pockets™. The names of such toys, designed with their diminutive and repetitive sounds for a female audience, are not only cloyingly winsome and suggestive of baby talk, but they also reiterate the idea that even the ears of young girls are more delicate than those of young boys.

Barbie, a traditional girls' toy rife with implications for anticipatory socialization, warrants mention here because of her longevity. For more than 35 years, Barbie has presented various caricatures of the stereotypical female. The most noticeable features of Barbie are her inferiority-inducing attributes. Aerobics Barbie™ and Rollerblades Barbie™ assist us in understanding why, when Workout Barbie™ steps on to her Barbie Workout Scale™, her varyingly reported 36-20-32 (Renzetti and Curran, 1995: 96) or 40-18-32 (Hamilton, 1996: 197) form always registers the preset 110 lbs. (Mattel introduced a "new look" Barbie in 1998 featuring a smaller bust, thicker waist, slimmer hips, and reportedly, by the end of 1999, 6 of 24 versions of the 30-centimetre doll will have the new look). Although Barbie has been criticized as forwarding an image of idyllic feminine beauty that is largely unattainable for the vast majority of adolescent and adult women, she must be recognized as having her problems as well. As Zilbergeld (1992: 39) remarks in another context, "[i]t might be thought that the combination of slimness and big breasts would create a problem of balance." This problem might explain why Barbie is forever posed on her toes in precarious danger of toppling over. Barbie's sister, Skipper™, demonstrates even more unusual physical capabilities.

Box 4.2   Big Bucks Barbie

She's glamorous, she's rich and she's one of the highest-ranking women executives in corporate America. And she got there thanks to Barbie. Jill Barad, president and chief operating officer of Mattel, got to the top by figuring out how to more than double sales—in five years—of the high-fashion doll invented in 1959.

Many girls no longer own just one Barbie, for whom they buy endless clothes, cars and other accessories, she said during a recent visit to the Toronto area. Now there's a new doll for every occasion. There's the Olympic Barbie, the Holiday Barbie, the Totally Hair Barbie, the Bicycle Barbie, and so on.

"The average American child has eight Barbies, instead of one. The number of dolls purchased per year per child is three in the United States, it's just over two in Canada, and everywhere else it's one or less," Barad said. That leaves a lot of room for growth in 140 countries where Barbie is sold. That strategy, along with acquisitions in recent years, has propelled Mattel to the top of the toy-maker heap and pushed Barad's annual pay over $1 million....The company owns three other major toy brands: Fisher-Price, Hot Wheels and Disney. But sales of Barbie account for just over half the $3.2 billion in revenue Mattel reported last year.

Barbie has also become more relevant to today's woman, says Barad, who's 44 and the mother of two sons in their early teens. Originally modelled on a lascivious comic strip character in postwar Germany, the doll was created by Ruth Handler, whose husband Elliot co-founded Mattel in 1945 in California. Barbie was named after their daughter. She was the first modern doll modelled on an adult, instead of a baby. And she was an instant hit. In more recent times, women began asking questions about Barbie's relevance in the age of feminism.

When she first took over the brand in 1985, Barad heard the criticism from a lot of women. Barbie had, in fact, been an astronaut, a doctor and teacher, "but she never got recognition for it. So the first thing I did was send her to work, officially and formally, with a new advertising campaign that was started around the position that, "We girls can do anything, right Barbie?" She had a briefcase, a computer, a Wall Street Journal and a credit card. "But she wasn't just a businesswoman because that wasn't meaningful to a little girl and what was the point of putting her out there if no little girls were going to want to play with her?" she said. "So we had her outfit turn into this fabulous party outfit. And it was pink, of course," Barad said. "But it brought Barbie to a place where a little girl thought it was fun to play executive."

Two years ago, the company created a Doctor Barbie, who came with a baby patient, whose heartbeat could be heard on Barbie's stethoscope. Last year, there was a Teacher Barbie, who came with two ethnically mixed students and a math book — "because we girls love math," Barad said.

Source: Canadian Press. "Mattel CEO is no Barbie doll: Top-ranking U.S. executive makes more than $1 million a year." Reprinted in *Kitchener-Waterloo* (Ontario) *Record*, 24 May 1996: B5.

| Box 4.3 | **Virtual Pets and Gender** |

[In an attempt to redress the gender imbalance of virtual-pet purchases, toy manufacturers have introduced a product they feel is more appealing to male children. We draw your attention to the manufacturer's attempts at reframing wherein "nurturing" becomes "training," thus decontaminating virtual pet ownership for males from any gender-threatening connotations of babysitting and/or parenting].

There's a new, macho twist on virtual pets—those small, electronic creatures that beep when it's time for their owner to feed and nurture them. Playmates Toys Inc. of Costa Mesa, Calif., having realized that 85 per cent of its Nano Pals sold to girls aged eight to 12, has created a fighting version to attract boys in the same age category. Say hello to Nano Fighters, virtual pets which, when connected to each other after a proper period of "train-

ing," slug it out on tiny liquid crystal display screens.

"The original Nano is targeted at girls because it's patterned after doll-playing in the feeding and caring," says Tom McClure, marketing director for Playmates Toys. "There's a caring aspect to the Nano Fighter, because you have to feed the guy, train him and when he gets sweaty, you have to clean him up by selecting the bathing icon—and a little bathtub pops up. "But rather than saying nurturing, we look at it as more coaching and training—good macho stuff."

The virtual gladiator, which, like other Nano toys fits on a key chain, comes with four control buttons you use to check the jock's health (he has to be 18 years to fight) and fulfil all the coaching requirements. In addition to feeding, cleaning, giving him medicine and, yes, disciplining him should he misbehave, you also have to put him

"In one version a child can rotate Skipper's arm and she will grow breasts and develop a thinner waist." (Richmond-Abbott, 1992: 73). Doll makers have yet to introduce a comparable technique for an anatomically correct male companion.

The next most noticeable feature of Barbie is that she, in keeping with stereotyped beliefs, is a clothes-horse with hundreds of garments, shoes, and other fashion accessories. As Lindsey (1997: 67) observes, "[c]onsidering that over 250 million Barbie dolls have been sold in the last 25 years and that over 20 million outfits are bought for these dolls every year, the seeds for a clothing addiction in girls are sown early." When additional clothes are not required, other accessories are provided. Baywatch Barbie comes complete with all of the essential paraphernalia required for success as a lifeguard—a frisbee, a hairbrush, and a dolphin. Phone Fun Skipper™ who "loves to talk on the phone" comes with her very own cellular phone. Mermaid Barbie™ comes with a gold lamé evening gown that, with an add-on tail fin, makes life under water viable *and* fashionable. Depending upon your point of view, Barbie either promotes the stereotypically feminine qualities of neatness and cleanliness, or she has a severe problem with excess body odour and suffers from an obsessive-compulsive disorder to wash herself. No less than eight specialty sets have been designed to either help Barbie promote personal hygiene or solve her problem: Barbie's Bathroom™, Barbie's Bubbling Bathroom™ shower set, Barbie's Beauty Bath™, Barbie's Bathtub Fun™ (complete with slide and diving board), Barbie's Hollywood Bath Set™,

through a strict training regime that includes weightlifting and "brick hitting."

Nano Fighters come in three versions: Supreme Sumo, the urban Alley Rumble and the biker, Rough Rider. While only two of the virtual combatants can duke it out at any one time, others can be connected to wait their turn in a simulated elimination tournament. When a punch is thrown, it's seen as an energy burst on the screen. But once of [*sic*] the Nano Fighters is near victory, he actually crosses over into his opponent's space and finishes him by knocking him out with a few direct blows at close range. "It's not only beating the guy, but invading his space," explains McClure with relish.

The sheer brutality, though simulated, doesn't impress Liz Campbell, editor of Oakville, Ont.-based *City Parent*, a monthly publication affiliated with Capital Parent in Ottawa. "Why do we need another toy that fights? There are enough toys out there that do that already."

Playmates Toys also makes one of the originals: Teenage Mutant Ninja Turtles.

But inasmuch as the Nano Fighters can be rough and tough, they also have their sensitive side, needing attention—ideally every hour—to ensure they're fit enough to rumble. And unlike the Tamagotchis, none of the Nano cyber-creatures die. When ignored, they simply go away. "We figure that's plenty enough negative reinforcement for kids," says McClure. "It's a pretty heavy guilt trip to lay out for a kid if something dies. It's pretty morbid."

And more is on the way this spring. Your child might enjoy the less aggressive, but still sporting nature of Nano Racers. And other children just might enjoy playing with the "virtual makeover" that comes in Nano Salon.

Source: Christopher Guly, Southam Newspapers. "Nano Fighters into ring to match her Nano Pals." *Edmonton Journal*, 5 February 1998: A2.

Barbie Foam & Colour Bathtub Fun™, Barbie So-Much-To-Do! Bathroom™ and Barbie's Hollywood Shower Set™. Two other products can also aid Barbie's problem and/or support her obsession with her physical appearance, Barbie's Beauty Parlour™ and, perhaps most tellingly, Barbie's Vanity™. Based on the toy maker's implicit messages, the problem either runs in the family or is common to all females. Kelly, Barbie's most recent baby sister (or her illegitimate daughter according to scurrilous rumours), also has an array of furniture and gadgets aimed at assisting her in the performance of ablutions.

Ken, Barbie's anatomically challenged boyfriend, has never been advertised as a doll for boys. Instead, he along with Barbie exists to provide young girls with opportunities to "practice the rituals of courtship and romance with the perfect (though certainly not normative) couple" (Uchalik and Livingston, 1980: 92). The popular Cabbage-Patch Kids™ of the mid-1980s included some passive dolls designed for boys, but all of the Kids now seem to be relegated to the unfashionable used-doll lot, including the very short-lived hair- and finger-eating Christmas Kid™ of 1996. Indeed, one toy catalogue of the same time period featured more than 356 female dolls and 68 male dolls (Schwartz and Markham, 1985). The boys' "action figures" (the preferred name for male dolls)—supermasculine (albeit miniature) crime fighters, soldiers, and superheroes—could all be accessorized with weapons (e.g., bow and arrows, guns, grenade and missile launchers), fast cars, spaceships, and activity-oriented equipment such as mountain-climbing gear. Not a single hairbrush or bathtub is in sight. Both then and now, the doll play of Canadian boys is largely dictated by American-created action figures dedicated to supporting and further promoting the Warrior theme of masculinity.

It is possible, of course, to construct a fantasy "family" with boy's toys such as the masculine-sounding X-Men™, Street Sharks™, Beast Wars Transformers™, Primal Rage™ characters, and the Dinobots™, but their accompanying paraphernalia mitigates against easily using them in this fashion. While perhaps "the family that enters the fray together, stays together," there are no cosy kitchen appliance accessories with which to prepare meals in the Batcave™, no beds and vanity tables in the Jurassic Park Compound™, no nursery in the Ghostbuster™ headquarters, and no frilly curtains to dot the entrance way of the Slime Pit™. Talking G.I. Joe™ does not excitedly squeal, "Let's Go Shopping!" out of his voicebox (although saboteurs have been known to switch his voicebox with Barbie's in some toy stores) nor does the G.I. Joe "action kit" include a shopping buggy or even a curling iron so he can style Barbie's hair when she finally gets out of the bathroom. Real action men just do not appear to be homebodies. When boys and girls grow weary of destroying or creating family homes with their three-dimensional toys, they can switch their attentions and affections to genered toys of a two-dimensional computerized nature (see Box 4.3).

The majority of parents still tend to actively encourage their children to play with gender-stereotyped toys and discourage playing with toys earmarked for the other sex (Caldera et al., 1989; Etaugh and Liss, 1992). Although recent research suggests that some parents view gender-neutral toys as the most acceptable (Idle et al., 1993), most parents appear to succumb to a variety of symbolic inducements designed to increase the selection of toys marketed as being most acceptable for only one gender. Peretti and Sydney (1985) report that toys stereotyped for boys (e.g., cars, trains, chemistry sets, tool chests, action figures) almost invariably feature boys in the photographs used in advertisements, catalogues, and on toy packages. Similarly, photographs of girls accompany those toys stereotyped for their use. Shoppers immune to a visual sales pitch will find that salespeople act as gatekeepers, actively encouraging the purchase of gender-typed toys (Schwartz and Markham, 1985). Despite the efforts of feminists and consumer's organizations encouraging advertisers and retailers to become less stereotyped in their campaigns, little has changed in the marketing and purchase of toys. By two to four years of age, boys and girls demonstrate strong preferences for, and play with, quite different sets of toys that conform to gender stereotypes and promote the further development of different gender outcomes (Basow, 1986: 132; Robinson and Morris, 1987; Leaper, 1994). Children's judgments about their toys are also influenced by those gender-role stereotypes. Cann and Garnett (1984) report that children rate gender-role congruent dolls (e.g., a male doctor) as more competent than gender-role incongruent dolls (e.g., a female doctor).

Even though bicycles, skip-its, in-line skates, stuffed animals, and board games initially may be thought "unisex," here too stylistic details distinguish the more likely user. The pink or purple bicycle (even without the heart-shaped carrier basket) is unlikely to be selected as a gift for a boy; the sturdier, more durable in-line skates typically do not sport pink laces nor cuddly baby animals. By ages two or three, boys are actively discouraged, through teasing from parents, siblings, kin, and peers from toting around a beloved stuffed animal. Yet girls and women of all ages may be given a stuffed animal as a birthday, Valentine's Day, or anniversary present. Brides receive a stuffed bear (appropriately clad in a wedding dress) as a matrimonial day offering. Women athletes and accused female offenders are permitted to clutch the stuffings out of cherished miniature creatures. Young, and not so young, men attempt to successfully complete a rite of passage by dazzling their female partners at exhibitions or fair grounds with a manly display of tossing balls or rings through hoops in the quest for a cheaply made, sawdust-filled stuffed animal. Calculate how many stuffed animals prominently reside in your bedroom at this moment; a dozen or more (each with names) allows us to predict with a reasonable degree of confidence that you are female.

Clothing

If, as our folk wisdom proclaims, "clothes make the man" or woman, subtle gender socialization via wearing apparel begins at very young ages. Once a newborn's genital sex has been publicly proclaimed, the infant is typically and rapidly enveloped in blankets and toques, while Huggies™ and other disposable diapers engage the infant bottom, all in sex-appropriately coloured material. According to customs of our culture established early in the twentieth century (Pomerleau et al., 1990) blue has been designated for boys and pink for girls, although the observations of Shakin et al. (1985) suggest that the gender palette has been expanded to include yellow for girls and red for boys. While a pink flowered diaper emerging from a similarly coloured bikini bottom and matching bikini "bra" worn up under the arms may not transform a baby into a Baywatch "babe," this fashion statement is designed to inform all observers immediately as to the baby's sex. It also operates to guide perceptions of the infants along gender appropriate lines. Those perceptions in turn typically lead to observer comments that reinforce gender stereotypes.

Passersby seem to resent parents who dress their newborn in nongender-specific rainbow-coloured outer wear. Denied symbolic cues to prompt remarks on the beauty of a girl baby ("She's going to be a real heartbreaker!") or the body build of a boy baby ("Whoa, look at the muscles on this little guy!"), observers often flounder in search of an appropriate response. Gender-neutral remarks ("What a sweetie! How old is your baby?") are often posed in a cagey attempt to prompt a parent into furnishing an identifying pronoun ("*He's* two weeks old."). Failing all else, the observer is often reduced to asking "What's your name, little one?" However, as Shakin et al. (1985) have noted, so common is the colour coding of infant apparel, that more than 90 percent of the infants they observed in a shopping mall could be readily identified by the characteristics of their clothing as being male or female.

If colours are sometimes deceiving, other clothing hints are often more helpful. Even when an infant's first garments are hand-me-downs, impressionistic evidence suggests that considerable resistance exists among parents and others to garbing a newborn in outfits associated with the other sex. Clothing styles for infants imitate adult sex-linked fashions, only in smaller sizes. Frilly panties, miniature hair bows to clasp the one existing strand of hair, tiny pierced earrings, bikinis, spandex leggings, and tube-tops all announce the presence of a female infant. Sailor suits, baseball caps with "Slugger" across the brim, miniature hockey jerseys, and a vast profusion of garments decorated with cars and trucks mark the infant wearer as male. Sleepwear for infants and young children is also gender coded with girls dressed in pastel nighties trimmed in lace and ruffles and boys in "astronaut, athlete, or super-hero pajamas" (Renzetti and Curran, 1995: 93).

Seemingly unisex clothes for young children are still blatantly and subtly sex-linked through emblems, insignia, and design patterns. Sweatsuits featuring cartoon characters such as Thomas the engine, Hercules, Aladdin, or the Marvel™ characters of Spiderman,

Superman, the Hulk, and the X-men, all ribbed in blue or black are located in the "Boys" section, while Sailor Moon, Princess Jasmine, Pocahontas, Esmerelda, and Minnie Mouse, ribbed in pink are located only in the "Girls" section. The presence of absence of tasteful pink rosettes on the collar or the embossed pink ballet slippers on the pant legs differentiate denim shirts and jeans. Unlike pants designed for boys, girls' pants typically lack pockets thereby encouraging early adoption of a purse or handbag for carrying lunch money, facial tissues, or a favoured toy. Even footwear follows a gendered pattern; boys' athletic shoes are not only typically sturdier, with thicker soles and better overall foot support, but they also sport appropriate gender colours (blues rather than pinks) emblems (Simba rather than Nala) and endorsements from male rather than female professional athletes.

Clothing styles themselves also promote gender appropriate and inhibit gender inappropriate behaviour. Pointy-toed patent shoes, crinolined or straight-lined dresses, and a mass profusion of barrettes and ribbons to keep hair in place all discourage their wearer from engaging in boisterous physical activity. Similarly, admonitions against dirtying their dresses, ripping costly colour-coordinated pantyhose, or losing an earring constrain girls from engaging in carefree play. Young girls aspiring to ladyhood cannot blithely ascend the monkey bars in a short skirt lest they display their lacy underwear. Notice how the examples that come quickly to mind all pertain to the greater restrictiveness of female clothing. Another of the classic symptoms parents point to in proclaiming a "tomboy" in their family is a daughter's preference for donning the less restrictive garb of boys and a refusal to wear dresses. Conversely, one of the supposed indicators of sissyhood is a son's predilection for cross-dressing, especially when he's working in Barbie's Beauty Parlour or cooking on his Easy-Bake Oven.

Public occasions such as going to church, synagogue or temple, or attending a wedding, school concert, or party typically require "dressing up" in highly gendered formal wear that once again reflects adult fashions in miniature. Tuxedos, three-piece suits, and floor-length gowns reign supreme in appropriate settings. Another rite of passage into manhood for young males in our society involves discarding a clip-on tie for one they have learned to knot themselves. Class photographs of elementary-school-aged children almost invariably provides the sight of adult-looking young boys slightly strangulated in formal shirts, long ties or bow ties, and suit jackets or sports coats. Young girls are outfitted to look pretty and demure, not sexy, in party dresses (no "power" suits), lacey socks or pantyhose, and with preferably long hair styled forwards over their shoulders.

Even when wearing clothing purposefully designed to escape ordinary identities such as, for example, donning Halloween costumes, what is considered an appropriate children's outfit tends to vary along gender lines. Dressing one's son as a superhero, ghost, clown, or an eggplant is deemed more appropriate than dressing him as a princess, fairy, or butterfly. Sewing patterns for Halloween costumes prompt the purchaser to consider the gender of the wearer by using a male or a female model to illustrate how the costume will look upon completion. While certain costumes are marketed as gender-neutral (e.g., a giant M&M™ peanut), the vast amount are not. Animal costumes such as Baby Bunny and Panda Bear are depicted with girl models, while Tyrannosaurus Rex and Lion King costumes feature boys in their packaging. Ready-made costumes, such as plastic Princess Jasmines or Cinderellas mirror the same approach as they are unlikely to be marketed as suitable garments for aspiring drag queens. Thus, by limiting the range of clothing options children have to select from, manufacturers and advertisers, along with parents, subtly shape children's behaviours in appropriate directions.

The vast majority of research observations and theoretical speculations on the role of the family in gender socialization focuses upon the developmental periods of infancy and early childhood. For reasons to be noted momentarily, comparatively little attention has been devoted to family socialization during late childhood and adolescence. Parents continue to exert an influence upon the lives of their daughters and sons as they develop over their life courses but, shortly after the age of school entry, the relative influence of the family begins to wane and other agents of socialization become more influential. Evidence of later family socialization contributions will be integrated into subsequent sections.

THE PEER GROUP

Even though a child interacts with other children outside of the family from at least the age of three years, contacts with age peers during these early years remain predominantly at the level of playmates who exert minimal influences upon one another. At we noted earlier, the power of peer-group influence forms a fast-rising curve, usually beginning at ages seven to eight, peaking around ages fourteen to sixteen (Thornburg, 1982: 124), and only gradually dissipating into the adulthood years. Regardless of the precise timing of the group's beginnings and endings, peers constitute an important reference group through the social time periods of late childhood through middle adolescence, as young people seek to assert autonomy from their families. When "something great happens" or "something big goes wrong," Canadian teenagers are at least three times more likely to want to share that news with their friends than with their families. They also rank enjoying their friends far ahead of sports, sexuality, music, partying, or family activities (Bibby and Posterski, 1992: 11).

Pioneering research conducted during the 1950s upon the leading edge of the baby boom generation (Coleman, 1967) acknowledged that peer groups among high school adolescents espoused and supported values, norms, and styles of conduct noticeably different from those transmitted by parents and educators. Furthermore, the content of these values and norms varied for male and female peer groups. Subsequent research (e.g., Adler et al., 1992/1995; Dunphy, 1963; Fine, 1987; Thorne and Luria, 1986) now finds that these important gender differences are also characteristics of preadolescent elementary-school-age peer groups.

From Same-Sex to Cross-Sex Peers

Young children tend to congregate in loosely structured same-sex play groups beginning around the ages of two to three, and continuing through to the age of entry into the formal school system (Maccoby and Jacklin, 1987; Thorne and Luria, 1986). More highly structured peer groups evolving from younger play groups remain restricted, for the most part, to same-sex members until middle adolescence (Dunphy, 1963; Fine, 1987), at which point they are as likely to be composed of a mixed-sex group. Individual girls and boys may initiate and maintain cross-sex contacts at young ages, but a same-sex peer group remains their important source of reference and identification throughout older childhood and the early to middle adolescent years.

These same-sex peer groups create a way of life sufficient to meet most needs for their members, outside of the context of their families and their schools, and increasingly inside those contexts as well, to warrant the term **peer gender subcultures**, to modify the term initially used by Udry (1971:75). Within each subculture, relatively distinctive values, attitudes, and perspectives on the world of young people, the world of grown-up people, and in particular the nature and meaning of each gender are disseminated and reinforced. The dominant characteristics of masculinity and femininity in our society are modified by peer subcultures to fit the confinements and opportunities relevant to this transitional social-time construct between childhood and adulthood. Given the importance to young people of gaining acceptance among those considered to be more or less their equals, the influence of the norms, values, and viewpoints of one's peer group takes on particular significance.

A couple of cautionary notes must be introduced before we proceed further. The attention of researchers tends to focus more upon differences than upon similarities between the gender subcultures. The distinctive features identified for each subculture are derived primarily from observations of members as they interact within their own same-sex contexts and less from cross-sex interaction contexts. Reflective of a traditional assumption that the genders are essentially different, similarities between subcultures tend not to receive as much notice. Furthermore, values, norms, and behaviours operative within a subculture may be modified by individuals when they interact outside of the confines of their subculture. Both women and men often note that a friend, or they themselves, will act differently when in mixed company than when he or she is with a same-sex peer group. Finally, researchers have found that the themes and focal points of interest within the male subculture have remained relatively unchanged in content and emphasis over the course of examination during the past 30 years. In contrast, slight but noticeable changes are occurring in female subcultures (Adler et al., 1992/1995: 1338). These changes do not involve the elimination of themes found in previous generations, but rather the addition of relatively new dimensions reflecting larger-scale changes in women's lives within our society.

Boys to Men

Various studies (see Elkin and Handel, 1989:186) indicate that boys tend to develop a more extensive network of friendships among their same-sex peers than do girls. In contrast to girls, boys' same-sex friendships tend to be less intense, less intimate, and more superficial in nature. During mid-adolescence (Duck, 1975), and throughout adulthood, males describe and evaluate their friendships primarily by emphasizing the physical activities they mutually engage in such as playing sports, going to athletic events, or drinking and carousing together. We will return to the subject of friendships in Chapter 7.

We noted earlier that Udry (1971: 76) argues that the basic themes of the male peer group centre around "independence, emotional control, and conquest." Udry further asserts (1971: 76–81) that males informally teach and reinforce these dominant themes of masculinity through interactions surrounding three focal points of interest—sexuality, sports, and automobile mechanics—that are of paramount interest to boys and young men across all regions of the country and all social classes, throughout childhood and adolescence.

In their research on elementary school children, Adler et al. (1992/1995) focus upon the sources of popularity within gender subcultures. Similar to other researchers (Coleman, 1961; Fine, 1987; Thorne and Luria, 1986), Adler et al. find athletic ability and success in sports to be perhaps the most important dimension along which young boys are hierarchically arrayed within their subcultures. Being "cool" in physical appearance and demeanor, including repressing one's emotions, and expressing "toughness" and independence through defiance and challenging adult authority and existing rules (see also Thorne and Luria, 1986) also promote a higher rank within the subculture. As well, boys in the higher grades are considered to be more popular by their peers if they are, or appear to be, successful in cross-gender interactions, especially if those relations include success in sexual relations. Somewhat surprisingly, in light of the absence of other supportive research, Adler et al. also find that a male's popularity is influenced by the sophistication of his social and interpersonal skills, or "savoir faire" (1992/1995: 125) that enable him to relate successfully with girls, adults, and male peers, often by manipulating and controlling these individuals.

Girls to Women

As noted earlier, girls tend to form less extensive friendship networks than do boys. However, girls' same-sex friendships tend to be more exclusive and intimate (Elkin and Handel, 1989: 186). Duck (1975) finds that, whereas girls in early adolescence tend to stress the physical similarities between themselves and their friends in areas such as clothing and hairstyles, mid-adolescent females are more likely to stress psychological similarities with their friends such as being able to "really talk" with one another and share the same hopes and anxieties about the present and the future.

Whitesell and Harter (1996) suggest that females' expectations of one-on-one communication and intimacy with their friends may act to discourage them from demonstration of overt hostility or physical aggression for fear of social rejection. Bukowski et al. (1993) reports that aggression is more strongly associated with peer rejection for girls than for boys. However, girls consistently have been found to demonstrate higher levels of relational aggression than boys. Relational aggression, generally expressed in the form of indirect verbal aggression, typically has, as its goal, the damaging of another's peer relationships (Crick, 1995, 1997; Crick and Grotpeter, 1995). Bjorkqvist et al. (1992) report that while direct aggression (physical and verbal) was more common among boys than among girls, indirect or relational aggression (e.g., gossiping, spreading injurious rumours, or excluding another girl as a form of retaliation) was more common among girls. "Experts," both inside and outside the media, and parents alike have registered surprise and dismay at several widely publicized incidents across Canada of aggressive violence committed in the late 1990s by early and mid- to late adolescent girls and women upon their peers. These reactions are due, in large part, to the seeming rarity, but perhaps rising trend, of female-initiated overt violent aggression.

The central themes of female subcultural peer groups have been identified as "sociability, popularity, and attractiveness" (Udry, 1971: 82). These dominant themes of nascent femininity are stressed and reinforced through discussions surrounding the focal issues in girlhood and early womanhood of other women, men, and clothing and cosmetics (Udry, 1971:82). Adler et al. (1992/1995) find that physical appearance and attractiveness are a major source of popularity and a major topic of conversation among elementary-school-age girls. Developing and demonstrating sociability skills in same-sex and other-sex relationships further promote a girl's ranking on the popularity hierarchy. In contrast to boys, however, girl subcultures do not require participants to develop disdain for academic success in the early school years. Finally, a girl's popularity ranking in childhood and early adolescence in strongly influenced by her parents' socioeconomic status. Higher status parents can and do afford the expensive and fashionable clothing, other material possessions, and extracurricular activities such as skiing and horseback riding that are important for success, at least in middle- and upper-class hierarchies. Furthermore, higher status parents tend to be more permissive and tend to grant daughters greater freedom to pursue the ingredients vital to popularity success.

Adler et al. (1992/1995: 135) conclude that "boys' culture" is characterized by a "culture of coolness," an "orientation of autonomy," and an "expression of physicality," all characteristics congruent with Udry's (1971) earlier depictions of the masculine subculture. "Girls' culture" is characterized by a "culture of compliance and conformity," a "culture of romance," and an "ideology of domesticity" that stresses an indoor, emotionally intimate, expressive way of life (Adler et al., 1992/1995: 136; see also Thorne and Luria, 1986). While the boundaries of female subcultures are expanding to incorporate a greater (but not yet equal to boys') emphasis upon sports competition and achievement, autonomy, and initiative, and, perhaps, even overt aggression, the boundaries of male subcultures have not evidenced any comparable expansion to incorporate values and themes more traditionally characteristic of females (Adler et al., 1992/1995: 137–138). We turn now to two hallmarks of male and female subcultures that have substantial bearing upon masculinity and femininity, respectively, within our culture: sports and the emphasis upon physical attractiveness.

Peer Play and Games

Studies on activities in early and middle childhood are limited mainly to examinations of toys, clothing, and reading material availability and preferences, all subjects that we examined earlier. The few studies on gender differences in play and game activities yield inconsistent findings that may reflect a fairly recent shift in the nature of those experiences for girls in particular. Early research suggests that noticeable differences in the play activities of girls and boys appear from three to eight years of age and continue until the mid-teens. Girls spend more time in play activities with few specific rules and little emphasis on competition (Maccoby and Jacklin, 1974). Activities such as jumping rope and hopscotch, while containing a physically competitive component, tend to have greater emphasis placed upon relationship components, as well as how to negotiate and structure play time.

Lerner (1977), in her study of fifth graders, concluded that girls' games traditionally have been less organized in the sense of being less bound by abstract rules and less competitive in the sense of pitting one participant's skills against another's to attain an award. In contrast, boys' play activities are generally more complex and rule-bound, requiring more coordinated actions of participants who tend to be in direct competition with one another for scarce rewards. However, Hughes' (1988) study of fourth and fifth graders concludes that girls can, and do, participate in highly complex and competitive games that often require the development of conflict resolution skills. At the same time, she also finds that girls are more likely than boys to emphasize cooperation and the maintenance of close personal relationships among competitors.

Sports

Gender differences in play activities are carried through into, and strongly reinforced by, the realm of organized sports. The school, the family, the peer group, and the larger community all influence the structure and dynamics of sports in our society. Formal school systems in Canada provide a major organizing framework for competitive sports and athletic activities, along with contributions from local not-for-profit community clubs or leagues, and for-profit private organizations. Schools provide physical facilities and equipment, coaching, and either compulsory or optional opportunities for children and adolescents to participate in structured athletic activities. Families provide varying levels of financial support for purchasing necessary equipment, transportation to and from lessons and competitions, and either encouragement for, or pressure on, sons and daughters to participate in available opportunities. Peers are an important source of validation or discouragement for continued participation in sports. The larger community contributes financial support indirectly through paying property taxes that fund school programs, and directly through paid attendance at sporting events.

Gender Participation Levels

The degree of school and community fan support for competitive sports in Canada generally pales in contrast to our neighbours to the south. Within the United States, entire towns, small cities, and sections of large cities all grind to a halt on Friday evenings and Saturday afternoons throughout the fall and winter as peers, families, and other interested fans attend junior-high and high-school football or basketball games, whose individual and team outcomes dictate personal and community pride or shame. Attendance at American high school football games typically exceeds that found at Canadian university and even professional games, while attendance at American university and college sports events is frequently far beyond the capacity of most Canadian sports venues. Such differences between the two countries are only partly attributable to demographics. Despite sharing a similar overall orientation towards sports, Americans appear to place a greater value upon actual or vicarious participation in competitive team athletic activities than do Canadians.

Contributions of the various agencies of socialization to sports in our society are shaped by our dominant system of social values. Sports in general and competitive body-contact sports in particular have been more strongly linked, traditionally, to desirable images of masculinity than to femininity (Henning and Jardim, 1978; Rohrbaugh, 1979). Following a British tradition that credits England's success in business and war since the defeat of Napolean at Waterloo to lessons learned on the "playing fields of Eton," an exclusive upper-class private boys' boarding school, sports in our society have been lauded as the principal mechanism by which boys are transformed into men. According to this belief system, through sports participation, boys learn standards for excellence and values of teamwork, to coordinate their actions with those of others, to subordinate their own impulses for the greater good, and to take directions and orders. All of these qualities are believed to be necessary preparations for later success in the public sphere.

Given the importance of sports to masculinity development, it is not surprising to observe that concern has been traditionally expressed that extensive participation in sports, particularly competitive full-contact sports, would have a "masculinizing" effect on girls' personalities and behaviour (Rohrbaugh, 1979). The fear has been that sports could become a mechanism for transforming girls into men: masculine creatures devoid of essential elements of desired femininity. Consequently, women's participation has been restricted historically to sports highlighting the grace and beauty of the female form. Figure skating and the athletic movements of floor exercise gymnastics, while requiring strength, coordination, and agility, display the lines of a woman's body as she strives for individual achievement. Role models of excellence within these sports are typically described in a language of prototypical femininity such as the "graceful" Michelle Kwan, or the "diminutive" Tara Lipinski, or the "lithe" Camille Martens or Stella Umeh.

Women have been "permitted" over the present century to slowly expand their sport repertoires in competitive venues. For those of you who are keeping score, a stereotypically male tendency, Canada sent a contingent of 304 athletes to the 1996 Summer Olympic Games. For the first time in our history, more than half of our country's representatives (155 athletes) were women. New role models of athletic femininity such as Silken Lauman now represent courage, perseverance, and mental and physical strength. Reflecting the constraints placed upon women in sports, however, these new role models are still found in essentially individual, not team, amateur sports. Henning and Jardim (1978), in their examination of women and management, suggest that the lack of comparable emphasis on and experience in competitive sports can be detrimental for women's success in business organizations. The fact that our media frequently report news of court challenges as females attempt to gain parity of participation in many sports once reserved solely for males is indicative of both an increasing desire of girls and women, along with supportive parents, to gain access to the sports experience and the continued resistance of boys and men, and many parents, to preserve this traditional bastion of masculinity. The only recourse for many girls and women is to form their own competitive leagues, parallel to those of boys and men, at both the amateur and professional levels.

Forty-two percent of Canadian boys aged 10–14 and 37 percent of girls were engaged in competitive physical activities in 1988. Between the ages of 15 to 19, young men's participation rate increased slightly to 44 percent, while young women's rate declined to 28 percent (Gauthier and Haman, 1992: 20). Results of the 1992 General Social Survey (Corbeil, 1995) of Canadians aged 15 and over indicates that men are much more likely to participate in sports than are women. The sports gender gap is greatest among teenagers and slowly narrows with increasingly age. Female adolescents and adults dominate figure skating (97 percent) and comprise 74 percent of all equestrians. The other sports with a female participant majority are swimming, bowling, and cross-country skiing. In contrast, males comprise the majority of participants in approximately three-quarters of the 60 athletic activities recognized by Sports Canada (not including, for example, recreational cycling or hiking and jogging). Male adolescents and adults dominate in hockey participation (97 percent), and in rugby, football, soccer, squash, racquetball, baseball, softball, golf, and weight lifting (all more than 70 percent). While sports participation by males in comparison to females, lessens more dramatically with age (Corbeil, 1995), males, as a hallmark indicator of their masculinity, are expected to retain a high level of interest in sports throughout adulthood, if for no other reason than to be able to knowledgeably fill in those awkward conversational moments with comments such as: "So, how about them Oilers, eh?"

Socialization Lessons of Sports

Through sports, boys are also expected to learn to control their emotions, and particularly to suppress expressions of emotions culturally labeled as "feminine." Anger and feelings of aggression are to be channeled into appropriate actions designed to further individual or team goals. Fear and feelings of physical pain cannot be displayed, but must be contained behind a veil of stoicism ("tape an aspirin to it and get back out there") lest these feelings be exploited for competitive disadvantage. The image of European-trained athletes writhing on the soccer pitch or arena ice is widely regarded as an object of disdain for the truly masculine Canadian male. Athletes permanently disabled physically by their participation in sports are offered admiration and respect, but empathy and compassion for an opponent are generally forbidden. "Big boys" may cry at the thrill of victory but losers in the agony of defeat are supposed to weep only in private, and preferably not at all.

Competitive sports are also expected to reinforce the conquest theme for boys and men. Given the small size and low profile of our peacetime armed forces, sports has become one of the major socially acceptable contexts for instilling and reinforcing the Warrior image of masculinity in Canada. The language of a variety of sports, football in particular, contains numerous military references. One Canadian professional football team (Rough Riders) was named after a famous military fighting unit and one (Blue Bombers) implicitly maintains a military theme. Teams are typically divided into "offensive" and "defensive" "units" comprising many players who are "built like a tank." Opponents are described as the "enemy." The leader of an offensive team, often referred to as a "general," "earns his stripes" "marching" his team down the "battlefield" by following his "battle plan," including the judicious use of the "weapons" in his "arsenal," including an "aerial attack" composed of "short lob" passes and the occasional "long bomb." The defensive team attempts to thwart these efforts by "blitzing" the enemy in an attempt to "sack" the quarterback, particularly during a goal line "stand," to prevent the offence from achieving victory and thus "capturing" some coveted crown.

The weekend Warrior is aided in his task by wearing a uniform with a team name emblazoned on his chest that invokes the imagery of barely controlled aggression channeled into annihilating opponents. Young boys and older adolescents perform on teams that frequently model their names on professional sport franchises. The language of team logos, particularly in hockey and football (aside from the basketball Grizzlies and Raptors), is dominated by ferocious, masculine-identifying, animal names such as the currently existing: Panthers, Cougars, Jaguars, Tiger Cats, Bengals, Lions, Bruins, Falcons, Eagles, Ravens, Seahawks, Sharks, Broncos, and Coyotes. Even the Mighty Duck has an evil scowl on his face. Rarely do boys find themselves donning the uniform of the Pooh Bears, the Pussy Cats, or the Daffy Ducks. As an aside, we could ponder whether the nicknames of our professional hockey teams, devoted as they are to patriotism (Canucks or Canadiens) and politics (Senators) and gentle nature (Maple Leafs), are reflective of a more peacekeeping-Warrior spirit in Canada. Only the Flames sound threatening, but, since they have been consistently self-immolated throughout most of the 1990s, it is uncertain who should fear them.

Sports imagery and participation teaches boys directly and indirectly that competing is not sufficient in and of itself. According to our sports folklore, competition has no value unless competitors are prepared to conquer all obstacles, vanquish all opponents, and be proclaimed as winners. While our playing fields from Corner Brook to Victoria are supposedly governed by the noble sentiment of "it matters not whether you win or lose, it's how you play the game," other well-worn sports clichés offer an alternative philosophy more consistent with traditional and contemporary expectations of masculinity: "Winning isn't everything, it's the only thing"; "To the victors go the spoils"; "Nobody remembers who came in second." A giant billboard displayed in Atlanta, Georgia, during the 1996 Summer Olympic Games captured these sentiments with the phrase "You Don't Win Silver, You Lose Gold." These lessons, and the skills acquired to implement them, are promoted as being generalizable to success in business, or politics, or in selecting and keeping a mate. Masculinity becomes anchored not in simple participation in a process but in the achievement of a successful outcome. Following immersion in a peer sports subculture, men tend to treat almost any activity, such as playing a game with a child or a female partner, as a competitive challenge rife with implications for their masculinity.

In 1978, Gabe Mirkin, author of *The Sportsmedicine Book* (1978) found when he asked 100 runners if they would take a drug that would make them Olympic athletes—but, in doing so, kill them within a year—more than half of the runners stated they would do so. Disturbed by this report, Goldman et al. (1984) replicated this study and asked 198 athletes, the majority of whom were weight lifters, if they would take a drug that would enable them to win every championship competition for the next five years, with full knowledge that the drug would kill them at the end of the five-year period. Once again, approximately half (52 percent) of the athletes surveyed indicated a willingness to take the drug, despite awareness that doing so would give them an "unsporting" advantage over their competitors and in spite of the lethal nature of the drug. Experiencing the "thrill of victory" may be especially desired by male adolescents who attempt to achieve status through success at sports. Cowart (1990), reporting on a national American study of male high-school seniors records that approximately 7 percent had at least experimented with the use of steroids; in the same year, the U.S. Department of Health and Human Services documented that between 5 to 10 percent of male adolescents and 0.2 to 0.5 percent of female adolescents were using steroids. Interviews conducted with a subsample of the adolescent steroid users found that four out of five male users believe steroids "made them bigger, stronger, better-looking, and, as a result, more popular among their peers" (in Dolan, 1992: 32).

Denied opportunities to demonstrate their masculinity in arenas reserved for adults such as business success or providing for a family, young males invest a considerable amount of their masculine identity in being a successful sports competitor. They are rewarded for doing so by their peers (Adler et al., 1992/1995; Coleman, 1961; Fine, 1987) and by their parents (Berlage in MacGregor, 1995: 16), particularly their fathers. Nelson suggests that although a father may decline to bathe, or feed, or read a bedtime story to his son, "he will probably at one time or another play catch with his son, take him to a ball game, or quiz him about the current or past feats of male sports heroes" (in MacGregor, 1995: 286). "Sports become the bond between many fathers and sons, with games becoming the way in which the male child wins approval from the father" (MacGregor, 1995:286).

However, such approval from a father is most often contingent upon a son demonstrating that he is a winner (MacGregor, 1995:32, 314). Sports participation consequently promotes the development within young males of a sense of self-worth, conditional upon the success of their performance during the last game. Failure in athletics can be devastating to boys in childhood and early adolescence (Lester, 1976). As Orlick notes, "the outcome of the game becomes more important than the outcome of the child" (in MacGregor, 1995:33). Messner (1990) suggests that the tendency to develop a conditional sense of self-worth encourages young men to construct instrumental (useful, goal-directed, but not emotional) relationships with themselves and others. He further suggests that this tendency creates difficulties for young men in developing intimate relationships when they try to relate instrumentally to women who have been taught to construct their own identities on meaningful relationships, not competitive success.

At times it is difficult to determine whether fathers are intent upon promoting sports success by their sons as part of an initiation rite into manhood, or as part of a vicarious experience to replace the father's lesser actual participation in sports with increasing age. On one hand, fathers in the stands or on the sidelines of a soccer pitch, football field, baseball diamond, or hockey rink, are notorious for screaming instructions and insults at their sons, opposing and own-team players, referees, and coaches to promote a favourable outcome for their sons. On the other hand, we can witness events such as what occurred during a semi-final 400-metre track event at the 1992 Barcelona Olympics when British runner Derek Redmond tore a hamstring.

> He fell to the track, clutched his injury and valiantly rose again in tears to continue hobbling down the track, determined to finish....[Redmond's father] burst from the stands, wrestled past the security guards and ran to meet his injured son. Then, with Derek's head buried protectively in his massive shoulder, Jim Redmond half dragged, half carried his son to the finish line. (MacGregor, 1995: 115)

MacGregor attributes the senior Redmond's actions to a "parent's desperate urge to fix" a hurt suffered by the son, thus reiterating the strength of sports to forge a bond between males of different generations.

The meaning of success in sports differs by social class (Messner, 1990). For those within the lower socioeconomic classes, sports as a future occupation is often perceived as a male's pathway out of poverty or a marginally subsistent way of life. Dolan (1992: 51) notes that, in the wake of the drug scandal surrounding Canadian Olympic sprinter Ben Johnson in 1988, Dr. Roy Bergman of the Olympic Sports Medicine Council reported that, not infrequently, parents would exert pressure on physicians to prescribe steroids for their sons, explaining that while their son was talented, he was "a little on the small side." "If the youngster were just a bit bigger," they would argue, "he could possibly win a scholarship to play college football" and "talk a great deal about the financial advantages to be obtained for their son."

The gross earnings of professional male athletes continues to reach previously unheard of proportions with basketball and baseball superstars earning at least $10–15 million per year, hockey superstars earning $7–10 million per year, and American (but definitely not Canadian) football stars earning somewhere in between. Prior to the introduction of a rookie salary cap, Quebec-born Alexandre Daigle, at the age of 18, signed a five-year, $12.25 million NHL playing contract. First-year players are now restricted to earning less than a million dollars a year, but the salary ceiling for subsequent contracts, as in all other professional sports, shows no signs of being lowered. Despite the extremely high odds against ever attaining ordinary athletic success, let alone superstar status and salaries, and even though the parents of a working-class or lower-class boy may stress education over sports, an athletically-talented boy's experiences in his school, community, and peer group are likely to narrow his occupational aspirations. In addition to the potential economic rewards, MacGregor (1995: 12) suggests that the value system in the working-class in particular is one where Canadian families "would probably rather tell their friends that their boys are NHLers than neurosurgeons."

Although middle- and upper-middle-class boys in Canada also see sports achievement as highly desirable, this is only one path to pursue of many. Boys from these social classes find it easier to discard sports and invest energy and self-identity in a future nonathletic career (Messner, 1990). Pathways to financial success and security are noticeably more restricted for aspiring female professional athletes. Only "ladies" golf or tennis offer the possibility of significant economic gain. Participants in the newly-founded Women's National Basketball Association (WMBA, the summer league) and the American Basketball League (the winter league), play for teams such as the Xplosion, the Rage, Power, Reign, StingRays, Lasers, Glory, Blizzard, and Quest. However, they are unlikely to reap the rewards of their male counterparts. Within the value system of our society, women are less likely to acquire substantial financial gain from what their bodies do than they are from how their bodies appear.

Physical Attractiveness

Our bodies, our "personal billboard[s]" (Garner, 1997: 32), provide a central basis for the creation of first impressions. Every society constructs ideal-type standards of physical attractiveness for both women and men. These standards define and encapsulate what is considered to be desirable, meaningful, and aesthetically appealing. The standards themselves are the product of social and historical circumstances. Abraham and Llewellyn-Jones (1992:1) argue that for much of recorded history "it was fashionable to be fat": the uncertainty of food supplies in preindustrial and early industrial societies made plumpness a symbol of economic prosperity. However, over the course of this century, perhaps in response to increased general affluence and a basically stable food supply, fashions of beauty and physical attractiveness have changed in our society. In particular, our icons of female beauty have undergone a transformation. Content analyses conducted on the "vital statistics" of *Playboy* centrefolds and of contestants and winners of Miss America pageants over a 25-year period find not only a decrease in average bust and hip measurements, but also a notable decline in weight among these role-model women (Garner et al., 1980; Robinson, 1982). As our "Dream Girls" have become thinner, what has become notably fatter are the incomes of those who manufacture and market products designed to aid us in attaining the new ideal.

Our socially constructed standards of physical attractiveness stress two qualities over all others: youth and thinness. Entire industries invest billions of dollars annually to convince Canadian and American men and, particularly, women that the slightest departure from our monolithic standard should be cause for great personal alarm. Increasing age, increased weight (and width) are linked by advertisers to lonely nights spent alone with only feline or canine companionship, loss of promotions and power on the job, increased life-insurance rates and, ultimately, public ridicule and scorn. Consequently, Canadian and American women, and increasingly men, invest billions of dollars annually, purchasing books and magazines, lotions and potions, clothing, cosmetics, plastic surgery, diet plans, exercise plans, and torture machines devoted to the elusive search for physical attractiveness and all that it is believed to entail (Wolf, 1991).

A self-fulfilling prophecy exists within our culture. Our emphasis upon physical attractiveness appears to be socially validated. Whether as infants or adults, attractive persons are judged to possess more socially desirable personalities than less attractive persons. Physically attractive infants are more likely than others to be picked up, to be held, to be embraced frequently, and to have their needs tended to by both their mothers and their fathers (Hildebrandt Karraker and Stern, 1990; Langlois and Casey, 1984; Parke et al., 1980). Male and female college students, as well as pregnant women, all rate physically attractive infants as "more sociable, less active, more competent, more attractive, and physically smaller and more feminine," from just their photographs alone (Hildebrandt Karraker et al., 1987). Attractive adults are believed to be more sociable, poised, sophisticated, sexually warm, kind, and genuine. The assumption that attractive external qualities equate with desirable internal qualities is known as the "what is beautiful is good" stereotype (Dion et al., 1972). By virtue of the existence of this stereotype, appearance also becomes a route to social success, with physically attractive people receiving more social rewards. In our social context, close conformity to our standards of physical attractiveness becomes an important personal resource and a source of power (see Chapter 7).

Beauty thus serves not only to focus people's attention, but also acts as a master status from which stems other desirable attributions and positive responses. Moreover, because physical attractiveness is seen as a particularly salient quality for females, women who fail to evidence expected levels of attractiveness are described in more negative terms than are similarly unattractive men (Basow, 1992; Wallston and O'Leary, 1981; Wolf, 1991). Generally possessing greater status and power, men are less likely to have to use their physical attractiveness as a commodity or "bargaining tool" (Lindsey, 1997: 168) for success and are less likely to be judged as harshly when their appearance departs from our standards of physical desirability. As well, in a reversal of the "beautiful is good" stereotype, women who possess socially disapproved-of qualities, such as feminists and lesbians, are often stereotyped as being physically unattractive (Abu-Laban and McDaniel, 1995: 115).

Girls, at a very early age, are introduced to our societal emphasis upon physical attractiveness for women by comments from adults such as "My, how pretty you look today." "That's a really attractive dress," or "Doesn't your hair look cute!" Rarely are little boys bestowed with these or comparable genuine compliments. Along with, and from, their parents, girls are socialized into basking in their own beauty, or bemoaning their lack thereof. Eventually with the aid of friends and the ever-present mass media, girls learn how to observe and analyze themselves as "beauty objects" or "sex objects." By late childhood or early adolescence, they learn to add another dimension and to appraise themselves as "sexual objects." Physical standards of female beauty and sexuality are internalized by both women and men in our society. As a consequence of our relentlessly exacting standards, in combination with incessant reminders from mass media advertising, most girls and women find themselves lacking in one way or another.

Subtle messages about the importance of physical appearance are conveyed during girlhood in endeavours such as gymnastics, figure skating, and ballet where, despite possession of the requisite athletic ability, coordination, and desire, success or rejection is ultimately dependent upon possession of a "correct" body type. A young female who aspires to enter a prestigious dance school such as the National Ballet School of Canada or the School of American Ballet can be distressed to learn, as early as age six or seven, that her body appearance is "wrong." Her bone structure may be too "heavy," she may not be sufficiently ethereal in appearance; she may not possess the preferred delicate face with sharp, distinctive features, her feet may not possess a "good arch" or she may not have the capacity to present a pleasing "turnout" in first position, when her heels are pressed together back to back, with her toes pointed in 180-degree opposite directions (Gordon, 1983; Kirkland, 1986; Varley and Varley, 1971). Indeed, an aspiring dancer may be chagrined to find that rejection occurs after a mere stroll across the dance studio floor before she has even had a chance to perform.

Akin to demands placed upon hopeful fashion models, weight, or more accurately the relative lack of it, becomes an essential prerequisite to candidacy for aspiring ballerinas. Parents are often cautioned to "watch the baby fat" on four-year-old daughters. In North America, the "Balanchinian aesthetic" (the standard demanded by choreographer George Balanchine) remains salient and defines the essential body type of female ballet dancers. The ballet "look" is fluid, graceful, and super-thin. Mirrors surrounding ballet studio walls, and figure skating rinks, reinforce a continuous fascination with, and dependence upon, the attainment of a desired appearance. Coaches and teachers constantly direct attention to a female student's physical failings. In the words of a student "They'll say 'You have bad feet, they're so ugly'; or 'Can't you lift your leg higher, what's wrong with you?'" (in Gordon, 1983: 26). As a consequence, "[t]he constant focus on the body and execution creates a self-concept that is characterized by low self-esteem, and many dancers develop a 'me' that is negative and hypercritical" (Dietz, 1994: 71).

In her examination of exclusive ballet schools, Gordon (1983) observes that students not only compete with one another in terms of their technical proficiency, but in how much they weigh. "Because the ballet look idealizes the thin-hipped, flat-chested figure, young dancers feel that they will be favored if they are thin" (Gordon, 1983: 39). This perception is reinforced by such practices as unannounced "weigh-ins" during which teachers record and announce, to everyone in the class, the student's weight. Weight gain—even of as little as a pound or half-kilogram—can prevent a student from advancing into the main dance company (Gordon, 1983: 42). Discussions of diets and calories become staples within the ballet-school world, wherein students "debate the effectiveness of…diet…versus that of simple fasting. Abstinence is a virtue" (Gordon, 1983: 40). Around the ages of 10 or 11, and continuing into older ages, both aspiring and professional ballerinas frequently take up cigarette smoking as a means of weight control. These smoking and dietary patterns persist, and have enduring consequences, throughout many women's adult years, all in the pursuit of a certain look. The ballet world reflects a larger cultural view that "thin is beautiful, so the thinner you are, the more beautiful you must be" (Gordon, 1983: 148). It is, therefore, not surprising that eating disorders such as anorexia nervosa and bulimia feature prominently in the competitive worlds of ballet, gymnastics, and figure skating (Brooks-Gunn et al., 1988; Garner and Garfinkel, 1980; Szymanski and Chrisler, 1990/1991).

According to the American College of Sports Medicine, 62 percent of women competing in appearance (i.e., gymnastics and figure skating) sports suffer from an eating disorder; 51 percent of the women's gymnastic programs that responded to the 1992 NCAA survey reported eating disorders among their athletes (Starkman, 1994: C3). Among those who aspire to international status, the quest for slimness may be particularly acute. At five-foot-one-inches and 107.8 pounds, the average size of a member of a member of Canada's women's gymnastic team exceeded both the international average at the 1992 Olympics of four-foot-eleven-inches and 92.18 pounds, and the 1992 average size of four-foot-nine-inches and 88 pounds among the American women's team. A recent study conducted at Toronto Hospital showed that female athletes are still at risk of eating disorders after they retire. In a sample of about 50 female patients who had to be hospitalized with eating disorders during the three-year study, more than half of those women had been professional athletes. American gymnast Christy Henrich, who, in her athletic prime, had weighed 96 pounds, shrank to 47 pounds after retirement, and weighed a mere 61 pounds when she died in July 1994. Janet Morin, a former Canadian gymnastic champion who retired after competing for Canada at the 1992 Summer Olympics, has revealed that she routinely swallowed eight to ten laxatives on weekends preceding regular weigh-ins (Starkman, 1994: C1).

An emphasis upon weight control as a necessary element in achieving physical attractiveness is not, of course, unique to the subcultural worlds of those who aspire to the elite ranks of amateur or professional ballet, gymnastics, or figure skating. Preschoolers prefer thin children over children of average or heavier-than-average weight (Dyrenforth et al., 1980). Valette (1988:5) finds that when preschoolers are offered a choice between playing with two life size rag dolls, one of which is thin and the other fat, 91 percent of the preschoolers opt for the thin doll. Girls at ages six and seven will position themselves in front of mirrors and bemoan the perception that they are "too fat" (Neuman and Halvorson, 1983: 27–28). Concern has been raised over the increasingly younger ages at which females are expected to embrace and demonstrate the cultural requirements of feminine beauty. "Today's birthday parties for nine-year-olds take place in beauty parlors, where group makeovers include manicures, hairstyles, makeup, the works; top modeling agencies advertise videos for the youngest adolescents on 'How to Become a Model'" (Friday, 1996: 177).

The vernacular for the application of makeup in North America is "putting on one's face"—a phrase which suggests that a woman's self-image is in some way bound up with her makeup and that her natural face is somehow incomplete and insufficient on its own.

> Women in our culture frequently report feeling undressed without mascara or lipstick. Although they are literally dressed in their clothing, they feel undressed as women; that is, the process of "putting-on" one's face is a behavior through which some women *achieve* their gender. (Richardson, 1988: 8, emphasis in original)

With such an intimate link between physical presentation and gender, it is not surprising that advertisers and retailers promote the message that, if one's beauty is marred by natural imperfection, this possible exposure of a "fatal flaw" can be ameliorated by proper packaging. The underlying fear being promoted and capitalized upon is that Cinderella will once again be reduced to a scullery maid should a blemish appear in her veneer. The props of beauty (i.e., makeup, dress, jewellery) thus become an essential part of presenting oneself as a Dream Girl worthy of admiration. Women are more likely than men to acknowledge the importance of flattering clothing for their self-image (Garner, 1997: 38). Men are relatively unskilled in the use of clothing to achieve a complimentary end, as any woman knows who has had to take on the task of dressing her man before he walks out of the door. In contrast, women and girls are schooled in these techniques from very young ages.

The emphasis on slimness, fashion, and makeup is especially marked among adolescent females. Pipher (1994: 190) claims that "losing weight is probably the most common goal" of adolescent girls and the social consequences of deviating from the ideal slender feminine beauty may be especially traumatic for young women. "Being fat means being left out, scorned and vilified. Girls hear the remarks made about heavy girls in the halls of their schools. No one feels thin enough" (p. 184). She notes that approximately half of all teenage girls are currently on diets, while one in five suffers from an eating disorder. "Young women with eating disorders are not all that different from their peers," she remarks. "It's a matter of degree." (pp. 184–185). These concerns about weight and appearance are fostered and maintained by magazines oriented towards a young female audience. While adolescent boys are frantically trying to obtain magazines featuring pictures of women not wearing any clothes, adolescent girls seek magazines featuring models demonstrating how to wear clothes, apply makeup, and generally look physically appealing. Of course, how the models actually achieve a picture of stunning attractiveness in mass circulation magazines is subject to debate. Not only can photographic techniques enhance what a model does or does not look like, but computers can now morph composite pictures of nonexistent women, "technological female impersonator[s]" (Abu-Laban and McDaniel, 1995: 110). Even when magazines reveal some of the secrets of their trade, there is no guarantee that readers, in their quest for perfection, will fully understand what is involved. "In one of your past issues you said models and movie stars look like they have perfect skin because of air-brushing. What exactly is that, and can I do it at home? Anne" (in Abu-Laban and McDaniel, 1995: 110).

Peirce's (1990) content analysis of issues from the adolescent female-oriented magazine *Seventeen* in 1961, 1972, and 1985 finds that approximately 50 percent of the magazine's nonadvertising content was devoted to the topic of physical appearance. Our own observations in December, 1996, of *Seventeen*, *YM* (the acronym for "Young and Modern") and *(All About) YOU!*, find these magazines still implicitly and explicitly extol the rewards of being beautiful in general, and thin in particular. Intermixed with articles which educate adolescent females on the "5 Total Turn Ons Guys Can't Resist" or the "50 Ways to Look, Feel & Think Better," and test quizzes such as "Are You The Type Guys Get Serious About?" "Are You Boyfriend Material?" "Are You Queen of Makeup or Fakeup?" "Do Your Clothes Suit Your Bod?" or "Do You Need A Makeover?" are instructions on how to firm up "flabby" thighs and "fit into that knock-out dress for Christmas." Between these enlightening articles are an array of advertisements for cosmetics, perfumes, and pull-in or push-out, concealing and revealing undergarments.

Many of these products, as on television and in other print media, are marketed using variations on the theme that the product will make the purchaser feel truly, fully, attractive and "feminine." The overall emphasis in teenager magazines is on how to make oneself attractive to "guys" and on how to become a "natural beauty" through artful application of artificial cosmetics and conscientious adhererence to the rigorous diet-plan of the day. Although magazines are becoming more sensitive to the desirability of using non-European models and including makeover plans for women of colour, the still-dominant Eurocentric standard means that members of "visible minorities" often wish "we were otherwise. Skin whiteners, hair-straightening, and dressing with obsessive care, are all part of the same response" (Bannerji, 1993: 183; see also Pipher, 1994; Wolf, 1991).

Through these messages, women are socialized to believe that establishing a relationship with a man, a "guy," is central for their success as a woman. Appearance is offered as the key to getting and keeping a man's attention. Research indicates that men are much more likely than women to publicly stress the importance of physical attractiveness in a potential romantic partner (Berscheid et al., 1971; Buss and Barnes, 1986; Davis, 1990). As the title of a research article on personal want ads states: "Single, White Male Looking for Thin, Very Attractive..." (Smith et al., 1990). While this differential emphasis is substantially less evident when it comes to the actual dating behaviour of adolescent and young adult men and women (Feingold, 1990), Elder's (1969) classic longitudinal study illustrates how physical attractiveness can facilitate upwards social mobility for women through marriage. Comparing the relative influence of physical attractiveness, education, and intelligence on social mobility, Elder found women's opportunities to be "embedded in physical qualities." Physically attractive women were generally more likely to be upwardly mobile through marriage than were women rated as less attractive by a panel of observers connected to the Oakland Growth Study. Elder's study suggests that physical attractiveness in women is not merely instrumental in sexual or other interpersonal relations, but is also correlated with socioeconomic advancement. While increasingly more women today can offer other concrete resources to a potential marriage partner, a women's physical appearance is still a quality appealing to most men (Szymanski and Cash, 1995).

Abraham and Llewellyn-Jones (1984: 16) point out that, in magazines designed for adult audiences, but also avidly read by teenagers, recipes for "mouth watering desserts" are juxtaposed, somewhat ironically, with the "latest" or "most effective" diet plans. Research conducted by Silverstein et al. (1986; 1987) on 48 issues of popular women's magazines notes the presence of 63 ads for diet fads, and 96 articles focusing on body shape or size. The comparable number within popular men's magazines are one and eight. It is perhaps not surprising to find that the vast majority of North American women engage, to some degree, in a regimen of self-restraint and dieting (Silverstein and Silverstein, 1991: 14). Women's concern with dieting within North America has become a "normative obsession" (Rodin in Wolf, 1991: 187) and a "cultural obsession" (Gordon, 1990:68). In her discussion of the "eating arc," Squire (1984: 2, 12) suggests that very few women today in North America are "perfectly content with their bodies as they are" and that most fall along a continuum of "odd eating behaviors and attitudes."

Findings from three different *Psychology Today* surveys of predominantly white, highly educated, financially comfortable, heterosexual (the prototype composite for our culture's attractiveness standards), volunteer samples indicate that dissatisfactions with body weight have heightened over the past 25 years. The proportions of women dissatisfied with their body weight increased from 48 percent in 1972, to 55 percent in 1985, to 66 percent in 1997. Rates for men increased from 35 percent to 41 to 52 percent over the same time period (Garner, 1997: 42). Body weight is clearly an important element of body images, and unhappiness with one's body type is rampant in our society, more so among women than among men. Fully 89 percent of the women in the latest *Psychology Today* survey indicate that they want to lose weight (Garner, 1997: 36). Weight and thinness are more important for fostering a positive body image among women than they are among men (Garner, 1997: 38). Men seem to have a different agenda in which they are more likely to want to "bulk up" (through, for example, weight lifting, or the ingestion of steroids or pastoids) to achieve a positive body image.

Similar results were obtained from a 1984 mail-in survey by more than 33 000 respondents in a study by *Glamour* magazine (Brumberg, 1988; see also Nylander, 1971). "Perversely, the deadly practice of the relentless pursuit of thinness has been presented as desirable by associating the pursuit with rich and/or famous women" (Szekely, 1988: 32) such as Princess Diana, Jane Fonda, or ballerina Evelyn Hart. "Maybe we can't all afford designer clothes, but we can eat less, eat low calorie desserts, drink diet soda, take diet pills and get thinner, much much thinner" (Valette, 1988: 5). Just as researchers find that athletes would be willing to risk their lives if taking a performing-enhancing drug would guarantee record-setting performances (Goldman et al., 1984), the latest *Psychology Today* survey (Garner, 1997: 36) finds that women and men would give up three years (24 and 17 percent respectively) or even five or more years (15 and 11 percent) of their lives to achieve their desired weight goals. In the case of severe eating disorders, the price of life can be measured in lost weight.

Anorexia nervosa, self-imposed starvation initiated and maintained in an attempt to achieve a thin body and a low body weight, is characterized by a morbid fear of becoming fat and by a distorted body image; one is always "too fat" despite objective evidence to the contrary. Bulimia nervosa is a binge-purge pattern of eating and eliminating, most often by self-induced vomiting, frequently aided by the self-administration of large quantities of laxatives, purgatives, emetics, or diuretics.

> The medical effects of anorexia include hypothermia, edema, hypotension, bradycardia (impaired heartbeat), lanugo (growth of body hair), infertility and death. The medical effects of bulimia include dehydration, electrolyte imbalance, epileptic seizure, abnormal heart rhythm, and death. When the two forms are combined, they can result in tooth erosion, hiatal hernia, abraded esophagus, kidney failure, osteoporosis, and death. (Wolf, 1991: 183)

Just as adolescent boys and young men can abuse their bodies by taking steroids in the pursuit of athletic achievement and a desirable physique, girls, and young women in particular, can engage in practices that pose serious detrimental health hazards in pursuit of an elusive, seemingly unattainable, physical ideal.

Approximately 85 to 97 percent of those suffering from anorexia/bulimia are women, with the "typical sufferer" being a "white, middle-class woman under the age of 25" (Lips, 1993: 254). While men are not immune to problems with food, the "overwhelming preponderance of female patients confers on eating disorders the distinction of having the most lopsided sex ratio of any known to psychiatry" (Gordon, 1990: 32). Some writers, such as Orbach (1986), direct attention to the supposedly pathological relationships between ambivalent, needy, mothers and their suffering daughters as the "precondition" of eating disorders. Others, like Friedman (1985: 63), stress the "narcissistic injury" done to daughters within dysfunctional mother-daughter relationships. Since the 1980s, a number of researchers have suggested that patients with eating disorders reported high rates of sexual abuse (Schwartz and Cohn, 1996; Schwartz, 1990). Still others suggest that sociocultural factors, such as the emphasis placed on thinness as a defining feature of female attractiveness, should be considered as the most salient factor in the etiology of eating disorders. In a society in which "[d]ieting is a $35-billion industry," (Crook, 1991: 6) and in which the definition of female perfection hinges, most fundamentally, on weight, "Thin is Perfect," "Thin is Magic" and "[Only] Thin is Acceptable" (Crook, 1991: 6–8). Cartoonist Nicole Hollander remarks, when asked to describe what a world without men would be like, "There would be no crime. And lots of happy, fat women" (in Tavris, 1992: 29).

Men are not immune to our cultural emphasis upon attractiveness. We have already noted that adolescent steroid users ingest their chemicals as much for a desired effect upon their physical appearance as for enhanced athletic capability. Engulfed in a sports mystique, as we saw earlier in this chapter, men carry the lessons of childhood and adolescence into adulthood and are more likely to focus upon exercise as a means of losing weight, should they even become concerned about it, then upon dieting. With increasing age, men do become vulnerable to the blandishments of advertisers for products intended to forestall the ravages of age upon their physical appearance. However, a man's attractiveness typically does not carry with it the same consequences as does a woman's within our culture. Men rarely need to bargain their physical attractiveness for economic or intimate relationship security (Murstein, 1986). How men look is generally less important than what men do. Men, therefore, invest less of their body image in their overall self-concept than do women.

THE SCHOOL: FORMAL AND INFORMAL EDUCATION

In Canada, as in other industrialized nations, the school is of fundamental importance in the socialization process. Compulsory-education laws and the wide availability of kindergarten (despite provincial variations regarding whether kindergarten is compulsory and in the amount of available days of instruction per school year) has resulted in the vast majority of Canadian children aged 5–14 currently attending school; moreover, 46 percent of Canadian children aged four were enroled in some type of school setting in 1988, up from 28 percent in 1977 (McCann, 1995). As a socialization agency, the school, in addition to its other functions, is charged with transmission of a culture's values (Henslin and Nelson, 1996: 478–480). Consequently, the socialization provided is not gender neutral. Abbott and Wallace (1990: 49–50) claim that females within the educational system are socialized into subordinate roles, encouraged to accept dominant ideologies of masculinity and femininity, channeled into gender-appropriate subjects and, in consequence, face restricted opportunities in the labour market.

About a century ago, leading educators claimed that a female's womb dominated her mind. Because females are equipped for childbirth, some argued, education should be regarded as "unnatural" if not, indeed, "dangerous." Diverting blood flow to the brain to solve educational problems would weaken women's wombs. Dr. Edward Clarke of Harvard University's medical faculty expressed the dominant sentiment this way: "A girl upon whom Nature, for a limited period and for a definite purpose, imposes so great a physiological task, will not have as much power left for the tasks of school, as the boy of whom Nature requires less at the corresponding epoch" (in Anderson, 1987). Because women were so much weaker, Clarke argued, they should study only one-third as much as young men—and not at all during menstruation. Similarly, according to Hacker (1984), the idea that women were capable of being doctors themselves was once considered to be simply outlandish. She offers the following as exemplifying the common attitude of those times: "Young ladies have no need of higher education. They could learn the piano if they liked and perhaps a little literature, but medicine—what nonsense! The subject would be way above their heads and, even worse, it would soil their modesty." Such sentiments were often uttered by men in the misguided belief that they were "protecting" women's supposedly delicate nature. In this way, women would be free to devote themselves to the care of their homes, husbands and, most important of all, their children (none of which tasks could actually be performed by a delicate creature, but then inconsistencies and contradictions in logic abound in all cultures).

In various ways, the educational system has become a rival for some functions formerly fulfilled by the family. Schools now provide the skills and credentials for employment that were once acquired within the family home. Formal education performs a latent function of providing a vital childcare service, especially for families where the lone parent or both parents are currently employed. As the amount of education considered necessary has expanded, the importance of teachers as role models has correspondingly expanded. The Ontario government's Royal Commission on Learning recommended in 1994 that three-year-olds be sent to school, pointing to research which indicated that early education for children results in greater literacy and in a lower dropout rate later on (McCann, 1995). Early exposure to role models alternative to family members would consequently increase.

Evidence suggests that school-like settings outside of our now-traditional formal school system encourage stereotypical gendered behaviour (Ramsey, 1995; Serbin et al., 1994). For example, gender segregation occurs in preschools as the result of teacher expectations, the structuring of play or game activities, and the expressed interests of young children themselves (Maccoby, 1994). Paley (1984: xi) observes that a young girl *may* play out a fantasy, while in the "doll corner," that she is Sailor Moon or another cartoon heroine, but it is the more familiar play scenario of "mother and baby which reign supreme and will continue to do so throughout the kindergarten year." "Play centres" for girls (with minikitchens, sinks, and tiny ironing boards) in which girls may don such "feminine" garb as aprons, high heels, and feather boas are typically more enclosed and physically removed from the play centres designed for boys, which feature a "work*man*'s bench" and minia-ture bulldozers. Within the narrower confines of the "girls'" area, boisterous play is struc-turally discouraged (unless one borrows the bulldozer and knocks down a wall in the "cozy kitchen"). However, as Lips (1993: 286) suggests, it is likely that such attempts at architectural redesign by girls would be discouraged by early childhood education teachers. Despite as-sertions of gender-neutrality, teachers at this early level of education do reinforce and reward aggressiveness and assertiveness in boys and dependency and passivity in girls. When boys attempt to use the doll corner as a centre for "warrior narratives" (a "Batcave" or "space station" in which to plot the annihilation of the "enemy") or adapt domestic artifacts such as toy rolling-pins to serve as "pretend" swords, they will be informed that such play belongs "on the playground" rather than in the classroom (Jordan and Cowan, 1995). The domestic sphere is thus reestablished as the "turf" of females and gender segregation is subtly promoted.

Role Models in School

When Martha Hamm Lewis gained entrance to a training school for teachers in New Brunswick in 1849, the principal of the school cautioned her to "enter the classroom ten minutes before the male students, sit alone at the back of the room, always wear a veil, leave the classroom five minutes before the end of the lesson and leave the building with-out speaking to any of the young men" (MacLellan, 1972, in Schaefer et al., 1996: 282). Since that time, women have been more warmly welcomed into the teaching profession to the point where female educators now have numerical superiority at many levels. Indeed, as increasing numbers of very young Canadian children spend some portion of their preschool years in a variety of childcare settings (day care, preschool, or junior and senior kinder-garten), with teachers and/or childcare workers assuming the role of surrogate parent for portions of each week day, the predominance of women teachers within such early childhood education settings symbolically suggests that caring for children is a woman's role rather than one that could be filled equally well by a man. Moreover, although women currently constitute the vast majority of teachers at elementary schools, they account for only about one in four (26 percent) vice-principals and less than one in five (20 percent) principals at that level (Cusson, 1990).

At the secondary-school levels and higher, the numbers of women teachers and admin-istrators declines markedly. This overrepresentation of women at the primary level of edu-cation and their underrepresentation at higher levels is not unique to Canada. Sivard's (1995) research on 56 developed and developing countries reports that, in both 1980 and 1990, while women made up the majority of teachers at the elementary level, they accounted for less than half of second-level teachers, only a quarter of third-level teachers, and a minority of school principals and departmental heads. She remarks that this segregation "can have done little to banish sex stereotypes. Women teachers are clustered in the lower grades and ranks, teach the softer subjects, and in equivalent positions average lower pay than men." (p. 21)

Within institutions of higher learning, this pattern of vertical segregation is equally apparent. Women teachers are underrepresented within such fields as mathematics and engineering and overrepresented in the humanities and social sciences (Sivard, 1995). Throughout Canada, women are less likely to be found at the highest rank of full professors. As well, female full professors earn less on average than male full professors; women academics earn 82 percent of the salary of male academics of comparable rank (CAUT Bulletin, 1995, in Henslin and Nelson, 1996: 294). The higher the prestige of the university, the greater the discrimination. Women are most likely to be found in full-time, continuous, tenured positions in community colleges (see Conway, 1993; DePalma, 1993). In only some of these colleges are such positions accorded the prestigious title of "Professor." More often their occupants as "simply" referred to as "Instructor."

Elementary School and Middle School

Ishwaran (1979) notes that during the years of primary education, kindergarten to grade six, children spend approximately 7000 hours in school. Besides learning the formal curricula, they also learn gender-role distinctions through the informal hidden curricula, guidance counseling, and teacher-student interactions. Levy (1972) observes that even in "free schools" (a term used to described very unstructured school and curricula settings that became popular during the 1970s in both Canada and the United States and that still exist today, although less commonly), the policy of encouraging students to "follow their own interests" frequently results in condoning the stereotyped activities that children are encouraged to pursue outside of the school setting. In this way, the school, regardless of the amount of "freedom" permitted and promoted, reiterates stereotyped gender activities and interests.

Although schools in Canada are not typically segregated by sex any longer—a look at elementary schools in particular within your community built prior to 1960 will likely yield a large number with the designations "Girls" and "Boys" over separate entrances, reflecting attempts to keep the sexes apart—attitudes of gender-appropriate roles for girls and boys may create subtly different gendered psychological and social environments. For example, as children advance through the educational system, they typically become aware that certain subjects (English, art, music, history) are "girls' subjects" while others (math, physics, chemistry, computers) are "boys' subjects." Moreover, Eccles et al. (1990: 197) report that parents evaluate their children's competencies in areas such as mathematics, English, and sports on the basis of the sex of their child. Stereotyped beliefs holding that one sex is "naturally" superior or inferior to the other in terms of certain areas of study may be reinforced by school counselors and teachers in both subtle and blatant ways. In an early study conducted by Donahue and Costar (1977) of 300 school counselors, respondents were each asked to select "appropriate" occupations for six case studies. When the case study described a young woman, counselors selected occupations that paid less, required less education, and were more subject to direct supervision than when the same case study described a young man.

Richardson (1988: 56–61) argues that the transition from the home to the school is easier for girls than it is for boys because of the differential socialization they receive at home. Girls are raised to be more compliant and sensitive to the apparent needs of others and, therefore, have an easier time adapting to the demands of teachers and peers in the classroom setting. Boys, in contrast, are raised to be more independent, assertive, and even aggressive at home and have greater difficulty adjusting to the compliance demands from teachers and the competing claims for attention by their classmates. Not surprisingly, boys tend to be more often and more easily identified as disruptive forces in class and tend to be identified earlier as having "learning" (frequently a euphemism for "behavioural") problems. As we noted earlier, Adler et al. (1992/1995: 128) find that boys, around grade three, change from a positive to a negative orientation towards education and academic achievement, as part of their turning away from parents and other adult authority figures, such as teachers, and towards their own peer group. Such a change leads to a downplaying of one's academic abilities and an increase in disruptive, or at least distant ("cool"), behaviour in the classroom. Girls retain a more positive orientation towards learning and education, at least until the junior high school years.

Teacher's attitudes about gender-appropriate behaviour can create self-fulfilling prophecies. Sadker and Sadker (1991), in their three-year study of more than 100 fourth, sixth, and eighth grades classes in four American states, suggest that a variety of subtle but salient differences exist in the ways teachers respond to female and male students. "Teachers praise boys more than girls, give boys more academic help and are more likely to accept boys' comments during classroom discussions" (Sadker and Sadker, 1991: 43). The researchers note that while teachers tend to give boys detailed information on how to accomplish a task on their own, they are more likely to perform the task for girls rather than provide them with directions. Similarly, teacher feedback to male students is more precise and encouraging than feedback offered to girls (see also Acker, 1994). Sadker and Sadker suggest that this enforcement of girls' passivity in the classroom not only detracts from their learning experiences, but also results in lower college entry test scores (SATs) later in their educational careers.

Contrary to teachers' perceptions, Sadker and Sadker report that boys, not girls, vocally dominate the classroom, whether the subject is mathematics, science, or language arts. Boys are eight times more likely to call out answers than girls, and teachers are far more likely to accept and condone this behaviour in boys than in girls (see also Crawford and MacLeod, 1990; Spender, 1989). Moreover, the researchers also observed a behaviour they term "mind sex"; once a teacher calls on a student of one sex, the teacher tends to continue calling upon children of that same sex. Since boys tend to be called upon more in the first place, and are more apt to call out answers without being called upon, they receive a disproportionate amount of teacher attention and dominate class discussion. The Sadker and Sadker research documents the tenacity of gender differentiation in the process of education and suggests that, in various ways, teachers' behaviour works to foster dependence in girls and independence in boys.

Challenging sexism within the school system is increasingly recognized as being of fundamental importance in Canada. The 1970 Canadian Royal Commission on the Status of Women made the following recommendations: "adoption of textbooks that portray both sexes in diversified roles and occupations; provision of career information about the broad field of occupational choice for girls; improved availability of sport programs for both sexes; development of educational programs to meet the special needs of rural and immigrant women and of Indian and Inuit girls and young women; and the continuing education of women with family responsibilities" (quoted in Mackie, 1991: 158). Almost 30 years later, some improvement can be noted; however, difficulties remain. Although textbooks using gender-neutral language and images are being adopted, "[b]ecause of budget constraints, the shelf life of many text books is 15 to 20 years [and] [e]ven some of the new materials are disappointing in their portrayal of women (Gaskell et al., 1989/1995: 114).

Gaskell et al., (1989/1995) note a trend in Canada since the 1970s, towards a more integrated curriculum in which boys and girls learn, for example, both auto mechanics and cooking. In the early 1980s, the Toronto Board of Education appointed a women's studies representative to ameliorate specific aspects of sexism within elementary and secondary schools. Since that time, school boards in many (but unfortunately not all) other jurisdictions across Canada have made similar appointments. As well, new programs specifically designed to reduce gender stereotyping are slowly being implemented in many of our country's schools. Among the pioneering programs were "Boys for Babies" and "Snakes and Snails."

"Boys for Babies" began as a pilot project in 1982 at the Toronto Board of Education, sponsored by the Woman's Studies division of the Board and modeled after an American program "Oh, Boy! Babies!" The goal of this program was to enrich masculine roles in relation to nurturant behaviour and childcare. Run on a voluntary basis (and therefore most likely to appeal to boys already predisposed to reduced gender stereotyping) with a maximum enrolment of eight students, pre-adolescent boys learn to care for, feed, diaper, and bathe babies, two hours a week over a period of six weeks. According to the creator of the program, Nancy Hart, the program offers "a learning experience which effectively validates and rewards caring and nurturing feelings and behaviours, in a boys-only context, just at the age when boys are most urgently concerned with learning how 'to be a man'" (Toronto Board of Education, undated: 1). Pairs of boys are assigned as caregivers to each infant and sharing responsibility using a cooperative team approach is felt to be an important part of the learning experience. A spin-off program for children of both sexes was developed in the mid-1980s for the Scarborough Board of Education as part of the family studies component of the grades seven and eight curricula.

"Snakes and Snails" is a program aimed at boys and girls in grades four through eight, with the goal of encouraging students to think critically about sex and gender stereotypes and, ultimately, to create a broader vision of both male and female gender roles. The first component of the program focuses on males in nontraditional occupations with text interviews with a homemaker, a day-care worker, a dancer, and a nurse. Instructions are provided for group projects in which students locate and interview men and women in nontraditional fields. A second section, which focuses on sex stereotypes within the media, promotes discussions of stereotypes within popular songs, rock videos, television, advertising, magazines, and comic books.

Recently, "all-girl" math and science classes have been initiated within a limited number of school districts to encourage young women to enter, and excel at, nontraditional areas of study. For example, at O'Neill Collegiate and Vocational Institute in Oshawa, Ontario, the STEM (Science, Technology, English, Mathematics) program is designed to encourage more girls to pursue studies in these subject areas and to discourage them from dropping these courses as soon as they are no longer compulsory. Although still in the experimental stage, the girls involved report feeling more comfortable about asking ques-

Box 4.4	No Boys Allowed: The Linden School, a "Woman-Centered School"

The term "girls' school' conjures up images of privilege, comfort, and exclusivity, of a "prim, pious academy of obedience training designed to be a finishing school for the daughters of the rich" (Cannon, 1995:18). But the Linden School, Canada's first self-avowedly "woman-centered" school, proclaims itself a "girls' school" with a difference. If the early Canadian feminists sought to liberate women by achieving access to boys' schools, the "Linden promise" is "to listen to your daughter's voice, provide an excellent academic programme,...include the contributions of women in history, science, and the arts, and to give your daughter the benefits of current research in education for girls" (p. 18). At Linden, students study "herstory" as well as history, and all classes emphasize women's contributions to knowledge and experience. [The school currently has a small enrollment; in June

1996, there were approximately 100 students registered. Like other private] schools for girls from Victoria to Halifax [where the price of tuition ranges] from $7,000 to $11,000 (plus extras), the cost is high—[approximately $7,700 for the 1996/97 academic year. The] price of private education likely discourages many [families] and may involve hardship for others determined to enroll their children in a private school.

The school, which received seed money from, among others, feminist philanthropist Nancy Jackman, was founded in response to research conducted at the Ontario Institute for Studies in Education which showed that between [ages] 12 and 16, the self-esteem of young women decreased significantly. This lowered self-esteem, it was suggested, discouraged young women from school achievement and led to a host of problematic behaviours such as dropping out and engaging

tions and speaking out in class because they do not have to fear teasing or "put-downs" from boys. They also report that the same-sex environment is "less distracting" than co-ed classes and allows them to concentrate more fully on their work (White, 1996). Similarly, all-girl schools, such as the Linden School (discussed in Box 4.4) have been created to allow young girls to maximize the advantages they can reap from their educational experience. However, despite the introduction of such programs and facilities, it would be presumptuous to suppose that equal attentiveness to the issue of sexism marks every school in Canada, or that the process of education more generally provides identical messages to young women and men. To paraphrase Mark Twain, school may continue to interfere with an individual's ability to get an education.

Dummying Down During Early Adolescence

Developmentalists have long noted that the self-esteem of girls declines during late childhood and early adolescence (Gilligan, 1982; Gilligan et al., 1990). Similarly, academic performance (particularly in certain subjects such as mathematics and the physical sciences)

in early sexual activity. A major factor in young women's lessened self-esteem, it was suggested, stemmed from the "silencing" of women's voices. The founders noted research findings that reported male voices tended to dominate the classroom, that teachers respond more attentively to male students than to female students (offering males more constructive criticism as well as praise), and that teachers grade assignments submitted by males on the quality of their ideas—not, as in the case of females, on the neatness or attractiveness of their submission. Finally, girls' peer groups at co-ed schools often advised their own members to "play dumb" in class so that they did not "scare off boys." The message of co-education, they deduced, could be much less than truly liberating.

In Alberta, single-sex schools for girls [have emerged] as part of the charter school movement. Charter schools, directed by [a council of teachers, parents and others, but] financed by local boards of education, have been suggested as one way to ensure that the special wishes of parents are accommodated. [For example, in Edmonton, the Nellie McClung school offers girls in grades 7 and 8 the opportunity to learn about women (Mitchell, 1995).] However, is it necessary to send one's daughter to [an all-girls' school—or a feminist school—]to ensure gender equity in Canadian education? According to Myra Novogrodsky, coordinator of Women's and Labour Studies at the Toronto Board of Education,... private schools such as Linden offer only a partial answer to the problem of sexism: "It's easy to make the choice if you have the money, but [parents who send their children to Linden] are only postponing the problem, not solving it. The problem of gender equity is a problem of society at large. Girls can't stay in an expensive cocoon. The problem will appear later—in college or in their career. I just hope they'll be sufficiently empowered to deal with it" [in Cannon, 1995].

Source: Henslin and Nelson, 1996: 499–500.

begins to decline, resulting in an increased gap between average performance scores of males and females. As we have already seen earlier, much of the explanation for this dwindling has been located within the structure of the school system in general and, in particular, in the dynamics of teacher-student interactions within the classroom itself. In a later section we shall consider the influence of gender ideologies and students' aspirations for the future. However, other factors also contribute to the process, including relations between male and female peers.

One aspect of this phenomenon pertains to the sexual harassment of girls by their male peers. Larken (1993), for example, chronicles young women's complaints of crotch grabbing, breast pinching, and being publicly "rated" as they walk down the school corridors. According to Larkin, girls as young as 10 reported that imitation "gang bangs" had taken place on school playgrounds in Canada. Especially during the junior-high-school grades of seven to nine, but occurring even earlier, boys tend to impose their own sexual agendas upon girls. Their actions take the forms of staring at girls' breasts, commenting directly upon body sizes and shapes, sending notes asking for or demanding sexually explicit acts from girls, and physical touching behaviour, some of which is "accidental" and some of which is deliberate and conducted with full awareness of both the boys and the girls. These behaviours go beyond "harmless" flirting and teasing.

Certain activities have long been a part of the school system since at least the early 1950s. Snapping bra straps ("summer, winter, fall, spr-ing,") name calling, and writing comments on the washroom walls are nothing new to male-female interactions during junior high school days, both within and outside of actual classroom walls. Indeed, a not atypical explanation given to a young girl who complained that a boy was teasing her, tripping her, or acting towards her in a generally obnoxious manner has been to say, "Oh, he must like you or he wouldn't act that way" or, alternatively, the verbal shrug of "Boys will be boys." Until recently, the general nondirect advice given to young girls has been to "just ignore them and they will eventually go away (and harass someone else)." What appears to be new, part of a long-term progression, is the direct and explicit nature of the unwanted verbal and nonverbal sexual behaviour.

Such activities lead to an increased awareness on the part of girls about their "womanhood," and about the nature of power differentials between the sexes. Harassment is, of course, a means of "putting women in their place." Young girls learn that their bodies are potential magnets for attraction, wanted and unwanted, from boys and men. Such attention forces girls to contemplate the power of their bodies, the role of their physical attractiveness against other options, their own power relative to that of males generally, and to begin to actively consider their actual options. Harassment can contribute to dummying down insofar as it stresses the traditional stereotypes of femininity and the "place" of women even within an educational setting.

Future Aspirations

Boys and girls, throughout childhood and adolescence, are asked constantly by parents, kin members, personal friends, and well-meaning strangers as to what they plan to be or do when they "grow up." The questions are prompted by our achievement-oriented value system, which proclaims that anyone can be and do whatever he or she wants or dreams. With this freedom to be the person of one's choice comes the responsibility of selecting and planning one's future. While young children initially proffer wildly unattainable goals such as fictional heroes ("Superman"; "Barbie") or inanimate objects ("a fire truck"), increasingly more narrowly defined and potentially attainable outcomes are announced in late childhood ("Supreme Court judge"; "Miss Universe") and adolescence ("lawyer"; "sociologist").

Plans for the future slowly become based upon more accurate perceptions of past, present, and future personal and societal realities. Boys and girls examine the world in which they currently participate, try to anticipate what that world will be like in the future, attempt to envision their future selves in that world, and then try to determine ways of getting there from here. As their understanding grows regarding how our society actually operates, they begin to comprehend that our societal ideals of unlimited possibilities most often translate into actualities of more limited probabilities when social inequities of ethnicity, social class, sex, gender, and even age are taken into account. In other words, what boys and girls would ideally like to do and be increasingly becomes divorced from what they can realistically expect to do and be, especially for those who are members of disadvantaged social categories.

Traditional general theories of *vocational choice* (e.g., Ginzberg, 1972; Ginzberg et al., 1951; Super, 1967) suggest that occupational aspirations and actual selections progress through a series of stages throughout childhood, adolescence, and early (even middle, in the case of Super's theory) adulthood. Choices are made in response to evolving individual internal capabilities and changing environmental opportunities and experiences. More reflective of a male perspective, these theories examine vocational choice, and by implication educational aspirations, in isolation from other issues related to gender and to family aspirations. More recent theorizing specifically focusing upon women (e.g., Hochschild, 1990; Larwood and Gutek, 1987; Levinson, 1996) expands the scope of inquiry to include vocational choice as part of a more comprehensive series of choices.

Larwood and Gutek (1987) argue that women's pathways towards occupational success or towards a more traditional scenario differ depending upon varying combinations of the following: career preparation, occupational and marital opportunities, whether they work or not after marriage, whether they work or not after childbirth, and the timing of entry or re-entry into the paid-work sphere. These paths are obviously dependent upon decisions made at various points over the life course regarding education, paid work, marriage, and family, and the real or anticipated links between all of them.

Hochschild (1990: 15–18) argues that a key element in these decisions lies in the development during adolescence of a woman's **gender ideology**, wherein she decides whether she wants to identify principally with the home sphere or the work sphere, and whether she wants to have less, more, or the same amount of power in her marriage as her husband. By implication, this gender ideology also includes whether a woman envisions marriage, childbearing, and childrearing as central, peripheral, or nonexistence components of her future. Hochschild claims that ideologies are developed by synthesizing certain cultural ideals with feelings about what has been experienced thus far in life, at home and at school, and with opportunities expected in the future. Adolescents match their personal assets (as best as they can evaluate them) against the opportunities they perceive being made available to men or women similar to themselves and develop an ideology that makes sense of themselves in the world, both for now and for the foreseeable future. Consistent with a gender perspective, Hochschild's suggestions reinforce the notion that adult women and men are products of the combined interaction of socialization, structural opportunities within a society, and active selections made by individuals.

Hochschild (1990: 15–16) identifies three major types of ideologies. **Traditionals** want a woman to identify with her activities at home, want her husband to base his identification on his paid work, and want a wife to have less power than a husband. **Egalitarians** want husband and wife either to identify with the same sphere—mainly home or mainly work—or with the same balance between the two spheres, and also want power to be shared within a marriage. A **Transitional** woman wants to identify with both her work and home, but wants her husband to base his identity on work. A Transitional man is in favour of his wife working in the paid-labour force, but still expects her to take the main responsibility at home while he maintains his traditional orientation to paid work with little participation at home. The marital power expectations of Transitionals is presumably closer to those of Traditionals than Egalitarians, although Hochschild is silent on this point.

Levinson (1996: 39–40) documents the continuing strength of an ideology he entitles the *Traditional Marriage Enterprise,* wherein women and men are expected to identify femininity with participation solely or primarily in the domestic sphere, masculinity with the public (and particularly the occupational) sphere, and authority in both spheres with men. He claims that our society has evolved to the point where "it cannot allow women to remain full-time homemakers" and that, for individual women, such an option is becoming less feasible and less attractive (Levinson, 1996: 46). However, the internal image of the "Traditional Homemaker Figure" (Levinson, 1996: 49) still exerts a powerful influence over the wishes, dreams, and decision-making processes of North American women, beginning in early adolescence and throughout their adult lives.

The relatively new antithetical internal image of the "Anti-Traditional Figure" now provides a counterpoint ideology. Levinson argues that the relative power exerted by the two internal Figures waxes and wanes for most women in contemporary North America over the course of their adolescent and adult lives. The Anti-Traditional Figure stresses the need for women to become "more independent, seek more in life than domesticity, acquire occupational skills, defer having a family until you establish yourself as a responsible, competent adult, able to take care of yourself, especially financially" (Levinson, 1996: 55). This woman will invest less of herself and her sense of femininity in marriage and family life while seeking additional satisfactions and a meaningful sense of identity within the extradomestic sphere. The strength of the Anti-Traditional Figure's appeal appears to be somewhat weakened in our society by the lack of a consistently positive image of the successful, happy, career woman. One of the respondents in Levinson's sample states:

> My image was that she had to be cold-hearted...grasping...cruel...embittered, frustrated, wishing she had done anything just to be sitting by the fireside knitting in the evening with children. The fear of success isn't the fear of succeeding per se but the fear of what consequences it would have....total personal disaster. (Levinson, 1996: 54)

Such an image views marital and family success as being incompatible with career success. Adler et al. (1992/1995: 136) claim that elementary school-age girls today see their career-oriented mothers, who are successful primarily in traditionally defined "women's occupations," still being accorded secondary status within their family constellations. These perceptions place limitations upon a young female's aspirations.

Hochschild (1990: 17–18) suggests that once a personal gender ideology has been formulated, an individual then creates a **gender strategy**, by combining thoughts and deeply felt emotions about gender into a plan of action for attaining her or his goals. The strategy subsequently provides directions to an active self-socialization process designed to achieve a person's chosen ideology. Larwood and Gutek (1987) note that a young person who does not anticipate being self-supporting later in life is less likely to absorb, or even seek out, socialization lessons that could be obtained from observing the paid-work world or from paying attention to parents' discussions of their jobs or general employment conditions. In contrast, a young person who anticipates being self-supporting will pay more attention to whatever lessons are implicit or explicit in any socialization relevant to the paid-work sphere.

Boys and young adolescent males begin making decisions regarding their educational and occupational futures without directly considering future marriage and family possibilities. Within the Traditional Marriage Enterprise (Levinson, 1996) or the Traditional and the Transitional (Hochschild, 1990) ideologies, men are expected not only to identify most strongly with their occupational sphere but also to take care of their families, primarily via performing the provider role. Consequently, while the vast majority of males in Canada expect, eventually, to get married and to support a family through gainful employment, they do not anticipate that their marital and family lives will impinge significantly upon their educational or occupational career development. Plans for schooling and work are, therefore, constructed independently of plans for marriage and family (DiBenedetto and

Tittle, 1990). Simply put, men's educational aspirations are directly linked only to their occupational aspirations (Levinson, 1996: 77). To state a theme that recurs constantly through several of our chapters, the majority of Canadian and American males, past and present albeit to a lesser degree today, consider marriage and family life to be less central to their life plans and to their ongoing lives than do females.

In contrast, girls and adolescent women have traditionally created their educational and vocational choices in light of their anticipations of a future marriage and family life. School, paid work, marriage, and family are all planned interdependently (DiBenedetto and Tittle, 1990). Research on adolescents during the 1950s, 1960s, and 1970s (e.g., Clausen, 1972: 474, 507; Douvan and Adelson, 1966; Lowenthal et al., 1975: 16) found that a majority of females claimed they could not make long-range career plans as they intended to get married. The shape and direction of their lives after that would depend primarily upon the needs, wants, and plans of husbands and children. These women's educational aspirations were, therefore, linked only to their marital aspirations (Levinson, 1996: 77).

Recent research on university and college students (e.g., Machung, 1989; Spade and Reese, 1991/1995) reflects the orientations of a select group of young adults. These respondents have already made decisions to continue their education beyond the secondary school level, to postpone marriage and family life for an extended period of time, and to not participate full-time in the paid- labour market at that particular moment. The women interviewed by Machung (1989), while intending to have full-time paid-work careers, acknowledge that their work plans will likely be interrupted by the lives and plans of their husbands and children. Both male and female students in the Spade and Reese (1991/1995) study fully expect work and family life to play important roles in their lives. However, men are much more likely to expect their spouses to not work at some point in the future, than are women. Women are much more likely to place a greater emphasis upon the importance of family roles such as housework, marriage and kinship work, and childcare, than are husbands and the potential husbands agree this should be the case. Balancing paid work and family life is clearly a task more likely anticipated by university-aged women than by men.

Ellis and Sayer (1986) find that even though young Canadian female school children are aware that women can enter into nontraditional jobs, few indicate they have made or will make these choices for themselves. The vast majority of girls aged between six and fourteen in this national Labour Canada study anticipate that they will get married, be supported by their husbands, and "never need to have a full-time paying job." Even though these Traditional ideologies may well undergo significant revisions over the adolescent and adult years, their current existence will exert an influence on girls' life decisions, especially at school, during early and middle adolescence.

Diamond (1987) indicates that research finds gender differences in career decisions beginning to appear in the "value" stage of Ginzberg's vocational-choice framework (Ginzberg, 1972; Ginzberg et al., 1951). These differences manifest themselves by the ages of 14–15, typically around grades eight or nine, or the same time that gender ideologies are being constructed. Schools begin requiring students to select courses from a range of options during the middle school years, usually between grades seven to nine. Upon confronting these choices, young adolescents begin to lay the groundwork for their immediate and long-term plans in the areas of education, paid work, and even family life.

Not surprisingly, the educational and occupational aspirations (if any) of women will be directed towards different ends and take different paths depending upon the strength of their internal Traditional or Anti-Traditional Figures. If a girl elects to follow a traditional path, she will be more sensitive to what she perceives male expectations of females in general, and potential wives in particular, should be like. If the perceptions include an apparent male injunction against women appearing to be too intelligent, too competitive for grades or awards, or too interested in nontraditional educational and occupational streams, a girl may "dummy down," become less competitive, or select a more traditional set of educational and vocational aspirations.

Wilson (1996: 121) notes that young women in Canada generally do not receive, nor gravitate towards, nor utilize the same type of educational opportunities as do men. Young women tend to be found in secondary and postsecondary educational streams that restrict their future occupational choices as a consequence of the tendency, for example, to avoid taking sufficient studies in middle and high school in subjects such as mathematics. Sells (1980) refers to mathematics as a "critical filter" for the occupational choices of young people, particularly women. Without a substantial grounding in mathematics, a person is virtually excluded from professional careers in physics, chemistry, medicine, engineering, architecture, economics, business administration, electronics, and computer sciences, all highly prestigious and rapidly growing fields that typically offer lucrative salaries, career ladders for promotions, and the potential for decent pensions. Just as mathematics has served as a filtering device for all students, but particularly women, computer literacy and proficiency also performs a crucial filtering function today and will continue to do so for the foreseeable future.

As we have already noted, selection of education and training is also partially dependent on the real and perceived opportunities a student believes are now and will be available (Hochschild, 1990; Larwood and Gutek, 1987; Wilson, 1996). However, as Wilson notes (1996: 120–124), gender differences in ideologies and the types of education already completed have been used in the past by employers as screening devices for segregating females into certain jobs. Younger women, during adolescence and even young adulthood, after noting the apparent occupational distribution of older women, often make education and vocation selections that fit the existing, apparently unchanging, labour market. As a consequence of these dynamics, a vicious circle appears to operate, in which past opportunities restrict present preparations and present preparations restrict future opportunities.

As suggested by the gender perspective, neither a process focusing exclusively upon socialization, nor one focusing exclusively upon structural opportunities, will address the relevant issues adequately. Breaking the vicious circle requires, based upon our current understanding of the processes of vocational choice, interventions along a combination of different dimensions. Further desegregation of the occupational structure will provide greater opportunities to which females in childhood and adolescence can aspire. In-school interventions for grades six to nine to influence the vocational choice of both young women and men can take various forms, ranging from bringing successful female career role models in nontraditional business, academia, and science occupations into the schools to talk about their lives, revising the school curriculum in terms of textbooks, course offerings, and vocational counseling, to creating all-girl public middle schools (such as Emily Murphy Junior High school in Edmonton or the Linden School in Toronto as discussed in Box 4.4) designed to forestall the "dummying down" phenomenon. Out-of-school interventions can include "take your daughter to work" days and pressuring the mass media to provide more realistic, yet still positive, images of successful Anti-Traditional Figures.

While we are witnessing all of these changes on a small scale throughout Canada during the 1990s, their impact has yet to be determined. Programs of change oriented towards women only will provide partial solutions at best to the perceived problems. Unless and until programs are also aimed at men, in an attempt to alter not only their ideologies and strategies for their own lives, but also their preferred ideologies and strategies for women in general and potential wives and children in particular, the chances of meaningful change among both men and women are reduced. Young and older women and men currently living in Canada have already created educational, occupational, marital, and familial aspirations within the framework of choice and opportunity available in the recent past. Present participation levels in postsecondary education, paid and unpaid work, and in intimate relationships reflect those frameworks.

Postsecondary Education in Canada

Enrolments in Canadian elementary and secondary schools increased significantly over the period between the end of World War II and 1970–71, largely as a function of the increased fertility levels associated with our baby boom. While fertility rates can also account for much of the enrolment explosion in university and community colleges during the late 1960s and throughout the 1970s, the continued growth of post-secondary school enrolments since that time are largely unrelated to earlier fertility levels (McVey and Kalbach, 1995: 322). Within our "credential society" (Collins, 1979), the increasing ability of employers to demand a more highly educated work force—despite the lack of evidence in support of the notion that today's jobs actually require the requested levels of technical, specialized, and general knowledge sophistication—has created an academic credentials inflation where the economic value of certificates, diplomas, and degrees is declining. In consequence, more and more Canadians are staying in school longer to pursue even higher credentials.

As we have pointed out, social class membership exerts a significant influence upon the likelihood of individuals attending a postsecondary educational institution. Not only does social class influence whether a person will continue beyond secondary school, but social class also influences what type of schooling will be obtained. "Children from the upper classes cluster in the most costly and prestigious private schools. Middle-class young people are most likely to attend state colleges and universities, and those with the fewest resources are most likely to enroll in community colleges" (BacaZinn, 1993: 230). Although the quote is taken from an American source, the generalization applies within the Canadian context. Just as upper-class families are likely to enrol their offspring in a handful of selected private secondary schools scattered across our country, with more found in southern Ontario than any other region because of demographic and monetary reasons, so too are those families likely to pressure young adults to attend one of a limited number of universities in Canada, the United States, or Britain. While Canada does not have truly "private" universities such as are found in the United States, some universities in southwestern Ontario and Quebec have a reputation across the rest of the country of being "country clubs," known as much for the social-class locations and aspirations of their student members as their faculty and programs of study.

While the biggest growth rate of men's enrolment at community colleges and university occurred following the end of World War II, the most significant increases in women's enrolments have occurred since the early 1970s (Normand, 1995: 18). As can be seen in Table

4.1, women's proportionate contribution to full-time enrolments at universities has increased noticeably, particularly at the level of graduate studies, between the 1972–73 and 1992–93 academic years. In 1991–92, women accounted for 53 percent of undergraduate enrolments at universities and the same percentage of full-time enrolments at community colleges in the previous year (Normand, 1995: 21).

TABLE 4.1	Women as Percentage of Full-time Enrolment, by Education Level, Canada, 1972–73 to 1992–93		
Education Level	**1972–73**	**1981–82**	**1992–93**
Undergraduate	43	50	53
Master's	27	41	46
Doctoral	19	31	35

Source: Adapted from Normand, 1995: 18.

Despite their overall increases as part of the growing student body working towards the attainment of higher academic credentials, women are still concentrated in traditionally female-dominated fields of studies at universities (see Table 4.2), community colleges, and trade apprenticeship programs (Normand, 1995). Female students are most likely to be concentrated at both undergraduate and graduate levels in university programs related to health, education, fine arts, and humanities. Participation levels in mathematics, engineering, and the physical and applied sciences remain relatively low despite concentrated efforts both inside and outside of university settings to attract more female students to these fields.

TABLE 4.2	Women as a Percentage of Full-Time Enrolment, by Field and Level of Study, Canada, 1992–93		
Field of Study	**Undergraduate**	**Master's**	**Doctoral**
Health professions	68	62	43
Education	67	66	60
Fine and applied arts	62	59	46
Humanities	61	56	46
Agriculture/biological sciences	59	50	33
Social sciences	54	47	45
Mathematics/physical sciences	30	27	19
Engineering/applied sciences	19	18	11

Source: Adapted from Normand, 1995: 19.

The data presented in Table 4.2 also indicate that while women's proportional participation rates continue beyond attainment of an undergraduate degree to remain basically constant in master's degree programs, the proportions drop noticeably in most fields of study at the doctoral program level with the exception of the social sciences. Still, women constitute the majority of students in only one area, namely the traditional field of education. To the extent that possession of higher academic credentials is a qualification required for entry into the decision-making levels of power in related professions, women are still less likely to be able to exert a significant influence in fields other than education.

Of all full-time enrolments at community colleges, women constitute the primary student component in programs of study such as secretarial services (96 percent), educational and counseling services (90 percent) and nursing (89 percent), and are highly visible only for their relative rarity in programs related to the natural sciences (32 percent), mathematics and computing sciences (30 percent) and engineering and related technologies (12 percent) (Normand, 1995: 21). Of the 15 largest programs in 1992, women accounted for less than 2 percent of the trade-apprenticeship enrolments in automobile repairs and mechanics, brick laying, carpentry, construction or industrial electrician, heavy-duty equipment mechanics, millwrighting, plumbing, refrigeration, sheet metal work, pipe fitting and welding programs (Normand, 1995: 21). Women do dominate, however, in hair stylist programs and account for about 22 percent of those in apprentice cook programs.

In terms of full-time university enrolments, women constitute the statistical majority among students under the age of 25 and over the age of 29 (Normand, 1995: 20). About 40 percent of women and 30 percent of men at universities during the 1992–93 academic years were enrolled as part-time students (Normand, 1995: 19). Attending a university part-time is particularly common among women over the age of 25 (Normand, 1995: 20), suggestive of a range of motivations from upgrading previously-obtained skills to enhance present or anticipated employment to combining further education with other, most likely family-related, obligations. Regardless of the notable increases in full-time and part-time enrolments of women in post-secondary educational institutions, we must bear in mind that nearly 60 percent of Canadian men and women did not possess any formal education beyond the high school level in 1991 (McVey and Kalbach, 1995: 323; Normand, 1995: 21).

SYMBOLIC REPRESENTATIONS OF GENDER

For many Canadians, the June 1993 election of Kim Campbell as Conservative Party leader and, by ascension shortly after, as the first female Prime Minister of Canada, seemed testament to the equality of men and women in our society. However, despite this presumption, newspaper and magazine coverage of Campbell, both during and following the Conservative-party leadership campaign, suggested otherwise. Why was Campbell referred to in a familiar fashion as "Kim" while her male competitors were referred to with use of their surname only? Why did the media latch on to leadership candidate Jean Charest supporters' eagerness to identify Campbell as a "divorcée" who, "with the speed of a hummingbird...flits from marriage to marriage" and suggest in their presentations that her marital status constituted proof that Campbell was the type of woman who "can't seem to figure out where she's coming from or where she wants to go—aside from up" (Maclean's, 12 July 1993: 68)? Why did the media direct attention to Campbell's "mesmerizing" green eye-colour, while viewing such trivia as irrelevant in their reporting on her male competitors? Why did the media widely disseminate Campbell's studio photograph portrait in which she wore a lawyer's robe and, ostensibly, nothing else, and gush over her "exquisite shoulders" and "overt, flaunting sexuality" (*London Sunday Times*) and dub her "the new Canadian covergirl" (*National Enquirer*), but did not draw comparable attention to the lack of similar qualities in her male competitors? (Lest we think an undue emphasis upon physical appearance was unique only to political campaigning in 1993, see Box 5.1 for advice given to women politicians in 1997).

When asked to comment on Campbell's leadership victory, leader of the NDP, Audrey MacLaughlin, responded that she would have preferred the election of a man who was

Box 5.1 — A Woman's Guide To Success?

A Liberal election guide that recommends women candidates cover up fatigue with makeup while avoiding loud colours and baubles in their wardrobes is being panned as patronizing and sexist. The 42-page booklet *Women Working to Win* has gone out to Grit female candidates in preparation for the election expected in early June.…For example, it advises that a candidate's wardrobe is as important as her election policy, strategy and organization. It also warns against wearing sunglasses: "Don't create the impression that you have something to hide."…[Also o]n the outlist: flashy, expensive cars; shiny jewelry; dangle earrings and bracelets; loud and numerous rings. On the in-list: up-to-date makeup; broken-in shoes; classic-look hairdo (it gets more mileage).…Body language is important too: "You create a positive impression with firm handshakes, good eye contact, confident carriage and good posture.…Don't let it show that you are tired."…

Controversial How-Tos

- A classic (hair) look will always give you more mileage.

- Using sexist language is not a crime, but it is a mistake.

- Campaigns and politics are supposed to be fun. Remember to laugh.

- Patterns, checks and pinstripes tend to run together on the screen causing a moire effect. However, large patterns can be worn.

- Don't canvass with a purse; it will get in your way.

- You want the audience to notice you, not your accessories…

Quotable

"On a brighter note, when all candidates are exhausted, concealing the circles under your eyes will convince perspective voters that you have unlimited (and untapped) resources and energy." … "Your wardrobe is a reflection of you; therefore it should be planned with the same care that you define your policy, develop your strategy, and plan the organization of your campaign team."

Source: Jack Aubry, "Election guide offers Liberal women hair tips."*Kitchener-Waterloo* [Ontario] *Record*, 5 April 1997: A4.

concerned with "women's issues" to the election of a woman who was not. The identification of some issues (day care, reproductive rights, violence) as being of concern to only women, while other issues (the economy, crime, globalization and international relations) are identified of concern to all Canadians, is a commonly used, but vexatious, linguistic tactical device. Why, within our supposedly egalitarian society and *despite* Campbell's election, are issues such as pay equity, the feminization of poverty, childcare, and the right to protection from physical and sexual violence commonly expressed as "women's" rather than fundamental "human" rights issues? Why was Campbell's identification as either a "profeminist" or an "antifeminist" a continuing issue of contention and debate? R.E.A.L. Women gleefully reported in 1991 that, according to a Decima Research poll, 66 percent of women across Canada did not consider themselves to be feminists (*Reality*, 1991: 1). What is a R.E.A.L. woman and what is a "feminist," both in the minds of survey respondents and in the minds of their avowed enemies, R.E.A.L. women? Since the acronym R.E.A.L. stands for "Realistic-Equal-Active-for Life," are we to assume that "feminists" stand for "unrealistic-unequal-passive-for death"? Why are "feminist" and "feminism" associated with unlovely and unloveable characteristics and why are both terms "four-letter" sneer words in the minds of so many Canadians?

LANGUAGE

At first glance, you might conclude that we seem overly concerned with words being bandied about as part of the conventional jockeying for position and general nastiness that attends political and social-movement campaigns. However, these are not "just" words. Two linguists in the 1930s, Edward Sapir and Benjamin Whorf, concluded that the common sense ideas of words being merely labels that people attach to things, and languages being simply different inventory systems for the same reality, are both wrong. Building upon the work of Sapir, Whorf developed the hypothesis that conception and perception are not only *expressed* through language, but are actually *shaped* by language. Since a way of looking at the world is embedded within a language, learning a language involves learning not only words, but also particular ways of thinking and seeing (Sapir, 1949; Whorf, 1956). Expressed in somewhat extreme terms, language determines what we come to understand as reality. Labeling a politician as a "feminist" or an "antifeminist" shapes our understanding of her. Drawing more attention to her eye colour or her exquisite shoulders than to her party platform suggests that gender form is more important than political content. Identifying some issues as relevant only to women directs men's attention away from them and towards issues of importance to humans.

The implications of the *Sapir-Whorf hypothesis*, which alerts us to how extensively language and other symbolic representations affect us, are far reaching. Language is the "inescapable socializer" (Richardson, 1988: 16), since, regardless of the amount and kind of exposure an individual has to any particular agency of socialization throughout life, most socialization occurs on a verbal level. Language thus becomes the principal means of disseminating a society's ideology on gender. Acquisition of our language provides the basis for developing the gender schema identified by Bem (1983/1995, see Chapter 2) as an integral part of encoding, and gendering, our social and physical worlds, and developing actions, feelings, and thoughts about those worlds. Our images of women and men are an outcome of a process of judgment and evaluation that distinguishes certain forms of behaviour as appropriate or inappropriate, acceptable or unacceptable (see also Berryman-Fink and Verderber, 1985; Rowland, 1984, 1986). These processes and resulting sentiments are all shaped by and conveyed by our system of language. To change a person's mind and his or her conception of reality, we have to change that person's language.

As we noted in an earlier chapter, English is a very sexist language (Eichler, 1984). A major contributor to the sexism systemic in Canadian society is the gender imagery embedded in our language. Attitudes towards, and beliefs about, women and men are encoded in our symbolic vocabularies so as to preserve our patriarchal heritage. Sometimes our attitudes and beliefs are expressed directly; most often they are expressed subtly and indirectly via the words we select to express ourselves in everyday speech. Individuals may deny being self-consciously sexist in their deeds, yet remain unaware of the extent to which they convey sexist sentiments in their words. Basow (1986: 129) suggests that our language promotes inequalities between men and women through the processes of ignoring, stereo-typing, and deprecating.

Ignoring

To be ignored means to be excluded, to be rendered invisible. The major difficulty in at-tempting to grasp hold of techniques of ignoring is that, by definition, we are trying to focus upon that which is not present. The only way to become aware of what is invisible is to concentrate first upon what is visible and then attempt to ascertain what is missing. One of the most common techniques for ignoring women occurs with reference to the use in English of the so-called generic noun (and sometimes verb) *man* and the related pronouns of *he, him,* and *his.* As a generic noun, "man" is supposedly a synonym for *human being* and its use is designed to include the entire human race. Read the following paragraph and judge whether you feel included or excluded.

A legislator is often described, by men of letters who hold bachelor's or master's de-grees, as being a "man of the people." We are also told by his supporters at a rally in front of the Family of Man sculptures in downtown Calgary (following an invocation offered by a man of the cloth) that he is the "best man for the job." Attempting to understand what his constituents desire, and to become a man for all seasons, the legislator hires pollsters to act as middlemen, charged with the task of surveying his fellow man. As a statesman, the leg-islator relies upon those who devote their manpower and manhours posing questions, man-to-man, to the man in the street. Pollsters solicit the views of the thinking man, the Renaissance man, the rational economic man, the working man, the common man, as well as the self-made man. In cases where the interests of big business or big government (some-times known as "Big Brother") threatens the interests of the little man, the legislator, as a man of good will, speaks up for the forgotten man. If re-election is to occur in a system of one man-one vote, every schoolboy knows that John Q. Public has to be satisfied. The legislator is eager to prove himself man enough to meet the challenge of office. As a man of action and a man of his word, he is concerned to demonstrate his commitment to mankind, to the brotherhood of man; after all, all men are created equal and it would be unsports-manlike to neglect some countrymen in favour of others. Indeed, to counter such sugges-tions, the legislator is quick to announce the appointment of an ombudsman to handle, for example, accusations of wrongdoing among the boys in blue. The legislator can dispatch spokesmen—or henchmen—to deal, in workmanlike fashion, with those critics who think themselves tough guys. As we all know, every man has his price, even though man does not live by bread alone. In the worst case scenario, the legislator, being a man of the world, re-alizes, as did his forefathers ever since the beginning of Father Time, that dead men tell no tales. Being an elected official is a man-size task, and in the cutthroat world of politics, it's every man for himself.

A generic language is an exclusionary language. As Basow (1986: 130) notes, use of the supposedly generic term has the effect of making men the visible norm and women the ex-cluded exception. "Man" becomes interchangeable with biological male and woman be-comes invisible, a finding documented in empirical research on students from grade one through postsecondary education, and on respondents outside of the educational system (see Basow, 1992; Gastil, 1990; Hamilton, 1991; Khosroshahi, 1989; Miller, 1994; Miller and Swift, 1993). Miller and Swift (1993: 73) suggest that, upon reading statements such as

Box 5.2	**Project Surname: Names and Inuit Culture**

In Inuit culture, names insure the continuity of the lives of individuals, families, and communities. Names are passed from one generation to the next without regard for gender. The same namesake can live through several new people, male or female. The ties are so strong that until puberty, kinship terms, dress and behaviour often follow the namesake relationship, rather than biological sex or conventional gender identification.

> No child is only a child. If I give my grandfather's *atiq* [soul-name], to my baby daughter, she *is* my grandfather. I will call her *ataatassiaq*, grandfather. She is entitled to call me grandson....

"Discovered" by seventeenth-century explorers, the Canadian Arctic has known traders, governments, and European religion since the early 1900s. Since then, visitors have continued to interfere with the ways Inuit define and experience genders and families, and name themselves and their land....The various missionaries and public officials gave religious or bureaucratic explanations for changing Inuit names. They sought to baptize and bring Inuit into the faith (whichever faith it happened to be). Or they found the absence of surnames "confusing" and the Inuktitut names difficult to pronounce and impossible to accurately record....

Census-taking was filled with inconsistencies and absurdities. Lists followed official standards for "the Canadian family," with no attempt to understand Inuit family structures or traditions. Such understanding would have made it clear that much of the census structure was irrelevant for Inuit. Some of the "standard" categories have no parallels in Inuit culture. There are no titles such as "Dr.," "Mr.," or "Ms." There are no gender-specific pronouns—an "Inuk" is a male or female per-

"man is the highest form of life on earth," a young boy may feel proud and think "wow!" The response of a young girl, however, may be "Who? Does that mean me, too?" As you undoubtedly noticed in the previous paragraph, many other exclusionary generic terms such as "fellow," "brother," and the names of two university degrees, are interwoven into our common everyday vocabulary. All of these generic words present variations upon a male theme. The introductory lyrics of our national anthem proclaim: "O Canada, our home and native land,/True patriot love in all thy sons command." Only "sons" are commanded to be "true patriots." These words implicitly suggest that women can neither be patriots nor, if you recall the rest of the lyrics, be permitted to "stand on guard" for our country (Ontario Women's Directorate, 1992: 1). Canada is man's country.

Some women feel ignored (and/or stereotyped and/or deprecated) by the fact that the word "woman" contains the generic term "man." The "wo" prefix implies that woman is nothing more than a modified man. Of course, as we all know from our understanding in Chapter 2 of the process of fetal development, males are a biologically modified form of females. Our language, largely as a consequence of root derivations from ancient Indo-Latin languages, suggests otherwise. In an attempt to create a separatist language that supports and promotes

son. Children who were full family members according to Inuit practice were designated "boarders," "step," or "adopted" by census-takers....The concept of "head of family" or "head of household," essential to government documentation, is alien. In an Inuit extended family, the "father/husband" is not necessarily the central or most powerful person....Inuit families feature close ties, grounded in the intricate, intimate naming system. The distinction between a "real" and a "common-law" spouse is meaningful only in non-Inuit terms, for southern law....

In western tradition, a women's renaming at marriage represents the transfer of "property" (the woman) from father to husband. Inuit tradition does not include this kind of marriage tie or reidentification of the woman through the husband's identity....Inuit in the Northwest Territories were given surnames out of a misguided idea this would give them more power by making them like other Canadians....In a culture without gender-specific naming, titles, or other status designations, surnaming was absurd. Despite assurances that all was "voluntary," many people had no say in their renaming. In fact, many of them were not even present for the program in which they presumably participated....

Women were renamed in their absence, by men. One Elder remembered her confusion when her husband came home and announced their new name. It made no sense. Women didn't take their husbands' names, yet suddenly, both she and her husband had his father's last name. The new name was not just a confusion or an inconvenience, it undercut the relationship between name, name avoidance, and respect in the family. In many communities, a woman may not speak the name of her husband's father. To follow traditional practice, a woman surnamed for her husband's family would now have to avoid speaking her own last name.

Source: Abridged from Valerie Alia, "Inuit Women and the Politics of Naming in Nunavut," *Canadian Woman Studies/les cahiers de la femme*, 14 (4), 1994: 11–14.

women's distinct and independent existence, some women prefer to use the designations of "wommon" (singular form) and "wimmin" (plural form) or the all-purpose term "womyn."

Smith (1987) suggests that women's historical exclusion from the public sphere resulted in the production of both a language and culture that effectively ignores their existence. Nilsen (1993), in her analysis of "Who's Who" dictionaries of famous people, notes that famous women traditionally have been listed under their married names even when they were not commonly known under that name (e.g. Charlotte Brontë as "Mrs. Arthur B. Nicholls"). She comments that, while creating their entries, the dictionaries' editors may have believed that it "was almost indecent to let a respectable woman's name march unaccompanied across the pages of a dictionary" (Nilsen, 1993: 162). Subsuming a woman's identity under that of her husband is a practice still with us today, although it is slowly changing with the passing of older generations. It is not uncommon to hear a woman identified as, for example, "Mrs. Jean Chrétien," leaving us to assume that the Jean Chrétien with the breasts is the missus. Slowly, over the course of this century, women's total "symbolic annihilation" (Tuchman, 1978) has been replaced by only a partial annihilation (e.g., "Mrs. Aline Chrétien").

The social custom of women retaining their birth (more on the implications of that label later) names is relatively recent and has become more noticeable since the time of the latest women's movement in Canada. Historically, European folkways, and sometimes laws, dictated that women should drop their family surname upon marriage and adopt the family surname of their husband (see Box 5.2 for illustrations of the havoc caused within Inuit culture by this dominating European practice). As pointed out in Box 5.2, the European name-change custom symbolizes the exchange of property (a woman) from her parent's home and family to that of her husband and his family. While, as we noted in Chapter 3, a series of legal changes in the nineteenth and early twentieth centuries eventually granted women the right to exist as independent beings, the custom of name changing upon marriage remains a vestige of earlier traditions and contributes to a form of ignoring women's independent existence. Name changing upon marriage is a social custom, not a legal requirement, in most provinces and territories in Canada. Since 1981, women in Quebec have been legally required to retain their birth names for legal documentation purposes throughout their entire lifetimes. A woman in Quebec may use whatever name she chooses for social purposes, but in legal matters such as wills, contracts, or lawsuits, she must be identified by the name registered for her at birth.

Unfortunately, from a sociological perspective, departments of vital statistics in the provinces and territories neither tally nor publish the frequency with which women in Canada either retain or change their surnames upon marriage. Impressionistic evidence suggests that the vast majority of Canadian women still adopt their husband's surname, thus symbolically ignoring their own, or, at least traditionally, their father's family history. Some unknown, but smaller, proportions of the married female population choose to retain their birth name only, hyphenate their birth surname with the surname of their husband to form a new identifying label (which begs the question of what happens in the future when the daughter of Mr. and Mrs. Silverstein-Utumchandandi marries the son of Mr. and Mrs. Zawadowski-Papadopoulis?), or retain their birth surname in the position of a "middle" name and place their husband's surname last. Men rarely, if ever, drop their family surname and adopt the surname of their wife. Few also incorporate their wife's surname as a new "middle" name. The vast majority of men appear to simply carry on postmarriage without any symbolic changes to their identity (and frequently wonder what the fuss over names is all about anyway).

Kaplan and Bernays (1997: 139) report that women who retain their birth names "tend to be achievers and individualists who have already established their names professionally, or wish to, and see no reason to surrender them." They observe that the likelihood that a woman will retain her birth name is positively correlated with her level of education and note that, according to a 1994 survey, "[f]ewer than 5 percent of wives who do not have a college education use something other than their husband's name, compared with 15 percent of those with bachelor's degrees and more than 20 percent of those with postgraduate degrees" (in Kaplan and Bernays, 1997: 139). Empirical research on marital naming is also available from a study of 258 American-born students attending a small college in the Midwest region of the United States (Scheuble and Johnson, 1993). As in most of Canada, women in the United States are not required by any state to change their surnames upon marriage. Just more than 80 percent (81.6) of the women students in the Scheuble and Johnson study indicate they plan to change their last names to that of their husband if they marry. A small minority (7 percent) indicate having plans to adopt a hyphenated last name. Unfortunately, the researchers did not ask men about their own plans. While the majority of women (91.8 percent) agree that it is all right for a married woman to keep her "maiden" (a term we shall explore in the next section) name, only a slight majority (57 percent) of the men agree with this principle. Both men and women give similar rankings for the top-three circumstances, selected from a limited list, under which a woman can acceptably retain her maiden name, including when a woman is in a profession, likes her maiden name, and wants to keep her family name alive. However, the proportions agreeing with each of these reasons are significantly higher among women than among men. The difference in proportions agreeing that a woman can retain her birth name if she doesn't like her husband's surname (40.5 percent for women; 24 percent for men) is statistically significant. This study indicates the presence of a fairly wide agreement, in principle, that women can retain their surname selfhood. However, few women intend to do so. The vast majority of women plan to symbolically merge their identity with that of their husband and consequently run the risk of being ignored, at least linguistically. It may be, as Kaplan and Bernays (1997: 138) argue, that "[t]he woman who refuses to submit to conventional practice of taking her husband's name risks having her loyalties questioned and, except in relatively sophisticated communities, being viewed as a subversive."

When individuals talk with one another, they exchange ideas—that is, they exchange perspectives. Their words are the embodiment of their experiences of events, distilled and codified into a readily exchangeable form, mutually intelligible for people who have learned that language. However, akin to Virginia Woolf's (1977: 3) suggestion that "men's sentence is unsuited for a woman's use," feminists such as Cameron (1985), Lorde (1984), and Spender (1980) argue that the "language of patriarchy" does not allow the vantage point of women to be expressed. A male-created language neither facilitates discussion of experiences that are unique to women, nor describes the range, depth, and complexities of women's lived-in reality. Women in a male-defined culture learn to "speak the language of patriarchy, we [learn to] translate our experience in a form foreign and deprecative of us" (Martel and Peterat, 1984: 44). In the absence of an appropriate language, women become a "muted group" (Spender, 1980). "Silence has been a major weapon in men's arsenal which has prevented women and children from talking about their experiences" (Kelley, 1994: 34).

As we noted in Chapter 3, Friedan (1963) struggled to identify and discuss "the problem that has no name." Hobbes observed long ago that "[t]he power to name and diagnose, the power to make definitions is the ultimate authority." Women traditionally have lacked the "power to name." Since the 1970s, feminists have attempted to "experiment inventively with ways of wrestling linguistic domination from patriarchal control" (Frith, 1990: 158). Recent efforts to build an *inclusive language* are based on the recognition of how our language currently either excludes women, or gives unequal prominence to men. Towards this end, when the intention is to refer to the entirety of the human species, speakers are reminded that words such as "humankind," "humanity," or the "human race" all serve to "count women in." In reference to job titles, emphasis should be placed upon the work performed, rather than the gender of the person traditionally assumed to occupy the work role (e.g., fire fighter versus fireman, worker versus workman, police officer versus policeman, postal worker versus postman).

Some successes in gender-inclusivity have been achieved. In 1976, Dr. Benjamin Spock's classic *Baby and Child Care*, was reissued in gender-neutral language; in 1978, the federal Manpower and Immigration and Unemployment Commission was renamed

Employment and Immigration Canada; in 1981, feminists were successful in having the word "person" replace the generic "man" within the Canadian *Charter of Rights and Freedoms*; in 1986, the National Museum of Man was renamed the National Museum of Civilization (later, the Canadian Museum of Civilization); in 1988, the Toronto City Council voted to replace the term "alderman" with the inclusive term "councillor" (Ontario Women's Directorate, 1993: 28–29). Other city councils across Canada have moved slowly towards adopting this convention.

There are, admittedly, difficulties in constructing a neutral, yet, inclusive language. First of all, unlike Inuktitut (see Box 5.2), English lacks a truly gender-neutral pronoun aside from the objectifying word "it." Shears (1985) suggests 14 ways we may avoid the dominant use of a masculine singular pronoun such as "him" including: combining both the masculine and feminine pronouns (e.g., "he/she" or "s/he"); using the first person (e.g., I, me, we, ours); deleting, relocating or repeating the noun or using a new noun in place of a pronoun; using the plural form of a noun (they, them, their); inserting words such as "a," "an," "but" or "the" as an article or conjunction; and using the passive voice. However, Kramarae (1980: 64) earlier observes that some "gender-neutral" words have already become other than truly neutral. She notes, for example, that when the term "chairperson" is used, it is used most often in reference to a woman, while the term "chairman" is still employed to refer to incumbents who are male. Moreover, she points out that gender-neutral words are often subject to derision and quotes a letter addressed to a leader in which the writer fumes that "[i]t was interesting to see how a group with obviously *personagled* egos were able to *personipulate* an organization the size of ours into looking like a pack of fools. Chairperson indeed!" (p. 64). The fight for an inclusive language often must contend with attempts to ridicule or trivialize, especially from conservatives who either wish to further enshrine patriarchy or simply retain comfortable and comforting traditions.

It is evident that, for some conservatives, inclusive language seems contrived and ridiculous, the latest in what is decried as a campaign of "political correctness" (for example, see Fekete, 1994). The Ontario Women's Directorate (1994: 5) observes, "By replacing 'man' with 'person' wherever it appears…[those who lampoon inclusive language have] devised such clunkers as 'personipulate' and 'Personitoba.' In fact, 'manipulate' and 'manacle' are here to stay because their root is not 'man', but the Latin for hand, 'manus.'" Of course, the term "person" also strikes purists as objectionable inasmuch as the ending "son" seems to give preference to male offspring (perone, anyone?).

Objectors query whether it is really that essential to rename a "manhole cover" as either a "utility hole cover" or a "personnel access structure." While the unfamiliarity of inclusive terms may lend themselves to comic exaggeration, the consequences of sexist language are not a laughing matter. The use of male pronouns is not gender neutral. Each word is like a single drop of water, perhaps inconsequential in and of itself, but constant exposure to exclusionary words, like a steady flow of water drops, can eventually have a destructive impact upon any object.

Stereotyping

Language is the principal means by which stereotypes are conveyed and maintained. Words highlight boundaries between women and men by *selectively* drawing attention to supposedly essential gender characteristics. Some words or phrases are simple and to the point.

For example, consider the oft-heard phrase "woman driver." In that simple phrase alone, driving behaviour is accounted for solely by the femaleness of the person holding the wheel. Women drivers are supposedly different from all other kinds of drivers. Men drivers are not, since we never hear specific reference to them. The phrase "career girl" makes a twofold distinction. First, one rarely hears career "boy" and, therefore, females dedicated to a career are presented, in a deprecating fashion, as the possessors of a childlike set of qualities; second, the phrase distinguishes the referent both from all men (every hear of a "career man," except within the military?) and from all other types of women. Creation of this special phrase signifies that some women are different, atypical from the norm, and our society needs to single them out with a specific identifying label.

Other words or phrases are more complex and reverberate throughout many dimensions of gendered social life. Graham (1977: 1) asserts that the word "woman" has "been defined as something less than a lady and something more than a girl." "Lady" and "woman" are neither semantic nor symbolic equivalents according to the strictures of our language. The word "lady" is classist in its origins and like "gentlewoman" (and "gentleman"), originally referred to a person who was "well-bred" with an attendant suggestion that distinguished ancestry and pedigree were all-important to the determination of a person's moral and/or social character. While use of the word "lady" is no longer strictly used to signify a woman's social rank (witness the signs on washroom doors), it still remains an evaluative term that measures conformity to a narrow definition of femininity and to its stereotypical, stylized enactment. The naming of the "Ladies Professional Golf Association," like the term "lady golfer," suggests that, while women cannot aspire to become part of the "Professional Golf Association," they are distinguishable from, and superior to, the hoi polloi that play golf in more plebeian venues. The injunction to "act like a lady" suggests that the standards to be met are much higher than those applicable to "ordinary" women. Imagine what your reaction would be if you were asked to join the Ladies Liberation Movement. The term "little old lady" conveys images of fragility, childlike dependency, yet refinement (even in her tennis sneakers). The phrase "lady of the evening" provides a glamorous euphemism for the word "prostitute." The phrase also deflects attention from the heightened risk of violence prostitutes experience; "prostitutes are 100 times more likely to be murdered than others" (*Kitchener-Waterloo* (Ontario) *Record*, 24 May 1996: A3). The condescending term "little lady," when addressed to an adult woman, infantilizes her and suggests that she is being viewed as a child who might become a big adult lady, if, and only if, the men allow it.

The importance of participation in the paid-work world and financial success for men and of physical attractiveness and marriage for women are reinforced through referencing men by their occupational roles or titles, while describing women by their appearance and/or their relationships (e.g. "Dr. Smith and his lovely wife Stella") (Foreit et al., 1980). We are given no clue as to Dr. Smith's appearance; tellingly, adjectives describing him as either "balding, fat, and knock-kneed" or as an Antonio Banderas look-alike are seen as unnecessary. The achieved occupational status of "Dr." is considered primary for defining the male Smith (identified only by his formal last name)—not his looks. Stella's (identified only by the familiar use of her first name) major achievements apparently are those of getting married and looking lovely.

Sports Illustrated once depicted figure skater Katerina Witt thusly: "She's so fresh-faced, so blue-eyed, so ruby-lipped, so 12-car-pile-up gorgeous, 5'3" and 114 pounds of peacekeeping missile." The *Toronto Star* highlighted the 1992 space flight of Canadian astronaut Dr. Roberta Bondar with the headlines "Canadian in space does 'housework'" and "Bondar spends hour tidying up shuttle" (in Ontario Women's Directorate, 1992: 9). On 6 April 1997, radio commentators congratulated Canada's national team for winning the Women's World Hockey Championship by referring to the team as the "Maple Leafettes" and describing Lesley Reddon and Danielle Dubé as both having looked "fetching" in goal. The professional accomplishments of these women are muted and clearly considered to be of secondary importance. Witt accomplished being beautiful and Bondar's housekeeping accomplishments were so compelling that she was dispatched by Molly Maid to tidy up the space shuttle, while her male colleagues concerned themselves with more challenging scientific-breakthrough tasks. Reddon's and Dubé's singular accomplishments appear to have been that they, unlike any male goaltenders anywhere in the world who helped their team to win a championship, looked "fetching." Patrick Roy has never accomplished this feat throughout his illustrious career.

The term "Mr." does not mark a man as being either never-married (single) or ever-married (currently married, divorced, or widowed). The terms "Miss," "Mrs.," and the more recent "Ms." announce important symbolic boundaries that supposedly signify different socially meaningful "types" of women. Marital status is a more significant master status for women than for men in our society. In their survey of news stories, Foreit et al. (1980) find that, while women's marital status was reported 64 percent of the time, the marital status of men was referred to only 12 percent of the time. We noted in the previous section that women traditionally have, upon marriage, taken the surname of their husband. In Canada and other English-speaking countries, a woman's surname was referred to conventionally as her maiden name. The term "maiden" designated a never-married virginal female; that is, her "maidenhead" or hymen was intact. At least in theory, in accordance with our ideal social mores, a female "surrendered" her maidenhead and the title of maiden upon marriage and the assumption of sexual relations. Given the significant changes in sexual behaviour prior to marriage in our society (see Chapter 7), many females "lose" their maidenhead much earlier than their maiden name. The term "maiden" has now become archaic and present-day preferences are to replace that term with "birth" name to designate an ascribed name status that may or may not be altered over the course of a woman's lifetime. Any continued efforts today to invoke the stereotyped maiden image for women is also an attempt to circumscribe a female's social and sexual life.

Along with a surname change, the transformative wedding ceremony that traditionally turned her into a wife, but left him unchanged ("I now pronounce you man and wife"), also granted her the right, even the social obligation, to adopt the prefix of "Mrs.," a prefix she would retain throughout her widow years, or, frequently, after divorce. In this way, our society made an important linguistic division between never-married and at-least-once-married women. The term "Ms." arose in an attempt to avoid or cease defining and differentiating women through their relationships to men. Ms. "established 'women' as a linguistic category in its own right.…[and] symbolically elevated women to personhood from their previous commodity status in the marriage market where 'Miss' meant 'for sale,' and 'Mrs.' meant 'sold'" (Davy, 1978: 47). However, Stewart et al. (1990) note that only since 1987 would major North American newspapers such as the *New York Times* print the term "Ms." if a woman expressed this as her preference. Many women resist adopting Ms., since it might be seen as equivalent to identifying oneself as a "feminist," an identification disfavoured by many women, or an embarrassing admission that one currently lacks a relationship with a man. Adoption of Ms. can have additional consequences in our society, as researchers note that women distinguished by the titles of Miss or Mrs. are perceived as being more likeable, stronger in expressive traits (e.g., tactful, gentle), and lower in instrumental traits (e.g., leadership, competence) that identically described women differentiated only by the title Ms. (Dion and Cota, 1991). Ms. women tend to be categorized as unlikeable, tough, roughshod, strong, independent women capable of making their own way, who either do not need or do not want relationships with men. Marital status semantics stereotype women one way or another.

The stereotypes linger even after divorce, as formerly married women are customarily still referred to as Mrs., especially if a woman has children (Ehrlich and King, 1993). Although it might rankle a woman to be tied, through the conventions of language, to her former spouse, resuming her birth name can create a linguistic discontinuity between herself and her children ("My name is Mary Smith and these are my children, Harvey and Myrtal Brown"), and legally altering the surname of one's children requires the consent of the other parent. That discontinuity, combined with a desire to avoid raising the spectre of illegitimacy over her children's births, encourages most women to retain both their married surname and the prefix of Mrs. The greater likelihood of remarriage among divorced men may create multiple "Mrs. Nelsons," most of whose social identities are that of "ex- wife," all linked by a common surname to a singular "Mr. Nelson." Mr. carries no connotations of a man's present marital status, nor his marital history, suggesting that our society deems such details to be of little social importance.

Stereotyping in language also promotes an active/passive dichotomization of men and women. Generally, men are more often described in the active voice ("he seduced her; "he swept her off her feet;" "he took her hand in marriage") and women described in the passive voice ("she was wed on June 4 in a candlelit ceremony"; "she was swept away"; "she got laid"). The phrase "lost one's virginity," almost never used in reference to a male, conveys the impression of something accidental or unintentional about the process—as if a woman had inadvertently misplaced her virginity among the debris at the bottom of her handbag ("I could swear I had it with me this morning when I left the house"). The phrase also suggests that, while a woman may be chided for an act of *omission* (i.e., failing to keep her virginity in a safe place), she should not be faulted for a deliberate act of *commission* (i.e., setting out purposefully to rid herself of her virginity by seducing a man, against his wishes if necessary). In consequence, the phrase simultaneously conveys the ideas that virginity for females is important and should be safeguarded lest they "lose" it and, secondly, that women who do "lose" their virginity should not be held fully culpable for its absence.

Basow (1992: 142) provides us with another example of the active/passive distinction by noting that, "[W]hen a newspaper reports, 'Blonde found murdered,' the reader knows that the corpse is a female (men rarely are referred to solely by their hair color)." Such headlines also implicitly suggest that victimization is somehow consistent with femininity. In contrast, the subject of a headline reading "Teenager arrested for arson" is understood implicitly to be male. The construction of passive female (victim) and active male (offender) is evident. One major exception to the passivity stereotyping of women can be found in the naming of *Mother* Nature. However, this analogy is predicated not upon emphasizing the power of women, but rather upon stereotyping the unpredictability and uncontrollability of women. Since the dominant orientation of men in Western societies is directed towards "taming" nature, a similar orientation towards women is encouraged by implication.

Stereotyping in language often means that men and women who perform identical tasks are subject to different representation and evaluation. The mandate of a police complaints officer requires the incumbent to review files on citizen complaints about police officers, inform the police commission if questions are still unanswered or warrant further attention and, if necessary, recommend that the complaint be filed with a provincial Law Enforcement Appeal Board. The appointment of a female in 1983 to be the Calgary Police Commission's first police complaints monitor illustrates how language is used to frame our ideas of the stereotypical depiction of women and men. Indeed, news reports tended to highlight the congruency of a delimited and demarcated occupational role with the selection of a female. Media accounts stressed that her involvement was limited essentially to that of a glorified secretary, conducting a paper review of files with no authority to interview police officers or complainants. One newspaper article noted that the "perky former alderman [*sic*]" had given up politics to "spend more time with her sons" and a police complaints monitor was presented as the type of part-time job that facilitated her continuing education (attending Mount Royal College), motherhood, and a wide gamut of recreational pursuits (including her interests in motorcycling, hiking, skiing, kayaking, etc.). In stark contrast, when a male was selected to be Edmonton's police complaints monitor, attention was directed rather flamboyantly to his administrative and military background. Such a background, media reports suggested, would allow him to "take charge" and to act as a vigilant "watchdog" (*Edmonton Journal*, 25 February 1991: B1). Same job, different-sex occupants, vastly different language depictions promoting and reinforcing a multitude of different gender stereotypes.

Solutions to the problem of gender stereotyping via language require breaking down stereotypes by exposing their limited generalizeability and by using gender-neutral terms to emphasize the actions, thoughts, or feelings themselves, rather than the gender of the person experiencing or expressing them. As with attempts to create an inclusive language to end ignoring, the search for a nonstereotyped language has also yielded attempts that ridicule and trivialize the process. Hurricanes are renamed "himmicanes," humans become "hufems," testimony becomes "ovarimony," seminal becomes "ovarian," a seminar is turned into an "ovular," and the classic patriarchal phallocentric distinction between the "hard" (masculine) and "soft" (feminine) sciences becomes a vaginocentric distinction between the "dry" and "wet" sciences. Politically correct dictionaries and fairy tales swap one set of stereotypes for another and, somewhat depressingly, manage to become international best sellers.

Deprecating

Deprecating occurs when a term in our language carries a derogatory connotation. How often have you heard "woman driver" used in a congratulatory fashion? Deprecations can be expressed in a *direct* form such as "all men are pigs," or "dumb broad." Most often, however, deprecations are expressed in an *indirect* form that encourages sexism via subtle means. The disparaging term "sissy," a diminutive form of the word "sister," not only condemns males for being unmasculine, but also implies that sisters are of a lesser status than brothers (one never hears the greeting on streetcorners "What's happenin' sis?"). A person with a liberal or compassionate orientation towards individuals, events, or social issues is disparagingly referred to in Canada as a "bleeding heart," a two-word combination derived from female menstruation and women's supposedly emotional nature caused from being lead by their hearts and not their heads. The connotations of the term suggest that the person is thinking "just like a woman" and is to be disparaged for that fault.

The priority ordering of males and females in such common phrases as "man (or husband) and wife," "Mr. and Mrs.," "males and females," or "boys and girls" reflects the historical primacy accorded to men in our society (Itons-Peterson and Crawford, 1985; Miller, 1994: 268). Henley et al. (1985: 171) remark that "this order is not coincidental, but was urged in the sixteenth century as the proper way of putting the worthier party first." During World War II, Stouffer (1949) reports that officers used feminine terms as insults to motivate soldiers. To show less-than-expected courage or endurance was to risk the charge of not being a man: "Whatsa matter, bud—got lace on your drawers?" A generation later, accusations of femininity were still being used as motivating insults to prepare American soldiers to fight in Vietnam. Drill sergeants would mock their troops by saying, "Can't hack it, little girls?" (Eisenhart, 1975). The worst insult one can hurl at male recruits in the United States Marines today is comparing their performance to a woman's (Gilham, 1989). During the ritual foot-stomping ceremony that opens weekly meetings of Beavers, leaders in Canada routinely exhort their young male charges to greater enthusiastic participation with "What are you— a bunch of Brownies?"

Foley (1993) notes that football coaches insult boys who don't play well by saying they are "wearing skirts," and Stockard and Johnson (1980), observing boys playing basketball, report that boys who missed a basket were called a woman. Coaches in all sports at all age levels regularly attempt to motivate male players with a sarcastic "come on, ladies" admonition. The commonly used term "wuss" is a polite form of "puss" (as in "pussy") and is always used to demote a male to female status. All of this name-calling embodies the generalized devaluation of women in our society: "There is no comparable phenomenon among women, for young girls do not insult each other by calling each other 'man'" (Stockard and Johnson, 1980: 12).

Deprecation also occurs through the intentional or unintentional use of words that trivialize or infantilize adult women in a condescending fashion (e.g., "Now dear/little lady/girls, you're overreacting"; "women and children will be evacuated first"). Secretaries of all ages are commonly referred to as the "girls in the office." Efforts have been made over the past 30 years to educate men in particular, and our society in general, to substitute the preferred term of "woman/women" (an effort that sometimes borders on the ludicrous as in the case of birth announcements proclaiming "It's a Baby Woman!") and thus properly acknowledge the independent adult status of most females. However, a particular usage of the term "girl" has been seeping slowly over the past four to five years from the black subculture, where it has long been an acceptable mainstream term, into white dominant culture wherein "girl" has been rehabilitated to apply under select circumstances to adult females (as in the popular exhortation "You go, girl!"). Our present gender politics of semantics appears to be one in which a female of any age can call another female of any age a "girl," but a male of any age calling any postpubsecent female a "girl" does so at his peril of being labeled as a deprecator.

Deprecatory words often ally women with animals (Nelson and Robinson, 1994: 29). Whether being supposedly praised as a "chick," "fox," or "Mother Bear" or being condemned as a "bitch," "bowser," "dog," "pig," "sow," "old hen," or an "old nag," the imagery is all animal reductionist. A man dominated by his wife is referred to as "henpecked" or "pussy whipped." However, women are additionally likened to food items (sugar, honey, tomato, hot tamale, sweetie pie, sweetcakes, cupcake) with the attendant suggestion being made that they look "good enough to eat" and are a "toothsome morsel." However endearing at first, such images reduce women to commodities intended for male consumption and sustenance. They also remind women that they have only a short shelf life before turning stale and unappealing.

The verbs and adjectives applied to women and men often convey different meanings. For example, we noted in Chapter 2 that women perceived to constitute a threat to men are often deprecated with words containing sexual imagery (ballbreaker, castrator, emasculator). No comparable words are used to deprecate men (ever heard of an "ovary crusher"?) A "breast beater" conjures up an archetypal Tarzan, take-charge, positive image while "studmuffin" and "hunk" invoke delectable images of men's sexual prowess and desirability. Women conversing together are described as "gossiping," "chattering," "nattering" or "cackling away," engaging in "girl talk" and having a "hen party." The implication in all of these terms is that the contents of such communications are unimportant, trivial, and of little consequence. In contrast, men conversing among themselves engage in "brainstorming," "manly talk," or "male bonding." The closest thing to an insulting phrase is to refer to such conversations as "pissing contests," but, even here, the phrase pays subtle positive homage to men's competitive endeavours. Once again, men and women can engage in essentially the same activities, but the descriptive terms used suggest not only a qualitative divide, but also a hierarchical evaluation.

In like fashion, he is described as "persistent," while she "nags"; he is "cautious," she is "hesitant"; he is "choosy," she is "picky"; he is "forceful," she is "bitchy" and "opinionated"; his face has "character lines" showing "maturity;" she is "wrinkled" and has "let herself go"; he is a "carefree bachelor," a "ladykiller," or a "playboy," while she is an "old maid" or "spinster," a "slut," a "slag," or "has been around." Stanley (1977) reports that at least 220 terms are used to refer to sexually promiscuous females in comparison to a relatively meagre 22 words to refer to sexually promiscuous males (see also Baker, 1993). Generally, the more terms a culture or subculture creates to refer to something, the more important that phenomenon is (think of the number of terms college and university students create for drinking, getting drunk, and vomitting). In this case, deprecating women for being sexual is more important culturally than disparaging men (if indeed the later even occurs without an accompanying nudge, nudge, wink, wink).

Sex-marked suffixes, such as the "-ess" (e.g., waitress, poetess, actress, stewardess), "-(en)ne" (e.g., comedienne and heroine) and "-ette" (e.g., majorette, jockette, suffragette, Leafette), set apart women who perform equivalent, if not identical, roles to men, yet the presence of these suffixes diminishes or devalues a woman's performance as being lesser than a man's. An inclusive language either replaces the so-called "masculine" and "feminine" forms with gender-neutral terms such as food server, flight attendant, comic, and suffragist, or attempts to "de-sex" the adjective thus making it neutral (an "actor" is simply one, either male or female, who acts).

LANGUAGE AND SPEECH PATTERNS

Language is a very powerful tool in the gender construction toolbox. Words create images and understandings of gender, yet the impact of what we say can be either reinforced or undermined by how we say it. Women and men tend to use different styles of verbal communication. These speaking styles reflect, and in many ways serve to maintain, comparative imbalances in gender social power. As we shall see, positions of relative advantage and disadvantage are represented in different means of expression.

Men and women use language in a different manner (Bodine, 1975; Brend, 1975; Cameron, 1985; Thorne et al., 1983). Adams and Ware (1983: 483) report that "one of the most consistent findings of those who have studied sex-based variations in English has been that women, no matter what their socioeconomic level, race, or age, use more grammatically correct forms than men and pronounce words in more acceptable ways." Trudgill (1972) finds that women are more likely than men to claim that they use "standard English," although women tend to underreport the extent to which they deviate from this pattern. Men, in comparison, are more likely to acknowledge swearing and using expletives that contain sexual meanings.

Various explanations have been advanced for these differences in grammatical patterns. On one hand, Trudgill (1972) contends that the traditional importance placed on women's appearance as a primary vehicle by which to achieve upwards social mobility and prestige (Elder, 1969) has made women, as a group, "status conscious." He argues that where presentation is central to the acquisition of recognition and reward, women become acutely aware of the impressions conveyed through the artful manipulation of symbols, including language use. Much as Eliza Doolittle in Bernard Shaw's *Pygmalion* (or its cinematic version *My Fair Lady*) was able to transform herself from one who sold flowers for pennies in the marketplace to a fashionable "society lady," women may shape the image they convey by tending more rigorously to demonstrating "proper speech." On the other hand, Adams and Ware (1983: 484) suggest that male socialization into such "core traits" as "competitiveness, independence, and toughness" encourages a cavalier attitude towards demonstrations of correct speech. They argue that prototypical speech patterns of working-class males "becomes a way for all males to be tough and independent." Similarly, they note that males find greater incentive to purposely adopt language patterns featuring various forms of slang, including swear words. A desire to establish oneself as "cool," "tough," or "macho" favours adopting terms of defiance to express disdain for verbal conventions dictating styles of speaking and words to use in day-to-day communications. A third explanation focusing upon power will be presented later in this section.

Slang

Carl Sandburg once offered a definition of slang as "…language that rolls up its sleeves, spits on its hands and goes to work." Thorne (1990: iii–iv) observes that the word "slang" is derived from "sling" in such archaic expressions as "'to sling one's jaw' (to speak rowdily or insultingly)." Much slang today, he observes, involves "the substitution of more forceful, emotive or humorous forms for standard words" (p. v). On the "spectrum of formality," he remarks, "[s]lang is at the end of the line…where language is considered too racy, raffish, novel, or unsavoury for use in conversation with strangers" (Thorne, 1990: iii). According to Kramarae (1975), slang reflects societal changes and is of critical importance within the evolution of language. She contends that the bulk of slang in North American society is created and adopted by men (see also Selnow, 1985). Adams and Ware (1983: 484) additionally note that "[n]ot only is its usage more frequent in the speech of males, but also many of the terms used for swearing, such as *son of a bitch*, vilify women" (emphasis in original). They report that women are more likely to define swearing as objectionable and to limit themselves to milder swear words such as "hell and damn" (see also Bailey and Timm, 1976; Crawford, 1996).

It can be argued that, in avoiding slang and other expletives, a speaker with a some- what abbreviated selection of terms to convey strong feelings is left at a distinct disadvan- tage, especially when the conversational other is not bound by similar concerns and sensibilities. Disparate verbal playing fields are constructed if one's conversational part- ner attempts to select from a relatively tepid vocabulary of standard words, or is forced to capture nuances of meaning through the adoption of polysyllabic, arcane words. Although a strict avoidance of slang may result in a loss of words to forcibly and graphically convey one's meaning, Eakins and Eakins (1978: 115–116) observe that women who use exple- tives are viewed negatively for doing so. When women do use expletives, they are more likely to use them in a way to "maintain a degree of politeness" (Lindsey, 1997: 79), such as the commonly heard "Oh sugar/shoot/shucks/fudge/darn!" Bear in mind that the *gender slang gap* is based upon relative, not absolute, measures. Impressionistic evidence gath- ered from unsupervised settings such as playgrounds, school corridors, campus watering holes, and washroom walls all suggests that gender slang parity, especially among the young, may be fast approaching.

Conversation Patterns

The conversations of men are more likely to focus upon external events (sports, politics, sexuality, paid work, and other men) than are the conversations of women (Johnson, 1966; Walker, 1996; West, 1994). Men are more likely to speak louder, to use more forceful state- ments ("You tell that guy to take a hike"), and to impose their viewpoints on others ("This is how you handle it") (Spender, 1989). According to Wood (1997: 173), giving advice functions on two levels: first, it establishes the speaker as the knowledgeable expert who "knows" what should and should not be done; second, it directs attention to instrumental ac- tivity. As we shall see in Chapter 7, women are more likely than men to speak on the top- ics of feelings, to make personal disclosures, to relay anecdotes, to show support for others ("I know just how you feel. I've done the same thing myself a hundred times"), and to re- veal their psychological or physical state ("I'm so mad I could just scream") (Hall and Langellier, 1988; Tannen, 1990; Wood and Inman, 1993).

Tannen (1990: 77) refers to the speaking style preferred by men as "report-talk" and the style preferred by women as "rapport-talk." *Report-talk* is a language of hierarchy, sep- aration, independence, and action. *Rapport-talk* is a language of connection, compromise, mediation, and emotion. "Each sex finds the other's style of speech uncomfortable. Men see women's speech as consisting of illogical recitals of feelings and women see men's speech as wearing and competitive" (Richmond-Abbott, 1992: 94). When men employ the emotional language associated with femininity, they are likely to be perceived as effeminate; when women adopt the assertive language associated with masculinity, they are likely to be perceived as arrogant, haughty, and uncaring (Rasmussen and Moley, 1986).

Men and women also differ in how they manage conversations and in the amount they speak within mixed-sex groups. Although the stereotype of woman-as-chattering-magpie sug- gests that it is woman's voice that dominates conversation, usurping the voice of her "strong, but silent" partner, the reverse is actually more accurate (Kimble et al., 1981; Leeft-Pellegrini,

1980). As Adams and Ware (1983: 487) remark, "the 'talkative' woman may be one who talks nearly as much as a man." Edelsky (1981) observes that men speak more often than women within mixed-sex groups, blithely interrupting women to make a point and answering questions directed to other people in the group (see also McConnell-Ginet, 1989; Mulac et al., 1988). Brooks (1982) notes that male university students interrupt their instructors more often than do female students, especially if the instructor is female.

Zimmerman and West (1975) in a study of two-person conversations between 20 white college-educated individuals ages 20 to 30, report that interruptions occurred in approximately 15 percent of same-sex conversations, but in 99 percent of mixed-sex conversations. With the exception of one conversation involving two interrupters, males were the sole interrupters in mixed-sex conversations (see also Spender, 1989: 9). Adams and Ware (1983: 486) note that "this pattern is parallel to the interruptions found in adult-child interactions, where it is overwhelmingly the adult who interrupts the child." In other words, interrupting is a function of power. Since men are more likely to interrupt conversations and to control changes in topics, sociologists and linguists conclude that talk between a man and a woman is often more like that between an employer and an employee than between social equals (Smith-Lovin and Brody, 1989; Tannen, 1990). Edelsky (1981) notes that, in "overlaps," when a man and woman start to speak at the same time, it is customary for the man to continue speaking and the woman to fall silent. Such deference also appears to be a silent acknowledgment of the power imbalance between men and women.

According to Lipman-Blumen (1984), the stereotype of the pushy, loud female functions as a form of informal social control, directing women to be solicitous of male speakers and to be deferential and nonassuming within mixed-sex groups. Within mixed-sex dyads or larger groups, women do most, if not all, of the conversation-work. Conversation-work involves a host of techniques designed to maintain a conversation and move it along smoothly. Thus, women often orient their comments towards the men in a group, encouraging them by various means to speak when, or if, they fall silent (Aries, 1976). Women are more likely to express agreement than disagreement with voiced statements and to build on another speaker's comments. They are more likely to cajole male speakers into continuing through the use of compliments ("That's incredible. I didn't know breeding iguanas was so complicated"), verbal prompts ("You must have a hundred fascinating stories to tell us about reshingling roofs"), head nods (even when a woman does not agree with the speaker's remarks), verbal reinforcements ("right!"; "awesome!"; "amazing!"), and other fillers and "spontaneous" laughter (Beck, 1988; Tannen, 1990; Wood, 1993). Generally, women nurture conversations and direct their energies towards its maintenance.

Men are more likely to monopolize a conversation and to dispute or disparage another's argument. Within all-male groups, men adopt a "competitive style" of speaking characterized by giving only limited reinforcement to the comments and observations of other speakers (Aries, 1976). Jockeying-for-position takes place as men engage in "brain picking to see who knows the most…telling jokes at each other's expense, and…telling stories about such physically threatening topics as castration and riots" (Adams and Ware, 1983: 486). Similarly, men are likely to employ techniques that discourage others in the group, particularly women, from speaking. The "delayed response" is perhaps the best well known of these. "The woman says something like 'You'll never guess what happened to me today.' Only after a long pause does her male companion say, 'Oh, what?' At other times the only response to the woman is silence" (Richmond-Abbott, 1992: 95). At other times, a woman may find her comments responded to with a noncommittal expression and/or grunts of disinterest ("Really?"; "That's nice"; "A-hmm"; "Mm-mmm"). We will return to these conversational styles under the heading of relationship styles in Chapter 7.

Predating Tannen's (1990) distinction between report-talk and rapport-talk, Lakoff (1975) argued that the speech of men and women is motivated by contrasting goals. Based on introspection ("I have examined my own speech and that of my acquaintances, and have used my own intuitions in analyzing it" [Lakoff, 1975: 4]) rather than a more formal research design, Lakoff suggests that while men's speech is motivated by a desire for the "pure transmission of factual knowledge" (p. 71), women's speech is motivated by the goal of "politeness" (p. 51). These contrasting goals, she suggests, results in distinct verbal styles. Drawing upon the work of Grice (1968), Lakoff characterizes the first of these two styles as seeking to impart information to one's listener "by the least circuitous route" (p. 71). This typically male style of speech is characterized by short, succinct, unambiguous sentences. Within this mode of speech, information is conveyed as a series of unqualified propositions of fact, which are ordered in accordance with a linear logic. These features, Lakoff argues, convey the authority and autonomy of the speaker.

In contrast, the "polite" style, which Lakoff suggests is typical of the speech patterns of women, is crafted to sustain connection with the listener. Polite speech does not announce the authority of the speaker to make truthful statements about the world; rather, it is characterized by a deferential and tentative quality. While speaking, the speaker attempts by intuition to gain clues about the listener's feelings towards both the speaker and the statements being uttered. In so doing, the speaker cedes to the listener the power to determine the message that the speaker actually means to convey (Lakoff, 1975: 70). Polite speakers use various "hedges" including a rising question intonation that ends a sentence on a high note, "tag questions" ("I think I've gained weight, don't you?"; "We're having a great time, aren't we?"), hyper-polite circumlocutions ("Don't you think it would be better if you just didn't bother me anymore?"), semantically ambiguous qualifiers ("I guess that might be sorta OK with me"), and empty adjectives ("What a divine darling little dress!"). Hedges effectively allow listeners "great linguistic latitude to determine" what the speaker is seeking to convey and "undercut the claim to authority that is implicit in declarative syntax" (White, 1991: 406). Although Lakoff acknowledges that social change rather than linguistic change is necessary to improve women's position in society, she suggests that women should adopt the speech forms more typically associated with men to advance their quest for equal treatment. If women wish to command the attention of their listeners, she suggests, they must adopt the speech patterns of men and avoid linguistic styles that are interpreted as confessions of their lack of power and dominance (for a similar line of argument directed specifically towards women in the paid-work sphere, see Tannen, 1994b).

White (1991: 423) has observed that "[v]irtually every linguistic and political claim of Lakoff's has stimulated further research." Dubois and Crouch (1975) challenge Lakoff's claim that women are more likely than men to use tag questions following statements. Kramarae (1975) suggests that "women's language" contains, in embryo, alternative values which should be reassessed, recognized as positive, and embraced. For Kramarae, the "polite" form of speech typically associated with women should be the *preferred* model of communication. Human social life, she suggests, is *not* concrete and uni-dimensional, nor best expressed as if the speaker's views are definitive. No statements of opinions, she argues, should be delivered as if they possess claim to a singular higher truth and are being magnanimously revealed to a hitherto ignorant audience. Women's language incorporating ambiguity, she suggests, allows for the adoption of multiple perspectives and is addressed in a tentative fashion ideal for promoting negotiation between conversants. Indeed, Kramarae contends that feminists should analyze the norms and values embodied in "women's language" and should translate these ideals into feminist campaigns for social change.

Gender Differences or Power Differences?

Researchers (e.g., Nichols, 1980; Stanbeck, 1982) focusing on the speech patterns of economically and "racially" subordinate groups in North America suggest that what Lakoff depicted as "women's language" is better reconceptualized as "powerless speech" (Erickson et al., 1978) since these linguistic strategies are shared by all powerless people when dealing with more powerful people (see also Conley et al., 1978, Lind and O'Barr, 1979; White, 1991). Thorne and Henley (1975) claim that those who are placed in subordinate positions in society demonstrate a vigilance and care towards rules—including those surrounding language use—that are more easily broken or ignored by people located in positions of high social status. Women's greater tendency to utilize proper "standard English" and men's greater tendency to break all the rules of grammar and syntax are, therefore, as much, if not more, a function of power than gender itself.

In his research on courtroom testimony, O'Barr (1983) finds that, while women are more likely than men to adopt powerless speech patterns, these verbal features are more strongly correlated with the social status of the speaker than with the speaker's gender. Minority men, working-class men, and others who occupy "relatively powerless social positions" (O'Barr, 1983: 104), all adopt the same patterns. Those who lack social power do not enjoy the linguistic luxury of speaking in a manner that may be perceived as authoritarian, confrontational, or opinionated. Rather, their language style anticipates and seeks to defuse potential antagonism and the possible risk of retaliation. Clarity of expression is forfeited as the speaker attempts to convey a readiness to have her or his assertions challenged or rejected. That outcome is a real possibility since O'Barr reports that jurors in simulated trials evaluate speakers using powerless language as "less credible, competent, intelligent, or trustworthy than speakers who use typically 'male' speech patterns" (in White, 1991: 406). As we noted earlier, while analysts agree that the speech patterns of women and men reflect and reinforce unequal gender statuses, strategies for change issuing from liberal feminist and cultural feminist perspectives vary from suggesting that women should become more like men to arguing that men should become more like women.

NONVERBAL COMMUNICATION

Language, of course, is not the only means by which we communicate. We also communicate through the use of *gestures*—movements of our bodies, in whole or in part, that convey meaningful messages. Facial expressions; hand, arm, and leg movements; body posture or demeanor; eye movements such as gaze, contact, and avoidance; spatial behaviour; touch; all of these are imbued with culturally shared meanings (Argyle, 1988). Researchers ignore idiosyncratic, unique and/or erratic, gestures and focus instead upon socially patterned movements shared in common by members of a social category. Even though these movements are learned, most of us remain essentially unaware we are performing them. Body language, therefore, provides an important source of information used to either verify or challenge the veracity of verbal communication. Considerable research has been devoted to identifying gender differences in nonverbal communication and to analyzing how these movements not only reinforce presentations of gender in everyday life, but also underlie the unequal status of women and men in our society.

Guess which sex is more likely to have sore facial muscles from smiling throughout an evening of social entertaining? Which sex is more likely to raise one or both hands to their mouth immediately following an excited utterance (swearing, crying, screaming for joy) or experiencing some form of excitation they are afraid or embarrassed to utter (using their hand to prevent themselves from speaking)? Who is more likely to gaze intently into another person's eyes or upon their face both while talking and listening to them, yet more likely to break off eye contact first if an approaching person is a stranger? Which sex is more likely to bow their head slightly and look up at another person through their eyelashes? Who controls more space—men or women—and how do they accomplish this feat?

A central issue in the study of gendered nonverbal communication centres upon whether observed differences reflect essential gender characteristics or situational status and power differentials. The findings presented next reflect generalizations derived from gender tendencies. Increasingly, analysts suggest that power is more explanatory than is gender per se. Women are more likely to find themselves in subordinate positions and, as a consequence, to adopt nonverbal communication patterns commonly found among members of other subordinate groups in our society. For example, women smile more often than do men (Halberstadt et al., 1987). Henley et al. (1984) suggest that the act of smiling is "women's badge of appeasement," a means of placating or appearing nonthreatening to others. Ekman et al. (1980) opine that crying may be a culturally acceptable way for women to mask anger, especially in those situations where an expression of anger might be construed as disruptive or inappropriate for one occupying a subordinate status.

In addition to finding parallels between nonverbal styles of women and members of other subordinate groups, research also finds that both men and women can adopt similar styles when conditions require them to do so. Our cultural folklore bestows unique status upon what is commonly referred to as "women's intuition." Intuition is generally understood to refer to an immediate perception, and accurate interpretation, of available cues. As such, intuition is a form of empathy. Despite cultural feminist claims that women are "naturally" more empathetic than men, no evidence exists to suggest that differences in empathy are the result of innate or biological predispositions (Tavris, 1992: 64).

Lips's research on men in occupations requiring heightened interpersonal sensitivity finds that men are "as good as women at decoding nonverbally expressed emotions. Whether this finding can be attributed to the effects of practice or to the self-selection of unusually sensitive men for such occupations is difficult to know" (Lips, 1995: 92). Even if these men were unusually sensitive prior to receiving their training, the fact remains that men can be as empathetic as women. Whether they choose to be, or need to be, is another matter. Snodgrass (1985) varied the sex of persons assigned into either superordinate or subordinate roles in a series of laboratory experiments and finds that people in subordinate positions, regardless of their sex, are more sensitive to the nonverbal signals provided by superordinates than the reverse. Snodgrass concludes that the phrase "women's intuition" more fittingly should be termed "subordinate's intuition." Tavris (1992) stresses that empathy should be considered a learned trait that demonstrates not a "female" skill, but a "self-protective" skill characteristic of those who have lesser amounts of power. Puka (1990) notes that prisoners, slaves, and members of other oppressed groups all demonstrate an interpersonal sensitivity considered "typical" of women.

Power, in combination with socialization, appears to account for women's tendency towards greater sensitivity to nonverbal cues. Chodorow (1978: 167) claims that the bonding between girls and their mothers, not found in relations between boys and their mothers, gives women a "stronger basis for experiencing another's needs or feelings as one's own (or of thinking that one is so experiencing another's needs and feelings)." A major source of information from which to intuit another person's thoughts and feelings is derived from visual cues. Compared to men, women are more likely to engage in a greater degree of eye contact with conversational partners (Podrouzek and Furrow, 1988; see Chapter 7 for the distinction between "face-to-face" and "side-by-side" friendship and intimacy styles). Women more often "read" other individuals' facial expressions in everyday interactions, and are more accurate in their readings of these nonverbal cues (Noller, 1980).

Feminists since the 1970s have drawn attention to the hidden sexist meanings underlying many nonverbal acts subsumed under the heading of *chivalry*. The chivalrous act of opening a door for a woman, for example, invites the assumption that women need to be "helped" by men (despite the fact that doors in modern times are substantially lighter and easier to open than in days of yore). In similar fashion, such seemingly innocuous acts as opening and closing a woman's car door, warming a car up in mid-winter for a waiting female passenger, lighting a woman's cigarette, taking her arm when crossing a street, walking between a woman and the edge of the sidewalk closest to the curb, and holding an umbrella over a female partner's head (but not necessarily over his own), and numerous other acts all cast men into active roles and women into passive protected roles. Traditionalists argue that such acts are common courtesies that should not be disdained. Tradition-oriented women often comment: "What's wrong with men acting like gentlemen and showing some manners? I like to be treated as a lady." There is, of course, nothing inherently disrespectful in being helpful or courteous; however, feminists draw attention to the gendered nature of etiquette rituals, along with their underlying assumptions and social meanings.

Such gestures might appear at first glance to be inconsequential and frivolous in contrast to larger life-and-death issues of gender, yet constant and continual participation in these routine nonverbal rituals of daily life reinforce unequal gender statuses. To demonstrate their underlying power for yourself, we invite you to "breach the rules" (Garfinkel, 1967) of nonverbal social etiquette and monitor your own reactions and those of others around you. If you are a female, move quickly, but not too obviously, ahead to open a door for a male partner (and avoid the temptation to add a sweeping flourish of your arm to guide him through— such dramatics trivialize the effect); carry his backpack to his next class; brush the snow off his car; walk slightly ahead of him; take his elbow to guide him across the street or trail your arm protectively to ward off other people; hold hands with him keeping your arm in front, with your hand on top facing outward towards oncoming traffic and his hand underneath facing backward. Idly caress your date's buttocks in movie lineups; once seated, place one arm across his knees and the other one around the back of his shoulders. Keep the popcorn box on your lap. If you are a male, keep your arms at your sides and your knees together while walking or sitting; do not initiate any form of touching behaviour—wait for her to make the "first move"; wait expectantly for her to open, and close, your car door (especially if it is her car) and stand beside all other doors waiting for them to be opened by others; while she is talking, reach over and remove pieces of lint or hair from a female friend's sweater; and constantly look onto the face and into the eyes of every woman who is talking to you and to whom you are speaking (do not just glance in her direction at the beginning and the ending of your speech).

Space

Some of the examples in the exercise above utilize spatial and touching behaviours, both of which express and reinforce dominance-submission patterns. Within our society, men command more personal space, that protective "bubble" that surrounds each of us, than do women. Women, along with members of other minorities, are expected to contain themselves in minimal space. When seated, women typically keep their feet flat on the floor and their knees touching or cross their legs either at their ankles or thighs. Elbows are usually tucked in towards the body, with arms either folded across or beneath the breasts or hanging straight down their sides to be joined in a V-shape, with wrists or hands touching in the middle of their laps (Spain, 1992; Weisman, 1992). In contrast, males consume more space. When sitting, men tend to "sprawl" with their knees wide apart or, if their legs are crossed, resting one ankle on the opposite knee or thigh, thus pointing their knees in different directions and exposing their genital region (a serpentine intertwining of their legs, with crossed knees and one foot tucked behind the calf or ankle of the other leg, is not considered masculine in our culture). Elbows either point away from the body in opposite directions with hands resting apart on each thigh or, along with armpits, face up and out with hands clasped behind the head, or arms are opened and extended in both directions on the backs of chairs on either side. When standing, men are more likely to stand "at ease" military fashion—with feet planted (firmly) apart. Women, in contrast, are more apt to stand with their legs together and the inside edges of their feet touching or with their legs crossed and the outside edges of their feet touching.

Richmond-Abbott (1992: 96) suggests that women's restricted use of space attests most fundamentally to their relative lack of power and dominance. When the spatial bubbles of men and women overlap, men are more likely to invade the personal and intimate zones (the two closest spatial layers surrounding our bodies, see Hall, 1969) of women than the reverse. Willis' extensive experimental research indicates that:

(1) women have more tolerance for invasion of their personal space than men have;

(2) women stand closer to other women than men stand to other men, and when women get as close to men as they do to other women, the men retreat;

(3) when men get as close to other men as they normally do to women, the male subjects "fight" (accuse the experimenter of being pushy or homosexual); and

(4) both men and women stand closer to women than they do to men. (Willis 1966 in Richmond-Abbott, 1992: 96–97)

Despite the existence of folkways requiring that a man move aside to let a "lady" pass, women are more likely to take evasive measures and move to one side to allow a man to pass, whenever a man and woman approach each other in a narrow hall or passageway (Richmond-Abbott, 1992: 97).

Touch

The shorter the physical distance between two people, the greater the potential for touching behaviour to occur. Reaching out to physically touch another person typically reflects power differentials. Generally, high-status individuals initiate touch more frequently and engage in touching subordinates more often than the reverse (Leathers, 1986; Spain, 1992); it is considered unseemly for lower-status individuals to put their hands on superiors. Touching behaviour in interpersonal gender relations follows the same general principle, with males more likely than females to initiate touch. Females are more likely to be touched than are males, and are likely to be touched over a greater proportion of their bodies by strangers, friends and acquaintances, and intimates than are males (Jourard, 1971; 1968).

Burgoon et al. (1989) contend that how we interpret a touch involves not only such incident-specific factors as the duration, intensity, and frequency of touch, and/or the site touched, but the meanings of touching learned through gender socialization as well. One experiment (Thayer, 1988) finds that brief touching of patients by a female nurse during presurgery information sessions lowered blood pressure and anxiety levels of females, both before the surgery and for more than an hour afterwards. Women patients experienced being touched as therapeutic and reassuring. Male patients in identical circumstances, in contrast, responded with rising blood pressure and anxiety levels both before and following surgery. Instead of a comfort, men appeared to interpret being the recipients of touch in this situation as a threatening reminder of their vulnerability and dependence. Perhaps this is why men tend to be more likely to use the disdainful label "touchy-feely" to refer to any real or potential touching they themselves neither initiate nor control.

Nonverbal communication is linked to a complex web of other assumptions about women and men and their "right" to choreograph how interaction will proceed in various social settings. Many observers have suggested that, in our essentially no-touch culture, interpersonal tactile contact is permeated with sexual meanings. Even if a specific touch is not directed towards an intimate portion of a man's or a woman's anatomy, nonintimate touching often either precipitates further sexual touching or signals a desire for more intimate physical contact. Many women (see Hite, 1976: 384–391) acknowledge that sexual involvement is often the only way they can obtain touching from a male partner. Conversely, many women fear that unwanted nonsexual touching from a male is a portend of more explicit sexual touching to follow. If not necessarily sexual, touch may signal physical, psychological, or emotional coercion. Wood (1997: 196) suggests that "[b]ecause masculine socialization encourages men to enter the private spaces of others, particularly women, and to use touch to establish power, they may engage in touching that women co-workers will perceive as harassing." In response to such unwelcome gestures, she remarks (1997: 196), "[w]omen's training to be nice to others may make them reluctant to speak forcefully to a boss or co-worker," especially if the offending party is intimidating by virtue of their height, weight, or seeming assuredness that they can do just as they please. A common male response that such touching is "harmless" reflects either an intention to mask other motivations or a lack of awareness than nonverbal gestures are meaningful.

THE MEDIA

As we have seen, words comprising the English language, speech patterns, conversational styles, and nonverbal communication patterns symbolically construct, represent, and compel men and women to present themselves in different ways. Ongoing debate focuses upon how much and how many of the gender differences are actually functions of the sex-linked distribution of power within our society. Regardless of the eventual outcome of those debates, symbolic representations of gender in the media are acknowledged as unquestionably salient sources of gender socialization. As we mentioned in Chapter 4, the media are unique agencies, as socialization messages are transmitted in a uni-directional fashion, without an immediate or direct feedback mechanism. As well, the media lack an ability to differentially reward and punish recipients for consequent appropriate or inappropriate behaviour. The media operate solely through the transmission of symbols (words and/or visual images) that represent gender in various ways. As with all other agencies of socialization, the media also exist for other purposes in addition to socialization, in this case entertainment and information transmission in the pursuit of profit. As with other agencies, the socialization implications of media messages are often accidental and unintentional.

Books and Magazines

Children's Books

Weitzman et al. (1972) examined children's books that had won the American Library Association's prestigious Caldecott Medal for best illustrations. Selection of a book as a Caldecott Medal winner is significant in that winning books are almost always routinely ordered by all children's libraries, in both the United States and Canada. Despite the fact that females accounted for more than half of the population in both countries, female characters were virtually invisible in the books examined. Almost all of the books told stories about male adventures and featured boys, men, and even male animals. For every one female animal, 95 male animals were depicted. Girls were portrayed in passive and doll-like ornamental roles, while boys were portrayed as active and adventurous. The majority of the girls were shown as trying to please their brothers or their fathers; the boys, in contrast, were depicted as engaged in tasks requiring independence and self-confidence. Subsequent replications of the Weitzman et al. research (e.g., Clark et al., 1993; Williams et al., 1987) find that, while female characters now appear in equal numbers to male characters, depictions of females have remained essentially unchanged. Males are still more active and independent, while females are still basically passive, dependent, and intent upon pleasing others.

Feminists have attempted to encourage publication of nonsexist books that allow "Dick...[to] speak of his feelings of tenderness without embarrassment and Jane...[to] reveal her career ambitions without shame or guilt" (Williams et al., 1987:154). Although females became more visible within both award-winning and nonaward-winning print books for children in the 1980s (Doughterty et al., 1987; Heintz, 1987), both male and female characters remain depressingly unidimensional.

> Not only does Jane express no career goals, but there is no adult female model to provide any ambition....How can we expect Dick to express tender emotions without shame when only two adult males in this collection of books have anything resembling tender emotions and one of them is a mouse? (Williams et al., 1987: 155)

The content of children's storybooks provides a blueprint for behaviour that either conforms to or challenges gender-role stereotypes. Research notes that children as young as nursery-school age evidence greater diligence in completing a task after listening to a story in which a same-sex character is depicted as achieving that task (McArthur and Eisen, 1976), and are more apt to select a nonstereotypical toy to play with after being read a non-stereotypical picture book (Ashton, 1983). Since most children are exposed only to conventional storybooks, conformity to traditional gender expectations is more often the result than is challenge.

Recent books, such as *The Paper Bag Princess* (1994), *Angela's Airplane* (1992), and others by Robert Munsch, an adjunct professor at the University of Guelph, offer young readers an assortment of unconventional gender messages. For example, *The Paper Bag Princess* embarks on a mission to save her fiancé, Prince Ronald, after he has been abducted by a fire-breathing dragon. Demonstrating ingenuity and cunning, the Princess bests the dragon and rescues the prince. Prince Ronald, however, shows little appreciation for her efforts and chides her for the appearance of her clothes and for having "messy hair." In response to this traditionalist emphasis upon her appearance, the princess replies "You, Prince Ronald are a bum." Eschewing the usual fairy-tale "happily ever after" ending, the story ends by noting that the Prince and Princess do not get married after all. Series such as *The Berenstain Bears* by Stan and Jan Berenstain; Joanna Cole's *The Magic School Bus;* Phoebe Gilman's (1994) *Jillian Jiggs To The Rescue;* and works such as Shirley Kurtz's (1991) *The Boy and the Quilt*, in which a young boy learns from his mother how to construct a quilt; Beverly Allinson and Barbara Reid's (1990) *Effie*, about an ant who is admonished for her loudness until her voice keeps all the other insects from being squished by an elephant; and Charlotte Zolotow's (1985) *William's Doll*, in which a boy desires a doll to take care of, feed, and love, so that he can practise being a father, all provide nonsexist depictions of their characters. Such books portray males and females in a greater variety of roles and suggest to young readers that heroic qualities are not exclusively "masculine" nor are nurturant behaviours solely "feminine" (see also Purcell and Stewart, 1990).

A variety of nonsexist books are available for preteenagers, such as Ethel Johnston Phelp's *Tatterhood And Other Tales*, a collection of 25 cross-cultural tales featuring female heroes; Canadian Marlene Nourbese Philip's *Harriet's Daughter*, the winner of the Casa de Las Americas Prize, Latoya Hunter's *The Diary of Latoya Hunter: My First Year In Junior High*, a nonfictional account of a young Jamaican immigrant's life; Marie Lee's *Finding My Voice*, a story of a young Chinese girl dealing with prejudice, parental pressure, and the search for self-identity; Scott O'Dell's *Black Star, Bright Dawn*, a story of a young Inuit girl competing in the thousand-mile Iditarod sled dog race. Unfortunately, a jarring discontinuity exists between the new nonsexist material designed for a very young audience and reading materials that purposefully target older readers.

Comics

Robbins (1996: 2) observes that, since the 1933 introduction of *Superman* in *Action Comics™* no. 1, "superheroes [have] entered the world's consciousness" through syndicated comic strips and the production of comic books. "The success of the Superman character naturally led to imitation, and new superheroes popped up almost faster than a speeding bullet" (Robbins, 1996: 2); *Batman* left the Batcave in 1939 to embark on the quest to avenge his murdered parents, and *Flash*, the "fastest man alive," *Hawkman*, the *Human Torch,* and *Captain Marvel* (a 12-year-old boy, Billy Batson, who became invincible upon uttering the word "Shazam!"), all appeared in 1940. While the first female superhero (Peggy Allen aka

The Woman In Red) also entered the scene that same year, and periodically reappeared over the next five years within the pages of *Thrilling Comics™*, her fate was interchangeable with the majority of most comic book female action characters: "None…ever appeared in her own book, and they were invariably short-lived, rarely lasting for more than three appearances before fading into permanent obscurity. Often they were merely sidekicks of the more important male hero…relegated to the role of girlfriend, and their purpose was to be rescued by the hero" (Robbins, 1996: 3).

The creation of *Wonder Woman* (initially known as *Amazon Princess Diana*) in 1941 represented a purposeful attempt by her creator, psychologist William Marston, to provide female readers with a same-sex superhero. Marston (1943) commented that his suggestion that girls might wish to read about and identify with a strong female hero character was "met by a storm of mingled protests and guffaws." He chronicled his reasoning for creating a female superhero thus: "It seemed to me from a psychological angle, that the comics worst offence was their blood-curdling masculinity.…It's smart to be strong. It's big to be generous, but it's sissified, according to exclusively male rules, to be tender, loving, affectionate, and alluring. 'Aw, that's girl stuff!' snorts our young comics reader, 'Who wants to be a girl?' And that's the point: not even girls want to be girls so long as our feminine archetype lacks force, strength…" (in Robbins, 1996: 7).

In her original incarnation, *Wonder Woman* was depicted as a muscular, flat-chested, and only mildly attractive young woman with a strong chin, who made villains (the majority of whom were other women) see the error of their ways, not through the exercise of super powers, but through "the message of love and humanitarianism" (Robbins, 1996: 10). Robbins (1996: 10) claims that "[t]he most powerful humanistic message in Wonder Woman, and the one most consistently repeated, is that super powers are not necessary for a girl to become a superheroine" and notes that this message was re-emphasized in a feature box appearing in every issue of the comic book identifying and relating stories about real-life heroes such as Florence Nightingale and Amelia Earhart. While *Wonder Woman*, along with other female American superpatriots such as *Black Cat*; *Miss Fury*; the *Spirit of Old Glory*; *Pat Patriot, America's Joan of Arc*; *Miss Victory*; *Commandette*; *Yankee Girl*; *Black Angel*; and *Black Venus* (often storied and drawn by women who had replaced male artists drafted into wartime service), "fought Germans and Japanese on land, on sea, in the air, and on the pages of America's comics" (p. 37), these androgynous role models were substantially challenged by 1947 with the emergence of Romance comics. *My Date*, for example, featured "true love stories" about adolescent characters and *Venus: Romantic Tales of Fantasy* followed "a love story between two girls and a guy." Although female superheroes re-emerged briefly in the 1950s with the 12-year-old *Tomboy* character and, more durably, with the introduction of *Supergirl*, the decline of the comic book industry during the 1950s saw a marked decrease in the number of superhero books and "by 1953, only the strongest supercharacters—Green Arrow, Aquaman, Superman, Batman, and Wonder Woman [now drawn as a curvaceous bombshell]—were left at DC Comics" (Robbins, 1996: 104).

While the 1960s saw the introduction of a series of superhero groups, female members of these groups are dubious candidates for the title "superhero." Sue Storm (aka the *Invisible Girl* of the Fantastic Four) personified the term "wimp," with a repertoire of behaviours consisting largely of fainting, bursting into tears, and becoming hysterical. Jean Gray (aka *Marvel Girl* of the first incarnation of the X-Men) alternated between serving meals and fainting whenever she attempted to telekinetically move large objects. Janet Van Dyne (aka

The Wasp whose "superpowers" allowed her to become the size of an insect and annoy archvillains) was the only member of the Avengers who was preoccupied with facial powder, lipstick, shopping, and going to the hairdresser. *Batgirl* could become distracted from crime fighting by a run in her nylons (Robbins, 1996). While "[f]eminism, in a slightly addled form" had an impact upon the comic book world of the 1970s, with characters such as Jungle Queen *Shanna: the She-Devil, Valkyrie, Ms. Marvel,* and *The Cat,* who voiced the buzz words of the woman's liberation movement while garbed in costumes that drew attention to their melon-sized breasts, "by the eighties…with the original feminist influence weakened or forgotten, they were getting sillier" (Robbins, 1996: 138). While the *She-Hulk* attempted to charge after her opponents while carrying 650 pounds on a six-foot-seven-inch frame, the *Dazzler*, a disco diva, was a crime fighter on roller skates, whose singular power was the ability to blind and bemuse villains with a psychedelic light show.

"By the nineties," Robbins (1996: 166–167) remarks, "comic books had become not merely a boy's club, but a Playboy Club.…[L]eading the way in sales" are "bad girl" superheroes like *Lady Death* (who wears a skull and crossbones on her thong and little else) described by Samuels (1995: 14) as "buxom characters who a) have had their families murdered by a psycho; or b) were abused as children and are now planning on controlling the world wearing only a string bikini while getting soaked by blood."

Not surprisingly the demographics of the comic book audience have shifted substantially. A 1946 survey reported that, among 8- to 11-year-olds and 18- to 34-year-olds, females were more likely than males to read comic books. Similarly, in 1948, when 26 of 49 Marvel Comics "were of obvious appeal to women and girls" and 17 featured a female name in the title (e.g., *Annie Oakley*, *Tessie the Typist*, *Sun Girl*, *Millie the Model, Nellie the Nurse*, etc.), one survey reported that among adults 21 to 30, 42.9 percent of men and 51 percent of women identified themselves as comic book readers. The comic book audience has become overwhelming male over time (Robbins, 1996: 193–192). Currently, Robbins (1996: 166) observes, "[t]he 92 percent male comic book readership of the nineties expect, in fact demand that any new superheroines exist only as pinup material for their entertainment."

While the observation that "chick books don't sell" has become the standard explanation offered by the comic book industry for the dominance of male comic book heroes, whose athletic abilities and powers are stressed more than their physical perfection, and for masterful female characters, who are most notable for the size of their mammary glands, Robbins (1996: 166) suggests that a circular logic is being employed. "Of course, as long as female comic characters are insulting to the average woman, she won't read comics." Female readers too old for *Sailor Moon* and *Barbie* comics may, of course, opt for such traditional "girl" comics as *Archie, Betty and Veronica,* and *Betty,* which offer sexually aseptic permutations on the two-girls-in-love-with-one-boy formulaic story. Like the message forwarded within longer, noncartoon counterparts, the emphasis within such "girl comics" places primary emphasis on contrasting the dating strategies employed by good girl Betty (e.g., baking a cake to win a boy through his stomach, being sweet, agreeable, and virtuous) and those of the rich, scheming Veronica. Traditional female-oriented comics depicting teenagers reinforce a theme that the central events of every young woman's life involve attempts to capture the attention and affection of a young man. Without him, a woman is incomplete. As we have seen, and will see momentarily, this theme runs throughout children's storybooks, comic books, and reading materials intended for older female audiences.

Teen Romance Novels

Girls who find the comic picturebook world either unappealing or too "childish," often gravitate towards the Juvenile-Young Adult section of local bookstores. Once heavily saturated with novels featuring the *Black Beauty*, *Nancy Drew* and *Hardy Boys* mysteries, and the everyday adventures of the *Bobbsey Twins* and *Cherry Ames*, bookshelf stock began changing by the 1980s to accommodate a greater variety of reading fare for young, predominantly female, readers. The old standards are still available for purchase, particularly by adults who wish to recreate their childhood among their own children, but are increasingly being outsold by novels purchased by young females themselves, focusing upon apparently more appealing themes of love and romance. While romance novels for adolescents date back to the 1940s and 1950s, "[w]hat is new…is the transposing of adult romance formats from Harlequin Romances to young adult publishing…big-budget marketing campaigns and…the use of the series format in which several books each month are issued" (Christian-Smith, 1988: 78). Teen romance novels now consistently rank in the top three types of books read and purchased by girls aged nine to fifteen. One leading educational publishing house, Scholastic Books, developed its first teen romance series, "Wildfire," early in the 1980s and sold 2.25 million books by 1982 (Christian-Smith, 1988: 78).

Christian-Smith finds consistent message themes in her analysis of 34 American adolescent romance novels written between 1942 and 1982: femininity is defined through "devotion to home, heart, and hearth, that a woman is incomplete without a man, that motherhood is women's destiny, and women's rightful place is at home" (Christian-Smith, 1988: 78). Utilizing central characters who can be identified with easily as peers, these primers for the future convey a basic message that romance shapes femininity. The links portrayed between love and (hetero)sexuality also act as informal mechanisms of social control upon women. Dominant ideologies surrounding sexuality in general, and female heterosexuality in particular, are reiterated "by privileging romance as the only legitimate context for sexual expression" (p. 83), and by excluding or ridiculing all other forms of sexual attraction. A female teenage reader is taught to know she is in love by the presence of various physical sensations, such as a throbbing head and fluttery feelings in her stomach (somewhat akin to the 'flu) "once that special boy has sealed his love for her with a kiss; her capacity for sexual feelings released when she is assured of her boyfriend's undying love and commitment" (p. 84). "Romance ultimately involves the construction of feminine identity in terms of others, with boys in the powerful position of giving girls' lives meaning.…While teen romances run counter to the realities of many women's and girls' actual lives, they nevertheless serve to maintain traditional views of what should constitute those lives" (Christian-Smith, 1988: 92–93).

Teen Magazines

The overwhelming majority of general magazines published for a preadolescent or adolescent audience, such as *Teen Beat, 'Teen, Sassy, Seventeen*, and *YM,* are aimed towards female purchasers and readers. Since no general-market teen magazine is published presently in our country, Canadian teenagers must generally select from American publications at their neighbourhood newsstands, or industriously seek out such self-distributed underground publications (or "zines") as *Riot Grrl, Girl Germs, Bikini Kill*, or *Goddess Juice*. Commercially available teen magazines, such as the American *New Moon: The Magazine for Girls and Their*

Dreams and the Canadian *Reluctant Hero* (advertised as "written by girls for girls 13 to 16"), featuring avowedly feminist messages entitled "Fun things to do on your period," "As good as the guys," "Hairy legs don't attract flies," "The Rush of Power Tools," and "The Look: Wear your self-esteem" (*Reluctant Hero*, vol.1, issue 2, n.d.), appear to be the exception rather than the rule. Undeniably more common to the vast majority of Canadian teenagers are the celebrity-laden magazines which predominantly feature headlines, interviews, and articles about young male stars of American television and movies and the standard narrowly defined beauty, diet, lifestyle, and relationship tips.

For example, *Teen Beat* (August, 1996) offers readers the challenge of completing a "20 Years of Hunks Star Search Puzzle," discovering "what's it gonna take" for "teen heart-throb" Andrew Keegan "to fall hard for a girl," and "Where to Find" Brad Pitt and win his heart. This one issue contains 15 colour pin-up photographs, only one of which features a female. Utilizing a formula developed by adult-oriented tabloids, the story related to a provocative headline of "JTT [Jonathan Taylor Thomas] & Devon! [Sawa] Doin' The 'Wild' Thing!" informs readers that the actors are to star in a movie, *Wild America*. Interviews with each actor furnish sufficient details on their awards and accomplishments, industry in researching their roles, and their "exciting, adventurous lives" to provide fodder for readers' romantic fantasies. Each actor pronounces the other "a real nice guy"—heady manly praise indeed.

Female celebrities typically occupy less prominent positions; when they are featured, attention is almost invariably directed to their appearance and their celebrity is often based upon their links as sisters or girlfriends of prominent male actors. A short article (*Teen Beat*, August, 1996: 22) on Josie Bissett, "Josie Smell Sweet," comments that "[p]retty, perky Josie" is "sweet to look at, and projects a fresh girl-next-door quality." A one-paragraph article on Justine Priestley, entitled "Jason's sis," describes her as "pretty...with honey brown hair, blue eyes, and dimples." In contrast to depictions of male actors' adventure-some lives, the one article featuring a female emphasizes the social costs of being a celebrity ("like I kind of missed out on high school"). Photographs of female stars typically occupy less than one-fifth of a page, feature headshots in black and white, or show the woman holding a stuffed animal. Photographs of male stars are more likely to be full-body colour shots, occupying a page or more of the magazine, and depicting the hunk-of-the-day engaging in some sports activity, such as surfing or playing basketball. A cover of *Sassy* (June 1996) entices readers with a "goof proof guide to getting gorgeous," feature articles on "love rehab: how to heal when you're hurting," and a "guy magnet quiz: is your romance for real?" Not to be outdone, *'Teen* (June 1996) announces on its cover that it will provide readers with information on "Hot Zones: what to wear, how to look, gotta-haves," an article on the "10 warning signs" that identify "loser guys," and an assortment of score-yourself quizzes ("What's your friend type?"; "Do you like your looks?"; "Problem skin: Are you to blame?"). None of these articles are intended for male readers.

Many magazines also include a "Real Life True Story," contemporary morality tales chronicling the disasters faced by young women who stray from the "good girl" role. "Busted for Pot" (*'Teen*, June 1996), ostensibly written by an anonymous teenage female, records her suspension from school and court-imposed community service sentence for possession of a minute amount of marijuana. The occasional-but-disinterested user emphasizes how lucky she was to escape the devastating life of a "pot-addict," while providing readers (p. 52) with horror stories of other female drug experimenters ("a girl at my school was doing some acid. It was laced with a blood thinner. She ended up in the hospital with a blood clot in her brain. She can't talk"). "Letters to the Editor" sections give thanks for the messages contained in such cautionary tales ("Thanks for the article on *Pregnant*…in your April issue. My boyfriend and I were thinking about becoming sexually active., but after reading the article, I'm going to wait until I think I'm ready to handle all the responsibilities that go with becoming sexually active"). Good girls, it seems, are best off staying at home, keeping their knees together, avoiding illicit (but not diet) drugs, reading about celebrity boys becoming men, while fantasizing about romance.

Romance Novels

Upon graduation from teen magazines and the Juvenile-Young Adult sections of local bookstores, many women gravitate towards what has been designated as "a pornography just for women" (Stoller, 1985: 37): romance novels. The dominant theme of male-oriented erotica is "a fantasy story of women who are sexually insatiable and are thus incapable of resisting any type of male sexual advance" (Reiss, 1986: 193). Strong female erotic desire, in combination with a lack of resistance, precludes the possibility of a male's sexual advances being rejected. The counterpart female fantasy story features a male who is "romantically obsessed.…He must pursue her, give her what she desires, and treat her properly" (Reiss, 1986: 195). In this scenario, the male is helpless to resist the allure of romantic involvement with an enchanting woman. Not only can he not be rejecting but, in keeping with traditional masculine stereotypes, he must also be relentless in pursuit of his desired love object. Readers of romance novels, almost exclusively female, are also typically relentless in pursuit of their desired books.

A Canadian company dominates the production and sales of romance novels worldwide. Harlequin Enterprises of Toronto, on its own or through joint ventures with other companies, "sells 176.5 million books a year in 23 languages in more than 100 international markets…a total of three billion books in less than half a century" (Grescoe, 1996: 3). Supposedly, "the average romance reader spends $1,200 a year on books" (Grescoe, 1996: 16), with readers consuming from three to twenty books a month. "[F]emale consumers are the reason the $855-million (U.S.) per year romance industry exists" (Laframboise, 1996: 255, emphasis in original), with the United States and Canada accounting for approximately $750 million alone (Grescoe, 1996: 1).

Since their contemporary beginnings in the late-1940s, romance novels published in North America have undergone a number of transformations. In the beginning years, Harlequin Romances were, avowedly, "clean, easy to read love stories about contemporary people, set in exciting foreign places" (Jensen, 1984, in Kaplan, 1991: 324). These stories followed a formula well known to even the most casual reader: "girl meets boy, girl and boy resist each other's allure, boy finally meets girl's expectations, and by the final page they either wed or bed—all told from the heroine's point of view" (Grescoe, 1996: 2). The range of romantic fantasies captured in print has expanded from a contemporary focus upon white middle-class characters to include historicals (set in the 1800s and often referred to as "bodice rippers" due to the provocative pictures on the front cover), westerns, medieval and ancient fantasies, supernaturals, gothics, contemporary mysteries, New Age, time travels, speculative fictions, New Reality stories dealing with chemical (but not romance-novel) addictions and sexual abuse, and multiculturals including nonwhite and explicitly gay themes and characters (Grescoe, 1996: 7–8).

In addition to varying temporal and geographical settings, ethnicities, and sexual orientations of the main protagonists, one of the most noticeable changes has been an increasingly explicit eroticism in romance novels. While the traditional genre depicting essentially chaste characters locked in passionately romantic, but euphemistically phrased, sexual embraces still exists, more and more "romantic fiction is for women who move their hips when they read" (Grescoe, 1996: 6). At least seven different Harlequin subseries (Kaplan, 1991: 325) cater to different audience tastes for varying degrees of sexual explicitness, in combination with differential emphases upon romantic ideals. Even though love is still required to conquer all, women are now often explicitly sexual conquests and conquerors from the beginning, through the middle, and at the end of romance novels today. According to Laframboise (1996), the consumption of sexually explicit romance novels by a female audience demonstrates "that the female erotic imagination is as varied as the male one" (p. 267), and that women are "capable of feeling desire as powerfully as any man" (p. 264).

The other noticeable change in romance novels since the 1980s has been a general trend towards depicting more balanced gender-power alignments and the development of more self-motivated autonomous female central characters. These women are increasingly portrayed as successfully asserting their needs and desires economically, erotically, and romantically. No longer are women solely defined by the more powerful men in their lives. However, one important imbalance remains. Akin to the formula in male-oriented materials, wherein his masculinity unleashes her sexuality, within female-oriented novels her femininity tames his masculinity and releases his previously dormant "desperate need for romance" (Grescoe, 1996: 7). Romance novels provide female readers with the opportunity "to fantasize about what it would be like to be so attractive that men view you as a 'prize' to be sought after, fought over and worth breaking laws to get their hands on" (Laframboise, 1996: 262). At the end of the story, most Harlequin and other erotic romances provide the central female character with a husband. The imagery and importance of the message for women, namely the need for an intimate relationship, remains a constant feature.

Reactions of analysts have varied over the years as romance novels increased in popularity. Some (e.g. Douglas, 1980) argue these novels offer escapist fare from the oppressiveness of women's everyday lives and, in allowing readers to avoid their harsh realities even temporarily, foster inaction over changing their circumstances. Others (e.g., Modleski, 1982) offer grudging approval insofar as the novels bestow some dignity on the state of surviving under oppressive circumstances. These reactions were crafted at a time when "historicals" (historical romances) were at the peak of popularity, featuring themes of blatant male domination, female submission, bondage, sado-masochism, and torture. The back cover of an acknowledged "classic" of the times (Karen Robard's [1985] *To Love A Man*) promises:

> Sam would make her his captive, his woman, taunting her, teasing her, treating her no better than a slave. He would take her when and where he chose, hurting her pride even as he healed her wounds. She would love him, hate him, fight him, need him… (in Laframboise, 1996: 247)

Even though the specific details of readers' lives are unlikely to parallel those depicted in the novels, sales figures indicate that themes of dominance and submission fall frequently upon receptive eyes. Other analysts (e.g., Radway, 1984) began to view reading romance novels as both an escapist protest against conditions that yield unfulfilled lives, and the first steps towards increased independence from, and the developing strength to try and change, those conditions. The current development of more autonomous female characters is now considered by some analysts (e.g., Thurston, 1987) to appeal to, and provide role models for, women who no longer need to be defined solely in terms of a man. Today's romance novels can provide a blueprint for a realignment of gender and gender relations. If more men were to read these novels, they might be inspired to actions that could alleviate problems in intimate relations that apparently drive many women to the bookstore. While romance novels hold the potential for changing gender and the conditions under which gender operates, consumption patterns of 10 to 20 novels a month leave little time for meaningful change.

Television

Noting that children in contemporary North American society spend, on average, about three hours of each day watching television and that, between the ages of 6 and 18, the average person will spend more time in front of the television set than at school (15–16 000 versus 13 000 hours), Schaefer et al. (1996: 69) remark that "[a]part from sleeping, watching television is the most time-consuming activity of young people." Chidley (1996: 30) notes that, [b]y the time most Canadian children reach high school, they each will spend between 10,000 and 15,000 hours watching TV—more time than is spent going to school, playing sports or talking to parents." According to Statistics Canada, Canadian children and young teenagers (ages two to eleven) spend less time watching television than do adults; in 1994, adults spent 22.7 hours per week compared with 17.1 hours for children and young teens. Although the hours spent watching television by teenagers and children have declined since 1986 (when teens watched 20.3 hours and children aged two to eleven watched twenty-two hours on a weekly basis), these numbers do not include the number of hours spent viewing videos nor playing video games (Chidley, 1996: 40–41).

Recognizing its primary importance in forwarding role models and guidelines for behaviour, McLuhan identified television as the "first curriculum" for young people in contemporary society (in Chidley, 1996: 40). Regarding the content of that curriculum, television has traditionally perpetuated and reinforced traditional stereotypes of men and women. Children's television shows overwhelmingly feature more males than females, while males outnumber females by four or five to one in the animated world of cartoons (Morgan, 1982, 1987). This "symbolic annihilation" (Tuchman, 1978) of women continues in prime time, where male characters outnumber female characters by two to one, with male characters also more likely to be portrayed in high-status positions (Davis, 1990; Vande Berg and Streckfuss, 1992). Content analysis research (Davis, 1990) reveals that men represent 65.4 percent of all prime-time television characters and are more likely to be cast in dramatic roles. Women, in contrast, are not only less visible, but are also found primarily in comedies, implicitly suggesting that they are not to be taken very seriously.

Role Models

The early research of Sternglanz and Serbin (1974) notes the pervasiveness of gender-stereotyping within programing directed at children. They report that males are typically cast as adventurous, aggressive, and heroic figures who rescue others from danger; females are likely to be depicted as submissive and passive characters. While male characters engage in a wide variety of behaviours and receive rewards for their accomplishments, the conduct of females is more limited and less likely to result in positive consequences. Various researchers (Alcock and Robson, 1990; Gerber, 1993; Hansen and Hansen, 1988; Kahan and Norris, 1994; Lott, 1989) have commented more recently upon the still relative scarcity of female characters in children's and family programs, and the narrowness of the roles in which female characters are portrayed. Signorielli (1991) reports that, in the world of animation, males (including anthropomorphized animals) outnumber females at a ratio of approximately five to one, while Pollitt (1991: 22) observes that cartoons often render females completely invisible or cast them into token roles such as the "little sister" (see also Thompson and Zerbinos, 1995).

Meehan (1993) finds that male and female characters on television tend to be gender-typed from an early age. Boy characters are portrayed as significantly more active, assertive, rational, sarcastic (especially towards parents), and engaging in more diverse activities than are girl characters. Young girls are more apt to be presented talking on the telephone, reading books and magazines, and helping out with household chores. Boys play sports, take trips, and get into many different kinds of trouble. On the wider screen, while the McCauley Caulkin young-boy hero of *Home Alone* and *Home Alone II* is portrayed as capable of taking care of himself in his family's absence and, along the way, of foiling the plans of would-be thieves, the Olsen twins, in *It Takes Two* are preoccupied with engineering a liaison between one young character's father and the other young character's caregiver. Like the dual characters portrayed by Hailey Mills 20 years earlier in *The Parent Trap*, their energies and ingenuity are solely directed towards the stereotypically feminine task of managing intimate relationships.

Inasmuch as children as young as two years of age have been found to model their behaviour on what they see on television (Comstock and Paik, 1991; Wood et al., 1991), particularly as exhibited by same-sex characters (Evans, 1993), concern has been expressed over the fact that children's programing is especially likely to feature stereotyped gender roles. Signorielli (1991, 1989) reports that children who spend the greatest amount of time watching television are more likely to hold values that are the most gender-typed and stereotypical. Similarly, in a study of children in grades six to eight, Morgan (1987) reports that expressed beliefs that "women are happiest at home raising children" and "men are born with more ambition than women" are correlated with the amount of time spent watching television.

One analysis of prime-time television shows from 1950 to 1983 (Meehan, 1993) identifies 11 types of female characters: (i) the Imp: rebellious and rowdy; (ii) the Goodwife: a banal, but beneficent, character; (iii) the Harpy: an aggressive, single woman; (iv) the Bitch: a strong-willed, self-absorbed, and destructive woman; (v) the Victim: a woman suffering from pain, injury, imprisonment, or disease; (vi) the Decoy: described as "bait in chic clothing"; (vii) the Siren: sexy and sinister; (viii) the Courtesan: a female entrepreneur/clotheshorse; (ix) the Witch: a woman portrayed as having some form of special power; (x) the Matriarch: a competent, brave, and socially prominent older woman; and (xi) the Androgyne: a strong, autonomous female who combines both "masculine" (instrumental) and "feminine" (expressive) traits and behaviours. A classic rare androgyne in the 1970s was the character of "Mary Richards" portrayed by Mary Tyler Moore on *The Mary Tyler Moore Show,* which ran from 1970 to 1977 (still appearing in syndicated reruns on the Women's Television Network in the mid-1990s). The androgyne became more common in the 1980s, when the newsroom torch was passed from "Mary Richards" to *Murphy Brown* and strong female characters in other employment venues (e.g., *Kate and Allie, The Golden Girls, Cagney and Lacey,* and, arguably, several characters in *Star Trek: Next Generation*).

Meehan (1993: 49) contends that the role of the androgyne is "more popular than ever" in the 1990s. *Murphy Brown* broke new ground by combining never-married parenthood with successful paid work, although she continued the tradition in television of featuring women in situation comedies. Mid-1990s science-fiction drama (e.g., "Captain Janeway" in *Star Trek: Voyager*) and fantasy (e.g., *Xena*) characters might not count, since they were deliberately located outside of a contemporary time frame and can, therefore, be termed "unreal," although the qualifications of "Dana Scully" as a contemporary androgyne are beyond debate. The current reality of females in prime-time television is more complex than ever before, especially with the increasing tendency towards ensemble casts with widely varying characters. Significantly more female lead characters in mid-1990s comedies and dramas are gainfully employed in a range of working-class and small-business occupations (and a smattering of barracudas in the boardrooms and corporate bedrooms), with a large proportion concentrated in some facet of medicine (and other helping professions, such as angels) and law or law enforcement (see Vande Berg and Streckfuss, 1992). Marital statuses are mixed, although the predominant demographic formula for the 1990s unrealistically dictates that dependent children be cared for by women, only occasionally by divorced or (preferably) widowed men, and must come in threes (even though the average family in Canada and the United States has had only one or two children since the early 1970s). Although a few openly gay or lesbian characters became part of the periphery casts of many television shows during the 1990s, *Ellen* was the first lead character in a continuing series to come out of the closet (amidst major media hoopla) in mid-1997, although in the spring of 1998 the series was canceled. Gay male leads are nonexistent and househusbands are rare.

Despite Meehan's (1993) claims, other observers are less sanguine about the presentation of women within the media. "As we approach the turn of the century, despite massive real-world changes in gender roles, the world of television persists in…stereotyped and sexist images" (Lindsey, 1997: 71). Even if *Roseanne* was no one's idea of a frail, helpless female and the *Nanny* is no *Mary Poppins*, females are more likely than men to be portrayed as passive and indecisive, depicted as being dominated by men rather than the other way around, unlikely to be found in truly egalitarian intimate relationships, and less likely than men to be found in leadership and decision-making positions affecting the lives of others outside of their family constellations. Rather, they are frequently found pursuing altruistic goals in betterment of home and family, or seeking protection or rescue from homicidal stalkers or others seeking to do them physical, psychological, or emotional harm (Davis, 1990; National Commission on Working Women, 1990; Wood, 1994). Signorielli (1991: 89, 94) observes that women of colour, older women, and foreign women are especially likely to be depicted as the victims of violent crime.

Daytime soap operas are a notable exception to the limited and limiting portrayals of women in television (Larson, 1996). Akin to romance novels, women are not underrepresented in the world of soap operas, nor are their lives portrayed as revolving solely or even largely around the private sphere of homemaking and parenting. Rather, the reverse seems true. In the world inhabited by soap opera characters, houses only need cleaning when a murder or an affair has been committed and a coverup is taking place. While parents may emotively proclaim children to be the centre of their lives, men and women are only occasionally depicted in active parenting roles, schlepping their children to extracurricular activities or to orthodontist appointments; even pregnancy requires less energy—but is more time-consuming, especially when paternity is uncertain (see also Larson, 1996). Female characters afflicted with the common soap opera problem of amnesia often forget who, and where, their children are. Parents of any soap opera child are also likely to be divorced, to maintain separate residences with their new true love, to be perpetually fearful of having their child kidnaped by some evil person (especially rejected fathers and deranged mothers or equally-deranged women who cannot conceive children), and to employ a retinue of housekeepers and nannies to deal with such mundane matters as childcare, meal preparation, house-cleaning, and gardening. In soap opera families, young children are usually seen only as extensions of adults, being mentioned more often than shown except for occasional birthday parties that provide convenient excuses for the adults to converse and connive, and only become prominent as the subject of custody battles. When the dust settles, children are sent back to their bedrooms to play until they become adolescents and can resurface, all grown up, during the summer months when students are more likely to be watching.

The breakup of a relationship, a common event on most soap operas, is typically portrayed in a highly gendered way. Regardless of who is depicted as being at fault, the soap-opera woman is much more likely than the soap-opera man to spend lengthy amounts of time crying and wringing her hands over the involuntarily loss of her man; men on soap operas rarely wring their hands for long periods of time. In a composite script, we would not be surprised to find that Ned marries Lois under an assumed name, and then marries Katherine one week later under his real name. Months later, Lois finds out about Ned's duplicity and throws him out. She then devotes herself to months of agonizing, ranting, crying, and hand-wringing. Ned, in contrast, continues his life as a successful millionaire businessman and vows to win back Lois. (Katherine, in case you were wondering, has been poisoned and is conveniently lying in a coma, where she only appears on the screen once a week, and possibly spends the remainder of her time wondering if she soon will be collecting unemployment insurance or, more likely, appear in an arc [a brief recurring, role on a nighttime soap], which may become permanent). Ned does not cry, agonize, or rant; he remains unrepentant and un-bowed. Such commonly occurring depictions reinforce stereotypes of male stoic fortitude and female emotionality.

When men in Port Charles, Genoa City, or Pine Valley do get emotional, they are likely to punch a hole in the wall or, in take-charge fashion, hire a killer. Women, in contrast, throw things at the object of their wrath and typically miss. Male anger, it seems, is considered understandable and acceptable, while female anger becomes a form of slapstick comedy. Similarly, male grief is shown as expelled in one brief burst of anguish, while female grief is incapacitating, forcing even the most powerful woman to take to her bed, lost in paroxysms of tears. Lesser women attempt suicide. Both powerful men and powerful women often take to the bed of someone else in search of solace. As a consequence of the shifting tides of marriage-divorce-remarriage-redivorce-re-remarriage, women in soap-opera land often have lengthy multiply-hyphenated surnames.

We noted in Chapter 4 that male given names in our society tend to have a harsher sound than female given names. One interesting manipulation of this pattern occurs within the soap opera, where females with masculine-sounding names are presented as powerful. For example, "Victoria Lord Buchanan" is the head of a successful and influential city newspaper; her sister, "Tina," is portrayed as having no business sense whatsoever. While exceptions do appear (e.g., "Tiffany" is the owner of a television station and the boss of the news department despite her fluffy-sounding name), women with harsher, male-sounding names are generally portrayed as being more successful than those with softer, more feminine names: "Erica" (All My Children) has established several successful major enterprises over the years; "Monica" (General Hospital) is a brilliant cardiologist; "Alex" (One Life To Live) is a nightclub owner and a former mob boss; "Dorian" (One Life To Live) runs a national gossip paper; but "Bobbie" (General Hospital) the most talented operating-room nurse in the hospital, has never been promoted.

Women may become important and powerful in business, but their careers tend to be in areas considered gender-appropriate or gender-linked; doyens within the business worlds of fashion, cosmetics, and the hospitality industries. Women are often depicted as acquiring their power through their personal ties to powerful men or through exercising their devious "feminine wiles." "Victoria Lord Buchanan" (One Life To Live) inherited her newspaper business from her father after he had disinherited his only son; "Dorian" (One Life To Live) blackmailed her former lover into selling her a tabloid business; "Erica" (All My Children) became rich enough to purchase a business after wily divorce settlements; "Alex" (One Life to Live) stole the paperwork for her business while her companion was sleeping. Regardless of how they came to attain power, women are often portrayed as less likely than men to maintain positions of power; "Opal" may develop the concept for a business, but her husband "Palmer" provides the clout to develop it into a multimillion dollar corporation. "Lucy" may invent the perfume, establish the company and market the product, but she is sure to surrender control to the men in the front office or the boardroom at the first sign of trouble. Images of men rescuing the interests of weaker females reinforce the stereotype of women's unsuitability for the high pressure world of business. Moreover, women who demonstrate stereotypical femininity are often presented as being morally superior to those who are more masculine or androgynous. Strong women who are successful, assertive, and highly determined to survive without men are portrayed as hydras and "villains" (Benokraitis and Feagin, 1995).

Advertising and Commercials

By the time an adolescent reaches the age of 18, he or she has watched approximately 360 000 commercials on television (Bretl and Cantor, 1988; Garst and Bodenhausen, 1997; Harris, 1992). Stereotypical idealized images of women and men are reinforced through advertising (Barthel, 1987; Kilbourne, 1992). An early study of gender in advertising noted that women were typically portrayed as either demented housewives, pathologically obsessed with cleanliness and cleaning products, or as wannabe sex objects driven to purchase a never-ending array of cosmetics (Courtney and Lockeretz, 1971). Shortly thereafter, Venkatesan and Losco (1975) reported a decline in the "most obnoxious" types of gendered advertising although they noted that the messages being conveyed remained markedly consistent. Three years later, Tuchman et al. (1978) reported that more than three-quarters of the television ads featuring women still were for products employed in the bathroom or kitchen. Even today, women's voices are rarely used as voice-over commentators in television advertising; the narrative voice of expertise is male in roughly 90 percent of commercials (Bretl and Cantor, 1988). Signorielli (1990, 1989) contends that the significance of such voice-castings is not lost on viewers; the more people watch television, the more they tend to hold restrictive ideas about the "proper" role of women in society. Although the rigidity of gender stereotypes has declined over the past 15 to 20 years, the roles occupied by women in advertising bear only a nodding acquaintanceship with the breadth and depth of women's lives outside of television (Garst and Bodenhausen, 1997; Hunt and Ruben, 1993; Sullivan and O'Connor, 1988; Timson, 1995).

Feldstein and Feldstein (1982) observe that male dominance also exists within commercials intended to influence young children; with the exception of advertisements for dolls, male characters are numerically overrepresented in children's commercials and girls are presented as being more passive than boys. The gender of the targeted purchaser of an advertised toy is identified not only by the explicit content, but also by the presentation style of commercials. Welch et al. (1979) note that commercials targeting boys are distinguished by such features as "rapid action, frequent cuts, loud music, sound effects, and many scene changes," while, in contrast, those for girls feature "background music, fades and dissolves, and female narrations" (in Lips, 1993: 273). Huston et al. (1984) find that six- to twelve-year-old children are able to indicate which forms are appropriate for advertising toys targeting young female or male consumers. "It is possible...that the form of presentation of various objects and activities on television influences children's attention and interest in subtle ways, cueing them as to the gender-appropriateness of particular content...[and] that television can act as a powerful agent of gender-role socialization even in the absence of content that explicitly defines certain activities as appropriate only for girls or only for boys" (Lips, 1993: 273). A positive relationship between extensive television viewing and the holding of rigid gender stereotypes has been reported in studies conducted on children (Eisenstock, 1984; Frueh and McGhee, 1975; Zuckerman et al., 1980), adolescents (Morgan, 1982) and adults (Lanis and Covell, 1995; St. Lawrence and Joyner, 1991; Walker, Rowe and Quinsey, 1993).

The increase in nudity and near-nudity in advertising in Canada and the United States perpetuates a stereotypical portrayal of women as decorative sexual objects (Lazier-Smith, 1989; Wiles, 1989). One 1997 advertisement for a hand-held pocket video game, for example, features a woman clad in a lacy baby doll pajama bound by her wrists to the headboard of a bed, legs spread apart, and the caption "The New Game Boy Pocket: Seriously distracting." While the faces of men are shown more often than their bodies ("face-isms"), women's bodies ("body-isms") or parts of their bodies ("partial-isms") prominently appear. Thus, a 1997 advertisement for White Label PC CD-ROM Games features a portion of a woman's body (from mid-rib to upper-thigh) clad only in a small white thong bikini. The caption reads: "It's the quality in the box that counts."

Belknap and Leonard (1991: 105) observe that the "selling [of] products that depict more traditional cultural patterns has been slow to change." Only with the mid-1990s obsession with abdominal muscles (abs) have men's bodies been featured more prominently and often reduced to a six-pack partial-ism. The depiction of minority women has been particularly resistant to change. If, in general, minorities are likely to appear as simply part of a crowd, or as "walking away from the camera"—as jazz musician Oscar Peterson remarked in describing the presence of black musicians on beer commercials—minority women appear to be notable only for their absence or for their depiction as "exotic" decorative adornments. MacGregor (1995) finds that women of colour were largely invisible in Canada's national newsmagazine *Maclean's,* when measured by their number of appearances in both advertisements and articles during a 30-year time period. Ageism is notable with the relative general invisibility of older women in advertising, except for their confinement largely within ads for adult diapers, hair dyes, dentures (Jamieson, 1995), and wrinkle creams. A 1997 advertisement for Osmotics advises: "See your mother on holidays. Not every time you look in the mirror."

There can be little doubt that advertising creates images of men and women stressing their differences rather than their similarities, and suggesting that these differences must be regarded as both mysterious and immutable. Reflecting our society's anti-body orientation, television advertising promotes an attitude of revulsion towards the natural excretions and secretions of the human body, women's bodies more so than men's. The mysterious and immutably different fluids emanating from women's bodies provide the foundation for millions of advertising dollars designed to first heighten anxiety about these emanations and then to provide a specific product to allay any concerns. Consider, for example, advertising surrounding "feminine protection products" and the significant cultural meanings they convey. Such ads are particularly interesting for the manner in which they promote products for a bodily function that has typically been treated as "taboo" within our own and other societies. Implicit within advertising are numerous messages reinforcing stereotypical conceptions of women in our society.

The idea that women in general, and menstruating women in particular, are unclean, contaminated, or cosmically dangerous is neither new nor unique to North American society (Hays, 1964). Many cultures, both historically and currently, have created normative prohibitions surrounding what women can or cannot do during the time of their menses, ranging across cultures from seclusion in a "menstrual hut," avoidance of contact with weapons for hunting and warfare, temporary suspension of aircraft-flying privileges, restriction from washing one's hair, to curtailment of strenuous physical activity in gym class and swimming pools, and abstention from sexual activity. That menstruation is both a subject and experience to be avoided is captured in our language that either refers to the phenomenon directly as "the curse" (a monthly stigmatic reminder of women's responsibility for the human fall from grace, according to Christian religious beliefs), or prefers to acknowledge the phenomenon only indirectly via an immensely varied euphemistic language having to do with, for example, invisible relatives ("Aunt Flo is visiting me") and playmates ("my little friend"), punctuation marks ("period"), a secular version of the Christian belief ("fallen off the roof"—an archaic phrase common in eastern parts of Canada and the United States), or marketed products ("riding the cotton pony"). Being indirect references, euphemisms are subject to varying interpretations and resulting misunderstandings and confusion over their meanings (Ernster, 1975; Hays, 1987).

In addition to the prohibitions mentioned above, women have been confronted with the pragmatic tasks of dealing with their menstrual flow and abdominal cramps. Elaborate layers of petticoats worn by women in previous generations, represented an attempt to conceal visible evidence of homemade diapers and pads. "Women in the 1890s carried some fifteen pounds of skirts and petticoats, hanging from a tightly corseted waist" (Rothman and Cashcetta, 1995: 71). The first menstrual pad appeared in 1920, shortly after the development of cellucotton products designed for use as surgical dressing during World War I. The "sanitary belt" at that time was a relatively simple contraption worn around a woman's waist with dangling clips, similar to a garter belt, to which one attached the "sanitary" menstrual pad or "napkin." While the invention of the menstrual pad allowed the "flapper" to forego the use of petticoats and don dresses that were straight and streamlined, the naming of the "sanitary pad" or "sanitary napkin" is significant. The symbolic alignment of these products with being "sanitary" clearly promotes the message that women during menstruation are unsanitary, or unclean, and in need of an artificial product to decontaminate them and render them pure and clean.

Increasingly, providing for "*that* time of month" (a phrase that not only bewilders young males who cannot find any such reference on any calendars, but also makes females appear even more mysterious—"they've got their own special calendars!") has become Big Business. Friday (1996: 195) reports that, while in 1986, "$23,974,600 was spent on magazine advertising for feminine hygiene products," this figure soared, in 1994, to $40 931 300. The commonly used phrase "feminine hygiene products" carries a double message. Menstruation is characterized as being both unhygienic and unfeminine (a marvelous stroke of advertising illogic wherein possession of a sex-linked irreducible difference causes a woman to become unfeminine). Fortunately, one product can restore a woman's hygiene *and* her femininity. Unfortunately, from a consumer's perspective, advertisers expound on the virtues of a veritable cornucopia of different products from which women may choose: napkins for "heavy days," "medium days" and "light days," tampons ("slim line," "baby powder scented" and/or with environmentally friendly disposable wrappers), maxipads (including the oxymoronic "ultra-thin maxis") and minipads (scented and unscented varieties), pantyliners, and the newly marketed reusable vaginal cup. The aim of advertisers is to keep all women padded, tampooned, pantylined, and cupped for all 28 days of each and every (theoretically constructed) menstrual cycle for approximately 40 years of menses (give or take a pregnancy or two).

Advertising has become somewhat more direct over the past 20 years. Friday (1996: 190) writes: "When I was growing up, the only references to feminine hygiene were the full-page ads of beautiful women in elegant gowns and in a corner the discreet message, 'Modess Because.' Because what?" Some advertisers now see fit to coopt the language of the women's movement (e.g., a 1996 ad for "Always Maxi-Wings" proclaims: "Women in the '90s have definite Advantages. Advantage #1. Comfort! Comfort! Comfort!" The message is clear: menstruation is discomforting; by "Always" using "Maxi-Wings," women can achieve their true advantage over men—comfort). Many advertisers align their products with freedom, such as the entitled *Stay-Free* line, thereby implying that menstruation constrains women's freedom. Television ads frequently depict female characters enjoying their freedoms in wide-open spaces by engaging in various forms of vigorous exercise, all made possible by an advertised product.

Other advertisers prefer to market their products under the term "feminine protection." We learn from their ads that femininity is a precarious commodity constantly under attack. An intriguing ad instructs women "For feminine protection everyday, use..." a police whistle, pepper spray, martial arts? No, a tampon. One product offers women "funnel dot protection." Does this mean that women need to be protected from "funnel dots," or that the only thing between femininity and unfemininity is a thin protective line of funnel dots? Sanitary napkins, we are informed, are designed to protectively address the mysterious problem of "excess moisture." If, as our old adage claims, "horses sweat, men perspire, and women glow," one might reasonably ask, who "moists"? Apparently only women, since men are not offered this product by advertisers.

The visual aids provided in television and print advertising are rarely helpful since the product's effectiveness is most often demonstrated by their ability to "absorb" (a key word in many ads) copious quantities of a blue liquid. To complicate matters further, this appears to be the same blue liquid that manufacturers of diapers use to advertise the effectiveness of *their* product. Nowhere in advertising do we hear or see references to blood or blood-red colouring. What we do see are advertisers directing our attention to the apparently aerodynamic construction of their product and its "wing design folds" (Initial slogan: "The darn things has wings!"). The "wings" versus "tabs" debate promises to extend into the next millennium, much to the perplexity of most men and to those women wondering what all of this has to do with protecting their femininity. Adding to the confusion is the conundrum over distinguishing precisely between "light" versus "heavy" days. It would seem that femininity has something to do with weight and gravity—a suggestion promoted by advertising comments that women should use certain products so they can feel "free as a bird." On "light days," women can fly around on their mini-winged personal hang gliders snubbing their noses at poor women heavily grounded by wearing tabs.

Other products "for women" are often similarly couched by advertisers in the language of euphemism and implicit references. Perhaps the most blatant of such ads are those designed to promote "feminine hygiene sprays" or "feminine deodorant sprays," not to be confused with douches or underarm deodorants ("strong enough for a man, but made for a woman"—the gender consequences of using the other sex's deodorant are unclear, but presumably dire). Viewing audiences are allowed to eavesdrop on secret "intimate discussions" between two women wearing lots of white clothes, often a mother and daughter, as they walk alone along a beach or through fields of cornflowers, or sit alone in an airy sunlight room, under no danger of intrusion from ignorant trespassers (i.e., men) as they discuss how to feel "really clean inside." Casual male observers of these ads are lead to believe that mothers pass along the secrets of cleanliness to daughters during conversations that feature such dialogue as "Sometimes I don't feel fresh enough. Did you ever have this problem?" the daughter tentatively asks. "Of course," the mother responds in a gentle all-knowing voice. "Oh, mom," the daughter gratefully replies. Then they hug and the ritual exchange of information is over. Exactly *what* problem both women suffer from is never clearly identified, but its solution has something to do with the shape of a bottle in relation to an unidentified body orifice and the chemical concentration of a magical fluid contained in the bottle. Other solutions to this mysterious problem are found in aerosol spray cans.

The ads implicitly suggest that women have infinitely more problems than do men, and also that their problems are so overwhelming that they cannot be discussed in a straightforward fashion. Women, apparently, have a unique odour problem to go along with their excess blue moisture problem. Such ads tell us that women cannot be feminine on their own; hygienic products are required to protect women from being women. Apparently, men do not suffer from these problems. Only one serious attempt was made to cajole men to try a "masculine deodorant spray," also not to be confused with an underarm deodorant. In the early 1980s, Brute came out with a product designed to make men feel really clean outside— *PUB: Below the Belt*. However, like more conventional pubs, PUB contained a high alcohol content that proved to be damaging, and stinging, to men's sensitive scrotal skin. In response to numerous complaints, the product was quickly taken off the market in less than a year. In stark contrast, ads for feminine protection sprays—"when you want to feel like a woman" (just use femininity in a can)—are still being strongly promoted despite possible linkages to vaginal cancer.

In our last word on advertising, we draw your attention to another short-lived product manufactured in 1994 and directed at a male market. Designed to parallel the successful marketing of home pregnancy tests for women, *Fertility Score* was intended to facilitate men's taking their own sperm counts at home. Advertising explicitly suggested that men could keep score of their fertility counts, presumably rewarding themselves for achieving personal bests. Implicitly, ads suggested that test scores could be used to establish competitive bragging rights ("Hey, I scored 20 billion per micro litre. Top that! Loser buys the beer.") For some unknown reason, the product quickly disappeared from store shelves and television advertising.

Popular Music

Popular music, particularly rock, was initially aimed at and supported by "war babies," who became teenagers in the early to mid-1950s, and then increasingly by baby boomers (who became teenagers starting in 1959). As Frith (1981) points out, prior to the 1950s, young people used to adopt the music preferences of their parents (who were actually the targets of the "family audience"). "There were adult records and children's records, and nothing in between" (Palmer, 1995: 17). Industry and advertising began targeting their marketing of products at the emerging teen population in the late 1950s primarily because they were so many of them. Targeting a music market at teenagers was simply an extension of a new trend towards segmented marketing (individuals in families rather than whole families). While mom and dad tuned into the *Gisele MacKenzie Show* or the *Don Messer Show* (later to be renamed *Don Messer's Jubilee*), their children could listen to the sh-boom sound of The Crew Cuts (or the Canadairs as they were known in the early 1950s) do the "Stroll" (one of the earliest dance-step crazes) to the music of the Toronto doo-wop group The Diamonds, harmonize along with The Four Lads, or become part of the filmed audience at a Paul Anka concert that prompted Chuck Barry to write "Sweet Little Sixteen" and other songs ("School Day," "Almost Grown") celebrating the newly emerging teen culture (Melhuish, 1996:62; Palmer, 1995: 30).

Many already in the music industry, especially performers of adult-oriented music like Frank Sinatra, were skeptical about the durability of this new genre of music. "Rock 'n roll," Sinatra commented in 1957, "smells phony and false. It is sung, played, and written for the most part by cretinous goons and by means of its almost imbecilic reiteration...it manages to be the martial music of every sideburned delinquent on the face of the earth" (in Palmer, 1995: 130). It was believed that old standards, and old (from a teenager's point of view) adults would continue to hold power over and control musical tastes. No one anticipated the amount of catering that baby boomers would receive in adolescence, nor how prolonged adolescence would become as a social age category in the postwar years.

The television, movie, advertising, and marketing industries had already reaped enormous financial rewards with the successful marketing to baby boom children of more than 3000 different types of Davy Crockett items, ranging from raccoonskin caps to toothbrushes and lunchboxes (Jones, 1980: 50–51). These industries now combined forces with the music industry to target the adolescent market. The growing economic prosperity of the postwar years put more money into the hands of those no-longer-children-but-not-yet-adults. In many ways, adolescents have more discretionary income than any other age group, since they do not have responsibilities for homes and appliances and family food and major clothing items and insurance and all the other fun things adults spend their money on. Combine a large target audience, the development of a mind-set in business and advertising that was used to catering to an enormous population bulge and wanted (and still does) to follow that group to their graves, discretionary income, and an elaboration of the belief that adolescence was a unique period in the social-time continuum with special needs, wants, anguish, and ecstasy, and the formula for a new and continuing music form was born.

Frith (1981) observes that an active attempt was made in the 1950s by the music industry to produce "bland, well-crafted songs" for the teenage market, and to purposefully groom chosen performers as "teenage entertainers." Palmer (1995: 42) suggests that the initial casting of teen idols as the white "boy next door" was strategic and stemmed from an attempt to quell "the specter of…miscegenation…a black man fondling daddy's little white girl." Those fears stemmed from the fact that the roots of rock and roll were firmly planted in earlier rhythm and blues music created and performed by black musicians. Rock music was initially condemned within white communities in both Canada and the United States as "jungle music." Little Richard, the self-designated King *and* Queen of Rock and Roll, writes in his autobiography that his pompadoured, gender-bending, madman image was deliberately crafted "so that adults would think I was harmless" (Szatmary, 1996: 24–25). The desirable new teenage heartthrob of the 1950s was to embody the appealing image of the white boy from either the new middle-class suburbs or the old working-class neighbourhood. Canadian singers such as Bobby Curtola and Paul Anka, along with American stars such as Bobby Rydell, Fabian, Frankie Avalon, and Cliff Richards, all "squeaky clean and perfect for the whitebread market" (Szatmary, 1996: 67), emerged as the fantasy boyfriend of young girls. Buttressed by the efforts of astute managers, fan club organizers (Salamon, 1984) and bi-weekly or monthly music magazines (which, in Canada, began in the late 1950s with the publication of *Music World*, then billed as "Canada's Only Publication Devoted to Popular Music"), the "pop charts were dominated by manufactured [white] 'teen idols'" (Palmer, 1995: 42), many of whom were further packaged as material objects for economic consumption. For example, Szatmary (1996: 53) notes that "[i]f a loyal fan so desired, she could put on Elvis Presley bobby socks, Elvis Presley shoes, skirt, blouse and sweater, hang an Elvis Presley Charm bracelet on one wrist, and with the other hand smear on some Elvis Presley lipstick—either Hound Dog Orange, Heartbreak Hotel Pink, or Tutti Frutti Red." She could carry an Elvis Presley handkerchief in her Elvis Presley purse, don Elvis Presley jeans, Bermuda shorts, or toreador pants, curl up in her Elvis Presley pajamas and write in her diary with her Elvis Presley pencil (inscribed "sincerely yours"). As Szatmary (1996: 53) observes, "All told, the fan could buy 78 different Elvis Presley products that grossed about $55 million by December 1957."

While a teen idol's ability to sing was desirable, it was not, in and of itself, essential. Consider that in creating the Monkees, "a prefabricated American version of the Beatles," executives from Raybert Productions purposively placed an ad in major Hollywood trade papers for "four insane boys, age 17-21" for an *acting* role in a television series and, after auditioning 437 hopefuls (which included future mass-murderer Charles Manson), they selected those that struck them as the most "photogenic" and "energetic" (Szatmary, 1996: 132–133). "[T]he group attracted 10 million viewers every Monday night for their television program, received 5000 fan letters a day and sold over $20 million in Monkees merchandise.…'We're advertisers,' enthused selected "actor" Mickey Dolenz at the time, 'We're selling a product. We're selling Monkees'" (in Szatmary, 1996: 133). This practice of manufacturing designer musical groups for the marketplace has continued from the time of the Monkees, through Minudo, to present-day groups, such as the Backstreet Boys and the Spice Girls.

Such technological innovations as the growing popularity and affordability of television sets (and with it shows such as *The Ed Sullivan Show, American Bandstand, Rock 'n Roll Dance Party, Soul Train,* and countless after-school imitators at every local television station across Canada), the increasing availability of both AM and eventually FM radio waves for a wider variety of recording artists (especially blacks), and the introduction of car radios, portable transistor radios, and inexpensive 45-rpm records (manufactured almost exclusively for teenagers), all made rock and roll easily accessible to a young generation living in comparatively prosperous times. By the 1960s, adolescence was extolled within the world of pop music as *superior* to adulthood and the suggestion made that if one could not help but grow old chronologically, one should strive to retain the *ideology of youth* (Frith, 1981: 34) "free from the narrow routines of maturity…sexually vigorous and emotionally unrestrained."

Although folk singer Bob Dylan was later to comment that "There's other things in this world besides love and sex that're important, too" and rhetorically ask, "How is this world ever going to get better if we're afraid to look at these things?" adolescence was romanticized in the song lyrics of the day and "[t]he music of the Dick Clark era, the Brill Building songwriters, the Beach Boys, the Motown artists, and the early Beatles showed a preoccupation with dating, cars, high school and teen love" (Szatmary, 1996: xii). Songs delivered by early all-female (referred to then as all-*girl*) groups such as the Crystals, the Ronettes, the Supremes, and the Shirelles (whose plaintive "Will You Still Love Me Tomorrow?" became the first number-one hit by an all-female group) especially tended towards the maudlin "limited language of sentiment, in the rhyming simplicities of moon and June" (Frith, 1981: 35). The sudden rise to fame, with attendant wealth and previously unknown lifestyles of the rich and adolescent, created role models out of both male and female young rock stars. "The rags-to-riches success stories of the girl groups added to the romantic appeal of the music for thousands of school-aged girls…[served] to create the fantasy among many young girls that they too could become famous…[and] the fantasies of teenage girls helped…establish a music-publishing empire" (Szatmary, 1996: 74, 77–78).

Over time, the singular "wholesome" whitebread image of rock and roll gave way to alternative visions created partly by the musicians themselves and partly by the music marketers. "[M]usic travels along with other forms of commerce and, as it collides with other cultures, changes" (Santoro, 1994: vi). The initial rebellion of rock in sound, shaded over into rebellion expressed in words and images. Elvis' hips, once banned on television, acknowledged the underlying sexual energy of the music and the musicians. The Rolling Stones, the original "bad boys of rock," were marketed by publicist Andrew Oldham to contrast with "the clean-cut choirboy image" of the Beatles and "to establish that the Stones were threatening, uncouth and animalistic"—an image that was furthered by a 1964 headline article in *Melody Maker* entitled "Would You Let Your Daughter Go Out With A Rolling Stone?" (Szatmary, 1996: 137). While the Beatles had sung "I Wanna Hold Your Hand," the music of the Stones featured an more overtly sexual and, not unoccasionally, misogynistic message with songs such as "Just Make Love to Me," "Under My Thumb," and "Stupid Girl." While "cock-rock performers" (Frith, 1981: 227) offered "a masturbatory celebration of penis power," the connection between "sex, drugs, rock-

'n'roll" (rapidly becoming youth's pledge of allegiance) was fostered by the emergence of acid rock, psychedelic rockers such as Jefferson Airplane, and the self-characterized "erotic politician" Jim Morrison and The Doors and attested to in such song titles as "Boobs Alot," "Group Grope," "Dirty Old Man," "Touch Me," "Love Me Two Times," and "Light My Fire."

The splitting of rock into a host of subgenres also demonstrates marketing attempts to identify and target even more specific adolescent and older target audiences (a more segmented market) based upon ethnicity and lifestyle. Szatmary (1996: 192) observes that "while white youths listened to the Beatles, acid rock, or British bands...African-Americans took pride in a gritty soul sound performed by fellow African-Americans." Soul music, which black disc jockey Magnificent Montague described in the 1960s as "the last to be hired, the first to be fired, brown all-year-round, sit-in-the-back-of-the-bus feeling" and songs such as Aretha Franklin's "Respect" and "Think" (which ends with the repetition of the word "freedom"), were to attract greater mainstream interest following the Detroit in-nercity riots of the late 1960s and renewed civil rights activism. For others, the pronounced pessimism and antiwar sentiment of heavy metal music, as embodied in groups such as Led Zeppelin and Black Sabbath, was more appealing. "'I don't profess to be a messiah of slum people,' insisted vocalist John ("Ozzy") Osbourne, 'but I was a back-street kid, and that little demon is still in there, shoving the hot coal in. The aggression I play is the aggression I know. And it's obviously aggression a lot of people have'; as punk singer Johnny Rotten was later to remark, 'You don't sing about love to people on the dole'" (in Szatmary, 1996: 206–207, 251).

The nascent gay liberation movement of the 1970s encouraged a variety of rock performers to publicly experiment with a gender-bending style, and a greater openness about bisexuality and homosexuality. From the pink boas of Elton John, the changing personas of David Bowie (who, in 1972, declared his bisexuality to the press), the self-mutilation and psychodrama of Iggy Pop, the transvestite hero of Lou Reed's "Walk on the Wild Side," and the makeup and macho of The Artist Then Known As Prince, at least theatrical androgyny was "in." "[T]here was the make-up wearing, fishnet-hose-and-spandex-sporting 'glam' movement [which was considered in Britain to be teeny-bopper music], spearheaded by the likes of Pink Floyd founder/singer/guitarist Syd Barrett, in his frilly lace cuffs and eye shadow, T. Rex main man Marc Bolan, with his fey androgyny, and the early David Bowie, warbling 'Space Oddity' and posing for the cover of his *The Man Who Sold The World* in a dress" (Palmer, 1995: 176). The 1970s gender-bending affectation of glam-rockers such as the Dolls—"in lipstick and powder, cellophane tutus, feather boas, and fishnet stockings, with or without combat boots," writes Palmer (1995: 266–267) "were giving rock and roll back to the kids, though not everyone understood why they had to wear dresses and lipstick to do it." Nor did every one appreciate this avowedly androgynous style; if David Bowie was to profess his admiration for Queen vocalist Freddie Mercury with the comment that "I always admired a man who wears tights" (in Szatmary, 1996: 261), punk bandleader Wayne County opinioned that "Alice Cooper had to stop wearing ladies' sling-back shoes and false eyelashes and dresses and get more into horror because people in America could understand horror and blood and dead babies, but they couldn't understand male/female sexuality, androgyny, or...as little American boys would say, fag music" (in Palmer, 1995: 186). The 1980s also spawned gender-bender Boy George and the fusion of androgynous makeup or dress (or undress), and the macabre continues to be popularized in the 1990s by groups such as Marilyn Manson and Fear Factory.

Surveying the state of popular music at the end of the 1970s, Frith (1981: 227) concludes that the world of rock music was strongly gendered. Female fans attended mainly to the lyrics of songs and less to the rhythms via which they were conveyed. Male fans generally ignored the lyrics (unless they were scrambling to find a good seduction line or a rallying call for drinking and partying) and focused mainly upon musical sounds and rhythms. Although not stated by Frith, it appears, both then and now, that performing or listening to such music, akin to actual or vicarious participation in sports, provides a socially acceptable and often-used opportunity for males to experience and express a wide range of emotions either alone or in the company of others. Females were overwhelmingly attracted to "teeny-bop" music and its performers who plaintively expressed vulnerability and need. Sexuality within the teeny-bop genre was presented "as a kind of spiritual yearning, carrying only vague hints of physical desire. The singer wants someone to love—not as a bedmate, but as a soul mate" (Frith, 1981: 227). In sharp contrast, males were overwhelmingly attracted to "cock-rock" music and its performers who expressed a raw, unabashedly physical, aggressive sexuality. "Their bodies are on display (plunging shirts and tight trousers, chest hair and genitals), mikes and guitars are phallic symbols (or else caressed like female bodies), the music is loud, rhythmically insistent built around techniques of arousal and release" (Frith, 1981: 227). The teeny-bop-cock-rock distinction still exists today (compare Roch Voisine, Boyz II Men, and Hanson with Metallica and Aerosmith, both in terms of their musical and stage presentation styles and the demographics of their respective audiences). However, the continually increasing diversity of all popular music forms, partly an attempt by the music industry to reflect social changes affecting adolescence over the past 25 years, and partly an attempt to find new sources of income, somewhat complicates a Frithian type of summary classification.

Some performers themselves blur the distinctions. The biggest stage act and airplay group at the time this book was being written, U2, performs like cock-rockers, but are widely lauded for their sensitive, spiritually soulful lyrics. Country music star Garth Brooks produces a cock-rock sound and stage performance closer to classic rock than that created by most of his contemporaries in mainstream rock, yet he also identifies himself in support of gay rights and sings about the devastating effects of domestic violence ("Thunder Rolls") and date rape ("Face-to-Face"). The distinction is blurred further in relatively new music genres such that, for example, while techno-disco and party/dance music is close to teeny-bop, they both focus more upon rhythm than upon lyrics. Rap, hip hop, and reggae contain potent lyrics, but require a strong underlying rhythm to aid their delivery, and to keep people dancing, or at least moving parts of their bodies in time. Cock-rockers shave their chest hairs (and sometimes their heads) before going on stage, and penis-powered gangsta rappers cover their bodies in voluminous layers of sweatsuits and jogging outfits. Some "girl" groups (e.g., En Vogue) present a rocking in-your-face sexuality while others (e.g., TLC with "Waterfall") dispense thoughtful advice to guide a woman's journey through life.

Despite a blurring of the lines between cock-rock and teeny-bop music, the proliferation of new popular musical genres (e.g., punk, grunge, garage, alternative music) geared to even smaller segments of the listening and buying audience, important gender distinctions remain regarding the production, performance, and content of rock music. The bulk of rock performers receiving air- and, more recently, video-play time, both past and present, have been and are male. Three-quarters of the music videos shown on MTV in the 1980s, and presumably the similarly-formatted MusicMusic, featured only male performers (Vincent et al., 1987). Women are generally portrayed in music videos as decorative, most often sexual, background ornaments for male action. Ten percent of the videos in the 1980s featured violence against women, and an additional 74 percent either "put women down" or tried to "keep them in their place" (Vincent et al., 1987).

The sounds of rock music that attract male attention tend not to become issues of social concern, aside from the early 1950s fears that listening to "jungle rhythms" could lead to dancing that could "inevitably" lead to fornication among white teenagers. Cock-rock stage performances now rarely lead to more than raised eyebrows by even the most conservative segments of the population unless, as occasionally happens, a performer deliberately exposes her breasts or (more often) his genitals on stage, or urinates on the paying customers standing near the stage. Biting the heads off bats, holding mock executions, creating unsafe conditions in the mosh pit that contribute to too many bodily injuries, or failure to provide sufficient crowd control when audience members rush the stage all lead to momentary concerns from public officials and social critics about health and safety issues, but these concerns tend to be fleeting. While music purists might complain that new musical forms are atonal or grating to the ears, or that present-day musicians lack sufficient formal training or do not pay sufficient homage to their earlier roots, and while parents and neighbours may complain that rock music is played too loud, the form of rock music is rarely a social issue.

In contrast, the lyrical content of popular rock music frequently is the recipient of social scrutiny and expressed concern. These lyrics, attended to more by females than by males, still contain dichotomous images of males and females and their respective ideal roles within relationships. Seidman (1992) argues that these messages are especially pronounced within music videos, in which males are more likely to be portrayed as aggressive and domineering, females as affectionate, dependent, and nurturing. Males are visually and auditorally provided with messages that they should dominate heterosexual relationships and females are reminded that they should be sexy and submissive. The ability of popular music to provide vicarious romance for its listeners remains among its myriad functions, appearing sometimes in the seemingly most unlikely of sources. Pascual (1997: 40) critically suggests that the most notable contribution of the Seattle grunge bands such as Nirvana, Soundgarden, Pearl Jam, and Alice in Chains was in "influencing plump starryeyed pubescent girls to fantasize about rainy miserable weather and unbathed heroin addicts who plagiarize Black Sabbath and Black Flag."

One major issue continues to be the depiction of women in rock songs. Teenage females hear women being portrayed as either saints or sinners capable of causing men's salvation through love and devotion or men's downfall through treachery and disloyalty. In one song, women are placed on a pedestal; in the next they reside in the gutter. Political and social-action groups over the years typically have been and are concerned only with the negative images of women (protests are never raised over a too-lofty image). Repeatedly over the past 25 years, rock has been condemned for, and various attempts have been aimed at censorship of, lyrics describing or advocating violence in some form against women. Occasionally, art work found on the covers of vinyl albums on CD jewel boxes or images presented in rock videos will be condemned for displaying women bound, battered, or betrayed by male physical or sexual force. That the issue of degrading portrayals of women recurs continually over the years is testament to the failure of previous efforts at change. Concerns over lyrical odes to illicit drug use, teenage sexuality, and suicide are more likely to lead to some form of censorship in the form of either removal of products from store shelves and music station playlists, or the application of a warning sticker regarding "offensive lyrics." Rarely are extremely negative or positive lyrics about women or men deemed sufficient cause to warrant affixing of a warning label. Gender is most often left to fend for itself.

While rap in general, and "gangsta" rap in particular, has been criticized as being male-dominated, for its characterization of women as "bitches" and "hos," and "for graphic lyrics boasting about the abuse, rape, and murder of women" (Burk and Shaw, 1995: 437), it is simultaneously heralded as a "vehicle for trenchant social protest," which is inherently political, addresses serious themes, and gives voice to unpalatable social truths (Palmer, 1995: 284; Santoro, 1993: 112–124). In addition, individual rappers themselves have offered stinging retorts to their critics. For example, Ice-T, hailed by *Rolling Stone* as "the man who invented L.A.-style gangsta rap," maintains in his autobiography that criticisms of rap and rappers as misogynistic and/or sexist are misplaced. According to Ice-T, "[i]f women want to be treated equally, earn equal wages, and attain equal status in the workplace, then I'm a feminist." (1994: 86–87). He argues that the "war" that exists is not between women and men, nor between women and rappers; rather, he claims that "[t]he real war is between the feminists themselves, between the woman who wants to wear a miniskirt and the woman who finds that demeaning." He suggests that women who find the unabashed sexuality of rap offensive are those who would be unappealing in a miniskirt and opines that "[t]he truth is, most hardcore feminists I've seen are ugly, and that's just the bottom line" (Ice-T, 1994: 86–89).

Despite the obvious flaws in Ice-T's defence of gangsta rap, any suggestion that all rap is inherently and solely sexist would seem overly bold. Surely Queen Latifah's chanting of "Stereotypes they got to go" in "Ladies First" or Salt-n-Pepa's boldly stating "Don't try to tell me how to party. It's my dance and it's my body" on "Shake Your Thang" are scarcely interchangeable with the "Wild and Lose (We Like It)" message of Oaktown 3.5.7. (Wallace, 1990). As in other forms of popular music, what one finds within rap is not a singular image of men and women, but rather something qualitatively akin to a hall of mirrors.

Unlike the country, soul, or light-pop music genres that have always had a fairly large representation of female lead performers, only a few women such as Janis Joplin, Pat Benetar, Joan Jett, and Tina Turner broke through into the higher echelons of rock music in the 1970s and 1980s. Helen Reddy received her 15 minutes of fame from performing the soft-rock tune "I Am Woman," which became the unofficial national anthem for the women's movement. By the mid-1980s, females still comprised less than 10 percent of the performers in rock (Groce and Cooper, 1990) and less than a quarter of the performers on music videos (Vincent et al., 1987). Female-star performers were notable in part because they were exceptions to the male-ruled rock music scene and, frequently, in part because they possessed or were marketed with some unique quality to their public performing or private life style. Janis Joplin was controversial as much for her alcohol-fueled private and public performances as her jagged lyrics about womanhood and her raw sexual sound. The mantle of controversy was eagerly coopted and managed by middle-of-the-road-singer, provocative stage performer, and video creator Madonna in the late 1980s and 1990s (Faith, 1993).

Canadian female popular music performers over the past 15 years have been relatively uncontroversial. In accepting her Juno award for Female Vocalist in 1984, out-of-the-closet lesbian Carole Pope (lead singer for Rough Trade) thanked CBS, True North Records, "and my creator, Max Factor." The following year, still-in-the-closet k.d. lang, clad in a frothy white wedding dress and bridal veil, dashed for the stage to accept her Juno award as Most Promising Female Vocalist (Melhuish, n.d.: 143, 147). The country-punk star eventually became controversial, not for coming out of the closet, but for extolling vegetarianism in a "Meat Stinks" campaign, a move that did not sit well with her former neighbours in Alberta's cattle country. Few high-profile Canadian women in mainstream popular music, such as Anne Murray, Rita MacNeil, Allanah Miles, Susan Aglukark, Jann Arden, Carla Marshell, Shania Twain, Celine Dion, and Alanis Morissette, almost all of whom are multiple Juno and Grammy award winners, could be called feminist in their lyrical or performance orientation. However, Sarah McLachlan, *Chatelaine* magazine's 1998 "Woman of the Year" and driving force behind and headliner of the most financially successful North American concert tour of 1997 (Lilith Fair featuring 80 female performers), is quoted as stating that the main idea behind the tour was "working toward a time when we're not referred to as women musicians, [but] we're called musicians [period]" (*Edmonton Journal*, 4 December 1997: C7).

A certain growth towards independence (occasionally expressed in four-letter terms) can be found in the angst-filled lyrics of Alanis Morissette and her transformation from a teenage heavily made-up airhead dance-pop queen to an adult minimalist-look life-wise authenticity. Morissette currently stands in sharp contrast to the glitzy, carefully packaged and promoted, glamorous appeal of other international stars, such as Celine Dion or Shania Twain (controversial only for her highly displayed belly button). Overall, the pains and joys of traditional heterosexual love relationships predominate in the lyrics of mainstream Canadian female performers in keeping with a formula for success, measured in airtime and product sales and carefully monitored and controlled by music-label executives, dependent upon appealing to the masses, while dressed most often in a sexually provocative manner and singing lyrics laced with time-honoured themes. Alternative female rock groups such as Ultra Vulva, with tunes such as "Twist in Bed" and "I'd Love To Be Bulimic," can only break into a spotlight initially located either on the margin or outside of the mainstream music scene. However, beginning with 1970s "underground" music, rock music has a history of first spawning alternative musical and presentation styles arising out of protest against the mainstream, and then coopting those styles to become an integral part of the mainstream. This history appears to be repeating itself in the 1990s regarding what has been referred to as "women's music."

Lont (1997: 127) observes that "[w]omen's music was originally defined as music by women, for women, about women, and financially controlled by women. By this definition, a song written by women, about women, and for women would not be considered a part of women's music if it were recorded on a major label." She notes that knowledgeability about women's music served in earlier decades as "a key into the lesbian community" (Lont, 1997: 126–127); "[i]f a woman mentioned certain performers such as Cris Williamson or Meg Christian, it identified her as a lesbian" (Lont, 1997: 126–127). It is obvious, however, that current lesbian performers, such as Michelle Shocked, Holly Near, Tracy Chapman, and k.d. lang, have achieved popularity with a broader audience and that many other contemporary young lesbian artists and groups such as Phranc and 2 Nice Girls "don't want to be in the ghetto of the women's music bin: 'we want to be in your face.'" (Lont, 1997: 133). Lont notes that the difficulty of reconciling profit and politics has "continually plagued women's music" and put tremendous pressure on women performers who were conscious that, as their music became more "mainstream," the possibility for retaining control of their message, music, and image could decline (p. 133). In particular, concern has been expressed that lesbian performers would be considered "so chic" that they would be considered "not really lesbians at all" or interchangeable with "the production of absolutely fake lesbianism à la Madonna and her simulacra" (Cottingham, 1996: 3).

Recognition that commercial success and getting one's music out to a wider audience often entails a loss of control over both one's image and message has also been noted in relation to other genres of women's music including punk rock and Riot Grrl bands, such as Bikini Kill, Heavens to Betsy, Bratmobile, Huggy Bear, and Excuse 17, where the "Do-It-Yourself ethic is a crucial element...[and] more freedom [exists] to explore expression through music...[and] to broach issues formerly untouched, such as rape, abuse, assault and other intensely personal themes" (Blofson and Aron, 1997: 15). They remark that while "[t]he media were quick to capitalize on the 'fashion' and Grrls became media darlings" in the early 1990s, when magazines such as *Seventeen*, *Newsweek*, and *Rolling Stone* ran stories about them and the fashion industry "turned that 'grrl-thang' into a commodity [complete with plastic barrettes and "Girls Rock" T-shirts]...Riot Grrl was virtually split between those who wanted to keep it underground and those who were willing to talk in the press and sacrifice secrecy to reach out to other girls" (p. 16). As with symbolic representations in other media, traditional gender images are transmitted by mass distribution while alternative images receive only limited distribution. The price to be paid for increasing access to mainstream audiences is frequently paid in the form of a dilution of the alternative visionary message.

Computers and the Internet

Since the first personal computer was introduced in 1975 (the MITS Altair 8800), followed by the Apple II series in 1977, and the IBM PC in 1981), the use of computers has grown exponentially. In 1989, almost half (47 percent) of Canada's adult population indicated that they knew how to use a computer, while 82 percent of Canadian teenagers possessed such knowledge (Lowe, 1994: 315–316). In 1993, just less than one-quarter of Canadian households owned home computers (23.3 percent), up from 16.3 percent in 1990 (Columbo, 1994). The phrase *infobahn* or *information superhighway* attempts to capture the way in which messages can now be transmitted at high rates of speed between computers in homes and businesses throughout the world. Wilkie and Riblett (1993) reported that at least 20 million people worldwide were able to communicate by Internet; more recently, a Neilsen random-household survey in December 1996 and January 1997 found that nearly one-quarter of all people in Canada and the United States over age 16 had surfed the Internet in the previous month. Of the 50.6 million people wired into the Internet, 42 percent were women, an increase from 35 percent in a 1995 survey (*Edmonton Journal*, 14 March 1997: H1). In addition, a host of minor and major service providers such as Prodigy,

Box 5.3   Gender Software

I am at a slumber party of some kind, as a group of high school girls giggles over a yearbook. Brandon, one girl gushes, is "a total charmer," but his friend Derrick is "big-time gorgeous in a completely natural way." The girls are ready to provide extensive advice on how to catch one of the class's hunks. "Sit next to him Monday. He'll be eating out of your hand." Talk about gender roles; I have entered the world of girl software and feel a bit uncomfortable, as if I've stumbled into the wrong locker room. The images are different, the words are different, and my thinking seems alien. Mouse clicks don't fire off laser weapons. I don't find myself zooming through tunnels, barely escaping garroting. Instead, I look in Kim's bedroom mirror, apply lipstick, eyeshadow or blush, altering the unblemished face staring back; or else, like the character Cher in the movie *Clueless*, click on different outfits to find one that will attract Derrick's attention in math class. For boys, this play would be a bit of a drag.

But that's the point. *McKenzie & Co.* (from Her Interactive) is a participatory computer game about high schoolers directed specifically at girls. Its five CD-ROMs full of video clips provide a model for the genre: Create a fantasy world that is unmistakably girlish. Here classmates share advice, commiserate on failure and rely on each other to propel them into romance. And nerve-wracking conversations with desired males can be replayed with different girlish responses, teaching, again and again, that kindness, consideration and charm work far more effectively than cranky aggression.

The same idea—an education in sugar, spice and everything nice—guides *Let's Talk About Me* (Simon and Schuster Interactive), which is a kind of teenage magazine on a CD-ROM, combining self-help with self-display, mixing the spice of liberating lessons with the sugar of traditional girl counsel, offering lessons in beauty along with biographies of women who are called "mentors." There are even true confessions: one boy was a "dream

AOL Canada, and CompuServe provide computer access to a seemingly infinite number of information and entertainment sources.

Given their very nature, computer representations of gender are truly symbolic. As with virtually ever other new advance in technology over the past 100 years, computers initially appear to possess the potential for transcending previous limitations imposed on gender, yet while computer technology is theoretically gender neutral, existing rules and roles pertaining to gender in our society seem to have been maintained with respect to anticipated and actual use of both computers and the Internet. School-aged children in California were asked to describe how they would use computers when they were 30-years-old. While young boys in the study reported that "they would use them for finances, data processing, and games," young girls said "they would use them for housework. Wrote one sixth grade girl: 'When I am thirty, I'll have a computer that has long arms and that can clean the house and cook meals, and another to pay for groceries and stuff'" (Kolata, 1984: 25). In a study conducted by the Center for Children and Technology, men and women in technical fields were requested to envisage machines of the future. It was noted that while men tended to imag-

date" except that he was "the worst kisser in the world." What, the game asks, should the poor pucker-picker do: deal with it, dump him, or develop his potential? The answer is clear enough, though the disk itself fails to provide appropriate lessons for how such potential is to be developed. The gender differences are evident even in the latest *McKenzie and* [*sic*] *Co.* narrative game: *The Vampire Diaries*. The teen heroine must help save her young sister and find out who her real friends are before she too becomes part of the living dead. The emphasis is on social interaction, betrayal, sexual threat: the female gothic novel, one of the staples of literature during the past two hundred years, has made it to the PC. The archetype though, may still be Barbie—Mattel's $1.7 billion industry—as she enters the digital age. New Barbie software turns the PC into another doll accessory. Using *Barbie Fashion Designer* — a CD-ROM that has sold 500,000 copies since it was introduced in October—a girl can make Barbie clothes using patterns on the PC and printing them on sheets of special fabric.

These games take little notice of any of the debates of recent decades—that the differences between girls and boys are socially conditioned and environmentally created. Girl software insists on those differences, and the market provides support. Boy software is never melancholy and introspective, but aggressive and fervent. Boy software is not concerned with personality and charm, but with action and achievement. Boy software doesn't incorporate friends, it requires allies. The goal of girl software is, well, girlish: not to combat boy software on its own turf, blowing it up or demolishing its terrain, but to approach it in a way that the high school girls of "McKenzie" might recognize. With its preferences for introspection, personality, friendship and dreamy fantasy, girl software gently alleviates the solitude, stubborn technicalities, and uncompromising grunts of the PC universe, trying to seduce and transform it, in the hopes of some future union.

Source: Edward Rothstein, *New York Times*. "Ill at ease in girl software." Reprinted in *Edmonton Journal*, 20 February 1997: H4.

ine machines that would allow them to "conquer the universe" and "transcend physical limitations," women were more likely to dream up machines that fulfilled the role of the "perfect mother," meeting individuals' needs (in Kantrowitz, 1994: 55).

Wajcman (1991: 153) points out that advertisements for home computers "are aimed at a male market and often feature pictures of boys looking raptly at the screen." She notes that the first video game designed by MIT in the 1960s, with the militaristic title of *Space War*, and more recent offerings "are simply programmed versions of traditionally male non-computer games, involving shooting, blowing up, speeding, or zapping in some way or another" (p. 154). Similar in orientation to *Doom* and *Command and Conquer*, the advertising blurb on the cover of *Mech Warrior 2* invites its inevitably male players into a mindset where "War is Life...Death is the only True Peace" (see Box 5.3 for more on gender software). Wajcman (1991: 154) also contends that the gender experience of leisure time, with males exempted from and females expected to participate in housework, promotes the greater likelihood that adolescent and older males will spend time at a computer surfing the Net or playing games. Moreover, she notes that greater parental restrictions on where daughters (but not sons) are and are not allowed to go further decreases the likelihood of female involvement within such relatively structured activities as afterschool computer clubs or within the unsupervised environment of the video arcade (Wajcman, 1991: 154–155).

Computers and the video arcade, like the pinball arcade and the pool halls before them, remain the turf of the male hobbyist (Brown et al., 1997; Haddon, 1988). After all, a hand-held computer game was not named *Game Boy* by accident. Based on ethnographic research conducted at MIT, Turkle (1984) describes the world of computer hackers as the ultimate representation of the male subculture's emphasis on "mastery, individualism, non-sensuality." "Though hackers would deny that theirs is a macho culture, the preoccupation with winning and of subjecting oneself to increasingly violent tests make their world peculiarly male in spirit, peculiarly unfriendly to women." (Turkle, 1984: 216).

Debate exists regarding whether males and females possess different styles of relating to computers. Based on her own observations of young children, Turkle (1984) contends that young boys prefer a "hard" mastery programing style that attempts to "control" the computer in a structured linear manner. In contrast, girls prefer a "soft," more "interactive" "relational" programing style. "While the hard master thinks in terms of global abstractions, the soft master works on a problem by arranging and rearranging these elements, working through new combinations" (Turkle, 1984a: 103). Even though Turkle maintains that neither style is inherently superior or inferior, teachers may evaluate female efforts as "getting the right results by the wrong method" and hence inferior (Wajcman, 1991: 157). It is also Tannen's (1994a: 53) contention that males are more likely than females to become enamoured by computer technology: "Boys are typically motivated by a social structure that says if you don't dominate you will be dominated. Computers, by their nature, balk: you type a perfectly appropriate command and it refuses to do what it should." According to Tannen, while males will view this as a situation to demonstrate mastery ('I'm going to whip this into line and teach it who's boss! I'll get it to do what I say!'), "[g]irls and women are more likely to respond: 'This thing won't cooperate. Get it away from me!'"

Although Tannen acknowledges that there undoubtedly are "plenty of exceptions," it is her contention that women are less likely than men to become "excited by tinkering with the technology, grappling with the challenge of eliminating bugs or getting the biggest and best computer" and suggests that "my relationship to my computer is—gulp—fairly typical for a woman....E-mail appeals to my view of life as a contest for connections to others. When I see that I have 15 messages I feel loved." Hollander has depicted this postulated difference between male and female styles of relating to computers in a cartoon in which a woman, standing behind a computer screen depicting a fat contented cat comments "My friends and I are teaching dolphins to communicate through E-mail." A man, standing behind a nearby computer screen featuring a rocket aiming at a Martian with antennae growing out of its head, remarks, "I like to blow stuff up."

Kantrowitz (1994: 50) claims that men are more likely than women "to be seduced by the technology itself" and to become absorbed by the "faster-race-car syndrome"—"bragging about the size of their discs or the speed of their microprocessors." Noting that computers are more likely to be purchased and used by men, Kantrowitz (1994: 50) suggests that "[i]t may be new technology, but the old rules still apply. It's that male-machine bonding thing, reincarnated in the digital age." Hackett (1994: 54) reports that men are more likely than women to use their computers to talk to others about the capacities of their software and computers and/or to purchase the very latest versions of the programs they do use "even if the update does nothing new besides correcting the faulty handling of annotated footnotes on certain Korean color inkjet printers." "What do women want? Who knows. What do men want? Something bigger, faster and cooler than yours" (Hackett, 1994: 54).

Skeptical of the claim that males and females have distinctive computing styles, Wajcman (1991: 157) acknowledges that a self-fulfilling prophecy, comparable to confidence in mathematical ability (Kelly, 1981; Walkerdine, 1989), may exist with regard to young women and computers. The social construction of computers as a "male domain" may mean "that girls approach the computer less often and with less confidence than boys" (Wajcman, 1991:158). Ironically, the first computer programers were women and programing was viewed initially as "tedious clerical work of low status." Ada Lovelace, who worked with Charles Babbage in the 1880s on his mechanical computing machines, is considered to be "the very first computer programmer" (Kantrowitz, 1994:51). However, with increasing recognition of the complexity and value of programing, "it came to be considered creative, intellectual and demanding 'men's work'" (Wajcman, 1991: 158). As with so many other areas of social life, the sex of the worker eventually dictates the power and prestige of the work itself and sets another self-fulfilling prophecy in motion. Kantrowitz (1994: 52) notes that while "there are no women CEOs [currently] running major computer-manufacturing firms and only a handful running software companies," a noteable exception occurs in the development of software designed for use by children. For example, Davidson & Associates, begun by Jan Davidson, a former teacher, is one of North America's largest developers of "kids' software" with revenues in excess of $58.6 million.

Spender (1995) claims that access to, and actual navigating on, the information superhighway is influenced by gender since men make the rules of the road even in cyberspace. Spender (1995: 193) contends that the same patterns of male dominance within real-world mixed-sex conversations apply, with a vengeance, in cyberspace. She notes the research of Herring et al. (1992), which found that, on various electronic discussion lists, men contributed between 70 to 80 percent of the postings or conversational space and that when a "feminist topic" was raised, "[a]ccusations came from the men that they were being silenced" with some threatening to unsubscribe the list and one man writing a 1098 word protest (in Spender, 1995: 193–194). She additionally notes that a 1993 study of the newsgroup alt.feminism discovered that here too, men dominated the conversational space with 74 percent of the postings made. Wylie (1995: 197) also observes that, "[w]hen men attack women's posts (by flaming, intellectualizing, or posting lengthy line-by-line rebuttals of women's messages), women retreat into silence." Akin to patterns observed in face-to-face mixed-sex exchanges, Wylie claims that women's ideas online are more apt to be received with silence, that female-initiated subjects generate less than one-third of the responses made to male-initiated subjects, that male postings are typically lengthier than female postings, and that female-initiated postings tend to be usurped by male voices online. She additionally reports that when professional women host online discussions, they may find their area of expertise ignored and themselves inundated with irrelevant queries as to their looks, their marital status, and whether or not they are menstruating.

The anonymity of the Net may encourage individuals to behave in ways that are more offensive and intimidating than they would when engaged in face-to-face interaction. Kramarae and Taylor (1993: 56) report that "[s]exual harassment on the networks is a problem being reported by many women at many sites" and Spender (1995: 202–211) provides numerous examples, including cases of women who logged onto a board with a feminine name and were "pounced upon by requests to go out and fill in my registration in order that the boys can 'fuck me,'" to messages sent to a female user that informed her that she "would have...[her] throat cut and be gangbanged."

D'Amico (1997: 32) reports that the first temporary restraining order has been issued in the United States to curtail the actions of an online "cyberstalker" and suggests that "the Internet has become another weapon in the stalker's arsenal because it enables users worldwide to find personal information about you in a few simple keystrokes." Stephens (1997: 75), in a discussion of "cyberstalking," reports that "[c]yberspace vengeance" may take various forms, which range from "ruining credit records and charging multiple purchases to the victim to creating criminal records and sending letters to employers informing them of the 'shady background' of the victim." While Sinclair (1996, 1997: 71) argues that women should not be fearful of going online: "You're not going to get on the Internet and end up attacked in some dark alley," the existence of "cyber-rape" (Michals, 1997) or "data rape" (Spender, 1995) may be sufficiently vexatious to encourage some women either to pose as a male when online or to turn off their computer entirely.

A study of women's participation on computer networks reports that women were more likely to violate "long-established net etiquette" rules by "asking too many basic questions," which anger male users (in Kantrowitz, 1994: 54–55). Recognition that the "language of the road rules" may, in itself, be offputting to women, with "the use of such terms as 'abort,' 'chaining,' 'execute,' 'head crash,' and 'kill'" (Spender, 1995: 201), and that "newbies" (the term used to refer to beginning users of the net) in general and female newbies in particular may be especially liable to intimidation and bullying ("flaming"), has led some to provide "netiquette guides for novices" (Holderness, 1994) that encourages them to stay logged on.

Logging on to networks run by or exclusively for women, such as Women's Wire for example, represents another way women attempt to avoid these types of situations. For example, Janis Cortese, a physicist at Loma Linda University in California and a longtime "Star Trek" fan, found the Trekkie discussion group on the Internet dominated with discussions of whether Troi or Crusher had bigger breasts. She was "chased off the net by rabid hounds" when she posted lusty comments about male crew members and queries as to why almost all the female crew members were young, white, and skinny. In response, Cortese launched "the all-female Starfleet Ladies Auxiliary and Embroidery/Baking Society" online (Kantrowitz, 1994: 48). Inspection of any of a number of so-called cyberguides yields a wide variety of Websites dedicated to women—from (**http://feminist.com**), the "United Nations of the Women's Movement," which houses the Web pages for various national feminist organizations, provides tips to assist social activism and, among other things, features an interactive "Question and Answer" column, to Systers, an online network for women with technical careers, which functions as part of an online mentoring and consciousness-raising effort, to *Power Surge* (**http://members.aol.com/dearest/intro.htm**), which focuses on the menopause, to *Canadian Woman* (**http://www.mediacity.com/canadianwoman**), which provides a directory of personal and business pages of women, to *On The Homefront* (**http://home.istar.ca/~mprovost/homefrnt.htm**), a quarterly forum for stay-at home women by stay-at-home women, to *Women's Wire* (**http://www.women.com/guide/#top**), which includes a Women's Hall of Fame, daily headlines about women making the news, relationships, business, and healthy living, to *Advancing Women* (**http://www.advancing-women.com**), which gives top priority to women in the news and workplace, to the riotgrrls site at (**http://www.riotgrrl.com**) to *Cosmopolitan Online* (**http://www.cosmomag.com**), to *Toronto Webgrrls* (**http://www.webgrrls.com/toronto**), a networking organization for women interested in learning about the opportunities of the Internet and multimedia.

In contrast to advocating a separatist response, techno-feminists like Cherny and Weise (1996) advise women to "turn the tables and hold their ground" or even to reconceptualize hostile cybersex Web sites "as an opportunity to assert themselves by creating a woman-friendly climate that provides a more accurate representation of women's sexuality and humanity" (Michals, 1997: 72). Cyberfeminists acknowledge male dominance of network culture and design historically, but proclaim that today "cyberspace is out of *man's* control" (Plant, 1996: 191–193, emphasis added). Whether cyberfeminists and nonfeminist women will have any significant impact upon computers and the Internet in the future, and if so what Brave New CyberWorld they will create, is unclear at the moment.

WORK

Gender in our society is inextricably intertwined with work and the family or intimate relations. These social institutions create and sustain gender as much as they are created and sustained by gender. Our focus in the next chapter will be upon intimate relations. Our focus in the present chapter lies upon both paid and unpaid work.

THE WORK-ROLE MODEL

Pleck (Pleck and Corfman, 1979) argues that men in our society are strongly influenced by a pervasive *male work-role model*. Implicit in this concept is an association between paid work and ideal stereotypical masculinity, an association formed at least since the creation by industrialization of the so-called separate spheres (see Chapter 3). The work-role model is not a formal blueprint knowingly and deliberately taught as part of the formal task of each major agency of socialization. Rather, an accumulation of messages transmitted subtly from these and other sources all promote the development, within most men in our society, of a set of three interrelated beliefs regarding paid work, which becomes an integral part of their taken-for-granted world. "The male work-role model in our society calls for full-time, continuous work from graduation to retirement, subordination of other roles to work, and actualization of one's potential through it" (Pleck and Corfman, 1979: 409).

Survey the males in your life and you will find that the vast majority hold an unquestioned belief shared by the rest of our society that, of course, men should and must work at a paid occupation. Unless they possess significantly noticeable physical, psychological, or emotional disabilities, men work. Even if they do possess any such disability, most men feel they should perform some form of paid work. In accordance with our social traditions, paid labour (often eulogized in our society as "honest labour") is endowed with the power to bestow a sense of worth and dignity upon the labourer. Our society does not readily grant men the option of becoming financially dependent upon others, especially as a long-term arrangement. Men are expected to become self-supporting, and possibly other-supporting, in a financial sense.

> Men are neither supposed nor allowed to be dependent. They are expected to take care of both others *and* themselves. And when they cannot do it, or "will not" do it, the built-in assumption at the heart of the culture is that they are *less than men* and therefore unworthy of help. (Marin, 1991/1995: 490, emphasis in original)

Marin's comments are directed towards identifying an underlying dimension that accounts for the hostility currently aimed at homeless men in our society. While homeless women and children are most often treated in Canada as victims of unjust circumstances, homeless (usually unemployed) men are most often treated as objects for scorn, derision, and even violence. A society that grants men agency, or the power to act, also demands agency from men. Even if men should become recipients of a huge lottery windfall or an inheritance that defies the imagination, men should work. Such beneficence may provide the freedom to indulge in a fairy-tale lifestyle and the opportunity to amass every material possession, but, in between holidays and shopping forays, men should work. The notion of an adult lifestyle based upon permanent nonparticipation in the labour force is completely foreign to most men, something only the European nobility find attractive and seem capable of indulging. In our society, men should work.

According to the first tenet of the male work-role model, as long as they are physically able to do so, men are expected by others and by themselves to labour in a paid occupation, from the moment they graduate from, or drop out of, secondary or postsecondary education, throughout their adulthood years, until they voluntarily or involuntarily retire (or die, whichever comes first). Then and only then do men have societal and personal permission to refrain from labouring for pay. The predominant attitude of most Canadians towards the unemployed, especially the male unemployed, is contained in three simple words: get a job. Whereas female employment has often been, and still is, considered to constitute a social problem, male unemployment has been, and still is, considered to be both a social and a personal problem. However, not just any form of paid work will meet the requirements of the male work-role model. A lifetime of seasonal, or part-time, casual, or intermittent work will not suffice. A young man anticipating filling his adult years as a lifeguard each summer at an outdoor swimming pool in Saskatoon, will find that prospective spouses, in-laws, the Employment Insurance commission, and Social Assistance (welfare) are highly unlikely to bestow social approval or additional financial support upon such a plan. In the absence of an available full-time continuing job, men are expected to take on a less-than-desirable, possibly part-time or seasonal McJob, but only as a temporary solution. A proper solution should take the form of permanent, full-time, continuous employment.

Our society sends a message to Canadian men to the effect that, if they do well in their paid-work role, everyone will benefit. The worker will benefit from monetary, prestige (both self-respect and respect from others), and power (both self-determination and power over others) payoffs. Others dependent upon the worker, such as children and a spouse, will also share those benefits to some degree. Even our society as a whole will supposedly benefit from a productive work force. Workers, in accordance with the second tenet of the work-role model, are expected to make their employment a central focus of their adult lives. All other roles are, therefore, to be made subordinate to the demands of the work role. The last point has been and is a source of family tensions. As we shall soon see, men often stand accused of focusing so much upon their paid-work role that they neglect other, especially childrearing and intimacy-related, roles (see Chapter 7), yet within the internally generated logic of the male work-role model, only through paid labour can men best serve the needs of their families.

The work-role model forms the philosophical basis for the notion of the breadwinner-provider. Paid labour is supposed to provide the material means for fulfilling the principal demands of the husband-father role. The model contends that men must give priority to the demands of the public paid-work sphere to be successful in the private family sphere. As a consequence, men's family role is reduced to that of a money-making machine and financial-success object. The male work-role model is a self-serving device forged by and designed to promote the interests of government, business, and industry. Some of the criticisms addressed towards a supposedly essential characteristic of men in our society, that they care more about their jobs and making money than about the psychological and emotional welfare of their families, or that important family decisions are made by men on the basis of job, but not family priorities, are actually misattributions. Men, successfully socialized into the work-role model, do care about their jobs. It is their jobs that do not care about their families. "The family is controlled not by the male but by his job" (Pleck and Corfman, 1979: 394).

The demands of the workplace exert expectations and demands independent of and regardless of the personal wishes of the worker. Work as an institution has not been, and largely today still is not, family friendly. Work only accommodates the demands and schedules of families and intimate relationships when it is in the best interest of work to do so. As we shall see later in this chapter, such accommodations are relatively rare and, even then, are brought about primarily in the employment of women, but not men. By and large, the institution of work expects the institution of the family to make most, if not all, of any required adjustments. In terms of negative impacts of one sphere upon the other, paid work is more likely to exert a negative effect upon family life than the other way around. Paid work exerts that influence via its effect upon time, energy, and psychological demands upon a worker, which detracts from the amount of each of these factors that a worker has left for his or her family at the end of each working day (Small and Riley, 1990). Observers, analysts, and everyday participants themselves often do not differentiate between attitudes and behaviours that are a function of gender and those that are a function of the nature of the institution of work. Work in many ways causes gender, which in turn causes certain triumphs and tribulations in gender relations.

The independent influence exerted by the paid-work sphere upon gender becomes more apparent as observers and analysts also attend to the impact of work organizations upon women and their family and intimate relations. It becomes readily apparent that work organizations are relatively impersonal, equally demanding of both male and female workers, and responsible for many outcomes that have previously been attributed solely, and improperly, to men and their gender. However, as we shall see in detail later, available data also clearly indicate that full-time employed women do make the time and create the energy to take care of homes, marriages or cohabiting relationships, and responsibilities associated with childrearing to a significantly greater extent than do men. Men still conduct themselves in the home in accordance with the expectations of the work-role model and attend less to family and intimate relationship responsibilities. Men generally still appear to believe that, by giving a greater portion of their physical and psychological time and energy to paid employment, they will best fulfill the obligations of the breadwinner-provider family role. The social requirements of gender also exert an influence independent of the paid-work model.

The third tenet of the male work-role model, as presented in the Pleck and Corfman quote, is expressed in the language of the human-potential movement dominant in the 1970s. Self-actualization (Maslow, 1970; 1968) refers to the condition of maximizing one's human potential. The male work-role model extols paid labour as providing the optimal conditions for men's self actualization. To paraphrase an advertising slogan created to convey just that message, through work men "can be all that they can be." Women, according to societal messages, are expected to actualize their potential through wife/mother roles. As noted in Chapter 4, the ever-present question asked of young males, "What are you going to be when you grow up?" is always asked in anticipation of an occupational answer—what kind of paid work he intends to do. Men in our society are expected to, and actually do, invest a considerable amount of their social, personal, and masculine identity in and, in turn, derive a considerable sense of their personal and masculine worth from, their paid work. In simple terms, for males, you are what you do and what you do is work for a living.

As we noted in Chapter 3, males are not the only sex to engage in paid labour from the time of the industrial revolution. Females, particularly from the lower- and working-classes, have always been employed in the paid-labour force. Statistics, presented later in this chapter, indicate that one of the major social trends in Canada in the post-World War II era has been the significant increase in the numbers of employed women from all adult age groups, all social classes and, particularly, all marital and family statuses. However, despite the increased tendency of women to follow a male pattern of employment, women generally have not been socialized into, nor have adopted, a work-role model identical to that of men in our society. We noted that men, as a consequence of their adoption of the male work-role model, view paid employment, at least in part, as meeting the needs of a breadwinner or provider role. Breadwinning in our society has been a "critical gender boundary" (Potuchek, 1992: 549), not only differentiating men's behaviour from women's behaviour, but also possessing important implications for gender identity. While the significant increase in female labour-force participation could in theory pose a challenge to the gender boundary surrounding the provider/breadwinner role, such has not been the case.

Based on their analysis of the results of the Most Admired Men and Women polls conducted annually by Gallup (from 1946 to 1994) and *Good Housekeeping* magazine (from 1970 to 1995), Young and Harris (1996) report that, while men were likely to be admired for their service in the military, politics, religion, and economics, women were more likely to be admired because they belonged to a royal or political family, or because of their work as activists and reformers, or in the area of entertainment and culture. While the proportion of "autonomous women" (i.e., women recognized for their personal activities or achievements) was higher in the 1980s and 1990s than previously, men were significantly more likely than women to have achieved their prominent status without the sponsorship of a family member and/or spouse. Their analysis of the activities or occupations of the most admired men and women also revealed large gender differences consistent with gender-role stereotypes of men as autonomous and independent and women as relatively dependent and passive.

As we shall see later in this chapter, the conditions of employment experienced by most women make participation in the workplace less appealing and less rewarding for them than for men. In addition, internalized social expectations for women, vis-à-vis marriage and children, circumscribe women's desire to be breadwinners or primary providers. Few women in our society, both in the past and today, anticipate being employed on a full-time, continuous, basis from the moment of graduation until the moment of retirement. Few women expect to place their paid-work role ahead of all other roles. Finally, few women believe that employment will provide the optimum conditions for them to actualize their potential as human beings. As we will see in this and later chapters, never-married women express ambivalence over whether the costs of their employment, usually defined in terms of lost marital and parenting opportunities, outweigh their considerable benefits. While female lone parents often find they need to adopt one or two of the tenets of the male work-role model to ensure family survival, this is typically an unanticipated situation, one for which they have received little preparation. Employed women in dual-earner marital or cohabiting relationships tend not to consider themselves as breadwinners.

Based upon the findings from the female portion of her sample of predominantly white American dual-earner couples, Potuchek (1992) derived an eight-fold typology of employed women's orientations to breadwinning. The largest and most common orientation (21 percent of the total) is that of **employed homemakers**, who view their husbands' jobs as being more important than their own and view their own employment as designed primarily to furnish income for the purchase of extras, not essentials, for family living. Nineteen percent of the women in the sample define themselves as **helpers**, whose employment is designed to literally "help out" their husbands in meeting their family's economic needs. Fifteen percent of the women consider themselves to be **co-breadwinners**, whose employment, by design, equally contributes to the provision of basic essentials for their families. Fourteen percent of the women are **reluctant providers**. "These are women who are behaving like breadwinners not because they want to or think that they should, but because they have no choice" (Potuchek, 1992: 552). If they were granted the power of choice, none of these women would chose to be either coproviders or sole providers.

Twelve percent are **supplementary providers**, who consider themselves to perform an important provider function within their families, but who also define their husbands as being the primary provider and consider his job to be more important than their own. Another 12 percent are what Potuchek (1992: 553) terms as **reluctant traditionals**. These women would like to see the provider role being based ideally upon some criterion other than gender but, in their own case, are only rarely employed full-time and only use the proceeds from their employment to furnish their families with extras. Their behaviour is similar to that of the employed homemakers, but their ideology is comparable to co-breadwinners. The remainder of the women are either **family-centred workers** (5 percent of the sample), who believe providers should be male and who reserve the right to quit employment whenever their families need them at home, or **committed workers** (3 percent) who derive enormous nonmaterial satisfactions from being in the labour force, are committed to particular jobs, and who, almost incidentally, find their families dependent upon the income they provide.

Of these eight different orientations, only the co-breadwinners (15 percent of the sample) knowingly challenge, via beliefs and deeds, the traditional gender boundary that designates and protects men as the family provider. These women perceive themselves to be breadwinner/providers as fully as are their husbands. Others either might wish to issue such a challenge, but do not do so in terms of their behaviour, or might implicitly issue a challenge by their behaviour, but have no desire to do so in terms of their beliefs. The latter women, who constitute the greater majority of the sample, still think that men should ideally be the family breadwinner. Potuchek's empirical analysis concludes (1992: 557) that situational, rather than socialization, factors account for women's different orientations to breadwinning. Although not explicitly addressed by the researcher, it appears that few adult women today have received or sought out a preparatory socialization, such as that contained in the male work-role model.

A longitudinal study illustrates how decisions about paid work and family responsibilities are based upon gender understandings and, in turn, how those decisions reaffirm or "cement" gender. Zvonkovic et al. (1996) collected data on the process of "work" decisions from 61 predominantly middle-class couples, over a period of one-and-a-half years. Thirty-six of the couples made decisions concerning a wife's job. In all cases, the topic for discussion focused upon whether she should increase or decrease her paid-work hours, but not whether she should become a breadwinner or equal partner coprovider, even temporarily. Nineteen of the couples focused upon decisions surrounding whether husbands should change jobs, but not whether he should increase or decrease his paid-work hours. A husband's role as sole breadwinner was not subject to debate or discussion. All decisions firmly supported existing constructions of gender, both in the workplace and in the homeplace. Decisions regarding wives' hours of employment were most often (15 of 36 couples) initiated and determined by family circumstances, pertaining to children's ages, outside of her control. Neither age of children nor other family circumstances played a part in decisions regarding husbands' employment.

Couples give higher priority to husbands' work decisions and husbands involve themselves more in decisions directly influencing their own futures, while they are more often "bystanders" in decisions regarding their wives' changing circumstances. While a husband comments: "She went to work. It was her choice. She arranged day care"; his wife states: "My job *had* to be part-time. The hours *had* to coincide with the children's school and day care....I pay so much money out just to be able to work" (in Zvonkovic et al., 1996: 95, emphasis in original). These statements illustrate how wives often have to purchase their freedom to work and have to construct and coordinate their own employment within family-schedule guidelines. Wives', not husbands', paycheques are most often used to purchase childcare and house cleaning services to accommodate her employment. According to a couple's constructions of gender, a woman's responsibilities still include taking care of the home and children and being responsive to children's changing needs. Husbands' paycheques are earmarked for family "necessities," thus preserving his family-provider gender image. Part of that image involves leaving childcare and homemaking responsibilities to women.

All of these work-family decisions appear, on the surface, to reinforce pre-existing gender ideals and realities. Most couples in Zvonkovic et al.'s study emphasize how their decisions are based upon consensus and mutual support. Beneath the surface, however, consensus is more apparent than real, with husbands enjoying support from wives, but not always the reverse (Zvonkovic et al., 1996: 96–97). Wives attempting to alter gender constructions within their marriages most often meet with passivity, occasionally opposition, on the part of husbands who fail to recognize the extent to which their wives require, but do not receive, support. As a consequence of decision-making processes, such as those experienced by these couples, male gender boundaries are maintained consistent with their expectations and desires. Female gender boundaries are maintained, but not necessarily consistent with wives' expectations and desires. As we shall see in a later section of this chapter, many women in our society feel they can only construct an alternate gender model for themselves outside of the traditional confines exerted by marriage and family responsibilities.

PAID WORK

The greatest single change to the face of the Canadian labour force since 1961 has been a substantial growth in the numbers of employed women in general and, in particular, employed married women with children. While the size of the female labour force has increased, the proportion of the male population over the age of 14 currently employed at any point in time has declined from the early 1980s (approximately 75 percent employed) to the mid-1990s (65 percent in 1993; Best, 1995: 31). This decline in male employment has been a consequence of a number of factors, the primary one being a growing tendency of men in their middle to late fifties to take early retirement (Krahn and Lowe, 1993: 63) or accept buy-outs from employers, sometimes voluntarily, but recently, more often involuntarily as a result of business and government downsizing. In addition, young men in the 15- to 24-year age category have been delaying their entry into the labour market by staying in school longer to attain higher credentials, and men of all ages have experienced layoffs (particularly in goods-producing industries; Best, 1995: 31), either as a consequence of technological change, or in response to a series of economic recessions in the early and middle 1980s and early 1990s. The overall result has been a greater gender mix in the employed population of this country.

Growing female labour-force participation since 1961 is attributable to a combination of changing opportunities in Canada's occupational structure (particularly an expansion of the service sector of the economy in the 1960s and 1970s), inflationary pressures necessitating higher family incomes, and changing gender expectations and beliefs affecting women's motivations vis-à-vis employment, marriage, parenthood, and parenting. Social gender expectations that once exerted a depressing effect upon paid employment among married women, and especially married women with dependent children in the home, have attenuated and no longer have the same impact. "Between 1971 and 1981…women without children accounted for 52% of the increase. In contrast, between 1981 and 1991, mothers with children at home were responsible for most of the rise (60%) in the number of women in the labour force" (Logan and Belliveau, 1995: 25).

Findings from the 1995 General Social Survey (GSS) indicate that 86 percent of adult Canadian men and 64 percent of adult women believe that being able to have a paying job is either important or very important for their personal happiness (Ghalam, 1997: 16). These findings are consistent among men across all age and educational levels, but higher among younger (age 44 and under) versus older women, and higher with increasing levels of education among women aged 25 to 64. Women aged 15 to 24 rate the importance of paid work of highest importance for personal happiness about equally, regardless of their attained educational level. Participation in the paid- labour force provides an important source of not only personal and social identity, but also personal happiness for men. Women under age 25 appear to have adopted this same expectation, while older women appear to have either alternative or additional sources of personal happiness for men. Fifty-five percent of women, as opposed to 49 percent of men, either agree or strongly agree that having a job is the best way for a woman to be an independent person (Ghalam, 1997: 16). Acquiring a sense of independence has become an important source of personal happiness among women.

More women than men (73 and 68 percent respectively) agree or strongly agree that both spouses should contribute to household income, with support for the proposition among men highest for those with less than high-school education and lowest among university-educated men (Ghalam, 1997: 16). Men with the lowest educational attainment levels appear to be the most aware of the necessity of having an additional income to support a family, possibly because their earning power has declined over the past three decades. However, the value of having another wage earner in the family still appears to conflict with other values and beliefs. For example, while 67 percent of women and 59 percent of men agree or strongly agree that employed mothers can maintain warm relationships with their children of any age, 59 percent of men and 51 percent of women agree or strongly agree that preschool age children are likely to suffer if both parents are employed (Ghalam, 1997: 16). Women appear to be almost evenly divided on the latter issue, while men are slightly more definite in their beliefs that young children need the attention of a nonemployed parent. Ghalam (1997: 16–17) further observes that 78 percent of women currently employed or seeking employment believe that employed mothers can maintain warm relations with children, but 64 percent of women who were mainly homemakers agree or strongly agree that preschool age children suffer if both parents are employed. Whether these beliefs lead to decisions of women either being or not being employed, or whether these beliefs were developed after the fact to support and justify prior employment decisions is impossible to determine from the GSS data.

Since the wording of the question on the GSS was gender neutral ("both parents"), we can only guess who respondents had in mind as the most desirable nonemployed parent. However, 46 percent of women and 44 percent of men agree or strongly agree (substantially more the former than the latter) that a "job is all right, but what most women really want is a home and children" (Ghalam, 1997: 16). These findings indicate the continuing presence among both men and women of substantial support for a Modified Traditional Marriage Enterprise (Levinson, 1996), which, while including employment for women, still places greater priority upon home and family. However, economic necessity often overshadows the impact of personal beliefs upon decisions of whether or not married women with children should remain in or re-enter the labour force.

As we noted earlier, inflationary pressures over the past three decades have reduced the likelihood that a Canadian family can survive with only one income provider. Employers no longer pay a "family living wage" to the average working Canadian. Earnings of men under the age of 35 (adjusting for inflation) have declined, while average earnings for men over age 35 have remained substantially unchanged since the 1980s (Best, 1995; Morissette, 1997; Rashid, 1994). Through the 1980s and into the mid-1990s, the wage gap between top- and bottom-earner men has widened as a function of top earners working more hours on average per week and bottom earners working fewer hours (Morissette, 1997: 11). Declining wages among younger male workers have also been influenced by changing technology. Machines have replaced humans and displaced semiskilled and unskilled workers have been forced to seek employment in lower-paying jobs (Morissette, 1997: 10). Cost-cutting measures adopted by employers, such as shifting more employees from full-time to part-time hours, are another contributing factor, although data are not yet available to test how important this factor is. The longer young male workers work for low real wages, the less likely they will be able to attain the earning levels currently enjoyed by older workers. Particularly among younger male workers and those in semiskilled and unskilled occupations, family survival increasingly requires the combined incomes of themselves and a spouse or cohabitation partner.

Age and Sex Differentials in Labour-Force Participation Rates

We noted earlier that male labour-force participation rates have declined generally since the mid-1970s. These declines have been manifested in all age categories. In 1975, 60 percent of

all males in Canada between the ages of 15–24, 91 percent of 25–44-year-olds, 89 percent of
45–54-year-olds, and 76 percent of 55–64-year-olds participated in the labour force. In 1993,
52 percent of 15–24-year-olds, 82 percent of both 25–44 and 45–54 age categories, and only
55 percent of 55–64-year-olds were participating in the labour force (Best, 1995: 31).
Participation rates declined about evenly among men aged between 15 and 54 (ranging from
7 to 9 percent), but dropped dramatically (21 percent) among men aged 55–64. In contrast,
as is evidenced by data presented in Table 6.1, labour-force participation rates increased
among women of all ages between 1961 and 1991, with the exception of women over 65
years of age, and then declined for most ages between 1991 and 1996, in response to the
same factors that have contributed to the decline among men (Krahn and Lowe, 1993: 63).

TABLE 6.1	Female Labour Force Participation Rates by Age, Canada 1961-1996				
Age Group	**1961**	**1971**	**1981**	**1991**	**1996**
15-19	34.2	36.9	44.3	47.5	46.6
20-24	49.5	62.5	77.1	81.1	72.1
25-34	29.6	44.5	65.7	78.5	77.6
35-44	31.1	43.9	64.1	79.6	78.6
45-54	33.4	44.5	55.7	71.9	71.9
55-64	24.4	34.4	35.4	39.2	36.9
65+	6.7	8.2	5.5	5.6	3.5
Total	29.7	39.9	51.0	59.9	57.6

Source: 1961-1991. Adapted from McVey and Kalbach (1995: 251) and based upon *1971 Census of Canada*, vol. 3, Part 1,
Economic Characteristics, Table 2; *1981 Census of Canada*, Labour Force Activity. Canada, Provinces, Urban Size Groups, Rural
Non-Farm and Rural Farm, Cat. 92-91, Table 1; *1991 Census of Canada*, Labour Force Activity, *The Nation*. Cat. 93-324,
Table 1. 1996: estimates from *Labour Force Annual Averages*, Cat. No. 71-529, 71-001, and 71-220.

At the beginning of the 1960s, female labour-force participation was characterized by a
bimodal pattern. The participation rate for women of typical early childrearing age (25–34)
drops off dramatically from the younger age group (20–24). The next highest participation
level is found among 45–54 year-olds, when most women have completed active childrearing and their children are beginning to leave home. Reading down the columns of Table 6.1
for subsequent census years reveals that the bimodal pattern has disappeared. Comparing 1991
and 1996 reveals a minimal decline in participation rates for most age categories, but a substantial decline for women in the 20–24 age group, reflecting a combination of young
women staying in school longer, downsizing based upon a last-hired first-fired philosophy,
and a general lack of available employment opportunities. Rates still remain high throughout the childbearing and childrearing years and only begin to drop off significantly among
women 55–64 years of age (as is found for previous years). This latter group represents
women socialized in earlier eras to anticipate never having to seek paid employment following
the birth of their children. Even if they had sought employment, they likely faced gender, perhaps also age, discrimination in that employers were reluctant to hire married women with
children in the home. Consequently, most of these women probably never did return to the

labour force after their childbearing and childrearing years. Higher rates of participation for women of all ages across the decades also reflect both increasing numbers of women who never marry, and increasing numbers of women who have voluntarily or involuntarily combined motherhood and employment (see Table 6.2).

TABLE 6.2	Percentage of the Population 15 Years of Age and Over in the Labour Force by Marital Status and Sex, Canada: 1971, 1991, 1996			
Sex and Marital Status	**1971***	**1981***	**1991****	**1996****
Males:				
Single	63.5	69.6	72.9	69.7
Married	84.4	83.6	79.6	75.5
Separated / Divorced	—	—	76.9	73.0
Widowed	46.8	57.5	22.9	17.6
Total	76.4	78.2	76.4	72.4
Females:				
Single	53.5	61.8	66.4	63.6
Married	37.0	51.9	63.2	61.6
Separated / Divorced	—	—	68.2	64.7
Widowed	26.6	31.3	14.5	11.4
Total	39.9	51.8	59.9	57.6

Note: *1971 and 1981: Separated are listed with married; figures listed for widowed include both widowed and divorced combined
**1991 and 1996: married includes persons in common-law unions

Source: 1971: Kalbach and McVey, 1979: 274. 1981: *Census of Canada*. Cat. 92-915. Population. Labour Force Activity. Canada, Provinces, Urban Sized Groups, Rural Non-Farm, and Rural Farm. Ottawa: Minister of Supply and Services Canada. 1984. 1991: *1991 Census of Canada*. Cat. 93-324. Labour Force Activity. The Nation. Table 1. 1996: *Labour Force Annual Averages 1996*. Cat. 71-220-XPB. Table 3.

Marital Status and the Presence of Children

You can see in Table 6.2 that the most significant increases in labour-force participation between 1971 and 1991 are found among married women. In 1961, 68.3 percent of Canadian husband-wife families were characterized by a husband-only, sole-provider pattern (McVey and Kalbach, 1995: 253). By 1991, only 19 percent of husband-wife families were characterized by that husband-only, sole-provider pattern, while 61 percent had dual-earners, 15 percent had no earners, and 5 percent had a wife-only sole-provider (Oderkirk et al., 1994: 19). Traditional-earner husbands-only families tend to be older on average or, among younger families with husbands under age 40, have more children than do dual-earner families (Oderkirk et al., 1994: 20). We can see from Table 6.2 that married women in the labour force have increased in proportion from 37 percent in 1971 to 62 percent in 1996, an actual increase of 67 percent that reflects the decline in traditional-earner families.We can also see in Table 6.2 that the lowest labour-force participation figures are recorded by widowed females. These low participation rates are a function of two factors: (1) the typically older age of these women contributes to the greater likelihood that, following age/gender norms of an earlier generation, they are unlikely to have stayed in the labour force if they had any children and likely also faced age discrimination if they desired to enter the labour force after becoming widowed; (2) the financial circumstances of widowed women typically differs from that of, for example, separated and divorced women, in that the former are typically left in a relatively better financial state than the latter women following their marital disruptions. One final note: the decline in participation rates for both males and females of all marital status categories recorded in Table 6.2 for 1996 primarily reflects the impact of downsizing upon the labour force during the first half of the 1990s. While most marital status categories demonstrate a decline averaging 3 to 4 percent, separated/divorced women participation rates declined more than 6 percent.

Table 6.3 presents data on the different labour-force participation rates of married women with a husband present at home, listed according to the women's age groups and the age groups of their dependent children. Married women with dependent children generally have lower participation rates than do women without children present. Not included in the table is the fact that 70 percent of mothers aged 25–34 in 1991 with children of all ages still at home were employed, while 91 percent of women without children at home were employed. Among women aged 35–44, participation rates were 78 and 85 percent, respectively (Logan and Belliveau, 1995: 25, 26).

TABLE 6.3 **Labour Force Participation Rates of Married Women* by Age and Presence of Dependent Children, Canada: 1981 and 1991**

Age of Married Female	All Women		With Children Under 6 Years of Age Only		With Children Over 6 Years of Age Only		With Children Under and Over 6 Years of Age	
	1981	1991	1981	1991	1981	1991	1981	1991
All Married Women	51.4	63.4	49.4	69.0	55.0	71.6	44.6	65.3
15-24	68.4	77.1	43.9	57.4	64.4	78.2	39.0	49.2
25-34	60.9	76.9	51.6	70.9	65.2	78.6	45.1	64.2
35-44	61.7	79.0	51.8	72.5	63.4	80.4	44.7	67.8
45 and over	34.7	43.3	44.1	61.9	44.5	60.3	33.3	56.8

Note: * includes only married women with husband present

Source: McVey and Kalbach, 1995: 254; based upon the 1986 and 1991 Census of Canada.

As you examine Table 6.3, notice that labour-force participation rates have increased substantially for all married women with children during their prime childbearing and childrearing years, over the 1980s. The most dramatic increase in Canada has occurred among women with preschool-age children (Logan and Belliveau, 1995). The presence of dependent children of any age no longer acts as a major inhibiting agent preventing labour-force participation by mothers. By 1991 (the last year for which data were available at press time), a majority of women of all ages, approaching almost three-quarters of women aged 25–44, with all of their children under the age of six, still manage to participate in the Canadian labour force. These figures are higher than comparable figures for American women (see Bird, 1997: 821). Despite the persistent presence of gender expectations encouraging women to place a lower priority upon paid-work careers to give much higher priority to childcare, having children under the age of 18 living in the home significantly increases the sense of economic burden and accompanying sense of psychological distress experienced not only by fathers, but also mothers (Bird, 1997), and becomes an economic incentive among mothers promoting continued or new participation in the paid-labour force. That employed mothers with children living at home are more psychologically distressed than are fathers is not surprising, given that such women are also responsible for shouldering the burden of responsibility and work involved with housework (to be explored later in this chapter) and childcare (see Bird, 1997).

American Current Population Survey data for selected years between 1971 and 1990 also indicate a dramatic rise in the employment of married mothers with preschool age children (Leibowitz and Klerman, 1995). These researchers find that two sets of factors operating together account for almost half (45 percent) of the increase over the 20-year period. Changes in the mothers' demographic characteristics, such as age, education, and number of children, account for about one-fifth of the increase, while expanding employment opportunities for women, coupled with declining wages for men, account for another fifth. Regarding the latter set of factors, increasing economic opportunities available for women are more important to women's decisions to seek employment than are deteriorating paid-work conditions experienced by their husbands. In other words, mothers are more likely to seek employed based upon their own personal circumstances rather than being stimulated by or reacting to their husbands' circumstances. Leibowitz and Klerman (1995) claim that the presence of very young children, aged three months and younger, no longer presents a major impediment to their mothers joining the labour force, as mothers are able to obtain satisfactory or at least acceptable alternative infant-care arrangements.

Despite the claims by Leibowitz and Klerman (1995) that children under the ages of three months no longer impede their mothers' participation in the labour force, mothers of very young children who prefer to breast feed their infants face particular difficulties. While a 1989 Supreme Court of Canada decision ruled that employers who discriminate against employees on the basis of pregnancy violate sex discrimination laws, a related issue currently being raised in our country is whether that ruling extends, or should extend, to postpartum breast feeding. Lindberg (1996), analyzing data derived from the National Survey of Family Growth, examines relationships between employment and breast feeding among American women between 1980 and 1986. She finds that significantly more women employed part-time also breast feed their children, and continue to do so for longer periods of time than do women employed full-time. As well, women are significantly more likely to cease breast feeding the same month as they commence full-time employment. These findings suggest that existing conditions of full-time employment typically are incompatible with mothers' desires for breast feeding, and that employers, should they wish to increase their full-time female labour force, must make accommodations for women who wish to combine employment and breast feeding. In the absence of any such compromises, women who wish to continue breast feeding are more likely to make their own adjustments by seeking part-time employment only. Currently, some provinces in Canada (such as British Columbia) have ruled that breast feeding in public is a public right. These rulings have been prompted in part by complaints raised by employed mothers who previously had been denied the right to breast feed their infants while on the job, and who were inconvenienced further, both physically and psychologically, by having to leave their work sites to breast feed.

Perhaps not surprisingly, the lowest participation rate in 1991, and almost the lowest percentage increase over the 1980s, is found among women aged 15–24 with at least two children, one of whom is under the age of six and one of whom is over the age of six. These women obviously began childbearing and childrearing at a young age, and are most likely to have among the lowest educational and occupational levels of all women. Consequently, their prospects for employment are among the lowest faced by women, especially under the age of 44. As well, across Canada generally, unemployment levels for both men and women aged 15–24 consistently remain higher than for older age groups. The highest labour-participation rate in 1991 among married women with a husband present who have dependent children in the home is found in the 35–44 age group, with all children over the age of six, although their rate is not significantly higher than those found for younger women with children of similar ages. Participation rates for women with children over the age of six are higher than are participation rates for women who have all or only some of their children under the age of six. While all women with dependent children in the home confront problems with arranging for alternate childcare, the problems are more acute for women with preschool-age children as we shall see shortly.

Employment Continuity and Discontinuity

Substantial discontinuities or interruptions in a person's employment career influence employers' attitudes towards a worker's commitment to his or her work, current earnings, lifetime earnings (in the form of lost wages and foregone pay raises), postretirement income, opportunities for advancement, and future employability. Generally, women experience more and longer discontinuities over the course of their paid-work histories than do men. The greater work-career interruptions of women undoubtedly are partly the result of individual personal decisions. Viewing such discontinuities as solely the responsibility of female workers, however, can become a misleading case of "blaming the victim," when a generalized psychological explanation is applied to what is often determined more by structural conditions associated with the nature of paid employment and societal expectations for differential gender priorities regarding employment, parenthood, and childcare.

Fast and Da Pont (1997) find that women in Canada are less likely to interrupt their paid work today and, where interruptions do occur, return to gainful employment more quickly than have women in the past. Younger workers experience a different set of social expectations regarding employment and motherhood than did women in the 1950s and 1960s. Today, as in the past, women also confront expectations different from those faced by men. Based upon findings from the 1995 General Social Survey, Fast and Da Pont find that employment interruptions (defined as "stopping working for pay for a period of six months or more") are more likely to be experienced by women (62 percent) than by men (27 percent) (Fast and Da Pont, 1997: 3). Paid-work interruptions most often occur during a woman's early twenties (43 percent), with the frequency of occurrence declining for subsequent age groups. Employment discontinuities among young female workers are more likely to be a consequence of changing vagaries of employment conditions faced by people with little work experience, periods of unemployment occasioned by searching for a more desirable line of work to settle into, or attempts to acquire higher educational credentials, than due to changing family circumstances

associated with childbearing and childrearing. Among workers over age 25, fertility and consequent family responsibilities are the most likely cause of discontinuities in employment.
"Marriage, maternity leave and care of children or elderly relatives (family-related reasons) were
the reasons for 62% of women's interruptions of paid work" (Fast and Da Pont, 1997: 5).

Fast and Da Pont (1997: 4) also find that 71 percent of the women sampled in the 1995 GSS
returned to paid work following a period of interruption. Forty-seven percent of those who
previously held full-time jobs returned to full-time employment, approximately one quarter returned to part-time work only, and the remainder had yet to return to employment at the time
of the survey. As we will see in a later section of this chapter, many women employed on a part-
time basis claim to be doing so as a consequence of the demands of their family responsibilities. Still, as indicated by Fast and Da Pont (1997:5), the impact of family responsibilities
upon women's work patterns is declining among younger workers, and the impact of economic factors (from forced layoffs to expanded opportunities) are increasing in importance.

Generally, women with higher levels of education experience the lowest likelihood of
work discontinuity and, where interruptions do occur, are likely to return to work more
quickly than are women workers with lower educational levels. More highly educated
women tend to possess highly marketable skills that receive high levels of remuneration, in
addition to other intangible rewards that are more characteristic of careers than hourly wage
jobs. Similar to findings produced from earlier research, Marshall's analysis of Canadian
women in male-dominated professions finds these women are "more likely than women in
other occupations to have never married, or if married, to have had fewer children or to be
childless" (Marshall, 1987: 7). Being single and childfree obviously removes two major
causes of career disruptions among employed women.

"Regardless of their age, mothers working full-time all year (49–52 weeks) earn less
than women without children at home" (Logan and Belliveau, 1995: 28). This earning differential is attributable in large part to discontinuities in employment histories occasioned by
childbirth and time devoted exclusively to childrearing. Prior to relatively recent innovations
in worker-protection policies, a vicious circle characterized most women's working environments. Employers used to justify paying women less than men by claiming that there
was no point in investing in female employees by paying them more, since they would "just
get pregnant and leave anyway." The low pay received by many women made their decision
to leave the labour force upon childbirth much easier, since they would only be foregoing a
minimal income. It was much easier to quit one job, stay at home for a period of time devoted
to childrearing, and then eventually look for another readily available low-paying job with
the same or another employer. If employers paid higher wages, or guaranteed an uninterrupted
pay scale upon early return to the workforce, decisions on the part of women (with or without input from partners) to quit employment for an indeterminate period of time would have
been more difficult to make in light of higher foregone earnings.

That the length of work-history disruptions is declining for younger women today, in contrast to longer periods characteristic of women in the past, is partly attributable to the en-
trenchment of paid maternity leave into Canadian government public policy (see Chapter 8 for
current details regarding maternity and parental leaves). Unlike Canada, the United States
does not have a federal government program guaranteeing paid maternity leave for mothers of
recently birthed or adopted children. However, available evidence indicates that, by 1989, 80
percent or more of full-time American female employees in companies of 100 or more workers had access to some form of paid maternity leave, although the amounts of pay and length

of leave varies across companies (Joesch, 1997: 1009). Upon analyzing data collected in 1988 from a representative American national sample as part of The National Survey of Family Growth, Joesch finds that "work behavior changes when women have the option of a paid, instead of an unpaid, leave. Although women were more likely to take time off from work during the birth month if their leave was paid, they also interrupted work later during pregnancy and started to work sooner once their infant was at least 2 months old" (Joesch, 1997: 1018). Paid leave programs, whether sponsored by business or government, appear to make an important contribution towards not only shortening employment discontinuities among women, but also to a diminution of the earnings gap between male and female workers.

Employment continuities and discontinuities have an impact not only on employers' conceptions of an employee's sense of commitment, with possible repercussions for continued employment and promotion, but also on present levels of personal, and perhaps family, income as well as future income (Fast and Da Pont, 1997: 6–7). Canada/Quebec Pension Plans, private pension plans, and registered retirement savings plans all depend upon contributions made over an extended period of time. Government pensions are determined by the amount of earnings upon which contributions are based. Lengthy interruptions in the present mean that pension earnings in the future will be reduced. The fact that women are more likely than men to experience employment discontinuities due to a heavier burden of family responsibilities jeopardizes their economic futures, especially when no guarantees exist that the families they were once responsible for will assume a reciprocal responsibility to support women in their old age (see Chapter 9 on women and poverty). It is possible that growing numbers of young women today are aware of the long-term implications of any lengthy departures from the paid-labour force, thus accounting, in part, for the present-day pattern of women workers taking fewer and shorter leaves.

Overtime and Underutilization of Family-Friendly Benefits

Hochschild (1997: 175–193) notes the increasing incidence of overtime (unpaid for salaried workers and paid for wage workers) among employees in the 1990s. The same phenomenon can be observed in Canada. According to a 1997 *Perspectives on Labour and Income* report, 17 percent of the Canadian labour force work overtime during a typical week, with the most common occurrences found within communication industries, educational services, consumer durables, manufacturing, and mining industries (*Edmonton Journal*, 11 December 1997: A1, A18). Increasing rates of overtime appear to be motivated by two forces operating simultaneously: an increased cost of living necessitates the need for higher income, while business, industry, and government downsizing typically requires more work from the existing workforce, thus necessitating more overtime to produce the same or even a greater output once contributed from a larger labour pool. Within downsizing sectors of our economy, workers fear they might be next to be laid off and consequently work harder and longer to preserve their jobs. While in agreement with the impact of these two motivating factors, Hochschild (1997) argues that an additional, perhaps more important, factor involves the increasing attractiveness of the workplace coupled with the decreasing attractiveness of the familyplace.

Inflationary and downsizing pressures, along with a changing balance of workplace/familyplace attractiveness, also account for a significant reluctance evidenced by employees to take advantage of any of the several "family friendly" programs made available by busi-

Box 6.1	Can the Workplace Make Room For Daddy?

Based on his Canadian research on thirty-two fathers from intact families, Kerry Daly (1994: 179) reported men often viewed their own fathers as an "anti-hero or negative role model" and were confronted with an absence of strong male parental role models. He observes that, on occasion, his respondents would identify a television character (such as the Dr. Huxtable role played by Bill Cosby on The Cosby Show) rather than a known person, as furnishing their ideal of what a "good father" should be. However, while Dr. Huxtable found it simple to combine childcare with high-status employment, an obstetrician working from his own home, Daly's sample of men reported a number of structural barriers which discouraged them from pursuing active involvement in childrearing responsibilities. These structural disincentives included: work policies which discouraged paternity leaves or taking time off from work for childcare duties and negative reactions from colleagues and supervisors.

INTERVIEWER: Would you say that one of you was the main parent?

FATHER: The parent at home, which definitely is the mother. In fact, our benefits government structure really makes that happen, doesn't it….I mean, I bet dollars to doughnuts, if I called the UI [now EI] people and asked how many males participate in the paternity benefits, it would be less than one percent. Why is that?…My own perspective is that men really… need to have the other things in place to convince them…they need to see that what they're thinking is okay, and it's reinforced by the fact that their employers says, "You want to take six months off to care for your newborn child, the government is going to provide you some support, so that you can do it with dignity.…

INTERVIEWER: Do you think that the responsibilities that you carry as a father are acknowledged at your work place?

FATHER: No. I don't think so.…When Sarah was born and in the hospital, they wanted to use her for the demo baby for the bath. The fathers were welcome to come. Well I'm excited of course, I'm up on cloud 9½. I say to my boss "I'm taking Friday morning off" [as vacation time].…I did give a reason (which I don't any more) because I'm going to see my child getting bathed because she's the demo baby and I want to see how it is supposed to be done. Well he just thought this was the funniest, biggest joke in the whole wide world—"We never had this and that and everything else!" When I happened to mention this to my co-worker that I was taking a morning off this past week to go see her get her eyes tested he said, "For God's sake don't tell the boss because it was like four months and that's all we heard of." He just couldn't believe you would be going, a man would be going to see how the baby is being bathed.…Okay, so like I say, no one at work appreciates it; I don't really think so." (p. 184)

ness, industry, or government employers. Flextime, flexplace, reduced hours, and parental leave programs are available to limited degrees throughout the workplace in both Canada and the United States today. Of these options, Hochschild (1997) finds that reduced hours (with reduced pay) and parental leave programs, particularly paternity leave, are the least likely to be selected by today's workers particularly among those with the most attractive higher income, high-safety, white-collar jobs. The lack of acceptance accorded paternity leave demonstrates the continued centrality of the provider role for men, who believe they best serve their families by staying on the job and earning an income. As well, the corporate mindset has advanced little beyond making family-friendly policies available, at least on paper. Commitment to those policies and the ends to which they are intended is lacking,(see Box 6.1). While the concept of "quality time" has apparently seeped into the lexicon of most Canadian and American families, no comparable concept of "quality time" has been developed in the workplace. Employers, including managers and supervisors who implement and oversee employers' demands, appear to be steeped in the notion that "quantity time" provides the best indicator of employees' dedication to their present and future jobs. The greater or longer hours male and female employees devote to working within the eyesight of managers and supervisors, the most likely they are to be rewarded.

Paid Work and the Costs of Parenting

In Chapter 3 we noted that in seeking to establish women's rights to participation in the public sphere, first-wave feminists in the early twentieth century confronted an entrenched "separate spheres" ideology, which maintained that women's anticipated or actual role within the family as wives, childbearers, and mothers, disqualified them for the world of paid work. Mr. Justice Barker in the 1873 decision of the United States Supreme Court in *Bradwell v. Illinois*, wrote:

> the civil law, as well as nature herself, has always recognized a wide difference in the respective spheres and destinies of man and woman. Man is, or should be, woman's protector and defender. The natural and proper timidity and delicacy which belongs to the female sex evidently unfits it for many of the occupations of civil life. The constitution of the family organization, which is founded in the divine ordinance as well as in the nature of things, indicates the domestic sphere as that which properly belongs to the domain and functions of womanhood." (Friedman, 1993)

Similar reasoning prevailed in Canada. Mr. Justice Tuck remarked in 1905 that "if I dare to express my own views I would say that I have no sympathy with the opinion that women should in all branches of life come in competition with men. Better let them attend to their own legitimate business." The "legitimate business" of married women and/or mothers was seen to reside outside of the paid workforce and even such liberals as John Stuart Mill "considered that equal rights of education, political life, and the professions could be granted only to single women without the responsibilities of family" (Mossman, 1997: 50).

Pleck (1977) directs attention to a "differential permeability of work and family boundaries" (in Mortimer and London, 1984: 28) for men and women that continues to exist today. Women, Pleck notes, are expected to disrupt their paid-work roles to accommodate their families. Obversely, it is viewed as acceptable for men to disrupt their families (through job transfers, commuter lifestyles, and long hours spent away from home) to accommodate their careers. Because women are commonly assigned primary caregiver tasks in Canadian society, those who seek to combine a career with motherhood must often address the issue of motherhood in a way that is qualitatively dissimilar from the issue of fatherhood for men. We noted earlier that, prior to 1989, women in Canada could be fired from their jobs simply because they became pregnant. Men were not fired simply because they contributed to a pregnancy. Until 1983, most women were denied the right to claim pregnancy benefits under the old Unemployment Insurance Act (Atcheson et al., 1984: 20–21). Beyond the obvious alterations to their present and future marriage and family lives, impending motherhood had, and still has, significantly greater implications for employment than fatherhood did and does.

The costs of parenthood upon paid work begin soon after the birth of a child. As we noted in Chapter 4, 15 percent of children twelve years of age and under were accommodated by licenced care facilities in 1991 (Baker and Lero, 1996: 93). The costs of such care for children of preschool age may, despite government financial support, prove prohibitive for many parents. Ontario's Childcare Review noted that, in August 1996, fees could range from approximately $10 000 to $12 000 per year for an infant, and $6000 to $7000 per year for preschoolers (Government of Ontario, 1996: 15).

Cleveland et al. (1996) report that high costs of childcare have a significant negative effect on the labour supply of women with children, and on women's decisions to purchase childcare. They confirm findings reported earlier in American studies examining this issue (Connelly, 1992; Nakamura and Nakamura, 1985). However, Cleveland et al. find that a mother's expected wage, if sufficiently high, has a significant positive impact on both the decision to purchase market forms of childcare and the decision to engage in paid work. In other words, if childcare costs exceed or equal women's wage income, mothers will likely either have to stay at home or else seek other, less expensive, alternative childcare arrangements. If a mother's wages exceed childcare costs by an amount deemed satisfactory, women are more likely both to work for pay and to purchase the more expensive forms of licenced childcare. All of these decisions appear to be based upon a mother's income, not a father's income. One way or another, childcare still remains a mother's responsibility and that responsibility has a significantly greater impact upon her employment than upon a father and his employment.

Parenting has other employment-related financial costs still unrecognized by official government policy in our society. Consider, for example, the case of Beth Symes. Ms. Symes faced the challenge of negotiating her roles as a self-employed lawyer and the mother of two preschool-age daughters by engaging the services of a nanny to provide in-home care for her children on weekdays, while she, as well as her spouse, both pursued their respective careers. The nanny was paid $13 359 for her services in 1985. However, the maximum allowable childcare deduction, under section 63 of the federal Income Tax Act that year, was $2000 per child up to the age of seven, or less than one-third of Symes' actual childcare expenses.

Rather than directly challenge the limit specified under section 63, Symes attempted to deduct the full cost of her childcare as a business expense (as outlined within section 18 of the Act), arguing that her childcare expenditures were incurred "for the purpose of gaining or producing income from…business." The Minister of National Revenue rejected this claim and Symes, in turn, argued that the Minister's interpretation of section 18 constituted discrimination on the basis of sex, contrary to the equality guarantee in section 15 of the Canadian *Charter of Rights and Freedoms*. Symes' arguments were accepted initially by the Federal Court (Trial Division), but that ruling was subsequently overturned by the Federal Court of Appeal. In delivering a unanimous decision, Mr. Justice Decary maintained that the costs incurred in relation to childcare by Symes were not legitimate business expenses. Macklin (1992) observes:

> This assertion failed to acknowledge that as long as business has been the exclusive domain of men, the commercial needs of business have been dictated by men who [think they] need to spend in order to produce income.…[T]he courts have in the past permitted businessmen to deduct club fees because men like to conduct business with each other over golf.…Because some men be-

lieve expensive cars enhance their professional image, driving a Rolls Royce has been held to be an incident of a professional expense. Similarly, it is difficult to sustain the claim that making charitable contributions to enhance one's reputation is a community inheres in the business of manufacturing boxes. It seems closer to the truth to suggest that these practices inhere in the way men, or some men, engage in business. Of course, since men have (until very recently) been the only people engaging in business, it is easy enough to confuse the needs of businessmen and the needs of business….[O]ne might reasonably demand a reconceptualization of "business expenses" that reflects the changing composition of the business class.

The Supreme Court of Canada, in 1993, upheld the decision of the Federal Court of Appeal, with both women members of the Supreme Court dissenting (Mossman, 1994). Although the income- tax maximum childcare deduction was raised in 1998 to $7000 for each child under the age of seven, the Income Tax Act of Canada still refuses to regard the cost of childcare as a legitimate "business deduction." In effect, childcare costs are viewed officially as part of the process of parenting, mothering in particular.

Once alternative childcare has been arranged, mothers' primary responsibilities for home and family continue to impinge upon their employment in ways less often found among fathers. Home and family obligations contribute substantially to higher employee absenteeism rates among women than among men (Akyeampong, 1992). Employee absenteeism rates, not including absences for vacations, rose between 1977 and 1990 in Canada across all "industries, occupations and provinces" (Akyeampong, 1992: 26), as a consequence of improved parental leave programs and increased numbers of employed mothers. In those cases where absenteeism results in lost wages, the lower wage-earner in a dual-earner family, typically the mother, will be designated by a couple as the one who will disrupt paid-work hours to meet childrearing obligations (Akyeampong, 1992: 27). During an average week in 1991, 3 percent of all employed women, but only 1.2 percent of employed men, were absent from paid work because of these reasons (Ghalam, 1993/1995: 6).

In 1991, 11 percent of women in two-parent families with at least one child under age six, and 6 percent of comparable lone mothers, missed time from work each week because of family responsibilities. Absentee rates dropped to around 2 percent for both lone mothers and mothers in dual-parent families whose youngest child was aged 6–15. In contrast, the presence of young children had little effect on the work absences of fathers. Only 2 percent of fathers in two-parent families with preschool-age children and 1 percent of those whose youngest child was aged 6–15 lost time from work. (Ghalam, 1993/1995: 6).

Absenteeism is disruptive to employers' general expectations for worker productivity and for workers' expectations for their own productivity. As well, absenteeism and other family-related situations (e.g., refusing to work overtime to be home with children) can have a negative impact upon a worker's chances for promotions and pay raises. Concerned with the "inconvenience" that women sometimes posed to organizations because they were mothers and with the need for companies to find an efficient way to deal with such women, management consultant Felice Schwartz (1989) suggested that business and industry should create two "streams" of career mobility for women: a fast track for career-primary women, who would not allow their children to interfere with their career pursuits, and a separate "mommy track" (a term coined by journalists, not Schwartz), a lower-paid, less-pressured, career path into which other career-and-family women would be placed. The fast track would be comparable to the male career pattern upon which all business and industry is modeled, while the "mommy track" would be a compromise solution for both female employees and employers wishing to accommodate women's responsibilities both inside and outside of the home. How, precisely, employers and women employees themselves were to determine which women would fit on which track, and when, remained unclear. No apparent need for a "daddy track" was seen to exist.

If some see a "mommy track" as furnishing an admirable and sensible solution, allowing women to have the best of both spheres, others were less enthusiastic in their response. Thus, Ehrenreich and English (1989/1995: 215) argue that "[b]umping women—or just fertile women, or married women, or whomever—off the fast track may sound smart....[but] it is the corporate culture itself that needs to slow down to a human pace....Work loads that are incompatible with family life are...a kind of toxin—to men as well as women, and ultimately to businesses as well as families." From the perspective of Ehrenreich and English, this is not just a "women's issue," but rather is a larger issue pertaining to both genders, to the structural organization and mindset of both paid-work organizations and families, and to the better integration of gender, work, and the family. However, changing the entire structural organization of work, family, and gender responsibilities appears to be beyond the scope, and perhaps even the capabilities, of most problem-solvers. Instead, answers are sought in more limited solutions.

Strategies such as flextime and flexplace have been advanced as alternative possibilities and will be described in a later section of this chapter. *Job-sharing* has been described as an arrangement that "lets women enjoy the best of both worlds" (*Kitchener-Waterloo Record*, 17 July 1997: E3). According to Statistics Canada, which released the first national data on job-sharing in 1997, although "still not a widely practiced work arrangement...[job-sharing] is becoming an increasingly important work option." In 1996, approximately 8 percent (or 171 000 Canadians) shared a job; the vast majority being women over the age of 35 with college or university degrees and with children at home. Approximately one-quarter of sharers are teachers and nurses and one-fifth have worked in their jobs for more than 10 years. The average hourly pay of job-sharers is three dollars an hour more than that earned by regular part-time workers. Job-sharers identify the strategy as allowing them to attain a better balance between work and family demands, reduce stress, and increase their energy and job satisfaction. Employers report that the strategy increases worker productivity, efficiency, job commitment, and enthusiasm, and decreases absenteeism. However, the report notes that drawbacks of job-sharing are, for the worker, a lesser likelihood of career advancement and, for the employer, an increase in paperwork. According to the report, the number of Canadian collective agreements with provision for job-sharing increased from 3 percent in 1986 to 12 percent in 1993; the Royal Bank of Canada, with 1100 employees sharing a job as part of its work-family program, has the largest program of any Canadian corporation (*Kitchener-Waterloo Record*, 17 July 1997: E3).

Occupational Distributions and Segregations

An employee's current location in a particular occupation is the result of a combination of factors including early educational and occupational aspirations, choices made regarding specific education and training, and eventual selection of employment from opportunities currently available in the occupational structure. As we noted in Chapter 4, educational and occupational aspirations and educational and occupational choices are themselves influenced by gender socialization expressed in the contexts of families, peers, schools, and the mass media. These socialization experiences, in addition to expectations for a desired paid work-family configuration, shape the employment dreams of both men and women.

TABLE 6.4	Full-Time Wage Earners by Occupational Category, Canada: 1991				
Occupational Category	**Males**			**Females**	
(Population 15 Years of Age and Over)	**Number**	**%**		**Number**	**%**
Managerial, Administrative	1 093 785	13.50		666 135	9.80
Natural Sciences, Engineering & Mathematics	464 240	5.73		116 895	1.72
Social Sciences	125 710	1.55		201 460	2.96
Religion	25 835	0.32		7 150	0.11
Teaching & Related	231 535	2.86		418 070	6.15
Medicine & Health	152 805	1.89		586 970	8.63
Artistic, Literary, Recreational & Related	141 170	1.74		115 030	1.69
Clerical & Related	574 780	7.09		2 101 415	30.90
Sales	721 450	8.90		639 605	9.41
Service	828 880	10.23		1 087 720	16.00
Farming, Horticultural, Animal Husbandry & Related	335 000	4.13		120 075	1.77
Fishing, Trapping & Related	45 730	0.56		7 425	0.11
Forestry, Logging	77 995	0.96		7 430	0.11
Mining, Quarrying (incl. Oil & Gas)	64 040	0.79		1 865	0.03
Processing Occupations	312 035	3.85		113 165	1.66
Machinery & Related	251 610	3.10		17 315	0.25
Product Fabricating, Assembling & Repairing	693 395	8.56		206 770	3.04
Construction Trades	832 830	10.28		23 685	0.35
Transport Equipment Operating	468 900	5.79		47 975	0.71
Material Handling and Related	179 680	2.22		55 250	0.81
Other Crafts and Equipment Operating Occupations	119 440	1.47		37 060	0.54
Occupations n.e.c	244 325	3.01		62 155	0.91

Note: Percentages will not add to 100 due to missing data.

Source: *Employment Income by Occupation*. The Nation. Cat. 93-332. Ottawa: Minister of Industry, Science and Technology, 1993. Table 1.

Fewer Canadian men and women are now employed in goods-producing industries, such as agriculture, construction, fishing and hunting, forestry, mining, and manufacturing in contrast to pre-World War II eras (Best, 1995: 33). While men have slowly been increasing their participation in service industries, women's proportionate participation in clerical occupations has declined, even though clerical work still remains one of the occupational categories in which female employees are highly concentrated (see Table 6.4). Women's participation levels in the professions and in managerial and administrative occupations has increased substantially since the 1970s and 1980s, although they still fall well behind men's participation levels in those occupations. For example, the proportion of doctors and dentists who were female rose to 26 percent in 1993, from 18 percent in 1982 (Best, 1995: 33), while the proportion of women in managerial and administrative positions rose to 42 percent in 1993 from 29 percent in 1982 (Best, 1995: 33) and 16 percent in 1971 (Wilson, 1991: 90).

Table 6.4 presents the distribution of full-time male and female workers by their major occupational categories. The data were collected in the 1991 Census and reflect respondents' identified occupations for the previous year. Men in the paid work force are almost evenly distributed across all occupational categories. Only a few occupational categories account for a concentration of more than 10 percent of male workers and the three largest general occupational categories (Managerial, Administrative; Service; Construction Trades) account for slightly more than one-third (34 percent) of all full-time male workers. These categories span a wide range of occupations varying in terms of their pay, prestige and power.

Women in the paid work force are not evenly distributed across all occupational categories. Data collected in the 1994 General Social Survey indicate that Canadian women who have completed university or community college are three times more likely than comparably educated men (24 percent and 8 percent, respectively) to have a clerical or service job (Kelly et al., 1997: 12). Three categories (Clerical, Sales, and Services) account for more than half (56.31 percent) of all full-time employed females, according to the 1991 Census. These three categories combined constitute what is often referred to as the "pink collar ghetto" and are characterized by relatively low levels of pay, prestige, and power. The concentration of women in the pink collar ghetto has declined since 1981, when clerical, sales, and services occupational categories accounted for 62.7 percent of all females in the full-time labour force (Krahn and Lowe, 1993: 74). While participation levels in the "managerial, administrative" ranks increased for both men and women between 1981 and 1991, the proportional increase was more substantial for women. The general trend for women since 1981 has been a contraction of participation in pink collar occupations and an expansion into other, particularly management, "nontraditional" occupations.

While Table 6.4 focuses upon general occupational categories, Tables 6.5 and 6.6 provide a more detailed examination of the top 10 specific occupations in which Canadian women workers are found most frequently in 1991 and 1996, respectively. As can be seen from these tables, most of the specific occupations are concentrated in the clerical, sales, service, nursing, and elementary-school teaching categories. Despite the importance of their contributions to their professions and to the clientele for whom they provide services, both the nursing and teaching occupations are also characterized by lower prestige, pay, and power relative to other specific occupations (e.g., doctors, high-school and university teachers) within their same professions. Statistics Canada notes (*Daily*, 17 March 1998: 6) that retail sales ranked as the most frequently occurring occupation in 1996 for women in all Canadian provinces except New Brunswick and Quebec. In both of these provinces, as well as in both of the territories, secretarial positions ranked as the more frequently occurring.

Unfortunately, for our purposes, precise comparisons cannot be made across 1996, 1991, and earlier time periods, due to differences in Statistics Canada's method of classifying and identifying occupations. However, some observations can be made. Over a 35-year period, the concentration of women in their 10 most frequently occurring occupations has been lessening. Available data from 1961 (Wilson, 1996: 106) indicate that the top 10 most frequent occupations for women accounted for 62.7 percent of the female labour force. This concentration had lessened by 1991 (Table 6.5) to 40 percent, and by 1996 (Table 6.6) to 32.5 percent. Such a decline suggests that women are spreading out into a wider range of occupations by the mid-1990s.

TABLE 6.5   Top Ten Most Frequent Occupations of Women in the Labour Force, Canada: 1991

Occupation	Number of Female Workers	% of Female Labour Force
Secretaries & Stenographers	449 580	7.1
Salesclerks	379 820	6.0
Bookkeepers	337 185	5.3
Cashiers and Tellers	296 965	4.7
Registered Nurses	242 170	3.8
Food Servers	222 345	3.5
Office Clerks	186 015	2.9
Elementary Schoolteachers	166 885	2.6
Receptionists	132 060	2.1
Child-Care Workers	127 215	2.0

Source: adapted from McVey and Kalbach, 1995: 330; based on 1991 Census data.

TABLE 6.6   Top Ten Most Frequent Occupations of Women in the Labour Force, Canada: 1996

Occupation	Number of Female Workers	% of Female Labour Force
Retail Salespersons	339 025	5.2
Secretaries	311 835	4.8
Cashiers	235 585	3.6
Registered Nurses	220 625	3.4
Accounting Clerks	219 895	3.4
Elementary Schoolteachers	187 070	2.9
Food Servers	176 310	2.7
General Office Clerks	173 175	2.6
Babysitters, Nannies	134 560	2.1
Receptionists	118 985	1.8

Source: adapted from Statistics Canada, *Daily,* 17 March 1998: 6; based on 1991 Census data.

Still, office workers (such as stenographers, typists, office clerks, and receptionists), sales clerks, bookkeepers (identified as accounting clerks in 1996), cashiers, nurses, and possibly food servers (identified as waitresses in the 1961 data) remain in the top 10 over a 35-year period. The 1961 data list only school teachers and does not distinguish between grade levels, whereas data for 1991 and 1996 specify elementary-school teachers as among the top 10. By 1996, women outnumbered men in elementary and kindergarten teaching positions by approximately four to one, were approximately equal in number to male teachers at the

TABLE 6.7   Top Ten Most Frequent Occupations for Men in the Labour Force, Canada: 1991

Occupation	Number of Male Workers	% of Male Labour Force
Sales Clerks and Salespersons	325 280	4.2
Truck Drivers	270 560	3.5
Sales and Advertising Managers	170 750	2.2
Motor Vehicle Mechanics & Repairers	165 530	2.1
Carpenters	148 555	1.9
Farmers	148 040	1.9
Janitors and Cleaners	146 260	1.9
General Managers	122 990	1.6
Accountants and Auditors	121 760	1.6
Chefs and Cooks	112 815	1.4

Source: 1991 *Census of Canada. Occupation.* The Nation. Cat. 93-327. Ottawa: Minister of Industry, Science and Technology. 1993.

TABLE 6.8   Top Ten Most Frequent Occupations for Men in the Labour Force, Canada: 1996

Occupation	Number of Male Workers	% of Male Labour Force
Truck Drivers	222 795	2.9
Retail Salespersons	215 345	2.8
Janitors	185 035	2.4
Retail Trade Managers	179 645	2.3
Farmers	176 985	2.3
Sales Representatives, Wholesale Trade	131 225	1.7
Motor Vehicle Mechanics	127 185	1.6
Material Handlers	119 135	1.5
Carpenters	112 965	1.5
Construction Trade Helpers	104 110	1.3

Source: Adapted from Statistics Canada, *Daily,* 17 March 1998: 6

secondary-school level, but were outnumbered by males as university professors by approximately two to one (*Daily*, 17 March 1998: 7). Gone from the 1961 top 10 list are maids, farm labourers, and sewers/sewing machine operators. A new specific occupation, childcare workers (who presumably are employed mainly in centralized, outside-of-the-home locations), was added to the list in 1991, but is absent from the top 10 list of 1996. However, babysitters and nannies (typically employed inside of a home) moved into ninth position in 1996. The existence of all these occupations reflect the growing demand for specifically trained workers to provide services for the children of women otherwise occupied with their own employment.

Tables 6.7 and 6.8 provide lists of the 10 specific occupations in which men were most frequently found in 1991 and 1996, respectively. The first thing to notice in both tables is that the percentages of male workers in each list are generally lower in comparison to the leading occupations for women presented in Tables 6.5 and 6.6. All together, the 10 occupations listed for 1991 (Table 6.7) account for just more than 20 percent (22.3) of the total male labour force, while the top 10 for 1996 (Table 6.8) account for 20.3 percent. In contrast, as noted above, the top 10 occupations for women in 1991 account for 40 percent of the total female labour force and 32.5 percent in 1996. Men are distributed more evenly across a larger range of occupations than are women, who tend still to be more highly concentrated or segregated into fewer occupations overall.

Differences in identifying and classifying occupations hampers our ability to make direct comparisons, in some instances, across the two time points for men. Two types of managers are listed for men in 1991 (sales and advertising; general), while only one (retail trade) makes the list for 1996. While retail trade would appear to be a more specific subset of the "general" managers category, it is difficult to determine whether "sales representatives, wholesale trade" (in 1996) is in anyway comparable to "sales and advertising managers" (in 1991) Sales representatives appear to be lower on a prestige ranking than are sales managers. Truck drivers have increased in numbers between 1991 and 1996 to supplant retail salespersons as the more frequent job for men in 1996. Similarly, janitors have increased in both numbers and percentages of the male labour force. Accountants and auditors, as well as chefs and cooks, found in the 1991 list, are absent from the 1996 list, while new frequently occurring occupations of construction trade helpers and material handlers have been added.

Some of you might be surprised to observe that many, if not most, of the employment categories in which men are most frequently found are not glamorous, powerful, highest-paying, high-prestige occupations. Five of the 10 most frequent occupations for men in 1996 are found in the blue-collar, often manual labour, broad occupational categories of trades, transportation, and equipment operators (truck drivers, mechanics, material handlers, carpenters, and construction trade helpers). The largest single concentration of white-collar workers among employed males across Canada are found in retail sales. None of the top 10 occupations for 1996 warrants the label of a profession. In marked contrast to female workers, most frequently occurring occupations vary noticeably for male workers by geographical region across our country (*Daily*, 1 March 1998: 6). Truck drivers are the most frequent occupation in 1996 among men in Quebec and New Brunswick. Fishermen (as they prefer to be called) are the most frequent in Newfoundland and Prince Edward Island, and farmers are the most frequent in the Prairie provinces of Manitoba, Saskatchewan, and Alberta. While retail salesmen are the most commonly found male occupation in Nova Scotia, Ontario, and British Columbia, heavy equipment operators are most frequent in the Yukon and carpenters the most frequent in the Northwest Territories.

Multiple Jeopardies

As we shall see shortly, four groups of people have been identified by the federal government of Canada as "disadvantaged because of their labour force participation and unemployment rates, their income levels, and their persistent occupational segregation" (Moreau, 1991: 26):

women, First Nations people, visible minorities (i.e. people of colour and Non-Caucasians, non-First Nations), and people with disabilities. Unemployment rates for First Nations men (24 percent) and women (22 percent) are more than double those for all Canadians. In contrast to visible minority men, who are found concentrated in either professional occupations or service jobs (in both cases at higher proportions than Canadians overall), visible minority women are more likely than Canadian women as a whole to be concentrated in manual labour work. While employed First Nations men are concentrated in manual occupations, First Nations women are found mainly in service or clerical work. First Nations, visible minority, and men and women with disabilities earn average yearly incomes well below the Canadian average (Moreau, 1991: 28). Closely paralleling the general population, women with disabilities aged 15 to 64 are less likely than men with disabilities (41 percent versus 56 percent) to be employed (Shain, 1995: 10). Despite substantial improvements in medicine and technology, people with disabilities continue to confront problems of lower educational qualifications generally, lack of access to and lesser ease of use of facilities within work environments (i.e., greater barriers to education and employment), greater concentrations in lower-paying jobs, and higher incidences of unemployment (Shain, 1995).

Women possessing multiple memberships in disadvantaged categories are in jeopardy of experiencing double, triple, or more forms of discrimination simultaneously. Since multiple jeopardies are difficult to disentangle, it is almost impossible to isolate which disadvantaged status has been accorded primary discrimination (e.g., is it because the actual or potential worker is female, or a person of colour, or of First Nations descent, or a person with a disability that is the primary reason for not being paid equal wages, not being promoted, or not being hired?). These jeopardies are frequently compounded by additional ones in the form of spoken language (especially problematic for persons for whom English or French is a second, or later, language; allophones—speaking neither English nor French—face additional problems) and/or source of formal education or training (foreign certificates, diplomas, or degrees might either not be recognized or may be depreciated in value within Canada; see Boyd, 1990).

Earnings Differentials

By 1991, employed wives's wages accounted for 30 percent, on average, of total family incomes in Canada, with slightly higher average contributions (33 percent) among families with husbands under the age of 40, and slightly lower contributions (25 percent) in families with husbands aged 55 or older (Oderkirk et al., 1994: 24). Among low-income families, wives' earnings play a major role in keeping families above the "poverty line." Fourteen percent of husband-only earner families in 1991 had incomes below the Low-Income Cut-Offs established to identify people living in "straightened circumstances" (to use governmental terminology for what is known unofficially as poverty), while only 4 percent of dual-earner families had incomes below those cut-off points (Oderkirk et al., 1994: 24).

Despite the fact that more than 50 percent of wives are in the labour force, their contributions to family income remain below 50 percent, due to a combination of three major reasons: (1) greater discontinuities in employment histories in comparison to husbands; (2) occupational segregation; and (3) the gender-pay gap. All of these contributing factors are based on long-standing gender expectations that women are not and should not be providers for their families, but rather should perform an economic "helper" role and be paid accordingly. With employment disruption histories becoming fewer and shorter, a lessening of occupational segregation and a more general dispersal of female employees throughout the occupational structure, particularly into traditionally male-dominated professions, and the resulting narrowing of the pay gap, all indications favour employed women increasing their contributory share of family income.

Best (1995: 33) argues that the gender-earnings gap is narrowing partly because men's earnings have remained relatively constant, while women's earnings have increased. More recently, Morissette (1997) has found that the earnings of men under the age of 35 have declined. Wilson (1996: 115–117) notes that the earnings of young, university-educated women in particular have increased noticeably. Among those employed full-time, women's earnings as a proportion of similarly employed men has increased from 60 percent in 1975 to 66 percent in 1989, to 72 percent in 1993 (Best, 1995: 33), to 73 percent in 1995 (*Canadian Social Trends*, 1998, 48 [Spring]: 27).

For full-time employees in 1993, the women's earnings gap widens with increasing age, with women acquiring 91 percent of men's earnings among 15–24-year-olds, 76 percent among 25–34-year-olds, 72 percent among 35–44-year-olds, 67 percent among 45–54-year-olds, and only 66 percent among 55–64-year-olds (Best, 1995: 33). This widening gap partly reflects employment discontinuity patterns experienced by women who left the labour force for varying lengths of time to attend to family obligations. As well, the earnings histories of older male and female workers differ significantly. When they were younger, social expectations of the time permitted and promoted sex discrimination in base-pay scales. Early in the twentieth century, legislation in Canada dictated that women were to be paid a minimum wage to enable them to be self-supporting, while men were to be paid a "living wage" to enable them to support a family. "This kind of differential calculation led to the pernicious habit of setting women's wages at a level of about two-thirds the amount set for men" (Niemann, 1984 in Wilson, 1996: 128). Young men and women started out at different pay levels and subsequent increments over time typically failed to redress any earlier imbalances, even when increments were distributed equally. As a consequence, from the turn of the century until the 1980s, women continued to earn approximately two-thirds that of men per year. Many young workers today, thanks mainly to pay equity legislation and union bargaining in some employment sectors, begin their earning histories on a more level playing field.

The gender-earnings gap varies not only by age, but also by education, with a narrower gap between university-educated men and women, and a wider gap between workers with less formal education within all age groups. For example, in 1993, female university graduates' full-time earnings averaged 75 percent that of male university graduates, while females with only some secondary education earned, on average, 64 percent of the earnings of males with comparable education (Best, 1995: 33). Combining age and postsecondary education we find that, in 1993, university-educated women aged 25–34 earned 84 percent of the earnings of comparably aged, comparably educated, men. The proportions for similarly educated, but older, women dropped to 77 percent among 35–44-year-olds and 72 percent among 45–54-year-olds (Best, 1993: 33). Once again, we see the impact among older workers of differential employment histories affecting yearly earnings.

As we have seen, the gender-earnings gap is partly attributable to occupational distributions, attained education, and differential gender employment histories. Age is an important contributing factor in that younger people benefit from social and legal expectations promoting greater equality in wage and pay scales. Expectations, as we have seen, were quite different in earlier times and conditions of those times are reflected in larger earnings gaps among older workers. All of the factors identified thus far still do not fully account for existing disparities in the earnings of men and women. "Most analysts suggest that between 15 to 20 percent of the variance in pay is due to discrimination. But, as Skolnick (1982: 117–118) points out, because education, occupation, and hours worked are also the effects of discriminatory practices, the total effect of discrimination is much greater" (Wilson, 1996: 122). While various attempts in a variety of forms have been directed towards reducing gender differences in educational aspirations and attainments, occupational aspirations, and responsibilities for housework and childcare, attempts have also been made via legislation to eliminate sex discrimination in pay scales.

Pay equity is a term used to refer to equal pay for work of equal or comparable worth or value, and focuses upon the compensation given to employed workers. In the 1980s, Great Britain and Australia adopted pay-equity policies to counteract the historical double-standard that defined women's work as being of lesser value than work performed by men. In Canada, most provinces and the federal government have pay-equity legislation. For example, Ontario's Pay Equity Act, which came into effect on 1 January, 1987, was designed to address part of the wage gap that exists between men and women. Employers are required to determine the proportion of male and female employees in jobs and job classes, compare the jobs usually performed by women with different jobs usually done by men and group similar jobs together into a job class. The term "job class" is defined as those positions within a business that are marked by similar duties, responsibilities, and qualifications, filled by similar recruiting procedures, and compensated by the same wage schedule, salary grade, or range of salaries. "For example, in an assessment of municipal government jobs, the work of nurses (female) would be compared with that of police constables (male)" (Lowe, 1995: 10–16). Under the Act, if a female job class has the same value as a male job class, it must receive similar rewards in terms of pay. In Manitoba, some groups of female government workers have received pay equity adjustments in the range of 15 percent (Lowe, 1995: 10–16).

Legislation on pay equity was designed to address the fact that, historically and into the present, women workers are most often found in jobs which have been undervalued (e.g., secretarial work and work in retail sales) and, as a result, have received lower pay than for jobs held by men. The Pay Equity Commission of Ontario employs the following simple analogy to explain the logic underlying pay equity: "Comparing female and male job classes is similar to comparing apples and oranges to assess how they are similar or comparable, rather than how they are different. Apples and oranges are both fruits, are both round and colourful, produce juice, and contain vitamins and fibre. The characteristics are different in each fruit, but the total value of each fruit is about the same" (Government of Ontario, nd: 3).

Nevertheless, observers have noted that pay equity as a policy cannot be applied to firms in which the labour force is exclusively female and that the method of establishing the comparable worth of two jobs is based upon a system of a evaluation that "does not correct for the a priori understandings of certain skills" (Boyd, 1995: 3–24). Lowe (1995: 10–16) additionally notes that the pool of workers covered by pay equity legislation is limited and typically covers workers who already hold relatively good jobs in the public sector, and its highly technical procedures are cumbersome to apply. Even when pay equity legislation is in place, enforcing compliance and achieving financial redress for past and present inequities is typically a long, drawn-out, process spanning many years, even decades. Employers, including federal and provincial governments, have demonstrated a willingness to tie up equity cases in the courts for protracted periods of time, all the while still paying workers inequitable wages. During this time, employers reap benefits, in the form of either higher profits or lower costs, from differential pay scales and final court judgments against employers are viewed simply as a "cost of doing business."

The Chilly Climate: Gender Bias and Sexual Harassment

The term "chilly climate" underscores the notion that equality of access does not, in and of itself, guarantee equality within workplace institutions. It recognizes that even when, and if, workplaces are populated with equal proportions of men and women, what George Orwell (1984) referred to in *Animal Farm* as a "funny sort of democracy" may prevail. That is, a land in which "all animals are equal, but some animals are more equal than others."

The widespread distribution of Sheila McIntyre's 1986 memorandum, "Gender Bias Within a Canadian Law School," known colloquially as the "McIntyre Memo," was perhaps the first detailed analysis of how the chilly climate creates an inhospitable environment, especially for women. McIntyre chronicles the "patterns of stereotyping, sexualization, overt harassment, exclusion, and devaluation" (*The Chilly Collective*, 1995: 1) she experienced during her first year of teaching law at Queen's University. The events recounted within the McIntyre Memo do not read like a detective novel in which a single, heinous incident disrupts normal, daily existence and a single individual is victimized by the actions of a single culprit. Rather, the mechanisms involved were, indeed, much more subtle as the processes "managed" and maintained gender differences. The climate described by McIntyre points to the presence of systemic misogyny (a hatred of women) within the everyday fabric of the Queen's Law School workplace at that time, affecting both male students and faculty members alike.

Among the incidents McIntyre records in her memo are: (i) being told by male students that her attempts to use "gender neutral language in lieu of the generic male idiom represented 'shoving my politics down students' throats'" (McIntyre, 1995: 224); (ii) having a cohort of male students act "deliberately disruptive, uncooperative, interruptive and angry" in class and, on occasion, shouting that the questions she raised were "irrelevant and a waste of time" (p. 224), or that she was a "bourgeois feminist" (p. 227); (iii) receiving a visit from a student claiming to be "the delegate" for others who informed her "not only how they wanted material taught and discussed in future, but…[who] warned me…that if I did not want to be attacked again, I had better not raise gender again" (p. 225); (iv) being told by students that she was "incompetent" and/or "unqualified" to teach (McIntyre is a graduate of Queen's Law School and possesses three degrees); (v) being informed by the student president that he and others "knew" that she had been hired only because the hiring process was "stacked" by a "feminist conspiracy"; (vi) being described on the walls of the men students' public bathrooms with such phrases such as "Sheila McIntyre sucks clits and tits" (p. 233); (vii) being "dressed…down publicly in the halls, and then rebuked, insulted, and threatened…in my office for about 45 minutes"(p. 235) by a senior male colleague; (viii) treated as an "over-reacting female" when she recounted her colleague's conduct to others.

In breaking the silence about her experiences at Queen's, McIntyre recognized that her action could be construed by some as an "act of violence on my part. The polite thing to do, the collegial thing to do, the safe thing to do, is suffer abuse privately rather than to urge recognition of its existence" (p. 237). Nevertheless, as she remarks, "[p]erhaps nothing can ensure it stops, but at least we could name this pattern of conduct for what it is—bullying, rank-pulling, cowardly abuse of hierarchy, and intimidation—and take an institutional and public stand that such conduct is unacceptable." Other evidence suggests that McIntyre's experiences are neither anomalous nor limited to one place and time (see the CBA Task Force on Gender Equality in the Legal Profession, 1993; The Chilly Collective, 1995).

Epstein (1981: 194) has suggested how an increase in numbers alone may not dispel hostility towards and bias against women in what are viewed by some as "gender-inappropriate" work roles:

> Like white cells surrounding offending matter, the dominant group may continue to regard women as something different and unacceptable, perhaps tolerated but not assimilated. The new entrants may be sabotaged as the majority group, protecting its community..., musters its forces to control its culture and its boundaries. When outsiders manage to establish themselves, strong but subtle forces may come into play to keep them from taking positions of command.

The experience of Canadian police departments provides an instructive example. Until 1975 the RCMP was exclusively male; it was only in that year that the organization began accepting women as regular members (*Winnipeg Free Press*, 13 May, 1980: 3). However, even after women became eligible for service, police departments were notably reluctant to hire and/or promote female officers or to deploy them in the full range of policing roles. The research of Linden and Minch (1982) reports that principal objections to female police officers included: (1) a perception by male police officers that the image of the police and policing would suffer should women be hired; (2) a belief that women were less committed to the career of policing; (3) a view that women threatened the social world of male police officers; and (4) a feeling that women were incapable of coping with the violent and/or physical aspects of police work. Although research in North America suggests that these objections are largely unfounded, Linden (1980: 30) notes that male general duty officers gave evidence of strongly negative attitudes towards females, which, he suggests, was succinctly summarized in the comment of one respondent: "Eliminate females!" Linden (1983, 1980) also notes that the majority of male general duty officers in both the Vancouver Police Department and Royal Canadian Mounted Police felt that the scope of the female police role should be curtailed to handling juveniles, questioning rape victims, searching females, and other traditionally "female" activities.

What is striking about the Linden study is how closely the comments of surveyed police officers parroted the "mythology of respect and decorum" that was historically used to deny women the vote and bar them entrance into certain professions and institutions of higher learning (Armstrong and Armstrong, 1984; Edwards, 1981; Porter, 1965; Report of the Royal Commission on The Status of Women in Canada, 1970). That is, although the police officers surveyed did not actually preface their comments by saying that some of their best friends were women, they were persistent in their emphasis that respect and concern underlay their belief that women were not "really" suited to a career in policing; the fallacious abstraction of female delicacy and the need to protect women from the harsh vicissitudes of policing the streets were used to defend their position. As Millett (1970: 37) remarks: "While a palliative to the injustice of woman's social position, chivalry is also a way of disguising it."

More recently, Nelson's (1992) examination of 22 Western Canadian municipal police departments notes that 18 evidenced, on average, an absence of women, First Nations people, and minorities and that even within larger departments, these groups were proportionately marginalized in terms of the rank structure. Of 326 women employed as sworn officers within the 22 departments, 290 or almost 89 percent were constables; the highest rank achieved by a female was that of an inspector. She reports that although, at the most basic level, a con-

Box 6.2	**Foreign Domestic Wins Sexual Harassment Suit Against Boss**

[The following recounts the history of the first precedent-setting case wherein a particularly vulnerable group, foreign domestic workers in Canada, were accorded protection from sexual harassment by employers.]

A Filipina nanny who was sexually harassed by her employer has been awarded $8,000 in damages by the B.C. Council of Human Rights. The complainant's lawyer…said that as far as she knows, "there have been no previous human rights decision in which a foreign domestic worker has brought forward a complaint of sexual harassment in the home and been successful in receiving damages. She explained that the West coast Domestic Workers' Association (an advocacy organization that represents foreign domestic workers particularly Filipina nannies) is quite concerned about incidents of sexual ha-

rassment and has been encouraging women to bring complaints…. Many of the women, however, are afraid to file any kind of complaint out of fear it will affect their immigration status.…[She also noted] that immigration regulations which allow domestic workers into Canada requires them to work as nannies and to reside in their employer's home. To obtain landed immigrant status in Canada, they have to work for two years as a live-in domestic worker.…

[The complainant] came to Canada from the Philippines at the age of 34 in 1991. She began working for a…[B.C. couple], looking after their one-year-old daughter in their home in February 1992 at a salary of $1,135 a month, less $250 a month for room and board.…[S]he lived with her employer during the week but spent weekends with a friend.… [The Human Rights Council's hearing offi-

sciousness of employment equity in recruiting typically manifested itself with the purposeful displaying of members of the target groups in recruiting posters and related material, even this type of cosmetic recognition was often lacking. If employment equity functions to allow persons of an infrequent status set into the ranks of police membership, this procedure alone, critics warn, will not serve to quell an inhospitable welcome, which may cause an applicant to face a "revolving door" of discrimination. Thus, it may be noted that although the RCMP had hired 800 women officers by 1986, women had resigned at five times the rate of male officers as the result of "sexual harassment and rampant sexism" (Conway, 1990: 93).

In *Breaking the Glass Ceiling*, a three-year study of factors that contribute to the success or failure of women executives in the 100 leading companies in the United States, the authors report that, while they found very little difference between the actual competence of women and men managers, the most marked difference they found was one of perception: no matter how well they performed, women were often rated less good at their jobs than were men. A seminar conducted to help 20 of the most senior managers of a large textile manufacturer in the Southeastern United States grapple with the issue of gender noted how perceptions of managers had barred women from advancement. Assumptions of a woman's

cer] said the incidents of harassment began about two months after she began working for the couple. "[The husband] made suggestive remarks to the complainant when she dressed up for church, touched her knees, suggested that she work as a prostitute, pulled her bra strap, referred to his past sexual experiences and fondled himself in the bedroom in her presence."

[The nanny] testified she was upset by the incidents but was scared to testify because of her immigration status. She said she began staying out all night to avoid being in the house with [the man]. In October 1992, [the woman] decided she could no longer tolerate [the man's] conduct and told [his wife] she was quitting. She did not tell [her] the real reason she was leaving because she was afraid she would not believe her. When [the wife] told her she could not leave without giving notice she agreed to work for another two weeks. [She] said she was unable to find work until November 1993 because [the couple] gave unfavourable

references when prospective employers called. The hearing officer rejected testimony from [the couple] that the complainant fabricated her evidence in retaliation for the bad job references. She also noted that [the couple] did not dispute two of the incidents complained of and that they confirmed the complainant's testimony about staying out all night.

In addition [the hearing officer] found that [the complainant] told [the husband] on a number of occasions that his suggestive comments and sexual advances were unwelcome and that [he] knew or reasonably ought to have known that his conduct was unwelcome. "[The man's] conduct interfered with the complainant's work performance and created an intimidating, hostile, and offensive working environment contrary to [the *Human Rights Act*]. I accept that the complainant was effectively forced to terminate her employment because [the man's] unwelcome conduct was so intolerable," the hearing officer held.

Source: Daisley, 1996: 21.

inability to do the job, the inability of women to handle big projects if they were married and had a family, caused managers to act "as if" these assumptions were unequivocally true.

> They realized they'd stalled women in staff jobs, kept them from moving into line jobs— that is, jobs that would give them some authority over subordinates involved in production, sales or finance. Most of the men in the organization had strong mentors, but they realized that those crucial mentorships were far less available to women because of men's fear of sexual innuendo. (Morrison et al., 1987: 61)

In his study of Fortune 100 multinational corporations, White (1987) observed that 15 percent of executive men, but only 5 percent of executive women, had been asked to fix a broken company; 15 percent of the men had had the opportunity to start up a new factory or division, as compared with only 0.5 percent of women (in Nelson, 1992: 257). If it is assumed that women are not "tough" or competent enough to take on certain challenges, if they are presumed unequal, the perceptions are real enough in their consequences (Thomas, 1928).

Presumptions and perceptions of equality do not lead only to ignoring, or acting chivalrous towards, or differentially evaluating women. All too frequently, they lead to outright harassment. Aggarwal (1987: 1) remarks that sexual harassment "may be an expression of power or desire or both." Canadian case law has recognized that sexual harassment is a multifaceted phenomenon that may include sexual assault; unwanted touching or patting; leering; sexually suggestive gestures; demands for sexual favours; derogatory or degrading remarks directed towards members of one sex or sexual orientation; repeated offensive sexual flirtations/advances/propositions; verbal threats or abuse; questions about or comments upon an individual's sexual life; the use of sexually degrading words to describe a person; sexist jokes that cause embarrassment; and displaying sexually offensive material. In identifying this nonexhaustive list of behaviours that has been held to constitute sexual harassment by the courts, the Law Society of Upper Canada acknowledges that "[w]hether a particular type of conduct constitutes sexual harassment is sometimes difficult to determine" and that although "the severity of the conduct may be the most conclusive factor...what is determinative is a combination of frequency, severity and persistence" (in Mossman, 1997: 244).

Although a host of difficulties are faced in defining acts of sexual violence, we can distinguish two general "types" of sexual harassment. The first, *quid pro quo*, which refers to situations wherein demands for sexual favours are linked to threats of adverse employment conditions for noncompliance, is perhaps the most obvious and recognizeable of the two forms. The second, a "poisoned work environment," is more subtle and "describes situations in which the conduct creates a working environment that is intimidating, uncomfortable or offensive to any employee," even though the offensive behaviour engaged in by a coworker, supervisor, or employee, is not necessarily directed to a specific person (Law Society of Upper Canada, 1991). The Supreme Court of Canada in *Janzen v. Platy Enterprises et al.* (1989) established as a point of law that sexual harassment can constitute discrimination on the basis of sex. Chief Justice Dickson's judgment on the *Janzen* case noted that, although *quid pro quo* tends to be regarded as a more serious form of sexual harassment than the form evidenced within a poisoned work environment, drawing a distinction between the two is myopic: "The main point in allegations of sexual harassment is that unwelcome sexual conduct has invaded the workplace, irrespective of whether the consequences of the harassment included a denial of concrete employment rewards for refusing to participate in sexual activity" (in Mossman, 1997: 246; see also Box 6.2).

While Dickson suggests that we abolish the distinction between the two "forms" of harassment and regard both as equally pernicious, others have suggested that the term sexual harassment is a misnomer and/or that attention directed to how workplaces can create a "poisoned work environment" are misplaced. For example, the early research of Backhouse and Cohen (1978) notes that, if one were to give substance to office gossip, successful women owed the majority of their promotions to the dispensing of "sexual favours." Complimenting this perception, Bradford et al. (1980: 22) in their discussion of the "seductress" depict the career woman as actively seeking out "affirmation that she is sexually desirable and wants to have men respond to her as highly attractive."

In their study of 218 recent business-school graduates, Anderson and Fisher (1991) address whether women are perceived as entering into "office romance" relationships for motives different from men, particularly in terms of exploiting sexuality for gain. Although few instances are found where relationships are formed for personal advancement, such motivations are far more commonly attributed to women. The researchers note, regarding these general perceptions, that "[m]en were perceived to enter into relationships for ego satisfaction, excitement, adventure, and sexual experience, whereas women were more likely to see a romantic involvement or job advancement." Placing the onus of responsibility upon women's supposedly improper motivations readily contributes to blanket denials that sexual harassment even exists.

The suggestion that women seek to "sleep their way to the top" not only leads to lowered morale among women employees and the disparagement of women as legitimate professionals, but, in addition, the perception of women as "seductresses" can erode opportunities for women to establish important mentoring relationships. As Salamon (1984) notes, if having a "mentor" has traditionally assisted in the career development paths of male employees, it may be difficult for a woman to establish a mentor relationship with a male employer or sponsor, because there are no appropriate precedents or role models to follow. Acting as a sponsor for a woman may be more closely tied to sexual than platonic role models, and persons with male-female mentor relationships may be "suspected of hanky-panky by jealous spouses and nosy colleagues" (Bowen, 1985: 31). Possible allegations of sexual impropriety are likely to cause either the mentor or the protegé to hesitate. Since "a very few women hold senior positions (and)…thus the number of women available to mentor other women is minuscule" (Anderson and Fisher, 1991: 177), women may find themselves denied access to mentoring because of all-too-popular inaccurate stereotypes about their own gender.

Approaching the problem of sexual harassment anthropologically, Mead (1980: 55) suggests that what is needed is an "organizational incest taboo," which "will operate within the worksetting as once they operated with the household." "Taboos," or "deeply and intensely felt prohibitions against 'unthinkable behaviour'"(p. 54), she argues, would "protect and nurture the most meaningful human relations…you don't make passes at or sleep with the people you work with" (p. 55) and result in "new ways that allow women and men to work together effortlessly and to respect each other as persons" (p. 56). However, if the power hierarchy of the workplace remains structured along gender lines, with males assuming the majority of authoritative positions and females the lower echelons, Mead's suggestion seems somewhat unrealistic. In addition, statistics on the phenomenon of incestuous abuse suggest that, perhaps, the most notable function of the incest taboo has been in curtailing its discussion rather than its practice. Accordingly, it has been suggested that until the gender-linked power imbalances within major societal institutions are altered, the costs and consequences of sexism will not be eradicated, but may be ameliorated through policies and programs which mandate a "zero tolerance" of sexual harassment in the form of a poisoned work environment (Sumrall and Taylor, 1992).

Under the Canadian Human Rights Act and/or provincial human rights codes, businesses may be held liable for acts of sexual harassment committed by their employees. The concept of "vicarious liability," as outlined within Section 65(1) of the Canadian Human Rights Act, R.S.C. 1987, c.H-6, as amended, specifies that "any act or omission committed by an officer, a director, an employee or an agent of any person, association or organization in the course of the employment of the officer, director, employee or agent shall, for the purposes of this Act, be deemed to be an act or omission committed by that person, association or organization." Section 65(2) stipulates that an exemption to the above will be noted to exist "if it is established that the person, association or organization did not consent to the commission of the act or omission and exercised all due diligence to prevent the act or omission from being committed and, subsequently, to mitigate or avoid the effect thereof." Accordingly, the Act specifies that employers are obliged to give evidence of their attentiveness to the possibility that sexual harassment *may* occur within their workplace by, for example, creating policies which define the prohibited conduct and assert the employer's commitment to ensuring a workplace free of harassment and discrimination (due diligence), and by demonstrating that procedures exist and penalties are imposed for those who contravene these policies (mitigation). In consequence, sexual harassment has become a high-priority item in many executive education programs, with attempts made to specify which behaviours will be regarded as intolerable (Adler, 1991). General Motors, Ford, Chrysler, and the Canadian Auto Workers announced a "woman's advocate program" in December 1994, specifically designed to provide assistance to women experiencing problems such as sexual harassment (*Toronto Star*, 6 December 1994: A2).

Within the province of Ontario, the *Human Rights Code* (R.S.O., 1990, c.H.19) asserts that freedom from sexual harassment is a human right and Subsection 7(2) asserts the general right of employees to freedom from sexual harassment in the workplace: "Every person who is an employee has a right to freedom from harassment in the workplace because of sex by his or her employee or agent of the employer or by another employee." Subsection 7(3) declares that: "Every person has a right to be free from (a) a sexual solicitation or advance made by a person in a position to confer, grant or deny a benefit or advancement to the person where the person making the solicitation or advance knows or ought reasonably to know that is unwelcome; or (b) a reprisal or a threat of reprisal for the rejection of a sexual solicitation or advance where the reprisal is made or threatened by a person in a position to confer, grant or deny a benefit or advancement to the person." Sexual harassment is also defined in Ontario as "a compensable injury under the provisions of the Ontario Worker's Compensation Act" (DeKeseredy and Hinch, 1993: 127).

Despite the existence of legal provisions within the province of Ontario and like provisions elsewhere, it would be presumptuous to assume that the problem of sexual harassment has been largely contained. It would be a mistake to assume that sexual harassment is exclusively a female problem. One study in 1981 and a second in 1992 reported that 15 percent of male respondents had been sexually harassed (Lawlor, 1994; Merit Systems Protection Board, 1981). Even though male victims also report feeling powerless and used in such situations, they are even less likely than female victims to receive a sympathetic ear. The commonly held belief that men are sexually rapacious and welcome *any* opportunity for sexual activity weakens the perception that the harasser has engaged in act of moral trespass—particularly when coupled with Hollywood castings of actresses such as Demi Moore as the "typical" harasser.

It is becoming increasingly evident that chilly climates are not restricted to the workplace, but also infect those settings where individuals prepare for entering the workplace. McDaniel and Roosmalen (1992), in a two-phase study of women students conducted at the University of Waterloo in the mid-1980s, find that sexual harassment is a common experience among female university students and one structured by power differentials. Their findings note that 74 percent of their female university-student sample had experienced sexual insults ("an uninvited, sexually suggestive, obscene or offensive remark, stare or gesture"), 29 percent had received a sexual invitation ("a sexual proposition without any explicit threat or bribe by a person in a position of power or authority"), 7 percent reported sexual intimidation ("a threat or a bribe by a person in a position of power of authority to coerce sexual contact"), and that 10.8 percent had been sexually assaulted ("sexual contact through the use of force, threatened force or a weapon, without consent as inferred from refusal, helplessness or incapacitation"). They further note that reactions to allegations of sexual harassment may be dismissive, "laughing it off as humorous and flattering, or broadening the definition to the point of absurdity" (p. 5). However, citing McKinnon, they emphasize how sexual harassment undermines women's potential for social equality in two important ways: "[B]y using her employment position to coerce her sexually, while using her sexual position to coerce her economically" (p. 5).

In stark contrast to suggestions that sanctions are necessary for those individuals whose actions create an inhospitable work or learning environment (*The Chilly Collective*, 1995), Fekete (1994) suggests that we face greater danger from the "politically correct" than the "politically incorrect." He argues that the "flat and flatulent formula of zero tolerance" (p. 198), along with "political correctness" more generally, should be seen as stemming from a "biofeminist" cabal, whose doctrine "is organized around abstractions like equity and inclusion" (p. 203) and who have identified a list of "biolabels" (p. 203), such as sexism, racism, and ablism, which they seek to "exorcise" (p. 200). For Fekete (1994: 207), the "real victims" are those who have stood accused of acting or speaking in a manner that is sexist, racist, ablist, or homophobic, or who have made "innocent remarks that happened to cause displeasure." From this perspective, those who are offended or displeased are the problem, not those who offend or give displeasure. Such a status-quo, conservative argument offers testimony to the obstacles faced by those who wish to thaw the chilly climate currently characterizing many workplace and educational settings.

Employment Equity: Solution or Problem?

Canadian case law documents the court's efforts to dissuade various organizations in business and industry, conducting business with the federal government, and particularly government itself, from engaging in a broad range of discriminatory behaviour, ranging from intentionally "chilling" females from applying for employment, discriminatory hiring procedures, unequal rates of pay, exclusion from certain duties, and dismissal from employment (Nelson, 1991). The courts have not rejected professionally recognized standards; rather, they have simply attempted to ensure that the requirements are meaningful and not merely pretexts for excluding qualified personnel who are marginalized via discrimination as "outsiders" (Hughes, 1958).

Weinfeld (1981) notes that the origin of "affirmative action" in Canada can be traced to the attempts of the Royal Commission on Bilingualism and Biculturalism in 1960 to augment francophone participation within federal government services. In forwarding a clear outline of affirmative action principles as a basis of policy-making, the identified principles marked a threefold shift in policy emphasis in relation to human rights. To wit:

> (1) a shift from an emphasis on individual discrimination to an emphasis on institutional and structural forms of discrimination; (2) a shift from an emphasis on individual rights to an emphasis on collective entitlement (categorical rights)…(which involved) a shift from the individual merit principle (earned rights) to a modified merit principle which took into account the differential nature and impact of collective linguistic and broader cultural considerations; (3) a shift toward the employment of statistical indicators of under-representation (re: population proportions) as a measure of group equality. Thus, under-representation of social categories at higher positional levels were taken as indicators of structural discrimination necessitating affirmative action programs. (Kallen, 1982: 236)

The passage of the Canadian Human Rights Act in 1977 provided the legal foundation for employment equity/affirmative action policies. Section 16(1) of the Canadian Human Rights Act asserts that it is not a discriminatory practice to adopt or carry out a special program, plan, or arrangement designed to prevent, eliminate, or reduce disadvantages suffered by persons or groups because of race, national or ethnic origin, skin colour, religion, age, sex, family status, marital status, or disability, by improving their opportunities in respect to goods, services, facilities, accommodations, or employment. Thus, the Act implicitly suggests that "employment equity" does not constitute "reverse discrimination." Indeed, under the terms of reference of the Canadian Human Rights Commission, charged with administering the Act, an affirmative action/employment equity program may be required as part of the settlement of a complaint of discrimination, as a strategic attempt to forestall the future recurrence of discriminatory practices.

The 1986 proclamation of the Employment Equity Act in Canada, akin to the guidelines established in 1983 for the federal Public Service, requires all sizable employers (varyingly defined as having either 50 or 100 or more employees) within the federal sector to ensure that their procedures for hiring, firing, promoting, and training are equitable to all groups. The overall employment data are to be compiled and submitted to the Canada Employment and Immigration Commission and, through this procedure, to the Canadian Human Rights Commission. This body of data is made public to allow accountability of employers' attempts to ensure equality for the underrepresented groups within the workforce: women, visible minorities, people with disabilities, and First Nations persons.

The framework of equal employment opportunity embraces as integral components equal opportunity to advance to all positions of responsibility and nondiscriminatory preparation to positions of authority. Employment Equity programs—such as the Treasury Board's (1978) Native Participation Plan, designed to increase the participation of aboriginal persons within the Canadian public service, and the Northern Women's Credit Union Limited's development of a special training program purposefully designed "to provide native (aboriginal) women with adequate skills, through academic training and field placements, to ensure that they find and keep employment in banks, credit unions, and the financial departments of business and government" (Affirmation 1981 03)—evidence recognition that the eradication of discrimination in employment requires that sensitivity to systemic discrimination must be of paramount concern.

Although the 1990 Annual Report of the Canadian Human Rights Commission suggests that the establishment of guidelines for the implementation of employment equity within the federal public sector in 1983, and the proclamation of the Employment Equity Act in 1986 have not been unqualified successes, they are forwarded as palliatives, whose implementation will direct attention to the eradication of structural and systemic discrimination. The report acknowledges the continuous underrepresentation of First Nations people and people with disabilities; it additionally observes a phenomenon that Mannheim (1940) termed *negative democratization*, that is, an inverse relationship between the power, rank, or prestige of an employment position and the presence of visible minorities, women, people with disabilities, and First Nations people.

Opponents of affirmative action/employment equity have argued that, despite the intentions of their supporters, these strategies will not quell or cause the attenuation of discrimination in North American society, and may well lead us back to the degrading colour/racial/gender consciousness of the past. These opponents further advance three specific counter-arguments. First, they claim that the policy itself denies individuals their full humanity and that, in labeling a person by the master status of his/her historic oppression, the labeler contributes little to an appreciation of the individual as a human being worthy of dignity or respect. Rather, it is suggested that the campaign itself is essentially invidious because, although it purports to be humanistic, it offers little more than a "technical" description of those who are thought to require society's paternalistic *largesse*.

Second, it is suggested that an examination of the American experience in implementing "affirmative action" policies in the 1970s is illuminating and illustrates the fallibilities of attempting to ensure justice and equality through the imposition of numerical abstractions in the form of quotas (Decker, 1980; Leinen, 1984). It is maintained that an integrated nation is ill-served by governmental policies that seek to subdivide the population into groups that are thought to warrant or not warrant differential treatment. (These critics tend, rather selectively, to ignore the extent to which their society is wrought with already existing subdivisions and prefer instead to take a Pollyanna stance and to insist that their society is indeed already fully "integrated.") Critics of affirmative action argue, furthermore, that employment equity/affirmative action policies are underwritten by an inadequate view of the nature of minority-group membership within society, and an implicit suggestion that the groups are in themselves so easily identifiable and delimited, so uniform in their condition, as to facilitate policy implementation. This premise, it is maintained, is erroneous. For example, it has been suggested that racial and ethnic groups make poor categories for the design of public policy inasmuch as they include a broad range of persons who have different legal bases for claims for redress and remedy of grievances stemming from injustices of the past.

The categories themselves have provided fodder for those who would deny the policy legitimacy. As Cicero cautioned long ago, the "freer utterances of poetic license" may latently dissuade individuals from sombre reflection of past injustices as would-be wits speculate on how employment equity might be illegitimately extended in increasingly marginal, and perhaps absurd, cases (e.g., left-handed, vertically-challenged people). Lampooned and lambasted, the reality and ravages of discrimination, and the need for its amelioration becomes trivialized and muted. As such, the policy is thought to ill-serve those whom it would propose to protect. During the mid-1990s, many affirmative action laws, policies, and programs have been repealed and dismantled at the federal level and in numerous states (California, the most populated state, in particular) of the United States. Will Canada follow suit in the near future?

Third, it has been suggested that the implementation of a policy which mandates statistical parity on the basis of, for example, skin colour or sex, may latently function to create resentment of and hostility towards those groups that it would avowedly help. Garcia et al. (1981) note that minority-group applicants to American colleges are seen by others as *less* qualified when the college is committed to an Affirmative Action policy; more recently, the CBA Task Force on Gender Equality in the Legal Profession (1993) in Canada notes that "even when admitted under the regular admission policy, minority [law] students frequently felt forced to defend affirmative action policies, given the ever present assumption that such students have inferior abilities and, therefore, do not deserve to be attending law school" (in Mossman, 1997: 25). The social-psychological effects of "tokenism" may function to deny the legitimacy and authority of those who might theoretically stand to gain from it (Boserup, 1970; Coser, 1975; Epstein and Coser, 1981). You might recall from our earlier presentation on the McIntyre Memo that her male students marginalized McIntyre's abilities and qualifications by asserting that her presence on faculty was only a consequence of an implicit affirmative action policy foisted on the Queen's Law School by a "feminist conspiracy."

Finkelstein (1981: 204–205) notes regarding the performance evaluation of a minority group member:

> There are two divergent expectations for the rare case.… Either of these expectations can be activated at the appropriate time and result in undermining the achievement or emphasizing the failure of one who has a statistically infrequent status set. The first expectation is that the individual will be like all other members of his/her minority group be they women, blacks or the elderly. The second is that the individual is the rare exception, unlike all others who share the particularly problematic status. When a female executive is clearly doing a superior job, her performance is explained by the fact that she is unlike other women. Here, she is essentially defeminized. However, if she slips up in some way or loses her temper, she is seen as very much like all other women (i.e. highly emotional or hysterical). Thus, what we see is an effective means of maintaining stereotypes and fortifying the barriers that keep women out of the executive suite.

Kanter's (1976) research finds special difficulties attendant on being a token member of an occupation: highlighted visibility within an organization creates special performance pressures; difficulty in sharing confidences with colleagues; and hesitation or avoidance of added responsibility or promotion—stemming from a fear of alienating coworkers who ostensibly have enough difficulty accepting tokens at less lofty positions—that may become defined as symptomatic of "laziness" or "lack of ambition." While Kanter focused on "number-balancing" as a strategy for social change, she ignored the broader issue of sexism (Zimmer, 1988) as well as how increased numbers can precipitate a "backlash" of discrimination in forms ranging from the blatant (e.g., sexual harassment, wage inequities) to the subtle (e.g., blocked mobility, female-dominated job "ghettos" within high-status occupations [Reskin, 1988]). Yoder (1991: 178) argues that an emphasis upon numbers alone "neglects the complexities of gender integration."

Research suggests that men who are tokens in a group dominated by women appear to be less adversely affected by their numeric underrepresentation (Johnson and Schulman, 1989; Ott, 1989). Williams (1992) suggests that token men may find themselves advantaged rather than disadvantaged in token situations. As Yoder et al. (1997) suggest, "what defines token-difference makes a difference. When the token is different by virtue of an ascribed status that privileges (e.g., being male), rather than subordinates (e.g., being female), negative outcomes seem to be avoided or reduced."

It is evident that Employment Equity is not, in and of itself, a panacea. Shrill cries of "reverse discrimination" against white male job applicants have been heard, leading to the development of a "whitelash" wherein white Anglo Saxon males, once considered by themselves and others to be a privileged group, now try to portray themselves to the court of public opinion as a suffering disadvantaged minority group. In this instance, one group's solution (employment equity) becomes another group's problem (reverse discrimination). Critics of the equity policy, showing unprecedented enthusiasm for the parable of Horatio Alger, have waxed rhapsodical of the benefits of a "nonintervention" policy towards those historically disadvantaged, with justification grounded firmly in a tradition of Social Darwinism. Nevertheless, as Cohen (1974) has remarked in another context, "nonintervention can become a euphemism for benign neglect, which in turn is another euphemism for simply doing nothing."

Part-Time Work

In less than 20 years, the number of Canadians employed part-time (less than 30 hours per week) increased 113 percent, from 988 000 in 1975 (Burke, 1986:10) to 2.1 million workers in 1993 (Best, 1995: 32). Whereas 6 percent of all employed persons worked part-time in 1975, that proportion rose to 17 percent by 1993 (Best, 1995: 32). Young people between the ages of 15 and 24 used to constitute the bulk of part-time workers in Canada. Currently, 60 percent of all part-time workers are 25 years of age or older (Best, 1995: 33). Between 1975 and 1993, the proportion of employed men who work part-time increased from 5 to 10 percent, while the proportion of part-time employed women increased from 20 to 26 percent (Best, 1995: 32). Women have consistently comprised approximately 70 percent of all part-time workers (Best, 1995: 32; Ghalam, 1993/1995: 202; Parliament, 1989: 5) from the mid-1970s to the present.

The rising numbers and proportions of male and female part-time employees are a consequence of "the increased globalization of the Canadian economy and the downsizing and restructuring of businesses and industry in the face of a persistent recession and increasing international competition for markets" (McVey and Kalbach, 1995: 319) as well as cost-saving public-service employee cutback measures adopted by provincial and federal governments. The effects of these large-scale changes in our economy are partly reflected in labour-force surveys conducted between 1975 and 1993 on reasons why individuals engage in part-time work only (Table 6.9). The findings are also partly reflective of the influence of other factors such as age, marital status, and gender. Respondents in these labour-force surveys are asked to select the single best reason for their participation in part-time work. Unfortunately, for a research standpoint, the reasons provided are not mutually exclusive. "Did not want full-time work" is not incompatible with either "going to school" or having "personal or family responsibilities," since either of the latter could give rise to the former as the best, but oversimplified, explanation for a person currently working part-time. Nonetheless, these findings provide us with the best data and insight available.

TABLE 6.9	**Reasons For Working Part-Time, in Percentage, by Sex, Canada: 1975, 1988, 1993**					
	Men			**Women**		
Reason	**1975**	**1988**	**1993**	**1975**	**1988**	**1993**
Could only find part-time	11	24	38	11	24	33
Did not want full-time	n/a	18	15	46	41	32
Going to school	62	54	43	21	22	21
Personal or family responsibilities	1	1	1	17	12	11

Note: Numbers will not add to 100 due to "other reasons, unspecified" not included

Sources: 1975 and 1993: Adapted from Best (1995: 31, 33). 1988: Adapted from Parliament (1989: 4, 5).

"Could only find part-time work" provides a clear indication for those individuals who are working less than full-time hours due solely to a lack of choice. As can be observed from Table 6.9, this reason accounts for significantly increasing proportions of both male and female part-time workers over the period from 1975 to 1993. Due to changes in Canada's economy that are beyond the control of individual workers, slightly more than one-third of the men and women engaged in part-time work in the first half of the 1990s are willing, but unable, to find full-time employment and must, consequently, settle for less.

"Did not want full-time" suggests an element of choice on the part of the individual worker. The proportion of men offering this reason appears to remain relatively unchanged over time, while the proportions for women have declined, particularly between 1988 and 1993. Women are noticeably more likely to offer this reason than are men, perhaps partly a consequence of our gender-role norms. Why individual women and men "did not want full-time" work remains unanswered in these labour-force surveys. However, as we saw in an earlier section in this chapter, the ideal male work-role model does not permit men to choose whether they will be employed or not. This prescriptive model demands full-time, continuous, employment. As of yet, no comparable work-role model has developed for women, although a trend in that direction is evident. At the moment, subject to constraints of real economic need, greater variations in types of employment, or lack thereof, are permitted to women. A greater proportion of women than men appear to have rejected full-time work in favour of part-time employment.

Men have been and are more likely than women to offer "going to school" as the main reason for being employed part-time. From 1975 to 1993, school responsibilities continue to be the most frequently cited reason by men for working part-time. While the proportion of men selecting this response has declined substantially over time, the proportion of women doing so has remained constant. Even though, as we saw in Chapter 4, the proportion of women students in postsecondary educational institutions has increased substantially over the same time period, attending school has dropped from second to the third most common reason offered by women for their employment pattern.

In contrast to the gender differences regarding school responsibilities, men are much less likely than women to offer "personal or family responsibilities" as the important reason for working part-time (Table 6.9). Another study finds that less than one percent of married men offer "family responsibilities" as their reason for working part-time (Burke, 1986: 13). Our media-driven perception of "new" men supposedly altering their employment practices nowadays to accommodate greater family responsibilities are not confirmed in these examinations of men's reasons for part-time work. If men are changing their paid-work experiences in response to family obligations, they are doing so in other ways, perhaps in the area of accepting shift-work more often. It is unlikely than men are reluctant to admit to labour-force surveyors that they select part-time work to participate more meaningfully in their family life. Instead, in their own minds, family appears to be irrelevant to the issue of part-time work among men.

While women are much more likely than men to cite "personal or family responsibilities" as an explanation for their part-time work, the proportion of women doing so has declined, particularly between 1975 and 1988. This change is less likely to be a consequence of family responsibilities being less onerous than in the recent past and more likely to be indicative of women's need for paid work despite their family work. Working part-time can be an act of necessity for many women born out of increased financial demands associated with a growth in the size of their family, requiring more food, clothing, and a larger shelter. A more refined analysis of another labour-force survey finds that 53.4 percent of married women cite "did not want full-time," followed by 24.9 percent who claim they "could only find part-time" and 19.2 percent who offer "personal and family responsibilities" as their major reason for working part-time (Burke, 1986: 13).

Keeping in mind that the first and the third responses are not mutually exclusive of one another, the impact of family responsibilities upon women may change over a family's career. As we shall see in our section on housework, being employed part-time may be a consequence of cutting back from full-time employment in response to the time crunch many women experience when they find themselves trying to live up to a seemingly impossible "superworkingmom" ideal when their children are young. These mothers are most likely to claim that they "did not want full-time" work or that "personal and family responsibilities" necessitated only part-time employment. Later, as children age, attain more independence, and are in less need of constant monitoring and nurturing, many mothers experience their changing family responsibilities as providing the freedom to pursue full-time employment.

Among married men, the most frequently cited reason (43.8 percent) was "could only find part-time work" (Burke, 1986: 13). We find that significantly more than one-third, approaching one-half, of the married men surveyed indicate that they are working part-time, not because they want to, but because this form of employment is all that is available. At first glance, this finding would appear to be in keeping with the historical influence of the "good provider" ideal, and the related male work-role model, where marital and family responsibilities are supposed to provide an impetus for men to become and remain employed full-time to adequately perform the role of provider. However, in the same survey, the second most commonly offered reason (38.8 percent of married men) for working part-time is "did not want full-time" (Burke, 1986: 13). That more than one-third of the married men seemingly chose part-time work is surprisingly high, in light of the previous argument. Unfortunately, due to the fact that selecting one answer does not necessarily preclude the influence of other answers, and due to the lack of other information on the economic family circumstances of these married men, we cannot offer an explanation for the high frequency of this response.

Single men (62.3 percent) and women (57.7 percent) are most likely to cite "going to school," followed by 29.3 and 30.1 percent, respectively, who claim they "could only find part-time work" (Burke, 1986: 13). Ghalam (1993/1995: 202–203) indicates that 66 percent of younger women, under the age of 25, are most likely to cite "going to school" as their most important reason. The similarity of these findings appears to reflect common gender experiences of a young single person's lifestyle.

Regardless of the stated reasons for their participation levels, we can see that approximately 90 percent of employed men work full-time and men comprise somewhat less than one-third of all part-time workers. In contrast, three-quarters of employed women work full-time, while more than two-thirds of all part-time workers are women. Part-time jobs are typically low paying, do not offer benefits such as dental, supplementary or basic health care, or pension plans, and provide limited opportunities for promotion. As well, most part-time work is nonunionized and, consequently, offers little in the way of job security. Of all classes of the employed, part-time workers are the most vulnerable to exploitation. If the downsizing and streamlining government and corporate mentality of the middle and late 1990s continues to hold sway into the next century, we can anticipate even more significant increases in the numbers and proportions of men and women who will be working part-time and doing so because they "could not find full-time" work.

Self-Employment

The proportion of the Canadian population who are self-employed has declined dramatically since the early 1930s (Gardner, 1995: 26). This decline is due primarily to the rapid decrease in agricultural workers, once the principal source of the self-employed, from 30 percent of all workers in 1931, to 4 percent in the 1990s. Over the same time period, non-agricultural-based self-employed workers have remained essentially constant, representing approximately 8 to 9 percent of all workers. The 1.2 million self-employed persons in 1991 constitute 10 percent of the working population in Canada (Gardner, 1995: 26). Nine percent of all women workers in Canada are self-employed, in contrast to 19 percent of working men. Women currently account for 29 percent of all self-employed workers (Ghalam, 1993/1995: 206).

The self-employed can be divided into two categories: those who employ other workers and independent workers who work solely by themselves. While their numbers are equally distributed in 1991, those who employ other workers (e.g., construction contractors) have doubled since the early 1930s, while the numbers of independent trades people (e.g., shoe makers) have declined (Gardner, 1995: 27). Regardless of the type of work, self-employment typically requires an extended educational background, such as that necessary for dentists, lawyers, and engineers, as well as considerable training and/or expertise acquired through many years of work experience. Many types of self-employment also require the investment of considerable financial capital. Consequently, it is not surprising to find that self-employed workers tend to be older on average (43 years for employers and 42 years for independent workers) than the rest of the working (36 years) population (Gardner, 1995: 27). Part of that greater average age may be due to the tendency of self-employed workers to defer retirement longer than do other workers.

Being self-employed offers many advantages including being one's own boss and having a degree of flexibility over working hours typically not experienced by other types of workers. The disadvantages pertain primarily to pressures to succeed, since the self-employed do not have access to unemployment insurance, private health and dental plans, holiday pay, or other fringe benefits commonly associated with other form of full-time employment. As we noted earlier, men currently comprise just more than 70 percent of the self-employed in Canada; "three-quarters of employers and two-thirds of independent workers" (Gardner, 1995: 27). However, women have increased their share substantially since 1981, from 26 percent to 34 percent of independent workers, and from 17 to 24 percent of employers (Gardner, 1995: 27). About 4.8 percent of Canadian women without children in the home were self-employed in 1991, as were 7.6 percent of mothers with children in the home (Logan and Belliveau, 1995: 27). Whether children are of preschool or school age does not influence the incidence of mothers in the self-employed work force (Logan and Belliveau, 1995: 28). Being self-employed appears to offer these mothers time flexibility for balancing work and family commitments.

The most frequently occurring occupations among those self-employed who have others working for them are sales supervisors and general managers for men, and sales supervisors and bookkeepers/accounting clerks for women. Among the independently self-employed, sales clerks and carpenters are the most frequently occurring occupations for men, followed closely by truck drivers, with childcare workers and sales clerks most frequent for women, closely followed by barbers/hairdressers (Gardner, 1995: 28). As well, four occupations of an artistic nature, including writers and editors, painters, sculptors, and interior designers are found among the 10 most common occupations for independently self-employed women, while physicians and lawyers are found in the 10 most common occupations for self-employed men who also employ others.

In 1991, self-employed employers earned the highest average incomes, followed by workers who were not self-employed, followed by independently self-employed workers (Gardner, 1995: 29). Men earned more on average than did women across all three categories of employment. Part of this discrepancy might be attributable to the fact that self-employed women are almost three times as likely as self-employed men (31 percent versus 11 percent) to work only part-time (Gardner, 1995: 27). Not surprisingly, the highest incomes are gathered by self-employed employers such as doctors, dentists, and lawyers. The lowest income among the independently self-employed is earned by childcare workers.

Home-Based Employment

Advances in technology, changes in the way many employers conduct business, along with desires or necessities of employees and other workers to accommodate other priorities along with employment have combed to produce innovations in not only how, but also where, income is earned. Over the past two decades, many employers have permitted workers to adopt a **flextime** arrangement, where daily work hours can be manipulated, within limits, to accommodate other demands, as long as the weekly work hours remain constant. More recently, we have seen the advent of **flexplace** arrangements where employees are either required or permitted to work some or all of their hours within their own homes. Self-employed workers are also taking advantage of newly created opportunities to combine their workplaces within their own homes.

Employer desires to cut overhead costs, in tandem with the availability of affordable personal computers and telecommunication devices such as modems and fax machines, permit many employees to simply "telecommute" or "telework" (Nadwodny, 1996: 16). The employer saves office space and the employee saves time, money, and energy costs associated with physically commuting from a homeplace to a workplace on a daily basis. The advantages to home-based workers also include a greater flexibility and comfort of working conditions and less over-the-shoulder direct supervision. The disadvantages of such an arrangement include the distractions posed by potentially twinning work and household-related demands (e.g., "Let's throw in a load of laundry while waiting for that document to print"), the necessity to remind others that one is "at work" even if "at home" (e.g., "Can you colour with me?") and a greater sense of isolation from other workers. As well, while the fact that one need not "go to work" may be uplifting, one may, simultaneously, have the nagging sense that he or she never truly "leave work" either. (One of the authors of this textbook, being both self-employed and home-based, is well aware of both sides of this coin.)

Doubling in size since 1981, the 1.1 million employed people working at home in 1991 account for approximately 6 percent of all Canadian workers. The home-based working population is currently composed of 53 percent men and 47 percent women. However, the increase among women since 1981 is substantially greater (69 percent) than for men (23 percent) (Nadwodny, 1996: 17). At the present rate of growth, it is conservatively estimated that at least 1.5 million Canadians will be involved in home-based employment by the turn of the century (Nadwodny, 1996: 201). About three-quarters of home-based employed people currently have nonagricultural jobs and that proportion is likely to increase in the future.

Approximately one-third of all Canadians currently working at home are self-employed, while the rest are paid by employers located elsewhere. Home-based workers are more likely to work part-time (27 percent) than are non-home-based workers (17 percent). This greater tendency for home-based than elsewhere-based workers to work part-time is found among both women (40 percent versus 26 percent) and men (16 percent versus 9 percent) (Nadwodny, 1996: 17). As we saw in the previous section on self-employment, home-based workers are more likely to be older than younger, probably due to the necessity of first acquiring both the knowledge and financial capital for most home-based jobs.

According to the 1991 Census, men are most likely to work at home in managerial and administrative occupations (22 percent), followed by construction and sales (15 percent each). All of these are higher than the proportions for men employed outside of the home, ranging from 7 percent higher in managerial and administrative work, to about 5 percent higher for both sales and construction work. In contrast, women working at home are most likely to be found in clerical (29 percent), service (25 percent), managerial and administrative (12 percent), and sales (10 percent) occupations. The proportions in clerical work are lower (by 4 percent), higher in service work (by 10 percent), and in managerial, administrative, and sales work are essentially the same as those found in non-home-based female labour-force distributions (Nadwodny, 1996: 19).

Self-employed workers, regardless of whether they work part- or full-time, and paid full-time employees who work at home, typically earn less than their counterparts who work outside of the home. "For example, 29% of self-employed women who worked at home full time earned $20,000 or more, compared with 44% of those who worked outside the home" (Nadwodny, 1996: 19). The only group of home-based workers earning more than the non-home-based are male and female paid employees who work part-time only. Judging from the available statistics on occupational distributions and incomes, the trend towards home-based employment does not appear to provide a significant solution to the quest for financial independence among Canadian women. Home-based employment might provide a partial solution to some of the problems associated with attempting to balance the needs of work and family among those women who either choose or are obliged to seek their own solutions.

Unfortunately, the available data do not enable us to determine how much of self-employment, or of home-based employment, is due to choice and how much is due to necessity. As in the case of part-time work, the effects of downsizing and restructuring policies in government, business, and industry are likely to be found in an increase of self-employed workers and workers who operate from inside of their own homes. As more men and women experience workplace policies that either prevent their continued employment or seriously limit their opportunities for advancement and success, we are likely to see a further increase in the numbers and proportions of women and men who become self-employed or home-based out of a lack of choice. The financial futures of men, and particularly women, in low-income independent employment situations will remain shaky. For every Mary Kay cosmetics entrepreneur, or Barbara Cartland writing empire success story, there are hundreds of low-income earning childcare workers and telecommuting telephone information operators.

HOUSEWORK

As we noted in Chapter 3, the industrialization process beginning in the 1800s firmly gendered women's work sites. A woman's place was ideally to be bounded by the family home, within which she was to perform unpaid labour for her husband, her children, and herself. These labours were believed to benefit not only individual women, men, and families, but also the larger society. Despite the uneven pace of change over the course of the century, greater and greater proportions of men and women conformed in practice to these evolving cultural beliefs about women's and men's proper place. The consequences of these beliefs and practices were only occasionally questioned and challenged.

"Material feminists" (Hayden, 1981) in the latter part of the 1800s argued that women benefited least from existing social arrangements and identified the isolation of housework in individual homes as a major factor contributing to women's subordination. Their proposed solution lay in collectivizing housework through the establishment of women-controlled and operated communal kitchens, dining halls, nurseries, and laundry facilities. Not only would women's isolation be reduced, but individual household maintenance would be reduced significantly and women would be freed to benefit from enjoying recreational and companionship activities with their families in their own homes on an equitable basis. For example, "kitchenless houses," linked by covered walkways were suggested as a way to free women from the ties of cooking. By altering the actual design of houses, material feminists believed they could create utopian communities that would provide an alternative to individualized housework in single-family homes.

These ideas were perfectly in keeping with the times as a large number of religious-based communes were established in the Midwestern and Northeastern United States during the 1800s. Practising variations upon the theme of "Biblical Communism," groups such as the Shakers (Roberts, 1971) and the Oneida community (Carden, 1969, Robertson, 1970) created communal kitchens and other facilities. While the Shakers practised a strict sex-linked division of labour, with women solely controlling domestic sites, the Oneidans promoted "mingling of the sexes" (Robertson, 1970: 58) in their facilities and a sharing of all forms of work. Only a small number of women in the United States attempted to put the non-religious-based material feminist theory into practice (Wilson, 1996: 66) during the late 1800s and very early 1900s. Aside from a brief flirtation with communes in both Canada and the United States during the 1960s (Roberts, 1971) and early 1970s, a communal solution to the isolating oppression of housework essentially ceased being promoted and practised by the turn of the present century. One reason this "lost feminist tradition" floundered was due to the difficulties of overcoming sex and class divisions in both urban and rural communities. "The problem of domestic service versus domestic cooperation could not be resolved" (Wajcman, 1991: 125). Hayden (1982: 201) notes that "[f]eminists with capital who could afford the new physical environment for collective domestic work never thought of voluntarily sharing that domestic work themselves." Accordingly, the liberation of professional, middle-class women from domestic drudgery often meant the exploitation of lower-class women.

Liberal feminists in the 1960s and 1970s assumed that creating equality of economic opportunity outside of the home and then motivating women to pursue those opportunities were key elements for improving the status of women within our society. To that end, significant alterations were proposed for our public economic, educational, and political institutions. The private institution of the home and family, and particularly domestic labour

Box 6.3	1991 and 1996 Census of Canada Questions

1991 Census:

Q. 30. Last week, how many hours did this person work (not including volunteer work, housework, maintenance or repairs for his/her own home)?

Include as work:

- *working without pay in a family farm or business (e.g., assisting in seeding, doing accounts);*

- *working in his/her own business, farm or professional practice, alone or in partnership;*

- *working for wages, salary, tips or commission.*

1996 Census:

HOUSEHOLD ACTIVITIES

Note: **Last week** *refers to Sunday, May 5 to Saturday, May 11, 1996.*

In Question 30, where activities overlap, report the same hours in more than one part.

Question 30

Last week, how many hours did this person spend doing the following activities?

(a) Doing **unpaid** housework, yard work, or home maintenance for members of thishousehold, or others.

Some examples include: preparing meals, doing laundry, household planning, shopping and cutting grass.

❑ None   ❑ 15 to 29 hours
❑ Less than 5 hours ❑ 30 to 59 hours
❑ 5 to 14 hours   ❑ 60 hours or more

(b) Looking after one or more of this person's own children, or the children of others, **without pay**.

Some examples include: bathing or playing with young children, driving children to sports activities or helping them with homework, and talking with teens about their problems.

❑ None   ❑ 15 to 29 hours
❑ Less than 5 hours ❑ 30 to 59 hours
❑ 5 to 14 hours   ❑ 60 hours or more

(c) Providing **unpaid** care or assistance to one or more seniors.

Some examples include: providing personal care to a senior family member, visiting seniors, talking with them on the telephone, and helping them with shopping, banking or with taking medication.

❑ None   ❑ 5 to 9 hours
❑ Less than 5 hours ❑ 10 hours or more

[Note: Subsequent questions pertaining to "Labour Market Activities" refer to paid employment]

centring around home care and childcare, were essentially overlooked from this viewpoint (Oakley, 1974; Vanek, 1974). Marxist and socialist feminists initially focused our attention upon housework as an important support system for sustaining workers in the formal economy and for developing the next generation of labourers. Domestic labour was now recognized as an important source of women's social inequality due to the lack of socially valued rewards accorded to housework within our society. Feminists from all frameworks now acknowledge that the organization of housework within the work site of the home exerts a key influence upon women's meaningful participation in the world of paid labour, eventual gender equality, both within and outside of the boundaries of the home, and the continued construction of gender (Lero, 1996: 36; Luxton, 1983/1995: 288; Thompson and Walker, 1995, 1989).

Housework has been transformed in many ways over the course of this century. Bradbury's (1994) analysis of the impact of technological changes on working-class women in nineteenth-century Montreal has indicated how the availability of running water, cast-iron stoves, improvements in lighting fuels, and the introduction of steam laundries and commercial bakeries with modern equipment and store-bought bread served to lighten the load of responsibility for those who could afford to indulge in these new commodities. While the provision of running water and toilet facilities eased the domestic duties of women married to skilled workers, much of the day of a working-class wife remained consumed with the onerous duties of domestic labour. "Chickens were usually bought unplucked, fish unscaled....Wood or coal...had to be carried inside, and....[w]hile men may have chopped the wood, lack of storage space within houses meant that carrying the wood or coal, often up one or two flight of stairs, usually fell to the wife or children" (Bradbury, 1994: 38–39).

As a consequence of technological innovations, some work previously done within the home has shifted to outside work sites and the household has become more a site of consumption, rather than production (Cowan, 1993). Most of the foods on our tables today are prepared, processed, and packaged outside of the home and hunted or gathered only in the aisles of neighbourhood supermarkets. Almost all of our clothing is manufactured, and often cleaned, in establishments distances removed from where we live. New appliances, powered not by human muscles, but by electricity and natural gas, are continually being introduced into our homes to alter the way housework is performed. Originally advertised following World War I as devices to "liberate" the homemaker from domestic labour, this message has been featured less and less prominently (Fox, 1993: 154, 1990). Appliances and other household products are now marketed as aides for better equipping the houseworker to more efficiently and sufficiently meet modern-day standards of hygiene, sanitation, nutrition, and appearance.

Early this century, "[t]he phrase 'Cleanliness is next to godliness,' which had originally referred to moral cleanliness, was applied to housework contexts" (Ahlander and Bahr, 1995: 55). Keeping a neat, clean, and tidy home became a woman's moral duty and the state of her home an outward indicator of her inner moral purity. The development of the domestic science movement, the germ theory of disease, and the idea of "scientific motherhood" in the early years of the 1900s remodeled the ideology of housewifery. Standards of cleanliness and appearance have constantly been "inflated" (Fox, 1993: 151) over the course of the century. Unfortunately, the products and appliances designed to supposedly help in their attainment often become hazardous to the physical and mental health of the houseworker (Rosenberg, 1986).

Estimates conclude that the actual amount of labour required to maintain a home has not changed significantly since the latter part of the eighteenth century (Cowan, 1984; Ogden, 1986). It is true that brooms have been replaced with vacuum cleaners larger and small, wood-burning stoves with microwaves, paring knives with food processors, kneading hands with bread-making machines, and scythes with electric and gas-powered stand-up or sit-down lawn mowers, hedge trimmers, whipper snippers, and leaf and snow blowers. These home appliances may save time, but the sizes of the homes being maintained today are much larger on average than they were 200 years ago. Not only have standards of household maintenance been raised, but the amount of help available for performing required tasks has been substantially reduced. Disappearing, except from all but the wealthiest homes today, are butlers, maids, nannies, governesses, charwomen, kitchen and scullery aides, gardeners and groundskeepers, and that general class of workers once common to even the most average of middle-class homes—the domestic.

The introduction of new appliances appears at times to be a mixed blessing. Rocks and washboards used down by the river along with clotheslines strung inside and outside of the home were replaced first by single-cycle washing machines, most often filled with water boiled on a stove, complete with a hand-cranked clothes wringer. Eventually, these devices were replaced by multiple-cycle, variable-temperature, washers and dryers. Whereas only one in six Canadian households had an automatic washer and dryer in 1961, these appliances were found in more than three out of every four homes by 1992 (Statistics Canada, 1995a). In addition to alleviating some of the muscle power and much of the drudgery associated with washing clothes, these machines now have to accommodate the greater accumulated numbers and arrays of clothes by individual household members, who now hold higher standards for their care. New fabrics require different methods of cleaning and increased levels of knowledge to not only comprehend washing instructions, but also to decipher the supposedly beneficial ingredients of a plethora of cleaning products. Yet, whereas Canadian houseworkers in the first half of this century commonly devoted one full day a week to washing and another day to ironing clothes (Luxton, 1980: 152–158), appliances now provide the opportunity for reorganizing these events at variable times over the course of a day, week, or month (Ogden, 1986; VanEvery, 1995).

Similarly, dishes must be washed, but the timing of the task (daily, weekly, monthly, biannually) is discretionary and limited by the number of dishes owned and, increasingly, a subjectively defined "best" time for running a dishwasher (often while everyone is sleeping). The autonomy of scheduling afforded by many new appliances contributes to the sense of freedom that constitutes one of the few most appreciated qualities associated with housework (Thompson and Walker, 1989). However, more income is needed to acquire new home appliances and their attendant advantages (Armstrong, 1990: 72). This income need, in conjunction with greater freedom over the scheduling of household tasks, combine to promote the movement of women from the home into the paid-labour force. Finally, the development of new task-specific technologies may lead to women taking over tasks that were previously performed by other members of the household (Bose, 1984). Thrall (1982) notes that in households possessing a garbage disposal unit, husbands and children are significantly less likely to perform garbage duties, and wives are more likely to be assigned exclusive responsibility for the task (presumably because the unit is now part of the kitchen sink and the sink is defined as part of women's domain).

Defining and Measuring the Social Worth of Housework

According to the first question in the 1991 Census of Canada section on "work" (see Box 6.3), only paid labour, but neither volunteer work nor housework, qualified for inclusion under the provided definition. This disqualification reinforced the lack of social recognition accorded to the value of both household workers themselves and the labour they perform, yet based upon results obtained from a General Social Survey of more than 9000 respondents, Statistics Canada estimates that Canadians performed at least 25-billion hours of unpaid work in 1992, the equivalent of almost 13 million full-time jobs, 95 percent of which was devoted to home and childcare (Statistics Canada, 1995a). This household labour had a conservatively estimated worth of $234 billion, equal to approximately 40 percent of Canada's gross domestic product (the value attached to all of the goods and services produced in our officially recognized economy).

The worth of household labour is typically estimated using one of two different methods (Statistics Canada, 1995a). The **opportunity cost** method assigns a monetary value to housework based upon what a houseworker having a specified education and paid work history would earn if the worker were employed in the job market. Using this method, all household tasks are accorded the same, usually the highest, hourly wage of the worker. The more conservative **replacement cost** method assigns the wages that each task would be worth if performed in the job market. This method is more difficult to calculate as housework comprises more than 80 different tasks (Renzetti and Curran, 1995: 206), many of which are frequently performed simultaneously. As a consequence, summing the actual number of hours to be "charged" at various hourly rates is somewhat problematic. These methods are used not only to estimate the contribution of housework to our gross domestic product, but also become part of the process involved in establishing settlement payments in disability or loss-of-life lawsuits.

Attaching a dollar value to household and childcare has long been resisted within our society, which insists that housework is a personal service, a "labour of love" (Luxton, 1980) willingly and selflessly done as a testimony of women's fundamental nature. Many aspects of housework are indeed performed as an expression of caring (Ahlander and Bahr, 1995; Mederer, 1993; Shaw, 1988; Thompson, 1991) and are described by houseworkers as having only a personally rewarding value. These emotional intangibles cannot easily be quantified and are typically ignored within government or other research calculations. However, within our materialistic society, value is equated with a dollar sign and measuring the important and heretofore unrecognized contributions of housework to the formal economy of Canada not only increases the visibility, but also elevates the prestige of housework and houseworkers. It also may increase the value of paid occupations viewed as formal extensions of labour performed within the household (e.g., childcare work).

Studying Housework: Basic Research Issues.

For well over 30 years, researchers have attempted to map expected and actual patterns of who does what, when, and how often, within Canadian and American households. Contemporary findings indicate that, similar to the way in which the "culture" of fatherhood has changed significantly more than has actual fathering behaviour (LaRossa, 1988/1995), the "culture" of housework has changed more rapidly than has behavioural reality within the home. As we shall soon see, "in spite of all the talk about egalitarian ideology, abstract beliefs about what women and men 'ought' to do are not connected with the division of family work" (Thompson and Walker, 1989: 857). Research suggests that the development of domestic technology has reinforced both the privatization of housework, as well as the traditional sex-linked division of labour within the home (Bose et al., 1984; Rothschild, 1983). Before examining general and specific empirical findings, we must first briefly explore a number of research issues that also shed light on gender and gender relations within our society.

Sharing, Responsibility, and Helping Out

Public opinion polls conducted from the mid-1970s to the mid-1980s (Luxton, 1983/1995: 288; Wilson, 1991: 56) document an increase from slightly more than 50 percent to just more than 80 percent of adult Canadians who agree that husbands should "share" in domestic duties. While **sharing** is a noble concept, it is also an elusive one to define. Our traditional folk wisdom popularizes the phrase that "marriage is a 50-50 proposition." This sentiment cannot be applied to housework easily, because of the absence of a calculus for computing the comparable worth of, for example, cooking one entire meal versus putting one night's dirty plates in a dishwasher or taking out the garbage for one week. Within the research literature, household labour is generally considered to be shared if neither of the spouses or cohabitation partners performs less than 40 percent or more than 60 percent of the tasks examined in the studies (Smith and Reid, 1986, in Mandell, 1989: 246). More realistically then, our folk phrase could be modified to a less catchy: "marriage is somewhere between a 40–60 and a 60–40 proposition."

Still at issue, however, is the question of what is actually being shared: performance of the task or responsibility for the task? As we shall soon see, most studies focus only upon the allocation of the number of tasks assigned to a partner and the amount of time each partner devotes to his or her allotted domestic chores. Mederer (1993) argues that this research orientation does not adequately capture the concept of household labour. In addition to the actual performance of the tasks themselves lies the processes of "defining them as necessary, creating standards for their performance, and making sure that they are done in an acceptable manner" (Mederer, 1993: 133). This "orchestration" of family work is best captured with a concept of responsibility for "household management" (Mederer, 1993: 133). **Responsibility** includes "anticipating, planning and organizing what needs to be done and managing people, resources and time" (Marshall, 1993/1995: 307). Most studies appear to focus upon the more visible sharing of tasks and ignore the less visible and harder to measure orchestrating responsibilities of home management.

The distinction between sharing and responsibility can be illustrated in the following example. A person sharing in the task of grocery shopping might limit his or her participation to skillfully manoeuvring the grocery cart down the aisles during rush-hour dinnertime traffic, picking out the necessary supplies, and transferring them with flair from the cart to the conveyor belt at the checkout counter. In contrast, responsibility for grocery shopping includes financial budgeting, menu planning (taking each household members' tastes and distastes into account), monitoring existing supplies at home, clipping coupons, watching advertised sales, comparison pricing, mastering metric conversions, and making a shopping list congruent with store floor plans. Many a man has said that he is willing to "share" shopping if his partner will "just" give him a grocery list.

Into this mix we should also add the concept of **helping out**. As we shall see later, helping out appears to involve less time and effort than sharing. A person helping out around the home is one who participates only minimally and not sufficiently to qualify as sharing in task performance and certainly does not assume responsibility for that task. Although rarely operationalized, our general reading of the available literature leads us to the conclusion that helping out involves performing a task less than 40 percent of the time, while sharing involves a participation rate of between 40 and 60 percent of the time. Involvement more than 60 percent of the time means the person has primary responsibility for that task. Typically, responsibility goes beyond primary task performance and includes planning and management of the task as well.

Time Estimate Problems

Many methods have been used to obtain measurements of the number of hours householders devote to domestic tasks. These range from the hourly keeping of detailed daily or weekly diaries, to creating snapshots of activities performed at variably scheduled specific moments during a day, to respondents' general impressions of the overall distribution of their tasks and responsibilities and those of their partners on an average day or week. To capture more households within their sample, some researchers ask only one respondent to estimate the housework hours of all household members. Others ask both husbands and wives, or cohabitation partners, to indicate their own time use to permit comparability of couple estimates. Regardless of the method used, certain problems exist regarding the estimates obtained.

For example, *husbands* typically *underestimate* their wives' hourly or weekly involvement in house and childcare and *overestimate* their own. Using an American sample of dual-earner marriages, Galinsky et. al (1993) find that, even when women do 81 percent of the cooking, 78 percent of the cleaning, and so on, their husbands are likely to see themselves as splitting the work fifty-fifty. Studies repeatedly find that husbands think they are helping out at home far more than their wives think they are, that husbands judge their participation levels and effects as positive, while their wives judge these results as being less satisfactory or even negative, and that husbands tend to grossly underestimate their employed wives' role overload and stress (Mandell, 1989: 249). Hochschild (1990) finds that upper-middle-class professional women commonly *overestimate* their husbands' participation in household labour, often claiming their husbands participate at a "shared" 50 percent level despite obvious and objective evidence to the contrary.

Furthermore, *wives* typically *underestimate* the amount of time they devote to household chores, in large part due to their frequent tendency to perform a number of tasks simultaneously (multitasking), such as, for example, doing a load of laundry and hand washing a few dishes, while cooking a meal (Hochschild, 1990: 8; Luxton, 1980; Shaw, 1988). Simultaneous task performance is frequently necessary, since women typically have a greater number of tasks to perform in a limited time frame. It is made possible in large part because of the much greater tendency of women in our culture to adopt a **polychronic** time orientation, which encompasses the possibility of engaging in multitasking. This approach defies reduction to the dominant North American **monochronic** time orientation of doing one thing at a time in a linear fashion. The monochronic orientation is preferred by men in the business world and brought with them into their own homes (Hall, 1984: 44–54). As a consequence of their time orientation and handling of multiple tasks, women tend to underestimate the amount of actual time they devote to each separate task. On the basis of these findings, you are always wise to be cautious when interpreting specific time estimate findings from housework studies.

Household Work or Household Leisure?

Very few studies have examined the meaning for the participants of tasks being performed within a household. Implicitly accepting existing stereotypes and values, researchers overwhelmingly tend to assume that all such tasks are conceived of as tedious drudgery, essentially devoid of pleasure, choice, or any other leisure characteristic (Ahlander and Bahr, 1995). We have already noted that many household tasks are experienced as expressions of caring (Thompson, 1991). In her study of 60 married couples in Halifax, Shaw (1988) finds a number of gender differences in conceptions of household tasks as being work, leisure, or a combination of the two (see Table 6.10). While more than half of the married women were employed in the paid-labour force and almost two-thirds had children living at home, respondents' age, family size, paid-work status, and occupational level had no influence upon the meanings respondents attached to household tasks.

TABLE 6.10   Definitions of Specific Housework and Childcare Activities by Gender, in Percentage

Activity	Gender	Work %	Mixed Work and Leisure %	Leisure %
Cooking*	M	20.3	22.0	57.6
	F	56.1	31.8	12.2
Home Chores*	M	44.4	35.6	20.0
	F	83.5	13.1	3.5
Laundry	M	33.3	66.7	0.0
	F	80.2	15.6	4.2
Gardening*	M	32.1	19.6	48.2
	F	0.0	29.4	70.6
Shopping	M	21.7	30.4	47.8
	F	38.0	32.0	30.0
Household Obligations*	M	31.3	28.4	40.3
	F	61.5	15.4	23.1
Childcare*	M	20.4	28.6	51.0
	F	33.0	39.1	27.8
Other Child Obligations*	M	13.3	16.7	70.0
	F	5.8	36.5	57.7

* Chi-square significant at $p \leq .05$

Note: percentages may not add to 100 as events defined as "neither work nor leisure" have been excluded.

Source: Adapted from Shaw, 1988: 335.

Husbands scheduled about 65 percent of their household tasks for weekend days, while only approximately 46 percent of the tasks performed by wives occur on weekend days, with 54 percent requiring a week day performance (Shaw, 1988: 336). As well, males are much less likely to do their household-related tasks either alone or with only a child present (Shaw, 1988: 336). In other words, husbands are more likely to have their wives physically present, and, therefore, sharing to some extent, while the men perform their housework. In contrast, wives are more likely to engage in housework in isolation, bereft of adult company.

In addition to these differences in scheduling and companionship, the events themselves are experienced differently by husbands and wives. We can see from Table 6.10 that significant gender differences exist regarding the meanings attached to cooking, home chores, gardening, household obligations (upkeep of the home or banking activities), and childcare (physical care in the form of feeding, dressing, or bathing children). With the exception of gardening, these tasks are significantly more likely to be defined as "work" by wives than by husbands and more likely to be defined as "leisure" by husbands than by wives. Wives are significantly more likely to define gardening, with its elements of greater freedom of choice, fresh air, and escape from the confines of the home, as a leisure activity than are husbands, a bare majority of whom are more likely to define this activity as either strictly work or a combination of work and leisure. Since only three of the 60 husbands were actually involved in doing any laundry (a low level confirmed in other Canadian studies: e.g., Brayfield, 1992: 25; Marshall, 1993/1995), meaningful tests for statistically significant differences could not be performed. We can safely presume that married men's aversion to the laundry room is based more upon its perception as an aversive work site than upon any act of gender solidarity with a Maytag repairman. Neither shopping nor "other child obligations" (playing with children) demonstrate significant gender differences in meaning.

Overall, husbands are more likely to define the activities they participate in as leisure "(44.5% of all male events…seen as leisure as opposed to 15.7% of all female events) and far less frequently as work (26.3% for males compared to 58.0% for females)" (Shaw, 1988: 334). The findings from this study caution us to avoid regarding housework as an activity having a uni-dimensional "work-only" meaning. In addition, these findings suggest that any attempts to redesign the household division of labour must address the meaning of such activities for the participants. "Sharing" ideally must include not only an equitable distribution of tasks and time requirements, but also essentially equal participation in work-like and leisure-like activities.

Tasks and Times

Finally, we must note that comparing findings across a number of different empirical studies is hampered by variations in how the dependent variable—housework—is measured. As you may have noticed already, two analytically distinct dimensions are present in the study of housework. One involves the *number and nature of tasks* to be examined. Not all studies include the same tasks and, as we have just seen, not all of these tasks have the same meaning to respondents. Only some studies include childcare under the rubric of housework, and even then attention is usually focused upon physical care and not playful or explicit socialization activities, while elder care and managing relationships with friends or members of an extended kinship network (e.g., sending gifts of special occasion cards, arranging celebrations or reunions) are virtually never considered. In keeping with that convention, we will be discussing child, elder, and friendship care in other chapters.

The second dimension involves the *absolute or proportional amount of time* devoted to housework by the subjects under study. Once again we observe variation across studies in terms of whether the focus is upon the absolute number of hours women and men devote per day or week to household labour (an absolute measure), or upon the relative contributions of men and women to the total daily or weekly hours devoted to housework by a couple (a proportional measure). The absolute-proportional distinction becomes important particularly when making statements about possible changes in the distribution of household labour over the time span of a marital or cohabiting relationship, or over the past few decades as women significantly increase their participation in paid labour. We shall return shortly to provide illustrations and examine implications of these distinctions.

Research Findings

Research in both Canada and the United States finds that wives and women cohabitors, whether employed full- or part-time or not employed, consistently devote more absolute and proportional time to household duties, performing approximately 75 to 80 percent of all housework (Berardo, Shehan, and Leslie, 1987; Coltrane and Ishii-Kuntz, 1992; Marshall, 1993/1995; Shelton and John, 1993). Despite an overall trend towards a more egalitarian distribution of paid labour-force participation, Canadian dual-income couples are not more egalitarian than other couples when it comes to the distribution of housework. Data compiled from a national sample of 2577 Canadians in 1983 indicates that "women in dual-employed couples perform over 76% of…feminine-typed tasks, while men in dual-employed couples do less than 30% on average" (Brayfield, 1992: 25).

Women are typically assigned or assume primary responsibility for tasks performed within the home, while men are assigned or assume responsibility for tasks outside of the home itself, with the notable exception of indoor household repairs. An American study (Berk and Berk, 1979, in Blair and Lichter, 1991: 93) finds that wives perform more than 96 percent of the cooking, 92 percent of the dish washing, 90 percent of the vacuuming, 94 percent of the bed making, and 94 percent of the diapering of children. In contrast, husbands perform more than 80 percent of the household repairs, 80 percent of the disciplining of the children, 75 percent of the lawn mowing, and 77 percent of the snow shoveling. Although not included in their study, it appears safe to assume that, if we were to move the kitchen outdoors and call it a barbecue, we would probably find that men do most of the outdoor cooking (although not preparation of the entire meal) and limit their indoor cooking to mainly preparing "gourmet" meals (but leave the clean-up chores to their wives). Finally, in one of the few studies to consider this variable, Demo and Acock's (1993: 325) analysis of an American national sample finds that divorced and never-married mothers with at least one child under the age of 18 still at home are responsible for driving other household members to work, school, or other activities at least 90 percent of the time, while both first-married and stepfamily mothers in similar circumstances are responsible for driving at least 67 percent of the time. Chauffeuring, now an essential component of childrearing among the middle- and upper-middle classes living in Canadian cities, appears to be one of the few outdoor duties where women have the greatest proportional responsibility.

The differential use of technologies also reflects the gendered division of household labours. For example, Cockburn (1985) observes that within her sample of respondents, few women used a hammer or screwdriver for more than the occasional hanging of a picture, and only a small amount used a lawnmower or electric drill because "men were proprietorial about these tools and the role that goes with them" (p. 219). Women, she observes, were likely to use utensils and appliances (e.g., the stove, the washing machine, blender, toaster) rather than tools per se. When Gray (1986) asked women to envisage pieces of domestic equipment as "pink" or "blue" or "neutral lilac," irons were uniformly pink and electric drills uniformly blue. Home-entertainment technologies were other than lilac; the timer switch and control switch were depicted as deep blue, indicating male objects of control. She observes that a new piece of technology within the home arrives replete with gendered meanings and that men are more likely to assume themselves capable of installing and operating items associated with the domain of domestic leisure. Reinforcing male dominancy over such objects, she suggests that women may develop "calculated ignorance" over how a video machine is installed and operated, lest it become an additional task expected of them.

Most of men's tasks are seasonal in nature, or nonroutine tasks performed at intervals rather than routinely, and offer considerable discretion over the timing and nature of their performance (Coleman, 1988). Except among the most competitive of neighbourhoods, it matters not whether the grass grows an additional centimetre before cutting. In contrast, it matters considerably more whether the dust bunnies on the living-room floor grow more feet. Women's tasks tend to be daily, more repetitive, isolating, boring and monotonous, invisible (both in terms of being unnoticed until and unless they are not performed, as when a houseworker goes "on strike" to draw attention to her taken-for-granted labour, and in terms of their required, but unobservable thinking and planning), and more time consuming (Oakley, 1974). Research in Canada (Frederick, 1995: 24), the United States (Hochschild, 1990: 9), and Australia (Gowland, 1983) finds that women devote more hours per week to housecare than to childcare, thereby reinforcing the symbolism inherent in the term "housewife." As an aside, it is noteworthy how employers often cite childrearing responsibilities ("after all, she'll probably miss work when her child gets sick or has a doctor's appointment"), but rarely cite homecare responsibilities ("she'll probably be exhausted from cooking and cleaning and ironing") as a rationale for limiting female employees' options—another testimonial to the invisible and taken-for-granted nature of housework and houseworkers.

Men's tasks also tend to be more discrete in the sense of having a definite beginning and ending (Coleman, 1988), in contrast to the continuity of women's tasks, where one activity shades into the next in an interconnected fashion. This difference, as well as the difference between sharing and responsibility, is often illustrated when husbands help out with certain tasks within the home. To most husbands or male cohabitation partners, helping out with meal clean-up by putting away the dishes means just that—putting away the dishes. Despite ample visual evidence that the counter and stove surfaces need wiping and the kitchen floor needs sweeping, men typically assume the task is finished when the dishwasher or drainer is empty and the dishes are in their (it is hoped) proper place. If asked by his wife or cohabitation partner why he didn't continue cleaning-up, his most likely reply is, "But you didn't tell me to!"

Until Statistics Canada releases findings from the three-part 1996 Census question specifically devoted to how much time people aged 15 and over devote to "household activities" (see Box 6.3), we have to fashion a picture of housework in Canada from either limited geographical studies (e.g., Shaw's 1988 research on married couples in Halifax or Luxton's 1980 Flin Flon sample) or data gathered from national surveys focusing primarily upon other issues (e.g., Brayfield, 1992). Findings on housework responsibilities from the 1990 General Social Survey—a random sample of approximately 13 500 Canadians—are presented in Table 6.11. More than two-thirds of all Canadian married or cohabiting couples between the ages of 15 and 64, with at least one child under age 19 living in the household, had both partners working (51 percent of wives full-time and 19 percent part-time) in the paid-labour force during 1990 (Marshall, 1993/1995: 302). As can be seen within the table, the findings for Canadians closely parallel those obtained from studies of American couples, which consistently have noted that women in all household situations do more housework than men (South and Spitze, 1994).

TABLE 6.11	Primary Responsibility for Housework, Couples Aged 15-64 with Children under Age 19, Canada, 1990, in Percentage			
Household chore and type of couple	Wife Only	Husband Only	Wife and Husband Equal	Other
Meal preparation				
Dual-earner, both full-time	72	13	12	2
Dual-earner, wife part-time	86	7	6	-
Single-earner, husband full-time	89	5	5	-
Meal clean-up				
Dual-earner, both full-time	59	16	15	6
Dual-earner, wife part-time	72	9	10	3
Single-earner, husband full-time	78	7	8	3
Cleaning and laundry				
Dual-earner, both full-time	74	7	13	3
Dual-earner, wife part-time	86	4	6	-
Single-earner, husband full-time	86	4	7	-
House maintenance and outside work				
Dual-earner, both full-time	7	79	4	9
Dual-earner, wife part-time	9	80	3	6
Single-earner, husband full-time	8	77	5	9

Notes: Percentages may not add to 100 due to rounding and exclusion of Not Stated.
"Other" means someone other than the wife or the husband holds primary responsibility for the chore.
In "Dual-earner, wife part-time," the husband is employed full-time.

Source: Adapted from Marshall, (1995) Errata for 1993: 12.

Wives have primary responsibilities for housework tasks in 80 percent of the couples. About 10 percent of full-time dual-earner Canadian couples share housework, while husbands have most or all of the responsibilities in 10 percent of the couples (Marshall, 1993/1995: 303). While the 20 percent rate of sole or shared responsibility, along with a 1990 estimate that househusbands can be found in approximately four percent of all Canadian couples (Nett, 1993: 264), might give optimism to promoters of beliefs about men's changed roles, the fact remains that the vast majority of men still do not participate meaningfully in domestic chores.

Slightly more than half of all full-time employed married or cohabiting women have sole responsibility for housework, while just more than 25 percent have most of those responsibilities (Marshall, 1993/1995: 303). Younger wives with higher education, fewer children, and greater income are generally less likely to have sole responsibility for housework and more likely to have a partner who shares. Being employed full-time is associated with a lesser likelihood of having primary responsibility for domestic chores among married and cohabiting women. However, only minimal differences exist between part-time employed and nonemployed women, suggesting that part-time employment among these women is structured, either willingly or unwillingly, so as to accommodate household responsibilities. We shall return to this latter possibility shortly.

TABLE 6.12   **Average Hours Per Day Spent on Unpaid Work by Canadians, Aged 25–44, Employed Full-Time, 1992**

	Males			Females		
	Unmarried no children	Married* no children	Married* with children	Unmarried no children	Married* no children	Married* with children
Cooking	0.3	0.4	0.4	0.4	0.8	1.2
Housekeeping	0.2	0.2	0.2	0.6	0.6	1.0
Maintenance/repairs	0.2	0.3	0.4	0.1	0.1	—
Other**	0.1	0.3	0.5	0.3	0.3	0.3
Shopping	0.5	0.3	0.6	0.9	0.6	0.8
Childcare	—	—	0.9	—	—	1.3
Volunteer	0.2	0.2	0.3	0.4	0.2	0.2
Total***	1.5	2.0	3.2	2.6	2.4	4.8

Notes: * Includes cohabitors
     ** Includes gardening/ground maintenance, pet care, paying bills
     *** Totals may not add due to rounding

Source: Adapted from Frederick, 1995: 24.

Table 6.12 presents findings from the 1992 General Social Survey on Time Use (Frederick, 1995). Data were collected over the course of that year from telephone interviews of a representative sample of 9000 Canadians aged 15 and over. Each respondent provided detailed information accounting for all time spent in the previous 24 hours. Generally, the data contained in Table 6.12 illustrate significant differences between men and women regarding the actual amount of time they devote to unpaid labour. The greatest similarity is found in volunteer work, while men's hours exceed those of women's in the area of maintenance and repairs. In all other areas, women devote more hours to housework activities than do men. Notice how the data regarding "housekeeping" suggest support for our popular stereotypes about the comparative neatness and order of single women's versus single men's households.

Placing the general daily findings into a long-term perspective, the gap in total hours between married fathers and mothers of 1.7 hours a day (total unpaid hours minus "volunteer" time) would, assuming the gap remained constant over time, yield a difference of 620.5 hours a year. This would mean that Canadian mothers between the ages of 25 and 44 work the equivalent of an *additional* 25.9 full 24-hour days per year doing housework than do Canadian fathers of the same age. At first glance, it would be tempting to suggest that these findings are just a few days short of Hochschild's claim (1990:3) that American women work an *"extra month of twenty-four-hour days a year"* (emphasis in original). However, Hochschild's conclusion is based upon the findings of several studies from the 1960s and 1970s that combine paid and unpaid work hours of men and women. If we examine the total hours-per-day expenditure on paid and unpaid labour for full-time employed Canadian mothers and fathers between the ages of 25 and 44, the closest equivalent to the American analysis, we find that the gap is 0.4 hours, or 24 minutes per day (10.3 hours for women; 9.9 hours for men: Frederick, 1995: 22) or the equivalent of 6 extra days per year. While we cannot conclude that Canadian women are hardier or more selfless, or more overworked and oppressed, than American women, we can conclude that significant disparities exist in the Canadian gender distribution of hours devoted to housework alone.

Table 6.13 provides a brief comparative summary of the unpaid labour time-use patterns of husbands and male cohabitors ages 25 to 44, by whether their female partners are employed, either full- or part-time, or are not employed (Frederick, 1995: 28). Findings indicate that male partners of employed women spend about 18 minutes a day *less* on overall unpaid work than do males whose partners are not in the paid-labour force. A further examination of the data finds that men with full-time-employed partners devote significantly more time to the "deadline" (Frederick, 1995: 28) chores associated with cooking (which include cleaning-up after meals), so named because they cannot easily be put off until a later time. It appears that when these men spend more time in the kitchen, they overcompensate for this increased time expenditure by decreasing nonkitchen time to such an extent that their overall time contribution to housework chores becomes less than that of men whose partners are not in the labour force.

Regardless of whether we examine responsibilities or time expenditures, the burdens of household labour fall overwhelmingly upon the shoulders of Canadian women. While the data presented here demonstrate a need for men to increase and redistribute their household participation levels significantly before gender "parity" (Marshall, 1993/1995: 302) is achieved, these findings do not directly address the question: "How much, and where?" Blair and Lichter (1991) apply the **Index of Dissimilarity** to distributions of time men and women devote to the tasks of meal preparation, doing dishes, ironing and washing, house cleaning, outdoor tasks, auto maintenance, managing bills, and grocery shopping. This summary measure indicates the extent to which existing dissimilarities would have to change to achieve an equitable distribution. Data from the 1988 American National Survey of Families and Households indicates that wives devote approximately twice the amount of time (33 hours) to household labour than do their husbands (14 hours). The approximately 40 percent of household time men spend on outdoor tasks (their largest single focal point) and auto maintenance exceeds the combined amount of time they devote to meal preparation, doing dishes, and house cleaning. In contrast, more than two-thirds of women's combined time is spent on meal preparation, cleaning house, and doing dishes, in that order. The only area of equal proportional time sharing lies in the lesser time-consuming task of grocery shopping (but who gets to drive the cart? And while we're on the subject, how come men become the instant experts once the cart arrives at the meat aisle, while women become the experts among the fruits and vegetables? Is this a vestige of the ancient hunting versus foraging and gathering division of labour?).

TABLE 6.13	Average Time Spent on Unpaid Labour by Husbands* Aged 25–44, by Labour Force Status of Wives*, Canada, 1992	
	Unpaid work Hours per day	Cooking Minutes per day
Spouse employed full-time	2.8	28
Spouse employed part-time	2.8	16
Spouse not employed	3.1	16

Note: *Includes cohabitors

Source: Adapted from Frederick, 1995: 28.

The researchers conclude that "the average male would have to reallocate 61% of his family labor to other chores before gender equality was achieved in the percentage distribution of labor time across all domestic tasks" (Blair and Lichter, 1991: 99). Bear in mind that this redistribution does not involve an increase in the absolute amount of time men would devote to household tasks. It pertains only to where men should perform their household labour to create a more equitable distribution of existing proportional time expenditures. Men would be required to shift their investment from the tasks most visible to the neighbours into the less publicly noticeable chores being performed by women within the home.

Shifting men's housework time to include greater participation in chores typically performed by their wives has the pragmatic benefit of increasing wives' sense of fairness about the division of household labour (Benin and Agostinelli, 1988). A husband increasing his participation in "her" tasks is much more impressive to his wife than one increasing his participation in "his" tasks. Devoting time to cleaning the toilet bowl is more likely to increase her feelings of fairness than spending more time on cleaning the sidewalk. Not only does contributing his time to her usual responsibilities lighten her work load, but it also visibly demonstrates caring about those responsibilities. However, his contributions must be *tangible* to increase her sense of fairness about the division within the home. Blair and Johnson (1992: 578) find that employed wives view the division of labour as being less fair if their husbands contribute only a few hours per week to tasks they define as "female." From a wife's perspective, it is apparently better for a husband to contribute nothing at all than to be seen as making only a "token" contribution of one to four hours a week to within-home labour. We shall address the issue of why men resist moving indoors a bit later.

Shifting Responsibilities over Relationship Time

Moving in together in a heterosexual marital or cohabiting relationship appears to promote adoption of a gendered division of household labour. Bridal shower, wedding, and house-warming gifts rarely include executive briefcases and snowblowers for her, and a set of cookware and a subscription to Martha Stewart's *Lifestyle* for him. Regardless of the skills either partner possesses prior to establishing a common household, being the "woman of the house" carries its own gender imperative of primary housework responsibility in a way not found to accompany becoming the "man of the house." According to the logic of our culture, "housework" is to be done by a "housewife," and, therefore, housework is an integral part of the implicit job description of wifework.

While household labour is more equitably "shared" among spouses without children, the arrival of the first child brings about a further noticeable shift in both allocations of time and assignment of responsibilities within the home (Blair and Lichter, 1991: 107; Coltrane and Ishii-Kuntz, 1992: 44; Rexroat and Shehan, 1987). Becoming a mother typically involves more than the assumption of primary responsibilities for childcare and childrearing for most women. It also signals the acquisition of even more time-consuming responsibilities for house care and house rearing. Substantial inequities in housework time and responsibilities continue to exist between husbands and wives until the children leave home when, once again, participation in domestic chores becomes almost as equitably distributed as in the prechild phase of the relationship (Rexroat and Shehan, 1987).

Perhaps not surprisingly, wives' satisfaction with the division of household labour in their homes demonstrates a pronounced U-shaped curve over the marital life course, with the lowest point associated with the presence of preschool age children (Suitor, 1991). While her satisfaction is greatest in the prechild and the postchild stages, his satisfaction remains essentially constant over time and is relatively unaffected with changes in his family's size and composition.

Wives' Changing Strategies

As part of the dynamics of ongoing relationships, marital and cohabitation partners use a variety of techniques, ranging from persuasion and joking, to playing dumb, to intimidation or violence in their attempts to either alter or maintain existing divisions of household labour (Mackie, 1995: 58–61). Overall, Hochschild (1990: 258–259) suggests that women currently adopt three basic strategies over time to deal with their responsibilities. The majority of full-time employed married women with children initially adopt the strategy of attempting to live up to the media-created image of the **supermom**, the woman who can do and be all things for all people. In trying to scale the heights of supermomdom, these employed-married women with children significantly reduce the time they devote to leisure activities such as gardening, visiting with friends and relatives, watching television, eating, sleeping, and, perhaps most frequently, time for oneself. "Nearly 50% of full-time employed [Canadian] boomer mothers reported they would like to spend more time alone. The proportion for men never rises much above 25%" (Frederick, 1995: 58). Since husbands do not reduce their time expenditures in these areas in any significant amounts, the result is a substantial gender **leisure gap** (Hochschild, 1990: 4). Supermoms are often depicted as if they were born with the personal attributes of boundless energy and enthusiasm, an innate sense of good time management, and a heartfelt desire to "have it all" in the realms of paid employment, marriage, motherhood, and homemaking (Nelton and Berney, 1987). Little thought is given to the possibility that supermoming is a forced adaptation to a highly demanding set of traditional and modern gender beliefs about what women "should" want in today's society.

Hochschild (1990: 127) suggests that the arrival of a second child provokes a real crisis in the marital division of labour. Supermoms realize that, indeed, they do "have it all"—all of the responsibilities, that is. According to the 1992 General Social Survey, more than 28 percent of Canadian women and slightly less than 16 percent of men in full-time-employed dual-earner relationships feel severely time crunched (Frederick, 1993: 8). Acknowledging that demands exceed available time and energy precipitates selecting from among what are perceived to be a limited number of possible alternatives. *Cutting back at work*, either shifting from full-time to part-time hours or scaling down aspirations and productivity levels, is one strategy adopted where family economics permit. This adaptation to the supermom time crunch demonstrates how family and household responsibilities can constrain women's ability to attain equality in the paid-work force as well as jeopardize their economic futures. Where cutting back at paid work is either not economically feasible or not desirable, and since the frequently uttered lament from women of "I need a wife" is not a viable option, many women reassess their ideal standards, modify them, and then adopt a third strategy of *cutting back on housework, marriage,* and *children*, typically in that order.

Cutting back on marriage is a phenomenon commonly associated with the shift from a marital to a family relationship. Studies in both Canada and the United States typically find that marital satisfaction is lowest during the years when children are present in the home (e.g., Hochschild, 1990: 197; Lupri and Frideres, 1981; Rollins and Cannon, 1974). In large part, the decline in satisfaction is due to spending less time together as a couple, frequently as a consequence of exhausted physical and emotional energy. Cutting back on childcare often involves a reduction in the physical care provided for children in the form of, for example, shorter or fewer baths, or changing and washing clothing apparel less often. The strategy may also take the form of reduced time spent with children or less attention paid to meeting children's emotional needs (Hochschild, 1990: 197–198). The shift of focus in parenting from quantity time to *quality time* in part reflects adaptive strategies to the time crunch phenomenon experienced by Canadians over the past few decades.

The most frequently adopted strategy, cutting back on household labour usually takes the form of lowering standards (such as dusting and washing floors less frequently), buying help (housekeeping services, sending laundry to the cleaners), or obtaining assistance from family, friends, or neighbours (particularly regarding looking after children, although small-scale cooking communes are becoming popular in the mid-1990s). Couples are rewriting the Canadian *Food Guide* to include five new basic food groups: take-out; delivery; frozen; meals-in-a-cup or pouch; and eating out. Coltrane and Ishii-Kuntz (1992: 54) suggest that a wife's willingness to lower her standards for house cleaning or to cut back on housework hours is influenced by how long she delays childbearing. Rather than moving directly from being someone's daughter to being someone's mother, postponing childbearing allows a woman to establish a more independent, usually work-related, identity. Less likely to derive her sense of identity and self-worth from being a wife and homemaker, these women are also less likely to view an immaculate house as a reflection of their essential femininity. While acknowledging that Coltrane and Ishii-Kuntz (1992) might be correct, Pittman and Blanchard (1996) argue that the more relevant fact explaining the lesser housework participation of women who delay childbearing is attributable mainly to their fewer number of children on average and, subsequently, the lesser amount of housework to be done.

When married or cohabiting mothers cut back on housework, the resulting household labour gap is not filled by married or cohabiting fathers or by children. Rather than picking up the housework slack, many men appear to feel that their main contribution will be to "suffer" more or less silently (at least while they are at home). Demo and Acock (1993: 328) find that all mothers in the paid-labour force for at least 30 hours per week, regardless of whether they are in first or subsequent marriages, divorced, or never-married, devote significantly less time to housework per week than do mothers not in the labour force. Furthermore, even though children of divorced mothers participate more in household labour than do children in other types of families, particularly in comparison to children in first-marriage families, children still contribute only a minimal fraction of the time required to run a household.

In terms of children's contributions, age is not a factor (Demo and Acock, 1993: 327), but gender is. Goldscheider and Waite (1991) find an inverse relationship between the housework contributions of fathers and children. The less fathers do, the more children do, and vice versa. Berk (1985) notes that daughters are more likely to do assigned housework duties than are sons and, even when both sons and daughters do housework, daughters do more. Not only do daughters generally do more than sons, but the differences are most noticeable in families where both parents are employed full-time (Benin and Edwards, 1990), raising questions about dual-earner families being potential training grounds for future egalitarian gender relations.

When employed mothers adopt the strategy of cutting back, they perform less housework overall than do nonemployed mothers and the amount of overall time a dual-earner family devotes to housework is thereby reduced. As the proportional contribution to housework of wives and mothers lessens, the proportional contribution of husbands and fathers *appears* to increase significantly, even when men's actual housework participation remains constant or increases only marginally. Changes in *proportional measures* misleadingly attributed to significant increases in men's participation may only reflect significant decreases in women's contributions (Pleck, 1985, 1979). Consequently, the use of proportional measures by researchers can foster a false impression of egalitarianism. In terms of general social trends, we have seen that the *trend towards convergence* in paid-labour participation levels is due primarily to an increase in women's economic behaviour. Conversely, the trend towards convergence in unpaid labour distributions is due primarily to a decrease in women's housework behaviour. In both cases, the most significant agents of change are women, not men.

Why Don't Men Do More?

As we have noted, about 10 percent of Canadian men in dual-earner relationships have primary responsibility for household tasks, and an additional 10 percent fully share responsibilities with their spouses (Marshall, 1993/1995). Husbands of full-time employed wives do not participate more in housework than do husbands of nonemployed wives (Fox and Nickols, 1983; Frederick, 1995). Illustrating the uneven progress of change in gender behaviour, Canadians and Americans today generally accept women's right to expand their domain to encompass paid employment, but, despite their lip-service support of "sharing" in response to public opinion pollsters (Willinger, 1993: 127), are still more reticent in supporting men's right to expand their domain to include meaningful involvement in housework (Meissner, 1985). A number of social structural and social-psychological reasons have been offered on why men in general resist increasing their participation in household labour (e.g., Gilbert, 1985; Goode, 1982/1995).

For example, men do not receive sufficient social and public support for significantly expanding their domestic skill levels or for using those skills within the home. Even though many wives privately engage in bragging contests over whose husband "helps out" the most, the primary purpose of such contests lies in determining which wife is the "luckiest," not in distributing public accolades to men. Husbands and wives are more likely to "collude" in creating an atmosphere to support men's justifications for their lack of participation in housework (Thompson, 1991) such as "he works hard at his job, he was not brought up to do housework, [or] his standards for cleanliness are low" (Thompson and Walker, 1995: 850).

Domestic skills are not considered within our historical legends to be part of men's intrinsic "nature," nor are these instrumental skills positively attributed to any masculine "labour of love." Within the military, assignments to kitchen patrol (KP) or cleaning lavatories are intended as punishments and are designed to demean a military man's self-concept. For the most part, **Father's Day** still celebrates men's provider role, their skill with a lawn mower and screwdriver, and perhaps even their visible presence along the sidelines at their children's sporting and recital events, but not their tireless work with a vacuum and a spatula. In comparison to wives, husbands obtain little moral support or logistical help from their peer networks for help with childcare and housework tasks (Lein, 1979). Wives can and do call upon neighbours, families, and friends for physical and emotional help and advice. In conformity with the masculine theme of independence, husbands are less likely to willingly admit to their peers that they need help in selecting a fabric softener or floor-cleaning product (despite the "brotherhood" appeal of *Mr.* Clean). Furthermore, should they be willing to ask for moral support or task advice, they are unlikely to be positively rewarded in their search for laundry tips from their friends gathered around the water cooler, in the locker room, or on a "Wild Man" weekend retreat. As well, publishers are not lining up to print "how-to" books containing tips for superhousedads.

Men are also unlikely to perceive any positive intrinsic personal gain from increasing their participation in household tasks. By being placed outside of the market economy, housework is denied equivalence with paid work. A houseworker can not easily measure his or her worth by the size of a lovecheque. A desired, yet rarely attained, outcome for substantial numbers of women saddled with the major responsibility for housework would be to receive "gratitude" (Hochschild, 1990: 205–206) or "appreciation" (Thompson, 1991; Thompson and Walker, 1995: 850) from their spouses and children. Domestic-labour studies report that women typically feel negative, or at best ambivalent, about housework (e.g., Oakely, 1974). Not only is housework unappealing, but it has long been socially trivialized as "women's work," thereby devaluing both the work and the worker. Despite attempts to elevate the prestige of houseworkers through the invention of linguistic devices such as "professional homemaker" and "domestic engineer," the lingering image of being "just" a housewife and stay-at-home mom remains. Even though the "job" of houseworker may provide some economic fringe benefits (at the discretion of the provider), emotional satisfactions, and yearly platitudes of public recognition (a **Mother's Day**, but no **Homemaker's Day**), it also carries the liabilities of "no job security, no retirement, and no pension" (Wilson, 1991: 57). Consequently, most men feel their own worth will be diminished, not enhanced, if they participate more in housework. As a result, men have little incentive to increase their participation.

Hochschild (1990: 215), while acknowledging that housework has been devalued historically, suggests that "one way to reverse this devaluation is for men to share in that devalued work, and thereby help to revalue it." This suggestion leads to an intriguing question. If men were to increase their housework participation levels significantly, what would change: the prestige of the men themselves (down) or the prestige of the work itself (up)? Within a patriarchal culture, one could expect that the prestige value of the work should increase, gaining from a spillover effect attributed to the sex of the worker. However, since we currently live within a cultural transition period, where behaviours anointed with the label of "men's work" are no longer automatically accorded higher prestige, the outcome is far from clear.

When men, due either to choice or necessity, take on the tasks typically associated with a wife, the social response received by these men is rarely positive (Rosenwasser et al., 1985). These researchers find that students notably devalue the "housewife" role when it is performed by men. Lutwin and Siperstein (1985), in their research on "househusbands," find that these men, the majority of whom are white, middle-class, managers/professionals who left the paid-labour force after becoming disabled or being fired, become more appreciative of their families, the *work* formerly performed by their spouses, and of their former jobs. The men who best adjust to a househusband role are those who become househusbands voluntarily, are committed to an alternative lifestyle, have firm plans for the future (i.e., househusbanding is a temporary role), do not experience any stress from boredom or alienation, and receive support for their role from both friends and extended family members (see also Beer, 1983).

Our cultural beliefs about gender attempt to justify different priority agendas for men and women in relation to paid work relative to unpaid housework. These same beliefs also contribute to the development of structural conditions within the public paid-work world that serve as barriers to further limit men's participation within the supposedly private world of the home. Success in advancing up the professional career ladder, based upon a traditional model established for and by men, is predicated upon the requirement of working long, uninterrupted, hours to such an extent that little time or energy is left over for anything else except recuperative leisure activities. The demands of professional occupations are viewed by their practitioners as being structurally incompatible with anything beyond minimal involvement in family tasks. No rewards are offered to male workers for taking unpaid or even paid paternity leave, or for rearranging their work schedules to accommodate childcare and homecare responsibilities. Neither government nor major corporations appear to be willing to institutionalize a "daddy track." Perhaps for many of the reasons mentioned above (e.g., loss of prestige or lack of public reward), the men who control and shape business and government policy, and occupational models for success, have been unwilling to alter the paid-work world to remove obstacles preventing greater accommodation to the necessary demands of house and childcare. These changes could facilitate significantly greater involvement of men within the household.

Explanatory Models for Housework Participation

Three major models have been offered as partial explanations for the current gendered division of labour in the household: **time availability**, **resource power**, and **gender ideology**. All of these models argue that factors existing outside of the home account for the dynamics of work done inside the home. While we have already woven elements of these three models into our housework presentation thus far, it is worthwhile to consider each model separately and explicitly. Before proceeding further, it is important to note that empirical research exists in support of each model (Blair and Lichter, 1991; Coltrane and Ishii-Kuntz, 1992; Ferree, 1991; Harrell, 1985; Thompson and Walker, 1989). To simplify matters, we suggest that you consider gender ideology as providing the general cultural setting within which operate each of the factors identified by the other models. A more comprehensive model will be created eventually that integrates elements from the more limited models and explains how the division of labour within households is the product of a complex interacting set of factors.

Time Availability Model

This model focuses upon structural or situational constraints. One explanation for the unequal distribution of household labour focuses upon which partner has more, or less, time available to perform the necessary tasks. Some researchers (e.g., Coverman and Sheley, 1986; Kamo, 1988) claim that husbands' involvement in housework is determined not by their type of job or by their levels of education and income, but by the number of hours they devote to paid employment. As we saw in the previous section, this argument suggests that, ignoring shift work, men's work schedules are generally not conducive to extensive participation in household labour. "Husbands, rather than wives in dual-career families, work on weekends more often, start their jobs earlier and end them later on the average work day, work more hours and more days per week, and more often hold second jobs" (Mandell, 1989: 244). This same line of argument is applied to explain women's participation in the household since, "the more time Canadian women spend in market work as compared to their husbands, the smaller their share of housekeeping tasks" (Brayfield, 1992: 28).

One problem with the time availability, or lack thereof, model is that it introduces a chicken-and-egg, cause-effect conundrum. Do husbands do less housework because they have less available time, while wives do more housework because they have more time available for household chores? Or, do wives make more time available because they have greater responsibilities for household duties, while husbands devote more hours to paid employment because they do not have, or do not want to have, as much responsibility for household labour? In addition to this conundrum, the time availability model in itself does not easily explain the existing segregation of household tasks documented in many studies. While the model may partially explain men's tendency to select tasks that require less time and permit greater control over their scheduling, the model cannot explain why women have the responsibility for so many chores that they are significantly more likely to feel time crunched. As well, if time availability were a sufficient explanatory model, unemployed men would perform more than an equal share of household tasks. As we shall see later, such is not the case. Clearly, time availability provides only a partial explanation and additional factors must be explored.

Resource Model

This model argues that who does what around the home, and how much, is determined in an inverse fashion by the amount of power possessed by each partner in a relationship: the greater the power, the lesser the amount of housework performed. Power, according to the model, is determined primarily by the economic resources a marital or cohabitation partner brings into the relationship (Blood and Wolfe, 1961). Although many studies have confirmed a general relationship between power resources and housework participation levels (e.g., Blair and Lichter, 1991; Blumstein and Schwartz, 1983; Brayfield, 1992; Coltrane and Ishii-Kuntz, 1992; Marshall, 1993/1995; Pittman and Blanchard, 1996), specific findings are somewhat inconsistent, ambiguous and, at times, difficult to interpret.

The difficulties in achieving a coherent synthesis of research findings are partly attributable to methodological variations across studies. The resources examined most frequently are either employment status (nonemployed versus employed full- or part-time) or the correlates of employment, such as income earned and/or educational level attained. These correlates are sometimes measured in absolute terms and sometimes in relative terms as a proportional difference between the partners. Some studies focus solely upon the impact of an individual's resources upon his or her own housework participation levels, but other studies focus upon the impact of one person's resources on another person's housework performance.

In terms of the latter, Blair and Lichter claim that wives with greater resources are "better able to 'extract' labor from their husbands as well as influence the types of family work these men do" (1991: 94). In contrast, two Canadian studies (Frederick, 1995; Meissner et al., 1975) find that wives' employment has no effect upon husbands' allotment of time devoted to housework. While one could initially suggest that being employed is not a sufficiently powerful resource in itself to influence or "extract" increased husband's behaviour, Marshall's (1993/1995) finding that employed full-time wives have less sole responsibility for housework, while their husbands tend to share responsibilities more (see Table 6.11) suggests that her employment influences his proportional responsibility within the household. While some of the inconsistencies in these findings may be attributable to differences between studies that simply observe an increase in men's contributions in contrast to studies that claim these increases are not of a significant nature, clearly more research is needed to specify the influence of one person's resources upon the behaviour of another person. Even though the influence of one's own resources upon another person's behaviour is somewhat uncertain, increased resource power appears to result in a decrease of one's own participation in housework. Canadian data indicate that a wife's sole responsibility for housework, and a husband's "propensity for doing housework," both decline as each individual's income level increases (Marshall, 1993/1995: 305). Absolute income appears to be a resource that permits "'buying out' of household tasks" (Brayfield, 1992: 28) in the form of reducing one's own participation levels, hiring someone else to perform certain tasks, or both.

Marshall (1993/1995: 306) notes that women with higher educational levels are less likely to have sole responsibility for household tasks, while husbands with higher educational levels are more likely to share responsibilities, a conclusion that essentially states the same thing in two different ways. The higher the educational level attained, the greater the sharing of household responsibilities. Marshall attributes these findings to higher education producing less of an income differential between spouses, despite the fact that no income differential measure is included in her data base. It could be argued that education is more likely to influence ideological beliefs about gender in general and about housework in particular, but these beliefs are not part of the resource power model.

Noticeable disparities between spouses in their income levels appear to influence housework differently for men and women. Canadian data indicate that a large income gap in favour of a working wife has no effect upon significantly reducing her share of participation in household tasks, regardless of the couple's income level, while an equally large income gap in his favour reduces a husband's share of task participation among low-income, but not high-income, couples (Brayfield, 1992: 25–26). Income differentials appear to interact with other factors, perhaps gender ideologies, influencing a couple's decision-making processes about housework participation levels.

We have seen that research provides at least partial, but not consistent, support for the influence of resource power upon the distribution of household labour. Part of the lack of consistency may be attributable to researchers not carefully controlling for the impact of resources at different stages of relationship development. Based upon their own findings, Coltrane and Ishii-Kuntz (1992: 54) suggest that wives' income resources may exert a greater influence early in a family's development when family income levels are generally low, and her proportional contribution is comparatively high. Her income resources may not exert as significant an influence over the division of labour later in a couple's relationship, when her proportional economic contribution is comparatively less.

While the general pattern of gendered income inequality outside of the home may account for the general pattern of gendered housework inequality inside of the home, we must bear in mind that almost all of the existing research has been conducted on heterosexual couples. The motto of "whoever brings home the most bacon doesn't have to cook it" (Brayfield, 1992: 20) appears to be equally applicable to gay couple relationships, but not to lesbian couple relationships (Blumstein and Schwartz, 1983: 53–61, 151). Blumstein and Schwartz suggest that what we have referred to here as a resource power model is male created and supported by heterosexual males, gay males, and by most heterosexual females as well. In contrast, lesbian couples make a successful concerted effort to ensure that the economic values of the market place equating worth with income do not intrude into the equitable context of their home place. This finding indicates that application of the logic underlying a resource model is not inevitable and is subject to subcultural modification or even neutralization.

Male cohabitation partners and husbands who control a greater share of resources and who, given the operating of the mating gradient to be discussed in the next chapter, are often selected as mates for just that reason, also perform a significantly lesser share of labour within the home. Despite making significant gains in the world of paid work, women have generally been unable to translate those economic gains into an equitable division of household labour. As we have seen, instead of husbands volunteering to take over more responsibility for and substantially increasing their hours devoted to housework, wives typically find themselves scaling back their own participation levels. Hochschild (1990: 244–253) suggests that wage or income inequality and a fear of divorce are two factors constraining women from pushing for more help around the home from their husbands. Both of these factors suggest that, from an economic point of view, women generally need marriage more than do men and further suggest that, lacking an equal resource power base, women are generally unable or unwilling to exert sufficient leverage upon their male partners to establish an equitable sharing in household labour.

One of the limitations of resource theory is that it ignores the fact that resources obtained by husbands and wives are themselves a function of a more fundamental power imbalance; namely, the imbalance attributable to being born either male or female within our society (Lero, 1996: 42). Among her admittedly small sample of 50 couples, Hochschild (1990: 218) could not find a single male earning less than his wife who performed any housework. She suggests that a principle of "balancing" operates in which men who lose power over women in one area make up for it in another way (Hochschild, 1990: 221). Men who earn much more than their wives already have power and need not attempt to make up for power lost elsewhere. They are, therefore, more willing to contribute to housework. However, the more a man's sense of power is threatened by his wife's greater financial power, the less he can afford to have his basic power base further threatened by doing what has traditionally been defined as "women's work." That basic power base is founded not upon control of economic resources *per se*, but rather upon being a male in a patriarchal society. According to Hochschild, in asserting their male power in the form of refusing to do housework, these men balance their relative lack of financially based power.

While Hochschild's "balance" hypothesis is founded primarily upon resource theory, it blends in features of existing gender ideologies with its reference to the distinction between "women's" and "men's work," and the anchoring of men's power within a patriarchal base. The impact of these ideologies will be described in more detail in the next section, but some aspects can be noted here. The "balance" hypothesis is compatible with the notion that, with the division of gendered spheres, housework among other activities comes to serve an important function as a "gender boundary" (Gerson and Peiss, 1985). Housework may become a more important gender boundary as the "provider" boundary becomes increasingly blurred. Men who feel they are losing some gender distinctiveness by no longer being either the sole or the primary provider may draw the boundary line of housework even more firmly to maintain their sense of masculinity. In other words, having lost some "gender points" by no longer being providers, they attempt to ensure they will not lose further points by crossing another important boundary and doing a greater share of housework.

The "balance" or "boundary" hypothesis may help to explain why unemployed Canadian husbands of employed wives, while contributing more than employed men, still perform only 40 percent of the household tasks traditionally assigned to women (Brayfield, 1992: 29). Men's perceptions of powerfulness and powerlessness, based not just in economics, but also in a sense of maleness reinforced by maintaining the gender boundary properties of housework, appear to be important variables mediating the extent of their housework participation. However, attempts to maintain gender boundaries within the home are not all one-sided. Mederer (1993: 143) notes that, while women may feel the allocation of housework tasks and the responsibility for those tasks is unfair, they are more likely to demand a redistribution of tasks than management responsibility. Mederer (1993: 143) also suggests that household and family management is a firmly "embedded" element of women's gender definition and furthermore that women resist sharing management responsibilities for fear of losing an important source of power. Based upon our culture's beliefs about gender, housework, therefore, becomes an important contributing factor in the construction of gender. These beliefs about whether housework is gender appropriate or inappropriate labour are part of the third model that has been used to explain housework distributions.

Gender Ideology

Two ideal-typical gender ideologies currently dominate Canadian society today: the **traditional** and the **egalitarian**. The traditional belief system, carrying with it the weight of an established history, divides the social world into two separate and distinct spheres of "men's work" and "women's work," whose boundaries are circumscribed largely by the walls of the family home. Each sex is then assigned to his or her area of supposed expertise. For women, "[i]t starts when you sink into his arms and ends with your arms in his sink" (Jackson and Scott, 1996: 13). Despite the functionalist theory claim (Parsons and Bales, 1955) that husbands and wives coexist in equal and complementary worlds, our society has granted considerably more power and privilege to men's instrumental work as breadwinners than to women's work as homemakers. By redefining essentially instrumental activities as services willingly performed out of love to meet the needs of others, and by placing those activities outside of the crass commercialism of the market economy, housework becomes expressive activities within both the functionalist and our traditional societally endorsed belief paradigms. One consequence of a traditional ideology is that, "it seems more acceptable to do without certain amounts of kinds of unpaid labor than to have it done by the person of the 'wrong' gender" (Ferree, 1990: 876).

The more recently developed **egalitarian** ideology, born of the 1960s and 1970s, but with roots in earlier historical periods, claims that paid and unpaid work assignments inside and outside of the home should be determined not by sex or gender, but rather by "desirability, availability, capability, and turntaking" (Mandell, 1989: 239). Following the principle of equity, responsibilities for work and family management, income provision, domestic chores, childcare, and emotional intimacy are to be equally divided between the genders. The emotional interdependence of a heterosexual couple is expected to support and promote flexibility and sharing. While the traditional ideology maintains (despite all evidence to the contrary) that the spheres of men and women are separate, but equal, the egalitarian ideology maintains that the domains of men and women are integrated and equitable. Within the latter ideology, the concepts of gendered "domains" or "spheres" are rendered meaningless and nonexistent.

Mandell (1989: 241) argues that "most Canadian marriages do not fit neatly into either the traditional or the egalitarian model." Instead, she suggests that marriages, and presumably cohabiting relationships, in Canada could best be characterized as either **neotraditional** or **pseudoegalitarian**. These terms, similar to Hochschild's (1990: 15) **transitional** ideology, characterize most relationships as still being essentially asymmetrical and male dominated, where his work status and patterns dictate the pace and rhythm of couple and family life, and his perceptions of himself as primarily a breadwinner and his wife as primarily a homemaker still prevail despite any proclamations of equity or objective evidence to the contrary (see Livingstone and Luxton, 1989/1995). In other words, we are currently somewhere in between the positions depicted by the two dominant gender ideologies.

Weiss (1990) identifies three principles that shape men's involvement in housework. The **traditional principle** (Weiss, 1990: 121) divides household chores into "men's work" and "women's work" and essentially proscribes men's involvement within the home except for maintenance and repair tasks. The traditional principle has been augmented recently by **the principle of helping out** (Weiss, 1990: 122). According to this principle, a husband should be willing to participate in some daily household activities to "help out" his wife if needed. The principle of helping out reinforces the traditional principle, since it does not alter the fundamental allocation of gender responsibilities. "Helping out" does not mean assuming a partner's primary responsibility for a task. A direct challenge to these principles is posed by the most recently developed **principle of equity** (Weiss, 1990: 122) which proclaims that all of the work of a marriage and family, both inside and outside of the home, is to be divided fairly and evenly between spouses and cohabiting partners. Characterizing our current condition as "neotraditional," "pseudoegalitarian," or "transitional," as we did in the previous paragraph, would appear equivalent to suggesting a shift from the "traditional principle" to the "principle of helping out," with the "principle of equity" as yet unattained. All of the various authors we have just reviewed appear to characterize the same condition with different names.

The lingering effect of tradition and helping out not only aids us in understanding why men are slow to increase their participation within the household, but also why Marshall (1993/1995: 306) finds that 75 percent of Canadian dual-earner wives who have sole responsibility for almost all housework are satisfied with their arrangements, or why Demo and Acock (1993: 328) find that American "mothers typically respond that the work is 'fair to both.'" Older, lesser educated, and lower-income couples are more likely to endorse a traditional helping out ideology. Despite any aggravations experienced by an inequitable arrangement, conforming to a comfortable set of traditional expectations can produce an overall sense of satisfaction. Support for a truly egalitarian ideology is most likely to come from "younger, better educated, and employed women" (Mandell, 1989: 243). As well, men with higher educations are likely to endorse a more equitable arrangement. Coltrane and Ishii-Kuntz (1992: 54–55) find that husbands' ideology plays a greater role in creating a more equitable division of labour among those couples who have their first child later in life and who have higher incomes and higher educations.

To the extent that the inequitable distribution of housework found within most Canadian families is considered to be a social and not just an individual couple problem, solutions will have to take many factors into account, including the distribution of available time, the balance of power between men and women, and the underlying ideologies surrounding the concepts of "women's" and "men's" work. To avoid the time crunch currently experienced by supermoms and superdads, these solutions will have to be sought not only within the private sphere of the household, but also within the public sphere of paid work.

Brayfield (1992) finds that French-Canadian couples tend to allocate housework more equitably than do either English-Canadian or recently arrived nonFrench, nonEnglish, immigrant couples. The differences exist independent of employment patterns and family characteristics. Francophone women's groups since the time of the Quiet Revolution of the 1960s (Krull, 1996; Burt, 1986) have focused upon implementing changes in both public and private spheres simultaneously, while anglophone groups have tended historically to focus more upon the public sphere of equality of economic opportunities. As we noted at the beginning of this section, only recently have anglophone feminists acknowledged that housework itself and the nexus between the private world of housework and the public world of paid work hold the key for producing a more equitable division of labour between women and men in our society.

INTIMATE RELATIONS

FRIENDSHIP

Rubin (1985: 59) notes that friendships between men have traditionally been offered as our societal model for what friendship is and ought to be. Male bonding has been placed on a social pedestal and extolled as a necessary precondition for individual and social survival (e.g., Tiger, 1969). Current laments about men's inability to sustain emotionally rich relationships with other men (e.g., Farrell, 1974; Levinson et al., 1978; Pittman, 1993; Pleck, 1981) reflect more modern times and more modern concerns. In contrast, women's same-sex friendships have tended to be ignored, except perhaps by historians of the nineteenth century (e.g., Smith-Rosenberg, 1975). Theorists now debate whether "romantic friendships" of women in the nineteenth and early twentieth centuries can or cannot be classified as lesbian relationships (see Martindale, 1995: 69–72 for an overview and see Rotundo, 1993, for romantic friendships among men). Only recently, due in large part to the influence of cultural feminists, have women's same-sex friendships been extolled as an ideal relationship form.

We noted in Chapter 4 that girls' friendship networks tend to be less extensive, but more intensive than boys'. This pattern carries through into adolescence and adulthood. Partly as a consequence of their use of more selective criteria for defining friendship (Rubin, 1985: 61), women usually name fewer people among their list of friends than do men. Men, in contrast, tend to have different friends with whom they pursue different activities, and the basis for these friendships tends to be more restrictive in scope than are the friendships of women (Buhrke and Fuqua, 1987). For example, Wright and Scanlon (1991) observe that men's friendships generally revolve around some type of specific and limited sphere of interaction; a man's "drinking buddies" may be distinct from the "guys" he plays basketball with on Tuesday nights, or those he "crams with" for an examination. Generally, the basis for and the content of same-sex friendships appear to be different for each gender. Similar to patterns formed in adolescence, adult "women's friendships are based primarily on emotional sharing and men's friendships on engaging in common activities" (Brehm, 1992: 365). All friendships probably contain elements of both, but women and men tend to stress different features (Duck and Wright, 1993; Jones, 1991; Monsour, 1992; Sherrod, 1989).

Women are more likely to spend time with a friend talking about themselves, their feelings for each other, and about other people (Aries and Johnson, 1983; Aukett et al., 1988; Caldwell and Peplau, 1982). These discussions can comprise either "deep talk" (focusing upon powerful feelings and worries) or "small talk" (focusing upon daily life events) or both (Tavris, 1992: 252). Rubin (1985: 61) argues that women's same-sex friendships rest upon "shared intimacies, self-revelation, nurturance and emotional support." Similarly, Becker (1987: 65) suggests that women's friendships can be seen as an "evolving dialogue" in which "each woman brings important parts of her life into the friendship, [and] a world of shared meanings and understanding is created." Wright (1982) characterizes women's friendships as being more "face-to-face," while men's tend to be "side-to-side." The latter phrase captures the fact that only rarely do men engage in deep talk with one another (see also Becker, 1987; Paul and White, 1990; Riessman, 1990; Wright and Scanlon, 1991).

The basic gender difference appears to centre primarily upon different levels of self-disclosure typically occuring among same-sex friends. Women tend to be more self-disclosing with other women than men are with other men. Both women and men are more comfortable confiding in a woman than in a man (Buhrke and Fuqua, 1987). Wright and Scanlon (1991) note that friendships among women are likely to have considerable breadth of knowledge, with women inviting each other to learn, in detail, of the many and varied aspects of their lives. In contrast, shared activities, and particularly sports, rather than verbal intimacies, are likely to form the centre of men's friendships (Duck, 1988; Monsour, 1992; Paul and White, 1990; Riessman, 1990; Wood and Inman, 1993). Swain (1989) suggests that male friendships are based on "closeness in the doing." In his study, more than two-thirds of his male respondents reported that the most meaningful times spent with friends were occupied with activities other than talking. Moveover, Swain proposes that men's friendships emphasize a reciprocal giving and receiving of help, assistance, and expertise. He contends that the bond that grows out of shared activities provides men with an alternative path to closeness, and concludes that men's friendships are as intimate as women's, even though "men generally do not express intimacy through self-disclosure" (p. 168).

In part, this difference is a function of the internalized injunction for emotional control boys and adolescent men receive as part of their early socialization (Rubin, 1980; Udry, 1971). Men, consequently, tend to downplay in public the importance of emotions in their friendships with other men. When confronted with a troubled friend, men are more likely to provide him with an opportunity for a diversionary activity rather than a shoulder to cry on or an ear to bend. Riessman (1990) suggests this preferred technique may be more effective in relieving men's stress and more promotive of close feeling between men than simply talking about the problem. Rohlfing (1995) argues that the instrumental, activity-based emphasis within male friendships explains why women's friendships are more likely to survive barriers of geographic distance while men's friendships tend to dissolve. Even though disclosures may continue via the mail, telephone lines, and e-mail communications, "[i]t's more difficult to shoot hoops or go to concerts with someone who lives miles away" (Wood, 1997: 225). Part of the message and the current appeal of the mythopoetic movement (see Chapter 3), lies in its emphasis upon breaking down the emotional barriers that characterize men's interpersonal relationships with one another. "Warrior Weekends" not only provide participants with opportunities to share their feelings directly with other men about past and present same-sex relationships, but also give men permission to acknowledge publicly that an emotional dimension is an important component of their friendships.

Since research indicates that the apparent gender difference in importance of self-disclosure and emotionality may be as much a function of social expectations as of the content of gender friendships themselves. Reis et al. (1985), in a series of studies, conclude that men are as capable as women of forming intimate friendships with men, but that men choose not to relax their learned social expectations and inhibitions. Our homophobic social climate pressures men to either de-emphasize or to disguise the emotional component, lest they raise the spectre of homosexual attachment, and instead emphasize the more superficial, but also valued, activities they share in common with close male friends (Lehne, 1976). Joking, teasing, laughing at one another, and mock acts of aggression (Swain, 1989) become means of expressing affection according to the male subculture. For explicit verbal and emotional intimacy, especially during times of interpersonal crisis, men most often turn to the women in their lives (Rubin, 1985: 74, 78), if they turn to anyone at all.

Rubin (1985: 62–64, 170), finds that more than three-quarters of her adult working-, middle-, and upper-middle-class sample of single women (regardless of whether they were straight or lesbian) between the ages of 25 and 55 had no difficulty in identifying a best friend, almost always another women. More than two-thirds of a similarly aged sample of single men (straight and gay) could not name a best friend, and those who did most often named a woman. "About two-thirds of the women who were named by a man as a close friend disavowed that definition of the relationship" (Rubin, 1985: 159), indicating once again that women tend to be more selective in their definitions of friends and friendship. While almost all of the single women who could not name a best friend characterized this condition as indicative of something missing in their lives, very few of the men identified this absence as being regretable.

Davis (1985) reports that when asked the gender of their best friend, and explicitly asked to exclude those with whom they were in a romantic relationship, slightly more than a quarter (27 percent) of respondents identified someone of the other gender. When asked to identify the gender of their close friends, more than half of the males sampled (56 percent) and 44 percent of the female respondents identified at least one person of the other sex (Davis, 1985: 26). Evidence suggests that cross-gender friendships are less intimate and stable and offer less emotional support than do same-gender friendships (Wright and Scanlon, 1991; Rawlins, 1993). West et al. (1996) suggest that, although cross-gender friendships can be rewarding in many ways, obstacles to their longevity include negotiating the line between a platonic and a romantic relationship (see also Ambrose, 1989; Bingham, 1996; Johnson, Stockdale and Saul, 1991). Gender socialization patterns with peers, from childhood through adolescence, reinforce the likelihood that same-sex friends will be more enduring than cross-gender friendships (Leaper, 1994). Despite the difficulties posed by cross-gender friendships, benefits can be obtained. West et al. (1996: 123–124) report that cross-gender friendships provide each member insight into the psychological and social orientations of the other gender and often offer an "insider's perspective" on how to deal with dating partners.

They additionally suggest that women in cross-gender friendships are able to provide their male friends with emotional and expressive support, while men are able to provide their women friends with the companionship developed through shared activities.

Married men in Rubin's (1985) sample were even less likely than single men to be able to name a best friend and, when they did, they most often named their wives. In contrast, regardless of whether or not they were employed outside of the home or whether or not they had primary childrearing responsibilities, married women in her sample had no difficulties naming one or more best friends, and rarely named their husbands among them. Rubin (1985: 60) concludes that women are more likely to "make time" for the creation and maintenance of friendships than are men, in large part because women rate friendship more highly than do men.

Reissman (1990) suggests that marriage, for most women, is considered to be just one of their close relationship ties. In contrast, most men consider marriage to be an exclusive primary relationship with someone who is both a mate and a best friend combined into one person. These findings could account for the difficulties most married men appear to have in naming someone other than their wives as being their best friend. Johnson and Aries (1983) find half the wives in their sample acknowledging they value their friendships with other women because they can talk to these women friends in ways they cannot with their husbands. In a similar vein, Rubin (1985: 140) notes that women value their conversations with women friends precisely because of a lack of verbal involvement with the men in their lives who seem to prefer "for her to come sit by me, nice and quiet." Such a preference by men reminds us why a dog is often referred to as "man's best friend."

A number of observers (e.g., Rubin, 1983: 70; Tavris, 1992: 252) note that when men talk to other men, or to women, they tend to either discuss relatively impersonal topics such as work, sports, community or world events, or to intellectualize their feelings ("Like most people, I think I feel…" rather than "I feel…") about themselves, as if the purpose of the discussion was to analyze and to solve the issues or problems at hand. This problem-solving orientation of men (Gilligan, 1982; Farrell, 1986: 305) tends not to be congruent with women's preferences for simply sharing problems, without necessarily worrying about solutions (Tavris, 1992: 252–253). Levinson (1996: 42) notes that men are extremely reluctant to talk, especially with a woman, about their experiences of failure, disappointment, anxiety, or confusion, since these all involve feelings on his part that he has somehow failed to live up to the mandates of masculinity in our culture. In a man's mind, opening these topics for discussion could pave the way towards a judgment on the part of his audience that he is somehow less of a man, more "girlish, more babyish" (Tavris, 1992: 267); in other words, a wimp. In light of such an anticipated response, most men prefer not to "share" their innermost thoughts and feelings just for the sake of sharing. For sharing and disclosing intimate thoughts and feelings, most women find they have to turn to their women friends.

HETEROSEXUAL COURTSHIP
AND MATE-SELECTION PRACTICES

Our heterosexual relationship focus here reflects the preponderance of information available at present. Whether these observations and findings can be generalized to the formation of intimate relationships within the gay and lesbian population is unclear at the moment. Because of a tendency of researchers, observers, and participants to focus upon other, more pressing issues within the gay and lesbian communities, we must await further investigation of the nature of their courtship rituals and mate-selection practices. Such investigation will build upon a limited, but potentially insightful, developing research literature (e.g., Wood and Duck, 1995).

During the sixteenth and seventeenth centuries, relationships between family members within the domestic home were most often characterized by "respect, deference, obligation, and fear rather than by sentiment and attachment" (Anderson, 1987: 33). As family and home life became increasingly privatized over the course of the next two centuries, domestic relations came to be characterized more by personal sentiments. Romantic love (to be defined momentarily) slowly became intertwined with marriage. First as a desired outcome of marriage and eventually as a basis for marriage, love became fashionable in Europe and North America during the nineteenth century (Branden, 1980: 42–45; Rotundo, 1993: 110). As part of a growing emphasis upon individualism, older adolescents and young adults began to assert greater independence from their parents. The system of courtship and mate selection in North America evolved slowly towards placing greater powers of choice in the hands of those seeking to form marital partnerships. The emergence this century of dating as an activity relatively independent of the influence of parents marked a significant transition in the system governing the formation of intimate relationships that may or may not lead to marriage (Saxton, 1990).

The degree of personal choice now exercised by young people in comparison to their parents varies significantly by social class within North America (Baca Zinn and Eitzen, 1993: 227–228). Generally, the higher the social class, the greater the amount of influence exerted by parents and related kin in controling and regulating the intimate relationships, particularly potential marital relationships, of their children (Cavan, 1969; Langman, 1987). Working- and lower-class parents apply the least amount of supervision and control over the various intimacy activities of their children. Parents in only some ethnic groups in Canada are able to exert considerable influence over their children's selection of a mate (Peters, 1990). Many families immigrate to Canada from various parts of the world arrange the marriages of sons or daughters to a mate currently living in Canada or in the family's country of origin (Hobart, 1996: 144).

The customs of the **bride price** or the **dowry** (see Goode, 1982: 57–60), once common in European societies until after industrialization, are still common in many parts of Africa and Western and South Central Asia. A bride price is a negotiated amount of valued goods (money, precious gems or metals, land, or animals) the groom, or most often his family, pays to the bride, or most often her family, to cement an alliance between the two families. In contrast, the dowry involves an exchange of valued goods from the bride, or her family, to the groom or his family. Some of these bride-price or dowry goods may be passed along to the newly married couple. Only rarely are the bride or groom involved directly in the negotiation process of establishing the value of a prospective marital partner. Whether, how, and why a culture establishes a bride-price or a dowry system is still unclear (Goode, 1982). However, the nature of the custom appears to be determined, at least in part, by cultural beliefs about the comparative value of each sex. In a bride-price system, a woman is valued more; in a dowry system, a woman is valued less than her partner.

European societies used to be characterized by the presence of a dowry system, in which a prospective bride's value was enhanced by the amount of material possessions her family could provide to the groom or his family. With the growing emphasis upon individualism and romantic love, the dowry system has gradually declined over time although vestigial elements may still be found in the *trousseau* that some women are expected to accumulate, tucked away in a "hope" chest prior to their possible marriage, and the folkway etiquette that the bride's parents should absorb the cost of the wedding gala. The trousseau, mainly comprising household items such as linen, china, and flatware, along with personal items of clothing, was designed to defray the costs of establishing an independent household for at least the first year, if not longer, of the marriage. Similarly, the custom of females-only theme showers for the prospective bride provides an opportunity for a woman to bring to her matrimonial home a wide assortment of colour-coordinated linens and kitchen items that the bride herself may have indicated a desire for at a bridal registry. Bridal showers contrast with stags given for prospective grooms, at which, most typically, either no gifts, or else gifts more notable for their raunchy, humorous, qualities than their domestic utility, are given.

A formal bride-price system has never existed in Canada, although the social expectation that a prospective husband should possess the stability to financially support his wife and their children implies the existence of an informal bride price system. The engagement ring provides not only a tangible expression of an intangible emotional commitment, but the purchase of such a ring also, and perhaps more importantly, demonstrates the ability of a man to economically support the relationship at a certain standard of living. Advertising from diamond merchants today (Farrell, 1986: 27–30) capitalizes on this spend-money-to-prove-your-love theme and, in the process, also reinforces the success-object status of men and their earning power. Despite the dramatic increases in the numbers of women in the labour force over the past 25 years, and their slowly escalating earning power, the merchants of love-in-a-sparkling-form have yet to embark upon trying to convince Canadians that men too are worthy of receiving a diamondic symbol, suitably priced to accommodate the wage gap, of their female partner's affection and earning potential.

Courtship Practices

"Courtship" is an archaic term still used by family sociologists to refer to the entire system of dating (itself another archaic term often replaced by adolescents and young adults today with vague-meaning phrases such as "hanging out," "going with," and "seeing") and eventual mate selection. Norms developed during the late-nineteenth and early-twentieth century established a script familiar to most Canadians today. Men were, and to a large extent still are, expected to be the initiators of all phases of intimate relationship development (Asmussen and Shehan, 1992; McCormick and Jesser, 1983: 67–69). Men were granted the power (a concept we shall explore more thoroughly later in this chapter) to formally initiate contact with women of their choosing. Men were expected to dominate and channel conversations (even though women actually do most of the conversation work), initiate touching and sexual contact, determine the level of emotional commitment prevailing in the relationship, and formally make any proposal for marriage. Men were also expected to assume all financial responsibilities for the couple's activities.

In contrast, women were expected to remain observably passive and await the attentions of potential suitors. At the level of superficial appearances, women were to be the pursued, not the pursuers. The most noticeable power of women was that of a gatekeeper role, exercising the right to pick and choose between her pursuers. Supposedly the most potent weapon in her mate-selection arsenal was the power of refusal; the right to say "no."

Unfortunately, due largely to their socialization surrounding the conquest theme, and a culturally sanctioned belief that men should dominate women, men often either refuse to acknowledge women's power or attempt to persuade or coerce women to change "no" into "maybe" and "maybe" into "yes." Beneath the level of superficial appearances, women were permitted to utilize subtle means of initiating pursuit of a desirable mate. Our culture disparagingly refers to these subtle means as "feminine wiles." Regardless of whether these practices are condemned or admired, they are frequently effective, as is often demonstrated in any discussion between a woman and a man over who *actually* initiated their relationship.

Our socially constructed rules of courtship and mate selection were, and to a large extent still are, embedded in the notion of separate spheres. Men sought physically attractive women who exhibited the potential to run a household efficiently and competently, to bear and rear children, to be an interpersonally skilled companion, and to be a knowledgeably exciting sexual partner. The desired rank ordering of these qualities has varied over the course of this century. Women, being denied equal access to well-paying occupations, power, and prestige on their own, evaluated potential males primarily in terms of whether or not they could be a good provider. No woman could have afforded the luxury of entertaining thoughts about entering a relationship with a man of no visible means of support no matter how many other endearing qualities he may have possessed. A woman's husband would "determine where she lived, what level of wealth and status she attained, and how she might structure her life" (Rotundo, 1993: 113). Despite the greater permeability of selective aspects of the boundaries between the separate spheres since the 1970s, most of the sought-after characteristics of a mate remain the same today.

However, some supplementary characteristics have been added to the job descriptions of potential intimate partners now being sought by men and women. South (1991), in a random sample of Americans between the ages of 19 and 35, finds that men are unwilling to marry a woman who does not currently have steady employment, or at least possess the promise of having such employment at a future point in time. This requirement appears to indicate an awareness among men of the growing impossibility of being a sole provider, and the necessity of having an economic coprovider of some sort. As well, perhaps now more than ever, women seek mates who are also capable of providing emotional contact and interpersonal support. The following shopping list of desired male qualities may be a bit extreme, but the underlying sentiment is not uncommon today.

> We dream of a world full of men who could be passionate lovers, grounded in their own bodies, capable of profound loves and deep sorrows, strong allies of women, sensitive nurturers, fearless defenders of all people's liberation, unbound by stifling conventions yet respectful of their own and other boundaries, serious without being humorless, stable without being dull, disciplined without being rigid, sweet without being spineless, proud without being insufferably egotistical, fierce without being violent, wild without being, well, assholes. (Starhawk, 1992: 27–28)

Regardless of whether the quest is for a marital or a cohabitation partner, most mates today, as in the past, are selected from within the general confines of similar ethnic backgrounds, as well as similar, but not identical ages and social-class locations (based upon occupational ranking and educational achievement). The phenomenon of "like selecting like" is also known as **endogamy** or **homogamy** (Ramu, 1989: 37) and, despite a declining emphasis upon national origins and religion, still remains prevalent (Kalmijn, 1991; Surra, 1991: 57; Tucker and Mitchell-Kerman, 1990; Whyte, 1990: 110). However, some important common variations do occur even within the confines of those general boundaries. Individuals who select partners possessing higher qualities than themselves experience **hypergamy**, while individuals selecting partners possessing lower qualities than themselves experience **hypogamy**. The most frequently occurring scenario within our society involves female hypergamy wherein a woman marries, or becomes involved in a relationship with, a man of slightly higher social characteristics (Murstein, 1991). The "Cinderella-Prince Charming" myth of two people from vastly different backgrounds being drawn to one another to form a mystical relationship is just that—a myth. Mates come from generally similar backgrounds with only slight, but often important, differences in the status characteristics they each possess.

Homogamy, hypergamy, and hypogamy are measured with reference to the **marriage gradient** (Bernard, 1973: 35–36), a concept that has also been applied to dating relationships and referred to as the **dating differential** (Saxton, 1990: 191). The gradient involves a rank ordering, from low to high, of all the objectively and subjectively measured qualities that are considered important in the selection of a mate or intimate partner in our society. Both men and women can be, and are, ranked or located, by themselves and others, on the gradient, by virtue of their possession of these various qualities. In the case of hypergamy, in accordance with our relationship formation norms, women tend to mate "up" in the sense of selecting intimate partners who possess, for example, a greater amount of or a more prestigious education, a higher occupational prestige, higher income (real or potential), and are heavier, taller, and older. We will explore some of the ramifications of our mate-selection system for power in intimate relationships a little later in this chapter.

Having an "older" and supposedly "wiser" man to literally look up to, one who offers physical, social, and monetary protection, is the cultural ideal held up to women in our society from their earliest exposure to fairly tales and childhood stories (Buss and Barnes, 1986; Uchalik and Livingston, 1980: 92). These cultural ideals were fashioned upon the once-presumed ideal model of the breadwinner-homemaker separate-spheres marital arrangement. Within that arrangement, married adult women were, and unfortunately to a large extent today still are, socially evaluated according to the social status of their male partner. In other words, what matters most is not her own accomplishments, abilities, or even family history, but rather that of her boyfriend, lover, cohabitation partner, or husband. Women, therefore, have a lot to gain by being hypergamous and marrying or mating upwards. Men, in contrast, are not as strongly influenced by the social status of their female partners, although men in the upper class are more carefully monitored by parents and kin to prevent their being "dragged down" by selection of an "inappropriate" mate. Men in other social classes can afford to be hypogamous in their selection of an intimate partner.

In their study of personal ads, Smith et al. (1990) find that, while men continue to specify that their potential partners be physically attractive—a finding that is consistent across race and social class lines—thin, and sexy, women's ads frequently emphasize a desire that their partner be "secure," "professional," "successful," and "ambitious." Melton and Lindsey (1987) observe that when they compare the criteria of college students for prospective intimacy partners in the 1980s with those reported in the 1970s, women continue to place greater emphasis upon men's instrumental behaviours, while men remain more likely to place substantial emphasis on the sexual and physical attractiveness of their prospective mates. Although a large proportion of the women surveyed in this research were pursuing nontraditional careers, including engineering and pharmacy, which offer the prospect of higher than average earnings and career advancement, they continued to place considerable emphasis upon men's employment prospects and their ability to save money and pay bills. The researchers speculate that even though these women wished to combine a career with marriage and children, they might have believed it advantageous to plan ahead for career disruptions caused by childbearing and childrearing and, in consequence, continue to prefer prospective partners who will be "good providers."

Hypergamy and hypogamy result in two different pools of undated and unmated men and women in our society. Women located at the upper echelons of the gradient or differential find few eligible men to look "up" to and form partnerships with. Somewhat similarly, men located at the lowest echelons of the gradient find few eligible women to look "down" on and select as a relationship partner. Thus, the most likely candidates to be found disproportionately among the essentially involuntarily unmarried in our society are "cream of the crop" women and "bottom of the barrel" men (Bernard, 1973: 36). Partial confirmation of problems associated with our society's emphasis upon some degree of hypergamy in mate selection can be found in the fact that, as we have already noted in Chapter 6, women located at the top of their professions tend to be unmarried.

LOVE AND INTIMATE RELATIONSHIP STYLES

As you read earlier regarding friendships, women and men have comparatively distinct styles of relating to others. These styles are partly the product of changing historical circumstances, and partly the product of differential socialization designed to prepare women and men for their primary participation in somewhat separate social spheres. Industrialization removed economic production from the home, established a physical boundary between the paid workplace and the homeplace, and established another social-psychological boundary between men and women by firmly gendering those physical places. Newly developing ideal images of men and women stressed different personal qualities necessary, and supposedly best suited, for the differential responsibilities women and men would assume within an industrialized society.

Prior to industrialization, relationships in the combined home/work place were simultaneously personal and impersonal. As the boundaries between the home place and the work place became more firmly entrenched, relationships within these places became comparatively more differentiated. The workplace and other public spheres outside of the home became more rational and impersonal over time, while the increasingly private world of the home became more personal and intimate. In keeping with their allotted paid-work duties, an existing stereotype was reinforced that men themselves were impersonal and rational creatures. These characteristics were believed to be ideally suited to survival and success in business and industry. Since men were to adopt an economically rational, business-like, orientation towards the world, they were also believed to be ill-suited for the day-to-day running of the family home.

Women were, and are, assigned primary duties as guardians of the private home, responsible for managing and maintaining the physical and emotional lives of all who dwelled within, and performing all or most of the tasks required to sustain those lives both inside and outside of the home place. Personal, or what are now referred to as intimate, relationships within the home became all the more important over time by way of contrast with relationships dominating the world outside of the home. The home place, and the women responsible for its maintenance, were called upon to provide a "haven" in an increasingly impersonal and "heartless" world (Lasch, 1977). Part of women's duties involved monitoring and anticipating every family member's feelings about themselves and about their lives. In keeping with their allotted duties, the existing stereotype was reinforced that women themselves were interpersonally sensitive, emotional, creatures. The ideal woman was to be "attentive, compassionate, comforting, and cooperative [while the] ideal man was ambitious, independent and self-made" (Thompson, 1993: 559). Her qualities were deemed to be ideally suited for survival and success in love, marriage, and intimate family relationships. One outcome of the processes associated with industrialization is that love became "feminized" during the nineteenth century (Cancian, 1987). Women's preferred expressions of love were, and still are, established as the accepted norm (Cancian, 1987: 69–71; Tavris, 1992: 248). Women also became the "love experts" (Safilios-Rothschild, 1977: 3). We shall explore some of the consequences of the feminization of love in a later section.

Love

Throughout most of the present century, love has been one of the most important preconditions for marriage in industrialized societies (Crosby, 1991; Goode, 1959; Walster and Walster, 1978). While homogamous and hyper- or hypogamous considerations (e.g., ethnicity, social class, age) all play important roles, a dominant expectation exists in Canada and the United States that the selection of an intimate partner should be based first and foremost upon a mutual experience of "being in love" (Hendrick and Hendrick, 1992; Benokraitis, 1996). While the emphases within definitions of what is generally referred to as **romantic** love within sociology (Kephart, 1966; Robinson, 1980) and as **passionate** love (Walster and Walster, 1978) within psychology vary somewhat, they both refer to essentially the same phenomenon. A classic definition of romantic love is: "(1) a strong emotional attachment toward a person of the opposite [*sic*] sex; (2) the tendency to think of this person in an idealized manner; and (3) a marked physical attraction the fulfillment of which is reckoned in terms of touch" (Kephart, 1966: 311).

Empirical research on love began in earnest during the 1950s and reached a peak from the late 1970s through the 1980s. Not surprisingly, researchers tend to focus upon identifying gender differences in experiences and expressions of love and tended to ignore, or give little attention and meaning to, any similarities. The vast majority of empirical studies conducted on love utilize middle-class, predominantly European-origin, Canadianized or Americanized, college- and university-student samples. In their quest to identify characteristic gender differences regarding love, researchers have, for the most part, essentially neglected to explore fully the possible range of variations associated with social class, ethnicity (cf. Simmons et al., 1986), sexual orientation, and lesser educational qualifications. A predominant assumption in both past and present studies has been that any differences found are a function of the properties of gender (Brehm, 1992: 110, 116) and not other factors.

Studies in both the United States and Canada find that males tend to be more idealistic about love than are females (e.g., Brehm, 1992; Dion and Dion, 1991; Hatfield and Sprecher, 1986; Lester et al., 1984; Robinson, 1980; Rubin et al., 1981; Sprecher and Metts, 1989). Males are more likely to believe in love "at first sight," to believe that love has the power to overcome all practical obstacles facing a relationship, that love cannot be rationalized, and that an ideal mate exists somewhere for everyone. Researchers and interpreters of existing research (e.g., Larson et al., 1994: 195) tend to conclude that males are generally naive and idealistic when it comes to love, while females are more realistic, pragmatic, or practical about the nature and power of love.

Research on relationship development (e.g., Hill et al., 1976; Huston et al., 1981; Kanin et al., 1970; Rubin et al., 1981) finds that males are more likely to admit, at least to themselves, that they are "in love" earlier in a relationship than are women. In addition to being slower to acknowledge falling in love, women are more likely to "fall out" of love earlier in a relationship than are men. Consequently, women are more likely to break off a relationship that has, as far as they can see, no future. Harris (in Walster and Walster, 1978: xi) summarizes the findings of these studies by suggesting that women tend to be the last in and the first out (LIFO) of relationships, while men are the first in and the last out (FILO). Since, as we noted above, men are more likely to believe in love "at first sight," the findings that men appear to "fall" in love faster are not surprising. A quick search of your own experience, or that of people close to you, will confirm that men are generally the last ones to know that a relationship is actually over. The four most dreaded words to adolescent and young adult men in our society are those uttered by a female relationship partner: "we have to talk." Upon hearing those words, most men begin mentally or physically packing their bags in preparation for an imminent departure even though they have been totally oblivious to earlier signs that the future of the relationship was in serious jeopardy.

In comparison to men, women appear to make finer discriminations between like, love, and romance (Rubin, 1973: 220–221). Once they have acknowledged being in love, women tend to experience the emotions of their relationship more intensely than do men (Dion and Dion, 1973; Kanin et al., 1970). Furthermore, women tend to feel that they give more than they receive within marital and nonmarital relationships than do men—and men tend to agree (Rubin, 1970). Hill et al. (1976) find that, at the breakup of a relationship, men tend to suffer more and take longer to get over a relationship than do women. Money (1980) summarizes these and other findings to suggest that men tend to suffer more "love sickness" after a relationship is over than do women.

Structural Explanations

Explanations for most of these findings from research on love focus primarily upon the different structural locations of women and men within our society. As we noted above, since the development of the separate spheres and the creation of the provider-homemaker ideal family type, women have a greater vested interest in the rewards to be gained from intimate partnerships. A man is looking for a wife, mother of his children, housekeeper, and companion. A woman is looking for a husband, father of her children, companion, financial provider, standing in the community, and a standard of living (Eichler, 1981). Intimacy, social and personal identity, and financial survival issues are all fused for women in society. "As long as most women still must depend on their husbands for income, economic security, and social status, they cannot afford to rely primarily on love as the basis for marriage" (Safilios-Rothschild, 1977: 3). Economic and social status considerations, therefore, circumscribe love for most women.

Not having to depend as much upon the financial and social contributions from an intimate partner, men are permitted to be caught up with their feelings and can allow themselves to believe that love is more important than practical issues. They can afford not to examine the potential implications of being carried away with feelings of love for another person. Consequently, men tend to be more idealistic about love, tend to fall in love faster, and tend to be less likely to realize a relationship's future is problematic. Generally, women must harness their emotions to more practical considerations. Only when circumstances appear to portend a good "match" can women permit themselves the luxury of indulging in their feelings. Not surprisingly, one of the dominant romantic fantasies of women involves allowing themselves to be "swept away" with a rush of feelings, without consideration of any practical necessities of life (Masters, Johnson, and Kolodny, 1985: 346). It is a functional survival necessity for women to be less idealistic about the power of love, to be more cautious about falling in love, and to constantly monitor the potential future of a relationship.

Only upper-class women could literally afford, at least in theory, to marry strictly for love. However, upper-class women tend to marry within their own class when marriage is more an issue of the sharing of wealth and position and, therefore, partner selection is limited by concerns of the entire family clan rather than the purely personal concerns of the individuals involved (Baca Zinn and Eitzen, 1993; Langman, 1987). Unfortunately, researchers in the 1990s have turned their attentions to other aspects of intimate relationships and have not revisited the issue of whether changing social circumstances have altered women's relationship with love. Would women who have chosen to establish themselves first in a career, thereby creating their own independent social and financial standing in the community, be free of the necessity to be as practical about love?

Emotion Work

While a structural explanation partially accounts for findings of gender differences regarding love, that explanation is not sufficient. An important additional factor contributing to these findings pertains to what has been labeled as **emotion work**, or **feeling work** (Hochschild, 1983). Doing emotion or feeling work involves monitoring one's emotional state, correctly identifying current feelings, and then ensuring that the feelings are appropriate for present objective circumstances. Ensuring appropriateness may involve either manufacturing new feelings or suppressing existing ones.

As a consequence of their socialization experiences, women tend to pay closer attention to their own emotional state and are better able to identify and analyze their ongoing feelings. In contrast, men are less likely to be able to tune in and identify their emotional states:

> Stop a woman in mid-sentence with the question, "What are you feeling right now?" and you might have to wait a bit while she reruns the mental tape to capture the moment just passed. But, more than likely, she'll be able to do it successfully....The same is not true of a man. For him, a similar question usually will bring a sense of wonderment that one would even ask it, followed quickly by an uncomprehending and puzzled response. "What do you mean?" he'll ask. "I was just talking." (Rubin, 1983: 69)

Men often appear to possess a less extensive vocabulary of emotions and, perhaps as a consequence, make less refined discriminations between emotions than do women (Christensen and Heavey, 1990; Wamboldt and Reiss, 1989; Wood, 1993; Wood and Inman, 1993). In response to a "what are you feeling now?" question from a female intimate partner, a male will usually run through a short mental checklist of general feeling states ("Am I hungry? Angry? Anxious? Horny? Depressed? Lonely?") and, if none of the above readily appear to be accurate, frequently answer with the ubiquitous, "nothing."

As we noted earlier, men appear to make fewer distinctions between like and love (Rubin, 1979: 220–221). When combined with a less extensive vocabulary, men are more likely to define their feeling state as "love" earlier in a relationship than are women and are also more likely to retain that definition, despite all objective evidence to the contrary, even after the relationship is over. Emotion work accounts for the tendency of women to be slower to acknowledge feelings as "love" early in a relationship, and to be quicker to discount feelings as love in a relationship deemed inappropriate. If a woman realizes that her feelings of love for a particular man are inappropriate since the relationship has no future (e.g., he has no chance of ever holding down a steady job, he is currently married, gay, dead) and the future is the overriding criterion of the moment, she will likely "work" to suppress the positive feelings, create appropriate feelings of indifference, and attempt to end the relationship. As long as women need marriage for economic reasons more than do men, emotion work will remain an important ability, vital to women's personal and social survival.

Men, however, do acquire a limited socialization regarding emotion work. As we have noted, men are expected to learn how to control their emotions. Emotion work for men traditionally takes the form of learning how to suppress not so much the experience but, more important, the expression of emotions that may make them seem vulnerable. Appearing dependent or in a state of need is still believed within our culture to be incompatible with the stereotype of the strong, stoic, independent male. Socially designed as a strategy to reinforce those qualities needed for success in the public sphere, suppressing emotions tends to not lead to success in the private sphere.

Intimate Relationship Styles

In keeping with their differential participation in the separate social spheres, women and men demonstrate different relationship styles in their heterosexual intimate partnerships. Women prefer, and are more comfortable with, a style stressing emotional closeness, verbal expressions of feelings, and sharing of mutual vulnerability (Cancian, 1987; Hite, 1987; Tavris, 1992). "The image of feminine love gives women responsibility for love and defines love as self-sacrifice, emotional warmth, expressiveness, vulnerability, and sensitivity" (Thompson, 1993: 559). Men, in contrast, prefer, and are more comfortable with, a relationship style reflecting "work world" values (Levinson, 1996: 42) or "action" values (Tavris, 1992: 250), including providing instrumental aid such as money, practical help or problem solving, spending time together, and sexuality. These preferences have a common underlying theme of allowing men to deny their dependence upon women in a relationship. Consequently, men can maintain a façade that they are still independent beings, powerful and in control.

Within lesbian couples, partners tend to assume joint responsibility for nurturing the relationship and providing the other with emotional support—a finding which is thought to reflect the fact that both women have absorbed the socialization message that females are responsible for the nurturing of intimate relationships (Eldridge and Gilbert, 1990; Wood, 1994). Eldridge and Gilbert (1990) contend that lesbian relationships have the highest level of equality of all types of intimate relationships. In contrast, Wood (1993) reports that men in gay relationships are the least likely to have a relational partner who takes care of the relationship and cultivates the development of the couple as a unit. While both lesbian and gay relationships resemble the relationships of "best friends" with the added dimension of sexuality and romance (Huston and Schwartz, 1996), the relationships of gay men rank lower than those of lesbians and heterosexuals in terms of expressiveness and nurturance (Wood, 1993).

One consequence of gendered lovestyle preferences is that both women and men in heterosexual relationships fail to appreciate fully the contributions flowing from the other gender's relationship style. Supported by feminist theorists such as Chodorow and Gillian (Cancian, 1987: 71–72) and by family therapists, who generally have uncritically adopted a feminized notion of love, women tend to take men's contributions for granted and instead focus upon what men do not provide. "It is not enough that he supports us and takes care of us. I appreciate that, but I want him to share things with me. I need for him to tell me his feelings" (in Cancian, 1987: 76). Measuring men's behaviour according to a "feminine ruler" (Cancian, 1987: 74) has lead scholars to unwittingly create a **deficit model of manhood** (Doherty, 1991). Lamenting "why can't a man be more like a woman," men are often criticized by wives, cohabitation partners, therapists, feminists, segments of the men's movement, and family-studies scholars as being deficient in intimacy skills (Beach and Tesser, 1988; Fowers, 1991). Men have been accused of suffering from "stunted emotional development" (Balswick, 1988), enjoined to learn how to converse openly about their emotions (Tognoli, 1980), or depicted as feeling "threatened by intimacy" (Mazur and Olver, 1987: 533). Whitbourne and Ebmeyer (1990: 15) claim that, in their research on married couples, husbands who are unable to participate in the "intense emotionality of a long-term close relationship" not only forfeit their opportunity to experience true intimacy, but as well, cause a reduction in their wives' capacity for intimacy and lessen the likelihood of their well-adjustment within marriage.

Dressel and Clark (1990) find that women define anticipation of another's needs as an important element of caring behaviour. The women in their study believe they are more likely than men to perform actions to please or serve their partners. Not only will they do things because their husbands like or want them, they also do things for their husbands that the men could do for themselves. While the authors conclude that women's care reflects deference to men's power in marriage, they did not actually assess power in their study. Equally plausible is the fact that women are more aware of social expectations that require them to anticipate and meet an intimate partner's needs, especially within the home. Performing actions to please another is not limited to only one gender, however. Some of these actions may become so taken-for-granted as to be ignored or may be given another meaning. "A wife washing her husband's shirt is seen as expressing feelings, while a husband washing his wife's car is seen as doing a job" (Cancian, 1987: 79). The latter act is more often explained away as a demonstration of a man's fascination with automobiles rather than an expression of affection for his wife (see Wills et al., 1974).

Men are at best ambivalent about women's relationship styles. As noted by Levinson, some demonstrations of women's love and care are appreciated, particularly by traditional men:

> He can appreciate her efforts to provide for his rest, nourishment, and comfort, to keep the household orderly and attractive, to share certain leisure activities and to allow him other activities that he prefers to do with men. He feels cared for when she inspires and supports his heroic occupational quest. She does this by admiring his intellectual and physical prowess, enjoying his success, finding him a valued source of knowledge and authority, by being a supportive player but not a hero in her own right. (Levinson, 1996: 42)

However, since most men tend to be uncomfortable and even fearful about discussing their own doubts and anxieties, they tend to be unappreciative of women's requests for greater expressiveness and self-disclosure of their innermost thoughts. "Wives push for more attention, responsiveness, communication, and closeness; husbands withdraw and withhold. This scenario renders women unhappy with husbands who are silent and insensitive and men unhappy with wives who do not recognize their best efforts at care" (Thompson, 1993: 560). As we have mentioned before, men's instrumental focus within relationships results in their placing greater emphasis on what they do for and with their partners, rather than on what they say. For men, "talk is not the centerpiece" (Riessman, 1990: 24).

This "demand-withdraw" (Christensen and Heavey, 1990) or "pursuer-distancer" (James, 1989) pattern *may* reflect gender preferences for desired levels of autonomy and connection. Wood (1997: 236) argues that, while all individuals seek both, masculine individuals typically desire greater autonomy and lesser connection than do feminine persons "whose relative priorities are generally reversed." As she observes regarding heterosexual intimate relationships, "[t]he irony is that the very thing that creates closeness for one partner impedes it for the other." The pattern of "demand-withdraw" is less likely to surface in gay and lesbian relationships, since "both partners tend to have congruent desires for autonomy and connection" (Wood, 1997: 237). However, as we shall see shortly, autonomy and connection are not the only factors that can account for the demand-withdraw pattern.

Men's Silence

The "strong silent" type has been an icon of masculinity extolled by our folklore and mass media over the course of this century. This type supposedly embodies a central quality of men most admired by women and men alike. Yet, as is often the case, the very qualities of another that so attract us in the first place, typically become major points of contention and even repulsion later on. "Women may be attracted to men's independent, self-contained ways because it reassures them of strength. Yet as relationships develop, women often resent men for being distant and invulnerable" (Baca Zinn and Eitzen, 1993: 253). Male inexpressiveness has not only been identified by women as the major problem in heterosexual love relationships (e.g., Hite, 1987: 5), but also as ultimately being hazardous to men's health (e.g., Balswick and Peek, 1971; Goldberg, 1976).

Many analysts trace male inexpressiveness to a socialization stressing the centrality of emotional control (e.g., Udry, 1971). According to this line of thinking, men are taught to believe that, since most emotions are unmasculine, they are not worth analyzing or discussing and are essentially best left ignored. The same logic is then applied to talking about emotional relationships. In contrast, many women believe that talk, particularly about feelings present or absent, offers a sound strategy through which to forestall the development of relationship problems. This strategy will not be appreciated by men who view such conversations as simply unnecessary. As one man states:

> We can have a minor problem—like an issue between us, and it's really not serious stuff. But can we let it go? No way....She wants "to talk about it." And I mean talk and talk and talk and talk. There's no end to how long she can talk about stuff that really doesn't matter. I tell her that she's analyzing the relationship to death and I don't want to do that. She insists that we need "to talk things through." That may work for her, but, honestly, it makes no sense to

me. Why can't we just have a relationship, instead of always having to talk about it? (in Wood, 1997: 215)

Gottman (1994; Gottman and Levenson, 1988) concludes that men are likely to be the ones who withdraw into silence and "stonewall" their partner during intense moments in a relationship. His conclusion is based upon more than 10 years of research using videotaped observations of, and physiological measurements taken from, heterosexual couples interacting in controlled laboratory situations. Withdrawal is precipitated by being "flooded" (Gottman, 1995: 110) with stressful emotions, which elevate both blood pressure and heart rates to higher levels in men than in women. Retreating into silence is a defensive technique used by men to protect themselves from being overwhelmed by the emotions of the moment. "Talking about the relationship as she wants to do will feel to him like taking a test that she has made up and he will fail…he is likely to react with withdrawal" (Cancian, 1987: 93). Gottman (1995: 95, 116, 138–140) vaguely attributes men's withdrawal response to a biological, evolutionary-based "fight or flight" stress reaction combined with emotion-control socialization that renders men inexperienced and uncomfortable with emotions.

Others argue that men's attempts to control their own emotions provides only a partial explanation. Sattell (1976) suggests that men withhold their emotions as a means of trying to control the emotional intensity of a relationship, as well as retaining power and control over their female partner. To lose one's cool is to risk giving up control to another. Silence is not only less risky, but it also tends, for a while at least, to make one's partner work harder to find what lies under the silent veneer. While Sattell envisions silence as a deliberate power strategy used by men, Tavris (1992: 271) notes that a silent partner may not wish to be powerful, nor actually feel powerful. Rather than being a sign of power and control, men's silence can be the sign of a limited coping mechanism in the face of out-of-control feelings, as has been demonstrated by Gottman's (1994) studies.

Contributing to the common pattern of male withdrawal and silence is the importance of the independence (or "autonomy," Wood, 1997: 236) theme of masculinity operating in our culture. Impressionistic evidence indicates that men are often seemingly impervious to their partner's request for some action or verbalization, because such requests challenge their sense of independence. Rather than simply comply with the request from a friend or lover (e.g., "tell me you love me," or "why don't you buy me a romantic card on Valentine's Day?"), men prefer to instigate action on their own initiative. To the frustration of their female partners, men will often appear to ignore a request, withdraw for a period of time, and then meet the request as if responding to their own inspiration. (Could this be why your mother told you: "Always let him think it was his idea"?) Empirical evidence is lacking as to whether this withdrawal in the service of preserving independence is somehow related to men's tendency to refuse to ask for road directions or to prefer to wander aimlessly around a department store rather than asking a clerk for help.

Essential or Situational Differences?

The feminization of love reinforces the primacy of the private sphere for women and the primacy of women in the private sphere. On the surface, the feminization of love and the deficit model of manhood, with its implication that men should become more like women, suggests that women in the private sphere have more power than do men. However, that surface impression is misleading, since, even though men's styles of loving may be found deficient, men do not lose power because of their "deficiency." To the contrary, our dominant cultural ideals still do not positively reward men for altering their relationship style. "Instead, most men who weep, speak their feelings, and reveal fears and passions are denigrated as being too weak, shrill, feminine, and emotional. The male norm of emotional suppression continues to be held up as the public ideal of adult behavior" (Tavris, 1992: 270).

Furthermore, responses to the deficit model of manhood have often taken the form of calling for greater recognition of men's traditional ways of loving, rather than for suggestions for altering men's preferred style (Levant, 1992; West, 1994). These responses implicitly reinforce the notion that existing relationship styles reflect essential gender differences that cannot, and should not, be changed. It is important to stress, however, that observed differences in romantic love idealism, the timing of "falling in love," emotion work, the withdrawal into silence, and various means of expressing love are all based upon average scores and tendencies. In other words, these differences are neither absolute nor essential. Either gender is capable of responding in alternative ways depending upon the requirements of the social situation with which they find themselves confronted. In support of this assertion, we will point to just two of many possible examples.

Lombardo et al. (1983) find that women acknowledge crying more often and over a greater range of situations than do men. However, according to their self-reports, these same women and men share very similar perceptions about what conditions—people, situations, objects—could evoke tears. The findings suggest that women and men are equally emotionally responsive to stimuli, but differ instead in their emotional expressiveness. Men are more likely to conform to the social demands for stoicism, and women are more likely to conform to the social expectations for demonstrative outlet.

Laboratory experiments varying the sex of the person pushing for change in a relationship indicates that, when confronted with demands for change from men, women as the person of whom change is required, are as likely to withdraw into silence as are men (Christensen and Heavey, 1993, 1990; Klinetob and Smith, 1996). The fact that men are more frequently the ones who withdraw is a consequence of the fact that women, charged with the responsibility for maintaining relationships, are most often in the position of asking men to change to explore or consolidate some aspect of the relationship. That demand-withdrawal is not an essential gender difference is demonstrated when men push for change in areas of relationships that are important to them, and their wives retreat into silence. Within the power dynamics of intimate relationships, the "spouse with the most to gain by maintaining the status quo is likely to withdraw" (Klinetob and Smith, 1996: 945). Once again, congruent with the precepts of the gender perspective, situational expectations appear to account for many of the differences often wrongly attributed to essential characteristics of gender. What men and women often do in intimate relationships is not necessarily an expression of what they are capable of doing.

POWER IN INTIMATE RELATIONSHIPS

Power is a multifaceted phenomenon. In part, power refers to the ability to exert one's will, to be able to translate one's wishes into meaningful action. **Empowerment** has become one of the buzzwords of the 1990s most often used regarding a process of enabling members of groups who have had less power (e.g., women, the poor, visible minorities) to find the means to control their own destinies by exerting their will. Power also refers to the ability of one person to influence the behaviour of another person, and to resist the influence of another person, regardless of that other person's wishes. This form of power is more **coercive** (French and Raven, 1959) than is empowerment. Relationships vary in terms of how explicitly or obviously power is expressed but, even in the most intimate relationships supposedly governed by an egalitarian ethic, a power dimension is always present. "Gender relations are basically power relations" (Osmond and Thorne, 1993: 593). According to the principles of **exchange** (also referred to in Chapter 6 as *resource theory*) **theory**, an individual's power is determined by a number of factors all operating simultaneously (Foa and Foa, 1980).

The first major factor involves the amount of actual or perceived control a person has over resources. We will examine types of resources shortly, but the general principle is that the greater amount of resources one possesses, or is seen to possess, the more power one has in a relationship.

Second, but equally important, is the extent to which one's partner values those resources. If the other person has no interest in the resources one controls, they will be of no consequence for the relationship. Only valued and desired resources confer power.

The availability of alternative sources of desired resources is the third factor. Our folk wisdom proclaims, "Why buy a cow when there is plenty of free milk in the market?" However, when marketplace milk is scarce, the value of having access to one's own cow increases significantly. The fewer the available alternatives, and, therefore, the more scarce the valued resources possessed by one's partner, the greater the amount of power that partner has. The availability of alternatives provides an indicator of one person's *dependence* upon another. Simply put, the fewer the alternatives, the greater the dependence.

Dependence and power are inversely related. The lesser one's dependence upon another person, the greater one's power over that person. Waller (1938) enunciates this fourth factor as the "principle of least interest." According to the principle, the person with the least interest in maintaining a relationship has the most power within that relationship. Having less or "least" interest in a relationship is related to a greater real or perceived availability of alternative sources of satisfaction. If one's needs are not being met in a current relationship, and one believes that those needs could be met in an alternative relationship, then one will be less willing to make major sacrifices or concessions to maintain the current relationship.

Conversely, the more one wants or needs a current partner—for what they are, or what they have, or what they can do—and the fewer the alternatives, the more dependent and the less powerful one is in that relationship. Making oneself appear to be indispensable for the happiness and life satisfaction of a partner—convincing the person that he or she cannot live without you — is one way to attempt to keep the other partner dependent and interested in maintaining the relationship. Of course, the more you have to work to make yourself indispensable, the more you must acknowledge privately that you have more interest in maintaining the relationship and are actually in the position of, at least initially, less power. Studies of both marital (Safilios-Rothschild, 1976) and heterosexual dating (Sprecher, 1985) relationships find that women who report loving their partners less than they are loved in return also perceive themselves as having more power in those relationships.

Eichler (1981) argues that "frontier families" were probably relatively egalitarian, because they were based upon a mutual or symmetrical dependency of husband and wife. With the evolution of the breadwinner-housewife family, dependency became asymmetrical. While wives came to depend upon their husbands for the income needed to procure food, shelter, clothing, and other necessities of life, husbands could simply purchase from an increasing variety of sources those services a wife could provide. Since wives apparently needed husbands more so than the reverse, the system of asymmetrical dependency resulted in men having more power in marital and family relationships.

The "second wave" of feminism, as we saw in Chapter 3, arose in support of the principles of decreasing women's dependence upon men, increasing women's access to resources external to the home, and consequently promoting more symmetry in the distribution of power within marital relationships. In response to the growing influence of the women's movement in the late 1960s and early 1970s, a counterwave of antifeminist publications (e.g., Andelin, 1974; Baker, 1975; Morgan, 1973) and related instructional seminars swept North America. Mixing tenets of fundamentalist Christianity with primitive understandings of a supposed biological basis for gender, these publications stressed the necessity of women remaining in the home, to exercise what all of the authors argued was women's most priceless, yet too-often denigrated, asset: domestic power. Promoting a variety of techniques of submissive manipulation, authors and seminar leaders stressed that the secret to women's happiness lay not in political, economic, or educational equality, but rather in making themselves indispensable to their husbands in the family home, bolstering men's egos, and reaffirming the belief within men that men were truly the superior sex as God and nature intended. By appearing submissive, coy, incompetent at any "masculine" task, "truly feminine" women could manipulate their big, tall, handsome brutes into worshipping the ground women walked on, protecting women from the harsh vicissitudes of life in a cold, cruel, public world, and enshrining women as domestic queens. Some authors eschewed discussions of sexuality (e.g., Andelin, 1974), while others (e.g., Morgan, 1973) encouraged women to utilize their sexuality to keep their men sexually satisfied, yet eager for more, anxious to hurry home every night to learn what new fleshly delights awaited them (such as Morgan's suggestion that a woman meet her man at the door wearing nothing but clear plastic wrap), and willing to meet their wives' every nonsexual wish and demand.

This form of antifeminist flurry receded into the background by the early 1980s. However, a new variation surfaced in the mid-1990s in the form of *The Rules*, a best-selling book (Fein and Schneider, 1995), with related workshops, that is an homage to an earlier era. Boasting such supposedly impressive credentials as being a married "magazine-writer" and being "married with two children," the authors proclaim that the 35 rules (originating around 1917, but more characteristic of advice to the lovelorn in the 1950s) provide "a simple working set of behaviors and reactions that…invariably serve to make most women irresistible to desirable men" (Fein and Schneider, 1995: 2). In a society that designates women to be the love experts, and consequently blames women if they make foolish choices in love, a call to return to old-fashioned techniques guaranteed to "make Mr. Right obsessed with having you as his by making yourself seem unattainable" (Fein and Schneider, 1995: 5) appears to have found a receptive audience, judging by publication sales. Playing hard-to-get and (almost) unattainable are designed, by the authors, to foster the false impression that a woman has options other than devoting herself, and making herself easily available, to one particular man. Even though the book's authors are oblivious to existing empirical research, such techniques designed to reduce apparent dependency can actually alter the balance of power in an ongoing or potential intimate relationship.

Power does not exist in a vacuum. The sociocultural context not only determines what is considered to be a valuable resource, but also strongly influences the manner and degree to which individuals have access to those resources. The fifth factor in determining an individual's power lies in the fact that patriarchal societies grant greater power to males simply by virtue of the fact they are male. Furthermore, the basic institutional structures of those societies are constructed in such a way that males have greater access to those positions that garner a greater share of socially valued rewards and resources. As a consequence of their higher locations in the structures of our economic, political, and legal institutions, males in general have greater **structural** power (Guttentag and Secord, 1983: 26) than do women within patriarchal societies.

We noted earlier in this chapter that our courtship norms have traditionally granted men the power to initiate all phases of intimate or potentially intimate relationships. While Kelley (in Kelley and Rolker-Dolinsky, 1987) finds that males are increasingly more likely to report being asked out on a date by females, female-initiated dates among university students tend not to lead to a relationship lasting beyond the third date (Kelley and Rolker-Dolinsky, 1987). It appears that an apparent loss of the control granted to them by tradition leads males to reassert control by terminating relationships they themselves have not initiated. But it may not be only men in our society who are eventually uncomfortable with female-initiated relationships. Initiation is often perceived to be an indicator of dominance and, even in the 1990s, "female dominance in a heterosexual relationship is less acceptable *to both parties* than is male dominance" (Brehm, 1992: 244, emphasis in original).

Types of Resources

Many types of resources are important for the experience and expression of power within intimate relationships. The simplest list would include the resources of material possessions in general and money in particular, social status, love, and sexuality (Foa and Foa, 1980). These resources differ in more than just the most obvious ways. Money is a **concrete** resource (Johnson, 1976) that can be quantified in the sense that it can be counted and amounts can be compared. As well, money can quite easily be transferred from one person or relationship to another. Social status is less concrete in and of itself, but most of its indicators are found in concrete forms such as material possessions. While most Canadians cannot describe the nature of our social-class hierarchy in precise detail, they can readily identify their position relative to those who are higher or lower in social status than themselves. As we saw earlier in this chapter, it is possible for one person to confer their own status onto another person and, therefore, possible for one person to transfer that status from one intimate partner to another. As well, both money and high status can be used to provide access to other valuable resources, such as higher education or a career in politics, which are in themselves sources of power.

Love, in comparison, is a **personal** resource (Johnson, 1976) that is not easily quantified, as anyone who has ever tried to "count the ways" can readily attest. As well, love is particularized and cannot readily be transferred to other persons or relationships. It is very difficult to determine if you will be likely to find another person who can and will love you in the ways your current intimate partner does. Finally, love cannot as easily provide access to other forms of power, although it is not incapable of doing so. While sexuality shares common properties with love, particularly within a society that idealistically equates the two, sexuality can provide a means of access to other forms of power, particularly when sexuality is deemed to be a valuable, scarce resource. While often we are easily aware that many people may want our money or high social status, it is not always obviously apparent who might want our love or even our sexuality. Similarly, while it is relatively easy to determine if another person offers more money or a higher standing in the community than what we can obtain from a current partner, it is not as easy to determine if another person offers more love or better sexual experiences.

Males, both currently and historically, generally control the resources of money and social status, while females generally control the resources of love and sexuality. Even though this distribution is slowly being transformed, current conditions set the stage for a bargaining or exchange of resources within intimate relationships. Unfortunately, the exchange is not necessarily one between equals. Lipman-Blumen (1976: 16–17) notes that "in relationships between the sexes, males have a disproportionate amount of resources under their control. They could bargain their power, status, money, land, political influence, legal power, and educational and occupational resources (all usually greater than women's) against women's more limited range of resources consisting of sexuality, youth, beauty, and the promise of paternity." Since the resources being exchanged are not equally valued within our materialistic society, with socioeconomic resources valued more than love or sexuality (Blood and Wolfe, 1960), resulting relationships are unlikely to be egalitarian. As well, conformity to the heterosexual mating gradient discussed earlier in this chapter promotes the pairing of two basically unequal partners (Cooney and Uhlenberg, 1991; Szinovacz, 1987).

An underlying principle of resource and exchange theory, that monetary resources derived from the world outside of a couple's home will determine the nature of relationships within their home, appears to be equally applicable to men in gay intimate relationships. Blumstein and Schwartz's large-scale empirical study of heterosexual, gay, and lesbian married and cohabiting couples find that "[m]oney establishes the balance of power in relationships, except among lesbians" (Blumstein and Schwartz, 1983: 53). The findings for lesbians demonstrate that resource theory offers a useful, but not fully explanatory, understanding of power. Blumstein and Schwartz (1983: 55) argue that women in our society are not used to judging their own self-worth in monetary terms and, consequently, do not measure an intimate female partner's worth (but will measure a male partner's worth) according to that standard. Men measure their own, other men's, and, increasingly, an intimate female partner's worth according to a monetary resource yardstick. The lesbian experience captured by these researchers illustrates the second point of our earlier discussion of factors influencing the distribution of power within intimate relationships. If one's partner doesn't value a particular resource, that resource has no consequence. "By noting that even gay male couples gain advantage over one another when one partner has a high income, we see that money may create inequality even when there is no gender difference. But we also see, by looking at lesbian couples, that money need not have that effect" (Blumstein and Schwartz, 1983: 55; for similar findings see Kurdek, 1993). Belief systems, or ideologies, can moderate the influence of resources as we shall soon see.

Power Techniques

Not only do men and women differ in terms of their access to and possession of resource power, but they also differ in terms of the different techniques with which they use the power they possess. "When the dominant group controls the major institutions of society it relies of *macromanipulation* through law, social policy, and military might when necessary, to impose its will and ensure its rule. The less powerful become adept at *micromanipulation* using intelligence, canniness, intuition, interpersonal charm, sexuality, deception, and avoidance to offset the control of the powerful" (Lipman-Blumen, 1984: 8, emphasis in original). Macromanipulation is a more direct and forceful set of techniques, while micromanipulation techniques tend to be more indirect and less blatantly forceful. Their differential use typically reflects the extent to which the user has access to structural power.

Men generally tend to use the macro, while women generally tend to use the micro, also known as "feminine wiles," means of influencing others. However, these are typical tendencies only. Men are not adverse to using micromanipulation techniques when it suits their purposes. For example, men often use a form of "playing dumb" as an excuse for avoiding many housework duties. Regardless of their capabilities prior to the development of a relationship, many men in domestic relationships pretend to be confused and/or totally incapacitated when confronted with the complex chemistry of laundry detergent, modern fabrics, and multistage washers and dryers—especially when they believe their female partner will rescue them from this task rather than risk having an entire wardrobe reduced to small all-pink garments. Nor are women adverse to using macromanipulation techniques when the opportunity is presented. Women's groups have successfully marshalled the force of law to either promote or prohibit certain actions within our society. On a more personal level, women have used the power of their own money to knowingly and deliberately purchase the services of a gigolo companion for relationships of variable duration (Nelson and Robinson, 1994). The differential use of manipulation or power techniques is as much a function of opportunity or necessity as it is preference.

Within a society where men possess greater structural power and women are unable to have independent access to the means for forging their own social standing, sexuality becomes one of their few, if not their only, resources to exchange for social status and a standard of living (Safilios-Rothschild, 1977: 2). Women born to high status in these conditions would not have to bargain their sexuality, but could negotiate with other attributes, such as their family's name or wealth. As will be noted later in this chapter, both men, and particularly women, have increased their participation in sexual relations prior to marriage since the 1970s. This increase suggests that sexuality is no longer considered to be as necessary a "bargaining chip" for women to use in forming or maintaining a potential partnership. While love is still important for relationships, women's possession of other resources such as education, employment, and increased income permits them to become less dependent upon marriage and less dependent upon the use of their own sexuality as a means of physical and social survival.

Resources, Control, and Ideologies

We saw in the previous chapter that the distribution of housework responsibility is altered when women possess higher amounts of or increase their occupational and monetary resources. Wives' employment promotes a greater equalization of the balance of power in marriages and cohabitation relationships, for at least three interrelated reasons (Blumstein and Schwartz, 1983). In itself, money provides women with greater financial independence and bargaining power to either alter or leave a relationship. Both money and employment confer a greater sense of self-worth and confidence upon women, which they bring into an intimate relationship. As well, husbands understand and respect paid employment with its stresses and achievements and, therefore, give employed wives credit for their additional resources. As we saw also in the previous chapter, an increase in resources permits women to either purchase more services from others (e.g., eating out more, hiring a cleaning service and/or a nanny), or to perform fewer tasks within the home. However, it does not appear from the existing research that an increase in a wife's resources leads to a meaningful increase of household task performance on the part of her husband. The effect of female employment *per se* on male housekeeping, childcare, and relationship care responsibilities and involvements appears to be minimal.

While structural power exerts an important influence, it does not necessarily determine **dyadic** (Guttentag and Secord, 1983: 26) or interpersonal power in intimate relationships. Possession of resources provides only a partial explanation for the power exerted in a relationship. According to **cybernetic** theory (Stets, 1993), individuals will attempt to assert or to reassert control over a relationship partner if they perceive that current conditions threaten to lower their own degree of control below a desired level. Based upon resource theory alone, we would anticipate that men would attempt to control relationships only when they possess more concrete resources than their partners. However, as we saw in the last chapter, despite a lack of socioeconomic resources, unemployed married men typically refuse to shoulder the greater burden of housework responsibilities. It appears that substantially increasing their "share" of housework poses a threat to their sense of masculine entitlement and desired level of control within their own homes. Stets (1993) finds that women are more likely to attempt to control their partners regardless of the level of commitment in a dating relationship. He attributes this finding (Stets, 1993: 682) mainly to women's greater control over love in the private sphere (Lipman-Blumen, 1984) and the fact that women feel they have more to lose when a love relationship is threatened. Issues of real or perceived control can exert as much influence in relationships as do differential possessions of resources.

In addition to resources and desired levels of control, ideologies can exert some influence over power relations between men and women and the management of tasks associated with relationships. Ever since the institution of marriage and other intimate relationships within North America began to emphasize the greater centrality of love and companionship over more prosaic socially prescribed functions (Burgess and Locke, 1950), and the feminist movement began to stress the importance of equality for improved gender relations, researchers have found more respondents in Canada and the United States endorsing an egalitarian ideology. A majority of dating or married couples now proclaim together that their relationships are egalitarian, wherein power is equally distributed between the partners (e.g., Blaisure and Allen, 1995; Peplau et al., 1976; Sexton and Perlman, 1989; Zvonkovic et al., 1996). However, such public declarations are usually found to be at odds with what actually occurs beneath the level of superficial impressions.

Egalitarian Relationships

Researchers find that most "egalitarian" relationships are male dominated (Blaisure and Allen, 1995; Sexton and Perlman, 1989; Schwartz, 1994). Kompter (1989) argues that many incidents of "apparent consensus" in intimate relationships are actually reflections of males' "hidden" power and prestige. Women's compliance with an apparently consensual decision-making event is frequently based upon a sense of "resignation" that the outcome is a foregone conclusion anyway, so why bother to disagree, or is a superficial agreement based upon anticipation of a negative reaction from a man if a woman should disagree (Kompter, 1989). In both cases, women defer to men's power and present the appearance of egalitarian mutuality. As well, whether they be wives or lovers, women often comply with their partners in large and small decisions and often misconstrue their own compliance as a sign of their love rather a sign of their lesser power. Marriage and family life has been referred to as a "tangle of love and domination" (Thorne, 1982: 12) and the two are often not easily disentangled.

The exercise of power may be manifested in major areas of concern such as each partner's paid work and family responsibilities (see Zvonkovic et al., 1996), or in such seemingly minor areas, such as who controls the remote control for the television set (see Box 7.1). Discerning who has the power in a relationship is sometimes obvious and sometimes fraught with difficulties. The following exchange is commonplace among intimate partners: Question "What do you want to do tonight?" Answer: "I don't know. You decide." Who has the power here—the person who will now make the formal decision or the person who designated the other to be the decision-maker? One clue might be obtained by observing how often the person who has just supposedly handed over the reins of power to the other still retains the right to veto all suggestions until the "designated decider" finally comes up with an acceptable one. More often than naught, veto power remains in male hands despite appearances of power equality.

The existing research literature indicates that it is much easier for individuals and couples to talk egalitarian talk than it is to walk an egalitarian walk. The small purposive-sample study by Blaisure and Allen (1995) is instructive not only for its further demonstration of this disparity between ideology and practice but, more importantly, for its findings regarding characteristics of couples who are able to translate beliefs into congruent behaviour. We offer their findings here not as a prescriptive blueprint for future action, but primarily as an illustration of several issues relevant to intimate gender relationships. Respondent couples in the Blaisure and Allen sample were all committed to feminism and the principle of gender equality, either prior to forming their relationship or prior to becoming married, and remained committed to egalitarianism in their marriages of a 10-year median duration. Ninety percent of the married couples had children. Husbands and wives in the all-white, mid-30s, sample possessed approximately equal educational, occupational, and monetary income resources. In all cases, wives acknowledged they could leave the marriages should they so desire and could survive on their own in an essentially comfortable manner. Individual members of all couples remained in their relationships by their own choosing.

Sixty percent of the couples evidenced discrepancies between their egalitarian ideologies and the actual outcomes of their housekeeping, childcare, or marital relationship practices. Forty percent of the couples essentially practised what they believed. All of the couples engaged in what the researchers term as **vigilance** and define as "an attending to and a monitoring of equality, within and outside of their relationship" (Blaisure and Allen, 1995: 10).

Box 7.1   Power by Remote Control

[A] new study from Oregon State University confirms what many women have known for years; the guy still controls the clicker. "He just flips through the channels," one woman told researchers. "It drives me crazy because you can't tell what's on."

The study was conducted by the president of the National Council on Family Relations, who found evidence that channel-surfing men rule the roost, systematically driving their wives and girl-friends bonkers. Alexis Walker did not have to look any further than her own parents for a living example of her research. "My parents bought a second TV set because my mother said to me, "I will not watch TV with your father any more because of the way he uses that remote control," Walker said.

As a daughter, it was funny. As a sociologist, it was confirmation that the balance of power at home is still tilted toward men. In fact, the women in the study said they saw nothing unfair about their men's control over time in front of the TV—typically the biggest chunk of time any couple spend together besides sleeping. "This fits with the gender pattern in family life," Walker said. "We think of men as primary breadwinners. They deserve leisure. They deserve to relax more. It's a way to compensate for going out to the salt mines every day and ensuring family survival," she said. "But many of these women out there are working and they still thought their jobs less important."

The women told researchers they had to plan programming in advance or resort to videotape to see shows they liked. Otherwise, they had to put up with annoying channel surfing to be with their men. "I usually start a couple of days ahead of time when I see them advertised," one woman told researchers. "I tell him to 'get prepared!' I have to be relatively adamant about it. When the time comes up, I have to remind him ahead of time that I told him earlier that I want to watch the program." Carolyn Hannesson of Davis, Calif., said her husband, John, was much the same way, "I don't watch much TV," Hannesson said. "It all depends on my mood. With him, it's sports. His mood doesn't matter."

The men in the study and those interviewed about its results appeared to have no idea they had charge of the remote control. "I guess I don't think about it, I just switch the channel," said Chuck Rhyne of Tracy, Calif.

The Consumer Electronics Manufacturers Association estimates almost 400 million remote controls are in use [in the United States] today. Those numbers—and the three hours a day the research showed most couples averaged in front of the TV together—give the study a serious side that shows women are giving up hard-won equality at home.

"Power dynamics among couples are rarely conscious," said Stephen Marks, who teaches at the University of Texas in Austin and at Maine. "He gets to watch it the way he wants to watch it, whether she's there or not. She has to watch by herself or the way he watches it. To put it in the most simple way, it's not fair. But by thinking it's fair, women make it easier for their husbands to get their own way."

Source: William McCall, Associated Press. "Television clickers still in male hands." Reprinted in *Edmonton Journal*, 3 July 1996: D6; (see also Walker, 1996).

Vigilance began for both men and women with the selection of a partner whose principles and practices appeared to be congruent with one's own and who offered the potential for creating a relationship "superior" to that found in traditional marriage. More specifically, this superiority would be demonstrated with women having their own separate identities within their marriages, and men being emotionally connected to their wives and children (Blaisure and Allen, 1995: 11). The researchers conclude that vigilance comprises five different processes. All of the couples practised three of the processes, while only those couples with congruent ideas and behaviours practised another two vigilant processes.

Common to all the couples were (1) critique of gender injustices; (2) public acts of equality; (3) support of wives' activities. Critiques of gender injustices involved both partners feeling free to note, comment upon, and discuss instances of sexism, harassment, and rigid gender expectations encountered in their daily lives. By pointing out examples of these "injustices" and working together to negate their influence in their own lives, couples were able to maintain a commitment to their preferred ideology. As well, the women in the sample noted that one of the benefits of feminism was the provision of a "language to help them clarify their experiences of injustice, and [to] make sense of their world and define themselves" (Blaisure and Allen, 1995: 11). Men noted they were now better able to empathize with their wives and also better able to express their frustrations with the restrictiveness of the traditional male role.

Public acts of equality included women retaining last names different from those of their husbands, financial decisions, including separate bank accounts and the establishment of separate credit ratings, and joint decision-making in public to reflect their equal input into events affecting their interdependent lives. As one husband states regarding the latter: "So people ranging from a car salesman to everything else expect me to make any decision that is confronting what we should do. They talk to me, and I don't like that. I don't want them to talk to me. I want them to talk to both of us" (in Blaisure and Allen, 1995: 120). Husband's support of wives' activities included giving priority to her employment opportunities, including areas of residential location, arranging his work schedule to accommodate demands upon her time, and various "behind the scenes" activities in support of various feminist organization work wives may wish to pursue.

As noted earlier, only couples whose beliefs and behaviours were congruent practised two additional processes of vigilance: reflective assessment and emotional involvement. Couples who were found to have an imbalance in the distribution of various domestic and relationship tasks not only did not practise these two additional processes, but also tended to explain away their discrepancies with reference to either gender or personality differences (e.g., "she has a higher standard"). Reflective assessment involves the constant monitoring of each partner's contributions to the relationship to identify and correct any imbalances that might be detected. This differs from traditional, and from feminist-discrepant, marriages where any such monitoring is usually done only by wives, and even then imbalances might not be corrected or might result in the demand-withdrawal syndrome noted in an earlier section of this chapter. In discrepant marriages, the unit of comparison is other members of one's own gender (i.e., what other wives or other husbands do or do not do). In congruent marriages, the unit of comparison is one's marital partner.

Finally, the emotional involvement vigilant process refers to couples stressing the importance of verbally communicating emotions, even in the face of disagreement or outright conflict. Continued emotional involvement maintained feelings of interpersonal closeness between the intimate partners. Among those couples who did not emphasize expression of emotions, wives often noted they turned to their friends to fill this important need. Others noted that emotional inexpressiveness created more relationship-work for themselves. As one wife states: "…we'll go through this, 'Well, how are you feeling?' and I try to drag things out of him at times when I know he should be depressed and he should be upset" (in Blaisure and Allen, 1995: 16). Feminist-congruent couples, in contrast, made emotional expressiveness a responsibility of both partners. To use a concept we introduced in an earlier section of this chapter, married couples who attempt to put their feminist beliefs into practice appear to have accepted and adopted a "feminized" conception of love that stresses the importance of shared feelings for maintaining an intimate relationship.

SEXUALITY

Sex, gender, and sexuality are intimately intertwined. However, as we noted in Chapter 1, the interconnections between these variables are neither natural nor inevitable. Our society labours to construct only two sexes, only two genders, and reluctantly acknowledges the existence of two, possibly three (hetero-, homo-, and bi-), sexual orientations, even though the seven-point continuum devised by Kinsey suggests the existence of even finer gradations. Sexual orientations can be distinguished by somewhat different sexual identities, practices, and desires for the other, same, or both sexes. Across all sexual orientations, individuals vary in their interests in all manifestations of sexuality along a (strong positive) erotophile-erotophobe (strong negative) continuum (see Byrne, 1977; Saxton, 1996: 130–131), in whether they prefer to take a dominant (initiating, controlling, "top") or a submissive (passive, receptive, "bottom") stance in sexual encounters, and in whether they incorporate fetishes into their preferred sexual scripts and, if so, what those fetishes might be (e.g., leather, bondage). The combinations and permutations of links between sex, gender, and sexuality defies easy explications. Consequently, generalizations about "male sexuality" or "female sexuality" must be tempered by an acknowledgment that sexuality does not devolve solely to a person's biological sex, but is the product of a complex construction of a variety of factors. Given the extremely brief history of research on sexuality in the United States, and its briefer history in Canada, it is not surprising to learn that social scientists, feminist and nonfeminists alike, have yet to untangle the independent contributions of various factors that together comprise human sexuality.

We are still trying to learn whether sexuality in males is more different from or similar to sexuality in females; whether gender overrides sexual orientation to produce common patterns of sexual desires, meanings, and practices among women and among men regardless of their sexual orientation; whether sexual orientation overrides gender, such that lesbians and gay men are uniquely different from heterosexual women and men. Central questions that focus research and theory on the subjects of sex and gender can also be raised regarding sexuality: "Is sexuality governed by biology or culture? Is it fixed, an identity that is set early and endures through life? Or is it fluid, shifting with time and temptation?" (Toufexis, 1992). Even though a large proportion of the people in our society display constancy in their sexuality, the sexual identity, sexual orientation, and sexual behaviour of substantial proportions do evidence changes in varying directions over time.

As we noted in Chapter 1, avowed heterosexuals can, and do, fantasize about sexual contacts with members of the same sex, and may have occasional same-sex sexual contacts during portions of their lives. Similar, but reversed, patterns are found among avowed homosexuals. Bisexuals can, and do, "swing" both ways, either demonstrating approximate equality in the numbers of sexual partners of either sex, or showing somewhat greater interest in and behaviour oriented towards one sex, while defying attempts to force them into "either or" classification as heterosexuals or homosexuals. Attempts to dismiss a current interest as a temporary passing "phase," a description leveled more often against departures from heterosexual norms, do an injustice to the heartfelt commitment of the moment. "Lesbian chic" is a contemporary phase designed to dismiss the challenge to our society's assumptions of "normality" and strength in heterosexual numbers posed by increasingly more women "coming out" of their closets in the mid- to late 1990s, and publicly proclaiming an erotic interest in other women.

While other cultures, both historical and contemporary, institutionalize periods of homosexual and heterosexual contacts into a bisexual life history (Bird and Melville, 1994: 152; Ford and Beach, 1951; Kinsman, 1996), Western cultures, including Canada, do not provide such guidelines. Women and men are not completely free to select repeatedly from an equally evaluated cafeteria of sexual choices comprising sex, gender, orientation, and interests for self and partners. Rather, sex, gender, and sexuality within our society exist within a sociocultural framework that shapes preferences and describes them as if they were natural, inevitable, lifelong, and the only possible outcomes. Lesbians, gay men, and bisexuals are often described as if they lack sufficient feminine and masculine qualities to qualify as "real" women and men. The sexualities of women, homosexual males, and homosexual females have all been subject to greater scrutiny and policing (both literally and figuratively) than has the sexuality of heterosexual men, which has been taken as the unquestioned norm throughout most of our social history.

Visible, and not so visible, anatomical differences between the sexes, coupled with an underlying assumption that sexuality equals reproduction, easily lead to a belief that male and female sexuality must be different and essentially reducible to, and embodied by, a penile versus a vaginal sexuality. If, as Freud held, "anatomy is destiny," then gender sexualities must be different. Positing the existence of a "'natural sexuality' uncontaminated by cultural influences" (Jackson and Scott, 1996: 11) is of limited value, since such a proposition is untestable. No examples of "pure" male or female sexuality can be found. Nor can the existence of such a sexuality account for historical, cross-cultural, and individual variations in sexual expression. As we indicated in Chapter 2, researchers thus far have been unable to isolate specific genetic or hormonal bases for human sexuality that dictate heterosexuality, bisexuality, or homosexuality or that clearly differentiate and determine male sexuality from female sexuality in terms of behaviour, attitudes, meanings, desires, and fantasies. Rather than being driven purely by human biology (doing what comes "naturally"), observable differences in human sexuality appear to be socially constructed through both active and passive participation in differential life-long socialization processes within variable sociocultural contexts. Part of this socialization, as we shall see later, involves being exposed to social definitions that distinguish the sexual from the nonsexual, privileging some forms of sexuality as acceptable and others as disreputable, and constructing sexuality scripts for women and men. These social definitions are all shaped, conveyed, and reinforced via language.

Languages of Sexuality

All of the English languages of sexuality are male-made. Three separate, yet interrelated, language systems pertaining to sexuality exist within our society: a technical-medical terminology; a socially proscribed language of profanity (the majority of our swear words are sexual in reference, with the remainder being either irreligious or excretory in nature); a vast vocabulary of euphemisms. Most of the technical-medical terms used to identify internal reproductive parts of the human body (e.g., Fallopian tubes, Mullerian and Wolffian systems) and components of sexual physiology (e.g., Cowper's glands) honour their male discoverers. The remainder of the technical names for hormones, for genitalia, for hetero-, homo-, bi-, and autosexuality are all derived from Latin, a male-created language system. We noted in Chapter 5 that most of our forbidden, impolite, vocabulary of swear words is male created and reserved predominantly for male use (although the gender gap in usage is narrowing). Even our lexicon of sexuality euphemisms are controlled overwhelmingly by, and reflective of, male experiences and desires. Through controlling the languages of sexuality, males control their own and female sexuality.

> This means that women's feelings and experience remains unspoken, because it is, quite literally, unspeakable. There are, in fact, very few words for women's genitals...whereas there are a great many other terms for the penis....[W]hen she wants to talk about what she feels, she will discover that there is a poverty of language to describe clitoral sensation....The term "vagina" comes from the Latin for "sheath" or "scabbard." This male encoding represents the vagina as a passive receptacle awaiting penetration as a scabbard awaits a sword. If women had the power to name and give meanings, the images associated with the vagina might well be much more active, creative and strong. (Kitzinger, 1985: 36, 38)

Implicit within the quote from Kitzinger is a question of whether important elements of sexuality of and for women have yet to enter into our individual and collective consciousness because of a lack of identifying names or terms. As suggested by the Sapir-Whorf hypothesis (see Chapter 5), a vicious circle exists, whereby a lack of terms prevents thinking and discussion about missing elements of women's sexuality, and the lack of thinking and discussion prevents the introduction of new terms.

Meaning: Sexuality and the Theme of Penetration

Thinking and communicating about sexuality is constrained by our understandings of what constitutes sexuality. Throughout the following pages, we use the term "sexuality" and "sexual" to refer to a wide inclusive spectrum of actions, thoughts, and feelings of an erotic nature. Whole societies, and specific subcultures therein, tend to narrow their focus to a more exclusive set of referents. Whether specific acts are given a sexual meaning depends upon the defining language available. In our society, for example, an erect penis may or may not be attributed a sexual meaning, depending upon the situation; erections in the womb, during early infancy, and during or upon waking from the REM sleep phase correctly are not given a sexual meaning. Female breasts are not defined as sexual when exposed in a "natural" outdoor setting in Ontario, but are defined as sexual when exposed indoors. Erect nipples of both males or females may be a response to cold weather, rather than an indicator of sexual desire. As we shall see later in this chapter, the social and legal definition of "rape" has been redefined in Canada from a purely sexual act stemming solely from sexual motives, to a physical assault stemming from nonsexual power-based motives. The sexually stimulating components of breastfeeding are essentially ignored or downplayed, while the nonsexual nurturant components are emphasized. Despite remarkable parallels between physiological changes in the female body during undrugged childbirth and during sexual orgasm (Newton, 1973, in Walum, 1977: 84), giving birth is not defined as a sexual act within our society.

What constitutes "real" sexuality, according to our belief systems, reflects male standards expressed in a male-controlled language system. Within the context of our historically pronatalist society (a society oriented towards promoting a high birth rate), heterosexuality is privileged, while homosexuality (incapable of reproduction without artificial aid) is marginalized and stigmatized. Penile penetration of the vagina (a description that reinforces active-male-passive-female stereotypes, as opposed to "vaginal envelopment of the penis"), is the defining characteristic of real sexuality, according to our predominant heterosexual model. This limited form of sexual behaviour is bracketed by two related, but lesser evaluated, categories of activities symbolically distinguished by their own distinctive terms. The three categories are presented in our society as forming a sequential continuum of interpersonal sexual activities.

Foreplay refers to activities engaged in prior to actual intercourse and includes talking, hugging, kissing, as well as manual and oral stimulation of erogenous zones. Over the course of the twentieth century, oral sexuality increasingly has become part of the sexual repertoires of women and men (Michael et al., 1994: 140; Rubin, 1990: 33–39) and has been acknowledged by social definers in the medical and therapeutic communities as an acceptable practice, so long as it does not become a substitute for penetrative sexuality, thus reinforcing a reproduction theme. Indulging only in oral and manual activities, but not actual intercourse, permits many women to retain their status, technically, of being a "virgin," a status necessary in a society still retaining vestiges of a gender-based double standard for evaluating sexual behaviour.

Afterplay refers to post-intercourse activities such as talking and hugging, although many males expand the definition to include lighting a cigarette, reaching for the remote control or their clothing, sleeping, or asking "Was it good for you?" or "How many this time?" (women rarely ask these questions of men since the answer is presumed to be a foregone, self-evident conclusion, not a subject for debate). Afterplay typically commences following his orgasm, the event signaling the end of intercourse, not hers. If one set of activities is characterized as foreplay, and another set of activities as afterplay, then real play (real sexuality) is characterized only by intercourse (coitus, copulation)—a penis penetrating and thrusting into a vagina. "Almost all resources that deal with sex[uality]—medical books, textbooks, popular books, and articles, as well as erotic materials—treat sex[uality] and intercourse as if they were the same" (Zilbergeld, 1992: 51; see also Michael et al., 1994: 135).

Hite (1981: 570–571) finds in her survey of men and sexuality that most men feel foreplay should lead quickly and inevitably to intercourse and orgasm. Although enjoyable, foreplay for most men is a means to an end, not an end in itself. Female respondents in Hite's (1976: 200–220) survey of women and sexuality express dissatisfaction both with intercourse and with a lack of sufficient foreplay. Since Hite's studies did not ask the same questions of male and female respondents, comparative findings across the surveys may be as much a function of research design as of actual gender differences. However, identical questions were asked of both male and female respondents in a small sample of American heterosexually experienced university students (Denney et al., 1984). More than two-thirds of the male respondents identified intercourse as the aspect of a sexual experience they most enjoy, followed by one-third identifying foreplay. No males identified afterplay as a most enjoyable experience. In contrast, almost two-thirds of the female respondents identified foreplay as the most enjoyable, followed by intercourse and then afterplay (Denney et al., 1984: 241). Halpern and Sherman (1979 in Denney et al., 1984) find that significantly more men prefer not to engage in lengthy expressions of affection, nor touch or be touched by their female partner, following intercourse and orgasm. Women are consequently much more likely to express feelings of being ignored following intercourse and experience feelings of being used by a male partner only for his sexual pleasure.

Penetration (or envelopment), if invited, is not loathsome for most women as it can satisfy any number of physical, psychological, and emotional needs. However, penetration rarely meets orgasmic needs and available studies suggest that, even if women overall prefer and enjoy foreplay more, the amounts they receive are often less than sufficient. In the most comprehensive, methodologically sound, survey of sexuality conducted to date, Michael et al. (1994: 135, 139) find that 95 percent of respondents had coitus during their last sexual encounter. Sometime during that occasion, only 20 percent of female respondents received cunnilingus. Men generally emphasize and prefer intercourse more than foreplay or afterplay. Whether this preference is indicative primarily of simple conformity to our dominant sexual script, or a reflective assessment of a primary source of physical enjoyment, is unclear. Regardless of the derivation of men's attitudes, the penetrative model of sexuality reflects male, more so than female, definitions, preferences, and satisfactions.

This male-shaped equation of sexuality equals heterosexuality equals masculine penetration was reinforced historically by Freud's prescriptive assertion at the turn of the century, without any supportive empirical validation, that "mature" female sexuality centred upon a vaginally induced orgasm (see Koedt, 1972). Freud's contention eventually was discredited by the laboratory research of Masters and Johnson (1966; Masters et al., 1994: 51–52) demonstrating and confirming that female orgasm originates with the clitoris and that intercourse typically fails to provide women with sufficient orgasm-inducing stimulation. More than 50 percent, perhaps up to 75 percent of women (exact figures vary by researchers), require direct manual or oral clitoral stimulation to orgasm (Reinisch, 1990: 201). Although Michael et al. (1994: 128) report that 29 percent of women regularly orgasm during intercourse, the researchers failed to ask how these orgasms were attained (e.g., possibly with additional manual stimulation). Furthermore, of those women who do attain orgasm during penile thrusting, the majority typically prefer other forms of clitoral manipulation (Masters et al., 1994). The timing of the Masters and Johnson (1966) research coincided with a societal attitude shift, amidst concerns about overpopulation and women's rights to control all aspects of their bodies, away from our strong pronatalist orientation of the past, and towards an orientation emphasizing, among other things, women's right to sexual pleasure. Sexuality featuring reproduction yielded to a sexuality featuring erotic enjoyment, including orgasm (D'Emilio and Freedman, 1988).

In feminist circles generally, and certain lesbian-feminist circles in particular, penetrative sexuality has been equated with an oppressive, exploitive, sexuality—a metaphor for all aspects of male-female relations in the context of a male-dominated society. If "real" sexuality should be defined by a new criterion of what is most likely to yield orgasmic pleasure, then foreplay sexuality that comprises manual and oral clitoral stimulation is more real, more central, than is intercourse sexuality for women. Such a shift in the meaning of real sexuality also renders the penis less central and, at best, only peripheral to women's orgasmic satisfaction, a daunting possibility in a society with a strong patriarchal heritage. Redefining sexuality in this way would be threatening to men and possibly also to the women who love and support them. Perhaps not surprisingly, our society generally continues to insist that proper sexuality ultimately involves a penetrative method of stimulation guaranteed to provide men with orgasmic satisfaction and typically guaranteed to deny women that same satisfaction. Our standards for and definitions of acceptable sexual behaviour and attitudes are still constructed predominantly by white, middle-class, heterosexual men (Baca Zinn and Eitzen, 1993: 247; Vance, 1984: 19), although Zilbergeld (1992: 9) argues that the definition of sexuality is on its way to becoming femininized.

Comparative Images of Male and Female Sexuality

Throughout history, until the late nineteenth century, images of sexuality conveyed by a variety of sources focused only upon heterosexual males and females, who were perceived and prescribed as normative. In the prescience era, sexuality was presumed to be ordained by reigning deities who, in their infinite wisdom, bestowed essentially different sexualities upon men and women. Science later began searching for organic, body-based, origins for male and female sexuality. In the past and the present, understandings of male sexuality has been shaped by the "belief in a sometimes overpowering male sex drive and the belief that men have immutable sexual needs that are manifested over and above individual attempts at repression" (Blumstein and Schwartz, 1990, in Bird and Melville, 1994: 139). According to our folklore, a "real man is someone who's always interested in sex and ready for it" (Zilbergeld, 1992: 46). This Western notion of a powerful, often uncontrollable, male sexuality has remained unchanged for centuries. What has changed over time has been the attributed source for this sexuality. In contrast, our cultural images of female sexuality have undergone a number of significant transformations over time.

Some of the earliest images in Western society of female sexuality were developed within a religious framework constructed to establish social and sexual morality. The Christian church propagated two differently evaluated images of women: the nonsexual Virgin Mary and the sexual temptress Eve (Laws and Schwartz, 1977: 13–14; Daly, 1973: 76–82). Evaluations of the sexuality, or lack thereof, of these women was based not upon their outcomes for women themselves, but rather upon their outcomes for men. The good, nonsexual woman, epitomized by the Virgin Mary, did not tempt men to lustful preoccupations with sexuality, but instead aided men in focusing their attentions and energies upon their own spiritual salvation. The bad, sexual woman, epitomized by Eve, turned men away from matters of the spirit towards matters of the sexual flesh, and in so doing condemned men to fall from a state of spiritual grace. Women's sexuality was thereby held accountable for men's status as saints or sinners. Implicit within these images of women lies a notion of female sexuality as a powerful force that must be curtailed, lest men succumb to evil temptation. Extolling a desirable image of, at best, a passive female sexuality represented an attempt to constrain women into a restricted sexual role to gain social acceptability.

Religious injunctions against an active female sexuality were eventually reinforced in the latter half of the nineteenth century, by an almost exclusively male medical profession of general practitioners, gynecologists, obstetricians, and psychiatrists, who claimed the responsibility for pronouncing judgments on sexuality and physical and mental health (Blumstein and Schwartz, 1983: 41). The terms *heterosexuality* and *homosexuality* were coined during this time and members of the medical profession provided politicians, lawyers, and judges with "scientific" evidence to justify the regulation of homosexual (Kinsman, 1996) and various pleasure-motivated heterosexual (Katz, 1995) practices. By now, the norms of chastity before marriage and fidelity within marriage confined socially acceptable female sexuality within narrowly constrained limits. Any deviations from this restricted sexuality script outside of marriage, and any dispositions towards an active, lustful sexuality within marriage, led to diagnoses of women in the nineteenth century as suffering from various forms of physical or mental ill health (Edwards, 1994; Ehrenreich and English, 1978).

Opinions and beliefs began to change over the first half of the twentieth century. "Marriage manuals" written largely, but not exclusively, by males with medical training continued to define and shape female sexuality. Typically, without providing any empirical evidence, and in a sincere-yet-condescending fashion, the experts of the time granted good and virtuous women a right to be actively sexual within marriage (Gordon and Shankweiler, 1971). Female sexuality was described and prescribed with two major qualities: **monogamy** and **dormancy**. Females were proclaimed to be monogamous by nature, unlike men who were held to be polygamous. Females naturally "saved" or conserved their sexuality for one man and one man only—namely, their husbands. In addition, female sexuality was held to be essentially dormant, quietly residing under a surface veneer of asexuality, until awakened in true Sleeping Beauty fashion by a man—a husband. In contrast to prevailing views in previous centuries, a good woman could now be sexual and enjoy erotic interest, desire, activity, and perhaps occasional aggressiveness, but only in her marital bed. Females were not granted an autonomous sexuality with their own independent sense of desire but, instead, required a sexual awakening at the instigation and control of a man. Marriage manuals provided medical approval for casting men into the role of "sexpert," charged with the responsibility of initiating and teaching women about female sexuality. At the same time, the qualities of monogamy and dormancy decreed as essential characteristics of female sexuality reinforced, and made seemingly natural, the social conventions extolling chastity and fidelity for women.

The norms of chastity and fidelity remained firmly in place until challenges to these standards began to arise in the 1960s. However, vestiges of the historical orientation towards female sexuality can be found in numerous dichotomous images still available within our culture for classifying women based upon their restrained or unbridled sexual conduct. Attitudes towards female sexuality held by both males and females have been characterized by ambivalent feelings of attraction and repulsion. The traditional notion of sexual man and nonsexual woman underlies a double standard of evaluation, with women who conduct themselves in a sexual manner comparable to men being publicly condemned although, often simultaneously, privately lusted after. A woman is often still described, by both men and women, as being either a "madonna" or a "whore," a "princess" or a "prostitute," a "good" girl or a "tramp"; she deserves to be placed on a "pedestal" or condemned to live in the "gutter," the dwelling place of a "fallen woman." No extensive comparable imagery is available to describe men in terms of their sexuality.

Women's sexuality continues to be defined in terms relative to men. A woman who is "too" sexual according to the standards of either her male partner or males generally (i.e., a woman who desires sexual acts more often than does her partner or wants a sexual relationship with someone else) is identified as a "nymphomaniac," "promiscuous," a "slut," a "bimbo," or tagged with the very euphemistic label of being "boy crazy." A woman who is deemed to be not sufficiently sexual (i.e., a female who either wants sexual acts less frequently than her male partner or does not want to have a sexual relationship with a particular male) is "frigid." In contrast, men are not evaluated sexually according to female standards. A man who desires to be sexually active more often than his female partner is identified as "normal." "Stud" is a term of endearment and positive evaluation, not condemnation. A man who is not sufficiently sexual around women is presumed to be "gay." Women's standards of behaviour essentially are irrelevant to these evaluations of men.

Throughout most of the twentieth century, our belief system has assumed that women do not possess an active, self-determined and self-initiated sexuality. Our socially constructed model depicts and judges female sexuality as essentially reactive to male sexuality. At the same time, our social beliefs construct a self-fulfilling prophecy, wherein sexuality should receive a lower priority in the consciousness of women than in men. While men are often accused of thinking with their genitals, the same claim rarely is registered for women. The image of penis-with-man-attached (*Erectus Homo*) is common; not so for clitoris-with-woman-following. "[A] boy's penis becomes the pole around which his consciousness revolves" (Keen, 1991: 71). "For most women, the 'essence of womanhood' would not lie in their genitals or in this experience of their sexual powers" (Rubin, 1983: 108).

We lack words in the English language to depict a positive and rewarding image of an independent and assertive female sexuality; "studette" has never been part of our everyday language system. Concepts of a female sexual predator generally are limited to the Criminal Code (e.g., the disproportionate emphasis placed upon policing female prostitutes rather than their male patrons) or, alternatively, psychiatric manuals. For example, a highly debatable explanation for childhood sexual abuse in females, derived from psychoanalytic theory, posits that young girls are supposedly acting out unresolved Oedipal fantasies with fathers or father-figures and, consciously or not, "seek out" or "invite" such treatment. However, generally, proclamations by rapists and sexual abusers that "she made me do it" are simply seen as wholly self-serving. Our society still commonly presumes that women's sexuality is inherently and ideally passive, not active.

A key issue of debate over the past 25 years concerns whether female sexuality was, and is, "repressed or socially constructed" (Jackson and Scott, 1996: 6). The notion of a repressed sexuality implies the existence of an internal "authentic" sexuality or sexual potential (presumably biologically based) that is not permitted full expression. External social forces deny women an opportunity to gratify their desires or translate their desires into reality. However, evidence of such repression can only be ascertained by comparisons with the supposed freedom of male sexual expression. Not only is male sexuality also constrained, but such comparisons imply that the meaning and nature of female sexuality is still to be derived from its contrast to male sexuality. Once again, male sexuality becomes normative, and attempts to remove constrains upon female sexuality deliberately, or inadvertently, become designs to bring female sexuality to a point of conformity with male sexuality. A repression argument ultimately becomes phallocentric. In contrast, a social-construction argument contends that women's sexuality has been and is created in such a way that women are unaware that certain sexual wants, desires, or expressions are possible. The language of sexuality prevents women from experiencing and articulating any desires for anything other than those circumscribed by the prevailing sexuality script. That script restricts women's sexual role and opportunities for sexual expression more severely than men's, although the script also places constraints and pressures on men.

The Sexual Script

As we indicated in Chapter 1, sexuality scripts are composed of culturally created guidelines defining appropriate sexuality and delineating roles to be performed by participants in a sexual encounter. While each seemingly casts performers into different roles, these scripts typically involve variations upon the same underlying themes. For example:

> In one [script]…he is expected to get an erection from her naked beauty, keep his erection, arouse her passions, and hold off his orgasm until she reaches hers. He's required to do all this without any information about what really turns her on. The woman is passive, beautiful, and graceful while she waits for this incredible experience called orgasm, and when nothing happens, she concentrates on the romance. In another [script], the poor woman is responsible for the man's erection. She does oralsex [*sic*] to get him hard and remains focused exclusively on his pleasure. He gets on top and does what feels good for him and she accommodates him, going into her act of passionate sounds to excite him all the more. He comes, she fakes it, and he dozes off holding her in his arms. She's happy because she has pleased him, and she loves the closeness. He's happy because her response has proved he's a good lover, and he loves her loving him. (Dodson, 1996: 16)

This description attempts to portray two variations upon the central heterosexual script. Unlike same-sex couples, who lack an institutionalized script prescribing "who does what to whom," "[a]mong heterosexual couples, the content of sexual behavior in the relationship is guided by gender. Men direct the couple's sexual life and women modify what happens by what they choose to accept" (Blumstein and Schwartz, 1983: 244). Since marriage manuals of the early part of the twentieth century granted men the right and obligation of awakening women's, preferably their wife's, sexuality, our sexuality script has mandated that, within sexual encounters, men be assigned the roles of choreographers and teachers, and women the role of willing, perhaps naive, students. Men, therefore, were and are expected to be more knowledgeable about sexuality, to be competent and, since they possessed a powerful sexuality, ever-ready. The commonly prescribed and adopted "missionary" position for heterosexual encounters of man on top and woman on the bottom reinforces a stereotypical theme of active, dominant, male and passive, submissive, receptive female.

Our culture's presumption that women possess a less powerful sexuality contributes to women being assigned a gatekeeper role as regulator of the progression of intimacies permitted within any sexual relationships. This role requires a woman to "engage in sexual behavior only to the extent necessary to satisfy her boyfriend's needs, not her own" (Lott, 1994: 120). If her needs are less than his, she can focus her attention upon a male partner, rather than the other way around. If men's sexual (and other) needs are deemed more important than women's, women need not consider what their own needs, wants, wishes, or desires actually are. The two script variations presented in the quotation form Dodson (1996) depict women performing either a completely passive or an active, but still supporting, role. Both scripts prescribe that female sexuality should be constructed and presented according to the needs of male sexuality.

Our predominant sexual script is not only a set of guidelines for shaping and attaining sexual pleasure, but also becomes a testing ground for masculinity and femininity. Success or failure affirms or threatens one's own and one's partner's sense of gender, which is particularly meaningful since it occurs within an intimate context. Using a circular form of logic, our culture decrees that to be masculine is to be sexual and to be sexual is to be masculine. Failure at one is, therefore, indicative of failure at the other. Men consequently have a considerable ego and gender investment in successful performance of their sexual role, a fact not unknown to women who learn during adolescence and confirm during adulthood that males pursue sexuality with more at stake than simply sexual pleasure, a theme we shall return to in a later section.

Men are required to attain and maintain an erection throughout the entire time period of a sexual encounter. In addition, men are now expected to take responsibility for women's orgasms. "You can't consider yourself a good lover unless you give your partner an earth-shaking experience" (Zilbergeld, 1992: 53). Failure to either attain or maintain an erection (commonly referred to as "impotence") and "premature" ejaculation (a deficiency in timing whereby his ejaculation and orgasm occurs prior to her orgasm) constitute "failures" on his part ("dysfunctions" in the language of sexual therapy). Worry over one or both frequently contribute to *performance anxiety* in men. Performance anxiety in men, in turn, can lead to a lessening or loss of desire for interpersonal sexual encounters (rarely does a man complain about premature ejaculation or erection problems when masturbating).

Even though our culture has not equated sexuality with femininity comparable to the equation for men, women are tested upon their sexual performances, and are expected to meet certain requirements. "Failure" to achieve orgasm can lead to a woman being negatively labeled as "frigid" ("preorgasmic" in the language of sexual therapy) and also cast doubts upon the expertise and masculinity of her supposedly sexpert male partner. Faking orgasms to please male egos and avoid negative labeling is not unknown among women, although presumably the practice was more common in the past than today. Even being slow to orgasm can have negative repercussions on a sense of femininity, particularly as women's sense of femininity becomes more strongly anchored in performance expectations for their own sexual bodies.

At a moment of sexual contact, both men and women share some concerns about their appearances and body images. In the past, men have only been concerned about penis size, but with the continuing greater emphasis, courtesy of the advertising industry, upon the desirability of attaining a level of muscular development unrelated to anything other than a visual aesthetic, men now also have concerns about their overall physical appearance. Concern over male body appearance is more recent and more limited, in comparison with our long history this century of demanding that women conform to an unattainable, youthful, slender, proportional or top-heavy (see Barbie) standard of physical attractiveness. Men are socialized to a strong visual component of sexual desire via countless years of exposure to media images of clothed and unclothed women. While advertisers gleefully proffer a variety of products to aid women in presenting a close approximation of the ideal sexualized body when clothed, nudity becomes the enemy of clothing artifice. Even though most men cannot recognize the enhancing appearance offered by a WonderBra™, a push-in-and-up underwire bra, or a full-body girdle when these items are covered by other clothes, they can acknowledge that they are not getting everything that was advertised when a female partner removes her clothes. Disrobing thus becomes a major area for concerns for most women who cannot count upon a male partner's awareness of the gap between fashion-industry fiction and naked reality.

Women in general face an additional concern not confronted by men. Both historically and currently, as we shall see in a later section, strong negative stereotypes abound regarding the sight, smell, and taste of women's genitals. Most women do not receive a positive introductory orientation during childhood towards their own genitals. Considerable effort is required to undo negative associations acquired during early years of life. Consequently, to literally expose oneself to a new male sexual partner requires a greater act of courage for women than for men.

Gender and Experienced Sexuality

From a physiological standpoint, male and female bodies respond in very similar ways as they proceed through the same four (excitement, plateau, orgasm, resolution) phases of the human sexual response cycle. The bodies of both sexes undergo similar changes in localized blood flow (vasocongestion), muscle tension (myotonia), heightened blood pressure, heart, pulse, and respiration rates (Masters and Johnson, 1966; Masters et al., 1994). Furthermore, male and female bodies are capable of proceeding through all four phases at the same speed (Masters and Johnson, 1970, 1966). That females are often slower than males demonstrates the greater inhibiting influence of dangers associated with sexuality, to be presented later, that can intrude upon women's physiological responses. Some gender differences exist in body-based experiences at certain times during the first two phases of the sexual response cycles, such as "ballooning" of the vagina, which creates a sensation of an inner "void," greater awareness of vaginal, as opposed to penile, lubrication, or greater awareness of a penile, as opposed to a clitoral, erection. However, the subjective experience of orgasm is the same for men and women (Saxton, 1996: 119).

Males typically experience ejaculation coincident with, yet independent of, orgasm. Once ejaculation occurs, male bodies enter a refractory phase of variable duration (Masters and Johnson, 1966) during which they are essentially insensate to further stimulation for a period of time and incapable of another ejaculation. During this time, vasocongestion and myotonia abate relatively quickly. Should orgasm (and ejaculation in males) not occur, tissues remain swollen with blood and muscles remain tense for longer periods of time, producing feelings of discomfort for both males and females. Cultural myths about male sexuality allow men to use these feelings (referred to in the vernacular as "blue balls") as an excuse to plead for or demand orgasmic relief lest they suffer permanent tissue damage. No equivalent claims ("a clitoral crisis"?) have been granted to women to justify female demands for orgasmic release. Despite ardent proclamations to the contrary, no tissue damage occurs if orgasmic release is not forthcoming, and both male and female bodies eventually return to pre-excitement states.

Females typically do not ejaculate near or during orgasm, although Ladas et al. (1982) contend that some unknown proportion of the female population possess a G-spot (named after the German physician Ernest Grafenberg, supposedly the first male researcher to discover its existence) on the upper wall of the vagina that, if properly stimulated, could induce orgasm and ejaculation. Even though the contention set off a short-lived treasure hunt among women, alone and in sexually active couples, the findings of Ladas et al. remain essentially unsubstantiated (Masters et al., 1992; Tavris, 1992). Without ejaculation, female bodies do not enter into a refractory phase and are, therefore, capable of responding continuously to further sexual stimulation. Women consequently are capable of "multiple" (more accurately "serial") orgasms during a single sexual encounter. Although posited earlier by Kinsey and his associates (1953), this capacity had not been observed, or if observed had not been acknowledged, by medical sexuality science prior to the late 1960s. Speculation holds that approximately one-quarter to one-third of all North American women have been multiorgasmic with a partner and an unknown, likely larger portion, with self stimulation only (Masters et al., 1994: 68).

This difference in orgasmic potential may not be sex-irreducible. Sexuality therapists claim to have been able to teach men to become "multiorgasmic" by delaying their ejaculation until achieving a final desired orgasm (Hartmann, 1991, in Rice, 1996: 166), although the veracity of these claims has been challenged (Masters et al., 1994: 68). It appears that the only training females need to become multiorgasmic is experimentation via self-exploration. If orgasms-per-encounter is to be taken as a hallmark indicator of sexuality, a highly debatable proposition, women are likely more sexual than men. The implications of this capacity potentially challenge our society's construction of sexuality, which, as we have already seen, has traditionally assumed that females are "less sexual" than males. While women *can be* multiorgasmic, whether they *actually are* at any precise moment in their lives or over their life course is another matter and the consequence of a host of other social and psychological factors.

Vance (1984) argues that sexuality for women comprises a powerful juxtaposed "tension" between *pleasure* and *danger*:

> For some [women], the dangers of sexuality—violence, brutality, and coercion, in the form of rape, forcible incest, and exploitation, as well as everyday cruelty and humiliation—make the pleasures pale by comparison. For others, the positive possibilities of sexuality—exploration of the body, curiosity, intimacy, sensuality, adventure, excitement, human connection, basking in the infantile and non-rational—are not only worthwhile, but provide sustaining energy. (Vance, 1984: 1)

Individually and collectively, women alternate over their lifetimes between these two perceptions of sexuality, in response to either actual or perceived changes in their life circumstances. The imagery of pleasure and danger has been applied in feminist literature exclusively to women, contributing to an assumption that sexuality for men is all pleasure and no, or only little, danger, yet sexuality poses a significant danger for a man's sense of his own (and a female partner's sense of his) masculinity. However, the dangers of sexuality appear to be greater for women. Ambivalence towards sexuality, consequently, is greater and more pronounced for women than for men.

Sexuality for women is associated with the dangers of a loss of reputation in a society maintaining a double-standard of evaluation for sexual experience, exploitation or coercion into sexual involvement against their will, unplanned or unwanted pregnancy, and discomfort, or even death, via sexually transmitted diseases (a danger shared with men). Feminists argue that it is not sexuality *per se*, but sexuality with men (i.e., heterosexuality) that constitutes the actual source of danger for women, a danger supposedly absent in lesbianism (Jackson and Scott, 1996: 17). Sexuality with men poses dangers for women, insofar as power is typically distributed unequally in heterosexual relationships. However, the connection between gender, sexuality, and power is neither simple nor straightforward.

Sexuality and Power

Sexual behaviour often springs from nonsexual motives, and often satisfies nonsexual objectives among both men and women. It appears, at first glance, that sexuality and power are configured into different pathways for each gender in our society. Among men, power begets sexuality; among women, sexuality is power. The social, political, and economic power enjoyed by men often acts as a symbolic aphrodisiac wherein many men, devoid of other physically appealing attributes, find that their power alone provides them with sexual access to women. Despite the fact that these men are often grossly overweight by any objective standards, ugly by an honest appraisal of human beauty, severely lacking in intimacy skills of charm and sensitivity, and even sexually inept, captains of industry, leading politicians, and men of significant economic wealth are often referred to by women as being "very sexy." Many of these, and other, men also, by virtue of their sense of entitlement associated with being the superior sex within a patriarchal society, often believe their sexual will should be acceded to by any women they desire. In other words, many men feel that they have the basic right to impose their sexuality upon women simply by virtue of the fact that they are the more powerful sex possessing the more powerful sexuality. To complete the circle, imposing their sexuality demonstrates their power. A large proportion of sexual harassment and sexual assault acts are based upon this sense of male entitlement anchored in social power.

In contrast, for centuries, in Western and many other societies, sexuality has been an important resource for women as a means of gaining power itself, or at least access to power, in various forms. Where

> women have little direct access to money, prestige, and power, they are not only tempted but are even forced to use sex[uality] as their only weapon, their only resource. Only by using sexuality as a tool can they diminish the social distance between themselves and men and gain access to money and prestige and occasionally also to power. (Safilios-Rothschild, 1977: 47)

The actual power wielded by women here is debatable, since standards of physical and sexual attractiveness are controlled by men, shaped to appeal to men's fanciful desires. Women's power largely resides in deciding whether or not to comply with these standards, not in creating and implementing the standards themselves. Women who, through a combination of nature and nurture, achieve male-defined standards of sexual attractiveness, often find that they can exchange their sexuality for other commodities controlled by men. Men, the supposedly powerful setters of standards, often find that women's compliance with those very standards can lead men to succumb to women's power and yield various material and nonmaterial advantages to women.

Sexuality can be utilized for both tangible (money and other material artifacts, marriage, occupational status) and intangible gain. "Girls and women learn that sex[uality] can be exchanged not only for commodities, but also for intimacy or commitment" (Lott, 1994: 118). Girls and women were, and are, taught to believe that their sexuality, if packaged in an appealing form, contains a powerful force, giving them an advantage at the intimate-relationships bargaining table. Especially during adolescence, when females have few other available resources (e.g., no meaningful occupation or income), becoming aware that one's sexual desirability can be translated into other positive outcomes (e.g., being wanted and sought after, deciding when and where to go out on dates, receiving gifts, enhancing status with peers) can produce a heady sense of power.

Often, women experience a sense of disillusionment and disappointment upon discovering that such packaging reduces them to sexual commodities, composed of attractive body components in which the whole person is often ignored by men who prefer to focus only upon a female's sexual parts (a "sex" object), and that promises fueled by lust often fail to materialize once a man's desire is satiated. In a society such as ours that has viewed love, commitment, and sexuality as interdependent with one another, boys and men also learn that promises of love and commitment can be exchanged for sexuality. That not all men bargain in good faith is indicated by the many adolescent and adult women who wonder if they have been sexually exploited by false promises.

The power of sexuality to provide nonsexual gain for women is declining in our society. Women have other means of access to power via education, occupation and income, legal change, and general social change. In addition, love, commitment, and sexuality are becoming more independent of one another within our society. Both men and women in Canada are increasingly more likely than in the past to require lesser levels of affectionate commitment before permitting themselves to become sexually involved (Hobart, 1996). Sexuality, consequently, becomes less of a powerful commodity of exchange for women, a change much lamented by sexual conservatives (e.g., Fein and Schneider, 1995). These changes have not in themselves, however, reduced the proclivity of men to use their own power to obtain sexuality.

Answers to questions about who has the power and what motives are being served in any specific sexual encounter are not always easily available. Men sometimes use power to obtain sexuality, and sometimes use sexuality to express power. However, as you might recall from an earlier section of this chapter, sexuality is also one of the principal means by which men communicate love, affection, and caring for their intimate partner. Power vulnerability, pleasure, and danger coexist in a sometimes uneasy and sometimes easy mixture. In expressing her feelings of exposure and vulnerability, one respondent in a study stated:

> …there's…that instant when he's about to enter me when I get this tiny flash of fear. It comes and goes in a second, but it's almost always there. It's a kind of inner tensing up. There's a second when instead of opening up my body, I want to close it tight. I guess it's like being invaded, and I want to protect myself against it for that instant. Then he's in and it's gone, and I can get lost in the sexual excitement. (Rubin, 1983: 10)

Demonstrating a commonly found admixture of danger and power, that same respondent also notes further that there is a "moment in sex when I know I'm in control, that he really couldn't stop anymore because his drive is so great, that I feel wonderful. I feel like the most powerful person in that instant" (Rubin, 1983: 109). Both women and men feel powerful when they have stimulated a partner to the point when orgasm is either eagerly sought or inevitable. Both can experience various feelings of being vulnerable to various dangers and both can experience intense physical, psychological, and emotional pleasures during a sexual experience. That women more often than men experience and emphasize the dangers more than the pleasures of sexuality is partly attributable to their differential histories of sexuality socialization within a society such as ours.

Contemporary Gender-Sexuality Socialization and Development

Our society has a strong antisexual heritage (Saxton, 1986: 110–113) and a history of believing that sexuality is "natural," instinctive, or biologically determined. Not surprisingly in such a society, little formal sexuality socialization occurs, since it is believed to be unwarranted and unwanted. However, considerable accidental, unintentional, and subtle socialization does occur. In simplified form, socialization messages direct a prosexual message at boys and men and a more antisexual message at girls and women. The messages are different in part because of the placement of more restrictive conditions that must be met before women are permitted to adopt a more prosexuality stance. As well, girls and women have few positive sexuality role models to draw upon. Most of those currently available are generated by a male-controlled, male-oriented media, and depict women solely in terms of what is most pleasing to men sexually. As we noted in Chapter 5, adult romance novels written by women for women now provide more explicit models should girls be able to gain access to them; however, even here, women's sexuality is depicted entangled with love and husband-hunting.

Females in our society are taught a script emphasizing the relational components of sexuality. As noted in several places earlier, socialization from family, peers, and the media directed towards females conveys a message that sexuality for women should be fused with love and intimacy. Only marriage sanctifies full and free expression of a woman's sexuality. However, given the restrictions operative prior to that relationship, and the lack of anticipatory socialization, most women have been uncertain what such expression can mean. An old joke depicts a mother congratulating her daughter following her wedding and informing her than now she can do "it." The daughter replies: "Fine, but what is 'it'?" While sexuality provides a "rite of passage" from girlhood to womanhood, the premium once placed in our society on virginity prior to marriage has declined noticeably over the past three decades. Even though the restrictiveness of waiting until marriage has been replaced with waiting until a stable, affectionate, respectful, relationship develops, sexuality initially becomes an intimacy-driven, not orgasm-driven, activity for women. Rubin (1983: 103) claims that "for men, the erotic aspect of any relationship remains forever the most compelling, while, for women, the emotional component will always be the more salient." Over time, most women do acquire a more genital focus for their sexuality (Kaplan, 1974: 110–111).

Sexuality for males is, as noted earlier, closely tied to masculinity (Udry, 1977; Simon and Gagnon, 1969). Sexual experience provides a series of important "rites of passage," symbolizing the transition from boyhood into manhood, with manhood initially symbolized by the first heterosexual intercourse experience. Like gender itself, sexual manhood, once attained, must constantly be demonstrated and reaffirmed. Male sexuality socialization in childhood, adolescence, and early adulthood emphasizes qualities necessary for fulfilling this role in the predominant heterosexuality script. Since, as we shall see later, most males learn about their own sexuality through masturbation, success and satisfaction in sexuality initially becomes measured in orgasm, not intimacy. With further input from female partners and changing social expectations over time, most men learn, by middle age or sooner, to acquire a greater sensitivity towards interpersonal components of sexual intimacy, as well as less of a genital focus and a greater sensate or sensual focus for their sexuality (Kaplan, 1974: 107; Starr and Weiner, 1981).

Families

Simon and Gagnon (1970; 1969) argue that the most important processes of childhood sexuality socialization occurring in the context of the family involve acquiring gender identities and learning general gendered patterns of behaviour. Gender provides the framework within which later sexuality socialization experiences and expressions of sexuality are embedded. Of particular importance is an overall emphasis upon male activity and female passivity that eventually accords well with our traditional heterosexuality script. An important facet of socialization occurring in the home that has important implications for later male and female experiences of their own sexuality, and for heterosexual relationships, pertains to the process of *naming genitals*.

Gartrell and Mosbacher (1984) gathered introspective data from a sample of college students, physicians, and mental health professionals on the earliest names they were taught as children for the genitalia of both sexes. Responses obtained from this highly educated, presumably middle-class or higher, group were classified according to whether they were anatomically correct names, anatomical names incorrectly applied (e.g., vagina instead of vulva for the entire female genital region), nonanatomical names (i.e., euphemisms), or no names at all. Males typically acquired either euphemisms (41.6 percent) or anatomically correct names (39.8 percent) for their own genitals. The euphemisms learned by males typically revolved either around the urinary function of the penis (e.g., Piddler, Pipi, Wee-wee), or around commonly used derivatives of penis (e.g., Dick, Dink, Peter). No males received an incorrectly applied anatomical name, and only slightly less than one-fifth of the sample (18.5 percent) were never given a name for their genitals.

In contrast, the largest single group of women (44.3 percent) was never given a name for their genitals, followed closely (41.7 percent) by those given euphemistic names. Parents are clearly more creative when it comes to euphemistically naming a daughter's genitalia using many terms whose meanings are idiosyncratic and obscure (e.g., Dee-dee, Christmas, Munghee, Pocketbook), explicit and negative (e.g., Nasty, Shame), extremely vague (e.g., Yourself), or equivalent to an anatomical geography lesson (e.g., Down there, Virginia). None of these names demonstrate any link to the principal erotic sexuality organ of the clitoris. Less than 10 percent of the female respondents were given either anatomically correct (6.1) or anatomically incorrect (7.8) names. As well, females were more likely to be provided with either no name (36.4 percent) or a euphemistic name (30.9 percent) for male genitalia, although almost one-third (29 percent) were provided with anatomically correct names. Likewise, males were most likely (56.1 percent) to receive no name for female genitalia, which, given parental inventiveness, may not be a bad thing since it might give a whole new meaning to a young boy working on his Christmas Wish List. The remainder of males were almost evenly distributed across all other categories of names learned for female genitalia (no examples of euphemistic names used in this regard were supplied by the researchers).

If the Sapir-Whorf hypothesis (see Chapter 5) is correct and words dictate thought and communication, euphemistic names serve only a limited communication value, particularly outside of the context in which the name is generated. Learning a unique or negative name is likely to make subsequent communication either difficult or embarrassing. Acquiring a negative name directs negative thoughts towards genitalia and, upon eventually learning that the genitalia are involved with sexuality, also towards sexuality generally. Leaving an entire region of the body unnamed clearly implies that something negative or unmentionable is involved with that region. Overall, assuming that naming sets a stage for subsequent encounters with sexuality, females receive a much more negative orientation than do males. Males are more likely to be able to build upon information imparted by their parents, while females are more likely to have to first undo initial damage done via early naming before they can begin to construct a more positive orientation towards their own sexuality and sexuality in general.

On average, both males and females in the research sample learned correct anatomical names for their own and the other sex's genitalia between 10 and 15 years of age, with names for male genitalia acquired by both males and females earlier than names for female genitalia, and with males learning correct names for female anatomy earlier than did most females (Gartrell and Mosbacher, 1984: 872). This finding suggests that male bodies (and implicitly their sexuality) receive a greater priority, while female bodies and sexuality receive a lesser priority, especially among girls and young women. In other words, somehow a message is acquired that learning about males and male bodies should take precedence. As well, males are more specifically interested in female sexual anatomy at an earlier age than are females. This finding accords with the more generally acknowledged initial genital focus to sexuality on the part of males.

The hallmark indicator of biological maturity is the ability to reproduce (Perlmutter and Hall, 1985: 5) and is first indicated in females by the onset of menses, although actual ability to conceive typically does not occur until approximately two years later, and in males by the ability to ejaculate, although orgasm can, and does, occur among boys at earlier ages (Masters et al., 1994; Reinisch, 1990). Even though this is only one of many simultaneously occurring processes, the capacity to reproduce is most often in our society, and in the minds of parents in particular, equated with puberty. While no historical records have been kept regarding the average age at onset of ejaculatory ability in boys, records do indicate that the onset of menses has commenced at ever-younger ages for girls in Western societies over the course of the past century. "In 1860, the average girl first menstruated when she was 16 or 17 years old. By 1920, this age was 14.5 years, and now it is about age 12.5, about two years earlier than when boys reach puberty" (Baca Zinn and Eitzen, 1993: 235–236). Boys genitals are stimulated to further growth around ages 11–12 and typically attain adult size and shape around ages 14–15 (Masters et al., 1994). While the mechanisms controlling the pubertal clock are still largely uncertain at the moment, body fat-lean ratios influenced by nutritional levels appear to be the most important.

The sexuality of sons can be, and typically is, ignored by parents, since evidence of ejaculatory capability is easily hidden from even the most vigilant prying eyes, and, even if discovered, is unlikely to become the cause for discussions about masturbation or other activities leading to ejaculation or the reproductive consequences of ejaculation during coitus (Nolin and Petersen, 1992). The myth of the father-son chat about "the birds and the bees" is just that—a myth. In contrast to ejaculatory ability, the appearance of a menstrual cycle cannot be ignored. Evidence indicates that the presence of a menstrual cycle forces parents, usually mothers, to acknowledge the real or incipient sexuality of daughters, and to initiate limited discussions about sexuality (Fox and Inazu, 1980; Nolin and Petersen, 1992). That sexuality, however, is typically framed initially in terms of reproductive, not erotic, sexuality.

Socialization messages aimed at early adolescent females in our society typically focus upon the potential negative reproductive consequences of being sexual (in the limited penetrative sense). Rarely do parents extol the alternative pleasures to be obtained from manual, oral, or anal sexuality. Instead, the message of males as dangerous sexual predators is reinforced at this time. Women currently in their thirties express a wish that their mothers had been more explicit and detailed regarding sexuality, and particularly, had been more positive about sexuality instead of presenting negative, mostly nonverbal messages (Brock and Jennings, 1993). Parents today who do present more positive messages about sexuality are usually unprepared for the early age at which their children become sexually active, and, in the rare case where children feel sufficiently comfortable informing parents of their ongoing sexual interest and activities, typically react in a negative fashion (Rubin, 1990: 80–83).

Since parents generally are still either too ignorant or too embarrassed to provide detailed and explicit information about sexuality, and school "family life" education courses tend to provide too little information too late, young males and females typically turn to the media (entertainment more so than educational) and to their peers for information (but most often receive misinformation), role models, and depictions of the prevailing sexuality scripts for sexually active men and women (Moore and Davidson, 1990). In addition to meeting these needs to varying degrees, both male and female peer groups also provide additional sexual vocabularies.

If the findings from an extremely limited-sample survey (Cameron, 1992) can be generalized, males can develop a more elaborate language for male genitalia, specifically the penis, than can females. Under competitive conditions, male college students identified or created 144 penis terms compared to only 50 generated by female students. Male terms focused upon rhapsodizing the penis, in descending order of frequency, as a person (e.g., his Excellency, the chief, Cyclops, The Lone Ranger, Mr. Happy), a tool (e.g., pole, garden hose, drill, jackhammer), an animal (e.g., King Kong, Cujo, snake, weasel), a weapon of conquest (e.g., passion rifle, heat-seeking moisture missile, destroyer, purple-helmeted love warrior), a foodstuff (e.g., love popsicle, wiener, tube steak, Whopper), or other miscellaneous items (e.g., pussy pleaser, male member).

Even though college women's responses were not as easily categorized, most noticeable by their absence were terms depicting a penis as a symbol of authority, tool, ferocious animal, or weapon. "One might generalize by saying that women find the penis endearing, ridiculous, and occasionally disgusting, but not awe-inspiring or dangerous" (Cameron, 1992: 374). Although many terms generated by the female sample overlapped with terms provided by males, some distinctive terms evidenced familiarity with romance novels (e.g., throbbing manhood, swelling hardness, growing desire), or were classified as either "nonsense" terms (e.g., dickhead, prickola, doodad), or miscellaneous (e.g., god's gift to women). While males appear to invest penises with positive-association masculine qualities, a penis by any other name is still just a penis for most females. No counterpart study appears to have been conducted regarding female genitalia.

Attitudes towards and practices of **masturbation** provide key indicators of societal and individual orientations towards erotic, pleasure-oriented, nonreproductive sexuality (Saxton, 1986: 113). Although infants and young children often engage in manually exploring their genitals or rubbing their genitals against inanimate objects (Kinsey et al., 1953; 1948), their motives are most likely to be pleasure-seeking, not sexual. Only after acquiring an awareness of the meaning of sexuality in our society, and learning which actions are considered to be sexual and which are not, can an individual's actions accurately be labeled as masturbation—actions stemming from a sexual motive and designed intentionally and explicitly to provide sexual pleasure (Gagnon, 1977; Simon and Gagnon, 1970).

While females typically learn to masturbate through their own experimentation (Saxton, 1996: 117), most males learn how to masturbate from another boy (Saxton, 1996: 111).

Girls tend to masturbate alone, while boys, in early adolescence, often gather in groups (Elkin and Handel, 1989: 294) to validate one another's right to be sexual and to express their sexuality initially in masturbation. It is not uncommon for boys to engage in mini-Olympic contests (generically referred to as "circle jerks"), wherein each contestant demonstrates his masturbation prowess in terms of knowledge, technique, and frequency. The competitive nature of such games ties in with the emphasis upon sports occurring at the same age, and contributes to a male fascination with keeping their peers informed about the frequency (real or imaginary) of their ability to "score" with girls and women, and with using sports metaphors (particularly baseball) to chart their progress in a sexual relationship. Males are more likely to publicize among their peers the nature and frequency of their recreational, non-intimate, sexual experiences, but less likely to discuss their sexual relationship with an intimate partner.

An early introduction to their own sexuality through masturbation promotes within males "a capacity for detached sexual activity—activity whose only sustaining motive is sexual. This may be the hallmark of male sexuality in our society" (Simon and Gagnon, 1970: 32). Such an orientation establishes a model for male sexuality of "conquest with orgasm, but with as little tenderness, intimacy, and emotionality as possible" (Baca Zinn and Eitzen, 1993: 252). A capacity for detached sexual activity also allows males to more easily compartmentalize physical sexuality from emotional intimacy in the same relationship. Many women are amazed when a male partner seeks or insists upon a sexual ending to an intense, highly emotional, argument. Sometimes this desire is based upon a male's limited means of expressing love and a wish to make up, and sometimes it reflects an ability to separate the sexual from the emotional, such that they are two separate issues. Just because emotional intimacy issues are not resolved does not preclude the pursuit of sexual desire for many men. This capacity is also frequently operative when males become sexually involved with someone other than their intimate partner. Husbands tend to have their first affair within the first five years of marriage (Seagraves, 1989) and generally claim their affairs were either motivated by a search for, or an attraction to, the availability of sexual novelty only ("But honey, she didn't mean a thing to me!").

Most males establish a consistent pattern of masturbation during early adolescence, while females typically do not begin to masturbate until their dating or early married years (Kinsey et al., 1953; 1948; Reinisch, 1990). Even then, female incidence patterns of masturbation demonstrate more variability than do male patterns. As part of the general movement towards taking greater control of their bodies, some early second-wave feminists created a vaginal art form (e.g., Betty Dodson, Judy Chicago) designed to acquaint women with the variability in female genitalia, and to desensitize women to the negative imagery they have received. Others (e.g., Dodson, 1996; 1974) not only advocated masturbation, but also created "self-love" workshops to aid women in becoming more comfortable with their genital sexuality. Despite these controversial efforts, researchers since the time of Kinsey et al. (1953) continue to document significantly lower rates of masturbation among females during childhood and adolescence (e.g., Michael et al., 1994). In contrast to boys' experiences with their peer groups, girls and young women do not receive the same amount and degree of validating and encouraging messages about genital sexuality in general, and masturbation in particular, from their peers. Adolescent females are more harsh in their judgements about a peer's apparent sexual activity levels than are adolescent males.

Female peer groups in childhood and early adolescence maintain a continuity with socialization received from their families and the media, by emphasizing love and the importance of establishing intimate relationships prior to becoming sexually involved. Generally, "girls appear to be well-trained precisely in that area in which boys are poorly trained—that is, a belief in and a capacity for intense, emotionally-charged [*sic*] relationships and the language of romantic love" (Simon and Gagnon, 1970: 36). Whereas a typical male relationship script reads "sexuality first, love later, whenever," a typical female relationship script reads "love first, sexuality later." "It is not that men are not attracted by romance, but, for them, they often say, romance is a means to an end and the end they are striving towards is sexual intercourse. Women, in contrast, often say that what is arousing about the sexual ending is the romantic beginning" (Michael et al., 1994: 150). This female script applies to premarital, marital, and extramarital sexual relationships. The frequency of extramarital affairs decreases with age for husbands, but increases, up to a point, with age for wives (Seagraves, 1989). Wives typically indulge in extramarital affairs later in marriage than do husbands and usually claim that tenderness, caring, and sensitivity is what they first found most appealing in either their female (Cameron, 1997) or male partner (Seagraves, 1989), and that emotional involvement paved the way to a later sexual involvement, not the reverse.

Contemporary Sexual Behaviour

An oft-repeated claim propagated in the media and perpetuated in everyday conversations pertains to a supposed immutable difference regarding when men and women attain their sexual "peaks." Women supposedly reach the peak of their sexuality in their mid-30s, while men peak in their mid to late teens. This belief is anchored in the research of Kinsey et al. (1953, 1948), identifying the points in the average male's and female's lifetimes when the frequency of orgasms (or "outlets" as Kinsey and his research team preferred to call them) reached its highest point. What the Kinsey researchers actually documented was not an immutable feature of male and female sexuality, but rather a set of responses to the prevailing double standard of opportunities permitted for sexual expression in the first half of the twentieth century.

Benefiting from their greater freedom, males, then and now, typically become sexually active in late childhood or early adolescence. Males establish a regular frequency of orgasm and ejaculation during adolescence that is maintained, relatively undiminished, into old age (Kinsey et al., 1948; Masters and Johnson, 1966; Reinisch, 1990). Ejaculations are initially obtained almost exclusively from masturbation from early to middle adolescence, and then through a varying combination of self-stimulation and manual, oral, or coital partner stimulation throughout late adolescence, adulthood, and old age. The sources of stimulation may vary, but the frequency of orgasm and ejaculation maintains a highly consistent lifetime pattern. The notion of a "peaking" of male sexual expression is almost useless, unless we focus only upon orgasms obtained by a specific method of stimulation, such as from intercourse.

In contrast, females do not follow this same pattern. Female orgasmic patterns are more subject to situational contingencies than are those of males. Females, during the first half of the twentieth century, were severely restricted from engaging in sexual behaviour until they were married, after which time most women had to be resocialized to learn about their sexual bodies, and to learn how to express their sexuality freely and comfortably. Consequently, orgasm-outlet frequencies increase significantly among older married women, in contrast to unmarried younger women. The "peaking" of women's sexuality documented by Kinsey was a function of socially constructed opportunity, not biology. Women, then and now, can, and do, change their orgasmic frequency and their sexual responses over their lifetimes (Kinsey et al., 1953; Masters and Johnson, 1966; Reinisch, 1990).

Building on the pioneering work of Kinsey et al. (1948, 1953), social scientists continue to document changes in the sexual behaviour of women and men. Darling et al. (1989: 238) claim the major trends in sexual behaviour in the twentieth century include an increase in coitus prior to marriage for both men and women, particularly a dramatic increase in nonmarital coital behaviour by women since 1970, and a resulting general trend towards convergence in the sexual behaviour of women and men. Not only are participation rates in oral, anal, and coital sexual behaviours increasing among teenagers at higher levels than ever recorded in the history of empirical sexuality research, but the onset of sexual activity is occurring at younger and younger ages, resulting in a notable increase in the average number of lifetime sexual partners for adolescents and young adults (Pratt, 1990; Sonenstein et al., 1989). In other words, it appears that women and men are becoming more sexually experienced at younger ages than ever before. Since culture, not biology, shapes sexuality behaviour, the gender difference in peak sexual activity has been converging over historical time towards a norm previously identified with males only.

Available evidence indicates that teenagers born in the mid-1960s had their first intercourse experience around the age of 17 (Michael et al., 1994: 90). Among adults of all ages, women are most likely (48 percent) to cite "affection for partner" as the major reason they had their first intercourse experience followed by 24 percent who cited "curiosity/readiness for sex." Fifty-one percent of males cite "curiosity" and only 25 percent "affection" as their primary reason (Michael et al., 1994: 93). "Virtually *no* women said that they wanted or went along with sex for physical pleasure" (Michael et al., 1994: 94, emphasis in original). Regarding oral sexuality, Michael et al. (1994: 139) find that 77 percent of adult men state they have performed cunnilingus and 79 percent have received fellatio; 68 percent of women have performed fellatio and 73 percent have received cunnilingus. While the recent study finds that 26 percent of the men and 30 percent of the women in a predominantly heterosexual sample claim they have sexual relations two or three times a week, an earlier study reports that 67 percent of gay couples, 45 percent of heterosexual married or cohabiting couples, and 33 percent of lesbian couples have sexual relations three or more times a week on average (Blumstein and Schwartz, 1983: 196).

Findings from other research on preferred social activities helps us place sexuality into a broader context of competing alternatives. A limited-sample survey (Robinson, 1968) of leisure patterns among respondents living in three suburbs of Winnipeg finds that no respondent selected "sex" from a detailed list of preferred leisure activities. A reluctance to identify sexuality as a favoured leisure activity can be interpreted as the product of shyness among Canadians in the mid-1960s to acknowledge their participation in sexual activities. However, the more recent Bruskin/Goldring Research study (1994 in Saxton, 1996: 131) inquiring into preferred relaxation activities of adult men and women in the United States was conducted in a social climate less bashful about sexual matters. The favourite activity for men in the American study was exercising (48 percent), while the favourite activity for women (38 percent) was taking a bath. Thirty-nine percent of the men and 19 percent of the women identified having "sex" as a favourite method of relaxing. Women would much prefer, following taking a bath, to call a friend (44 percent), exercise (42 percent), go shopping (35 percent), or eat (28 percent). In other words, "most women would rather do al-most anything other than have sex" (Saxton, 1996: 131).

Kinsey et al. (1953) found that 3 percent of the women in his white sample had ex-perienced intercourse by age 15, and about half were sexually experienced by age 20; most of them with their fiancé. In contrast, 71 percent of white never-married males (Kinsey et al., 1948) were sexually experienced by age 19, only some of them with their fiancée. A convenience sampling of American teenagers finds that two-thirds have ex-perienced sexual intercourse and, of those who had not, "fellatio and cunnilingus had be-come a significant part of sexual activity for close to half of them" (Rubin, 1990: 65). A summary of surveys conducted in Canada over the past three decades finds that 62 percent of teenage males and 49 percent of teenage females in 1992, and approximately three-quarters of both university-aged males and females in 1988 were sexually experienced and concludes that the proportions of sexually experienced adolescent and young adult men and women has doubled in Canada since the 1970s (Hobart, 1996: 150). The most dramatic increases in permissiveness standards and actual sexual behaviour in Canada have oc-curred among francophone women and men in Quebec over the past 20 years (Hobart, 1996). Based on his 1995 national, random-sample research, Bibby (1995: 65) reports that people in Quebec not only appear to be sexually active more often than individuals liv-ing in other regions of Canada, but also hold the most liberal attitudes towards sexuality, including approval of premarital and extramarital sexuality and, along with people in British Columbia, express the highest approval level of homosexuality.

Accompanying the increase in sexual experience over the past 30 years has been the virtual disappearance of the double-standard among university students and a noticeable decline of that standard among high-school students. Canadian young-adult men (51.9 per-cent of francophones and 36.4 percent of anglophones in 1988) are more willing than young-adult women (37.1 percent of francophones and 19.7 percent of anglophones) to endorse a casual, recreational, "fun" orientation towards heterosexual involvement. Canadian women of comparable ages (48.9 percent of anglophones and 47.4 percent of francophones) are more likely than men (39.1 percent of anglophones and 33.9 percent of francophones) to en-dorse a love standard (Hobart, 1996: 149). We can see from these figures that, while slightly more anglophone male students endorse a love standard than a fun standard (a difference that is not statistically significant), substantially more anglophone female students believe that an underlying level of affection, trust, and respect must be established prior to engaging in sexual intimacies. For men, sexuality is pleasurable, with or without emotional involve-ment. For women, sexuality is pleasurable with emotional involvement, but potentially dan-gerous without it.

Overall, in Canada, if changes in sexual attitudes and behaviour can be called a "revo-lution," the revolution has occurred in women's sexuality, not men's. Along with other changing power alignments in politics, education, employment, and families, women ef-fected change in their own sexual behaviour and in sexual relations with and without men. The greater availability of a highly effective oral contraceptive in the 1960s allowed women to have greater power and control over their bodies, their reproductive destinies, and their own sexuality. Reiss (1986: 212) notes that "the greater the power of one gender, the greater that gender's sexual rights in that society." Women continue to challenge conventional wis-dom about their sexuality created and distributed by male-dominated medical and therapeutic professions, and propagated via male-dominated media. Part of that challenge involves writing a new sexual script.

In simple terms, the desired new sexual script is highlighted by equality. The right to equality in sexual relations also carries an additional, different, set of responsibilities for women. A new script requires women to take greater responsibility for their own sexuality by becoming more knowledgeable about their sexual minds and bodies. It requires women to become more assertive about their own wants and desires, thereby relieving men of their burden of responsibility as teachers, sexual guides, and mindreaders. Before any of these requirements can be met, however, women must first explore their minds and bodies to identify their own wants, desires, and fantasies. This exploration must be self-initiated and autonomous, not guided by male-defined principles and evaluations as in the past, wherein male pleasures received first priority.

The search for new script guidelines and a new sense of female sexuality has taken the form in the 1990s of an increasing emphasis being placed upon the pleasures of sexuality. From the time of the second-wave women's movement of the 1960s, considerably more energy has been expended by feminists upon identifying and emphasizing the dangers of sexuality, particularly heterosexuality, for women. These dangers have been, and will continue to be, well documented, even although solutions remain elusive. Until recently, comparatively less attention has been focused upon identifying and emphasizing the pleasures sexuality can, and does, yield (e.g., Hollibaugh, 1984).

One arena in which explorations of the breadth and depth of female sexual potential and pleasure are being conducted pertains to pornography. From the 1960s through the 1980s, feminists waged war against pornography, guided in part by Steinem's (1978) distinction between **erotica**, characterized by depictions of mutually consenting adults participating in egalitarian sexual encounters and **pornography**, sexual relations characterized by dominance, exploitation, and violence. "Good" sexuality is thus differentiated from "bad" sexuality by virtue of the distribution of power between participants. Women presented in pornography were held to be without power, while male participants in and viewers of pornography possessed power. Fueled by a strong belief that pornography, broadly and vaguely defined, causes men to commit sexual and nonsexual violence against women, feminists lead by Dworkin (1981) and MacKinnon (1987) fought to ban, by legal or other means, virtually all explicit depictions of sexuality.

The efforts of the antipornography movement have met with resistance from both outside and inside feminism, since the issues involve more than the objectification and commodification of women depicted in positions of unequal power, but also issues of censorship generally and censorship of sexuality in particular. Some feminists are against censorship, but not necessarily pro-pornography (see Burstyn, 1985), while others are pro-pornography (see Matrix, 1996). The latter groups of feminists use the term "pornography" to refer to any explicit depictions of sexuality, and do not consider power to be either a central or a contentious issue. Any objections they raise against existing pornography pertain to poor quality in all facets of production and an orientation directed solely towards promoting and satisfying male interests in sexuality. Pro-pornography feminists advocate support for a better-quality pornography, written, produced, and directed by women for women designed to appeal to, explore, and extend female sexual fantasies, along with discussion and debate about female sexuality—in other words, females literally writing, performing, and disseminating their own sexuality scripts.

The pro-pornography movement emphasizes the importance of women gaining power and control over their sexuality and their roles in sexual scripts. Without having the power to explore their own sexuality, to name, understand, and express sexual desire, women's sexuality will remain bound by limitations created and enforced by men and, through socialization conditioning, women themselves. The "feminist sexuality wars" between anti- and pro-pornography adherents, and between feminists who insist that only egalitarian, consensual, nondirective sexuality constitutes an acceptable sexuality for women, and other feminists who reject such "vanilla" sexuality and argue that women should be encouraged and permitted to pursue any and all forms of sexual pleasure including sadomasochism (e.g., Califia, 1997: 1996), have persisted for more than two decades and promise to continue into the next millennium. As well, how successful women will be in renegotiating existing heterosexuality scripts or gaining acceptance of new scripts is debatable. "The reality of heterosexual relationships, however, works against women redefining sexual practices" (Jackson and Scott, 1996: 19). Clearly issues surrounding sexuality, gender, and power have yet to be resolved.

VIOLENCE IN INTIMATE RELATIONSHIPS

It has long been a central tenet of family sociologists that one of the major functions of the family is to provide **protection** for family members from bodily harm by outsiders (Ogburn, 1922). Even though this function has increasingly been assumed by the state (e.g., the police and the courts) and private organizations (security systems), families are and have been expected to be governed by the motto of "to preserve and protect." Sociologists, and the general public (Begin, 1991: 1), have blithely assumed until relatively recently that family members or intimate relationship partners did not require protection from one another. The *Journal of Marriage and the Family*, the principal journal for the sociological study of the family, does not contain a single article on husband-wife violence between the years of 1939 to 1969 (O'Brien, 1971). As a consequence, even though violence against intimate partners is not a "new" phenomenon, "the terms 'battered wife' and 'wife abuse' were not available as ways to think about the experience" (Walker, 1990: 97) prior to the 1970s. These terms, along with "battered husbands" and "husband abuse" have now been added to our intimacy lexicon. The more sociologists, feminist and otherwise, and other social scientists examine intimate relationships inside and outside of the traditional framework of the family, such as gay and especially lesbian relationships (Lobel, 1986) and the phenomena of what are referred to as "courtship violence" and "date rape" (Makepeace, 1981; 1986), the more we become aware of the magnitude of **intimate violence** (Gelles and Straus, 1988), a term designed to differentiate this form of violence from that committed by strangers or even casual acquaintances. Our focus in this section is on violent actions committed by one partner upon another, within the context of an ongoing intimate relationship. Sex, gender, or sexual harassment and stalking or criminal harassment have been or will be a focus in other chapters.

Defining Intimate Violence

Defining intimate violence is not a simple task. Drawing a linguistic boundary to capture the essence and extent of the phenomenon and creating a definitive conceptual name is complex and highly contested. Supposedly gender-neutral terms such as "family violence," "domestic violence," "marital violence," "conjugal assault" or "spousal abuse," and more gender-specific terms such as "violence against women," "wife abuse," "battered wife," "battered husband," and "husband abuse," all reflect the theoretical, empirical, or political orientations of their creators and/or users. Existing definitions and their meanings become even less precise when variant terms are created (such as "data rape"; Spender, 1995), or metaphysical links are forged, for example, between wife beating and sexism in language, or between sexual assault and the "symbolic annihilation" of women on television (Tuchman, 1978).

A number of writers argue that the use of gender-neutral terms is misleading. Based upon available evidence, to be explored briefly in the next section, and upon "historical and political justifications," Neidig and Friedman (1984: 3) contend that we should adopt the "male-as-perpetrator view of spousal abuse," and the subsequent view of females as the recipients of violence. Freedman (1985: 44) suggests that the use of terms such as "marital violence" should not be employed, since such terms ignore "the direction [male to female] in which most of this violence flows." Gender-specific terms are, therefore, preferred by these and other writers over gender-neutral terms that pretend the phenomena are gender-blind. In a series of contradictions, Wood (1997: 331) proposes that the issue should be framed neutrally as "gendered violence," yet specifically defined as "physical, verbal, and visual brutality that is inflicted disproportionately on members of one sex" including "gender intimidation, sexual assault, violence between intimates, sexual harassment, genital mutilation, and selective murder of women."

At present, both narrow and broad definitions have been applied by sociologists to measure and conceptualize terms such as "abuse" and "violence" (Gelles, 1989; Straus, 1991). Indeed, Gelles (1989: 19) observes that "one of the major problems that confronts investigators who attempt to study domestic violence has been the quagmire of conceptual dilemmas encountered." Straus (1990: 23) argues that the term "abuse" covers a variety of acts including "verbal abuse or verbal battering, physical abuse, sexual abuse, and fiscal abuse." Emotional and psychological forms of abuse typically leave no visible evidence of abusive conduct; in other cases, the physical evidence of the abuse is more graphic. Initial studies by feminists on violence against women focused on the physical nature of abuse (e.g., Martin, 1976; Pizzey, 1974). For Pizzey (1974), an "abused woman" was one who experienced physical abuse at the hands of her husband. Martin (1976) only applied the term "battered wife" to married or cohabiting women who were physically abused by their male partner. Other researchers broaden the scope of the term. Walker (1984: 27–28) argues that we are myopic if we fail to consider psychological abuse as equally pernicious, and suggests that a modification of the definition of torture used by Amnesty International, can be employed to define and measure psychological abuse. Not only do writers disagree upon the defining characteristics of intimate violence, but researchers also vary in the indicators they select to provide measurements of violence and abuse.

The Incidence of Intimate Violence

The 1970s Royal Commission on The Status of Women in Canada did not examine the phenomenon of violence against women. In 1991, the federal government document *The Status of Women*, notes the "gravity of the problem and the degree to which violence harms the lives of women" *(The Status of Women*, 1991: 1). We have witnessed a knowledge explosion on the topic of intimate violence generally, and violence against women in particular, during the intervening two decades. Violence against women within intimate relationships has been transformed from a "private trouble" into a "public issue" (Mills, 1959) commanding the attention of academics, lobbyists, the media, the public, and collective action groups (Ursel, 1991; Walker, 1984). As Johnson (1996: 133) notes, "there is now a substantial body of literature available about the correlates and consequences" and the incidence of intimate violence.

The Violence Against Women Survey (VAWS) was undertaken by Statistics Canada in 1993, upon the request of Health Canada, as part of its federally funded four-year Family Violence Initiative. Police incident reports and victimization surveys, such as that contained within a General Social Survey in 1988 (Statistics Canada, 1990), consistently note that women are overwhelmingly more likely than men to be the victims of police-reported conjugal violence and domestic homicide. Analysis of data obtained from 15 Canadian police departments for the year 1991 points out clear gender differences among the victims of the most violent crimes, as well as noting that men and women tend to be the victims of different types of offences (Trevethan and Samagh, 1992). Seventy-five percent of the reported adult violent-crime victims were victims of assault. Women were more likely to be victims of assault at the hands of their husbands or ex-husbands (52 percent), while men were more likely to be assaulted by strangers (44 percent).

A law against "criminal harassment" (Section 264 of the Criminal Code) enacted in 1993, is directed against "stalking" behaviours that stem from a variety of motives. "For example, in a marital or dating relationship, perpetrators may be motivated by their refusal to believe that the relationship has ended. In other relationships, like friendships or acquaintanceships, perpetrators may believe that their victims are equally in love with them, or that the victims might return their affections if they would only get to know the perpetrator better" (Kong, 1997: 30). Stalking or criminal harassment includes repeatedly following, communicating via cards, letters, telephone, faxes, e-mails, or gifts, watching a person's home or workplace, and/or uttering direct or indirect threats or promises of violence or forcible intimacy.

According to research conducted by the Canadian Centre for Justice Statistics that analyzed the relationship of the victim and the stalker in 5023 incidents (more than 90 percent of which came from Ontario and Quebec), 8 out of 10 of the victims of criminal harassment were women, and more than half (58 percent) were stalked by an ex-husband, boyfriend, or current husband (Kong, 1997). Another one-quarter of the women victims were stalked by casual acquaintances, and the rest by other family members, strangers, or coworkers. In contrast, almost half of the 977 male stalking victims were stalked by a casual acquaintance, usually another male, while 11 percent were stalked by coworkers. Few of the male victims of criminal harassment were stalked by an ex-wife or girlfriend. Similarly, official statistics collected from a nonrepresentative sample of police agencies in Canada indicate that "80% of almost 7,500 victims during 1994–1995 were female and that 88% of about 5,400 persons accused of criminal harassment were male. A large proportion of these women (57%) were stalked by an ex-husband or (ex-) boyfriend" (Kong, 1997: 30). Male victims were more likely (48 percent) to be stalked by a casual acquaintance than by (13 percent in total) an ex-wife, girlfriend, or ex-girlfriend (Kong, 1997: 32).

While the vast majority of criminally harassing acts are of a nonviolent nature, with approximately 5 percent of the reported cases involving physical injury and less than half of a percent involving attempted or actual homicide (Kong, 1997: 32), all constitute invasions of privacy and can easily initiate fear over one's own physical safety or the safety of closely related persons. In approximately 20 percent of the cases where the stalker is known and identified to police, victims preferred not to pursue their cases through the courts by laying charges against their harasser. Coworkers and male victims of stalking by their ex-wives are the most reluctant to go beyond informing the police of stalking incidents, followed by women being stalked either by former husbands or by former or current boyfriends (Kong, 1997: 32). Of those cases that proceed through the full court process (less than two-thirds do), limited available data indicate that most perpetrators receive either probation or light (less than six month) sentences—far less than the maximum penalty of five years imprisonment (Kong, 1997: 33). Such sentencing is unlikely to have much deterrence value.

Unlike the previously mentioned surveys that focus solely upon officially reported events, the VAWS study utilized a nationally representative sample of 12 300 adult (18 years of age and older) women only (Rodgers, 1994), and expanded the scope of violence beyond homicide and generic "assault" to include a large number of specific events all of which transgress the Criminal Code of Canada, but were not necessarily reported by victims to the police. The survey finds that 3 out of every 10 Canadian women (29 percent) currently or previously married, or living in a common-law relationship, have experienced at least one incident of physical or sexual violence at the hands of an intimate partner. Counting each victim only once, the survey finds that 29 percent of ever-married women have experienced wife assault; 16 percent have been kicked, hit, beaten, choked, had a gun or knife used against them, or have been sexually assaulted; and 11 percent have been pushed, grabbed, shoved, or slapped. Two percent have experienced nonphysical assaults such as being threatened or having something thrown at them. "[F]or about 20% of women who had been in abusive relationships, the violence continued during or after the couple separated; furthermore, in 35% of these cases, the violence actually became more severe at the time of separation" (Kong, 1997: 31). Half of all Canadian women have experienced some type of physical or sexual violence since the age of 18 (Rodgers, 1994). Children witness violence against their mothers in about 40 percent of violent marriages, including more than 50 percent of the cases in which the women fear for their lives. As well, women of partners who witnessed marital violence in their youth endure more severe and chronic violence than women whose partners were not exposed to marital violence in their youth (Rodgers, 1994).

Findings from analyses of police reports and surveys of only women, such as the VAWS, lend support to proponents of gender-specific terms, who feel that neutral terms such as "domestic violence" fail to acknowledge specific gender differences in perpetrator and victim statuses. However, not all sociologists agree that it is necessarily women who are more likely than men to be abused in an intimate relationship. For example, Brinkerhoff and Lupri's (1988) study of 562 married or cohabiting relationships in Calgary finds wife-to-husband violence to be more prevalent than husband-to-wife violence, as measured by both an overall violence scale and a severe violence scale. The rate for the former is found to be more than double the rate of the latter. Straus and Gelles (1990: 110) claim that "assaults by women on their male partners occur at about the same rate as assaults by men on their female partners, and women initiate such violence about as often as men." Given the low rates of violence committed by women outside of the context of the family, it is more than likely that violent assaults by wives against their husbands are either acts of self-defence or acts of retribution (see also Flynn, 1990a).

Gelles (1993: 32) claims that "more women [are] using violence towards men that what shelter data indicate." Male victims of female violence may not be as willing to publicly admit their experience. Most men also possess sufficient financial resources to seek private solutions to their predicament and need not rely upon shelters or government programs for aid. They consequently do not come to the attention of public authorities. A reliance upon official police statistics, data gathered from shelters and abuse hotlines, and single-sex surveys can lead to a significant underestimation of the extent to which men are battered and/or psychologically and emotionally abused. The search to establish the full parameters of all victims of intimate violence, aside from the apparent desire of some men's rights groups to seek gender equality primarily in terms of claims for victimization status, need not detract, as many feminists fear (Flynn, 1990b), from acknowledging the high numbers of female victims, nor from "giving first attention to *wives as victims* as the focus of social policy" (Straus, 1980: 43, emphasis in original).

Any notion of gender equality vanishes when it comes to the effects of violence (Pagelow, 1992). As Straus (1992) emphasizes, even though she may throw the coffeepot first, it is generally he who lands the last and most damaging blow(s). Many more wives than husbands need medical attention as a consequence of marital violence (Dobash and Dobash, 1979, 1992, 1995). In accordance with the mating gradient, most husbands are taller, bigger, and stronger than their wives. While these may be attractive male features initially, women are subsequently placed at a disadvantage when marital conflict becomes physical. Furthermore, adherence to the traditional model of a homemaker-wife and sole or primary child-care-giver roles, and the typical wage gap experienced by employed women, force many female victims of intimate violence to rely upon publicly funded programs and public or private shelters. Unfortunately, increased awareness of male victims of intimate violence has been used by politicians and antifeminists as a cause for reducing funds and programs for women.

Empirical research on heterosexual married or cohabiting couples additionally finds that intimate violence follows certain "social channels," thus making some men and women more likely to be abusers—or victims—than others. The highest rates of marital violence are found among families with low incomes and low education levels; blue collar workers, and individuals under age 30; families in which the husband is unemployed; families with above-average numbers of children; families living in large urban areas; individuals who have no religious affiliation; and individuals who believe in and uphold traditional gender roles (Gelles, 1980). As well, cohabitators tend to have higher rates of intimate violence than do married and dating couples (Stets, 1991; Stets and Straus, 1989). One longitudinal study (O'Leary et al., 1989) finds that the likelihood of abuse occurring in a marriage is three times greater if abuse also occurred during the courtship phase of a relationship than if abuse did not occur during courtship. In addition, according to statistics provided by the DisAbled Women's Network (DAWN) in Toronto, disabled women face an increased risk of both sexual and physical abuse and find their emotional and physical safety jeopardized by the inaccessibility of support services (Coalition of Provincial Organizations of the Handicapped (1987: 1). Future research will attempt to quantify how the statuses of income, occupation, education, age, employment status, religion, gender-role orientation, and geographic region interact, and how much each of them contribute independently to the likelihood of being involved in intimate violence. It is important to remember that, while the incidence may be more highly correlated with some statuses than others, intimate violence is found across all social class, ethnic, ability, and sexual-orientation lines.

Despite the research findings proclaiming lesbian relationships to be the most egalitarian of all forms of intimate partnerships (Blumstein and Schwartz, 1983; Eldridge and Gilbert, 1990), violence between partners is not uncommon even here. Waterman et al. (1989), in their study of a nonrandom sample of 34 gay and 36 lesbian college students in New York, find that 18 percent of the gay men and 40 percent of the lesbians report having experienced violence within their current or most recent relationship. A third of the lesbians report they have been subject to forced sex by their current partner. Two-thirds of Chesley et al.'s (1991) nonrandom sample of 189 women in Toronto, the majority (87 percent) of whom are white, middle-class lesbians possessing some college or university education (76 percent), report knowing lesbians who have experienced abuse within an intimate relationship. One in five respondents perceive themselves as "survivors of some form of psychological, physical and/or sexual violence in their lesbian relationships" (Ristock, 1991: 76) and three out of four feel abuse is a problem within the lesbian community.

Violence and sexual exploitation have been called the "darkside" (Lloyd, 1991) of courtship and dating. Although specific figures vary from one study to another, generally between 15 and 40 percent of university-student samples indicate they have either inflicted or received violence, while dating (e.g., Stets and Straus, 1989), while the figures for sexual aggression alone are usually much higher (e.g., Burke et al., 1988). Barnes et al. (1991) find that almost 43 percent of their all-male University of Manitoba sample have perpetrated some form of physical abuse in their dating relationships. Pushing, slapping, and threats of violence are much more common than physical assault with a weapon or an object, and emotional abuse is more common than physical abuse. Research from an American national representative sample of never-married men and women between the ages of 18 and 30 indicate that women are at least as likely, if not more likely, to be physically aggressive than men in dating relationships (Stets, 1993; Stets and Henderson, 1991). Drinking alcohol prior to a conflict between dating partners is associated with physical aggression among both men and women. Violence can also be found, although on a lesser scale, among high-school students. One in 10 last- and next-to-last-year high-school students in Michigan are found to have a direct experience with violence in a dating relationship, while 3 in 10 report knowing someone else who had such an experience (Roscoe and Callahan, 1985). The finding that a higher proportion of respondents supposedly know of violence experienced by others than acknowledge violent experiences for themselves is also obtained in studies of university and college students (Barnes et al., 1991; Makepeace, 1986).

The boundaries of intimate violence must be expanded in the case of "date rape" to include actions perpetrated by acquaintances, and even "strangers" on a first date, as well as intimates (see Shotland, 1989, for the distinction between "beginning date," "early date," and "relational date" rape, and Ward et al., 1991 for the distinction between "stranger," "party," "acquaintance," and "date" rape). University women report a higher incidence of having been raped by a steady date than by an acquaintance or a stranger (Koss et al., 1988). Johnson et al. (1992) find that 20 percent of the women in one American university indicate they have been raped while on a date. The incidence of actual rape itself is just the tip of the sexual-aggression-violence iceberg. A review of studies conducted in the 1980s concludes that "fully one half to three quarters of college women report experiencing some type of sexual aggression in a dating relationship" (Lloyd, 1991: 17). Ward et al. (1991) find that, in dating situations during the current year only, 34 percent of their American female university students have experienced some form of forced sexual contact, 20 percent have had a partner forcibly attempt intercourse, and 10 percent have experienced completed forced vaginal, oral, or anal intercourse.

An all-female Ontario university study indicates that, while less than 1 percent of the sample acknowledge being "raped" on a date during the previous year, 22 percent acknowledge having intercourse when they did not want to because they felt "it was useless to attempt to stop him," and an additional 9 percent had intercourse when they did not want to because they "felt pressured by his continual arguments" (DeKeseredy et al., 1993: 267). Being raped by a stranger is more likely to be defined as a criminal act and reported to authorities (Hills, 1980/1995) than is being raped by an acquaintance or, especially, by a partner in an ongoing intimate relationship (Russell, 1982; Finkelhor and Yllo, 1983, 1989). Since women are held responsible socially for the maintenance and regulation of intimate relationships (Belensky et al., 1986) and are still likely to be blamed when an encounter exceeds acceptable boundaries, many women are reluctant to acknowledge to themselves or others that the unacceptable has happened. The figures noted above from available studies are likely underestimates of the full extent of "date rape."

Prior to changes in the Canadian Criminal Code effective in 1983 and 1987, **rape** was legally conceptualized in a very narrow sense as an act of sexual lust perpetrated by a male upon a female, who was not his wife, and who did not consent to the act in question. In keeping with traditional limited definitions of sexuality, provisions of the old Section 143 of the Code legally defined rape as the penetration of a vagina by a penis; a forced oral sexual act constituted "gross indecency," forced penetration of a vagina either manually or with a foreign object constituted "indecent assault against a female," while anal penetration alone constituted "buggery." In all cases, the old laws emphasized the sexual components of the acts involved over the violence or threats of violence accompanying them. Our new **sexual assault** laws shift the focus, emphasizing the violence components of the acts involved, over a more widely defined inclusive set of sexual acts. These changes attempt to both reflect and educate general beliefs that sexual assault first and foremost is motivated by, and is an expression of, power and intimidation, acted out through a sexual realm.

The tripartite laws contained in Section 271–273 of the Criminal Code (sexual assault, sexual assault with a weapon causing bodily harm, and aggravated sexual assault), are differentiated on the basis of the violence committed, not on the sexual acts themselves. The new laws are gender neutral and both males and females (including wives) can now be legally defined as victims, and both males and females can now be charged and convicted for perpetrating any and all three types of sexual assault. Despite attempts in 1992 to precisely define "consent" in Section 273.1(1) of the Criminal Code as "voluntary agreement of the complainant to engage in the sexual activity in question" (Comack, 1996: 151), the issues of voluntary and involuntary consent, the relevance of a complainant's prior sexual history, access to a complainant's therapeutic records, and a defendant's right to a fair trial all remain contested subjects of debate between individuals personally involved, the police, lawyers, as well as provincial and Supreme Court judges. An underlying hope of lawmakers is that eventual resolution of the issues just mentioned and changes in public perceptions of the nature of sexual assault will motivate more victims to publicly acknowledge their status and then seek legal redress for intimate assaults perpetrated upon them.

Explanations

It is not surprising to find that researchers and theorists have attempted to provide explanations, to varying degrees of completeness, more for women's violent victimization by men than for any other forms of intimate violence. Straus (1979) identifies three factors as being particularly salient in directing academic attention to the various forms of violence perpetrated upon women, and to the phenomenon of "battered women" in particular. First, in the aftermath of social protest, political assassinations, and rising rates of violent crime that marked the 1960s and 1970s, sensitivity was heightened to the issue of violence generally. Second, among sociologists during that same time period, conflict theorists began to challenge functionalism's idealized view of the family, which suggested that women and men led harmonious and complimentary lives (see also Cheal, 1991). Third, the second wave of the women's movement increasingly rejected traditional societal and academic understandings of and explanations for violence against women. Feminists maintained that there was "more to the story of 'battered women' than their experiences with violence and the relationship in which violence is enacted" (Kirkwood, 1993: 1). The women's movement raised the consciousness of women, and our entire society, regarding the extent of violence against women.

> In the early 1970's, it sometimes seemed as if the issue of battered women came out of nowhere. Suddenly feminist lawyers, therapists, and women's crisis and anti-rape workers were reporting hundreds of calls and visits from abused women desperately in need of assistance. No mere accident, this groundswell was the result of the changing political consciousness and organizing activity of women. The emerging feminist movement painstakingly detailed the conditions of daily life that would allow women to call themselves battered. A fundamental assertion of the movement, women's right to control their bodies and lives, and one of its practical applications, women's hotlines and crisis centres, provided a context for battered women to speak out and ask for help. (Schecter and Gary, 1989: 249)

The full magnitude of the meaning of this shift in perspective can only be appreciated when viewed against the backdrop of history.

Historical Overview

In chronicling the history of violence against women in European societies, Thorne-Finch (1992: 110) contends that "[f]or centuries, male violence against women was viewed as something completely normal, often necessary." Husbands in ancient Rome

> had the legal right to chastise, divorce, or kill their wives for engaging in behaviour that they themselves engaged in daily. But it did not take something as extreme as marital infidelity to rouse the man of the house to raise club and boot—or sandal—to the erring wife. If she were caught tippling in the family wine cellar, attending public games without his permission, or walking outdoors with her face uncovered, she could be beaten. (Dobash and Dobash [1979] as cited in Thorne-Finch, 1992: 110)

An adulterous Spanish woman could be killed with impunity during medieval times, while in France, "[i]t was legal for a Frenchman to beat his wife when she wronged him by committing adultery, or by preparing to do so, or by refusing to obey him" (Dobash and Dobash, 1979, as cited in Thorne-Finch, 1992: 111). Husbands in sixteenth-century Siena were advised as follows regarding the circumstances under which they were morally obliged to physically discipline their erring wives:

You should beat her…only when she commits a serious wrong; for example, if she blasphemes against God or a saint, if she mutters the devil's name, if she likes being at the window and lends ready ear to dishonest young men, or if she has taken to bad habits or bad company, or commits some other wrong that is a mortal sin. Then readily beat her, not in rage but out of charity and concern for her soul, so that the beatings will rebound to your merit and good. (Dobash and Dobash (1979) cited in Thorne-Finch, 1992: 111)

Husbands in England were "enjoined not to inflict bodily damage other than that 'which pertains to the office of a husband for lawful and reasonable correction'"(Dobash and Dobash (1979) as cited in Thorne-Finch, 1992: 111). That "which pertains to the office" refers to a right granted in law to husbands known as the "rule of thumb," that is, the right to beat or "correct" their wives with a rod, so long as that stick did not exceed the thickness of a man's thumb. It was only during the latter part of the nineteenth century that this right of husbands to inflict corporal punishments upon their wives was gradually eroded by changes in the law and, still much later, in the enforcement policies of the police and the courts (Ursel, 1992).

Dobash and Dobash (1979: 31–32) maintain that Western "history is littered with references to, and formulas for, beating, clubbing, and kicking [women] into submission" and conclude that "[w]omen's place in history often has been at the receiving end of a blow." The marriage licence has been referred to as a "hitting license" (Stets and Straus, 1989). There is little to indicate that this institutionalized violence against women was perceived as a socially problematic condition in need of explanation or analysis.

To be a wife meant becoming the property of a husband, taking a secondary position in a marital hierarchy of power and worth, being legally and morally bound to obey the will and wishes of one's husband, and thus, quite logically, subject to his control even to the point of physical chastisement or murder. (Dobash and Dobash, 1979: 33)

Even though, as pointed out by Walker (1990), church-sponsored shelters for the homeless have, in some Canadian communities since the 1930s, also housed women seeking sanctuary from abusive husbands, "wife battery" *per se* lacked social definition. Despite social and legal changes this century that now define abuse, assault, and battery, the legacy of wives as the property of men still lingers on. Married men in Canadian society today still commonly refer to their spouse as "the wife," a linguistic device that symbolically reduces a woman to the status of an object similar to "the house" and "the car," and do so in a context that clearly defines all of them as property he owns. Only rarely, and most often in a facetious manner, do we hear married women referring to "the husband." Such a counterpart objectification and ownership device lacks historical grounding in our society.

Laws and informal social norms granting men the right or obligation to inflict physical punishment upon their wives were buttressed historically by dominant social ideologies that supported the *sanctity* of "private" family life, and the home as a man's inviolable "castle." Social mores dictated that what went on behind closed doors was solely a family matter that could not, and should not, be interfered with by such outsiders as the courts, police, or nosy neighbours. Under these conditions, it is not surprising that myriad forms of family violence went largely unexamined. The "illusion of domestic tranquillity" (Karmen, 1990: 240) began to crack with the earliest empirical studies on marital conflict in the late 1960s. Even then, "in these early inquiries, the unreported acts of violence that were uncovered tended to be dismissed as the peculiar disorders of pathological couples" (Karmen, 1990: 240). These acknowledged acts of violence were considered to be "extremely rare" (Fattah, 1991:

168). Alternatively, the emerging phenomenon of violence directed against wives was often portrayed as unique to the lower-class, and a byproduct of poverty, low education, and marginalized status. By defining intimate violence as the "exception," or as something limited to a small segment of the largely invisible underclass, or as a product of a pathologically disturbed mind, the socially constructed romantic illusion of marriage and the family home as a safe haven for women and men could be maintained. Increasingly, however, awareness of the extent of intimate violence grew and explanations grounded in rare pathologies of poor people no longer sufficed.

Feminism and Family Violence

Feminist scholarship has been credited with directing the greatest amount of attention to the issue of intimate violence against women (Besharov, 1990; Dobash and Dobash, 1979; Fagan, 1990; Macleod, 1994; Walker, 1984). Feminism "explains and articulates the ways in which violence against women in the home is a critical component of the system of male power" (Yllo, 1993: 54). Feminists, who regard a patriarchal system as one that affirms male control and promotes the suppression of women, argue that violence against women is employed as a tool of social control at both the personal and institutional levels (Brownmiller, 1975). Restrictions placed upon women's personal and physical freedom are enforced by the fear and the threat of male-orchestrated violence (Schecter and Gary, 1989). Feminists offer not only explanations for intimate violence, but also, stemming from their own perspectives, direct attention to solutions for the problem.

Although all feminists would agree that "men and women are not evaluated similarly in a society such as Canada, and, therefore, that women live under conditions of oppression that are neither natural nor inevitable" (Nelson and Fleras, 1995: 214), feminist writings on violence against women often appear to be ideologically diverse, yet an underlying common ground exists beneath their search for answers. Bograd (1988: 13) claims that, while "there is no unified feminist perspective on wife abuse," all perspectives still attempt to answer the fundamental question, "why do men beat their wives?" Schecter (1985: 45) notes that early feminist activists in the Canadian battered-women's movement often held a "women's rights" or liberal feminist perspective which assumed that no radical restructuring of the basic institutions in Canadian society was necessary to help battered women. Early writers often emphasized that not all women were equally likely to experience violence within their homes. McAfee and Wood (1970: 421) claimed that *"few* [middle- class]…women really know the worst of women's condition.…*Few* have experienced the constant violence and drunkenness of a brutalizing husband or father" (emphasis added). These comments implicitly suggest that violence at the hands of abusive husbands and fathers was not viewed as the universal condition of *all* women; rather, such behaviour was held to be rare in the background experience of middle-class women, the core constituents of the second-wave women's movement. For these early activists, "making society better through winning concrete changes in the law and within institutions" (Schecter, 1985: 45) were thought to be sufficient solutions to the problem.

In contrast, others framed the problem in quite disparate ways. For "women's liberation" feminists (Schecter, 1982: 31), whose ideas reflected the influence of socialist feminist and radical feminist groups, violence against women was viewed as firmly entrenched within society and would require more to eradicate it than could be effected by limited changes made to individual laws or specific social policies. Schecter (1982: 31) observes that the goals of women's liberationists encompassed those of women's rights activism, "but went far beyond it, exploring the unequal division of labour and women's lack of control over their bodies, sexuality, and lives." To "end the violence," she notes, "women's liberation [writers] demanded a total, egalitarian restructuring of male/female relationships and society."

Women's liberationist writers on the phenomenon of battered wives drew upon the earlier work and writings of feminists involved in the antirape movement. These activists had argued that "profound social struggle would have to attack the sexism, racism, and class domination in capitalist society in order to end rape" (Schecter, 1982: 37), a view consistent with socialist feminism, or alternatively that "[r]ape is not an isolated act that can be rooted out from patriarchy without ending patriarchy itself...No simple reforms can eliminate rape" (Griffin, 1971: 36), a viewpoint consistent with radical feminism. Feminists in the antirape movement were instrumental in changing our society's perception, realizing that rape, ultimately, is not about sexuality per se, but about power and control.

The feminist perspective in general, and the radical perspective in particular, posits that violent acts against women, including rape, are not isolated incidents precipitated by circumstances unique to each woman. Rather, all women in our society share "something fundamentally in common" (Eisenstein, 1983: 132). In seeking to draw attention to those shared circumstances, essentially those associated with living in a patriarchal society, some feminists may have been guilty of hyperbole in their generalizations. For example:

> No matter what social and economic class a woman's husband belongs to, when she leaves her husband she is leaving the money behind. In this sense all women are of one class; they receive no money for their work, put in unlimited hours of service, and can be beaten mercilessly on the whims of their masters. (Leghorn, 1977: 29)

The basic message is that violence is a mechanism by which an individual male exerts or maintains his control over an individual female. When these individual acts are added together, the collective reality appears to support a conclusion that violence is the last line of defence, more accurately of offence, men use to preserve male privilege. Although derived from a different theoretical perspective, Straus' conclusion is appropriate here: "Violent acts by violent persons may generate positive feedback; that is, these acts may produce desired results" (in Gelles, 1993: 37). At least in the short term, violence works for the perpetrator. Dworkin (1976) coined the term **gynocide** to refer to the "systematic crippling, raping, and/or killing of women by men...the relentless violence perpetrated by the gender class men on the gender class women." For Dworkin, "under patriarchy, gynocide is the ongoing reality of life lived by women" (Dworkin, 1976: 16, 19).

Several relatively simple and related questions flow from a feminist perspective to demonstrate the gender issue regarding violence. One, are women ever abused, assaulted, or even killed simply because they are women? Two, are men ever abused, assaulted, or even killed simply because they are men? Unfortunately, the answer to the first question is "yes,", while the answer to the second appears to be "no." We noted in a previous chapter that each member of our society occupies a number of statuses simultaneously. Our questions here ask if sex is ever the only active status relevant to acts of violence. For an illustration of the answer to the first question we have only to recall the infamous events of what is now referred to as the Montreal Massacre, where 14 women were carefully selected and killed simply because they were women. Try as we might, we have been unable to find a comparable example where men were the recipients of violence simply because they were men and not because of other, more relevant, related statuses they happened to possess at the same time such as, for example, their occupations or their location in a particular physical setting, such as a bar or on a street late at night. Even then, our societal reaction is unlikely to blame these men for being men as the cause of the violence they received.

Many Canadians prefer to think that the events in Montreal on 6 December 1989 were orchestrated by a deranged madman, and that the victims, the events, and the assailant were not representative of any underlying conditions in our society. A feminist interpretation challenges the wisdom and accuracy of that line of thinking as simply an attempt both to deny the reality of patriarchy and to preserve a belief in the uniqueness of individual acts of violence against women. Of course, our two guiding questions could be altered to shift the focus from a victim to a perpetrator orientation. Do women ever abuse, assault, or kill solely because they are women? Do men ever abuse, assault, or kill solely because they are men? Answers from a feminist perspective would be, respectively, "no" and "yes." MacKinnon would phrase our questions: "When do you kill, or die, as a member of your gender and when as whoever else you are?" (MacKinnon, 1982: 703). We leave you to debate the questions among yourselves, while we move on to consider other issues.

Feminists, along with observers from other perspectives, have established that violence against women is systemic to a patriarchal society. Your answers to our (we hope) provocative questions in the previous two paragraphs likely support a feminist position (whether you wish to publicly admit this is another question). However, our use of an infamous incident as an illustration did not directly address the issue of intimate violence. The events in Montreal involved individuals who were strangers to one another and were not involved in an intimate relationship. Feminists argue that violence in intimate relationships essentially reflects conditions in the larger society. Intimate relations, such as marriage, are, consequently, based upon societal understandings of gender and power, and imbalances between the two (Bograd, 1988: 13) particularly under the influence of sexism or patriarchalism, which feminists argue is *the* factor underlying violence directed at women in intimate relationships (Dobash and Dobash, 1979; Pagelow, 1984; Russell, 1982; Stanko, 1985; Yllo, 1988). However, Thompson (1991), in a study of 336 undergraduates, reports that both men and women who abused their intimate partners had strong masculine gender orientations that valued control and dominance and weak feminine gender orientations that esteemed harmony within interpersonal relationships. This research suggests that gender orientation is more salient than the biological sex of the violent person.

Proponents of an alternative perspective agree that sexism or patriarchalism is *a* factor, but argue that certain other features of intimate relationships play more important, or at least equally important, roles. The sociologically oriented family-violence perspective "emphasizes the family as a system embedded within the larger society" (Coates and Leong, 1988: 177). For those writing from a family-violence perspective, wife abuse "is only one aspect of the general pattern of family violence, which includes parent-child violence, child-to-child violence, and wife-to-husband violence" (Straus et al., 1980: 44). Proponents of this perspective claim that violence is learned in the context of families living with exposure to violent role models, including parents, siblings, children, and those seemingly omnipresent in the mass media (Straus, 1973).

Gelles (1993: 35) identifies numerous factors that contribute to making the family, and by extension, all intimate relationships, a "violence-prone institution." Within this framework, it is the nature of family or intimate relationships themselves, rather than the gendered relationship between men and women, that is seen as the central violence-generating condition. These factors include: (i) a high frequency of interaction between partners, which serves to increase a "time risk" (Straus and Gelles, 1978) for conflict and violence; (ii) a wide array of activities engaged in by intimates that increase the likelihood that disagreements and tensions will surface (Brinkerhoff and Lupri, 1988); (iii) the intensity of involvement demanded within intimate relationships may "render one partner vulnerable if the other remans uninvolved, distant, and aloof" (Brinkerhoff and Lupri, 1988: 411); the combination of (iv) "built-in structural conflicts" and (v) the hierarchical structure of the family, such that interactions between family members are based upon, and influenced by, power and dependence (Brinkerhoff and Lupri, 1988); (vi) the privacy surrounding intimate relations in our society. The last factor refers to our social belief in the sanctity of the family and other intimate relationships that we mentioned earlier. While that sanctity serves to minimize outsider interference, it also increases pressures upon participants in the relationship itself. Brinkerhoff and Lupri (1988: 412) contend that the "norms of the nuclear family dictate that couples solve their own problems regardless of their origin, nature, and extent." Violence is frequently selected as a problem-solving mechanism in our society.

The phenomenon of violence within lesbian relationships poses a challenge to those feminists who argue that the abuse of power and the use of violence is uniquely and essentially "male" (Kelly, 1988; Schilit et al., 1990). Ristock (1991) argues that breaking the silence surrounding violence in lesbian relationships has been discouraged among lesbians in the past out of fear that negative stereotypes would be promoted and exacerbated. She suggests that violence in lesbian relationships can be understood as part of "a continuum of violence against women, the roots of which are in the hierarchical, oppressive nature of our society" (Ristock, 1991: 75). Through the mechanism of socialization, lesbians learn to hate and despise women and to "accept violence as a form of power and control." Lesbian violence is, therefore, internalized misogyny resulting from "institutionalized and internalized homophobia and heterosexism" (Ristock, 1991: 75). A similar viewpoint is forwarded by Renzetti (1992) who, observing that intimate abuse among lesbians is associated with the dynamics of power and dependency, suggests that lesbians, like heterosexuals, are raised to recognize families as hierarchical social units and to appreciate that the person who has the greater amount of resources holds the greater amount of power. As White and Kowalski (1994: 485) have observed, "to the extent that power corrupts men, it may also corrupt women."

Explanations for courtship violence in general and date rape in particular, focus upon a combination of gender expectations and the sociosexual norms comprising our dominant courtship and sexuality scripts (see Hills, 1980/1995). Males are socialized to be conquerors and winners who overcome any obstacles confronting them. Men are more likely to have learned that they can use physical force and sexual aggression as a means of intimidating their partners and getting their own way (Stets and Pirog-Good, 1990). Some male students at Queens University in Ontario reacted to a sexual abuse "No Means No" campaign by posting signs in dormitory windows boldly proclaiming that "No Means Tie Her Up" and "No Means More Beer" and by selling boxer shorts that read "No Non" in the daylight, but "Yes Oui" in the dark (Motherwell, 1990, in Benokraitis, 1996: 222); (Benokraitis, an American sociologist, wrongly attributes the incident to Queens College in New York City.) At least some of these students felt they had the support of their male peers, or felt they needed such bravado to seek support from their peers, in denigrating a campaign designed to heighten sensitivities to women's rights of refusal and to lessen men's perceived right to force their will. In similar fashion, in October of 1990, 20 to 30 male students who lived in the all-male Caribou House residence at the University of British Columbia, sent "party invitations" to 300 women in another nearby UBC residence. The invitation-writing, which turned into a competition among the male students, featured such "enticements" as: "What's the best thing about fucking an advisor? Killing her afterwards and giving her 2 points for screaming"; "We'll crush your cervix to oblivion" (Hookham and Merriam, 1991: 58). Anyone tempted to downplay these incidents, such as "lighten up, it's just guys havin' fun," are reminded that such a reaction is similar to the responses offered to female complainants of sexual harassment in junior-high schools.

Russell (1975: 206) has long argued that rape is not so much a deviant act as it is an **overconforming** act. From this perspective, rape can be viewed as an exaggerated form of "normal" gender relations in actual or potential sexual situations. Our general courtship script calls for men to initiate and control dating activities, while women maintain the interpersonal relationship. "The male theme of control justifies the use of force; it is the prerogative of the male to demand compliance from his partner by whatever means necessary" (Lloyd, 1991: 16). Our specific sexuality script calls for males to take the initiative in sexual relations and to continue pressing for greater intimacies until he achieves his goal. Females are assigned the gatekeeper role of determining just how far a male, and consequently the couple, can proceed sexually. Our traditional script permitted females to offer token resistance to preserve their reputations, but also encouraged males to engage in tactics designed to overcome such resistance. Male use of force to attain a sexual goal was an act of conformity with the sexuality script. Current sexuality norms have changed to reduce the necessity for token resistance and to insist that any resistance is of a heartfelt nature that should and must be respected (i.e., "No Means No"). However, male gender socialization in general and sexuality socialization in particular, has not kept abreast of our changing sexuality script. Some portion of the male population continues to use any means possible, including persuasion, threats of violence, and violence itself to attain their sexuality goals within relationships of variable degrees of intimacy.

MARRIAGE AND PARENTING

Our creation of a separate chapter on marital and family relations is not meant to suggest that these relationships are not intimate. Unlike many other types of intimate relations in our society, husband-wife and parent-child relationships are governed by law in addition to other unique informal expectations and conventions. Contemporary legal and historical common-law influences add important dimensions that necessitate these relationships and their social contexts be considered separately. Even though cohabiting heterosexual couples share many of the experiences common to married couples, research evidence in both the United States and Canada indicates that cohabitation tends to be a temporary arrangement of relatively short duration, ending in either separation or marriage (Le Bourdais and Marcil-Gratton, 1996). Due to its more enduring quality, and to the fact that marriage partners bring a different level and kind of commitment to their relationship (Bumpass et al., 1991) that manifests itself in many ways pertinent to the study of gender, we focus in the following pages upon marriage rather than cohabitation.

Unlike divorce law, which is under federal jurisdiction, marriage laws in Canada fall under the control of individual provinces and territories. At present, no province or territory in Canada sanctions marriage between individuals of the same sex. "A wedding ceremony between persons of the same sex produces not a marriage which is invalid, but one which is non-existent" (Canadian Family Law Guide, 1991, in Larson et al., 1994: 237). Gay and lesbian domestic partners and heterosexual cohabiting partners increasingly, over the past decade, have gained access to numerous social, financial, and legal benefits formerly available only to legally married spouses. However, bestowal of such benefits has been, and is, based on a premise that the former exist only *as if* married, but such bestowal does not, in and of itself, also constitute any conferral of legally married status upon a relationship. Marriage is, therefore, a heterosexual legal, as well as social, institution within our society and, as a consequence, our comments in the following pages will focus primarily upon gender in that context. As we shall see, marriage and gender create and recreate one another in a continually interacting fashion.

First-wave feminism around the turn of the twentieth century did not focus upon women's location and experiences in the family, since women's very dependence upon husbands and fathers precluded envisioning alternative arrangements at that time. Attention instead focused upon challenging "limitations on women's activities in the public sphere" (Hamilton, 1988: 15). Generated in a new and different historical timeframe, with changed social, political, and economic circumstances, second-wave feminism from the late 1970s onwards continues to examine women's experiences in the public sphere, but has also extended its analysis into the supposedly private sphere of marital and family arrangements.

The nuclear family initially (e.g., Firestone, 1970; Mitchell, 1984) came to be conceived of, and is still conceived of by some (e.g., see Stacey, 1993), as "the primary site for the constitution and perpetuation of male domination and female subordination" (Hamilton, 1988: 16). Such conclusions lead to calls for abolishing marriage and family as currently constituted, and for developing or legitimizing alternative arrangements designed to address themes of gender equality.

Continuing examinations since the 1970s and 1980s have lead to a partial shift in focus. "While many feminists in the 1970s movement regarded marriage as an inherently oppressive institution for women, many now recognize that it is the inequality of the sexes rather than marriage itself that is the problem" (Skolnick, 1996: 273). These inequalities bleed into and are intensified on an intimate scale by existing marital arrangements and relations.

MARRIAGE

An overwhelming majority of the populations in Canada and the United States have participated, and continue to participate, in legal marriage for a substantial portion of their adult lives. Ninety to 95 percent of the adult American population eventually marry (Norton and Miller, 1992). Varying in response to changing economic and political circumstances, 85 to 95 percent of the population born in Canada between the mid-1800s and the mid-1900s married at least once before reaching the age of 50 (Oderkirk, 1994). Of the total population aged 15 and older living in Canada in 1991, about one-quarter (29.8 percent of the males and 23.2 percent of the females) were currently single and had never been married, more than half (62.6 percent of males and 59.2 percent of females) were currently married, and approximately 10 percent (7.6 percent for males and 17.6 percent for females) had been married at least once and were currently separated, widowed (especially women), or divorced (Statistics Canada, 1992a: 19). As a sign of the times, considerable change occurred in our society over the first half of the 1990s. Comparable statistics for 1996 indicate that, of our population aged 15 and over, close to one-third (35.7 percent of the males and 28.9 percent of the females) have never been married, barely half (52.7 percent of the males and 49.7 percent of the females) are currently married, and approximately 15 percent (11.7 percent of the males and 21.4 percent of the females) have been married at least once, but are currently separated, divorced, or widowed (Statistics Canada, 1997b). Between two-thirds and three-quarters of the Canadian population in the 1990s are, or have been, involved in a legal marital relationship at some point during adulthood. However, orientations towards, and experiences of, marriage vary significantly for men and women.

Reasons for Marrying

Marriage provides a significantly more important legal stamp in the passport to adult femininity than it does in the passport to adult masculinity. As we noted in previous chapters, from the time of the "cult of true womanhood" in the 1800s and even earlier, the Traditional Marriage Enterprise (Levinson, 1996) extolled the centrality of marriage for women's lives. The Modified Marriage Enterprise (Levinson, 1996) of today still emphasizes marriage, albeit sharing centre stage with paid employment. Hopes of obtaining economic security used to be one of the chief reasons for marrying among women (Saxton, 1996: 239). Traditional gender roles decreed that only men should engage in paid work. Denied opportunities to be financially self-supporting, women were, therefore, forced to rely upon marriage and husbands as a means of economic survival. With greater employment opportunities now available for women, economic motivations for marrying are not as compelling today as in the past but, given the persistence of the wage gap, marriage still offers significant financial incentives for many women.

Men used to derive direct economic benefits from marrying, in the form of dowries, during that period of history where such transfers of money or property accompanied a bride. Today, with the significant increases in female labour-force participation, men can now anticipate improving their own standard of living via marrying an employed woman. As well, upon marrying, men, both in the past and present, obtain indirect economic benefits in the form of essentially unpaid services of a wife to do his cooking, cleaning, ironing, nurturing, and sexual servicing. "A man could not look after himself nearly so well as he could be looked after by a wife" (Saxton, 1996: 239). Marriage provides more physical comforts than singlehood for men and a husband provides a higher standard of living than does singledom for most women.

Women also married, and still marry today, for protection for themselves (although such protection is not always forthcoming from an intimate partner) and for their children (also not guaranteed). Women, more so than men, marry as a means of obtaining independence from their parental homes and from restrictive parental supervision. Since male lives are not monitored as closely, nor are they as constrained, marriage as a means of seeking independence and control of one's own household does not appear to be as compelling among males. Living more constricted and constrained adolescent and young adult lives, many females seek marriage as a visa to freedom. Both women and men also marry in an act of social conformity. Despite the rising incidence of cohabitation, especially in Quebec, but also generally throughout the rest of Canada (Dumas and Bélanger, 1997), marriage in our society is considered to be one of the hallmark indicators of, and part of the taken-for-granted pathway to, adulthood. A special form of approval from family (especially parents whose values were formed in a pre-cohabitation era), friends, employers, and society in general is generated towards those who finally "settle down" and get married.

Orientations Towards Marriage

Despite all of the objective advantages it offers, as we shall see later, to men marriage is a destination surrounded with ambivalence at best and fear at worst. While the vast majority of males in our society readily accept getting married as a fact of adult life, phrases such as "the old ball and chain" and "the tender trap," commonly used to refer both to a wife and to marriage, give expression to a male fear of committing themselves to something defined as not unremittingly good. As we saw in Chapter 7, part of males' fear lies in making a commitment to a love relationship whose rules and standards are feminized, and for which he is inadequately prepared and ill-equipped to succeed. Another part of the fear lies in making a commitment to a traditionally defined provider role when, as we saw in Chapter 6, men have eschewed the "good provider role" since the late 1970s or early 1980s (Bernard, 1981/1995; Ehrenreich, 1984).

Women's orientation is more optimistic than pessimistic, with marriage tending to be defined as an essential means of fulfilling one's gender destiny. Long embedded in our cultural folklore is the belief held out for every woman of the existence of a "Mr. Right," a carefully nurtured, constantly reinforced image of an ideal man to pursue, or hopefully be pursued by, for the sole objective of matrimony. No comparable historical image pertains to a "Miss" or "Ms. Right" for men except for the notion of a "good woman" suitable for marrying. Once found, men are expected to marry this good woman, who will retain the desired characteristics for the duration of a marriage. In contrast, if Mr. Right possesses a few flaws, common belief holds that a prospective wife has a legitimate right to expect that either he will change by himself as a consequence of love and marriage, or in response to her marital duty and obligation to try to transform him. Our cultural folklore also contains a somewhat cynical evaluation of these prospects: "Women marry believing that their husbands will change; Men marry believing that their wives will not change: They're both wrong" (Anonymous, quoted in Saxton, 1996: 228).

As we shall see in more detail in Chapter 9, a variety of circumstances combine to produce an uneven ratio of males to females during younger ages of the human life span. Between the ages of late teens to early thirties typical of first marriage, men outnumber women, and the demographics of availability within our society in recent years favour female choice (see McVey and Kalbach, 1995: 219; Nelson and Robinson, 1995; 1994: 74–87). Changing sex ratios with age shift the balance of demographic power towards equality during the mid-thirties to early fifties, and then into men's hands by mid-fifties onwards, when women outnumber men by a wide margin. Popular magazines in the mid-1980s elevated to the level of an urban myth a belief that an unmarried woman of age 40 faced a greater likelihood of being killed by a terrorist than of finding a man to marry (see Faludi, 1991: 9–19; Nelson and Robinson, 1994). A misinterpretation of data from one study lead to a frenzied cultural debate over whether all unmarried women over 40 were "doomed" to eternal spinsterhood as a caretaker of cats. That lead well-intentioned families, especially mothers, and friends to pressure unmarried younger women to stop being so "picky" or "particular" and to marry young, before it was "too late." Despite the existence of denials regarding the sensationalism of the preliminary study, and the consequent rebuttal of that study by a subsequent analysis (see Faludi, 1991; Nelson and Robinson, 1994), the "terrorist more likely than husband" scenario remains a popular belief still disseminated, both inside of and outside of the media.

Differing gender orientations towards marriage can be observed in the performed rituals leading up to a wedding. As we noted in previous chapters, males demonstrate their capability as providers by making one of the first material investments in the marital relationship in the form of purchasing an engagement and a wedding ring for the bride; brides today are likely to demonstrate a financially supportive role by purchasing a, typically less expensive, wedding ring for the groom. Other than remembering to show up at the wedding venue on time, preferably sober, grooms' further participation traditionally has been limited to a gender-conformity task of arranging for vehicular transportation.

The greater symbolic importance of weddings for women than for men is captured in our typically sequenced phrasing of the words "bride and groom," not the other way around. The bride, her family, and female friends are involved extensively in preparations for the wedding (most often paid for by her family/father), including booking the wedding and reception venues, official announcements, catering, decorations, photography, and clothing items such as the centrepiece wedding dress. Our folk wisdom claims that the three most important days in a woman's life are: the day she gets engaged; the day she gets married; the day she gives birth. Of these three, the wedding day is the most public and calls for the most elaborate costuming. Grooms are typically expected by custom, although fashion restrictions are loosening somewhat, to be costumed in such a manner as to blend in with the background and not distinguish themselves in any manner that might detract from the centrestage presence of the bride on this, her most special day. While he may be encouraged to rent his tuxedo, she is encouraged to purchase the gown.

Differing orientations towards marriage are also reinforced by the ritual events of *stags* and *showers*. The basic underlying theme of stags emphasizes a "last night of freedom" for the prospective groom. This age-homogeneous "boys' night out" typically involves little in the way of gift giving, but instead is characterized by excessive consumption of alcoholic beverages and/or illicit narcotics, cigars, sloppy foods that make dietitians and cleanup staff cringe, and female strippers and/or hardcore sexually explicit videos. Stags are intended to remind the groom (the "condemned" man) and other attendees of all the things he supposedly will be forced to do without once he gets "tied down" by a wife, who puts a real ring on his finger, a symbolic ring through his nose (although current fashion often requires the latter to be real also), and a restrictive clamp of domesticity upon his freedom.

In contrast, prospective brides are showered with gifts and positive reinforcements for a much-anticipated joyous transition into respectable femininity. Typically, an age-heterogeneous "girls night in," complete with moderate consumption of mildly alcoholic or non-alcoholic beverages, carefully arranged ribbon sandwiches and dainty foodstuffs, no live or video entertainment, but plentiful games and gift-giving, takes place. It is expected that the bride will be showered with comments of support and concern from her female friends, family members, and coworkers. The expression of good wishes for her future well-being are intended to validate a positive orientation towards marriage among women, and accent the supposed gains brides will attain upon completing this rite of passage. Elaborately wrapped gifts typically include items intended for display on her person (e.g., tasteful, but not raunchy, lingerie), for display to make her new house into a "home" (e.g., cups and saucers, bathroom and bedroom linens, and stemware and crystal), or utilitarian items for her housework (e.g., bread and pasta makers, measuring cups and spoons and toasters, but neither snow shovels nor garbage cans). Often these gifts are accompanied by storytelling about how handy the giftgiver found the item to be, or how and when the items will be found useful or image-saving. All of these gifts and accompanying anecdotes function as anticipatory socialization into feminine wifehood and constitute an important part of the initiation ritual that often culminates in the bride-to-be donning a paper-plate hat laden with the ribbons and bows that have decorated the gifts. Further socialization often takes a form wherein attendees each write some few words of advice to the new bride, sometimes humorous, sometimes serious, almost always optimistic and rarely cynical, that are combined into book form by the mother of the bride and presented to the bride-to-be.

Our society has witnessed, over the past two decades, a growing androgyny of prenuptial rituals as a consequence of a number of factors, including desires to break from tradition, changing gender roles in general, increasingly later ages for first marriage, with a consequent greater accumulation of finances permitting lesser dependence upon parents (i.e., fathers) and greater assumption of more financial input and decision-making on the part of both brides and grooms, and an increasing incidence of remarriages, when the traditional rituals no longer appear to be as appropriate (but gifts are appreciated to replace items worn out during previous marriages). A trend towards egalitarianism is demonstrated in the greater participation of grooms in the planning and preparations for weddings, "stagettes" for brides, complete with male strippers and other reminders that a bride's freedom also will be curtailed by marital roles, and "Jack-and-Jill (combined) showers," usually without strippers of either sex.

Marital Roles

Gender becomes an organizing principle in heterosexual marriages, as does gender inequality. Blumstein and Schwartz (1983: 324) note that "gender provides a shortcut and avoids the decision making process" when it comes to assigning roles, such as who takes out the garbage, initiates sexual contact, or does housework. "Research shows...that gay and lesbian relationships rarely pattern themselves after heterosexual husband-and-wife roles. They are more likely to follow a best friends or roommates model that emphasizes similarity of experiences and equal sharing of resources and responsibility" (Shehan and Kammeyer, 1997: 154). Gays and lesbians must be innovative, otherwise only 20 percent of inside housework would ever get done in gay households, and lesbian households would be impossible to access because of snow or grass accumulations. Any inequities of role responsibilities existing in gay and lesbian relationships are not organized around gender.

At the same time, marriage provides a cultural blueprint for gender. Marriage is more than just "a piece of paper," to quote a commonly uttered phrase and widespread belief. External, and internalized, cultural expectations for the roles of husband and wife dictate gender performances. "Wife" has been explored more (e.g., Bernard, 1973; Heyn, 1997) than has "husband." Adoption of these roles brings about scripted changes in thoughts, feelings, and actions that often are misattributed as essential characteristics of gender, when they should be understood more accurately as the products of the marital construction of gender. Prior to the 1970s, a well-established gender blueprint existed for marriage and for marital roles. "She'd subordinate her life to his, and wouldn't even notice it; her needs for achievement and mastery would be met vicariously through his accomplishments or those of the children" (Rubin, 1983: 266). Since the 1970s, this blueprint has been smudged by general social, and specific gender, changes.

The heterosexual institution of marriage, in all nine anglophone provinces (Quebec is governed by its own *Civil Code*) and in the territories of Canada, is anchored in English common law. Pertinent legislative and judicial systems, many, if not most, governmental and nongovernmental organizations, as well as the implicit (rarely stated nor fully understood) contract binding husbands and wives, are all embedded in common-law traditions pertaining to the gendered "bed and board" privileges and obligations of marriage. According to English common law, a man, upon marriage, automatically became designated as the head of the household and in that capacity was expected to provide protection, security, and financial maintenance in the form of food, shelter, and clothing for his wife and their children. In return, a woman, upon marriage, was expected to assume domestic responsibility for household and childcare, and make herself sexually available to her husband. Women's responsibilities expanded over time to include providing nurturance and affection for her husband and children as well.

Even though marriage and divorce laws in the United States lag behind changes in gender roles (Saxton, 1996: 232), Canada has attempted, in some ways, to keep abreast of changing gender expectations and behaviours. We saw in Chapter 3 that a series of laws were enacted in our society, over the latter half of the nineteenth and the early portion of the twentieth centuries, to give married women independent control over their own wages, property, and rights to inheritance. More recently, to provide just a few contemporary examples, husbands since the 1981 Census of Canada are no longer automatically presumed by the government to be the head of the household; banking and business organizations are slowly changing their practices to allow married women to establish their own independent credit ratings (although examples still abound of wives discovering they cannot make major transactions without their husband's cosignature); changes in divorce laws regarding what was once termed "alimony" now limit a man's financial responsibility to his former wife; mothers since 1985 have been expected to assume joint responsibility with their former husbands for the financial welfare of their children; the Canadian parliament created a crime of "marital sexual assault" in 1983, acknowledging that wives were no longer unquestioningly obligated to make themselves sexually available to their husbands; since the implementation of the *Charter of Rights and Freedoms,* wives are no longer legally required to follow a husband and establish domicile with him should he undertake a geographical move.

Over the course of the twentieth century, bed and board responsibilities have been elaborated into a greater number of roles incorporating heightened social expectations for marriage and marital relationships. Nye and Berardo (1973) argue that marriage and the family is composed of at least six distinguishable adult roles: **provider, childcare, child socialization, housekeepers, sexual, therapeutic**. To this list we could also add an additional, somewhat distinct, role of **kinkeeper**. Of course, Martha Stewart (aka the dominatrix of domesticity) has singlehandedly (with the help of a large unseen number of background helpers) elevated the bar in the 1990s to expand domestic roles to include architect and interior designer, landscaper, wood and sheetmetal crafter, and animal husbandry, but since even she cannot perform all these tasks by herself, we shall not consider the latter additions. The roles of childcare and socialization will be considered later in a separate section of this chapter.

Provider, Housekeeper, and Sexual Roles

We have already presented material on these roles in previous chapters. It is sufficient to note here that the majority of marriages in the 1990s are characterized by the presence, in some form, of two providers, as opposed to the more traditional middle-class division of labour, since the time of the Industrial Revolution, of only one financial provider. The housekeeper role was and still is performed primarily by wives, while husbands are still most likely to be prime initiators of sexual contact within marriages today and, as a result, the sexual rhythms of a marriage conform mainly to his preferences. Husbands are still known to seek legal redress, by suing for "loss of *consortium*" should a wife's housekeeping, childcare, or sexual services become unavailable, as a consequence of the negligent actions of a third party. These suits are based upon a premise that such services are owed to a husband by a wife, and someone else should compensate a husband for the loss of his wife's services. Wives rarely, if ever, attempt to sue for loss of consortium if a husband is unable, through the actions of a third party, to perform housekeeping, childcare, or sexual services.

Therapeutic Role

The therapeutic role refers to a bundle of activities oriented towards the maintenance and care of the spousal relationship, and spouses' physical, emotional, and mental health. "The therapeutic role for women appears to be clearly recognized….Women should listen to their husbands' frustrations, serve as a 'sounding board' for their novel ideas, build them up when they are discouraged, and reassure them when they feel insecure" (Nye and Berardo, 1973: 258). Although in theory either spouse could perform this role, social expectations surrounding marriage and other interpersonal relationships dictate that this role be allocated to wives. In part, assignment of this role to women is based upon the traditional hierarchical arrangement of marriage, whereby the inferior partner is expected to nurture the superior partner. Heilbrun (1981 in Heyn, 1997: 173) notes that "man's superiority must not be challenged….At the same time, that superiority is so frail that women must contrive with man to sustain it." In their performance of the therapeutic role, wives are expected to pay special attention to the care and nurturing of the supposedly "frail" or "fragile" male ego. Care and feeding of the female ego are not contained in a husband's job description.

In part, assigning the therapeutic role to wives is based upon a presumption that women are better qualified than men, either innately or via specialized socialization, to perform the part. "A husband may notice a new dress or a drop of perfume behind his wife's ear, but it is rare for him to be as sensitive to her shifting moods as she is to his" (Drummond, 1979, in Baca Zinn and Eitzen, 1993: 274). Regardless of the underlying reasons for the assignment, most women understand this role will become part of their implicitly contracted duty upon marriage. In the words of one respondent, "I understood that I was the relationship pro. That it was 'our' marriage, but my emotional responsibility. I was the one who would end the fight, manage the emotional stuff, keep the marriage on an even keel….I was the one who was better at relationships, so my new position sort of codified that responsibility" (in Heyn, 1997: 37).

The therapeutic role embodies the quality of "selflessness" long attributed to the "good woman," who would make an ideal "good wife" (Heyn, 1997: 89; Laws, 1979) and subsume her self and her identity under that of her husband and, eventually, her children. Preoccupation with self-development not intended solely for the purpose of providing better service to husband and children has been, and still is, deemed as "selfishness" on the part of married women and as anathema to the good-wife role (Rubin, 1979); yet proponents of the human-potential movement during the late 1960s to early 1980s (e.g., O'Neill and O'Neill, 1972; Rogers, 1972; Satir, 1970) argued that marriages and marital roles should be constructed to permit and promote self development of both partners. The legacy of that movement, along with the corresponding initial influence of the second-wave of feminism, influenced significant portions of the population in Canada. Consequently, whether self-ishness is a vice or a virtue becomes a focal point for debate between those who champion "traditional family values" and the good-wife role, and those who champion alternative visions. Contemporary wives often feel that they have a right to be selfish, yet experience guilt over asserting that right.

As we noted in the previous chapter, women are much more likely to seek out female friends to attend to their own emotional and communication therapeutic needs, and to discuss, analyze, or commiserate about relationships with a particular man or men in general (Filion, 1996: 18–19), while men are more likely to identify their wives as their best friends and the ones to whom they turn when in need of emotional nurturance. "A man finds companionship in marriage when he finds a woman in whom he can confide his emotions and his troubles. This woman—his wife—is, in most cases, the only such person in his life....Being accepted and emotionally supported engendered a sense of security for...husbands" (Stebbins, 1988: 34). In addition to the fact that men have their emotional needs met in the private confines of their own homes, "the traditional economic dependency of women on men in an industrial society has obscured the extent to which men are emotionally dependent on women" (Skolnick, 1996: 271). Emotionally dependent men are enabled by their wives to maintain the belief that emotional expertise is part of women's, not men's work. In addition to emotional therapy, wives are also expected to provide physical care and therapy.

Upon assumption of the role of wife, a woman typically begins immediately to monitor her husband's diet (restricting and/or redirecting his food and beverage intake) and general lifestyle, all in the name of his physical health (Ross, 1995). Such monitoring frequently extends also to his language and public commentaries and his clothing styles ("Are you going out wearing that?"), this time in the name of social appearances. Except for men with a high possessiveness-jealousy quotient, husbands usually do not monitor or try to change their wives as extensively. Wives also monitor their own voices, and modulate them where necessary, and modify "their dress, their mannerisms, their entire self presentation" to become "less playful, less flirtatious, less ambitious, less assertive, less sexual, less open, and less honest with their partners, their families, their friends, and themselves" (Heyn, 1997: 26). The decrease in honesty is practised upon everyone, except, perhaps, a closest confidant, in the name of preserving and protecting both the public and private images of a marriage, a husband, and oneself.

Another facet of the therapeutic role typically required of, and performed by, wives pertains to anticipating, creating, and maintaining marriage and family rituals. Women, more so than men, are likely to be in charge of the calendar of events holding important meaning to marital partners and other family members. Wives typically are expected to invest greater amounts of time and energy in orchestrating the myriad details associated with birthdays, anniversaries, quiet evenings at home, couple or family holidays, meal times, and special events associated with accomplishments (career moves and promotions, passing exams) made by partners, all of which shared experiences are designed to provide the glue promoting marital and family cohesion. Deciding upon who will participate and the timing, dress codes, specific activities, desired and necessary sustenance and libations, gift-wrapping, and reminders about events are part of a therapeutic role performed, overwhelmingly, by wives to enhance feelings among the other celebrants of being cared for and special. A possible exception in our culture pertains to the rituals associated with Valentine's Day. In this instance, advertisers and the media perform the functions of providing reminders of the upcoming events, suggesting desirable means of expressing specialness in a material form, and hinting that efforts on the part of the husband will be amply rewarded by an appreciative wife.

Sharing recreational activities (e.g., watching favourite TV programs together, bowling, going to concerts) can become important rituals that aid in binding marital partners together. While enjoyable in and of themselves, such activities also serve a therapeutic function. Nye and Berardo (1973: 259) suggest that husbands in the 1970s "probably" did not place as great an emphasis upon shared recreational activities as did wives. Implicit within their presentation is the notion that wives conforming to the "traditional" housewife role experienced isolation in their day-to-day activities and, therefore, welcomed shared recreation as a means of gaining and maintaining interpersonal contacts with another adult. Husbands, for the most part surrounded by coworkers throughout the work day, preferred recreational activities that provided a needed component of privacy. As we noted in Chapter 6, husbands typically have more time for leisure than do wives, and also participate more in leisure activities outside the home. Stebbins (1988: 37–38) contends that findings from more recent research indicate that substantial numbers of men are shifting their search for self-fulfilment away from paid employment and towards, not their family and marital relationships, but rather, their serious, nonfamilial leisure pursuits, which neither require nor invite participation of other family members (e.g., astronomy, music, hunting or fishing, amateur archaeology). "[L]eisure, once a supplementary form of relaxation between sessions of work, is now becoming a central, if not the central life interest of many men" (Stebbins, 1988: 40).

Research has yet to address whether this work-leisure shift is more commonly associated with the midlife transition, to be presented in the next chapter, experienced by most men. Nor is it clear whether a retreat from intimate relations to leisure is related to feelings, noted in the last chapter, on the part of men that marital intimacy relationships are a foreign terrain filled with uncomfortable expectations requiring unfamiliar negotiation skills. For many men, the solitary activity of building a better birdhouse becomes more appealing than building a better marital relationship through joint exploration and expression of interpersonal feelings. Regardless of the timing and the motivations for development of these solitary consuming leisure interests, wives and children are relegated to a peripheral role, where primary emphasis is placed upon the activities, and participants become secondary. A major exception to this formula pertains to the tradition of "men only" fishing, golfing, or gambling expeditions. At other times, wives who value joint recreational activities are more likely to make the necessary compromises, spending time with their husbands in activities pleasing to him. One wife states that "I found I had either to take up fishing or find a new husband, so I took up fishing" (in Nye and Berardo, 1973: 260). Husbands rarely invoke similar explanations for their newly developed interest in bird watching.

Kinkeeper

The kinkeeper maintains formal and informal ritual ties with real or fictive kin, who are all considered to be members of an extended family. Typically a wife's responsibility, the kinkeeper is in charge of buying, expressing appropriate sentiments in, and sending cards, along with appropriate gifts, acknowledging special occasions, such as births, weddings, and anniversaries of both, graduations, special holidays, and deaths. If the kinkeeper does not perform these tasks directly, she usually is in charge of prompting other family members to perform them. Failing that, husbands and children usually turn to the kinkeeper to learn what cards, gifts, and appropriate sentiments were sent on their behalf to kin members on these special, but almost forgotten, occasions. Kinkeepers also maintain informal ties through telephone and e-mail contacts, shopping trips, shared meals or coffee breaks, and other forms of interpersonal contacts. When necessary, kinkeeping may also require provision of physical care and emotional sustenance to aging, ill, or infirm members of the extended family (Walker and Pratt, 1991).

Viewed from one standpoint, therapeutic, recreational, and even kinkeeper services comprise "companionship." Viewed from another standpoint, therapeutic and kinship roles comprise "community service." Wives' services are a counterpart of governmental social services and, as federal, provincial, and municipal governments continue to cut back on services in the politically expedient name of fiscal responsibility, wives and mothers are increasingly being called upon to provide a compensatory level of service. The new fiscal and social conservatism places a number of additional burdens upon wives. Not only are women predominantly employed, as we saw in Chapter 6, in the fields of education, social services, and healthcare, but they also tend to be the greatest users of those services, either on their own or on behalf of other family members. These women are more likely to lose employment at the hands of government cutbacks, and also likely to lose access to valued services that are no longer provided by the government. At the same time, wives are expected to replace those missing services as part of their own unpaid labour.

Armstrong (1996: 223) argues that "cutbacks in health care are accompanied by [an] attempt to resurrect 'the family' and make into family responsibilities many of the services that have, for years, been provided by paid female workers in the public sector." Such expectations conveniently ignore the fact that a large percentage of wives and mothers are still employed, despite the cutbacks, and are already performing a "double shift." Calls to return family members' care into the hands of women acknowledge neither the increasing length of time (especially for the elderly) such care may be required, nor the significant differences between care provided in the past and the kinds of care demanded today. Women no longer learn many skills needed to perform various kinds of homecare (how many women today can prepare a body for burial, properly change dressing on surgery wounds, or dispense numerous medications?), nor can they reasonably be expected to learn what have become increasingly technical procedures often requiring access to, and knowledge of, sophisticated technologies. If present trends continue into the future, the ideal kinkeeper role will expand substantially.

Marital Interaction

Despite the fact that all marriages are unique in some respects, they also demonstrate sufficient similarities in many other respects that they can be categorized into between three and five major types (Crosby, 1991; Cuber and Harroff, 1965; Fitzpatrick, 1988). Certain gendered patterns of marital interaction, however, are found consistently across all types.

After summarizing existing research findings, Epstein et al., (1994) conclude that wives, during times of marital conflict, are more likely than husbands to engage in direct negative communication patterns of making belittling, complaining, derogatory, or critical fault-finding comments, often referred to by participants as "nagging" behaviour. Part of this gender difference is attributable to the greater likelihood of men either retreating into silence or leaving the scene of a conflict, especially when a discussion focuses upon emotional issues. The physical and emotional withdrawal of husbands constitutes indirect negative communication. At the same time as being more likely to engage directly in negative communications, wives are also more effective and more frequent in communicating positive, complimentary, or loving messages. As we noted in the previous chapter, husbands typically attempt to convey positive messages indirectly, via activities whose intentions and meanings are subject to misinterpretation, such as proffering advice, washing cars, or initiating something sexual. Wives perform instrumental activities as well, but typically also extend unambiguously soothing words to bridge disrupted harmony or (re)establish emotional intimacy.

During an exchange of traditional vows in wedding ceremonies, wives promise to "obey" their husbands and husbands promise to "cherish" their wives, a difference that establishes a basis for patriarchal marital relationships. Since the time of the 1947 wedding of then-Princess Elizabeth to Prince Philip, women in our society have been released from automatically taking a vow of obedience and few women today incorporate the traditional wording into their wedding ceremonies. However, despite that deletion of a symbolic affirmation of inequality, the vast majority of marriages today are still characterized by an imbalance of power stemming from other sources. The "bride and groom" are linguistically transformed into "husband and wife" and "Mr. and Mrs. (insert his family last name here)," wherein he immediately acquires temporal and other forms of priority. Resource power derived from income and benefits, pensions, occupational prestige, age, height, weight, body mass, and strength are unequally distributed in favour of husbands in most marriages. In accordance with social expectations and limited available alternatives, wives typically have more of a social, psychological, and economic stake in marriage than do husbands, thus granting husbands, according to the "principle of least interest," an additional source of power.

As we saw in the last chapter, and will observe at the end of the present chapter, husbands usually hold the balance of coercive physical power within marriage and even beyond the boundaries of a legally dissolved marriage. Wives typically hold the balance of sexual power in marriage, and are much more likely than husbands to use sexuality as a bargaining chip, either withholding sexuality as a form of punishment, or bestowing sexuality as a reward for desired behaviour in nonsexual realms of marital relations (Blumstein and Schwartz, 1983). Udry (1968) finds that relationship satisfaction precedes sexuality satisfaction for wives, but the converse holds for husbands. These findings conform to the typical sexuality socialization experienced by men and women in our society. Unless a marital relationship provides a desired level of stability and security, wives are less likely to commit themselves sexually in a wholehearted fashion. In contrast, husbands judge sexual satisfaction to be a most important barometer of how satisfying a marital relationship is overall.

A constant finding of research over the past three decades has been the noticeable decline in marital quality, occurring earlier and more precipitously among wives than husbands, associated with the arrival of children and the intrusion of parenting upon marital relationships (e.g., Belsky, 1990; Glenn, 1990; Kurdek, 1993a; Rollins and Feldman, 1970). Mothers assume the vast majority of responsibilities and duties associated with children's care and socialization. Wives/mothers also perform, and are responsible for, most duties associated with housework, and the majority are also gainfully employed. These tremendous demands upon time and physical and emotional energy typically leave wives/mothers with fewer, usually depleted, personal resources to devote to the care and maintenance of their husbands. While other marital dynamics are also involved, husbands' evaluations of marital quality also deteriorate following the birth of each child, partly as a consequence of feeling rejected and no longer being the sole focus of wifely attention. Even though young couples today claim to be in favour of a more equitable distribution of labour in their homes, empirical evidence indicates these couples actually replicate and perpetuate traditional patterns of inequality (Baker, 1995: 308).

His and Hers Marriages

Bernard (1973) was one of the first sociologists to argue that marriage has such different meanings and consequences for women and men that generalizations about marriage *per se,* which ignore gender differences, are almost meaningless. Within each legal union, his marriage differs anywhere from a little to a lot from her marriage. Paradoxically, both sexes demonstrate contradictions between their public evaluations of marriage and their experiences within marriage. Despite the negative orientation of men towards marriage evidenced by their public complaints about restrictions upon their economic and sexual freedom and discomfort with issues surrounding love and emotions, being married is extremely beneficial to men in terms of their physical, emotional, and mental health. Despite the positive orientation of women towards marriage, and their positive evaluations of their marriages, being married is detrimental to women's physical, emotional, and mental health.

Research findings indicate that married men are healthier than are never-married, widowed, and divorced men, while married women are less healthy than never-married, widowed, and divorced women. Married men are also generally healthier than married women, while rates of physical, emotional, and mental illness among men and women who are never-married, widowed, and divorced are found to be either comparable or slightly higher among men (Bernard, 1973; Gove and Tudor, 1973, Gove et al., 1990; Ross et al., 1991). The most striking differences are found between married men and stay-at-home housewives, between housewives and women not currently married, and between housewives and employed wives (Gove, 1984; Waldron and Jacobs, 1988).

Two major types of explanations have been offered for these findings. The *selectivity* explanation holds that only certain kinds of people are selected to either enter into, or remain within, marriage, while other kinds of people are found wanting (either prior to or during marriage) and are rejected as potential or current legal mates. While evaluations of the selectivity hypothesis find some moderate support for this position, selectivity fails to provide a sufficient explanation for the consistent findings regarding marriage and health (Ross, 1995; Waite, 1995). The alternative explanation suggests that the institution of marriage, as traditionally and presently constituted, causes the observed outcomes. We earlier noted that men benefit from wives' performance of a therapeutic role in marriage. No such benefits accrue to wives themselves.

Arguments have been advanced to suggest that the disadvantages of marriage for women are built into the transformative process of becoming a wife. Bernard (1973: 43), who initially (1942) proposed the "shock" theory of marriage for women, cites research indicating the presence of an almost reverse "Pygmalion effect," whereby traditional housewives gradually lose their sense of independence, become more submissive and accommodating, and slowly become much like their husbands. Eventually, in keeping with words often intoned during wedding ceremonies, the "two shall become as one" and that one is the husband. Problems experienced by many women are exacerbated by the isolating elements of the wife/mother role, where meaningful contacts with other living beings are most often limited to only young children and one's spouse (Baca Zinn and Eitzen, 1993: 271–272; Gove and Tudor, 1973; Skolnick, 1996: 272). Despite role-strain pressures experienced by employed "'double shift' wives and mothers" (Moen, 1992), evidence indicates that accumulating multiple roles in addition to that of housewife provides additional sources of satisfaction for women, which manifest themselves in improved scores on indicators of physical, emotional, and mental health (Barnett, 1994; Baruch and Barnett, 1986; Hobart, 1996: 166). Such benefits are not automatically forthcoming, but are derived from developing effective role-balancing techniques (Marks and MacDermid, 1996).

Despite a socially constructed wife role that contains elements deleterious to their health, wives generally evaluate their marriages as being very to mainly satisfying overall, even during the pressure-filled childrearing years. Bernard (1973: 54–58) argues that this apparent paradox is partially explained by the high value our society places upon conformity. Marriage is held to be part of women's gender destiny. Having conformed by getting married, women are expected to consider themselves successes, not failures. Only women who never marry and women who divorce should, according to our societal norms, consider themselves as failures. Married women must be successes and, therefore, must, and do, evaluate themselves and their marriages as successful and satisfying. Even though the "division" of labour within marriage tends to be heavily tilted against wives, accepting this imbalance as simply part of women's "lot" in life tends to influence women's sense of fairness and their evaluations of marital relationships (Hobart, 1996: 167–169; Thompson, 1991). Bernard offers an additional possible explanation:

> For to be happy in a relationship which imposes so many impediments on her, as traditional marriage does, a woman must be slightly ill mentally. Women accustomed to expressing themselves freely could not be happy in such a relationship; it would be too confining and too punitive. We therefore "deform" the minds of girls, as traditional Chinese used to deform their feet, in order to shape them for happiness in marriage. It may therefore be that married women say they are happy because they are sick rather than sick because they are married."
> (Bernard, 1973: 56–57)

Changing Demographics of Marriage

In 1972, the marriage rate in Canada per 1000 population reached a level (8.7) previously attained only immediately following World War II, and the actual number of marriages performed exceeded 200 000 for the only time in Canadian history (Nault, 1996: 39). Demographers anticipated that baby boomers would continue existing trends upon reaching marriageable ages. Such anticipations proved groundless, as the trends from 1972 to 1995 have been in the opposite direction, with decreases in both yearly marriage rates and the numbers of marriages performed (with a slight exception in the later 1980s). The number of marriages rose slightly between 1993 and 1995, still well below levels attained in the early 1970s, but marriage rates remained essentially the same at 5.4 in 1995 (Nault, 1996; Statistics Canada, 1996). The average age at first marriage in our society reached an all-time low, in 1972, of 22.2 years for brides and 24.7 years for grooms (Nault, 1996). By 1995, the average age for those entering their first marriage had risen to 27.1 for brides and 29.0 for grooms (Statistics Canada, 1996), with average-age differentials between brides and grooms reflecting the operation of the marriage gradient. From a strictly demographic perspective, we note that marriage rates have declined over time, partly because the population available for marriage, especially among younger ages characteristic of first marriages, is now smaller in the 1990s.

Other reasons for the decline in marriage rates are many and varied, including "changing values that made divorce and nonmarital childbearing more acceptable; widespread access to and use of contraception; women's growing participation in higher education and the workforce and their resulting financial independence; an unpredictable job market; and a generation pursuing self-fulfilment and avoiding long-term commitments" (Nault, 1996: 40). Single women's earnings are increasing, while, given present rates of unemployment and underemployment for young males, single men's earnings are either remaining stable or declining. Oppenheimer (1994) concludes that women are, therefore, less dependent upon men's financial support, and men, especially younger men, are less able to provide such support. These conditions reduce the numbers and proportions of women actually marrying, or at least substantially increase women's waiting time before getting married. The changes over time in average ages demonstrate a lessening of the rush into marriage among younger age groups. Contributing to this hesitation is the fact that both permanent singlehood and cohabitation have become increasingly appealing alternatives to legal marriage. In addition to these oft-cited reasons, however, some of the decline must also be attributed to a decreased willingness on the part of Canadian women to commit themselves to an institution that, upon increased scrutiny, appears not to offer an attractive gender bargain.

Standing on the outside looking in, 85 percent of Canadian adolescents expect to marry (Bibby and Posterski, 1992: 30). However, if patterns existing in 1990 hold, statistical projections for the future suggest that only 63 percent of men and 67 percent of women born in Canada are expected to marry prior to age 50, down from the 85–95 percent characteristic of Canadians earlier in this century (Oderkirk, 1994: 5); projected rates are 44 percent for males and 48 percent for females in Quebec, and 70 percent and 74 percent respectively for males and females residing in the rest of Canada (Le Bourdais and Marcil-Gratton, 1996: 422). The significantly lower projected rates for Quebec are attributable to cohabitation being more institutionalized in that province than in other parts of Canada (La Bourdais and Marcil-Gratton, 1996), with, perhaps, the exception of the territories. Not only do projections suggest that the proportions of our population entering marriage will decline, but also the proportions who will stay married will decline in the future as a consequence of divorce. These latter predictions forecast the continuation of a trend begun during the late 1960s in our society.

DIVORCE

Almost all of the reasons offered earlier in partial explanation for declining marriage rates apply also as partial explanations for why many Canadians do not remain married. Based on an exhaustive review of available research, Lewis and Spanier (1979) theorize that whether a marriage remains intact or not depends upon an extensive series of factors some of which pertain to the quality of the marital relationship itself, and some of which pertain to conditions existing outside of marriage. Quality of marriage is influenced by factors such as "marital adjustment, satisfaction, happiness, conflict and role strain, communication, and integration" (Lewis and Spanier, 1979: 287). The balance of attractions and tensions internal to a marriage determine its judged quality.

One additional factor occurs outside of contemporary family boundaries, but exerts an important influence within the family. We earlier noted the significant increases in married women's labour-force-participation rates since the mid-1960s. In addition to making a necessary contribution to the financial survival of a marriage and family, income provision among women also creates or sustains an understanding that their own economic self-sufficiency at some level is possible. "[A]s more women participate in the labour force and all women have access to social assistance, they are partly freed from their former dependency on their husbands and now have an alternative not available to women in the past....[A] relatively low income or even poverty is often preferable to living in an unhappy or violent relationship" (Richardson, 1996: 216). In some cases, income provision leads women to an awareness that divorce is possible; in other cases, awareness of a possible divorce leads women to a decision to acquire employment income. Skolnick (1996: 270) argues that "[w]ith the likelihood of divorce approaching 50 percent or more, a woman who enters marriage assuming she will be supported for life, and with no thought for how she might support herself, is much more foolhardy in a statistical sense than someone who smokes three packs of cigarettes a day." Hobart (1996: 171) claims that

> [t]he recent rapid increase in the Canadian divorce rate is the result, in part, of two sources of increased marital conflict...paid employment has greatly reduced the time available to wives for domestic work, and having paycheques has empowered them, giving them increased influence and independence. Conflict has resulted, over (1) husband's reluctance to share the domestic work fairly, and (2) wives' refusal to be traditionally subservient.

Waite (1995: 499) also claims that "employed wives have less time and energy to focus on their husbands, and are less financially and emotionally dependent on marriage, than wives who work only in the home." Employed wives appear to find that the benefits of being married are decreasing, while the emotional, psychological, and physical costs are increasing, a combination that augments their propensity to divorce. Wives' employment can also lead to a greater willingness on the part of husbands to end an unhappy marriage, armed with the knowledge that their wives are no longer dependent upon a husband's income for survival.

Important factors external to the marital dyad include the influence of, and adherence to, religious doctrines (all of which positively evaluate intact marriages), the availability and valuation of nonmarital alternatives, the strength of the stigma attached to divorce and divorced persons, and legal accessibility to divorce (Lewis and Spanier, 1979: 287). Singlehood, as well as cohabitation, have become more socially acceptable and positively evaluated alternatives to marriage over the course of the past three decades. Divorce traditionally carried a strong stigma connoting "failure" on the part of one or both marital partners. This stigma was more readily applied to a wife than a husband, since she was held responsible for maintenance of a marital relationship. Even if a marriage ostensibly broke apart as a consequence of his drinking, gambling, or infidelity, family, friends, and the general community still maintained that, if only she had been a better wife, he would not have needed to drink, gamble, or seek out the sexual or companionship affections of other women. Consequently, a wife was held more culpable for a marriage dissolving than was a husband. Over the past three decades, the stigma attached to divorce has interacted with the incidence of divorce, such that as divorce becomes more common, the stigma attached to both partners, but especially to wives, lessens. A more negative stigma is still attached to those who redivorce than to those who divorce only once. "Oscar Wilde once quipped that to lose one's wife is unfortunate; to lose two is merely careless" (Richardson, 1996: 243).

Canada had one of the lowest divorce rates of all industrialized societies prior to the liberating reform of our Divorce Act in 1968. However, by 1976, a greater proportion of the population were informally separated than were formally divorced (McVey and Robinson, 1981), suggesting that legal access to divorce was still not easily available, or readily acceptable. Marriages that remain intact are not necessarily happier than are marriages that dissolve via separation or divorce, since many intact marriages can be characterized as "empty shell" (Goode, 1982: 149) relationships, held together for the sake of appearances rather than intrinsic satisfactions. Furthermore, intact marriages in our own and other societies can also be held together with the aid of either an institutionalized or idiosyncratic tolerance of kept mistresses (Salamon, 1984) and gigolos (Nelson and Robinson, 1994), as well as other forms of extramarital affairs. Until the 1980s, more marriages ended with the death of one of the partners than with divorce, although the situation is now reversed in both Canada (Robinson and McVey, 1985) and the United States (Glick and Lin, 1986b). In addition to long-term trends towards greater longevity, this change is partly accounted for by changes to our divorce laws in 1985, through which the government of Canada attempted to make divorce more accessible.

Divorce Law in Canada

At the time of Confederation, Canadian divorce law was based primarily upon the British *Divorce and Matrimonial Causes Act* of 1857. Prior laws, or lack thereof, in the colonies were still in force following Confederation, but divorce now came under federal jurisdiction and, unlike the United States where each state controls its own divorce laws, provinces and territories in Canada could no longer independently enact new legislation on the grounds for divorce (although they have retained control over marital property, financial support awards, and child custody determinations). The *Divorce and Matrimonial Causes Act* contained a sex-linked double-standard regarding divorce. Whereas a husband was entitled to petition for divorce on the grounds that his wife had committed adultery, a wife could only petition for divorce if she could prove that her husband's adultery was coupled with incest, or bigamy, or rape, sodomy or bestiality, or cruelty, or desertion for at least two years. Encoded in law was the notion that her adultery constituted a major transgression against a marriage, while his adultery was but a minor transgression, unless it was joined with some other more unacceptable offence. This double-standard was removed from Canadian divorce law by the deletion, in 1925, of the additional requirements imposed upon a wife, and both spouses thereafter could and can petition for divorce on the same grounds (Report of The Joint Committee of The Senate and House of Commons on Divorce, 1967: 52).

Until 1968, provincial courts in Quebec (anchored in the French *Civil Code*) and Newfoundland (when it joined Canada) could not grant divorces. Between 1867 and 1968, adultery was the only grounds for divorce across the rest of Canada, except for Nova Scotia, which additionally recognized cruelty as grounds, and New Brunswick, which also included frigidity, impotence, and consanguinity (Report, 1967: 49). New Brunswick was the only province in Canada to ever acknowledge sexual and reproductive "failure" on the part of either spouse as a "fault" or an "offense" against marriage. The 1968 Divorce Act expanded the list of "fault grounds" under which a divorce could be granted in all provinces, and also introduced a number of "no fault, no-blame" grounds under the heading of "marriage breakdown."

The 1985 Divorce Act (effective in 1986) of Canada simplified divorce procedures further, in the spirit of our values of individualism and gender egalitarianism (Peters, 1987). Essentially, the power to decide if a marriage should be terminated has been placed in the hands of the couple themselves, with the courts relegated mainly to an administrative role of ensuring that proper form is followed in legally dissolving the relationship, as well as an adjudicative role in instances of contested issues. Having lived separate and apart for a period not less than one year, or one partner having committed adultery, or one partner having treated the other with mental or physical cruelty are all viewed in the eyes of the court as indicative of a marriage having broken down irreparably and not indicative of either partner's "fault." These legal grounds for divorce seldom, and then only loosely, accord with the actual psychological, emotional, interpersonal, and social reasons for a couple's decision to seek legal dissolution of their marriage. Grounds for divorce are best thought of as a legal convention rather than as indicators of the actual state of a marriage prior to a divorce.

The new divorce law was intended to be gender neutral. Regardless of the gendered nature of a former marriage, gender was no longer to be a major basis for dividing financial assets, for awarding financial support, or for determining custody of any dependent children. As we shall see later in this chapter, gender differences in terms of consequences of divorce are most noticeable in cases where dependent children are involved. Childfree couples evidence few gender effects. "Prior to the Divorce Act, 1985, most provinces and territories reformed their legislation so that marital property is divided equally between spouses" (Richardson, 1996: 232), although inconsistencies exist across provincial and territorial jurisdictions (with regard, for example, to pensions), and debates can occur between divorcing spouses as to what actually constitutes the sum total of "marital property" to be divided. In theory, only those tangible assets accrued jointly over the course of a marriage constitute property to be divided equally. Upon divorce, a husband typically "retains the major intangible assets of the marriage—his career assets, future earning power, education, and insurance" (Skolnick, 1996: 317). While these intangibles may or may not have a bearing upon the issue of spousal support, they do have a significant bearing upon the respective standards of living of former husbands and wives, especially when dependent children are involved.

Spousal Support

The notion of continued financial provision following divorce has undergone several trans-formations over time, from the notion in our divorce law prior to 1968 of **alimony**, to spousal **maintenance** between 1968 and 1985, to the present concept of **spousal support** embedded in the Divorce Act of 1985. Alimony was rooted in English common law and a tra-ditional division of labour, whereby women in general, and married women in particular, could not, and did not, seek paid employment. Upon marriage, a husband gained control of his wife's assets and typically reaped financial benefits as a consequence of that control. A husband was, therefore, expected to assume responsibility to not only support his wife financially over the course of a marriage, but also to continue providing such support following the dissolution of a marriage (Weitzman, 1985). It was not uncommon in divorces granted prior to 1968 in Canada for a husband to be ordered to pay a monthly sum of alimony to his wife, either in perpetuity (i.e., until the death of either spouse) or until she remarried, when the obligation of financial provision would be transferred legally to her new husband. Although it was theoretically possible for a husband to be awarded alimony from a former wife, instances of such awards were extremely rare. The concept of alimony consequently reaffirmed traditional gender roles, particularly the provider role, beyond the years of marriage.

Beginning with the introduction of the concept of "maintenance" in 1968, and intensi-fying with the concept of "support" in 1985, alimony was essentially eliminated and re-placed with an egalitarian gender-neutral ethic mandating that both men and nonmarried women should attain economic self-sufficiency as quickly as possible following a divorce. Spousal support is intended to be an interim measure to provide a "reasonable" grace period, typically limited to four or five years at most, during which time the recipient is expected to take significant steps (e.g., further education, training, or retraining) towards economic self-sufficiency. Depending upon a particular couple's circumstances, support can be awarded ei-ther in the form of a lump-sum once-only payment at the outset, or a monthly instalment of payments over a fixed duration of time. Current law recognizes that middle-aged and older women from traditional marriages face significant additional barriers to economic self-suf-ficiency, such as ageism in addition to sexism, and, therefore, may require spousal support for an extended or even an unlimited time period.

These new support laws both reflect, as well as attempt to create, new conceptions of gender and gender roles. However, feminists frequently argue that divorce law cannot mandate equality in the workplace and, therefore, spousal support laws fail to acknowledge conditions of employment and pay inequity still confronting women today (Ahrons, 1994; Demo and Ganong, 1994). Whether limited-term spousal-support periods are awarded for sufficiently long time periods, and whether support payments are themselves of sufficient magnitude, are debatable issues. The issues are made murky by the fact that some women also receive child support awards for their dependent children. Government-collected sta-tistics, to be presented in a later section, focus upon total incomes acquired, and do not distinguish between amounts derived from spousal support and amounts derived from child support. The latter typically have been found insufficient, while the sufficiency of the former is less clear.

Only 16 percent of divorcing women in Canada currently request spousal support and only 6 percent are actually awarded such support (Richardson, 1996: 238). The scant number of applications suggests numerous possibilities. Most younger divorcing women, especially those without any dependent children, probably consider themselves to be sufficiently self-supporting. Some women may have little faith that any support awarded by the court would actually be provided by their former spouse; making an application would, therefore, be considered a waste of time. Newman (1988 in Skolnick, 1996: 316) finds that whereas older divorced women feel entitled to financial support from former husbands as compensation for an earlier gendered marital division of labour, younger women prefer to be economically self-sufficient and resent any notion of maintaining protracted links with a former husband forged by his continued financial support.

Incidence of Divorce

Social changes external to marital dyads, in the form of a reduced impact of religious ideologies regarding the sanctity of marriage vows; the lessening stigma attached to divorce and divorced persons; the expansion and greater ease of access to formal divorce procedures; the growing acceptance of singlehood and cohabitation as alternatives to marriage; and the significant rise of women's labour-force participation, enabling greater economic self-sufficiency, can all be measured. More difficult to quantify are the contributions over the past three decades of two ideologies: the ideology of rising expectations, which places great demands upon marriage and marital partners to become major sources of personal satisfaction and growth; and the ideology of feminism, which demands a restructuring of the marital bargain to produce a different, more equitable, interpersonal arrangement. While the impact of these two ideologies cannot be ascertained in any simple cause-effect relationship, they, along with the other social changes mentioned above, have undoubtedly contributed to the significant increase in divorce since the mid-1960s in our society.

The number of divorces per 100 000 population in Canada, known as the *crude divorce rate*, has risen from 36.0 in 1961 to 137.6 in 1971, 278.0 in 1981, reaching a peak of 307.8 in 1989, and declining to 282.0 by 1991 (McVey and Kalbach, 1995: 23) and by 1995, to 262.2 (Statistics Canada, 1997a). The decline in divorce rates since the late 1980s is linked, in large part, to the declining marriage rate in Canada that consequently places fewer married couples at risk for divorce. If recent patterns remain constant, it is estimated that approximately 40 percent of marriages contracted recently in Canada will end in divorce (Dumas and Peron, 1992), even though 86 percent of Canadian adolescents idealistically anticipate they will stay with the same marital partner for life (Bibby and Posterski, 1992: 31). This estimate is substantially lower than American calculations from the 1980s (Castro, Martin and Bumpass, 1989) suggesting that between one-half or two-thirds of all marriages in the United States entered into during that decade would end in either separation or divorce. More recent estimations by the United States Census Bureau have cautiously lowered the prognosis to suggest that approximately 40 percent of American marriages contracted during the 1990s will end in formal divorce (Skolnick, 1996: 304). Neither the more recent American forecast nor the Canadian estimate include the likely incidence of married couples informally separating.

The Decision to Divorce and Postdivorce Adjustments

The fact that women file the majority of petitions for divorce (Kitson, 1992; Wallerstein and Blakeslee, 1989) has been seen by contemporary writers (Heyn, 1997) to infer that women most often initiate the dissolution of marital relationships in response to oppressive conditions inherent in marriage as presently constituted. However, both Hopper (1993) and Vaughan (1986) point out that the issue of who actually instigates a divorce is far from obvious. Selection of which partner will file the formal petition is often unrelated to who makes the final decision to seek a divorce, or who initiates the decision-making process leading to the final decision, or who most contributes to the conditions that precipitate the decision-making process. Rather, formal filing of a petition or application for divorce is more often related to convenience, or availability, in cases where the whereabouts of the other spouse is currently unknown, or perhaps to a lawyer's advice regarding which partner is most likely to receive a speedy and sympathetic hearing from a presiding judge. Conventions associated with the adversarial nature of our court system typically requires that only one person actually file a divorce application. Only 4 percent of divorces are jointly petitioned in Canada (Richardson, 1996: 231). Present conformity to one-person-filing conventions is now more of an administrative expediency than an indicator of the state of a marriage.

Research (Albrecht, 1980: 76; Kelley, 1982: 318; Kitson, 1992) suggests that women who do initiate the decision to divorce are more likely to experience the period prior to actual separation as the most physically and emotionally stressful time, while men are more likely to experience the immediate postdivorce period as the most stressful. The period following divorce tends to be met with a sense of relief and freedom among these women. Kitson (1992) finds that approximately half of former husbands claim they had no warning that their marriages had deteriorated to a point where their wives not only wanted out, but were willing to take the legal steps necessary to terminate what had become an unsatisfactory relationship. These men, who were the last to know their marriages were over, were the most likely to experience negative effects, such as depression, loneliness, and other emotional or physical disturbances, following the divorce. "Men have much more difficulty replacing what a wife and family provided. Divorce creates expressive hardships for men that it does not create for women" (Riessman, 1990: 209). The now-antiquated term of the "gay divorcee" was never applied to men, perhaps for good reason. The greater number and intensity of men's physical and emotional difficulties experienced following the breakup of a marriage is due in part to their lack of a supportive network of family and friends to rely upon (Baker, 1980), and in part to their internalization of a masculinity role demanding stoicism and independence in the face of crisis.

Some rejected husbands who fail to comprehend or accept the finality of separation or divorce have been known to stalk, verbally or physically harass, or even kill their former partners. While this response to rejection is by no means exclusively male, it is more common to men than to women. Other men more frequently exhibit a frenzied social and sexual life immediately after divorce (Hetherington et al., 1976: 426), while also trying to cope with a disorganized household and, for some, the loss of daily contact with their children. Divorced wives may reduce their contacts with friends, but they typically have a more extensive support network to call upon should they desire (Baker, 1980). Gender differences are least observable among childfree spouses, who have the smoothest adjustment in coping with the emotional roller coaster, alterations to their standard of living, and establishing a new household.

REMARRIAGE

Approximately 10 percent of all marriages entered into in 1971 in Canada involved at least one previously married partner (Richardson, 1996: 243). That proportion increased until the early 1990s, when one-third of all marriages were remarriages for one or both partners, and has since declined by the mid-1990s to now comprise about one-quarter of all marriages (Nault, 1996: 43; Statistics Canada, 1996). Remarriage rates for all marital statuses have declined. Among all Canadians aged 15 and over, marriages per 1000 population for previously divorced people declined from 148.0 in 1975 to 40.5 in 1995, and for the previously widowed from 13.5 to 6.0 (Statistics Canada, 1996).

During the early 1970s, about 85 percent of divorced men and 79 percent of divorced women remarried. These proportions decreased to 76 percent for men and 64 percent for women by the mid-1980s (Adams and Nagnur, 1990, in Richardson, 1996: 243), and continued to decline into the 1990s. Nault (1996) reports the incidence of remarriage in 1991 at 46 and 34 percent, respectively, for divorced men and women in Quebec, and 69 and 58 percent, respectively, for men and women in the rest of Canada. Similar to first marriage, some unknown proportion of the overall decline in remarriage is accounted for by increasing numbers of divorced men and women choosing to remain in a single lifestyle, and a larger proportion establishing cohabitation rather than marital relationships (see Wu and Balakrishnan, 1994, on cohabitation in Canada). Despite the decline, remarriage is still the most frequent likelihood following divorce, for both men and women, everywhere in Canada except in Quebec.

As a consequence of mortality differentials associated with aging that result in higher death rates for men, and the influence of the mating gradient, the pool of eligibles for women interested in remarriage declines with age, but that pool expands in both age directions for men interested in seeking a new mate. In addition, men's emotional dependence on women's therapeutic and companionship skills, and their physical dependence upon women's housekeeping skills increases divorced men's motivation to remarry. Thus, a combination of motivation and opportunity appear to account for the consistent findings over the years that men are more likely to remarry than are women, in both the United States (Glick and Lin, 1987) and Canada (Nault, 1996), and to do so sooner after a divorce than do women (Glick and Lin, 1987). Men between the ages of 45 and 64 are twice as likely to remarry, in comparison to women of comparable age (U.S. National Center for Health Statistics, 1994 in Saxton, 1996: 425).

Younger divorced women are more likely to remarry than are older divorced women, although some evidence exists to suggest that younger childfree divorced women are now postponing remarriage (Glick and Lin, 1986b). American data indicate that less than half of the women who divorce while in their late thirties eventually remarry, and the proportions of divorced women in their forties and older who remarry decline significantly (Norton and Miller, 1992, in Saxton, 1996: 452). As with first marriages, possession of very high levels of income are associated with high probabilities of remarriage for men and, along with very high levels of education, low probabilities of remarriage for women. This difference between "cream of the crop" men and women may be due to a more limited number of eligibles available for women to choose from, in combination with, unlike most other women, their having little or no financial incentive to remarry. Remarriage appears to lose a significant amount of its appeal or lustre for women when it is no longer a visa to financial security.

Decisions to remarry or not, or to stay married, can be based wholly or largely upon inter-personal attraction and anticipated gender-based marital-role bargains.

Glick and Lin (1987) estimate that two-thirds of ever-divorced parents eventually remarry while their children are still at home. The presence of children reduces the likelihood of re-marriage among women, but not men, with the greatest impact noticeable among divorced women with three or more children (Glick, 1989: 126). These women will, on average, be older than women with fewer children and, consequently, have fewer eligibles to choose from should they desire to remarry. At the same time, men may be reluctant to take on the additional burden associated with becoming a **dual-provider father**, who must act as a provider or coprovider for his former spouse and their children via support payments, as well as a provider or coprovider for his current wife and their children. The financial re-sponsibilities associated with an "instant family" composed of a divorced women and three or more children might become too prohibitive for many men. As well, custodial children of a divorced mother may not want any man, or a particular man, to become emotionally and physically involved with their mother. Courtship is a more complicated process for the for-merly married, especially among those with children.

Remarriage Dynamics and Stability

In a follow-up study of divorced and separated individuals who remarried, Furstenberg and Spanier (1984: 71–77) find that remarried women describe themselves as less submissive and more willing to assert themselves, even if this means that their second or later marriage is characterized by more discussion, debate, or conflict than was their previous marriage. This assertiveness is partly a consequence of reflection upon a past marriage, wherein they con-cluded they should have been more assertive of their rights and vowed to correct this defi-ciency in any future relationships, and partly, for some, as a consequence of having been the head of a solo-parent household in the interval between marriages. Remarried women are also more likely to be employed, and to have a lengthier employment history than women in first marriages, which increases their resource power in marital relationships. Remarried men describe themselves as being less assertive and more accommodating than they were in their previous marriage. Couples generally agree that decision-making and overall partici-pation levels in decision-making are more egalitarian in remarriages. Similar findings have been reported in more recent American (Ganong and Coleman, 1994) and Canadian studies (Hobart, 1991). Even though men claim greater involvement in housework, their wives dis-agree. Remarriages are not more egalitarian, with wives still bearing the brunt of responsi-bilities and actual participation in housework and childrearing (Demo and Acock, 1993).

Cherlin (1978; 1992: 86) argues that remarriage is still an "incomplete institution" with insufficient normative guidelines and shared meanings regarding how men and women should function as spouses and parents or stepparents in remarried families. As a conse-quence, remarriage partners and their relationships may flounder as they attempt to con-struct a new married unity all on their own. Furstenberg and Spanier (1984) argue that, having already experienced and survived at least one divorce, most remarried individuals are predisposed to do so again rather than remain in a second or subsequent remarriage if it should become unsatisfying. Despite claims suggesting that the likelihood of redivorce is higher in remarriages than is divorce in first marriages, Castro Martin and Bumpass (1989) contend that differences between divorce and redivorce rates are minimal when the effects of age, education, and age at first marriage are taken into account. If correct, their contention means that approximately 40 percent of remarriages in Canada are likely to end in redivorce, the same rate estimated for first marriages (Dumas and Peron, 1992).

PARENTING

In Chapter 5, we noted that our cultural grammar imposes boundaries around what women and men are perceived capable of doing, and that language itself plays a role in reinforcing a differentiated and oppressive pattern of gender relations. We recognize the terms "good mother" and "unfit mother" as common evaluative descriptors of women who have children and understand "mothering" to encompass a wide range of nurturing behaviour. In contrast, a "good father" is most often narrowly associated with a man's ability to fulfill the role of provider, while the term "unfit father" seems forced, contrived, and without any immediately discernible referent. As David (1985: 22) maintains, "[m]otherhood is a social concept, fatherhood barely recognised. To father a child refers only to the act of procreation."

The "ideology of motherhood," which places central emphasis on the biological mother assuming the care and responsibility for her child, especially during the child's early years, has been translated into the "tender years doctrine" within child custody law. However, the assumptions on which this doctrine is based, have an impact upon a broader constituency than petitioners seeking to obtain child custody. The "natural" sex-irreducible fact that women "menstruate, gestate and lactate" encourages a belief that motherhood is simply a biological fact, governed only by what is called "Nature" (or "Mother Nature"), and, as such, constrained from any fundamental reorganization. However, as Virginia Woolf (1978: 203) cynically remarked in another context, "[n]ature is now known to vary greatly in her commands and to be largely under control."

We have previously noted that for both functionalists in general and sociobiologists in particular, the division of labour between men and women is grounded in the argument that women, because of their biological role as potential mothers, must depend upon men, the fathers of their children, to provide them with protection and support. Similarly, we earlier noted that psychoanalytic theory suggests that all "normal" women desire a child (if only as a vicarious way of obtaining the desired-for penis) and that, without two "opposite"-sexed parents *in situ* in the family home, acquisition by a developing child of a mature gender identity will be impossible. Implicit within all these theoretical formulations is a **naturalistic** theory of heterosexual motherhood containing four interrelated assumptions. First, all "normal" women desire to be mothers. Second, mothering takes place within a heterosexual family. Third, women and men will play complimentary rather than functionally equivalent roles within the family. Fourth, motherhood takes its shape as a response to a biological imperative and, as such, is largely a biological, rather than a social, role. Women who disdain to bear children, or are childfree by choice, or who opt to limit the number of children they have through practices such as contraception or abortion, are often portrayed as acting in a "unnatural" or "selfish" manner (Gairdner, 1992; Faludi, 1991: 55). Luker (1984) suggests that the current conflict over abortion is, most fundamentally, a debate over motherhood as central or optional within women's lives.

The second wave of feminism has been accompanied by a reconceptualization of motherhood from a social conflict framework. Marxist feminists, for example, direct attention to the social structural arrangements of motherhood within the nuclear family as one of principal mechanisms for excluding women from full participation within the public sphere. Similarly, it has been argued that motherhood, as institutionalized within the social role of the housewife, is oppressive to women (Oakley, 1974). McMahon (1995: 9) notes that feminist analysis during the 1960s and 1970s set itself the task of debunking "'the feminine mystique'; the motherhood 'myth'; [and exposing] the real work of housework and childrearing; the compulsory nature of childbearing; the lack of access to abortion, contraception, and reproductive health information women faced; and so on." In consequence, she remarks "the 'demon texts' of this period of feminism are falsely read as antimotherhood. The target…was patriarchy, not mothers" (p. 9). She observes that, since that time, feminists have attempted to examine motherhood through analyses that "validated women, and their work, qualities, and experiences" (p. 9) by focusing on such diverse topics as women's experiences of birth and "maternal thinking" in a "revalorization of maternity that was both radical and feminist.…The challenge facing feminist analysis became one of valuing women's social capacity to care and/or their biological capacity to give birth while resisting having these capacities considered definitive or 'essential' or best in what it is to be a woman" (pp. 9–10).

Birth rates have been falling in Canada since the middle of the nineteenth century, with the exception of the baby-boom years following World War II. One of the most notable changes pertains to the decline of large families constructed through continuous pregnancy and birthing by women during the 1800s. While families with eight to 13 or more children were once not at all uncommon, by 1991, only 1 percent of all families in Canada had five or more children (La Novara, 1993). Due to children becoming economic liabilities with the rising costs of raising a child, greater survivorship of those children already born, less need for children as labourers and as insurance for their parents' old age, increased availability of more effective contraception, and increased participation of women in the paid-labour force, the average number of children born to the average woman (known as the Total Fertility Rate or TFR) has declined over the course of this century, from 3.54 in 1921 to 2.83 in 1941, increasing during the boom years to 3.84 in 1961, then moving down again to 1.70 in 1981, rising slightly to 1.80 by 1991 (McVey and Kalbach, 1995: 270), and declining again in 1993 to 1.7 (Grindstaff, 1995: 13). Canadian fertility rates are now lower than American rates, in very large part due to low fertility rates among francophone women in Quebec (up to 1.7 in 1990 from a low of 1.4 during the mid-1980s), and high fertility rates among black women in the United States (Le Boudrais and Marcil-Gratton, 1996: 421).

Not only has the average number of births per woman declined, but the timing of childbearing has also changed in recent times. Since the 1970s, most Canadian women have been delaying their first childbirth until they reach their late twenties and early thirties. "By 1989, women aged 30 to 34 had higher fertility rates than did those aged 20 to 24, although women aged 25 to 29 had the highest rates of fertility.…[T]he proportion of all births that were to women aged 20 to 24 declined, falling to less than 20 percent in 1993.…[T]he proportion of all births that were to women aged 30 to 34 doubled, rising to 29 percent in 1993 from 14 percent in 1971" (Grindstaff, 1995: 14). Unlike women in previous generations, who gave birth to a third or fourth child during their thirties, many women in Canada giving birth in their thirties today are having their first child. While the mass media provide more than sufficient publicity to celebrities having first children in their forties to suggest that such fertility patterns are common, the proportion of all births occurring to Canadian women in their forties accounted for only 1 percent in 1993 (Grindstaff, 1995: 15).

Existing indicators suggest that the numbers and proportions of women choosing to remain childfree are increasing. "Of women who had ever been married, the proportion aged 35 to 39 who had never given birth grew to 13% in 1991 from 7% in 1971, and 9% in 1961 and 1981" (Grindstaff, 1995: 16). Demographers typically focus their data gathering upon the married population and do not calculate proportions of the never-married female population who do or do not ever give birth. Nor, since paternity is uncertain barring a DNA test, are calculations provided for the male population. Some proportion of the married female population desire to have children, but are unable to conceive. Some other proportion of these women may be postponing childbearing for what in their estimation is a more propitious time. With the advent of new assisted reproductive techniques, to be considered later, we will have to wait until all of these women have died before we can determine exactly what percentage of all women in Canada born after World War II did not become biological mothers. Our safest conclusion is to note that a large majority of women do become mothers at some point in their lifetimes. Having children adds still another stamp in the adult passport to both masculinity and femininity. Based on his national Canadian survey of 1995, Bibby (1995: 4) reports that although "some observers have been inclined to think that women who value careers do so at the expense of valuing family life, it's not the case. If anything, women in the 90s are somewhat more likely than men to place a very high value on *both* family *and* a rewarding career. *Both are coveted*" (emphasis in original). As well, the vast majority of elementary-school-aged children and older adolescent females expect and/or desire to have children eventually (Mackie, 1991: 84).

Inventing Motherhood

Although the "sanctification of motherhood" (Heilbrun, 1973: 16) is built upon an iconology or symbolic representation of the "ideal mother" that is assumed to be both timeless and universal, social expectations placed upon mothers vary markedly over both time and space. Dramatic differences exist in how societies respond to the biological fact that women give birth to children. Ambert (1994: 530–531) points out that cross-cultural research suggests that "the Western focus on individual mothers at the core of children's development is not universal," and that in many agrarian and gathering societies, for example, practices such as multiple mothering, multiple parenting, and sibling parenting are common. Basow (1992: 236) reminds us that in times past and present, women have been expected to abandon or murder their children when a child was perceived as a financial liability, of the "wrong" sex, or in possession of a physical or mental disability. Similarly, Fildes (1988: 152–167) suggests that in Catholic countries in early modern Europe, the social practice of wetnursing (wherein upper-class women were expected and obliged to place their newborn infants with a lower-class woman to be breastfed) stemmed from strong beliefs that, while a lactating woman should not engage in sexual intercourse, a husband's conjugal rights to his wife's body took precedence over the needs of a suckling child. Early in this century, the expectation that an unwed mother would place her child up for adoption was similarly held as the responsible and "correct" way for these mothers to respond to the biological fact of their motherhood.

Unlike some tribal societies in which childrearing is seen to be the responsibility of everyone and the role of "mother" occupies only a peripheral part of women's social identity, Moore (1994) observes that in the West, since the eighteenth and nineteenth centuries, considerable overlap has developed in the identity of "women" and "mothers." These changes are partly due to changes in the organization of our society as a whole, and partly due to cultural changes in conceptions of children and childhood. Generally, the importance of mothers for child development waxes and wanes over history in response to general economic conditions: when a mother's labour outside of the home is required, the mother-child bond is de-emphasized; when a mother's labour outside of the home is not required, mothers and mothering are glorified and deemed essential for optimal child development (Margolis, 1984). Parenting, prior to the eighteenth century, was devoted primarily to breaking a child's will and inherent selfishness. By age of six or seven, a child was expected to act as a little adult in family relations. Consequently, parenting, as understood by and expected of people at that time, was limited to only the first few years of a child's life.

The concept of an indulgent and extended childhood did not emerge and become part of our cultural ethos until sometime during the industrializing eighteenth and nineteenth centuries in North America (Anderson, 1987; Demos, 1970). As children were deemed to require more intensive extended care and nurturing, and women were presumed to not have a place in an industrial labour force, the role of women as mothers changed correspondingly. Whereas fathers once assumed responsibility for socializing and integrating their sons into adult life as soon as basic infancy care had been completed, with industrialization taking men out of the home, parenting now became the almost exclusive responsibility of women in the home. Women also came to be defined solely as keepers of the hearth and heart. Over time, as children became economically useless, they—at least on a symbolic level—came to be defined as socioemotionally priceless and "gradually acquired a culturally sacred value" (McMahon, 1995: 27).

That the developing images of ideal childhood, as well as those of womanhood and motherhood, were both classist and racist are notable. Valverde (1991), for example, has noted that the historical representations of motherhood and gender within social purity movements in Canada were robustly racist and relied upon symbols that were both white and Protestant. Similarly, Green (1986) and Sher (1983) note that the history of Canadian immigration policies is based on stereotypes of disparaged groups that depicted them as "coming in swarms" and breeding like "insects." Then, as now (Gairdner, 1992), only children of certain racial or socioeconomic groups were viewed as "priceless" or as inherently valuable and to be protected, both by their devoted mothers and, on a broader scale, by members of the larger society.

Beginning as early as the 1820s in the United States, the maternal role became romanticized and defined as "somewhat other-worldly and sublime" (Light and Prentice, 1980: 134). The "motherhood mystique" (Hoffnung, 1989), which emerged in the eighteenth century, puts forward a romanticized vision of motherhood and suggests that "only by having a child can a woman actualize her full potential and achieve the ultimate meaning of her life" (Lips, 1993: 314).

> In the Victorian period motherhood came to have the emotional and semisacred connotations that tempt one to write it with a capital "M." The mother's task was to care for her children physically, preserve their moral innocence, protect them from evil influences, and inspire them to pursue the highest spiritual values....This glorification of motherhood...was as new an element in Anglo-American culture as the opinion that females were particularly virtuous. Indeed, the two ideas evolved together and reinforced one another in eighteenth and nineteenth century thought. (Harris, 1979: 71)

The image of the "all-loving, kind, gentle, and selfless" mother (Anderson, 1997: 163) suggested that motherhood brought about a culmination of feminine fulfillment for all "normal" women. A "want of maternal feeling" was thought to characterize only "unnatural" women or criminal women who "psychologically and anthropologically...belong more to the male than to the female sex," and within whom "that love of dissipation...is necessarily antagonistic to the constant sacrifices demanded of a mother" (Lombroso and Ferrero, 1895: 153).

The "Motherhood Mandate" (Basow, 1992: 234) and its attendant suggestion that all "normal" women possess a deep-rooted "maternal instinct" that motherhood alone can fulfill effectively renders invisible the labour that mothering entails. As Graham (1984: 153–154) observes, the work involved in mothering "is most in evidence when it is not done, when clothes and faces are left unwashed, rooms and hair are untidy, and children are ill-disciplined and noisy. When a mother works successfully to maintain the standards of dress, decor and decorum her labour is at its most invisible." Nevertheless, the Motherhood Mandate remains a powerful part of many secular and religious ideologies, and "[w]omen who cannot bear children tend to be pitied, and women who are voluntarily child-free are viewed by others as misguided, maladjusted, or selfish" (Basow, 1992: 234).

As we noted in Chapter 4, the socialization girls receive often places considerable emphasis on "playing house" and occupying the role of mothers. Given the consistency of messages which reiterate that caring for children is a "feminine" role, it is not surprising that babysitting is one of the first jobs promoted for earning money among preadolescent and early adolescent girls (but not boys). Nor is it surprising that 98 percent of those who provide "surrogate" mothering as day-care workers are women (Ontario Women's Directorate, 1995: 19). Links between femininity and motherhood are reinforced by the mass media, when a modern-day celebrity, such as actor Gena Lee Nolan of *Baywatch* fame, is widely quoted as saying, following the birth of her son two days earlier: "I feel so complete as a woman, wife, and mother" (*Edmonton Journal*, 6 June 1997: C7).

In addition, cultural models of "good girl" sexuality, which link love and romance to married intercourse and procreation, implicitly serve to refurbish the Motherhood Mandate. Although birth-control measures have been legal in Canada since 1969, cultural inhibitors remain that discourage women from acknowledging their current participation in sexual activities, or their desire to become sexually active in the near future, and from ensuring they take responsibility for contraception. The mystique of spontaneous sexual combustion in a first encounter, being swept away by a romantic and passionate sexual current, does not encode contraception as part of the script. Hacker (1992: 16) has observed that "most teenage pregnancies occur in the first six months of sexual activity...[while] seeking contraception typically is delayed from nine to 12 months after intercourse has been initiated." As Nelson and Robinson (1994) note, at least part of the failure to use contraceptives may stem from a woman's discomfort in acknowledging her sexual behaviour to pharmacists, doctors, parents, or herself. Ireson (1984), in a study of sexually active teenagers, found that those young women who became pregnant were more traditional in their gender-role orientation than their counterparts who did not. A traditional orientation accepts, even desires, pregnancy as an affirmation of femininity and an opportunity to get an early start on fulfilling one's gender destiny.

Motherhood as Institution

Rich (1986: 58) suggests that women's experience of motherhood has been coopted by "motherhood as institution"—an interlocking power structure of legal, medical, and cultural expertise, which has functioned to create an "invisible institution" of male control. For example, it had long been the custom in Canada, and elsewhere, for midwives to deliver babies; pregnancy and childbirth were viewed as "natural" events for which women, whether or not they were trained as midwives, were best suited for assisting other women. It was considered indecent for men to know much about pregnancy—far less to participate in the birthing process—and even after physicians gained entry to the rooms in which women were giving birth, concerns with maintaining decency necessitated that the physician fumble "blindly under a sheet in a dark room, his head decorously turned aside" (Henslin and Nelson, 1996: 547).

Throughout the eighteenth century, the professionalization of medicine, the movement of childbirth from home into newly established hospitals, the increasing power vested in the medical establishment, and the development of obstetric forceps (which allowed their user to shorten the period of labour and deliver live infants in circumstances in which mother and/or child would otherwise have died) encouraged physicians in Canada and elsewhere to assert their control over childbirth (Donnison, 1977; Ehrenreich and English, 1979). They maintained that pregnancy and childbirth were not "normal," but "medical conditions" and potentially pathological events that required the assistance of an able professional (man) and not a "dirty, ignorant and incompetent" midwife. In Canada, the Victorian Order of Nurses, founded in 1897 by the National Council of Women to assist rural women who otherwise lacked access to medical care, originally included midwifery in their work. However, as Mitchinson (1993: 396) observes, "the opposition of the medical establishment in Canada was so great to what it saw as an infringement of its prerogatives that the idea was to die."

Over the course of this century, childbirth has become increasingly medicalized and managed through the use of new technological developments and new practices, such as anaesthesia, forceps delivery, episiotomies, artificial inductions of births, and increasing use of Caesarian sections, all to be performed in hospital, not home, settings. The list of indicators favouring performance of a Caesarean section has expanded from purely physical reasons (difficult labour, fetal distress, an abnormal fetal presentation) to now include precautionary concerns (older maternal age, previous performance of a Caesarean section), as well as reasons of convenience (accommodating the attending obstetrician's vacation or hospital schedule). While Caesarean-section deliveries used to be reserved for emergencies, they have now become so routine that Canada has the second-highest rate of Caesarean-section births in the world, rising from a rate of 5.8 per 100 hospital deliveries in 1970, to 19.5 in 1988–1989 (Nair, 1991). The fact that more Canadians are currently born between Tuesday and Thursday than on any other days of the week (Dumas, 1993) reflects the extent to which childbirth has become a medically managed event. While medicalization has resulted in a decrease of the dangers associated with childbirth for both mothers and their newborn infants, it has also decreased the degree of autonomy women themselves exercise over their reproductive lives, and has increased the degree to which childbirth is managed and regulated by professionals, the majority of whom are men.

Martin (1989) argues that the terms employed in obstetrical discourse reflect the logic of **Fordism**—a postwar form of industrial economy based on mass production and consumption. She suggests that childbirth is regulated as if it was equivalent to factory labour, with only a certain amount of time allotted to each stage; as a result, she remarks, the role of the shop steward (obstetrician) is elevated and the role of the worker (mother) devalued. Rothman (1989: 16) argues that in births which occur within hospitals, "[t]he women may be more or less awake, more or less aware, more or less prepared, and more or less humanely or kindly treated, but within the medical model the baby is the product of the doctor's services." Queniart (1992: 164–165) suggests that pregnancy and childbirth are increasingly viewed within a "risk factor ideology" which directs attention to the dangers posed to a fetus by "not just the mother's genetic background, but other variables such as age, weight, blood pressure, overall health, etc., as well as data related to personal habits and lifestyle" (e.g., consumption of drugs or alcohol during pregnancy, smoking, etc.). She argues that this ideology, coupled with advances in technology which allow for fetal monitoring and surgery, reinforces the belief that "the mother's interests and personal needs should automatically be second to those of her offspring....Being pregnant (and then giving birth) is increasingly becoming a private matter that takes place between a woman and her physician, in a relationship increasingly mediated by technology" (Queniart, 1992: 170).

Since the 1978 birth of "test-tube baby" Louise Brown, the first child to be conceived from *in vitro* fertilization techniques, it has become increasingly possible and common to engage in methods of conception that are not, by necessity, limited to heterosexual intercourse. The growth of infertility clinics and sperm banks seem to simply offer the possibility of reproductive choice to women who desire to become pregnant and otherwise would be unable to do so. However, feminists are notably divided among themselves as to whether the new reproductive technologies are a liberating force, as radical feminists had originally hoped, or simply a Trojan Horse. For example, while noting the history of women's reproductive and sexual oppression, Shalev (1989) views female autonomy within the field of surrogacy as crucial to women's liberation. In stark contrast, Spallone (1989) argues that the new reproductive technologies simply present a new opportunity for patriarchy to devalue women, while Hamner and Allen (1980) suggest that the increasing availability of artificial reproduction is "the ushering in of the female apocalypse" that may promote femicide, with reproductive engineering serving as the "final solution" to the "woman problem."

In less flamboyant fashion, Maier (1992: 149–150) cautions that the development of new reproductive technologies and the concepts of "fetal rights" and "the best interests of the child" may lead to "reproductive wrongs" in which a woman's "right to bodily integrity, that is, her security of the person," is denied and her basic human rights coercively violated "under the guise of child protection." She emphasizes that, in both Canada and the United States, "[w]omen with the least power and who are the most oppressed by virtue of their socioeconomic or racial status are the most vulnerable to having their fetuses apprehended or their pregnancies policed" (p. 153). Whatever one's position on the desirability of the new reproductive technologies, it is noteworthy that the costs involved are considerable and that, in consequence, they are unlikely to be an equally viable option for all women (Mackie, 1991). Some feminists have voiced concern that arrangements such as surrogate mothering can be classist and result in poor women being exploited to serve as "baby farms" for those who are either well-off or who seek to become so. French (1992: 149) observes that "[t]he mothers...are paid a small fee; the lawyers, doctors, and middlemen who arrange the implantation are paid a large fee."

It is evident that, while technological change may stimulate social change, the introduction of any device or set of procedures does not, in and of itself, necessitate changed social attitudes or behaviours. For example, in 1993, a lesbian couple sought, and were refused, insemination in Vancouver, B.C., by the only doctor whose practice made available the artificial insemination of frozen sperm. The couple, a lawyer and a doctor, then complained to the B.C. College of Physicians and Surgeons. Their appeal was rejected in a letter stating that since "the service you sought was not urgent nor emergent," the doctor's refusal to take them as patients was justified. In drawing media attention to their experience, the couple stated that they sought to draw attention to discrimination against lesbians as potential users of the new reproductive technology. Their claims would seem valid. As the Federal Royal Commission on New Reproductive Technologies reported in 1991, "being a lesbian was probable or possible grounds for being refused artificial insemination in 28 out of 49 Canadian fertility programs" (*Vancouver Sun*, 22 July 1993: A1).

In 1994, a 60-year-old woman provided doctors at The University of Southern California's Program for Assisted Reproduction with multiple forged medical documents claiming she was 10 years younger. She received *in vitro* fertilization, in which an anonymous donor's egg was fertilized with sperm from her husband, and, in 1996 at age 63, gave birth via Caesarean section to a healthy baby girl. The woman needed forged documents since the USC program has a set age limit of 55 for receiving assisted reproductive help, a limit determined by doctors who developed the program and could not find data on any women having conceived "naturally" and given birth beyond that age. Canada's Federal Royal Commission on New Reproductive Technologies similarly advocates that artificial techniques should not be made available to women beyond the age of menopause, arguing, essentially, that conception beyond that event is "unnatural." Following the birth to the 63-year-old American woman, controversies erupted on a variety of different issues. Some public opinion argued that the woman would be too old to provide effective parenting for a teenager. Other opinion noted that many grandparents today raise their grandchildren through adolescence and do so effectively. The outcry over the "unnaturalness" of a woman "mothering" a child in her sixties typically overlooks the not-infrequent occurrence of men between the ages of 60 and 80 biologically and socially "fathering" children.

As a consequence of this "reproductive revolution" (Eichler, 1989), new questions about motherhood and fatherhood are being posed. For example, "what does parenthood mean when artificial wombs are being developed by which men can be pregnant through the implantation of an embryo in the male abdomen? When women are impregnated from semen which combines donations from their husbands and strangers? When babies conceived through artificial insemination from the husband are carried by surrogate mothers?" (Mackie, 1991: 118). These questions raise issues regarding the nature and meaning of "mother" and "father," in both biological and social senses of these terms. It is currently possible for a person to have at least three mothers—an egg mother; a womb and birth mother; and a parenting mother—or some combination of the three as well as at least two fathers—a sperm father and a parenting father—and possibly even a womb father. (Think of all the Mother's and Father's Day cards we might need in the future.) Both gay and heterosexual men could, at some point in the near future, seek artificial insemination for themselves. Issues of real or fictive kinship links pale in contrast to the questions raised as to the "natural" or "unnatural" connections between sex, gender, sexual orientation, and parenting.

Conservative voices provide answers which reiterate conventional images of men and women. For example, the La Leche League, an organization "dedicated to 'good mothering through breastfeeding'" was founded in the 1950s by "seven Catholic women committed to extended, on-demand breastfeeding, natural childbirth, and large families, literally embodying the assumptions of exclusive, intensive motherhood and female economic dependence" (Blum and Vandewater, 1993: 4–5). The conservatism of this officially nonsectarian group is suggested by the fact that it was named after "Our Lady of Happy Delivery and Plentiful Milk," Nuestra Señora de la Leche y Buen Parto (Blum and Vandewater, 1993: 5). Andrews (1991), in her study of La Leche League's composition in Canada notes that few low-income or single mothers are attracted to the movement and suggests that this is due to the League's emphasis on the importance of the "intact" family unit. Similarly, Blum and Vandewater (1993: 6) report that, within their admittedly nonrepresentative sample of American women in the La Leche League, the majority fell "on the high side" of the "racialized gender/class divide" and were all in intact marriages. They note that, while the La Leche League is notable for its nonmedicalized, woman-centred approach to mothering, emphasizing the "sensual pleasures" involved in breastfeeding, it reiterates the patriarchal message that a husband/father holds the "ultimate rights" to the wife/mother's body and the notion that sexuality is to be confined within the sphere of the heterosexual marriage.

According to the La Leche League, the father/husband is to be "the instrumental leader, the protector and provider, standing outside (and above) the mother-child dyad," and men's inability to breastfed is used to justify their contention that men are "naturally" unsuited for assuming a nurturant, expressive role within the family (p. 8). Although Blum and Vandewater note that the bimonthly members' magazine contains a "Focus on Fathers" column, that one book, *Becoming A Father*, is devoted to the topic of fatherhood, and that new norms promote increased fatherhood involvement and/or "valorize token efforts at 'involved fathering'" (p.18), they suggest that these changes may simply contribute to a "restabilization of male dominance in a modified, partial form" (p. 3). Women in the La Leche League are encouraged to "remain married…to diffuse resentment towards their husbands, who may fall short of new and old constructions of ideal masculinity, by diminishing their expectations and inflating the value of their husbands' contributions" (p. 18).

The Good Mother

The promotion of motherhood since the 1800s has been accomplished both by exhortation and prescription. Badinter (1981), in an analysis of advice to mothers from Rousseau on, observes how practical advice (e.g., do not swaddle your baby, do breastfeed your baby) was interspersed with identification of the deep and powerful feelings that women should or ought to experience as mothers. The development of "scientific motherhood" (Ehrenreich and English, 1979: 4) allowed "experts" to pontificate on "woman's true nature…to prescribe the 'natural' life plan for women," and to use their authority "to define women's domestic activities down to the smallest details of housework and child raising" (see also Margolis, 1984). "Parental" responsibility became a misnomer as gender divisions in parenting emphasized maternal responsibility and privatized care of a child by the mother within the family. Done correctly, motherwork is to produce a "marketable product…an adjusted and achieving child" (Epstein, 1988: 197).

As expectations of the "good mother" broadened from the simple physical maintenance of a child to an idealized role model who created the optimal physical, social, and emotional environment for her child, they were accompanied by a burgeoning likelihood that a mother would be labeled as deficient in at least some way, and assigned culpability for the production of a less-than-perfect child. As Epstein (1988: 197) remarks, "idealization and blame of the mother are two sides of the same belief in an all-powerful figure." It is, therefore, not surprising that Tavris (1992: 275) notes that even today, "[m]others are held responsible for almost any disorder that their offspring might develop, including bedwetting, schizophrenia, aggression, learning problems, and homicidal transsexualism. The concepts of competent motherhood and incompetent fatherhood are almost nowhere to be seen in the clinical literature."

Caplan and Hall-McCorquodale (1985), in an analysis of 125 articles in major clinical journals written in 1970, 1976, and 1982, report that "mother-blaming" remains common within the fields of both family therapy and clinical psychology. Caplan (1989) additionally reports that a double-standard is used by clinicians in their evaluations of mothers and fathers; behaviour that is labeled as "cold and rejecting" in a mother is simply viewed as "normal" in a father. She reports that when parents are described by clinicians, attention is directed to the occupational roles of fathers and the presence or absence of emotions displayed by mothers (e.g., "the father is a bricklayer and the mother is nervous") (in Tavris, 1992: 276). As Chodorow and Contratto (1982: 65) argue, pervasive within the "blame-the-mother" literature is "the unrealistic expectation that perfection would result if only a mother would devote her life completely to her child and all impediments to doing so were removed."

Employed mothers are often faulted for spending "insufficient" time with their children (e.g., Gairdner, 1992) even though research now suggests that children of employed mothers are not, on the whole, neglected or adversely affected by their mother's employment (Clarke-Stewart, 1989; Scarr et al., 1990; Van Horn, 1989). Studies comparing the children of employed and nonemployed mothers find that when differences emerge, the benefits accrue to children of employed mothers. For example, these children are more likely to receive more training in independence, to have higher career goals and motivation to achieve, to evaluate female competence more highly, and to hold less rigid and traditional conceptions of gender roles. While daughters in particular are likely to benefit from the existence of a positive model of female achievement, research also suggests that middle-class sons of employed mothers are less likely to hold stereotyped gender roles and to exhibit better social adjustment than the sons of nonemployed middle-class women.

Generally, children benefit from having mothers who have positive attitudes towards their multiple roles. Accordingly, the employment of mothers is not, in and of itself, deleterious to their children. Rather, the impact of mothers' employment upon children is influenced by such intervening variables as the mother's attitude towards her job, the family environment, and the quality of childcare secured. Women are encouraged to view themselves as inadequate or guilty for being other than full-time, stay-at-home mothers to their children (Hoffnung, 1989), while, simultaneously, full-time, stay-at-home mothers are disparaged for their "obsessive" and "overprotective" demonstration of "smother love" or "momism" (Wylie, 1942).

"The reality of mothering is frequently very different from the romantic ideal of feminine fulfilment" (Parton, 1990: 48). A new mother typically has no or little previous experience of breastfeeding, responding to a newborn, preparing bottles, giving baths, and so on (Mercer, 1986). Indeed, Blum and Vandewater (1993: 5) identify one reason behind the remarkable success of the La Leche League as stemming from their role as "the major source of practical breastfeeding advice." They observe that, although breastfeeding is currently advocated by medical practitioners "and popular among the white middle-class, breastfeeding remains outside the expertise of most physicians" (p. 5). While breastfeeding a child may seem a most "natural" act, the fact that more than two million copies of the La Leche League's manual, *The Womanly Art of Breastfeeding* have been sold would suggest otherwise.

The privatization of motherhood also provides additional explanations of women whose feelings about their day-to-day involvement with their children do not accord with the romanticized ideal mother. A belief in the existence of a "maternal instinct" may discourage a woman from acknowledging to others that she requires assistance or has ambiguous or negative feelings about being a mother, while the structural conditions of the nuclear family, compared to the extended family, discourage the likelihood that support will be provided (Power and Parke, 1984). Anderson and Leslie (1991) report that a mother of a young child is likely to be under greater stress than her husband, regardless of whether or not she participates in the labour force. Isolation and a lack of support may be particularly acute for single mothers. Various authors have suggested that addictions to cigarettes and alcohol represent the aftermath of attempts to cope with the stresses involved in caring for preschool-age children. For example, Graham (1984) has argued that for working-class women, the time spent sitting down to smoke a cigarette may be "the one peaceful time they have" (Abbott and Wallace, 1990: 91). Similarly, the description of gin as "mother's helper" has a long history.

Rosenberg (1987/1995: 311–312) argues that because childbirth and childrearing are seen as "natural," we fail to recognize the structural origins of women's emotional problems such as depression following childbirth or adoption. She notes that, although between 60 and 90 percent of women in Western societies experience emotional problems following the birth of a child and that depression and anxiety are also reported by men and women who adopt a child (p. 312), "the psychiatric literature still characterizes women with postpartum depression as infantile, immature, having unresolved conflicts with their mothers, failing to adjust to the feminine role, and having penis envy" (p. 314). Rosenberg likens motherhood to the highly stressful, low-control, high-demand jobs performed by industrial workers. She suggests that, although the organization of motherhood within contemporary society produces the psychological and physical symptoms of "burnout," the dominant explanations of "postpartum depression" and infanticide are "explicitly asocial."

Boulton (1983) reports that nearly one-third of her sample neither enjoyed the daily tasks of childcare nor achieved much sense of meaning or purpose from their children. An additional 30 percent noted the tiring, repetitive, and irksome nature of childcare and domestic work, and the social isolation and loss of financial independence motherhood entailed. She observes that these problems were particularly acute for working-class and single mothers, who often lacked an attractive environment in which to care for their children, or who simultaneously had to cope with the challenges of poverty, unshared parenting, and inadequate housing. Ong (1986) argues that isolation within the home is a major factor underlying the physical abuse of children by their mothers; child physical abuse is more common where mothers have been unable to develop or maintain links with supportive friends or family because of the costs posed by travel, telephone, or babysitting. As Ambrose (1989: 535)

notes, "[p]overty and deprivation make parenting problematic because they increase obstacles,…risk factors, and the simultaneous presence of both."

As Okin (1989: 4) observes, "an equal sharing between the sexes of family responsibilities, especially childcare, is 'the great revolution that never happened.'" Douthitt (1989)
reports that, on average, married women with a child under the age of five will devote 47
hours a week to home-production tasks, with approximately 40 percent of this time devoted directly to childcare. Approximately 17 hours a week are spent on childcare by nonemployed mothers with a child under age five, versus 14 hours by employed mothers.
Both employed and nonemployed women with children over the age of five spend, on average, five hours a week in direct childcare. In contrast, fathers of young children spend, on
average six to seven hours per week in childcare activities, regardless of the employment
status of the child's mother, and the majority of this time occurs on weekends (Douthitt,
1989). According to Statistics Canada, in 1992, employed women with at least one child
under the age of five spend, on average, 5.3 hours a day on housework, childcare, and
shopping; in contrast, the average husband spends approximately three hours per day on these
activities (Philip, 1996: A8).

Homemaker Mothers

Although the husband-provider/housewife-mother family remains celebrated by the New
Right as the traditional and ideal family form, it is increasingly becoming the exception
rather than the rule among Canadian families. While predominant during the 1940s and
1950s, this family form now accounts for only 22 percent of all husband/wife families
(Conway, 1990: 24). While the majority of women's adult lives in the past were occupied
with rearing dependent children, "[t]oday…a couple might spend two-thirds of their married
life free of the responsibility for young children, and a third without any children at home"
(Robertson, 1980: 269; see also Davis and van den Oever, 1982). Fewer children per family, combined with increased longevity, account for the significant reduction in the proportion of adult lives devoted to childcare today. Especially since the 1970s, women who
envision devoting their adult lives to raising children eventually confront an unanticipated
reality of having to decide what to do with a very lengthy period of adult life without children in their houses.

Although nonemployed mothers are generally viewed by student evaluators as being
more family-oriented, less competent professionally, and rank less highly on instrumental
qualities than employed mothers (Etaugh and Nekolny, 1990), being a homemaker mother
is often, due to financial constraints, a role that is limited in its tenure. The term **transitional family** refers to a work-family pattern in which women attempt to stagger the demands of work and family through a sequential patterning of motherhood and paid labour.
According to Daniels and Weingarten (1984: 211), this type of accommodation pattern is also
termed an **employment brackets motherhood sequence**. It occurs when a woman interrupts
her education or employment for a period of time and then returns to continue her role as student or employee. In this way, "some period of parenthood is cordoned off, as it were, insulated and protected from the competing demands of other work" (Daniels and Weingarten,
1984: 211).

Due to the financial hardship incurred by a woman's absence from the paid-labour force,
the time spent as a nonemployed mother may be limited to that period of time allowed for

under provisions of maternity leave. While Employment Insurance allows women 15 weeks (the first two of which are nonpayable) of pregnancy benefits, it requires that they have worked at least 700 hours during the previous year, and provides them with only a percentage of their normal weekly pay. For those earning in excess of $375 a week, benefits are calculated at 55 percent of the individual's gross earnings over the past 26 weeks; for those earning less, benefits are calculated at 60 percent. Although either parent may apply for parental benefits for an additional 10-week period following the birth of the baby, existent provisions seem to encourage mothers, rather than fathers, to pursue primary parenting. That is, should the father decide to seek the 10-week parental benefits, he would not receive benefits for the first two of the 10 weeks. Similarly, if the couple decides to split the parental benefits, two of the five weeks during which the father assumes primary care of the child will not result in payable benefits. In contrast, if the mother cares for the child continuously following its birth, she will receive payment for the entirety of the 10 weeks, since she would have already satisfied the two-week nonpayable period. The length of time devoted to full-time nonemployed homemaker motherhood consequently varies from as little as 15 weeks to more than 25 years, depending primarily upon the sufficiency of an available partner's performance as a provider and a woman's desire, if indeed she makes this decision on her own, to focus solely upon homemaking and childrearing.

Employed Mothers

As we saw in Chapter 6, since the 1960s, Canadian women with children increasingly have been entering the workforce. By 1991, 63 percent of mothers with children under the age of 16, and 57 percent of mothers with children under the age of six were employed. Reflective of this, current ads for cellular phones and paging systems aimed at employed mothers suggest that the contemporary supermom can reassure herself that she is only a phone call away from her child in the event of a crisis or emergency. We also noted that employed mothers operate with a more permeable boundary between paid work and family than do employed fathers, such that greater responsibilities for childcare result in higher work-absentee rates for mothers. Primary caregivers also frequently scale back career aspirations, refuse promotions carrying increased work responsibilities, resist transfers that might unsettle stable family life, and ultimately face flatter career trajectories, as a consequence of trying to balance employment with motherhood. At the same time, paid employment alters the organization of mothering. Just as they have to see to the reorganization of housework, mothers, upon entering or re-entering the labour force, typically assume, or are shouldered with, the mantle of responsibility within a married couple for securing acceptable alternative childcare arrangements and, typically, paying for those arrangements out of their own earnings.

Technological "fixes," such as cellular phones and pagers, are, in themselves, unlikely to substantially dissipate women's feelings of ambivalence towards paid employment or towards their own childrearing practises, while their children are still very young. Worrying and wondering about a child's daily life often detract from optimal performance on the job. When at their place of employment, many mothers' thoughts turn to what might be happening at home, and thoughts and feelings of fear, wistfulness, and guilt are likely to arise: fear that something extremely negative might befall a child during their absence; wistfulness over possibly missing a child's developmental milestones, such as the first word or first unaided steps; and guilt, since scientific research maintains that a constant presence of *someone* is a vital component of early child development and our dominant cultural ethic translates that evidence to mean that "someone" should be "mother." These feelings suggest to many an employed mother that she is, despite her best efforts, failing to provide adequate mothering in a variety of ways. It appears that, for women, learning to balance and manage employment and childrearing involves, most of all, learning how to manage guilt.

In coining the term "motherguilt," Eyer (1996) argues that the image of the "good mother" must be retired, since it is embedded in the notion of the stay-at-home mother (who is now an antiquated anachronism), and replaced with the notion of the "honourable parent," a term that can, and should, refer to both mothers and fathers. However, she acknowledges that the concept will face an uphill battle in gaining acceptance, since work institutions still do not bend sufficiently to enable fathers to take on a more active parenting role. In this vein, it is notable that virtually all the advice columnists in our media world still proclaim that the stresses of "employed motherhood" could best be reduced via women learning better stress- and time-management techniques, and almost always neglect to mention more shared parenting. Rarely do ads suggest that fathers purchase pagers so that day cares can easily reach them in the event that their child is running a fever or is suffering from constipation.

Hochschild (1997: 220–238) finds that employed mothers, confronting major "time binds," stemming from excessive demands of full-time employment and exclusive or primary responsibility for childrearing, develop a number of strategies to accommodate their limited time resources. Perhaps the most common strategy involves "downsizing" expectations for what both parents and children really need in their daily lives. If the level of needs can be pared down and prioritized, guilt can be assuaged and beliefs maintained that quality time is superior, for both parent and child, to quantity time. If hot noontime meals are available to workers at a restaurant and children at day care or school, then evening meals need not be. The necessity for daily baths and/or complete wardrobe changes can be questioned and reduced in number. Instead of lavishing constant time and attention upon children, employed mothers (and fathers) now emphasize a child's need for "independence." "Smother love" is replaced with the life-enhancing experience of autonomy granted by allowing a child to stay home alone after school.

Another strategy practised by growing numbers of employed mothers involves "outsourcing" many aspects of parenting. "Instead of trying to meet these needs themselves, they paid others to do it for them and detached their own identities from acts they might previously have defined as part of being 'a good parent'" (Hochschild, 1997: 221). Ironically, a substantial proportion of the increase in female employment involves women providing, for a fee, services that could be provided by mothers if they were not employed. Instead of planning a child's birthday party, an employed mother can hire a service (typically comprised mainly of women) to provide a full birthday party experience, complete with cake, goody bags, entertainment, decorations, invitations, and even gifts. "As the idea of the 'good mother' retreats before the time pressures of work and the expansion of 'motherly services,' actual mothers must continually reinvent themselves" (Hochschild, 1997: 233). In some eyes, a "good mother" saves time by outsourcing the planning and preparation for a party, and instead is available for participating, relatively unstressed, in the party itself. Hiring nannies or *au pairs*, arranging for relatives and neighbours to babysit or drive children to a full spectrum of planned activities, buying prepared foods, videotapes, and computer-entertainment games, are all examples of a revised definition of a "good mother," who, under time limitations, purchases help with the tasks of parenting. Children's needs are acknowledged, only the means of meeting them are altered, while still allowing a parent to consider herself a good mother.

A third strategy involves mothers (and fathers) splitting themselves into a "potential" and a "real" parental self (Hochschild, 1997: 235–238). The potential parent becomes an ideal parent, filled with ideas about what she or he will do with a child when time constraints produced by work problems brought home in briefcases or in executive minds or via telephones, faxes, and e-mail, are not an issue. Extended camping trips, vacations to major amusement centres, entire evenings or weekends devoted to child-centred activities, devoid of outside interference, comprise some of the favourite fantasies spun by employed parents, who promise themselves and their children that their ideal selves will be actualized someday. In this case, the road to good parenting is paved with the best of intentions. In the mean time, real selves continue to make do with less by downsizing, outsourcing, or expending what limited energies they possess within the limited time they can make available for hands-on parenting.

Solo Mothers

As we noted in an earlier chapter, 14.5 percent of all Canadian families in 1996 were headed by a lone parent (Statistics Canada, *Daily*, 14 October 1997: 2). Whereas lone-parent families in the first half of the twentieth century were primarily the product of the death of a parent (Oderkirk and Lochhead, 1992) occasioned by wars, mortalities associated with childbirth, and generally more hazardous living conditions, widowed people raising children alone accounted for only 20 percent of lone-parent families in 1996 (Statistics Canada, *Daily*, 14 October 1997: 3). Over the course of this century, increasing numbers of women have chosen to give birth and raise children on their own, without undertaking marriage. As a consequence of this trend, 24 percent of solo mothers in 1996 had never been married. Solo parenting currently, however, is most likely the product of marital dissolution (either separation or divorce), after which child custody is typically granted, either informally or formally, to one parent only (mothers overwhelmingly). Approximately 83 percent of all lone-parent families are headed by women, as of 1996, an increase from 74 percent in 1941 (Ram, 1990: 52). Lone-parent mothers are more likely to be younger, less well educated, have lower earnings, and less income, and typically are responsible for younger-aged children than are lone-parent fathers (Oderkirk and Lochhead, 1992).

Child Custody

Examination of annual divorce statistics indicate that at least half of all divorces awarded each year in Canada involve married couples with dependent children. In addition to decisions about which spouse will keep the house, car, cat, and dishes, partners must also come to an agreement, eventually, over custody of their children. Canadian law is, in many ways, less clear on resolving disputes over child custody than it is on the division of material assets. Upon divorce, or a judicial separation (in provinces where such can be obtained), or an interim order issued prior to divorce, the law usually only becomes involved in child-custody decisions when parents cannot resolve the matter on their own. As agents of the law, judges may overturn or choose to disregard private parental arrangements, if judges believe that such arrangements will be detrimental to the children. Even though no official statistics are published, it appears that judges seldom overturn mutually agreed upon private arrangements.

Prior to the mid-to late 1800s, custody decisions in Canada were based on the English common-law rule, which held that a father was the sole legal guardian of children. A mother could only become the legal guardian of her children in the event of their father's death and his previous appointment of her as testamentary guardian. Following a separation, a mother had no legal right, under common law, of either custody or of visitation. Even in cases where a father gave his former wife signed consent allowing her to retain custody of the children, such documents were held to be unenforceable and "contrary to public policy" (McBean, 1987: 184). Mothers, opined legal scholar William Blackstone, were entitled only to "reverence and respect," while the power of fathers "continues even after his death for he may by his will appoint a guardian to his children" (in Lowe, 1982: 27). Children were held to be the "natural property" of their fathers, a position reflecting the fact that women did not have rights as independent persons before the law and could not take legal action on their own before the court. Only in cases of gross neglect, or where a child over the "age of discretion" (generally set at 16 years of age for girls and 14 for boys) indicated a strong desire to live with their mothers, would a court allow a child to remain with its mother.

While the passage of the first custody act, Talfourd's Act (also known as the Custody of Infants Act of 1839), allowed mothers a limited likelihood of custody rights and, in the case of paternal custody, allowed mothers a certain degree of access (provided that the grounds for the divorce had not been the woman's adultery), mothers were only eligible to obtain custody of a child under the age of seven; after this age, children would be awarded to or ordered to be returned to the residence of their fathers. Dissatisfaction with **absolute privilege** held by fathers later prompted a slight shift in child-custody determinations to one of **paternal preference**. Both, however, were based on the assumption that fathers needed the labours of their children (especially older children) for family survival and, as well, the belief that children needed to be trained and raised by a firm hand. Since fathers were stereotyped as strong and mothers as weak, a father's hand was believed to be required to accomplish the necessary preparation of the young for eventual adult life.

Towards the latter portion of the nineteenth century, a combination of the influence of the newly developing psychoanalytic theory, and the increasing recognition of women's (including the Married Women's Property Act of 1882) and children's rights led to a gradual replacement of the paternal preference doctrine, which was purely parent-oriented, with a supposedly child-oriented principle known as the **tender years doctrine**. As child development theories evolved that recognized emotional development as being of equal, or perhaps even greater, importance than physical development, and that further recognized the importance of nurturance from the "emotional" sex, judicial opinion shifted towards a belief that, all things being equal, children during their tender years should be raised by their mothers. The logic underlying the tender years doctrine is illustrated more recently in the 1955 case of *Bell v. Bell,* in which the judge ruled that:

> No father, no matter how well intentioned or how solicitous…can take the full place of the mother. Instinctively, a little child, particularly a little girl, turns to her mother in her troubles, her doubts and her fears.…The feminine touch means so much to a little girl; the frills and flounces and the ribbons in the matter of dress; the whispered consultations and confidences

on matters which to the child's mind should only be discussed with Mother, the tender care, the soothing voice; all these things have a tremendous effect on the emotions of the child. (in McBean, 1987: 186)

The tender years doctrine became a euphemism for **maternal preference**. The "tender years" themselves were never precisely defined, but usually ranged from birth to ages 7–12. Adolescent children were believed to be best served if they were placed into the custody of the same-sex parent.

The tender years doctrine has supposedly been supplanted in the Divorce Act of 1985 with a new principle known as the **best interests of the child**. Section 16, subsection 8, of the Divorce Act of 1985 states that: "In making an order under this section, the court shall take into consideration only the best interests of the child of the marriage as determined by reference to the condition, means, needs, and other circumstances of the child."

The subsection does not define what the best interests of a child actually are and, therefore, considerable discretion is permitted to the judiciary. Richardson (1987) suggests that, based upon various judgments, the principle appears to include such factors as the wishes of the parents, the child's relationship to the parents, the child's current state of adjustment, the length of time the child has lived with one parent (thus establishing the importance of possession), and the relative emotional and financial ability of each parent to raise the child. Although, theoretically, the expressed wishes or preferences of the child could be taken into account, they apparently rarely are. In addition to the above mentioned factors, the conduct of a parent is considered to be an important influencing factor if that conduct is believed to be directly relevant to the best interests of the child. Adultery is no longer considered to be important, but substance addiction, and particularly child abuse are. The courts have held that a husband's commission of assault upon his wife does not invalidate his application for custody or his claim of being a "good father."

The *friendly parent rule*, created in the Divorce Act of 1985, additionally requires the court to take into consideration which parent would be most likely to provide the other with "liberal and generous" access to the children. Based on the belief that children benefit from as much contact with both parents as possible, a judge is required to consider the willingness or likelihood of each parent to facilitate the potential noncustodial parent with access. If one partner is hypothesized to be relatively unwilling to or "uncooperative" about providing such access, it is unlikely that he or she would be granted custody. For example, in the case of *Peterson v. Peterson*, 1985, the refusal of the mother to give her children's father liberal access was seen as the height of selfishness and of putting her own needs before those of her children. Ironically, the friendly person rule may create a situation in which a former spouse who has been battered may be obliged to continue in a relationship of sorts with her batterer, lest she be considered "uncooperative." In those situations in which a restraining order prohibits the abusive partner from establishing contact with the former spouse, the order itself is breached and rendered inoperative if and when the abused spouse voluntarily allows the abusive partner into the home to pick up or deliver their children.

According to Richardson (1987: 178) custody was defined by a judge as:

"[T]he full responsibility and control in providing physical nurture as well as mental and emotional nurture of children—for providing physical care, educational training and guidance in all matters that are considered of importance in the healthy rearing of a child."

The alternatives available to the courts are those of sole custody to one parent, joint custody, split custody, or custody to neither parent. A central issue for men's rights groups in Canada during the 1990s has been promotion of a "presumption" of joint custody (i.e., the presumption that joint custody would become an automatic preference in the mind of the court unless, and only if, compelling evidence dictates otherwise). That joint custody is far from a forefront presumption is indicated by official published statistics. For example, regarding all divorces granted in 1995, the courts of Canada, either through decisions in contested cases or simple ratification of informal uncontested arrangements, awarded legal custody of children to the mother in 67.6 percent, to the father in 10.9 percent, to the mother and father jointly in 21.4 percent, and to neither in 0.2 percent of the cases (Statistics Canada, 1997a: 20). Bear in mind that these statistics reflect only judicial decisions and do not necessarily reflect the actual living relationships that exist between parents and children. A mother with sole custody may still involve the father in almost all dimensions of a child's life and, therefore, parenting is shared. Similarly, joint custody may not really be shared in terms of equal parenting participation by both mothers and fathers, and children of joint custody typically live with one parent only. "Split" custody, dividing up the children (usually along sex lines) between parents, is so rarely awarded that it does not warrant specific mention in official published statistics.

In theory, the best-interests-of-the-child principle is gender neutral and allows judges to make a custody decision that is based solely on what is perceived to best serve the child's welfare. However, examination of actual court decisions suggests that the tender years doctrine and maternal preference still underlie judicial understandings of what custody arrangements serve the best interests of a child. When a husband (as he is referred to in the published statistics) applied for custody in 1995, that petition was granted in 20.1 percent of the cases, with the wife receiving custody in 51.3 percent, and the husband and wife receiving joint custody in 28.4 percent of those cases. When the wife applied for custody, she was awarded custody in 74.7 percent of the cases, with the husband granted custody in 7.2 percent, and the husband and wife receiving joint custody in 17.9 percent of the cases. When husband and wife applied for joint custody, the custody was awarded only 28.3 percent of the time, with the husband receiving sole custody in 13.2 percent and the wife granted sole custody in 58.2 percent of those cases. In all cases, awards to neither parent were less than 1 percent (Statistics Canada, 1997a: 20). Regardless of who applies for custody, husbands either alone (quite rare) or in a joint petition (slightly more often) are significantly less likely to be awarded custody of their children than are wives alone. If it is the judgment of the court that a child's best interests are to be met in emotional nurturance, then fathers are stereotypically seen by the family court system as being less capable of parenting.

A concern has been raised that judgments based on the "best interests of a child" may also exhibit a subtle bias against some women by reinforcing the ideology of "good" motherhood. Boyd (1987: 172) argues that "[t]he ideology is a double-edged sword for women in custody battles because the bias it creates in favour of mothers only operates where the mother's conduct of life-style accords with the assumptions and expectations of the ideology of motherhood. If they do not, the chances are good for a father who wishes to challenge the 'unfit' mother for custody." Chesler (1991) offers numerous illustrations, based on American custody cases, in which women lost custody because, among other things, they were employed (too ambitious), were not employed (too lazy), were involved with a man (immoral), or with a woman (even more immoral), or were not involved with a partner (did not offer the

Box 8.1	In The Child's Best Interest?

A killer who won custody of his 11-year-old daughter because his former wife is a lesbian said...he can give the girl a better home. John Ward, who murdered his first wife, won custody of his daughter in August from a judge who wanted to give the girl a chance to live in a "non-lesbian world." The mother, Mary Ward, asked a state appeals court to return their daughter, Casey, to her. "Her home life since we separated changed a lot and I feel I can give her a better environment," John Ward, 44, said on ABC's *Good Morning America*. "I can give my baby a home and I think she deserves that." Mary Ward, 46, has refused interviews. She was represented on the program by Kathryn Kendell, legal director for the San Francisco-based National Centre for Lesbian Rights.

Casey had been in Mary Ward's custody since her parents' divorce in 1992. Shannon Minter, a lawyer for the lesbian-rights centre, said laws in Florida, and most other states clearly say evidence must show a child has been harmed to change a custody order. "It presents a very stark example of how irrational it is to take a child from a stable, committed parent because of sexual orientation," Minter said. John Ward's lawyer, Ted Stokes, said Thursday his client has been rehabilitated since he fatally shot his first wife, Judy, in 1974. He served eight years in prison after pleading guilty to second-degree murder. He married Mary Ward, his second wife, in 1988. Circuit Judge Joseph Tarbuck granted the father's request for a custody change, citing the mother's lesbianism. He gave Mary Ward standard visiting privileges.

Source: Associated Press/*Ottawa Citizen*, "Judge gives killer custody because wife is a lesbian." 3 February 1996: A2.

*[Authors' note: Mary Ward died of a heart attack in 1997; at the time of her death, she was in the planning stages for taking her case, requesting sole custody, to Florida's Supreme Court (*Lesbian Connection*, March/April, 1997: 3).]*

child a stable family). A father's ability to offer a "mother substitute" is often viewed more positively by the court than a mother's ability to offer a "father substitute," especially if the biological father convincingly argues that he can provide the child "a family set-up which most closely resembles the traditional nuclear family, including 'female care'...[in the shape of] a new female partner, a grandmother or other female relative who...[is] willing to perform the stay-at-home motherly functions which accord with the ideology of motherhood" (Boyd, 1987: 179).

It appears that, in the minds of judges, a child's best interests are protected when the custodial parent does not veer far from traditional gendered expectations. Accordingly, while the working father who takes an "interest" in caregiving may be successful in his claim for child custody, the "househusband" is likely to meet with disappointment. For example, in the 1987 case of *Peterson v. Peterson*, the presiding judge ruled that "he would never award custody of a boy to a house-husband because with such a role model the child would be 'socially crippled when he is an adult'" (in Wikler, 1993: 49). Similarly, Yogis et al. (1996: 56) observe that, although "[n]othing in Canadian law stops a homosexual parent from applying for custody," they acknowledge that "the courts will often take judicial notice (that is recognize that it could easily be proved) of the fact that some harm might arise from living with a homosexual parent." In *Case v. Case*, a 1974 custody case heard in Saskatchewan, the judge remarked that "I greatly fear that if these children are raised by the mother [a lesbian], they will be too much in contact with people of abnormal tastes and proclivities." Judicial evaluations of the best interests of a child not only help to create public opinion, but they also reflect selective interpretations of what is presumed to be public opinion and dominant ideologies on gender and sexuality (Boyd, 1987: 171; see also Box 8.1). Canadian case law, however, does indicate that "custody is awarded to discreet, nonmilitant homosexual parents who do not flaunt their sexual orientation" (Yogis et al., 1996: 56).

Financial Support

Canadian Divorce Acts distinguish between court orders issued for support payments for spouses and support payments for children. We earlier noted the evolution of spousal payments from "alimony" to limited-term "support" and suggested that the latter often does not allow women, especially those with child custody, sufficient time to acquire the job skills or education necessary to become self-supporting (Galarneau, 1993). Prior to 1997, child support payments were negotiated between parents and/or their lawyers and then ratified or altered by the courts. Even though amendments to the Divorce Act of 1985 proclaimed that both spouses had a joint financial obligation to maintain their children, and that this obligation should be proportioned between the spouses according to the relative abilities to contribute, payment amounts awarded by court order varied greatly from one case to another. While such diversity was partly reflective of economic circumstances unique to each formerly married couple, it was also partly reflective of either power imbalances within a couple's relationship (with one partner coercing the other into giving or receiving greater or lesser amounts of support), or imbalances created by whomever obtained the services of a more powerful lawyer. Regardless of the amount of the ordered or ratified award, payments typically flowed from the noncustodial father to the custodial mother.

A government study examining family income (adjusted for the number of family members) following separation or divorce spanning the period from 1987 to 1993 finds that, one year after a marital union dissolves, women, on average, experience a 23 percent loss in after-tax income, while men register a 10 percent gain in income (Galarneau and Sturrock, 1997: 20). These differences are attributable partly to the fact that women generally earn less than men and partly to the fact that women typically have custody of any children following the dissolution of a marriage. Men without children to support increase their income by 14 percent one year following separation and by a total of 16 percent five years after separation. Women without children experienced a decrease in their incomes of 32 percent in the first year that lessened to 19 percent five years later. Female heads of lone-parent families experienced a 31 percent loss in family income in the first year following separation. While these women also recovered some portion of their financial losses, five years after separation lone-parent women were still 21 percent below their preseparation adjusted family income. In contrast, lone-parent fathers increased their income by 1 percent a year following the separation and by 5 percent after five years. The only women to improve their financial situation following separation were those forming new marital or cohabiting (most likely heterosexual) relationships whereby their income increased by 8 percent in the first year and by 14 percent five years later.

Galarneau (quoted in the *Edmonton Journal*, 10 April 1997: A7) notes that 40 percent of divorced or separated fathers in Canada make support payments. We are unaware of any data indicating what proportion of divorced or separated mothers make support payments. A support order, in and of itself, does not guarantee that payments, in whole or in part, will be made. For example, according to a 1991 estimate, 90 000 support orders, representing $470 million in delinquent payments, are unpaid in Ontario alone (in Galarneau, 1993: 9). During the 1990s, more than half of the provinces and territories in Canada enacted slightly differing forms of legislation intended to enforce greater and more timely compliance with existing support orders. These legislative acts focus upon varying combinations of suspending driver's licences, downgrading credit ratings, confiscating lottery winnings, and garnisheeing wages. For example, Ontario's Bill 17 in 1992 implemented stricter support-payment measures, requiring employers to withhold portions of the paycheques of employees who were found by the courts to be delinquent in their payments. Similar to Employment Insurance or the Canadian Pension Plan, such deductions are obligatory upon employers' receipt of a court order. However, comparable provisions have not been passed uniformly throughout all the provinces and territories, nor are they enforceable throughout the United States, should the delinquent elect to seek employment elsewhere to escape support payments. While estimates claim that Ontario's new system of enforcing child-support orders will generate an additional $410 million in tax revenues, it has been argued that "in most cases there will be less money available for the two parents" and, at least in some cases, "remove one incentive to comply with the child support order" (Wichman, 1996: 50).

According to the Survey of Consumer Finances during the late 1980s (presented in Oderkirk and Lochhead, 1992), almost two-thirds (65 percent) of all lone-parent families had at least one child under the age of 18 living at home. According to this survey, the major source of income for the majority of lone-parent families (71 percent of fathers and 57 percent of mothers) was wages and salaries, followed by income transfers from the government, such as Social Assistance or Unemployment Insurance (as it was known then). Reporting upon his own more recent research and additional data provided by the Canadian Department of Justice, Richardson (1996: 238) claims that approximately 40 percent of solo-parent custodial fathers and more than 60 percent of solo-parent custodial mothers now have incomes below Statistics Canada's LICOs (Low Income Cut-offs, comparable to "poverty lines"), with solo-parent mothers often being well below those cut-off points.

The lack of access to affordable childcare has been noted as one explanation for both the high unemployment rates of lone-parent mothers (16.8 percent versus 9.6 percent for wives in two-parent families) and their high rate of poverty. A 1991 survey conducted by the Daily Bread Food Bank in Toronto finds that 22.4 percent of sole-support mothers identified childcare responsibilities as the reason why they were not working. According to Statistics Canada (1993), 52 percent of lone-parent mothers in Canada are in paid employment, 20 percent are working part-time and half of those working part-time desire full-time work.

In an attempt to address a variety of inequities in the existing system, major changes in the tax rules for child support in Canada became effective in May of 1997. Under previous tax law, the payer was allowed to deduct child support (and spousal support) payments as legitimate expenses where a written agreement or a court order was in effect. The recipient or payee was required to declare payments received as income and was taxed accordingly. As part of the changes, under child support agreements or court orders established after

May 1, 1997, the payer no longer receives a tax deduction and the recipient pays no income tax on any monies received. As this legislation was tabled in the federal government's budget in March 1996, child-support agreements made prior to March 1996 remain unaffected by the new rules (unless both parties agreed to have the new rules apply or one party receives a court order to that effect). Mutual agreements or court orders made between March 1996 and 1 May 1977 could specify that the new rules would apply. Taxation of spousal-support payments is unaffected by these new rules.

In addition to these changes, the federal government introduced standardized formula guidelines, based on the income of the noncustodial parent only and the number of children involved, to establish the amount of payment mandatory for child-support orders granted effective 1 May 1997 onwards under the Divorce Act. These guidelines were created to provide more consistency across support orders, to establish more realistic awards, and to reduce the effect of power imbalances between separating and divorcing spouses or their lawyers. However, slight variations from the new guidelines for awards are permitted to exist between provinces to reflect cost-of-living differences, including provincial income taxes and sales taxes. As well, judges may increase support payments to accommodate childcare expenses for preschool children, medical expenses not covered by provincial healthcare plans, educational expenses, and "extraordinary" expenses (e.g., extracurricular activities) or evidence of demonstrated hardship (to any party), and decrease payments in joint custody situations where the noncustodial parent is responsible for a child at least 40 percent of the time.

Various self-named "educational" and political-pressure groups sprang up in Canada during the middle to late 1990s, protesting many of the changes in tax laws, the formulas for determining child-support awards, and the variety of techniques proposed or imposed to enforce greater compliance with existing orders. Comprising mainly divorced fathers and remarried fathers and their current wives, these groups protest that recent legislation at the federal and provincial levels is directly solely towards noncustodial fathers and ignores custodial mothers. The focus of the legislation, it is argued, reduces fatherhood (but not motherhood) to financial provision alone and fathers (but not mothers) to "money-making" machines. These groups want the federal and provincial governments also to address the issue of access awards, which they feel is in need of more forceful enforcement techniques. Members argue that noncompliance with support orders is closely related to noncompliance with access awards.

Although access to visitation and financial support are technically separate and independent dimensions of postdivorce childrearing, anecdotal accounts suggest that custodial and noncustodial parents wield the dimension over which they have more control as a power lever to influence the dimension over which they have less control. Custodial parents supposedly deny access when they are dissatisfied with the amount or timing of support payments received or not received, while noncustodial parents supposedly delay payments when they are dissatisfied with the amount or timing of visitations permitted or denied. The loss of custody supposedly becomes synonymous in many men's minds with both a real and symbolic loss of power and control over their children and over their former wife's childraising goals and techniques. Both parents are reported to manipulate access or payments to express displeasure over other issues, such as a former spouse's current lifestyle, including choice of intimate partner and real or imagined sexual activities; money management practices (or lack thereof); and comments passed along to children about the former partner.

While either parent can bring access or support issues back to the courts for reassessment or enforcement, such procedures are often time-, money-, and energy-consuming, and no data are available to indicate the prevalence and accuracy of many of the currently popular anecdotal accounts offered as reasons for denied payments or access. Much of the research on fathers' postdivorce relations with their children is actually based upon data collected from mothers' reports. However, mothers have been found, typically, to underestimate and underreport both visitation contacts and support payments, while fathers may overestimate both (Arditti and Keith, 1993: 702).

The amount of contact with noncustodial parents also appears to be gendered, with nonresident mothers maintaining a greater degree of contact with their children than nonresident fathers (Seltzer and Bianchi, 1988; Santrock and Sitterle, 1987). Empirical research indicates that high visitation frequency on the part of fathers is associated with joint custody, living nearby, high levels of father-child closeness predivorce, and higher socioeconomic status (Arditti and Keith, 1993). Visitation frequency positively influences visitation quality. Even though intuitive reasoning might suggest that the quality of visits should influence their frequency, empirical analysis (Arditti and Keith, 1993) indicates that such reasoning is not supported, and the lines of cause and effect run from frequency to quality. The nature of the postdivorce relationship between former spouses is positively related to the quality of fathers' child visitations. Compliance with informal agreements or court-ordered awards for financial support is positively linked to higher socioeconomic status of fathers and living nearby. However, neither visitation frequency nor visitation quality have been found empirically to be significantly related to compliance with financial agreements (Arditti and Keith, 1993; Berkman, 1986; Pearson and Thoennes, 1988).

Fatherhood

It has been cynically observed that "[f]atherhood has a long history, but virtually no historians (Demos, 1982: 425). Both popular and scholarly interests in the topics of fathering and fatherhood have fluctuated throughout the twentieth century. In their examination of popular magazine articles published from 1900 to 1989, Atkinson and Blackwelder (1993) find that fathers, prior to the 1940s, were more apt to be portrayed as providers than as nurturers. Such portrayals may have been more a reflection of beliefs in the desirability of a rigid gender division of family labour than a reflection of an actual absence of nurturing behaviour from fathers (LaRossa and Reitzes, 1995). Since the 1940s, depictions of fathers have fluctuated between these two images (Atkinson and Blackwelder, 1993). It is arguably only since the mid-1960s that, as Fein (1978: 242) has observed, discussions of fatherhood have become "fashionable" within academic literature. Coincident with significant increases in mothers' labour-force participation came a societal shift of emphasis from "mothering" to "parenting" (now transformed into a verb), and the concomitant discovery by society and academics alike of fathers and fatherhood.

McKee and O'Brien (1982: 4–7) attribute this focusing of academic attention upon fathers to a combination of social and structural changes including, but not limited to, the impact of second-wave feminism and its questioning of women's domestic and maternal roles; the rise in single-parent families; the increase in male unemployment; the decrease in average family size; the shortening of the work week and the concomitant rise in leisure time; the nascent men's movement; and the continuance of a child-centred ideology that places emphasis upon the nuclear family providing care. Blum and Vandewater (1993: 4) note that "because gender is always relationally constructed,…ideologies of motherhood that have powerfully shaped women's subordination must be seen in relation to equally powerful ideologies of masculinity, fatherhood, and dominance." LaRossa (1988/1995: 365, emphasis in original) has additionally suggested that to fully understand fatherhood, we must recognize the distinction between what he terms the "*culture of fatherhood* (the shared norms, values, and beliefs surrounding men's parenting)" and the "*conduct of fatherhood* (what fathers do, their parental behaviors)." LaRossa contends that "the culture of fatherhood has changed more rapidly than the conduct" (p. 365).

In their discussion of the history of fatherhood, McKee and O'Brien (1982: 13–14) observe that a wide range of materials exists, including "the Bible, the writings of moral theologians…catechisms…, religious and royal edicts, marriage contracts, inheritance settlements, portraits, photographs and paintings of family scenes…, census material…, tax records, parish registers…memoirs and biographies…legal statutes and cases, and literary evidence" that have been used by scholars to understand the social role of fathers in times past. Analysis of the meanings assigned to the word "family" within archaic dictionaries of the sixteenth through seventeenth centuries reveals that the power of fathers "was not necessarily restricted to his biological offspring, or even just to those living with him," but rather was viewed as akin to the "natural" power a king commanded over his subjects which rendered both "king and the father…accountable for their governance to God alone" (Flandrin, 1979, in McKee and O'Brien, 1982: 15). According to Flandrin (1979), until the mid-1500s, societal emphasis was placed upon the duties of children to their parents, with negligible attention directed towards the duties parents owed their children. McKee and O'Brien (1982: 17) conclude that paternal authority prior to modern times was "uncontested" and absolute, and "reflected the social reality that itself was characterized by hierarchical social relations and by the governance of the father, the husband, the master, and the lord" even though the way in which this absolute power was exercised varied by class.

According to McKee and O'Brien (1982: 19), examination of fatherhood in the modern period continues to reveal variation by such variables as social class, occupation, and geographical region. Roberts (1978), examining the memoirs of 168 Victorians born between 1800 and 1850, suggests that the development of a "self-conscious" and "admonitory" form of fathering stemmed from both increased urbanization and the rise of Puritanism and evangelism. Within the eighteenth and early nineteenth centuries, fathers were viewed as playing an important role in both the moral and vocational education of their sons, in particular, and children in general. Among the "well-born," the concept and code of the gentleman required that a man's behaviour be governed by an essential integrity towards his obligations and duties and, at least theoretically, the **paterfamilias** would ensure that his dependants were treated well—if not because of a generous nature then at least from a consciousness of proper form. If not loving husbands and fathers, the expectation was that a gentleman should be an attentive guardian. More complex images of fathering emerge from Thomson's (1977) analysis of 500 men and women selected from the 1911 census in England. He notes, for example, that in textile districts where female employment was high, male participation in housework and childcare was much greater than in those areas of heavy industry where men were employed in physically exhausting labours. In like fashion, Medick (1976) notes that in families dependent on a cottage industry form of economy, the roles of husbands/fathers and wives/mothers became considerably more blurred.

It was not until after World War II that the employment-dictated absence of fathers from the family home was re-evaluated and found wanting by scholars and social critics who decried the unavailability of a gender role model necessary, not only for sons, in particular, but also for daughters as well (Basow, 1992: 246). A new model of the "nurturant father" (Lamb, 1987) or "androgynous father" (Pruett, 1987) emerged during the middle of the 1970s. This new father was expected to become intimately involved from the moment of his partner's announced pregnancy, perhaps even strapping on a device called the "Empathy Belly" to approximate his female partner's feelings of being pregnant, and to perform an active and nurturant role towards his children from birth onwards. Childrearing guru Dr. Benjamin Spock advised fathers in 1945 to get involved and "prepare a formula on Sundays," but changed with the times and advised fathers in 1985 to do half the work involved in baby care (Shehan and Kammeyer, 1997: 220). While Jump and Haas (1987: 111) suggest that fatherhood is "in a state of transition—moving from the traditional perspective of fatherhood towards a more egalitarian model," no one singular ideology governs the culture of fatherhood at present and we witness a uneasy blending of the new with vestiges of older models.

Survey evidence suggests that a high proportion of males assign importance to becoming fathers. Over 80 percent of Bibby's (1995: 4) representative sample of Canadian men place a very high value on having a family and 83 percent of Canadian teenage males in the early 1990s anticipate having children in the future, including 30 percent who plan on staying home for at least a few years to raise their children (Bibby and Posterski, 1992: 33, 32). Male college students report that they desire having children as a means of building family ties, expressing love for their partners, and growing as human beings (Gormly et al., 1987). However, men are more likely than women to conceive of the roles of parent, spouse and worker as conflicting with one another, to view having children as a leading cause of adult's declining life satisfaction, and to doubt their ability to be able to interact effectively with their children. Men are also less likely than women to view the prospect of parenthood as an important means for achieving adult status (Baber and Dreyer, 1986; Ross and Kahan, 1983). This latter finding is most likely attributable to the wider variety of options available to men, both historically and currently, in the public sphere. Despite their ambivalence, however, Owens (1984) suggests that their own infertility is viewed by men as a major disruption to their envisaged "natural" adult career plan, a threat to their self-definition as masculine and virile, and a circumstance likely to lead men to define themselves as failures vis-à-vis their wives, because they are unable to "provide" their wives with a motherhood career.

Experiencing Fatherhood

We noted in Chapter 4 some of the gender differences which characterize the parenting of young children. At present, it is estimated that married fathers are the primary caretaker in only about 2 percent of families and their assumption of this role tends to be short in duration (Radin, 1988). While fathers, particularly in the middle-class, are now increasingly likely to attend birth classes with their partners and to be present at the birth of their children (Buie, 1989), Cox (1985) observes that, even in supposedly egalitarian marriages, assignment of childcare responsibilities tends to become markedly more traditional immediately following the birth of a child. Pedersen (1987) reports that fathers of infants devote less time to caretaking activities than do mothers. Entwisle and Doering (1988) find that many fathers feel unskilled in infant care and, by way of compensation, tend instead to emphasize their abilities as protectors and providers. These roles, Harris and Morgan (1991: 532) point out, require men to assume "some paternal responsibilities for training and discipline," but do not require that the father-child relationship be especially close or compassionate.

Basow (1992: 251) notes that a number of factors favour the likelihood that a father will experience satisfying involvement with his infant child, including the father's satisfaction with the marital relationship and with marital decision-making; the birth order and sex of the child (with first-born sons commanding greater attention than first-born daughters or subsequent children); the father's possession of child-centred parenting attitudes and predicted involvement in the provision of childcare; positive relations in the father's family of origin; good self-esteem; and specific instruction in traditionally female-assigned tasks such as feeding and diapering a child. However, Basow notes that the involvement of fathers is "best predicted by the wife's encouragement of such involvements" and observes that "[a] father's participation is greatest when an employed mother works long hours, earns more than the father, and supports the father's involvement in child care" (pp. 251, 254).

According to conventional wisdom, children "need their mothers" during infancy and toddlerhood and, as they grow older, increasingly need involvement with their fathers. However, actual paternal involvement with children beyond toddlerhood varies depending upon such factors as the constraints or freedoms provided by his employment, his gender ideology, the support he receives from a child's mother as well as family friends, and personal factors relating to his own motivation, self-confidence, and skill (Lamb, 1987). The best predictors of paternal involvement are a wife/mother's employment and fathers' possession of a flexible definition of the masculine role (Basow, 1992: 251–252). Overall, while the proportion of childcare provided by fathers does increase with maternal employment, the actual time spent by fathers in direct care for a child under the age of five increases by less than half-an-hour a week and, as we earlier noted, occurs primarily on weekends (Douthitt, 1989). When mothers are employed in night-shift work, fathers spend more time with children; when fathers are employed on the night shift, their contact with children declines dramatically (Nock and Kingston, 1988). Husbands of women employed in the professions are the most likely of all husbands to share equally in young children's physical care (Darling-Fisher and Tiedje, 1990), and higher-social status, higher-education fathers offer more "assistance" in general childcare (Seward et al., 1996).

LaRossa (1988/1995: 370) cautions that the actual amount of time fathers spend with their children may be inflated by both fathers and researchers, and rhetorically asks:

> If we took the time to scrutinize the behavior of fathers and mothers in public would we find that, upon closer examination, the division of childcare is still fairly traditional? When a family with small children goes out to eat, for example, who in the family—mom or dad—is more accessible to the children; that is to say, whose dinner is more likely to be interrupted by the constant demands to "put ketchup on my hamburger, pour my soda, cut my meat"?

Paternal childcare most often reflects the father as recreational specialist—reading to or playing with children, taking them to the park, movie theatre, or sports events—while mothers remain the parent charged with the bulk of such mundane, repetitive, physical-care tasks, such as feeding, dressing, and bathing (Burns and Homel, 1989; Thompson and Walker, 1989). Basow (1992: 252) notes that, while males voice a preference for sons prior to the birth of a child, express greater involvement with and attachment to their sons than to their daughters from infancy onwards, and are less likely to divorce in families of sons than in families

| **Box 8.2** | **A Gold-Medal Father in the 1990s** |

Four years ago, Jack Lipinski's family left him for a gold medal. His wife, Pat, and his only child, Tara, then 11, went to Delaware for the summer to take figure-skating lessons from a hot new coach, and they just never quite came back. Since then Pat and Tara have made what amounts to three trips around the world, become famous and moved again, this time to suburban Detroit, but Jack is still by himself, knocking around like a pinball in the family's 5,000-square-foot house....He shuffles around the only three rooms he uses, dutifully calling his wife and daughter twice a day, sending out the cheques, being the good dad.

He has law and engineering degrees and is vice-president of refining for a Houston-based oil company, but he still had to refinance the house to pay for the condo outside Detroit and the coaches and the ballet teacher and the tutors and the trainers and the travel and the clothes. Pat and Tara are grateful but they don't call him in Houston and ask him what he thinks about adding a triple toe loop or more sequins or the competition in Munich. You ask long-time skating writers about Lipinski's father, and they say, "are they together" or "what dya mean,

father?" You open Tara's autobiography and see the dedication to her mom: "You have...sacrificed so much....Without [you] I know I couldn't have gone this far." No mention of you-know-who....But he doesn't complain and he doesn't re-gret it and he doesn't even call it a sacri-fice. He figures a certain fireman and seamstress...worked like dogs to get him his two degrees, and now it's his turn....The phone bill is almost $1,000 a month, but sometimes the calls only make him lonelier....

After Tara almost knocked down the boards in Nagano [at the 1998 Winter Olympic Games]...the Lipinskis finally had that precious medal, fair and square, and were on their way to the doping con-trol station [for mandatory drug testing] to prove it. As usual Jack trailed along at the end of the entourage-escorts, officials, coaches, Tara and Pat. All of them were allowed in. Except one. "It's okay," he said, "I'm her dad." "*Nai*," the Japanese guard said. "Father," he argued, "Daddy." "*Nai*," the guard said....He gave up....It was well after midnight, which meant it was his 47th birthday. You wonder if he made a wish.

Source: Rick Reilly, "Tara's dad makes gold-medal sacri-fice."*Globe and Mail*, 28 February 1998: A22.

of daughters, the relationship between sons and fathers may become particularly thorny be-cause of issues of competition and dominance.

LaRossa (1988/1995: 370) notes that the majority of books and articles heralding the ar-rival of "new and improved" fathers are written by upper-middle-class professionals, who hardly constitute a representative sample of North American fathers. He suggests that even when "putting in time" with their children, many fathers may be characterized as "technically present, but functionally absent" or, more prosaically stated, "'there' in body, [but]...some-place else in spirit" (LaRossa, 1988/1995: 371). In this vein, we are reminded of a divorced father of our acquaintance who prided himself on the "quality time" spent with his young chil-dren: shopping for a new bicycle for himself, paying his bills at the bank, and having them watch him perform an oil change on his vehicle. Expressing these behaviours in a vocabulary of "quality time" suggests that this man embraced the rhetoric of the culture of fatherhood, but demonstrably little else. As LaRossa (1988/1995: 373, 375) remarks, "[t]oday…the culture and conduct of fatherhood appear to be out of sync. The culture has moved toward (not to) androgyny much more rapidly than the conduct.…Fatherhood is different today than it was in prior times but, for the most part, the changes that have occurred are centered in the culture rather than the conduct of fatherhood."

Basow (1992: 252) suggests that, due to the limited involvement of fathers with their children, "it is not surprising that most children and teenagers report a closer and better relationship with their mother than with their father." Bibby and Posterski (1992: 11) find that "when something big goes wrong," 61 percent of Canadian teenagers want to tell their friends and 22 percent want to tell someone in their family. Ten percent want to share this news with their mother, 10 percent with a sibling or grandparents, but only 2 percent want to share with "dad." When "something great happens," 15 percent of teenagers want to share the news with family, 9 percent with "other" family members, 5 percent with mom and only 1 percent with dad (Bibby and Posterski, 1992: 11). An American study (Fairbank et al., 1995, in Stacey, 1996: 140) finds that 44 percent of a sample of preteens and teens would turn first to their mothers for advice, 26 percent would seek help from friends, and only 10 percent would seek their father's advice first. Whether good news or bad, support or advice, fathers are the least likely to be approached and appear to be perceived as the least approachable member of Canadian and American families. In some ways, a father really is a forgotten man (see Box 8.2).

Lamb (1987 in LaRossa, 1988/1995: 368) divides the concept of "parental involvement" into three components: **engagement**, defined as time during which parents engage in one-to-one interaction with their children, regardless of whether that time is spent in play, assisting with homework, or feeding an infant; **accessibility**, a lesser form of involvement in which a parent is occupied with one task or activity, but is available to tend to a child in the event that it is required; and **responsibility**, the most intense form of involvement requiring planning, organizing, and decision-making about tasks necessary for a child's well being, ranging from making sure a child has winter boots that fit to scheduling a child's semi-annual visit to the dentist. Based upon a review of existing research, Lamb concludes that in dual-parent families where only fathers are employed, fathers are less involved with children than are mothers in terms of engagement (devoting only one-fifth to one-quarter as much time) and accessibility (about a third); when mothers are employed, fathers devote approximately a third of the time mothers spend in terms of engagement with their children, and two-thirds of what mothers devote in terms of their accessibility. Regardless of whether mothers are employed or not, fathers do not assume the component of responsibility for childcare. Only in the absence of a mother, will fathers be forced to take on the parental responsibility role.

Solo Fathers

Much of the research on solo parenting has focused on families headed by women (Price-Bonham, 1988) and, to date, research on father-headed lone-parent families remains limited (Meyer and Garasky, 1993: 74). However, the available research suggests that single-fathers are, in the main, not the ineffectual *Mr. Mom,* nor the superdad *Mrs. Doubtfire,* or the almost real Santa Claus depicted in *The Santa Clause.* Conway (1990: 20) observes that "studies of single parent fathers suggest they are quite successful at parenting, and they express more satisfaction than single-parent mothers." As he notes, their success may reflect the fact that, as we noted earlier, solo fathers in comparison with solo mothers tend to be older, better off financially and, due to vestiges of the tender years doctrine, more likely to be parenting older than younger children. Findings that solo fathers are more authoritative than solo mothers may be explained with reference to a greater familiarity with traditional parenting roles (Thomson et al., 1992) which assign responsibility for discipline and control to fathers. However, Hetherington et al. (1982) observe that when the behaviour of mothers immediately after divorce was compared with their behaviour two years later, mothers were found to exert greater control over the passage of time as a consequence of their assumption of "paternal behaviours." When confronted with an "all roles fit one" person situation, a tendency towards eventual congruency in parental role performance appears to characterize both female and male solo parents.

Stepfathers

The General Social Survey of 1995, conducted by Statistics Canada, reports the existence of approximately 430 000 stepfamilies in Canada, comprising about one in ten of the country's 4.165 million families. Not surprisingly, given the custody arrangements most commonly observed following divorce, slightly more than half of all stepfamilies are composed of a mother, her children, and a stepfather; about 10 percent are a father, his children, and a stepmother; and about a third of the families were composed of a mother and "her" children, a father and "his" children, and/or children of the new couple (*Toronto Star*, 20 June 1996: A2). While research on stepfamilies is still in an early stage of development, concern has been raised that various forms of child abuse are more likely to occur in this type of family because of the lack of early bonding between children and stepparents (particularly stepfathers) and to the related perception that a stepchild is other than one's own "flesh and blood."

Finkelhor (1979) reports that father-"daughter" incest is almost five times greater in families with stepfathers than in families with biological fathers. Russell (1984) finds that 2 percent of women with biological fathers present during their childhood years were incestuously abused. In comparison, 17 percent of American women whose stepfathers became principal figures in their childhood years were sexually abused by these men. Stepfathers who are sexually involved with children they did no sire appear to be even more likely to believe that the culturally normative injunctions against incest are not relevant to their situation. The "relative stranger" (Beer, 1988) explanation for sexual abuse appears to be applicable here, especially during the early stages of new stepfamily formation. Thomson et al. (1992) find that stepmothers, stepfathers, and cohabiting male partners (informal stepfathers) report having significantly less activities with, and less positive responses to, children than do biological parents. Herman (1981) argues that being absent during the early years of children's lives reduces the likelihood of viewing stepdaughters as "children," increases the likelihood of viewing them instead as female sexual beings, and thus increases the probability that stepfathers will act in a sexually abusive manner. She argues further that the gender gap (Russell and Finkelhor, 1984) in incestuous abuse is at least partly attributable to women's typical assumption of the principal child-nurturer role within the family. Months or years spent washing and diapering infants, and later assisting in wiping children's genitalia and anuses effectively discourages most women from envisaging children as particular "alluring" or "sexual" (Herman, 1981). Herman contends that greater participation of fathers and stepfathers in physical care and nurturing of children would reduce the likelihood of men becoming sexually abusive towards their "own" children. While some research suggests that relationships between stepfathers and stepchildren become warmer over time, stepfathers have been found to withdraw from attempts to establish close relationships with stepdaughters after initial attempts to assert authority are rebuffed or prove unsuccessful (Amato, 1987).

ULTIMATE VIOLENCE

We ended the previous chapter on intimate relations with an examination of intimate violence. We conclude the present chapter by noting that coercive and brutal behaviour between intimates sometimes escalates into an ultimate act of violence resulting in death. Presently or previously married partners commit spousal homicide and parents commit filicide. Even though some of the circumstances surrounding each death are unique to the participants involved, many gender characteristics of perpetrators and victims of these homicidal acts are consistent and, unfortunately, persistent.

Spousal Homicide

Silverman and Kennedy (1993) observe that approximately 40 percent of all homicides that occurred in Canada over the past 30 years involved family members. Annual rates of spousal homicide in Canada remained relatively constant between 1974 and 1992, with the ratio of wives killed by their husbands to husbands killed by their wives being 3.2 to 1. A married woman was 9 times more likely to be killed by her spouse than by a stranger. While women in Canada are more likely to be killed by husbands or ex-husbands (48 percent), men are more likely to be killed by acquaintances (53 percent) rather than by a wife or ex-wife, another family member, a friend, a business relation, or a stranger (Trevethan and Samagh, 1993). During the 1974–1992 time period, men also committed 94 percent of all *familicides* in Canada. Familicide refers to a form of spousal homicide in which the offender not only kills a spouse, but also kills one or more of a couple's children at the same time (Wilson and Daly, 1994). More recently, of 164 women murdered in Canada in 1993, 77 (47 percent) were killed by a current or past partner. In Ontario alone, 64 women were murdered in 1993 with more than half (55 percent or 35 women) killed by a partner or former partner (*Toronto Star*, 6 December 1994: A12). Crawford and Gartner find that, between 1991 and 1994, an average of 40 women died each year in Ontario, 71 percent of them (159 out of a total of 224 homicides) at the hands of a current or former husband, a cohabiting partner, or a boyfriend (*Edmonton Journal*, 29 April 1997: A5).

Silverman and Kennedy (1993) note that most spousal homicides are the culmination of an escalating sequence of spousal violence and not a sudden isolated event. One of the most common legal defences offered by men charged with homicide of a spouse, where both partners are still living together, is the defence of "provocation." Section 232 of the Criminal Code allows for a charge of murder to be reduced to manslaughter if a defendant suffers an insult or wrongful act sufficient "to deprive an ordinary person of the power of self-control" that also causes the person to react "before there is time for his passion to cool." This defence has been used successfully by men who found their wife in bed with another man, and by men who claim they were provoked by slogans on a T-shirt worn by a wife or by verbal commentaries proffered by a wife upon a husband's virility, fertility, or masculinity.

Many other issues, if not present during a marriage, are particularly likely to erupt when a couple separate, especially if a wife appears to be the initiator of the relationship breakup. "Homicide statistics [show]…that women are generally at greater risk of being killed by their spouse after separation; between 1974 and 1992 women were six times more likely to be murdered by their husband after leaving him than when living with him" (Kong, 1997: 31). Many of these homicides appear to be motivated by expressed or unexpressed sentiments such as "love me or I'll kill you" or "if I can't have you, nobody else can either." As noted in an earlier section of this chapter, due to an often unstated emotional dependence, men appear to have greater difficulties dealing with rejection psychologically and emotionally than do women. Within this context of rejection, issues of masculinity, power, control, and possession of women as property come to the surface for many men and are given expression via ultimate violence. An unknown, but significant, proportion of these spousal homicides are subsequently followed by the perpetrator's taking of his own life following the murder of his current or former intimate partner.

A relatively new defence has been offered in some recent cases of wives charged with murdering their husbands. The term **battered woman syndrome** was originally popularized by Walker (1979) to describe a pattern of "learned helplessness" (Brodsky, 1987) acquired by abused women as a consequence of the cycle of violence perpetrated upon them within intimate relationships. Having become conditioned to believe themselves incapable of effecting change to their circumstances and to feel that any efforts on their part to leave would be both futile and painful, many women perceive themselves to be trapped and consequently will remain within an inhumane situation. In the precedent-setting case of *Regina v. Lavallee*, a trial court in Manitoba allowed expert testimony to be given on the battered woman syndrome in support of a self-defence claim by Angelique Lavallee to a charge of second-degree murder. In the wake of the Lavallee case and a 1990 Supreme Court of Canada ruling, battered woman syndrome is now recognized in law as a modified form of the doctrine of self-defence. Expert witnesses may testify on this syndrome and explain why, given a woman's past, she may have believed her life to be in danger in light of an escalating cycle of violence against her. Feeling unable to change the conditions of her life otherwise, a woman might believe she has no choice other than to take the life of her batterer as the only way to protect herself from becoming a victim of ultimate violence.

Self-defence pleas require (as set out in Sections 34 to 42 of the Canadian Criminal Code) that the use of force should be no greater than one might expect a "reasonable man" to use to defend himself when there are "reasonable and probable grounds" to believe that his life is threatened. Faith (1993: 105) observes that "a woman cannot be a reasonable man"; the use of a generic term here ignores the different realities of men and women. Proving that one's actions are "reasonable" may be problematic in the case of battered women who kill, since "in many of these cases the homicide occurs when the victim is incapacitated (e.g., sleeping), sometimes following a physical confrontation, or in anticipation of a confrontation" (Gillespie, 1989 in Kasian et al., 1993: 290). In such circumstances, difficulties exist in convincing a judge and/or jury that it was reasonable for the defendant to believe that her life was in "imminent danger of death or serious bodily harm at the time of the incident" (Kasian et al., 1993: 290). Unfortunately, "once a man has established himself as a nonlethal wife beater, some judges and juries will presume that he will always be a nonlethal wife beater" (Gillespie in Bannister, 1991: 409). The defendant has to convincingly argue that on the occasion in question, she "reasonably" believed that the abuser's next actions would be lethal. For these reasons, "[t]he battered woman's claim is most likely to be successful if she killed the batterer during an acute battering incident" (Silverman and Kennedy, 1993: 150).

In 1995, Judge Lynn Ratushny of the Ontario Court (general division) was appointed by the federal government to re-examine the cases of 98 women who claimed they killed their intimate partners in self-defence, but were still convicted of murder or manslaughter. Ratushny recommended in 1997 that only seven of those cases warranted reopening. In response to these recommendations, the federal government of Canada pardoned two women, erased the remainder of the sentences of two others, awarded one woman a new hearing, but refused to alter the sentences currently being served by two others (*Edmonton Journal*, 27 September 1997: A3). The federal government reserved judgment of Ratushny's other recommendations that juries and judges be allowed greater discretion in sentencing women found guilty of second-degree murder when the killing occurs in "exceptional circumstances," such as those pertaining to battered women.

The battered woman syndrome, as it is presently constructed, contains certain dangers and limitations. First, the term "syndrome" refurbishes the notion that women who kill are pathological rather than normal individuals forced to live in abnormal circumstances. Schneider (in Faith, 1993: 104) remarks that "to successfully plead a Battered Woman Syndrome defense, a defendant must be presented as a defeated woman, a passive helpless victim whose irrational behaviour was the desperate act of a trapped animal." Second, the introduction of a "syndrome" to explain why women kill their abusive partners ignores the ways in which society generally, and the criminal justice system in particular, fail to protect such women—and their husbands—from lethal violence. A focus upon the woman in question deflects attention away from larger issues pertaining to gender and gender relations as presently constructed in our society.

Filicide and Infanticide

"Only 11 percent of child homicides between 1980 and 1989 [in Canada] were committed by strangers. Two-thirds of child victims were killed by their parents (one-third each by mothers and fathers), while a further 10 percent were killed by stepparents, foster parents, or other relatives" (Sacco and Kennedy, 1994: 191). In two-thirds of the child murders which occurred during 1991 to 1994, one or both of the child's parents were charged with the crime. Of 53 Canadian homicides of children under the age of 12 in 1996, the perpetrator in 85 percent of these cases was the child's parent (*Edmonton Journal*, 31 July 1997: A4). While Canadian homicide rates have been relatively low for children as a group, the rate for infants within the first year of life—5.6 homicides per 100 000—is five times the rate for children overall, and more than twice the rate for adults and the accused is nearly always the child's parent (Holtz, 1997: 98). Our presentation to follow will focus primarily upon biological parents. Three terms are used to refer to ultimate violence perpetrated by a parent upon his or her own child. Each term focuses upon a more general or more specific age range for the victim of the violent act. **Filicide** is the generic term used to refer to the killing of one's own child of any age; **infanticide** is the term generally used to refer to the killing of one's own child aged one year or less; **neonaticide** (Resnick, 1969) is the term used to refer to the killing of one's own child during the first day of its life. Of these three terms, only infanticide is specifically mentioned in the Canadian Criminal Code, with the other two found primarily within social science literature. Individuals accused of murdering a child over the age of one year are charged under appropriate sections of the Criminal Code dealing with murder or manslaughter as warranted by details of each case.

The legal definition of infanticide, first introduced within the Criminal Code in 1948 as a form of culpable homicide, is notable in that it renders the offence as one of the last remaining gender-specific crimes within the body of Canadian statutory law. Section 233 of the Canadian Criminal Code defines infanticide as follows:

> A female person commits infanticide when by a wilful act or omission she causes the death of her newly-born child [*sic*], if at the time of the act or omission she is not fully recovered from the effects of giving birth to the child and by reason thereof or of the effect of lactation consequent on the birth of the child her mind is then disturbed.

For purposes of this section, "newly-born child [*sic*]" refers to a child under the age of one year and, therefore, includes both infanticide and neonaticide as referred to earlier. Under Canadian law, specified within section 223(1) of the Criminal Code, a "child becomes a human being...when it has completely proceeded, in a living state, from the body of its mother whether or not (a) it has breathed, (b) it has an independent circulation, or (c) the navel string is severed." Accordingly, the act of "procuring a miscarriage" for another or for oneself (as defined within section 287[1] and 287[2], respectively), is considered to be separate and distinct from the Criminal Code offence of infanticide.

Two points become immediately obvious upon examining Section 233 above. First, only women are specified as the perpetrators of infanticide. A male person suspected of killing an infant cannot be charged under this section, but must be charged under a culpable homicide section. Infanticide is, therefore, considered, at least in law, to be a female crime for which women only are liable to imprisonment for five years. Second, Section 233 clearly states that causing the death of one's own "child," or infanticide, is a consequence either of giving birth or of lactation, both of which cause a mother's mind to become "disturbed." Over the course of the nineteenth century, both statutory and case law increasingly reflected medico-legal assumptions that infanticides as well as other acts of female deviance stemmed from gynecological disturbances caused, in part, by women's reproductive cycles (Edwards, 1981: 95). England, in 1922, and Canada, in 1948, introduced legislation that reduced a charge of murder to infanticide if it could be demonstrated that the defendant had, at the time of the act, been suffering from a form of temporary insanity incurred by childbirth or lactation.

Clarke (1987: 166) observes that difficulties soon arose with the infanticide provisions of the code since a woman could claim, by way of defence, that she had, at the time of murdering her child, fully recovered from the effects of giving birth or had never suffered from a "disturbed mind." If such a plea was accepted, a woman could be acquitted of the charge of infanticide and, due to the rule of "double jeopardy" which prohibits trying a person twice for the same offence, never be charged for the killing of her child. Recognizing that the Crown could potentially prove part of the offence (i.e., that a child was killed), but not the other part of the offence (i.e., her state of mind at the time of the offence was disturbed), a further provision was added to Canadian law. Section 663 of the Criminal Code stipulates that:

Where a female person is charged with infanticide and the evidence establishes that she caused the death of her child but does not establish that, at the time of the act or omission by which she caused the death of the child, (a) she was not fully recovered from the effects of giving birth to the child or from the effect of lactation consequent on the birth of the child, and (b) the balance of her mind was, at that time, disturbed by reason of the effect of giving birth to the child or of the effect of lactation consequent on the birth of the child, she may be convicted unless the evidence establishes that the act or omission was not wilful.

In cases where neither murder nor infanticide are likely to be proven, either men or, most often, women can be charged under a section of the Canadian Criminal Code dealing with concealing the dead body of a child. Section 243 specifies that "every one who in any manner disposes of the dead body of a child, with intent to conceal the fact that its mother has been delivered of it, whether the child died before, during or after birth" has committed an indictable offence, punishable by a two-year term of imprisonment. Boyle et al. (1985) point out that the Crown makes the final decision as to which charge(s) a woman who kills her infant will face and few women in Canada have faced charges of infanticide.

Available summary statistics on the incidence of filicide and infanticide in Canada fail to provide a clear picture as the time periods being reported on frequently overlap. Silverman and Kennedy (1993: 77,155) indicate that between 1974 and 1990, of the 298 cases in Canada of mothers killing children, police laid charges of infanticide in 69 cases. In their earlier analysis of homicide statistics between 1961 and 1983, Silverman and Kennedy (1988) report that 230 children over the age of one year were killed by their mother. While we lack statistics on the number of maternal filicides for the entirety of this time period, Silverman and Kennedy report that from 1974 to 1983, 45 children under the age of one were killed by their mothers. Between 1991 and 1994, an annual average of 22 newborns were killed, with two-thirds of these murders committed by a child's parents (Johnson, 1994: 13).

In comparison to the maximum penalty of life imprisonment available for other types of culpable homicide, such as first- and second-degree murder and manslaughter, the maximum sentence of five years imprisonment upon conviction for infanticide is comparatively light. As Chunn and Gavigan (1995: 163) point out, "in practice, women charged with infanticide are often acquitted and serve no sentence at all." Chunn and Gavigan (1995: 163) additionally report that, according to an analysis of child deaths due to abuse or neglect from 1973 to 1982, of 11 women charged with infanticide, only two were sentenced to a term of imprisonment and both women received sentences of two years or less. Greenland (1988) notes that of the 37 women and 32 men who faced filicide criminal prosecution for either manslaughter or homicide in Ontario cases of child abuse and neglect deaths, women were more likely than men to face less serious charges and to receive shorter prison terms upon conviction. However, women were less likely than men to receive a nonpenal disposition of their cases. We should not conclude that courts consider a woman's killing of a child as less serious than a man's killing of a child. As Chunn and Gavigan (1995: 196) point out, female defendants typically possess less lengthy criminal records than do male defendants, and past criminal histories influence the nature and severity of charges laid and sentences imposed. The wide range of variation in sentencing defendants convicted of child-abuse related deaths (Ruby, 1987: 413) caution against making broad generalizations as to which, if either, receives more lenient treatment.

Wilcynski's (1991) study of 22 English cases of mothers who killed their children found that distinctions were drawn between women who were "good" and "bad" women/mothers. Women who were perceived as acting in a manner inconsistent with normative femininity and idealized visions of devoted maternity (e.g., those who were sexually active, self-centred, cold or aloof, lacking in nurturant qualities) could expect little sympathy from the judiciary and were likely to be described in press accounts of their cases as "evil," "callous," or "vile." Wilcynski additionally observes that those mothers who failed to safeguard their children from the violence of their partners were also likely to be labeled as "unnatural" and/or "bad" mothers. Consider, for example, the 1985 case of *Gregory* in which a child's father received a sentence of four years imprisonment after his two- month-old daughter died of brain injuries when he struck her several times in a fit of stress-induced uncontrollable rage. "The court noted the accused's excellent background and that he had been left with the care of his daughter at a time when his wife *was neglecting to perform her share of the parental duties.*" (Ruby, 1987: 414, emphasis added). A dissenting judgment in this case proposed that a two-year sentence be considered more appropriate than the four-year sentence imposed.

Carlen (1985: 10) suggests that a woman who commits a crime has already violated society's gendered expectations about women and will be viewed as deficient to at least some degree. Carlen further argues that certain women, most notably those who commit a criminal act and whose noncriminal behaviour also contravenes normative gender roles, especially in relation to domestic arrangements and motherhood, are particularly likely to experience "judicial misogyny.…[T]hose who fall within the 'bad' category because they are assertive, unemotional, promiscuous, divorced or have children in care can expect to be judged more severely than defendants who, at the time of their court appearances, are living at home with their husbands and children, and who are prepared to 'soften' [their image]…to conform with the judge's stereotype of appropriate motherhood by presenting an image of docility" (Carlen, in Ballinger, 1996: 2).

In her analysis of psychiatric and social inquiry reports prepared on men and women convicted of serious violent offences, Allen (1987) observes that, while reports on men focused upon their lifestyles and behaviour, the focus in reports prepared on women almost invariably focused upon the woman's mental state. Allen suggests that because violence is seen to be contrary to women's "essential nature," women who commit violent acts may be viewed as more mad than bad or, in other words, as being "pathological" in some way. Ruby (1987: 415) reports that "young mothers who have shown a serious inability to cope with the stresses of childrearing [and whose conduct results in the death of their children]" have received short or suppressed sentences involving conditions regarding psychiatric treatment in preference to sentences of lengthy incarceration." Psychiatric treatment is tantamount to an indeterminate sentence, since it ends only when, and if, a determination is made that the "patient" is sufficiently well enough to be released.

Morris and Wilcyznski (1994: 206) argue that the "very existence of the infanticide charge," and the suggestion that women kill their children while suffering some form of psychosis, stem from twin beliefs in (1) women's essential passivity and (2) an inherent gentleness and natural nurturance in mothers. Both of these beliefs, central tenets of cultural feminism today, were illustrated in one highly publicized trial (immortalized in the film *A Cry in the Dark*), when Australian mother Lindy Chamberlain, claiming that her infant daughter had been abducted and killed by dingoes, was charged with the murder of her child. In his summation to the jury, Chamberlain's defence attorney made pointed reference to the supposed nature of women-as-mothers and why his client could not have possibly have killed her child. "Ladies and gentlemen, women do not usually murder their babies, because to do so would be contrary to nature. One of the most fundamental facts in nature is the love of a mother for her child....A mother will make all manner of sacrifices for her baby. A mother will die for her baby" (in Wood, 1994: 68–69). Chamberlain was initially found guilty of murder, but upon retrial and the introduction of new evidence, was eventually acquitted of the charge.

Unlike the case of Chamberlain, women defendants most often argue some form of temporary "insanity" defence. Morris and Wilcyznski (1994: 215) point out that the "dominant discourse on mothers who kill their children is rooted in the belief that *all* women are potentially mad at certain times in their lives—for example, during, before and after menstruation, childbirth, lactation and the menopause." They observe that, while "the amount of time that women spend in one or other of these 'ordinary states'" should, on the basis of common sense alone, be "enough to reject such claims as generalizations," the "myth of motherhood" (Oakley, 1986) with its attendant notions that all normal women long for motherhood and are "naturally" caring, altruistic, and skilled within the role becomes effectively insulated by a medico-legal discourse which suggests that women who are not, are "obviously" sick (Scutt, 1981; O'Donovan, 1984). Ironically, naturally nurturing mothers are described in that discourse as being driven temporarily sick or insane by their naturally reproductive bodies. "Nature" is made to appear as a force driving women in two different directions simultaneously. The Law Reform Commission of Canada recommended in a 1984 report that the criminal offence of infanticide be repealed, observing that "a mother who has not recovered from giving birth could also kill their [*sic*] other children, not just her newly-born [*sic*] child" and that "it was doubtful that mental disturbance due to childbirth was ever the real cause of infanticide" (in WGAGO, 1992: 85). This recommendation was not acted upon and the crime of infanticide in Canada, as of 1998, remains anchored to notions that a woman's gynecology is riddled with deviance-producing tendencies—a tenacious viewpoint Weininger (1906: 39) captured when he wrote: "Man possesses sexual organs; her sexual organs possess woman."

GENDER
AND AGING

Although members of a youth-oriented society such as ours might prefer not to think in these terms, it can be argued that the processes of aging begins at birth. While the precipitants, processes, and outcomes of physical aging demonstrate more similarities than differences for women and men, the social processes of aging exhibit more gender differences than similarities. Our focus in this chapter will be upon selected events associated with aging and, more important, upon the social meanings of aging for each gender.

SEX-RATIO AND LIFE-EXPECTANCY DIFFERENTIALS

Sex-Ratio Differentials

The sex ratio of chromosomal male (XY) conceptions to chromosomal female (XX) conceptions is approximately 140 to 100 (Money and Tucker, 1975). In other words, in the absence of technological interventions, 140 male embryos are created at moments of conception for every 100 female embryos. From conception onwards, the sex ratio begins to decline. As a consequence of misfortunes over the typical nine-month period of fetal gestation, such as miscarriages or spontaneous abortions and stillbirths, the ratio of male to female births is generally around 106 (McVey and Kalbach, 1995: 56) or 105 (Saxton, 1990: 26) to 100. Immediately following birth, the likelihood of survivorship for women and men to various points over the human life span, and the resulting sex ratio, varies from one society to an-

Box 9.1   Deadly Bias Against Girls Increasing

[Authors' note: Once again, we ask for your tolerance with a journalist display of ignorance, this time in explicitly assigning decision-making responsibility for family size to women only and implicitly suggesting furthermore that decisions to abort or to commit infanticide in one form or another are made solely by women. We suggest you focus first and foremost upon the summary of research findings and their implications and then, secondarily, upon the implications of the writer's gender-biased and misleadingly inaccurate presentation style.]

The long-standing custom in some Asian countries of allowing girls to die soon after birth, either by neglect or by outright infanticide, appears to have become increasingly common in recent years as women opt for smaller families. New research on demographic data from India, China and Taiwan suggests that biases against girls are not disappearing even as those countries' birth rates approach those of Western nations. The work also indicates that women are increasingly using prenatal sex-determination tests and selective abortions to ensure that they give birth to boys. "As fertility has declined, sex preferences have stayed constant," said Nancy Williamson, director of the women's studies project at Family Health International a Durham, N.C.-based non-profit organization specializing in reproductive health in developing countries. As a result, Williamson and others said recently in New Orleans at the annual meeting of the Population Association of America, the latest figures show that boy-to-girl ratios are continuing to increase in such countries as China, South Korea, India and Taiwan.

Sex selection is an old practice in many Asian countries, reflecting the significantly higher value those societies place on boys and men. While male-female ratios among children in Western countries are roughly one to one [*sic*], those in several Asian countries range from 106 to 114 boys for every 100 girls. Because countries such as China and India are so populous, such differences can add up to millions of "missing" girls. The details of what happens to these girls are often vague. In some cases the girls are killed soon after birth, but in many cases their demise is more subtle—the result of deeply ingrained cultural practices that increase female death rates during their first few years of life. In India, for example, women and girls traditionally do not eat until the men and boys have had their fill. When food is short, that can lead to reduced survival of girls compared with boys.

Harvard University researchers Monica Das Gupta and colleague Mari Bhat used census data and hospital records to calculate the rate of sex discrepancy in India, and to determine how much of it is likely to be due to prenatal testing and abortion. Such testing allows women to learn the sex of their fetus during the second trimester by ultrasound, and then to have a late-stage abortion if the sex is not to their liking. Das Gupta's analysis indicates that more than one million girls were lost due to selective abortions between 1981 and 1991, chiefly during the second half of that decade since the technology was not widely available before then. In addition, however, about four million girls "disappeared" during their first four to six years of life, or about

36 girls for every 1,000 born. That's about the same rate documented during the previous decade, suggesting that selective abortion is not substituting for female infanticide, but supplementing it. "It has been an additive effect," Das Gupta said. "And in 1991 to the year 2000 we should expect to see more of it."

Judith Banister, of the U.S. Census Bureau, described a new analysis of data from China, a country with a long history of skewed sex ratios. Using Chinese census figures from the past decade, she calculated that about 1.5 million female fetuses had been selectively aborted between the mid-1980s and 1990. By the beginning of this decade, she said, such abortions were responsible for about 50 percent of that country's annual shortfall of girls, which has been estimated by others at half a million. "We see a rising number of girls missing for this reason, but it doesn't stop the other categories," including infanticide, abandonment and selective neglect, Banister said.

Shelley Clark, of Princeton University, presented evidence that sex selection is also widespread in Taiwan. Along with that country's steady eco-nomic development, she said, the average number of children per family has dropped from 5.75 in 1960 to 1.7, mostly as a result of contraceptive use. The ratio of boys to girls is 107 to 100. Clark's analysis of birth-order and family size data indicates that contraceptives are being used to shape the sex ratios in families. Women who already have a couple of sons are likely to start using contraceptives, she and her colleagues found, while those who keep having daughters do not. The result is a peculiar pattern of small, son-heavy families and larger, daughter-heavy ones. The researchers said more highly educated Asian women are less likely to express strong preferences for boys, suggesting there is hope that the trend may eventually decline. But the cultural and economic roots of male preference run deep. Meanwhile, they said, the growing availability of prenatal testing and abortion—long a rallying cry for feminist concerned about reproductive rights in the Third World—may be working against the interests of female children.

Source: Rick Weiss, *Washington Post*. "Research shows bias against girls in Asian countries." Reprinted in *Edmonton Journal*, 14 May 1996: E8.

other across historical time periods, as well as across ethnic and social-class lines within each society (Guttentag and Secord, 1983).

Social practices, such as active or passive infanticide (see Box 9.1), not only significantly alter the ratio of males to females during infancy, but also reverberate over time throughout the entire age structure of a society. While popular culture and folklore often entertain the possibilities of a society of Amazons or Wonder Women who survive capably without the presence of men, except for the necessity of an occasional sperm extraction, no known society has practised male infanticide. Instead, where infanticide has been, and still is, incorporated as part of a culture's traditions, the victims of such practices are almost always females. A possible exception to the more common practice of sex-specific infanticide is the little researched practice of infanticide committed in some cultures upon those born with visible physical disabilities, a practice that does not necessarily discriminate between female and male infants in a purposeful fashion.

As can be seen in Box 9.1, demographers examine and attempt to explain sex-ratio differentials, both within and between different societies over time. To help put the journalistic presentation of Box 9.1 into perspective, and to permit a quick comparison with the Canadian experience, Table 9.1 presents United Nations data on sex ratios by selected age groups for one European and a number of Asian societies. (Unfortunately, data for Taiwan are unavailable from our United Nation sources.) Neither Canada nor Switzerland (an historically neutral country, but the last in the industrial world to grant women even partial rights of franchise) have ever been identified with the practice of female infanticide, while countries such as Bangladesh, China, India, and Pakistan have been known to engage in this practice.

TABLE 9.1 Sex Ratios[1] by Age Groups, Selected Countries

| | Canada | Switzerland | Bangladesh | China | India | Pakistan |
Age Groups	1991	1990	1990	1990	1990	1990
All Ages	97.2	95.5	106.2	106.0	107.0	108.8
0-4	104.8	104.6	105.6	106.6	106.0	105.6
5-9	105.2	104.8	106.6	107.0	107.1	105.9
10-14	105.2	104.3	103.0	106.5	107.7	110.6
15-19	105.3	105.4	103.4	106.1	109.0	111.8
20-24	100.9	101.6	116.4	106.4	109.2	110.9
25-29	99.1	101.8	103.0	107.8	109.5	111.0
30-34	98.7	103.1	93.6	107.9	110.2	111.8
35-39	98.5	102.8	104.5	106.3	110.3	111.8
40-44	99.8	102.8	101.8	109.6	106.6	112.1
45-49	100.9	103.0	113.5	112.4	103.4	106.5
50-54	100.2	99.5	107.7	112.7	102.0	106.4
55-59	98.9	96.3	120.6	109.8	102.4	106.3
60-64	94.6	88.1	106.0	106.0	102.5	99.5
65-69	84.8	80.7	125.2	97.3	101.1	106.3
70-74	77.5	76.7	108.1	87.1	98.8	109.2
75+	60.2	54.9	135.8	67.2	96.2	116.0

[1] Number of males per 100 females

Sources: For Switzerland, Bangladesh, China, India, and Pakistan: United Nations. *The Sex and Age Distribution of the World Populations*. The 1992 Revision. New York: United Nations, 1993: 358, 100, 138, 218, 305.
For Canada: Statistics Canada. 1991 Census of Canada. *Age, Sex and Marital Status. The Nation.* Cat. 93-310. Ottawa: Minister of Industry. 1992. Tables 1 and 3.

Reading down the sex ratio columns in Table 9.1 is akin to journeying through the past of each society. The older the age group, the greater the number of accumulated social and individual experiences such as infanticide, immigration, emigration, wars, epidemic diseases, and other events that sometimes selectively, and sometimes randomly, affect the distribution balance of men and women within a society at a particular point in time. The general pattern observable in Table 9.1, for both Canada and Switzerland, involves a gradual lowering of the sex ratio for each successive five-year age group, from the youngest to the middle-aged. More abrupt and substantial declines begin to appear when men and women reach their mid-fifties and beyond.

The data are markedly different for the four Asian societies. Only China, and to a lesser extent India, parallel the European and Canadian experience among the very oldest age groups, and even then the sex ratios for these older groups are higher. For some Asian societies, the sex-ratio imbalance of earlier historical periods was so great that events which generally and cumulatively contribute to a gradual attrition of men fail to reduce the sex ratio to anything approaching parity. The fact that sex ratio imbalances are now smaller among the youngest age groups suggests that the practice of infanticide may be lessening. However, as indicated in the presentation found in Box 9.1, new medical technologies now play an important part in influencing the sex-ratio imbalance at birth in many of those countries. Renteln (1992) reports that 99.9 percent of the abortions performed in India following amniocentesis are performed when the fetus is found to be female. Henslin and Nelson (1996: 583) note that the use of amniocentesis as part of a sex-selection process led to a public outcry in India only because of an incident in which, following an amniocentesis test, "a physician mistakenly gave the parents wrong information and aborted a *male* baby!" Regardless of whether such practices occur in Asia or Canada, and regardless of the ethnic origins of the practitioners, a rather cruel irony exists whereby a woman is asked, or required, to abort or let die a fetus or infant of her *own* "wrong" sex as defined by cultural beliefs.

While infanticide is prohibited by law in Canada, as we saw in the previous chapter, the same techniques of ultrasound, amniocentesis, and CVS, coupled with the selective use of "menstrual flushing" (an advertising euphemism for abortion) or therapeutic abortion, can easily culminate in female **feticide** in our country. Several new genetic and asexual reproductive technologies carry with them the potential for altering our sex ratios at birth. For example, gene splicing or the artificial insemination of "washed" sperm (using a special solution to separate those sperm bearing X-chromosomes from those bearing Y chromosomes, then collecting and implanting in the fallopian tubes only the sex-preferred sperm) can be used to create sex-specific "designer" embryos.

Great concern was expressed in Canada during the early 1990s as American medical practitioners from, for example, Buffalo, New York, and Blaine, Washington, began selectively advertising in certain ethnic newspapers in southern Ontario and the lower mainland of British Columbia regarding sperm-washing services and other technologies, specifically controversial ultrasound techniques that, supposedly, guaranteed fetal sex-identification by the twelfth to fourteenth week after conception (even though most medical practitioners in Canada contend that ultrasound sex-identification results are not reliable until approximately the thirtieth week). However, all of these same services are currently available from private for-profit health clinics located within our country (Eichler, 1996: 100).

The possible use of various genetic and reproductive technologies to shape a sex-selected family is by no means limited to Canadian couples of Asian or South Asian heritage. The general trend in Canada since the early 1970s has been for married and cohabiting couples to limit their families to one or two children (McVey and Kalbach, 1995: 270). Such a trend is possible only with the availability of birth-control technologies. New reproductive technologies further permit a couple to design their ideal family in terms not only of sex composition (e.g., all boys, all girls, or only one of each), but also sex birth order (e.g., a first-born son, a second-born daughter). While such designer families might be appealing to individual couples for their own personal reasons, the impact of such immediate decisions upon the overall sex ratio, and the longer-term consequences for our society as a whole, has lead to serious discussions about the ethical use of reproductive technologies.

At this text went to press, a government-sponsored bill was about to be placed before Parliament prohibiting the use in Canada of sex-selection technologies for *nonmedical* purposes. The intention of the bill was to deny Canadians access, within our country, to technologies that would enable them to satisfy a purely personal desire to procreate only a son or daughter. The fate of sex-selection for medical reasons, such as to prevent the conception of a fetus likely to possess an inherited life-threatening medical condition, is still unclear. However, the use of selective reproductive techniques for medical purposes will remain contentious with regard to both the eugenics and gender issues involved in these decisions. As our awareness increases of the sex-linked genetic contributions to various diseases (e.g., hemophilia, certain types of muscular dystrophy, and prostrate cancer in males only; breast cancer in men and women; and ovarian cancers in women only), the possibilities of preventing male or female births or conceptions for medical reasons, and whether these are, indeed, purely medical reasons rather than masks for ableism and/or sexism, will remain subjects of considerable debate.

Sex ratios of our entire population have slowly, and somewhat erratically, declined in Canada over the twentieth century from a level of 106 in 1921 to a parity level of 100 in 1971 (Statistics Canada, 1972) to the 1991 level presented in Table 9.1 of 97.2. As of 1996, the sex ratio in Canada had declined further to 96.5 (calculation based on data provided by Statistics Canada, *Daily*, 29 July 1997: 9.)Men currently constitute 49 percent of the total Canadian population. Our declining sex ratio is primarily a consequence of three combined factors. First, with the notable exception of the post-World War II baby boom, our fertility levels have been gradually declining since the middle of the nineteenth century (McVey and Kalbach, 1995). Second, proportionately more men die at all ages than do women (Wilkins, 1996). Third, significantly more women live to older ages than do men. The ratio of surviving men to women in our society declines rapidly among older age groups, as can be seen in the overview of selective age groups since 1931, presented in Table 9.2. We will return to some of the implications of the changing age-specific sex ratios later in this chapter.

Life Expectancy Differentials

The upper-age limits to human longevity were established with the evolution of modern-day humans more than 100 000 years ago. Accordingly, the maximum human **life span** is approximately 120 years (Perlmutter and Hall, 1985: 61). Journalistic reports occasionally surface claiming that individuals, or even entire villages of people living in isolated regions of the world, have exceeded the maximum limit, but scientific investigations inevitably discount these extravagant claims. Examinations of successive editions of the *Guinness Book of Records* reveal that accurately documented and verified holders of the title as the world's oldest living human being have been, and continue to be, women.

	Age Group				
Year	**55+**	**55-64**	**65-74**	**75-84**	**85+**
1921	109	112	109	97	84
1931	111	117	108	100	80
1941	111	117	109	96	80
1951	105	107	108	87	76
1961	98	103	96	93	77
1971	89	97	87	74	66
1981	82	91	83	76	49
1991	82	97	82	66	44

TABLE 9.2 Sex Ratios[1] of Selected Age Groups, Canada, 1921 to 1991[2]

[1] Number of males per 100 females   [2] Excludes Newfoundland prior to 1951

Source: Adapted from Gee, 1995: 78.

Only a very exceptional few ever reach the upper limits of the human life span. Despite our attempts to live according to current fashions of diet, nutrition, and exercise, virtually all of us will fall short of achieving our human potential in this regard. Based upon known mortality rates for males and females at certain ages, and assuming these rates will remain constant in the future (i.e., no major catastrophes occur or miracle cures for high-incidence life-threatening illnesses or diseases are found), average **life expectancies** can be estimated for individuals as they attain specified ages. As we noted in Chapter 3, life in pre-Confederation Canada was nasty, brutish, and short, with early European pioneers living an average of approximately 30 to 35 years (Lavoie and Oderkirk, 1993: 3), a marked improvement over early Roman times, almost two thousand years earlier, when the average citizen lived only 22 years (Perlmutter and Hall, 1985: 6). Women and men born in Canada during the twentieth century have benefited significantly from our rapidly improving conditions of life, to the point where average life expectancies are now at least three and a half times greater than those of early Romans, and at least double those for Canadians born only 200 years earlier.

Table 9.3 illustrates increases in life expectancy for both men and women born in Canada during the twentieth century. Before directing your attention to specific gender-related issues, a few general comments about the table are required. Each of the columns in the table indicate the number of additional years an individual can be expected to live upon achieving an identified age, once again assuming that existing death rates will remain constant. Up to a point, the longer a person lives, the longer that person can be expected to live. If a person survives the hazards to life associated with a specific portion of their lifetime during an historical period, their chances of living longer increase. As you read the table from left to right, you can examine the increases in life expectancy made possible as individuals achieve certain specified milestone older ages.

TABLE 9.3 Life Expectancy by Age and Sex, Canada, Selected Years: 1926–1991

Year	at birth		1 year		20 years		40 years		60 years	
	m	f	m	f	m	f	m	f	m	f
1926	56.9	58.9	63.1	63.7	48.5	48.7	31.5	32.3	15.8	16.5
1941	63.0	66.3	66.1	68.7	49.6	51.8	31.9	34.0	16.1	17.6
1951	66.3	70.8	68.3	72.3	50.8	54.4	32.5	35.6	16.5	18.6
1961	68.4	74.2	69.5	75.0	51.5	56.7	33.0	37.5	16.7	19.9
1971	69.3	76.4	69.8	76.6	51.7	58.2	33.2	39.0	17.0	21.4
1976	70.2	77.5	70.2	77.4	52.1	59.0	33.6	39.7	17.2	22.0
1981	71.9	79.0	71.7	78.7	53.4	60.1	34.7	40.7	18.0	22.9
1986	73.0	79.7	72.7	79.3	54.3	60.7	35.5	41.2	18.4	23.2
1991	74.6	80.9	74.1	80.4	55.6	61.7	36.8	42.2	19.4	24.0

Sources: 1926–1986: Adapted from McVey and Kalbach, 1995: 202.1991: Statistics Canada. *Life Tables, Canada and Provinces, 1990–1992.* Cat. 84-537. 1992: 2–5.

This general principle is easily illustrated by comparing the column presenting life expectancies at birth, with that of expectancies at one year. Particularly during the early part of this century, surviving the first year of life posed a major obstacle for infants in Canada (King et al., 1991). Males and females born in 1926 could be expected to live about 57 and 59 years respectively. However, should they be able to endure to the first anniversary of their birth, in an historical period of high infant mortality, males could then be expected to live an additional 63.1 years for a total of approximately 64 years. Females, upon reaching their first birthday, could be expected to live for an additional 63.7 years for a total of between 64 and 65 years. Surviving that first year increased the life expectancy of Canadians another five or six years.

Increases in life expectancy over the course of the present century can be observed by reading down any specific column. Significant improvements in diet, nutrition, and sanitation, as well as new medical technologies and greater availability of healthcare-delivery systems have all lead to noticeable increases in life expectancy at birth, between 1926 and 1991, of approximately 17.5 and 22 years, respectively, for men and women. The first year of life is not as hazardous as it once was, even though the death rate for infants is still relatively high (King et al., 1991; Wilkins, 1996), especially in comparison to those of the Scandinavian countries. Those born in Canada in 1991 who survive that first year now increase their life expectancy by only half a year approximately. Generally, the greatest advances this century in improving our quantity of life have reduced the likelihood of mortality over the first 45 years, more so than the later years, of the life span (McVey and Kalbach, 1995: 91). Consequently, you can observe that increases in life expectancy are not as dramatic as you read down the columns towards the right side of the table.

While perusing Table 9.3, you might want to pencil in (near the bottom left hand corner), additional information for the first column to indicate that life expectancy at birth for Canadians born in 1996 is now 75.7 years for men and 81.4 years for women (Statistics Canada, *Daily*, April 16, 1998: 2). As life expectancies for specific older ages as of 1996, unfortunately, were not available as this text went to press, we can note only that men have now added an increase of 18.8 years since 1926 to their at-birth life expectancy, while women have added 22.5 years to theirs. You should be able to locate the row indicating the historical time period most closely associated with your own year of birth, and the column closest to your current age, or the rows and columns for your parents, and possibly even your grandparents. You can observe the life expectancies for yourself and for other significant individuals in your environment. You might wish to photo-reduce and laminate a copy of this table for insertion into your wallet, pocketbook, or backpack for handy reference during those times when you meet a potential "life-long partner" and you want to ascertain quickly just how long that life might last. Just bear in mind that life expectancy figures are conditional probabilities, not lifetime guarantees.

As can be seen in Table 9.3, the gender *life expectancy gap* first increased and then decreased over the twentieth century in Canada. Science has not advanced sufficiently to enable us to determine precisely how much of the gender gap is due to genetic factors and how much is due to social factors. The difference in life expectancy between men and women born during 1926 was two years. Since the basic genetic factors of biological sex have not changed between 1926 and 1996, differences in the life expectancy gap over these 70 years must be attributed mainly to changes in social gender-related factors. Reading down the first column, you can observe that the gap in life expectancy increases until 1976 where the difference is 7.3 years. While both men and women gained extensions of their life expectancy since 1926, women attained a little more than five more probable years than did men. Major factors contributing to women's increased gains over this time period were the significant reductions in health hazards associated with pregnancy, childbearing, and childbirth (Gee, 1984: 12). Following 1976, the gap has narrowed somewhat, so that women born in 1996 can expect to live an additional 5.7 years beyond that of men born in the same year (Statistics Canada, *Daily*, 16 April 1998: 2). Reasons for the declining life expectancy gap will be addressed shortly.

The lack of equal life-expectancy gains for men has generally been attributed to the fact that, within economically developed countries, such as Canada and the United States, proportionally more men are likely to die at all ages than are women. This fact would appear to be attributable to a more hazardous lifestyle (deathstyle?) associated with masculinity in our society. Former radical profeminist, and now leading men's rights activist, Warren Farrell (1993, 1986) laments that this fact of life, or death, has become so acceptable as to marginalize men now as the "disposable" sex. He questions our society's priorities and commitment to equality by pondering what would happen if "we cared as much about saving males as saving whales" (Farrell, 1993: 229). Following a tradition established by earlier analysts (e.g., Goldberg, 1976), Farrell (1993) explores the stresses of masculinity, the unhealthy and unsafe hazards of many male-dominated occupations and work settings, including the military, the causes and consequences of men's greater likelihood of becoming victims of violence, and how precepts of masculinity frequently precipitate suicide. Many leading causes of mortality, such as motor-vehicle accidents, suicide, lung and other smoking-related cancers, and HIV/AIDS account for significantly more deaths among men than among women in Canada.

However, while Farrell offers some useful insights, the facts of life and death for men are not all grim. Between 1976 and 1996, men's gain in life expectancy at birth (5.5 years) was greater than the gain for women (3.9 years). The more recent decrease in the life-expectancy gap appears to be attributable to a growing equality of the lifestyles of women and men, with a greater increase of health among males and a slight increase of ill-health among females. This ill-health appears to be a consequence of women increasing their participation in life-threatening activities (including formerly male-dominated occupations) and using coping mechanisms for stress, such as alcohol and tobacco, that can become self-defeating over time (Gee, 1984). Regardless of specific causes, if the two-year gap between men and women born in 1926 reflects a not yet fully understood female biological advantage associated with possessing an extra X chromosome, it is unlikely that we will be able to observe gender equality in the graveyard until, or unless, we arrive at an ethical and practical level of genetic engineering. Currently, solutions to the problem of gender inequality in life expectancy must be sought in the realm of contributing social factors.

Canada is one of 16 nations, out of 30 examined, to have a similar pattern of changes in gender life expectancies between 1970, 1980, and 1990 (Travato and Lalu, 1996). These 16 highly industrialized countries, located in Northern and Western Europe and the "Anglo-Saxon overseas" societies of Australia, Canada, New Zealand, and the United States, all have increasing life expectancies for both men and women between 1970 and 1990, an increasing gender life-expectancy gap between 1970 and 1980, and a decreasing gender life-expectancy gap between 1980 and 1990. Another group of seven Western European countries demonstrate a continuous increase in the gender life-expectancy gap into 1990, but the magnitude of the gap slows down between 1980 and 1990. A third group of Eastern European nations, as well as Greece, Spain, and Japan demonstrate an unabated increase in the gender gap between 1970 and 1990, with men in many of these countries actually undergoing a decrease in life expectancy, and women expected to live even longer. Travato and Lalu (1996: 119) predict that nations in the second group will soon demonstrate a pattern similar to that found for the nations in group one, which includes Canada, of a gradual decrease in the gender life-expectancy gap.

Further examination of the group of 16 highly industrialized nations, including Canada, for changing patterns of the leading causes of death between 1970 and 1990 (Travato and Lalu, 1996) reveals that male rates for heart disease have been decreasing faster than female rates, and so have male rates of death due to accidents and violence, excluding suicide. As a consequence of these two factors, expectations for male life expectancy have risen proportionally more than have expectations for females, and the gap between the two has narrowed. Also contributing to a narrowing of the gap are the facts that female lung-cancer rates are increasing, while male rates are either decreasing or remaining stable, and that rates for breast cancer among women are increasing at a faster rate than are rates for prostate cancer in men (Travato and Lalu, 1996). The findings of Travato and Lalu focus upon the changing impact of leading causes of death among all 16 countries. We turn now to an examination of the leading causes of death for men and women of all ages, for one single year in Canada.

Gender Mortality Differentials

Of the 204 912 deaths occurring in Canada in 1993, males accounted for 109 407 and females accounted for 95 505 (Wilkins, 1996: 12). Table 9.4 presents the leading causes of death in Canada for males and females, by age, in 1993. We first need to clarify the meanings of some of the terms used in the table before examining the findings themselves. Registries of vital statistics across Canada enter on each person's death certificate all identified causes contributing to their death. Following classification rules established by the World Health Organization, "a single underlying cause of death is then selected for each decedent" (Wilkins, 1996: 12). Even though this information is no longer made available on public death certificates, the information is gathered from all the provincial and territorial registries by the federal government. For purposes of reporting the collected information, Statistics Canada notes the specific cause and then groups these specific causes into larger broad cause categories (e.g., lung cancer and prostate cancer into a general "cancer" category). These broader cause categories are then differentiated into external or nonexternal causes. "*External* causes include events such as suicide, poisoning, and motor vehicle and other types of accidents. *Nonexternal* causes of death, in contrast, arise from natural physiological processes" (Wilkins, 1996: 12, emphasis added).

These causes are presented in Table 9.4 as a rate of incidence per 100 000 population, enabling you to compare the relative contributions of each cause to the deaths of Canadian men and women of various ages in 1993. As you can see, the order of leading causes is remarkably similar for almost every age grouping, but the rates themselves are usually significantly different. These rate differentials reflect the fact that, with the exception of certain causes that tend to be more sex-specific (e.g., breast cancer), a higher proportion of men die of each cause than do women, across all ages. Generally, the leading causes of death for men and women are noticeably different during the early to middle adult years of 20 to 44, and noticeably similar for all younger and all older ages (Wilkins, 1996: 11).

Almost three-quarters (72 percent) of infant deaths in Canada in 1993 are due either to causes associated with premature births, or to congenital birth anomalies, such as structural heart defects (percentage figures not shown in Table 9.4 are all from Wilkins, 1996). The leading single specific cause of death among both boys and girls aged one to nine, namely motor-vehicle accidents, is presumably the consequence of the actions of their parents and other adults. Still, within this age group, nonexternal causes account for a greater proportion of all deaths for both sexes. Among boys aged 10 to 14, we find that external events for the first time become a proportionally greater cause of death, perhaps due to a noticeable increase in the contribution of motor-vehicle accidents.

Of all age groups presented in the table, it is only among 15- to 19-year-olds that we find that rates for external causes are higher than rates for nonexternal causes for both boys and girls. Motor-vehicle accidents are not only the highest leading single cause for both sexes, although the rates are noticeably higher for young men than for young women, but the rates for this external cause are higher here than for any other age grouping in the table. Bear in mind that these rates are based upon their incidence of occurrence among the total population within that age range. If we limit our attention to only those who died, we find that motor vehicle accidents account for almost the same proportion of deaths (40 percent of male and 42 percent of female) among 15- to 19-year-olds (Wilkins, 1996: 13). Suicide accounts for a much higher proportion (23 percent) of male deaths than of female (13 percent) deaths in this age range. Suicide rates are noticeably higher for males in all age ranges where their numbers are sufficiently high enough to register as a leading cause of death. The frequency of suicide for men tends to be highest between the ages of 15 to 44 years, and highest for women between 25 and 55 years of age (McVey and Kalbach, 1995: 205). While women are more likely to attempt suicide, men are more likely to achieve a "successful" outcome.

TABLE 9.4 Leading Causes of Death in Canada, 1993

	Deaths per 100 000	
	Males	**Females**
Age under 1 – All causes	685.0	557.4
Perinatal mortality	302.5	227.9
Obstetric complications	66.1	54.2
Other respiratory conditions	54.6	42.2
Congenital anomalies	188.8	172.1
Anomalies of circulatory system	75.0	55.8
Sudden infant death syndrome	70.0	65.2
Age 1 to 9 - All causes	26.1	19.9
External causes	10.9	7.7
Motor vehicle accidents	3.8	3.5
Drowning	2.5	-
Non-external causes	15.2	12.2
Cancer	3.6	2.8
Congenital anomalies	3.4	2.1
Age 10 to 14 - All causes	21.8	15.3
External causes	11.8	6.9
Motor vehicle accidents	6.0	2.9
Suicide	2.6	1.9
Non-external causes	10.0	8.4
Cancer	3.1	2.8
Age 15 to 19 - All causes	84.5	36.4
External causes	66.7	24.7
Motor vehicle accidents	33.5	15.1
Suicide	19.4	4.6
Non-external causes	17.8	11.7
Cancer	5.4	3.7
Age 20 to 44 - All causes	151.2	67.2
Non-external causes	76.6	46.1
HIV	18.0	-
Cancer	17.5	23.8
Breast cancer	-	7.3
Lung cancer	-	3.0
External causes	74.5	21.2
Suicide	28.2	6.5
Motor vehicle accidents	20.8	7.7

TABLE 9.4 Contined

	Deaths per 100 000	
	Males	**Females**
Age 45 to 64 - All causes	735.9	424.7
Non-external causes	671.1	400.6
Cancer	272.9	225.6
Lung cancer	101.9	55.5
Colorectal cancer	28.8	-
Breast cancer	-	53.5
Diseases of the circulatory system	248.2	89.2
Ischaemic heart disease	177.1	47.9
External causes	64.8	24.1
Suicide	26.2	7.9
Motor vehicle accidents	14.6	6.9
Age 65 and over - All causes	5333.9	3934.0
Non-external causes	5199.7	3838.9
Diseases of the circulatory system	2260.9	1799.5
Ischaemic heart disease	1360.1	924.3
Stroke	389.2	419.2
Cancer	1497.3	896.9
Lung cancer	482.3	169.7
Prostate cancer	231.1	-
Breast cancer	-	
Respiratory diseases	624.9	142.2
Pneumonia and influenzia	-	179.8
External causes	134.2	95.0
Falls	56.0	58.8
Suicide	24.4	-
Motor vehicle accidents	-	12.0

Source: Adapted from Wilkins, 1996: 15.

Beginning with the adult age group of 20- to 44-year-olds onwards, the leading causes of death for both women and men in Canada are, once again, those classified as nonexternal. According to the data presented in Table 9.4, cancer is the leading broad cause of death for women in the 20 to 44 age group, but only the fourth leading broad cause for men. Cancer is three to four times more likely to be a leading cause of death among women of this age. In contrast, suicide is the leading broad cause for men, followed by motor-vehicle accidents and then HIV/AIDS, a broad cause that did not register among the leading causes for women in that year. In 1993, "HIV/AIDS caused 1,077 deaths among men aged 20 to 44, compared with only 68 among women that age (1 death per 100,000 women)" (Wilkins,

1996: 13). It is possible that the knowledge they had acquired HIV or AIDS may have been one of the significant contributors to the high incidence of suicide among men in this age group, although no empirical data are available to support this assertion.

The leading causes of death once again converge among the older age groups. Cancer and circulatory diseases combined account for 71 percent of male deaths and 74 percent of female deaths in 1993 among the 45- to 64-year-old group, and 70 percent of male deaths and 69 percent of female deaths among those aged 65 and over (Wilkins, 1996: 13–14). While cancer is the leading broad cause for both men and women aged 45 to 64, circulatory diseases of the heart and the cerebrovascular system (strokes) become the leading broad causes over the age of 65. The predominance of these causes is attributable mainly to the fact that our bodies simply degenerate, or wear out, over time. External causes account for only a very small proportion (3 percent among men and 2 percent among women) of all deaths of senior citizens in Canada (Wilkins, 1996: 14), even though the actual rates of these events are noticeably higher here than among much younger age groups. Generalizations about this last age category are limited by the fact that it spans a much wider age range than any of the younger categories.

A comparison of death rates by age from 1950 to 1993, standardized to take variations of the age composition of our population into account, reveals that, while overall rates have noticeably declined in Canada for both sexes, the drop has been more dramatic for women (51 percent) than for men (35 percent) (Wilkins, 1996: 14). Once consequence of these changes is reflected in the overall greater increase in life expectancy for women than for men over this time period, as we saw in Table 9.3. Comparisons of changes in the rates for circulatory diseases, cancer, respiratory diseases, and external causes, the four leading causes of death, provided by Wilkins (1996) offer some insights into changes in the life-expectancy differential between women and men.

The largest single contributor to the decline in overall death rates since the 1950s has been the decline in deaths due to circulatory diseases. The gender gap in death rates due to circulatory diseases increased noticeably between 1950 and the mid-1970s, when the rates fell steadily for women, but only very gradually for men. Since that time, the rates for men have declined more sharply, thus narrowing, but not eliminating, the gap. Death rates due to cancer, particularly lung cancer, increased sharply for men between 1950 and 1988, largely as a consequence of their increases in smoking in earlier decades (Villeneuve and Morrison, 1995), and then declined slightly by 1993. In contrast, overall female cancer death rates declined between 1950 and the mid-1970s (despite a rapid increase in lung cancer rates), then rose slightly and have been fairly constant throughout the 1980s and early 1990s. Breast cancer death rates among women have remained essentially constant from 1950 through 1993. The same general pattern occurs for the deaths of men and women due to respiratory diseases, with the largest gap appearing in the mid-1970s, followed by a slight narrowing by the early 1990s.

Between 1993 and 1996, adjusted rates for men of all ages demonstrate further declines in mortality from the major causes of death, particularly lung, prostate, and colorectal cancers; heart and cerebrovascular disease; accidents; suicides; and HIV infection (Statistics Canada, *Daily*, 16 April 1998: 2). While women also experienced declines in mortality due to heart and cerebrovascular disease and accidents, mortality rates due to suicide and to lung cancer increased. Lung cancer has now become the most lethal form of cancer for women since 1993 (Statistics Canada, *Daily*, 16 April 1998: 2). This overall pattern of declining mortality rates for males from the major causes, but increases in mortality rates for females from certain causes that outnumber declines in mortality from other causes (thus contributing to an overall increase in female mortality), further contributes to a gradual overall narrowing of the gender life-expectancy gap.

Morbidity Differentials

Morbidity relates to disease, sickness, and disability (McVey and Kalbach, 1995: 180). Morbidity data come from two sources: subjective self-reports provided by respondents to surveys, and "objective" incidence data reported by health agencies. The National Population Health Survey began in Canada in 1994 and will collect self-reported data every two years for the next two decades, from the same panel of more than 26 000 individuals aged 15 and over, drawn from all provinces, to establish a profile of health and health-related issues for Canadians. Preliminary analysis of data collected from the first panel survey during 1994 and 1995 (Millar and Beaudet, 1996) reveals some gender differences along a variety of dimensions that have implications for disease, sickness, disability, and gender itself.

Self-reported health is positively associated in our country with social class as measured by household income. Defining their health as either excellent or very good are approximately 75 percent of women and men from the highest-income households, 68 percent from upper-middle, 56 percent from lower-middle, and 51 percent of men and women from the lowest-income households. Men are only slightly more likely than are women to report their health as being excellent or very good, with a range of gender differences in responses varying across the four household-income categories, from 1 to 4 percent (Millar and Beaudet, 1996: 25).

According to the initial Health Survey, women are more likely than men to report experiencing chronic health problems associated with allergies, back ailments, arthritis and rheumatism, and high blood pressure, and to report experiencing a multiplicity of chronic conditions at one time (Millar and Beaudet, 1996: 25). Although the proportions reporting a major episode of clinically diagnosed depression is small overall, women outnumber men by a ratio of two to one (8 versus 4 percent, respectively; unless stated otherwise, all statistics come from Millar and Beaudet, 1996). More women than men (83 percent compared to 71 percent, respectively) had taken at least one prescription or over-the-counter drug in the month prior to completing the Health Survey. Women also consumed more legal drugs (an average of 1.9 versus 1.3 drug doses per month) than did men. Excluding birth control and menopause-related medications, the monthly intake rates for women still exceed that for men (1.7 versus 1.3). Our knowledge of the extent of greater experienced physical-health problems among women than among men is due, at least partially, to the fact that women are more likely to report having consulted a physician than are men (83 percent versus 72 percent, respectively). Findings from the Health Survey indicate no noticeable gender differences in reported contacts with dentists, physiotherapists, occupational therapists, or psychologists.

Some of the greater contact with physicians demonstrated by women can be attributed to visits associated with pregnancy and to a growing responsiveness to increasingly widespread campaigns exhorting women beyond the age of 40 to seek regular examinations for early detection of various forms of cancer, in particular breast cancer (while the detected incidence of breast cancer among women has increased approximately 11 percent since the mid-1980s, mortality rates due to breast cancer have declined an equal amount according to the

National Cancer Institute of Canada and the Canadian Cancer Society [*Globe and Mail*, 8 April 1998: A6]). "Approximately one woman in nine can expect to develop breast cancer during her lifetime; about one in 25 will die of it" (Gaudette et al., 1998: 19). Contributing to the early detection rate is the fact that mothers are more likely than fathers to be responsible for scheduling children's visits to doctors and, as a consequence, are more likely to include themselves in a yearly round of consultations with their own physicians.

Despite impressionistic evidence suggesting that many men fully embrace a "sick" role (one of the few times they can acknowledge vulnerability and dependency) for minor ailments when they can actively bid for pampering from their own "Dr. Wife" at home, the lesser number of physician contacts reported by men appears to be attributable largely to the strength of masculinity stereotypes in our society requiring toughness and stoicism when confronting sickness and illness. "Toughing it out" in the face of seemingly minor aches and pains leads men to be less likely to seek out professional medical help and, as a consequence, also be less likely to receive early diagnosis of, and treatment for, serious maladies (for example, despite wide availability of detection tests and successful treatment regimens, an estimated 16 100 new cases of prostate cancer will be detected in 1998, leading eventually to 4300 male deaths [*Globe and Mail*, 8 April 1998: A6]).

While more men (33 percent) than women (29 percent) overall smoke cigarettes, the finding that slightly more women between the ages of 15 and 19 smoke than do men of the same age (30 percent versus 28 percent respectively) continues to worry health professionals concerned about increasing rates of lung cancer occurring among older adult women, as well as worsening problems with asthma and other problems stemming from debilitating coughing and wheezing found in both adult women and men. Whereas the Health Survey finds a slight gender difference in smoking incidence among late adolescents, the 1994 Youth Smoking Survey in Canada finds no gender differences in the proportions of young Canadians between the ages of 10 and 19 who smoke (about 15 percent), but has found gender differences in typical cigarette usage, with young men being heavier smokers, consuming more cigarettes per day on average (Clark, 1996: 3).

Canada's Alcohol and Other Drugs Survey, conducted in 1994, finds that more than 40 percent of 15- to 19-year-old smokers also engage in heavy drinking, and 28 percent also use marijuana or hashish at least once a month (Clark, 1996: 6). Using a rather weak measure, namely consuming alcoholic beverages at least once a month, the initial Health Survey finds that men (69 percent) are more likely than women (47 percent) to be drinkers. Drinking behaviour is monitored in surveys as a possible means of predicting future incidences of alcoholism (more prevalent in men than in women), liver disease, fetal alcohol syndrome, depression, diabetes, and other alcohol-related problems. The peak age of drinkers for men is 25–29 (79 percent), while women have two peak ages: 20 to 24, and 35 to 44 (both at 54 percent). The first peak for women may be attributable, in part, to women associating with men a few years older than themselves, and the valley between the two peaks for women may be associated with abstaining from drinking between ages 25 to 34, which are prime periods for childbearing among women in our society. We leave you to speculate on whether having primary responsibility for childrearing, housework, and marriage management drives women in the second peak-age group to drink.

Men are more likely than women (25 percent compared with 20 percent) to be classified by researchers using a Body Mass Index as being overweight (Millar and Beaudet, 1996). Please note that this finding is not based upon self-perceptions. Keeping in mind that only respondents aged 15 and over were surveyed, women in general, and young women in particular, are more likely to be classified as underweight. Among those aged 20 to 24, 25 percent of women, but only nine percent of men, are classified by the Health Survey as being underweight. The greater incidence of underweight women compared to men appears to offer further testimony that our thin, or at least slender, standard of physical attractiveness is directed more at females than at males. Findings that the likelihood of being overweight increases with age for both men and women also appear to offer a contributing cause for concerns, voiced by both men and women in later years, about "growing invisible" and feeling an increasing need to adopt various measures to bring themselves back in line with our limited social standards for physical attractiveness.

Dementia, characterized by "severe losses of cognitive and emotional abilities" (Burke et al., 1997: 24) that eventually interfere with a person's ability to function in daily life, is significantly more common in elderly women than in elderly men. Of those Canadians classified as having dementia in 1991, 68 percent were women (Burke et al., 1997: 25). Early reports suggested that Alzheimer's disease (a specific and most prevalent form of dementia) affected twice as many women as men (Spar, 1982 in Gee and Kimball, 1987: 44). However, more careful and refined subsequent analyses indicate that, while nearly twice as many women die as a consequence of Alzheimer's, the actual incidence of this disease occurs only slightly more frequently in women than in men (Dumas and Bélanger, 1997: 50). The imbalance in death rates is largely a function of women's greater longevity, and the fact that Alzheimer's tends to become more prevalent among older populations, and is not due to a significant imbalance in the prevalence of the condition itself. In contrast, osteoporosis, a loss of bone mass that weakens bones and contributes significantly to skeletal shrinking, curvature of the spine associated with aging (leading to both a "hunchback" appearance and shrinking height), and to broken limbs, vertebrae and either fractured hip joints or upper thigh bones, is a condition almost exclusively found among women, particularly older women. Osteoporosis (Gee and Kimball, 1987: 44–46) has been linked to inadequate weight-bearing physical exercise among women when they were younger, a dietary loss of calcium among women of all ages, and reduced estrogen production among older women following menopause.

Overall, available data (and we have been selective and limited in our presentation above) indicate that adult women have higher rates of most forms of morbidity than do adult men in our society (with the exception of sex-specific forms), a pattern consistently found in previous decades in Canadian and American research. A number of hypotheses have been offered as possible explanations for gender morbidity differentials. Each hypothesis has supporters and critics and none has yet emerged as *the* most compelling, suggesting that the issue of morbidity itself is highly complex. The **social acceptability** hypothesis (Gee and Kimball, 1987: 34) contends that, as a consequence of gender socialization and existing gender expectations, both of which provide greater social permission, women are more likely to report experiencing symptoms of illness and disease and are more likely to act upon these experiences by seeking medical help early. In contrast, as suggested earlier, men are socialized to deny, both to themselves and to others, including members of the health professions, early symptoms of illness and disease, and only seek out professional help when their symptoms are impossible to ignore. Women, consequently, receive earlier and more treatment, thus figuring more prominently in health statistics, while men receive later and possibly less treatment. The social acceptability hypothesis may contribute to an understanding of why men have lower rates of morbidity, but higher rates of mortality. Some portion of men's mortality statistics may be a consequence of not seeking treatment until it is too late. Early detection and treatment may increase women's morbidity, but decrease, or at least delay, their eventual mortality.

The **role compatibility** hypothesis (Gee and Kimball, 1987: 34) suggests that, because women's roles are less demanding than are men's, women can more easily find more time both to be "sick" and to seek out treatment. The least compelling of the four hypotheses, this hypothesis was based initially upon an old sexist assumption that nonemployed women do not really "work," and, therefore, have more free time during an average day or week than do men. However, as we saw in an earlier section on housework, time-budget research indicates that nonemployed women labour as many, if not more, hours per day and week than do employed men. The somewhat related **fixed role obligations** hypothesis (Gee and Kimball, 1987: 34) argues that women are more likely to have role obligations that are not locked into a fixed timetable, but rather are more flexible and can be rescheduled thus allowing women the "luxury" of being sick and acting out a sick role such as confining themselves to bed for a longer period of time, or significantly reducing their performance of selected roles. Men, in contrast, supposedly experience greater time constraints, especially in relation to employment and, therefore, have less freedom to define themselves as "sick" or to engage in sick-role behaviour.

Some support for these two hypotheses, combined into one, can be found from an earlier Canada Health Survey (Gee and Kimball, 1987: 37–38) indicating that employed women are "healthier" than homemakers as measured by fewer reported health problems, fewer days spent in bed annually, fewer days when they are disabled and unable to perform their duties, fewer visits to a physician within a year, and a lower percentage using three or more prescription and nonprescription medicines, pills, or ointments in a specified time period. However, as noted by Gee and Kimball (1987: 39), available data, for the most part, are unable to determine whether employment selects or attracts healthier women to venture out of the homemaker role, or whether employment, with its attendant benefits of income and social support, bestows greater health. You might recall from Chapter 6 that women typically experience higher absenteeism rates from employment, using up more "sick" days, than do men. Gender differences in absenteeism are more likely an indicator of greater family responsibilities among women and less likely to provide indications of actual health differences.

All three of the hypotheses mentioned thus far suggest in one way or another that women's higher morbidity is more a function of other, related factors and not a true indication of health or lack thereof. All suggest, in one way or another, that higher morbidity statistics for women are mainly a function of opportunity. A fourth, **nurturant** hypothesis (Gee and Kimball, 1987: 34), suggests that stresses and strains associated with performing a role nurturing or caring for others, in both familial and nonfamilial contexts, contributes to greater ill-health among women, literally making them sick (e.g. see Bernard, 1973, for effects of the nurturing role in marriage upon women). This hypothesis argues that women actually suffer more ill-health than do men as a consequence of at least one role women are socially expected to, and are more likely to, perform within our present gender system.

Gee and Kimball (1987: 38–40) suggest that further light might be shed on these hypotheses and morbidity differences themselves by focusing research in new directions. Since no one hypothesis can account for all of the differences in both reported and actual health differences, it may be that certain hypotheses are better suited as explanations for differences in more limited areas of, for example, physician visits only. As well, the role of physical and mental-health professionals vis-à-vis women and men still needs to be explored in more depth. The finding, from the initial National Population Health Survey of 1994–1995 (noted above), that women take more legal and prescription drugs than do men, may be a consequence of the medical profession's greater predisposition to prescribe medicines to women than to frequency of visits and available time, severity of symptoms, or nature of role obligations (see Armstrong, 1995: 298–299 for supportive evidence). The same explanation may hold true for clinical diagnoses of depression. Finally, drug prescription or ailment diagnoses may separately or additionally be more a function of women's clearer ability to express and communicate experienced symptoms than a consequence of the nature of the symptoms themselves or medical professionals' predispositions towards different genders.

ADULT DEVELOPMENT

A largely unexplored consequence of the noticeable increases in life expectancy this century for both women and men is the effect such increases have upon individual development during adulthood and old age. We noted in Chapter 4 that women and men in our society are expected, by their late teens or early twenties, to have decided what they want to do and be when they "grow up." This social requirement of making early decisions regarding the rest of one's life developed during a period in our history when lives were comparatively short. Social expectations have not kept in pace with the scientific, medical, and technological advances prolonging our longevity. Asking someone during the 1800s to make plans during the teen years for the remaining 20 or 30 years is quite different from asking a teenager in the 1990s to make lasting plans for the next 50 or 60 years of their adult life.

The current adult population of Canada began planning their lives somewhere between the early 1920s and the late 1980s. Most could not realistically anticipate the form and content of their lives beyond the early adulthood years. Many middle-aged and older Canadians found themselves living in an unanticipated future, and confronted the necessity or freedom of reinventing themselves by making new life plans. Research now indicates that change is a dominant characteristic of adulthood and old age, recently more so among women than men.

Adulthood, arbitrarily defined chronologically as spanning the years from 18 to 65, had been relatively neglected from a developmental research perspective until the late 1960s for two major reasons. First, the prevalence of an oversimplified model of biological development stressing the existence of only three major phases in human development—growth, stability, and decline—contributed to a belief that not much of developmental significance occurred during adulthood. "An adult…is an individual who has *completed his [sic] growth*" (Hurlock, 1968 in Troll, 1975: 1; emphasis added). Second, influenced by Freud's psychoanalytic theory, many psychologists blithely asserted that basic human personality structures were established firmly by the age of five. Since these personality traits were presumed to be highly resistant to change, any apparent modifications observable during "normal" adulthood were believed to be superficial and of no significant consequence. A leading textbook on child development and personality stated, as a fundamental matter of fact, that much of the normal adult's predominant personality characteristics and behavior patterns can be traced to factors in his [*sic*] earlier life....All these characteristics are the outcome of...the intimate experiences of his [*sic*] childhood....Most sophisticated people take it for granted that the events of early childhood affect the individual's later social and psychological adjustment. (Mussen et al., 1969: 6)

However, "sophisticated people" in the fields of study known as **life span** (in psychology) or **life course** (in sociology) **development** now challenge the veracity of previously held simplistic beliefs about adulthood. In general, our current understandings of adulthood, particularly from the ages of 18 to the mid-forties or early-fifties, are more descriptive than explanatory. One of the crucial issues confronting developmental theory concerns whether chronological age is **intrinsic** (deterministic) or **extrinsic** (arbitrarily associated) to human development (Looft, 1973). In keeping with our largely social-constructionist position in this text, we offer age markers in the following sections for illustrative purposes only. We must also note the presence of an implicit heterosexist bias in the existing literature (Allen and Demo, 1995: 121). With the exception of recent research on the lesbian "family cycle" (Slater, 1995), which does not focus directly upon lesbian adult development per se, studies of the life course rarely examine the lives of gay men and lesbians from an adult developmental perspective.

Adulthood is now viewed as comprising a number (varying according to the age span under examination) of sequential stages of development. Periods of instability, transition, or passages (numerous terms have been used), are interspersed between, and interrelated in a dialectical fashion with, periods of stability or relative tranquility. Although the content of each stage varies, the processes underlying movement from one to the next appear to be quite similar. During a transition stage, certain life decisions are made by individuals, and commitments are forged to future courses of action. Available resources such as time, energy, and personal qualities are shaped to fit the commitments which are then lived out in the ensuing stage. Towards the end of each stability stage, the presence of some dissatisfactions and the absence of certain satisfactions prompt individuals to assess both the external and internal dimensions of their lives. This assessment leads to, and becomes part of, the next transition stage during which future commitments are made (either in the form of rededication to previous lines of action or the creation of commitments to new lines of action), which lead to the next stage of stability and the process continues.

Before turning to some of the more intriguing gender-related findings, we must note that most existing studies utilize a **cross-sectional** research design, where a number of sub-samples comprising respondents of different ages are studied at one point in time. Researchers then compare these respondents along several measured dimensions and attempt to identify changes associated with the passage of time. Since researchers often lack objective information and must rely upon subjects' subjective memory recall of their younger lives, it is difficult to determine sometimes if older respondents were, indeed, once similar to younger respondents and, therefore, if reported differences are associated with aging and not with having lived in somewhat different historical time periods. Very few studies utilize a **longitudinal** design, where one sample of respondents is repeatedly measured at different periods over time. Regardless of the underlying causes of reported differences, findings from this growing body of studies provide further insights into the lives of adult men and women in our society.

Young Adulthood

Men

We consider men first, since research findings are highly consistent and male patterns of development are comparatively simple. Perhaps not surprisingly, male adult development in general has been found to be linked closely with occupational development. Reflecting commitments formed during late adolescence (see Chapter 4), when occupation began to form the central component of future masculinity, the most significant events shaping men's lives from early adulthood through to their middle years, are those pertaining to the progress of their paid-work careers. The timing and nature of periods of stability and change in men's lives are found to be most strongly influenced by what does, or does not, occur on the job front.

A number of researchers have noted the existence among men of what has been referred to as the "Dream" (Levinson et al., 1978: 91–97), the "career clock" (Kimmel 1980: 303), or the "work clock" (Newman and Newman, 1975: 317). The Dream is a more general concept that encompasses a set of images of what one's adult life will be like in the future. Included in the Dream are anticipations of an intimate relationship, perhaps children, a desired type of living accommodations, a general lifestyle, and ownership of various material possessions. However, a component central to men's Dreams is their career or work "clock." The clock includes not only an image of obtaining employment in a particular kind of job but, more important, also contains a picture of progress over time towards achieving a specific job or occupational goal, such as owning one's own business, or becoming a shop foreman, a Chief Executive Officer, Nobel Prize winner, or Prime Minister. Embedded within the clock is an anticipated timetable schedule of specific milestone events, such as promotions or income levels or amounts of power, whose accomplishment will mark one's progress towards achieving the ultimate goal.

At various points during their adult years, men pause for a period of reflection to assess their progress and to determine if they are ahead of, on, or behind schedule. Clausen (1972: 477) suggests that men in managerial positions and in the professions initiate their initial assessment during their early forties. Gould (1978, 1975, 1972: 525) and Levinson et al. (1978; 1977: 283), studying primarily middle- and upper-middle-class men, suggest that an initial, and somewhat superficial, review occurs earlier, somewhere between ages 28 and 32, with the most typical result being one of rededication to the original career choices and occupational Dreams. During their late thirties and early forties, according to these researchers, most men undertake a more extensive occupational life review forced by the added pressure of an increasingly urgent sense of time running out.

Most men at this time are forced to confront a sense of disparity between their Dreams and their current reality (Levinson et al., 1977: 288). As relatively few men achieve their Dreams, let alone exceed them, most find they have fallen short in some way (Drebing and Gooden, 1991). Their perceived options typically include: scaling down their aspirations and learning to settle for what they have; devoting themselves to a period of even more intense involvement in their careers by putting their energy pedal to the career metal before time completely runs out (after all, they are still relatively young); or changing jobs in the hopes of finding another occupational venue in which to capture either an old or a newly revised Dream (what Brim [1968: 204] refers to as "repotting"). According to the available research, the options most likely selected are in the order just presented. Bear in mind that most of the research on male adult and occupational development occurred prior to the downsizing frenzy of the middle 1990s, when large numbers of workers were fired in the name of debt reduction and greater profit-making efficiency. Whereas the period of assessment and selection among various alternatives referred to above was found by adult development researchers to be voluntary and self-initiated, many men in the 1990s find their decisions to search for a new line of work being made for them by their former employers.

Men who choose to scale back their occupational Dreams also typically hope to involve themselves more directly in their family life. Partly out of a desire to seek compensations no longer found in work, and partly out of a desire to make up for previously missed opportunities, these men claim they are seeking to establish or re-establish intimate connections with their wives and children. As one respondent in the Grant longitudinal study states: "At age 20 to 30, I think I learned to get along with my wife. From 30 to 40, I learned how to be a success at my job. And at 40 to 50, I worried less about myself and more about the children" (Vaillant, 1977b: 206).

We should be somewhat wary of accepting such claims at face value. It has become increasingly common in the 1990s for male politicians, athletes and coaches, and some business leaders to proclaim they are leaving public office or some high profile occupation to "spend more time with their families", while their "children," most often now adolescents, are "still young." Much of the time, these proclamations are prompted by anticipations of being voted out of office, forced resignations to avoid scandal, failures to renew contracts because of poor past performances, or other unpublicized motives. The public face-saving reasons offered dovetail with the 1990s emphasis upon the importance of the "new family man." Some of these men sincerely seek to become more than just an economic provider for their families. Claiming they now want to play a greater role in their families' lives is a tacit admission that any earlier intentions to do so did not translate into fact. The available evidence indicates that their chances of finding meaningful involvement in their families are limited (Harry, 1976). Men frequently turn to their families at a time when other family members are moving away from husbands/fathers and family life and seeking their own satisfactions elsewhere.

Women

Women's adult development has not been charted as extensively as that of men. The comparative lack of available research findings appears to be due to a combination of two factors: androcentrism and complexity based on plurality. A still-lingering androcentric assumption is that men's lives represent human lives. The most comprehensive studies of the stages of adult development have focused either exclusively (e.g., Levinson et al., 1978; Vaillant, 1977a; 1977b) or primarily (e.g., Gould, 1978, 1972) on men. When attempts are made to generalize the findings from men's to women's lives, the results are frequently less than satisfactory (Roberts and Newton, 1987). Most research on adult women (e.g., Baruch et al., 1983; Livson, 1981, 1976; Rubin, 1981) has tended to focus either primarily upon one portion of the life course (e.g., middle age or menopause), or upon only one dimension of women's lives (e.g., Livson's 1976 research on traditional versus independent orientations to femininity). Based upon the findings from his, admittedly small, female sample, Levinson (1996) concludes that the processes of sequential stage development for women and men from early to late adulthood are very similar, but the contents and central issues demonstrate significant differences.

In addition, women's developmental paths appear to exhibit a greater plurality that defies easy reduction into one general path. The marked increase in women's paid-labour-force participation rates since the middle 1970s, and the resulting influence of employment conditions, has complicated the lives of adult women, most of whom are also strongly influenced by their marriage and family responsibilities. Skrypnek and Fast (1993) conclude that Canadian women's labour-force-participation patterns are increasingly becoming more like those of men's. In contrast, Jones et al. (1990) conclude that women's patterns do not match those of men's, but are more individualized and highly diversified. We will return to this momentarily.

Not surprisingly, research conducted during the late 1960s and early 1970s concluded that female adult development closely paralleled marriage and family development. The most important turning points in adult women's lives were found to be those occurring within the context of their families in general, and in the development of their children in particular. Childbirth, school entry, puberty, school leaving, and "launching" from the family home all had greater impact on the lives of women than on the lives of men. A pioneer in the study of middle age notes that:

> Women, but not men, tend to define their age status in terms of timing of events within the family cycle. For married women, middle age is closely tied to the launching of children into the adult world, and even unmarried career women often discuss middle age in terms of the family they might have had. (Neugarten, 1968a: 95)

In contrast to men, who are expected to break away from their families of origin and establish their identities independent of their subsequent marital and family relations, women have been expected to "find themselves" within the context of their marital and family ties (Baruch et al., 1983; Chodorow, 1978; Gilligan, 1982; Hochschild, 1990; Levinson, 1996). Given the high level of conformity to our social mandates that assign primary responsibility for childrearing and maintenance of the marital relationship to women, it is not surprising to learn that research confirms the importance of family-life events for women's lives during the early to middle adult years. For most women, but not for most men, identity issues and intimacy issues have been conflated or fused together.

However, the significant events in women's adult lives today are not solely confined to those occurring within the context of their marriages and families. We have repeatedly noted that one of the most significant changes in the lives of women since the mid-1970s involves labour-force participation. Not only has the proportion of employed wives and mothers increased significantly, but women's patterns of attachment to the labour force have also undergone change. The former bimodal M-shaped pattern of higher participation rates prior to the birth of the first child and following the launching of children from the parental home, and significantly lower participation rates during the childrearing years, has given way to a consistently higher participation rate for women over the complete length of their marital and family careers (Fast and Da Pont, 1997; McVey and Kalbach, 1995; Skrypnek and Fast, 1993). However, as opposed to continually working full-time throughout their adult lives, most women still exhibit some form of a discontinuous work pattern, with entry and exist points determined by a combination of desire and necessity.

Employment conditions influence these patterns in a number of ways. As we have seen in previous chapters, pay scales, the presence or absence of maternity-leave programs, employers' attitudes towards female workers with children and their willingness to accommodate a worker's family demands, and possibilities for promotions and pensions can either push or pull women into or out of the labour force. Family conditions, such as children's health and current stage of development, also influence women's different occupational paths over their adult years. Varying numbers of women return to the labour force when all of their children are launched, or are in high school, or in elementary school, or are old enough to participate in available day care. The general trend since the mid-1970s has been for women to re-enter the labour force at younger ages. Women who are separated, divorced, or widowed (the latter being a relatively rare event prior to age 50) typically must remain in, or re-enter, the paid-labour force without having the luxury of choice. The larger variety of combinations of family life and paid-work careers evidenced by women, and the stronger impact of family life upon women because of their greater share of family responsibilities, creates a more complex picture for female adult development. Generalizations about men's lives are easier to create, since, as we noted in an earlier chapter, men's decisions and events regarding their paid work are usually more independent of conditions within their marriages and families.

The limited available research on unmarried or married, but childfree women (Levinson, 1996) suggests that their lives follow a pattern, during the years between young and middle adulthood, very similar to that of most men, wherein adult development closely parallels occupational development. Married women's careers appear to be more influenced by the career decisions of their husbands than the reverse. The ideology of the Traditional Homemaker Figure still exerts an influence over many decisions these women make with regard to their careers, in terms of whether or not to accept increased responsibilities and promotions or whether to stay in or leave a particular career path. For many women today, choosing a full-time continuous occupational career feels like having to choose simultaneously not to have children or even a marital relationship.

Middle Adulthood

This portion of the adult life course has been referred to in the scientific and popular literature variously as middle age, mid-life, midolescence, middlescence, the menopausal years, and second adulthood. We have selected "middle adulthood" partly because it is becoming the most commonly used referent, and partly because "middle age" increasingly has become a pejorative term for many Canadians. Identifying the chronological marker ages for this portion of the adult life career is subject to considerable debate. Suggested age ranges have varied anywhere from 31 to 50 (Newman and Newman, 1975), 30 to 54 (Beaujot et al., 1995), or 40 to 65 (Hunt and Hunt, 1975; Levinson, 1996; Levinson et al., 1978). The majority of writers focus upon the period from the late forties to early sixties (e.g., Buhler, 1968; Clausen, 1986; LeShan, 1974; McMorrow, 1974; Lowenthal et al., 1975; Livson, 1981, 1976; Sheehy, 1995, 1976). The existence of disagreements and debates clearly indicates that middle age is influenced more by a social than by a biological clock or calendar.

The age of entry into the middle years appears to vary by social class, with an earlier age identified by lower classes and a later age by higher classes (Neugarten, 1968b: 144–145). Popular journalist Gail Sheehy (1995) suggests that baby boomers, as they approach their fifties sometime during the 1990s, are attempting to push the entry age marker to an even later portion of adult life. The self-perceptions of boomers is one that rejects any parallels between themselves and their parents at a comparable chronological age. Most of the events associated with entry to middle age (e.g., physical appearance, strength and stamina, the "empty nest" family, peaking of occupational careers, intimations of mortality) appear to be under greater personal control today than ever before and, consequently, occur at more variable times than they used to. Only a limited number of events, such as menopause, are largely biologically determined and, therefore, essentially unalterable with regard to timing. Generally, the greater the degree of real or apparent control, the greater the tendency of individuals today to push those events back and to deny that they have entered middle age. We turn now to a brief consideration of some of the events and phenomena associated with middle age, specifically noting some relevant gender similarities and differences.

The Empty Nest

Prior to the middle 1960s, clinicians claimed that many, or most, middle-adulthood women in our society suffered from "empty nest syndrome" (Rubin, 1981: 13). The term referred to a period of depression experienced by women who had difficulty coping with the departure of their children and the attendant loss of an active parenting role. For women who had dedicated themselves to the role expectations of the Traditional Marriage Enterprise (Levinson, 1996), confronting an empty family nest, with only the prospect of taking in stray cats as substitute children, was akin to men's difficulties upon confronting retirement. No longer was a major source of life's meaning and social rewards available. The problem was what to do with oneself. Since role expectations for adult life were created from an earlier historical context in which most women would not experience an empty nest (having died before their last child left home), no social guidelines were provided to women for a life after children, except, perhaps, to become a "meddlesome mother-in-law" (Leslie, 1967: 670) or a doting grandmother.

One solution often offered to women by the clinical community in particular, and our society in general, and described uncritically by family sociologists of the time (e.g., Leslie, 1967: 669), was to adjust to their primary-role loss by taking up "charity" work. Paid work was not considered to be a viable option for most middle-adulthood women, due to a combination of a lack of training or possession of rusty occupational skills and having to confront ageism in the labour market: "They *are* middle-aged and have lost the fresh appeal of younger women" (Leslie, 1967: 669; emphasis in original). For those women whose husbands' incomes could sustain a married couple, volunteer work was offered as the best solution for filling in the empty hours that would inexorably toll away within a now-empty house. "And in the lulls in between there are always shopping, lunch and the ubiquitous bridge games" (Leslie, 1967: 669).

However, research from the late 1960s and beyond began reporting middle-adulthood women's descriptions of the empty nest period as a time not of loss, but of increased options and freedom (e.g., Borland, 1982; LeShan, 1974; Long and Porter, 1984; Neugarten, 1968b; Rubin, 1981), particularly for more highly educated women. Gone were the days when almost all women felt they had to live for, and vicariously through, other family members (Laws, 1979). Present were the days when many women could gain greater control of their lives and, as intimidating as it might seem initially, make decisions about what they wanted to do with the remaining years of adulthood.

Most of the women in these studies began to explore jobs, careers, and other options (e.g., writing, painting, or sculpting) that could not easily be accommodated with child-drearing and homemaking responsibilities. However, Rubin (1981) finds that many of her female subjects experienced difficulties in making a mid-life transition from their previous stay-at-home roles of wife and mother to outside-of-the-home commitments primarily because of a lack of psychological and emotional support from their husbands. Despite these obstacles, middle adulthood increasingly came to be viewed by women as the beginning of a period of time when previously unused talents and abilities could be put to use. The sense of freedom expressed by women stands in contrast to the experiences of husbands and fathers at this same point in time. Since many fathers are seeking to make up for lost time with their children, "it may be fathers more often than mothers who are pained by the children's imminent or actual departure" (Rubin, 1981: 31). These men are more likely to experience "empty nest syndrome" than are most women, an issue not yet addressed in the research literature.

Research also began to note that improved mental health and a sense of well-being is associated with multiple role experiences outside of the home (Clausen, 1976: 105). Baruch et al. (1983), from their study of 298 women between the ages of 35 and 55, identify two basic criteria for determining mental health: mastery and pleasure. Mastery refers to the degree of control a woman feels she has over her life and pleasure refers to her degree of enjoyment during that life. The best single predictor of mastery is participation in a challenging and well-paid job that allows a woman to use her skills and make decisions; the best single predictor of pleasure is a positive experience with a husband (including an active and satisfying sexual life) and children. The highest scores of overall well-being are found among employed married women with children present in the home and the lowest scores are obtained from unemployed childfree (including empty-nest) married women. Despite the stresses involved, women's well-being seems to be enhanced through taking on multiple roles. Being uninvolved is apparently more stressful and hazardous to one's mental health.

Associated with the desire among many middle-adult women to seek change and new directions is a growing awareness of the necessity of making plans for a life of one's own. Women in their late forties, typically married to men in their early to mid-fifties, become more aware of a husband's concerns about his own physical health. Just as men become increasingly sensitized to intimations of their own mortality, so too do wives confront the reality of their husbands' eventual deaths, however near or far away that may be. Concern for a husband's health and awareness of the demographic reality of life-expectancy differentials becomes part of a "rehearsal for widowhood" (Neugarten, 1968b) that begins for many women in middle adulthood. While this might appear to be unduly morbid, we must bear in mind that until age forty Canadian "women are more likely than men to be married; afterwards it is men who are more likely to be married" (Beaujot, 1995: 39) and women who are more likely to be widowed and living alone. In addition to preparing for the (presumably) mournful loss of one's life partner, lies the necessity of preparing for a life on one's own.

Women's search for sources of satisfaction outside of the home during middle adulthood may be instigated additionally by the fact that marital satisfaction tends to be at its lowest ebb around the time when children are still in the home and about to be launched (Burr, 1970; Rollins and Feldman, 1970; Rollins and Cannon, 1974; Steinberg and Silverberg, 1987). Middle-adult women tend to be the least satisfied with their marriages and most critical of their spouses (Lowenthal et al., 1975: 26; Thurnher, 1976: 131). At a time when many men are turning to their families to seek more satisfaction than they are currently experiencing from their paid work, many women are seeking sources of satisfaction outside of marriage. "Some of these women describe this sense of freedom coming at the same time that their husbands are reporting increased job pressures or—something equally troublesome— job boredom" (Neugarten, 1968b: 97).

Marital satisfaction generally increases among couples in the postparental (i.e., all children launched) phase of the marital career (Rollins and Feldman, 1970; Rollins and Cannon, 1974). For those marital partners who have survived the childrearing years, a return to couple-only status appears to have an ameliorating effect upon their relationship. A combination of reduced child-related responsibilities for women, reduced economic-provider responsibilities for men, and satisfactions derived by women from participation in the public sphere, all contribute to an enhanced marital quality for those couples who remain together. While the empty nest phenomenon is no longer a negative experience for most women, it now appears than an unwillingness or inability of children to leave home "on schedule" is creating a problem for parents of both sexes. Increasing educational requirements and an unstable job market for young adults, or the return of children (known as "boomerang" children) to the nest following job loss or a dissolved marriage, contribute to the creation of a "cluttered nest" (Heer et al., 1985; Boyd and Pryor, 1989) that is increasingly becoming a major source of stress for parents, particularly mothers, impatient to get on with their childfree lives (Glick and Lin, 1986a).

Gender Depolarization

An intriguing phenomenon in adult development has been noted repeatedly by researchers since studies began in the late 1960s: specifically, previously polarized sex-linked personality and behavioural characteristics show a significant decline sometime during the middle-adult years (Cytrynbaum et al., 1980; Hyde et al., 1991; Lowenthal et al., 1975; Neugarten, 1968b; Sheehy, 1995; 1976; Vaillant, 1977a). "Men seem to become more receptive to affiliative and nurturant promptings: women, more responsive towards and less guilty about aggressive and egocentric impulses" (Neugarten, 1968b: 140). Lowenthal et al. (1975: 71), based upon a comparison of self-administered Adjective Rating Lists for different age groups of men and women find men in their late fifties and sixties to be characteristically more "mellow," with less hostility and drive and more reasonableness than any of the younger men in their sample. Older women, in contrast to younger women, see themselves as "less dependent and helpless and as more assertive" (Lowenthal et al., 1975: 71). Levinson et al. (1977: 289) note that "the emergence and integration of the more feminine aspects of the self are more possible at mid-life" for men during their early to late forties. Journalist Gail Sheehy (1995: 318–341; 1976: 286–287) claims to have observed a tendency for women in their forties and fifties to incorporate aggressive and achievement-oriented characteristics within themselves, while men become more comfortable with emotional expressiveness, especially tearfulness, and a willingness to show vulnerability. At least superficially, these findings offer support for Jung's (1968; 1933) contention that the second half of life requires that men get more in touch with their **anima** and women with their **animus**.

While a number of researchers and observers have noted the existence of this phenomenon, they have not been able to identify when the process begins, as the discovery of depolarization has been largely an accidental byproduct of research designed to examine other facets of adult life. Only a narrowly focused longitudinal design, following a number of different age cohorts, will enable us to pinpoint both the precise age of onset and the contributing causes of the phenomenon. Such research should also determine whether depolarization is a constant element in adult development ("the normal unisex of later life," [Brim, 1974]) within our society, or is characteristic of only certain historically shaped age cohorts. Existing studies of women and men who were in their forties and fifties during the 1970s and 1980s focus upon individuals born between the late 1920s and the early 1940s. These baby boomer parents moved through young adulthood during the 1950s and the early 1960s, when social norms strongly endorsed strict gender divisions in personal qualities and behaviours. They entered middle adulthood during the 1970s and 1980s, when the women's and men's movements, along with the human potential and therapeutic movements (Rubin, 1990: 6–7), all proclaimed the desirability and necessity of breaking down rigid gender expectations and behaviours. Will members of younger age cohorts, raised in a time context of somewhat less rigid gender constraints, demonstrate the same degree of early adulthood polarization, followed by depolarization as they move into middle adulthood?

Assuming for the moment that research has identified a central process of adult development, the findings suggest an interesting overview of the human life course. The first "half" of life is devoted to a process of gender polarization. By the middle years, a trend towards depolarization begins. Men begin evidencing more "feminine" characteristics and women evidence more "masculine" characteristics. In alarmist fashion, despite a lack of supportive empirical evidence, journalistic reports extrapolate these findings to suggest that a role reversal occurs in the middle years, producing a gender "crossover crisis" (e.g., Sheehy, 1995: 329) where men become like women and women become like men. While maintaining that the genders "cross over," and experience the crossover as a "crisis," Sheehy (1995: 318; 1976: 304) further confuses the issue by insisting that the polarization-depolarization process is best captured by the imagery of a "sexual diamond" (which actually suggests either an imaginative position for sexual acts or another marketing ploy from rare-gem merchandisers). Despite these proclamations of a "crossover crisis," based upon the findings of gender depolarization among respondents in the Baltimore Longitudinal Study, Costa et al. (1983) claim that it would take an "average" 75-year-old man 136 years to reach the average femininity scores of a 75-year-old woman. In other words, the overall trend is *towards* greater gender convergence, neither achieving actual convergence nor gender reversal.

Even if confined to only one generational cohort, the existence of a life course trend from polarization to depolarization gives rise to competing explanations. Social constructionists view polarization and depolarization as reflective of different gender age-related, situationally normative scripts that compel individual adjustments. Levinson (1996: 38–39) argues that rigid gender divisions are a consequence of what he terms **gender splitting**. This gender splitting operates in a number of interrelated domains; the domestic sphere is split from the extradomestic sphere; the economic-provider role is split from the homemaker role; "women's work" is split from "men's work," and masculinity is split from femininity. Social forces operate to reinforce gender splitting in all domains for individuals from earliest childhood through middle adulthood. Following Levinson's lead, we could further postulate that, from middle adulthood onwards, a process of **gender splicing** is permitted wherein depolarization of gender characteristics occurs to some degree.

Cameron (1976) finds that age-sex norms vary over the life course. Adults in his study perceive social pressures to demonstrate gender differences in personality and behaviour as increasing during young adulthood and decreasing during middle adulthood through older adulthood, which is perceived as a time period subject to relatively minimal gender pressures. Turner and Turner (1991) also find that middle-adulthood and older men are viewed as being less aggressive, less autonomous, and consequently as less "masculine." Early adulthood years are characterized by individuals placing a strong emphasis upon compliance with social expectations (Gould, 1972: 525; Kimmel, 1974: 305; Sheehy, 1976: 84). Personal energy is directed towards demonstrating apparent conformity with gender roles, work and family roles, and the acquisition of material possessions indicative of success. Inner qualities are shaped and displayed towards attainment of the "proper" external trappings of life in our society. It appears that greater freedom of behavioural and personality expression is socially granted to persons at a stage in life when they have typically discharged the bulk of their gender duties of being economic providers or childbearers and childrearers earlier in life. With reduced social pressures to conform to rigid gender expectations, inner qualities either never acquired or once acquired, but previously left dormant, a "return of the repressed" (Gutman et al., 1982) can now be explored and displayed. The result is an apparent depolarization process.

Furthermore, the changing situations of men and women in the second half of life call for the development of new qualities. Dictates of economic employment promote more assertive achievement-oriented qualities among women. An increasing likelihood of being alone also requires a greater focus upon self-preoccupation and meeting personal needs by one's efforts alone. No longer can an individual "piggyback" (Sheehy, 1976: 27) one's needs on to the abilities provided by a partner in an intimate relationship. Similarly, the increasing desire of men to seek satisfactions from relationships with their wives and children requires them to develop more affiliative and nurturant qualities. Since, as we have suggested in earlier chapters, basic social institutions create gender as much as gender creates institutions, the earlier in life that men meaningfully participate in the domestic sphere and women participate in the extradomestic sphere, presumably the earlier depolarization will occur.

In contrast, biological reductionists claim that women and men are "hard-wired" (genetically or hormonally programed) to develop in two different directions over the first half of the life course. Depolarization requires an explanation of how this programing is rewired at some point during or following middle age. Researchers consequently search primarily for hormonal changes associated with the general phenomenon of the climacteric that could account for alterations in the balance of, for example, aggressive and nurturant qualities among women and men.

Menopause and Men's Pause

Biological changes occurring during middle adulthood, particularly those associated with changes in hormone production from the ovaries, testes, pituitary gland, and hypothalamus, are generically referred to as the **climacteric**. While the term "climacteric" is often, and incorrectly, used as a synonym for the term *menopause*, "menopause" has a more specific referent and should be linked only to changes associated with reduced production of hormones from the ovaries. As with many other areas that comprise the focus of this text, we have an abundance of terms used in both the scientific/scholarly and the popular/mass media press with considerable confusion resulting over proper use of the terms themselves. Terms used to refer to women in this phase of life are often used interchangeably and in a misleading fashion. Terms properly used with reference to women are often used with reckless abandon to refer to men and create confusion regarding any possible similarities and differences between females and males.

As we noted in Chapter 2, women's periodic menstrual cycle is the outcome of rhythmic or cyclical hormone (estrogen and progesterone) production centred primarily in the ovaries, and linked into a feedback loop with the pituitary gland and the hypothalamus. With physiological aging (except for women who have earlier had the ovaries removed via hysterectomy), women's bodies, at some time during their forties or early fifties undergo a series of changes precipitated mainly by significant declines in the production of estrogens by their ovaries (Consumer Reports on Health, 1993; Gee and Kimball, 1987; Masters et al., 1994). Estrogen production continues to decline, typically for about four years, but with a wide range of variation, until reaching a lower plateau level.

A number of short-term physiological consequences attributable to declining estrogen production include changes to menstrual periods, such as length (sometimes longer than usual, eventually dwindling to shorter, with occasional incidents of "false alarms" or breakthrough bleeding), rate of flow (sometimes heavier than usual, eventually lighter than usual), and variable timing (occasionally shorter time between periods, missing periods, increasingly longer time between periods, eventually no period). As well, many women experience all or some of the following: hot "flashes" (a sudden rush of internally experienced heat, often accompanied by reddening of the skin and drenching perspiration) or "flushes" (when they occur during sleep they are referred to as "night sweats"), insomnia, weight gain, vaginal "dryness" (or reduced levels of vaginal lubrication), "stress" incontinence (occasional involuntary release of urine), and, frequently, an increased need to urinate. Long-term effects of reduced estrogen production can include increased incidence of bladder infections, rising cholesterol levels, and bone-density loss, leading to osteoporosis.

The time period of declining estrogen production and associated short-term physiological consequences is referred to as **perimenopause**. The English word "menopause" initially appears to be misleading as "pause" as usually used to refer to a temporary disruption of ongoing events. However, "pause" in this case is derived from *pausis*, meaning cessation, and *menopause*, therefore, refers specifically to the cessation of menses. **Menopause** is technically defined as that point in time following one full year in an adult woman's life without a menstrual period, that is, when she is no longer menstruating and the cause cannot be attributable to pregnancy or lactation. The convention of adopting a time frame of one full year without a menstrual period is somewhat arbitrary, but this provides a convenient and relatively obvious benchmark that does not require extensive physiological testing and measurement of, for example, estrogen levels or ova viability. Since one of the hallmarks of perimenopause involves a lengthening of the time between menstrual periods, leading some women to falsely conclude they have reached menopause (and finding themselves, to their surprise, to be fertile still and pregnant, thus producing a "second" or "oops," as in "oops, I thought I was in menopause" generation of children for their families), a full year without a menstrual period is considered to be indicative that perimenopause is over and a woman has reached menopause. Among women in North America, the average age when reaching menopause is 51, with a range varying from 40 to 55 (Saxton, 1996: 116). The lower figure of that range is suspect and in all likelihood refers to the onset of perimenopause and not menopause itself.

Within our everyday language use, and occasionally even within the scholarly press, the latter term is used incorrectly as, for example, in the oft-heard phrase, "I'm going through menopause." The proper technical term to be used here is, "I'm going through perimenopause," admittedly not as easy a phrase to roll off one's tongue. Adding to the confusion has been the introduction of the term "postmenopause" and "postmenopausal," sometimes used interchangeably with perimenopause, most often used interchangeably with menopause. For purposes of technical accuracy, if we limit use of the term "menopause" to refer only to that specific moment in time when a woman has gone a full 12 months without a menstrual period, than **postmenopause** can be one of the terms used to refer to the remaining portion of an adult woman's life. The resulting sequence is one of perimenopause-menopause-postmenopause. Unfortunately, we currently live in a time period characterized by a sloppy, interchangeable, use of the terms, a condition you should be aware of as you read other materials in the scholarly and the popular press.

Most, but not all, women also experience some changes of a sexual nature, attributable in large part to changing levels of estrogen production, that manifest themselves during the perimenopausal or postmenopausal years (Masters et al., 1994: 469–479; Sarrel, 1990). Reduced vaginal lubrication and possible thinning and reduced elasticity of vaginal lining can contribute to discomfort or pain during intercourse. A few women report delayed and/or reduced responsiveness to clitoral stimulation and some women report a reduced or less intense physiological experience of orgasm. However, in contrast, many women report heightened sexual interest, responsiveness, and orgasmic frequency after menopause. These latter changes are due indirectly to physiological changes, in that these women report they no longer worry about becoming pregnant and, consequently, are less inhibited in their sexuality.

The full experience and meaning of perimenopause, menopause, and postmenopause for women appears to be strongly influenced by the social context in which this series of events occur. Few "symptoms" of a disruptive nature have been observed among women in China, a finding that has been attributed to that society according women greater respect as they age and, consequently, not viewing menopause as a woman's critical loss of social significance (noted in Knox and Schacht, 1994: 387). In contrast, the various events associated with the menopause sequence are still surrounded in Canada and the United States by substantial amounts of negative mythology and misinformation attributable largely to the strength of existing stereotypes centring upon womanhood as being encapsulated by, and limited to, potential (**fecundity**) or actual (**fertility**) reproductive capacity and, to a lesser extent, sexual capacity. Therefore, according to this reductionist line of thinking, any minor or major disruption of these capacities signals the end of womanhood as we know it.

Medical doctors, in the early part of the twentieth century, referred to menopause as the "death of the woman in women" (Ehrenreich and English, 1978) and the terms "castrate" and "postmenopausal" were often used interchangeably. During the first few decades following World War II, perimenopause and menopause were thought to provoke a "crisis" in women as they tried to cope with their loss (before the advent of new reproductive technologies) of the ability to conceive children and become mothers (Barbach, 1993; Bart, 1971 and Penfold, 1981, in Gee and Kimball, 1987: 49). Images of estrogen-starved postmenopausal women still abound. Stereotypical images of these hysterical, irrational, or at least irritable, frightening women are perhaps best captured by Sheehy (1995: 202) in her subheading phrase: "I'm Out of Estrogen and I've Got a Gun."

Empirical evidence belies these images and concerns. Research from the time of Neugarten et al. (1963) finds that only a very small minority of women during perimenopause or shortly thereafter actually experience a process of mourning at the thought of losing their potential or actual reproductive capacity. Other findings indicate that anywhere from a low of 10 to 15 percent to a high of 50 percent of female respondents (Posner 1979, in Gee and Kimball, 1987: 49) experience some degree of difficulty during their perimenopausal years. Unfortunately, research investigations vary in terms of their operationalization of experienced problems with some studies including occasional and minor difficulties, thus yielding a higher reported incidence rate, while others focus only upon frequent and disabling problems, thus yielding small frequencies of experienced difficulties. Regardless of the measuring devices used, it appears from available research that approximately half of the women in our society experience perimenopause and menopause as being free of any "symptoms" (Gee and Kimball, 1987: 50). For one-fifth of women, no difficulties or apparent changes are experienced until menstruation suddenly and completely stops (Boston Women's Health Book Collective, 1984, in Gee and Kimball, 1987: 49). A cautious interpretation of the available research findings suggests that only a small minority, perhaps 10–15 percent, of women are severely affected by the physiological changes associated with perimenopause.

However, perimenopausal "problems" of women have recently become a major focus for drug manufacturers, as well as advertising and marketing businesses in North America. Seizing upon the opportunities presented by the currently large demographic, baby-boom bulge in our population between the ages of 40 and 55, "marketing menopause" has become a lucrative source of income for product makers and advertisers in both Canada and the United States. Braud (1993) quotes a president of a major health care consulting firm in the United States as indicating that marketing interest in PMS (premenstrual syndrome) products peaked in the mid-1980s, and manufacturers and advertisers then refocused their sights in the 1990s largely upon women either facing, or actually experiencing, their perimenopausal and postmenopausal years. Advertisers attempt to raise women's anxieties in not only middle adulthood, but also in young adulthood, about current or potential bone-density loss, painful experiences of vaginal intercourse, stress incontinence, hot flashes, irritability, and insomnia, and then offer to provide solutions in the form of exercise classes and videos, calcium supplements, vaginal lubricants, diapers or "feminine" pads, and both nonprescription and prescription drugs to replace declining hormone production and forestall the development of any of the foregoing "symptoms." Premarin™ (an artificial or synthetic estrogen) was the second most prescribed drug in 1991 in the United States (Braud, 1993: 47). A major American pharmaceutical company currently markets a low-dosage birth control pill to women in the 35- to 51-year-old age group, as a preventative measure to reduce estrogen loss, maintain menstrual cycle regularity, and prevent any surprise pregnancies among women in middle adulthood experiencing menstrual irregularity (Braud, 1993: 47). For-profit and not-for-profit health centres feature carefully marketed educational classes and "support groups" for women interested in, or experiencing, a broadly defined concept of "menopause" and "menopausal problems."

Of the products being marketed and used, those containing replacement hormones are the most controversial and contentious, with opinions being expressed both pro (e.g., Sheehy, 1992, 1995) and con (e.g., Greer, 1991). Hormone replacement is predicated upon a perspective that medicalizes a natural process and views perimenopause, menopause, and (particularly) postmenopause primarily as conditions of "deficiency," requiring long-term medical intervention. Initially called ERT (estrogen replacement therapy) when essentially only one hormone set was the focus of attention, the intervention is more often now referred to by a generic term of HRT (hormone replacement therapy). HRT is also a more accurate term when the focus of intervention includes other hormones, such as progesterone. Replacement therapy is designed to counteract a loss of ovarian-produced estrogens by adding synthetic estrogens, via injections or pills, to prevent calcium loss and reduce the likelihood of osteoporosis, restore or retain vaginal lubrication and vaginal wall thickness and elasticity, reduce or eliminate hot flashes, and reduce the likelihood of heart disease among postmenopausal women as a consequence of rising cholesterol levels.

Estrogen replacement therapy alone has been linked to possible increases in breast cancer, gall bladder problems, fluid retention, blood clots, ovarian and endometrium cancers, and possibly even migraines. While debates continue over the questions of whether estrogen replacement therapy alone, and in what dosages, are directly responsible for these outcomes, additional questions have been raised about the possibility of preventing these negative effects by adding synthetic progesterone to the therapeutic mix. While progesterone may have a counteractive effect, the drawback of its inclusion is that, unless carefully monitored and moderated, progesterone can lead to a resumption of menstrual periods (Masters et al., 1994: 470–472). Since ERT and HRT are relatively new interventions, the full long-term effects of continuous synthetic hormone intake among women in middle and older adulthood is unknown and will not be known until all women currently on various regimens of replacement therapy are dead.

Almost three million prescriptions were written for Canadian women for some form of HRT during 1996, although only slightly less than two million of those prescriptions were filled (Beaudet et al., 1997: 11). Previous research has suggested that some of the benefits attributed to HRT might be due not to the use of synthetic hormones themselves, but to a greater likelihood that healthier women were more likely to be attracted to HRT use than were less healthy women. This selection process could account for HRT users demonstrating better health at later ages than do nonusers. However, data collected in the 1994–1995 National Population Health Survey in Canada finds female HRT users are no different from nonusers in terms of marital status, educational attainment, income, cigarette smoking, alcohol consumption, regular exercise, high blood pressure, cancer, diabetes, migraine headaches, heart disease, or urinary incontinence (Beaudet et al., 1997). HRT users were more likely to have consulted physicians in the previous year and had mammograms and high blood pressure checks, but such physician visits are typically required before a prescription can be written. A significantly higher proportion, more than double, of HRT users also report taking antidepressants, in comparison to non-HRT users. According to the findings of the National Population Health Survey, slightly more than 22 percent of women aged 45–64 and 33 percent of women aged 50–54 in Canada report using some form of hormone replacement therapy (Beaudet et al., 1997: 13).

Men do *not* experience a series of events or processes comparable to the biologically based perimenopause-menopause-postmenopause sequence experienced by women. To use words commonly found in the popular press, "male menopause" does not exist (Consumer Reports on Health, 1993/1995; Keogh, 1990 in Knox and Schacht, 1994: 387; Money, 1980; Starr and Weiner, 1981). The term "male menopause" does a disservice to both men and women, as it suggests the presence of similarities that do not exist. While men do undergo and experience biological changes in their reproductive and sexual capacity associated with the process of physical aging, the changes are highly variable across all men and very gradual within each man (Starr and Weiner, 1981). In contrast to the precipitous decline in estrogen experienced by women, testosterone production declines only gradually among men beyond the ages of the mid-forties or mid-fifties, even then on a highly variable scale, and eventually reaches a lower plateau level, typically when men are in their seventies, that is only slightly below their previous higher plateau (Consumer Reports on Health, 1993/1995).

Whereas women's ovaries eventually cease releasing ovum or eggs, men's testes continue to produce viable sperm throughout the entire adult male postpubertal lifespan. Although total sperm counts do decline over time, the amount of decline is highly variable across men and many men, subject to both opportunity and interest, can, and do, contribute their needed share to the conception process when they are well into their seventies and beyond (frequently, in the case of media celebrities, making news headlines in doing so). With no observable marker event, short of a sperm count, to demarcate infertile from fertile men, no obvious method exists to determine when men during middle or older adulthood cease walking around with a "loaded gun," to use an old analogy between fertility and the phallic potency associated with firearms. Men do lose a small amount of muscle mass and bone density between the ages of 40 and 70, but the amounts typically do not place men at high risk, compared to women, for osteoporosis-related bone injuries during older adulthood. These physiological changes bear only a slight relationship to gradually declining testosterone levels (Consumer Reports on Health, 1993/1995: 164).

Associated with aging among men during late phases of middle and in older adulthood, erectile tissues in the penis may be slower to engorge with blood upon stimulation and, among some men, may retain their swollen state for shorter durations of time (Masters et al., 1994: 409). As well, a gradual decline in penile sensitivity may develop and, for some, an enlargement of the prostate gland can occur, such that it presses more firmly upon surrounding tissues and can slow down urination and weaken the strength of ejaculation. Ejaculation typically is delayed and most men during middle adulthood, and well into older adulthood, are capable of sustaining an erection for a considerably longer period of time. Men also typically experience a more generalized and diffuse sense of pleasure they define as sexual and become less genital and orgasm focused in their sexual expression (Masters et al., 1994; Starr and Weiner, 1981). Once again, we must note that all these changes are highly variable both in terms of their timing and severity of impact.

Despite the lack of marked biologically based changes in men, drug and medical companies in Europe and North America are preparing and marketing, through public advertising in the mass media, as well as specialized advertising to physicians, an HRT for men in the form of testosterone booster shots and patches to supposedly "rejuvenate" aging men, especially, but not exclusively, targeted at men over the age of 65, who, the marketers claim, have gone through "male menopause," "andropause," or "viropause" as it is often referred to in Europe, and are in need of being restored to their "premenopausal" state. Synthetically boosting testosterone in middle and older adulthood men appears to benefit only the drug manufacturers, marketers, and health practitioners involved. Any possible benefits to male recipients themselves appear to be far outweighed by the risks, as increased synthetic testosterone has been found to either exacerbate or initiate prostate cancer in men (Consumer Health Reports, 1993/1995: 163–164).

We can see from the foregoing that the concept of a "male menopause" is a figment of the journalistic media's imagination. So too is the related, and often interchangeably used, concept of a male "midlife crisis." Popular mass-media fiction and modern urban legends abound with stories and stereotypes of men in middle adulthood suddenly, and without warning, purchasing a new red sports car or abandoning a successful business, home, and family life and running away to Tahiti with a 20-year-old secretary. If not trying to recapture their youth through purchasing shiny inanimate or animate artifacts, popular stereotypes then portray middle adulthood men as being mired in major episodes of depression. While these stereotypical images supposedly provide us with concepts (male menopause and midlife crisis) to describe men in a random and indiscriminate fashion, empirical research fails to confirm their existence (e.g., Clausen, 1976; Rosenberg and Farrell, 1976; Vaillant, 1977a). More recent clinical research fails to find evidence of an increase in depression among men during middle adulthood (Consumer Reports on Health, 1993/1995: 164).

We noted in an earlier section that some adult-development research finds supportive evidence indicating that many men during middle adulthood experience a period of reflection as they assess their life's progress to that point and either decide to maintain their earlier-crafted Dreams for the remainder of their foreseeable lives, or decide to make minor changes in the balance of their occupational and marriage-family priorities. This period of contemplation and stock-taking, sort of a *men's pause*, while providing the fodder for unsubstantiated claims of a major life change in men, typically leads only to relatively minor changes, if any at all. Trying to fashion a link between this portion of men's lives and women's peri- and postmenopause experiences is unwarranted and misleading.

In summary, the decline in estrogen production among women experiencing perimenopause leads, in the absence of ERT, to a new balance level of estrogen and testosterone during the menopause years. Hypothetically, this new balance could account for an increased influence of testosterone and a decreased influence of estrogen upon women's behaviour. As a consequence, women in menopause could become more aggressive or assertive. None of these hypothesized biologically based relationships have been supported by empirical research. The decline in testosterone production among men as they age leads, in the absence of HRT, to a new balance level of testosterone and estrogen. Hypothetically, this new balance could account for a lessened influence of testosterone and an increased influence of estrogen upon men's behaviour. As a consequence, men could become less aggressive and more "mellow." None of these hypothesized relationships have been supported by empirical research.

Departing Beauty and Stealing Beauty Back

Aging in a youth-oriented society such as ours means, in part, departing from our socially constructed rigid standards of physical attractiveness. Departing from beauty is not a "fade to ugly" process, but rather a process of growing invisible, becoming one of the nondescript masses, blending into the background, becoming a nonperson according to the standards by which we measure and evaluate beauty. For some people in our society, departing beauty is greeted with relief as attention can now be focused upon more important qualities. For many others, it becomes a source of concern and provides motivation for action. As insulting or uncomfortable as it may be to be appraised by bystanders, given the "once over," as one walks down a shopping mall or sidewalk or enters a classroom, an equal sense of discomfort may arise when one becomes aware that appraisers no longer notice one's passing. The real or feigned anger, generated from knowledge that one has just been reduced solely to an object of physical beauty and found wanting or desirable, pales by comparison, for many people, to the knowledge that one is no longer noticeable enough or worthy enough of being evaluated.

While it is our physical bodies that age, the meanings and experiences of that process are interwoven with social interpretations. Our society is characterized by a double standard of aging (Sontag, 1972) wherein women are judged by a much younger and narrower standard than are men. As a consequence of this double standard, women are said to "grow old" and depart beauty at an earlier chronological age than do men. "Physical appearance is a key indicator of aging and old age...standards of beauty are...narrow, restrictive, and set impossible expectations for most females all of the time, and by virtue of human aging, are impossible for all women at least some of the time" (Abu-Laban and McDaniel, 1995: 107, 108). Our social adages proclaim, "women grow old; men become distinguished" or "women grow age lines; men develop character lines." According to our social criteria, women are "girls as long as possible, who then age humiliatingly into middle-aged women and then obscenely into old women" (Sontag, 1972, in Abu-Laban and McDaniel, 1995: 110). A long-time feminist comments that "[m]en may find their sexual attractiveness actually increasing with age....The commonest image of a middle-aged woman is someone who is lumpy, dumpy, and frumpy" (Greer, 1991: 295). To the extent that physical appearance "becomes a measure of personal value" (Abu-Laban and McDaniel, 1995: 108), observable departures from beauty standards lead many women (and, to a lesser, but now increasing extent, men) to take sometimes extraordinary, sometimes ordinary, steps designed to steal beauty back from the ravages of time. These measures are intended to turn faces and bodies back to younger-looking appearances that will, they hope, belie a person's actual age.

Becoming invisible, having the mirror on the wall no longer inform that "you're the fairest of them all," being inundated by commercial advertising messages that subtly or blatantly suggest age is the natural enemy of beauty, or being aware of commonly held beliefs that departing beauty signals an inner moral weakness, resulting in "letting oneself go" are not the only instigators of attempts to regain or retain a young attractive appearance. Another event over which men and women in our society have no direct control, becoming a grandparent, often triggers a desire to present a physical image to the public that emphasizes one's still-youthful outer, and by implication, inner self. "The *transition* to grandparenthood is a middle age, not an old-age phenomenon" (Connidis, 1989: 51, emphasis in original) and has been so throughout the twentieth century in Canada and the United States. The word "grandparent" typically brings to mind a stereotypical visual image of white hair, eyeglasses, lined and fallen face and neck wattle, loose-skinned upper arms, apple or pear body shape with sagging male or female breasts, thick ankles supported by sturdy sensible shoes, and slow mobility. An urge to deny that grandparent image from becoming their reality motivates many women and men to initiate or intensify efforts to steal beauty back.

Stealing beauty takes many forms involving a variety of techniques or methods. A large gamut of physical fitness activities ranging from walking, jogging, running, stationary and mobile bicycling, swimming, triathaloning, aerobic exercising with or without an accompanying video demonstration, weight lifting, through to participating in sporting activities and square dancing appeal to increasing numbers of women and men in middle and older adulthood. Less strenuous approaches involve increased use of an abundant array of widely advertised cosmetic products to present either a more youthful, or at least a less aged, appearance. Some products promote the use of artificial ingredients with the promise of decelerating or even reversing aging in a "natural" way. Other products promise to camouflage or "vanish" wrinkle lines and age spots or, at the very least, to "keep him guessing" about a woman's real age. If hair dyes and face/hand/body lotions and creams are deemed insufficient or too temporary and physical exercise too exhausting or time-consuming, elective and invasive cosmetic surgery may entice. Breasts can be tilted up and either augmented or reduced, every portion of the face and neck can be lifted and/or peeled, lips and wrinkle lines can be filled in with either artificial or natural ingredients, tummies and derrieres can be tucked in, eye size and shape and vision can be altered, and body fat can be removed or moved around to more visually pleasing locations.

Generally, as a consequence of our double standard of aging, men have been less interested, and slower to participate, in the techniques and methods listed in the previous paragraph. The major area of concern for men during middle adulthood and older ages appears to be centred upon their hair, most notably its absence and to a lesser extent its greying presence. Hair products for men in the form of colouring agents, growth promotion lotions and prescription potions, cover-ups such as wigs and toupées, along with surgical implants, seem to constitute the bulk of artificial aids targeted at a male audience interested in denying possession, or loss, of aging hair follicles. However, counterarguments abound in our culture over whether natural balding in men, but not women, is actually beautiful and a symbol of virility and potency.

Wolf (1991: 17) indicates that the American cosmetic industry for women has product sales of approximately $20 billion a year, while the cosmetic surgery industry grosses around $300 million a year. Estimates suggest that one out of every 225 women in the United States has had some form of cosmetic surgery (Morgan, 1991). Not being completely immune from the "peacock" syndrome, men in the United States account for almost 13 percent of the cosmetic surgeries in 1990 including "28 percent of nose jobs, 16 percent of eyelid surgeries, 10 percent of liposuction procedures, and 9 percent of facelifts" (Cutler, 1993: 49). While many of the purchasers of cosmetic products and surgeries are adolescents and young adults, increasingly large numbers are women and men in middle adulthood seeking to forestall the appearance of having departed too far from our Eurocentric standards of youthful beauty. Most cosmetic lotions and potions lie within the economic budgets of all Canadians and Americans, but surgeries are typically beyond the economic means of most working-class and even middle-class women and men (Abu-Laban and McDaniel, 1995).

While one segment of our middle-adulthood population seeks to steal beauty back, another segment, particularly aging baby boomers, focuses their energies on pushing back the upper-age limits of our narrowly defined standards of beauty, literally "advancing beauty into a new time period" (Friday, 1996: 493), especially for women. To appeal to this large consumer group, advertisers and the popular mass media now incorporate an increasingly larger proportion of older (i.e., beyond age 40 in appearance) models and spokespersons, some famous and some unknown, some with real and some with dyed grey hair (typically worn in a long sweeping "youthful" style), as visual images used to sell a wide variety of both age-related and age-irrelevant products. However, all of these poster adults for aging baby boomers still closely approximate the slender, physically fit standard of body and facial attractiveness. Finally, still another segment of our population, lead by a variety of spokeswomen (e.g., Banner, 1992; Friday, 1996; Friedan, 1993; Greer, 1991) attempt to de-emphasize beauty as a measure of a woman's personal worth and instead re-emphasize other qualities to be more positively evaluated with increasing age, such as knowledge, wisdom, experience, and power. As part of this banishing beauty approach, attempts are also being made to re-habilitate and positively value the image and role of the crone, the witch, and the wrinkled old wise and powerful woman.

Adult-Elder Caregiving

Many women and men during middle adulthood find that, in addition to providing some degree of care for their own children, similar attention must also now be extended to one or both of their own elder parents and/or parents-in-law. Journalists describe these adult women and men as belonging to the "sandwich generation," or even the "clubhouse sandwich generation" in four-generation families, when adults must care not only for their own children, but also their parents and grandparents. Using the word "generation" here is both inaccurate and misleading, since that term implies a unique cohort of people whose experiences will never be repeated (such as, for example, as implied by the phrase "baby-boom generation"). Having caregiving responsibilities for both one's own children and one's own parents, and perhaps even grandparents, is created by the combined actions of a number of people relative to their ages at marriage, ages at giving birth, their longevity, and their dependency. These combinations are unlikely to be limited to only one generation of Canadians near the end of the twentieth century, but likely will be repeated for other cohorts well into the first half of the twenty-first century as well.

Rather than use the term "sandwich generation," and assuming that the journalistic term "sandwich" should be retained for its descriptive value, a concept of *sandwich phase* is more appropriate for two reasons. First, the term is applicable only with reference to those middle-adulthood males and females who have caregiving responsibilities towards both their own children and their parents at the same time. Not all members of the present middle-adulthood Canadian cohort meet those qualifications, either because they do not have any dependent children, or do not have any surviving dependent parents. Second, the term "phase" denotes something temporary and is more accurate since presently "sandwiched" middle-adulthood males and females will be so only until either their children or their parents no longer are in need of caregiving. Our focus of attention in this section lies upon the eldercare portion of the caregiving sandwich phase when adults are involved with the often awkward role reversal involved in "parenting" (admittedly not a verb) their parents.

How many Canadian women and men in middle adulthood actively engage in caring for their parents or parents-in-law is partly determined by definitions of caregiving activities. Most empirical research focuses upon and counts instances of **instrumental** activities such as meal preparation and clean up, house cleaning, grocery shopping, yard work, provision of transportation, bill payment, and banking, and **personal care** activities such as bathing, dressing, and toileting. Findings from the 1990 General Social Survey (Dumas and Bélanger, 1994: 26) suggest that less than 25 percent of adults between the ages of 35 and 64 provide instrumental and/or personal care for their parents. The 1996 General Social Survey (Cranswick, 1997) adds another category of **caring about** activities such as providing emotional support, keeping a parent's feelings and spirits up, and providing reassurance and encouragement. Research in the United States finds this latter category constitutes an important, but little studied, component of adult caregiving activities (Piercy,

1998). However, as noted by Dumas and Bélanger (1994: 126), since emotional support can be provided on an episodic basis, such as when taking a parent out for dinner or celebrating birthdays, Mother's Day, or Father's Day, this component may not always be thought of by respondents or counted by researchers as a caregiving activity. Findings from the 1996 General Social Survey (Cranswick, 1997: 3) indicate that elder caregiving in all forms occurs most frequently among the 45- to 64-year-old age group (19 percent of women and 11 percent of men).

Regardless of what activities are included, research consistently finds that primary caregivers are most likely to be women, in their roles as wives, daughters, or daughters-in-law (e.g., Cranswick, 1997; Chappell, 1987 in Connidis, 1989: 50; Dumas and Bélanger, 1994; Piercy, 1998; Starrels et al., 1997). "Most services to the elderly are provided by their families and, in the absence of a spouse, the key person in this role is a daughter who is probably middle-aged" (Connidis, 1989: 49). Families in the past were known to designate one daughter who would remain unmarried, perhaps even live continuously with her parents, and, therefore, be on call as insurance to provide caregiving to parents should they eventually require it. As in the past, sons become primary caregivers for elderly parents today most likely because they have no sisters. Among today's smaller families, few, if any, daughters are designated to become the "spinster" elder caregiver. All, or almost all, daughters over the past few decades, from personal choice, are likely to marry, to have their own children, to be employed, and to live geographically apart from their parents. Yet, elder caregiving still remains part of the kinkeeper role assigned to women in our society. and extends beyond a woman's own immediate family to include also the family of her husband. Daughters-in-law during the middle-adulthood years provide more elder caregiving help than do sons-in-law (Connidis, 1989: 50).

Aside from more likely being female, caregivers share few other distinguishing characteristics. Results from the 1996 General Social Survey indicate that female caregivers are about equally as likely to be living with a spouse and children, living with a spouse only, or living with children only. Female caregivers are also equally likely to be employed, unemployed, or full-time homemakers, and male caregivers are equally as likely to be either employed or unemployed (Cranswick, 1997: 3). To compensate for their lesser amounts of available time, employed daughters tend to use a more "managed" (Connidis, 1989: 50) caregiver style, by arranging for the provision of paid-for services to meet some elder parents' needs, although they still manage to provide more caregiving services personally. Men, perhaps stemming from an awareness of their more limited repertoire of housekeeping and other caregiving skills, are also generally more likely than women to purchase necessary help. As we noted in Chapter 8, changes to our physical and mental healthcare systems, in the form of shorter hospital stays, greater use of outpatient treatments, and increased emphasis upon home rather than institutional living, have added more medicalized responsibilities for Canadian caregivers beyond the typical cooking, cleaning, and ensuring the bills are paid (Armstrong, 1990; Cranswick, 1997). Findings from the 1996 GSS indicate that, although the percentages reported are small, women (15 percent) today are more likely than are men (9 percent) to change their geographical location to live closer to a person requiring their caregiving aid (Cranswick, 1997: 6). About equal numbers of men and women actually move in with the person being aided. Working-class daughters are more likely than are middle- or upper-class daughters to leave employment to better meet the needs of aging parents (Connidis, 1989: 50).

Most caregivers in the 1996 GSS experience few problems associated with caring for others, and only a small minority of caregivers find their responsibilities to be onerous (Cranswick, 1997: 4). However, while that general pattern exists among both men and women, some gender differences are noteworthy. Sixty-five percent of male and 55 percent of female caregivers indicate they never feel that helping others results in not having time for themselves, while 12 percent of females and 9 percent of males indicate they nearly always feel that way. Fifty-five percent of male and 41 percent of female caregivers never feel stressed about helping others while also trying to meet their own employment and family responsibilities, but 18 percent of females and 12 percent of males nearly always feel stressed. While gender differences obtained from the 1996 GSS research are modest overall, these findings do indicate that women are more likely to feel burdened by their caregiving responsibilities than are men, which appears to be attributable largely to the differential distribution of the caregiving burden. As well, other research indicates that caregivers experience greater stress when coping with an elder who suffers from cognitive-behavioural problems associated with some form of dementia, than when coping with an elder who suffers from physical impairments only (see Starrels et al., 1997). In conformity with prevalent gender stereotypes emphasizing supposedly different gender skills, women caregivers are more likely to assume responsibility for a cognitive-behaviourally impaired elder than are men, who are more likely to confine themselves mainly to providing instrumental aid for a physically impaired elder.

Barely more than half (55 percent) of women caregivers and just less than half (45 percent) of men caregivers report that caregiving responsibilities have affected their employment situations in the form of coming in later, leaving early, or missing days of paid work (Cranswick, 1997: 5). Starrels et al. (1997: 869) find that taking time off from paid employment is more stressful for male caregivers. They attribute this finding to a combination of men "having a larger social investment than women in their employment roles," thus becoming more stressed when family obligations interfere with their paid work routines, and employers being less sympathetic towards, or tolerant of, men deserting the workplace for family reasons. Finally, even though men and women in Canada are about equally likely to find their caregiving activities affecting their holiday plans, sleep patterns, and current financial situation, women (27 percent) are more than twice as likely as men (12 percent) to report that caregiving has had a negative affect upon their health (Cranswick, 1997: 6). In support of the "nurturant role" hypothesis (Gee and Kimball, 1987: 34) we presented in our earlier section on morbidity, caregiving may be one component of women's roles that literally makes them sick.

One way to interpret findings such as those obtained from the 1996 GSS is to conclude that caregiving responsibilities are not considered by caregivers generally to be onerous, with only small percentages of men and women reporting significant or severe dislocations to their lives caused by assuming these duties. Another way of interpreting these findings is to suggest that men are less likely to feel burdened, since they assume a lesser share of caregiving responsibilities, while women are much more accepting of our culture's gender expectations that caregiving, in all physical and emotional forms (except perhaps for the directly financial), is an integral part of the female role in our society. Such responsibilities tend to be accepted without question and only in cases of extreme hardship are women allowed to complain or acknowledge the extent to which such responsibilities have become burdensome.

Displaced Genders

Among Canadians now in the late phase of middle adulthood are two categories of people deserving special note. Of the two, the better known have been generally referred to in the literature as **displaced homemakers**. Less well known, and essentially unstudied, is a comparatively new category created in the 1990s, which we choose to refer to as **displaced providers**. These women and men between the ages of 55 to 64 were born between the mid-1930s to mid-1940s and spent their formative years of childhood and adolescence within social institutions supporting and supported by a social climate of traditional, even rigid, gender norms. They followed their respective gender scripts until middle adulthood, when, for different reasons, they have been prevented from continuing with what they believed were their gender destinies.

Women. The term "displaced homemakers" refers to women who have devoted their adult lives to being full-time homemakers (comprising the roles of wives, mothers, and housekeepers), but who, typically due to divorce, but also to separation and to desertion, suddenly find themselves in late middle adulthood without a "job." No longer married, lacking employment histories and the skills and credentials necessary to generate sufficient income to support themselves, sometimes having dependent children to support, a home to maintain, and likely facing age and sex discrimination from employers, many of these women have little or no opportunity to continue their gender Dreams into old age. We noted in previous chapters that Divorce Acts in Canada of 1968 and 1985 allowed for special long-term alimony or spousal maintenance payments to be accorded to displaced home-makers in this stage of life. Courts often feel they have an obligation to ensure that divorcing husbands continue to financially provide for the well-being of these women, either for the remainder of their middle-adulthood, and even older-adulthood, years or until they re-marry. Not all women of this age choose to rely upon the court-ordered or voluntarily proffered kindness from former husbands, but many women must, because of a lack of perceived alternatives. Remarriage is possible, but becomes increasingly unlikely given the combination of sex-ratio imbalances in the numbers of available suitors, and mate-selection gradient norms that provide men with greater latitude in selecting much younger mates.

Burke and Spector (1991) note that the Council of Aging in Canada have portrayed women aged 55–64 who are living on their own as being "too young, yet too old." These women are too young to receive old-age income benefits, but typically are viewed as being too old for the labour market. In 1986, 29 percent of all Canadian women aged 55–64 were living on their own (unless stated otherwise, all statistics in this paragraph come from Burke and Spector, 1991). Between the end of World War II and the middle 1980s, the proportions of widows declined, while the proportions of separated and, particularly, divorced women increased. While 56 percent of divorced women in 1986 were in the labour force, 44 percent of these women living on their own were not (including just less than 10 percent who were seeking employment, but had been unable to find any). Women living on their own had incomes approximately 25 percent below that of men living in comparable circumstances (and more than 50 percent lower than average family incomes), with separated women having the lowest average and divorced women just-above-average incomes. Close to half of separated and divorced women relied on either alimony or government transfer (typically social assistance) payments for financial survival. Women in this age category who were still lone parents faced an imminent prospect of their children leaving home with one result being a cessation of child-support and family-allowance payments, as well as perhaps a loss of subsidized housing. These children were unlikely to become a major source of mothers' financial support in the immediate future.

Even though increases in divorce rates over the past two decades, in combination with slowing rates of remarriage, will likely produce larger numbers of women between the ages of 55 of 64 living on their own in the next two decades, the proportions of these women who qualify for the label of "displaced homemakers" likely are, and will be, smaller, but still substantial, in the period between the mid-1990s and the following two decades. Thirty-four percent of women aged 45 to 54 participating in the 1994 General Social Survey (Beaujot et al., 1995: 61) and 63 percent of women between the ages of 55 and 64 in 1996 (according to *1996 Labour Force Annual Averages*) were not employed. Since the general trend among younger women is to retain close ties to the labour force (Fast and Da Pont, 1997), we should anticipate that the proportions of nonemployed women in their late middle-adulthood years will decrease in the future. Larger portions of younger women are earning higher educational credentials and demonstrating a greater likelihood of utilizing those credentials in the labour force (and not just to provide sparkling conversation around their carefully prepared dinner tables). The long-term trend towards smaller families, including fewer children, means lesser, while still onerous, childrearing responsibilities for many women, and greater opportunities to combine marriage, family, and employment. As well, growing awareness of the likelihood of divorce, as well as personal experiences within their own families of orientation while they were growing up, has created a, perhaps necessary, skepticism within many women to not expect that they will be financially supported until death parts them from their husbands. Whether employment is viewed as "life insurance," or as an ingredient of a desired lifestyle, higher employment levels mean that fewer women are likely to find themselves in a displaced and disadvantaged position during late middle adulthood. However, many women continue to follow the Traditional Marriage Enterprise and some will find their Dreams do not come to full fruition.

Men. The corporate and government restructuring and downsizing frenzy that swept the Canadian economy during the early to mid-1990s resulted in large numbers of men being laid off, fired, "outsourced," or induced to take early retirement before they were ready to leave the labour force. Some of the younger, suddenly unemployed men were products of a "last-hired-first-fired" policy, but the same criteria were not applicable for most older-aged workers. Younger unemployed workers tend to have shorter periods of being without work than do the older unemployed. Best (1995: 32) notes that, while men aged 15–24 had an average duration of unemployment lasting 18 weeks, men over the age of 44 in 1993 were unemployed for an average of 35 weeks. These unemployment figures represent workers who are actively seeking, and typically find, employment, and do not include "discouraged workers," individuals who have given up their search for employment and have effectively dropped out of the labour force. Approximately 18 percent of males between the ages of 45 and 54, and 45 percent of males between the ages of 55 and 64 in 1993, were not in the labour force (estimations derived from Best, 1995: 31).

An unknown proportion of these men represent a new category of men, displaced providers, who no longer find themselves able to fulfill an important element of what they believed was their gender destiny. While unemployment, underemployment, and nonemployment have been part of our economic institution since industrialization, with the exception of the Great Depression of the 1930s, it appears that the mid- to late 1990s has the largest proportion of men who would also fit the Council of Aging's description of being "too young, yet too old." They are too young to give up their male work-role Dreams of being providers for their spouses and children, and, therefore, too young to consider themselves as "retired," yet they have been deemed too old, and too expensive, to be of value to their former employers. The commitment and desire to remain a provider is still present, but the opportunity to do so, similar to displaced homemakers, has been taken away from them.

It is unlikely that all displaced providers face the same obstacles. Social class, measured primarily by (former) occupation, but also by education, will play a crucial role. Working-class and lesser-educated men, possibly men of certain visibly different ethnic groups as well, are more likely to find themselves displaced from the workplace with only a minimal severance package, if any, unless they are among the minority enjoying union protection. These displaced providers face continued age discrimination and, perhaps, also a credential-based discrimination, in that both former and potential employers are likely to choose to ignore seasoned, experienced workers who possess fewer degrees, diplomas, or certificates, in favour of less experienced, but more highly credentialed workers. As well, older and more experienced workers typically command higher salaries and wages and their skills are less portable. Employers, in an era of budget cutting and "bottom line" downsizing prefer to hire less expensive employees. These older displaced providers will continue to face discrimination against the very qualities they possess that led them to being downsized out of economic existence in the first place. Displaced providers in professional, managerial, and administrative locations within organizational structures, who also tend to possess higher credentials, are more likely to receive severance or early retirement packages that enable them to enjoy a smoother ride into nonemployment on their golden parachutes. Since their credentials and experiences tend to be more portable, they are likely to find greater opportunities for employment and a continuation of their provider role in the future.

The outcome of taking forcible early retirement is not clear as yet, although postretirement data (to be presented later in this chapter) are suggestive of a pattern. Approximately 40 percent (see Monette, 1996b) of these men will attempt to return to the labour force to take part-time, or contract, or self-employment paid work. More highly credentialed men are more likely both to seek and to find subsequent employment. Eventually, after a few years, the largest proportion of displaced providers are likely to be working-class, lesser-credentialed, men living in financially straightened circumstances. Today, all displaced providers were born, raised, and socialized in social institutions characterized by more rigid and fixed gender norms, although more highly educated men and women profess greater gender-role flexibility than do lesser-educated men and women. While we know little about the fate of displaced providers, we know even less about the reactions of their spouses to losing a provider, but still retaining a companion in the home.

Do spouses, as many of the displaced providers themselves are likely to do, equate his displacement with a diminution of his masculinity? Or, will they embrace a notion, and try to convince their husbands of this, that an opportunity exists to rethink and re-evaluate the central basis of masculinity and use displaced providership as a new transitional event leading into a later phase of adult male, possibly even female, development? Since the displaced provider phenomenon is a consequence of the Canadian economy of the 1990s, only history will tell if this is to be a unique and temporary phenomenon or something more enduring. Only research will tell us the outcome of the displaced provider experience upon gender.

Marital Status in Late Middle Adulthood and Older Adulthood

Table 9.5 presents data for five-year age groups, from ages 50–54 through to ages 90 and older, collected from the 1996 Census in Canada. Findings presented in the columns under the headings of "never-married," "separated," and "divorced" demonstrate great similarities between the genders with increasing age. Percentages for never-marrieds decline between the ages of 50–54 to the late seventies or early eighties and then increase for older age groups. For the most part, these variations reflect differing economic circumstances from earlier historical eras, when males in particular could, more or less, easily afford to marry and financially support a spouse and family. Given that females were not expected to take any overt initiative in decisions to marry during these earlier times, female rates partly reflect differing opportunities to marry as a consequence of male circumstances. Some unknown portion of all never-marrieds are gay or lesbian and have never had an opportunity to marry legally in our society. Another unknown portion of the never-married population includes individual males and females who chose never to marry for personal reasons. A smaller, yet also unknown, number of gays and lesbians are, or were, involved in heterosexual marriages and will be located in the married or formerly married categories.

TABLE 9.5	Legal Marital Status*, By Selected Five-Year Age Groups, in Percentage, Canada: 1996									
	Never Married		Legally** Married		Separated***		Divorced		Widowed	
Age	Male	Female	Male	Female	Male	Female	Male	Female	Male	Female
50–54	8.4	7.0	73.8	69.2	4.1	4.1	12.5	14.5	1.3	5.2
55–59	7.2	5.9	76.4	69.4	3.6	3.4	10.7	11.8	2.2	9.5
60–64	6.8	5.6	77.7	66.0	3.1	2.8	8.5	9.2	3.8	16.3
65–69	6.9	5.8	77.4	58.8	2.8	2.4	6.5	6.8	6.4	26.1
70–74	6.6	6.1	76.1	48.4	2.5	1.9	4.6	4.8	10.2	38.8
75–79	6.1	6.9	73.0	35.4	2.2	1.5	3.2	3.2	15.5	53.0
80–84	6.6	8.4	65.6	22.2	2.1	1.1	2.4	2.0	23.4	66.4
85–89	6.9	9.4	54.7	11.9	2.1	0.7	1.7	1.3	34.6	76.8
90+	7.7	10.3	38.7	4.8	1.7	0.4	1.4	0.8	50.4	83.9

Note: *individuals in common-law arrangements are listed by their legal marital status
   **legally married and still living together
   ***physically living apart but still legally married

Source: Percentages derived from Statistics Canada. *Age, Sex, Marital Status and Common Law, Canada, Provinces and Territories, 1996.* Electronic media Release. 14 October 1997b.

Declining proportions for both males and females down the columns of "separated" and "divorced" statuses reflect changing social mores where younger men and women were more likely to take advantage of increasingly available options to either separate or divorce should their relationships become unsatisfying or unworkable. Older men and women faced greater social and personal pressures in earlier times to remain together "until death us do part." As census data do not in themselves provide information on the number of marital status transformations any particular individual has undergone over his or her lifetime, some unknown proportion of the Canadian population currently aged 50 and beyond has previously divorced (at least once), subsequently remarried (at least once), and are currently listed under the heading of "married."

The most striking gender differences are found in the columns under the headings of "legally married" and of "widowed." The majority of men between the ages of 50 and 89 are still legally married and living with a spouse. The decline with age for now-married men is gradual, except for the sharp drop between the age 85–89 group, and the last group of men aged 90 and over. This more precipitous decline is attributable to the fact that the last category includes an age-grouping with no upper limit (i.e., is not limited to only a five-year age span). Only among men aged 90 and over do we find that less than 50 percent, but still close to 40 percent, are currently married. In contrast, the proportions of females currently married decline dramatically over the ages considered in Table 9.5. By ages 70 to 74, fewer women, proportionally, are still married and living with a spouse than are men over the age of 90. By ages 80 to 84, only around one-fifth of all women that age are still married. By ages 90 and over, just under five percent of Canadian women are legally married and presumably have a partner with whom to relate on a daily basis.

The declines of currently marrieds across increasingly older ages are accounted for primarily by noticeable increases in the proportions of each age group who are widowed. The last columns in Table 9.5 readily demonstrate gender differences in mortality described at the beginning of the present chapter. The commonly used term to refer to surviving men is "widowers," but the word itself implies "one who widows" and implicitly raises questions as to how these men came to attain their status. We prefer to use the less suspicious gender-neutral term of "widow" to refer to both men and women. The proportions of men who are currently widowed are very small among the younger age groups considered in the table. Only at ages 70 to 74 do we first find more than 10 percent (10.2) of the men occupying that status. These low figures reflect a combination of both greater female longevity and a greater likelihood of previously widowed men remarrying. By ages 85 to 89, slightly more than one-third (34.6 percent) of the men are presently widowed, and not until ages 90 and over do we find that more than 50 percent (50.4) of men identify themselves as widowed. In sharp contrast, more than a third of all women (38.8 percent) between the ages of 70 to 74 are widowed, reflecting the combined effects of lower male longevity and a lesser likelihood of female remarriage after becoming widowed. More than 50 percent of all Canadian women beyond age 75 are widowed.

Between the ages of 50 and 64, what could be termed as the late phase of middle adulthood, 75.7 percent of men and 68.4 percent of women were married in 1996 (figures derived from Statistics Canada, 1997, see Table 9.5 source). Viewed another way, 24.3 percent of men and 31.6 percent of women between the ages of 50 and 64 either have never been married or, more commonly, were among the formerly married. For ages 65 and beyond, what can be termed as older adulthood, 73.1 percent of men and 40.7 percent of women were married in 1996. More than one-quarter (26.9 percent) of the men and more than half of the women (59.3 percent) were either never married or among the formerly married. About one-tenth (13.3 percent) of older men, but close to one-half (46.5 percent) of older women were widowed. The percentage distributions in 1996 of married and widowed men and women over the age of 64 are very similar to findings obtained from the 1981

Census of Canada, and comparable to distributions found in the 1921 Census (Connidis, 1989: 7). Over the long term, the most noticeable change pertains to higher proportions of divorced persons among all age groups and slightly lower proportions of currently married individuals.

With the exception of a larger divorced population among Canadians in middle adulthood, the proportionate distributions of men and women by marital status demonstrate a continued persistence of stable social patterns since the 1920s, resulting in older-adulthood men, but not women, being almost assured that spousal companionship will remain part of their lives until their own deaths. Just as census data do not provide information on how long a person has occupied a particular marital status, they also do not inform us as to what proportions of nonmarried men and women are involved in heterosexual unmarried couple relationships, what proportions have relationships or friendships confined solely or mainly to same-sex age peers, and what proportions, essentially, are alone. The statistical sex-ratio imbalance described earlier in this chapter, along with impressionistic evidence gathered from observing the sex composition of travel tour groups, concert attendees, midweek shopping-mall walkers, coffee shop- and restaurant-goers, and participants at other public functions suggests that substantially more women than men lack a heterosexual companion. While this represents a personal and desired choice for some, an absence of male companionship for many other women is due simply to a lack of available opportunity.

Older Adulthood

According to the United Nations, a society can be classified as "aged" if 8 percent or more of its population is 65 years of age or older (McVey and Kalbach, 1995: 75). Relative to that index, Canada was officially classified as an "aged" society in 1971. Since then, the number of people in our society aged 65 and over has more than doubled. Viewed from a longer-term perspective, the growth of this age cohort has been remarkable. Approximately 178 000 people aged 65 and over lived in Canada in 1881 (McVey and Kalbach, 1995: 75). The 1996 census registered slightly more than 3.5 million people in our country aged 65 and over, who, as a consequence of smaller younger-age cohorts and the large size of this older age cohort, now comprise 12.2 percent of our total population (Statistics Canada, *Daily*, 29 July 1997: 9).

Varyingly referred to as "seniors," "the elderly," "golden agers," or "old folks," people in older adulthood will, in all likelihood, continue to comprise a substantial proportion of our population in the first few decades of the twenty-first century (McVey and Kalbach, 1995: 75–76). At the moment, older adulthood is still an emergent stage in the human life course of Canadians, in that specific age-related gender norms are vague, amorphous, and principally an extension of earlier, particularly middle-adulthood, expectations and enactments brought by the participants themselves into this new stage. The life-course stage of older adulthood is, literally, a "work in progress" at the individual, societal, and scholarly levels, with a complete, well-integrated, life-course perspective integrating older adulthood with earlier adulthood years and stages yet to be established.

As more of our population moves into older adulthood, it is still unclear whether this stage will ultimately be composed of two or three subphases, demarcated roughly by chronological age boundaries such as "young olds" (between the ages of 65 and 80) and "old olds" (beyond the age of 80), or "young olds" (between ages 65 and 75), "middle olds" (between ages 75 and 85), and "old olds" (aged 86 and over). We must allow for the passage of time and a more complete social construction of old age before we can determine the best means of capturing relevant age groupings meaningfully differentiated by experiences, challenges and solutions, and distinctive lifestyles, and then isolating pertinent gender issues. In the interim, we focus very briefly upon three major experiences common to many or most people aged 65 and over: **retirement**, **poverty**, and **widowhood**.

Retirement

In earlier eras characterized by comparatively shorter life expectancies, the concept of *retirement* from the paid-labour force did not exist within our society. Prior to industrialization, women and men laboured to provide for their own and their families' survival until such time as they were physically unable to continue. Even though industrialization altered the meaning of "work" itself and the nature of the tasks being performed, paid workers generally continued to seek employment until such time as they were physically incapable, since neither government nor business nor manufacturing companies provided any kind of financial compensation for older Canadians unable to labour for pay. "Most North Americans prior to the Second World War worked until disability or death, or depended upon their children for assistance" (Baker, 1988: 78). Even though old-age and postretirement programs had long been part of many European countries, and began to emerge in nascent form in our society during the late 1920s, not until the postwar prosperity of the 1950s and 1960s did national large-scale social safety net programs for older citizens come fully into being in Canada. These programs, current versions of which are outlined in the next section, contributed significantly to the notion that employed persons could actually retire from their jobs once they had reached a certain length of employment service or a defined age, and still receive some form of income during their post-paid-labour years (for a history of retirement in Canada, see McDonald and Wanner, 1990: 17–37).

As an event, retirement "involves the formal end of employment and the beginning of life without a job" that does not carry with it the stigma of unemployment (McDonald and Wanner, 1990: 4). Retirement has become a major transition event, demarcating movement from middle adulthood into older adulthood, although more so for men than for women in our society, as we shall soon see. Age 65 has been set arbitrarily (first by Otto von Bismarck in Germany of the 1880s and eventually copied by most industrialized nations) as the minimum age of eligibility for collection of pension and social security benefits. Canada initially established an arbitrary age of eligibility at 70, but in 1966 gradually began to lower the age to 65 (Oderkirk, 1996a: 3). Age 65 also became the expected time of retirement. Prior to the establishment of universal social security and old-age pensions, nearly half of the male population in Canada over the age of 65 in 1946 were still in the labour force; forty years later, only 11 percent of men aged 65 and over remained actively employed (McDonald and Wanner, 1990: 42). Since the mid-1970s, actual age of retirement in Canada has become more variable, particularly among men.

Lowe (1992) notes that although Canadian women are less likely than men to have an employer pension plan, they are more likely than men to opt for early retirement. Lowe additionally notes that, while health-related reasons are identified by both men and women as an important factor influencing their decision to retire, women are more likely than men to identify marriage and/or family responsibilities as important in their decision to retire early.

Conducted prior to the downsizing frenzy of the 1990s, Canada's 1989 General Social Survey finds that women are more likely than men to retire before age 65 (65 percent of women compared to 61 percent of men) or age 60 (43 percent of women compared with 28 percent of men). As Townson (1995: 7) suggests, "it seems reasonable to assume that many women left the paid-work force because they wanted to retire at the same time as a spouse or because they had to care for older spouses." It would appear that traditional messages still hold considerable sway over Canadian women even if and when the aftermath of adhering to them may prove financially perilous. While being married *may* provide a protective buffer against poverty, "the need to depend on a spouse for support in retirement raises issues of women's financial autonomy. And married women may experience serious financial hardship if the relationship ends" (Townson, 1995: 2).

Findings from the 1994 General Social Survey (Monette, 1996a: 9) indicate that 14 percent of men aged 55–59 in Canada were retired as were 45 percent of men aged 60–64, 78 percent of men aged 65–69, 87 percent of those in their early seventies, 89 percent of those in their late seventies, and 92 percent of those aged 80 and older. The average age of retirement among men who participated in the survey was 61.4 years. The most common reasons offered by men of all ages in 1994 for having retired from the labour force were (Monette, 1996a: 9): for their health (25 percent); strictly personal choice (24 percent); as a consequence of mandatory retirement policies (16 percent); simply feeling old enough (11 percent); the availability of early retirement incentives (10 percent); and becoming unemployed (10 percent). Whereas men who retired for reasons of mandatory retirement policies or because they felt old enough left the labour force in their mid-sixties, men who retired for health or personal choice reasons tended to retire on average in their late fifties or very early sixties. Even though "health reasons" suggests that retirement is involuntary, some degree of personal choice is still involved in a decision to cease being employed to preserve an existing level of personal health. Men who retired due to unemployment or the availability of early retirement incentives also retired in their late fifties or early sixties, primarily as a consequence of policies implemented to downsize the work force. The former group of men appear to have had little choice over whether to retire, while the latter group chose to retire (and receive extra benefits) rather than look for employment elsewhere. Presumably, men who avail themselves of early retirement packages are more likely to have been employed in managerial or professional positions, while unemployed men are more likely to have been employed in lesser skilled, less transferable, and more vulnerable positions.

The concept of retirement is more complex among older women in Canada. Predictive models, based upon male experiences, appear to be less effective when trying to explain and predict decisions to retire among women (Gee and Kimball, 1987: 76; McDonald and Wanner, 1990: 116). The 1994 General Social Survey (Monette, 1996a: 10) finds that, while many older women share a definition with men of retirement meaning a recent severance of ties from the paid-labour force, some women define themselves as "retired" even though they actually left the paid labour force for the birth of their first child many years, even decades, ago and never returned. Within this latter group, which has been separated from the labour force for many years, some women do not label themselves as "retired" until such time as their husbands begin collecting a pension cheque (in order words, their self-definition is dependent not upon their own behaviour, but upon the situation of their spouses). Regardless of the circumstances surrounding their self-definition, 2 percent of women aged 50–54 identified themselves as retired, as did 9 percent of women 55–59, 22 percent of women 60–64,

33 percent of women 65–69, 42 percent of women in their early seventies, 49 percent of women in their late seventies, and 46 percent of women aged 80 and older (Monette, 1996a: 10). All of these percentages are substantially lower than those obtained from comparably aged men in the same survey and is, perhaps, an indication, consistent with gender norms from an earlier era in Canada's history, of these women's weaker attachment to labour-force participation as a central or important component of their social and personal identity. If other, more important, sources of identity are available, retirement from the labour force becomes a less meaningful event for self-definition. Paid work is, and has been, a central component of masculine identity for men in our society, but is only now becoming an important component of feminine identity.

While 13 percent of women participating in the 1994 General Social Survey indicate they retired for "family reasons," such as raising children or caring for a spouse or relative (Monette, 1996a: 10), family considerations rarely appear to influence men's retirement (among the 3 percent of "other" reasons given). Obviously, women who "retire" to care for their children do so at a much earlier age than do women who leave the labour force to care for a spouse or another relative, either of whom are typically much older when they are in need of such care. Overall, women who retired for family reasons did so at an average age of 48 (Monette, 1996a: 10). Seven percent of women who labeled themselves as "retired" claim they retired because their spouses retired. Given that women typically marry men older than themselves, it is not surprising to find that women who retired because of their husband's retirement were an average of 59.2 years old (Monette, 1996a: 10), approximately two years younger than the average age of retirement for men.

Early writings on the retirement experience promoted a notion that, since paid employment provides a major source of accomplishment, identity, and income, as well as being a major force structuring time use among adults, a loss of such benefits upon retirement would precipitate a "crisis" for men (Friedmann and Havighurst, 1954). This trauma was equivalent to the "empty nest crisis" supposedly experienced by women upon the departure of children from the family home and the attendant loss by women of their meaningful role and identity as a childrearer. Research findings on the retirement-as-crisis hypothesis have been largely inconsistent (Beck, 1982). These inconsistencies lead to a conclusion that some men find retirement to be a difficult experience initially, but many, if not most, men do not (Martin Mathews et al., 1982). Health, finances, anticipatory socialization and actual preparedness and attitudes towards retirement all influence how the event and the transition into postretirement life are experienced (see McDonald and Wanner, 1990; Chapter 5, for a review).

Social relationships, particularly their quality, are positively correlated to satisfaction with retirement (McDonald and Wanner, 1990: 90–91). Men's social relationships in adulthood, being connected mainly to their occupations and employment-related organizations, appear to decline in number following retirement, while women's social relationships, particularly those derived from involvements in religious and volunteer activities, tend to increase. To the extent to which social relationships provide an alterative source of life satisfaction following retirement, women appear to be able to adjust more satisfactorily than do men. Contacts with relatives and neighbourhood friends remain essentially the same for both men and women following retirement (Keating and Cole, 1980).

Retirement is more likely to bring about a sense of discontinuity or disjuncture in the lives of men than in the lives of women. This disjuncture is experienced as a major break from the past, with few continuities from a life characterized by employment. The central tasks facing men upon retirement lie in finding alternative activities that not only provide meaning and satisfaction, but also fill in the significantly greater amounts of time now available. While retiring women must also confront similar issues, their lives are characterized by underlying continuities not experienced by men. Women's caregiver role, especially towards husbands, continues after retirement and may become intensified as their husbands age and typically experience an increase in health problems. As well, since men tend to drift away from friendships with former coworkers, wives often find their husbands to be even more emotionally dependent upon them following retirement and wives' marriage-maintenance role continues, perhaps becoming even more important. Men's greater dependency can become a source of either greater closeness or increased irritation (Connidis, 1989: 24) among wives in particular.

Similar to findings for the previous adult years, women also perform the great majority of household tasks during the postretirement years, even though men's participation levels do increase somewhat (Brubaker and Hennon, 1982; Connidis, 1989: 23). Even if such labour held or holds little in the way of intrinsic satisfactions, the continuity of such responsibility prevents development of a major personal sense, among older women, of dislocation or disjuncture from earlier stages of adult life. Ironically, housework, once the scourge of life, becomes a stabilizing factor in the transition to the postretirement years (although retired men's sudden fascination with either doing or supervising housework, as a means of filling in their time, may become a source of dissatisfaction among women or conflict between couples).

Even though the concept and practice of retirement has become institutionalized in Canada, a portion of our population first experience the transition out of the workforce into retirement status, and then later transit back into paid-worker status. According to the 1994 General Social Survey (unless indicated otherwise, all statistics presented here are from Monette, 1996b), 13 percent of all respondents, and presumably the same percentage of all Canadians, aged 50 and over who retire, return to the workforce later on. Sixteen percent of men and 8 percent of women who have ever retired have returned to working for pay. These returnees retired at an average age (57.9 years) younger than all other retired people (average age at retirement of 60.6 years). It appears that the younger the age at retirement, the greater the likelihood of returning to the labour force at a later time. Twenty-six percent of those who retired between the ages of 55 and 59 returned to the labour force, in comparison to 16 percent of those aged 60 to 64, 12 percent of those 65 to 69, and only 8 percent of those who retired at age 70 or older.

The major reasons behind a decision to retire (Monette, 1996a) are also related to the decision to return to the labour force (Monette, 1996b). Individuals induced to retire by the availability of early retirement incentives were the most likely (25 percent) to return to paid work at a later time, followed by those who retired because of losing their previous job (15 percent), those who felt old enough to retire (14 percent), and those who retired simply out of personal choice (13 percent). People who retired for health, family care, because a spouse retired, or mandatory retirement reasons were the least likely to return later to the workforce. Simultaneously, a number of factors in postretirement life have become added reasons contributing to decisions to return to paid work. Additional identified reasons include the 25 percent of retirees who return to the labour force for financial reasons, 20 percent for a way of filling in their spare time, 21 percent because they simply desired to, and lesser proportions who felt they were too young to retire in the first place, or moved to a new location and became aware of new paid-work opportunities.

A person was more likely to return to the labour force if he or she was not living alone or was living in a household comprising three or more people. Financial reasons became a more compelling reason to return to paid work among those living in larger households (45 percent) than for those living alone (24 percent) or with one other person (17 percent). Having a partner who was also in the labour force added another important incentive to return to paid work (48 percent). Higher education is positively correlated to the decision to return to the labour force; 23 percent of university-educated people, 13 percent of persons with high-school diplomas or nonuniversity postsecondary certificates or diplomas, and nine percent of persons with less than high-school credentials have returned to the labour force. People who returned to the labour force were also more likely to have backgrounds in professional or managerial occupations, and much less likely to have been employed previously in semiskilled occupations. Women were more likely than men (68 percent versus 51 percent) to take on part-time employment following an earlier decision to retire, and were also more likely to take on temporary (with or without a specified-term contract) employment than were men (45 percent versus 36 percent, respectively). In comparison, men were more likely to consider themselves employed full time.

That men were twice as likely as women to return to the labour force appears to reflect men's historically greater attachment to the labour force, as well as their greater difficulties in finding satisfying alternatives to paid work. All or a majority of their adult lives were structured around the hours and demands of full-time employment, and their social and personal identity was derived mainly from their jobs. Neither housework nor marriage maintenance and caregiving are sufficiently appealing ways of filling in a major increase in the amount of free time suddenly available to them, following initial retirement. An initial flurry of travel activities, new "hobbies," wandering around shopping malls or having coffee and conversation with old workmates quickly leaves some men unfulfilled. An identity of "retired" appears to be less satisfactory than their previous work-related identity. Substantial numbers of these men were employed during historical periods in our country when company-based pension plans and private registered retirement plans were not available. Their personal savings and government pension plans do not produce sufficient income for a viable postretirement lifestyle. Since they had devoted their adult years to being a provider, many of these men returned to being a provider and, in addition, to enjoying the familiar identity and activities offered by employment.

Women of retirement age today have not been conditioned or socialized to derive their major sense of identity from being attached to the labour force. Most of these women derive more of their sense of identity from being a wife and mother and can continue with wifely activities and mothering, albeit on a reduced scale, throughout their adult years, until the deaths of their husbands, children, or themselves. As well, housework responsibilities continue to exert demands upon their time. Returning to the labour force has less appeal for these women than it does for men of comparable age, especially given older women's comparative lack of credentials or paid-work experience, and the limited kinds of employment available to them in their postretirement years.

Whether younger generations of men and women will follow in the same footsteps as their elders when they enter their retirement years remains to be determined. Increasingly, more younger men proclaim, although their behaviour is not consistent with those declarations, they are less attached to paid work for their sense of identity and masculinity, and are more attached to marriage and family and to nonemployment activities. Should these marriages and families last into their retirement years and should they continue to be able to afford participation in favoured activities, men's retirement experiences may well be different in the future and may converge with experiences more common to retired women.

As with many other areas of social life, women's lives relative to retirement promise to be less patterned in the near future than are men's. Younger women, including those in middle adulthood today, have a stronger and longer attachment to the labour force than have any previous cohorts of women since the end of World War II. Employment has become integrated with their own conceptions of femininity. We can anticipate that women currently in the professions and managerial occupations will be less likely to retire simply because their husbands are, and more likely to base their decisions on personal pension and job-related considerations. As well, women today, especially those under the age of 65, are distributed more variably across all marital statuses than in the past. Widowed and never-married women typically face fewer financial constraints on their decision to retire than do divorced and separated women. All of these women are more likely to make retirement decisions independently than are currently married women, who have a relationship partner to take into consideration. However, given changes of the past 30 years, currently married women are less likely to base their decisions solely or primarily upon a husband's needs or desires. Whether all of these younger women's retirement experiences will converge with currently older men's experiences remains to be seen.

Poverty

For many Canadians, including the near-elderly, the issue of financial security during retirement seems remote and of only distant concern. As Townson (1995: 6) remarks, "[s]urveys indicate a wide gap between the optimistic expectations of Canadians for retirement and the reality of inadequate final resources that most will face." She observes that, according to a 1992 Canadian survey, while three-quarters of the respondents recognize that they will be personally responsible for a significant portion of their retirement income, "three-quarters are also doing little or no planning for retirement" (p. 6). Although a retirement income of $50 000 per year would require a lump sum deposit of $500 000 (or, alternatively, for a person with 20 years remaining until retirement, depositing $11 000 yearly at a 7 percent rate of return), the savings of most Canadians are far more modest. Including contributions made to an employer's pension plan, 50 percent of Canadians in the paid work force save less than $2000 on a yearly basis (Townson, 1995: 6).

We noted earlier that, after the age of 50, women are less likely than men to be currently married. This demographic fact becomes important because marital status has a significant impact on the likelihood of poverty during old age (The National Council of Welfare, 1990). While the rate of poverty among the Canadian elderly declined from approximately 22 percent in 1980 to 9 percent in 1991, married seniors have a much lower poverty rate than seniors living alone or with nonrelatives (Poverty Profile Update for 1991, 1993). Part of the answer for why this occurs lies in the fact that, while federal income-security programs are effective in protecting most senior couples from poverty, they are less effective in safeguarding seniors who live alone.

At present, Canada's retirement income system is composed of three tiers: governmental benefits such as Old Age Security (OAS) and the Guaranteed Income Supplement (GIS) designed to forestall the likelihood of poverty by furnishing all seniors with a taxable, flat rate benefit (adjusted every three months as the Consumer Price Index increases), which is paid monthly regardless of their work histories or life circumstances; the government-sponsored Canada (CPP)/Quebec (QPP) pensions plans, which are designed to provide workers with a retirement income based upon their preretirement earnings from ages 18 to 65; and private savings, which include employer-sponsored private pensions plans, private investments, and Registered Retirement Savings Plans (RRSPs) (Townson, 1995: 27). While, generally, both men and women become eligible to receive OAS benefits at age 65, some exemptions do exist. For example, since 1989, Canadian seniors whose yearly net incomes exceed $50 000 are required to repay all or some of their OAS benefits, depending upon the full amount of that income. Subject to the total income requirement, only Canadians who, from the age of 18, have lived in our country for a period of not less than 40 years qualify for full OAS benefits. Individuals who have lived here for 10 or more years, but less than 40 years, may apply for and receive partial benefits and persons who have lived in Canada for less than 10 years may receive even smaller partial benefits. However, under a series of reciprocal arrangements with certain other countries, a person residing in Canada can add their years of residency in one of those countries to their years of Canadian residency to qualify for some form of OAS pension (Oderkirk, 1996a). As well, if a person has at least 20 years previous residency in Canada after reaching age 18, an OAS pension will be paid to him or her for an indefinite period of time even if the person currently resides permanently outside of the country (in, for example, Florida, Texas, Arizona, or Mexico).

The GIS is designed to assist those seniors whose incomes (excluding the OAS) fall below a specified level and provides benefits that are graduated by income (current assets, such as the value of an owned home, are not taken into consideration) and marital status. As of 1994, the maximum GIS benefit available for a single elderly person was $458.50 monthly; a single person who had an income in excess of $917 a month from other sources was not eligible for this supplement. For married couples, eligibility was determined by a ceiling of family income, excluding OAS, that was less than $1194 a month. For those who qualified, the maximum monthly benefit available in 1994 was $597.30 per couple (or $298.65 per person). Unlike the OAS, GIS payments are not taxable and have, over the years, been increased on an ad hoc basis (Townson, 1995: 29). Taken together, these benefits furnished single individuals with a maximum guaranteed annual income of $10 132, and couples with a maximum annual income of $16 427 in 1994 (Townson, 1995: 30). Consider, however, in 1993 that the low-income cut-off line for a single person living in an urban area with a population of 500 000 or more was $16 482; for a two-person family in an urban area of that size, it was $20 603 (Columbo, 1996: 83).

Spouse's Allowance (SPA) is available to a spouse between the ages of 60 and 64 with 10 years residency in the country, as long as her or his married partner is 65 years of age or older and is collecting GIS. SPA is subject to an income test similar to the GIS. Widowed SPA is available to any widowed person between the ages of 60 and 64 with at least 10 years residency in this country. SPA payments to spouses in couples are based on couple income, while Widowed SPA payments are based on the surviving person's income. The upper limit for eligibility among couples in 1994 was $20 688; for the widowed, that limit was $15 168. In 1994, the maximum monthly SPA payment was $687, while the maximum monthly Widowed SPA was $758. Ninety-one percent of SPA recipients in 1994 were women, reflecting age differentials at marriage. Women also accounted for 93 percent of Widowed SPA recipients (Oderkirk, 1996a: 4)

As we noted earlier, unlike GIS and OAS benefits, which are unrelated to an individual's prior income history, CPP/QPP benefits are directly based upon a person's income earned between the ages of 18 and 65, and proportionately reflect their prior income patterns. Although full benefits do not begin until age 65, partial CPP/QPP payments can be received by retired persons between ages of 60–64, or a person can wait until age 70 to begin receiving enhanced payments. Reduced or enhanced payments can deviate from basic payments to a maximum of 30 percent (Oderkirk, 1996b: 9). In recent times, many federal politicians and economic advisors have advocated moving the age for full-benefit coverage up to age 67 or even 70, as a means of reducing the total payout to Canadians in the face of increasing numbers of eligible seniors. Not only is our age-65-and-older population increasing, but the number of formerly employed, formerly contributing, and now pension-eligible (in their own right) women are increasing at a dramatic rate and will continue to increase (Oderkirk, 1996b: 10). Raising the age of eligibility for full payments may happen soon.

Townson (1995: 31) observes that the CPP is, in many ways, "an ideal pension plan for women," since, for example, it accommodates women's often-interrupted employment histories with a "child-rearing drop-out provision" that allows women to exclude from their calculation of preretirement earnings those typically reduced-income years when they had a child under age seven. As well, in that the CPP/QPP does not discriminate between full-time and part-time workers, the plan is "ideally suited to women, who are much more likely than men to be employed part-time (Townson, 1995: 33). In these ways, the CPP/QPP indirectly makes allowances for women's unpaid work responsibilities within the home, which contribute to lower preretirement earnings. Generally, the level of benefits available from the CPP/QPP is low relative to earnings, with the retired worker receiving 25 percent of his/her average annual lifetime earnings, up to a maximum that is adjusted yearly with increases in the Consumer Price Index. "[T]o the extent that women have low [preretirement] earnings, an income replacement pension plan will give them low benefits" (Townson, 1995: 31) and women, on average, receive a monthly retirement benefit that is much lower than that paid to men. Whereas women who retired in 1993 received, on average, a monthly CPP benefit of $263, men received an average monthly CPP benefit of $478 (Townson, 1995: 33). As in preretirement years, many women in their retirement years are dependent for financial survival upon a spouse's (pension) income.

Women may receive additional CPP benefits through a spouse in three ways: sharing of benefits at retirement; division of pension credits upon divorce; or, upon death, survivor benefits. While sharing benefits upon retirement is not available to members of the QPP, the CPP can provide an independent form of income for a woman who has been a full-time housewife throughout her adult years and has not contributed to the pension plan. However, as Townson (1995: 34) points out, "pension assignment" occurs only on a voluntary basis and, since the inception of this program in 1987, only 50 000 couples have made application for credit-sharing at retirement.

Since 1991, a division of credits may also occur in most provinces at formal dissolution of a marriage, when pension credits earned during the course of a marriage can be equally divided between the spouses upon divorce (except in the provinces of Saskatchewan, British Columbia and Quebec where provincial family law allows couples to waive credit-splitting in the event of a divorce). Townson (1995: 35) reports that a lack of awareness of this provision has resulted in many eligible formerly married women forfeiting this opportunity to gain CPP credits. Others "traded" this benefit for other, perhaps more immediately tangible assets. In consequence, she reports, "[t]he data indicate that, unless their divorce took place within the past year or two...divorced women who are now 45–54 are unlikely to have benefited from a share in a husband's CPP/QPP credits" (1995: 35) with divorced women in Quebec more likely than women in other parts of Canada to have benefitted from this option. Couples who have lived common-law may also apply for credit-splitting when their relationship ends, but can do so only after they have resided separately for a minimum period of one year, but less than a maximum of three years.

Survivor benefits are available to the spouses of contributors to the CPP/QPP provided that the deceased contributed to the plan for at least 10 years or one-third of his or her "eligible years." About 90 percent of those receiving survivor benefits are women. The benefit to the spouse is calculated as 60 percent of the amount that would have been payable to the deceased had the spouse turned 65 on the date of his/her death and had, in 1994, a ceiling of $416.66 per month for a surviving spouse aged 65 and older, and $384.59 per month for surviving spouses who were less than 65 years of age; these benefits are payable even in the event that a survivor remarries. The amounts paid to survivors in Quebec are considerably more generous than in the rest of Canada (see Townson, 1995: 35).

While CPP/QPP, OAS, and GIS provisions forestall the likelihood of individuals falling into poverty during their retirement years, the risk of poverty for elderly women remains significant in that relatively few have access to additional private-sector (i.e., nongovernment) pensions such as those provided by employers to employees. Findings derived from Statistics Canada's Labour Market Activity Survey and prepared specifically for a Canadian Advisory Council on the Status of Women (Townson, 1995) indicate that slightly more than one-third (35.3 percent) of all women in 1992, versus 41.0 percent of all men, in the Canadian labour force were covered by company pension plans; when the unemployed are excluded, 42.5 percent of women versus 51.8 percent of men in paid employment were covered by such plans (Townson, 1995: 37). Approximately half (53 percent) of Canadian women, compared to 77 percent of men, in the 45–54 year age group were covered by private pension plans in at least one of the jobs they held between 1988 to 1990. Certain groups, such as First Nations women and women with disabilities, are particularly unlikely to be covered by a private pension plan, and the likelihood of poverty is particularly pronounced among elderly women with disabilities (Ross et al., 1994: 41; DAWN, 1987).

To a large degree, women's lack of company-sponsored pension coverage reflects their relative absence from employment in sectors such as manufacturing, construction, transportation, communication, and government services where pension coverage is quite high, and their overrepresentation within the areas of retail trade and community, business, and personal service where coverage is low. A woman employed as a secretary or as a salesperson for a small business is unlikely to receive a benefits package and, if she does, it is unlikely to be as comprehensive as those provided to workers whose pension plans are negotiated by trade unions on their behalf. Accordingly, the low percentage of women workers who are unionized (28 percent of women workers versus 36 percent of men) becomes significant (Townson, 1995: 39). Boyd (1989/1995: 217) reports that substantial numbers of Asian, Caribbean, and South European women immigrants are self-employed as seamstresses, domestics, or other marginally paid roles within the "invisible economy," and likely receive no benefits for their years of underground employment.

While having any type of pension is advantageous, differences in pensions plans undoubtedly influence an individual's financial future. "Defined contribution plans" or "money purchase plans," which are typical of many small businesses, refer to a type of pension plan in which both employer and employee make contributions to a fund, but in which only the contribution—and not the benefit—is guaranteed. Rather than a providing a benefit linked to earnings or years of employment, the monies received by a worker upon retirement simply reflect the investment performance of the fund. "Defined benefit" pension plans, which provide benefits upon retirement that are linked to a worker's salary and years of service, may or may not require contributions to be made by the worker. Townson (1995: 43) notes, however, that employers who provide such plans are more likely to be public sector or large businesses or institutions. Although only Ontario currently has provisions which guarantee that pensions will be paid (up to $1000 monthly) in the event that a company undergoes bankruptcy, various reforms made in the past decade protect workers covered under this system of benefits, including "vesting" or a decrease in the number of years of employment required before an employee is guaranteed the right to retirement benefits. In addition, persons who change jobs may now transfer the benefits accumulated under an old employer to a new pension plan, or place the funds accrued into a locked-in RRSP. However, while such provisions allow employees a greater range of options than was previously available to them, they are not retroactive.

In consequence, as Townson (1995: 43) points out, Canadian women who are now 45–54 may find their financial future based upon an admixture of systems and old and new rules. Given that, until the late 1970s and early 1980s, pension plans often contained discriminatory provisions which stipulated, for example, that women were required to retire at an earlier age than men or were ineligible to join an employer-sponsored plan until they reached an older age than that stipulated for men, "there are undoubtedly women in the age group 45–54 today whose financial future will be affected by this kind of past discrimination in their employer's pension plan" (Townson, 1995: 44). Although women born between 1937 and 1946 are participating in the Canadian paid-labour force in record numbers, their financial security upon retirement will be hampered by both their typically low earnings and their shorter length of service. Statistics Canada's 1991 Survey of Aging and Independence reports that workers aged 45–54 with incomes less than $20 000 annually are the most likely to face financial hardship during retirement. The survey additionally notes that 44 percent of women in this age group have incomes below this level. While women who possessed a university education in this age group earn, on average, an annual income of $45 000 (compared to $19 000 among those with less than a high school education), "only about 11% of employed women over age 45, compared with 16% of men in the same age group, have a university degree" (Townson, 1995: 51). In that "housework brings no work-related benefits, no disability or unemployment insurance, no health benefits, and, most importantly, no pension coverage" (Wilson, 1996: 54), women will continue to be penalized for their interrupted labour-force-participation rates and patterns.

If the old stereotype of financial decision-making in the household placed men at the helm, it is evident that the majority of women today, regardless of their current marital status, will have to handle their own finances at some point in their lives. Although a 1993 survey conducted by Trimark Investment Management reports that 78 percent of women did not know what a mutual fund was, while one-quarter of women did not know what was held in their RRSPs (Monsebraaten, 1996), financial institutions in the 1990s are increasingly attempting to tap this huge and potentially lucrative market. Canada's first financial magazine directly specifically at the female market, *Financial XPress*, emerged in 1994, while investment seminars, such as Midland Walwyn Inc.'s "Women and Wealth," have begun to specifically target females as potential investors. To some extent, change has already been notable. Between 1981 and 1991, the number of female contributors to RRSPs rose to 42 percent from 31 percent. It has also been estimated that 40 percent of women own common or preferred stocks, and 50 percent own mutual funds (Monsebraaten, 1996).

Although the term "mandatory retirement" is, in itself, misleading, in that Canadian law does not specify an age at which all Canadians must retire, the Supreme Court of Canada has ruled that, although forcing a worker to retire at a specific age is discrimination, it is legal under the Canadian *Charter of Rights and Freedoms*. Dissenting justices noted in the case of *Dickason v. University of Alberta* (24 September 1992: 67) that involuntary or mandatory retirement must be recognized as particularly disadvantageous to women:

> Women are penalized, in particular, because they tend to have lower paying jobs which are less likely to offer pension coverage and they often interrupt their careers to raise families. These socio-economic patterns combined with private and government pension plans which are calculated on years of participation in the workforce, in some ways make mandatory retirement at age 65 as much an issue of gender as of age discrimination.

The majority of women today who are 65 and over did not anticipate that it would be their financial responsibility to provide for their children or themselves. Rather, they were likely to accept the traditional model, which suggested that women invest in a marriage rather than in a RRSP and optimistically forecasted that their husbands would always provide for them financially. Despite this assumption, many of these women are now finding that their husbands did not or could not. In 1990, elderly Canadian women aged 65 and over had a median income of approximately $11 000, suggesting that a majority of these women live below the "poverty line" (Crompton, 1994). While 35.0 percent of elderly unattached Canadian men are poor, 53.1 percent of elderly unattached Canadian women are living in poverty (Ross et al., 1994: 119).

Widowhood

One of the most stressful life events that individuals experience, typically occurring in later life, is the death of a spouse (Martin Matthews, 1991; 1987). The vast majority of research conducted to date on the experience of widowhood has focused primarily on women for several reasons. First, gender differences in life expectancy in combination with the mating gradient, increase the likelihood that a husband will predecease his wife. As a result, we have a gender widowhood gap. "After 30 years of marriage a woman, compared with a man, runs three times the risk of widowhood" (Novak, 1997: 267). Of all marriages involving men or women aged 65 or over that dissolve due to the death of a partner, 72 percent end with a husband's death and only 29 percent end as a consequence of a wife's death (Norland, 1994: 25). About seven out of ten Canadian widowed women are currently 65 years of age or over. Given their greater longevity, women can expect to remain in a widowed state for longer periods of time than ever before. A woman widowed at the age of 65 can expect to live for almost two decades following the death of her spouse, while a woman widowed at the age of 80 may expect to live for an additional nine years (Novak, 1997: 267–268).

Second, among all those legally eligible for remarriage or marriage (the widowed, divorced, and never-married), the widowed have had the lowest remarriage rates in Canada from the mid-1870s through the mid-1990s, and those rates have declined substantially over time throughout Canada in general, and Quebec in particular (Nault, 1996: 42–44; Statistics Canada, 1996: 22). Male remarriage rates are generally higher than female remarriage rates at any given age and the rates for widowed elder adults are no exception. Wu (1995) notes that, five years following the death of a spouse, 12 percent of men who are widowed have remarried, compared to less than 4 percent of women who are widowed. Ten years after being widowed, 35 percent of men versus 11 percent of women have remarried. The remarriage rate among widowed Canadians aged 65 to 69 between 1985 and 1987 "was almost seven times higher" (Norland, 1994: 25) for men than for women. Using figures obtained from the National Advisory Council, Novak (1997: 267) reports that, among Canadians seniors 70 years of age and over, the remarriage rate of men was nine times that of women.

Not surprisingly, since widowhood occurs most likely at older ages, the mean age at remarriage for widowed grooms and brides continues to increase, slowly reaching 61.3 years of age for grooms and 55.0 years of age for brides in 1995 (Statistics Canada, 1996: 24). As Canadian women move into their senior years, our socially constructed double-standard age norms surrounding a desirable potential mate have a particularly harsh impact upon their probability of remarrying. Brecher et al. (1984: 70) note that "autumnal" remarriages are often viewed askance, with, reportedly, comments such as: "Why on earth do you want to remarry at *your* age?" not infrequently expressed. These researchers asked a sample of 4246 women and men aged 50 to 93 about their level of agreement with two statements: "I think it's a mistake for an older man to marry a much younger woman" and "I think it's a mistake for an older woman to marry a much younger man." Female and male respondents were almost evenly divided on whether they agreed, disagreed, or were neutral about the idea of a much-younger-woman marriage, with men being slightly more likely to disagree that such a marriage would be a mistake. However, the possibility of a much-older-woman marriage brought forth decidedly more negative reactions with 41 percent of the men and 45 percent of the women agreeing that such a marriage would be a mistake. In partial conformity with attitudes such as these, available data indicate that the age gap between intimate partners increases with age in Canada (Wu and Balakrishnan, 1992) as older men select from a wider and younger age range of women, which leads, in part, to a lesser likelihood that senior women will find an "older" man available for marrying should they be interested in doing so. Among married Canadian men aged 65 to 69 in 1991, more than over half (55 percent) had a spouse younger than age 65, slightly more than a third (37 percent) had a spouse in the same age group, and less than one-tenth (9 percent) had a spouse who was 70 years of age or over (Norland, 1994: 24–25). As a result of their greater longevity, in combination with the social constraints contained in the mating gradient reducing their likelihood of getting remarried, Canadian women are not only more likely to become widowed than are Canadian men, but they also are more likely to remain in this social role for the remainder of their lifetime.

Che-Alford et al. (1994) report that, while the vast majority of Canada's seniors maintained their own household in 1991, "over three-quarters of the 818 110 seniors who maintained their household and lived alone were women," with elderly women aged 75 and over being especially likely to do so. Preliminary data from the 1996 census indicate that of the 933 675 Canadians living alone "most of them (71%) were widows" (Statistics Canada, *Daily*, 14 October 1997: 5). With increasing age and the higher mortality rate of men, widowed women are the more likely marital partner to find themselves living alone in the family home. However, despite the onus placed upon men in our society to continue providing "after you're gone" for their wives via life insurance benefits and savings accounts, the National Council of Welfare (1990/1995: 214) claims that encroaching poverty often necessitates that widowed women eventually sell their family home and move to rental or institutional settings. Such moves are more often necessitated not by failing health nor by required mortgage payments (since the vast majority own their homes), but because widowed women lack sufficient money to live day-to-day and still keep up with the inexhaustible expenses home ownership entails (roofs, furnaces, and windows that need replacement, property taxes, driveways that require repaving, etc.). Geographically moving away from long-time neighbours and friends who provide emotional support and advice, and frequently act as a "family comforter" (Rosenthal, 1987/1995: 348), often leads to an increase in social isolation among widowed women which may partially explain research findings that older women tend to have less stable mental health than do older men (Nett, 1993). While most older men "have built-in housekeepers and nurses—their wives" (National Council of Welfare, 1990/1995: 214), elderly widowed women may, due to a combination of having no money and no spouse, be unable to benefit from the comforts that services such as visiting nurses and homehelp provide. If older individuals are apt to identify living independently as an important measure of personal autonomy (Mutchler, 1992), having the financial ability to do so would seem as important here as physical health per se.

Although women in Canada are statistically more likely to face the problem of adjusting to widowhood and living alone, little doubt exists that Canadian men also experience widowhood as a markedly stressful life event. McPherson (1994: 249) reports that, while men who are widowed "are not often faced with economic burdens, they apparently have more difficulty in adapting to their new role, as evidenced by higher suicide rates, higher rates of remarriage, and higher rates of mortality following bereavement." An early study conducted by Benjamin and Wallis (1963) finds that in the months following the death of their spouse, the mortality rate of men showed a sharp increase and that, on occasion, the deaths were due to suicide. More recently, Datan (1989: 16) reports that "if a man is widowed, his mortality rises by 67 percent in the first year after the death of his spouse, while if a woman is widowed, her mortality rises by only about 3 percent." Findings from other American research (Helsing et al., 1981, in Lott, 1994: 319), suggest that men can forestall higher mortality effects following widowhood by remarrying. In effect, remarriage keeps men well.

Lund (1989) claims that approximately 75 percent of males and females report that loneliness is the most serious problem they face after becoming widowed. Loneliness and intense feelings of isolation following widowhood are associated with a relative lack of social supports (DiGiulio, 1992; McDaniel and McKinnon, 1993). Men's greater likelihood of identifying their spouse as their "best friend" often means that "[w]idowed men are doubly bereft—they have lost both a helpmate and confidante....Conversely, the widowed woman is unlikely to be entirely devoid of close friends" (Hess and Soldo, 1985 cited in Novak, 1997: 269). Particularly among senior men, whose identity is no longer tied to a "career anchor" (Salamon, 1984), the loss of a best friend/spouse can be experienced as extremely stressful. Even though Wister and Strain (1986) suggest that men require fewer social supports than do women to feel satisfied, and that men who are widowed may feel content with the camaraderie and companionship that is offered within more casual rather than close friendships, the search for companionship, a sexual partner, and someone to provide needed housekeeping, cooking, and laundry services (Connidis, 1990) explains, in part, the greater likelihood of widowed men remarrying and doing so within a relatively short period of time. In contrast, both women's kinship network, kept vital through performing the kinkeeper role, and their more intensive network of friendships provide a larger array of supportive individuals to help buffer the loss of spousal companionship. Widowed women, although easily retaining their command of housekeeping skills, oftentimes find themselves confronting difficulties with yard work, transportation, and house maintenance tasks but, finances willing, can purchase those services and rarely end up marrying their handyman chauffeur.

For both men and women, the death of a spouse involves a wrenching away of identities that have merged over the years (DiGiulio, 1992). McPherson (1994: 249) suggests that widowed men and women typically go through a series of stages, beginning with a period of mourning that may last up to two years, in which the person attempts to build a network of others who will provide him or her with social support. He reports that the process of adjustment is easier if the bereaved has a group of same-age friends who themselves have experienced widowhood (see also Connidis, 1990: 30). Although the presence of a greater number of social supports may ease the transition into widowhood for women (Connidis and Davies, 1992), those women survivors whose primary identity for an extended period of time has been "Mrs. Bob Smith" must wrestle with the perplexing question of "who am I?" now that Mr. Smith has gone. If all widowed women must attempt to come to terms with living without a partner with whom they have shared daily living, meals, bed, financial fortunes, and burdens, those women whose identity has been forged in the "Wife of" role (Salamon, 1984) will feel particularly unsettled by the death of a spouse. Indeed, it appears that, for some women, commitment to the role of "wife" continues even after the death of their spouse. Norris (1980) reports that, among her sample of respondents whose husbands had died ten years earlier on average, many women "remained emotionally committed to being wives." For these women, widowhood alters their identity now to being a "Former Wife of." Other women must grapple with defining themselves as an independent person in their own right. For the many women whose marriages have been characterized by abuse, violence, drudgery, or complete boredom, widowhood provides a liberating relief from the status of wife, and an independent identity, although still difficult to attain, is likely to be readily embraced. Whether future cohorts of widowed women will attempt to cling to a former married past is uncertain, but less likely.

While death is not unknown among people at younger ages, it is a more common occurrence among men and women during older adulthood. Due to its comparative rarity, research notes that younger women experience a greater degree of anguish, as well as other more intense emotions, and a more difficult adjustment to widowhood upon the death of their spouse than do older women (Caine, 1974; Hiltz, 1989; Novak, 1997: 270). The sudden death of a young spouse may be experienced as an unanticipated tragedy for which one is totally unprepared, while the death of an elderly spouse tends to be experienced as a sad, but predictable, event. Older survivors, who know that death is impending and have the experiences of age-mates to draw upon, can, and do, make preparations that smooth the transition from married to widowed status by, for example, arranging or rearranging finances or preplanning funerals and eventual disposal of a spouse's personal effects, or preparing them-selves psychologically for the prospect of living alone. What, in our culture, is typically unthinkable becomes more readily thinkable among those confronting the prospect of an intimate partner's death. Saying goodbye and cultivating treasured last memories become im-portant parts of adjusting to imminent widowhood. As we have noted repeatedly in the past few pages, these adjustments are more common to older women than to either younger women or to older men in our society.

In summary, aside from some relatively minor specific problems pertaining to daily liv-ing such as housekeeping and yardwork, research focusing upon social and psychological well-being, life satisfaction, or indices of physical or psychoemotional distress (e.g., McCrae and Costa, 1990; Rodeheaver and Datan, 1988) finds few significant gender differences following widowhood, except for income-related outcomes stemming from the fact that women are more likely than men to experience poverty following the death of spouse. Since poverty touches the lives of so many widowed elderly women, particularly in the working and even middle classes and among women of colour, our culture's popular stereotype of the "merry widow" appears to be class- and ethnicity-bound in its application.

EQUALITY AND SOCIAL GENDER MOVEMENTS

Social movements involve "the conscious attempts of masses of people to bring about change deliberately in the social structure by collective action" (McKee, 1969: 580) and, since at least the nineteenth century, "have become an increasingly common means of bringing about social change" (Staggenborg, 1998: 5). From the mid nineteenth to the mid twentieth centuries, women's movements emerged in 32 different countries. The size of each movement was positively related to higher levels of urbanization, industrialization, education, and available leisure time (Staggenborg, 1998: 7). The women's movements of this early period did not advocate radical changes to the structure of gender roles, nor did they attract a substantial following. Rather, they largely remained a white, middle-class movement, with demands for women's suffrage often couched in the language of moral reform rather than equality *per se*.

WOMEN AS GUARDIANS OF SOCIETY

Suffragettes in various countries argued that society would benefit from their participation in the public sphere, as "women's nature" was one of heightened piety, goodness, and morality. "Maternalist movements" based on "ideologies that exalted women's capacity to mother and extend to society as a whole the values of care, nurturance and morality" were common within many Western countries (Koven and Michel, 1990: 1079). For example, in France, advocates of women's suffrage argued that granting women the right to vote was "a way to bring the nurturing influence of mothers to the political arena" and to ensure that policies benefiting children and families would be promoted (Staggenborg, 1998: 9). In a similar fashion, Bacchi (1983: 123) observes that, in Canada, the suffrage movement "was less a 'woman's movement' than an attempt on the part of particular men and women, predominantly urban professionals and entrepreneurs, to supervise [the moral development] of society."

As part of the "progressive-reform impulse that gripped North America between…1880 and 1920…thousands of upper-class and middle-class women, increasingly educated, with their children in schools and new labour-saving devices and servants in their homes…were propelled out of their homes by a sense of religious duty and a spirit of expanding opportunity, which combined with their growing apprehension about the state of Canadian society and their special place within it" (Errington, 1993: 73). First at the local, and later at the national and provincial levels, these women sought to ameliorate a "host of social ills" and became active in the temperance movement, in campaigns for religious instruction, better workplace conditions, improvements in public health and child welfare, and in the development of living facilities for single women. Women's early activism in these areas was often linked to "women's auxiliaries, institutes and missionary societies to spread the word of God" (Errington, 1993: 73) established by Christian churches and forwarded as the philanthropic extension of women's "natural" expertise as wives, mothers, and "guardians" of moral virtue. Such efforts were later buttressed by secular organizations (often not entirely divested of church-sponsorship and/or a religious ethos), such as the Girls' Friendly Society, the Dominion Order of the King's Daughters, the Federation nationale Saint-Jean-Baptiste, and the British Young Women's Christian Association.

The Women's Christian Temperance Union (WCTU), founded in Ontario in 1874, became the "largest and perhaps the most influential women's organization" of this early period (Errington, 1993: 74). Initially formed to combat the sale of alcohol, it became a national union in 1883 with thousands of members. Alcohol was believed to be the harbinger of a large number of social ills, including crime and juvenile delinquency, prostitution, sexual immorality and debauchery, low intelligence, poverty, child neglect and abuse, and the destruction of the family as a viable social unit. The prohibition of alcohol, temperance workers argued, was vital to saving society and its innocents from perdition. The participation of women within the temperance movement was advanced in the lexicon of women's "difference" and moral superiority. Nellie McClung, one of Canada's foremost maternal feminists and an activist in the WCTU believed that the women's movement was

> a spiritual revival of the best instincts of womanhood—the instinct to serve and save the race.…Women are naturally guardians of the race, and every normal woman desires children.…It is woman's place to lift high the standard of morality. (McClung, in Adamson et al., 1988: 31)

Maternal feminists such as McClung believed that "[w]omen had an obligation to use their moral superiority and ability to bear children to make the world a better place for everyone" (Adamson et al., 1988: 31), as guardians of the home, angels of the hearth, and defenders of moral propriety. However, the quest for women to broaden their social role, "from guardians of family morality to guardians of public morality" (Adamson et al., 1988: 32) drew the ire of conservatives, especially in Quebec, where nationalists and the church denounced the increasingly visible presence of women within the public sphere as corrosive of traditional values and the stability of the family.

In her autobiography, McClung (1945: xii) reflected that "I have been accused, attacked, and maligned. Once I was burned in effigy.…I have been caricatured, usually as a mosquito or other disagreeable insect, under the caption of 'Calamity Nell.' I have engaged in hot controversies, been threatened with violence and with libel suits." However, the challenges and demands that early Canadian female activists posed to Canadian society were hardly revolutionary. With the exception of such small groups as the Dominion Women Enfranchisement Association, which demanded equality with men and suffrage as the "right" of women, "few reform-minded women advocated a revolutionary change in the social or political order or desired any involvement in politics" (Errington, 1993: 76). When compared to their counterparts in England and the United States, women activists in Canada were more apt to engage in a "battle of rhetoric" (Wilson, 1996: 137) than in militant action. McClung's much-quoted motto, "Never retract, never explain, never apologize, get the job done and let them howl," suggests a flouting of "ladylike" decorum; however, McClung believed that women were "natural peacemakers" (Wilson, 1996: 138) who would "cleanse and purify the world by law" (as cited in Savage, 1979: 26).

THE FACES OF FEMINISM

Theorists note that social movements are composed of an "indefinite and shifting membership…with leadership whose position is determined more by the informal response of the members than by formal procedures for legitimizing authority" (Turner and Killian, 1972: 246). Even during the early period of first-wave feminism in Canada, at least three traditions or "three faces of feminism" (Banks, 1981) were nurtured during this early time period: **moral reform**, **liberalism**, and **socialism**.

In contrast to maternal feminism, which exemplifies the "face" of moral reform, equal-rights feminism argued that certain rights, including the rights to vote, to own property, to be awarded guardianship of one's children, and to gain access to higher education, were human rights that should not be denied on the basis of gender. "The first organizational expression of equal-rights feminism in Canada was Dr. Emily Howard Stowe's Toronto Women's Literary Club, founded in 1876; in 1883 it took a name more revealing of its politics: the Toronto Women's Suffrage Association" (Adamson et al., 1988: 33). Forced to provide for herself, her invalid husband, and their three children on a teacher's salary, Stowe attempted to obtain training in a higher-paying profession. Barred from attending medical school in Canada because she was a woman, Stowe was accepted by an American medical school and graduated from the New York Medical College for Women in 1867. On her return to Canada, Stowe practised medicine illegally until being a granted a licence in 1880 (Stowe's daughter, Ann Stowe-Gullen was later to become the first woman in Canada to graduate in medicine).

Along with others, Stowe launched a campaign to demand the franchise for women at every political level and for women's right to obtain entrance to and education within the prestigious occupations. A woman, argued Stowe, should be "as free to choose her vocation as her brother…tethered by no conventionalities, enslaved by no chains either of her own or man's forging" (in Adamson et al., 1988: 33). In like spirit, Flora MacDonald Denison maintained that the "real suffragists" were equal-rights feminists, who "did not succumb to the dominant view that the women's vote represented a vote for purity" (Adamson et al., 1988: 33).

The First Wave

"In the first wave most women who were socialists made a clear separation between themselves and the women's movement" (Adamson et al., 1988: 33–34). Nevertheless, certain commonalities are evident. Like maternal feminists, women who were socialists believed that women could "clean up public life." Like equal-rights feminists, socialist women maintained that women deserved to have the same rights as men. Although socialist women viewed capitalism as a barrier to women's full equality, and regarded class alliances as more important than alliances among women against men, they pressed the Socialist Party of Canada to adopt a pro-suffrage position at their 1909 convention. The following year, "the Women's Labour League of Winnipeg endorsed woman suffrage 'as a practical political necessity to secure the other objects of the league,' among them equal pay for equal work, the abolition of 'the evils that promote woman's degradation,' the active participation of women in the trade-union movement, and improved education in domestic and health matters" (Adamson et al., 1988: 34).

In the decades between the first and second waves of the feminist movement, the position of women did improve, if most notably for white woman. While Clare Brett Martin became, in 1897, the first woman lawyer in the Commonwealth, it was not until 1946 that the first Asian-Canadian woman graduated from law school in Ontario. The first black female in Ontario was admitted to law school in 1960, and only in 1976 did the first woman from the First Nations graduate (Mossman, 1994: 216). Although legislation entitling women to vote was enacted in 1916 in the provinces of Manitoba, Saskatchewan, and Alberta, and in 1917 in Ontario and British Columbia, "prior to 1960, Aboriginal women (and men) in Canada were entitled to vote only if they gave up their Indian status...[although] an Aboriginal woman became automatically 'enfranchised' if she married a white man...[I]t was only in the 1970s that Aboriginal women's claims to equality in marriage were tested in the Supreme Court of Canada" (Mossman, 1994: 212). While Mary Ellen Smith became, in 1918, the first women to be elected to the Legislative Assembly in British Columbia and the first woman in the British Empire to serve as a cabinet minister, it was not until 1972 that a black woman, Rosemary Brown, won a seat in that province; in Ontario, it occurred in 1991, when the first black woman, Zanana Akande was elected to the Ontario legislature. Akande was also the first black woman to become a cabinet minister in the province of Ontario (Mandell, 1995: 347).

The Uneven Path of Progress

Following enfranchisement, Black (1993: 153) observes that, although "organized women were engaged in fewer concentrated campaigns, had less publicity and less success...[f]eminism and women's groups had not simply died off." In 1922, Agnes Campbell Macphail became the first woman elected to Canada's House of Commons and was, for 15 years, the only woman within it. Macphail serves as a notable example of how some Canadian women attempted to pursue feminists goals, despite formidable odds. Although derided as "mannish," a "lesbian," a "troublemaker," a "socialist," or as "'poor Aunt Aggie' who was too peculiar or too ugly to catch a man," Macphail became Canada's foremost advocate of women's rights and championed the provision of family allowances, the financial support of deserted wives, income-tax deductions for working wives, the establishment of daycares, and Canada's first attempts at equal-pay legislation.

Macphail had little patience for those whom she termed "white-glove feminists." "If women are exclusively interested in private life and not in a place in the world, then they are not worthy of the franchise. I am fed up with auxiliaries. Join with the men. Be adults together" (in Robertson, 1992: 229). A feisty combatant, it is reputed that on one occasion, when a heckler jeered at her, shouting "Don't you wish you wish you were a man?" Macphail coolly responded, "Don't you?" On a second occasion, when a man repeatedly interrupted her speech with shouts of, "Aw, get a husband!" it is reported that Macphail "made him stand up, looked him scornfully up and down and asked the crowd in mock despair, 'How could I be sure that someone I married might not turn out like this?'" (in Robertson, 1992: 224). According to Macphail, "[a] women's place is any place she wants to be."

In the 1930s, female students at the University of Toronto voted Macphail the woman that they would most like to be (followed by silent-screen actress Mary Pickford). However, other Canadians were far less admiring. Reflecting on her initial reception by MPs in the House of Commons, Macphail observed that: "Some of the members resented my intrusion. Others jeered at me. Everything I said was wrong, everything I wore was wrong, everything I did was wrong,...The men did not want me in Parliament and the women had not put me there" (in Robertson, 1992: 219). It is perhaps disheartening that, more than 70 years later, a 1997 Angus Reid survey, which polled 102 of the 180 women in legislatures across Canada, reported that approximately one-third have been sexually harassed (i.e., been the object of unwanted sexual advances or propositions) by their male colleagues, 60 percent have been the target of inappropriate or demeaning remarks relating to their gender, 30 percent felt that they have been held back because they are women, and 75 percent believed that women face greater pressures than men in relation to how they dress, their physical appearance, their family responsibilities, and their weight. *Plus ca change?*

Like Macphail, who maintained that "[t]o have part of life can never be enough. One must have all" (in Robertson, 1992: 219), more than 85 percent of the women politicians surveyed said that they would "do it again," and would encourage their daughters to participate in politics (*Kitchener-Waterloo* (Ontario) *Record*, 10 May 1997: A4). However, unlike Macphail, these women were not forced to regard the troubles that beset them as solely "private troubles." Indeed, as "public issues," the results of the Angus Reid survey formed the basis of a one-hour documentary on a *CBC-Newsworld* program and made headlines across the nation. By the 1990s, the vocabulary of the women's movement, which included the introduction of such terms as "male chauvinist," "sexism," and "sexual harassment," had acquired widespread currency and intelligibility. As Wine and Ristock (1991: 1) remark, "[p]erhaps the most impressive impact of the [women's] movement is the massive shift in the consciousness of the Canadian public in terms of affirmation of women's right to equality, including reproductive freedom, equal treatment in the workplace, and freedom from violence."

The first-wave and the second-wave women's movements demonstrate all of the characteristics of a classic social movement, with a genesis in social conditions deemed intolerable for women; a strong underlying belief that such conditions are neither natural nor inevitable; eventual development of an ideology or set of ideologies; the coherent articulation of the grievances, frustrations, goals, and aspirations of its members; the development of a social base to support and attempt to implement the defining ideology; and the emergence of leaders, either self-anointed or appointed in some manner (see Decker, 1983; Marshall, 1984/1987; Prentice et al., 1988; Steuter, 1992/1995). Both waves of feminism sought to effect change, either through converting increasingly larger masses of people to their ideologies and values, or through pursuing and accumulating power, and using that power to influence other powerful people to instigate change or by instigating legitimate change themselves (McKee,

1969; Turner and Killian, 1972). Members of the first-wave women's movement essentially lacked social power and more often emphasized the conversion pathway. Members of the second-wave women's movement, because of changed circumstances, were able to pursue both avenues for social change with specific groups within the larger movement.

The Second Wave

In the 1950s and early 1960s, Black observes, many of the problems women faced appeared to be, at worst, "temporary disadvantages:"

> Women were increasingly getting the education needed for better-paying work, and public opinion supported their right to work and to get equal pay....There were still few women in the federal Parliament, but the tradition of having one woman in the cabinet seemed secure, while local women politicians....were highly visible and vocal—often objecting to any specific concern for the status of women. (1993: 51)

As Black's comments implicitly suggest, this period was characterized by a lack of "minority group consciousness" (Hacker, 1951) among women, including those who occupied positions of relative power and prestige. As Betty Friedan observed in creating her "three-sex theory" (i.e., "there's men, there's women and there's me"), "it was quite possible [for women]…to share the socially accepted prejudices against women without ever drawing the appropriate conclusions" (Freeman, 1975: viii). "For the generation of women who came of age in the 1940s and 1950s feminism as an intellectual tradition was virtually invisible. The few authors who raised feminist concerns in those years went unread until they were rediscovered in the 1960s" (Ferree and Hess, 1985: 35). During this period, popular wisdom was based on Freudianism and functionalism, both of which suggested that fundamental differences between men and women were attributable to "nature" and were natural, desirable, and immutable.

The "second wave" of the women's movement in Canada emerged cresively and somewhat unexpectedly in the 1960s . Originally viewed by many as an "American import" that was "simply another, relatively unimportant part of an era of activism" (Black, 1993: 151), this time period also saw the rise of the civil-rights movement, the Quebec nationalist movement, the American Indian or "Red Power" movement, the student movement, and the antiwar movement. The three major sociopolitical movements of the 1960s—the New Left, Black Power, and Feminism—did share certain values and were interrelated in a variety of ways. However, if their common critique of society may have, in retrospect, proven significantly greater than the sum of their parts (Rorabaugh, 1996), each independently challenged the legitimacy of existing social conditions, institutions, and relationships and "created a belief in, and an enthusiasm for, the possibilities of change unparalleled in recent history" (Adamson et al, 1988: 257).

Black (1993: 165) observes that "the Canadian women's liberation groups in their first years disliked and rejected the very term 'feminist'" for several reasons. First, feminism was seen as intricately bound up in an ideology that subordinated a critique of capitalism and gave prominence to a critique of the family. Second, early members of the women's movement in Canada identified the term feminist as part of a movement that, they felt, promoted antagonism between men and women. Third, the Canadian women's movement was both "[p]roudly socialist and proudly nationalist" and sought to distance itself from an American social movement that was seen to promote American cultural imperialism.

Fourth, in Quebec, the first francophone group, le Front de liberation des femmes du Quebec, was formed in 1966 as "a response to the marginalization of women in the independentist Front de liberation du Quebec (FLQ)," with efforts made to position the demands of women "squarely in the context of independentism" and to promote the status of women in the province (Black, 1993: 162).

In anglophone and francophone Canada, the second wave of the women's movement in Canada drew vigour from a new, radicalized constituency—younger women, students or former students—who "brought with them, from the student movement, a significant commitment to a Marxist or at least an economic, class-oriented analysis of women's situation" (Black, 1993: 154) and was fueled by two types of overlapping grievances. The first set of grievances identified the **differential and discriminatory treatment** of women, which still existed within the public sphere of work and the private sphere of the home, as unjust and as something that had to change. "While the barriers were officially down and women shared in 'male' activism they did without the rewards men could expect" (Black, 1993: 152). Women, who were increasingly participating in the labour force or experiencing the "radicalizing force" (Lipman-Blumen, 1984: 205) of higher education, experienced a sense of relative deprivation as they realized that a "glass ceiling" limited their career aspirations, while a "wage gap" differentially rewarded their work and the equivalent or identical work performed by men. Whether entreated to "dress for success" in a way that downplayed their femininity (e.g., a grey flannel suit, a business-like hairdo, and an absence of makeup or jewellery) or to learn the games "that mother never taught you," it grew increasingly evident that women who wished to "make it in a man's world" were expected to act like men. The role conflicts that "acting like men" posed, especially for full-time working mothers, were summarily ignored. "As the tension between family and work, and between domestic and wage labour, increased, women came to feel that their situation was unjust" (Adamson et al., 1988: 37). The second set of grievances identified **specific qualities**, "characteristics that they valued and thought society appreciated insufficiently. Women wanted to stay different without being disadvantaged. More positively, they wanted credit for their valuable female qualities, as well as protection from their vulnerabilities in a male-dominated world" (Black, 1993: 153).

The two sets of grievances that Black identifies can be distinguished, at least analytically, as emanating from two types of feminism. The first set of grievances are consistent with the goals of "equity," "political," "equal rights," or "women's rights" feminism, while the second are consistent with "social feminism," "emancipation," or "women's liberation" feminism. According to Black (1991), "equity feminism" would include those variants of feminism earlier identified in Chapter 3 as liberal feminism, Marxist feminism, and socialist feminism, as well as the broader ideological traditions of liberalism, Marxism and Socialism. **Equity feminists** forwarded their demands in the language of "equal rights" and sought to redress inequality between men and women through such measures as enhanced educational and employment opportunities, reform of the divorce law, and pay equity provisions. In contrast, **social feminism** (Black, 1991), which includes both the "maternal feminism" of the nineteenth century and, more recently, radical feminism, ecofeminism, and cultural feminism, directs attention to values and experiences identified with women. While a substantial segment of the second-wave women's movement was composed of equal-rights feminists, it was the social feminists who were the most conspicuous, challenging the desirability of beauty pageants, drawing attention to the experiences of battered women, and calling for the recognition and valorization of women's qualities.

ORGANIZING FOR CHANGE: MAINSTREAMING AND DISENGAGEMENT

Although the metaphor of a "wave" suggests a movement propelled forward by a singular, momentous force, the contemporary women's movement can be seen as composed of at least two types of women's organizations that differ in terms of their origin, structure, and the composition of their membership. Adamson et al. (1988: 12) suggest, that for purposes of simplicity these two types of feminist activism can be termed **grassroots feminism** and **institutional feminism**. "Institutional feminism operates within traditional institutions— inside political parties and government ministries, for example—while grass-roots feminism is more community based, emphasizing collective organizing, consciousness-raising, and reaching out to women 'on the street.'" These two organizational styles are comparable with Rothschild-Whitt's (1979) suggestion that the "fabric" of feminism woven during this period was composed of a "bureaucratic strand" and a "collectivist strand," and with Cassell's (1977) distinction between "women's rights" and "women's liberation" groups.

Following Weber's (1947) ideal-type, the essential characteristics of a bureaucracy include: a hierarchy with assignments flowing downwards and accountability flowing upwards, a division of labour, written rules, written communication and records, and impersonal relationships. In contrast, the ideal collectivist organization can be characterized as a community in which there are few specific rules or roles, relationships are personalized, and decisions are reached through consensus. For many second-wave feminists, collectivism was an ideal to be pursued; "hierarchy" was trounced as a "male" form of organization. Women were urged to **sisterhood**, "generally understood as a nurturant, supportive feeling of attachment and loyalty to other women that grows out of a shared experience of oppression" (Dill, 1983: 132). Sisterhood, as a horizontal rather than a vertical relationship, was lauded as a female mode of equality and as a superior organizational structure.

Although the ideal of sisterhood and collectivism may seem attractive, it has been a difficult ideal to put into practice. Ristock's (1991) examination of feminist social-service collectives reports that individuals participating in these groups often found them to be chaotic. Although eschewing formal systems of leadership, covert forms could nevertheless emerge that were as prescriptive as those in the most despotic bureaucracy. Ferree and Hess (1985: 65) report that feminist collectives have, on occasion, evolved into bastions of mediocrity. A refusal to create a hierarchy within the "sisterhood" by acknowledging expertise and, in particular, academic credentials, could result in women with credentials being chastised for their accomplishments and discouraged from displaying initiative.

> Women who violated the unwritten rules of egalitarianism…could be subject to 'trashing,'…a particularly vicious form of character assassination…accused of using the movement and other women's oppression for their own personal gain, and…either openly condemned or subtly excluded from group activities. (Ferree and Hess, 1985: 65)

According to Ferree and Hess (1985: 48), the term women's rights groups refers to "those formal, structured organizations established to pursue equality through legislation, the courts, and the lobbying; that is, to fight a political battle on political turf." In contrast, the term women's liberation groups is applied to those "relatively informal, loosely structured networks of women in the community, struggling for feminist goals outside of the conventional political system, through consciousness-raising (CR) and support groups, self-help projects, [and] media-directed actions,...to construct more egalitarian relationships in their personal lives." Regardless of the specifics, these terms attempt to identify variations in the structure of women's groups by the extent to which they pursue a bureaucratic or collectivist mode of organization, and by whether the preferred vehicle for change was through mainstreaming or disengagement. **Disengagement**, according to Briskin (1991), "operates from a critique of the system and a standpoint outside of it, and a desire, therefore, to create alternative structures and ideologies." In contrast, **mainstreaming** "operates from a desire to reach out to the majority of the population with popular and practical feminist solutions to particular issues, and therefore references major social institutions, such as the family, the workplace, the educational system and the state." Both types of activist effort, she observes, carry strategic risk. "Disengagement can easily lead to marginalization and invisibility; mainstreaming to co-optation and institutionalization" (Briskin, 1991: 31).

Grassroots Feminism

In tracing the nascent development of the grassroots women's movement of the late 1960s and early 1970s, Adamson et al. (1988: 42) comment that

> it is difficult to capture the intensity and the strength of the almost spontaneous eruption of feminist ideas and questions....The grass-roots women's liberation movement was activist, optimistic, and externally focused. Feminists talked about, wrote about, made speeches about, demonstrated about, had meetings about everything....Those years had an almost evangelical tone to them....[w]e were ready to take on the world and male chauvinism in all its manifestations."

From its inception, women were active in the peace movement in Canada (Adamson et al., 1988: 39). The Canadian branch of the group Voice of Women (VOW) was originally formed in July 1960, in response to a newspaper column written by *Toronto Star* columnist Lotta Dempsey. In her column, Dempsey challenged women to address their energies to the threats posed by the possibility of nuclear war. The result spawned a grassroots voluntary association of thousands of women whose stated purpose was "to unite women in concern for the future of the world...[and] to provide a means for women to exercise responsibility for the family of mankind" (in Adamson et al., 1988: 39).

"VOW was premised on the belief, and operated on the assumption, that women's historic distance from official power and women's common involvement in child rearing gave women a particular outlook on issues of war and peace" (Pierson, 1995: 377). In the decades that followed its emergence, VOW expanded their focus to include such issues as environmental protection, women's health and safety, biculturalism and bilingualism, and reproductive choice. In support of their goals, members of VOW wrote letters, participated in and sponsored international conferences, and organized protest marches and antinuclear vigils. They were credited, by then Secretary of State for External Affairs, Howard Green, "for Canada's delay in joining the missile alert at the time of the Cuban Missile Crisis (Black, 1993: 156). On occasion, the tactics employed by VOW were flamboyant. For example, Black (1993: 156) reports that "Voice members presented the government with thousands of baby teeth documenting how strontium-90 in fallout from nuclear testing had got into the food chain and into the bones of children." VOW did not simply encourage women to organize at the community level; their efforts "helped to shape public opinion about Cold War and environmental issues" (Black, 1993: 156–157) for a broader Canadian constituency.

Most members of VOW were married women with children who, like maternal feminists of an earlier time and ecofeminists of a later generation, believed that women were "instinctively" tied to the earth, to life-giving processes, and to humanistic values. However, indicative of the cross-fertilization that may exist between the memberships of the two kinds of feminism, Black (1993: 157) notes that many women within VOW were later to become active in mainstream politics in Canada.

Like the peace movement, the native-rights, civil-rights movement, and New Left activist groups such as the Student Union for Peace Action (SUPA), Students for a Democratic Union (SDU), the Young Socialists, and League for Socialist Action, served as important training grounds for those Canadians who were later to assume important roles within the women's movement. Marsden and Harvey (1979: 195) note that, within broader activist organizations, women often found themselves "asked to do the cooking and cleaning, the licking of stamps, and the stuffing of envelopes…but never to advance their own ideas or become leaders themselves." Over time, women's groups emerged from Vancouver to Fredericton, extending far beyond the ivory walls of universities that had originally housed them. Consciousness-raising or CR groups, typically made up of eight to ten women who met regularly in deliberately nonhierarchical groups, allowed women to discuss topics that included sex and sexuality, personal relationships, battering, rape, and differential treatment within the workplace. While consciousness raising was mocked by some who charged that "women were 'naval gazing' while the real revolution was going on without them" (Ferree and Hess, 1985: 64), Adamson et al. (1988: 45) argue that CR groups served as a "powerful tool for grass-roots organizing" and, that "[b]y focusing on the reality of each woman's life, it was able to reach and, ultimately, activate women in a way that more abstract calls to organize around an issue would not have done."

As a practice, consciousness raising typically consists of a four-stage discussion. In the first stage, self-revelation, each woman talks about herself and her feelings, while others engage in "active listening" (i.e., encourage the woman to speak and extrapolate on her observations). In the second stage of CR, experiences are assembled into larger patterns. In the third stage, an attempt is made to understand the structural causes for these shared patterns of experiences. In the fourth stage, abstraction, group members link the theories they have arrived at in their own analyses with other theories of oppression. "[R]ather than starting with theory, as in Freudian or Marxist analysis, and then attempting to fit contemporary experience into the theoretical framework…women started with their own experience, developed theory from that, and ended up criticizing the 'master'" (Ferree and Hess, 1985: 64).

In this early stage of the contemporary women's movement, grassroots feminists were themselves divided on whether it was more advantageous to focus attention on one or many issues "With hindsight we can see that single-issue organizing can make it appear that women's oppression is an isolated problem: for example, if women had full access to abortion, then they would no longer be oppressed" (Adamson et al., 1988: 47). However, Adamson et al. note that, while multi-issue organizing has the benefit of stressing the interconnectedness of the challenges that face women and "the systemic character of women's oppression," a broad critique of society's institution can alienate those who may find themselves in only partial agreement with the issues and goals pursued.

In seeking to please everyone, one often winds up satisfying no one. Adamson et al. (1988: 5) point out that, as the women's movement grew, both in terms of the "staggering" numbers of organizations it included and in the range of issues it sought to address, "the unity of the women's movement was…splintered as factions pitted themselves against one another: radical feminists against socialist feminists, supporters of a 'Wages for Housework' analysis against those of traditional marxism [*sic*], unaligned feminists against revolutionary vanguard parties, and heterosexual feminists against lesbians." By 1970, "the francophones in women's liberation in Quebec [had] expelled the anglophones, dividing up even the referral services. The struggle for independence, central among leftist issues in Quebec, meant that linguistic barriers were symbolic of Quebec's identity; anglophone feminists were seen as representative of the federalist 'colonizers'" (Black (1993: 162).

Radical and Socialist Currents

While much of grassroots feminism in Canada has been marked by its "anti-theoretical stance," Adamson et al. (1988: 65–78) suggest that two currents can be identified within it: (i) **radical feminism**, the dominant grassroots politic of the 1970s, which emphasized the goals of obliterating gender roles "as a basis of oppression," and of transforming society to reflect women's values and priorities, and (ii) **socialist feminism**, which sought to integrate the issues of gender and class.

In the early 1970s, the radical grassroots women's movement in Canada organized around the issue of abortion and women's limited access to birth control. While amendments to the criminal law in August 1969 allowed for the legal distribution of information about birth-control, for the sale of birth-control devices, and for abortions that were approved by a hospital's "therapeutic abortion" committee, these measures were felt to be inadequate. On Valentine's Day, 1970, the first demonstration calling for the repeal of the new law governing abortion in Canada was held in Vancouver. A month later, the Vancouver Women's Caucus asked women across Canada to participate in an abortion caravan traveling across the country with a coffin, symbolizing the women who had been forced to rely on the services of underground abortionists and who had died as a result. In calling for the repeal of the abortion laws, grassroots activists "chained themselves to seats in the visitors' gallery, and disrupted the proceedings of Parliament." Buoyed by such measures and displays of collective strength, other women's groups were encouraged to form and to expand their focus of concern (Adamson et al., 1988: 46).

By the late 1970s, radical feminists had made violence against women a focus, with rallies and demonstrations held to direct attention to the issues of battering, rape, and pornography. Their accomplishments include the 1977 formation of Women against Violence against Women (WAVAW), and Take-Back-the-Night marches, which began in 1978 to protest street violence and stranger rapes. Radical feminists are additionally credited with the development of feminist therapy "as a political extension of a radical-feminist analysis" (Adamson et al., 1988: 73) and the establishment of women's centres, battered-women hostels, and rape-crisis centres, information, and counselling services across Canada. In addition, the promotion and growth of "women's cultural events"—music festivals, art exhibits, and writing workshops—all stemmed from attempts by radical feminists to extend the focus of grassroots activities to recognize and attend to the heterogeneous needs, issues, and interests of Canadian women. For some radical feminists, embracing a "feminist lifestyle" included adopting the viewpoint that "feminism is the theory, lesbianism is the practice." As Ferree and Hess (1985: 39) observe, "[a]dvocates of the lesbian alternative present this as part of a continuum of female solidarity, with the most highly 'woman-identified woman' expressing her commitment in a physically loving relationship."

During the same period, socialist feminists, who drew upon the writings of such Canadians authors as Charine Guettel, Dorothy Smith, and Roberta Hamilton, focused their attention on issues of class and coalition politics. "[B]y the end of the seventies,...[a] 'working class feminism' based in the trade unions...[had become] a distinct current in the women's movement" (Adamson et al., 1988: 124). Among the more successful socialist-feminist organizations formed during this time was the Toronto International Women's Day Committee (IWDC), which identified itself as "an anti-capitalist, anti-patriarchal organization," and which forged alliances with various unions such as the Ontario Federation of Labour, the Ontario New Democratic Party, and Organized Working Women. A second organization, the Saskatchewan Working Women (SWW) similarly made contact with a number of unions including "the Saskatchewan Government Employees Association, the Canadian Union of Postal Workers, the Canadian Union of Public Employees hospital workers, and the Public Service Alliance of Canada" (Adamson et al., 1988: 80). Socialist feminists have found political affinity with the NDP, in which there exists "a strong, organized, and relatively successful movement of union women, heavily influenced by a socialist-feminist politic" (Adamson et al., 1988: 124). In Canada, socialist-feminist activists have joined with liberal feminists in campaigning for the adoption of such reformist strategies as employment equity, the wages-for-housework movement, equal pay for work of equal value, and improved daycare. Their focus on the issues of class and gender has made them particularly sensitive of the need to establish links and to tend to the concerns of women who face "multiple jeopardies," including women who are differently abled, women of colour, and lesbians.

Institutional Feminism

In 1979, Lynn McDonald, then president of the National Action Committee on the Status of Women (NAC) described the "distinctive characteristics of the Canadian Women's Movement" as including:

> [F]irst, a political position slightly left of centre, progressive/reformist...but with little questioning of capitalist institutions....Second, solidarity across class lines, and, to a lesser extent, across ethnic and religious barrier...[and third] a commitment to the ordinary political process, public education and persuasion of politicians and parties within the system. (in Adamson et al., 1988: 62)

While Adamson et al. (1988: 62) emphasize that McDonald's description refers to the "institutionalized feminist Canadian women's movement" rather than a "Canadian Women's Movement," McDonald's comments endorse a view of the women's movement that is more "reformist" than "radical," that seeks to avoid, rather than to embrace "partisan politics and radical political theory," and that adopts a "mainstreaming" agenda of "advocating *greater* state intervention (short of state ownership of the means of production) by ways of protective legislation, equal pay, and the creation of a broad range of social services" (McDonald, in Adamson et al., 1988: 62, emphasis added).

The establishment of a Royal Commission on the Status of women, with Florence Bayard Bird as its chair, is often heralded as "the first success of Canada's re-emerging feminist movement" (Mackie, 1991: 256) that "inaugurated 'second wave feminism' in Canada" (Mandell, 1995: 338). Laura Sabia, a popular talk-show host, city councillor in St. Catherines, Ontario, and president of the Canadian Federation of University Women, had earlier requested that all established women's organizations send delegates to a conference that would meet and discuss the status of women. A 32-member Committee on Equality for Women was formed, "made up of representatives of the large voluntary and professional women's organizations, including the most vocal and consistent campaigners for woman suffrage" (Black, 1993: 158). An official delegation of five women from this group, accompanied by approximately 60 observers, presented a brief requesting a Royal Commission on the status of women. After the Pearson government "virtually ignored the group's first mildly posed request," Sabia threatened to "march two million women on Ottawa" and to use "every tactic we can" to obtain an official inquiry into women's rights in Canada (Black, 1993: 159). In 1967, the Royal Commission was appointed, with the mandate to inquire into the situation of women in Canada and to "recommend what steps might be taken by the Federal Government to ensure for women equal opportunities with men in all aspects of Canadian society" (in Mackie, 1991: 256).

In its published report of 1970, the Royal Commission made 167 recommendations for alleviating inequalities in Canadian criminal law, education, taxation, poverty, public life, immigration and citizenship, the economy, and the family. It also identified four principles: "women are free to seek employment outside the home; the care of children is a shared responsibility for mother, father, and society; society has a responsibility for women because of pregnancy and childbirth, and so special treatment for reasons of maternity is necessary; and women in certain areas need special treatment to overcome adverse effects of discriminatory practices" (Mandell, 1995: 339). Inadvertently, "the Royal Commission on the Status of Women strengthened the network of women's organizations across Canada as many worked to prepare briefs for the public hearings held in 14 cities across the country " (Wilson, 1996: 147). A conference held in 1972, "Strategy for Change," to discuss the findings of the royal commission led to the creation of an Ad Hoc Committee that, in 1972, became the National Action Committee on the Status of Women (NAC).

The accomplishments of institutional feminists, although distinct from those of grassroots feminists, are no less notable and include efforts to ensure the inclusion of an equal-rights clause within the Canadian constitution. In 1981, as a result of efforts by the Ad Hoc Committee of Canadian Women, Section 28 of the Canadian Constitution was amended to read: "Not withstanding anything in this charter, all the rights and freedoms in it are guaranteed equally to male and female persons" (Wilson, 1996: 148). In 1985, the Women's Legal Education and Action Fund (LEAF), was founded. LEAF acts as a watchdog group and attempts, through Charter litigation, to seek equality for women and to ensure that the guarantees of equality in Section 15 of the *Charter of Rights and Freedoms* are not ignored in Canadian courtrooms, nor interpreted restrictively (Razack, 1991).

Chunn and Brockman (1993: 215) observe that "[h]istorically, feminists in Canada and other Western market societies have placed great emphasis on law as an important vehicle for establishing formal equality between women and men." Throughout the 1980s, the efforts of institutional feminists were consequential in the establishment of task forces to investigate "gender bias" in law, in judicial education initiatives, in the establishment of such journals as the *Canadian Journal of Women and the Law*, and the formation of such committees and subcommittees as the Manitoba Association of Women and the Law, the Law Society of Alberta's Committee on Gender and Inequality in the Legal Profession, the Working Group on Gender Equality in the Canadian Justice System, the National Steering Committee of the National Association of Women and the Law, the Women in the Legal Profession Sub-Committee of the Law Society of Upper Canada, and the Law Society of British Columbia's Subcommittee on Women in the Legal Profession (Brockman and Chunn, 1993).

National Action Committee on the Status of Women

The goal of NAC is to "unite women and women's groups from across the country in the struggle for equality." In 1996, NAC spoke "for almost 600 women's organizations" (Wilson, 1996: 148). In 1998, NAC represented more than 800 women's groups in Canada (Monsebraaten, 1998).

In its first two decades, the second wave of the feminist movement did not always nor consistently recognize, include, or champion the needs of all Canadian women equally. For example, women who were differently abled often found their needs excluded or marginalized within the agenda of institutional feminists, even though "[f]or women with disabilities, unemployment and/or unequal pay for work of equal value, lack of union protection, of equality of services and public benefits, and outright exploitation in the name of charity, undoubtedly play a role in determining their destinies" (Barile, 1995: 406). Driedger (1993) notes that until relatively recently, women with disabilities have been largely excluded from meaningful participation in the women's movement and in organizations campaigning for the rights of the differently abled. Similarly, Wine and Ristock (1991: 13) point out that "though women's organizations provided some support,...[t]he activist work of Native women to change section 12(b) of the Indian Act, and its denial of treaty rights to Native women who married non-Native men...[was a] battle fought almost entirely by Native women." As Cassidy et al. (1998: 26) acknowledge in their discussion of "silenced and forgotten women"— First Nations women, black women, immigrant women, women with disabilities, and poor women—it is only recently that the second wave of the women's movement "has finally begun to address criticisms that white, middle-class feminists have denied, dismissed, and denigrated the experiences of differently raced, abled, and classed women."

The leaders of NAC, in the 1990s, have explicitly shifted the focus of the organization to one of greater inclusivity, particularly by addressing the needs of women of colour and of women in poverty. In 1993, Sunera Thobani, a woman of colour, became the president of the NAC. Mandell (1995: 348) notes that Thobani's bid "was unopposed by the more than 200 delegates at the annual meeting as an effort to heal a long-standing rift over the role of 'minority' women in the feminist movement" and that more than "a quarter of the NAC's executive [is] composed of women from visible minorities." However, while a more inclusive focus is supported by academic feminists (see Lucas et al., 1991/1995), critics charge that the movement towards inclusivity has been accompanied by a fragmented and increasingly atomized women's movement.

Willis (1992: xv–xvi) argues that, throughout the 1980s and 1990s, we have been witnessing the emergence of "a cultural politics...[in which] hopes for equality were increasingly displaced onto affirmation of group identity as an end in itself, a form of community and a ritual moral protest." According to Willis, "[t]he most obvious drawback of identity politics" is in the fragmentation of social movements "into ever smaller and more particularist groups." She asks, "Do we simply defer to the authority of whoever is more oppressed, relinquishing our own moral autonomy (and what if the more oppressed change their minds, or disagree with each other, as they have the inconvenient habit of doing)?" Willis charges that at best, identity politics has produced a "rich body of scholarship and criticism," but more commonly has devolved into "a stale, pious rhetoric of comparative victimhood."

In addition to challenges posed about the direction that institutional feminism should take as we approach the millennium, there can be little doubt that decreased government funding will have an impact on the ability of NAC and other feminists to lobby for change. As Monsebraaten (1998) points out, "[o]ver the past decade, women's groups have seen federal funding drop to $8.25 million this year from a high of $13 million in 1988. No new women's groups have received core funding from Ottawa since 1989." Recent changes to the federal government's Women's Program Fund no longer furnishes women's organizations with money for core administrative or ongoing activities. Rather, federal funding is linked to activities that must fall under one of three broad categories: improving women's economic status, eliminating violence against women and girls, and achieving social justice. Although Status of Women Minister Hedy Fry maintained that these changes will allow more women's groups to get federal help and provide greater flexibility, others are less optimistic about the impact these changes will have. At the 1998 annual meeting of NAC, Joan Grant Cummings, president, announced that NAC is boycotting the Women's Program Fund until core funding is reinstated (in 1997, NAC received $248,673 from Ottawa, about a third [30 percent] of its $800,000 budget). NAC is asking Ottawa to spend at least $30 million to help women achieve economic and social equality in Canada (Monsebraaten, 1998).

RESISTANCE TO FEMINISM

As any social movement gains adherents and experiences small successes, counter-movements develop in the form of either **resistance movements**, intended to forestall any further changes to existing social conditions, or **regressive movements**, intended to restore social conditions and structures, to a state existing prior to any changes made. Both the first-wave and the second-wave women's movements spawned a series of counter-movements of both kinds (see Marshall, 1984/1987; Steuter, 1992/1995).

"Success" is an outcome not easily measured. The more specific and narrowly focused the goals and aspirations of a movement, the easier it is to measure whether they have been achieved or accomplished. The more general and multifaceted the goals and aspirations, the more difficult it is, for insiders and outsiders alike, to agree upon what qualifies as success and to determine whether the movement has achieved or accomplished it. Some portion of the leadership and the membership may feel that goals and aspirations attained eventually are sufficient, while another portion may not be satisfied. Splinter groups may then develop, who dedicate themselves to further pursuit of as-yet-unachieved goals and who accuse the satisfied leaders and members of the larger movement of having "sold out" and lost their sense of commitment.

Success, in whole or in part, also begets both legitimacy and opposition. Legitimacy comes in the forms of new laws, new policies, and changed circumstances, all of which address previously unmet needs. Legitimacy also comes in the forms of transforming the movement into an official mainstream social institution and of installing some leaders and members as officers and workers of a formal organization. The first-wave and second-wave women's movements were, and are, successful in having new laws and social policies passed and implemented. The present women's movement is represented at an official level by the National Organization of Women (NOW) in the United States and by the National Action Committee (NAC) on the Status of Women in Canada.

Opposition can also be found in individuals who do not belong to counter-movements, but who express a sense of alienation from the mainstream, legitimate, organizational women's movement. Mostly women, they express a sense that the women's movement no longer "speaks" for them (Fox-Genovese, 1991, 1996; Kamen, 1991; Mansbridge, 1986; Willis, 1992). In some cases, alienation leads some women to cease identifying with the women's movement. In other cases, alienation leads to attempts to articulate the shortcomings of the now-mainstream movement and to give voice to alternative visions of where feminism should be headed.

Official opposition to feminism in Canada can be found in a number of self-styled "profamily" organizations (Steuter, 1992/1995). R.E.A.L. Women (Realistic, Equal, Active, and for Life), is the most visible and well known of Canada's antifeminist women's organizations. Erwin's (1988) Canadian survey of 1200 members of R.E.A.L. Women and other avowedly "profamily" organizations suggests that those active in these organizations are largely women over the age of 40, who are either Catholic or Protestant fundamentalists with a high degree of religious commitment, who may come from poorer families, but who have achieved a relatively high degree of financial success. These characteristics would seem typical of people who actively oppose feminism more generally. Various studies have reported that antifeminists are disproportionately likely to be married, to be religiously and politically conservative, to support a fundamentalist view of biblical truth, and to deny that poverty is caused by structural (versus individual) factors (Brown, 1984; Morgan and Wilcox, 1992; Mueller and Dimieri, 1982, Salecl, 1992; Smith and Kluegel, 1984).

Of pivotal importance to R.E.A.L. Women is the reprivatization of the family by limiting forms of government assistance (see also David, 1984). R.E.A.L. Women, and the Christian Heritage and Family Coalition political parties state their goal as the restoration of "traditional family values," upon which, they argue, Canada as a nation and as a society was founded and to which Canada must return if it is to regain its former greatness. R.E.A.L. Women explicitly, and the other political parties implicitly, blame feminism for a decline in "family values" and, therefore, the moral and social decline of our society. Akin to arguments advanced by biological and moral conservatives in the conservative men's perspective, these regressive opposition groups argue for a return of the "natural," heterosexual, breadwinner-homemaker family. The same basic tenets of a "profamily, antifeminist" orientation are shared informally by other federal and provincial political parties and political pressure groups in our country. Shehan and Scanzoni (1988) claim that the long-term goal of conservative family policies is to remove women from the paid-labour force and return them to the family home, where their primary obligations are to care for children, homes, and husbands. Accordingly, conservative opposition groups in Canada and the United States are in favour of paying men a sufficient "family wage" that would no longer require women to help out with income provision, increase tax exemptions for dependent spouses to make stay-at-home wives and mothers financially viable, withdraw government financial support of daycare centres, increase tax credits and deductions for dependent children to encourage more women to stay home and raise their children, prevent sexuality education from being taught in schools, promote chastity outside of marriage and fidelity inside of marriage, severely restrict access to contraception and abortion, and reduce or even elimi-nate access to divorce.

Antifeminist Feminism

In the 1980s and 1990s, a variety of writers identified what they regarded as the "failure of feminism." Although criticism of those who seek to advance women's social position is hardly new or limited to these decades (Coutinho-Wiggelendam, 1983; McLachlan and Swales, 1980), what makes this period notable is the outpouring of grievances that stemmed from those feminists who were identified, by themselves or others, as "neofeminists" (Faludi, 1991: 282), "feminists without illusions" (Fox-Genovese, 1991), "feminist fatales" (Kamen, 1991), "family feminists" (Fox-Genovese, 1996), "second-stage feminists" (Friedan, 1963), "dissident feminists" (Laframboise, 1996), "antifeminist feminists" (Paglia, 1990, 1992), "free-speech feminists" (Schwartz and Rutter, 1998: 178), or "power feminists" (Johnson, 1996; Wolf, 1993, 1998). These individuals were eager to distance themselves from "main-stream feminists" who, they charged, had "failed" feminism (Sommers, 1994) or led women along the wrong path. For purposes of convenience, we shall use the term **antifeminist feminism** to refer to this body of writings.

The writings of antifeminist feminists are characterized by certain stylistic commonal-ties. First, the authors actively attempt to establish themselves as people who can speak knowledgeably as "insiders" in the women's movement. It seems customary for these writ-ers to make elaborate reference to their personal biographies and, not infrequently, offer family genealogies identifying their mothers, grandmothers, and assorted relatives as ac-tive in the first or second wave of the women's movement. For example, Laframboise (1996: 4–5) informs her readers that, while in her twenties, she lined up to obtain Gloria Steinem's autograph at a book-signing session, attended an information evening on midwifery, and participated in various pro-choice events to support free-standing abortion clinics. In a sim-ilar vein, Roiphe (1993: 5) begins her book by identifying her mother as the author of the six-ties' novel, *Up the Sandbox*, "an early feminist novel recounting the elaborate escape fantasies of a bored housewife." Not to be outdone, Paglia (1992: 255–156, emphasis in original) maintains that "I began my revolt when I was just a little child…[F]rom my earliest years I had this burning desire to *do* something for women, to do something *so massive* for women, to demonstrate that women should be taken seriously."

Second, akin to the exposés penned by former members of religious movements or "cults" and those who chronicle "my life in the Mob," antifeminist feminist books are rou-tinely marketed as the act of the "broken but unbowed," the altruistic crusader who, de-spite personal peril, dares to challenge the powerful to ensure the safety of society. The author is identified as a renegade, an iconoclast, a "free-thinker" who has resisted the "brain-washing" and coercive "thought control" of feminists. For example, the book jacket of *Feminism Is Not The Story of My Life* (Fox-Genovese, 1996) proclaims that its author dares to "say out loud what many women have only whispered." In like fashion, Canadian "dis-sident-feminist" Donna Laframboise is lauded on the back cover of her book, *The Princess At the Window*, for her "courage" in daring to tackle a mainstream women's movement that is "extremist, self-obsessed, arrogant and intolerant."

Third, there is an outpouring of allegations of wrongdoing on the part of the "women's movement" or those whom the author identifies as its "spokespersons." Drawing upon a typology developed by Bromley and Shupe (1981) in another context , these allegations can be summarized as taking one or more of six basic forms. The first are allegations of **mental manipulation and coercion**. The author charges that members of the women's movement are gullible dupes whose minds have effectively been controlled by the edicts and "dogma" disseminated by key spokespersons. Supposedly, adherence is maintained through the censorship efforts of a "thought police."

> At Harvard, and later at graduate school…I was surprised at how many things there were not to say, at the arguments and assertions that could not be made, lines that could not be crossed, taboos that could not be broken…and the list of couldn't went on and on. (Roiphe, 1993: 5)

The second are allegations of the **illegitimacy and inadequacy of beliefs**. The author charges that the core contentions advanced by feminists are based on the faulty reasoning of mediocre theorists who "can't think their way out of a wet paper bag" (Paglia, in Faludi, 1991: 319), on flawed concepts, and on inadequate research. The back cover of Hoff Sommers's *Who Stole Feminism* carries an endorsement that proclaims, "Christina Hoff Sommers has done something lethally deflating to the pretensions of the shriller sorts of feminists: she looked at their evidence and found it lacking." In like fashion, Paglia charges:

> The disaster of women's studies today is that women are being…forced to read these very narrowly trained contemporary women. And most of it is *junk*! It's *junk*! It's appalling!…Trying to build a sex theory without studying Freud, women have made nothing but mud pies. (1992: 259–260, 243, emphasis in original)

Allegations of **sexual perversion or inadequacy** are the third kind. The sexual orientation of noted feminist writers becomes the object of speculation, derision, or attack. Although accusations of lesbianism are common (with the insinuation that lesbians are "man-haters"), mainstream feminists may also be derided as sexually repressed women with a prurient fascination with sex. For example, Roiphe (1993: 5) suggests that "the fascination with sexual harassment had to do with more than sexual harassment." Alternatively, mainstream feminists are depicted as women who have fallen victim to "the insatiable demands of female machismo." Friedan (1981: 113–114) offers the following depiction of one such "young feminist:"

> [S]he strips her life clean of all these unmeasured, unvalued feminine tasks and frills—stops baking cookies altogether, cuts her hair like a monk, decides not to have children.…She does not feel grounded in life. She shivers inside.

It seems that a common strategy employed by antifeminists to distinguish themselves from such "bad" and "unnatural" feminists is to proclaim both their heterosexuality and marital status. For example, Naomi Wolf lapses into lyricism in describing herself as a "radical heterosexual feminist: Male sexual attention is the sun in which I bloom. The male body is ground and shelter to me, my lifelong destination" (in Chesler, 1994: 58). Maudlin dedications and acknowledgment pages that note, in lugubrious detail, the "wisdom, encouragement, and unfailing assistance of my husband, Fred" (Sommers, 1994: 8) or "the generosity of my mother-in-law"(Laframboise, 1996) are fairly routine.

The fourth are allegations of **financial wrongdoing or wastage**. Commonly, mainstream feminists are derided as subverting funds that are spent in frivolous, irrelevant, and unscholarly ways. Laframboise claims that

> Canadian taxpayers paid $10 million for a study [the Violence Against Women Study] that was supposed to be about female anguish. Instead, it turned out to be, first and foremost, about something else: male misconduct. This is where extremism leads. (1996: 46)

The fifth kind of allegations are of **political subversion**. Mainstream feminist writers are accused of promoting communism, seeking to subvert key institutions in society and, if left unchecked, of bringing on a sociopolitical-educational apocalypse.

> It would be difficult to exaggerate the extent of the difficulties we now face. The gender feminists…hold the keys to many bureaucratic fiefdoms, research centers, women's-studies programs, tenure committees, and para-academic organizations. It is now virtually impossible to be appointed to high administrative office in any university system without having passed muster with the gender feminists. (Sommers, 1994: 273)

Sixth are allegations of **promoting tension between the sexes** "that never existed." The authors claim that hostilities between the sexes have been manufactured, engineered, and promoted by feminists themselves.

> [T]he so-called male establishment, sensitive as it is, will not sit back and let its books be banned. It will not accept the accusations without a fight…[Feminism] will force the…old guard to defend itself, its jobs, and its books against the timid, inarticulate, even dull…who has risen to power on the crest of the multiculturalist wave. (Roiphe, 1993: 107)

According to Wolf (1993, 1998), not only have "victim" feminists alienated many men, they have encouraged women to pursue goals that are both unhelpful and unnecessary.

If the charges raised by antifeminist feminists largely echo those that have been made against women's rights activists since the turn of the century, they are now amplified by the mass media. Unfortunately, it often seems that those who are best able to phrase their critique into a vicious sound bite are heralded as *the* spokesperson for the "new feminism," the "third wave of feminism," or a "postfeminist" world. It is somewhat odd, to say the least, that "[w]e've managed to enter a postfeminist world without ever knowing a feminist one" (Kaminer, 1990: 1).

The Promise Keepers

Images of gender social movements are multifocal. The evaluation of theories and organizations that seek to change or return us to earlier-held models of masculinity and femininity are neither simple nor consensually defined. Rather, the meanings, implications, and functions of social movements that focus attention on gender are subject to confusion and disagreement.

Consider, in this context, the controversy that surrounds the men-only Promise Keepers, who describes themselves as a "Christ-centered ministry dedicated to uniting men through vital relationships to become godly influences in their world" (in Stodghill, 1997: 40). The Promise Keepers began in the spring of 1990, when founder Bill McCartney, then coach of the University of Colorado Buffaloes and a born-again Christian, received a vision "of stadiums filled with men willing to become deeply committed Christians" (Ostling, 1997: 38).

The evangelical gatherings of the Promise Keepers attract a substantial degree of support and of criticism. The Promise Keepers are denounced by the president of the National Organization of Women (NOW), Patricia Ireland, as a group that offers men a "feel-good form of male supremacy with...dangerous political potential" (Gergen, 1997: 78); NOW has also passed a resolution declaring the Promise Keepers "the greatest danger to women's rights" (in Stodghill, 1997: 36). The Keepers are lampooned for having a "Jesus-goes-to-Sears aesthetic," attacked by Equal Partners in Faith, a coalition of liberal clergy as "divisive and potentially dangerous," and by the Center for Democracy Studies as "steeped in political ideology and the third wave of the religious right—after Jerry Falwell's Moral Majority and Pat Robertson's Christian Coalition" (Phillips, 1997: 53). The Promise Keepers are also praised by such diverse figures as Hillary Clinton, James Dobson of Focus on the Family, and Robert Wuthnow of Princeton's Center for the Study of American Religion. According to supporters, the Promise Keepers provide a "new model of manhood for our times," and are ushering in "a generation of freshly sensitive husbands who are not afraid to unload the dishwasher—or their tears" (McDonald, 1997: 29). According to their critics, however, the Promise Keepers are "something more sinister: a nostalgic throwback to the days of unchallenged male supremacy, or even another bid by the religious right to impose a fundamentalist agenda on [North] American life" (Phillips, 1997: 52).

McDonald (1997: 28) notes that surveys conducted by the Promise Keepers indicate that "one of the top three reasons men offer for attending is that their wives prodded them to go" and that "despite NOW"s contention that Promise Keepers is designed to foster a new breed of swaggering misogynists,...scores of...wives indicate the movement is more likely to produce the opposite." Following conferences, Promise Keepers frequently ask their wives if they may perform the "biblically inspired ritual" of washing their wives' feet (Phillips, 1997: 30). However, although Promise Keepers declare that "it has no political agenda...it makes no attempt to hide its allies on the religious right" who have provided it with both financial support and strategic publicity (Stodghill, 1997). Similarly, while Promise Keepers as a group does not take an official position on the issue of abortion, its founder has attacked abortion as "a violation of the heart of God."

Based on her examination of the two books that form the foundation of the Promise Keeper's ideology, Griffith's (1992), *What Makes a Man? 12 Promises That Will Change Your Life* and Jansen's (1994) *Seven Promises of a Promise Keeper*, Beal (1997) contends that the Promise Keepers use images and metaphors of sport to construct a type of masculinity that promotes patriarchal ideology and the accompanying notion that men are superior. There is no doubt that the images of sports abound within the rhetoric of the Promise Keepers. As Phillips (1997: 53) observes, "[u]sing stadiums is no coincidence. McCartney (known as 'Coach' in Promise Keeper circles) uses a blend of sports metaphors and military language to reach his all-male, overwhelmingly white audience. Men, he says, "have dropped the ball; they have to get back on Christ's team." However, given the centrality of sports within male socialization, and McCartney's professional background, it may be the case that this group is simply using the images and lexicon with which men in general, and McCartney in particular, are comfortable.

Leaders of gender social movements, as we have previously noted, are often the objects of impassioned commentary. McCartney is no exception to this pattern of response. He has been denounced by his critics as a "raving lunatic" (Gergen, 1997) and as a "homophobe" who describes homosexuality as "an abomination against Almighty God" (in Phillips,

1997: 53), and as a "racist," who, as a coach, disciplined a disproportionate number of black players with suspensions. However, to his supporters, McCartney is a sage who supports "traditional values," and who proudly and prominently displays pictures of his two biracial grandchildren—one Samoan, the other African-American—in his Denver office. They note that "speakers at Promise Keeper gathering are exceedingly racially diverse…[and that] racial reconciliation is invariably addressed from the podium." At the first Promise Keepers gathering, McCartney told his audience that he believed the Lord told him that if only whites attended, "I ain't coming"—a message that he regularly repeats to his audiences (Cose, 1997: 30). It is reported that "[currently] minorities constitute 38% of [the Promise Keepers'] staff and a growing share of the attendance at…rallies" (Stodghill, 1997: 38).

The number of men belonging to or active within the Promise Keepers varies widely within published reports. Within four articles appearing in *Time, U.S. News & World Report, Maclean's,* and *Newsweek* within the first week of October 1997, quite disparate figures are given. Stodghill (1997: 34) writes that approximately 20,000 Promise Keepers fellowship groups exist throughout the United States and that, in 1996, an average of 50,000 men congregated at each of the 22 events held by the group "for a total of 1.1 million souls." Gergen (1997: 78) states that, while the Promise Keepers were able to attract 4,200 men to their rallies in 1991, by 1996, 1.3-million men had congregated at their 22 events. Cose (1997: 30) reports that the movement boasts that no fewer than 2.6-million men. In Canada, Phillips (1997: 52) reports that "a separate and smaller" Promise Keepers group has existed since 1995, with headquarters in Burlington, Ontario, and offices in Kitchener, Ontario, Winnipeg, Manitoba, and Langley, British Columbia. According to Phillips, the Canadian branch of the Promise Keepers "has a mailing list of 70,000 and…[has drawn] as many as 11,500 men in Vancouver and Hamilton," while buses and chartered planes reportedly transport "several hundred" Canadian men to rallies in American cities such as Washington, D.C.

Although the exact number of Promise Keepers is disputable, there is consensus that the only women who attend their stadium rallies are those who volunteer to sell souvenirs. "The reason, say Promise Keepers, has nothing to do with chauvinism (Phillips, 1997: 53). Promise Keepers maintain that men, because of concerns with pride and ego, would be loathe to admit their failings and embrace Christ, if women were in attendance at their rallies. For others, however, the reason goes "to the heart of Promise Keepers' most controversial belief that men must reclaim leadership of their families, and wives should submit to their husbands. McCartney says that is not debatable—the Bible says the man is head of the family and that is that" (Phillips, 1997: 53).

A STALLED REVOLUTION

Noting the differential rates and speed of change for men, women, their respective roles, and the institutional contexts in North America within which the players perform their parts, Hochschild (1990: 12) introduces the concept of a "stalled revolution." She notes that men, and their roles, changed more dramatically than did women and their roles during the beginning years of the Industrial Revolution. The institution of the economy was changed simultaneously by the introduction of machine power and mechanization, and by the introduction of men into the roles of paid workers. However, since the time of the second-wave of the feminist movement in the middle to late 1960s, women and their roles have changed much more dramatically and much faster than have men and their roles. The substantial increase in the number of female paid workers has changed the gender balance of the economic institution. However, women have adapted more to fit the economy than the economy has adapted to fit women. Even though some changes have occurred within the institution of the family in terms of its average size and its structure, women still bear primary responsibility for housework, parenting, and relationship or family maintenance. The differential pace of gender and institutional changes produces a sense of strain within and between women and men. "This strain between the change in women and the absence of change in much else leads me to speak of a 'stalled revolution'" (Hochschild, 1990: 12).

Although not couched in the language of a "stalled revolution," the research findings and analyses of Chafetz and Hagan (1996) not only provide further supportive evidence that the insights of Hochschild are not limited to the United States alone, but extend the stalled revolution concept even further. Chafetz and Hagan (1996) compared 21 nations, nearly all of whom, including Canada, were industrialized prior to World War II. Each nation was examined over the decades from 1960 to 1990 for changes in both the economic and family institutions. The same general patterns occurred in all nations, varying only slightly in terms of their timing and in the magnitude of specific changes.

> During the three decades examined, with very few exceptions: 1) women's labour force participation rates expanded dramatically in response to increased demand for their labour; 2) post-secondary enrollment rates increased for women; 3) first marriage rates decreased, most notably, among young women; 4) divorce rates increased; 5) total fertility fell to below replacement level [2.1 children per women]; and 6) first births were increasingly deferred to the late 20s and beyond. (Chafetz and Hagan, 1996: 197)

Chafetz and Hagan use a **Modified Rational Choice** approach (Marini, 1992, in Chafetz and Hagan, 1996: 200) to explain these general patterns. "We argue that women increasingly behave as economically rational actors to the same extent as do men, yet are unwilling to abandon the socioemotional rewards of romantic relationships and children"(Chafetz and Hagan, 1996: 200). Women do so within social contexts that provide increasingly greater accessibility to educational and economic participation and rewards, while at the same time confronting them with relatively unchanged sets of expectations for familial and domestic obligations. Expanding economies, well-developed feminist ideologies or belief systems, and excessive demands that women shoulder the burden of responsibility for relationship maintenance, housework, and childrearing duties combine to promote an increasingly popular gender strategy among women that seeks to maximize self-fulfillment and monetary rewards in paid work, while decreasing, but not foregoing, participation in marriage, housekeeping, and raising children.

A rational modified model for "having it all" requires women to acquire educational credentials and to obtain satisfying employment that does not demand extra commitment such as overtime, geographical relocation, or promotions accompanied by extra workloads. While those educational and economic goals are being attained or set in motion, sexual relationships and romantic commitments through cohabitation are possible, but marriage and childrearing with overwhelming responsibilities for both, are not rational alternatives. Modified goals in these areas take the form of remaining childfree or having fewer children, purchasing domestic and childrearing services, and negotiating or renegotiating a new division of marriage, household, and childrearing labours. Intransigence from intimate partners to negotiate or renegotiate, in combination with a more equal balance of power resources between partners and greater legal accessibility, make divorce a more widely available, and a more frequently taken, option. Chafetz and Hagan (1996: 212) argue that, while younger and more affluent women may be the initial trendsetters for new behaviours, these new patterns "diffuse" throughout a society to reach older and even younger, less affluent women, and perhaps even men, eventually becoming "legitimated as normative changes."

Taken together, the observations, findings, and arguments of Hochschild and of Chafetz and Hagan suggest the uneven pace of gender change. Women, in our own and in other industrial societies, have changed much more than have men, and have gone about as far as they can on their own. On one hand, that statement appears to be an oversimplification and, as such, overlooks the lack of change in some women and the changes incurred or instigated by men. On the other hand, as a generalization, the statement unfortunately captures the state of gender today. We are, at best, still in the middle of a gender "revolution," or gender transformation process and until (or unless) men, on a mass scale, initiate substantial changes in their roles and in the institutions they still control (either formally or informally), the gender revolution will remain stalled.

Postgender Marriages

One of the factors contributing to a stalled revolution is an appearance of gender equality that masks an underlying reality of gender inequality. To paraphrase LaRossa's (1988/1995) contention regarding fatherhood, our culture of gender equality, as expressed in and by language, has changed faster than has our behaviour, particularly at the level of interpersonal, and especially intimate, cross-gender relationships. We have already noted that most heterosexual couples who proclaim their relationship to be egalitarian actually fall short of attaining that ideal (Blaisure and Allen, 1995; Hochschild, 1990; Zvonkovic et al., 1996). A more recent empirical investigation (Knudson-Martin and Mahoney, 1998) suggests that more couples speak a "myth of equality" than live in relationships actually characterized by equality. Couples are able to maintain their "myth" through the use of one or more types of equality talk (Knudson-Martin and Mahoney, 1998: 86). **Give-and- take** talk emphasizes mutuality (e.g., "she's going to be there for me and vice versa") without acknowledging which partner is actually "there" for the other most often. **Free-choice** talk obliterates inequalities under the guise of freedom of choice (e.g., "she chooses to do all the housework because she's better at it than I am"). **Oneness** talk emphasizes a couple unity in which what is good for one is, of course, good for the other and good for the relationship (e.g. "we all benefit when I stay late at work") without ever specifying which "one" of the intimate partners is the more frequent representative of the "us." **Partnership** talk implies mutual decision-making (e.g., "she can be assertive when I don't feel like being assertive, and I can be assertive when she doesn't feel like being assertive") without acknowledging who more frequently influences actual decisions made.

Expressing the rhetoric of equality is only one of the means by which couples maintain a facade of equality in relationships. A variety of other strategies can be and are used to avoid confronting actual relationship inequalities (Knudson-Martin and Mahoney, 1998: 86–87). **Benign framing/rationalization** involves labeling a condition of inequality as something else ("She has better judgment about the house," "It doesn't bother me to clean the house," "We each know our roles as mother and father"). **Not examining the consequences** is a strategy that focuses only upon the immediate present and ignores the long-term consequences of an arrangement for each partner individually ("We never discussed living any place else—my business is here"). **Settling for less** is a strategy in which, for example, one partner draws an imaginary line between what currently exists and what will not be permitted to exist, as if the two conditions represent a distinction between equality and inequality when both conditions represent only degrees of inequality ("I will not dust his books! I really can't deal with that!"). **Hiding the issues** requires a high degree of cooperation and coordination between intimate partners to maintain a facade of equality so that the reality of their inequality never intrudes upon their fantasy. Hochschild (1990) describes a couple who managed to maintain publicly that their housekeeping relationship was based upon a 50–50 sharing even though the "half" of the house he was responsible for was less than one-quarter of its actual size. Finally, **placing responsibility on the wife** is a commonly adopted strategy in which she is responsible for maintaining the illusion of equality by becoming more accommodating ("If I have decent arguments, he will listen," "If I'm not getting what I should from her, then I'm not going to give it myself").

Inequality stems from an imbalance of power in cross-gender relationships. However, not all power is immediately obvious. "*Invisible power* is the power to prevent issues from being raised. *Latent power* derives from the operation of dominant values and institutional procedures which shape a person's perceptions and preferences in such a way that they can see or imagine no alternative to the status quo or they see it as natural or unchangeable" (Knudson-Martin and Mahoney, 1998: 82 emphasis in original). A language of equality and the strategies referred to earlier all conceal the extent to which invisible and latent power imbalances continue to promote male domination and female subordination within intimate relationships. Relationships in which women more often accommodate themselves to men's desires and wishes only perpetuate those inequalities, even when the accommodations are made in the name of "love."

Empirical evidence obtained from a longitudinal study of marriage relationships finds that wives' love for their husbands is a major motivating force behind new mothers altering their own preferences to conform to the preferences of their husbands regarding childcare responsibilities (Johnson and Huston, 1998). Regardless of other personal resources they possess that could influence the balance of power effecting the decision-making process, "the more wives loved their husbands, the more their preferences changed toward their husbands' preferences, regardless of whether their husbands were more patriarchal or more egalitarian in preferences about the performance of child-care tasks" (Johnson and Huston, 1998: 200). In contrast, husbands' love for their wives does not lead husbands to alter their preferences to conform to or better accord with their wives' preferences. This study suggests that the distribution between mothers and fathers of childcare responsibilities and behaviours is not so much a preference imposed by fathers in a unilateral, patriarchal fashion, supported by possession of a greater share of personal resources (such as income or education), but rather is more the product of an active choice made by mothers whose other resources could have altered the direction of the childcare outcome, but did not.

This active choice by wives implicitly confirms the existence of an underlying invisible power dimension to the gendered relationships between marital partners. Johnson and Huston (1998: 202) argue that women, out of love for their husbands, children, and marriages, perform relationship work designed to minimize conflict and enhance harmony that will, they hope, benefit all members of a family. To this end, "keeping the peace may be more important to wives than husbands doing their fair share" (Johnson and Huston, 1998: 202). Even though women's decisions may result in their assuming an inequitable share of the burden of responsibilities and work for childcare and family maintenance, they are made as a means of furthering women's perceived best interests, namely a harmonious family environment. Still, should these decisions achieve a desired outcome, men's power in marital and family relationships is reinforced, since husbands and fathers are rarely aware of the extent to which their own wishes and desires are anticipated and provided for without negotiation. Inequality remains unchallenged.

Gottman and his colleagues (Gottman et al., 1998) present an impressive array of empirical evidence, obtained from detailed observations of newly married couples over a six-year period, which suggests that conflict-resolution styles significantly differentiate unhappy couples from happy couples. Although it is too soon to determine whether these findings can be generalized beyond the boundaries of marriage to include all heterosexual-couple relationships, two key elements clearly differentiate marriages that ended in divorce from marriages that remained stable and happy from unhappy, but still stable, marriages: **female "start-up,"** and **male willingness to accept influence from a female**. Women, in both laboratory and everyday life situations, typically initiate conflict discussions. We referred to this in an earlier chapter as the first part of a female-demand/male withdraw pattern. "Usually the wife brings marital issues to the table for discussion, and she usually brings a detailed analysis of the conditions in which this problem occurs, its history, and suggestions for a solution" (Gottman et al., 1998: 18). How a wife starts a conflict discussion appears to dictate its ensuing tone. A "soft" start-up comprising gentleness and neutral affect portends well for a positive outcome for both partners. A "hard" start-up, where an initial neutral affect on her part quickly escalates into a negative affective tone (such as contempt, belligerence, or defensiveness), almost always leads to a negative outcome for both partners.

Following the initial overtures of a conflict discussion, whether a male partner will respond with hard, high-intensity negative affect (including withdrawal) or with a more moderate, accepting, response will depend in large part upon whether he is willing to be influenced by a female, in this case his wife. Men whose marriages end up being stable and happy are willing to be influenced by their wives. Men whose marriages either end in divorce or in stable, but unhappy, relationships are not so willing. Preliminary analysis of data collected from unwilling husbands finds that these men do not differ in terms of age, income, occupation, or educational level, but do tend to be "rated by observers as dominating their wives...make the major decisions in the family, have suffered financial or emotional hardships in the marriage, are physically shorter...and are more physically active in one-on-one competitive sports than men who accept influence from their wives" (Gottman et al., 1998: 19). The thread of power appears to link these characteristics and the threat of a shift in the existing power relations appears to lie behind their rejection of their wives' influence. We have mentioned numerous times in the previous chapters that power based upon educational, occupational, and income resources appears to be becoming more equitable among heterosexual couples in the 1990s. However, power bestowed by virtue of a person's sex remains largely unchanged. Many men reject a woman's influence simply because she is a "mere" woman, regardless of any other power resources she may possess. One power resource she does not possess is the biological status of being male. Still, the fact that other men have overcome this sexist way of thinking and evaluating indicates that biological status power is not fixed and immutable.

Risman and Johnson-Sumerford (1998) collected data from a small sample of 15 married couples characterized by equitable, shared responsibilities for housework and childcare. The data reveal a number of different "paths" taken towards creation of a "postgender" marriage in which gender does not operate as a major organizing principle for the distribution of household labour. Partners in **dual-career** couples (the most frequently occurring of all couples in the study) are equally interested in attaining success in their professional careers and participating equally in co-parenting their children. **Dual-nurturer** couples place greater emphasis upon family and children than upon careers or paid-work jobs. **Posttraditional** couples had once experienced "traditional" gender-linked inequitable intimate partnerships, but changed to an equitable relationship. Finally, some couples are "pushed" into forming equitable relationships initially by circumstances perceived by the couple to be beyond their individual control (e.g., chronic illness of one partner; a highly demanding, inflexible, high-paying job held by a partner).

Traditional gender manifests itself among postgender dual-career couples in a common, but not universal, tendency for wives to hold higher standards for household cleanliness. In addition to learning at a very young age to notice other people's feelings, girls also learn to see dust. Boys, and most men, do not. "Men can't see dust. Men don't know what dust is. I still don't see it. I don't know it's there. I know that the nirvana of nonsexist male development is dust. If I get to the dust stage, I'll know that I've really made it" (male respondent, in Risman and Johnson-Sumerford, 1998: 31). However, even though dual-career wives were more likely to see dust and to hold higher standards for household cleanliness, their abilities and preferences did not translate into greater participation in housecleaning activities. The couples negotiated acceptable standards for cleanliness and for equitable participation in house-cleaning.

Traditional gender also manifests itself in the area of emotions. Six of the 15 couples were characterized by a woman-as-emotion-expert pattern, five couples shared emotion work, and four couples were characterized as being "parallel emotion workers" (Risman and Johnson-Sumerford, 1998: 36) in which both partners continually attended to both their own emotions and the emotions of others in the family. In all of these couples, each partner described the other as an irreplaceable best friend. As well, both partners in all couples devoted approximately equal time in parenting activities and in assuming responsibility for childcare scheduling and monitoring. Only in the first group was a mother described as having a more intense emotional connection with children and as being more likely to monitor the emotional health of the marital relationship. This emotional ability was described by both partners as an idiosyncratic personality characteristic and was not considered to be a basis for delegating an inequitable share of emotion responsibilities to wives. The findings of Risman and Johnson-Sumerford demonstrate that participation in a gendered world outside a family's boundaries need not translate inevitably into differential, gendered behaviour inside a family.

A number of researchers (e.g., Blaisure and Allen, 1995; Risman and Johnson-Sumerford, 1998; Schwartz, 1994) argue that the chances of establishing intimate partnerships organized on the basis of principles other than sex and gender are enhanced by, perhaps even predicated upon, certain conditions. Risman and Johnson-Sumerford (1998: 27) contend that "women in our society don't have the clout or self-assurance to seek a postgender marriage unless they are highly educated, income-producing professionals." As is indicated by the statistical rarity of postgender outcomes, being highly educated, high income-earners will not automatically propel women to construct nonmarital or marital, family, and economically productive lives not governed by gender. Many, if not most, highly edu-cated, comfortably incomed women and men in our society seek and find marital and fam-ily arrangements that follow either traditional or modified-traditional gendered divisions of labour inside and outside the home. However, possession of that education-income back-ground does appear to be a necessary condition for women who are successful in achiev-ing "postgender" arrangements. Higher education provides the potential, but by no means the guarantee, that women and men can overcome the latent power limitations imposed by our existing gender system and can conceive of alternative possibilities. As well, fi-nancial and material survival are not the foremost issues governing daily life for high-in-come dual-income couples. Income equality removes one important basis for an inequitable distribution of power in couple relationships.

Does this mean that a postgender life will be limited only to a highly educated, com-fortably incomed, elite few? As we noted earlier, Chafetz and Hagan (1996) argue that, while social change typically originates within these groups, these changes are felt through-out society. Until such time as change becomes more general, some people may suggest that a postgender goal is utopian and beyond the reach of those individuals who have less ed-ucation and lower incomes.

THE UNFINISHED JOURNEY:
HOW DOES CANADA COMPARE?

As anyone living in this country during the middle to late 1990s is aware, Canada has been ranked by the United Nations as the number one nation in which to live, based upon what is euphemistically referred to in the media as our "quality of life." Beginning in 1990, the United Nations began seeking analytical tools and methods useful for comparing nations in terms of how well each nation creates a living environment that will promote "long, healthy and creative lives" (United Nations Development Programme, 1995: 11) among all of its cit-izens. The simplest method used previously by various individual researchers and research organizations focused upon measures such as national economic growth or per-capita Gross National Product (GNP). The GNP is usually calculated by adding the total dollar (ex-pressed in US currency equivalents) value of all goods and services produced in one year by a nation, and then dividing that total by the total number of citizens living in the nation that same year. Such measures provide some international comparability, but ignore important issues of the actual distribution of national wealth or standard of economic living among all the citizens of a country. Many nations foster higher economic growth or have high per-capita GNPs, but actual wealth frequently is concentrated in a small proportion of the pop-ulation, while the vast majority of the populace experience lives of mere subsistence. In addition to these drawbacks, comparing countries solely upon economic indicators fails to acknowledge many other essential elements of social life.

In 1990, the United Nations Development Programme began using the composite **Human Development Index** (HDI) as a way of measuring national development using indicators of longevity (based upon life expectancy), knowledge (based upon adult literacy rates and, initially, mean years of schooling in the population), and income or PPP (purchasing power parity, the per-capita GNP adjusted for local cost of living). The selection of these specific indicators was based primarily upon pragmatic groups; data for each indicator were readily available and in a form permitting comparability across nations. The United Nations

Development Programme acknowledges that deriving average figures for measures, such as mean years of schooling and per-capita GNP, conceals ranges of variation that may be indicative of inequality for specific segments of a nation's total population. Mean years of schooling was eventually replaced by a more comprehensive measure indicating the proportion of a population enrolled in primary, secondary, and tertiary levels of education. The composite HDI does not measure well-being, nor happiness, among the residents of a country, but it does provide an indication of a nation's progress towards promoting long life, good health, and informed choices among its citizenry (United Nations Development Programme, 1995: 12).

The Development Programme further sought to refine its measures to allow for identification of how nations treat, or promote the human developmental growth of, significant groups. These groups could then be compared with other groups within a nation and with other similar significant groups in other nations. In 1995, the Human Development Report introduced two new measures designed to highlight the status of women within nations (United Nations Development Programme, 1995: 72–86). The **Gender-related Development Index** (GDI) uses the same measures as does the HDI, but applies them to indicate the extent of inequality between men and women within a nation. "In other words, the GDI is the HDI adjusted for gender inequality" (United Nations Development Programme, 1995: 73). Disparities between women and men in terms of, for example, life expectancy, adult literacy, or purchasing power parity lower a country's GDI ranking. Typically, a nation will attain one ranking for its overall national score on HDI, but will receive a lower ranking on GDI, thus indicating that existing human development growth factors are unequally distributed between women and men within a country, a distribution that favours men more so than women.

A third measurement device, the **Gender Empowerment Measure** (GEM), focuses upon women's advancement within a nation in terms of political, economic, and professional life. More specifically, GEM focuses upon the extent to which women are able to participate in political and economic decision making so they can take advantage of a nation's opportunities. Three indicators are used to construct a nation's GEM ranking: (1) women's share of seats in parliament or share of seats in parliamentary caucus, (2) women's share of administrative and managerial jobs, as well as professional and technical jobs, (3) women's earning power, which indicates their access to jobs and wages. Taken together, these indicators provide information on the extent to which women are able to use their capabilities within a nation. As with other indices, GEM indicators were selected primarily because data for them are more readily available from more nations than would be data on, for example, women's power within households. In general, the ranking for most nations drops dramatically when comparing their HDI to them GEM, thus indicating a nation's underutilization of women's capabilities.

Rankings are based upon results from weighted indicators that are combined within statistical formulas to produce final outcome scores or "values." In theory, scores for each of the HDI, GDI, and GEM indices can range from a low of 0.0 to a high of 1.0. No society has attained a "perfect" score of 1.0, indicating that room for improvement exists even within the "best" countries. "The HDI value for each country indicates how far that country has to go to attain certain defined goals: an average life span [*sic*] of 85 years, access to education for all and a decent level of income. The closer a country's HDI is to 1, the less the remaining distance that country has to travel" (United Nations Development Programme, 1995: 18). The GDI value indicates how far a country has to go to achieve gender equality in those same three areas. The GEM value indicates how far a country has to go in empowering women to enable them to participate meaningfully in decision making in the public sphere relative to selected aspects of economic and political life.

As we noted at the outset of this section, Canada has fared well according to HDI comparisons, ranking as the number one nation of 174 countries compared in 1995 and 1996 and of 175 countries compared in 1997. However, our prominence typically declines when rankings are computed for GDI and GEM. In 1995, Canada was ranked first on HDI, but ninth of 130 countries on GDI, and fifth of 116 countries on GEM (United Nations Development Programme, 1995). In 1996, Canada was second of 137 countries on GDI, and sixth of 104 countries on GEM (United Nations Development Programme, 1996). Table 10.1 provides HDI, GDI, and GEM rankings for a number of selected countries, based upon information contained in the *Human Development Report* of 1997. In 1997, Canada ranked number one of 146 countries on GDI, but number six of 94 countries on GEM (United Nations Development Programme, 1997). Over the three-year period of these Reports, Canada's GDI ranking has improved, but our GEM ranking has worsened.

Data available to the United Nations Development Programme permitted GDI comparisons for 79 countries from 1970 to 1992. GDI values increased in all countries over that time period (United Nations Development Programme, 1995: 80). However, comparisons of country rankings for 1970 to 1992 reveal that both Canada and the United States dropped in their comparative rankings: Canada from second to ninth, and the United States from first to fifth. While gender equality (as measured by the GDI) improved in both countries over the 1970s and 1980s, the pace of change was slower than in many other societies. Nordic countries in particular, such as Sweden, Finland, and Norway, made even greater strides in promoting and implementing gender equality in those areas measured by the GDI, especially regarding earned income. Canada's ninth-place ranking in the 1992 survey was due primarily to a low value assigned for women's share of earned income compared with men's share (United Nations Development Programme, 1995: 79).

The fact that GDI values for all 79 countries increased between 1970 and 1992 suggests that, even though the pace of change may be uneven over time within and between societies, once normative policies, programs, and general expectations are put into place, trends towards greater gender equality are difficult to reverse. Even though regressive social movements may attempt to return a society to "the good old days," the prognosis for the successful reversal of social trends appears to be slim. Perhaps only armed overthrow of existing governments, in the name of religious fundamentalist purity and hegemony (e.g., the Taliban in Afghanistan in the late 1990s), can reverse these trends.

Rank-orderings of countries conceal as much as they reveal. More insight can be obtained from examining the HDI, GDI, and GEM values obtained from the United Nations analyses. Table 10.2 provides a summary of the values on each of these three measuring devices for 25 selected (out of a possible 94) countries (United Nations Development Programme, 1997). A quick examination of the GDI values in the table demonstrates the evidence that leads the United Nations to observe, repeatedly, that "no society treats its women as well as its men" (United Nations Development Programme, 1997: 39, 1995: 75). Even though Canada scored the highest GDI value in the 1997 analysis, our country still falls short of the maximum and still scores lower than on the HDI index. We have noted on numerous occasions in previous chapters that the terms "men" or "man" are often used as generic synonyms for "human" and the terms "woman" or "women" often stand for something less.

TABLE 10.1	Selected Countries+, Ranked According to HDI, GDI, and GEM, 1997*		

Country	HDI Rank	GDI Rank	GEM Rank
Canada	1	1	6
France	2	5	40
Norway	3	2	1
USA	4	4	7
Netherlands	5	10	10
Japan	6	11	34
Finland	7	6	4
New Zealand	8	7	5
Sweden	9	3	2
Spain	10	18	21
Austria	11	14	8
Belgium	12	13	15
Australia	13	8	11
United Kingdom	14	12	20
Switzerland	15	19	12
Denmark	17	9	3
Germany	18	15	9
Barbados	23	16	14
Cuba	53	48	23
Philippines	60	55	35
China	63	58	28
Guatemala	70	69	29
India	80	75	86
Pakistan	81	76	92
Mauritania	86	79	84

* HDI refers to Human Development Index; GDI refers to Gender Development Index; GEM refers to Gender Empowerment Measure
+ Rankings based upon 94 countries from whom complete data for all three measures could be obtained.
Source: Adapted from United Nations Development Programme (1997). *Human Development Report 1997*. Text Table 2.9, p. 41.

In similar fashion, we could conclude from the HDI and GDI values contained in Table 10.2 that "Canadians live in the best place in the world; female Canadians live someplace else."

As can be seen in Tables 10.1 and 10.2, the countries with the highest HDI and GDI rankings and values tend to be found in Northern and Western Europe, and in what were referred to in an earlier chapter as the "Anglo-Saxon overseas" (Travato and Lalu, 1996)

TABLE 10.2 Selected Countries, HDI, GDI, and GEM Values, 1997*			
Country	**HDI Value**	**GDI Value**	**GEM Value**
Canada	**0.960**	**0.939**	**0.700**
France	0.946	0.926	0.452
Norway	0.943	0.934	0.795
USA	0.942	0.928	0.671
Netherlands	0.940	0.901	0.660
Japan	0.940	0.901	0.465
Finland	0.940	0.925	0.719
New Zealand	0.957	0.918	0.718
Sweden	0.936	0.932	0.784
Spain	0.934	0.874	0.542
Austria	0.932	0.890	0.667
Belgium	0.932	0.891	0.591
Australia	0.931	0.917	0.659
United Kingdom	0.931	0.896	0.543
Switzerland	0.930	0.874	0.642
Denmark	0.927	0.916	0.728
Germany	0.924	0.886	0.661
Barbados	0.907	0.885	0.602
Cuba	0.723	0.699	0.523
Philippines	0.672	0.650	0.459
China	0.626	0.617	0.481
Guatemala	0.572	0.510	0.476
India	0.446	0.419	0.228
Pakistan	0.445	0.392	0.189
Mauritania	0.355	0.341	0.177

* HDI refers to Human Development Index; GDI refers to Gender Development Index; GEM refers to Gender Empowerment Measure.
Source: Adapted from United Nations Development Programme, (1997). *Human Development Report 1997.* HDI values are found in Tables 2.10 and 2.11 (pp. 44–45); GDI values are found in Appendix Table 2 (pp. 149–151); GEM values are found in Appendix Table 3 (pp. 152–154).

societies of Australia, Canada, New Zealand, and the United States, and in Japan. However, examination of the tables reveals considerable variation within and between countries in terms of their HDI ranks and values and their GDI ranks and values. A high HDI rank and value do not predict an equally high GDI rank and value. The Netherlands, Japan, and Spain, for example, all register significant declines in their GDI rankings and values in comparison to their HDI rankings and values. In contrast, Australia, Denmark, Barbados, Cuba, the Philippines, China, India, Pakistan, and Mauritania all substantially improved their GDI rankings relative to their HDI rankings, even though their GDI values remain lower than their HDI values. These variations demonstrate that "gender equality does not depend on the income level of a society" (United Nations Development Programme, 1995: 75). Other factors, such as health-care and education systems and a society's commitment to ensuring equality of gender access to these systems are equally, if not more, important. A society that shapes its social policies solely upon economic indicators will not be able to guarantee a gender equality outcome. A commitment to gender equality itself can have a meaningful impact, independent of the state of a country's economy.

The most telling indicator of gender equality, or lack thereof, can be found in a country's GEM ranking and values. The columns in tables 10.1 and 10.2 under the GEM headings illustrate the distance women still have to travel, with or without the help of men, to receive an equitable share of power in important areas of public-sphere decision making. A cursory examination of Table 10.2 reveals that GEM values are typically much lower than either HID or GDI values for all countries, although the drop is more precipitous in some countries (e.g., France, Japan, the United Kingdom) than in others (e.g., Norway, Sweden, Denmark). Canada and the United States are in a middle range with GEM values, which indicates that considerable work must still be done before women's empowerment is equal to that of men. Some developing countries are ahead of developed countries in terms of providing women with more opportunities to participate in economic and political decision making at the highest levels (e.g., Barbados is ranked higher than the United Kingdom, Spain is well ahead of Japan and France). Once again, we see that gender equality, and particularly women's empowerment, is not solely dependent upon a country's standard of living. The Nordic countries generally have demonstrated the greatest commitment to women's empowerment.

An even better understanding of where we stand in Canada now, and of some areas in which we still have significant room for improvement, can be obtained from examination of Table 10.3. As noted earlier, the GEM index is composed of three main variables: access to political power, access to economic decision-making power, and earned-income share. Earned-income share represents not only purchasing power, but also indicates women's access to jobs and wages. Due to limitations of data currently made available to the United Nations, access to political power can only be measured regarding women's representation at the national, but not at the local, level of government. Generally, women in Canada tend to participate more on the provincial and municipal levels than on the national level (Mackie, 1991: 271; Sharpe, 1994; Wilson, 1996: 144–145).

The United Nations Development Programme has identified a five-point strategy for "accelerating progress" towards gender equality. Point three states: "A critical 30% threshold should be regarded as a minimum share of decision-making positions held by women at the national level" (United Nations Development Programme, 1995: 9). This point, initially recommended in 1990, pertains to political representation in parliament and, where applicable, in caucus or cabinet, and to participation within government and economic institutions at the administrative and managerial level. While employment at the professional and technical level is also important, these positions typically do not carry the same responsibilities for decision making that is likely to have as strong a bearing upon women's lives as are decisions made in parliament or at the administrative and managerial levels. We must also bear in mind that women who attain positions of power in parliament, and in administrative and managerial levels in government, business, and industry, do not necessarily wield their power in ways that are beneficial to all women, and that women outside the corridors of official power, such as the numerous female philanthropists in our country, also wield influence that benefits both men and women (Nowell, 1996). However, their presence in positions of power provides a tacit acknowledgment of the extent to which avenues to power are relatively open or closed to women in our society. The 30 percent "threshold" identified by the United Nations is not to be considered an end-point objective demonstrating gender equality, but rather is a minimum requirement level on the road to equality.

TABLE 10.3 **Comparison of Selected Countries Ranked According to Gender Empowerment Measures, 1997**

Country At 1 January 1997	GEM Rank	GEM Value	Seats in Parliament %	Admin & Management* % Women	Prof. & Tech.+ % Women	Income Share¶ % to Women
Norway	1	0.795	39.4	30.9	57.5	42.0
Sweden	2	0.784	40.4	38.9	64.4	45.0
Denmark	3	0.728	33.3	20.0	62.8	42.0
Finland	4	0.719	33.5	26.4	62.3	41.0
New Zealand	5	0.718	29.2	32.3	47.8	39.0
Canada	6	0.700	19.3	42.2	56.1	38.0
USA	7	0.671	11.2	42.0	52.7	41.0
Austria	8	0.667	25.1	19.2	48.6	34.0
Germany	9	0.661	25.5	19.2	43.0	35.0
Netherlands	10	0.660	28.4	15.0	44.2	34.0
Australia	11	0.659	20.5	43.3	25.0	40.0
Switzerland	12	0.642	20.3	27.8	23.8	30.0
Barbados	14	0.602	18.4	37.0	52.1	40.0
Belgium	15	0.591	15.4	18.8	50.5	33.0
United Kingdom	20	0.543	7.8	33.0	43.7	35.0
Spain	21	0.542	19.8	12.0	48.1	29.0
Cuba	23	0.523	22.8	18.5	47.8	31.0
China	28	0.481	21.0	11.6	45.1	38.0
Guatemala	29	0.476	12.5	32.4	45.2	21.0
Japan	34	0.465	7.7	8.5	41.8	34.0
Philippines	35	0.459	11.5	33.7	62.7	31.0
France	40	0.452	6.1	9.4	41.4	39.0
India	86	0.228	7.3	2.3	20.5	26.0
Pakistan	92	0.189	3.4	3.4	20.1	21.0
Mauritania	94	0.177	0.7	7.7	20.7	37.0

* Administrators and managers
+ Professional and technical workers
¶ Refers to earned income only. Income share would reach equality at 50 percent, indicating that earned income was shared equally between women and men.
Source: Adapted from United Nations Development Programme. (1997). *Human Development Report 1997.* Appendix Table 3, pp. 152–154.

TABLE 10.4	Women in National Legislatures in Selected Countries, in Percentage				

Legislature %	Cabinet %	Country	Legislature %	Cabinet %	Country
41.0	52.0	Sweden	17.0	14.0	Switzerland
39.0	39.0	Norway	15.0	13.0	Belgium
34.0	39.0	Finland	14.0	13.0	Guatemala
33.0	35.0	Denmark	13.0	14.0	Philippines
30.0	31.0	Netherlands	11.0	29.0	United States
29.0	4.0	New Zealand	10.0	8.0	United Kingdom
26.0	12.0	Germany	9.0	4.0	India
23.0	30.0	Austria	8.0	0.0	Japan
23.0	12.0	Cuba	7.0	3.0	Russia
21.0	8.0	China	5.0	13.0	France
19.0	**23.0**	**Canada**	2.0	7.0	Pakistan
18.0	13.0	Australia	0.0	4.0	Mauritania
18.0	27.0	Spain	0.0	0.0	Kuwait

Note: Dates of data collection unstated in source.
Source: Adapted from Neft and Levine, 1997: 21–23.

"No gender-specific training is required to be a parliamentarian. Neither public speaking, nor the ability to represent the opinions of the electorate, nor the art of winning public confidence requires exclusively masculine traits. But politics remains an obstacle course for women" (United Nations Development Programme, 1995: 83). When you examine Table 10.3, you will find that only four countries (Norway, Sweden, Denmark, and Finland) have crossed the 30 percent "threshold" level recommended by the United Nations, with New Zealand and the Netherlands very close to attaining that mark. Canada, the sixth ranked country on the GEM index, is a considerable distance away, with women having achieved approximately two-thirds of the seats necessary to reach that threshold. Ten of the 25 countries identified in Table 10.3 have more female representation in parliament than does Canada. The United States, United Kingdom, Japan, and France are even further behind.

Table 10.4 provides a more detailed look at women's representation in parliamentary legislatures and in cabinet positions within those parliaments for selected countries (since data on Barbados were not available from our source, we have added Russia and Kuwait to the list).

Table 10.5 provides an overview of 25 countries, ranked according to the proportion of postsecondary-education students who are women. Participation in postsecondary education provides an important indicator of both women's present and future status. Within achievement-based societies, generally, the higher the obtained educational credentials, the higher the occupation and income to be obtained. However, within those societies where social standing is ascribed at birth, participation in postsecondary education is more often a function of present standing and, particularly for women, may have little bearing upon future occupation and income earned. For example, women constitute more than half (56 percent) of

TABLE 10.5	Female Enrolment in Postsecondary Education for Selected Countries, as a Percentage of the Student Body				
%	Country	%	Country	%	Country
75	United Arab Emirates	56	Poland	53	Denmark
74	Bolivia	56	Sweden	53	Finland
61	Kuwait	56	United States	52	Russia
60	Portugal	55	Dominican Republic	49	United Kingdom
59	Philippines	**54**	**Canada**	48	South Africa
58	Cuba	54	New Zealand	40	Japan
58	Panama	54	Norway	33	India
57	Bulgaria	53	Australia	8	Ethiopia
57	Jamaica				

Note: Dates of data collection unstated.
Source: Adapted from Neft and Levine,
1997: 42–43.

all university graduates in Saudi Arabia (not included in Table 10.5), yet constitute less than one-tenth (8 percent) of the paid-labour force in that country (Neft and Levine, 1997: 61). Women are permitted to participate in higher education, but are generally prohibited from participating within the labour force within Saudi Arabia (see Table 10.6).

According to data collected by the United Nations, Canada ties for 14th place among 125 countries, in terms of the proportion of all students in postsecondary education who are women (Neft and Levine, 1997: 42–43). Women in Canada constitute a bare majority of all students. These general enrolment figures do not provide information on the fields of study being pursued. As we noted in an earlier chapter, women in Canada, as in the United States, are concentrated in the humanities and social sciences, education, and the helping professions of social work and nursing, many of which are extensions of the housewife and mother roles assigned to women.

Table 10.6 provides a comparison of 46 countries based upon women's share of the paid-labour force. Canada, tied with six other countries, ranks 27th out of 140 countries from whom data could be collected by the United Nations (Neft and Levine, 1997: 51–52). Women constitute half of the paid-labour force in only one country (Slovenia) and close to half (45 to 48 percent) in only 32 other countries. Eastern European countries that were once integral parts of, or satellites to, the former Union of Soviet Socialist Republics have a lengthy history throughout most of the twentieth century of promoting women's employment in a wide range of occupations, following blueprints laid down by Frederich Engels and, to a lesser extent, Karl Marx. In sharp contrast, the lowest rates of female participation in the paid-labour force have traditionally been found in Muslim countries, where religious beliefs preclude women from participating in labour outside the home. As we saw in an earlier chapter, Canada discouraged female employment for much of the first half of the twentieth century, except in what were defined as "exceptional" circumstances. From the

TABLE 10.6 Women's Share of the Paid-Labour Force in Selected Countries, in Percentage

%	Country	%	Country	%	Country
50	Slovenia	46	Burkina Faso	45	Uzbikistan
48	Armenia	46	Estonia	44	United Kingdom
48	Moldova	46	Hungary	43	China
48	Russia	46	Jamaica	42	France
48	Sweden	46	Korea, North	41	Norway
47	Belarus	46	Niger	40	Germany
47	Benin	46	Poland	40	Japan
47	Bulgaria	46	Slovakia	36	New Zealand
47	Burundi	46	Ukraine	30	Ireland
47	Finland	**45**	**Canada**	25	India
47	Latvia	45	Central African	22	Iraq
47	Mozambique		Republic	19	Iran
47	Romania	45	Czech Republic	13	Pakistan
47	Rwanda	45	Denmark	8	Saudi Arabia
47	Tanzania	45	Georgia		
47	Vietnam	45	Lithuania		

Note: Dates of data collection unstated.
Source: Adapted from Neft and Levine, 1997: 51–52.

1960s onwards, women's participation levels have increased rapidly, particularly between 1960 and 1990, and have slowly diversified across a wider range of occupations.

One major factor that tends to keep women's share of the paid-labour force population to at or below 50 percent is the sex ratio of a population. As we saw in the last chapter, men tend to outnumber women between the ages of birth and 50. Consequently, men are more likely to outnumber women in the labour force, especially between the ages of 15 and 50. Typically, women begin to outnumber men in any society beyond the ages of 50 and, depending upon the level of a society's support for the employment of women, may or may not outnumber men in the labour force beyond the age of 50. Between the ages of 15 and 64, approximately 80 percent of women are in the labour force in China, Sweden, and several African countries; more than 70 percent are in the labour force in many Eastern European countries; 68 percent are in the labour force in Norway and the United States, and 58 percent are in the labour force in Canada. The lowest participation rates for women between the ages of 15 and 64 (10 percent or less) are found in Jordan, Libya, Saudi Arabia, Afghanistan, and Algeria (all figures from Neft and Levine, 1997: 55–56).

As you can see, total labour-force participation rates provide only a partial glimpse into the gender structure of a nation or society. The distribution of men and women within that labour force has a much greater impact upon each gender's life events and life chances. "Approximately 50% of the world's working women are employed in the service sector:

TABLE 10.7	Women in Professional and Technical Positions for Selected Countries				

Women per 100 Men	Country	Women per 100 Men	Country	Women per 100 Men	Country
194	Kazakhstan	127	Bulgaria	72	Japan
172	Philippines	**127**	**Canada**	71	France
170	Denmark	127	Sweden	69	Indonesia
159	Finland	115	Puerto Rico	61	Switzerland
157	Uruguay	108	Chile	59	Syria
152	Poland	103	Panama	47	Rwanda
147	Jamaica	103	United States	30	Bangladesh
137	Slovakia	86	Italy	26	India
133	Brazil	82	China	11	Saudi Arabia
130	Norway	78	United Kingdom	7	Angola

Note: Dates of data collection unstated.
Source: Adapted from Neft and Levine, 1997: 67

wholesale and retail trades, restaurants, hotels, communications, insurance, real estate, business services, and social and personal services" (Neft and Levine, 1997: 62).

As we pointed out in an earlier chapter, women have been increasing their participatory share in occupations formerly reserved, officially or unofficially, for men. The focus of attention for most observers of gender in Canada, has been the increasing numbers of women in professional, technical, administrative, and managerial occupations. These positions typically are accompanied by higher levels of power, prestige, and monetary rewards. Table 10.7 is derived from United Nations data and lists 30 selected countries, ranked according to the proportions of women in professional and technical positions. As you can see, Canada, along with Bulgaria and Sweden, is ranked 11th of all nations for whom data are provided. Included under the heading of professional and technical workers are "teachers, nurses, scientists, laboratory workers, medical and dental technicians. Women comprise 42% of professional and technical workers worldwide" (Neft and Levine, 1997: 66). The greatest concentrations of women in these occupations tend to be found in the developed nations, Latin America, and the Caribbean.

Generally, women are more likely to be found in professional and technical occupations than they are to be found in administrative and managerial positions. Table 10.8 provides a rank-order listing of 30 countries. Worldwide, women comprise only 14 percent of all managers and administrators (Neft and Levine, 1997: 62). The glass-ceiling phenomenon is not limited to Canada and the United States. Women managers and administrators are more likely to be found in the more developed, industrialized countries, while the lowest proportions tend to be found in developing, industrializing, countries. However, exceptions can be found among women in the Latin American and Caribbean countries, who rank significantly higher than do women in developed countries such as

TABLE 10.8	Women in Administrative and Managerial Positions for Selected Countries					
Women per 100 Men	**Country**	**Women per 100 Men**	**Country**	**Women per 100 Men**	**Country**
139	Hungary	40	Puerto Rico	10	France
91	Kazakhstan	37	Columbia	9	Japan
68	**Canada**	34	Australia	9	Rwanda
67	United States	34	Norway	7	Indonesia
64	Sweden	24	Mexico	6	Switzerland
49	United Kingdom	18	Zimbabwe	5	Bangladesh
		17	Denmark	4	Italy
48	Guatemala	15	Iraq	3	Syria
48	Haiti	13	China	2	India
48	New Zealand	11	Greece	0	Saudi Arabia
44	Bulgaria				

Note: Dates of data collection unstated.
Source: Adapted from Neft and Levine, 1997: 63.

Japan and Italy. As you can see from Table 10.8, Canada ranks third among all countries, just ahead of the United States.

THE UNFINISHED JOURNEY: WHERE DO WE GO FROM HERE?

As we approach the millennium, it would seem safe to conclude that, as Canadians, we can be proud, but not complacent, about the progress our country has made towards gender equality. However, the journey is not complete. The persistence of a "wage gap" between the earnings of men and women, substantial inequalities in the areas of housework and childcare, occupational segregation, the absence or underutilization of family-friendly benefits, and the social problems of intimate and ultimate violence, all suggest ways in which it has proven difficult to achieve equality or to remove inequality.

The question, "Where do we go from here?" is a difficult one to answer. A core issue, which may never be resolved—except with an agree-to-disagree solution—revolves around whether gender should or should not remain as a central organizing basis for the distribution of economic, political, and marital roles (to name just a few). For some, the "obvious," sagacious, response is that it should not. Recall, for example, that radical feminists once issued a clarion call for the abolition of gender as a central organizing principle of social life —a call echoed by researchers such as Risman and Johnson-Sumerford (1998) in their discussion of "postgender marriages." At the same time, however, the opposite conclusion is considered equally "obvious" and sagacious by others. Both right-wing conservatives, who believe that God and nature intended gender to remain central, and cultural feminists, who promote gender values (or, more accurately, one gender's values) concur that gender should or *must* remain central. It is likely that advocates on both sides will remain convinced of the correctness of their beliefs and approach, and that a lack of consensus on this issue will remain a facet of present and future Canadian life.

The question, "Where do we go from here?" is additionally complex, for while gender is created and recreated within the context of institutions such as the economy, the polity, and education, it is also acted out, shaped, and reshaped on the stage of everyday life. We have previously noted that marriage and gender create and recreate each other, as does paid work (Chapter 6) and parenting (Chapter 7). It would seem that, to reduce the inequalities of gender, we must redefine and reconstruct institutions such as marriage, paid work, and child-drearing, and the interconnections among all three, since all of them, as presently constituted for the majority in our society, contribute to perpetuating gender inequality.

REFERENCES

Abbott, P. and C. Wallace. 1990. *An Introduction to Sociology: Feminist Perspectives*. London: Routledge and Kegan Paul.

———. 1992. *The Family and the New Right*. London: Pluto.

Abraham, S. and D. Llewellyn-Jones. 1992. *Eating Disorders: The Facts*, 2nd ed. Oxford, UK: Oxford University Press.

Abramovitz, M. 1988. *Regulating the Lives of Women: Social Welfare Policy from Colonial Times to the Present*. Boston: South End.

Abu-Laban, S.M., and S.A. McDaniel. 1995. Aging Women and Standards of Beauty. In *Feminist Issues: Race, Class and Sexuality,* edited by N. Mandell. Scarborough: Prentice Hall Canada.

Abu-Laban, S.M., A. McDaniel, and R.A. Sydie. 1994. Gender. In *Sociology,* edited by W. Meloff and D. Pierce, 225–252. Toronto: Nelson.

Achenbaum, W.A. 1978. *Old Age in the New Land: The American Experience Since 1870.* Baltimore: John Hopkins University Press.

Achilles, R. 1995. Assisted Reproduction: The Social Issues. In *Gender in the 1990s: Images, Realities and Issues,* edited by E.D. Nelson and B.W. Robinson, 346–364. Toronto: Nelson.

Acker, S. 1994. *Gendered Education: Sociological Reflections on Women, Teaching and Feminism.* Buckingham, UK: Open University Press.

Adams, G.R. and R.M. Jones. 1983. Female Adolescents' Identity Development: Age Comparisons and Perceived Child-rearing Experience. *Developmental Psychology* 19: 249–256.

Adams, K.L. and N.C. Ware. 1996. Sexism and the English Language: The Linguistic Implications of Being a Woman. In *Women: A Feminist Perspective*, edited by J. Freeman, 5th ed., 331–346. Palo Alto, CA: Mayfield.

———. 1983. Sexism and the English Language: The Linguistic Implications of Being a Woman. In *Women: A Feminist Perspective*, edited by J. Freeman, 3rd ed., 478–491. Palo Alto, CA: Mayfield.

Adamson, N., L. Briskin, and M. McPhail. 1988. *Feminists Organizing For Change: The Contemporary Women's Movement in Canada.* Don Mills, ON: Oxford University Press.

Adler, L.L. 1991. *Women in Cross-Cultural Perspective.* Westport, CT: Praeger.

Adler, P.A., S.J. Kless, and P. Adler. 1992/1995. Socialization to Gender Roles: Popularity among Elementary School Boys and Girls. *Sociology of Education*, 65: 169–187. Reprinted in *Gender in the 1990s: Images, Realities and Issues*, edited by E.D. Nelson and B.W. Robinson, 119–141. Toronto: Nelson Canada.

Adler, S. J. 1991. Lawyers Advise Concerns to Provide Precise Written Policy to Employees. *Wall Street Journal*. October 9: B1, B4.

Aggarwal, A.B. 1987. *Sexual Harassment in the Workplace.* Toronto: Butterworths.

Ahlander, N.R. and K.S. Bahr. 1995. Beyond Drudgery, Power and Equity: Toward an Expanded Discourse on the Moral Dimensions of Housework in Families. *Journal of Marriage and the Family* 57: 54–58.

Ahrons, C.R. 1994. *The Good Divorce.* New York: Harper Collins.

Akyeampong, E.B. 1992. Absenteeism At Work. *Canadian Social Trends* Summer: 26–28.

Albrecht, S.L. 1980. Reactions and Adjustments to Divorce: Differences in the Experiences of Males and Females. *Family Relations* 29: 59–68.

Alcock, B. and J. Robson. 1990. Cagney and Lacey Revisited. *Feminist Review* 35: 42–53.

Alia, V. 1994. Inuit Women and the Politics of Naming in Nunavut. *Canadian Woman Studies* 14: 411–414.

Allen, H. 1987. *Justice Unbalanced: Gender, Psychiatry and Judicial Doctrine.* Milton Keynes: Open University Press.

Allen, I.L. 1984. Male Sex Roles and Epithets for Ethnic Women in American Slang. *Sex Roles* 11: 43–50.

Allen, K.R. and D.H. Demo. 1995. The Families of Lesbians and Gay Men: A New Frontier in Family Research. *Journal of Marriage and the Family* 57: 111–127.

Allen, L.S. and R.A. Gorski. 1992. Sexual Orientation and the Size of the Anterior Commissure in the Human Brain. *Proceedings of the National Academy of Sciences* 89: 7199–7202.

Allinson, B. and B. Reid. 1990. *Effie*. Richmond Hill, ON: Scholastic Canada.

Amato, P.R. 1987. Family Processes in One-Parent, Stepparent, and Intact Families: The Child's Point of View. *Journal of Marriage and the Family* 49: 327–337.

Ambert, A.M. 1994. An International Perspective on Parenting: Social Change and Social Constructs. *Journal of Marriage and the Family* 56: 529–543.

———. 1990. Marriage Dissolution: Structural and Ideological Changes. In *Families: Changing Trends in Canada,* edited by M. Baker, 2nd ed., 192–210. Toronto: McGraw-Hill Ryerson.

Ambrose, S.F. 1989. Men and Women Can be Friends. In *Male/Female Roles: Opposing Viewpoints*, edited by N. Bernards and T.O'Neill. San Diego, CA: Greenhaven.

Andelin, H.B. 1974. *Fascinating Womanhood,* rev. ed. New York: Bantam.

Anderson, C.J. and C. Fisher. 1991. Male-female Relationships in the Workplace: Perceived Motivations in Office Romance. *Sex Roles* 11: 277–287.

Anderson, E.A. and L.A. Leslie. 1991. Coping with Employment and Family Stress: Employment Arrangements and Gender Differences. *Sex Roles* 24: 223–237.

Anderson, K.L. 1987. Historical Perspectives on the Family. In *Family Matters: Sociology and Contemporary Canadian Families,* edited by K.L. Anderson et al., 21–39. Toronto: Methuen.

Anderson, M.L. 1997. *Thinking About Women,* 4th ed. Boston: Allyn & Bacon.

Andrews, F.K. 1991. Controlling Motherhood: Observations on the Culture of the La Leche League. *Canadian Review of Sociology and Anthropology* 28: 84–98.

Archer, J. 1989. The Relationship between Gender-role Measures: A Review. *British Journal of Social Psychology* 28: 173–184.

Arditti, J.A. and T.Z. Keith. 1993. Visitation Frequency, Child Support Payment, and the Father-Child Relationship Postdivorce. *Journal of Marriage and the Family* 55: 699–712.

Argyle, M. 1988. *Bodily Communication,* 2nd ed. London: Methuen.

Aries, E. 1976. Interaction Patterns and Themes of Males, Females, and Mixed Groups. *Small Group Behavior* 7, 1: 1–18.

———. 1976b. Male-female Interpersonal Styles in All Male, All Female, and Mixed Groups. In *Beyond Sex Roles,* edited by A. Sargent, 292–299. St. Paul: West.

Aries, E.J. and F.L. Johnson. 1983. Close Friendship in Adulthood: Conversational Content Between Same-Sex Friends. *Sex Roles* 9: 1183–1197.

Armstrong, L. 1993. Connecting the Circles: Race, Gender, and Nature. *Canadian Woman Studies,* 13, 3: 6–10.

Armstrong, P. 1996. Resurrecting 'The Family': Interring 'The State.' *Journal of Comparative Family Studies* 27 Summer: 221–247.

———. 1995. Women and Health: Challenges and Changes. In *Feminist Issues: Race, Class, and Sexuality,* edited by N. Mandell, 294–313. Scarborough, ON: Prentice Hall Canada.

———. 1990. Economic Conditions and Family Structures. In *Families: Changing Trends in Canada,* edited by M. Baker, 2nd ed., 67–92. Toronto: McGraw-Hill Ryerson.

Armstrong, P. and H. Armstrong. 1978. *The Double Ghetto: Canadian Women and Their Segregated Work.* Toronto: McClelland and Stewart.

Arnup, K. (ed.). 1995. *Lesbian Parenting: Living with Pride & Prejudice.* Charlottetown, PI: gnergy books.

Ashmore, R.D. and F.K. Del Boca. 1979. Sex Stereotypes and Implicit Personality Theory: Toward a Cognitive-Social Psychological Conceptualization. *Sex Roles* 5: 219–248.

Ashmore, R.D., F.K. Del Boca, and A.J. Wohlers. 1986. Gender Stereotypes. In *The Social Psychology of Female-Male Relations,* edited by R.D. Ashmore and F.K. Del Boca, 69–119. Orlando: Academic Press.

Ashton, E. 1983 Measures of Play Behavior: The Influence of Sex-role Stereotyped Children's Books. *Sex Roles* 9: 43–47.

Asmussen, L. and C.L. Shehan. 1992. Gendered Expectations and Behaviors in Dating Relationships. *Proceedings: Family and Work* 2: 32. Orlando, FL: National Council on Family Relations.

Atcheson, E., M. Eberts, E. Symes, and J. Stoddart. 1984. *Women and Legal Action*. Ottawa: Canadian Advisory Council on the Status of Women.

Atkinson, M. and S. Blackwelder. 1993. Fathering in the 20th Century. *Journal of Marriage and the Family* 55 November: 975–986.

Aukett, R., J. Richie, and K. Mill. 1988. Gender Differences in Friendship Patterns. *Sex Roles* 19: 57–66.

Ayim, M. 1987. Wet Sponges and Band-aids: A Gender Analysis of Speech Patterns. In *Women and Men: Interdisciplinary Readings on Gender*, edited by G. Hofmann Nemiroff, 418–430. Montreal: Fitzhenry & Whiteside.

Baber, K.M. and A.S. Dreyer. 1986. Gender-role Orientations in Older Child-free and Expectant Couples. *Sex Roles* 14: 501–512.

Baca Zinn, M. and D. Stanley Eitzen. 1993. *Diversity in Families*, 3rd ed. New York: Harper Collins College.

Bacchi, C.L. 1983. *Liberation Deferred? The Ideas of the English-Canadian Suffragists, 1877–1918*. Toronto: University of Toronto Press.

Badinter, E. 1981. *Mother Love: Myth and Reality*. New York: Macmillan.

Baik, D.E. 1994. *Adolescent Development: Early Through Late Adolescence*. Pacific Grove, CA: Brooks/Cole.

Bailey, L.A. and L.A. Timm. 1976. More on Women's—and Men's—Expletives. *Anthropological Linguistics* 18, 9: 438–449.

Baker, M. (ed.) 1995. The Future of Family Life. In *Families: Changing Trends in Canada*, 3rd ed., 299–317. Toronto: McGraw-Hill Ryerson.

———. 1988. *Aging in Canadian Society: A Survey*. Toronto: McGraw-Hill Ryerson.

———. 1980. Support Networks and Marriage Breakdown. In *Helping Networks and the Welfare State*. Toronto: University of Toronto, School of Social Work, Conference Proceedings, May.

Baker, M. and D. Lero. 1996. Division of Labour: Paid Work and Family Structure. In *Families: Changing Trends in Canada,* edited by M. Baker, 3rd ed., 78–103. Toronto: McGraw- Hill Ryerson.

Baker, O. 1975. *Be A Woman!* New York: Ballantine.

Baker, R. 1993. 'Pricks' and 'Chicks': A Plea for 'Persons'. In *Gender Basics: Feminist Perspectives on Women and Men*, edited by A. Minas. Belmont, CA: Wadsworth.

Baldus, B. and V. Tribe. 1995. Children's Perceptions of Social Inequality. In *Everyday Life: A Reader*, edited by L. Tepperman and J.E. Curtis, 2nd ed., 161–169. Toronto: McGraw- Hill.

Baldwin, A. L. 1967. *Theories of Child Development*. New York: John Wiley.

Balk, D.E. 1995. *Adolescent Development: Early Through Late Adolescence*. Pacific Grove, CA: Brooks/Cole.

Ballinger, A. 1996. The Guilt of the Innocent and the Innocence of the Guilty: The Cases of Marie Fahmy and Ruth Ellis. In *No Angels: Women Who Commit Violence*, edited by A. Myers and S. Wright, 1–28. San Francisco, CA: Pandora.

Balswick, J. and C. Peek. 1971. The Inexpressive Male: A Tragedy of American Society. *The Family Coordinator* 20: 363–368.

Bandura, A. 1986. *The Social Foundations of Thought and Action: A Social Cognitive Theory*. Englewood Cliffs, NJ: Prentice-Hall.

———. 1977. *Social Learning Theory*. Englewood Cliffs, NJ: Prentice-Hall.

———. 1965. Influence of Model's Reinforcement Contingencies on the Acquisition of Imitative Responses. *Journal of Personality and Social Psychology* 1: 589–595.

Bandura, A. and R.H. Walters. 1963. *Social Learning and Personality Development*. New York: Holt, Rinehart and Winston.

Banks, O. 1981. *Three Faces of Feminism*. New York: St. Martin's Press.

Banner, L. 1992. *In Full Flower: Aging Women, Power and Sexuality*. New York: Alfred A. Knopf.

Bannerji, H. 1993. *Returning The Gaze: Essays on Fascism, Feminism and Politics*. Toronto: Sister Vision Press.

Bannister, S.A. 1991. The Criminalization of Women Fighting Back Against Male Abuse, Imprisoned Battered Women as Political Prisoners. *Humanity and Society* 15: 400–416.

Bar-Haim, G. 1989. Actions and Heroes: The Meaning of Western Pop Information for Eastern European Youth. *British Journal of Sociology* 40, 1: 22–45.

Barbach, L.G. 1993. *The Pause*. New York: Dutton.

Bardwell, J.R., S.W. Cochran, and S. Walker. 1986. Relationship of Parental Education, Race and Gender to Sex-Role Stereotyping in Five-Year-Old Kindergartners. *Sex Roles* 15: 275–281.

Barile, M. 1995. Disabled Women: An Exploited Underclass. In *Social Problems In Canada Reader*, edited by A. Nelson and A. Fleras, 403–406. Scarborough, ON: Prentice Hall Canada.

Barnes, G.E., L. Greenwood, and R. Sommer. 1991. Courtship Violence in a Canadian Sample of Male College Students. *Family Relations* 40: 37–44.

Barnett, R.C. 1994. Home-to-Work Spillover Revisited: A Study of Full-Time Employed Women in Dual-Earner Couples. *Journal of Marriage and the Family* 56: 647–656.

Barnett, R.C. and C. Rivers. 1996. *She Works, He Works: How Two-Income Families are Happier, Healthier and Better-off*. San Francisco: Harper.

Barry, K.L. 1989. Tootsie Syndrome, or 'We Have Met the Enemy and They Are Us.' *Women's Studies International Forum* 12, 5: 487–493.

Bart, P. 1971. Sexism and Social Science: From the Gilded Cage to the Iron Cage, or the Perils of Pauline. *Journal of Marriage and the Family* 13: 734–735.

Barthel, D. 1987. *Putting on Appearances: Gender and Advertising*. Philadelphia: Temple University.

Baruch, G.K. and R.C. Barnett. 1986. Role Quality, Multiple Role Involvement and Psychological Well-Being in Midlife Women. *Journal of Personality and Social Psychology* 51: 578–585.

Baruch, G.K., R.C. Barnett, and C. Rivers. 1983. *Lifepoints*. New York: McGraw-Hill.

Basow, S.A. 1992. *Gender: Stereotypes and Roles*, 3rd ed. Pacific Grove, CA: Brooks/Cole.

———. 1986. *Gender Stereotypes: Traditions and Alternatives,* 2nd ed. Monterey, CA: Brooks/Cole.

Beach, S.R.H. and A. Tesser. 1988. Love in Marriage: A Cognitive Account. In *The Psychology of Love*, edited by R.J. Sternberg and M.L. Barnes. New Haven, CT: Yale University.

Beal, B. 1997. The Promise Keepers' Use of Sport in Defining 'Christlike' Masculinity. *Journal of Sport and Social Issues* 21, 3 August: 274–284.

Beal, C.R. 1994. *Boys and Girls: The Development of Gender Roles*. New York: McGraw-Hill.

Beard, H. and C. Cerf. 1992. *The Official Politically Correct Dictionary & Handbook*. New York: Villard Books.

Beaudet, M.P., W. Walsop, and C. Le Petit. 1997. Characteristics of Women on Hormone Replacement Therapy. *Health Reports* 9, 2: 9–18.

Beaujot, R., E.M. Gee, F. Rajulton, and Z.R. Ravanera. 1995. Family over the Life Course. *Current Demographic Analysis Series,* 37–75. Ottawa: Statistics Canada, Minister of Industry.

Beck, A.T. 1988. *Love Is Never Enough*. New York: Harper and Row.

Beck, E.T. 1992. From 'Kike' to 'Jap': How Misogyny, Anti-Semitism, and Racism Construct the 'Jewish American Princess.' In *Race, Class and Gender: An Anthology*, edited by M.L. Anderson and P. Hill Collins, 88–95. Belmont, CA: Wadsworth.

Beck, S.H. 1982. Adjustment to and Satisfaction with Retirement. *Journal of Gerontology* 37: 616–624.

Bee, H.L., S.K. Mitchell, K.E. Bernard, S.J. Eynes, and M.A. Hammond. 1984. Predicting Intellectual Outcomes: Sex Differences in Response to Early Environmental Stimulation. *Sex Roles* 10: 783–803.

Beer, W.R. 1983. *Househusbands: Men and Housework in American Families*. New York: Praeger.

———— (ed.). 1988. *Relative Strangers: Studies of Stepfamily Processes.* Totawa, NJ: Rowman & Littlefield.

Berscheid, E., K. Dion, E. Walster, and G.W. Walster. 1971. Physical Attractiveness and Dating Choice: A Test of the Marching Hypothesis. *Journal of Experimental Social Psychology* 7: 173–189.

Belenky, M.F., B.M. Clinchy, N.R. Goldberger, and J.M. Tarule (eds.). 1986. *Women's Ways of Knowing: The Development of Self, Voice and Mind.* New York: Basic Books.

Belknap, J. 1996. *The Invisible Woman: Gender, Crime and Justice.* Belmont, CA: Wadsworth.

Belknap, P. and W.M. Leonard II. 1991. A Conceptual Replication of Erving Goffman's Study of Gender Advertisements. *Sex Roles* 25, 3–4: 103–118.

Bell, D. 1988. Television Sex Roles in the 1980s: Do Viewers' Sex and Sex Role Orientation Change the Picture? *Sex Roles* 19, 5/6: 387–394.

————. 1972. On Meritocracy and Equality. *The Public Interest* 29: 29–68.

Bell, J.P. 1989. The Double Standard: Age. In *Women: A Feminist Perspective*, edited by J. Freeman, 4th ed., 236–244. Mountain View, CA: Mayfield.

Belsky, J. 1990. Parental and Nonparental Child Care and Children's Socioemotional Development: A Decade in Review. *Journal of Marriage and the Family* 52: 885–903.

Bem, S.L. 1993. *The Lenses of Gender: Transforming the Debate on Sexual Inequality.* New Haven: Yale University Press.

————. 1983/1995. Gender Schema Theory and Its Implications for Child Development: Raising Gender-Aschematic Children in a Gender-Schematic Society. *Signs* 8: 598–616. Reprinted in *Gender in the 1990s: Images, Realities and Issues*, edited by E.D. Nelson and B.W. Robinson, 83–99. Toronto: Nelson Canada.

————. 1981. Gender Schema Theory: A Cognitive Account of Sex-Typing. *Psychological Review* 88: 354–364.

————. 1978. Beyond Androgyny: Some Presumptuous Prescriptions for a Liberated Sexual Identity. In *The Future of Women: Issues in Psychology*, edited by J. Sherman and F. Denmark, 1–23. New York: Psychological Dimensions.

————. 1975. Sex-Role Adaptability: One Consequence of Psychological Androgyny. *Journal of Personality and Social Psychology* 314: 634–643.

————. 1974. The Measurement of Psychological Androgyny. *Journal of Consulting and Clinical Psychology* 42: 155–162.

Bem, S.L. and E. Lenney. 1976. Sex-Typing and the Avoidance of Cross-Sex Behavior. *Journal of Personality and Social Psychology* 331: 48–54.

Bem, S.L., W. Martyna, and C. Watson. 1976. Sex-Typing and Androgyny: Further Explorations of the Expressive Domain. *Journal of Personality and Social Psychology* 345: 1016–1023.

Benin, E.H. and E. Edwards. 1990. Adolescents' Chores: The Difference Between Dual and Single Earner Families. *Journal of Marriage and the Family* 50: 349–361.

Benin, M.H. and J. Agostinelli. 1988. Husbands' and Wives' Satisfaction with the Division of Labor. *Journal of Marriage and the Family* 50: 349–361.

Benjamin, B. and C. Wallis. 1963. The Mortality of Widowers. *The Lancet* 2 August: 454–456.

Benjamin, H. 1966. *The Transsexual Phenomenon.* New York: Julian Press.

Benokraitis, N.V. 1996. *Marriages and Families: Change, Choices, and Constraints,* 2nd ed. Upper Saddle River, NJ: Prentice Hall.

Benokraitis, N.V. and J.R. Feagin. 1995. *Modern Sexism: Blatant, Subtle and Covert Discrimination*, 2nd ed. Englewood Cliffs, NJ: Prentice-Hall.

Benston, M. 1969. The Political Economy of Women's Liberation. *Monthly Review* 21: 13–27.

Berardo, G.H., C.L. Shehan, and G. Leslie. 1987. A Residue of Tradition: Jobs, Careers, and Spouses' Time in Housework. *Journal of Marriage and the Family* 49: 381–390.

Berch, D.B. and B.G. Bender. 1987. Margins of Sexuality. *Psychology Today* December: 54–57.

Bergen, D.J. and J.E. Williams. 1991. Sex Stereotypes in the United States Revisited: 1972–1988. *Sex Roles* 24: 413–23.

Berk, S.F. 1985. *The Gender Factory: The Apportionment of Work in American Households*. New York: Plenum.

Berkman, B.G. 1986. Father Involvement and Regularity of Child Support in Post-divorce Families. *Journal of Divorce* 9: 67–74.

Bernard, J. 1981/1995. The Good-Provider Role: It's Rise and Fall. *American Psychologist* 36, 1: 1–12. Reprinted in *Gender in the 1990s: Images, Realities, and Issues*, edited by E.D. Nelson and B.W. Robinson, 156–171. Toronto: Nelson Canada.

———. 1973. *The Future of Marriage*. New York: Bantam.

———. 1942. *American Family Behavior*. New York: Harper.

Berryman-Fink, C.L. and J.R. Wilcox. 1983. A Multivariate Investigation of Perceptual Attributions Concerning Gender Appropriateness in Language. *Sex Roles* 9: 663–681.

Berryman-Fink, C.L. and K.S. Verderber. 1985. Attributions of the term feminist: A Factor Analytic Development of a Measuring Instrument. *Psychology of Women Quarterly* 9: 51–64.

Berscheid, E., K.K. Dion, E. Walster, and G.W. Walster. 1971. Physical Attractiveness and Dating Choice: A Test of the Matching Hypothesis. *Journal of Experimental Social Psychology* 7: 174–189.

Best, P. 1995. Women, Men & Work. *Canadian Social Trends* 36, Spring: 30–33.

Betz, N. 1993. Career Development. In *Handbook on the Psychology of Women: Future Directions for Research*, edited by F.L. Denmark and M.A. Paludi. Westport, CT: Greenwood.

Bibby, R.W. 1995. *The Bibby Report: Social Trends Canadian Style*. Toronto: Stoddart.

Bibby, R.W. and D.G. Posterski. 1992. *Teen Trends: A Nation in Motion*. Toronto: Stoddart.

Binion, V.J. 1990. Psychological Androgny: A Black Female Perspective. *Sex Roles* 22: 487–507.

Birch, H. (ed.). 1994. *Moving Targets: Women, Murder and Representation*. Berkeley, CA: University of California Press.

Bird, C. 1997. Gender Differences in the Social and Economic Burdens of Parenting and Psychological Distress. *Journal of Marriage and the Family* 59: 809–823.

Bird, G. and K. Melville. 1994. *Families and Intimate Relationships*. New York: McGraw-Hill.

Birnbaum, P. and W. Croll. 1984. The Etiology of Children's Stereotypes about Sex Differences in Emotionality. *Sex Roles* 10: 677–691.

Bjorkqvist, K., K. Lagerspetz, and A. Kaukiainen. 1992. Do Girls Manipulate and Boys Fight? Development Trends in Regard to Direct and Indirect Aggression. *Aggressive Behavior* 18: 117–127.

Blachford, G. 1981/1995. Male Dominance and the Gay World. In *The Making of the Modern Homosexual*, edited by K. Plummer, 184–204. London: Century Hutchinson. Reprinted in *Gender in the 1990s: Images, Realities, and Issues*, edited by E.D. Nelson and B.W. Robinson, 58–72. Toronto: Nelson Canada.

Black, N. 1993. The Canadian Women's Movement: The Second Wave. In *Changing Patterns: Women in Canada*, edited by S. Burt, L. Code, and L. Dorney, 2nd ed., 151–176. Toronto: McClelland & Stewart.

———. 1989. *Social Feminism*. Ithaca: Cornell University Press.

Blair, S.L. and M.P. Johnson. 1992. Wives' Perceptions of the Fairness of the Division of Household Labor: The Intersection of Housework and Ideology. *Journal of Marriage and the Family* 54: 570–581.

Blair, S.L. and D.T. Lichter. 1991. Measuring the Division of Household Labor. *Journal of Family Issues* 12, 1: 91–113.

Blaisure, K.R. and K.R. Allen. 1995. Feminists and the Ideology and Practice of Marital Equality. *Journal of Marriage and the Family* 57: 5–19.

Bland, L. 1992. The Case of the Yorkshire Ripper: Mad, Bad, Beast or Male? In *Femicide: The Politics of Woman Killing*, edited by J. Radford and D.E.H. Russell, 233–252. London: Twayne Publishers.

Blau, P.M. and O.D. Duncan. 1967. *The American Occupational Structure*. New York: Wiley.

Blauberg, M.S. 1978. Changing the Sexist Language: The Theory behind the Practice. *Psychology of Women Quarterly* 2: 244–261.

Bleier, R. 1984. *Science and Gender*. New York: Pergamon Press.

———. (ed.). 1988. Sex Differences Research: Science or Belief? In *Feminist Approaches to Science*. New York: Pergamon.

Block, J.H. 1984. *Sex Role Identity and Ego Development*. San Francisco: Jossey-Bass.

———. 1978. Another Look at Sex Differentiation in the Socialization Behaviors of Mothers and Fathers. In *The Psychology of Women*, edited by J.A. Sherman and F.L. Denmark, 29–87. New York: Psychological Dimensions.

Blofson, B. and N. Aron. 1997. Riot Grrls. *Reluctant Hero*, n.d., 1, 1: 14–17.

Blood, R. and D. Wolfe. 1961. *Husbands and Wives*. New York: Free Press.

Blum, L. and E. Vanderwater. 1993. Mothers Construct Fathers: Destablized Patriarchy in Le Leche League. *Qualitative Sociology* 16, 2: 3–22.

Blumer, H. 1969. *Symbolic Interactionism: Perspective and Method*. Englewood Cliffs, NJ: Prentice-Hall.

———. 1951. Collective Behavior. In *Principles of Sociology*, edited by A.M. Lee, 167–222. New York: Barnes and Noble.

Blumstein, P. and P. Schwartz. 1983. *American Couples: Work, Money, Sex*. New York: William Morrow.

Bly, R. 1996. *The Sibling Society*. New York: Addison-Wesley.

———. 1990. *Iron John: A Book About Men*. Reading, MA: Addison-Wesley.

———. 1988. *When a Hair Turns Gold: Commentary on the Fairy Tale of Iron John, Part Two*. St. Paul, MN: Ally Press.

———. 1987. *The Pillow and the Key: Commentary on the Fairy Tale of Iron John, Part One*. St. Paul, MN: Ally Press.

Bodine, N. 1975. Sex Differentiation in Language. In *Language and Sex: Difference and Dominance: An Overview of Language, Gender, and Society*, edited by B. Thorne and N. Henley, 30–45. Rowley, MA: Newbury House Publishers.

Bograd, M. 1988. Feminist Perspectives on Wife Abuse: An Introduction. In *Feminist Perspectives on Wife Abuse*, edited by K. Yllo and M. Bograd, 11–26. Newbury Park, CA: Sage.

Boritch, H. 1997. *Fallen Women: Female Crime and Criminal Justice in Canada*. Scarborough, ON: Nelson Canada.

Borland, D.C. 1982. A Cohort Analysis Approach to the Empty-Nest Syndrome Among Three Ethnic Groups of Women: A Theoretical Position. *Journal of Marriage and the Family* 44: 117–28.

Bose, C. 1987. Dual Spheres. In *Analyzing Gender: A Handbook of Social Science Research*, edited by B. Hess and M. Marx Ferree, 267–285. Newbury Park, CA: Sage.

Bose, C., P. Bereano, and M. Malloy. 1984. Household Technology and the Social Construction of Housework. *Technology and Culture* 25: 53–82.

Bose, C.E., R. Feldberg, and N. Sokoloff. 1984. *Jobs and Gender: A Study of Occupational Prestige*. New York: Praeger.

Boserup, E. 1970. *Women's Role in Economic Development*. New York: St. Martin's Press.

Boulton, M. 1983. *On Being A Mother*. London: Tavistock.

Bowen, J. 1985. University Admission and Woman's Aspirations: A Century of Class Conflict in Australia. *Discourse* 5, 2 April: 1–18.

Bowles, S. 1977. Unequal Education and the Reproduction of the Social Division of Labor. In *Power and Ideology in Education*, edited by J. Karabel and A.H. Halsey. New York: Oxford University Press.

Boyd, M. 1995. Gender Inequality: Economic and Political Aspects. In *New Society: Brief Edition*, edited by R.J. Brym, 3.1–3.29. Toronto: Harcourt Brace & Company.

———. 1990. Immigrant Women: Language, Socioeconomic Inequalities and Policy Issues. In *Ethnic Demography: Canadian Immigrant, Racial and Cultural Variations*, edited by S.S. Hallik, F. Travato, and L. Driedger, 275–295. Ottawa: Carleton University Press.

———. 1989/1995. Immigration and Income Security Policies in Canada: Implications for Elderly Immigrant Women. *Population Research and Policy Review* 9, 1: 5–24. Reprinted in *Aging & Society: A Canadian Reader*, edited by M. Novak, 217–226. Scarborough, ON: Nelson.

———. 1975. English-Canadian and French-Canadian Attitudes toward Women: Results of the Canadian Gallup Polls. *Journal of Canadian Family Studies* 6: 153–169.

Boyd, M. and E.T. Pryor. 1989. The Cluttered Nest: The Living Arrangements of Young Adults. *Canadian Journal of Sociology* 14: 461–477.

Boyd, S. 1993. Investigating Gender Bias in Canadian Child Custody Law: Reflections on Questions and Methods. In *Investigating Gender Bias in Law: Socio-Legal Perspectives*, edited by J. Brockman and D.E. Chunn, 169–190. Toronto: Thompson Educational Publishing.

———. 1987. Child Custody and Working Mothers. In *Equality and Judicial Neutrality*, edited by S.L. Martin and K.E. Mahoney, 168–183. Toronto: Carswell.

Boyle, C., M.A. Bertrand, C. Lecerte-Lamontagne, and R. Shamai. 1985. *A Feminist Review of Criminal Law*. Ottawa: Minister of Supply and Services Canada.

Bradbard, M. 1985. Sex Differences in Adults', Girls' and Children's Toy Requests at Christmas. *Psychological Reports* 56, 3: 969–970.

Bradbury, B. 1994. Women's Workplaces: The Impact of Technological Change on Working-class Women in the Home and in the Workplace in Nineteenth-Century Montreal. In *Women, Work, and Place*, edited by A. Kobayashi, 27–44. Montreal: McGill-Queen's University Press.

Bradford, D.L., A. Sargent, and M. Sprague. 1980. The Executive Man and Woman: The Issue of Sexuality. In *Bringing Women into Management*, edited by E. Gordon and M. Strober. New York: McGraw-Hill.

Branden, N. 1980. *The Psychology of Romantic Love*. Los Angeles: J.P. Tarcher.

Braud, P. 1993. Facing Menopause. *American Demographics* March: 44–48.

Brayfield, A.A. 1992. Employment Resources and Housework in Canada. *Journal of Marriage and the Family* 54: 19–30.

Brecher, E.M. and the Editors of Consumer Report Books. 1984. *Love, Sex, and Aging: A Consumer's Union Report*. Mount Vernon, NY: Consumers Union.

Brehm, S.S. 1992. *Intimate Relationships*, 2nd ed. New York: McGraw-Hill.

Breines, W. 1986. The 1950s: Gender and Some Social Science. *Sociological Inquiry* 56: 69–92.

Breines, W. and L. Gordon. 1983. The New Scholarship on Family Violence. *Signs* 9: 490–531.

Brend, Ruth. 1975. Male-Female Intonation Patterns in American English. In *Language and Sex: Difference and Dominance*, edited B. Thorne and N.M. Henley, 84–97. Rowley, MA: Newbury.

Brenner, J.A. 1987. Feminist Political Discourses: Radical Versus Liberal Approaches to the Feminization of Poverty and Comparable Worth. *Gender & Society* 4, December: 447–465.

Bretl, G. and M. Cantor. 1988. Portrayal of Men and Women in U.S. Television Advertisements: Recent Content Analysis and Fifteen-Year Trends. *Sex Roles* 18, 4/5: 543–609.

Bridges, J.S. 1991. Perceptions of Date and Stranger Rape: A Difference in Sex Role Expectations and Rape-Supportive Beliefs. *Sex Roles* 24, 5/6: 291–307.

Bridges, J. and C. Etaugh. 1996. Black and White College Women's Maternal Employment Outcome Expectations and Their Desired Timing of Maternal Employment. *Sex Roles* 35, 9/10: 543–562.

Briere, J. and C. Lanktree. 1983. Sex-Role Related Effects of Sex Bias in Language. *Sex Roles* 9: 625–632.

Brim, O.G. Jr. 1968. Adult Socialization. In *Socialization and Society*, edited by J.A. Clausen, 182–226. Boston: Little, Brown.

Brinkerhoff, M.B. and E. Lupri. 1988. Interspousal Violence. *Canadian Journal of Sociology* 31, 4: 407–434.

Briskin, Linda. 1991. Feminist Practice: A New Approach to Evaluating Feminist Strategy. In *Women and Social Change*, edited by J.D. Wine and J.L. Ristock, 24–40. Toronto: James Lorimer & Company.

Brock, L.J. and G.H. Jennings. 1993. Sexuality Education: What Daughters in Their 30s Wish Their Mothers Had Told Them. *Family Relations* 42: 61–65.

Brockman, J. and D. Chunn (eds.). 1993. Gender Bias in Law and the Social Sciences. In *Investigating Gender Bias: Law, Courts, and the Legal Profession*, 3–15. Toronto: Thompson Educational Publishing.

Brod, H. (ed.). 1987a. Introduction: Themes and Theses of Men's Studies. In *The Making of Masculinities*, 1–17. Boston: Allen & Unwin.

———. (ed.). 1987b. The Case for Men's Studies. In *The Making of Masculinities*, 39–62. Boston: Allen & Unwin.

Brodsky, D. 1987. Educating Juries: The Battered Woman Defense in Canada. *Alberta Law Review* 25, 3: 461–476.

Bromley, D.G. and A.D. Shupe Jr. 1981. *Strange Gods: The Great American Cult Scare*. Boston: Beacon Press.

Bronstein, P. 1988. Father-Child interaction. In *Fatherhood Today: Men's Changing Role in the Family*, edited by P. Bronstein and C.P. Cowan. New York: John Wiley.

Brooks-Gunn, J. 1986. The Relationship of Maternal Beliefs about Sex Typing to Maternal and Young Children's Behavior. *Sex Roles* 14: 21–35.

Brooks-Gunn, J., C. Burrow, and M.P. Warren. 1988. Attitudes Toward Eating and Body Weight in Different Groups of Female Adolescent Athletes. *International Journal of Eating Disorders* 7: 749–757.

Broverman, I.K., S.R. Vogel, D.M. Broverman, F.E. Clarkson, and P.S. Rosenkrantz. 1972. Sex–Role Stereotypes: A Current Appraisal. *Journal of Social Issues* 28: 59–78.

Brown, R.M. 1984. In Defense of Traditional Values: The Antifeminist Movement. *Marriage and Family Review* 7 3/4.

Brown, R.M., L.R. Hall, R. Holtzer, S.L. Brown, and N.L. Brown. 1997. Gender and Video Game Performance. *Sex Roles* 36, 11/12: 793–812.

Brubaker, T.H. and C.B. Hennon. 1982. Responsibility for Household Tasks: Comparing Dual-Earner and Dual-Retired Marriages. In *Women's Retirement*, edited by M. Szinovacz. Beverly Hills, CA: Sage.

Bruch, H. 1978. *The Golden Cage*. Somerset: Open Books.

———. 1974. *Eating Disorders, Obesity, Anorexia Nervosa and the Person Within*. London: Routledge and Kegan Paul.

Brumberg, J.J. 1988. *Fasting Girls: The Emergence of Anorexia Nervosa as a Modern Disease*. Cambridge, MA: Harvard University Press.

Buhler, C. 1968. The General Structure of the Human Life Cycle. In *The Course of Human Life*, edited by C. Buhler and F. Massarik, 12–26. New York: Springer.

Buie, J. 1989. Course Helps Fathers Know Best. *APA Monitor* August: 28.

Bukowski, W., C. Gauze, B. Hoza, and A. Newcomb. 1993. Differences and Consistency in Relations with Same-sex and Other-sex Peers During Early Adolescence. *Developmental Psychology* 29: 255–263.

Bumpass, L.L., J.A. Sweet, and A. Cherlin. 1991. The Role of Cohabitation in Declining Rates of Marriage. *Journal of Marriage and the Family* 53: 913–927.

Burgess, E.W. and H.J. Locke. 1950. *The Family*. New York: American Book.

Burgoon, J.K., D.B. Buller, and G.W. Woodall. 1989. *Nonverbal Communication: The Unspoken Dialogue*. New York: Harper and Row.

Burk, M. and K. Shaw. 1995. How the Entertainment Industry Demeans, Degrades, and Dehumanizes Women. In *Issues in Feminism*, edited by S. Ruth, 3rd ed., 436–438. Mountain View, CA: Mayfield.

Burke, M. 1986. The Growth of Part-time Work. *Canadian Social Trends* Autumn: 9–14.

Burke, M. and A. Spector. 1991. Falling Through the Cracks: Women Aged 55–64 Living on Their Own. *Canadian Social Trends* 23 Winter.

Burke, M., J. Lindsay, I. McDowell, and G. Hill. 1997. Dementia Among Seniors. *Canadian Social Trends* 45, Summer: 24–27.

Burke, M., S. Crompton, A. Jones, and K. Nessner. 1991. Caring For Children. *Canadian Social Trends* Autumn: 12–15.

Burke, P., J. Stets, and M.M. Pirog-Good. 1988. Gender Identity, Self Esteem, and Physical and Sexual Abuse in Dating Relationships. *Social Psychology Quarterly* 51: 272–285.

Burns, A. and R. Homel. 1989. Gender Division of Tasks by Parents and Their Children. *Psychology of Women Quarterly* 13: 113–125.

Burr, W.R. 1973. *Theory Construction and the Sociology of the Family*. New York: John Wiley & Sons.

———. 1970. Satisfaction with Various Aspects of Marriage over the Life Cycle: A Random Middle-Class Sample. *Journal of Marriage and the Family* 32: 29–37.

Burr, W.R., R. Hill, F.I. Nye, and I.L. Reiss (eds.). 1979. Introduction to *Contemporary Theories About the Family*. Vol. 1, 1–16. New York: Free Press.

Burstyn, V. (ed.). 1985 *Women Against Censorship*. Vancouver: Douglas & McIntyre.

Burt, S. 1993. Changing Patterns of Public Policy. In *Changing Patterns: Women in Canada*, edited by S. Burt, L. Code, and L. Dorney, 2nd ed., 212–242. Toronto: McClelland & Stewart.

———. 1986. Women's Issues and the Women's Movenent in Canada since 1970. In *The Politics of Gender, Ethnicity and Language in Canada*, edited by R. Hamilton and M. Barrett, 111–169. Toronto: University of Toronto Press.

Burt, S. and L. Code (eds.). 1995. *Changing Methods: Feminists Transforming Practice*. Peterborough, ON: Broadview Press.

Buss, D. 1994. *The Evolution of Desire*. New York: BasicBooks.

Buss, D. and M. Barnes. 1986. Preferences in Human Mate Selection. *Journal of Personality and Social Psychology* 50: 559–70.

Butler, J.E. 1985. Toward a Pedagogy of Everywoman's Studies. In *Gendered Subjects: The Dynamics of Feminist Teaching*, edited by M. Culley and C. Portuges. London: Routledge & Kegan Paul.

Byrne, D. 1977. A Pregnant Pause in the Sexual Revolution. *Psychology Today* 11 July: 67–68.

Caine, L. 1974. *Widow*. New York: Morrow.

Caldera, Y.M., A.C. Huston, and M.O'Brien. 1989. Social Interactions and Play Patterns of Parents and Toddlers with Feminine, Masculine and Neutral Toys. *Child Development* 60: 70–76.

Caldicott, H. 1984. *Missile Envy*. New York: William Morrow.

Caldwell, M. and L. Peplau. 1982. Sex Differences in Same-Sex Friendship. *Sex Roles* 9: 1–15.

Califia, P. 1997. Dildo Envy and Other Phallic Adventures. In *Dick For A Day*, edited by F. Giles, 90–109. New York: Villard.

———. 1996. Femininism and Sadomasochism. In *Feminism and Sexuality: A Reader*, edited by S. Jackson and S. Scott, 230–237. New York: Columbia University Press.

Callender, C. and L. Kochems. 1983. The North American Berdache. *Current Anthropology* 24: 443–470.

Cameron, D. 1992. Naming of Parts: Gender, Culture and Terms For the Penis Among American College Students. *American Speech* 67, 4: 367–382.

———. 1985. *Feminism and Linguistic Theory*. London: Macmillan.

Cameron, E. 1997. *No Previous Experience: A Memoir of Love and Change*. Toronto: Viking.

Cameron, P. 1976. Masculinity/Femininity of the Generations: As Self-Reported and as Stereotypically Appraised. *International Journal of Aging and Human Development* 7, 2: 143–151.

Canadian Press. 1996. Mattel CEO is No Barbie Doll: Top-ranking U.S. Executive Makes More Than $1 Million a Year. Reprinted in *K-W Record*, May 24: B5.

———. 1996. Prostitutes Face High Murder Risk. Reprinted in *K-W Record*, May 24: A3.

Cancian, F.M. 1987. *Love in America: Gender and Self-Development*. New York: Cambridge University Press.

Cann, A. and A.K. Garnett. 1984. Sex Stereotype Impacts on Competence Ratings by Children. *Sex Roles* 11: 333–343.

Cannon, M. 1995. No Boys Allowed. *Saturday Night*. February: 19, 20, 22, 24.

Canter, R.J. and S.S. Ageton. 1984. The Epidemiology of Adolescent Sex-role Attitudes. *Sex Roles* 11: 657–676.

Caplan, P. 1989. *Don't Blame Mother: Mending the Mother-Daughter Relationship*. New York: Harper and Row.

Caplan, P. and I. Hall-McCorquodale. 1985. Mother-Blaming in Major Clinical Journals. *American Journal of Orthopsychiatry* 55: 345–353.

Caputi, J. 1989. The Sexual Politics of Murder. *Gender & Society* 3, 4: 437–456.

Caputi, J. and D.E.H. Russell. 1992. Femicide: Sexist Terrorism against Women. In *Femicide: The Politics of Woman Killing*, edited by J. Radford and D.E.H. Russell, 13–21. London: Twayne Publishers.

Caputi, J. and G.O. MacKenzie. 1992. Pumping Iron John. In *Women Respond to the Men's Movement*, edited by K.L. Hagan, 69–82. San Francisco, CA: Pandora.

Carden, M.L. 1969. *Onedia: Utopian Community to Modern Corporation*. New York: Harper Torchbooks.

Carlen, P. 1985. *Criminal Women: Autobiographical Accounts*. Cambridge: Polity Press.

Carlip, H. 1996. *Girl Power: Young Women Speak Out*. New York: Seal Books.

Carmody, D.L. 1989. *Women and World Religions*. Englewood Cliffs, NJ: Prentice-Hall.

Carter, C.S. and W.T. Greenaugh. 1979. Sending the Right Sex Messages. *Psychology Today* September: 112.

Carter, D.B. and G.D. Levy. 1988. Cognitive Aspects of Early Sex-Role Development: The Influence of Gender Schemas on Preschoolers' Memories and Preferences for Sex-Typed Toys and Activities. *Child Development* 59: 782–792.

Cassell, J. 1977. *A Group Called Women: Sisterhood and Symbolism in the Feminist Movement*. New York: McKay.

Cassidy, B., R. Lord, and N. Mandell. 1998. Silenced and Forgotten Women: Race, Poverty and Disability. In *Feminist Issues: Race, Class and Sexuality*, edited by N. Mandell, 2nd ed., 26–54. Scarborough: Prentice Hall Allyn and Bacon Canada.

———. 1995. Silenced and Forgotten Women: Race, Poverty, and Disability. In *Feminist Issues: Race, Class, and Sexuality*, edited by N. Mandell, 32–66. Scarborough, ON: Prentice Hall Canada.

Castro, G. 1990. *American Feminism: A Contemporary History*. New York: New York University.

Castro, J. 1990. *Get Set: Here They Come! Women, the Road Ahead*. Special issue of *Time* magazine. Fall: 50–52.

Castro M.T. and L.L. Bumpass. 1989. Recent Trends in Marital Disruption. *Demography* 26, 1: 37–51.

Cavan, R.S. 1969. *The American Family*, 4th ed. New York: Thomas Y. Crowell.

Chafetz, J.S. and J. Hagan. 1996. The Gender Division of Labor and Family Change in Industrial Societies: A Theoretical Accounting. *Journal of Comparative Family Studies* 27, 2: 187–219.

Che-Alford, C.A. and G. Butlin. 1994. *Families in Canada*. Toronto: Statistics Canada and Prentice Hall Canada.

Cherlin, A.J. 1992. *Marriage, Divorce, Remarriage*. Rev. and enlarged ed. Cambridge, MA: Harvard University Press.

———. 1978. Remarriage as an Incomplete Institution. *American Journal of Sociology* 84: 634–650.

Cherny, L. and E.R. Weise. 1996. *Wired Women: Gender and New Realities in Cyberspace*. New York: Seal Press.

Chesley, L., D. MacAulay, and J.L. Rostock. 1991. *Abuse in Lesbian Relationships: A Handbook of Information and Resources*. Toronto: Counselling Centre for Lesbians and Gays.

Chesler, P. 1994. *Patriarchy: Notes of an Expert Witness*. Monroe, ME: Common Courage Press.

———. 1991. *Mothers on Trial: The Battle For Children and Custody*. New York: Harcourt Brace Jovanovich.

Chilly Collective (eds.). 1995. *Breaking Anonymity: The Chilly Climate for Women Faculty*. Waterloo: Wilfred Laurier University Press.

Chodorow, N. 1978. *The Reproduction of Mothering: Psychoanalysis and the Sociology of Gender*. Berkeley: University of California Press.

Chodorow, N. and S. Contratto. 1982. The Fantasy of the Perfect Mother. In *Rethinking the Family*, edited by B. Thorne and M. Yalom. New York: Longman.

Christensen, A. 1990. Gender and Social Structure in the Demand/Withdrawal Pattern of Marital Conflict. *Journal of Personality and Social Psychology* 59: 73–81.

Christensen, A. and C.L. Heavey. 1993. Gender Differences in Marital Conflict: The Demand-Withdraw Interaction Pattern. In *Gender Issues in Contemporary Society*, edited by S. Oskamp and M. Constanzo, 113–141. Newbury Park, CA: Sage.

Christian-Smith, L.K. 1988. Romancing the Girl: Adolescent Romance Novels and the Construction of Femininity. In *Becoming Feminine: The Politics of Popular Culture*, edited by L.G. Roman, L.K. Christian-Smith, and E. Ellsworth, 76–101. London: Falmer Press.

Chunn, D.E. and J. Brockman. 1993. Running Hard to Stand Still?—Future Directions for Studying 'Gender Bias' in Law. In *Investigating Gender Bias: Law, Courts, and the Legal Profession*, edited by J. Brockman and D. Chunn, 215–219. Toronto: Thompson Educational Publishing.

Chunn, D.E. and S.A.M. Gavigan. 1995. Women, Crime, and Criminal Justice in Canada. In *Canadian Criminology*, edited by M.A. Jackson and C.T. Griffiths, 141–184. Toronto: Harcourt Brace.

Clark, L. and D. Lewis. 1977. *Rape: The Price of Coercive Sexuality*. Toronto: Women's Educational Press.

Clark, R., R. Lennon, and L. Morris. 1993. Of Caldecotts and Kings: Gendered Images in Recent American Children's Books by Black and Non-Black Illustrators. *Sex Roles* 7: 227–245.

Clark, W. 1996. Youth Smoking in Canada. *Canadian Social Trends* 43, Winter: 2–6.

Clarke, A.P. 1987. *Women's Silence, Men's Violence: Sexual Assault in England, 1770–1845*. London: Pandora

Clarke-Stewart, A. 1989. Infant Day Care: Malignant or Maligned? *American Psychologist* 44: 266–273.

Clatterbaugh, K. 1990. *Contemporary Perspectives on Masculinity: Men, Women, and Politics in Modern Society*. Boulder, CO: Westview.

Clausen, J.A. 1986. *The Life Course: A Sociological Perspective*. Englewood Cliffs, NJ: Prentice-Hall.

———. 1976. Glimpses into the Social World of Middle Age. *International Journal of Aging and Human Development* 7, 2: 99–106.

———. 1972. The Life Course of Individuals. In *Aging and Society: A Sociology of Age Stratification,* edited by M.W. Riley, M. Johnson, and A. Foner, Vol. 3, 457–514. New York: Russell Sage.

Cleveland, G., M. Gunderson, and D. Hyatt. 1996. Child Care Costs and the Employment Decision of Women: Canadian Evidence. *Canadian Journal of Economics* 24, 1: 132–147.

Cockburn, C. 1991. *In the Way of Women: Men's Resistance to Sex Equality in Organizations*. Ithaca, NY: ILR Press.

Code, L. 1993. Feminist Theory. In *Changing Patterns: Women in Canada*, edited by S. Burt, L. Code, and L. Dorney, 2nd ed., 19–57. Toronto: McClelland & Stewart.

Coker, D.R. 1984. The Relationships Among Gender Concepts and Cognitive Maturity in Preschool Children. *Sex Roles* 10, January: 19–31.

Coleman, M.T. 1988. The Division of Household Labor: Suggestions for Future Empirical Consideration and Theoretical Development. *Journal of Family Issues* 9: 132–148.

Collins, R. 1979. *The Credential Society*. New York: Academic Press.

———. 1975. *Conflict Sociology*. New York: Academic Press.

Coltrane, S. and M. Ishii-Kuntz. 1992. Men's Housework: A Life Course Perspective. *Journal of Marriage and the Family* 54: 43–57.

Columbo, J.R. 1996. *The 1996 Canadian Global Almanac*. Toronto: Macmillan Canada.

———. 1994. *The 1995 Canadian Global Almanac*. Toronto: Macmillan Canada.

Comack, E. 1996. *Women and Crime*. In *Criminology: A Canadian Perspective*, edited by R. Linden, 139–176. Toronto: Harcourt, Brace & Company.

Comstock, G. and H. Paik. 1991. *Television and the American Child*. San Diego, CA: Academic Press.

Condry, J. and D. Ross. 1985. Sex and Aggression: The Influence of Gender Labels on the Perception of Aggression in Children. *Child Development* 56: 225–233.

Condry, J. and S. Condry. 1976. Sex Differences: A Study of the Eye of the Beholder. *Child Development* 47: 812–819.

Conley, W., W.M. O'Barr, and E.A. Lind. 1978. The Power of Language: Presentational Style in the Courtroom. *Duke Law Journal:* 1375.

Connell, R.W. 1985. Theorizing Gender. *Sociology* 19: 260–272.

Connelly, P. 1978. *Last Hired, First Fired: Women and the Canadian Work Force.* Toronto: Women's Press.

Connelly, P. and L. Christiansen-Ruffman. 1977/1987. Women's Problems: Private Troubles or Public Issues? *Canadian Journal of Sociology* 2: 167–178. Reprinted in *Gender Roles: Doing What Comes Naturally?* edited by E.D. Salamon and B.W. Robinson, 283–295. Toronto: Methuen.

Connelly, R. 1992. The Effects of Child Care Costs on Married Women's Labour Force Participation. *Review of Economics and Statistics* 74: 83–90.

Connidis, I.A. 1989. *Family Ties and Aging.* Toronto: Butterworths.

Connidis, I.A. and L. Davies. 1992. Confidants and Companions: Choices in Later Life. *Journal of Gerontology: Social Sciences* 47, 3: S115–S122.

Consumer Reports on Health. 1993/1995. Do Men go Through Menopause? October: 105–108. In *Human Sexuality 95/96,* edited by S.J. Bunting, 163–66. Guilford, CT: Dushkin.

Conway, J.F. 1993. *The Canadian Family in Crisis,* rev. ed. Toronto: James Lorimer.

———. 1990. *The Canadian Family in Crisis.* Toronto: James Lorimer.

Cooley, C.H. 1902. *Human Nature and the Social Order.* New York: Scriber's.

Cooney, T.M. and P. Uhlenberg. 1991. Changes in Work-Family Connections Among Highly Educated Men and Women: 1970 to 1980. *Journal of Family Issues* 12: 69–90.

Corbeil, J.P. 1995. Sport Participation in Canada. *Canadian Social Trends* 36, Spring: 18–23.

Cose, E. 1997. Promises....Promises. *Newsweek.* October 15: 30–38.

Coser, L.A. 1975. *The Idea of Social Structure.* New York: Harcourt, Brace Jovanovich.

Costa, P.T. Jr, R.R. McCrae, and D. Arenberg. 1983. Recent Longitudinal Research on Personality and Aging. In *Longitudinal Studies of Adult Psychological Development,* edited by K.W. Schaie, 222–265. New York: Guilford.

Cottingham, L. 1996. *Lesbians Are So Chic...That We Are Not Really Lesbians At All.* New York: Cassell.

Cottle, C.E., P. Searles, R.J. Berger, and B.A. Pierce. 1989. Conflicting Ideologies and the Politics of Pornography. *Gender & Society* 3, 3: 303–333.

Cotton, N.S. 1979. The Familial Incidence of Alcoholism: A Review. *Journal of Studies on Alcohol* 40, 1: 89–116.

Courtney, A.E. and S.W. Lockeretz. 1971. A Woman's Place: An Analysis of the Roles Portrayed by Women in Magazine Advertisements. *Journal of Marketing Research* 8: 92.

Courtney, A. and T.W. Whipple. 1985. Female Role Portrayals in Advertising and Communication Effectiveness: A Review. *Journal of Advertising* 14, 3: 4–8, 17.

———. 1983. *Sex Stereotyping in Advertising.* Toronto: Heath.

Coutinho-Wiggelandam, A. 1983. Women's Emancipation around the Turn of the Century and the Opposition to It: A Comparative Study of Feminism and Anti-Feminism in the Netherlands from 1870 to 1919. *Netherlands Journal of Sociology/Sociologia Neerlandica* 19, 2 October: 113–131.

Coverman, S. and J.F. Sheley. 1986. Change in Men's Housework and Child-Care Time, 1965–1975. *Journal of Marriage and the Family* 48: 413–422.

Cowan, G. 1993. Pornography: Conflict Among Feminists. In *Women: A Feminist Perspective,* edited by J. Freeman, 4th ed., 347–364. Mountain View, CA: Mayfield.

Cowan, R.S. 1984. *More Work for Mother.* New York: Basic Books.

Cowart, V.S. 1990. Teenage Steroid Use Surveyed. *Facts on File* 14 September: 684.

———. 1990 Blunting 'Steroid Epidemic' Requires Alternatives: Innovative Education. *JAMA: The Journal of the American Medical Association* October 3: 1041.

Cowgill, D. 1974. The Aging of Populations and Societies. *Annals of the American Academy of Political and Social Science* 415: 1–18.

Cowgill, D. and L. Holmes (eds.). *1972. Aging and Modernization*. New York: Appleton- Century-Crofts.

Cox, M. 1985. Progress and Continued Challenges in Understanding the Transition to Parenthood. *Journal of Family Issues* 6: 395–408.

Crane, M. and H. Markus. 1982. Gender Identity: The Benefits of a Self-Schema Approach. *Journal of Personality and Social Psychology* 43: 1195–1197.

Cranswick, K. 1997. Canada's Caregivers. *Canadian Social Trends* 47, Winter: 2–6.

Crawford, M. 1996. *Talking Difference: On Gender and Language*. London: Sage.

Crawford, M. and M. MacLeod. 1990. Gender in the College Classroom: An Assessment of the 'Chilly Climate' for Women. *Sex Roles* 23: 101–122.

Crawford, M. and R. Gartner. 1992. *Woman Killing: Intimate Femicide in Ontario 1974–1990*. Toronto: Ontario Women's Directorate.

Creese, G., N. Gyppy, and M. Meissner. 1991. Ups and Downs on the Ladder of Success: Social Mobility in Canada. *General Society Survey Analysis,* Series 5, Cat. 11–612E. No. 5. Ottawa: Statistics Canada.

Creith, E. 1996. *Undressing Lesbian Sex: Popular Images, Private Acts and Public Consequences*. London: Cassell.

Crewdson, J. 1995. Second Thoughts about 'Gay Genes.' *The Edmonton Journal*. July 2: E7.

Crick, N. 1997. Engagement in Gender Normative versus Nonnormative Forms of Aggression: Links to Social-psychological Adjustment. *Developmental Psychology* 33: 610–617.

———. 1995. Relational Aggression: The Role of Intent Attributions, Feelings of Distress and Provocation Type. *Development and Psychopathology* 7: 313–322.

Crick, N., J. Casas, and M. Mosher. 1997. Relational and Overt Aggression in Preschool. *Developmental Psychology* 33: 579–588.

Crick, N. and J. Grotzpeter. 1995. Relational Aggression, Gender, and Social-psychological Adjustment. *Child Development* 66: 710–722.

Crisp, A. 1980. *Anorexia Nervosa—Let Me Be*. London: Academic Press.

Crompton, S. 1994. Facing Retirement. *Perspectives on Labour and Income* Spring, 5: 1.

Crook, M. 1991. *The Body Image Trap*. North Vancouver: Self-Counsel Press.

Crosby, J.F. 1991. *Illusion and Disillusion: The Self in Love and Marriage,* 4th ed. Belmont, CA: Wadsworth.

Cuber, J.F. and P.B. Harroff. 1965. *Sex and the Significant Americans*. Baltimore: Pelican.

Current Population Reports. 1993. *Population Profile of the United States, 1993*. Special Studies Series, 23–185. Washington: U.S. Government Printing Office.

Currie, D.H. and V. Raoul (eds.). 1992. *Anatomy of Gender: Women's Struggle for the Body*. Ottawa: Carleton University Press.

Cusson, S. 1990. Women in School Administration. *Canadian Social Trends* Autumn.

Cutler, B. 1993. Marketing to Menopausal Men. *American Demographics* March: 49.

Cytrynbaum, S., L. Blum, R. Patrick, J. Stein, D. Wadner, and C. Wilk. 1980. Midlife Development: A Personality and Social Systems Perspective. In *Aging in the 1980s*, edited by L. Poon. Washington: American Psychological Association.

Dahrendorf, R. 1959. *Class and Class Conflict in Industrial Society*. Stanford, CA: Stanford University Press.

Daisley, B. 1996. Foreign Domestic Wins Sexual Harassment Suit Against Boss. *The Lawyers Weekly* 15, 47, April 26: 21.

Dally, P. and J. Gomez. 1990. *Obesity and Anorexia Nervosa*. London: Faber.

Daly, Mary. 1978. *Gyn/Ecology: The Metaphysics of Radical Feminism*. Boston: Beacon Press.

————. 1973 *Beyond God the Father*. Boston: Beacon Press.

Daly, K. 1994. Uncertain Terms: The Social Construction of Fatherhood. In *Doing Everyday Life: Ethnography As A Human Lived Experience*, edited by M. Lorenz Dietz, R. Prus, and W. Shaffir, 170–185. Mississauga: Copp Clark Longman.

D'Amico, M. 1997. Cyberstalking via the Net. *NETGUIDE*. February 4, 2: 32.

Daniels, P. and K. Weingarten. 1984. 'Mothers' Hours: The Timing of Parenthood and Women's Work. In *Work & Family: Changing Roles of Men and Women,* edited by P. Voydanoff. Palo Alto, CA: Mayfield.

Darling, C.A., D.J. Kallen, and J. VanDusen. 1989. Sex in Transition, 1900–1980. In *Family in Transition*, edited by A.S. Skolnick and J.H. Skolnick, 6th ed., 236–244. Glenview, IL: Scott, Foresman.

Darling-Fisher, C. and L.B. Tiedje. 1990. The Impact of Maternal Employment Characteristics on Fathers' Participation in Child Care. *Family Relations* 39: 20–26.

Darwin, C. 1859. *The Origin of Species*. Chicago: Conley.

Datan, N. 1989. Aging Women: The Silent Majority. *Women's Studies Quarterly* 17, 1/2: 12–19.

David, M. 1985. Motherhood and Social Policy—A Matter of Education? *Critical Social Policy* 12: 28–43.

————. 1984. Teaching and Preaching Sexual Morality: The New Right's Anti-Feminism in Britain and the U.S.A. *Journal of Education* 166, 1 March: 63–76.

Davidman, L. 1995. Gender Play. *Qualitative Sociology* 18, 1: 105–107.

Davies, B. 1989. *Frogs and Snails and Feminist Tales: Preschool Children and Gender*. Sydney: Allen & Unwin.

Davis, D. 1990. Portrayals of Women in Prime-time Network Television: Some Demographic Characteristics. *Sex Roles* 23, 5/6: 325–332.

Davis, K. 1993. Class-Race-Gender: Sloganeering in Search of Meaning. *Social Justice* 20, 51/52: 56–71.

Davis, K.E. 1985. Near and Dear: Friendship and Love Compared. *Psychology Today* 19: 22–30.

Davis, K. and P. van den Oever. 1982. Demographic Foundations of New Sex Roles. *Population and Development Review* 8, 3: 495–511.

Davis, S. 1990. Men as Success Objects and Women as Sex Objects: A Study of Personal Advertisements. *Sex Roles* 23: 43–50.

Davy, S. 1978. Miss to Mrs: Going, Going, Gone! *Canadian Woman Studies* 1: 47–48.

Dawkins, R. 1976. *The Selfish Gene*. London: Oxford University Press.

de Beauvoir, S. 1961. *The Second Sex*, edited and translated by H.M. Parshely. New York: Bantam.

de Klerk, V. and B. Bosch. 1996. Nicknames and Sex-Role Stereotypes. *Sex Roles* 35, 9/10: 525–541.

Deaux, K. and L. Lewis. 1984. Structure of Gender Stereotypes: Interrelationships among Components and Gender Label. *Journal of Personality and Social Psychology* 46: 991–1004.

————. 1983. Components of Gender Stereotypes (Ms. no. 2583). *Psychological Documents* 13: 25.

Deaux, K. and M.E. Kite. 1987. Thinking About Gender. In *Analyzing Gender*, edited by B.B. Hess and M.M. Ferree, 92–117. Newbury Park, CA: Sage.

Decker, B.S. 1983. *The Women's Movement,* 3rd ed. New York: Harper and Row.

Decker, S. 1980. Criminology in Focus. *Criminology* 18, 1 May: 141–143.

DeKeseredy, W.S., M.D. Schwartz, and K. Tait. 1993. Sexual Assault and Stranger Aggression on a Canadian University Campus. *Sex Roles* 28, 5/6: 263–277.

DeKeseredy, W. and R. Hinch. 1991. *Woman Abuse: Sociological Perspectives*. Toronto: Thompson Educational Publishing.

Delgado, R. 1996. *Coming Race War? And Other Apocalyptic Tales of America After Affirmative Action and Welfare*. New York: New York University Press.

DeLisi, R. and L. Soundranayagam. 1990. The Conceptual Structure of Sex Role Stereotypes in College Students. *Sex Roles* 23, 11/12: 593–611.

Deloache, J.S., D.J. Cassidy, and C.J. Carpenter. 1987. The Three Bears are All Boys: Mothers' Gender Labeling of Neutral Picture Book Characters. *Sex Roles* 17: 163–178.

D'Emilio, J. and E.B. Freedman. 1988. *Intimate Matters: A History of Sexuality in America*. New York: Harper & Row.

Demo, D.H. and A.C. Acock. 1993. Family Diversity and the Division of Domestic Labor: How Much Have Things Really Changed? *Family Relations* 42: 323–331.

Demo, D.H. and I.H. Ganong. 1994. Divorce. In *Families and Change: Coping with Stressful Events*, edited by P.C. McKenry and S.L. Price. Thousand Oaks, CA: Sage.

Demos, J. 1986. *Past, Present and Persona; The Family and the Life Course in American History*. New York: Oxford University Press.

———. 1982. The Changing Face of Fatherhood: A New Exploration in American Family History. In *Father and Child: Developmental and Clinical Perspectives*, edited by S.H. Cath, A.R. Gurwitt, and J.M. Ross, 425–445. Boston: Little, Brown.

———. 1970. *A Little Commonwealth*. New York: Oxford University Press.

Denfeld, R. 1995. *The New Victorians: A Young Woman's Response to the Old Feminist Order*. New York: Warner Books.

Denney, N.W., J.K. Field, and D. Quadagno. 1984. Sex Differences in Sexual Needs and Desires. *Archives of Sexual Behavior* 133: 233–245.

DePalma, A. 1993. Rare in Ivy League: Women Who Work as Full Professors. *New York Times*. 24 January 1993: 1, 13.

Di Stefano, C. 1990. Dilemmas of Difference: Feminism, Modernity, and Postmodernism. In *Feminism/Postmodernism*, edited by L.J. Nicholson, 63–82. New York: Routledge.

Diamond, E.E. 1987. Theories of Career Development and the Reality of Women at Work. In *Women's Career Development*, edited by B.A. Gutek and L. Larwood, 15–27. Newbury Park, CA: Sage.

Diamond, M.I. 1982. Sexual Identity: Monozygotic Twins Reared in Discordant Sex Roles and a BBC Follow-Up. *Archives of Sexual Behavior* 11: 181–186.

DiBenedetto, B. and C.K. Tittle. 1990. Gender and Adult Roles; Role Commitment of Women and Men in a Job-Family Trade-off Context. *Journal of Conseling Psychology* 37: 41–48.

Dietz, M. Lorenz. 1994. On Your Toes: Dancing Your Way into the Ballet World. In *Doing Everyday Life: Ethnography As A Human Lived Experience*, edited by M. Lorenz Dietz, R. Prus, and W. Shaffir, 66–84. Toronto: Copp Clark Longman.

DiGiulio, R.C. 1992. Beyond Widowhood. In *Marriage and Family in a Changing Society*, edited by J.M. Henslin, 4th ed., 457–469. New York: Free Press.

Dill, B.T. 1983. Race, Class and Gender: Prospects for an All-inclusive Sisterhood. *Feminist Studies* 9, 1: 131–150.

DiLorio, J.A. 1989. Sex, Glorious Sex: The Social Construction of Masculine Sexuality In A Youth Group. In *Feminist Frontiers II: Rethinking Sex, Gender and Society*, edited by L. Richardson and V. Taylor, 261–269. New York: McGraw-Hill.

Dimen, M. 1984. Politically Correct? Politically Incorrect? In *Pleasure and Danger: Exploring Female Sexuality*, edited by C.S. Vance, 138–148. Boston: Routledge & Kegan Paul.

Dinnerstein, D. 1978. *The Rocking of the Cradle, and the Ruling of the World*. London: Souvenir Press.

———. 1976. *The Mermaid and the Minotaur: Sexual Arrangements and Human Malaise*. New York: Harper & Row.

Dion, K.L. and A.A. Cota. 1991 The Ms. Stereotype: Its Domain and the Role of Explicitness in Title Preference. *Psychology of Women Quarterly* 15: 403–410.

Dion, K., E. Berscheid, and E. Walster. 1972. What is Beautiful is Good. *Journal of Personality and Social Psychology* 24: 285–290.

Dion, K.K. and K.L. Dion. 1991. Psychological Individualism and Romantic Love. *Journal of Social Behavior and Personality* 6: 17–33.

Dion, K.L. and K.K. Dion. 1973. Correlates of Romantic Love. *Journal of Consulting and Clinical Psychology* 41: 51–56.

Dion, K.L. and R.A. Schuller. 1990. Ms. and the Manager: A Tale of Two Stereotypes. *Sex Roles* 22: 569–577.

Dobash, R.E. and R.P. Dobash. 1992. *Women, Violence and Social Change.* New York: Routledge.

———. 1979. *Violence Against Wives.* New York: Free Press.

Dobash, R.P., R.E. Dobash, M. Wilson, and M. Daly. 1992. The Myth of Sexual Symmetry in Marital Violence. *Social Problems* 35: 71–91.

Dodson, B. 1996. *Sex for One: The Joy of Selfloving.* New York: Crown Trade Paperbacks.

———. 1974. *Liberating Masturbation: A Meditation on Self Love.* New York: Betty Dodson.

Doherty, W.J. 1991. Beyond Reactivity and the Deficit Model of Manhood: A Commentary on Articles by Napier, Pittman, and Gottman. *Journal of Marital and Family Therapy* 17: 29–32.

Dolan, E.F. 1992. *Drugs in Sports,* rev. ed. New York: Franklin Watts.

Dominion Bureau of Statistics. 1968. Marital Status by Age Groups and Sex. *1966 Census of Canada.* Table 34. Cat. 92–613. Ottawa: Minister of Trade and Commerce.

Douglas, A. 1980. Soft-porn Culture. *New Republic* August, 30: 25–29.

Doughtery, W. Holden, and R.E. Engel. 1987. An 80s Look For Sex Equality in Caldecott Winners and Honor Books. *Reading Teacher* 40, 4: 394–398.

Douthitt, R.A. 1989. The Division of Labour within the Home: Have Gender Roles Changed? *Sex Roles* 20: 693–704.

Douvan, E. and J. Adelson. 1966. *The Adolescent Experience.* New York: Wiley.

Downes, D. and P. Rock. 1982. *Understanding Deviance: A Guide to the Sociology of Crime and Rule-Breaking.* Oxford: Clarendon.

Downey, D.B. and B. Powell. 1993. Do Children in Single-Parent Households Fare Better Living with Same-Sex Parents? *Journal of Marriage and the Family* 55: 55–71.

Doyle, J.A. 1989. *The Male Experience,* 2nd ed. Dubuque, IA: Wm C. Brown.

Doyle, J.A. and M.A. Paludi. 1995. *Sex and Gender: The Human Experience,* 3rd ed. Madison: WCB Brown & Benchmark.

Drakich, J. 1988/1995. In Whose Best Interest? The Politics of Joint Custody. In *Family Bonds and Gender Divisions,* edited by B. Fox, 477–497. Toronto: Canadian Scholar's Press. Reprinted in *Gender in the 1990s: Images, Realities, and Issues,* edited by E.D. Nelson and B.W. Robinson, 380–396. Toronto: Nelson Canada.

Drebing, C.E. and W.F. Gooden. 1991. The Impact of the Dream on Mental Health Functioning in the Male Midlife Transition. *International Journal of Aging and Human Development* 32: 277–287.

Dressel, P.L. and A. Clark. 1990. A Critical Look at Family Care. *Journal of Marriage and the Family* 52: 769–792.

Driedger, D. 1993. Discovering Disabled Women's History. In *And Still We Rise,* edited by L. Carty, 173-188. Toronto: Women's Press.

Dubbert, J.L. 1979. *A Man's Place: Masculinity in Transition.* Englewood Cliffs, NJ: Prentice- Hall.

Dubois, B.L. and I. Crouch. 1975. The Question of Tag Questions in Women's Speech: They Don't Really Use More of Them, Do They? *Language in Society* 4: 289–294.

Duck, S.W. 1975. Personality Similarity and Friendship Choices by Adolescents. *European Journal of Social Psychology* 5: 351–365.

Duffy, A., N. Mandell, and N. Pupo. 1989. *Few Choices: Women, Work and Family.* Toronto: Garamound Press.

Dumas, J. 1994. *Report on the Demographic Situation in Canada 1994.* Cat. 91–209E. Ottawa: Statistics Canada, Minister of Industry, Science and Technology.

———. 1993. *Report on the Demographic Situation in Canada 1993.* Statistics Canada. Cat. 91–209. Ottawa: Minister of Science and Technology.

Dumas, J. and A. Bélanger. 1997. *Report on the Demographic Situation in Canada 1996.* Cat. 91–2090XPE. Ottawa: Statistics Canada, Minister of Industry.

Dumas, J. and Y. Peron. 1992. *Marriage and Conjugal Life in Canada*. Cat. 91–534. Ottawa: Statistics Canada.

Dunkle, J.H. and P.L. Francis. 1990. The Role of Facial Masculinity/Femininity in the Attribution of Homosexuality. *Sex Roles* 23, 3/4: 157–167.

Dunphy, D.C. 1963. The Social Structure of Urban Adolescent Peer Groups. *Sociometry* 26: 230–246.

Durkin, K. 1984. Children's Accounts of Sex-Role Stereotypes in Television. *Communication Research* 11, 3: 341–352.

Dworkin, A. 1981. *Pornography: Men Possessing Women*. New York: Penguin.

Dyrenforth, S.R., O.W. Wooley, and S.C. Wooley. 1980. A Woman's Body in a Man's World: A Review of Findings on Body Image and Weight Control. In *A Woman's Conflict: The Special Relationship Between Women and Food,* edited by J.R. Kaplan. Englewood Cliffs, NJ: Prentice-Hall.

Eakins, B.W. and R.G. Eakins. 1978. *Sex Differences in Human Communication*. Boston: Houghton Mifflin.

———. 1975. *Sex Differences in Human Communication*. Boston: Houghton Mifflin Co.

Eccles. J.S., J.E. Jacobs, and R.D. Harold. 1990. Gender Role Stereotypes, Expectancy Effects and Parents' Socialization of Gender Differences. *Journal of Social Issues* 46, 2: 183–201.

Eccles, J.S. and P. Blumenfeld. 1985. Classroom Experiences and Student Gender: Are There Differences and Do They Matter? In *Gender Influences in Classroom Interaction*, edited by L.C. Wilkinson and C.B. Marrett. New York: Academic Press.

Echols, A. 1984. The Taming of the Id: Feminist Sexual Politics, 1968–83. In *Pleasure and Danger: Exploring Female Sexuality*, edited by C.S. Vance, 50–72. Boston: Routledge & Kegan Paul.

Edelsky, C. 1981. Who's Got the Floor? *Language in Society* 10: 383–421.

Editors of the Harvard Law Review. 1990. *Sexual Orientation and the Law*. Cambridge: Harvard University Press.

Edwards, S. 1984. *Women on Trial*. Manchester: Manchester University Press.

———. 1981. *Female Sexuality and the Law*. Oxford: Martin Robertson.

Ehrenreich, B. 1984. *The Hearts of Men: American Dreams and the Flight from Commitment*. Garden City, NY: Anchor/Doubleday.

Ehrenreich, B. and D. English. 1989/1995. Blowing the Whistle on the 'Mommy Track.' *Ms* Vol. 18, Nos. 1 & 2 (July/August 1989). Reprinted in *Gender in the 1990s: Images, Realities, and Issues*, edited by E.D. Nelson and B.W. Robinson, 211–215. Toronto: Nelson Canada.

———. 1979. *For Her Own Good: 150 Years of the Experts' Advice for Women*. Garden City, NY: Anchor Press.

———. 1978. *For Her Own Good*. Garden City, NY: Anchor-Doubleday.

Ehrensaft, D. 1990. Feminists Fight For Fathers. *Socialist Review* 20, 4: 57–80.

Ehrlich, S. and R. King. 1993. Gender-based Language Reform and the Social Construction of Meaning. In *Women's Studies Essential Readings*, edited by S. Jackson, 2nd ed. York: New York University.

Eibl-Eibesfeldt, I. 1970. *Ethology: The Biology of Behavior*. New York: Holt, Rinehart and Winston.

Eichler, M. 1996. The Impact of the New Reproductive and Genetic Technologies on Families. In *Families: Changing Trends in Canada*, edited by M. Baker, 3rd ed., 104–118. Toronto: McGraw-Hill Ryerson.

———. 1989. Reflections on Motherhood, Apple Pie, the New Reproductive Technologies and the Role of Sociologists in Society. *Society/Société* 13: 1–5.

———. 1984. Sexism in Research and its Policy Implications. In *Taking Sex Into Account: The Policy Implications of Sexist Research*, edited by J. McCalla Vickers, 17–39. Ottawa: Carleton University Press.

———. 1981. Power, Dependency, Love and the Sexual Division of Labour. *Women's Studies International Quarterly* 4, 2: 201–219.

———. 1980/1995. Sex Change Operations: The Last Bulwark of the Double Standard. From M. Eichler, *The Double Standard*, 72–88. London: Croom Helm. Reprinted in *Gender in the 1990s: Images, Realities and Issues,* edited by E.D. Nelson and B.W. Robinson, 29–37. Toronto: Nelson Canada.

Eisenhart, R.W. 1975. You Can't Hack It, Little Girl: A Discussion of the Covert Psychological Agenda of Modern Combat Training. *Journal of Social Issues* 31, Fall: 13–23.

Eisenstock, B. 1984. Sex Role Differences in Child's Identification with Counterstereotypical Televised Portrayals. *Sex Roles* 10: 417–430.

Eitzen, D.S. and M. Baca Zinn. 1994. *Social Problems*, 6th ed. Boston: Allyn and Bacon.

Ekman, P., W.V. Friesen, and S. Ancoli. 1980. Facial Signs of Emotional Experience. *Journal of Personality and Social Psychology* 39: 1125–1134.

El-Shiekh, M. and S. Reiter. 1995. *Children's Responding to Live Angry Interactions: The Role of Form of Anger Expression*. Poster presented at the biennial meeting of the Society for Research in Child Development, Indianopolis: Indiana, 30 March–2 April.

Elder, G. 1969. Appearance and Education in Marriage Mobility. *American Sociological Review* 34: 519–533.

Elkin, F. and G. Handel. 1989. *The Child and Society: The Process of Socialization,* 5th ed. New York: Random House.

Elliot, P. and N. Mandell. 1995. Feminist Theories. In *Feminist Issues: Race, Class, and Sexuality*, edited by N. Mandell, 3–31. Scarborough, ON: Prentice Hall Canada.

Elliott, J.L. and A. Fleras. 1992. *Unequal Relations: An Introduction to Race and Ethnic Dynamics in Canada*. Scarborough, ON: Prentice-Hall.

Ellis, D. and L. Sayer. 1986. *When I Grow Up: Career Expectations and Aspirations of Canadian Schoolchildren*. Ottawa: Women's Bureau: Labour Canada.

Ellis, L., D. Burke, and M.A. Ames. 1987. Sexual Orientation as a Continuous Variable: A Comparison Between the Sexes. *Archives of Sexual Behavior* 16, 6: 523–529.

Engels, F. 1884/1902. *The Origin of the Family, Private Property, and the State*. Chicago: C.H. Kerr.

Entwistle, D.R. and S. Doering. 1988. The Emergent Father Role. *Sex Roles* 18: 119–141.

Epstein, N., L. Evans, and J. Evans. 1994. Marriage. In *Encyclobedia of Human Behavior,* edited by V.S. Ramachandran, Vol. 3., 115–125. New York: Academic Press.

Epstein, C.F. 1988. *Deceptive Distinctions: Sex, Gender, and the Social Order*. New York: Russel Sage Foundation and Yale University Press.

———. 1981. *Women In Law*. New York: Basic Books.

Epstein, C.F. and R.L Coser. 1981. *Access to Power*. London: George Allen & Unwin.

Erickson, B., E.A. Lind, B.C. Johnson, and W.M. O'Barr. 1977. *Speech Style and Impression Formation in a Court Setting: The Effects of Power and Powerless Speech*. Law and Language Project Research Report no. 13. Durham, NC: Duke University; also in 1978 *Journal of Experimental Social Psychology*, 266.

Erikson, E. 1963. *Childhood and Society,* 2nd ed. New York: W.W. Norton.

Ernster, V.L. 1975. American Menstrual Expressions. *Sex Roles* 1: 3–13.

Errington, J. 1993. Pioneers and Suffragists. In *Changing Patterns: Women in Canada*, edited by S. Burt, L. Code, and L. Dorney, 2nd ed., 59-91. McClelland & Stewart.

Erwin, L.K. 1991. The Politics of Anti-Feminism: The Pro-Family Movement in Canada. *Dissertation Abstracts International, The Humanities and Social Sciences* 51, 9 March: 3237-A.

Erwin, L. 1988. REAL Women, Anti-Feminism, and the Welfare State. *Resources for Feminist Research/Documentation sur la Recherche Feministe* 17, 3 September: 147–149.

Etaugh, C. and K. Nekolny. 1990. Effects of Employment Status and Marital Status on Perceptions of Mothers. *Sex Roles* 23: 273–280.

Etaugh, C. and M.B. Liss. 1992. Home, School, and Playroom: Training Grounds for Adult Gender Roles. *Sex Roles* 26: 129–147.

Etaugh, C. and V. Hughes. 1987. Teacher's Evaluations of Black Students. In *Black Children: Their Roots, Culture and Learning Styles*, edited by J.E. Hale-Benson. Baltimore: John Hopkins University Press.

Evans, D. 1993. *Beauty and the Best*. Colorado Springs, CO: Focus on the Family Publishing.

Eyer, D.E. 1996. *Mother-Infant Bonding: A Scientific Fiction*. New Haven, CT: Yale University Press.

Faderman, L. 1992/1995. The Return of Butch and Femme: A Phenomenon in Lesbian Sexuality of the 1980s and 1990s. *Journal of the History of Sexuality* 2: 578–596. Reprinted in *Gender in the 1990s: Images, Realities, and Issues*, edited by E.D. Nelson and B.W. Robinson, 40–57. Toronto: Nelson Canada.

———. 1981. *Surpassing the Love of Men*. New York: William Morrow.

Fagot, B.I. 1986. Beyond the Reinforcement Principle: Another Step Toward Understanding Sex Role Development. *Developmental Psychology* 21: 1097–1104.

Fagot, B.I. and M.D. Leinbach. 1995. Gender Knowledge in Egalitarian and Traditional Families. *Sex Roles* 32, 7–8: 513–526.

———. 1989. The Young Child's Gender Schema: Environmental Input, Internal Organization. *Child Development* 60: 663–672.

Faith, K. 1993. *Unruly Women: The Politics of Confinement & Resistance*. Vancouver: Press Gang Publishers.

Faludi, S. 1993. Fatal and Fetal Visions: The Backlash in the Movies. In *Taking Sides: Clashing Views on Controversial Issues in Mass Media and Society*, edited by A. Alexander and J. Hanson, 2nd ed., 55–64. Guilford, CT: Dushkin Publishing Group.

———. 1991. *Backlash: The Undeclared Woman Against American Women*. New York: Crown.

Farrell, W. 1993. *The Myth of Male Power: Why Men are the Disposable Sex*. New York: Simon & Schuster.

———. 1986. *Why Men Are the Way They Are: The Male-Female Dynamic*. New York: McGraw-Hill.

———. 1974. *The Liberated Man*. New York: Bantam.

Fasick, F. 1994. On the 'Invention' of Adolescence. *Journal of Early Adolescence* 14, 1 Februrary: 6–23.

———. 1979. Acquisition of Adult Responsibilities and Rights in Adolescence. In *Childhood and Adolescence in Canada*, edited by K. Ishwaran, 119–135. Toronto: McGraw-Hill Ryerson.

Fast, J. and M. Da Pont. 1997. Changes in Women's Work Continuity. *Canadian Social Trends* 46, Autumn: 2–7.

Fasteau, M.F. 1975. *The Male Machine*. New York: Delta.

Fausto-Sterling, A. 1985. *Myths of Gender: Biological Theories About Women and Men*. New York: Basic Books.

Federation of Women's Teachers' Association of Ontario. 1986. *Inclusion in Language: A Sex Equity Issue*. Toronto: author.

Fein, E. and S. Schneider. 1995. *The Rules: Time-tested Secrets for Capturing the Heart of Mr. Right*. New York: Warner Books.

Fein, G., D. Johnson, N. Kosson, L. Stork, and L. Wasserman. 1975. Sex Stereotypes and Preferences in the Toy Choices of 20-Month-Old Boys and Girls. *Developmental Psychology* 11: 527–528.

Fein, R.A. 1978. Research on Fathering: Social Policy and an Emergent Perspective. *Journal of Social Issues* 31, 1: 122–135.

Feingold, A. 1990. Gender Differences in Effects of Physical Attractives on Romantic Attraction: A Comparison Across Five Research Paradigms. *Journal of Personality and Social Psychology* 59: 981–993.

Fekete, J. 1994. *Moral Panic: Biopolitics Rising*. Toronto: Robert Davies.

Feldstein, J.H. and S. Feldstein. 1982. Sex Differences on Televised Toy Commercials. *Sex Roles* 8: 581–587.

Ferree, M.M. 1991. The Gender Division of Labor in Two-Earner Marriages: Dimensions of Variability and Change. *Journal of Family Issues* 12: 158–180.

———. 1990 Beyond Separate Spheres: Feminism and Family Research. *Journal of Marriage and the Family* 52: 866–884.

Ferree, M.M. and B.B. Hess. 1985. *Controversy and Coalition: The New Feminist Movement*. Boston: Twayne Publishers.

Fildes, V.A. 1988. *Wet Nursing from Antiquity to the Present*. Oxford: Basil Blackwell.

Fillion, K. 1996. *Lip Service: The Truth About Women's Darker Side in Love, Sex and Friendship*. Toronto: HarperPerennial.

Findlen, B. (ed.). 1996. *Listen Up! Voices from the Next Feminist Generation*. New York: Seal Press.

Fine, G. 1987. *With the Boys: Little League Baseball and Preadolescent Culture*. Chicago: University of Chicago Press.

Fine, M.A. 1986. Perceptions of Steppanrets: Variations in Stereotypes as a Function of Current Family Structure. *Journal of Marriage and the Family* 48: 537–543.

Finkelhor, D. 1979. *Sexually Victimized Children*. New York: Free Press.

Finkelhor, D. and K. Yllo. 1985. *License to Rape: Sexual Abuse of Wives*. New York: Holt Rinehart.

Finkelstein, C.A. 1981. Woman Managers: Careers Patterns and Changes in the United States. In *Access to Power*, edited by C.F. Epstein and R.L. Coser, 193–210. London: George Allen & Unwin.

Firestone, S. 1970. *The Dialectic of Sex: The Case for Feminist Revolution*. New York: William Morrow.

Fisher, E. 1979. *Women's Creation: Sexual Evolution and the Shaping of Society*. New York: McGraw-Hill.

Fisher, H. 1992. *Anatomy of Love*. New York: Fawcett Columbine.

Fisher, W. and D. Byrne. 1978. Sex Differences in Response to Erotica? Love versus Lust. *Journal of Personality and Social Psychology* 36: 117–125.

Fiske, S.T. 1993. Controlling Other People: The Impact of Power on Stereotyping. *American Psychologist* 48: 621–628.

Fitzpatrick, M.A. 1988. *Between Husbands & Wives: Communication in Marriage*. Newbury Park, CA: Sage.

Fivush, R. 1991. Gender and Emotion in Mother-Child Conversations about the Past. *Journal of Narrative and Life History* 1: 325–341.

Flandrin, H.L. 1979. *Families in Former Times*. London: Cambridge University Press.

Flax, J. 1990. Postmodernism and Gender Relations in Feminist Theory. In *Feminism/Postmodernism*, edited by L.J. Nicholson, 39–62. New York: Routledge.

Fling, S. and M. Mansovitz. 1982. Sex Typing in Nursery School Children's Play Interests. *Developmental Psychology* 7: 146–152.

Flynn, C.P. 1990a. Sex Roles and Women's Response to Courtship Violence. *Journal of Family Violence* 5: 83–94.

———. 1990b. Relationship Violence by Women: Issues and Implications. *Family Relations* 39: 194–198.

Foa, E.B. and U.G. Foa. 1980. Resource Theory: Interpersonal Behavior as Exchange. In *Social Exchange: Advances in Theory and Research*, edited by K.J. Gergen, M.S. Greenber, and R.H. Willis, 79–94. New York: Plenum.

Foley, D.E. 1993. The Great American Football Ritual. In *Down to Earth Sociology: Introductory Readings*, edited by J.M. Henslin, 7th ed., 418–431. New York: Free Press.

Foot, D. with D. Stoffman. 1996. *Boom, Bust, and Echo: How to Profit from the Coming Demographic Shift*. Toronto: Macfarlane, Walter and Ross.

Ford, C.S. and F.A. Beach. 1951. *Patterns of Sexual Behavior*. New York: Harper.

Foreit, K.G., T. Agor, J. Byers, J. Larue, H. Lokey, M. Palazzini, M. Patterson, and L. Smith. 1980. Sex Bias in the Newspaper Treatment of Male-centered and Female-centered News Stories. *Sex Roles* 6: 475–480.

Fowler, M. 1993. *In A Gilded Cage: From Heiress to Duchess*. Toronto: Vintage.

Fox, B.J. (ed.). 1993. The Rise and Fall of the Breadwinner-Homemaker Family. In *Family Patterns, Gender Relations,* 147–157. Toronto: Oxford University Press.

Fox, B.J. 1990. Selling the Mechanized Household: 70 Years of Ads in *Ladies' Home Journal. Gender & Society* 4: 25–40.

Fox, G.L. and J.K. Inazu. 199x. Mother-Daughter Communication About Sex. *Family Relations* 29: 347–352.

Fox, K.D. and S.Y. Nickols. 1983. The Time Crunch: Wife's Employment and Family Work. *Journal of Family Issues* 4: 61–82.

Fox-Genovese, E. 1996. *Feminism Is Not The Story of My Life: How Today's Feminist Elite Has Lost Touch with the Real Concerns of Women*. New York: Doubleday.

———. 1991. *Feminism Without Illusions: A Critique of Individualism*. Chapel Hill: University of North Carolina Press.

Frederick, J.A. 1995. *As Time Goes By...Time Use of Canadians*. General Social Survey. Cat. 89–544E. Ottawa: Minister of Industry.

———. 1993. Tempus Fugit...Are You Time Crunched? *Canadian Social Trends* 31 Winter: 6–9.

Freedman, R. 1990. Myth America Grows Up. In *Issues in Feminism: An Introduction to Women's Studies*, edited by S. Ruth, 2nd ed., 397–406. Mountain View, CA: Mayfield.

Freeman, J. 1975. *The Politics of Women's Liberation*. New York: Doubleday.

French, J. and B. Raven. 1959. The Bases of Social Power. In *Studies in Social Power*, edited by D. Cartwright. Ann Arbour: University of Michigan, Institute for Social Research.

French, M. 1992. *The War Against Women*. New York: Ballantine Books.

Freud, Sigmund. 1933/1964. Femininity. In *New Introductory Lectures on Psychoanalysis*, 112–35. New York: Norton.

Friday, N. 1996. *The Power of Beauty*. New York: Harper Collins.

Friedan, B. 1993. *The Fountain of Age*. New York: Simon & Schuster.

———. 1963. *The Feminine Mystique*. New York: Dell.

Friedman, J. 1993. *America's First Woman Lawyer*. New York: Prometheus Books.

Friedman, M. 1985. Bulimia. *Women & Therapy* 2: 63–69.

Friedmann, E.A. and R.J. Havighurst. 1954. *The Meaning of Work and Retirement*. Chicago: University of Chicago Press.

Frieze, I., J.C. Parsons, P.B. Johnson, D.N. Ruble, and G. Zellman. 1978. *Women and Sex Roles: A Social Psychological Perspective*. New York: W.W. Norton.

Frith, G. 1993. Women, Writing and Language: Making the Silences Speak. In *Thinking Feminist: Key Concepts in Women's Studies*, edited by D. Richardson and V. Robinson, 151–176. New York: Guilford Press.

Frith, S. 1981. *Sound Effects: Youth, Leisure, and the Politics of Rock'n'Roll*. New York: Pantheon Books.

Frueh, T. and P. McGhee. 1975. Traditional Sex Role Development and Amount of Time Watching Television. *Developmental Psychology* 11: 109.

Furnham, A. and N. Bitar. 1993. The Stereotyped Portrayal of Men and Women in British Television Advertisements. *Sex Roles* 29, 3/4: 297–307.

Furstenberg, F.F. and G.B. Spanier. 1984. *Recycling the Family: Remarriage after Divorce*. Beverly Hills, CA: Sage.

Gaffield, C. 1990. The Social and Economic Origins of Contemporary Families. In *Families: Changing Trends in Canada*, edited by M. Baker, 2nd ed., 23–40. Toronto: McGraw-Hill Ryerson.

Gagnon, J.H. 1977. *Human Sexualities*. Glenview, IL: Scott, Foresman.

Gairdner, W.D. 1992. *The War Against The Family: A Parent Speaks Out*. Toronto: Stoddart.

Galarneau, D. 1993. Alimony and Child Support. *Canadian Social Trends* Spring: 8–11.

Galinsky, E., J.T. Bond, and D.E. Friedman. 1993 *The Changing Workplace: Highlights of the National Study*. New York: Families and Work Institute.

Ganong, L.H. and M. Coleman. 1994. *Remarried Family Relationships*. Thousand Oaks, CA: Sage.

Garcia, A.M. 1991. The Development of Chicana Feminist Discourse. In *The Social Construction of Gender*, edited by J. Lorber and S.A. Farrell, 269–287. Newbury Park, CA: Sage.

Garcia, M. 1997. *Affirmative Action's Treatment of Hope: Strategies for a New Era in Higher Education*. Albany, NY: State University of New York Press.

Gardner, A. 1995. Their Own Boss: The Self-Employed in Canada. *Canadian Social Trends* 37, Summer: 26–29.

Garfinkel, H. 1967. *Studies in Ethnomethodology*. Englewood Cliffs, NJ: Prentice-Hall.

Garfinkel, P.E. and D.M. Garner. 1983. *Anorexia Nervosa: A Multidimensional Perspective*. New York: Brunner Mead.

Gargano, Paul. 1997. Pat Boone: In A Metal Mood. *Metal Edge* May, 41, 12: 43.

Garner, D.M. 1997. The 1997 Body Image Survey Results. *Psychology Today* 30 January/February: 30–44, 74–80, 84.

Garner, D.M. and P.E. Garfinkel. 1980. Socio-Cultural Factors in the Development of Anorexia Nervosa. *Psychological Medicine* 10: 647–656.

Garner, D.M., P. Garfinkel, D. Schwartz, and M. Thompson. 1980. Cultural Expectations of Thinness in Women. *Psychological Reports* 47: 483–491.

Garst, J. and G.V. Bodenhausen. 1997. Advertising Effects on Men's Gender Roles. *Sex Roles* 16, 9/10: 551–583.

———. 1996. 'Family Values' and Political Persuasion: Impact of Kin-related Rhetoric on Reactions to Political Campaigns. *Journal of Applied Social Psychology* July, 26, 13: 1119–1137.

Gartrell, N. and D. Mosbacher. 1984. Sex Differences in the Naming of Children's Genitalia. *Sex Roles* 10, 11/12: 869–876.

Gaskell, J., A. McLaren, and M. Novogrodsky. 1989/1995. What's Worth Knowing? Defining the Feminist Curriculum. *Claiming an Education: Feminism and Canadian Schools*. Toronto: Our Schools/Our Selves Education Foundation. Reprinted in *Gender in the 1990s: Images, Realities, and Issues*, edited by E.D. Nelson and B.W. Robinson, 100–118. Toronto: Nelson Canada.

Gastil, J. 1990. Generic Pronouns and Sexist Language: The Oxymoronic Character of Masculine Generics. *Sex Roles* 23: 629–643.

Gaudette, L.A., J.F. Gentleman, and J. Lee. 1998. Breast Cancer and Mammography. *Canadian Social Trends* 48, Spring: 19–24.

Gauthier, P. and A. Haman. 1992. Physical Fitness. *Canadian Social Trends* 25, Summer: 18–20.

Gayle, N.A. 1992. Black Women's Reality and Feminism: An Exploration of Race and Gender. In *Anatomy of Gender: Women's Struggle for the Body*, edited by D.H. Currie and V. Raoul, 232–242. Ottawa: Carleton University Press.

Gecas, V. 1990. Families and Adolescents: A Review of the 1980s. *Journal of Marriage and the Family* 52: 941–958.

Gee, E.M. 1995. Families in Later Life. In *Families over the Life Course*, edited by R. Beaujot, E.M. Gee, F. Rajulton, and Z.R. Ravenera, 77–113. Current Demographic Analysis Series. Ottawa: Statistics Canada.

———. 1995b. Contemporary Diversities. In *Canadian Families: Diversity, Conflict and Change*, edited by N. Mandell and A. Duffy, 79–109. Toronto: Harcourt Brace Canada.

———. 1986. The Life Course of Canadian Women: An Historical and Demographic Analysis. *Social Indicators Research* 18: 263–283.

———. 1984. Mortality and Gender. *Canadian Woman Studies* 53: 12–14.

Gee, E.M. and M.M. Kimball. 1987. *Women and Aging*. Toronto: Butterworths.

Geis, F.L., V. Brown, J.J. Walstedt, and N. Porter. 1984. T.V. Commercials as Achievement Scripts for Women. *Sex Roles* 10, 7/8: 513–525.

Geller, S.E., M.I. Geller, and C.J. Scheirer. 1979. The Development in Sex Attitudes and Selective Attention to Same-sex Models in Young Children. Paper presented at the Eastern Psychological Association Convention, Philadelphia, April.

Gelles, R.J. 1974. *The Violent Home*. Beverly Hills, CA: Sage.

Gelles, R.J. and M.A. Straus. 1988. *Intimate Violence*. New York: Simon & Schuster.

Genevie, L. and E. Margolies. 1987. *The Motherhood Report: How Women Feel About Being Mothers*. New York: Macmillan.

Gerber, G. 1993. Women and Minorities on Television. A Report to the Screen Actors Guild and the American Federation of Radio and Television Artists. Philadelphia: University of Philadelphia.

Gergen, D. 1997. Promises Worth Keeping. *U.S. News & World Report*. September 20: 78.

Gerrard, N. and N. Javed. 1995. The Psychology of Women. In *Feminist Issues: Race, Class, and Sexuality*, edited by N. Mandell, 123–151. Scarborough, ON: Prentice Hall Canada.

Gerson, K. 1986/1987. Briefcase, Baby, or Both? *Psychology Today* 20, 11: 30–36. Reprinted in *Gender Roles: Doing What Comes Naturally?* edited by E.D. Salamon and B.W. Robinson, 206–212. Scarborough, ON: Methuen/Nelson.

Gerson, J.M. and K. Peiss. 1985. Boundaries, Negotiation, Consciousness: Reconceptualizing Gender Relations. *Social Problems* 32: 317–331.

Ghalam, N.Z. 1997. Attitudes Toward Women, Work and Family. *Canadian Social Trends* 46 Autumn: 13–17.

———. 1993/1995. Women in the Workplace. *Canadian Social Trends* 28, Spring: 2–6. Reprinted in *Gender in the 1990s: Images, Realities, and Issues*, edited by E.D. Nelson and B.W. Robinson, 201–210. Toronto: Nelson Canada.

Gilbert, L.A. 1985. *Men in Dual-Career Families: Current Realities and Future Prospects.* Hillsdale, NJ: Lawrence Erlbaum.

Gilbert, D. and J.A. Kahl. 1993. *The American Class Structure: A New Synthesis,* 4th ed. Homewood, IL: Dorsey Press.

Gilbert, L. 1996. *SurferGrrls*. New York: Seal Press.

Gilder, G. 1986. *Men and Marriage*. Gretna, LA: Pelican.

———. 1973. *Sexual Suicide*. New York: Bantam.

Giles, W. and S. Arat-Koc (eds.). 1994. *Maid in the Market: Women's Paid Domestic Labour*. Halifax: Fernwood Publishing.

Gilham, S.A. 1989. The Marines Build Men: Resocialization in Recruit Training. In *The Sociological Outlook: A Text With Readings*, edited by R. Luhman, 2nd ed., 232–244. San Diego: Collegiate Press.

Gillespie, C.K. 1989. *Justifiable Homicide*. Columbus, OH: Ohio State University.

Gilligan, C. 1982. *In A Different Voice*. Cambridge, MA: Harvard University Press.

Gilligan, C., N.P. Lyons, and T.J. Hanmer (eds.). 1990. *Making Connections: The Relational Worlds of Adolescent Girls at Emma Willard School*. London, UK: Cambridge University Press.

Gilman, P. 1994. *Jillian Jiggs to the Rescue*. Richmond Hill, ON: Scholastic Canada.

Ginzberg, E. 1972. Toward a Theory of Occupational Choice: A Restatement. *Voational Guidance Quarterly* 20: 169–176.

Ginzberg, E., S.W. Ginsberg, S. Axelrod, and J.L. Herman. 1951. *Occupational Choice*. New York: Columbia University Press.

Givens, D.B. 1983. *Love Signals: How to Attract a Mate*. New York: Pinnacle.

Glenn, N.D. 1990. Quantitative Research on Marital Quality in the 1980s: A Critical Review. *Journal of Marriage and the Family* 52: 818–831.

Glick, P.C. 1989. The Family Life Cycle and Social Change. *Family Relations* 38: 123–129.

Glick, P.C. and S. Lin. 1987. Remarriage After Divorce: Recent Changes and Demographic Variations. *Sociological Perspectives* 30: 162–179.

———. 1986a. More Young Adults are Living with their Parents: Who Are They? *Journal of Marriage and the Family* 48: 107–112.

———. 1986b. Recent Changes in Divorce and Remarriage. *Journal of Marriage and the Family* 38: 737–747.

Glossop, R. 1994. Robert Glossop on the Canadian Family. *Canadian Social Trends* 35, Winter: 2–10.

Godard, B. 1985. *Talking About Ourselves: The Literary Productions of the Native Women of Canada*. Ottawa: CRIAW/ICREF.

Goffman, E. 1979. *Gender Advertisements*. Cambridge, MA: Harvard University Press.

Gold, D., G. Crombie, and S. Noble. 1987. Relations between Teachers' Judgements of Girls' and Boy's Compliance and Intellectual Competence. *Sex Roles* 16, 7/8: 351–362.

Goldberg, H. 1976. *The Hazards of Being Male: Surviving the Myth of Masculine Privilege*. New York: Signet.

Goldberg, S. and M. Lewis. 1969. Play Behavior in the Year-Old Infant: Early Sex Differences. *Child Development* 40: 21–31.

Goldman, B. D. 1978. Developmental Influences of Hormones on Neuroendocrine Mechanisms of Sexual Behaviour. In *Biological Determinants of Sexual Behaviour*, edited by J.B. Hutchinson, 127–152. New York: John Wiley and Sons.

Goldman, B., P. Bush, and R. Klatz. 1984. *Death in the Locker Room: Steroids and Sports*. South Bend, IN: Icarus Press.

Goldscheider, F.K. and L.J. Waite. 1991. *New Families, No Families? The Transformation of the American Home*. Berkeley: University of California Press.

Goode, W.J. 1982/1995. Why Men Resist. In *Rethinking the Family: Some Feminist Questions*, edited by B. Thorne and N. Yalom, 287–310. New York: Longman. Reprinted in *Gender in the 1990s: Images, Realities, and Issues*, edited by E.D. Nelson and B.W. Robinson, 516–524. Toronto: Nelson Canada.

———. 1982. *The Family,* 2nd ed. Englewood Cliffs, N.J: Prentice-Hall.

———. 1959. The Theoretical Importance of Love. *American Sociological Review* 24: 38–47.

Gordon, L. and A. Hunter. 1977/1978. Sex, Family & the New Right: Antifeminism as a Political Force. *Radical America* 11/12, 6/1, November–February: 8–25.

Gordon, M.M. 1964. *Assimilation in American Life: The Role of Race, Religion, and National Origin*. New York: Oxford University Press.

Gordon, M. and P.J. Shankweiler. 1971. Different Equals Less: Female Sexuality in Recent Marriage Manuals. *Journal of Marriage and the Family* 33: 459–466.

Gordon, S. 1990. *Prisoners of Men's Dreams*. Boston: Little, Brown.

———. 1983. *Off Balance: The Real World of Ballet*. New York: McGraw-Hill.

Gormly, A.V., J.B. Gormly, and H. Weiss. 1987. Motivations for Parenthood among Young Adult College Students. *Sex Roles* 16: 31–39.

Gottman, J.M. 1993. The Roles of Conflict Engagement, Escalation, or Avoidance in Marital Interaction: A Longitudinal View of Five Types of Couples. *Journal of Consulting and Clinical Psychology* 61: 6–15.

Gottman, J.M., J. Coan, S. Carrere, and C. Swanson. 1998. Predicting Marital Happiness and Stability from Newlywed Interactions. *Journal of Marriage and the Family* 60: 5–22.

Gottman, J. with N. Silver. 1994. *Why Marriages Succeed or Fail*. New York: Simon & Schuster.

Gottman, J. and R.W. Levenson. 1988. The Social Psychophysiology of Marriage. In *Perspectives on Marital Interaction*, edited by P. Noller and M.A. Fitzpatrick, 182–202. Clevedon, UK: Multilingual Matters.

Gould, L. 1980/1995. X: A Fabulous Child's Story. *Ms.*Magazine. May: 61–64. Reprinted in *Gender in the 1990s: Images, Realities, and Issues*, edited by E.D. Nelson and B.W. Robinson, 75–82. Toronto: Nelson Canada.

Gould, R. 1976. Measuring Masculinity by the Size of a Paycheck. In *The Forty-Nine Percent Majority: The Male Sex Role*, edited by D.S. David and R. Brannon, 113–118. Reading, MA: Addison-Wesley.

Gould, R.L. 1978. *Transformations: Growth & Change in Adult Life*. New York: Simon & Schuster.

———. 1975. Adult Life Stages: Growth Toward Self Tolerance. *Psychology Today*. 8 Feb: 74–8.

———. 1972. The Phases of Adult Life: A Study in Developmental Psychology. *The American Journal of Psychiatry* 129, 5: 521–531.

Gove, W.R. 1984. Gender Differences in Mental and Physical Health: The Effects of Fixed Roles and Nurturant Roles. *Social Science and Medicine* 19: 77–84.

Gove, W.R., C.B. Style, and M. Hughes. 1990. The Effects of Marriage on the Well-Being of Adults. *Journal of Family Issues* 1: 34–35.

Gove, W.R. and J.R. Tudor. 1973. Adult Sex Roles and Mental Illness. *American Journal of Sociology* 78, 4: 812–835.

Government of Ontario. 1996. *Improving Ontario's Child Care System: Ontario Child Care Review.* Janet Ecker, M.P.P.

Gowland, P. 1983. *Women in Families: The Sexual Division of Labour and Australian Family Policy*. Melbourne: Knox Community Relations Centre.

Grabb, E. and J.E. Curtis. 1992. Voluntary Association Activity in English Canada, French Canada, and the United States: A Multivariate Analysis. *Canadian Journal of Sociology* 16 4: 371–388.

Graham, H. 1987. Women's Smoking and Family Health. *Social Science and Medicine* 25: 47–56.

———. 1984. *Women, Health and the Family*. Brighton: Wheatsheaf.

Graham, A. 1977. Words that Make Women Disappear. *Redbook,* March.

Grant, Karen R. 1994. Health and Health Care. In *Contemporary Sociology*, edited by P.S. Li and B. Singh Bolaria, 394–409. Toronto: Copp-Clark Pitman.

Grauerholz, E. and B.A. Pescosolido. 1989. Gender Representations in Children's Literature, 1900–1981. *Gender and Society* 3, 1: 113–125.

Gray, H. 1986. Television and the New Black Man: Black Male Images in Prime-time Situation Comedies. *Media, Culture and Society* 9: 223–242.

Gray, S. 1987. Sharing the Shop Floor. In *Beyond Patriarchy,* edited by M. Kaufman, 216–234. Toronto: Oxford University Press.

Greaves, L. 1991. Reorganizing the National Action Committee on the Status of Women, 1986–1988. In *Women and Social Change*, edited by J.D. Wine and J.L. Ristock, 101–116. Toronto: James Lorimer.

Green, M. 1986. The History of Canadian Narcotics Control: The Formative Years. In *The Social Dimensions of Law*, edited by N. Boyd. Scarborough, ON: Prentice Hall Canada.

Green, R. 1992. *Sexual Science and the Law*. Cambridge, MA: Harvard University Press.

———. 1987. *The Sissy Boy Syndrome and the Development of Homosexuality*. New Haven: Yale University Press.

———. 1969. Psychiatric Management of Special Problems in Transsexualism. In *Transsexualism and Sex Reassignment*, edited by R. Green and J. Money. Baltimore: John Hopkins University Press.

Greenglass, E.R. 1982. *A World of Difference: Gender Roles in Perspective*. Toronto: Wiley.

Greenland, C. 1988. *Preventing CAN deaths: An International Study of Deaths Due to Child Abuse and Neglect*. London: Tavistock.

Greer, G. 1991. *The Change: Women Aging and the Menopause*. New York: Fawcet Columbine.

Grescoe, P. 1996. *The Merchants of Venus: Inside Harlequin and the Empire of Romance*. Vancouver: Raincoast.

Grice, H.P. 1968. The Logic of Conversation. Unpublished manuscript, Department of Philosophy, Berkeley: University of California.

Griffiths, C.T. and J.C. Yerbury. 1995. Understanding Aboriginal Crime and Criminality: A Case Study. In *Canadian Criminology: Perspectives on Crime and Criminality*, edited by M.A. Jackson and C.T. Griffiths, 383–398. Toronto: Harcourt, Brace Canada.

Grindstaff, C.F. 1995. Canadian Fertility, 1951 to 1993. *Canadian Social Trends* 39, Winter: 12–16.

Groce, S.B. and M. Cooper. 1990. Just Me and the Boys? Women in Local-Level Rock and Roll. *Gender & Society* 2: 220–228.

Guppy, N. and B. Arai. 1993. Who Benefits from Higher Education? Differences by Sex, Social Class and Ethnic Background. In *Social Inequality in Canada: Patterns, Problems, Policies*, edited by J.E. Curtis, E. Grabb, and N. Guppy, 2nd ed., 214–232. Scarborough, ON: Prentice Hall.

Gutman, D. 1975. Parenthood: A Key to the Comparative Psychology of the Life Cycle. In *Lifespan Developmental Psychology: Normative Life Crises*, edited by N. Datan and L. Ginsberg. New York: Academic Press.

Gutman, D., B. Griffin, and J. Grunes. 1982. Developmental Contributions to the Late-Onset Affective Disorders. In *Life-Span Development and Behavior*. P.B. Baltes and O.G. Brim Jr., Vol. 4, 243–260. New York: Academic Press.

Guttentag, M. and P.F. Secord. 1983. *Too Many Women? The Sex Ratio Question*. Beverly Hills: Sage.

Hacker, C. 1984. *The Indomitable Lady Doctors*. Halifax, NS: Federation of Medical Women of Canada.

Hacker, H. 1951. Women as a Minority Group. *Social Forces* 30 October: 60–69.

Hacker, S.S. 1992. The Transition From the Old Norm to the New: Sexual Values for the 1990s. In *Human Sexuality 92/93*: 22–29. Guilford, CT: Dushkin.

Hackett, G. 1994. Online:alt.men.waste-time. *Newsweek*. May 16: 54.

Haddon, L. 1988. The Roots and Early History of the British Home Computer Market: Origins of the Masculine Micro. PhD thesis, Management School, Imperial College, University of London.

Halberstadt, A.G. and M.B. Saitta. 1987. Gender, Nonverbal Behavior, and Perceived Dominance: A Test of the Theory. *Journal of Personality and Social Psychology* 53: 257–272.

Hale-Benson, J.E. 1987. *Black Children: Their Roots, Culture and Learning Styles*, Rev. ed. Provo, UT: Brigham Young University Press.

Hall, D. and Langellier, K. 1988. Storytelling Strategies in Mother-Daughter Communication. In *Women Communicating: Studies of Women's Talk*, edited by B. Bate and A. Taylor, 197–226. Norwood, NJ: Ablex.

Hall, E.T. 1984. *The Dance of Life: The Other Dimension of Time*. New York: Anchor.

———. 1969. *The Hidden Dimensions*. Garden City, NY: Anchor.

Hall, G.A. 1977. Workshop for a Ballerina. *Urban Life* 6: 193–200.

Hamer, D. and P.F. Copeland. 1996. *The Science of Desire: The Search for the Gay Gene and the Biology of Behavior*. New York: Touchstone Books.

Hamer, D., P.F. Copeland, S. Hu, V.L. Magnuson, N. Hu, and A.M.L. Pattatucci. 1993. A Linkage Between DNA Markers on the X Chromosome and Male Sexual Orientation. *Science* 261: 321–327.

Hamilton, M.C. 1991. Masculine Bias in the Attribution of Personhood: People—Male, Male = People. *Psychology of Women Quarterly* 15: 393–402.

———. 1988. Using Masculine Generics: Does Generic 'He' Increase Male Bias in the User's Imagery? *Sex Roles* 19, 11/12: 785–799.

Hamilton, R. 1996. *Gendering the Vertical Mosaic: Feminist Perspectives on Canadian Society*. Toronto: Copp Clark.

———. 1988. Women, Wives and Mothers. In *Reconstructing the Canadian Family: Feminist Perspectives*, edited by N. Mandell and A. Duffy, 3–26. Toronto: Butterworths.

Hamm, M.S. and J. Ferrell. 1996. Rap, Cops, and Crime: Clarifying the Cop Killer Controversy. In *Taking Sides: Clashing Views on Controversial Issues in Crime and Criminology*, edited by R.C. Monk, 39–44. Guilford, CT: Dushkin/Brown & Benchmark.

Hammer, M. and J. McFerran. 1988. Preference for Sex of Child: A Research Update. *Individual Psychology* December: 486–492.

Hamner, J. and P. Allen. 1980. Reproductive Engineering: The Final Solution. In *Alice Through the Microscope: The Power of Science Over Women's Lives*, edited by S. Best and L. Birke. London: Virago.

Hansen, C.H. and R.D. Hansen. 1988. How Rock Music Videos can Change What is Seen When Boy meets Girl: Priming Stereotypic Appraisal of Social Interaction. *Sex Roles* 19: 287–316.

Hardesty, C., D. Wenk, and C.S. Morgan. 1995. Paternal Involvement and the Development of Gender Expectations in Sons and Daughters. *Youth and Society* 267, 3: 283–297.

Harmatz, M.G. and M.A. Novak. 1983. *Human Sexuality*. New York: Harper and Row.

Harrell, A. 1985. Husband's Involvement in Housework: The Effects of Relative Earning Power and Masculine Orientation. *Edmonton Area Studies*. Series #39. Edmonton, AB: Population Research Laboratory, Department of Sociology, University of Alberta.

Harris, B. 1979. Careers, Conflict and Children. In *Career and Motherhood*, edited by A. Roland and B. Harris, 55–86. New York: Human Sciences Press.

Harris, D. Wise. 1991. Keeping Women in Our Place: Violence at Canadian Universities. *Canadian Woman Studies* 11, 4: 37–41.

Harris, K.M. and S.P. Morgan 1991. Fathers, Sons, and Daughters: Differential Paternal Involvement in Parenting. *Journal of Marriage and the Family* 53, 3 August: 531–544.

Harris, S. 1992. Black Male Masculinity and Same Sex Friendship. *Western Journal of Black Studies* 16: 74–81.

Harry, J. 1976. Evolving Sources of Happiness for Men Over the Life Cycle: A Structural Analysis. *Journal of Marriage and the Family* 38: 289–296.

Hartley, R.E. 1959. Sex-Role Pressures and Socialization of the Male Child. *Psychological Reports* 5: 457–468.

Hartmann, E. 1991. *Boundaries in the Mind: A New Psychology of Personality*. New York: Basic Books.

Hartmann, H. 1981. The Unhappy Marriage of Marxism and Feminism: Towards a More Progressive Union. In *Women and Revolution*, edited by L. Sargent, 1–41. Boston: South End Press.

Hartouni, V. 1995. Reproductive Technologies and the Negotiation of Public Meanings: The Case of Baby M. In *Provoking Agents: Gender and Agency in Theory and Practice*, edited by J. Kegan Gardiner, 115–132. Chicago: University of Chicago Press.

Hatfield, E. and S. Sprecher. 1986. Measuring Passionate Love in Intimate Relationships. *Journal of Adolescence* 9: 383–410.

Hathaway, S. and J. McKinley. 1943. *The Minnesota Multiphasic Personality Inventory*. New York: Psychological Corporation.

Hay, D., C. Zahn-Waxler, M. Cummings, and R. Iannotti. 1992. Young Children's Views about Conflict with Peers: A Comparison of the Daughters and Sons of Depressed and Well Women. *Journal of Child Psychology and Psychiatry* 33: 669–683.

Hayden, D. 1981. *The Grand Domestic Revolution: A History of Feminist Designs for American Homes, Neighborhoods and Cities*. Cambridge, MA: MIT Press.

Hayford, A. 1987. Outlines of the Family. In *Family Matters: Sociology and Contemporary Canadian Families*, edited by K.L. Anderson et al., 1–19. Toronto: Methuen.

Hays, H.R. 1964. *The Dangerous Sex: The Myth of Feminine Evil*. New York: G.P. Putnam's.

Hays, S. *The Cultural Contradictions of Motherhood*. New Haven, CT: Yale University Press.

Hays, T. 1987. Menstrual Expressions and Menstrual Attitudes. *Sex Roles* 16: 605–614.

Hayward, F. 1987. A Shortage...of Good Women. *Single Scene Magazine.* September: 12.

Heavey, C.L., C. Layne, and A. Christensen. 1993. Gender and Conflict Structure in Marital Interaction: A Replication and Extension. *Journal of Consulting and Clinical Psychology* 61: 16–27.

Heer, D.M., R.W. Hodge, and M. Felson. 1985. The Cluttered Nest: Evidence that Young Adults are More Likely to Live at Home Now than in the Recent Past. *Sociology and Social Research* 69, 3: 436–441.

Heilbrun, C. 1973. *Reinventing Womanhood*. New York: W.W. Norton & Company.

Heiman, J.R. 1975. The Physiology of Erotica: Women's Sexual Arousal. *Psychology Today.* 8: 91–94.

Heintz, K.E. 1987. An Examination of Sex and Occupational-Role Presentations of Female Characters in Children's Picture Books. *Women's Studies in Communication* 10, 2: 76–78.

Helmreich, R.L. et al. 1981. Making It in Academic Psychology. *Journal of Personality and Social Psychology* 39: 896–899.

Hendrick, S.S. and C. Hendrick. 1992. *Romantic Love*. Newbury Park, CA: Sage.

Henley, N.M., B. Gruber, and L. Lerner. 1985. Studies on the Detrimental Effects of 'Generic' Masculine Usage. Paper presented at the Eastern Psychological Association, Boston, March.

Henley, N., M. Hamilton, and B. Thorne. 1984. *Womanspeak and Manspeak: Sex Differences and Sexisms in Communication, Verbal and Nonverbal*. St. Paul, MN: West.

Hennig, M. and A. Jardim. 1978. *The Managerial Woman*. Garden City, NY: Anchor/ Doubleday.

Henry, W.A. 1993. Born Gay. *Time*. 26 July. Reprinted in *Human Sexuality 95/96*, edited by S.J. Bunting, 20th ed., 63–65. Guilford, CT: Dushkin.

Henslin, J. and A. Nelson. 1996. *Sociology: A Down-to-Earth Approach*. Scarborough, ON: Allyn & Bacon.

Herman, J.L. 1991. Sex Offenders: A Feminist Perspective. In *Sexual Assault Issues: Theories and Treatment of the Offender*, edited by W.I. Marshall, D.R. Laws, and H.E. Barabee, 177–194. New York: Plenum Press.

———. 1981. *Father-Daughter Incest*. Cambridge, MA: Harvard University Press.

Herrig, S., D. Johnson, and T. Dibenedetto. 1992. Participation in Electronic Discourse in a Feminist Field. In *Proceedings of the Second Berkeley Women and Language Conference*, edited by K. Hall, M. Bucholz, and B. Moonwoman. Berkeley: University of California.

Hess, B.B. and M.M. Ferree. 1987. Introduction. In *Analyzing Gender*, edited by B.B. Hess and M.M. Ferree, 9–30. Newbury Park, CA: Sage.

Hetherington, F.M., M. Cox, and R. Cox. 1976. Divorced Fathers. *The Family Coordinator* 25: 417–428.

Hetherington, E.M., M. Stanley-Hagan, and E.R. Anderson. 1989. Marital Transitions: A Child's Perspective. *American Psychologist*. 33: 303–312.

Hetherington, E.M. and R. Cox. 1982. Effects of Divorce on Parents and Children. In *Nontraditional Families*, edited by M. Lamb. Hillsdale, NJ: Lawrence Erlbaum Associates.

Heyn, D. 1997. *Marriage Shock: The Transformation of Women into Wives*. New York: Villard.

Higginbotham, A. 1992. We Were Never on a Pedestal: Women of Colour Continue to Struggle with Poverty, Racism, and Sexism. In *Race, Class, and Gender: An Anthology*, edited by M.L. Anderson and P. Hill Collins, 183–190. Belmont, CA: Wadsworth.

Higginbotham, E. and L. Weber. 1992. Moving with Kin and Community: Upward Social Mobility for Black and White Women. *Gender & Society* 6, 3: 416–440.

Hildebrandt, K.A. and H.E. Fitzgerald. 1979. Facial Feature Determinants of Perceived Infant Attractiveness. *Infant Behavior and Development* 2: 329–339.

Hildebrandt, K. and T. Cannan. 1985. The Distribution of Caregiver Attention in a Group Program for Young Children. *Child Study Journal* 15, 1: 43–54.

Hill, C.T., Z. Rubin, and L.A. Peplau. 1976. Breakups Before Marriage: The End of 103 Affairs. *Journal of Social Issues* 32: 147–168.

Hills, S.L. (ed.). 1980/1995. Rape and the Masculine Mystique. In *Demystifying Social Deviance*. New York: McGraw-Hill. Abridged and reprinted in *Gender in the 1990s: Images, Realities, and Issues*, edited by E.D. Nelson and B.W. Robinson, 443–454.Toronto: Nelson Canada.

Hiltz, S.R. 1989. Widowhood. In *Marriage and Family in a Changing Society*, edited by J.M. Henslin, 3rd ed., 521–531. New York: Free Press.

Hinch, R. (ed.). 1992. Is Mandatory Retirement Justified? In *Debates in Canadian Society*, 298–300. Scarborough, ON: Nelson Canada.

Hinde, R. and J. Stevenson-Hinde. 1987. Implications of a Relationship Approach for the Study of Gender Differences. *Infant Mental Health Journal* 8: 221–235.

Hines, M. 1982. Prenatal Gonadal Hormones and Sex Differences in Human Behavior. *Psychological Bulletin* 92: 56–80.

Hite, S. 1987. *Women and Love: A Cultural Revolution in Progress*. New York: Alfred A. Knopf.

———. 1981. *The Hite Report on Male Sexuality*. New York: Alfred A. Knopf.

———. 1976. *The Hite Report: A Nationwide Study on Female Sexuality*. New York: Macmillan.

Hobart, C. 1996. Intimacy and Family Life: Sexuality, Cohabitation and Marriage. In *Families: Changing Trends in Canada*, edited by M. Baker, 3rd ed., 143–173. Toronto: McGraw- Hill Ryerson.

———. 1991. Conflict in Remarriages. *Journal of Divorce and Remarriage* 15: 69–86.

———. 1958. The Incidence of Romanticism During Courtship. *Social Forces* 35: 364–367.

Hochschild, A.R. 1997. *The Time Bind: When Work Becomes Home & Home Becomes Work*. New York: Metropolitan Books.

———. 1983. Attending to, Codifying and Managing Feelings: Sex Differences in Love. In *Feminist Frontiers: Rethinking Sex, Gender and Society,* edited by L. Richardson and V. Taylor, 250–262. Reading, MA: Addison-Wesley.

Hochschild, A.R. with A. Machung. 1990. *The Second Shift*. New York: Avon.

Hodgeon, J. 1985. A Woman's World? In *Alice in Genderland: Reflections on Language, Power and Control*, edited by Language and Gender Working Party. London: National Association for the Teaching of English.

Hoffman, L.W. 1977. Changes in Family Roles, Socialization, and Sex Differences. *American Psychologist* 32: 644–657.

Hoffnung, M. 1995. Motherhood: Contemporary Conflict for Women. In *Women: A Feminist Perspective*, edited by J. Freeman, 5th ed., 162–181. Mountain View, CA: Mayfield.

———. 1989. Motherhood: Contemporary Conflict for Women. In *Women: A Feminist Perspective*, edited by J. Freeman, 4th ed., 157–175. Palo Alto. CA: Mayfield.

Holderness, M. 1994. Netiquette for the Novices. *Guardian.* Repinted in *Age Green Guide* October 13: 25.

Hollibaugh, A. 1984. Desire for the Future: Radical Hope in Passion and Pleasure. In *Pleasure and Danger: Exploring Female Sexuality* edited by C. Vance, 401–410. Boston: Routledge & Kegan Paul.

Holmes, S.A. 1990. House, 265–145, Votes to Widen Day Care Programs in the Nation. *New York Times.* March 30: A1, A14.

Holtz, P. 1997. Society's Child. *Toronto Life.* 31, 13: 98–103.

Hookham, L. and N. Merriam. 1991. The Caribou House Incident: Sexual Harassment of UBC Women. *Canadian Woman Studies* 12, 1: 58–59.

hooks, b. 1992. Feminism: A Transformational Politic. In *Race, Class and Gender in the United States: An Integrated Study*, edited by P.S. Rothenberg. New York: St. Martin's.

Hopper, J. 1993. The Rhetoric of Motives in Divorce. *Journal of Marriage and the Family* 55: 801–813.

Hornacek, P.C. 1977. Anti-sexist Consciousness-raising Groups for Men. In *A Book of Readings for Men Against Sexism*, edited by J. Snodgrass, 123–29. Albion, CA: Times Change Press.

Horney, K. 1967. *Feminine Psychology*. New York: W.W. Norton.

Howe, H., J. Lyne, A. Gross, H. VanLente, A. Rip, R. Lewontin, D. McShea, G. Myers, U. Segerstrale, H.W. Simons, and V.B. Smocovitis. 1992. Gene Talk in Sociobiology. *Social Epistemology* 6, 2: 109–163.

Howe, N. and W.M. Bukowski. 1996. What Are Children and How Do They Become Adults: Child-Rearing and Socialization. In *Families: Changing Trends in Canada*, edited by M. Baker, 3rd. ed., 174–194. Toronto: McGraw-Hill Ryerson.

Hubbard, R. 1994. Race and Sex as Biological Categories. In *Challenging Racism and Sexism: Alternatives to Genetic Explanations*, edited by E. Tobach and B. Rosoff. New York: Feminist Press at City University of New York.

———. 1990. *The Politics of Women's Biology*. New Brunswick, NJ: Rutgers University Press.

Hughes, F.P. 1991. *Children, Play, and Development*. Boston: Allyn & Bacon.

Hughes, L.A. 1988. But That's Not Really Mean: Competing in a Cooperative Mode. *Sex Roles* 19: 669–687.

Hunt, B. and M. Hunt. 1975. *Prime Time: A Guide to the Pleasures and Opportunities of the New Middle Age.* New York: Stein and Day.

Hunt, T. and B.D., Ruben. 1993. *Mass Communication Producers and Consumers*. New York: Harper Collins Publishing.

Hurst, C.E. 1992. *Social Inequality Forms, Causes and Consequences*. Boston: Allyn and Bacon.

Huston, A.C. 1983. Sex Typing. In *Handbook of Child Psychology,* edited by P.H. Mussen and E.M. Hetherington, Vol. 4, 387–468. New York: Wiley.

Huston, T.L., C.A. Surra, N.M. Fitzgerald, and R.M. Cate. 1981. From Courtship to Marriage: Mate Selection as an Interpersonal Process. In *Personal Relationships: Developing Personal Relationships*, edited by S. Duck and R. Gilmour, Vol. 2, 53–88. New York: Academic Press.

Hutchinson, M. 1985. *Transforming Body Image*. New York: McGraw-Hill Book Company.

Hyde, J.S. 1995. *Understanding Human Sexuality,* 5th ed. New York: McGraw-Hill.

———. 1985. *Half the Human Experience,* 2nd ed. Toronto: D. C. Heath.

———. 1981. How Large are Cognitive Gender Differences? A Meta-analysis Using w^2 and d. *American Psychologist* 36: 892–901.

Hyde, J.S. and M.C. Linn. 1988. Gender Differences in Verbal Ability: A Meta-Analysis. *Psychological Bulletin* 104: 53–69.

Hyde, J.S., M. Krajnik, and K.S. Kuldt-Niederberger. 1991. Androgyny Across the Life Span: A Replication and Longitudinal Follow-up. *Developmental Psychology* 27: 516–519.

Ice-T and H. Siegmund. 1994. *The Ice Opinion: Who Gives a Fuck?* New York: St. Martin's Press.

Idle, T., E. Wood, and S. Desmarais. 1993. Gender Role Socialization in Toy Play Situations: Mothers and Fathers with Their Sons and Daughters. *Sex Roles* 28 June: 679–692.

Imperato-McGinley, J. and R. Peterson. 1976. Male Pseudohermaphrodites: The Complexities of the Phenotypic Development. *American Journal of Medicine* 61: 251–272.

Inglis, J. and J. Lawson. 1981. Sex Differences in the Effects of Unilateral Brain Damage on Intelligence. *Science* 212: 693–695.

Intons-Peterson, M.J. 1988. *Children's Concepts of Gender*. Norwood, NJ: Ablex.

———. 1985. Father's Expectations and Aspirations for their Children. *Sex Roles* 12, 7–8: 877–895.

Intons-Peterson, M.J. and J. Crawford. 1985. The Meanings of Marital Surnames. *Sex Roles* 12: 1163–1171.

Ireson, C.J. 1984 Adolescent Pregnancy and Sex Roles. *Sex Roles* 11: 189–201.

Ishwaren, K. (ed.). 1979. *Childhood and Adolescence in Canada*. Toronto: McGraw-Hill Ryerson.

Jacklin, C.N. 1985. *Stalking the Development of Sex Differences*. Invited address to the Canadian Psychological Association, April, Halifax, Nova Scotia.

Jackson, L.A., N. Ialongo, and G. Stollak. 1986. Parental Correlates of Gender Role: The Relations between Parents' Masculinity, Femininity and Child-Rearing Behaviors and Their Children's Gender Roles. *Journal of Social and Clinical Psychology* 4, 2: 204–222.

Jackson, S. and S. Scott. 1996. Sexual Skimishes and Feminist Factions: Twenty-Five Years of Debate on Women and Sexuality. In *Feminism and Sexuality: A Reader*, edited by S. Jackson and S. Scott, 1–31. New York: Columbia University Press.

Jacobs, S.E. 1983. Reply. *Current Anthropologist* 24, 4: 459–460.

———. 1968. Berdache: A Brief Review of the Literature. *Colorado Anthropologist* 1: 25–40.

Jacobson, M.B. and W. Insko. 1985. Use of Nonsexist Pronouns as a Function of One's Feminist Orientation. *Sex Roles* 13, 11/12, December: 1–7.

Jaggar, A.M. and P.S. Rothenberg. 1984. *Feminist Frameworks,* 2nd ed. New York: McGraw-Hill.

———. (eds.) 1993. *Feminist Frameworks,* 3rd ed. New York: McGraw-Hill.

Jamieson, K.H. 1995. *Beyond the Double Bind: Women and Leadership*. New York: Oxford University Press.

Jardin, A. 1978. *The First Henry Ford: A Study in Personality and Business Leadership*. Cambridge, MA: MIT Press.

Jensen, M.A. 1984. *Love's Sweet Return: The Harlequin Story*. Toronto: Women's Educational Press.

Joesch, J.M. 1997. Paid Leave and the Timing of Women's Employment Before and After Birth. *Journal of Marriage and the Family* 59: 1008–1021.

Johnson, D. 1996. What Do Women Want? *New York Review of Books,* November: 22, 24–26, 28.

Johnson, E.M. and T.L. Huston. 1998. The Perils of Love, or Why Wives Adapt to Husbands During the Transition to Parenthood. *Journal of Marriage and the Family* 60: 195–204.

Johnson, G.D., G.J. Palileo, and N.B. Gray. 1992. Date Rape on a Southern Campus: Reports from 1991. *Sociology and Social Research* 762: 37–41.

Johnson, H. 1996. *Dangerous Domains: Violence Against Women in Canada*. Scarborough, ON: Nelson Canada.

Johnson, M., T. Huston, S. Gaines, and C. Levinge. 1992. Patterns of Married Life among Young Couples. *Journal of Social and Personal Relationships* 9: 343–364.

Johnson, P. 1976. Women and Interpersonal Power: Toward a Theory of Effectiveness. *The Journal of Social Issues* 32: 99–110.

Johnson, R.A. 1989. *He: Understanding Masculine Psychology,* rev. ed. New York: Harper & Row.

Johnson, R. and E. Aries. 1983. The Talk of Women Friends. *Women's Studies International Forum* 6: 353–361.

Johnson, R.A. and G.I. Schulman. 1989. Gender Role Composition and Role Entrapment in Decision-making Groups. *Gender & Society* 3: 355–372.

Jones, C., L. Marsden, and L. Tepperman. 1990. *Lives of Their Own*. Toronto: Oxford University Press.

Jones, L.Y. 1980. *Great Expectations: America and the Baby Boom Generation*. New York: Ballantine.

Jordan, E. and A. Cowan. 1995. Warrior Narratives in the Kindergarten Classroom: Renegotiating the Social Contract? *Gender & Society* 9, 6: 727–743.

Jouard, S.M. 1968. *Disclosing Man to Himself*. New York: Van Nostrand Reinhold.

———. 1971. *Self Disclosure: An Experimental Analysis of the Transparent Self*. New York: Wiley-Interscience.

Jump, T.L. and L. Haas. 1987. Fathers in Transition: Dual-career Fathers Participating in Child Care. In *Changing Men: New Directions in Research on Men and Masculinity*, edited by M.S. Kimmel, 98–114. Newbury Park, CA: Sage.

Jung, C.G. 1968. *The Archetypes and the Collective Unconscious*. Bollingen Series 10, 2nd ed. Princeton: Princeton University Press

———. 1933. *Modern Man in Search of a Soul*. New York: Harcourt, Brace, and World.

Kahan, N. and N. Norris. 1994. Creating Gender Expectations Through Children's Advertising. In *Images of the Child*, edited by H. Eiss. Bowling Green, OH: Bowling Green State University Press.

Kalbach, W.E. and W.W. McVey. 1979. *The Demographic Bases of Canadian Society,* 2nd ed. Toronto: McGraw-Hill Ryerson.

Kallen, E. 1982. Multiculturalism: Ideology, Policy and Reality. *Journal of Canadian Studies* 17, 1: 51–63.

Kalmijn, M. 1991. Shifting Boundaries: Trends in Religious and Educational Homogamy. *American Sociological Review* 58, December: 786–800.

Kamen, P. 1991. *Feminist Fatale: Voices from the Twentysomething Generation Explore the Future of the Women's Movement*. New York: Donald I. Fine.

Kamin, L.J. 1985. Genes and Behavior: The Missing Link. *Psychology Today* 19, 10: 76–78.

———. 1975. *The Science and Politics of I.Q.* Hillsdale, NJ: Erlbaum.

Kaminer, Wendy. 1992. *I'm Dysfunctional, You're Dysfunctional*. Reading, MA: Addison- Wesley.

———. 1990. *A Fearful Freedom: Women's Flight from Equality*. Reading, MA: Addison- Wesley.

Kamo, Y. 1988. Determinants of Household Division of Labor. *Journal of Family Issues* 9: 177–200.

Kanin, E.J., K.R. Davidson, and S.R. Scheck. 1970. A Research Note on Male-Female Differentials in the Experience of Heterosexual Love. *The Journal of Sex Research* 6: 64–72.

Kanter, R.M. 1976. *Men and Women of the Corporation*. New York: Basic Books.

Kantrowitz, B. 1994. Men, Women & Computers. *Newsweek*. May 16: 48–55.

Kaplan, H.S. 1974. *The New Sex Therapy*. New York: Brunner/Mazel.

Kaplan, J. and A. Bernays. 1997. *The Language of Names*. New York: Simon & Schuster.

Kaplan, L.J. 1991. *Female Perversions*. New York: Anchor Books.

Karraker, K.H., D.A. Vogel, and S. Evans. 1987. Responses of Students and Pregnant Women to Newborn Physical Attractiveness. Paper presented at the August meetings of the American Psychological Association, New York.

Karraker, K.H. and M. Stern. 1990. Infant Physical Attractiveness and Facial Expression: Effects of Adult Perceptions. *Basic and Applied Social Psychology* 11, 4: 371–385.

Kasian, M., N.P. Spanos, C.A. Terrance, and S. Peebles. 1993. Battered Women Who Kill. *Law and Human Behavior* 17: 289–312.

Katz, J.N. 1995. *The Invention of Heterosexuality*. New York: Dutton.

Kaufman, M. 1993. *Cracking the Armour: Power, Pain and the Lives of Men*. Toronto: Penguin.

————. (ed.). 1987a. *Beyond Patriarchy*. Toronto: Oxford University Press.

————. (ed.).1987b. Masculinity, Sexuality, and Society. In *Beyond Patriarchy*, 1–29. Toronto: Oxford University Press.

Keating, N.D. and P. Cole. 1980. What Do I Do With Him 24 Hours a Day? Changes in the Housewife Role After Retirement. *The Gerontologist* 20, 1: 84–89.

Keen, S. 1991. *Fire in the Belly: On Being A Man*. New York: Bantam.

Kelley, J.B. 1982. Divorce: The Adult Perspective. In *Family in Transition,* edited by A.S. Skolnick and H.J. Skolnick, 4th ed., 304–337. Boston: Little, Brown.

Kelley, K. 1994. A Modern Cinderella. *Journal of American Culture* 171: 87–92.

Kelley, K. and B. Rolker-Dolinsky. 1987. The Psychosexuality of Female Initiation and Dominance. In *Intimate Relationships: Development, Dynamics and Deterioration*, edited by D. Perlman and S. Duck, 63–87. Newbury Park, CA: Sage.

Kelly, A. (ed.). 1981. *The Missing Half: Girls and Science Education*. Manchester: Manchester University Press.

Kelly, K. L. Howatson-Leo, and W. Clark. 1997. I Feel Overqualified for my Job… *Canadian Social Trends* 47, Winter: 11–16.

Kelly, L. 1988. *Surviving Sexual Violence*. Minneapolis: University of Minnesota Press.

Kendall, K. 1992. Sexual Difference and the Law: Premenstrual Syndrome as Legal Defense. In *Anatomy of Gender: Women's Struggle for the Body*, edited by D.H. Currie and V. Raoul, 130–146. Ottawa: Carleton University Press.

Kephart, W.M. 1966. *The Family, Society and the Individual,* 2nd ed. Boston: Houghton Mifflin.

Kerig, P., P. Cowan, and C. Cowan. 1993. Marital Quality and Gender Differences in Parent-Child Interaction. *Developmental Psychology* 29: 931–939.

Kessler, S.J. 1990/1995. The Medical Construction of Gender: Case Management of Intersexed Infants. *Signs* 16, 2, 1990: 3–26. Reprinted in *Gender in the 1990s: Images, Realities, and Issues*, edited by E.D. Nelson and B.W. Robinson, 8–28. Toronto: Nelson Canada.

Kessler, S.J. and W. McKenna. 1978. *Gender: An Ethnomethodological Approach*. New York: John Wiley and Sons.

Kettle, J. 1980. *The Big Generation*. Toronto: McClelland and Stewart.

Ketts, J.F. 1977. *Rites of Passage: Adolescence in America 1790 to the Present*. New York: Basic Books.

Khosroshahi, F. 1989. Penguins Don't Care, but Women Do: A Social Identity Analysis of a Whorfian Problem. *Language in Society* 18: 505.

Kilbourne, J. 1992. Beauty and the Beast of Advertising. In *Race, Class, & Gender In the United States: An Integrated Study*, edited by P.S. Rothenberg, 348–350. New York: St. Martin's Press.

Kimble, C.E. and J.I. Musgrove. 1988. Dominance in Arguing in Mixed-sex Dyads: Visual Dominance Patterns, Talking Time and Speech Loudness. *Journal of Research in Personality* 22: 1–16.

Kimmel, D.C. 1980. *Adulthood and Aging: an Interdisciplinary, Developmental View*, 3rd ed. New York: John Wiley and Sons.

————. 1974. *Adulthood and Aging: an Interdisciplinary, Developmental View*. New York: John Wiley and Sons.

King, M. J. Gartrell, and F. Travato. 1991. Early Childhood Mortality, 1926–1986. *Canadian Social Trends* 21 Summer: 6–10.

Kinsey, A., C. Pomeroy, and C. Martin. 1948. *Sexual Behavior in the Human Male*. Philadelphia: W.B. Saunders.

Kinsey, A., C. Pomeroy, W. Gebhard, and C. Martin. 1953. *Sexual Behavior in the Human Female*. Philadelphia: W.B. Saunders.

Kinsman, G. 1996. *The Regulation of Desire: Homo and Hetero Sexualities,* 2nd ed. Montreal: Black Rose.

———. 1987. Men Loving Men: The Challenge of Gay Liberation. In *Beyond Patriarchy,* edited by M. Kaufman, 103–119. Toronto: Oxford University Press.

Kirkland, G. with G. Lawrence. 1986. *Dancing on My Grave.* Garden City, NY: Doubleday.

Kirkwood, C. 1993. *Leaving Abusive Partners: From the Scars of Survival to the Wisdom for Change.* Newbury Park, CA: Sage.

Kitson, G.C. 1992. *Portrait of Divorce: Adjustment to Marital Breakdown.* New York: Guilford.

Kitzinger, S. 1985. *Women's Experience of Sex.* New York: Penguin.

Klapp, O.E. 1964. *Symbolic Leaders: Public Dramas and Public Men.* Chicago: Aldine.

Klein, M. 1957. *Envy and Gratitude.* London: Tavistock.

Klinetob, N.A. and D.A. Smith. 1996. Demand-Withdraw Communication in Marital Interaction: Tests of Interspousal Contingency and Gender Role Hypotheses. *Journal of Marriage and the Family* 58: 945–957.

Knox, D. 1970. Conceptions of Love at Three Developmental Levels. *Family Life Coordinator* 19: 151–157.

Knox, D. and C. Schacht. 1994. *Choices in Relationships: An Introduction to Marriage and the Family.* Minneapolis/St. Paul, MN: West.

Knox, D. and M.J. Sporakowski. 1968. Attitudes of College Students Toward Love. *Journal of Marriage and the Family* 30: 638–642.

Knudson-Martin, C. and A. Rankin Mahoney. 1998. Language and Processes in the Construction of Equality in New Marriages. *Family Relations* 47: 81–91.

Koedt, A. 1972. *Radical Feminism.* New York: Quadrangle.

Kohlberg, L. 1966. A Cognitive-Developmental Analysis of Children's Sex Role Concepts and Attitudes. In *The Development of Sex Differences*, edited by E. Maccoby, 82–172. Stanford, CA: Stanford University Press.

Kohn, M.L. 1977. *Class and Conformity: A Study in Values,* 2nd ed. Homewood, IL: Dorsey Press.

———. 1976. Occupational Structure and Alienation. *American Journal of Sociology* 82: 111–130.

———. 1963. Social Class and Parent-Child Relationships: An Interpretation. *American Journal of Sociology* 68: 471–480.

———. 1959. Social Class and Parental Values. *American Journal of Sociology* 64: 337–351.

Kohn, M.L. and C. Schooler. 1983. *Work and Personality: An Inquiry into the Impact of Social Stratification.* New York: Ablex Press.

———. 1969. Class, Occupation, and Orientation. *American Sociological Review* 34: 659–678.

Kohn, M.L., M. Kazimierz, M. Slomcznsky, and C. Schoenbach. 1986. Social Stratification and the Transmission of Values in the Family: A Cross-National Assessment. *Sociological Forum* 1, 1: 73–102.

Kolata, G. 1984. Equal Time For Women. *Discover*. January.

Kolbenschlag, M. 1979. *Kiss Sleeping Beauty Goodbye.* New York: Bantam.

Komarovsky, M. 1988. The New Feminist Scholarship: Some Precursors and Polemics. *Journal of Marriage and the Family* 50: 585–593.

Kompter, A. 1989. Hidden Power in Marriage. *Gender & Society* 3: 187–216.

Kong, R. 1997. Criminal Harassment in Canada. *Canadian Social Trends* 45, Autumn: 29–33.

Korsmeyer, C. 1981. The Hidden Joke: Generic Uses of Masculine Terminology. In *Feminism and Philosophy*, edited by M. Vetterling-Braggin, F.A. Elliston, and J. English, 138–153. Totawa, NJ: Rowan and Littlefield.

Koss, M.P., T.E. Dinero, C.A. Seibel, and S.L. Cox. 1988. Stranger and Acquaintance Rape: Are There Differences in the Victim's Experiences? *Psychology of Women Quarterly* 12: 1–24.

Koven, S. and S. Michel. 1990. Womanly Duties: Maternalist Politics and the Origins of Welfare States in France, Germany, Great Britain, and the United States, 1880–1920. *American Historical Review* 95, 4: 1076–1108.

Krahn, H.K. and G.S. Lowe. 1993. *Women, Industry and Canadian Society,* 2nd ed. Scarborough, ON: Nelson Canada.

Kramarae, C. 1981. *Women and Men Speaking*. Rowley, MA: Newbury.

———. 1980. Proprietors of Language. In *Women and Language in Literature and Society*, edited by S. McConnell-Ginet, R. Borker, and N. Furman, 58–68. New York: Praeger.

———. 1975. Women's Speech: Separate but Unequal? In *Language and Sex,* edited by B. Thorne and N. Henley, 43–56. Rowley, MA: Newbury House Publishers.

Kramarae, C., M. Schultz, and W.O'Barr (eds.). 1984. *Language and Power*. Beverly Hills, CA: Sage.

Kramarae, C. and H.J. Taylor. 1993. Women and Men on Electronic Networks: A Conversation or a Monologue? In *Women, Information Technology, and Scholarship*, edited by H.J. Taylor, C. Kramarae, and M. Ebben. Urbana-Champaign, IL: Center for Advanced Studies, University of Illinois.

Kreiger, S. 1982. Lesbian Identity and Community: Recent Social Science Research. *Signs* 8: 91–108.

Krull, C.D. 1996. From the King's Daughters to the Quiet Revolution: A Historical Overview of Family Structures and the Role of Women in Quebec. In *Voices: Essays on Canadian Families,* edited by M. Lynn, 370–396. Toronto: Nelson Canada.

Kurdek, L. 1993. The Allocation of Household Labor in Gay, Lesbian, and Heterosexual Married Couples. *Journal of Social Issues* 49, 3: 127–139.

———. 1993a. Nature and Prediction of Changes in Marital Quality for First-Time Parents and Nonparent Husbands and Wives. *Journal of Family Psychology* 6: 255–265.

La Novara, P. 1993. *A Portrait of Families in Canada*. Ottawa: Statistics Canada.

Lackey, P.N. 1989. Adults' Attitudes about Assignments of Household Chores to Male and Female Children. *Sex Roles* 20: 271–281.

Ladas, A.K., B. Whipple, and J.D. Perry. 1982. *The G Spot and Other Recent Discoveries About Human Sexuality*. New York: Holt, Rinehart and Winston.

Laframboise, D. 1996. *Princess at the Window*. Toronto: Penguin.

Laird, J. 1993. Lesbian and Gay Families. In *Normal Family Processes*, edited by F. Walsh, 2nd ed., 282–328. New York: Guilford.

Lakoff, R. 1975. *Language and Woman's Place*. New York: Harper Colophon.

Lamb, M.E. (ed.). 1987. *The Father's Role: Cross-Cultural Perspectives*. Hillsdale, NJ: Lawrence Erlbaum.

———. (ed.). 1986. The Changing Roles of Fathers. In *The Father's Role: Applied Perspectives*. New York: Wiley.

Lambert, R.D. 1971. *Sex Role Imagery in Children: Social Origins of Mind*. Royal Commission on the Status of Women in Canada. Study 6. Ottawa: Information Canada.

Landrine, H. 1985. Race x Class Stereotypes of Women. *Sex Roles* 13, 65–75.

Langlois, J.H., J.M. Ritter, L.A.V. Roggman, and S. Lesley. 1991. Facial Diversity and Infant Preferences for Attractive Faces. *Developmental Psychology* 27, 1: 79–84.

Langlois, J.H., L.A.V. Roggman, and L.A. Reiser-Danner. 1990. Infants' Differential Social Responses to Attractive and Unattractive Faces. *Developmental Psychology* 26: 153–159.

Langlois, J. and R. Casey. 1984. Baby Beautiful: The Relationship Between Infant Physical Attractiveness and Maternal Behavior. Paper presented at the fourth biennial International Conference on Infant Studies. New York.

Langlois, J.H. and S.C. White. 1981. Beauty and the Beast: The Role of Physical Attractiveness in the Development of Peer Relations and Social Behavior. In *Developmental Social Psychology: Theory and Research*, edited by S.S. Brehm. New York: Oxford University Press.

Langman, L. 1987. Social Stratification. In *Handbook of Marriage and the Family*, edited by M.B. Sussman and S.K. Steinmetz, 211–249. New York: Plenum.

Lanis, K. and K. Covell. 1995. Images of Women in Advertisements: Effects on Attitudes Related to Sexual Aggression. *Sex Roles* 22, 9–10: 639–649.

Lansky, L.M. 1967. The Family Structure Also Affects the Model. *Merrill-Palmer Quarterly* 13: 139–150.

Lapsley, D.K., R.D. Enright, and R.C. Serlin. 1985. Toward a Theoretical Perspective on the Legislation of Adolescence. *Journal of Early Adolescence* 5: 441–466.

Larken, J. 1993. *Sexual Harassment: High School Girls Speak Out*. Toronto: Second Story Press.

LaRossa, R. 1988/1995. Fatherhood and Social Change. *Family Relations* 37, October 1988: 451–457. Reprinted in *Gender in the 1990s: Images, Realities, and Issues*, edited by E.D. Nelson and B.W. Robinson, 365–379. Toronto: Nelson Canada.

LaRossa, R. and D.C. Reitzes. 1995. Gendered Perceptions of Father Involvement in Early 20th Century America. *Journal of Marriage and the Family* 57: 223–229.

Larson, L.E., J.W. Goltz, and C. Hobart. 1994. *Families in Canada: Social Context, Continuities and Changes*. Scarborough, ON: Prentice Hall Canada.

Larson, M.S. 1996. Sex Roles and Soap Operas: What Adolescents Learn About Single Motherhood. *Sex Roles* 35, 1/2: 97–110.

Larwood, L. and B.A. Gutek (eds.). 1987. Working Toward a Theory of Women's Career Development. In *Women's Career Development*, 170–183. Newbury Park, CA: Sage.

Lasch, C. 1977. *Haven in a Heartless World*. New York: Basic Books.

Lavoie, Y. and J. Oderkirk. 1993. Social Consequences of Demographic Change. *Canadian Social Trends* 31, Winter: 2–5.

Lawless, K. 1983. Confessions of a Copycat: The Economics of Originality in a Consumer Society. Paper presented at the New York State Sociological Association NYSSA Meetings, 1983.

Lawlor, J. 1994. Women Gain Power, Means to Abuse It. *USA Today*. January 17: 1A, 2A.

Lawrence, M. 1982. *Fed Up and Hungry*. London: The Woman's Press.

Laws, J.L. 1979. *The Second X: Sex Roles and Social Role*. New York: Elsevier.

Laws, J.L. and P. Schwartz. 1977. *Sexual Scripts: The Social Construction of Female Sexuality*. Hinsadle, IL: Drysden Press.

Lazier-Smith, L. 1989. A New Genderation of Images of Women. In *Women in Mass Communication*, edited by P.J. Creedon. Newbury Park, CA: Sage.

Le Boudrais, C. and N. Marcil-Gratton. 1996. Family Transformations across the Canadian-American Border: When the Laggard becomes the Leader. *Journal of Comparative Family Studies* 27, 2: 415–436.

Leaper, C. (ed.). 1994. Exploring the Consequences of Gender Segregation on Social Relationships. In *Childhood Gender Segregation: Causes and Consequences*. San Francisco: Jossey-Bass.

Leathers, D.G. 1986. *Successful Nonverbal Communication: Principles and Applications*. New York: Macmillan.

Lee, D. and J. Hertzberg. 1978. Theories of Feminine Personality. In *Women and Sex Roles: A Social Psychological Perspective*, edited by I.H. Frieze, J.E. Parsons, P.B. Johnson, D.N. Ruble, and G.L. Zellman, 28–44. New York: W.W. Norton.

Leghorn, L. 1977. Social Responses to Battered Women. *Feminist Alliance Against Rape Newsletter*. March/April: 22.

Lehne, G. 1976. Homophobia Among Men. In *The Forty-Nine Percent Majority: The Male Sex Role*, edited by D. Brannon and R. Brannon, 66–88. Reading, MA: Addison-Wesley.

Leibowitz, A. and J.A. Klerman. 1995. Explaining Changes in Married Mothers' Employment over Time. *Demography* 32, 3: 365–378.

Lein, L. 1979. Male Participation in Home Life: Impact of Social Supports and Breadwinner Responsibility on the Allocation of Tasks. *The Family Coordinator* 28: 489–495.

Leinbach, M. and B. Hort. 1995. *Do Young Children Sex-type Emotions?* Poster presented at the biennial meeting of the Society for Research in Child Development, Indianapolis, Indiana. 30 March to 2 April.

Lerner, G. 1977. *The Female Experience: An American Documentary*. Indianapolis: Bobbs- Merrill.

Lero, D.S. 1996. Dual-Earner Families. In *Voices: Essays on Canadian Families*, edited by M. Lynn, 19–53. Toronto: Nelson Canada.

LeShan, E. 1976. Patterns of Personality Development in Middle-Aged Women: A Longitudinal Study. *International Journal of Aging and Human Development* 7, 2: 107–115.

———. 1974. *The Wonderful Crisis of Middle Age*. New York: Warner Books.

Lesko, N. 1988. The Curriculum of the Body: Lessons from a Catholic High School. In *Becoming Feminine: The Politics of Popular Culture*, edited by L. Roman, L.K. Christian-Smith, and E. Ellsworth, 123–142. London: Falmer Press.

Leslie, G.R. 1967. *The Family in Social Context*. New York: Oxford.

Lester, D., N. Brazill, C. Ellis, and T. Guerin. 1984. Correlates of Romantic Attitudes Toward Love: Androgyny and Self Disclosure. *Psychological Reports* 54 April: 554.

Lester, J. 1976. Being a Boy. In *The Forty-Nine Percent Majority: The Male Sex Role*, edited by D.S. David and R. Brannon, 270–273. Reading, MA: Addison-Wesley.

Levant, R.F. 1992. Toward the Reconstruction of Masculinity. *Journal of Family Psychology* 5: 379–402.

Lever, J. 1978. Sex Differences in the Complexity of Children's Play and Games. *American Sociological Review* 43: 471–483.

Levinson, D.J. 1996. *The Seasons of a Woman's Life*. New York: Alfred A. Knopf.

———. 1977. Periods in the Adult Development of Men: Ages 18 to 45. In *Beyond Sex Roles*, edited by A.G. Sargent, 279–291. St. Paul: West.

Levinson, D.J. et al. 1978 *The Seasons of a Man's Life*. New York: Alfred A. Knopf.

Levy, J. 1972. Lateral Specialization of the Human Brain: Behavioral Manifestations and Possible Evolutionary Basis. In *The Biology of Behavior*, edited by J.A. Kiger, 159–180. Corvallis: Oregon State University Press.

Levy, M.J. Jr. 1989. *Our Mother-Tempers*. Berkeley, CA: University of California Press.

Levy, G.D. 1989. Relations among Aspects of Children's Social Environments, Gender Schematization, Gender Role Knowledge and Flexibility. *Sex Roles* 21: 803–811.

Lewis, R.A. and G.B. Spanier. 1979. Theorizing About the Quality and Stability of Marriage. In *Contemporary Theories About the Family: Research-Based Theories*, edited by W.R. Burr, R. Hill, F.I. Nye, I.L. Reiss, Vol. 1., 268–294. New York: Free Press.

Lewis, M. 1972. State as an Infant-Environment Interaction. *Merrill-Palmer Quarterly* 18: 95–121.

Light, B. and A. Prentice. 1980. *Pioneer and Gentlewomen of British North America, 1713–1867*. Toronto: New Hogtown Press.

Lind, E.A. and W.O'Barr. 1979. The Social Significance of Speech in the Courtroom. In *Language and Social Psychology*, edited by H. Giles and R. St. Clair. Oxford: Blackwell.

Lindberg, L.D. 1996. Women's Decisions About Breastfeeding and Maternal Employment. *Journal of Marriage and the Family* 58: 239–251.

Linden, R. 1983. Women in Policing: A Study of Lower Mainland R.C.M.P. Detachments. *Canadian Police College Journal* 7: 217–229.

———. 1980. *Women in Policing: A Study of the Vancouver Police Department*. Ottawa: Solicitor General of Canada.

Linden, R. and C. Minch. 1982. *Women in Policing: A Review*. Ottawa: Solicitor General of Canada.

Lindesmith, A.R. and A.L. Strauss. 1968. *Social Psychology,* 3rd ed. New York: Holt, Rinehart and Winston.

Lindsey, L.L. 1997. *Gender Roles: A Sociological Perspective,* 3rd ed. Englewood Cliffs, NJ: Prentice Hall.

———. 1996. Gender Equity and Development: A Perspective on the U.N. Conference on Women. Paper presented at the Midwest Sociological Society, Chicago.

———. 1994. *Gender Roles: A Sociological Perspective,* 2nd ed. Englewood Cliffs, NJ: Prentice Hall.

Linton, R. 1945. *The Cultural Background of Personality*. New York: Appleton-Century-Crofts.

Lipman-Blumen, J. 1984. *Gender Roles and Power*. Englewood Cliffs, NJ: Prentice-Hall.

————. 1976. A Homosocial Theory of Sex Roles: An Examination of the Sex Segregation of Social Institutions. In *Women and the Workplace*, edited by M. Blaxall and B. Reagan. Reading, MA: Addison-Wesley.

Lips, H.M. 1995. Gender-role Socialization: Lessons in Femininity. In *Women: A Feminist Perspective*, edited by J. Freeman. Mountain View, CA: Mayfield.

————. 1993. *Sex & Gender: An Introduction*, 2nd ed. Mountain View, CA: Mayfield.

Livingstone, D.W. and M. Luxton. 1989/1995. Gender Consciousness at Work: Modifications of the Male Breadwinner Norm Among Steelworkers and Their Spouses. *Canadian Review of Sociology and Anthropology* 26: 240–275. Reprinted in *Gender in the 1990s: Images, Realities, and Issues*, edited by E.D. Nelson and B.W. Robinson, 172–200. Toronto: Nelson Canada.

Livson, F.B. 1981. Paths to Psychological Health in the Middle Years: Sex Differences. In *Present and Past in Middle Age*, edited by D.H. Eichorn, J.A. Clausen, N. Haan, M.P. Honzik, and P.H. Mussen, 195–221. New York: Academic Press.

————. 1976. Patterns of Personality Development in Middle-Aged Women: A Longitudinal Study. *International Journal of Aging and Human Development* 7, 2: 107–115.

Lloyd, S.A. 1991. The Darkside of Courtship: Violence and Sexual Exploitation. *Family Relations.* 40: 14–20.

Lobel, K. (ed.). 1986. *Naming the Violence*. Seattle: Seal Press.

Loeber, R. and D. Hay. 1997. Key Issues in the Development of Aggression and Violence from Childhood to Early Adulthood. *Annual Review of Psychology* 48: 371–410.

Logan, R. and J. Belliveau. 1995. Working Mothers. *Canadian Social Trends* 36, Spring: 24–28.

Lohyn, M. 1994. Naomi Wolf and the New Feminism: Women's Power Revisited. *Australian and New Zealand Journal of Family Therapy* 15, 3 September: 143–149.

Lombardo, W.K., G.A. Cretser, B. Lombardo, and S.L. Mathias. 1983. For Cryin' Out Loud—There is a Sex Difference. *Sex Roles* 9: 987–995.

Lombroso, C. and E. Ferrero, 1895. *The Female Offender*. New York: D. Appleton.

Long, J. and K.L. Porter. 1984. Multiple Roles of Midlife Women: A Case for New Directions in Theory, Research and Policy. In *Women in Midlife*, edited by G. Baruch and J. Brooks- Gunn. New York: Plenum.

Lont, C.M. 1997. Women's Music: No Longer A Small Private Party. In *Feminist Frontiers IV*, edited by L. Richardson, V. Taylor, and N. Whittier, 126–134. New York: McGraw-Hill.

Looft, W.B. 1973. Socialization and Personality Throughout the Life Span: An Examination of Contemporary Psychological Approaches. In *Life-Span Developmental Psychology: Personality and Socialization*, edited by P.B. Baltes and K.W. Schaie, 25–52. New York: Academic Press.

Lopata, H. and B. Thorne. 1978. On the Term 'Sex Roles'. *Signs* 3: 718–721.

Lorber, J.A. 1991. Dismantling Noah's Ark. In *The Social Construction of Gender*, edited by J.A. Lorber and S.A. Farrell, 355–369. Newbury Park, CA: Sage.

Lorber, J.A. and S.A. Farrell (eds.). 1991. *The Social Construction of Gender*. Newbury Park, CA: Sage.

Lorde, A. 1992. Age, Race, Class and Sex: Women Redefining Difference. In *Race, Class, and Gender in the United States: An Integrated Study*, edited by P.S. Rothenberg. New York: St. Martin's.

————. 1984. *Sister Outsider: Essays and Speeches*. New York: Crossing Press.

————. 1983. The Master's Tools Will Never Dismantle the Master's House. In *This Bridge Called My Back: Writings of Radical Women of Color*, edited by C. Moraga and G. Anzaldna, 98–101. New York: Kitchen Table, Women of Color Press.

————. 1978. *Uses of the Erotic: The Erotic as Power*. Brooklyn, New York: Out and Out Book.

Losh-Hesselbart, S. 1987. Development of Gender Roles. In *Handbook of Marriage and the Family*, edited by M.B. Susman and S.K. Steinmetz, 535–563. New York: Plenum.

Lott, B. 1994. *Women's Lives: Themes and Variations in Gender Learning*, 2nd ed. Pacific Grove, CA: Brooks/Cole.

————. 1989. Sex Discrimination as Distancing Behavior, II: Primetime Television. *Psychology of Women Quarterly* 13, 3: 341–355.

Lott, B. and D. Maluso. 1993. The Social Learning of Gender. In *The Psychology of Gender*, edited by A.E. Beall and R.J. Sternberg. New York: Guilford.

Lovdal, L. 1989. Sex Role Messages in Television Commericals: An Update. *Sex Roles* 21, 11/12: 715–727.

Lowe, G.S. 1995. Work. In *New Society: Brief Edition*, edited by R.J. Brym, 10.1–10.25. Toronto: Harcourt Brace & Company.

————. 1992. Canadians and Retirement. *Canadian Social Trends*, 26, Autumn: 18–21.

Lowe, N.V. 1982. The Legal Status of Fathers: Past and Present. In *The Father Figure*, edited by L. McKee and M. O'Brien, 26–42. London: Tavistock.

Lowenthal, M.F., M. Thurnher, and D. Chiriboga. 1975. *Four Stages of Life*. San Francisco: Jossey-Bass.

Lucas, S., J.V. Persad, G. Morton, S. Albuquerque, and N. El Yassir. 1991/1995. Changing the Politics of the Women's Movement. *Resources for Feminist Research RFR/DRF*, 20 1/2: 3–4. Reprinted in *Gender in the 1990s: Images, Realities, and Issues*, edited by E.D. Nelson and B.W. Robinson, 534–536. Toronto: Nelson Canada.

Luebke, B.F. 1989. Out of Focus: Images of Women and Men in Newspaper Photographs. *Sex Roles* 20, 3: 121–129.

Luker, K. 1984. *Abortion and the Politics of Motherhood*. Berkeley: University of California Press.

Lund, D.A. 1989. *Older Bereaved Spouses: Research with Practical Application*. New York: Hemisphere Publications.

Lund, D.A., M.S. Caserta, and M.F. Dimond. 1986. Gender Differences Through Two Years of Bereavement Among the Elderly. *The Gerontologist* 26, 3: 314–320.

Lundberg, O. 1991. Causal Explanations for Class Inequality in Health—An Empirical Analysis. *Social Science and Medicine* 32, 4: 385–393.

Lupri, E. and J. Frideres. 1981. The Quality of Marriage and the Passage of Time: Marital Satisfaction Over the Family Life Cycle. *Canadian Journal of Sociology* 6: 283–306.

Lutwin, D.R. and G.N. Siperstein. 1985. Househusband Fathers. In *Dimensions of Fatherhood*, edited by S.M.H. Hanson and F.W. Bozett. Beverely Hills, CA: Sage.

Luxton, M. 1983/1995. Two Hands for the Clock: Changing Patterns in the Gendered Division of Labour in the Home. *Studies in Political Economy* 12, Fall: 27–44. Reprinted in *Gender in the 1990s: Images, Realities, and Issues*, edited by E.D. Nelson and B.W. Robinson, 288–301. Toronto: Nelson Canada.

————. 1980. *More Than A Labour of Love: Three Generations of Women's Work in the Home*. Toronto: Women's Press.

Lynn, D.B. 1976. Fathers and Sex-Role Development. *The Family Coordinator* 25: 403–428.

————. 1974. *The Father: His Role in Child Development*. Monterey, CA: Brooks/Cole.

————. 1969. *Parental and Sex Role Identification: A Theoretical Formulation*. Berkeley, CA: McCutchan.

————. 1959. A Note on Sex Differences in the Development of Masculine and Feminine Identification. *Psychological Review* 66: 126–135.

Lynn, M. and M. Todoroff. 1995. Women's Work and Family Lives. In *Feminist Issues: Race, Class, and Sexuality*, edited by N. Mandell, 244–271. Scarborough, ON: Prentice Hall Canada.

Lytton, H. and D. Romney. 1991. Parents' Differential Socialization of Boys and Girls: A Meta-analysis. *Psychological Bulletin* 109: 267–296.

MacAuley, D., L.C. Chesley, and J.L. Ristock. 1989. Coming Out About Violence. *Broadside* 10, 5: 14.

Maccoby, E.E. 1994. Commentary: Gender Segregation in Childhood. In *Childhood Gender Segregation: Causes and Consequences*, edited by C. Leaper. San Francisco: Jossey- Bass.

Maccoby, E.E. and C.N. Jacklin. 1987. Gender Segregation in Childhood. In *Advances in Child Development*, edited by E.H. Reese, 239–287. New York: Academic Press.

————. 1974. *The Psychology of Sex Differences*. Stanford, CA: Stanford University Press.

MacDonald, K. and R.D. Parke. 1986. Parent-Child Physical Play: The Effects of Sex and Age on Children and Parents. *Sex Roles* 15: 367–378.

MacGregor, R. 1995. *The Home Team: Fathers, Sons & Hockey*. Toronto: Viking.

Machung, A. 1989. Talking Career, Thinking Jobs: Gender Differences in Career and Family Expectations of Berkeley Seniors. *Feminist Studies* 15: 35–58.

Mackie, M. 1995. Gender in the Family: Changing Patterns. *In Canadian Families: Diversity, Conflict and Change*, edited by N. Mandell and A. Duffy, 45–76. Toronto: Harcourt Brace Canada.

———. 1991. *Gender Relations in Canada: Further Explorations*. Toronto: Butterworths.

———. 1987. *Constructing Women and Men: Gender Socialization*. Toronto: Holt, Rinehart and Winston of Canada.

MacKinnon, C.A. 1987. *Feminism Unmodified: Discourses on Life and Law*. Cambridge, MA: Harvard University Press.

———. 1982. Feminism, Marxism, Method, and the State: An Agenda for Theory. *Signs* 7, Spring: 515–544.

———. 1979. *Sexual Harassment of Working Women*. New Haven: Yale University Press.

Macklin, A. 1992. Symes v. M.N.R.: Where Sex Meets Class. *Canadian Journal of Women and the Law* 5: 498.

MacLeod, L. 1987. *Battered But Not Beaten...Wife Battering in Canada*. Ottawa: Canadian Advisory Council on the Status of Women.

Maglin, N.B. and D. Perry (eds.). 1996. *Bad Girls/Good Girls: Women, Sex, and Power in the Nineties*. Rutgers University Press.

Maier, K.E. 1992. Assessing Reproductive Wrongs. In *Anatomy of Gender: Women's Struggle for the Body*, edited by D.H. Currie and V. Raoul, 147–160. Ottawa: Carleton University Press.

Makepeace, J.M. 1986. Gender Differences in Courtship Victimization. *Family Relations* 35: 383–388.

———. 1981. Courtship Violence Among College Students. *Family Relations* 30: 97–102.

Malatesta, C. and J. Haviland. 1982. Learning Display Rules: The Socialization of Emotion Expression in Infancy. *Child Development* 53: 991–1003.

Mandell, N. 1989. Marital Roles in Transition. In *Family and Marriage: Cross-Cultural Perspectives*, edited by K. Ishwaran, 239–252. Toronto: Wall and Thompson.

——— (ed.). 1995. Introduction to *Feminist Issues: Race, Class and Sexuality*, vii–xxi. Scarborough: Prentice Hall Canada.

Mann, P.S. 1995. Cyborgean Motherhood and Abortion. In *Provoking Agents: Gender and Agency in Theory and Practice*, edited by J.K. Gardiner, 133–151. Chicago: University of Chicago Press.

Mannheim, K. 1940. *Diagnoses of Our Time: Wartime Essays of a Sociologist*. Oxford, UK: Oxford University Press.

Mansbridge, J.J. 1993. The Role of Discourse in the Feminist Movement. Paper presented at the annual meeting of the American Political Science Association, Washington, D.C.

———. 1986. *Why We Lost the ERA*. Chicago: University of Chicago Press.

Manski, C.E. 1992/1993. Incomes and Higher Education. *Focus* 14, 3: 14–19.

Maracle, L. 1996. *I Am Woman: A Native Perspective on Sociology and Feminism*. Vancouver: Press Gang Publishers.

Marchildon, R.G. 1991. The 'Persons' Controversy: The Legal Aspects of the Fight for Women Senators. *Atlantis* 6: 99–113.

Marcus, D. and W. Overton. 1978. The Development of Cognitive Gender Constancy and Sex Preferences. *Child Development* 49: 434–444.

Margolis, M. 1984. *Mothers and Such: Views of American Women and Why They Changed*. Berkeley: University of California Press.

Marie, S. 1984. Lesbian Battering: An Inside View. *Victimology: An International Journal* 9, 1: 16–20.

Marin, P. 1991/1995. The Prejudice Against Women. *The Nation*. 8 July. Reprinted in *Gender in the 1990s: Images, Realities, and Issues*, edited by E.D. Nelson and B.W. Robinson, 490–498. Scarborough: Nelson Canada.

Marks, S.R. and S.M. MacDermid. 1996. Multiple Roles and the Self: A Theory of Role Balance. *Journal of Marriage and the Family* 58: 417–432.

Markus, H., M. Crane, S. Bernstein, and M. Siladi. 1982. Self Schemas and Gender. *Journal of Personality and Social Psychology* 42: 38–50.

Marsden, L.R. and E.B. Harvey. 1979. *Fragile Federation: Social Change in Canada*. Toronto: McGraw-Hill Ryerson.

Marshall, K. 1993/1995. Dual Earners: Who's Responsible for Housework? *Canadian Social Trends*. Cat. 11–008E. Spring/Winter: 11–14. Reprinted in *Gender in the 1990s: Images, Realities, and Issues*, edited by E.D. Nelson and B.W. Robinson, 302–310. Toronto: Nelson Canada.

———. 1987. Women in Male-Dominated Professions. *Canadian Social Trends* Winter: 7–11.

Marshall, S.E. 1984/1987. Keep Us on the Pedestal: Women Against Feminism in Twentieth-Century America. In *Women: A Feminist Perspective*, edited by J. Freeman, 3rd ed., 568–581. Palo Alto, CA: Mayfield. Reprinted in *Gender Roles: Doing What Comes Naturally?* edited by E.D. Salamon and B.W. Robinson, 347–355. Toronto: Methuen.

Marston, W.M. 1943. Why 100,000,000 Americans Read Comics. *The American Scholar* Winter.

Martel, A. and L. Peterat. 1984. Naming The World: Consciousness in a Patriarchal Iceberg. In *Taking Sex Into Account: The Policy Consequences of Sexist Research*, edited by J. McCalla Vickers, 43–56. Ottawa: Carleton University Press.

Martel, R.E. 1996. What Mediates Gender Bias in Work Behavior Ratings? *Sex Roles* 35, 3/4: 153–169.

Martin, Carol L. 1990. Attitudes and Expectations about Children with Nontraditional and Traditional Gender Roles. *Sex Roles* 22: 151–165.

———. 1989. Children's Use of Gender-related Information in Making Social Judgements. *Developmental Psychology* 25: 80–88.

———. 1981. A Schematic Processing Model of Sex Typing and Stereotyping in Children. *Child Development* 52: 1119–1134.

Martin, C.L. and C.F. Halverson. 1983. The Effects of Sex-Typing Schemas on Young Children's Memory. *Child Development* 54: 563–574.

Martin, C.L and J.K. Little. 1990. The Relation of Gender Understanding to Children's Sex-typed Preferences and Gender Stereotypes. *Child Development* 61: 1427–1439.

Martin, D. 1976. *Battered Wives*. New York: Pocket Books.

Martin, D.R. 1996. The Music of Murder. In *Taking Sides: Clashing Views on Controversial Issues in Crime and Criminology*, edited by R.C. Monk, 4th ed., 34–38. Guilford, CT: Dushkin/Brown & Benchmark.

Martin, E. 1987. *The Woman in the Body: A Cultural Analysis of Reproduction*. Boston: Beacon Press.

Martin, S.E. 1984. Sexual Harassment: The Link between Gender Stratification, Sexuality, and Women's Economic Status. In *Women: A Feminist Perspective*, edited by J. Freeman, 3rd ed., 54–69. Palo Alto, CA: Mayfield.

Martin Matthews, A. 1991. *Widowhood*. Toronto: Butterworths.

———. 1987. Widowhood as an Expectable Life Event. In *Aging in Canada: Social Perspectives*, edited by V. Marshall, 2nd ed., 343–355. Markham, ON: Fitzhenry and Whiteside.

Martin Matthews, A., K.H. Brown, C.K. Davis, and M.A. Denton. 1982. A Crisis Assessment Technique for the Evaluation of Life Events: Transition to Retirement as an Example. *Canadian Journal on Aging* 1: 28–39.

Martindale, K. 1995. What Makes Lesbianism Thinkable? Theorizing Lesbianism From Adrienne Rich to Queer Theory. In *Feminist Issues: Race, Class, and Sexuality*, edited by N. Mandell, 67–94. Scarborough, ON: Prentice Hall Canda.

Martyna, W. 1980. The Psychology of the Generic Masculine. In *Women and Language in Literature and Society*, edited by S. McConnell-Ginet, R. Borker, and N. Furman. New York: Praeger.

———. 1980b. Beyond the 'He/Man' Approach: The Case for Nonsexist Language. *Signs* 5, 3, Spring: 482–493.

Marx, K. 1848/1964. *Selected Writings in Sociology and Social Philosophy*, edited by T.B. Bottomore and M. Rubel. Baltimore: Penguin.

———. 1867–1894/1967. *Das Capital*. New York: International.

Maslow, A.H. 1970. *Motivation and Personality*. New York: Harper & Row.

———. 1968. *Toward a Psychology of Being*, 2nd ed. New York: Van Nostrand Reinhold.

Masson, J.M. 1985. *The Assault on Truth*. New York: Penguin.

Masters, W.H. and V.E. Johnson. 1970. *Human Sexual Inadequacy*. Boston: Little, Brown.

Masters, W.H., V.E. Johnson, and R.C. Kolodny. 1994. *Heterosexuality*. New York: HarperPerennial.

———. 1992. *Human Sexuality*, 4th ed. New York: Harper Collins.

———. 1986. *Masters and Johnson on Sex and Human Loving*. Boston: Little, Brown.

———. 1985. *Human Sexuality*, 2nd ed. Boston: Little, Brown and Company.

———. 1966. *Human Sexual Response*. Boston: Little, Brown.

Matrix, C. (ed.). 1996. *Tales for the Clit*. Edinburgh: AK Press.

McAfee, K. and M. Wood. 1970. Bread and Roses. In *Voices From Women's Liberation*, edited by L.B. Tanner. New York: Signet.

McAninch, C.B., R. Milich, G.B. Crumbo, and M.N. Funtowicz. 1996. Children's Perception of Gender-Role-Congruent and -Incongruent Behavior in Peers: Fisher-Price Meets Price Waterhouse. *Sex Roles* 35, 9/10: 619–638.

McArthur, L.Z. and S.V. Eisnen. 1976. Achievements of Male and Female Storybook Characters as Determinants of Achieving Behavior by Boys and Girls. *Journal of Personality and Social Psychology* 33: 467–473.

McBean, J. 1987. The Myth of Maternal Preference in Child Custody Cases. In *Equality and Judicial Neutrality*, edited by S.L. Martin and K.E. Mahoney, 184–192. Toronto: Carswell.

McCann, W. 1995. Debate Rages Over Plan to Send 3-Year-Olds to School. *KW* (Ontario) *Record*. January 28: B10.

McClung, N.L. 1945. *The Stream Runs Fast: My Own Story*. Toronto: Thomas Allen.

McConnell-Ginet, S. 1989. The Sexual Reproduction of Meaning: A Discourse-based Theory. In *Language, Gender and Professional Writing: Theoretical Approaches and Guidelines for Nonsexist Usage*, edited by F.W. Frank and P.A. Treichler. New York: Modern Language Association of America.

McConnell-Ginet, S., S.R. Borker, and N. Ferman (eds.). 1980. *Women and Language in Literature and Society*. New York: Praeger.

McCormick, N.B. and C.J. Jesser. 1983. The Courtship Game: Power in the Sexual Encounter. In *Changing Boundaries: Gender Roles and Sexual Behavior*, edited by E.R. Algeier and N.B. McCormick, 64–86. Palo Alto, CA.: Mayfield.

McCrae, R. and P. Costa, Jr. 1990. *Personality in Adulthood*. New York: Guilford.

McDaniel, S. 1988a. Women's Roles, Reproduction and the New Reproductive Technologies: A New Stork Rising. In *Reconstructing the Canadian Family: Feminist Perspectives*, edited by N. Mandell and A. Duffy, 175–206. Toronto: Butterworths.

———. 1988b. Women's Roles and Reproduction: The Changing Picture in Canada in the 1980s. *Atlantis* 14, 1: 1–12.

McDaniel, S. and B. Agger. 1982. *Social Problems Through Conflict and Order*. Don Mills, ON: Addison Wesley.

McDaniel, S.A. and A.L. McKinnon. 1993. Gender Differences in Informal Support and Coping among Elders: Findings from Canada's 1985 and 1990 General Social Surveys. *Journal of Women and Aging* 5, 2: 79–98.

McDonald, K. and R.D. Parke. 1986. Parent-Child Physical Play: The Effects of Sex and Age on Children and Parents. *Sex Roles* 15: 367–378.

McDonald, M. 1997. My Wife Told Me To Go. *U.S. News & World Report.* October 6: 28.

McDonald, P.L. and R.A. Wanner. 1990. *Retirement in Canada.* Toronto: Butterworths.

McGlone, J. and A. Kertesz. 1973. Sex Differences in Cerebral Processing of Visual-spatial Tasks. *Cortex* 9: 313–320.

McIntyre, S. 1995. Gender Bias within the Law School: The 'Memo' and Its Impact. In *Breaking Anonymity: The Chilly Climate for Women Faculty*, edited by The Chilly Collective, 211–264. Waterloo: Wilfred Laurier University Press.

McKee, J.B. 1969. *Introduction to Sociology.* New York: Holt, Rinehart and Winston.

McKee, L. and M. O'Brien (eds.). 1982. *The Father Figure.* London: Tavistock.

McKie, D.C., B. Prentice, and P. Reed. 1983. *Divorce: Law and the Family in Canada.* Ottawa: Minister of Supply and Services Canada.

McLachlan, H.V. and J.K. Swales. 1980. Witchcraft and Anti-Feminism. *Scottish Journal of Sociology* 4, 2 May: 141–166.

McLaren, A. 1990. What Makes a Man a Man? *Nature* 346: 216–217.

McMahon, M. 1995. *Engendering Motherhood: Identity and Self-Transformation in Women's Lives.* New York: The Guilford Press.

McMorrow, F. 1974. *Midolescence: The Dangerous Years.* New York: Quadrangle/The New York Times Book Co.

McNeill, S. 1992. Woman Killer as Tragic Hero. In *Femicide: The Politics of Woman Killing*, edited by J. Radford and D.E.H. Russell, 178–183. London: Twayne Publishers.

McPherson, B.D. 1990. *Aging as a Social Process: An Introduction to Individual and Population Aging.* Toronto: Butterworths.

———. 1994. Aging: The Middle and Later Years. In *Sociology*, edited by L. Tepperman, J. Curtis, and J. Richardson, 230–266. Toronto: McGraw Hill Primus.

McVey, Jr., W.W. 1996. Department of Sociology, University of Alberta: Personal communication.

McVey, Jr., W.W and B.W. Robinson. 1981. Separation in Canada: New Insights Concerning Marital Dissolution. *Canadian Journal of Sociology* 6, 3: 353–366.

McVey, Jr., W.W. and W.E. Kalbach. 1995. *Canadian Population.* Toronto: Nelson Canada.

Mead, M. 1980. *Aspects of the Present.* New York: William Morrow.

———. 1949. *Male and Female.* New York: William Morrow.

———. 1935. *Sex and Temperament in Three Primitive Societies.* New York: Mentor Books.

Mead, G.H. 1934/1962. *Mind, Self, and Society*, edited by C.W. Morris. Chicago: Phoenix.

Mederer, H.J. 1993. Division of Labor in Two-Earner Homes: Task Accomplishment versus Household Management as Critical Variables in Perceptions About Family Work. *Journal of Marriage and the Family* 55: 133–145.

Medick, H. 1976. The Proto-Industrial Family Economy: The Structural Function of Household and Family During the Transition from Peasant Society to Industrial Capitalism. *Social History* October.

Meehan, D.M. 1993. The Strong-Soft Woman: Manifestations of the Androgyne in Popular Media. In *Taking Sides: Clashing Views on Controversial Issues in Mass Media and Society*, edited by A. Alexander and J. Hanson, 2nd ed., 48–54. Guilford, CT: Dushkin.

Meilaender, G. 1990. A Christian View of the Family. In *Rebuilding the Nest: New Commitment to the American Family*, edited by D. Blankerhorn, S. Bayme, and J. B. Elshtain, 133–148. Milwaukee, WI: Family Service Association.

Meissner, M. 1985. The Domestic Economy—Half of Canada's Work: Now You See It, Now You Don't. In *Women's Worlds: From the New Scholarship*, edited by M. Safiret et al. New York: Praeger.

Meissner, M.E., W. Humphreys, S.M. Meis, and W.J. Scheu. 1975. No Exit for Wives: Sexual Division of Labour and the Cumulation of Household Demands. *Canadian Review of Sociology and Anthropology* 12: 424–439.

Melhuish, M. 1996. *Oh What A Feeling: A Vital History of Canadian Music*. Kingston, ON: Quarry Press.

Melton, W. and L.L. Lindsey. 1987. Instrumental and Expressive Values in Mate Selection among College Students Revisited: Feminism, Love, and Economic Necessity. Paper presented at the Midwest Sociological Society, Chicago, April.

Meltzoff, A. 1988. Imitation of Televised Models by Infants. *Child Development* 59, 5: 1221–1229.

Mercer, R.T. 1986. *First-time Motherhood: Experiences from teens to forties*. New York: Springer.

Merton, R.K. 1968. *Social Theory and Social Structure*, enlarged ed. New York: Free Press.

Messner, M. 1990. Boyhood, Organized Sports, and the Construction of Masculinities. *Journal of Contemporary Ethnography* 18, 4: 416–444.

Meyer, D.R. and S. Garasky. 1993. Custodial Fathers: Myths, Realities and Child Support Policy. *Journal of Marriage and the Family* 55: 73–89.

Michael, R.T., J.H. Gagnon, E.O. Laumann, and G. Kolata. 1994. *Sex in America: A Definitive Survey*. Boston: Little, Brown.

Michals, D. 1997. Cyber-Race: How Virtual Is It? *Ms*. March/April: 68–72.

Michaud, J. 1997. On Counterhegemonic Formation in the Women's Movement and the Difficult Integration of Collective Indenties. In *Organizing Dissent: Contemporary Social Movements in Theory and Practice,* edited by W.K. Carroll, 2nd ed., 197–212. Toronto: Garamond Press.

Miles, A. 1985. *Feminist Radicalism in the 1980s*. Montreal: CultureTexts.

Miles, R. 1991. *The Rites Of Man: Love, Sex and Death in the Making of the Male*. London: Grafton Books.

Millar, W. and M.P. Beaudet. 1996. Health Facts from the 1994 National Population Health Survey. *Canadian Social Trends* 40, Spring: 24–27.

Miller, A. 1990. *Banished Knowledge: Facing Childhood Injuries*, translated by L. Vennewitz. New York: Doubleday.

Miller, B.D. 1993. Female Infanticide and Child Neglect in Rural North India. In *Gender in Cross-Cultural Perspective*, edited by C.B. Bretl and C.F. Sargent. Englewood Cliffs, NJ: Prentice Hall.

Miller, C. and K. Swift. 1993. Who is Man? In *Gender Basics: Feminist Perspectives on Women and Men*, edited by A. Minas. Belmont, CA: Wadsworth.

———. 1991. *Words and Women Updated: New Language in New Times*. New York: Harper Collins.

———. 1977. *Words and Women*. London: Victor Gollancz.

Miller, C. 1994. Who Says What to Whom. In *The Women and Language Debate: A Sourcebook*, edited by C. Roman, S. Jubasz, and C. Miller. New Brunswick, NJ: Rutgers University.

Miller, C. 1987. Qualitative Differences among Gender-stereotyped Toys: Implications for Cognitive and Social Development in Girls and Boys. *Sex Roles* 16, 9/10: 473–487.

Miller, J.B. 1974. *Psychoanalysis and Women*. London: Penguin.

Miller, M. 1993. Dark Days: The Staggering Cost of Depression. *Wall Street Journal*. 2 December 1993: B1, B6.

Millett, K. 1970. *Sexual Politics*. Garden City, NY: Doubleday.

Mills, C.W. 1959. *The Sociological Imagination*. New York: Oxford University Press.

———. 1956. *The Power Elite*. New York: Oxford University Press.

Minas, A. 1993. *Gender Basics: Feminist Perspectives on Women and Men*. Belmont, CA: Wadsworth.

Mirkin, G. 1978. *The Sportsmedicine Book*. Boston: Little, Brown.

Mischel, W. 1966. A Social-Learning View of Sex Differences in Behavior. In *The Development of Sex Differences*, edited by E. Maccoby. Stanford, CA: Stanford University Press.

Mitchell, G., S. Obradovich, F. Harring, C. Tromborg, and A.L. Burnes. 1992. Reproducing Gender in Public Places: Adults' Attention to Toddlers in Three Public Locales. *Sex Roles* 26 7/8: 323–330.

Mitchell, J.J. 1984. *The Longest Revolution.* New York: Pantheon.

———. 1975. *The Adolescent Predicament.* Toronto: Holt, Rinehart & Winston.

———. 1973. *Women's Estate.* Toronto: Random House.

Mitchinson, W. 1993. The Medical Treatment of Women. In *Changing Patterns: Women in Canada*, edited by S. Burt, L. Code, and L. Dorney, 2nd ed., 391–421. Toronto: McClelland & Stewart.

———. 1991. *The Nature of Their Bodies: Women and Their Doctors in Victorian Canada.* Toronto: University of Toronto Press.

Modleski, T. 1982. *Loving With A Vengeance.* Hamden, CT: Anchor.

Moen, E. 1991. Sex Selection Eugenic Abortion: Prospects in China and India. *Issues in Reproductive and Genetic Engineering* 4: 231–249.

Moen, P. 1992. *Women's Two Roles: A Contemporary Dilemma.* New York: Auburn House.

Mofina, R. 1993. Sex Harassment in RCMP for 60% of Women Officers. *The Edmonton Journal.* September 26: A3.

Mohr, R.M. and J.V. Roberts (eds.). 1994. Sexual Assault in Canada: Recent Developments. In *Confronting Sexual Assault: A Decade of Legal and Social Change*, 3–12. Toronto: University of Toronto Press.

Monette, M. 1996a. Retirement in the '90s: Retired Men in Canada. *Canadian Social Trends* 42, Autumn: 8–11.

———. 1996b. Retirement in the '90s: Going Back to Work. *Canadian Social Trends* 41, Autumn: 12–14.

Money, J. 1988. *Gay, Straight, and In-Between: The Sexology of Erotic Orientation.* New York: Oxford University Press.

———. 1980. *Love and Love Sickness: The Science of Sex, Gender Difference and Pairbonding.* Baltimore: John Hopkins University Press.

———. 1955. Linguistic Resources and Psychodynamic Theory. *British Journal of Medical Psychology* 20: 264–266.

Money, J. and A.E. Ehrhardt. 1972. *Man and Woman, Boy and Girl.* Baltimore: John Hopkins University Press.

Money, J. and P. Tucker. 1975. *Sexual Signatures: On Being a Man or a Woman.* Boston: Little Brown.

Monsebraaten, L. 1998. Women's Movement in Peril, Group Says. *Toronto Star.* June 7: A11.

———. 1996. Struggling on in the Wake of Cuts. *Toronto Star.* May 5: F6.

———. 1994. Female Investors Emerge at Last as a Huge and Lucrative Market. *Toronto Star.* September 28: B1.

Monsour, M. 1992. Meanings of Intimacy in Cross- and Same-sex Friendships. *Journal of Social and Personal Relationships* 9: 277–295.

Moore, M. 1994. Female Lone Parenting. *The Canadian Journal of Sociology* 14, 3: 335–352.

Moore, N.B. and J.K. Davidson, Sr. 1990. Sex Information Sources: Do They Make a Difference in Sexual Decisions. Paper presented at the annual meeting of the National Council on Family Relations, November, Seattle.

Moore, R. and D. Gillette. 1990. *King, Warrior, Magician, Lover: Rediscovering the Archetypes of the Mature Masculine.* New York: HarperSanFrancisco.

Moreau, J. 1991. Employment Equity. *Canadian Social Trends* 22 Autumn: 26–28.

Morgan, A. and C. Wilcox. 1992. Anti-Feminism in Western Europe, 1975–1987. *Western European Politics* 15, 4 October: 151–169.

Morgan, K.P. 1991. Women and the Knife: Cosmetic Surgery and the Colonization of Women's Bodies. *Hypatia* 6, 3: 25–50.

Morgan, M. 1987. Television, Sex-Role Attitudes and Sex-Role Behavior. *Journal of Early Adolescence* 7, 3: 269–282.

———. 1982. Television and Adolescents' Sex Role Stereotypes: A Longitudinal Study. *Journal of Personality and Social Psychology* 43: 947–955.

———. 1973. *The Total Woman*. London: Hodder and Stoughton.

Morissette, R. 1997. Declining Earnings of Young Men. *Canadian Social Trends*. 46, Autumn: 8–12.

Morra, N. and M.D. Smith. 1995. Men in Feminism: Reinterpreting Masculinity and Femininity. In *Feminist Issues: Race, Class and Sexuality*, edited by N. Mandell, 185–208. Scarborough, ON: Prentice Hall Canada.

Morris, A. 1987. *Women, Crime and Criminal Justice*. Oxford: Basil Blackwell.

Morris, A. and A. Wilczynski. 1994. Rocking the Cradle: Mothers who Kill their Children. In *Moving Targets*, edited by H. Birch, 198–217. Berkeley, CA: University of California Press.

Morrison, A.M., R.P. White, E. Van Velsor, and the Centre for Creative Leadership. 1987. *Breaking the Glass Ceiling: Can Women Reach the Top of America's Largest Corporations?* Reading, MA: Addison-Wesley.

Morris, D. 1969. *The Naked Ape*. Toronto: Bantam.

Morris, J. 1974. *Conundrum*. New York: Signet.

Mossman, M.J. 1997. *Readings on Law, Gender, Equality*. Materials prepared for the study use of students at Osgoode Hall School of Law of York University.

———. 1994. The Paradox of Feminist Engagement with Law. In *Feminist Issues: Race, Class, Sexuality*, edited by N. Mandell, 211–243. Scarborough, ON: Prentice Hall Canada

Motherwell, C. 1990. *Smart Money: Investment Strategies for Women*. New York: Simon & Schuster.

Moulton, J. 1981. The Myth of the Natural 'Man.' In *Feminism and Philsophy*, edited by M. Vetterling-Braggin, F.A. Elliston, and J. English, 124–137. Totawa, NJ: Rowan & Littlefield.

Mueller, C. and T. Dimieri. 1982. The Structure of Belief Systems among Contending ERA Activists. *Social Forces* 60: 657–675.

Mulac, A., J.M. Wiemann, S.J. Widenmann, and T.W. Gibson. 1988. Male/female Language Differences and Effects in Same-sex and Mixed-sex Dyads: The Gender-linked Language Effect. *Communication Monographs* 55: 315–335.

Murstein, B. 1991. Dating: Attracting and Meeting. In *Marriage and Family in Transition*, edited by J.N. Edwards and D.H. Demo. Boston: Allyn & Bacon.

———. 1986. *Paths To Marriage*. Beverly Hills, CA: Sage.

———. 1972. Physical Attractiveness and Marital Choice. *Journal of Personality and Social Psychology* 22: 8–12.

Mussen, P.H., J.J. Conger, and J. Kagan. 1969. *Child Development and Personality,* 3rd ed. New York: Harper & Row.

Mutchler, J.E. 1992. Living Arrangements and Household Transitions among the Unmarried in Later Life. *Social Science Quarterly* 73, 3 September: 565–580.

Nadwodny, R. 1996. Working at Home. *Canadian Social Trends* 40, Spring: 16–20.

Nair, C. 1991. Trends in Cesarian Section Deliveries in Canada. *Health Report* 33: 203–217.

Nakamura, A. and M. Nakamura. 1985. *The Second Paycheck: A Socioeconomic Analysis of Earnings*. Orlando, FL: Academic Press.

Nanda, S. 1990. *Neither Man Nor Woman: The Hijras of India*. Belmont, CA: Wadsworth.

Nardo, D. 1990. *Drugs and Sports*. San Diego, CA: Lucent Books, Inc.

National Council on Welfare. 1992. *The 1992 Budget and Child Welfare, 1992*. Ottawa: Supply and Services.

———. 1990. *Women and Poverty Revisited*. Ottawa: Supply and Services.

National Commission on Working Women. 1991–1992. *Women, Work and Family: Working Mothers—Overview,* Fall/Winter. Washington DC: Author.

Nault, F. 1996. Twenty Years of Marriages. *Health Reports* 8, 2: 39–46.

Neft, N. and A.D. Levine. 1997. *Where Women Stand: An International Report on the Status of Women in 140 Countries, 1997–1998*. New York: Random House.

Neidig, P.H. and S.H. Friedman. 1984. *Spouse Abuse: A Treatment Program for Couples*. Champaign, IL: Research Press.

Nelson, E.D. 1991. 'Employment Equity' and the Red Queen's Hypothesis: Recruitment and hiring in Western Canadian Municipal Police Departments. *Canadian Police College Journal* 16, 3.

———. 1992. *Il faut cultiver notre jardin: Employment Equity Within Western Canadian Municipal Police Departments*. Ottawa: Multiculturalism Sector, Secretary of State.

Nelson, A. and B.W. Robinson. 1994. *Gigolos and Madames Bountiful: Illusions of Gender, Power and Intimacy*. Toronto: University of Toronto Press.

Nelson, E.D. and B.W. Robinson (eds.). 1995. The Quest for Intimacy. In *Gender in the 1990s: Images, Realities and Issues*, 231–248. Toronto: Nelson Canada.

Nelton, S. and K. Berney 1987. Women: The Second Wave. *National Business* May: 18–27.

Nett, E.M. 1993. *Canadian Families: Past and Present*, 2nd ed. Toronto: Butterworths.

Neuburg, P. 1973. *The Hero's Children: The Post–War Generation in Eastern Europe*. New York: William Morrow and Company.

Neugarten, B.L. (ed.). 1968a. The Awareness of Middle Age. In *Middle Age and Aging*, 93–98. Chicago: University of Chicago Press.

———. (ed.). 1968b. Adult Personality: Toward a Psychology of the Life Cycle. In *Middle Age and Aging*, 137–147. Chicago: University of Chicago Press.

Neugarten, B.L. and E. Hall. 1980. Acting One's Age: New Rules for Old. *Psychology Today* 13 April: 66–80.

Neugarten, B.L., V. Wood, R.J. Kraines, and B. Loomis. 1963. Women's Attitudes Towards the Menopause. *Vita Humana* 6: 140–151.

Neuman, P. and P. Halvorson. 1983. *Anorexia Nervosa and Bulimia: A Handbook for Counselors and Therapists*. New York: Van Nostrand Reinhold.

Newman, B.M. and P.R. Newman. 1975. *Development Through Life: A Psychosocial Approach*. Homewood, IL: Dorsey.

Newton, N. 1973. Trebly Sensuous Woman. In *The Female Experience*, G. Lerner, 22–25. Del Mar, CA: Communication Research Machines.

Nichols, A. 1983. Linguistic Options and Choices for Black Women in the Rural South. In *Language, Gender and Society*, edited by B. Thorne, C. Kramarae, and N. Henley. Rowley, 38–53. MA: Newbury House Publishers.

Nichols, J. 1980. Women in their Speech Communities. In *Women And Language in Literature and Society*, edited by S. McConnell-Ginet, R. Borker, and N. Furman. Rowley, MA: Newbury.

Nicholson, L.J. (ed.). 1990. Introduction to *Feminism/Postmodernism*, 1–16. New York: Routledge.

Nielsen, L. 1991. *Adolescence: A Contemporary View*, 2nd ed. Toronto: Harcourt, Brace, Jovanovich.

Nilsen, A. 1972. Sexism in English: A Feminist View. In *Feminist Studies*. Old Westbury, NY: Feminist Press.

Nilsen, A.P. 1993. Sexism in English: A 1990s Update. In *Experiencing Race, Class and Gender in the United States*, edited by V. Cyrus. Mountain View, CA: Mayfield.

Nock, S.L. and P.W. Kingston. 1988. Time with Children: The Impact of Couples' Work-Time Commitments. *Social Forces* 67: 59–85.

Nolin, M.J. and K.K. Petersen. 1992. Gender Differences in Parent-Child Communication About Sexuality: An Exploratory Study. *Journal of Adolescent Research* 7: 59–79.

Noller, P. 1980. Misunderstandings in Marital Communication. *Journal of Personality and Social Psychology* 39: 1135–1148.

Noonan, S. 1993. Strategies of Survival: Moving Beyond the Battered Woman Syndrome. In *In Conflict With the Law: Women and the Canadian Justice System*, edited by E. Adelburg and C. Currie, 247–270. Vancouver: Press Gang Publishers.

Norland, J.A. 1994. *Profile of Canada's Seniors*. Scarborough, ON: Statistics Canada and Prentice Hall.

Normand, J. 1995. Education of Women in Canada. *Canadian Social Trends* 39 Winter: 17–21.

Norris, J. 1980. The Social Adjustment of Single and Widowed Older Women. *Essence* 4: 134–144.

Norton, A.J. and L. Miller. 1992. *Marriage, Divorce and Remarriage in the 1990s.* Current Population Reports, October, 23–180. Washington, DC: U.S. Bureau of the Census.

Novak, M. 1995. *Aging & Society: A Canadian Reader.* Scarborough, ON: Nelson Canada.

Nowell, I. 1996. *Women Who Give Away Millions: Portraits of Canadian Philanthropists.* Toronto: Hounslow.

Nye, F. I. and F.M. Berardo. 1973. *The Family: Its Structure and Interaction.* New York: Macmillan.

Nylander, I. 1971. The Feeling of Being Fat and Dieting in a School Population: Epidemiologic Interview Investigation. *Acta Sociomed* (Scandinavia) 3: 17–26.

Oakley, A. 1986. *From Here To Maternity: Becoming A Mother.* Harmondsworth: Penguin.

———. 1974. *The Sociology of Housework.* New York: Pantheon.

O'Barr, W.M. 1983. The Study of Language in Institutional Contexts: 2nd International Conference on Social Psychology and Language. Bristol, England. *Journal of Language & Social Psychology* 2: 241–251.

O'Barr, W. 1982. *Linguistic Evidence: Language, Power and Strategy in the Courtroom.* New York: Academic Press.

O'Barr, W. and C. Kramarae. 1984. *Language and Power.* Beverly Hills, CA: Sage.

O'Barr, W. and M. Atkins. 1975. 'Women's Language' or 'Powerless Language?' In *Women and Language in Literature and Society*, edited by S. McConnell-Ginet, R. Borker, and N. Furman, 93–103. New York: Praeger.

O'Bireck, G.M. (ed.). 1996. *Not A Kid Anymore: Canadian Youth, Crime, and Subcultures.* Scarborough: Nelson Canada.

O'Brien, C.A. and L. Weir. 1995. Lesbians and Gay Men Inside and Outside Families. In *Canadian Families: Diversity, Conflict and Change*, 111–139. Toronto: Harcourt Brace Canada.

O'Brien, J.E. 1971. Violence in Divorce-Prone Families. *Journal of Marriage and the Family* 33: 692–698.

O'Brien, M. 1987. Parent's Speech to Toddlers: The Effect of Play Context. *Journal of Child Language* 14, 2: 269–299.

———. 1985. Activity Level and Sex-Stereotyped Toy Choices in Toddler Boys and Girls. *Journal of Genetic Psychology* 146, 4: 527–533.

———. 1981. *The Politics of Reproduction.* London: Routledge & Kegan Paul.

Oderkirk, J. 1996a. Government Sponsored Income Security Programs For Seniors: Old Age Security. *Canadian Social Trends* 40, Spring: 3–7.

———. 1996b. Government Sponsored Income Security Programs For Seniors: Canada and Quebec Pension Plans. *Canadian Social Trends* 40, Spring: 8–15.

———. 1994. Marriage in Canada: Changing Beliefs and Behaviours 1600–1990. *Canadian Social Trends* Summer: 2–7.

Oderkirk, J. and C. Lochhead. 1992. Lone Parenthood: Gender Differences. *Canadian Social Trends* 27, Winter: 16–19.

Oderkirk, J., C. Silver, and M. Prud'homme. 1994. Traditional-Earner Families. *Canadian Social Trends* 32, Spring: 19–25.

O'Donovan, K. 1984. The Medicalization of Infanticide. *Criminal Law Review* 5: 259–264.

Offer, D., E. de Vito, and H.C. Triands. *The Teenage World: Adolescent Self-Image in Ten Countries.* New York: Plenum Medical.

Ogburn, W.F. 1922. *Social Change.* New York: Viking Press.

Ogden, A.A. 1986. *The Great American Housewife.* Westport, CT: Greenwood.

O'Keefe, E. and J.S. Hyde. 1983. The Development of Occupational Sex-Role Stereotypes. *Sex Roles* 9: 481–492.

Okin, S.M. 1989. *Justice, Gender and the Family.* New York: Basic Books.

O'Leary, K.D., J. Barling, I. Arias, A. Rosenbaum, K. Malone, and A. Tyree. 1989. Prevalence and Stability of Physical Aggression between Spouses: A Longitudinal Analysis. *Journal of Consulting and Clinical Psychology* 57: 263–268.

Olien, M. 1978. *The Human Myth*. New York: Harper and Row.

O'Neill, N. and G. O'Neill. 1972. *Open Marriage: A New Life Style for Couples*. New York: M. Evans.

Ong, B.N. 1986. Are Abusing Women Abused Women? In *Feminist Practice in Women's Health Care*, edited by C. Webb. London: Wiley.

Ontario Ministry of Labour, Women's Bureau. 1993. *Employer's Guide to Non-Sexist Language in the Workplace.*Ottawa: Ontario Ministry of Labour.

Ontario Women's Directorate. 1995. *Sex-Role Stereotyping: An Awareness Kit for Parents and Teachers*. Toronto: Ontario Women's Directorate.

———. 1994. *Words That Count Women In*. Ottawa: Ontario Women's Directorate.

———. 1993. *Words That Count Women In*. Toronto: Ontario Women's Directorate.

———. 1992. *Words That Count Women In*. Toronto: Ontario Women's Directorate.

Oppenheimer, V.K. 1994. Women's Rising Employment and the Future of the Family in Industrial Societies. *Population and Development Review* 20, 2: 293–342.

Orbach, S. 1986. *Hunger Strike*. New York: Norton.

———. 1980. *Fat Is A Feminist Issue*. New York: Berkley.

Osmond, M.W. and B. Thorne. 1993. Feminist Theories: The Social Construction of Gender in Families and Society. In *Sourcebook of Family Theories and Methods: A Contextual Approach*, edited by PG. Boss, W.J. Doherty, R. LaRossa, W.R. Schumm, and S.K. Steinmetz, 591–622. New York: Plenum.

Ostling, R.N. 1997. God, Football and the Game of His Life. *Time.* October: 36–37

Ott, E.M. 1989. Effects of the Male-female Ratio at Work: Policewomen and Male Nurses. *Psychology of Women Quarterly* 13: 58.

Owens, D. 1984. The Desire to Father: Reproductive Ideologies and Involuntarily Childless Men. In *The Father Figure*, edited by L. McKee and M. O'Brien, 72–88. London: Tavistock Publications.

Pagelow, M. 1992. Adult Victims of Domestic Violence. *Journal of Interpersonal Violence* 7, 1: 87–120.

Paglia, C. 1990. *Sexual Personae*. New Haven, CT: Yale University Press.

———. 1992. *Sex, Art and American Culture: Essays*. New York: Vintage Books.

Paley, V.G. 1984. *Boys and Girls: Superheroes in the Doll Corner*. Chicago: University of Chicago.

Palmer, R. 1995. *Rock & Roll: An Unruly History*. New York: Harmony Books.

Palmer, R.L. 1989. *Anorexia Nervosa*. Harmondsworth: Penguin.

Palmore, E. 1985. *The Honorable Elders Revisited*. Durham, NC: Duke University Press.

Paludi, M.A. 1996. *Sexual Harassment on College Campuses: Abusing the Ivory Power*. Albany, NY: State University of New York Press.

Paradise, L.V. and S.M. Wall. 1986 Children's Perceptions of Male and Female Principals and Teachers. *Sex Roles* 14: 1.

Parke, R.D. et al. 1980. Fathers and Risk: A Hospital Based Model of Intervention. In *Exceptional Infant IV: Psychosocial Risks in Infant-Environmental Transactions*, edited by D.B. Sawin. New York: Brunner/Mazel.

Parliament, J.B. 1989. Women Employed Outside the Home. *Canadian Social Trends* 13, Summer: 2–6.

Parsons, T. 1949. The Social Structure of the Family. In *The Family: Its Function and Destiny*, edited by R. Anshen, 173–201. New York: Harper and Brothers.

———. 1942. Age and Sex in the Social Structure. *American Sociological Review* 7: 601–616.

Parsons, T. and R.F. Bales. 1955. *Family, Socialization and Interaction Process*. New York: Free Press.

Parton, N. 1990. Taking Child Abuse Seriously. In *Taking Violence Against Children Seriously: Contemporary Issues in Child Protection Theory and Practice*, edited by The Violence Against Children Study Group, 7–24. London: Unwin Hyman.

Pascual, N. 1997. In A Metal Mood. *Heavy Metal.* May: 75.

Pearlin, L.I. and M.I. Kohn. 1966. Social Class, Occupation, and Parental values: A Cross-National Study. *American Sociological Review* 31: 466–479.

Pearson, J. and N. Thoennes. 1988. Supporting Children After Divorce: The Influence of Custody of Child Support Levels and Payments. *Family Law Quarterly* 22: 319–339.

Pedersen, F.A. 1987. *Men's Transition to Parenthood: Longitudinal Studies of Early Family Experiences.* Hillsdale, NJ: Lawrence Erlbaum Associates.

————— (ed.). 1980. *The Father-Infant Relationship: Observational Studies in the Family Setting.* New York: Praeger.

Peele, S. and R. DeGrandpre. 1995. My Genes Made Me Do It. *Psychology Today* 28, 4, July/August: 50–53, 62–68.

Peirce, K. 1993. Socialization of Teenage Girls Through Teen-magazine Fiction: The Making of a New Woman or an Old Lady? *Sex Roles* 29, 1/2: 59–68.

—————. 1990. A Feminist Theoretical Perspective on the Socialization of Teenage Girls Through *Seventeen* Magazine. *Sex Roles* 23: 491–500.

Peplau, L., Z. Rubin, and C. Hill. 1976. The Sexual Balance of Power. *Psychology Today.* 10: 142–147.

Pepler, D. and W. Craig. 1995. A Peek Behind the Fence: Naturalistic Observations of Aggressive Children with Remote Audiovisual Recording. *Developmental Psychology* 31: 548–553.

Peretti, P.O. and T.M. Sydney. 1985. Parental Toy Stereotyping and its Effect on Child Toy Preference. *Social Behavior and Personality* 12: 213–216.

Perlmutter, M. and E. Hall. 1985. *Adult Development and Aging.* New York: John Wiley & Sons.

Peters, J. 1990. Cultural Variations: Past and Present. In *Families: Changing Trends in Canada*, edited by M. Baker, 2nd ed., 166–191. Toronto: McGraw-Hill Ryerson.

—————. 1987 Changing Perspectives on Divorce. In *Family Matters: Sociology and Contemporary Canadian Families*, edited by K.L. Anderson et al., 141–162. Toronto: Methuen.

Phelan, S. 1989. *Identity Politics: Lesbian Feminism and the Limits of Community.* Philadelphia: Temple University Press.

Phillips, A. 1997. Christian Men on the March. *Maclean's.* October 6: 52–53.

Phillips, B. 1990. Nicknames and Sex Role Stereotypes. *Sex Roles* 23: 281–289.

Phillips, R. 1991. *Untying The Knot: A Short History of Divorce.* Cambridge: Cambridge University Press.

Piaget, Jean. 1968. *Six Psychological Studies*, translated by A. Tenzer, translation edited by D. Elkind. New York: Vintage.

—————. 1954. *The Construction of Reality in the Child.* New York: Basic Books.

—————. 1950. *The Psychology of Intelligence.* London: Routledge & Kegan Paul.

Piercy, K.W. 1998. Theorizing About Family Caregiving: The Role of Responsibility. *Journal of Marriage and the Family* 60: 109–118.

Pierson, R.R. 1995. Global Issues. In *Canadian Women's Issues: Volume II: Bold Visions: Twenty-Five Years of Women's Activism in English Canada*, edited by R.R. Pierson and M. G. Cohen, 360–401. Toronto: James Lorimer.

Pipher, M. 1994. *Reviving Ophelia: Saving The Selves of Adolescent Girls.* New York: Ballantine.

Pittman, F.S. 1993. *Man Enough: Fathers, Sons, and the Search for Masculinity.* New York: Perigee.

Pittman, J.F. and D. Blanchard. 1996. The Effects of Work History and Timing of Marriage on the Division of Household Labor: A Life-Course Perspective. *Journal of Marriage and the Family* 58: 78–90.

Placek, J. 1988. Why Do Men Batter their Wives? In *Feminist Perspectives on Wife Abuse*, edited by K. Yllo and M. Bograd, 133–157. Newbury Park, CA: Sage.

Plant, S. 1996. On The Matrix: Cyberfeminist Simulations. In *Cultures of Internet: Virtual Spaces, Real Histories, Living Bodies*, edited by R. Shields, 170–183. Thousand Oaks, CA: Sage.

Pleck, E., and J. Pleck (eds.). 1980. *The American Male*. Englewood Cliffs, NJ: Prentice-Hall.

Pleck, J.H. 1985. *Working Wives/Working Husbands*. Beverly Hills, CA: Sage.

———. 1981. *The Myth of Masculinity*. Cambridge, MA: MIT Press.

———. 1979. Men's Family Work: Three Perspectives and Some New Data. *The Family Coordinator* 28: 481–488.

———. 1977. The Work-Family Role Systems. *Social Problems* 24: 417–427.

Pleck, J.H and E. Corfman. 1979. Married Men: Work and Family. In *Families Today: A Research Sampler on Families and Children*, edited by E. Corfman, Vol. 1, 387–411. NIMH Science Monographs 1. Washington, DC: U.S. Department of Health, Education, and Welfare.

Podrouzek, W. and D. Furrow. 1988. Preschoolers' Use of Eye Contact While Speaking: The Influence of Sex, Age and Conversation Pattern. *Psycholinguistic Research* 17: 89–98.

Pollitt, K. 1991. The Smurfette Principle. *New York Times Magazine*. April 7: 22–23.

Pomerleau, A., D. Bolduc, G. Malcuit, and L. Cossette. 1990. Pink or Blue: Gender Stereotypes in the First Two Years of Life. *Sex Roles* 22, 5–6: 359–367.

Ponting, J.R. 1986. Canadian Gender-Role Attitudes. Unpublished manuscript. University of Calgary.

Pooler, W.S. 1991. Sex of Child Preferences among College Students. *Sex Roles* 25, 9/10: 569–576.

Porter, J., M. Porter, and B. Blishen. 1982. *Stations and Callings*. Toronto: Methuen.

Potkay, C.R. and B.P. Allen. 1986. *Personality: Theory, Research, and Applications*. Monterey, CA: Brooks/Cole.

Potuchek, J.L. 1992. Employed Wives' Orientations to Breadwinning: A Gender Theory Analysis. *Journal of Marriage and the Family* 54: 548–558.

Power, T.G. and R.D. Parke. 1986. Patterns of Early Socialization: Mother and Father Infant Interaction in the Home. *International Journal of Behavioural Development* 9: 331–341.

———. 1984. Social Network Factors and the Transition to Parenthood. *Sex Roles* 10: 949–972.

Pratt, W.F. 1990. Premarital Sexual Behavior, Multiple Sexual Partners, and Marital Experience. Paper presented at the annual meeting of the Population Association of America, Toronto, Canada.

Prentice, A., P. Bourne, G.C. Brandt, B. Light, W. Mitchinson, and N. Black. 1988. *Canadian Women: A History*. Toronto: Harcourt Brace Jovanovich.

Price-Bonham, S.J. 1988. *Divorce*. Newbury Park, CA: Sage.

Priest, L. 1990. *Conspiracy of Silence*. Toronto: McClelland and Stewart.

Pruett, K.D. 1987. *The Nurturing Father: Journey Toward the Complete Man*. New York: Warner Books.

Puka, B. 1990. The Liberation of Caring: A Different Voice for Gilligan's Different Voice. *Hypatia* 5: 59–82.

Purcell, P. and L. Stewart. 1990. Dick and Jane in 1989. *Sex Roles* 22, 3/4: 177–185.

Queniart, A. 1992. Risky Business: Medical Definitions of Pregnancy. In *Anatomy of Gender: Women's Struggle for the Body*, edited by D.H. Currie and V. Raoul, 161–174. Ottawa: Carleton University Press.

Radin, N. 1988. Primary Caregiving Fathers of Long Duration. In *Fatherhood Today: Men's Changing Role in the Family*, edited by P. Bronstein and C.P. Cowan, 127–143. New York: Wiley.

Radke-Yarrow, M., J. Richters, and W. Wilson. 1988. Child Development in the Network of Relationships. In *Relationships within Families: Mutal influences*, edited by R. Hinde and J. Stevenson-Hinde, 48–67. New York: Oxford University Press.

Radway, J. 1984. *Reading the Romance: Women, Patriarchy and Popular Literature*. Chapel Hill: University of North Carolina Press.

Ram, B. 1990. *New Trends in the Family: Demographic Facts and Features*. Current Demographic Analysis Series. Cat. 91–535E. Ottawa: Minister of Supply and Services.

Ramsey, P.G. 1995. Changing Social Dynamics in Early Childhood Classrooms. *Child Development* 66, 3: 764–773.

Ramu, G.N. (ed.). 1989. Courtship annd Mate Selection. In *Marriage and the Family in Canada Today*, 35–52. Scarborough, ON: Prentice Hall Canada.

Rapson, R.L. 1965. The American Child as Seen by British Travelers, 1945–1935. *American Quarterly* 17: 520–534.

Rashid, A. 1994. Changes in Real Wages. *Canadian Social Trends* 32, Spring: 16–18.

Rasmussen, J.L. and B.E. Moley. 1986. Impression Formation as a Function of the Sex Role Appropriateness of Linguistic Behavior. *Sex Roles* 14: 149–161.

Ravanera, Z.R. 1995. A Portrait of the Family Life of Young Adults. In *Family Over the Life Course*, edited by R. Beaujot, E.M. Gee, F. Rajulton, and Z.R. Ravanera, 7–35. Current Demographic Analysis Series. Ottawa: Statistics Canada.

Rawlins, W.K. 1993. Communication in Cross-sex Friendships. In *Women and Men Communicating*, edited by L. Arliss and D. Borisoff. Fort Worth, TX: Harcourt Brace Jovanovich.

Raymond, J. 1982. *The Transsexual Empire*. London: The Women's Press Ltd.

Razack, S. 1993. Exploring the Omissions and Silence in Law Around Race. In *Investigating Gender Bias: Laws, Courts and the Legal Profession*, edited by J. Brockman and D.E. Chunn, 37–48. Toronto: Thompson Educational Publishing.

———. 1991. *Canadian Feminism and the Law: The Women's Legal Education and Action Fund and the Pursuit of Equality*. Toronto: Second Story Press.

Reality. 1991. Real Women of Canada Policies Supported by Majority of Canadian Women Winter, 9, 5: 1. [R.E.A.L. Women of Canada.]

Reigel, K.F. 1975. Toward a Dialectical Theory of Development. *Human Development* 18: 50–64.

Reinharz, S. and L. Davidman. 1992. *Feminist Methods in Social Research*. New York: Oxford University Press.

Reinisch, J.M. 1990. *The Kinsey Institute New Report on Sex*. New York: St. Martin's Press.

Reis, J.T., M. Senchak, and B. Solomon. 1985. Sex Differences in the Intimacy of Social Interaction: Further Examination of Potential Explanations. *Journal of Personality and Social Psychology* 48, 1204: 17.

Reiss, I. 1986. *Journey into Sexuality: An Exploratory Voyage*. Englewood Cliffs, NJ: Prentice- Hall.

Rekers, G. and J. Varni. 1977. Fathers' Verbal Interaction with Infants in the First Three Months of Life. *Child Development* 42: 63–8.

Renteln, A.D. 1992. Sex Selection and Reproductive Freedom. *Women's Studies International Forum* 153: 405–426.

Renzetti, C.M. 1992. *Violent Betrayal: Partner Abuse in Lesbian Relationships*. Newbury Park, CA: Sage.

———. 1988a. Violence in Lesbian Relationships: A Preliminary Analysis of Causal Factors. *Journal of Interpersonal Violence* 34: 381–389.

———. 1988b. Building A Second Closer: Third Party Responses to Victims of Lesbian Partner Abuse. *Family Relations* 38: 157–163.

Renzetti, C.M. and D.J. Curran. 1995. *Women, Men, and Society,* 3rd ed. Boston: Allyn and Bacon.

Reskin, B.F. 1988. Bring the Men Back In: Sex Differentiation and the Devaluation of Women's Work. *Gender & Society* 2 March: 58–81.

Resnick, P.J. 1969. Child Murder by Parents: A Psychiatric Review of Filicide. *American Journal of Psychiatry* 126, 3: 325–334.

Rexroat, C. and C. Shehan. 1987. The Family Life Cycle and Spouses' Time in Housework. *Journal of Marriage and the Family* 49: 737–750.

Rheingold, H. L. and K. V. Cook. 1975. The Content of Boys' and Girls' Rooms as an Index of Parents' Behavior. *Child Development* 46: 459–463.

Rice, C. and L. Langdon. 1991. Women Struggles with Food and Weight as Survival Strategies. *Canadian Woman Studies* 12, 1: 30–33.

Rice, F.P. 1996. *Intimate Relationships, Marriages, and Families,* 3rd ed. Mountain View, CA: Mayfield.

Rich, A. 1986. *Of Woman Born: Motherhood as Experience and Institution*. New York: W.W. Norton.

———. 1980/1984. Compulsory Heterosexuality and Lesbian Existence. *Signs* 5: 631–660. Reprinted in *Desire: The Politics of Sexuality*, edited by A. Snitow, C. Stansell, and S. Thompson. London: Virago.

———. 1976. *Of Woman Born*. New York: Norton.

Richardson, C. J. 1996. Divorce and Remarriage. In *Families: Changing Trends in Canada*, edited by M. Baker, 215–248. Toronto: McGraw-Hill Ryerson.

———. 1987. Children of Divorce. In *Family Matters: Sociology and Contemporary Canadian Families*, edited by K.L. Anderson et al., 163–200. Toronto: Methuen.

Richardon, L. 1996. Gender Stereotyping in the English Language. In *The Meaning of Difference: American Constructions of Race, Sex and Gender and Sexual Orientation*, edited by K.E. Rosenblum and T.M.C. Travis New York: McGraw-Hill.

———. 1988. *The Dynamics of Sex and Gender: A Sociological Perspective*, 3rd ed. New York: Harper & Row.

———. 1977. *The Dynamics of Sex and Gender: A Sociological Perspective*. Chicago: Rand McNally.

Richer, S. and L. Weir (eds.). 1995. *Beyond Political Correctness: Toward the Inclusive University*. Toronto: University of Toronto Press.

Richmond-Abbott, M. 1992. *Masculine & Feminine,* 2nd ed. Toronto: McGraw-Hill Inc.

Riessman, C.K. 1990. *Divorce Talk: Women and Men Make Sense of Personal Relationships*. New Brunswick, NJ: Rutgers University Press.

Risman, B.J. and D. Johnson-Sumerford. 1998. Doing It Fairly: A Study of Postgender Marriages. *Journal of Marriage and the Family* 60: 23–40.

Ristock, J.L. 1991. Beyond Ideologies: Understanding Violence in Lesbian Relationships. *Canadian Woman Studies* 12, 1: 74–79.

———. 1991b. Feminist Collectives: The Struggles and Contradictions in our Quest for a 'Uniquely Feminist Structure.' In *Women and Social Change*, edited by J.D. Wine and J.L. Ristock, 41–55. Toronto: James Lorimer.

Robbins, T. 1996. *The Great Woman Super Heroes*. Northampton, MA: Kitchen Sink Press.

Roberts, D. 1978. The Paterfamilias of the Victorian Ruling Classes. In *The Victorian Family*, edited by A.S. Wohl. London: Croom Helm.

Roberts, L. 1988. Zeroing in on the Sex Switch. *Science* 239: 21–23.

Roberts, P. and P.M. Newton. 1987. Levinsonian Studies of Women's Adult Development. *Psychology and Aging* 2: 154–163.

Roberts, R. 1990. 'Sex as a Weapon'; Feminist Rock Music Videos. *NSWA Journal* 2, 1, Winter: 1–15.

Roberts, R.E. 1971. *The New Communes: Coming Together in America*. Englewood Cliffs, NJ: Prentice-Hall, Spectrum.

Robertson, C.N. 1970. *Oneida Community: An Autobiography*, 1851–1876. Syracuse, NY: Syracuse University Press.

Robertson, H. 1992. *More Than A Rose: Prime Ministers, Wives, and Other Women*. Toronto: Seal Books/McClelland & Stewart.

Robertson, I. 1987. *Sociology,* 3rd ed. New York: Worth.

———. 1980. *Social Problems,* 3rd ed. New York: Worth Publishing.

Robinson, B.W. 1982. Every Picture Has A Story: *Playboy* Playmate Biographies, 1956–1980. Paper presented at the Annual Meetings of the Pacific Sociological Association, April, San Diego.

————. 1980. *Love Counts: Romanticism in Canadian Undergraduate Students*. Unpublished doctoral dissertation, Department of Sociology, Edmonton, University of Alberta.

————. 1968. *Leisure: A Suburban Winnipeg Study*. Unpublished Master's Thesis. Department of Sociology, University of Manitoba.

Robinson, B.W. and W.W. McVey Jr. 1985. The Relative Contributions of Death and Divorce to Marital Dissolution in Canada and the United States. *Journal of Comparative Family Studies* 16, 1: 93–109.

Robinson, C. and J.T. Morris. 1987. The Gender-Stereotyped Nature of Christmas Toys Received by 36-, 48- and 60-Month-Old Children: A Comparison between Nonrequested and Requested Toys. *Sex Roles* 15: 21–32.

Rock, P. 1977. Review Symposium on Women, Crime and Criminology. *British Journal of Criminology* 17: 392.

Rodeheaver, D. and N. Datan. 1988. The Challenge of Double Jeopardy: Toward a Mental Health Agenda for Aging Women. *American Psychologist* 43: 648–654.

Rodgers, K. 1994. Wife Assault: The Findings of a National Survey. *Juristat Service Bulletin*. 14 9. Cat. 85–002. Ottawa: Minister of Industry, Science and Technology.

Rodgers, K. and G. Roberts. 1995. Women's Non-Spousal Multiple Victimization: A Test of the Routine Activities Theory. *Canadian Journal of Criminology* 37, 30: 362–392.

Rodin, J., L. Silberstein, and R. Striegel-Moore. 1985. Women and Weight: A Normative Discontent. In *Psychology and Gender: Proceedings of the Nebraska Symposium on Motivation, 1984*, edited by T.B. Sonderegger, 267–307. Lincoln: University of Nebraska Press.

Rogers, C.R. 1972. *Becoming Partners: Marriage and its Alternatives*. New York: Delacorte.

Rohrbaugh, J.B. 1979. Femininity on the Line. *Psychology Today*. August: 308.

Roiphe, K. 1993. *The Morning After: Sex, Fear, and Feminism on Campus*. Boston: Little.

Rollins, B.C. and S.J. Bahr. 1976. A Theory of Power Relationships in Marriage. *Journal of Marriage and the Family* 38: 619–627.

Rollins, B.C. and S.J. Bahr, and K.L. Cannon. 1974. Marital Satisfaction over the Family Life Cycle: A Reevaluation. *Journal of Marriage and the Family* 36: 271–283.

Rollins, B.C., S.J. Bahr, and H. Feldman. 1970. Marital Satisfaction over the Family Life Career: A Reevaluation. *Journal of Marriage and the Family* 26: 20–28.

Roman, L.G. 1988. Intimacy, Labor and Class: Ideologies of Feminine Sexuality in the Punk Slam Dance. In *Becoming Feminine*, edited by L. Roman, L.K. Christian-Smith, and E. Ellsworth, 143–184. London: Falmer Press.

Roopnarine, J.L. 1986. Mothers' and Fathers' Behaviors Toward the Toy Play of their Infant Sons and Daughters. *Sex Roles* 14: 56–68.

Rorabaugh, W.J. 1996. Challenging Authority: Seeking Community, and Empowerment in the New Left, Black Power and Feminism. *Journal of Policy History* 8, 1: 106–143.

Roscoe, B. and J.E. Callahan. 1985. Adolescents Self-Report of Violence in Families and Dating Relations. *Adolescence* 20: 545–553

Roscoe, W. (ed.). 1988. *Living The Spirit: A Gay American Indian Anthology*. New York: St. Martin's Press.

Rosenberg, H. 1987/1995. Motherwork, Stress, and Depression: The Costs of Privatized Social Reproduction. Originally in *Feminism and Politcal Economy*, edited by H.J. Maroney and M. Luxton, 181–196. Toronto: Methuen. Reprinted in *Gender in the 1990s: Images, Realities, and Issues*, edited by E.D. Nelson and B.W. Robinson, 311–329. Toronto: Nelson Canada.

————. 1986. The Home is the Workplace: Hazards, Stress and Pollutants in the Household. In *Through The Kitchen Window: The Politics of Home and Family*, edited by M. Luxton and H. Rosenberg, 181–196. Toronto: Methuen.

Rosenberg, S.D. and M.R. Farrell. 1976. Identity and Crisis in Middle Aged Men. *International Journal of Aging and Human Development* 7, 2: 153–170.

Rosenkrantz, P., S. R. Vogel, H. Bee, I. K. Broverman, and D. M. Broverman. 1968. Sex-Role Stereotypes and Self Concepts in College Students. *Journal of Consulting and Clinical Psychology* 32: 287–295.

Rosenthal, C.J. 1987/1995. The Comforter: Providing Personal Advice and Emotional Support to Generations in the Family. Originally appeared in *Canadian Journal on Aging* 6, 3: 228–239. Reprinted in *Aging & Society: A Canadian Reader*, edited by M. Novak, 342–351. Scarborough: Nelson Canada.

Rosenwasser, S.M., M.H. Gonzales, and V. Adams. 1985. Perceptions of a Housespouse: The Effects of Sex, Economic Productivity, and Subject Background Variables. *Psychology of Women Quarterly* 9: 258–264.

Ross, C.E. 1995. Reconceptualizing Marital Status as a Continuum of Social Attachment. *Journal of Marriage and the Family* 57: 129–140.

Ross, C.E., J. Mirowsky, and K. Goldstein. 1991. The Impact of the Family on Health: The Decade in Review. In *Contemporary Families: Looking Back*, edited by A. Booth, 341–360. Minneapolis: National Council on Family Relations.

Ross, D.P., E.R. Shillington, and C. Lochhead. 1994. *The Canadian Fact Book of Poverty*. Ottawa: Canadian Council on Social Development.

Ross, H., C. Tesla, B. Kenyon, and S. Lollis. 1990. Maternal Intervention in Toddler Peer Conflict: The Socialization of Principles of Justice. *Developmental Psychology* 28: 994–1003.

Ross, H. and H. Taylor. 1989. Do Boys Prefer Daddy or his Physical Style of Play? *Sex Roles* 20, 1–2: 23–31.

Ross, J. and J.P. Kahan. 1983. Children by Choice or by Chance: The Perceived Effects of Parity. *Sex Roles* 9: 69–77.

Rothman, B.K. 1989. *Recreating Motherhood: Ideology and Technology in a Patriarchal Society*. New York: Norton.

Rothman, B.K. and M.B. Caschetta. 1995. Treating Health: Women and Medicine. In *Women: A Feminist Perspective*, edited by J. Freeman, 65–78. Mountain View, CA: Mayfield.

Rothschild, J. 1983. *Machina Ex Dea: Feminist Perspectives on Technology*. New York: Pergamon Press.

Rothschild-Whitt, J. 1979. The Collectivist Organization: An Alternative to Rational-bureaucatic Models. *American Sociological Review* 44: 509–527.

Rotundo, E.A. 1993. *American Manhood: Transformations in Masculinity from the Revolution to the Modern Era*. New York: BasicBooks.

Rowland, R. 1986. Women Who Do and Women Who Don't Join the Women's Movement: Issues for Conflict and Collaboration. *Sex Roles* 14: 679–692

Royal Commission the New Reproductive Technologies, Patricia Baird, Chairperson. 1993. *Proceed With Care: Final Report of the Royal Commission on New Reproductive Technologies*. Ottawa: Canadian Communications Group.

Rubin, J. Z. 1974. From Liking to Loving: Patterns of Attraction in Dating Relationships. In *Foundations of Interpersonal Attraction*, edited by T.L. Huston, 383–402. New York: Academic Press.

Rubin, J. Z., F. J. Provenzano, and Z. Lurra. 1974. The Eye of the Beholder. *American Journal of Orthopsychiatry* 44: 512–519.

Rubin, L.B. 1990. *Erotic Wars: What Happened to the Sexual Revolution?* New York: Farrar. Straus & Giroux.

———. 1985. *Just Friends: The Role of Friendship in Our Lives*. New York: Harper & Row Perennial.

———. 1983. *Intimate Strangers: Men and Women Together*. New York: Harper & Row.

———. 1981. *Women of a Certain Age: The Midlife Search for Self*. New York: Harper Colophon.

Rubin, M. 1980. *Men Without Masks: Writings from the Journals of Modern Men*. Reading, MA: Addison-Wesley.

Rubin, R.T., J.M. Reinisch, and R.F. Haskett. 1981. Postnatal Gonadal Steroid Effects on Human Behavior. *Science* 211: 1318–1324.

Rubin, Z. 1973. *Liking and Loving: An Invitation to Social Psychology*. New York: Holt, Rinehart and Winston.

———. 1970. Measurement of Romantic Love. *Journal of Personality and Social Psychology* 6: 265–273.

Rubin, Z., L.A. Peplau, and C.T. Hill. 1981. Loving and Leaving, Sex Differences in Romantic Attachments. *Sex Roles* 7: 821–835.

Ruble, T.L. 1983. Sex Stereotypes: Issues of Change in the 1970s. *Sex Roles* 9, 3: 397–402.

Ruby, C.C. 1987. *Sentencing,* 3rd ed. Toronto: Butterworths.

Russell, D.E.H. 1987. The Nuclear Mentality: An Outgrowth of the Masculine Mentality. *Atlantis* 12, Spring: 10–15.

———. 1984. *Sexual Exploitation: Rape, Child Sexual Abuse, and Workplace Harassment.* Beverly Hills, CA: Sage.

———. 1982. *Rape in Marriage.* New York: Macmillan.

———. 1975. *The Politics of Rape.* New York: Stein and Day.

Russell, D.E.H. and D. Finkelhor. 1984. The Gender Gap. In *Sexual Exploitation*, edited by D.E.H. Russell. Beverly Hills, CA: Sage.

Russman, L. 1989. Survey of News Magazines Shows Little News Coverage of Women. *Media Report on Women* 17, 6: 1.

Sacco, V.F. and L.W. Kennedy. 1994. *The Criminal Event.* Scarborough: Nelson.

Sadker, M.P. and D.M. Sadker. 1991. *Teachers, Schools and Society.* New York: McGraw-Hill.

Safilios-Rothschild, C. 1977. *Love, Sex & Sex Roles.* Englewood Cliffs, NJ: Prentice-Hall.

———. 1976. A Macro- and Micro-Examination of Family Power and Love: An Exchange Model. *Journal of Marriage and The Family* 38: 355–362.

Safir, M.P. 1986. The Effects of Nature or of Nurture on Sex Differences in Intellectual Functioning: Israeli Findings. *Sex Roles* 14: 581–589.

Salamon, E.D. 1984. *Kept Women.* London: Orbis.

Salecl, R. 1992. Nationalism, Anti-Semitism, and Anti-Feminism in Eastern Europe. *New German Critique* 57, Fall: 51–65.

Sanday, P.R. 1996. *A Woman Scorned: Acquaintance Rape On Trial.* New York: Doubleday.

Santoro, G. 1994. *Dancing In Your Head: Jazz, Blues, Rock and Beyond.* New York: Oxford Unversity Press.

Santrock, J.W. 1987. *Adolescence.* Dubuque, IL: Wm. C. Brown.

———. 1981. *Adolescence: An Introduction.* Dubuque, IL: Wm. C. Brown.

Santrock, J.W. and K. Sitterle. 1987. Parent-Child Relationships in Stepmother Families. In *Remarriage and Stepparenting Today: Research and Theory*, edited by K. Pasley and M. Ihinger-Tallman. New York: Guilford.

Sapir, E. 1949. *Selected Writings of Edward Sapir on Language, Culture and Personality.* Edited by D.G. Mandelbaum. Berkeley, CA: University of California Press.

Sarbin, T.R. and V.L. Allen. 1968. Role Theory. In *The Handbook of Social Psychology*, edited by G. Lindzey and E. Aronson, 2nd ed., Vol. 1., 488–567. Reading, MA: Addison-Wesley.

Sarrel, P.M. 1990. Sexuality and Menopause. *Journal of Obstetrics and Gynecology,* 75: 26s–30s.

Satell, J.W. 1976. The Inexpressive Male: Tragedy or Sexual Politics? *Social Problems* 23: 469–477.

Satir, V. 1970. Marriage as a Human-Actualizing Contact. In *The Family in Search of a Future*, edited by H.A. Otto, 57–66. New York: Appleton-Century-Crofts.

Savage, C. 1979. *Our Nell: A Scrapbook Biography of Nellie L. McClung.* Saskatoon: Western Producer Prairie Books.

Sawyer, J. 1974. On Male Liberation. In *Men and Masculinity*, edited by J. Pleck and J. Sawyer, 170–173. Englewood Cliffs, NJ: Prentice-Hall.

Saxton, L. 1996. *The Individual, Marriage, and the Family,* 9th ed. Belmont, CA: Wadsworth.

———. 1990. *The Individual, Marriage and the Family,* 7th ed. Belmont, CA: Wadsworth.

———. 1986. *The Individual, Marriage and the Family,* 6th ed. Belmont, CA: Wadsworth.

Scarr, S., D. Phillips, and K. McCartney. 1990. Facts, Fantasies, and the Future of Child Care in the United States. *Psychological Science* 1: 26–35.

Schaefer, R.T., R.P. Lamm, P. Biles, and S.J. Wilson. 1996. *Sociology: An Introduction: First Canadian Edition*. Toronto: McGraw-Hill Ryerson.

Schafly, P. 1977. *The Power of the Positive Woman*. New York: Jove, HBJ Books.

Schecter, S. 1982. *Women and Male Violence: The Visions and Struggles of the Battered Women's Movement*. London: Pluto Press.

Schecter, S. and L. Gary 1989. A Framework for Understanding and Empowering Battered Women. In *Abuse and Victimization Across the Life Span*, edited by M. Straus, 240–253. Baltimore: John Hopkins University Press.

Scheuble, L. and D.R. Johnson. 1993. Marital Name Change: Plans and Attitudes of College Students. *Journal of Marriage and the Family* 55: 747–754.

Schilit, R., G. Lie, and M. Montagne. 1990. Substance Use as a Correlate of Violence in Intimate Lesbian Relationships. *Journal of Homosexuality* 9: 51–65.

Schlegel, A. and Barry, H. III. 1991. *Adolescence: An Anthropological Inquiry*. New York: Free Press.

Schneider, S.W. 1986. Jewish Women in the Nuclear Family and Beyond. In *All-American Women: Lines that Divide, Ties That Bind*, edited by J. Cole, 198–215. New York: Free Press.

Schulenberg, J. 1983. *Gay Parenting*. New York: Doubleday.

Schwartz, L. 1985 Sex Stereotyping in Children's Toy Advertisements. *Sex Roles* 12, 1/2: 213–216.

Schwartz, L. and W.T. Markham. 1985. Sex Stereotyping in Children's Toy Advertisements. *Sex Roles* 12: 157–170.

Schwartz, M.A. 1990. *A Sociological Perspective on Politics*. Englewood Cliffs, NJ: Prentice Hall.

Schwartz, M.F. and L. Cohn. 1996. *Sexual Abuse and Eating Disorders*. New York: Brunner/Mazel.

Schwartz, P. 1994. *Love Between Equals: How Peer Marriage Really Works*. New York: Free Press.

Schwartz, P. and V. Rutter. 1998. *The Gender of Sexuality*. Thousand Oaks, CA: Pine Forge Press.

Scutt, K. 1981. Sexism in the Criminal Law. In *Women and Crime,* edited by S. Mukherjee and J. Scutt. Sydney: Institute of Criminology/George Allen & Unwin.

Seagraves, K.B. 1989. Extramarital Affairs. *Medical Aspects of Human Sexuality* 23: 99–105.

Seidman, S.A. 1992. An Investigation of Sex-Role Stereotyping in Music Videos. *Journal of Broadcasting and Electronic Media* Spring: 210–216.

Sells, L.W. 1980. The Mathematics Filter and the Education of Women and Minorities. In *Women and the Mathematical Mystique*, edited by L.H. Fox, L. Brody, and D. Tobin. Baltimore: John Hopkins University Press.

Selnow, G.W. 1985. Sex Differences in Uses and Perceptions of Profanity. *Sex Roles* 12, 3–4: 303–312.

Seltzer, J. and S.M. Bianchi. 1988. Children's Contact with Absent Parents. *Journal of Marriage and the Family* 50: 663–677.

Serbin, L.A., L.C. Moller, J. Gulko, K.K. Powlishta, and K.A. Colburne. 1994. The Emergence of Gender Segregation in Toddler Playgroups. In *Childhood Gender Segregation: Causes and Consequences*, edited by C. Leaper. San Francisco: Jossey-Bass.

Seward, R.R., D.E. Yeatts, and L. Stanley-Stevens. 1996. Fathers' Changing Performance of Housework: A Bigger Slice of a Smaller Pie. *Free Inquiry in Creative Sociology* 24, 1 May: 28–36.

Sexton, C.S. and D. Perlman. 1989. Couples' Career Orientation, Gender Role Orientation and Perceived Equity as Determinants of Marital Power. *Journal of Marriage and the Family* 51: 933–941.

Shain, A. 1995. Employment of People With Disabilities. *Canadian Social Trends* 38, Autumn: 8–13.

Shakin, M., D. Shakin, and S.J. Sternglanz. 1985. Infant Clothing: Sex Labeling for Strangers. *Sex Roles* 12: 955–964.

Shalev, C. 1989. *Birth Power: The Case for Surrogacy*. New Haven: Yale University Press.

Sharpe, S. 1994. *The Gilded Ghetto: Women and Political Power in Canada*. Toronto: Harper Collins.

Shaw, M. 1991. *Survey of Federally Sentenced Women: Report of the Task Force on Federally Sentenced Women on the Prison Survey*. User Report 1991–4. Ottawa: Corrections Branch, Ministry of the Solicitor General of Canada.

Shaw, S.M. 1988. Gender Differences in the Definition and Perception of Household Labor. *Family Relations* 37: 333–337.

Shears, M. 1985. Solving the Great Pronoun Debate: 14 Ways to Avoid the Sexist Singular. *Ms*. October: 106–109.

Sheehy, G. 1995. *New Passages: Mapping your Life across Time*. New York: G. Merritt Corporation.

———. 1992. *The Silent Passage: Menopause*. New York: Random House.

———. 1976. *Passages: Predictable Crises of Adult Life*. New York: E.P. Dutton.

Shehan, C.L. and K.C.W. Kammeyer. 1997. *Marriages and Families: Reflections of a Gendered Society*. Boston: Allyn and Bacon.

Shehan, C. and J. Scanzoni 1988. Gender Patterns in the United States: Demographic Trends and Policy Prospects. *Family Relations* 37, October: 444–450.

Sher, J. 1983. *White Hoods: Canada's Ku Klux Klan*. Vancouver: New Star Books.

Sherman, J.A. 1978. *Sex-Related Cognitive Differences*. Springfield, IL: Charles C. Thomas.

Sherrod, D. 1989. The Influence of Gender on Same-Sex Friendships. In *Review of Personality and Social Psychology: Vol. 10. Close Relationships*, edited by C. Hendrick, 164–186. Newbury Park, CA: Sage.

Shotland, R.L. 1989. A Model of the Causes of Date Rape in Developing and Close Relationships. In *Close Relations*, edited by C. Hendrick, 246–270. Newbury Park, CA: Sage.

Sidorowicz, L.S. and G.S. Lunney. 1980. Baby X Revisited. *Sex Roles* 6: 667–673.

Signroielli, N. 1991. *A Sourcebook on Children and Television*. New York: Greenwood.

———. 1990. Children, Television and Gender Roles: Messages and Impact. *Journal of Adolescent Health Care* 11: 50–58.

———. 1989. Television and Conceptions about Sex Roles: Maintaining Conventionality and the Status Quo. *Sex Roles* 21, 5/6: 341–352.

Silverman, R. and L. Kennedy. 1993. *Deadly Deeds: Murder in Canada*. Scarborough: Nelson Canada.

———. 1987. *The Female Perpetrator of Homicide in Canada*. Edmonton: Centre for Criminological Research, University of Alberta.

Silverstein, B. and D. Perlick. 1995. *The Cost of Competence: Why Inequality Causes Depression, Eating Disorders and Illness in Women*. New York: Oxford University.

Silverstein, B., L. Perdue, E. Peterson, and E. Kelly. 1986. The Role of the Mass Media in Promoting a Thin Standard of Body Attractiveness for Women. *Sex Roles* 14: 519–523.

Silverstein, B., S. Carpman, D. Perlick, and L. Perdue 1990. Nontraditional Sex Role Aspirations, Gender Identity Conflict and Disordered Eating among College Women. *Sex Roles* 23: 687–695.

Simmons, C.H., A.V. Kolke, and H. Schimizu. 1986. Attitudes Toward Romantic Love among American, German and Japanese Students. *Journal of Social Psychology* 126: 327–336.

Simon, W. and J.H. Gagnon (eds.). 1970. Psychosexual Development. In *The Sexual Scene*, 23–41. Chicago: Trans-action Books.

———. 1969. On Psychosexual Development. In *Handbook of Socialization Theory and Research*, edited by D.A. Goslin, 733–752. Chicago: Rand McNally.

Sinclair, C. 1996. *Net Chick: A Smart Girl Guide to the Wired World*. New York: Henry Holt.

Sivard, R.L.. 1995. *Women...A World Survey,* 2nd ed. Washington, DC: World Priorities.

Six, B. and T. Eckes. 1991. A Closer Look at the Complex Structure of Gender Stereotypes. *Sex Roles* 24, 1/2: 57–71.

Skolnick, A.S. 1996. *The Intimate Environment: Exploring Marriage and the Family,* 6th ed. New York: HarperCollins.

Skrypenk, B.J. and J.E. Fast. 1993. Trends in Canadian Women's Labour Force Behavior: Implications for Government and Corporate Policy. In *Papers on Economic Equality Prepared for the Economic Equality Workshop.* Ottawa: Status of Women Canada.

Slater, A.S. and S. Feinman. 1985. Gender and the Phonology of North American First Names. *Sex Roles* 13, October: 429–440.

Slater, S. 1995. *The Lesbian Family Life Cycle.* New York: Free Press.

Small, S.A. and D. Riley. 1990. Toward a Multidimensional Assessment of Work Spillover in Family Life. *Journal of Marriage and the Family* 52: 51–61.

Smelser, N.J. 1981. *Sociology.* Englewood Cliffs, NJ: Prentice-Hall.

Smith, C. and B. Lloyd. 1978. Maternal Behavior and Perceived Sex of Infant Revisited. *Child Development* 49: 1264–1265.

Smith, D. 1974 Woman Perspective as a Radical Critique of Sociology. *Sociological Quarterly* 44: 7–13.

Smith, E.R. and J.R. Kluegel. 1984. Beliefs and Attitudes about Women's Opportunity: Comparisons with Beliefs about Blacks and a General Model. *Social Psychology Quarterly* 47, 1: 81-94.

Smith, G. 1957. *A History of England.* New York: Charles Scribner's Sons.

Smith, J.I. 1987. Islam. In *Women in World Religions,* edited by A. Sharma. Albany: State University of New York.

Smith, J.E., A.V. Waldorf, and D.L. Trembath. 1990. Single White Male Looking for Thin, Very Attractive...*Sex Roles* 23: 675–685.

Smith, P.A. and E. Midlarsky. 1985. Empirically Derived Conceptions of Femaleness and Maleness: A Current View. *Sex Roles* 12: 313–328.

Smith, P.M. 1985. *Languages, the Sexes and Society.* New York: Blackwell.

Smith-Lovin, L. and C. Brody. 1989. Interruptions in Group Discussions: The Effects of Gender and Group Composition. *American Sociological Review* 54: 424–435.

Smith-Rosenberg, C. 1975. The Female World of Love and Riual: Relations Between Women in Nineteenth-Century America. *Signs* 1: 1–29.

Snodgrass, S. 1985. Women's Intuition: The Effect of Subordinate Role on Interpersonal Sensitivity. *Journal of Personality and Social Psychology* 49: 146–155.

Snow, M.E., C.N. Jacklin, and E.E. Maccoby. 1983. Sex-of-child Differences in Father-Child Interaction at One Year of Age. *Child Development* 54: 227–232.

Snyder, M. 1982/1992. Self-Fulfilling Stereotypes. Originally published in *Psychology Today.* July: 60–68. Reprinted in *Race, Class, & Gender: An Integrated Study,* edited by Paula S. Rothenberg, 325–331. New York: St. Martin's Press.

Sommers, C.H. 1994. *Who Stole Feminism? How Women Have Betrayed Women.* New York: Simon & Schuster.

Sonenstein, F.L., J.H. Pleck, and L.C. Ku. 1989. Sexual Activity, Condom Use and AIDS Awareness Among Adolescent Males. *Family Planning Perspectives* 21, 3: 152–158.

Sontag, S. 1972. The Double Standard of Aging. *Saturday Review.* 23 September: 29–38.

South, S.J. 1991. Sociodemographic Differentials in Mate Selection Preference. *Journal of Marriage and the Family* 53: 928–940.

South, S.J. and G.D. Spitze. 1994. Housework in Marital and Nonmarital Households. *American Sociological Review* 59, 3: 21–25.

Spade, J.Z. and C.A. Reese. 1991/1995. We've Come a Long Way, Maybe: College Students' Plans for Work and Family. *Sex Roles* 24: 309–321. Reprinted in *Gender in the 1990s: Images, Realities, and Issues,* edited by E.D. Nelson and B.W. Robinson, 142–153. Toronto: Nelson Canada.

Spain, D. 1992. *Gendered Spaces.* Chapel Hill, NC.: University of North Carolina.

Spallone, P. 1989. *Beyond Conception: The New Politics of Reproduction*. Granby, MA: Bergin and Garvey Publishers.

———. 1987. Reproductive Technology and the State: The Warnock Report and its Clones. In *Made to Order: The Myth of Reproductive and Genetic Progress*, edited by P. Spallone and D. Steinberg. Oxford: Pergamon.

Spence, J. 1983. Androgyny versus Gender Schema. *Psychological Review* 88: 365–368.

Spender, D. 1995. *Nattering on the Net: Women, Power and Cyberspace*. Toronto: Garamond Press Ltd.

———. 1993. Language and Reality: Who Made the World? In *Women Studies Essential Readings*, edited by S. Jackson et al. New York: New York University.

———. 1989. *The Writing of the Sex: Or Why You Don't Have to Read Women's Writing to Know it's No Good*. New York: Pergamon Press.

———. 1983. *Man Made Language*. Melbourne: Routledge and Kegan Paul.

———. 1980. *Man Made Language*. London: Routledge & Kegan Paul.

Sprecher, S. 1985. Sex Differences in Bases of Power in Dating Relationships. *Sex Roles* 12: 449–462.

Sprecher, S. and S. Metts. 1989. Development of the 'Romantic Beliefs Scale' and Examination of the Effects of Gender and Gender-Role Orientation. *Journal of Social and Personal Relationships* 6: 387–411.

Squire, S. 1984. *The Slender Balance*. New York: Pinnacle.

St. Lawrence, J.S. and D.J. Joyner. 1991. The Effects of Sexually Violent Rock Music on Males' Acceptance of Violence against Women. *Psychology of Women Quarterly* 15, 1: 49–64.

St. Peter, C. 1989. Feminist Discourse, Infertility and Reproductive Technologies. *NWSA Journal*. Spring, 1, 3: 353–367.

Stacey, J. 1996. *In the Nature of the Family: Rethinking Family Values in the Postmodern Age*. Boston: Beacon Press.

———. 1993. Good Riddance to 'The Family': A Response to David Popenoe. *Journal of Marriage and the Family* 55: 545–547.

Stacey, J. and B. Thorne. 1985. The Missing Feminist Revolution in Sociology. *Social Problems* 32: 301–316.

Staff Writers. 1993. The Power and the Pride. *Newsweek*. July 21. Reprinted in *Human Sexuality 95/96*, edited by S.J. Bunting, 20th ed. (1995), 66–69. Guilford, CT: Dushkin.

Staggenborg, S. 1998. *Gender, Family, and Social Movements*. Thousand Oaks, CA: Pine Forge Press.

Stanley, J.P. 1977. Paradigmatic Woman: The Prostitute. In *Papers in Language Variation*, edited by D.L. Shores and C.P. Hines, 303–321. Tuscaloosa: University of Alabama Press.

Stanbeck, G. 1982. Language and Black Woman's Place: Toward a Description of Black Women's Communications. Paper presented at meeting of Speech Communication Association, Louisville, KY.

Starhawk. 1992. A Men's Movement I Can Trust. In *Women Respond to the Men's Movement: A Feminist Collection*, edited by K.L. Hagan. 27–38 San Francisco, CA: Pandora.

Stark, E. 1989. Friends Through It All. In *Marriage and Family in a Changing Society*, edited by J.M. Henslin, 3rd ed., 441–449. New York: Free Press.

Stark, R. 1992. *Sociology*, 4th ed. Belmont, CA: Wadsworth.

Starkman, R. 1997. Cashing In On Success. *Toronto Star*. March 30: B6.

———. 1994. Tragedy of Women's Gymnastics: Athlete's Death Reveals Grim Toll of Eating Disorders. *Toronto Star*. 5 October: C3.

Starr, B.D. and M.B. Weiner. 1981. *Sex and Sexuality in the Mature Years*. New York: Stein and Day.

Starrels, M.E., B. Ingersoll-Dayton, D.W. Dowler, and M.B. Neal. 1997. The Stress of Caring for a Parent: Effects of the Elder's Impairment on an Employed, Adult Child. *Journal of Marriage and the Family* 59: 860–872.

Statistics Canada. 1997a. *Divorce, 1995*. Cat. 84–213–XMB. Ottawa: Minister of Industry.

————. 1997b. *Age, Sex, Marital Status and Common Law, Canada, Provinces and Territories, 1996.* Electronic Media Release. 14 October.

————. 1996. *Marriages, 1995.* Cat. 84–212. Ottawa: Minister of Industry.

————. 1995. *Canadian Social Trends.* Summer 37. Cat. 11–008E. Ottawa: Minister of Industry.

————. 1995a. Unpaid Work of Households. *The Daily.* December 20. Ottawa.

————. 1993. *Canadian Child Care In Context: Perspectives from the provinces and territories.* Ottawa: Health and Welfare Canada.

————. 1992. *Families: Number, Type and Structure, The Nation, 1991 Census.* Cat. 93–312. Ottawa: Minister of Industry, Science and Technology.

————. 1992a. *Age, Sex and Marital Status: The Nation, 1991 Census.* Cat. 93–310. Ottawa: Minister of Industry, Science and Technology.

————. 1992b. *Lone-Parent Families in Canada.* Cat. 89–522E. Ottawa: Ministry of Supply and Services.

————. 1986. *Family Characteristics.* Cat. 71–533. Ottawa: Ministry of Supply and Services.

————. 1983. *Historical Statistics of Canada.* 2nd ed. Cat. 11–516. Ottawa: Ministry of Supply and Services.

————. 1972. *Population Sex Ratios.* 1971 Census of Canada. Cat. 92–714. Ottawa: Ministry of Supply and Services.

Stebbins, R.A. 1988. Men, Husbands and Fathers: Beyond Patriarchal Relations. In *Reconstructing the Canadian Family: Feminist Perspectives*, edited by N. Mandell and A. Duffy, 27–47. Toronto: Butterworths.

Steinbacher, R. and F.D. Gilroy. 1985. Preference for Sex of Child among Primiparouis Women. *Journal of Psychology* 119: 541–547.

Steinberg, L. and S.R. Silverberg. 1987. Influences on Marital Satisfaction during the Middle Stages of the Family Life Cycle. *Journal of Marriage and the Family* 49: 751–760.

Steinem, G. 1994. *Moving Beyond Words.* New York: Simon & Schuster.

————. 1978. Erotica and Pornography: A Clear and Present Difference. *MS.* November: 53–4; 75, 76.

Steinmetz, S. 1987. Family Violence: Past, Present and Future. In *Handbook of Marriage and the Family*, edited by M.B. Sussman and S.K. Steinmetz, 725–765. New York: Plenum.

Steinmetz, S. and M.A. Straus (eds.). 1974. *Violence in the Family.* New York: Harper and Row.

Stenberg, C. and J. Campos. 1990. The Development of Anger Expressions in Infancy. In *Psychological and Biological Approaches to Emotion*, edited by N. Stein, B. Leventhal, and T. Trabasso, 247–282. Hillsdale, NJ: Lawrence Erlbaum Associates.

Stephens, G. 1997. Computer Crimes Will Increasing Invade People's Privacy. In *Computers and Society*, edited by P.A. Winter, 71–78. San Diego, CA: Greenhaven Press.

Stern, M. and K.H. Karraker. 1989. Sex Stereotyping of Infants: A Review of Gender Labeling Studies. *Sex Roles* 20, 3: 501–511.

Sternglanz, S.H. and L.A. Serbin. 1974. Sex Role Stereotyping in Children's TV Programs. *Developmental Psychology* 10: 710–715.

Stets, J. 1993. Control in Dating Relationships. *Journal of Marriage and the Family* 55: 673–685.

————. 1991. Cohabiting and Marital Aggression: The Role of Social Isolation. *Journal of Marriage and the Family* 53: 669–680.

Stets, J. and D.A. Henderson. 1991. Contextual Factors Surrounding Resolution while Dating: Results From a National Study. *Family Relations* 40: 29–36.

Stets, J. and M. Pirog-Good. 1990. Interpersonal Control and Courtship Aggression. *Journal of Social and Personal Relationships* 7: 371–394.

Stets, J. and M.A. Straus. 1989. The Marriage License as a Hitting License: A Comparison of Assaults in Dating, Cohabiting and Married Couples. *Journal of Family Violence* 4, June: 161–180.

Steuter, E. 1992/1995. Women against Feminism: An Examination of Feminist Social Movements and Anti-Feminist Countermovements. In *Canadian Review of Sociology and Anthropology* 29, 3: 288–306. Reprinted in *Gender in the 1990s: Images, Realities, and Issues*, edited by E.D. Nelson and B.W. Robinson, 537–552. Toronto: Nelson Canada.

Stewart, L.P., A.D. Stewart, S.F. Friedley, and P.J. Cooper. 1990. *Communication Between the Sexes*. Scottsdale, AZ: Gorsuch Scarisbrick.

Stockard, J. and M.M. Johnson. 1980. *Sex Roles*. Englewood Cliffs, NJ: Prentice-Hall.

Stodghill, R. 1997. The Rise of the Promise Keepers. *Time*. October 6: 34–38.

Stoller, R. 1985. *Observing the Erotic Imagination*. New Haven: Yale University Press.

Stoneman, Z., G.H. Brody, and C.E. MacKinnon. 1986. Same-Sex and Cross-Sex Siblings: Activity Choices, Roles, Behavior and Gender Stereotypes. *Child Development* 56: 1241–1252.

Stoppard, J. M. 1992. A Suitable Case for Treatment? Premenstrual Syndrome and the Medicalization of Women's Bodies. In *Anatomy of Gender: Women's Struggle for the Body*, edited by D.H. Currie and V. Raoul, 119–129. Ottawa: Carleton University Press.

Storms, M.D. 1981. Sexual Scripts for Women. *Sex Roles* 7: 699–708.

Stouffer , S. 1949. *The American Soldier*. New York: Wiley.

Straus, M.A. 1992. Explaining Family Violence. In *Marriage and Family in a Changing Society*, edited by J.M. Henslin, 4th ed., 344–356. New York: Free Press.

———. 1990. The Conflict Tactics Scales and its Critics: An Evaluation and New Data on Validity and Reliability. In *Physical Violence in American Families: Risk Factors and Adaptations To Violence in 8,145 Families*, edited by M.A. Straus and R.J. Gelles, 49–73. New Brunswick, NJ: Transaction.

———. 1980. Wife-beating: How Common and Why? In *The Social Causes of Husband-Wife Violence*, edited by M.A. Straus and G.T. Hotaling, 23–36. Minneapolis: University of Minnesota Press.

———. 1979. Family Patterns and Child Abuse in a Nationally Representative American Sample. *Child Abuse and Neglect* 3: 213–225.

———. 1973. A General Systems Theory Approach to a Theory of Violence Between Family Members. *Social Science Information* 12: 105–125.

Straus, M.A. and R. Gelles. 1978. Determinants of Violence in the Family: Towards a Theoretical Integration. In *Contemporary Theories About the Family*, edited by W.R. Burr, R. Hill, F.R. Nye, and I.L. Reiss, Vol. 1. New York: Free Press.

———. 1990. *Physical Violence in American Families: Risk Factors and Adaptations to Violence in 8,145 Families*. New Brunswick, NJ: Transaction.

Strossen, N. 1995. *Defending Pornography: Free Speech, Sex, and the Fight for Women's Rights*. New York: Scribner.

Sturgeon, N. 1997. *Ecofeminist Natures: Race, Gender, Feminist Theory and Political Action*. New York: Routledge.

Suitor, J.J. 1991. Marital Quality and Satisfaction with the Division of Household Labor across the Family Life Cycle. *Journal of Marriage and the Family* 53: 221–230.

Sullivan, G.L. and P.J. O'Connor. 1988. Women's Role Portrayal in Magazine Advertising: 1958–83. *Sex Roles* 13, 3–4: 181–188.

Sumrall, A.C. and D. Taylor (eds.). 1992. *Sexual Harassment: Women Speak Out*. Freedom, CA: The Crossing Press.

Super, D.E. 1967. *The Psychology of Careers*. New York: Harper & Row.

Surra, C.A. 1991. Research and Theory on Mate Selection and Premarital Relationships in the 1980s. In *Contemporary Families, Looking Forward, Looking Back*, edited by A. Booth, 54–75. Minneapolis: National Council on Family Relations.

Swain, S. 1989. Covert Intimacy: Closeness in Men's Friendships. In *Gender in Intimate Relationships: A Microstructural Approach*, edited by B.J. Risman and P. Schwartz, 71–86. Belmont, CA: Wadsworth.

Switzer, J.Y. 1990. The Impact of Generic Word-choices: An Empirical Investigation of Age- and Sex-related Differences. *Sex Roles* 22, 1–2: 69–82.

Sykes, G.M. and D. Matza. 1988. Techniques of Neutralization. In *Down To Earth Sociology*, edited by J.M. Henslin, 5th ed., 225–231. New York: Free Press.

Symons, D. 1979. *The Evolution of Human Sexuality*. New York: Oxford University Press.

Szatmary, D. 1996. *A Time To Rock: A Social History of Rock'N'Roll*. New York: Schirmer Books.

Szekely, E. 1988. *Never Too Thin*. Toronto: The Women's Press.

Szinovacz, M.E. 1987. Family Power. In *The Handbook of Marriage and the Family*, edited by M. Sussman and S.K. Steinmetz, 651–693. New York: Plenum.

Szymanski, L.A., and J.C. Chrisler. 1990/1991. Eating Disorders, Gender-role, and Athletic Activity. *Psychology* 27, 4: 20–29.

Szymanski, M. and T.F. Cash. 1995 Body-image Disturbances and Self-discrepancy Theory: Expansion of the Body Image Ideals Questionnaire. *Journal of Social and Clinical Psychology* 14: 134–146.

Tannen, D. 1994a. Gender Gap in Cyberspace. *Newsweek*. May 16: 54–55.

———. 1994b. *Talking From 9 to 5: How Women's and Men's Conversational Styles Affect Who Gets Credit and What Gets Done at Work*. New York: William Morrow.

———. 1990. *You Just Don't Understand: Women and Men in Conversation*. New York: William Morrow.

Tavris, C. 1992. *The Mismeasure of Women*. New York: Simon and Schuster.

———. 1979. Freud and Female Inferiority. *International Journal of Women's Studies* 2: 287–304.

Tavris, C. and C. Wade. 1984. *The Longest War: Sex Differences in Perspective,* 2nd ed. San Diego: Harcourt Brace Jovanovich.

Thayer, S. 1988. Encounters. *Psychology Today*. March: 31–36.

Thomas, W.I. with D.S. Thomas. 1928. *The Child in America: Behavior Problems and Programs*. New York: Alfred A. Knopf.

Thompson, L. 1993. Conceptualizing Gender in Marriage: The Case of Marital Care. *Journal of Marriage and the Family* 55: 557–569.

———. 1991. Family Work: Women's Sense of Fairness. *Journal of Family Issues* 12: 181–196.

Thompson, L. and A.J. Walker. 1995. The Place of Feminism in Family Studies. *Journal of Marriage and the Family* 57: 847–865.

———. 1989. Gender in Families: Women and Men in Marriage, Work and Parenthood. *Journal of Marriage and the Family* 51: 845–871.

Thompson, M. 1987. *Gay Spirit: Myth and Meaning*. New York: St. Martin's.

Thompson, T.L. and E. Zerbinos. 1995. Gender Roles in Animated Cartoons: Has the Picture Changed in 20 Years? *Sex Roles* 32, 9/10: 651–673.

Thomson, E., S.S. McLanahan, and R.B. Curtin. 1992. Family Structure, Gender, and Parental Socialization. *Journal of Marriage and the Family* 54, May: 368–378.

Thomson, K. 1977. *To Be A Man: Developing Conscious Masculinity*. Los Angeles: Tarcher.

Thornburg, H.D. 1982. *Development in Adolescence,* 2nd ed. Montery, CA: Brooks/Cole.

Thorne, B. 1982. Feminist Rethinking of the Family: An Overview. In *Rethinking the Family: Some Feminist Questions*, edited by B. Thorne and M. Yalom, 1–24. New York: Longmans.

———. 1974. *Sex Differences in Language, Speech and Nonverbal Communication,* rev. ed. Rowley, MA: Newbury House Publishers.

Thorne, B., C. Kramarae, and N. Henley (eds.). 1983. *Language, Gender, and Society*. Rowley, MA: Newbury.

——— (eds.). 1975. *Language, Gender and Society*. Rowley, MA: Newbury.

Thorne, B. and M. Yalom. 1982. *Rethinking the Family: Some Feminist Questions*. New York: Longmans.

Thorne, B. and N. Henley (eds.). 1975. *Language and Sex: Difference and Dominance*. Rowley, MA: Newbury.

Thorne, B. and Z. Luria. 1986. Sexuality and Gender in Children's Daily Worlds. *Social Problems* 33: 176–190.

Thorne, T. 1990. *The Dictionary of Contemporary Slang*. New York: Pantheon.

Thorne-Finch, R. 1992. *Ending the Silence: The Origins and Treatment of Male Violence Against Women*. Toronto: University of Toronto Press.

Thrall, C. 1982. The Conservative Use of Modern Household Technology. *Technology and Culture* 23: 175–194.

Thurnher, M. 1976. Midlife Marriage: Sex Differences in Evaluation and Perspectives. *International Journal of Aging and Human Development* 72: 129–135.

Thurston, C. 1987. *The Romance Revolution*. Urbana and Chicago, IL: University of Illinois Press.

Tiger, L. 1969. *Men in Groups*. London: Thomas Nelson and Sons.

Tolson, A. 1977. *The Limits of Masculinity*. London: Tavistock.

Tong, R. 1989. *Feminist Theory: A Comprehensive Introduction*. Boulder, CO: Westview.

Toufexis, A. 1992. Bisexuality: What Is It? *Time* August 17: 49–51.

Townson, M. 1995. *Women's Financial Futures: Mid-Life Prospects for a Secure Retirement*. Ottawa: Canadian Advisory Council on the Status of Women.

Tracy, D.M. 1987. Toys, Spatial Ability and Science and Mathematics Achievement: Are They Related? *Sex Roles* 17: 115–136.

Travato, F. and N.M. Lalu. 1996. Causes of Death Responsible for the Changing Sex Differential in Life Expectancy Between 1970 and 1990 in Thirty Industrialized Nations. *Canadian Studies in Population* 23, 2: 99–126.

Trevethan, S. and T. Samagh 1993. Gender Differences among Violent Crime Victims. *Juristat Service Bulletin* 12, Winter: 21.

———. 1992. Gender Differences Among Violent Crime Victims. *Juristat Service Bulletin* 12, 21: 1–17.

Troll, L.E. 1975. *Early and Middle Adulthood*. Monterey, CA: Brooks/Cole.

Trudgill, P. 1972. Sex, Covert Prestige and Linguistic Change in the Urban British English of Norwich, *Language in Society* 1: 179–195. Reprinted in *Language and Sex*, edited by B. Thorne and N. Henley, 88–104. Rowley, MA: Newbury House Publishers.

Tuchman, G. 1978. *Making News: A Study in the Construction of Reality*. New York: Free Press.

Tuchman, G., A.K. Daniels, and J. Benet. 1978. *Hearth and Home: Images of Women in the Mass Media*. New York: Oxford University Press.

Tuck, B., J. Rolfe, and V. Adair. 1994. Adolescents' Attitudes Toward Gender Roles within Work and its Relationship to Gender, Personality Type and Parental Occupations. *Sex Roles* 31, 9–10: 547–558.

Tucker, M.B. and C. Mitchell-Kernan (eds.). 1995. *The Decline in Marriage among African Americans: Causes, Consequences and Policy Implications*. New York: Russell Sage Foundation.

Turkle, S. 1988. Computational Reticence: Why Women Fear the Intimate Machine. In *Technology and Women's Voices*, edited by C. Kramarae. London: Routledge and Kegan Paul.

———. 1984. *The Second Self: Computers and the Human Spirit*. London: Granada.

Turner, B.F. and C.B. Turner. 1991. Bem Sex-Role Inventory Stereotypes for Men and Women Varying in Age and Race Among National Register Psychologists. *Psychological Reports* 69: 931–44.

Turner, R.H. and L.M. Killian. 1991. *Collective Behavior*, 2nd. ed. Englewood Cliffs, NJ: Prentice-Hall.

Uchalik, D.C. and D.D. Livingston. 1980. Adulthood: Women. In *On Love and Loving: Psychological Perspectives on the Nature and Experience of Romantic Love*, edited by K.S. Pope and Associates, 89–103. San Francisco: Jossey-Bass.

Udry, J.R. 1994. The Nature of Gender. *Demography* 31: 561–573.

———. 1971. *The Social Context of Marriage,* 2nd ed. Philadelphia: J.B. Lippincott.

———. 1968. Sex and Family Life. *Annals of the American Academy of Political and Social Science* 376, March: 25–35.

Underwood, M., J. Coie, and C. Herbsman. 1992. Display Rules for Anger and Aggression in School-age Children. *Child Development* 63: 366–380.

Unger, R. and M. Crawford. 1992. *Women and Gender: A Feminist Psychology.* New York: McGraw-Hill.

United Nations Development Programme. 1997. *Human Development Report 1997.* New York: Oxford University Press.

———. 1996. *Human Development Report 1996.* New York: Oxford University Press.

———. 1995. *Human Development Report 1995.* New York: Oxford University Press.

Vaillant, G.E. 1977a. *Adaptation to Life.* Boston: Little, Brown.

———. 1977b. The Climb to Maturity: How the Best and the Brightest Came of Age. *Psychology Today.* 11 September: 34–41, 107–110.

Valette, B. 1988. *A Parent's Guide to Eating Disorders.* New York: Walker.

Valverde, M. 1991. *The Age of Light, Soap and Water.* Toronto: McClelland & Stewart.

Van Horn, J.E. 1989. Studies Find Latchkey Children are Doing Fine. *Morning Call.* 16 February: B10.

Van Kirk, S. 1986. The Role of Native Women in the Fur Trade Society of Western Canada, 1670–1830. In *Rethinking Canada: The Promise of Women's History,* edited by V. Strong-Boag and A. C. Fellman, 59–66. Toronto: Copp Clark Pitman

Vance, C.S. (ed.). 1984. Pleasure and Danger: Toward a Politics of Sexuality. In *Pleasure and Danger: Exploring Female Sexuality.* Boston: Routledge & Kegan Paul.

Vande Berg, L.H. and D. Streckfuss. 1992. Prime-time Television's Portrayal of Women and the World of Work: a Demographic Profile. *Journal of Broadcasting and Electronic Media* 36: 195–208.

Vanek, J. 1974. Time Spent in Housework. *Scientific American* November: 116–120.

VanEvery, J. 1995. *Heterosexual Women Changing the Family: Refusing To Be A Wife.* London:Taylor & Francis.

Vannoy-Hiller, D. and W. Philliber. 1989. *Equal Partners.* Beverly Hills, CA: Sage.

Varley, G. and P. Varley. 1971. *To Be A Dancer: Canada's National Ballet School.* Toronto: Peter Martin Associates.

Vaughn, D. 1986. *Uncoupling: Turning Points in Intimate Relationships.* New York: Vintage.

Vazquez-Nuttall, E., I. Romero-Garcia, and B. DeLeon. 1987. Sex Roles and Perceptions of Femininity and Masculinity of Hispanic women: A Review of the Literature. *Psychology of Women Quarterly* 11: 409–425.

Venkatesan, M. and J. Losco. 1975. Women in Magazine Ads: 1959–71. *Journal of Advertising Research* 15: 49–54.

Vetterling-Braggin, M. 1981. *Sexist Language.* New Jersey: Littlefield, Adams.

Villeneuve, P.J. and H.I. Morrison. 1995. Trends in Mortality from Smoking: Related Cancers, 1950 to 1991. *Canadian Social Trends* 39, Winter: 8–11.

Vincent, R.C., D.K. Davis, and L.A. Boruszkowski. 1987. Sexism on MTV: The Portrayal of Women in Rock Videos. *Journalism Quarterly* 64, 4: 750–755, 941–942.

Waite, L.J. 1995. Does Marriage Matter? *Demography* 32, 4: 483–507.

Wajcman, J. 1991. *Feminism Confronts Technology.* University Park, PA: Pennsylvania State University Press.

Waldron, I. and J.A. Jacobs. 1988. Effects of Labor Force Participation on Women's Health. *Journal of Occupational Medicine* 30: 977–983.

Walker, A.J. 1996. Couples Watching Television: Gender, Power, and the Remote Control. *Journal of Marriage and the Family* 58: 813–823.

Walker, A.J. and C.C. Pratt. 1991. Daughters' Help to Mothers: Intergenerational Aid versus Caregiving. *Journal of Marriage and the Family* 53: 3–12.

Walker, G. 1990. *Family Violence and the Women's Movement.* Toronto: University of Toronto Press.

Walker, L. 1979. *The Battered Woman.* New York: Harper Perennial.

Walkerdine, V. 1989. *Counting Girls Out.* London: Virago.

————. 1988. *The Mastery of Reason*. London: Routledge and Kegan Paul.

Wallace, M. 1990. Women Rap Back. *Ms.* 1, 3 November–December.

Waller, W. 1938. *The Family: A Dynamic Intepretation*. New York: Dryden.

Wallerstein, J.S. and S. Blakeslee. 1989. *Second Chances: Men, Women, and Children a Decade After Divorce*. New York: Ticknor & Fields.

Wallston, B.S. and V. O'Leary. 1981. Sex Makes a Difference: Differential Perceptions of Women and Men. In *Review of Personality and Social Psychology*, edited by L. Wheeler, Vol. 2, 9–41. Beverly Hills, CA: Sage.

Walsh, C. and C. L. Cepko. 1992. Widespread Dispersion of Neuronal Clones Across Functional Regions of the Cerebral Cortex. *Science* 255: 434–440.

Walster, E. and G.W. Walster. 1978. *A New Look at Love*. Reading, MA: Addison-Wesley.

Walum, L.R. 1977. *The Dynamics of Sex and Gender: A Sociological Perspective*. Chicago: Rand McNally.

Ward, K.B. and L. Grant. 1985. The Feminist Critique and a Decade of Published Research in Sociological Journals. *The Sociological Quarterly* 26: 139–157.

Ward, S.K., K. Chapman, E. Cohn, S. White, and K. Williams. 1991. Acquaintance Rape and the College Social Scene. *Family Relations* 40: 65–71.

Watchell, S.S. 1979. H-Y Antigen and Sexual Development In *Genetic Mechanisms of Sexual Development*, edited by H. Vakket and I. Porter, 271–277. New York: Academic Press.

Waterman, C., Dawson, L., and Bologna, M. 1989. Sexual Coercion in Gay and Lesbian Relationships: Predictors and Implications for Support Services. *Journal of Sex Research* 26: 118–124.

Watson, R.S. 1993. The Named and the Nameless: Gender and Person in Chinese Society. In *Gender in Cross-Cultural Perspective*, edited by C.B. Bretl and C.F. Sargent. Englewood Cliffs, NJ: Prentice-Hall.

Weaver, S. 1993. First Nations Women and Government Policy, 1970–92: Discrimination and Conflict. In *Changing Patterns: Women in Canada,* edited by S. Burt, L. Code, and L. Dorney, 2nd ed., 92–150. Toronto: McClelland & Stewart.

Weber, M. 1947. *The Theory of Social and Economic Organizations*, translated by A.M. Henderson and T. Parsons, edited by T. Parsons. Glencoe, IL: Free Press.

Weinfeld, M. 1981. Myth and Reality in the Canadian Mosaic: Affective Ethnicity. In *Ethnicity and Ethnic Relations in Canada*, edited by R.M. Bienvenue and J.E. Goldstein, 2nd ed., 65–86. Toronto: Butterworths.

Weininger, O. 1906. *Sex and Character: Authorized Translation from the Sixth German ed*. London: Heineman, AMS Press.

Weise, E.R. and D. Weise. 1996. *Wired Women: Gender and New Realities in Cyberspace*. New York: Seal Books.

Weisman, L.K. 1992. *Discrimination by Design: A Feminist Critique of the Man-made Environment*. Chicago: University of Chicago Press.

Weisner, T.S., H. Garnier, and J. Loucky. 1994. Domestic Tasks, Gender Egalitarian Values and Children's Gender Typing in Conventional and Nonconventional families. *Sex Roles* 30 January: 23–54.

Weisner, T.S. and J.E. Wilson-Mitchell. 1990. Nonconventional Families Life-styles and Sex-typing in 6-year-olds. *Child Development* 61: 1915–1933.

Weiss, R.S. 1990. *Staying the Course: The Emotional and Social Lives of Men Who Do Well at Work*. New York: Fawcett.

Weitzman, L.J. 1985. *The Divorce Revolution*. New York: Free Press.

Weitzman, L.J., D. Eifler, E. Hokada, and C. Ross. 1972. Sex Role Socialization in Picture Books for Pre-School Children. *American Journal of Sociology* 77: 1125–1150.

Weitzman, N., B. Birnes, and R. Friend. 1985. Traditional and Nontraditional Mothers' Communication with their Daughters and Sons. *Child Development* 56: 894–898.

Welch, R.L., A. Huston-Stein, J.C. Wright, and R. Plehal. 1979. Subtle Sex-role Cues in Children's Commercials. *Journal of Communication* 29: 202–209.

West, C. 1994. Rethinking 'Sex Differences' in Conversational Topics. In *The Women and Language Debate: A Sourcebook*, edited by C. Roman, S. Juhasz, and C. Miller. New Brunswick, NJ: Rutgers University.

West, C. and D. Zimmerman. 1987. Doing Gender. *Gender & Society* 1: 125–151.

Whitbourne, S.K. and J.B. Ebmeyer. 1990. *Identity and Intimacy in Marriage: A Study of Couples*. New York: Springer-Verlag.

White, L. 1996. No Boys Allowed in this Class. *Oshawa Whitby This Week*. November 17: 3.

———. 1987. Mobilizing on the Margins of Litigation. *Review of Law and Social Change* 16: 515.

White, L.E. 1991. Subordination, Rhetorical Survival Skills, and Sunday Shoes: Notes on the Hearing of Mrs. G. In *Feminist Legal Theory: Readings in Law and Gender*, edited by K.T. Bartlett and R. Kennedy, 404–428. Boulder, CO: Westview Press.

Whitehead, H. 1981. The Bow and the Burden Strap: A New Look at Institutionalized Homosexuality in Native North America. In *Sexual Meanings: The Cultural Construction of Gender and Sexuality*, edited by S.B. Ortner and H. Whitehead, 80–115. Cambridge: Cambridge University Press.

Whitesell, N. and S. Harter. 1996. The Interpersonal Context of Emotion: Anger with Close Friends and Classmates. *Child Development* 67: 1345–1359.

Whitla, W. 1995. A Chronology of Women in Canada. In *Feminist Issues: Race, Class and Sexuality*, edited by N. Mandell, 315–353. Scarborough, ON: Prentice Hall Canada.

Whorf, B.L. 1956. The Relation of Habitual Thought and Behavior to Language. In *Language, Thought and Reality,* 134–159. Cambridge: MA: Technology Press of MIT.

Whyte, M.K. 1990. *Dating, Mating and Marriage*. New York: Aldine de Gruyter.

Wichman, T. 1996. Child Support Rules—An Improvement? *Exchange Magazine for Business*. May: 48–51.

Wikan, U. 1977. Man Becomes Woman: Transsexualism in Oman as a Key to Gender Roles. *Man* NS 12: 304–319.

Wikler, N.J. 1993. Researching Gender Bias in the Courts: Problems and Prospects. In *Investigating Gender Bias: Law, Courts, and the Legal Profession*, edited by J. Brockman and D. Chunn, 49–62. Toronto: Thompson Educational Publishing.

Wilczynski, A. 1991. Images of Women Who Kill Their Infants: The Mad and the Bad. *Women and Criminal Justice* 2: 71–88.

Wiles, C. 1991. A Comparison of Role Portrayal of Men and Women in Magazine Advertising in the USA and Sweden. *International Journal of Advertising* 10: 259–267.

Wilkie, J.R. 1993. Changes in U.S. Men's Attitudes Toward the Family Provider Role, 1972–1989. *Gender & Society* 7, 2: 261–279.

Wilkins, K. 1996. Causes of Death: How the Sexes Differ. *Canadian Social Trends* 41, Summer: 11–17.

Williams, C.L. 1992. The Glass Escalator: Hidden Advantages for Men in the 'Female' Professions. *Social Problems* 39: 253–267.

Williams, J.A. Jr. 1987. Sex Role Socialization in Picture Books: An Update. *Social Science Quarterly* 68: 148–156.

Williams, J.A., J. Vernon, M. Williams, and K. Malecha. 1987. Sex Role Socialization in Picture Books: An Update. *Social Science Quarterly* 68, 1: 148–156.

Williams, J.C. 1991. Deconstructing Gender. In *Feminist Legal Theory: Readings in Law and Gender*, edited by K.T. Bartlett and R. Kennedy, 95–123. San Francisco: Westview.

Williams, J.E. and D.L. Best. 1982. *Measuring Sex Stereotypes: A Thirty-Nation Study*. Beverly Hills, CA: Sage.

Williams, J.E. and D.L. Best, and S.M. Bennett. 1975. The Definition of Sex Stereotypes via the Adjective Check List. *Sex Roles* 1: 327–337.

Williams, W.I. 1996. The Berdache Tradition. In *The Meaning of Difference: American Constructions of Race, Sex, and Gender, Social Class, and Sexual Orientation*, edited by K.E. Rosenblum and T.M.C. Travis. New York: McGraw-Hill.

Willis, E. 1992. *No More Nice Girls: Countercultural Essays*. Hanover, NH: Wesleyan University Press.

Wills, T., R. Weiss, and G. Patterson. 1974. A Behavioral Analysis of the Determinants of Marital Satisfaction. *Journal of Consulting and Clinical Psychology* 48: 802–811.

Wilson, M. and M. Daly. 1994. Spousal Homicide. *Canadian Centre for Justice Statistics. Juristat Service Bulletin* 14, 8: Cat. 85–992. Ottawa: Minister of Industry, Science and Technology.

Wilson, S. J. 1996. *Women, Families & Work,* 4th ed. Toronto: McGraw-Hill Ryerson.

———. 1991. *Women, Families, and Work,* 3rd ed. Toronto: McGraw-Hill Ryerson.

Wilson, E.O. 1978. *On Human Nature*. Cambridge, MA: Harvard University Press.

———. 1975. *Sociobiology*. Cambridge, MA: Harvard University Press.

Wine, J.D and J.L. Ristock (eds.). 1991. Introduction: Feminist Activism in Canada. In *Women and Social Change: Feminist Activism in Canada*, 1–18. Toronto: James Lorimer.

Winkler, A.E. 1993. The Living Arrangements of Single Mothers with Dependent Children: An Added Perspective. *The American Journal of Economics and Sociology* 52, 1: 1–18.

Wister, A.V. and L.A. Strain. 1986. Social Support and Well-Being: A Comparison of Older Widows and Widowers. Paper presented at the 21st Annual Meeting of the Canadian Sociology and Anthropology Association, Winnipeg, Manitoba.

Witelson, S.F. 1989. Hand and Sex Differences in the Isthmus and Genu of the Human Corpus Callosum: A Postmortem Morphological Study. *Brain* 112: 799–835.

———. 1976. Sex and the Single Hemisphere: Specialization of the Right Hemisphere for Spatial Processing. *Science* 193: 425–427.

Wittig, M. 1992. *The Straight Mind and Other Essays*. Boston: Beacon Press.

Wolf, N. 1998. *Power Feminism: How to Love the Women's Movement Again*. New York: Random House.

———. 1993. *Fire With Fire: The New Female Power and How It Will Change the 21st Century*. New York: Random House.

———. 1991. *The Beauty Myth*. Toronto: Vintage Books.

Wood, B. 1994. The Trials of Motherhood: The Case of Azaria and Lindy Chamberlain. In *Moving Targets: Women, Murder and Representation*, edited by H. Birch, 62–94. Los Angeles: University of California Press.

Wood, J. 1997. *Gendered Lives: Communication, Gender and Culture,* 2nd ed. Belmont, CA: Wadsworth.

———. 1993. *Gendered Lives: Communication, Gender and Culture*. Belmont, CA: Wadsworth.

Wood, J.T. and C. Inman. 1993. In a Different Mode: Recognizing Male Modes of Closeness. *Journal of Applied Communication Research* 21: 279–295.

Wood, J.T. and S. Duck (eds.). 1995. *Under-Studied Relationships: Off the Beaten Track*. Thousand Oaks, CA: Sage.

Wood, W., F.Y. Wong, and J.G. Cachere. 1991. Effects of Media Violence on Viewers' Aggression in Unconstrained Social Interaction. *Psychological Bulletin* 109: 371–383.

Woolf, V. 1978. *Books and Portraits: Some Further Selections from the Literary and Biographical Writings of Virginia Woolf*. New York: Harcourt, Brace Jovanovich.

———. 1977. *A Room of One's Own*. San Diego: Harvest/HBJ.

Worell, J. 1996. Feminist Identity in a Gendered World. In *Lectures on the Psychology of Women*, edited by J.C. Chrisler, C. Golden, and P.D. Rozee. New York: McGraw-Hill.

Wright, P.H. 1982. Men's Friendships, Women's Friendships and the Alleged Inferiority of the Latter. *Sex Roles* 8: 1–20.

Wroblewski and A. Huston. 1987. Televised Occupational Stereotypes and Their Effects on Early Adolescents: Are They Changing? *Journal of Early Adolescence* 7, 3: 283–297.

Wu, Z. 1995. Remarriage after Widowhood: A Marital History Study of Older Canadians. *Canadian Journal on Aging* 14, 4: 719–736.

Wu, Z. and T.R. Balakrishnan. 1994. Cohabitation After Marital Disruption in Canada. *Journal of Marriage and the Family* 56: 723–734.

———. 1992. Attitudes towards Cohabitation and Marriage in Canada. *Journal of Comparative Family Studies* 22, 1 Spring: 1–12.

Wylie, M. 1995. No Place for Women. *Digital Watch* 4, 8, January.

Wylie, P. 1942. *Generation of Vipers*. New York: Rinehart Pocket Books.

Yee, M. 1993. Finding The Way Home Through Issues of Gender, Race and Class. In *Returning the Gaze: Essays on Racism, Feminism and Politics*, edited by H. Bannerji, 3–44. Toronto: Star Vision Press.

Yllo, K.A. 1993. Through a Feminist Lens: Gender, Power and Violence. In *Current Controversies on Family Violence*, edited by R.J. Gellese and D. Loseke, 47–62. Beverly Hills, CA: Sage.

———. 1988. Political and Methodological Debates in Wife Abuse Research. In *Feminsit Perspectives on Wife Abuse*, edited by K. Yllo and M. Bograd, 28–50. Newbury Park, CA: Sage.

Yoder, J.D. 1991. Rethinking Tokenism: Looking Beyond Numbers. *Gender & Society* 9: 8–37.

Yoder, J.D., P. Aniakudo, and L. Berendsen. 1997. Looking Beyond Gender: The Effects of Racial Diferences on Tokenism Perceptions of Women. *Sex Roles* 35, 7/8: 389–400.

Yogis, J.A., R.R. Duplak, and J.R. Trainor. 1996. *Sexual Orientation and Canadian Law: An Assessment of the Law Affecting Lesbian and Gay Persons*. Toronto: Emond Montgomery Publications Limited.

Young, T. and M.B. Harris. 1996. Most Admired Women and Men: Gallup, Good Housekeeping, and Gender. *Sex Roles* 35, 5/6: 363–375.

Zahn-Waxler, C., P. Cole, and K. Barrett. 1991. Guilt and Empathy: Sex Differences and Implications for the Development of Depression. In *The Development of Emotion Regulation and Dysregulation*, edited by J. Garber and K. Dodge, 243–272. Cambridge: Cambridge University Press.

Zaretsky, E. 1976. *Capitalism, the Family, and Personal Life*. New York: Harper & Row.

Zelizer, V.A. 1985. *Pricing the Priceless Child The Changing Social Value of Children*. New York: Basic Books.

Zilbergeld, B. 1995. It's Two Feet Long, Hard as Steel, Always Ready, and Will Knock Your Socks Off; The Fantasy Model of Sex. In *Gender in the 1990s: Images, Realities, and Issues*, edited by E.D. Nelson and B.W. Robinson, 276–287. Scarborough, ON: Nelson.

———. 1992. *The New Male Sexuality: The Truth About Men, Sex, and Pleasure*. New York: Bantam Books.

Zimmerman, D. and C. West. 1975. Sex Roles, Interruptions and Silecnes in Conversation. In *Language and Sex*, edited by B. Thorne and N. Henley, 105–29. Rowley, MA: Newbury House.

Zimmer, L. 1988. Tokenism and Women in the Workplace: The Limits of Gender-neutral Theory. *Social Problems* 35: 64–77.

Zolotow, C. 1972. *William's Doll*. New York: HarperTrophy

Zuckerman, D.M. and D.H. Sayre. 1982. Cultural Sex-Role Expectations and Children's Sex-Role Concepts. *Sex Roles* 8, August: 853–862.

Zuckerman, D.M., D.S. Singer, and J.L. Singer. 1980. Children's Television Viewing, Racial and Sex-role Attitudes. *Journal of Applied Social Psychology* 10: 281–294.

Zvonkovic, A.M., K.M. Greaves, C.J. Schmiege, and L.D. Hall. 1996. The Marital Construction of Gender Through Work and Family Decisions: A Qualitative Analysis. *Journal of Marriage and the Family* 58: 91–100.

Name Index

Subject Index